# Foreword

**Andrew Holroyd**
President of the
Law Society

**Geoffrey Vos QC**
Chairman of the Bar

**Few professions offer the sheer variety of being a solicitor. Ever fewer are as vibrant, rewarding or intellectually stimulating. During your career you might find yourself in the overseas office of a commercial firm, working in the courts as a solicitor advocate or going in-house for any number of multinational companies.**

Our profession is in the midst of great change and it is you, the solicitors of tomorrow, who will see the greatest benefits from the opportunities that these changes will afford. The Legal Services Bill, which is likely to be passed in October 2007, will create a number of new ways to deliver legal services.

Just as the profession is changing, we at the Law Society are changing too. Gone are our responsibilities for overseeing complaints and acting as the industry regulator. Today we are focused on representing the best interests of solicitors up and down the country. This autumn sees the launch of our Junior Lawyers Division (JLD), which will offer a superb range of new services for trainees and new solicitors with up to five years' post-qualification experience. Membership to the JLD is also open to registered Law Society students.

As president of the Law Society, I am delighted to commend to you the 11th edition of *The Training Contract & Pupillage Handbook*. I wish you every success as you embark on your careers.

**I believe that the Bar must be equally accessible to talented people from all backgrounds. That does not, of course, mean that starting a career at the Bar is an easy matter. The profession is, by its nature, highly competitive, and only the most able can expect to succeed. My concern, however, is that everyone, whatever their origin or upbringing, should have an equal opportunity to compete on merit.**

Perhaps the greatest hurdle in joining the profession is obtaining a pupillage. This is because pupillage is an intensive period of apprenticeship, which requires dedication from both pupil supervisor and pupil alike. It is obviously important to undertake detailed research into the available pupillages and their suitability for your legal interests.

*The Training Contract & Pupillage Handbook 2008* provides information about training as a barrister and areas of practice. It also reproduces information provided by some chambers about themselves. Further information on qualification is available via the Bar Council's website at www.barcouncil.org.uk and from www.pupillages.com, which gives easy access to all vacancies.

I very much hope that you will find the information in the handbook useful. I wish you every success with your future career in the law.

# Becoming a Lawyer

# Work Experience

# Postgraduate Training

# Solicitors

# Training Contract Directory

# Barristers

# Pupillage Directory

# Useful Information

# Credits

| | | |
|---|---|---|
| **Managing Editor** | Sinead Dineen | sdineen@tcph.co.uk |
| **Editor** | Isla Grant | igrant@tcph.co.uk |
| **Assistant Editor** | Adam Smith | asmith@tcph.co.uk |
| **Sub-editor** | David Minto | |
| **Production Assistant** | Julia Browne | jbrowne@tcph.co.uk |
| **Publishers** | Matthew Broadbent | mbroadbent@tcph.co.uk |
| | and Amy Knowles | aknowles@tcph.co.uk |
| **Assistant Publisher** | Karly Last | |
| **Publishing Directors** | Guy Davis | |
| | Tony Harriss | |
| | and Mark Lamb | |
| | | |
| **Design** | Russell Anderson | randerson@tcph.co.uk |
| **Design Assistant** | John Meikle | jmeikle@tcph.co.uk |
| **Layout** | Roger Walker | |
| **Printer** | Pyramid Press, Nottingham | |

| | |
|---|---|
| **Published by** | Globe Business Publishing Ltd |
| | New Hibernia House, Winchester Walk, London Bridge, London SE1 9AG |
| **Tel** | 020 7234 0606 |
| **Fax** | 020 7234 0808 |
| **Email** | info@tcph.co.uk |

Copyright © 2007 Globe Business Publishing Ltd

All rights reserved

| | |
|---|---|
| **ISBN** | 978-1-905783-11-3 |
| **ISSN** | 1741-9395 |

Whilst every attempt has been made to ensure the accuracy of this publication, the publishers cannot accept responsibility for any errors, omissions, mis-statements or mistakes.

**Further copies of this book can be ordered at ww.tcph.co.uk.**

# Becoming a Lawyer

# *LawCareers.Net Basic Training*
# **Are you ready?**

*It's never too early to start planning your career in the law. Don't risk missing out! The LawCareers.Net Basic Training events will be coming to a campus near you in early 2008. Keep checking www.LawCareers.Net for further information.*

# Introduction

Welcome to *The Training Contract & Pupillage Handbook 2008*. This is the 11th edition of the handbook and, thus, is the product of over a decade of experience offering essential information to you would-be lawyers out there – so you needn't look anywhere else!

Over the past 12 months, we've surveyed hundreds of barristers, solicitors, graduate recruiters and others to get a sense of the current legal landscape. We've interviewed dozens of practitioners to form a detailed picture of their areas of expertise and what it really means to be a lawyer. We've expanded sections, added information and checked facts – all in an effort to make sure that you have every morsel of relevant information right at your fingertips.

If you're not sure where to begin your quest, then "Solicitor v barrister" is a great place to start. Hot on its heels follow "Getting the best careers advice" and "Choosing where to apply" – both useful guides to clarifying your search. Then we get down to the nuts and bolts of applying, with twin chapters on application and interview technique. We've also got a bumper section on work experience, including first-hand accounts from work placement veterans in the "Insider reports" section. And for how not to do things, take a look at the diverting – nay, hilarious – "Where did it all go wrong?".

The postgraduate phase is explained in full, with all manner of acronyms demystified (we've got your LPC, your GDL, your BVC…). There is also some timely advice on how to fund your studies and how to make the most of your postgraduate provider's careers service. And don't skip past our section on clerks and the important role they play in shaping the careers of young barristers.

Perhaps you're not even sure that it's a solicitor or barrister you want to be; in which case, read "Alternative careers" for an introduction to a host of related job paths that might just take your fancy.

Of course, it's not just paper-based help we offer – we also urge you to make full use of the handbook's online sister publication, www.LawCareers.Net. The website gives you access to recruitment literature, trainee profiles, application deadlines, legal news and so much more.

Finally, we would of course be delighted to hear from you if you have any views on the handbook, suggestions to make or generally just feel like dropping us a line. You can contact us via www.tcph.co.uk, www.LawCareers.Net or by emailing us direct at info@tcph.co.uk.

As ever, we wish you all the very best with your legal career and hope that the handbook can help you along the way. Happy reading!

# Solicitor v barrister: how to choose

One of the most fundamental questions you must address when considering a career in the law is whether to become a solicitor or a barrister. This decision rests on a number of factors concerning your abilities, temperament and – dare we say it – financial circumstances.

The chief difference between the two strands of the profession is widely perceived to be the contrast between the individualist (barrister) and the team player (solicitor). A barrister is (in almost all cases) self-employed and bound to other barristers only by convenience, while it is possible for a solicitor to be one worker in a strictly hierarchical law firm consisting of more than 1,000. In reality, the situation is less black and white; barristers are often involved in teamwork and some solicitors may spend many hours in a locked room devising gnomic opinions (and let's not forget that modern day push-me-pull-you: the solicitor advocate!). In this chapter we provide a general guide to help you to decide on the strand that suits you best. Just remember not to take it too seriously…

| SOLICITOR | | BARRISTER |
|:---:|:---:|:---:|
| | **ACHIEVEMENTS** | |
| 8 | Academic | 9 |

Fantastic academics are the ideal underpinnings of every fledgling legal career. You will generally find a pretty close correlation between the best academic scores and the best (or at least the best-paying) jobs in the legal profession. We've scored academics as being slightly more important for the Bar as it is smaller and consequently more selective. The Bar is also probably rather more weighted to the traditional universities, to which the Oxbridge-heavy tenant lists at many chambers testify (the Bar is doing its best to address this bias, however).

| | | |
|:---:|:---:|:---:|
| 8 | Positions of responsibility | 6 |

Again, having been the head prefect is an impressive achievement wherever you go. In most cases, though, positions of responsibility are concerned with keeping hierarchies in order and thus could be described as management training. For this reason they may be better valued by firms of solicitors.

| | | |
|:---:|:---:|:---:|
| 7 | Sporting prowess | 7 |

Even stevens on this one. Sporting prowess implies drive, teamwork, organisation and an aversion to sloth. Some sports may lend themselves better to one branch of the profession or the other (eg, team sports for would-be solicitors and individual sports for the Bar), but really all are good for both.

| | | |
|:---:|:---:|:---:|
| 7 | Acting/performing | 8 |

These are highly relevant skills for both branches of the profession. You will be in the business of conveying information and ideas whether you are a solicitor or barrister. The courtroom side of a barrister's work is directly equivalent to these attributes, so the Bar scores a little higher.

| | | |
|:---:|:---:|:---:|
| 9 | Commercial/business know-how | 7 |

Whatever you do in the law you will, at some level, be involved in running a business – be it as a small cog in a huge firm or as a self-employed person at the Bar. Furthermore, you will often be working to assist the businesses of others. Firms of solicitors no longer provide purely legal advice, but are employed almost as business advisers with an eye on overall strategy. Barristers are more typically 'hired hands' for advocacy or preparing highly specific legal opinions.

| | | |
|:---:|:---:|:---:|
| 8 | Legal experience | 8 |

At trainee level, nobody expects you to know the law inside out. What they do expect is for you to have a relatively sophisticated grasp of the profession, its activities, its imperatives and its rhythms, as a way of showing that you have thought sensibly about why you want to become a lawyer. One of the best ways of doing this is to find a law (or law-related) environment in which you can learn what it's all about.

| SOLICITOR | | BARRISTER |
|---|---|---|
| | **TEMPERAMENT** | |
| 8 | Eloquence | 9 |

As we saw above, the ability to communicate is *the* fundamental tool of the trade. The better you are at communicating, the better a lawyer you will be. Again, the advocatory aspect of a barrister's life means this skill is more important at the Bar.

| 9 | Sociability | 8 |
|---|---|---|

The law is a sociable profession in which you can expect to meet large numbers of people from all walks of life (depending on your practice area). Crucially, you must be able to get on with your clients and other lawyers with whom you work. The legal community is intimate and incestuous. It helps to be able to fit in and get on. Yes, there are legendary curmudgeons floating around (particularly at the Bar), but don't think it's advisable to become one of them. If you become a barrister you'll need social skills to stay onside with the clerks – they decide whether you work or not!

| 7 | Self-reliance | 9 |
|---|---|---|

You'll need a fair amount of self-reliance and self-belief whatever you do in law. The solicitor generally has a more definite career structure, but after a certain point (especially towards partnership) it's dog eat dog. As a barrister, though, you are literally on your own. It's your career and you've got to make it happen, make the most of it and deal with the quiet times. If you need more structure, then think again.

| 7 | Intellectual curiosity | 8 |
|---|---|---|

Sweeping generalisation time here. In reality, the area of law in which you end up will be the greatest driver of the intellectual content of your work. However, if you want to be a really serious analyst and provider of opinions on heavyweight points of law, then the Bar may be for you – especially as the 'backroom boys' at firms of solicitors are considered to be a dying breed.

| 8 | Drive | 8 |
|---|---|---|

In case you hadn't noticed, becoming a successful lawyer is hard work. Get used to some hard graft now and it won't hurt so much later on in your career.

| | **OTHER FACTORS** | |
|---|---|---|
| 2 | Affluence | 3 |

This may appear to be a facetious point. Quite clearly, it is right and proper that a career in the law should be available to all. That said, the relevant training (especially at postgraduate level) means that it is not uncommon for individuals to finish the LPC or BVC with over £20,000 worth of debt. Before you rack up this kind of bill, be realistic about your job prospects. In particular, take note that only around 25% of those who apply to take the BVC end up with a tenancy!

| 1 | Enthusiasm for dressing up | 10 |
|---|---|---|

Do you like wearing tights? Gowns? Wigs? Has the reign of Louis XIV always fascinated you? Do you feel that panto should be staged all year round? The Bar values tradition above virtually any calling and the outfits show. Fair play to them! Solicitors' dress is, by contrast, dull, dull, dull (even on Fridays).

| 10 | Love of modern architecture | 1 |
|---|---|---|

Modern firms of solicitors, especially in 'the City' (this now includes Docklands), work in BIG, IMPRESSIVE, MASCULINE buildings; ideally they have been built by Lord Rogers or that other bloke. Barristers work in charming Dickensian warrens. Both the previous statements are exaggerations.

| 0 | Commitment to social justice | 0 |
|---|---|---|

There remain many commendable organisations and individuals in the legal profession who work tirelessly to beat injustice and ensure that right prevails. Furthermore, the grandest and greatest may well be involved in something socially useful (usually trumpeted all round town as pro bono work), but don't be fooled; the law is an industry like any other and should be treated as such.

# The legal scene

We offer below a summary of some of the hottest news and most significant developments in the legal profession, which at the very least will give you something to talk about at interview.

## Legal aid

In July 2006 Lord Carter published his controversial report, suggesting methods to bring spiralling legal aid costs under control, primarily by introducing fixed or graduated fees. Many commentators immediately recognised that the proposed reforms could drive small legal aid practices out of business and that price competitive tendering could have a negative impact on ethnic minority firms. The Law Society and the Bar Council gave the report a cautious welcome.

However, criticism has since grown. At the Legal Aid Practitioners Group annual conference in October 2006, the group's then director Richard Miller said the reforms would leave legal aid in "meltdown". By January 2007 the Law Society's caution had developed into outright disapproval. In March 2007 roughly 1,000 lawyers descended on Parliament to demonstrate against the Legal Services Commission and the Department for Constitutional Affairs (DCA), which, alleged the lawyers, were ignoring the pleas of legal aid practitioners.

In April 2007 Andrew Holroyd, now president of the Law Society, said: "The government is living in cloud cuckoo land. How can their proposals serve access to justice?" The society held a debate for legal aid lawyers and frontbench MPs to galvanise opposition.

While the Black Solicitors' Network and the Society of Asian Lawyers joined together to fight the proposals, the Constitutional Affairs Select Committee published a report expressing concern that the reforms could breach the Race Relations Act. Lord Falconer, the outgoing lord chancellor, published a defiant response to this report, stressing that the system needed reforming. The Black Solicitors' Network and the Society of Asian Lawyers later settled the dispute when the government made several concessions.

The Bar Council finally created a working party to examine the reforms and report its findings in October 2007. In July 2007 the Law Society and the Legal Services Commission both claimed victory over a High Court decision that said the latter had breached EU rules in the way it had tried to implement fixed fees, but that the new system itself was lawful and would be implemented in October 2007.

## Postgraduate training

It has been a year of growth for postgraduate training. Cobbetts and Halliwells signed up to become the first two non-London firms to offer bespoke Legal Practice Courses (LPCs). Trainees will take the course at The College of Law in Chester. The University of Plymouth took over the University of Exeter's LPC and began offering the Graduate Diploma in Law (GDL), Bar Vocational Course (BVC) and some postgraduate degrees, forming its own law school.

The Law Society visited every College of Law campus and ranked them all with the 'commendable practice' grade, the highest rating. Professor Nigel Savage, chief executive of The College of Law, said: "We are delighted by the confidence shown by the Law Society in our courses. This reaffirms the college's standing as a leading legal education provider."

Having taken over the regulatory function of the Law Society, the Solicitors Regulation Authority (SRA) continued to assess law schools, awarding Staffordshire Law School the highest grade in all six assessment criteria. Meanwhile, a consortium of five City firms – Freshfields Bruckhaus Deringer, Slaughter and May, Herbert Smith, Lovells and Norton Rose – renewed its contract with BPP Law School to provide a bespoke City LPC.

Nottingham at Kaplan Law School announced the location of its new London campus, behind Borough Market and close to London Bridge station. CEO Giles Proctor said: "It's a fabulous location and we feel it gives something extra. We have great enthusiasm for the project because there's a real synergy between the ethos of Kaplan and Nottingham."

### Training review
The SRA invited responses to a discussion paper suggesting ways to make the training process more flexible. Proposals included: (i) replacing the current two-year training period with a more flexible approach; and (ii) allowing people to qualify who are not in a formal contract but can demonstrate the required skills and knowledge after having worked in a legal environment.

Although a pilot scheme was due to begin in September 2007, the SRA delayed the plans following analysis of the responses to its discussion paper. Jonathan Spencer, chair of the Education and Training Committee, said: "The challenge is to develop a system which is robust enough not to be seen as a second-class route to qualification… We have not yet quite cracked this dilemma."

### Money talks
In October 2006 the Law Society launched a consultation on whether to continue setting a minimum salary for trainee solicitors. In May 2007 the findings were published by the SRA, which had taken control of the consultation from the Law Society. Results showed widespread support from all corners of the legal profession. Thus, the minimum salary was set on 1 August 2007, with trainees in London to earn at least £17,660 and those outside the capital to earn at least £15,820.

Meanwhile, trainees and newly qualified solicitors (NQs) at large firms saw their salaries raised to new levels – far beyond the SRA minimum. Allen & Overy kicked off an early salary war in October 2006 by increasing the pay of final seat trainees to £40,000 and that of NQs to £63,250. Meanwhile, a survey indicated that one-third of the biggest civil sets offered pupils salaries of £40,000 or higher.

The following month, Slaughter and May hiked trainee salaries to £34,000 and NQ pay to £60,000, although Jones Day trumped these by offering a whopping £70,000 to NQs. All was quiet until April 2007 when Clifford Chance raised trainee salaries to £35,700 and NQ salaries to £62,500. By the end of the month, Allen & Overy had sneaked in a further 3% to its earlier pay hike, bringing NQ salaries close to £65,000. Suddenly, Linklaters put NQs up to £64,000 and trainees up to £36,000, while Freshfields splashed around a firm-wide 19% raise, putting its NQ salary up there with Allen & Overy's.

June 2007 saw salary hikes at SJ Berwin, CMS Cameron McKenna, Cleary Gottlieb Steen & Hamilton, White & Case, Olswang and Denton Wilde Sapte. Addleshaw Goddard broke the mould by announcing salaries for its regional offices months ahead of schedule in a retention strategy – a move followed by Pinsent Masons, which matched Addleshaw Goddard's £40,000 for regional NQs. Weil, Gotshal & Manges trumped them all; not only did the firm promise a £500 cheque for those in its 2009 intake who achieve a first-class degree, it raised NQ salaries by 20% to an overwhelming £90,000. This looked great until Paul Hastings Janofsky & Walker matched the salary. Indeed, it appeared the US firms had their own little skirmish. Cleary Gottlieb Steen & Hamilton announced an NQ salary of £92,000, while those at Latham & Watkins bagged a whopping £96,000.

### SRA launched

The SRA finally took over full regulation of the profession, with the Law Society focusing solely on representing the solicitors of England and Wales. At the launch of the SRA, its chief Antony Townsend confirmed the body's commitment to transparency and consumer focus. This was reflected in the new Solicitors' Code of Conduct, which came into effect on 1 July 2007.

In June 2007 the Law Society got comfortable in its purely representative role and launched a high-profile poster campaign in Tube stations across the City to say so.

### Diversity matters

Stonewall published its updated student guide, which included five new law firms in its list of workplaces that are safe for people of all sexual orientations. The firms that now appear on the list are Clifford Chance, Herbert Smith, Linklaters, Mayer Brown, Pinsent Masons and Simmons & Simmons. In December 2006 the DCA set up another working group to look into diversity issues, finding that firms should publish trainees' academic backgrounds and that bespoke LPCs may be too narrow in scope.

In March 2007 new figures published by the DCA showed how the proportion of female appointees to the judiciary has doubled since 1999. The proportion of ethnic minority appointees has increased by 5% over the last year alone and now stands at 14%.

The Law Society hosted a double whammy of diversity events at the end of April. First up was a careers day encouraging students from all backgrounds to enter the legal

profession. The event was organised in conjunction with the Association of Muslim Lawyers, the Black Solicitors' Network and the Society of Asian Lawyers. The following day, the Law Society hosted a conference providing a forum for black and ethnic minority lawyers to express their views.

An independent group headed by Sir Paul Kennedy published suggestions to make the Bar Council more representative and inclusive. Proposals included increasing the percentage of young and junior barristers on the council, using the first-past-the-post system to elect members of the council and making it easier for candidates to stand.

The fourth annual LawCareers.Net Training & Recruitment Awards were held in June, this time with a new honour: the Commendation for Diversity. Awarded in association with leading diversity magazine publisher Arberry Pink, the gong went to Herbert Smith. Meanwhile, Baroness Scotland took over the role of attorney general, becoming the first black woman to do so.

### Ministry of Justice

The Home Office was split in two, creating a new Ministry of Justice (which also swallowed up the DCA). The leaner Home Office was refocused onto police, counter-terrorism, ID cards and immigration, while the new ministry took control of prisons, judges and courts, and probation. Lord Falconer was in charge of the new ministry until Jack Straw took over the position of lord chancellor and secretary of state for justice. Some lords and judges – including the lord chief justice – criticised the reforms by saying that they were rushed and that the independence of the new ministry was not assured.

### Bar chief's mission

Chairman of the Bar Geoffrey Vos QC made his intentions to open up the profession very public, campaigning throughout the year for a more "inclusive and representative" Bar. On becoming chairman, he promptly launched a working party headed by Lord Neuberger to address concerns over the profession's diversity. Vos also spoke out in the national press to criticise the snobbishness of his profession. With almost 70% of barristers educated at private schools, he noted that the Bar discriminates against working class students. He said he was hoping to expand the pool of candidates.

In April 2007 Neuberger and his working party published an interim report to relate the group's progress. Suggestions included allowing pupils to earn money through evening and weekend work, capping the number of BVC places, increasing the academic requirements needed to enrol on the BVC and providing a voluntary aptitude test to help those considering the BVC ascertain their likelihood of succeeding at the Bar. The Bar Standards Board quickly rejected limiting the number of BVC places and requiring a 2.1 degree.

Vos spoke to the Social Mobility Foundation to reiterate his plans to create new loans to help fund the BVC and a placement programme designed to familiarise state school students with barristers and courts. He followed through in July by inviting 27 students from underprivileged backgrounds to spend time with barristers, watch judges in action, and generally have a good poke around courts and chambers for a week.

Tim Dutton QC takes over as chairman of the Bar on 1 January 2008.

## Firm trends
Lots of firms have leapt into the 21st Century in the past year. Watson Farley & Williams became the first City firm to start a blog with its new trainee intake in September 2006. It wasn't long before other firms followed suit –

Allen & Overy soon launched a flashy graduate recruitment site along with blogs from trainees and senior partners. Leeds firm Clarion Solicitors went live with its distinctive new website in February 2007, complete with a blog and X-ray photographs. Even the chairman of the Bar Council started a blog!

Field Fisher Waterhouse became the first firm to open an office in virtual reality; Second Life, an online three-dimensional world with its own economy and 6 million users. One of the firm's partners was even elected president of the virtual world's Bar association. Addleshaw Goddard branded a custom-made booth and installed a camera inside. The so-called VoxBox will appear at law fairs and record the thoughts of students, which will be assembled into a video podcast.

Turnover was, of course, on the increase. Clifford Chance finally broke the £1 billion barrier, reporting as it did a £1.19 billion turnover in 2007. Linklaters came close with £1.12 billion. Allen & Overy announced a whopping 20.5% increase in turnover to £887 million, just behind Freshfields which, at £986 million turnover, looks set to break a billion in the near future. The average magic circle profit per equity partner was £1 million.

A flood of firms converted to LLP on 1 May 2007, including Barlow Lyde & Gilbert, Clyde & Co, Linklaters, Lovells and Norton Rose.

## Cases and laws
Some noteworthy cases in the past year include the following:
- *Douglas v Hello!* and *Lord Browne v Associated Newspapers*: Two landmark privacy cases. In the former, the House of Lords' decision gave celebrities greater control over their photographs. In the latter, Mr Justice Eady decided that BP shareholders had the right to know that Lord Browne had lied in court, but that his

# The legal scene

private conversations with his ex-boyfriend will remain confidential.

- *Kevin Berwick v Lloyds TSB Bank PLC*: Berwick filed a claim for £1,982.37 against his bank, Lloyds TSB, to recover charges he'd paid which he claimed were unlawful. Developing from growing public cynicism over charges for overdrafts and late fees, *Berwick* was the first case against a bank and thus generated a substantial level of publicity. The judge decided against Berwick, saying that there was no ground in law which would allow him to recover the charges. However, in August 2007 a judge ordered Barclays to stop charging one of its customers until a test case on the legality of bank charges is tried in the High Court next year.
- *Case against the 21 July bombers*: Four of the six defendants charged with conspiracy to murder after having planned to detonate backpacks filled with explosives on London's transport network on 21 July 2005 were convicted and sentenced to life with a minimum of 40 years. The bombs had failed to explode and the men were later arrested in Birmingham. The jury returned a unanimous guilty verdict for the four after a six-month trial which was covered widely in the media. The remaining two defendants face a retrial.

Here is some headline-grabbing legislation:

- *Legal Services Bill*: This complex and controversial bill was introduced in the House of Lords in November 2006 and its main components remain largely intact. The bill creates a new oversight regulator named the Legal Services Board, and an Office for Legal Complaints, and allows alternative business structures, enabling firms to form partnerships with non-lawyers and some corporations to offer legal services.
- *Health Act 2006*: This act came into force in July 2007, banning smoking in all public

spaces and places of work in England. The government issued signage and new requirements to businesses to enforce the regulations. Fines for breaking the ban range from £30 for an individual to £2,500 for a business.
- *Pensions Act 2007*: Building on the proposals put forward in Lord Turner's report of 2005, this bill was introduced to the House of Commons in November 2006. It seeks to re-establish a link between earnings and the basic state pension, and thus will raise the retirement age to 68 by 2046. More women and carers will be able to claim a full state pension and the number of years any person needs to have worked will fall to 30, from 44 for men and 39 for women.

# Statistical analysis of the training market

In this chapter we consider the various trends affecting the legal profession. We examine how many jobs are out there, where they can be found and how well they pay. The information is gleaned from the Law Society's annual statistical report, the Bar Council's website and our own research. We have presented the most up-to-date statistics available.

## Pay

As ever, the profession is divided between the larger commercial players that offer hefty packages (especially in the City) and the rest, which don't. The Solicitors Regulation Authority sets a minimum wage that firms must meet and, in August 2007, raised this threshold to £17,660 for London trainees and £15,820 for those training elsewhere. These represent increases of 7% since the last minimum was set.

After several years of big rises, City salaries had stabilised until 2006-07, when firms battled over which of them could pay the most. First-year trainees receive around £29,000 to £35,000, rising by £4,000 to £5,000 in their second year. Qualifying salaries are usually £50,000 to £70,000, with the average salary in the City being £65,000. That said, the rates paid by many of the US firms now entrenched in London continue to have a potential inflationary effect as they peg salaries to the New York market. Qualifying salaries in excess of £80,000 are not common, but not unknown. Many firms are analysing and improving their bonus schemes, and considering abandoning the lockstep system of remuneration.

The Law Society has looked at the disparities in pay across the nation, as well as by gender. Men are paid over 3.6% more than women in the Northwest, and Yorkshire and Humberside. However, Southeast England overcompensates for this by paying women on average 4.2% more than the men in the region.

The number of pupillages has increased over the past two years, counterbalancing an initial reduction after it was ruled that chambers were obliged to pay pupils a minimum of £10,000 annually. In 2005-06 the number of pupillages available was 550, up from 527 in the previous year. Debate is currently raging within the profession as to how to pay for future generations. While in many cases income is supplemented by additional earnings, especially during the second six, a salary of £10,000 raises questions of access to the profession. At the opposite end of the scale, a number of the top sets boast pay rates commensurate with the large commercial firms.

## Training contracts

The number of trainees continues to increase and 5,751 trainees started their careers in 2004-05. While the number of contracts has increased modestly, so has the number of those completing the Legal Practice Course (LPC) and looking to join the profession. The number of full-time LPC places available is actually up by 16.8% to 10,325 (with an extra 2,948 part-time places). During 2005-06 there was a decrease of 3%, with 6,376 candidates completing the professional qualification. Comparing the number of LPC passes with the number of training contracts registered is a fairly crude measure because those who took the LPC in previous years may also be looking for training contracts and anecdotal evidence indicates an oversupply of candidates. And because up to a quarter of new additions to the Solicitors' Roll are conversions, primarily from either the Bar or other jurisdictions, firms are able to pick and choose between the most capable candidates.

As ever, most (57%) of trainee jobs are concentrated in London and the Southeast, with the City accounting for one-third of all contracts. However, these proportions have decreased by a few percentage points over the past two years as cities farther north expand, the Northwest region being the busiest after London.

The vast majority of training contracts are in private practice (ie, law firms), with firms of more than 26 partners accounting for almost half of them. In 2005-06 285 sole practitioners took on trainees.

## The Bar
The way in which the Bar gathers statistics makes an exact examination of them problematic. What is clear from the figures available is that the annual number of applicants to the Bar Vocational Course (BVC) is around four times greater than the number of tenancies offered. This further underlines the need for aspiring barristers to take a realistic look at their prospects before making career plans.

## Undergraduates in law
The most recent figures indicate that acceptances on law courses went up by 1.4% between 2004 and 2005 (much less than the 10% jump between 2002 and 2003). The National Admissions Test for Law introduced by some institutions is a testament to demand, with law continuing to be the most popular degree course – particularly at those institutions with a good reputation. The University of Nottingham, for example, receives over 17 applications for each of its 250 law course places. In 2005 21,373 potential students applied for places on undergraduate law courses. Of these, 13,693 accepted places. Nationwide, of those accepted onto law degrees, 61% are female, 15.6% are overseas students and 32% are from ethnic minorities.

## Graduates in law
In 2005 the total number of graduates was 12,084 – an 8.5% rise on 2004. Among these graduates, 586 achieved first-class degrees and 5,989 achieved an upper second. Thus,

nearly 55% of all law graduates achieved excellent marks. It should be noted that the Law Society believes it is possible that more than 4,000 students graduate each year with qualifying law degrees (from joint honours or modular degrees).

The total number of places offered on the LPC has risen over the past few years, reaching 10,325 full-time and 2,948 part-time places for 2006-07. But only 8,262 students were enrolled for 2005-06. However, when one considers the 12,000 or so law graduates, the 2,500 Graduate Diploma in Law graduates and some of the further 4,000 or so law students with qualifying law degrees, there could be as many as 19,000 students competing for the 10,000-plus LPC places and 1,745 BVC places. The fact that many LPC places remain unfilled is perhaps an indication of the difficulty many students face in financing the course.

## LPC success rate
In Summer 2006 8,153 students sat the LPC exams. Of these, 6,376 passed – a success rate of 78.2%. Moreover, 2,029 (25%) achieved a distinction and 2,700 (33%) received a commendation, proving just how competitive the market is.

## BVC success rate
The success rate for the BVC looks similar to that of the LPC. For the two years between 2001 and 2003, just over 85% of those enrolled ended up successfully completing it. In 2003-04 89% passed the course, but data is not yet available for 2004-05 onwards. The proportion of those who win a pupillage seems to fall dramatically year on year: from 68% in 2001-02 to 41% in 2003-04. Further data is not yet available, but the message is clear: it's a bloodthirsty business aiming for the Bar.

## Total number of training contracts registered 1989-2006

| Year | No | No of LPC passes |
|---|---|---|
| **1989-90** | 3,254 | 3,170 |
| **1990-91** | 3,841 | 3,828 |
| **1991-92** | 3,941 | 4,201 |
| **1992-93** | 3,681 | 4,319 |
| **1993-94** | 3,874 | 4,691 |
| **1994-95** | 4,170 | 4,755 |
| **1995-96** | 4,063 | 4,775 |
| **1996-97** | 4,739 | 4,338 |
| **1997-98** | 4,826 | 4,460 |
| **1998-99** | 4,827 | 4,627 |
| **1999-2000** | 5,285 | 5,007 |
| **2000-2001** | 5,162 | 4,990 |
| **2001-2002** | 5,385 | 5,467 |
| **2002-2003** | 5,650 | 5,721 |
| **2003-2004** | 5,708 | 6,258 |
| **2004-2005** | 5,732 | 6,558 |
| **2005-2006** | 5,751 | 6,376 |

## Training contracts 2005-06 by category of employment

| Employment category | Training contracts | % by category |
|---|---|---|
| **Private practice** | 5,480 | 95.3 |
| **Commerce and industry** | 94 | 1.6 |
| **Government department** | 15 | 0.3 |
| **Local government** | 78 | 1.4 |
| **Court** | 28 | 0.5 |
| **Advice service** | 24 | 0.4 |
| **Crown Prosecution Service** | 10 | 0.2 |
| **Other** | 22 | 0.4 |

## Training contracts 2005-06 by size of private practice firm

| Firm size | No | % by size |
|---|---|---|
| **Sole practitioner** | 285 | 5.2 |
| **2-4 partners** | 1,111 | 20.3 |
| **5-10 partners** | 743 | 13.6 |
| **11-25 partners** | 734 | 13.4 |
| **26-80 partners** | 926 | 16.9 |
| **81+ partners** | 1,681 | 30.7 |

## Training contracts 2005-06 by region

| Region | No | % by region |
|---|---|---|
| **Central London** | 1,585 | 27.6 |
| **Rest of London** | 1,114 | 19.4 |
| **Southeast** | 427 | 7.4 |
| **Southwest** | 233 | 4 |
| **Wales** | 156 | 2.7 |
| **West Midlands** | 401 | 7 |
| **Northwest** | 673 | 11.7 |
| **Northeast** | 173 | 3 |
| **Yorkshire and Humberside** | 385 | 6.7 |
| **East Midlands** | 245 | 4.3 |
| **Eastern** | 360 | 6.3 |

## Routes to admission 1993-94 and 2005-06

| | 1993-94% | 2005-06% |
|---|---|---|
| **Law graduate** | 64.3 | 53.6 |
| **Non-law graduate** | 19.4 | 16.4 |
| **Transfers** | 16.2 | 20.3 |
| **Unknown** | 0.1 | 9.8 |

**Training contract starting salaries by region 2005-06**

| Region | Mean salary | Salary as % of minimum | % male salary greater than female |
|---|---|---|---|
| **Central London** | 27,823 | 169 | 1.2 |
| **Rest of London** | 20,626 | 140 | 3.2 |
| **Southeast** | 17,829 | 121 | -4.2 |
| **Southwest** | 16,306 | 111 | 2.7 |
| **Wales** | 15,623 | 106 | -0.5 |
| **West Midlands** | 17,370 | 118 | 3.8 |
| **Northwest** | 16,969 | 115 | 3.6 |
| **Northeast** | 15,994 | 109 | 0.7 |
| **Yorkshire and Humberside** | 17,340 | 118 | 3.6 |
| **East Midlands** | 16,583 | 113 | 2 |
| **Eastern** | 16,396 | 111 | -1 |

**Law firm salaries 2005-06**

| | | 1st year | 2nd year | On qualification |
|---|---|---|---|---|
| **London** | Large | 27,000-33,000 | 29,000-45,000 | 45,000-70,000 |
| | Medium | 23,000-30,000 | 24,000-41,000 | 43,000-64,000 |
| | Small | 16,450-20,000+ | 16,450-25,000 | Up to 35,000 |
| **International** | | 28,000-39,000 | 34,000-45,000 | Up to 96,000 |
| **Regions** | | 16,450-23,000 | Up to 25,000 | Up to 40,000 |

**BVC participation, pupillages and tenancies**

| Year | BVC applicants | BVC enrolments | BVC successful | Pupillages commenced 1 Aug - 31 July 1st six | 2nd six | Tenancies 1 Oct - 30 Sep |
|---|---|---|---|---|---|---|
| **1998-1999** | 2,696 | 1,459 | 1,238 | | | 541 |
| **1999-2000** | 2,370 | 1,487 | 1,206 | | | 511 |
| **2000-2001** | 2,252 | 1,403 | 1,082 | 695 | 700 | 535 |
| **2001-2002** | 2,119 | 1,379 | 1,188 | 700 | 724 | 541 |
| **2002-2003** | 2,067 | 1,440 | 1,121 | 698 | 702 | 698 |
| **2003-2004** | 2,570 | 1,697 | | 518 | 557 | 601 |
| **2004-2005** | 2,883 | 1,745 | | 556 | 598 | 544 |

NB. More recent data is not comprehensive enough to be included in this table

# Getting the best careers advice

They say that forewarned is forearmed, and that is never more true than if you are considering a career in law. You will need the best advice you can get, given that competition for the legal profession is fierce and the outlay is high in terms of both time and money.

And it is never too early to seek careers advice. You really do need it from the very beginning in order to be in the know about careers fairs, open days, campus presentations and crucial work placement scheme/mini-pupillage deadlines.

## Available help
We suggest that you use every resource on offer at your university/college careers service in order to be as informed as possible. Usually, resources include:
- details of law fairs with visiting firms of solicitors and postgraduate course providers, and law firm open days;
- a programme of campus visits by firms;
- workshops on applications/CVs and interview technique;
- names of people in the profession who are willing to talk to you (eg, former students who are now practising law);
- up-to-date files on employers;
- information leaflets and brochures;
- recruitment literature for firms and prospectuses for postgraduate courses;
- copies of the trade press and *The Training Contract & Pupillage Handbook* to keep you abreast of the current legal scene; and
- computer facilities offering access to dedicated recruitment websites as well as employers' own websites.

Your adviser should also be able to give you some individual help with improving your CV, written applications and interview technique (eg, assisting with mock interviews). Careers advisers may also be able to help organise work experience.

Jane Elkins, careers adviser at the University of Warwick, has this to say: "Your careers service should usually be able to offer you the following: one-to-one advice to help you decide the direction you should take and when things need to be done; practical help and advice on applications and interviews; and opportunities to meet recruiters. If you are away from campus you can usually get advice from your careers service by email or telephone. Use the extensive information available to you – it's never too early to plan your legal career."

A significant minority of students don't come to the profession straight out of full-time education. In the first instance, they should contact their local university and see if they can get careers advice under the mutual aid scheme. Most universities are happy to provide any graduate with a period of assistance – in some cases, up to three years. They may find the careers service particularly useful in terms of receiving tailored advice on ways to present previous experience to the greatest effect.

Last, but by no means least, if you have a problem that's keeping you awake in the middle of the night, simply log on to www.LawCareers.Net and click on "The Oracle". As its name suggests, this section of the website is the bearer of advice and wisdom. Check out The Oracle's back catalogue of questions (chances are, someone has been troubled by the same issue) and see if the answers apply to you. If you have an original question, feel free to email us for individual careers advice. Click on "Ask the Oracle" or email oracle@lawcareers.net.

## Common advice
### Dates and deadlines
Jane stresses the need to be clued up about on-campus events and application deadlines: "Always check the events programme at your university early on in the

academic year. You should also keep an eye on departmental calendars and events organised by student societies, as they will often arrange things independently of the careers service. This will mean that you are covering all your bases in terms of getting along to all the presentations and talks by employers on campus. If employers are not visiting your university, look out for regional and national law careers events and fairs. Also, be aware that if you want to work for a big firm of solicitors, most of them recruit two years in advance."

### Don't rush

Dick Lidwell, careers adviser at the University of Oxford, advises against panicking if you're not immediately sure which legal path you want to take: "If you're not sure whether it's a barrister or solicitor you want to be, don't rush into it. Don't postpone the issue, but do take the time to explore; you can always come into the system a bit later. There's no point applying until you know, and this is where your careers service comes in. We can help and guide you right from the beginning – don't think that you can only go and see an adviser if you already know what you want to do! Obviously, we're also there to help at the next stage of actually applying: targeting, CVs/forms and interview technique." Dick's top tips are as follows: "Demonstrate clarity in your application, be yourself at interview and be honest at all times."

### Got what it takes?

Above all, what you want most from a careers adviser can be summed up in one word – honesty. Any careers adviser worth his or her salt should make it clear that you must have the following qualities and skills (without which you are going to find getting a training contract or pupillage much more difficult):

- Academic ability – The job is intellectually rigorous and demands that you be capable of clear and lucid thought, and can process and assimilate large swathes of information. Most top-paying employers require at least a 2.1 degree and excellent A-level grades.
- Interpersonal skills – It is vital that you are able to interact with colleagues and clients alike to engender confidence, form lasting relationships and clearly explain complex situations.
- Written and verbal communication skills – We know lawyers are famed for their ability to use 20 words when five would suffice, but that is changing. Lawyers spend a large amount of their time talking to clients and drafting documents. The use of clear and succinct language is appreciated by all.
- Personal responsibility and integrity – Be true to yourself.

And don't forget that most crucial of assets: commercial awareness. Almost every recruiter we surveyed mentioned this as being important. It is not enough just to know about strict legal principles; you have to be able to apply these to the commercial context within which your clients operate. It may also be important to have a sense of regional commercial issues.

Straight from the horse's mouth, these recruiters give examples of the outstanding attributes of their recent recruits:

- Janice Singleton, practice manager of Dorset-based firm Jacobs & Reeves, says that trainees "must be adaptable, able to work using their own initiative and not concerned about putting the hours in".
- Hannah King, graduate recruitment officer at international firm Trowers & Hamlins, says they found that "long-term vision and commercial focus help a trainee adapt quickly to his or her new role".
- Victoria Cox, deputy trainee resources manager at national firm Nabarro, says she has been particularly impressed by those people with "strong interpersonal skills,

commercial acumen and an entrepreneurial approach".

Financial commitment

Finally, we're going to put on our own careers advisory hat for a minute to give you this warning: if you don't have all of the above qualities and you're considering doing the GDL/LPC/BVC without the security net of a training contract/pupillage – think very carefully. For many postgraduate institutions, money is the bottom line. Putting it bluntly, they sometimes offer GDL/LPC/BVC places to students who don't have the remotest chance of getting a training contract/pupillage.

In *The Training Contract & Pupillage Handbook* Survey of the Bar 2007, we asked graduate recruiters at chambers nationwide what they thought of the BVC and its providers. Some of their replies are unprintable! Many called for a reduction in BVC places, others suggested raising entrance standards. One summed up the feelings of the majority, stating: "Many BVC institutions consider their course a licence to print money, forcing candidates into debt. They allow in students who are unlikely to ever get an interview, let alone pupillage." All we're saying is that it is worth bearing this in mind before committing your time and funds.

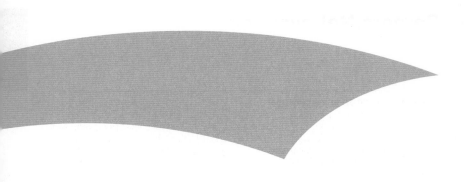

**Law Careers.Net**

*5750 training contracts*
*500 pupillages*
*8500 users every day*
*One address*
***www.LawCareers.Net***

# LawCareers.Net overview

As much as we love the feel of shiny pages hot off the printing press, we are also big fans of all things Internet! So let us introduce you to *The Training Contract & Pupillage Handbook*'s online sister, www.LawCareers.Net (LC.N). The website is the most sophisticated resource available to tomorrow's lawyers, today.

Designed to offer a one-stop guide to joining the legal profession, LC.N is relevant to candidates from their secondary education right up to the day they formally join the legal profession and beyond. On LC.N you can find vital information about what it means to be a lawyer, how to go about becoming one, where to apply and much more besides.

First things first – **LC.N Weekly** is our free email newsletter and provides high-quality, incisive information to over 18,000 happy subscribers every week. To join them, visit the site and follow the subscription instructions.

Some of the site's other key features are described below:

- **Search engine:** The site contains comprehensive directories of firms, chambers and law course providers, all searchable under a number of criteria, including size, location and type of work. There are details of around 1,000 firms, 200 chambers and 100 law course providers, and the site is the only resource with such broad scope and sophistication.
- **Exhaustive editorial:** LC.N contains information on every aspect of becoming a lawyer. Topics range from your first steps in the law to career paths and life as a solicitor or barrister.
- **Deadline calendar:** We offer an extensive list of application deadlines for training contracts and work placement schemes – a vital tool in helping to minimise the last-minute application submission scramble.
- **Immediate vacancies:** This is where firms and other organisations that need to recruit at short notice or on an ad hoc basis can advertise. Positions include those for trainees, paralegals, secretaries, voluntary case workers and more. It is constantly updated, so is a great place to check regularly if you find yourself somewhat under-employed!
- **News:** We provide an ongoing news service, highlighting key stories from the legal press and elsewhere. With you in mind, our particular emphasis is on training issues.
- **Burning Question:** This is a weekly Q&A written by a leading firm designed to get you thinking about the commercial issues that the modern lawyer must contend with, as commercial acumen is an essential quality that firms both big and small look for. Topics covered already include money laundering, the rising Chinese economy and whether VAT applies to pizza.
- **Meet the Recruiter:** Bearing in mind that the recruitment team is usually the first contact you will have with your desired firm, we have dissected that most powerful breed of legal professional – the recruiter. The resulting profiles are a great way for you to get a sense of the men and women who have the ability to welcome you to the profession with open arms or close the proverbial door in your face.
- **Trainee profiles:** Where better to find out what it's like to be a trainee than direct from the people doing it? We have interviewed over 40 current and former trainees at different firms (and are adding to this all the time) to give you a taste of how things could be if you were in their position.
- **LC.N Focus:** Each week we put at least one firm under the microscope. We analyse the various sources of information available (firms' own sites, the legal and business press, client guides and our own information) to produce an objective guide to the firms in question. We even give you a few questions to ask at interview that are designed to impress!

- **The Oracle:** We have always received requests for advice from future trainees and pupils, and decided to formalise this process in a 'problem page' format. The Oracle will help you solve all those tricky problems relating to the recruitment and training process. All letters are answered and those that raise vital issues are published in the LC.N Weekly newsletter and on the site.
- **Features:** Every fortnight we publish a new feature designed to increase your knowledge of the recruitment process or of the legal profession as a whole. Some are produced in-house, while others are written by experts from firms, chambers, universities and other organisations within the legal community.
- **Videos:** You can't really tell what life at a given firm is like until you have met the people who have lived it. Videos on LC.N allow you to do just this. Listen to individuals from all different levels at our featured firms tell the truth about their careers.
- **Podcasts:** Presentations from the LC.N Basic Training events (more on which below) are available for download and we plan on adding to this in the future.
- **Student law societies:** We provide a list of some of the many student law societies around the country. Where possible, we have added a link to the society's website so that you can gain a better insight into the focus of the society and how it functions and serves its members.
- **Diary:** Many firms travel the country to meet candidates and raise their profiles. Find out about law fairs and other events that are happening near you with our online diary.
- **Brochures:** Over 30 firms have given us their brochures to display online for your downloading pleasure! They are the first thing to look at when you want to identify which firms would be a good match for your personality and skills.
- **Deals:** We have put together a searchable database that lists thousands of deals and the firms involved. Use it to research the deals in which the firm you are targeting has been involved and you will be sure to impress at interview!
- **Book recommendations:** In this section we highlight law books that have been recommended by LC.N users. You can even click through to our friends at Amazon for an instant purchase!

## Basic Training

Now in its fifth year, LC.N's Training Contracts – Basic Training programme will once again be taking to the road, spreading vital information up and down the country (in 2007 we visited Birmingham, Bristol, Cambridge, Leeds, London, Manchester, Nottingham and Oxford). Aimed at first-year law students and penultimate-year non-law students, the skills sessions provide a thorough and robust grounding in how to secure a training contract. You arrive not knowing much about how it all works and leave armed with vital information and the beginnings of a plan of how to proceed.

Short presentations from four major law firms and a postgraduate law course provider offer advice on how the recruitment process works, the most effective ways to conduct your research, what firms are looking for and what to expect from life as a trainee. At the end, a mini-law fair gives attendees the chance to enjoy a glass of wine, nibble a sandwich, meet the guest speakers and start putting into practice what they've learnt so far!

Keep your eyes glued to LC.N for updates on the 2008 events. In fact, it's yet another reason to subscribe to **LC.N Weekly**, for this is where you will be kept posted on when and how to attend these crucial sessions.

## Awards

June 2007 saw the fourth annual LC.N Training & Recruitment Awards. The awards identify and reward those firms whose

LC<sup>N</sup>

**AWARDS
2007**

training and recruitment procedures are the best in the country. In order to uncover the best trainers and recruiters, we asked those who really know: the current crop of trainees and newly qualified solicitors. Nearly 3,000 of them responded. From these results we were able to identify the best-performing firms. And this year we added two new categories ('Best Recruiter – US Firm in the City' and 'Best Trainer – US Firm in the City') and a special Commendation for Diversity.

The winners were:

**ASHURST**
Best Recruiter – Large City Firm

**BAKER & MCKENZIE LLP**
Best Trainer – Large City Firm

**JONES DAY**
Best Recruiter – Medium City Firm

**SPEECHLY BIRCHAM LLP**
Best Trainer – Medium City Firm

**BURGES SALMON**
Best Recruiter – National/Large Regional Firm

**SHOOSMITHS**
Best Trainer – National/Large Regional Firm

**STEVENS & BOLTON LLP**
Best Recruiter – Medium Regional Firm

**THOMSON SNELL & PASSMORE**
Best Trainer – Medium Regional Firm

**PALMERS**
Best Recruiter – Small Firm

**FOLLETT STOCK**
Best Trainer – Small Firm

**CROWN PROSECUTION SERVICE**
Best Recruiter & Trainer Public Sector / In-House

**REYNOLDS PORTER CHAMBERLAIN LLP**
Best Work Placement Scheme – City Firm

**MILLS & REEVE**
Best Work Placement Scheme – Regional Firm

**SHEARMAN & STERLING LLP**
Best Recruiter – US Firm in the City

**SKADDEN, ARPS, SLATE, MEAGHER & FLOM (UK) LLP**
Best Trainer – US Firm in the City

**HERBERT SMITH LLP**
Commendation for Diversity

The following firms were also nominated:
Allen & Overy LLP
Beachcroft LLP
Berryman
Berwin Leighton Paisner LLP
Bird & Bird
Brabners Chaffe Street
Campbell Hooper Solicitors LLP
Charles Russell LLP
Clarkson Wright & Jakes
Cleary Gottlieb Steen & Hamilton LLP
Clifford Chance
Clyde & Co LLP
CMS Cameron McKenna LLP
Cobbetts LLP
Coffin Mew & Clover
Covington & Burling LLP
Debevoise & Plimpton LLP
Dickinson Dees LLP
DLA Piper UK LLP
DMH Stallard Solicitors
Dorsey & Whitney
DWF
The Endeavour Partnership LLP
Farrer & Co LLP
Fox Hayes LLP
Freeth Cartwright LLP
Freshfields Bruckhaus Deringer
Geldards LLP
George Green

Goodman Derrick LLP
Government Legal Service
Halliwells LLP
Hill Dickinson LLP
Howes Percival LLP
Hughes Paddison
Knight & Sons
Lanyon Bowdler
Latham and Watkins
Lawrence Graham LLP
Lodders
Lovells
Mace & Jones
Maples Teesdale
Mayer, Brown, Rowe & Maw LLP
McGrigors LLP
Morgan Cole
Mundays LLP
Nabarro
Olswang
Osborne Clarke
Pannone LLP
Penningtons Solicitors LLP
Powell Spencer & Partners
Pritchard Englefield
Reed Smith Richards Butler LLP
Robert Muckle
Royds
Smith Partnership
Stephenson Harwood
Taylor Wessing
Thackray Williams
Travers Smith
Vinson & Elkins RLLP
Walker Morris
Weil Gotshal & Manges
Wilsons
Withers LLP
Wragge & Co LLP
Wrigleys Solicitors LLP

Alastair Ferguson **joined Linklaters in 2006.**
You can read about his experiences on our website.

# 'So

## what's it really like?'

How is it, such a simple question can so often be avoided by employers? It's the one thing you probably want to ask – and definitely need to know. On our website we've included various features that are designed to give an honest flavour of Linklaters. There's really no substitute for the kind of exposure you get on a vacation scheme or by meeting people at campus events, but we've done our best to provide insights and information that come a close second. We hope you'll visit soon.

**What do you need to know?**
**www.linklaters.com/careers/ukgrads**

Linklaters LLP

# Linklaters

# Choosing where to apply

Don't even think about applying to a law firm or set of chambers until you've figured out your own criteria for applying and done the relevant homework. The trick isn't to apply to loads of firms aimlessly in the hope that one of them will take pity on you. Avoid being the candidate who answers the question "Why did you apply to us?" with "I couldn't get in at any of the firms I really wanted, so I thought I would apply here" – as one Leeds-based firm was told. Rather, identify the sort of organisation you want to work for and then target those that fit the bill.

## What type of law?

Many firms and chambers specialise in one or more areas of law (eg, family, banking or media). They're pretty proud of this fact and their number one complaint is when applicants fail to mention the specialism or, worse, get it entirely wrong. In other words, don't write to a firm that's known for its family law expertise telling it you want to be a banking lawyer. The head of graduate recruitment at one City firm says: "What drives me insane is when applicants talk about a practice area we don't have, for example 'your thriving media practice'! It comes across as sloppy and not well researched." A regional firm notes: "A candidate who had done a German degree told me that he was looking for a position where he could really use his German language. The problem was we are a law firm in the Midlands with no German clients. A glance at our website would have told him that. So it pays to match your comments to the firm and don't make it obvious that you've done zero research."

Think about what sort of lawyer you want to be: do you see yourself as a human rights barrister? A commercial solicitor? A criminal lawyer working in the inner city? Or something else altogether? As an example, let's say that you want to be a human rights barrister – the best way of going about the application process is as follows:

- First, find out which sets specialise in human rights law (searching www.LawCareers.Net and the legal directories at your careers centre will give you this info).
- Next, notice what's particularly special or exciting about the set and what places it apart from its rivals (look on its website to see if there's a particular line of cases or a niche area of law that its tenants are developing).
- Finally, see whether you match the criteria the set asks for from its applicants. Be realistic – if they ask for applicants with a first, you're not going to get in with a 2.2.

If you meet all the criteria and the set has grabbed your interest, you should apply. Otherwise, keep looking, using the same step-by-step approach. This approach applies for other sets, law firms and practice areas. Trust us, it's foolproof!

Those of you who don't know what sort of law you want to practise long term would be wise to focus on getting in with a firm or set that offers a well-rounded training contract/pupillage. Also focus on firms and sets that offer a variety of seats and experience, and that have a good reputation generally (scan the trade press for positive/negative coverage as well as looking at the glossy recruitment literature).

## Where do I want to work?

Once you've figured out the sort of firm you want to target, you need to consider whether you'll be happy with the location. It's no use applying to a firm in the City if you don't like London; your heart won't be in it and this will be apparent at interview.

Often, regional firms prefer applicants with local connections. This is because they'll be investing a lot of money in their trainees and, not unreasonably, they want to see a good return on their investment. In asking whether an applicant has local connections, they figure that those with ties to an area are less likely to leave for greener pastures after the training contract.

Also, regional firms want to be sure that you're not applying to them just because the London firms have passed you over. As one partner of a Yorkshire firm explains: "Does a candidate who has attended a prep school in Sussex, attended the University of Sussex and always lived in Sussex seriously expect us to believe that he or she wishes to move to Scunthorpe? There's clearly no long-term commitment and we've received the application for a training contract only because the candidate has been rejected by every practice in the Southeast."

## What sort of working environment?

Many students find it difficult to distinguish between the different types of firm. The problem is not as acute with chambers, which don't conform to a 'type' as such – all barristers are effectively self-employed and share chambers out of convenience rather than to market themselves as a certain sort of organisation. However, it is possible to do some generalising about firms and chambers, and the sort of working life they offer. We categorise them broadly as follows.

### Law firms
#### International/City/magic circle firms
Based in the City of London, these top firms are the world's major players. They handle all aspects of company and commercial law, with all the complications involved in multi-jurisdictional business. You will need to understand the workings of the global marketplace as much as you will need to be a very able lawyer. With offices throughout the world's major financial centres, you're unlikely to spend your career exclusively in the United Kingdom. You're also likely to be one of many trainees – how do you feel about the potential lack of individuality?

For a first-hand account of what it's like to be a lawyer in this type of environment, read the "Company/commercial and corporate" chapter of the "Solicitor practice areas" section in relation to Weil, Gotshal & Manges.

### National/regional firms
National and regional firms offer broad-based legal services to major clients from a number of regional commercial centres. Clients are mostly UK public and private companies, and local and public authorities, although many firms represent and advise international clients regarding their concerns in that particular region. National and regional firms also offer services to individuals. The smaller firms tend to concentrate on private client work. Your training contract will be domestic in outlook rather than European or international, with fewer trainees and potentially more responsibility early on in your career.

For a first-hand account of what it's like to be a lawyer in this type of environment, read the "Banking and finance" chapter of the "Solicitor practice areas" section in relation to Pinsent Masons.

### High street/legal aid firms
High street and legal aid firms usually act for individuals and sometimes for small private companies. Hours (and salaries) will be lower than their equivalents at other firms, but many such lawyers claim to work in the most rewarding practice area of law. The emphasis will be on teamwork, and you will most certainly get hands-on experience when it comes to marketing the firm locally and winning new clients.

For a first-hand account of what it's like to be a lawyer in this type of environment, read the "Human rights" chapter of the "Solicitor practice areas" section in relation to Hodge Jones & Allen.

### Barristers' chambers
#### Supersets
These are the barristers' sets equivalent of the magic circle. Birmingham's status as the home of the barrister superset is now firmly established, thanks to No5 Chambers (the largest set in the United Kingdom) and St Philip's Chambers; both have nearly 200 tenants. The thinking behind supersets is to keep work that is generated locally from disappearing down to London and to attract talent from the capital to the provinces. Supersets are increasingly run as state-of-the-art business practices, with multi-million pound offices, marketing arms and boards of directors taking care of administration.

#### Regional sets
According to the Bar Council, almost one-third of practising barristers work outside of London. Birmingham, Bristol, Leeds, Liverpool and Manchester are the main hubs outside London, but there are also sets in Brighton, Eastbourne and other smaller centres. While you may earn less outside of the capital, generally less expensive living costs mean that a pupil in the regions could end up better off than his or her London peers. In addition, young barristers may gain earlier exposure to more interesting cases.

For a first-hand account of what it's like to be a lawyer in this type of environment, read the "Civil" chapter of the "Bar practice areas" section in relation to Garden Court North Chambers (Manchester).

#### Niche sets
Some sets specialise in particular areas of law. Construction, IP and tax law are three such specialist areas. If you are absolutely committed to a specific practice area, then you might like to focus your energies on finding out which sets specialise in your field of interest.

For a first-hand account of what it's like to be a lawyer in this type of environment, read the "Revenue" chapter of the "Bar practice areas" section in relation to Gray's Inn Tax Chambers.

#### What other factors are important?
When considering making an application for a training contract or pupillage, you might also want to bear in mind the following factors:
- the nature of the training programme or pupillage;
- the way you'll be treated as a trainee/pupil;
- the firm or set's overall reputation in the legal market;
- any awards received (www.LawCareers.Net has a list of firms recognised for best training and recruitment);
- any impending changes such as mergers that may affect the firm or set's future;
- any financial help offered during postgraduate training;
- trainee/pupil retention rates;
- the firm or set's client base;
- the salary on offer and any benefits; and
- future opportunities and remuneration.

Many firms and chambers will hold events at your university/college campus in the nature of workshops or seminars, and/or a social occasion at which you can learn a little about their working culture. You can also view graduate recruitment videos, browse their websites, attend open days and go on work placement schemes and mini-pupillages.

Finally, let's leave you with a quick-fire checklist for easy reference:
- Type – commercial or high street?
- Size – law factory or local firm?
- Focus – highly specialist or a wide range of clients/practice areas?
- Location – London or regional?
- 'Feel' – pressured or relaxed?

# Application technique

By the time it comes to applying, you should have thoroughly researched the profession and know where it is you want to work. Wherever that is, mention why you're attracted to the firm or chambers in question (ie, the special/exciting things you've found out about it after following our advice in the previous chapter), and how your skills and qualities match what they're looking for.

Bear in mind the need to apply to a manageable number of firms or chambers. Ten well-researched and considered applications will serve you far better than 100 randomly fired-off CVs.

It goes without saying that applications should be your own work. One common law set recalls the candidate "who had provided a very good written answer, but upon discussion it became quite clear that she could never have written it!". Equally, we don't recommend getting your mum to apply on your behalf because you're enjoying a holiday in Greece, as one young man did.

## What's in a name?

Quite a lot actually. Imagine how peeved you'd be if you received a letter from a firm offering a training contract to someone else. Firms and chambers take offence when you get their name wrong. One graduate recruitment partner at a regional firm recalls one student who "sent an application and covering letter for a training contract stating that 'I would love to work at Withers'. Wrong firm!". Don't make this amateurish mistake. Equally, don't be like the applicant who admitted to one City firm, on being called for interview, that "she couldn't remember applying to us – we were not impressed!". Keep a handle on who you apply to.

## Timing

Many firms and chambers look to fill their training places two years in advance. For law students, this means applying during the summer vacation between the second and third year of your law degree. Non-law students should apply before starting the Graduate Diploma in Law (GDL).

While budding solicitors should apply directly to firms for training contracts, the recruitment process for the Bar is different. Certain applications must be made through the centralised online pupillage application system at www.pupillages.com. See "Training as a barrister" for further details.

Some smaller organisations accept applications just one year in advance. If you've left your application late or if you were unsuccessful in your first round of applications, use the "Immediate vacancies" section of www.LawCareers.Net to source up-to-date information and availability.

Many recruiters we spoke to for *The Training Contract & Pupillage Handbook* Graduate Recruiters Survey 2007 mentioned the importance of applying well before the official closing date: first, so you don't have to rush to get the application done; second, because the most popular firms may well fill their quota of trainees before the deadline.

## Getting it right

Make sure you know how the firm or chambers wants you to apply (CV and covering letter or application form?), and obtain the name of the person to whom your application should be addressed. Don't just send a CV in when the firm or chambers clearly wants you to tackle its application form.

Unless the employer's instructions state otherwise, you should send a short covering letter with the application form. A covering letter gives you the opportunity to highlight your unique selling points, provide extra information in support of your application and convey your motivation for the job. The golden rule of covering letters is to keep them brief. They should be no longer than one A4 page. The first paragraph should mention the position you're applying for, the year of entry and, if it was advertised, where you saw the vacancy.

The second paragraph should say why you want to work for the firm and what you can offer it (rather than what it can offer you).

The third (ie, final) paragraph should close on a positive note, saying you look forward to hearing from the recruiter at his or her convenience, with your mobile number and any dates on which you are not available for interview.

### Presentation
An application is usually the first contact you make with a prospective employer. Create a good impression by convincing them that you have the necessary skills, experience, qualifications and enthusiasm for the job in question.

We can't stress enough that the best applications are tailored to each individual firm or chambers. Tell a firm or set why you're choosing to apply to it rather than any of its competitors. In our survey, many recruiters again complained about applications that were littered with misspellings (one applicant somehow managed to misspell his own name) and flannel about the nature of the organisation. A head of chambers in the Southeast agreed: "We had an application recently from someone allegedly impressed by 'the ethos of our set and the fact that it had kept it touch with its roots'. Our advice? Don't write guff like that on your applications. Flattery will get you nowhere – it's just padding and it doesn't impress."

Peter Kay of the University of Nottingham has this advice: "Good applicants will make their text engaging and interesting to the reader. Avoid making claims that can't be evidenced and use plain English. You are marketing yourself, and if you want the recruiter to select you for interview then you have got to provide them with information that demonstrates that you meet their requirements."

Competition is stiff and some firms and chambers receive thousands of applications for just a few places. Whether you're applying by CV and covering letter or the firm's own application form, we have all the advice you need:

### Application forms
The content of your application should speak for itself without resorting to wacky gimmicks, flashy fonts or lurid coloured paper. Along with a CV done in the style of a lonely hearts ad, one partner in a high street firm says: "A female candidate sent an alluring photograph of herself in jeans and wearing a 'come to bed' smile." A little too intimate, we fear! We don't know whether these applicants were offered training contracts, but frankly, we doubt it.

Many students struggle with the open-ended or competency questions on application forms. These questions vary, but tend to focus on teamwork, problem solving, communication and judgement (eg, "outside of your studies, describe a situation where you have worked with a group of people to achieve a goal"). As a rule, the best answers are as significant and unique to you as possible, easy to discuss at interview and relevant to the job. Tackle the question by breaking it down into the situation or context, the task or problem faced and the outcome or result. Don't be like the student who, when asked to describe a major challenge they had faced and how they overcame it, responded "moving away from home".

Make sure you read instructions very carefully. Don't be like this candidate for a regional firm: "We ask people to list their strengths and weaknesses. One student obviously did not read the question properly and listed her strengths as being 'honest, competent and hardworking' – so far so good – but unfortunately went on to list her weaknesses as 'dishonest, incompetent and lazy'. Needless to say she was not invited for an interview."

Dick Lidwell, careers adviser at the University of Oxford, makes this point about what experience to include in your applications: "Students sometimes decide themselves what experience is relevant and only put down the legal stuff. That is a mistake – your other work experience is also relevant to firms. For example, a casual job at Sainsbury's demonstrates that you are able to work as part of a team and interact with real people. This is likely to reflect well on your ability to interact with clients. So don't be too narrow with your terms of relevance."

Don't underestimate the amount of time it takes to complete an application form (hours rather than minutes). Always read through the entire form including the small print, which may contain important instructions, and practise on a photocopy of the form first.

Small but important points to note: (i) never be tempted to include a CV with your application form and write on the application form 'See CV'; and (ii) be sure to use an envelope large enough to take the form unfolded. An uncreased form looks far better than one that refuses to lie flat.

Much of the above also applies to online application forms, especially when it comes to rereading everything, checking grammar and spelling, and spending the requisite time on answers. Plan to do them well in advance and don't leave it to the last minute on deadline day to submit. Caroline Walsh, head of graduate recruitment and trainee

development at Barlow Lyde & Gilbert LLP, discusses the firm's adoption of an online application system: "We've been really impressed with it. We were told we might suffer a drop in applications because of it, but in fact it has been the reverse. Doing it online really helps us as we can sort on screen and cut down on paperwork – we can see at a glance if that person is right for us. I was worried that people would just bash things out on screen and not pay attention, but I've been pleasantly surprised. Silly mistakes do get made, though! You must check your spelling – otherwise it just looks sloppy. Where there is a word count, make sure that you are succinct. It's all about attention to detail and presentation, which is of course what we're looking for in our future lawyers – we wouldn't send out something with mistakes in it to a client."

### CVs and covering letters

If one of your target firms requires a CV rather than its own form, use this to your advantage. Unlike application forms, a CV gives you the chance to create your own personal record of achievement in a format that you control. The end product should demonstrate that the next logical step in your career is a training contract with that particular firm.

Never write a standard CV or standard letter. 'Dear Sir or Madam' will not do. Use your letter to support your CV, not to repeat what is in it. Clarity, neatness and courtesy are all equally important. We've said it already, but we'll say it again: don't refer to a rival firm/chambers in your covering letter.

The content of your CV should comprise the following:

### Personal details

Include your name, address, telephone number and email address. Nationality and date of birth are optional.

## Education and qualifications

Set out your most recent achievements in some detail. Recruiters are more interested in how you performed in your year-end exams than how good you were at GCSE metalwork.

## Work experience/employment history

Use reverse chronological order. Include dates of work experience, including the name of the employer and the town/city they're based in (as one law firm recruiter put it, "we can't be expected to have heard of every firm in the country!"). Highlight the relevant experience you've gained. Mention any work experience, including any voluntary and seemingly less relevant jobs, as Dick advises above – for example, bar work can be sold as demonstrating your ability to work under pressure.

## Other skills and interests

Non-academic skills include leadership, teamwork, flexibility, judgement, commercial awareness, imagination, adventurousness and diligence. They are often best illustrated and reflected through cultural, social, sporting, travel, and independent activities and hobbies. But remember, the facts must ultimately support your application to become a lawyer. In particular, non-law graduates should highlight any legal work experience they have in order to prove their commitment to law.

List your qualifications and skills in areas that are not mentioned elsewhere, such as languages, computing and driving. List interests that you are involved in regularly and be ready to back them up with examples (unlike the 'keen cinemagoer' who couldn't recall the name of the last film she'd seen when asked at interview). If you've won awards in pertinent areas, such as writing or debating, mention them.

## Referees

It's standard practice to include two referees: one academic and one relating to work experience or general character. Check with your intended referees in advance that it's OK to mention them and offer to send them a copy of your application.

## 10 top tips for online apps

**At a time when everyone should be computer literate, there really is no excuse for submitting a bad application. You should approach an online form exactly as you would a paper form – take your time, carefully prepare your responses and pay attention to detail. Here are our top 10 tips for online apps:**

- Do read through the whole application form before you start, keeping a close eye on all instructions.

- Do plan where all your main boasts will be made. It would be a shame to work a slightly tangential skill or experience into one answer when you turn out to be questioned directly on the issue on the next page.

- Don't complete the form with your caps lock on except where specified. It's rude, as it looks as if you're SHOUTING.

- Do take care with the layout of your application. Consider writing the longer sections in Word and then copying the text over. Remember to check after copying, as some characters and symbols may not transfer properly (eg, bullet points).

- Do use the spell check, although not the US version, which will let annoying Americanisms through. Firms have been known to discard applications immediately on the basis of basic spelling, grammar and punctuation errors.

- Don't succumb to 'copy and paste' fatigue. This opens the door wide to calling the firm by the wrong name – recruiters' number one most hated thing.

- Don't be tempted to use email or text talk (eg, 'It wld be wkd to work 4 u'). Write in full sentences and do not abbreviate words.

- Do make sure there is some way of keeping a record of your application. Whereas previously you would have photocopied it, make sure you either save it, print it or copy it into a separate document.

- Do read through your completed application at least three times before you submit it. Boasting of your 'excellen eye for deetail' will not get you the training contract/pupillage.

- Do use a sensible email address that you will be able to access throughout the recruitment period. If you graduate in June, your university email address will be shut down, but firms will want to contact you throughout the summer.

# Interview technique

So you've taken on board all of our advice from previous chapters, submitted your applications and – hooray! – you've been invited to an interview. After five minutes of patting yourself on the back, the fears start to surface. What if I become a gibbering wreck? What do I wear? What sorts of question are they going to ask?

Never fear. It's all about transforming your 2D application persona into a 3D person. Read on to find out how best to present yourself on the day.

## Preparation

It's your application that has aroused the firm's/chambers' interest, so reread it. Try and imagine some of the things on which your interviewers might focus (eg, what you have gained from your experiences in terms of skills and personal development). Peter Kay of the University of Nottingham suggests: "Employers are interested in your past experience and achievements. No matter what you have been involved in and whatever the level (captain or team player) you can use this experience to answer their questions. All it takes is for you to understand what lies behind the question and for you to provide the appropriate information."

Read the firm's/chambers' recruitment literature and browse its website. Read the trade press, such as *The Lawyer*, *Legal Week* and *The Law Gazette*, as well as the law section of *The Times*, so that you are aware of current legal issues. If you can't face trawling through the broadsheets, log on to www.LawCareers.Net for its rolling news service. One northwest firm was less than impressed by the interviewee who "had not even a basic understanding of the law. Perhaps we should have guessed when he said that his only extracurricular activity was the Frisbee Society".

On the day itself, arrive with time to spare. Being late will be viewed as a sign of arrogance or rudeness, not confidence. Make sure you have a mobile phone and the number of the firm in case you are unavoidably detained, so you can let them know what's happening. Don't follow the example of the applicant from Leeds who turned up two hours late for an interview with a firm in London, armed with several Harrods shopping bags, or the candidate who failed to show up for an interview without explanation, then rang chambers a week later demanding to know why she hadn't heard from them.

Having done your preparatory homework and got yourself safely to the correct location, let's take a look at the sort of thing you can expect when you get there.

## Assessment days

Firms and sets are increasingly using a variety of ways to assess your suitability to be a lawyer. Selection procedures can range from a series of interviews to a day of group exercises and tests, devised to ascertain whether you have the skills and qualities for which a firm is looking. In some ways, assessment days are a bit like a mini work placement scheme – they are a chance for a firm to put you through your paces in a variety of different ways rather than just talking to you at an interview.

A typical assessment day (if there is such a thing) might include group exercises, ability tests, presentations and in-tray exercises. In a brutal twist, there may even be a cull at the lunch break where poorer performers are sent home while the remainder might have a formal panel interview in the afternoon. One recruiter mentions an incident that occurred during the chambers' assessment day: "We do a *Pop Idol*-type goodbye halfway through the day, inviting only a few to stay for lunch and second interview. We were joined at lunch one year by someone we had rejected but who could not understand the word 'goodbye'." The lesson here is to learn when to take a hint!

Remember that although they might sound intimidating, the exercises generally aren't set to trick you, but rather are intended to reveal what sort of person you are and the sort of lawyer you might become. One firm likes to test applicants' initiative by asking in a written assessment whether you know its address and phone number (the answers are on the pen you're given to write the answer!). Be your best self on the day and certainly don't let nerves get the better of you. One candidate for a northwest firm "arrived for an assessment day, realised she would have to make a presentation, turned tail and fled", according to its head of graduate recruitment.

Each firm/chambers will have its own way of going about things and with a bit of luck they will brief you properly in advance. If they don't, there's no harm in asking, but don't be too pushy as surprises might be a deliberate part of the day!

### Psychometric tests
Psychometric tests are supposedly the Holy Grail, bringing science into the recruitment equation. With employers looking for not only ability but also a candidate with an appropriate temperament and character profile, psychometric tests are designed to work this out. While they are somewhat imperfect and should always be used in conjunction with other methods, it is fair to say that they represent a useful tool for recruiters.

The key to psychometric tests is that there is no 'right' answer. Often, similar questions are asked in a number of ways. The aim is to discourage candidates from trying to guess what answer is expected and instead give a genuine picture of themselves. As such, it is hard to offer advice on how to approach them, beyond being honest. Some firms will even give an identical test immediately after the first, to ensure people are being honest – as one recruiter says: "Nobody can remember how they responded previously if they were trying to suppress their true nature!"

### Interviews
#### During
An interview is a two-way process, designed for both you and the interviewer to decide whether you meet each other's needs. Caroline Walsh, head of graduate recruitment at Barlow Lyde & Gilbert LLP, says: "Over and above good academics, when it comes to interview, the bottom line is that we're looking for someone who we would be happy to put in front of a client. That's important from day one because we don't tend to lock our trainees away! They take an active role in client functions and marketing from the beginning. When we see them at interview, we want them to have some understanding of the firm and the work we do. We also want to see that they are thinking like a commercial lawyer, so we ask a lot of scenario-based questions – for example, you're sitting next to the owner of a well-known company on the Tube; how would you sell Barlows to them?"

During the interview, you should do the following:
- Listen carefully to all questions and think for a moment before answering.
- Speak in a clear voice, and be positive and alert throughout.
- Remember your manners. One City firm recruiter mentions an interviewee who asked "whether there were any David Brent characters in the office – it might have been funny if the candidate hadn't been performing so badly".
- Be aware of your body language. Look the interviewer in the eye when speaking to

him or her, but without staring psychotically.

- If it's a panel interview, make eye contact with everyone, not just one person throughout. And do try to get people's names right – one interviewer recalls "making such an impression on the candidate that she called me David; my name is Robert!".
- Try to be relaxed and enthusiastic, without being too laid-back. One partner at a City firm recalls the candidate who swore during the interview but had no recollection of doing so: "It just goes to demonstrate that people are often oblivious to how they come across."

We mention eye contact for a reason. Judging by our graduate recruitment survey, it's an issue for many candidates. Whether you want to or not, you must make eye contact with the interviewer(s). Simply put, avoiding eye contact makes you look shifty, whereas making it projects confidence and self-assurance. One London recruiter, giving an example of how not to do an interview, recalled in horror "the candidate who spent 40 minutes staring at a speck on the wall because she just could not make eye contact with us". Equally bad was the interviewee who "listed effective communication as one of his main strengths but did not once make eye contact, rather disproving his claim".

Although there's no way of finding out the interview questions in advance, you can make an educated guess about some of them (eg, "Why do you want to work for this firm/chambers?", "Why should we offer you a training contract/pupillage?" and "Why do you want to be a solicitor/barrister?"). Prepare your answers accordingly and think about one or two clever questions to ask yourself.

We know it's hard, but do try to speak intelligently while thinking on your feet during the interview. Examples of how not to do it include: naming Victoria Beckham when asked who in the world you most admire; declaring that you don't know who Jeffrey Archer is or whether George Bush is left or rightwing; and mentioning the importance of presenting a professional appearance while sporting zebra-striped hair, a skirt with the hem hanging off, a creased jacket and scuffed shoes.

On the question of attire, matching green tights and nail varnish do not go down well with the rather staid legal profession. One regional recruiter gives this sartorial example: "One candidate arrived dressed more appropriately for nightclubbing than an interview. She wore a very orange, very short skirt and a low-cut pink top with a low-slung belt around her hips. When she stood up to leave her belt fell to the floor, leaving her face as pink as her top!"

Ask questions to which you genuinely want to know the answers – but not those for which you could have found out the answer beforehand. One northwest graduate recruitment adviser says: "As long as they don't ask a question that, had they done any research on the firm, they would have found out the answer. There are no brownie points for asking the obvious."

We asked recruiters what sort of questions would impress them. Most said anything that reflects an interest in and understanding of the commercial world, clients and their business needs, or something that demonstrates specific knowledge of the firm without merely parroting the graduate recruitment literature or the firm's/chambers' website. Paul Bennett, graduate recruitment partner at regional firm George Green, says: "We are impressed by any question that indicates thorough research of the firm. For example, 'I see you have recently acted for X in Y. What role could a trainee typically expect to play in such a transaction?'." While Hannah King, graduate recruitment officer at international firm Trowers & Hamlins, says: "One candidate asked about the developmental pattern in terms of training from newly qualified to partnership."

Some recruiters mentioned being both impressed and flummoxed by questions about why they like their job and what would make them leave!

### After

Try and end things on a positive note, shaking hands with your interviewer(s) and thanking them for their time. If you feel comfortable doing so, ask for some feedback. Ways not to end an interview? One candidate concluded by saying: "I like to try lots of things, but rarely succeed at any of them." We suspect that didn't leave a very positive impression. Another barged back into the room, interrupting another interview, to ask if the interviewers had his lost bus ticket.

As soon as you come out of the interview, it's a good idea to find somewhere quiet to sit and write down all the questions you can remember being asked. Then write down what you gave as an answer. Later, work through the questions again, this time writing out what you would have said, given time to think and no interview nerves. By taking time to reflect on the interview, you'll be making the most of the experience (whether good or bad), and preparing yourself for the next one.

### Offers

You'll hear back from most recruiters quickly. If you receive an offer, most firms will give you four weeks in which to respond. If you are certain that you want to accept, respond in writing as soon as possible. If you are unable to give a decision at the time of receiving an offer, let them know and give a date by which you should be able to give a final answer. Once you've accepted an offer, inform all other firms/chambers that have invited you for interview or that have made you an alternative offer. If no deadline is given, don't feel pressured to give an answer if you think that other offers may still be forthcoming.

Further advice appears throughout the handbook. In particular, be sure to read the profiles of individual solicitors and barristers in the practice area sections, many of whom offer their take on the application and interview process.

# How things work in Scotland and Northern Ireland

As we already have a firm handle on how things work in England and Wales, we thought it might be interesting to see how lawyers are trained in other parts of the Kingdom that is United. Here follows a brief explanation of what happens north of the border (that's Scotland to you) and over the sea (no, not France – Northern Ireland!).

## Scotland
### Undergraduate study

It is possible to study an LLB at 10 universities in Scotland. The ordinary degree takes three years, while the honours degree takes four. There are also accelerated degree options, which can be taken if you have a non-law first degree.

For those who do not wish to do an LLB, it is possible to do a three-year, pre-Diploma in Legal Practice training contract with a qualified Scottish solicitor, at the end of which you sit the Law Society of Scotland's professional exams. During the three years you must receive training in various prescribed areas.

### Vocational study

All those who intend to practise as a solicitor or advocate (the equivalent of a barrister) must sit the Diploma in Legal Practice. This is a 26-week course offered at a handful of Scottish universities. The course teaches knowledge and skills necessary for working life, with an emphasis on practical application and much of the teaching carried out by practising lawyers.

### Training
#### Solicitors

To qualify as a solicitor, individuals must complete a two-year training contract. Trainees are usually paid by the training firm as per agreed rates set by the Law Society of Scotland. Trainees must complete a logbook and have regular quarterly reviews. After six months of the contract, trainees must attend a Professional Competence Course. It is possible to be admitted as a solicitor after one year of training (especially useful if the trainee is to appear in court on behalf of clients), but normally, at the end of the two years – and provided all conditions have been met – the trainee is admitted as a fully qualified solicitor.

#### Advocates

The body that administers the Scottish Bar is the Faculty of Advocates. Currently, the process of becoming an advocate is under review. However, as things stand, having completed the diploma, a trainee advocate (or 'intrant') must undertake a 21-month period of training in a solicitors' office (as for a trainee solicitor above, although slightly shorter), followed by a nine-month period 'devilling' as an unpaid pupil to an advocate. The trainee must then pass an exam set by the Faculty of Advocates that covers written and oral advocacy. At this stage, he or she is admitted as an advocate.

Prospective students should note that a law degree from an English university will not form part of the qualification process in Scotland. Nor will a Scottish law degree be recognised by the Law Society of England and Wales as part of their qualification process. If you train in, say, Scotland, you'll have the retrain to practise in England, Wales or Northern Ireland, and the same applies for movement in the opposite direction.

For more details on this information, see www.lawscot.org.uk and www.advocates.org.uk.

## Northern Ireland
### Undergraduate study

Law degrees are offered at Queen's University Belfast and the University of Ulster in Northern Ireland. However, law degrees from a number of other institutions in England, Wales and the Republic of

Ireland are also accepted as qualifying law degrees for the purposes of passing on to the next stage.

Non-law graduates may study the two-year Bachelor of Legal Science at Queen's University Belfast and then do their apprenticeship.

### Vocational study/training

The vocational study and practical training aspects that are found separately in England, Wales and Scotland are combined in Northern Ireland. Note that both trainee solicitors and trainee barristers must study the one-year Certificate of Professional Studies at the Institute of Professional Legal Studies.

### Solicitors

Trainee solicitors must undertake a two-year 'apprenticeship' under a supervising solicitor called a 'master'. The practical component comes first, with a four-month period of office-based training. This is followed by one year studying for the certificate, followed by a further eight months of office-based work.

Yvonne Blackstock at the Law Society of Northern Ireland says: "Under the reciprocal arrangement this society has with the Law Society of England and Wales, English qualified solicitors may transfer to Northern Ireland without having to take any further qualifications or examinations. The procedure is simply to complete an application form, supply proofs asked for in the form and pay a fee of £150."

However, Scottish solicitors are required to take further examinations and a period of apprenticeship before they can be admitted in Northern Ireland.

### Barristers

Trainee barristers begin with a four-week stint working in a Citizens Advice Bureau or law centre, and one week shadowing a practising barrister. This is followed by one year studying for the certificate, followed by a further year in practice as a pupil.

For more details on this information, see www.lawsoc-ni.org and www.barlibrary.com.

# Where did it all go wrong?

As you may have already discovered, finding a training contract or pupillage involves careful planning and application. Clearly, if you are an A-grade student with a winning personality, a packed CV and a passion for the law that shines from your every pore, then finding a job should be easy enough. For everyone else, it's a case of ensuring that what you have to offer is presented as efficiently and attractively as possible, while avoiding the kind of *faux pas* that will haunt you for years after the event. Inevitably you will make mistakes but, rest assured, whatever has gone wrong for you has been trumped many times over. Here we look at some of the pitfalls encountered in the past, based on surveys of recruiters. We urge you not to reprise them!

### First impressions...

...or falling at the first hurdle. While it's important for your application to stand out from the pack, bear in mind that grabbing the interviewer's attention isn't always a good thing. You don't want your well crafted application to end up being forwarded around the firm for giggles.

One firm was dismayed to be confronted with an inspirational quote from *The Lion King* at the head of an application. A magic circle firm describes receiving an application couched entirely in (excruciating) rhyming couplets. Another City firm received a covering letter in which the applicant described himself thus: "I am the David Beckham of law, the Asian sensation, I am the artist and you are the canvas."

On a more mundane level, recruiters are adept at spotting mass applications, even if the candidate has managed to match up firm, recruitment contact and the type of work the firm does (apparently quite an achievement for many). They don't like them. Published example letters are likewise a

guide and shouldn't be copied out verbatim. You really aren't the only one that's found that wizard website, you know. Recruiters generally tire of the same letter once they've read it 20 or so times.

### Face to face

So you've made it to interview. Well done, but don't be complacent now. You can rewrite an application, but once you've got it very wrong in front of an interviewer there's not a lot you can do, so stay focused. There are three main ways that an interview can go awry on the interviewee's part: nervousness, rudeness and inappropriateness.

Lawyers are generally a sociable breed whose work involves a high degree of interaction with both colleagues and clients. This means that recruiters are looking for a modicum of social ability, confidence and grace. Nervousness at the interview is understandable, and any but the most callous interviewer will allow for this. However, nervousness shouldn't cloud common sense.

Before you go to the interview, think about your appearance. As with your application, it's best not to stand out for the wrong reasons: don't wear anything too outlandish and do check everything's done up properly!

Once in the interview room, remember all that experience you've had of sitting on – not falling off – chairs and drinking glasses of water rather than pouring them down your front. Similarly, it's best to wipe clean your specs if they've misted up (unlike one candidate who conducted his whole interview through a fog). And remember, the firm wants to interview you; if you bring your mother along it is unlikely that you, or she, will get a training contract.

Think about what you say, too; a candidate who claimed to have a lifelong love of shipping and the sea (in an application to a shipping firm) eventually revealed this 'love' amounted to a one-week family cruise 15 years previously, while the candidate who admitted to informing herself of current affairs via the tabloids (apparently she found broadsheets boring) was rather ill-advised.

There are lots of old interview chestnuts that you can expect to be asked, so have an answer ready. These include (with less than ideal answers): what is your greatest achievement? ("Stopping biting my nails.") What are your hobbies? ("Playing with my girlfriend.") What is your greatest weakness? ("I have no weaknesses.") Why do you want to become a lawyer? ("I used to be a doctor, but I'm tired of having to use my judgement.") Having something positive to say about the town or city you are in is helpful – definitely don't be like the candidate who, when asked why he wished to move to Norwich, replied: "This is Norwich?"!

It shouldn't be difficult to remember that a job interview is not the place to brush up on your speed-dating skills. One candidate who was asked if he had any questions inquired if the interviewer was free that evening. Even if you feel yourself about to make one such gaffe, it's arguably better than staying silent. A prospective barrister who had applied for a pupillage just froze when asked a simple question, despite several prompts. The silence lasted for five very long, awful minutes.

Outright rudeness will make you the stuff of legend at a firm or chambers, but won't get you a job. One City firm tells how an interview was interrupted by the candidate's ringing mobile phone (bad). The candidate answered her phone (very bad) and then asked for some privacy while she conducted her conversation (very, very, *very* bad). Another candidate, when asked why he had applied only to City firms bar the northern

firm interviewing him, replied: "You must have slipped through the net!"

Remember you're not in your living room. A Midlands practice describes a candidate who guzzled a can of fizzy drink he had been offered, belched loudly and then declared: "That stuff never agrees with me." And the interviewer certainly isn't your 'mate': especially not when you try to stretch a personal contact by saying: "I'm a great friend of your wife, you know."

### Accidental disaster

It happens. You've covered every angle, done your research, arrived hours early and while you're waiting, you manage to drop mustard on your blouse. Don't panic. Tell somebody what has happened. Don't be like the woman who walked into her interview in an inappropriate party dress for this reason, but only told the firm after the interview, or the man who arrived covered in blood from a stress-induced nosebleed and likewise gave no explanation. Pouring a cup of scalding tea into the groin of the interviewer can also be a tricky situation, as a candidate in Yorkshire discovered. As long as you apologise for any mistakes, you should be OK. One interviewee who arrived on the wrong day at the wrong time was still offered a training contract despite inconveniencing the firm.

Hopefully this chapter puts things in perspective. If you do have a rush of blood to the head and pull off something similar to the above, don't despair – just move on to the next application.

And remember, mishaps don't only happen to candidates. A recruiter in Bath conducted an interview using the wrong candidate's name throughout and then fell down the stairs while showing her out.

# Alternative careers

Nobody ever said that having a law degree condemns you to life as a lawyer – far from it, in fact! There are many alternatives to becoming a solicitor or barrister, and routes to qualification other than the standard training contract or pupillage. Employers will value the skills you have learnt through your legal training, such as the ability to research, collect and analyse large amounts of information, and to create a logical argument and reasoned conclusion from a set of facts. The ability to communicate clearly with the public and the profession alike is another sought-after skill. Discretion and a first-class memory are all highly valued in the general career market.

Read on to see if any of these alternative careers and/or routes to law tickles your fancy.

## Alternative professions
### Accountancy and taxation
Many accountancy firms recruit law students to specialise in tax work because, arguably, there are few differences between the job of a tax accountant and a tax lawyer. In addition, some large accountancy firms have launched their own law firms.

Accountancy exams are tough but the potential rewards – both professional and financial – are excellent. A move into accountancy also offers the opportunity to branch out into other careers (with positions in industry, management and consultancy). For further details of careers in accountancy, contact the Institute of Chartered Accountants in England and Wales or the Chartered Institute of Taxation (see "Useful addresses").

### Finance
Banks are keen to recruit law graduates, as are building societies, insurance companies, stockbrokers and related professions. Those who thrive in a competitive and high-pressure environment may find a financial services or City career attractive and well worth investigating. Most of the leading financial institutions offer summer work placement programmes, which are a good starting point for you to explore this as a career option.

### Civil service
There are opportunities throughout the civil service, some of which are particularly appropriate to holders of a law degree. Law graduates may wish to pursue a career in the Home Office, the Ministry of Justice, the diplomatic service or the Foreign Office. HM Revenue & Customs employs tax inspectors, and those with an ability to understand the intricacies of tax law are especially suited to such jobs. The Border & Immigration Agency also welcomes applications from candidates with a legal background. It is also worth investigating the Civil Service Fast Stream, an accelerated training scheme for graduates (www.faststream.gov.uk).

### Media
Writing about the law can be a creative way in which to use your legal knowledge. Specialist publishers occasionally advertise for law graduates or qualified lawyers to train as legal editors. There is a wide variety of potential employers, ranging from international publishing houses with large legal departments to small companies that produce legal news and features, reference works and directories. In addition, a number of international law firms have publishing departments that provide newsletters and briefings for clients.

Newspapers, and television and radio stations all employ legal correspondents. Here, an understanding of how the law works is invaluable.

## Police

Those with a keen interest in law and order may wish to consider joining the police force; opportunities abound for graduates to achieve accelerated promotion within it. For further details contact the police graduate liaison officer (see "Useful addresses").

## European Commission

The European Commission often advertises for law graduates to work in its directorates. To get a taste of what that might be like, the commission offers five-month periods of in-service training ('*stages*') for people who have recently obtained a university degree/diploma. The programme has been running for 45 years and more than 30,000 people have benefited – in fact, many of them have gone on to become European civil servants and even European commissioners! Traineeships run from 1 March and 1 October each year. For more information, contact the European Commission's London office (see "Useful addresses").

## Court reporting

Court reporters record verbatim court hearings for official transcripts of court proceedings. Increasingly, reporters use a computer-aided transcription system rather than traditional shorthand. Court reporters need not be legally qualified to enter the profession, although it is an advantage. Details of training and careers are available through the British Institute of Verbatim Reporters (see "Useful addresses").

## Conveyancing

A licensed conveyancer is a specialist property lawyer who is trained and qualified in all aspects of the law dealing with property. They advise on the transfer of ownership of property or land from one person to another and can act for buyers, sellers and lenders. They are regulated by the Council for Licensed Conveyancers (see "Useful addresses").

## Alternative qualification opportunities

### In-house lawyers

Almost 2,500 companies and non-governmental organisations employ around 7,000 lawyers to work in-house. The main characteristic of the in-house role is that lawyers deal exclusively with their employer's legal business. This close involvement enables the lawyers to develop detailed knowledge of all aspects of their employer's business and provide advice that is in tune with the employer's commercial needs. Most in-house lawyers agree that this working relationship is the most satisfying feature of such work.

Although commercial organisations are usually the main employers of in-house lawyers, an increasing number of non-profit making bodies (eg, charities and trade unions) are hiring legal advisers to work in-house. One interesting aspect of working as a lawyer within a non-profit making organisation is that many of its legal concerns relate to its own particular interests, in addition to the general laws that affect other companies.

However small, most in-house legal departments are expected to provide cost-effective, commercially attractive and legally correct solutions to problems. Common to most legal departments is a requirement to draft and maintain up-to-date standard contract documents. In-house lawyers may also be involved in planning business strategies with commercial colleagues and negotiating the terms of deals with customers or other lawyers. Other responsibilities could involve advising on the supply of goods and services, leases, mortgages, mergers and acquisitions, and cooperation agreements for research, production, distribution or marketing, as well as litigation stemming from disputes arising from any of these activities.

Ensuring the company's compliance with UK and EU law is an increasingly important part of the in-house lawyer's remit. Specialist knowledge of the law relating to the employer's business may be necessary (eg, financial services, pharmaceuticals or telecommunications). Besides a thorough and analytical approach to business and the relevant law, it is also important for in-house lawyers to have excellent communication skills, a flexible and confident attitude, an ability to work as part of a team and sound commercial awareness.

For more information contact the Law Society Commerce and Industry Group (www.cigroup.org.uk) or the Bar Association for Commerce, Finance and Industry (www.bacfi.org).

## Government Legal Service

The Government Legal Service (GLS) is the organisational name for the legal teams of about 40 central government departments, agencies and public bodies which between them employ over 2,000 qualified lawyers. The teams provide a comprehensive range of legal services to the government of the day.

The work carried out by lawyers in the GLS covers virtually all aspects of the law relating to the private sector (eg, advisory services, litigation and prosecution), as well as a wide range of specialisms (eg, company/commercial, charity, criminal, social security, land, property and trust laws). In addition, the GLS has unique responsibilities of national and international importance, including drafting subordinate legislation, instructing parliamentary counsel on primary legislation and advising ministers on policy or constitutional matters.

Jenny Underhill at the GLS Secretariat says: "The GLS is unrivalled in the opportunities it can offer those starting out in a legal career. We offer our trainees the opportunity to experience countless areas of advice, litigation and law making on a huge range of domestic and European affairs. Government lawyers are unique in that they advise not only on what the law is, but also on what it should be. The GLS recruits around 30 trainee solicitors and pupil barristers each year. The training that we provide is second to none. What many GLS trainees find attractive is that they are given a high level of responsibility at an early stage in their training/pupillage."

The GLS offers real career development and training opportunities combined with a clear grading structure that allows lawyers to progress to higher levels at a pace determined by their own performance. The GLS will pay LPC or BVC fees in full, and will provide a grant of between £5,000 and £7,000 during this year. More information on the GLS (including its work placement scheme) is available in the directory section of this book.

## Crown Prosecution Service

The Crown Prosecution Service (CPS) is the largest legal employer in England and Wales with around 2,500 lawyers who conduct criminal prosecutions on behalf of the crown.

Crown prosecutors weigh up evidence and public interest factors in all cases and decide those which should be heard by the courts. They also advise the police on matters relating to criminal cases. CPS caseworkers assist prosecutors in case management as well as attending court, dealing with post-court administration, assessing professional fees and liaising with witnesses and other organisations within the criminal justice system.

Lesley Williams, training principal at the CPS, says: "The CPS offers a varied, challenging and interesting career for those with an interest in criminal litigation. It's not just about prosecuting cases in court; but the opportunities for our lawyers to prosecute in the higher courts are greater than ever – the director of public prosecutions wants all prosecutors to aspire to higher rights (ie, up to the Crown Court) and his aim is to have as much advocacy as possible carried out in-house. This initiative, together with our work on charging and victim and witness care, is at the heart of the prosecutor's role."

Lesley adds: "We offer flexible working practices and award-winning training programmes. Our trainees receive comprehensive feedback and supervision, and we provide ongoing development opportunities for all staff through the Prosecution College. Lawyers say that they have come to us with a desire to work on the right side of justice and make a daily difference."

Applicants for the role of lawyer within the CPS must be solicitors admitted in England and Wales with a full current practising certificate, or barristers called to the English Bar who have completed pupillage. Contact the CPS directly for further details of career opportunities (see "Useful addresses").

## Law centres

For over 30 years law centres have provided an invaluable service to those in need of legal help and advice, often in deprived inner-city areas. With around 60 centres nationwide, the non-profit making service is free for clients and the centres are funded through local authorities. The nature of the work is dictated by local needs; workers are likely to need to know something about the law relating to immigration, employment, crime, and landlord and tenant. Jobs are advertised in the local and national press, and in specialist publications such as the *Legal Action Group Bulletin* or the *Law Gazette*.

Although not financially rewarding, law centre work is one of the most satisfying ways in which a lawyer can use his or her legal expertise. For more information, contact the Law Centres Federation (see "Useful addresses").

## Citizens Advice Bureau

The Citizens Advice Bureau Service is a professional national agency offering free, confidential, impartial and independent advice. In operation since 1939, the Citizens Advice Bureau provides a service similar to law centres at more than 3,000 locations throughout the United Kingdom.

Advisers can help fill out forms, write letters, negotiate on behalf of clients and represent them at courts or tribunals in matters ranging from debt and benefits to housing, employment and immigration. Most bureaux offer legal advice and some employ their own lawyers. Contact the Citizens Advice Bureau for further information (see "Useful addresses").

## Court work

Over 95% of all criminal cases are dealt with by magistrates. Her Majesty's Courts Service employs many qualified solicitors and barristers as justices' clerks. Clerks advise lay magistrates on law and procedure, and are key figures in the daily running of the courts and in the administration of justice. They also play a vital role in the management and administration of the service, organising the arrangement of court time, payment of fines and other related matters.

Stipendiary magistrates are largely chosen from practising solicitors and barristers, although it is possible for a lawyer to progress through the magistrates' courts to the circuit bench and beyond. Clerks who are interested in administration can work towards becoming a justices' chief executive, with responsibilities for

# Law **Careers.Net**

*5750 training contracts*
*500 pupillages*
*8500 users every day*
*One address*
**www.LawCareers.Net**

increasingly large groupings of magistrates' courts. Further information is available from the Magistrates' Association (see "Useful addresses").

Her Majesty's Courts Service also provides administrative support to the higher courts and tribunals. More information can be found at www.hmcourts-service.gov.uk.

### Alternative routes into law
### Paralegaling

There are opportunities to work in a law firm without completing a training contract; for example, as a paralegal or solicitor's clerk, or in some other administrative capacity. The Institute of Legal Executives (ILEX) offers a range of paralegal training, helping to make graduates more marketable and employable (see www.ilexpp.co.uk).

### ILEX legal executive

ILEX was established in 1963 with the aim of recognising the skills offered by lawyers' clerks in England and Wales. ILEX now represents over 20,000 individuals who are employed in various legal institutions in the United Kingdom, including private practice law firms, local government, and commerce and industry.

ILEX legal executives are qualified lawyers with at least five years' experience of working under the supervision of a solicitor and who have passed the ILEX exams. Their daily work is similar to that of solicitors. Depending on his or her area of specialisation, a legal executive may be called on to brief barristers, advise a party to a matrimonial dispute, draft a will or draw up documentation for the formation of a company. However, legal executives are not qualified solicitors and subsequently cannot become partners in legal practice.

Apart from some minimum qualification requirements, an introductory qualification course is provided for those who do not have the necessary grades. Special provisions are also available for mature students. Most trainee legal executives combine study for the ILEX exams (in evening classes, by day release or through a distance-learning course) with the practical experience of working in a firm, building up a client base and becoming a fee-earner.

Ray Barrowdale, press and media officer at ILEX, says: "ILEX gives people the opportunity to gain really worthwhile on-the-job experience while they are studying. Once you are at the end of your training, there is a clear career progression, from ILEX member to fellow, and then on to train as a solicitor if you want. Last year ILEX fellows were granted extended rights of audience that allow them to appear in criminal courts. This year, changes to legislation mean they can now apply to be considered for district judges, deputy district judges and tribunal chairmen appointments, which is great news for our members."

Most employers will pay for ILEX tuition and examination fees and, of course, the trainee is earning his or her living as he or she progresses. For further information contact ILEX (see "Useful addresses").

### Chartered secretaries

Chartered secretaries work as company secretaries and in other senior positions in companies, charities, local government, educational institutions and trade bodies. They are qualified in company law, accounting, corporate governance, administration, company secretarial practice and management. They are trained to deal with regulation, legislation and best practice, and to ensure effective operations. See the website of the Institute of Chartered Secretaries and Administrators at www.icsa.org.uk.

# University Law Fairs 2007-2008

| Date 07-08 | University | Notes | Contact name |
|---|---|---|---|
| 01/11/07 | Queen Mary, University of London | Queen Mary students only | Kate Reed |
| 02/11/07 | University of East Anglia | Open to all students | Marianne Bhavsar |
| 05/11/07 | University of Leeds | | Caroline Shingles |
| 08/11/07 | University of Reading | Open to all students, including those from other universities | Sally Pawlik |
| 10/11/07 | University of Oxford | Oxford students only | Susan Brand-Bui |
| 12+13/11/07 | London School of Economics | LSE students only | Jen Harris |
| 13/11/07 | University of Leicester | Non-Leicester students to obtain tickets | Rachel Beard |
| 14/11/07 | University of Liverpool | | Gill Graham |
| 15+16/11/07 | University of Bristol | Bristol and regional University students only | Michelle Carey |
| 19/11/07 | University of Newcastle upon Tyne | | Angela Smee |
| 20/11/07 | Cardiff University | | Charlotte Harris |
| 20/11/07 | University of Warwick | Warwick students only | Eleanor Davis |
| 21/11/07 | University of Birmingham | Birmingham students only | Rachel Quiney |
| 21/11/07 | University of Exeter | Exeter students only | Shirley Lovegrove |
| 22/11/07 | University of Manchester | | Jan Hewitt |
| 22/11/07 | University of Southampton | Southampton students only | Jill Elliott |
| 22/11/07 | University of Sussex | | Jocelyn Owen |
| 26+27/11/07 | University College London | UCL students only | Phil Howe |
| 26+27/11/2007 | University of Durham | Open to students from all universities | Susan Wilson |
| 28/11/07 | University of Sheffield | | Michelle Dexter |
| 15+16/01/08 | King's College London | Kings College and University of London students only | |

| Telephone | Email Address | Website |
|---|---|---|
| 020 7882 5065 | careers@qmul.ac.uk | www.admin.qmul.ac.uk |
| 01603 592483 | m.bhavsar@uea.ac.uk | www.uea.ac.uk |
| 0113 343 5293 | c.shingles@leeds.ac.uk | www.leeds.ac.uk |
| 0118 378 8359 | s.a.pawlik@reading.ac.uk | www.careers.reading.ac.uk |
| 01865 274733 | susan.brand-bui@cas.ox.ac.uk | www.ox.ac.uk |
| 020 7955 7134 | careers.events@lse.ac.uk | www.lse.ac.uk |
| 0116 252 2004 | rrb3@leicester.ac.uk | www.leicester.ac.uk |
| 0151 794 5825 | ggraham@liv.ac.uk | www.liv.ac.uk |
| 0117 928 8121 | g-r@bristol.ac.uk | www.bris.ac.uk |
| 0191 222 7768 | Angela.Smee@ncl.ac.uk | www.careers.ncl.ac.uk |
| 029 2087 4712 | harriscl5@cardiff.ac.uk | www.cf.ac.uk |
| 024 7652 3763 | eleanor.davis@warwick.ac.uk | www.warwick.ac.uk |
| 0121 414 6128 | r.j.quiney@bham.ac.uk | www.careers.bham.ac.uk |
| 01392 264418 | S.M.Lovegrove@exeter.ac.uk | www.exeter.ac.uk |
| 0161 275 2828 | jan.hewitt@manchester.ac.uk | www.man.ac.uk |
| 023 8059 2376 | jill.elliott@soton.ac.uk | www.soton.ac.uk |
| 01273 678429 | j.c.owen@sussex.ac.uk | www.sussex.ac.uk |
| 020 7866 3600 | careers.events@ucl.ac.uk | www.ucl.ac.uk |
| 0191 334 1439 | sue.wilson@durham.ac.uk | www.dur.ac.uk |
| 0114 222 0931 | m.l.dexter@sheffield.ac.uk | www.shef.ac.uk |
| 020 7848 4053 | careers@kcl.ac.uk | www.kcl.ac.uk |

# Work Experience

# Work experience

Here at *The Training Contract & Pupillage Handbook*, we like to tell it to you straight. The bottom line is that without relevant work experience, you are not going to get a training contract/pupillage.

You see, dazzling academics and personality aren't enough to satisfy recruiters in the legal profession. They also want hard evidence that you're committed to a career in law. This is for two reasons. First, they want to know that law isn't so much a passing fancy for you as a serious ambition. Second, they want your decision to be an informed one, based on your experience to date.

An ideal start to your career is to get a place on a formalised work placement scheme/mini-pupillage. You know the drill: they're run by the moneyed firms and chambers, and no expense is spared during your two weeks (they even pay you to be there!). In an ideal world, everyone who wanted a place on one of these would get one. They're the perfect foot in the door of a firm/chambers: you get to make crucial contacts and put across the real you, rather than the tongue-tied version that recruiters tend to meet at interview. However, there just aren't enough places to go round. Fear not, though, as we'll show you how to create your very own work placement.

## How do I get involved?
### Formal schemes
During the formal work placements and mini-pupillages, firms and chambers will make every effort to ensure that you get a wide range of experience and a real taste of life as one of their own. The two-week Jones Day work placement, for example, promises a chance to be involved with real legal work, to meet trainees, associates and partners, and to enjoy an array of social events. All this and you get paid as well – around £400 a week! On these sorts of scheme you're effectively becoming a trainee for two weeks, dipping your toe in the water, seeing if you like the firm and vice versa. The same goes for a good mini-pupillage, which will give you the chance to attend court and conferences with members of chambers, see barristers at their day-to-day work and get a feel for how the particular set operates. During assessed mini-pupillages, you may be asked to prepare a piece of written work in order to develop a feel for the practical application of law. Generally, you should see the two/three weeks as a time to get a feel for the work, the people and the culture, while being sure to make the best possible impression.

With any luck, your positive impression will lead to the offer of a training contract. A partner at a City firm says: "The best way to get into any firm is through its summer scheme. I think the process is like going to a dating agency, but it's very much a two-way process. It's not just about us finding the right people – it's also about the right people finding us." But can we suggest that you don't follow the lead of one work placement student at an international firm who "constantly posted his experiences with us on the satirical RollOnFriday website. Sadly, his efforts to remain nameless failed!" Equally, we think it may not be sensible to resort to violence, as one placement student did on a night out with a Newcastle firm: "The candidate picked a fight with one of our trainees on a social night during a work placement. We didn't take his application any further and he didn't ask for any feedback!"

### Work placement: case study
Daniel Natoff, a law graduate from the University of Bristol who is about to start a training contract at Norton Rose, completed a four-week placement at magic circle firm Linklaters. After a somewhat inauspicious start to proceedings following a fall down some stairs and three hours in an X-ray

department – "although I was joined by the very nice graduate recruitment woman" – Daniel spent two weeks in the firm's London office and two weeks in the Brussels office. He says: "In addition to the day-to-day research, writing and reading work, we were asked to do a project on a corporate takeover and then a group presentation in the style of a client pitch. We also attended lectures and departmental meetings, took documents to other firms (and, when in Brussels, to the European Commission building), enjoyed cake afternoons and a fortnightly Friday afternoon drinks trolley, and much more. And then there was the social side of things: we were treated to a welcome barbeque, treasure hunt, comedy club, bowling, swanky dinner, nice lunch, informal drinks – I could go on! The rule, I think, is that as long as you don't do anything overtly crazy, you should feel free to have a few drinks and a few laughs. These events are a chance to mix with people and show that you're able to socialise." It would of course be indiscreet to mention the time that Daniel was so socially able that he missed the last train home after a night out with some of his new Linklaters buddies!

Daniel has this advice to give: "Get stuck in to the work; you're not going to know what you're doing, but I was certainly made to feel that I could ask amateurish questions – people were just so kind and helpful. Also get to know the people, from your fellow schemers to the graduate recruitment team to the associates and partners. Go to as many of the social events as you can. You're trying to work out whether that firm is right for you, so make the most of your time there. The placement is a two-way process for them to impress you, as well as you to impress them. I found it extremely beneficial and really good fun." Daniel also makes the point that it takes you one step closer to a training contract, as most firms will

guarantee you an interview if you attend their work placement scheme.

*Mini-pupillage: case study*
One barrister-to-be says of his mini-pupillage experiences: "I did three different mini-pupillages at three different chambers, all of varying length. Broadly, I found myself reading different sets of papers, talking with the juniors you sit with (the QCs do say hi, although they are generally very busy), going to court, and sitting in on meetings/client conferences. We were also taken out for lunch on a couple of occasions, and at one set we had high tea every day at 4:00pm, which was extremely nice! I did have to sit a four-hour opinion-writing exercise followed by an interview for one of them. It doesn't really matter if you are there when not much is happening. It serves the purpose of opening a window into a world and getting a sense of what the daily life of a barrister is like – both the high drama and the more mundane aspects." He also notes that it is usually straightforward to apply – a polite cover letter and CV either to a barrister you have identified or the person responsible for mini-pupillages. Some large commercial sets also have separate application forms more in line with work placement applications.

Those of you who aren't lucky enough to get a place on one of the formalised programmes must be resourceful. It's not the end of the world if you don't get a place, but you will have to take the initiative and make opportunities for yourself. Try one of the following avenues.

Citizens Advice Bureau
One option is to volunteer at your local Citizens Advice Bureau (CAB). Maxine Cole, a solicitor at the Crown Prosecution Service, volunteered for about a year at the Barking and Dagenham CAB following her master's degree. She comments: "I provided advice

on housing law, landlord and tenant issues, claims for disrepair and welfare law. When it came to applying for training contracts, I was able to talk about some of my experiences at CAB – for example, when asked to discuss how I dealt with a difficult situation, I referred to an incident at the CAB involving a client with Alzheimer's. I would certainly recommend CAB work because the training was excellent: you are trained in all the areas that they expect you to advise on and in how to use their files to find information. It teaches you how to apply the law in reality, and hones your interview and advice skills."

Even a two or three-week stint at the CAB could work to your advantage. Like Maxine, you'll be able to include the experience on your CV and then talk about it at interview.

## Court work

Court work is another option. Fatim Kurji, a barrister at Birmingham superset No5 Chambers, talks about marshalling: "The point of marshalling is to spend some time with a judge to see the litigation process from a judicial perspective. I spent my time reading the skeleton arguments and papers before the court, and then watching the trial unfold. The process is immensely insightful: you quickly learn which advocacy styles are effective and which to avoid! When it came to applying for pupillages, my marshalling experience in particular helped me to answer those standard interview questions, such as 'what makes a good barrister?' I would recommend it as a good introduction into seeing how trials are run, and putting into perspective the roles of the advocates and the ultimate aim – that of persuading the judge."

## Free Representation Unit

Other options include volunteering for the Free Representation Unit (FRU), a charity that provides free legal representation to those who cannot afford it. FRU trains you to represent its clients at tribunals. Lots of barristers/solicitors look favourably on this practical experience, and it is invaluable when applying for pupillage and training contracts. Tom Croxford, a barrister at Blackstone Chambers, thinks that anyone interested in the Bar should join FRU, which he says is "a fantastic scheme that does a great public good and which should be encouraged by everybody".

The first step in volunteering is to attend an induction day for the area in which you are interested. They are usually held eight times a year, in March/April, June/July, September/October and December/January. Four of the days focus on training in employment law, the other four in social security. You can attend either employment or social security or both, depending on your level of experience. To undertake employment training, you must be at least a master's, Graduate Diploma of Law (GDL), Legal Practice Course or Bar Vocational Course student. To undertake social security training, you must be at least a final-year LLB or GDL student. Find out more about FRU at www.freerepresentationunit.org.uk or by ringing 020 7611 9555.

Sarah Curwen, formerly a trainee at Martineau Johnson, says she gained valuable practical experience in her final year working with FRU: "We handled employment disputes under supervision and I conducted a tribunal with a fellow student. That practical experience of having to stand up and present information was valuable in terms of transferring my skills to the workplace."

## Pro bono work

Many universities and postgraduate study providers operate pro bono clinics, which are a great chance to get involved in providing legal advice at the front line.

Richard de Friend, the board member responsible for pro bono work and director of College of Law London, talks about the college's schemes and the value of getting involved: "Our four main pro bono and clinical programmes comprise: (i) in-house legal advice centres offering written advice to members of the public; (ii) a tribunal representation service, which offers advice and representation to litigants before the residential property tribunals; (iii) placement clinics where students work in host organisations helping them to provide legal services to the community; and (iv) the Streetlaw programme, providing rights and responsibility awareness training for community groups. We encourage all our students to do some pro bono work – it's an opportunity to apply knowledge, skills and values in practice. It complements legal training and keeps students highly motivated – training sticks in the mind so much more when you put it into practice rather than just sitting listening in class – and helps you to recognise the importance of being a lawyer in the community. The end result is that everyone who's involved in pro bono work – from the student to the public – is a winner."

For more detail on getting involved and other schemes and clinics, see www.lawworks.org.uk.

## European Union

Graduates might also like to consider doing a *stage* at the EU institutions. The European Parliament, the Council, the European Commission, the European Court of Justice, the Social and Economic Committee, the Committee of the Regions and the European Ombudsman all organise traineeships, each lasting between three and five months. Traineeships may be paid or unpaid. For further details visit http://europa.eu/epso/working/training_en.htm.

## What else can I do?

Staying closer to home, you could send a speculative letter to local high street law firms asking to shadow a partner (or a trainee) for a few days or offer to answer the phones at a nearby legal advice centre. Court ushering at your nearest magistrates court or outdoor clerking are suggested for those unable to get on a formal mini-pupillage.

We asked graduate recruiters how non-law graduates in particular can get a foot on the ladder if they cannot get onto a formalised work placement. All said that non-law graduates should at least make the effort to research the profession, speak to solicitors/trainees about their experiences, and visit firms or attend open days. In addition, they suggest using personal contacts to obtain work experience, either in law or in a related field (eg, banking or accountancy). One recruiter for a Newcastle firm says: "I think we all know how difficult it is for students to get commercial legal experience, so I admire those who wangle it through their contacts (but not if they namedrop about it on their application form)." One recruiter talked about the non-law student candidate who was studying business management, joined his university law society and enjoyed the benefits it gave him. Best suggestion of all: write speculatively to firms for experience in some sort of support capacity (eg, legal secretarial work or paralegaling). Commercial, perhaps in-house, experience is also regarded as valuable.

Carly Butler, graduate recruitment assistant at international firm Stephenson Harwood, says in relation to work experience other than through a formal work placement: "Try and get other business experience in order to develop yourself in all areas. It's worth trying to make contact with the firm you're interested in (eg, attend a law fair or phone up the graduate recruitment team) so that your name is remembered positively. In relation to extracurricular activities, we like to see anything that demonstrates commitment and an ability to take something to a high level. Activities that show responsibility, leadership or team cooperation are also valued." Addleshaw Goddard says that in addition to the usual commercial and legal work experience, they encourage "a healthy balance between work and academics, and a range of activities outside of work, such as music, sport and culture may help your application".

Students with disabilities would do well to contact the Group for Solicitors with Disabilities. The group aims to achieve equality of opportunity for people with disabilities, whether they be qualified solicitors, trainee solicitors, law students, clients or members of the public. The group's Training Contract and Legal Education Working Party devises initiatives to assist students with disabilities in searching for training contracts. It asks firms to designate work placement places to students with disabilities and is pushing for firms to offer help in mentoring students. It collaborates with firms (including Herbert Smith in 2006) in organising open days for students with disabilities. For more details visit www.gsdnet.org.uk or write to gsd@equalability.com.

**When should I do it?**
It's never too early to start. In terms of formal schemes, law students should try to secure a placement in the summer before their final year at university at the latest; non-law students should apply during the summer following their third year. Most formal schemes last between two and three weeks. Check the directory a few pages on for the application deadlines of formalised work placements.

With regard to informal DIY experience, just get writing!

**How do I get the most out of it?**
Without a shadow of a doubt, most firms will use their formal and informal work experience schemes as part of the recruitment process. A solicitor at regional firm Freeth Cartwright says: "You can only learn so much from an application form and interview. However, a week or two spent with lawyers and support staff is the best way for both firm and student to make an informed decision about each other. Because they are so useful, I suggest you treat your applications for summer schemes as seriously as – if not more seriously than – your training contract applications."

As a result, this is your opportunity to show off your skills and charms to their very best advantage. So while there, make sure that you really do all you can to be your best possible self. That means:
• asking questions;
• showing enthusiasm and initiative;
• taking advantage of all opportunities that are offered;
• behaving professionally; and
• acting appropriately (so no getting drunk or being rude!).

Equally, if you are at a firm or chambers, you should be assessing whether it is the sort of place in which you can imagine working. If you are at one of the other voluntary schemes (eg, CAB or pro bono clinic), make sure you are taking some mental notes about how you respond to the type of work to which you are being exposed. What sparks your interest? What makes you switch off? What gives you a buzz? Don't forget it's a two-way process.

**What about afterwards?**
Send a brief letter thanking the recruiter for your placement/mini-pupillage/DIY work

experience. Add a personal touch along the lines of how you think the experience has helped you at the outset of your career and what you most enjoyed.

It may be worth jotting down some thoughts and impressions of the experience to focus your mind. This will allow you at interview to talk about how it helped in terms of your future plans and overall knowledge of the legal profession.

# LawCareers.Net
# Basic Training
## Are you ready?

*It's never too early to start
planning your career in the law.
Don't risk missing out! The
LawCareers.Net Basic Training
events will be coming to a
campus near you in early 2008.
Keep checking www.LawCareers.Net
for further information.*

# Insider reports

# ADDLESHAW GODDARD

# EAGER

**If you have the potential, we can take you as far as you want to go.**

As a fast expanding and innovative law firm, a career with Addleshaw Goddard means variety, early responsibility and exciting opportunities to develop with the firm. Training with us will mean working with top FTSE companies and other leading organisations.

But it's not just about hard work. We care about supporting our employees and maintaining a balanced culture. The proof? *The Sunday Times* and *The Times*

listing Addleshaw Goddard as one of the 'Top 100 Best Companies to Work For', and winning The Lawyer HR Award 2007 for 'Excellence in Training.' We offer quality training in each of our London, Leeds and Manchester offices.

To find out more about applying for a training contract with us and to download our innovative trainee podcasts, please visit our website:

**www.addleshawgoddard.com/graduates**

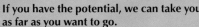

**Tessa Forge**, a Psychology graduate from the University of Manchester, attended a two-week placement scheme at Addleshaw Goddard in summer 2007. She will commence a training contract in the firm's London office in September 2009.

# Addleshaw Goddard LLP

If you are looking for a commercial firm which is open and friendly, I strongly advise the placement scheme at Addleshaw Goddard.

During these two weeks, you gain experience in two departments of your choice and you are assigned a personal supervisor for each week. The supervisor will give you a variety of work which will keep you constantly busy. Although you may be challenged by some of the work you will never feel out of your depth. You are also assigned a 'minder', who is one of the trainees. The trainee minder provides an incredible amount of support and keeps in contact with you throughout your placement.

Enormous efforts are made to enable you to experience the range of work that Addleshaw Goddard undertake. I was able to attend client meetings and conference calls, and I saw the signing of a major corporate finance deal. Court trips, case studies, workshops and client interviewing skills are also incorporated into the scheme so that a complete overview of life as a trainee is provided.

In addition, a variety of social activities are planned so that you can get to know the members of the firm on a more personal level. The go-karting evening and the trainee dinner definitely allow you to see the firm in its true colours. As well as the structured social activities for the placement students all attempts are made by your department to make you feel welcome with invitations for lunches and drinks. Addleshaw Goddard offer a variety of social activities whether it be cricket matches, table tennis tournaments or bowling, as well as encouraging your participation in their the pro-bono scheme, so you are bound to find something you want to join in with.

The firm's employees define its culture, so getting to know them on the placement scheme both in the office environment and in a more relaxed, social atmosphere allows you to get the best insight into what working at Addleshaw Goddard will be like and how you would fit in.

**No of scheme places**
75

**Location of schemes**
London, Leeds, Manchester

**Length of schemes**
1 or 2 weeks

**Remuneration (per week)**
£250 - London
£190 - Leeds/Manchester

**Dates of schemes**
Easter and June - August

**Closing date for applications**
31 January 2008

**Application procedure**
Applicants should complete our own online application form

For full contact information and details of Training Contract, see the firm's full entry in the main directory on page 343

Want to be in Star Wars? Forget it. It is illegal for ordinary UK citizens to launch space objects – let alone build Death Stars.

☐ Law *or* ☐ Non-law?

Law and business are full of surprises. Whether you are exploring the modern implications of existing laws, or working to find legal solutions to new situations, you'll need to be open-minded, creative and commercial. At Allen & Overy, we are working at the forefront of today's evolving legal landscape, helping to shape and frame the environment in which business, and life itself, is conducted.

# Outer space – out of reach?

You don't need to have studied law to become a lawyer, but business sense, curiosity and a commitment to excellence are essential.
www.allenovery.com/careeruk

Answer: Law

**Rebecca Copcutt** read Law at Exeter University. Rebecca attended a three-week summer vacation placement at Allen & Overy in 2006 and will commence her training contract with the firm in March 2009.

# Allen & Overy LLP

Selecting a training contract from the mass of law firms is not the easiest of tasks. Researching and attending presentations are certainly useful, but experiencing first hand the inner workings of any firm through a vacation scheme was, for me, priceless in helping to choose the right firm.

I chose to complete a vacation scheme with Allen & Overy for two reasons. Firstly, the firm's leading practices across the commercial spectrum and their international perspective make them instantly attractive. I was keen to see what role I could play in such a large City-based firm. Secondly, I was excited to apply the theory I was learning at university to a practical situation in an office environment.

The vacation scheme was a wonderful opportunity to experience working life in the firm and in the City. I spent time in the competition department (where the work my trainer was involved in was on the front page of the *Evening Standard* the following day!) and in Allen & Overy's leading banking department. I felt instantly welcomed and involved in both departments and enjoyed attending client meetings, completing research tasks and drafting letters. Alongside working with my trainer, I learned a great deal from my trainee buddy and worked with other 'vaccies' to prepare a presentation on one of Allen & Overy's key clients. As a result, I gained an excellent feel for the friendly and approachable atmosphere of the firm across their diverse practice areas.

Coupled with the work experience was the fun-packed social calendar which included evening boat trips along the Thames, exploring the new office location of Spitalfields, a trip to the Royal Courts of Justice and numerous suppers. I also made an effort to take part in the firm's thriving pro bono scheme.

Completing the 'hands-on' scheme at A&O left no doubt in my mind that this was the place to train. The vacation scheme offers exposure to an impressive client base and the opportunity to work with a leading firm in a friendly and professional environment where one would feel encouraged to take responsibility – and enjoy doing so.

**No of scheme places**
Approximately 120 places for Winter, Spring and Summer placements.

**Location of schemes**
London

**Length of schemes**
Winter: 10 days
Spring: 10 days
Summer: 3 weeks

**Remuneration (per week)**
£250

**Dates of schemes**
Winter:
10 - 19 December 2007
Spring:
2 April - 11 April 2008
Summer:
16 June - 4 July 2008
7 July - 25 July 2008
28 July - 15 August 2008

**Closing date for applications**
Christmas:
31 October 2007
Spring and Summer:
18 January 2008

**Application procedure**
Online application form
www.allenovery.com/careeruk

For full contact information and details of Training Contract, see the firm's full entry in the main directory on page 345

# Forget the competition

## At Ashurst we work as a team, which means less competition and more communication.

If you've got team spirit call Stephen Trowbridge, Graduate Recruitment & Development Manager, on 020 7638 1111, email gradrec@ashurst.com or visit www.ashurst.com

**Lindsey Roberts**, a Law graduate from Bristol University, completed a three-week summer placement with Ashurst in 2007. She will join the firm as a trainee solicitor in September 2009.

When deciding where to apply for a summer placement, the key factors for me were the quality of work that I would be doing as a trainee and the ability to work in a relaxing and sociable environment. Ashurst stood out as it immediately seemed to satisfy both of these criteria. As a leading international law firm, Ashurst has a diverse and impressive client list guaranteeing an equally diverse and impressive quality of work. However, it was their emphasis on recruiting well-rounded and down to earth individuals that was the major factor in putting Ashurst at the top of my application list.

On my summer scheme I had the opportunity to spend a week in three different departments: corporate, international finance and employment, incentives and pensions. The work included researching points of law, drafting documents, attending client and departmental meetings and preparing documentation for a completion. This gave me an insight into what life as an Ashurst trainee would be like. In addition, there were group projects to complete and a number of presentations that were given by solicitors about the different departments within Ashurst, the firm's pro bono activities and the secondment opportunities available.

However, I'm glad to say, it wasn't all work! There were numerous social activities including a trip to the London Eye, a game of "Ashopoly" (which involved a lot of running around London!) and the infamous "Big Night Out" on the final Friday, not to mention a fantastic day-trip to Paris to see another of the firm's offices in action. The opportunity to see the social side of Ashurst, and talk to trainees and lawyers more informally, was invaluable.

Overall, my summer scheme was a brilliant opportunity to experience what life in the legal profession would entail and provided me with the chance to see whether I would fit in with the firm's culture, both inside and outside work. I thoroughly enjoyed my time at Ashurst and all the people I came into contact with - trainees, associates and partners alike - were willing to help me and were happy to answer any of my questions. You can spend a great deal of time researching different law firms, but there is no substitute for actually being there in order to help you make up your mind. Spending three weeks at Ashurst convinced me that this is the firm I want to work for.

**No of scheme places**
90

**Location of schemes**
London

**Length of schemes**
2-3 weeks

**Remuneration (per week)**
£275 (May 2007)

**Dates of schemes**
March 2008
June - August 2008

**Closing date for applications**
31 January 2008

**Application procedure**
Online application accessed via the firm's website at www.ashurst.com

For full contact information and details of Training Contract, see the firm's full entry in the main directory on page 352

London

BAKER & M<sup>c</sup>KENZI

Baker & McKenzie in London offers unparalleled opportunities to become a first class lawyer in the world's largest global law firm.

Tel: +44 (0)20 7919 1000
Email: london.graduate.recruit@bakernet.com

# Expand your horizons

**www.ukgraduates.bakernet.com**

Baker & McKenzie LLP is an English limited liability partnership and is a member of Baker & McKenzie International, a Swiss Verein.

**Lauren Hurtley**, a Law student at King's College London, undertook an International Summer Placement with Baker & McKenzie LLP in London and Sydney in 2007.

# Baker & McKenzie LLP

I am eight weeks into a twelve-week international vacation scheme at Baker & McKenzie and am writing this report from the Sydney office with a view of the Opera House gleaming in the sunshine from my window. After spending six weeks in London I am now enjoying living in one of the world's most dynamic cities and experiencing Baker & McKenzie's international network first-hand.

I chose to apply to Baker & McKenzie for many reasons but what was most influential is the supportive culture and working environment that the firm is so well known for worldwide. Many firms offer interesting, cross-border work, but few place as much emphasis on training and development as Baker & McKenzie, as is evidenced by the firm's fourth consecutive win of the LawCareers.Net 'Best Trainer – Large City Firm Award'.

I have undertaken a fascinating range of work and feel a genuine effort has been made to make the scheme as valuable as possible. In London I was based in the corporate and IP departments and in Australia I am part of the taxation group. Highlights include attending client meetings for high-profile transactions, researching complex points of intellectual property law and reviewing key documents for associates and partners. Even more routine work such as proofreading has been interesting as it is usually of a multi-jurisdictional nature and always enables you to learn more about the firm's work and clients. Learning about the tax system in Sydney is proving to be intriguing and I am planning to visit as much of Australia as possible during my time here. I have also been able to get involved with some of the firm's pro-bono work and to see that the firm takes this seriously is encouraging in such a competitive legal marketplace.

An array of social events were organised by the London graduate recruitment team – a private film screening, a night at the Comedy Store, a City quiz, lunch at the Oxo Tower – and there were so many delicious lunches and drinks events that I quickly lost count! These are a great way to get to know other students and to meet people from all levels of the firm. In Sydney I have been treated equally well and have been given thorough induction training. At all times I have felt like a true member of the team, which reflects the high calibre and friendly attitude of the firm's people. I have really enjoyed my time here and have learnt a lot about Baker & McKenzie, made some good friends and developed firmer plans for my career and future. I would strongly advise anyone thinking of applying for a vacation scheme at Baker & McKenzie to do so.

**No of scheme places**
30 London Summer Placements
3-5 International Summer Placements

**Location of schemes**
London Summer Placement: London
International Summer Placement: London plus one of our locations overseas

**Length of schemes**
London Summer Placement: 3 weeks
International Summer Placement: 6-12 weeks

**Remuneration (per week)**
£270

**Dates of schemes**
June, July and August

**Closing date for applications**
31 January 2008

**Application procedure**
Candidates can apply online at www.ukgraduates.bakernet.com.

For full contact information and details of Training Contract, see the firm's full entry in the main directory on page 354

**Victoria Cooper**, a Jurisprudence graduate from Merton College, Oxford University, attended a two-week vacation scheme placement at Barlow Lyde & Gilbert LLP in June 2007.

Like many law students, I just didn't feel ready to start applying for vacation schemes in my second year at university. I had enough trouble trying to decide what to have for dinner, let alone trying to decide which firms to apply to from the seemingly unending list! Waiting another 12 months until I had a better idea of what I was looking for in a law firm meant I could better target my applications. However, what I hadn't banked on was being turned away by some firms even before I got to the application stage, all because I had waited an extra year. But not by BLG! There were plenty of people on my vacation scheme who, like me, had already finished finals, or had even completed the LPC. This is an indication of the welcoming and understanding nature of everyone at BLG.

BLG offered everything I was looking for in a law firm, so the decision to apply for the vacation scheme was not a difficult one; a medium-sized, but continually growing, city law firm, with a deservedly excellent reputation, quality work and top flight clients.

The two-week scheme itself was very well organised and every effort was made to ensure we all felt comfortable whilst getting to know the firm. We were given the opportunity to choose our seat a few weeks before and I opted for the commercial and technology department, one of the non-contentious departments at BLG. In addition, to increase our knowledge of the firm, we were given a presentation by a member of each department during the first week, which I found to be extremely helpful.

In terms of work on the scheme, I was assigned a trainee mentor and a supervisor to provide me with tasks over the two weeks. However, I found that I was given work to do by pretty much everyone in the department, including research for the head of department! This made me feel truly involved with the work that was happening in the CommTech department at BLG and I could see that my efforts were being put to real use. It's a crucial part of any vacation scheme to experience what life as a trainee at the firm would honestly be like and I felt that I definitely experienced this on the scheme at BLG.

Throughout my time at BLG, I was impressed by the friendly, approachable and encouraging atmosphere across the firm. Social events were well attended by trainees, associates and partners alike and I found everyone was happy to spend time answering any questions I had about the firm. Every effort was made to encourage us to get to know each other with plenty of social events, my particular favourites being softball in Regent's Park and the infamous 'Curry Night'.

I felt very settled at BLG by the end of the two weeks and was sad to leave. Little wonder that when I was offered a training contract, I couldn't wait to accept! I did another vacation scheme elsewhere, which I also enjoyed, but felt that BLG was definitely the firm for me. I enjoyed my experience of both the work and the people and can honestly say it lived up to all my expectations of the qualities which first attracted me to the firm.

**No of scheme places**
75

**Location of schemes**
London

**Length of schemes**
2 weeks

**Remuneration (per week)**
£230

**Dates of schemes**
June, July and August 2008

**Closing date for applications**
31 January 2008

**Application procedure**
Online application form

For full contact information and details of Training Contract, see the firm's full entry in the main directory on page 355

# more

emphasis on client contact
work/life balance
locations nationwide
approachable
variety of work

**Sam Rose**, a History of Art graduate from the University of London, completed a placement on the 2007 vacation placement scheme in the Bristol office of Beachcroft LLP. She will be starting her training contract with the Firm in Bristol in 2009.

# Beachcroft LLP

I decided to apply for a vacation scheme with Beachcroft whilst I was working as a researcher at a legal publishing company. Time and time again the Firm's name would come up in relation to pieces of work that I found particularly interesting and so it shot to the top of those firms that I was considering applying to for a training contract.

The vacation placement scheme lasted for a week, although it seemed much shorter as we were kept pretty busy! My time was split between the Employment and Professional Indemnity departments and my work was allocated and assessed by the trainees in those departments. I was set a range of tasks, the like of which the trainees were expected to handle on a day-to-day basis, such as writing up chronologies. This was obviously invaluable experience considering that I was applying for training contracts at the time. I was also lucky enough to accompany one of the partners in the Professional Indemnity department on a successful trip to court, which was the highlight of the week for me.

The placement also incorporated a relaxed lunch and an evening out with the current trainees, which, as well as being extremely enjoyable, allowed us to ask the trainees about the ups and downs of training with Beachcroft.

As well as giving us the opportunity to see behind the scenes, the vacation placement scheme was a chance for the firm to assess our suitability for a training contract and as a result of this our schedule was punctuated by assessments. Although taking tests is always a bit daunting I really appreciated the fact that the firm staggered them in this way, as it allowed us to approach each task as a part of a normal working day rather than having to face them in a stressful single sitting.

The week that I spent with Beachcroft was a fantastic experience. All of the staff, from the secretaries through to the partners were incredibly welcoming and the week offered an honest and enjoyable insight into working at the firm.

**No of scheme places**
28

**Location of schemes**
London, Bristol, Manchester, Leeds

**Length of schemes**
1 week

**Remuneration (per week)**
£175 (regions)
£225 (London)

**Dates of schemes**
Summer 2008

**Closing date for applications**
1 March 2008

**Application procedure**
Please visit
www.bemore.beachcroft.co.uk

For full contact information and details of Training Contract, see the firm's full entry in the main directory on page 359

**Caroline Ferrigan**, a History graduate from Durham University, participated in a two-week vacation scheme with Berwin Leighton Paisner in June 2007. He will commence a training contract with the firm in March 2007.

# Berwin Leighton Paisner LLP

Did you know that County Hall is powered by solar power? Neither did I until I went on a vacation scheme at Berwin Leighton Paisner. This was to be one of many things I found out during my two weeks with the firm. Okay, so this fact is rather irrelevant when it comes to choosing the law firm for you but it, in part, highlights the emphasis that the firm puts on taking time to enjoy yourself and get to know one another. I discovered this piece of trivia whilst taking part in a treasure hunt, one of a number of socials that the firm had organised. However, the activities didn't end there. In fact, the scheme was planned down to a tee, allowing every single student to take full advantage of the opportunities on offer, both to shine as an individual and to learn about the firm and whether it was right for them.

Striking a fine balance between spending time in departments and coming together for group activities, the scheme allowed every student to grasp what the firm is like, what its work involves and what it strives to achieve. With presentations on the past, present and future of BLP and the strengths of each of its core practice areas, the scheme could have been just a grand advertisement for BLP but there was a clear emphasis on allowing each student to find out exactly what he or she wanted to know about the firm. Something that certainly stood out for me was the way in which BLP did not shy away from allowing us to delve deeper. In fact, it was actively encouraged by giving us a significant amount of time with trainees to really find out their views and every trainee gave the same message – BLP is a great place to work.

I came away from the scheme feeling very positive about the firm. What I knew and believed about it previously had been confirmed and amplified. Whilst it is undoubtedly a large, well-established firm, it maintains a friendly, personable ethos – one that clearly encourages a warm, creative and enjoyable working environment.

**No of scheme places**
Easter: 10
Summer: 50

**Location of schemes**
London

**Length of schemes**
Easter: 1 week
Summer: 2 weeks

**Remuneration (per week)**
£250

**Dates of schemes**
Easter: March/April
Summer: Mid June to August

**Closing date for applications**
31 January 2008

**Application procedure**
Via our website
www.blplaw.com

For full contact information and details of Training Contract, see the firm's full entry in the main directory on page 362 .

# A late night at Bird & Bird

join the celebration

## BIRD & BIRD

www.twobirds.com/graduates

| Beijing | Brussels | Düsseldorf | Frankfurt | The Hague | Hong Kong | London |
|---|---|---|---|---|---|---|
| Lyon | Madrid | Milan | Munich | Paris | Rome | Stockholm |

**Luisa Zukowski**, who studied Neuroscience at Nottingham University, completed a three-week placement at Bird & Bird in Summer 2007.

I was initially attracted to Bird & Bird for several reasons. Not only did it fulfil my individual objectives as a non-law graduate but the firm also offered a broad and flexible training programme, a high standard of work, an enviable client list and a work-life balance. Having completed one of Bird & Bird's summer vacation schemes, my expectations of the firm have been confirmed and exceeded.

In contrast to other placements, Bird & Bird's scheme has a more unusual structure; students spend three weeks at the firm in one department. This allowed me to really integrate with my department, assisting many different people at all levels, and meant that I was assigned a significant amount of varied and valuable work. In addition to the departmental work, I was set a group presentation task. This involved participating in a presentation skills workshop and interviewing a range of people, from trainees to the Chief Executive, for their perspectives of the firm and the legal profession. The vacation scheme gave me an insight into working life at an international law firm.

The most impressive aspect was the balance of work and social activities. I was encouraged to take part in sporting events as well as various lunches and social drinks – including the Bird & Bird summer party – with members of the firm. This provided a great degree of exposure and gave me the opportunity to meet a variety of people in a less formal environment. It was striking how each person, whether trainee or partner, was genuinely enthusiastic about Bird & Bird and had a unified, positive perspective of their work and their colleagues. In contrast with other legal experience, I can confidently say that the supportive atmosphere and lack of barriers were extremely apparent and I was genuinely surprised by the level of interest shown in me as an individual.

My experiences at Bird & Bird have developed my confidence and proved that a career in a successful international law firm need not be daunting - it doesn't have to be 'all work and no play'.

**No of scheme places**
20

**Location of schemes**
London

**Length of schemes**
2 x 3 week schemes

**Remuneration (per week)**
£275

**Dates of schemes**
Summer 2008

**Closing date for applications**
31 January 2008

**Application procedure**
Online application

For full contact information and details of Training Contract, see the firm's full entry in the main directory on page 366

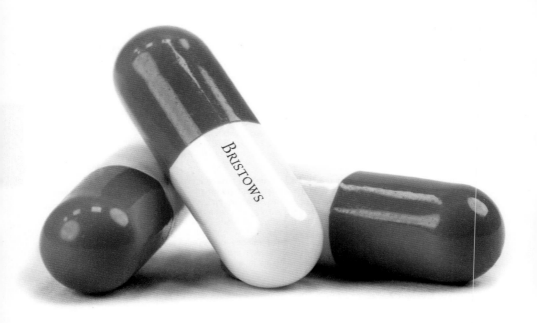

**Elizabeth Carter** studied Natural Sciences (Biological) at Cambridge and graduated with a 2.1 degree in June 2007. Elizabeth attended a placement scheme at Bristows in December 2006. She will commence her training contract with the firm in September 2009.

I was attracted to Bristows principally by its excellent reputation in intellectual property law. Its speciality in the field would guarantee me a seat in IP during my training and offer the enhanced possibility of working in IP after qualification. The placement was enlightening in this respect as we received interactive talks from partners from other departments of the firm, for example corporate and real estate, which showed me that Bristows' expertise was much wider than IP and I came out of each talk convinced I wanted to specialise in that area!

My favourite aspect of the placement was the case study. Each day, vacation students had an informative meeting with an associate to discuss a different aspect of intellectual property law. This equipped us with a sufficient understanding of the law to prepare a patent infringement case for a mock trial at the end of the week, which was very entertaining! The excellent feature of the case study was that it provided a basis from which to explore Bristows. I was sitting in the IP department during the day and was allowed to research past Bristows' case files in order to understand how to structure my argument. I was permitted to use the library or wander around to ask anyone in the firm questions if I needed help-a brilliant way to get to know people.

The friendly ethos of the firm was emphasised during an enjoyable lunch with the partners, and the value which Bristows places on achieving a work-life balance was striking. The trainees also treated us to lunch and to drinks after work-some of my most valuable question and answer sessions! Another highlight of the week was a tour of the law courts by two trainees, during which we attended a hearing to watch Bristows in action.

When I finished my placement, I really felt like part of the firm, which was testament to its extremely friendly atmosphere, a benefit of working at a medium sized firm where everyone interacts. At my subsequent interviews for a training contract, I had genuine answers to the questions, "Why law?" and, "Why Bristows?".

**No of scheme places**
24

**Location of schemes**
London

**Length of schemes**
Easter: 1 week
Summer: 2 weeks

**Remuneration (per week)**
£200

**Dates of schemes**
Easter 2008
Summer 2008

**Closing date for applications**
Easter and Summer:
28 February 2008

**Application procedure**
Application form and covering letter

For full contact information and details of Training Contract, see the firm's full entry in the main directory on page 380

# individuals required
## call us now

**Paul Olliff**, a graduate in Ancient History from the University of Nottingham, attended an open day at Browne Jacobson LLP's Nottingham office. He has recently joined the firm as a trainee.

# Browne Jacobson LLP

Browne Jacobson's consistent rating as a top five UK law firm to train with was what initially attracted me to the firm. Upon further investigation, my decision to apply was made easy. I found that they offer good responsibility at trainee level, have high quality clients and are a leading Midlands firm.

I applied for a training contract and subsequently attended an open day in the Nottingham office. Another 30 people were at the day and after an introduction to the firm, its history and core values, we participated in a group exercise. This involved building towers in teams, with a few 'land mines' thrown in to test your ability to communicate, lead and, well, build! It was a fun task which really helped to break the ice with everyone.

Next came interactive case studies, presented by Browne Jacobson trainees and solicitors. This was a great opportunity to see what type of work and responsibility you would be given as a trainee and also to find out what working within the firm would be like. Everyone came away with a feeling for how friendly Browne Jacobson people are.

At lunch the current trainees joined the group and it provided a chance to ask any small or seemingly bizarre questions which you would not feel comfortable asking a Partner. In the afternoon two trainees presented to us and told us about the departments that they were currently in. The day was then concluded by another group exercise in which we were asked to adopt the role of a department within Government and make a small presentation to the rest of the group, which is a last chance to impress with your advocacy and persuade others to agree.

When the day was over we were all invited to the pub - for an informal drink and chat with people from the firm.

The day was professional, relaxed, fun and highly informative and since starting at Browne Jacobson as a trainee I have found that it lives up to its excellent reputation and I am thoroughly enjoying it.

**No of open day places**
80

**Location of open days**
Nottingham and Birmingham

**Dates of open days**
Spring 2008

**Application procedure**
Online application form at www.brownejacobson.com/trainees.aspx

For full contact information and details of Training Contract, see the firm's full entry in the main directory on page 382

# sardines

# salmon

After a long day at work, where would you rather be? Battling through the rush hour on the tube, or sipping a drink at one of Bristol's many waterfront restaurants and bars?

And it's not just our quality of life that speaks volumes about us...

"The firm has managed to win work that other national rivals would kill for... with client wins such as EMI Group, Reuters and Coca Cola HBC, Burges Salmon has quietly built the elite firm outside London" LAWYER AWARDS.

"Work on deals of all sizes and complexity is praised as 'impeccable' by a client base that appreciates the firm's blend of technical excellence and commercial nous" LEGAL 500.

For further information, please contact our trainee solicitor recruitment team on 0117 902 2766.

www.sardinessalmon.com

**Natalie Jeffries** graduated from Oxford University with a degree in Law. She attended a two-week vacation placement with Burges Salmon and commences her training contract with the firm in 2009.

I applied for a vacation placement with Burges Salmon because the firm appeared to have the ideal mix of City-quality work, prestigious clients and an excellent reputation, with all the advantages of being based outside of London. I was therefore delighted to be offered a placement following the open day in February.

My two-week vacation placement took place in July and from the start it was an extremely positive experience. I chose to spend the first week in employment and the second in commercial disputes and construction (CDC), which gave me a really good introduction to two very different areas of the firm. Having been slightly dubious of the claims of 'real work' in the marketing literature, I was both surprised and excited to be whisked away to a meeting regarding the strategy for a client pitch within half an hour of arriving in the employment unit! I was asked to take attendance notes and this level of work and responsibility really set the tone for the rest of the placement. In CDC I experienced a wide variety of work which included attending a consultation with a QC in London, drafting a settlement agreement and accompanying a trainee to his first court application at Bristol County Court. In both departments I was treated as a valued member of the team and I really felt that my contribution mattered. Both of my supervisors were happy to answer questions and provide feedback, something I found very valuable.

Without exception, everyone I met at Burges Salmon was friendly and welcoming, and those I spoke to had a genuine interest in what I was doing. Although the atmosphere varied between departments, the balance between professionalism and good humour was consistent and the open door culture was evident throughout.

The social side of the placement proved to be just as varied and interesting and the trainees organised a fantastic two weeks of evenings out including a BBQ, pub quiz, volleyball and wine tasting. The small number of candidates (there were nine of us) meant that it was easy to get to know both the trainees and the other candidates. The social activities provided an excellent insight into the life of a trainee in Bristol with Burges Salmon.

The atmosphere at Burges Salmon can best be described as professional and friendly, with partners being just as approachable as trainees. Trainees undertake quality work and are given plenty of responsibility and are confident and highly competent as a result. Overall, I thoroughly enjoyed my time with the firm and it more than lived up to my expectations.

**No of scheme places**
40

**Location of schemes**
Bristol

**Length of schemes**
2 weeks

**Remuneration (per week)**
£250

**Dates of schemes**
23 June - 4 July 2008
7 July - 18 July 2008
21 July - 1 August 2008
4 August - 15 August 2008

**Closing date for applications**
31 January 2008

**Application procedure**
Selection incorporated into Open Day held in February. Application for Open Day places by Employer's Application Form available online via firm's website.

For full contact information and details of Training Contract, see the firm's full entry in the main directory on page 384

# What would you like for breakfast?

Waking up to something a little more exotic than toast is just one of the perks of a global network like ours. With 27 offices in 20 countries, there's a very real possibility you could spend six months of your training contract overseas. You might even qualify into one of our worldwide offices. If you're based in London, your scope will be no less international. As a trainee, the client work you'll contribute to will span countries and continents. With a whole range of vacation schemes and workshops on offer, we can give you the chance to dip a toe in the water before you make any commitment. As one of the world's most successful and respected law firms, it all comes with the territory.

Want to explore law? To find out more and apply, visit **www.cliffordchance.com/gradsuk**

Clifford Chance LLP

# C L I F F O R D
# C H A N C E

We have a global commitment to diversity, dignity and inclusiveness.

**Dawei Hu** attended the Easter vacation scheme at Clifford Chance in 2007.

For me, the vacation scheme at Clifford Chance was a good opportunity to get a feel for the direction I might take in the future. My experience was extremely positive; I really enjoyed it. I was based in Litigation and the work was so much more varied than I'd expected, including a pro bono case for a prisoner on death row in America who needed to be represented in a final appeal.

The prisoner had been charged with murder back in the 1970s. It was my job to put together a chronology of key events on the night of the murder by going through previous judgements. I was also lucky enough to attend client brunches with the prisoner's supporters.

The social side was good too – there were lots of opportunities to get to know people at events like lunches and drinks evenings. Having spoken to friends who'd been on schemes at other firms as well, the social scene at Clifford Chance came out tops.

Taking part in the vacation scheme was a big factor in deciding that Clifford Chance was the right place for me but it also works both ways. If I hadn't been on the scheme, I don't know whether I'd have been able to distinguish myself enough from all the other candidates. As it turned out I was confident about the way I felt about the firm – and really pleased to accept a training contract.

At the end of the vacation scheme I was offered the chance to do some paralegaling. I had to do my finals and dissertation at university but then returned to Clifford Chance for about a month's work in Litigation. Because of the confidential nature of the work, they wanted somebody who already been offered a training contract – but I also like to think it was thanks to feedback from my supervisor!

Starting my training contract is a long way off because I have to complete a conversion course and then the LPC. But I'm excited about becoming a trainee. If I hadn't been on the vacation scheme I'd have been nervous about what to expect, whether I'd get on with everyone, whether I'd fit the culture – but now I can't wait.

**No of scheme places**
85

**Location of schemes**
London; a number of international placements are available during the summer for those with relevant language ability.

**Length of schemes**
2-4 weeks (depending on scheme)

**Remuneration (per week)**
£270

**Dates of schemes**
Christmas, Easter and Summer

**Closing date for applications**
Christmas workshops:
16 November 2007
Easter and summer:
31 January 2008

**Application procedure**
Please complete the online application form available on our website at www.cliffordchance.com/gradsuk

For full contact information and details of Training Contract, see the firm's full entry in the main directory on page 396

# CLYDE&CO

what's the deal? why are you a lawyer? what gets you out of bed? why Clyde & Co? what should I know before I apply? what keeps you awake at night? what makes a good lawyer? got questions?

theanswers@clydeco.com

**Clyde & Co.** Major international law practice. Leaders in insurance and reinsurance, marine, aviation and transportation, international trade and energy, offering a full corporate and commercial service in these areas and businesses involved in international trade. Top clients in more than 100 countries. High-quality training. Excellent prospects on a worldwide basis ... and totally individual. For more information on a Clyde & Co training contract please visit our website at www.clydeco.com/graduate.

**Mark Frith** graduated with a History degree from Manchester University. He attended the summer vacation scheme at Clyde & Co LLP in June 2007. Mark is joining Clyde & Co LLP as a trainee solicitor in September 2009.

# Clyde & Co LLP

I had high hopes for the vacation scheme at Clyde & Co because I had read about the firm's ability to attract some of the best work whilst maintaining friendly working environment. From the first day, which included a refreshingly engaging ice-breaker, an introduction to the firm and a meet-and-greet with our supervisors and buddies, the group bonded well.

The support at Clyde & Co put me at ease. Our buddy, a current trainee, was on hand to answer any questions. My supervisor, too, took time to explain casework diligently and sometimes with the aid of unconventional props (bananas and tea cups). Sitting in the insurance department, I worked on court preparation for a major case of negligence and ensuing liability regarding asbestos contamination. I found that the variety – from researching about property insurance law to drafting letters to clients with claims at Lloyd's – and the intellectual and strategic challenges of casework meant there was never a dull moment. It was clear that the firm brought in some of the best international work. Moreover, the idea of spending some of the training contract abroad appealed.

Closer to home, the Guildford office is a city-like operation in a pleasant provincial setting. Following one of our team exercises, we left work at the office and enjoyed a BBQ in the summer sun at a pub nearby. Socialising across the firm up to the senior partner confirmed the notion of Clyde & Co. as a truly open-minded and friendly firm. Indeed, the fact that partners were keen to promote their working environment and interested in the direction of Clyde & Co. sat well with most on the scheme.

Other vacation experience I had entailed top financial-based legal work but without the sense of real responsibility and the support network in place to ensure a quality all-round training. If you are looking for some of the best international work in many fields of law with a firm culture that gives a work-life balance and training where you are not sidelined into obscurity by the photocopier, then Clyde & Co is certainly worth applying to.

**No of scheme places**
20

**Location of schemes**
London and Guildford

**Length of schemes**
2 weeks

**Remuneration (per week)**
£250

**Dates of schemes**
June and July 2008

**Closing date for applications**
31 January 2008

**Application procedure**
Online only via firm's website

For full contact information and details of Training Contract, see the firm's full entry in the main directory on page 397

C/M/S/ Cameron McKenna

**Vanessa** & **Shamila**: Both Trainee Reps, Vanessa and Shamila represent the views and concerns of their fellow trainees and work closely with Graduate Recruitment to design new initiatives. "I'm quite new to this, so Shamila is helping me understand my role and is showing me all the ropes."

# Our training & your hard work.
# A brighter future.
# www.law-now.com/gradrec

TRAINEE SOLICITOR OPPORTUNITIES WITH AN INTERNATIONAL LAW FIRM

**Great things come from great relationships**

**David Rutherford**, a Law graduate from Nottingham University, attended a two-week summer vacation placement at CMS Cameron Mckenna in 2007.

# CMS Cameron McKenna

Choosing one major international law firm over others is not an easy process at first because it depends so much on your intuition and from what you have read and heard about the firm from others. It gets easier. Once you have some of your own experience under your belt you can start to make informed decisions. In the end it was a simple choice for me. My vacation placement at CMS Cameron McKenna stood out amongst those of other firms, not only for the stimulating work in which I was involved, but also because of the people at the firm.

I spent my first week with the corporate department. I was delighted to be trusted with emailing clients on the first day. I was struck by how I was treated as part of the team, rather than 'someone who needs something to do'. My second week was in commercial litigation which I really enjoyed. I felt that the results of the research I was given were very much appreciated. My time in the departments was interspersed with presentations from trainees, associates and partners which were very useful for finding out about other areas of the firm and the experiences of others.

The social events were really good fun – and different – unless dining at Gary Rhodes' restaurant or being driven around London in an amphibious craft before being driven straight onto the Thames is something you do regularly!

Towards the end of the second week I could really see myself walking through the front doors every morning. The people I worked with had a confidence and an obvious enthusiasm for the work they were doing which is a reflection of a firm which supports and encourages those who work there. My impression of the firm after the two weeks was that it was more than a place in which to work but one with a deep appreciation of the work/life balance and a willingness to develop individual abilities in a happy work atmosphere.

If you are looking for experience in a firm with well-rounded individuals, intellectually engaging work and an excellent reputation, I would strongly recommend spending two weeks at CMS Cameron McKenna.

**No of scheme places**
60

**Location of schemes**
London

**Length of schemes**
2 weeks

**Remuneration (per week)**
£250

**Dates of schemes**
Please visit
www.law-now.com/gradrec
for further information.

**Closing date for applications**
Christmas 2007:
16 November 2007
Easter and Summer 2008:
28 February 2008

**Application procedure**
Interview with HR followed by an assessment centre

For full contact information and details of Training Contract, see the firm's full entry in the main directory on page 399

**Nell Pearce-Higgins**, an English graduate from Magdalene College, Cambridge University, attended a two-week vacation scheme at Cleary Gottlieb during Easter of 2007. She will commence her training contract with the firm in September 2009.

Having researched various different firms I was initially attracted by Cleary's long-standing position as a US firm in London, and on a practical level by the fact that the application process allowed me to apply by CV and cover letter. I found this incredibly appealing after the reams of endless boring and repetitive questions in the application forms required for vacation schemes elsewhere. Several lawyer friends had positive comments about the firm's work and people, all of which were confirmed by my own experiences during an open day and interview.

The open day was organised to be approachable to both law and non-law students. It involved a couple of group exercises in which we were introduced to some basic legal concepts and encouraged to discuss them, a talk about the history of the firm, and a short interview with a couple of partners or associates. Having interviewed elsewhere, I found Cleary's assessment and interview procedure by far the most interesting and insightful, and in fact rather enjoyable! We were given the opportunity to meet current lawyers and trainees of the firm over drinks at the end of the day, which enabled us to ask candid questions, get a real idea of the sort of people we might be working with, and get some insight into the firm as a whole. The swift response I received, with an offer of a vacation place waiting for me by the time I got home that evening, is one example of how smoothly and efficiently the whole process was conducted.

The scheme itself consisted of a neat balance between work and play. The work was varied and real, being anything from sitting in on conference calls and making notes, reading and drafting letters and documents, and researching specific legal and commercial details for different cases. The tasks we were given were occasionally daunting, but there were always people willing to be helpful and the challenging moments served to give a real sense of what it might be like to do such work on a permanent basis. As a non-law student, I had been concerned beforehand by my complete lack of legal education, but in reality I felt at no disadvantage to my peers in accomplishing what I needed to do, and I was thoroughly impressed by the brief legal education I received in the process. Daily seminars offering an introduction to different areas of practice served as useful insights into the work we were given at the time, and the responsibility and training that we would receive if we joined the firm at some stage in the future.

The scheme also incorporated a range of excellent social activities, including organised trips to the greyhound races, meals at smart restaurants, and an afternoon of archery and clay pigeon shooting in Hampshire, as well as more spontaneous lunches and trips to the pub after work. These gave the chance to meet numerous members of the firm at different levels, all of whom proved to be very friendly and welcoming, more than happy to discuss legal matters or help with queries, or simply offer interesting conversation. In comparison with other firms, I found Cleary's approach to be increasingly attractive as the scheme went on, and it became clear that the firm's lack of observed hierarchies and emphasis on intellectual vigour attracted a group of bright and interesting individuals who seemed genuinely to enjoy their work and the company of those they worked with.

I accepted a training contract with Cleary in preference to training contract offers from magic circle firms, which is the firmest demonstration of how highly I regard the firm.

**No of scheme places**
30

**Location of schemes**
London

**Length of schemes**
Easter: 2 weeks
Summer: 3 weeks

**Remuneration (per week)**
£500

**Dates of schemes**
Easter:
25 March - 4 April 2008
Summer:
30 June - 18 July 2008
28 July - 15 August 2008

**Closing date for applications**
28 January 2008

**Application procedure**
Cover letter and full CV

For full contact information and details of Training Contract, see the firm's full entry in the main directory on page 395

**Ben Sautelle-Smith**, who studied LLB Law at Exeter University, attended the vacation scheme at Covington & Burling LLP in June 2006. He will commence a training contract at the firm in September 2008.

Covington & Burling LLP is a law firm with a difference; working at the pinnacle of international legal development; but with an ethos firmly centred upon a co-operative collegiate environment. I was naturally attracted by the stellar nature of the firm's work, particularly their world-leading life sciences practice and intellectual property departments, and the relatively small trainee intake compared to other City firms.

The one-week placement embodied a broad spectrum of activities, including an individual research project, a team negotiation exercise, departmental talks, a visit to an employment tribunal, and several pre-arranged and ad hoc social events. The negotiation competition is something which I believe is unique to the firm, and is a fantastic way to gain an insight into professional practice. We were split into two teams with opposing agendas - and shrewd fictitious clients – in a corporate acquisition scenario. We spent time during the week researching and preparing our legal positions, and by Friday morning we were decidedly protective of our strategy. The negotiation itself was very exciting, with our supervisors allowing events to develop freely; for a brief hour or so we became corporate solicitors!

The individual research project provided an opportunity to produce a written piece of work; in my case a memorandum to a client concerning a topical redundancy situation. I was assigned a project supervisor who specialised in employment law. He guided me towards useful sources, and also provided feedback at the end of the week. The rest of our time was largely filled with comprehensive departmental talks, all of which proved highly informative and reassuringly informal. The life sciences presentation was a particular favourite not only because the area itself is fascinating, but also in view of Krispy Kreme donuts that were provided for the meeting!

Whilst the pre-eminent legal credentials of the firm are self-evident, perhaps more valuable is the sense of the working environment which I gained from the placement. In contrast to some of my other experiences in City and provincial firms, the people at Covington are both interesting and interested. From the continued support of the graduate recruitment team, to the fact that the managing partner deliberately took over an hour out of his schedule to speak to us personally; this is a law firm which values the individual. This was something which was consolidated at the social events, particularly the mid-week dinner and the pre-negotiation lunch.

Ultimately, my placement at Covington provided me with an invaluable insight into the firm's work and culture. Covington has a genuinely non-hierarchical and collegiate ethos. The vacation scheme is well structured and far more productive than many longer placements; a must for anyone who is interested in the firm. When the time came to leave on Friday afternoon, I had already decided that this was the firm for me and was thoroughly pleased when they offered me a training contract. Since accepting, the firm has been in regular contact and has invited me to a number of social events.

**No of scheme places**
16

**Location of schemes**
London

**Length of schemes**
1 week

**Remuneration (per week)**
£270

**Dates of schemes**
June and July

**Closing date for applications**
28 February 2008

**Application procedure**
Online application form

For full contact information and details of Training Contract, see the firm's full entry in the main directory on page 404

aspirational focused international
high profile **supportive** challenging
friendly growing award winning

# Interested?

Denton Wilde Sapte is a commercial law firm with over 700 lawyers and a network of offices in the UK, Europe, Middle East, Africa and the CIS. This gives us the scale and reach to secure some of the best instructions. With them come the best opportunities for our people. As a trainee, we'll give you as much responsibility as you can handle. You'll have direct access to partners and will work with the law – and with clients – in real business situations.

To find out more about our training contracts and vacation schemes, and how to apply, visit:
www.dentonwildesapte.com/graduates

## DentonWildeSapte...

**Anna Copeman**, a Law graduate from the University of Cambridge, attended a one-week vacation placement at Denton Wilde Sapte. She is a current trainee at the firm.

# Denton Wilde Sapte

I carried out a vacation scheme with DWS shortly after finishing my law degree. DWS attracted me because it offered the opportunity to work in a variety of strong sectors, in areas that are often merely 'corporate support' in other firms. I felt that this would allow me to experience really high quality work in numerous different departments (and would also offer me more choice on qualification!). Just as importantly, I had heard that DWS offered the all important 'work-life balance', and encouraged its employees to be well-rounded, approachable individuals.

On the vacation scheme, we spent the first couple of days doing business games and 'ice-breakers' run by different trainees and fee-earners. We also had talks from the different sectors. This enabled us to begin thinking about areas that interested us, and also meet more trainees and fee-earners. We then spent the rest of the time sitting with trainees in three different departments, but also managed to find time to have some cocktails with all the trainees on the Thursday night (and some of the other nights too)!

The vacation scheme confirmed to me that DWS was the firm for me. I really enjoyed the time spent in the three departments, and came away from the week wanting to work in all of them. Everybody in the departments made a big effort to explain to me the type of work carried out there, and really tried to get me involved. I was impressed at the strength of DWS in many different sectors, and the opportunities for trainees to experience these sectors.

While researching which firm to join, I carried out vacation schemes at four leading city firms. DWS stood out for me due to the variety of work it offered, and the friendliness of its employees. All the trainees, fee-earners and support staff I met during the placement seemed happy and enthusiastic about working at DWS. I was therefore very happy to accept an offer from DWS, and am currently really enjoying my training contract here.

**No of scheme places**
Christmas: 24
Summer: 35-40

**Location of schemes**
London

**Length of schemes**
Christmas: 1 day
Summer: 1 week

**Remuneration (per week)**
£300 (summer scheme only)

**Dates of schemes**
December 2007
June and July 2008

**Closing date for applications**
Christmas: 23 November 2007
Summer: 8 February 2008

**Application procedure**
By firm's application form available online or by request

For full contact information and details of Training Contract, see the firm's full entry in the main directory on page 415

# BE LOCAL – GO GLOBAL

**Dominic McKean** graduated with a Theology degree from Oxford University. He completed a two-week vacation placement at the Liverpool office of DLA Piper UK LLP in Summer 2007.

After a degree in theology from Oxford I thought that a career in law might enable me to deploy and further develop the skills I had learned over the previous three years. It was important to me to try to 'get a feel' for whether working for one of the best law firms in the country could help my ambition to serve and have a positive impact upon my local community. A vacation scheme at DLA Piper, a global law firm with strong local perspectives, offered me the perfect opportunity to make this assessment.

I had met one of the DLA Piper graduate recruitment team at the Oxford law fair and was greatly encouraged by what she had to say about the firm. After attending an interesting and relaxed interview for a place on their vacation scheme I was already starting to believe that this was a firm I would like to work for. However, not having previously had any experience in law I still saw the vacation scheme not only as a means to being able to gain a training contract but also as an opportunity for me to dig deeper into whether or not a career in law was in fact what I wanted to pursue. It was as much an opportunity for me to consider that big question as it was for the firm to be able to make their assessment of me.

The scheme itself lasted two weeks and every day of it increased my optimism, both about law as a career, and DLA Piper as a great place to work and keep on learning. Like all the students I was assigned to a different department in each week, which was a useful insight into the wide range of work the firm undertakes. It was especially useful to a non-law student such as myself to see the different opportunities that fall under the single broad umbrella of 'commercial' law. I spent my first week in the restructuring department, and my second working in employment, pensions & benefits. In both departments I worked closely with a solicitor, which was really helpful as they took the time and care to explain everything fully to me. Being still relatively newly qualified themselves, they appreciated how bewildering things might seem to a total novice and they went out of their way to help all the students. We were actively encouraged to ask as many questions as we wished concerning both our work and the firm itself, and the friendly atmosphere of the workplace appealed to me greatly. I was given a diverse range of tasks to do, and the two week placement gave me a thorough chance to see what life would be like as a trainee in this firm and confirmed my decision that I wanted to be a solicitor.

During the two weeks there were also organised group exercises and informative presentations from other departments, which enhanced our understanding of the multiple functions of a major law firm. The group exercises were an enjoyable means by which to get to know the other students undertaking the scheme and we had lot of fun taking part in a mock client meeting and a desert survival exercise! In addition, we spent a very interesting afternoon at the Crown Court, where we were given the opportunity to sit in on a high-profile trial.

An integral part of the two weeks was a range of social events, which were not only highly enjoyable but also gave us the opportunity to learn more about the firm at an informal level, and to get to know current employees. Such events included drinks with the partners, a dinner out with the trainees and a night out in town after our interviews. It became apparent throughout such events that DLA Piper is not only a driven and challenging place to work, but also a very friendly and sociable one. I thoroughly enjoyed my vacation scheme there, and would recommend it to anyone wanting to make up their mind about a career in law.

**No of scheme places**
200

**Location of schemes**
All UK offices (Birmingham, Edinburgh, Glasgow, Leeds, Liverpool, London, Manchester and Sheffield)

**Length of schemes**
2 weeks

**Remuneration (per week)**
£200 (Regions)
£250 (London)
(2007 figures)

**Dates of schemes**
June, July and August 2008

**Closing date for applications**
31 January 2008

**Application procedure**
Online application form

For full contact information and details of Training Contract, see the firm's full entry in the main directory on page 418

# In law there are no short cuts

*But there are fast tracks*

Eversheds is a major international law firm in the middle of an exhilarating phase of growth that will see us become a leading light on the global legal stage.

So, join us as a trainee and you are guaranteed a stimulating experience: opportunities and challenges will come thick and fast and our exceptionally talented team will involve you in diverse, high profile legal work.

We will give you the best possible start. And with good reason: by challenging and supporting our trainees in equal measures, we ensure that they stay on the fast track. Find out more by visiting our website.

www.eversheds.com

**Richard Green**, a History and Politics graduate from Exeter University, attended a one-week vacation scheme placement at Eversheds LLP. He commenced a training contract at the firm in 2007.

As I was nearing the end of my degree in History and Politics at Exeter University, I began to consider what career I wanted to follow once I graduated. I was interested in a career that would offer me a challenge, that would stimulate my mind and that would provide me job satisfaction as well as financial reward.

I came across the idea of a law conversion and decided to find out more. Following lots of research and discussions into the idea, I could see law being the career for me. Law offered an element of problem solving, where creative solutions were rewarded with the satisfaction of success. Key for me in my job was interaction, therefore knowing that an integral part of law is dealing with people, was reassuring and satisfying. So I started the Graduate Diploma in Law and half way through this I applied for places on various vacation schemes. These are run by law firms to help offer work experience for aspiring lawyers. Securing a training contract is a major achievement in a competitive market and I was very aware that the vacation scheme provided the candidate with an opportunity to make an impression on that firm and for that firm to make a more informed decision.

As I researched the different schemes I came across Eversheds. The more I read about the firm and what it had to offer, the more excited I became about their common sense approach, the drive to make the firm an enjoyable and exciting place to work, and the chance to get on board during a period of growth and improvement. Eversheds offered me a vacation scheme placement during the Easter period. It was a full weeks placement with introductory talks on all the practice groups in Eversheds, actual work experience in the various departments, social activities to meet lots of people in the firm as well as assessed pieces of work to do. I worked in the intellectual property department, where I was included in all of their meetings and discussions and felt involved from day one. I was amazed that they were able to provide the support and supervision to allow me to be involved in doing real work. It gave me a real insite into what being a trainee at Eversheds would be like.

When Eversheds offered me a contract the following week I did not hesitate. I knew it was the place for me. I had had a great experience at Eversheds and I knew that I would benefit from the training they offer and the investment that they put into their people.

**No of scheme places**
150

**Location of schemes**
All UK offices for Easter and Summer (except Newcastle and the East of England at Easter)

**Length of schemes**
Easter: 1 week (except London office scheme is 2 weeks)
Summer: 2 weeks

**Remuneration (per week)**
London £225
Other offices £175

**Dates of schemes**
Easter: April 2008
Summer: June and July 2008

**Closing date for applications**
31 January 2008

**Application procedure**
Online application form (doubles as a training contract application form) at www.eversheds.com

For full contact information and details of Training Contract, see the firm's full entry in the main directory on page 430

# FRESHFIELDS BRUCKHAUS DERINGER

# SERIOUSLY HIGH-RISE

## FEET ON THE GROUND

Freshfields is one of the world's biggest and most successful law firms. We have over 2,500 lawyers in 27 offices worldwide and are well known for handling large, complex and high-profile cases.

But it isn't the size of our deals or our impressive client list that makes us a special firm – it's our people. We have a friendly and inclusive culture in which making time for each other is important and everyone's contribution is valued. And while we take our work very seriously, we like to take ourselves less so. So if you're high on drive and ambition but down to earth, you might like to find out more.

www.freshfields.com/uktrainees

**Susan Wamanga-Wamai**, who will study the LPC at BPP Law School in London from September 2007, attended the two-week Easter vacation scheme with Freshfields Bruckhaus Deringer in 2007. She will commence a training contract with the firm in February 2009.

# Freshfields Bruckhaus Deringer

With most firms appearing to be exactly the same on the outside, the best way to find out what makes each of them unique is to do a vacation scheme. Freshfields appealed to me because of my experiences with members of the firm. I had met representatives at a law fair and was impressed by how helpful and easy to talk to they were. I was really glad when I was offered a place on the Easter Scheme.

I sat in the insolvency and restructuring team in the finance department with an associate and a trainee. A lot of the work I did was what a new trainee would do: preparing documents for clients, sitting in on meetings and a lot of research into specific legal areas. One of my 'highs' was seeing my research in an email to a client. It was good to know that the work I did was actually used.

A departmental fair was organised where trainees and associates from each department gave us an insight into the work they did. Because we spent all our time in one department, it was helpful for us to find out more about the firm's other practice areas. We also took part in a mock takeover where we were split into two groups and had to negotiate various issues. It was a great way for us to see how different departments can all be involved in the same transaction.

The social side was excellent and we had something to look forward to constantly! In addition to a comedy night, receptions and a fancy dinner, we went go-karting which was probably the highlight of the scheme (despite our bruises).

Since the placement, I have maintained that what makes Freshfields different from other firms is the people and culture of the firm. Even though everyone had a lot of work to do, they were still down to earth, relaxed and always up for a laugh, which really makes a difference at work. I had a brilliant two weeks at Freshfields, it confirmed my aspiration to be a City lawyer and showed me what I was looking for in a firm.

**No of scheme places**
100

**Location of schemes**
London

**Length of schemes**
2 weeks

**Remuneration (per week)**
£275

**Dates of schemes**
31 March - 11 April 2008
23 June - 4 July 2008
7 July - 18 July 2008
21 July - 1 August 2008
4 August - 15 August 2008

**Closing date for applications**
18 January 2008

**Application procedure**
Firm's online application form and interview

For full contact information and details of Training Contracts, see the firm's full entry in the main directory on page 445

**Jack Beech**, who is currently studying Law at the University of Leeds, attended a two-week vacation placement in the Manchester office of Halliwells LLP in July 2007.

# Halliwells LLP

I completed the placement scheme in the summer of 2007 at Halliwells' Manchester office just after my second year exams had finished. I was very lucky to be accepted by Halliwells because I knew its placement scheme was a very popular choice. This is because Halliwells is one of the biggest regional firms in Manchester and is one of the fastest developing legal practices in the UK outside of the Magic Circle. For me, Halliwells offered the chance of working in several specialised commercial services in the areas of law in which I have an interest.

During my two-week placement I was made to feel very welcome by all the staff, especially the trainees with whom I worked the closest. I found all the trainees to be very helpful and patient and more than happy to give their opinions of the firm. The trainees organised social evenings which were very entertaining and gave me a better chance to talk to the trainees openly and honestly, ask any important questions that I did not want to ask in the office and find out more about the trainees' daily routines and work.

Over the two weeks, I had the opportunity to work in four different departments within the firm. I was allocated two departments that I would not have chosen had I been given the choice. However, I did enjoy these departments and the experiences gained opened my eyes to new possibilities which will no doubt benefit me in the future.

Having completed two placement schemes before going to Halliwells I was in a good position to compare the differences between the firms. I found that the Halliwells' scheme proved to have the best balance between an in depth insight into individual departments and a broad overview of the firm as a whole. This allowed me to make a more informed decision about the firm and with regard to pursuing a career as a solicitor.

I would definitely recommend Halliwells' placement scheme to any other student in search of an accomplished law firm.

**No of scheme places**
63

**Location of schemes**
Manchester, Liverpool & London

**Length of schemes**
2 weeks x 3 blocks

**Remuneration (per week)**
£210

**Dates of schemes**
Summer 2008

**Closing date for applications**
29 February 2008

**Application procedure**
Online via
www.halliwells.com

For full contact information and details of Training Contract, see the firm's full entry in the main directory on page 458

# Financial odyssey.

**From Ireland to Africa via London and the British Virgin Islands. Tullow Oil's record-breaking reserve base financing deal was a voyage of discovery.**

Join us and make your own headlines.

Get the full story on our training programme and vacation schemes by requesting a brochure from the graduate recruitment team on 020 7374 8000 or graduate.recruitment@herbertsmith.com or visit our website at

**www.herbertsmith.com**

## Herbert Smith

**Maeve Lynch** studies Genetics at Queen Mary, University of London. She attended a vacation scheme in Spring 2007 and will be joining Herbert Smith LLP to start her training contract in September 2009.

# Herbert Smith LLP

Attracted by the prospect of a highly reputable firm that excels across the board, I applied for a vacation scheme at Herbert Smith. Right from the start, I was impressed by the interview process, which tested my aptitude for a legal career in a challenging, yet informal and friendly manner. Prior to commencing the vacation scheme, the graduate recruitment department was extremely helpful and always readily available if I had any queries.

Having expressed an interest in the intellectual property department, I was fortunate to spend the first week there. I gained an insight into previous cases the firm had been involved with and I was asked to undertake some research and attend client meetings. I sat with a partner and therefore gained a realistic insight into the work of a City lawyer. The idea of sitting with a partner was initially quite intimidating. However, I soon found out that I had nothing to worry about and there is no such thing as a stupid question! Additional support was provided in the form of a mentor and a trainee who both helped me to fit in well. I spent a second enjoyable week in the litigation division and despite the fact that it was quite busy, people always took the time to answer questions and take an interest in me. Again, I familiarised myself with past cases, undertook research and even attended a meeting with a top City barrister!

Both weeks were interspersed with seminars about different departments in the law firm that provided ample opportunities to ask questions. The seminars also afforded us an opportunity to meet with our fellow vacation scheme students every so often, and this regular contact provided yet another layer of support. In addition, a trip to the Royal Courts of Justice was both fun and insightful and some people got the opportunity to attend a pro bono legal advice centre.

Of course, some of the highlights of the vacation scheme were provided in the form of social events and included a trip to a comedy club, bowling, dinners and drinks. Many of the events were attended by trainees, giving us an opportunity to ask those probing questions that everybody wants to ask! These events were thoroughly enjoyable and allowed us to bond as a group. As a result, I now consider many of my fellow vacation scheme students to be firm friends.

Overall, I was thoroughly impressed by the calibre of the people at Herbert Smith. Everybody was extremely hospitable and down to earth. The vacation scheme was a great way to get to know the firm thoroughly and I can safely say that having spent time at Herbert Smith, I am safe in the knowledge that it is the firm for me.

**No of scheme places**
130

**Location of schemes**
London and some overseas opportunities

**Length of schemes**
2 weeks

**Remuneration (per week)**
£250

**Dates of schemes**
Winter 2007 (non-law only):
3-14 December 2007
Spring 2008:
31 March - 11 April 2008
Summer 2008:
16 June - 27 June 2008
7 July - 18 July 2008
28 July - 8 August 2008

**Closing date for applications**
Winter:
12 November 2007
Spring and Summer:
31 January 2008

**Application procedure**
Winter:
Online employer application form
Spring and Summer:
Online employer application form, case study and partner interview

For full contact information and details of Training Contracts, see the firm's full entry in the main directory on page 467

**James Emberton** attended a one-week vacation placement at Howes Percival LLP in the summer of 2005. He will commence a training contract with the firm in September 2007.

# Howes Percival LLP

As one of the regions largest firms I had already heard of Howes Percival before I applied but it was the recommendation of a friend who had enjoyed so much completing a vacation scheme the summer previously that was my reason for applying.

Having completed three other week long schemes with other firms I was not looking forward to another week of me and ten other candidates being told how good that firm was whilst watching yet another partner give me what seemed like another piece of homework, rather than allowing me to help them with their actual work. It was with this attitude that I began the week and was this attitude that was so completely obliterated during my week at Howes Percival.

Rather than being one of many candidates that the partners clearly could not find enough work for, I was the only one there. Plus, rather than one week of ten candidates, Howes Percival had one candidate per week for the summer, thus allowing the partners they worked under to actually explain and seek participation from the placement student in ongoing cases.

This hands-on approach really made me feel welcome. I got a real insight into the working life at a law firm. My planned timetable for the week was scrapped after the Wednesday so that I could continue to assist a partner with the preparation for a big case that had taken an unexpected twist. The work wasn't sugar coated though, it was an international client and some of the tasks we did were laborious but knowing that I was contributing to such a large case gave me a feeling of belonging. It was the staff that really made you feel welcome though. On one task I worked with the partner, a trainee and a secretary all together. There was never a feeling of 'them and us' that is glaringly prevalent in other firms I had been to.

The staff were genuinely interested in having you there with them. The office operated an open door policy and all the staff, whilst clearly dedicated to their work, were friendly and open.

Having spent a week seeing what life in a law firm was really like, and that it could be so intimate and friendly despite the size, I knew that Howes Percival was the place I wanted to do a training contract.

**No of scheme places**
48

**Location of schemes**
Leicester, Milton Keynes, Northampton, Norwich

**Length of schemes**
1 week

**Remuneration (per week)**
£120

**Dates of schemes**
June, July and August

**Closing date for applications**
30 April 2008

**Application procedure**
CV and covering letter

For full contact information and details of Training Contract, see the firm's full entry in the main directory on page 478

"I THINK MOST
OF MY FRIENDS
ARE ENVIOUS
THAT I HAVE MY
OWN OFFICE."

BEN

TRAINEE

AT JONES DAY YOU GET YOUR OWN OFFICE
FROM DAY ONE, WITH GREATER RESPONSIBILITY
AND INDEPENDENCE. TO GO BEHIND THE
SCENES OF A MAJOR GLOBAL LAW FIRM, WITH
A DIFFERENT APPROACH TO TRAINING, VISIT
WWW.JONESDAYLONDON.COM/RECRUIT/

**Adam Callaghan**, a graduate in Government from the London School of Economics, attended a two-week vacation placement at Jones Day in December 2006.

Having decided to pursue a career as a solicitor, the search began for a firm whose work would keep me constantly stimulated and motivated. First impressions matter; an imperative even more pronounced in a profession where there is seemingly so little to distinguish between the workings and remits of the city law firms. Having examined the literature, it struck me that Jones Day could be the 'elusive' firm I was looking for. Indeed a unique non-rotational training contract, with an emphasis on early responsibility, flexibility and individuality which also enables trainees to make a real contribution to the success of the firm, certainly made this a firm with a difference. The placement scheme seemed like the perfect opportunity to get some real experience of the profession I hoped to enter and, importantly, to gain an insight into what working for the firm was actually like.

The scheme, in essence, mirrors a Jones Day training contract and the emphasis is very much on undertaking real work rather than attending seminars or carrying out mundane tasks. Like trainees, placement scheme students are encouraged to find work by introducing themselves to trainees, associates and partners. As such there is an opportunity to gain exposure to all the firm's practice areas and the type of work central to them. The work placement is also a great way to meet a wide variety of people and learn their experiences of the firm. What really struck me was that every door was, quite literally, open and everybody was receptive to questions and approachable, whether trainee or partner. Almost immediately I felt like part of the team and it is certainly a nice feeling to be stopped several times on the way to your office in the morning by people asking how it is going!

The work I undertook not only gave me experience across a range of practice areas but was also varied and interesting. I attended client meetings, drafted letters and carried out the legal research necessary for certain deals. I was shocked by how much the work I did actually mattered and how valued my contribution was. I even attended a drinks reception at the German Embassy with an associate which, given my limited linguistic abilities, is demonstrative of the amount of trust the firm have in you!

Placement students are also encouraged to participate in the social life of the firm and an array of events were arranged including trips to the pub (one of which was to celebrate a trainee's birthday!) and some exquisite organised dinners. The ice skating trip was, for me, particularly memorable. It is a strange feeling to be desperately clinging to the side of the rink whilst an associate pirouettes past you! Throughout the scheme I was struck by how friendly, approachable and close-knit Jones Day is. The non-hierarchical ethic of the firm was also evident away from the office and it was refreshing to see a firm whose staff so obviously enjoyed each other's company.

The placement scheme served to confirm and even surpass my initial impression of the firm. Jones Day is an ambitious firm which promises a challenging and rewarding career working with high profile clients in an international arena. Alongside this exists a friendly and sociable atmosphere conducive with meeting the undoubted pressures of a legal career in the best possible manner. The prospect of training with Jones Day fills me with excitement and I cannot wait for my contract to begin.

**No of scheme places**
Christmas - 20 (non-law)
Easter - 10-20 (non-law)
Summer - 40 (law)

**Location of schemes**
London

**Length of schemes**
2 weeks

**Remuneration (per week)**
£400

**Dates of schemes**
December - January
2007/2008
April 2008
June - August 2008

**Closing date for applications**
Christmas:
31 October 2007
Easter and Summer:
31 January 2008

**Application procedure**
CV and letter online at www.jonesdaylondon.com/recruit. For applicants without internet access, please send in a CV and cover letter by post.

For full contact information and details of Training Contract, see the firm's full entry in the main directory on page 489

## Insider report
## Ince & Co

**Emmanuel Wedlock** undertook a BA Classics at St Hugh's College, Oxford University, before completing a M. St. Byzantine Studies at St Hugh's College, Oxford University. He attended the trainee recruitment placement scheme at Ince & Co in 2007 and will join the firm as a trainee in September 2009.

I applied to Ince for a trainee recruitment placement scheme because I had always wanted to learn and practice shipping law. Ince is one of the leading firms in this field.

The firm's reputation was vindicated during my placement. Activities over the two weeks included: a lunchtime presentation on charterparties; a departmental lunch followed by two wet-shipping partners talking about their experiences in South America and India; opinions to write on a possible case of cargo smuggling in Crete, and a yacht with a flawed hull design. To add to the maritime element, the office location in International House has a magnificent view overlooking St Katharine's Dock and the Thames.

However Ince is also a strong player in other areas of commercial law, such as insurance and energy, and the other activities I was involved in were correspondingly varied: a visit to the Technology and Construction Court to hear a case on tortious liability; preparation at the International Dispute Resolution Centre on a high-stakes reinsurance case; research on the trend of the nationalization of natural resources; drafting advice on a pharmaceutical supply agreement, among other things. In all of the work I did at Ince during the placement, I was working on real cases, with live and sometimes urgent issues, and my work was being made use of. This made my effort worthwhile and gave me a sense of what it would be like working there as a trainee.

I was attracted to Ince because as a trainee you are given a high level of responsibility and autonomy from very early on and you carry your case-load through your traineeship. The work is stimulating and challenging, and the opportunity exists to push yourself to new limits. At the same time you operate as a member of a highly efficient team, with other well rounded and interesting individuals. During my time there, the partners were always genuinely willing to help, and I was valued personally and supported throughout. This high standard of attentive care has applied in all my dealings with Ince from the moment I made my first application, and is a welcome contrast to the impersonal attitude at other bigger law firms.

I also felt the work ethos at Ince suited me. A high level of professionalism is encouraged, but in a friendly and relaxed atmosphere, without the stuffiness and excruciating consistently long hours one hears about in the Magic Circle firms. Outside of work the solicitors at Ince are very active, with events organized on a regular basis. The size of the firm makes for a healthy social environment, and is not too small to be stifling, nor too large so that you are lost in the crowd.

In conclusion, Ince is an excellent place to work and I am extremely happy to have been offered a training contract for 2009!

**No of scheme places**
15

**Location of schemes**
London

**Length of schemes**
2 weeks

**Remuneration (per week)**
£250

**Dates of schemes**
Easter and Summer 2008

**Closing date for applications**
14 February 2008

**Application procedure**
Apply online at
www.incelaw.com

For full contact information and details of Training Contract, see the firm's full entry in the main directory on page 483

**Rurik Jutting**, a History and Law student at the University of Cambridge, completed a two-week placement at Latham & Watkins in the summer of 2007.

I have been fortunate to attend a number of vacation schemes at various US and Magic Circle firms. At each, I have asked myself the same three questions: would I be proud to work alongside the current trainees, associates, and partners? will there be enough variety for me to remain stimulated and challenged in the years after I qualify? would I still be happy working there at the end of my career? After two weeks at 99 Bishopsgate, I'm happy to say that as far as Latham is concerned, all three answers are very much in the affirmative.

To begin with, the people at Latham are quite simply outstandingly good at what they do. A number of City firms (including, I believe, some from the US) appear to achieve results through a kind of personnel Blitzkrieg: an "if we throw enough highly specialised people at a deal it will get done somehow" mentality. Something which really struck me in my time in the structured finance and technology, media & telecommunications departments is how competent Latham lawyers are across a broad range of disciplines and, consequently, how they are able to handle transactions to an extremely high level with teams often half the size of those on the other side.

Even more important than the quality of individuals at Latham, however, is the collegiate atmosphere. This is one of those phrases which gets bandied around the recruitment literature in much the same way as do 'seamless service' and 'integrated global network'. However, having been through five vacation schemes at leading UK and US firms and attended open days at many others, I can honestly say that the office culture at Latham is the most pleasant and friendly I have encountered.

And of course the work Latham does is about as top tier as it gets (not for nothing was the firm recently named *Legal Business*' "Law Firm of the Decade"!). Of course a lot of firms can claim to participate in 'cutting-edge multijurisdictional transactions'; in a large City law practice that's pretty much par for the course. What distinguishes the elite US firms (of which Latham is a leading example) is that trainees and junior associates cut their teeth on the substance of these deals far quicker than their Magic Circle contemporaries.

The experience of one of my vacation scheme mentors provides a good example. He was hired by Latham one year after qualifying into a Magic Circle firm's IP department, where his time had almost entirely been spent doing corporate support due diligence. At Latham, along with a handful of other associates and a partner, he was given the mandate of building virtually from scratch the office's technology, media & telecommunications department. Two years later, the department has doubled in size and, in comparison with colleagues from his former firm, my mentor is working at a level equivalent to associates three or four years his senior.

Certainly Latham's London office isn't for everyone: the learning curve is steep and the levels of responsibility necessarily high. However, for those cut from a hardworking and intellectually curious cloth, the firm seems the ideal place to develop professionally. The question should perhaps not be "Is training at Latham a realistic alternative to the Magic Circle?", but rather "Is training in the Magic Circle a realistic alternative to Latham?".

**No of scheme places**
10-15

**Location of schemes**
London

**Length of schemes**
Easter: 1 week
Summer: 2 weeks

**Remuneration (per week)**
£300

**Dates of schemes**
March and August 2008

**Closing date for applications**
Easter: 31 December 2007
Summer: 31 January 2008

**Application procedure**
Online form at www.lw.com

For full contact information and details of Training Contract, see the firm's full entry in the main directory on page 502

# HAVE YOU EVER BEEN ON THE OTHER SIDE OF THE BAR?

## SHABNUM WAS. NOW SHE'S AN ASSISTANT LAWYER. WHAT KIND OF UNIQUE EXPERIENCES HAVE YOU HAD?

In the not too distant past, students went from school to university to law school to law firm. Now, you're more likely to spend a year out doing something that little bit different than you are to jump straight onto the great corporate conveyor belt. These days, qualifications plus life experience plus personality is the magic key. Which is why at LG we fully embrace that. We're after well-rounded people, not square pegs. Versatility, not predictability.

So bring us your experience, your colour, your humour and your vitality. We'll help you shine. To find out more about a career in law with us, simply visit **www.lg-legal/graduates**

**Frances Little** graduated in Jurisprudence from Pembroke College, Oxford University and completed the LPC at the College of Law. Frances attended a two-week vacation scheme at Lawrence Graham in July 2005 and will commence a training contract with the firm in September 2007.

# Lawrence Graham LLP

Doing a vacation scheme at LG appealed to me for several reasons. I knew that I wanted to work for a leading City firm with strengths across several practice areas and an impressive roll call of clients but I also wanted to experience life in a firm where individual contributions are recognised and valued. LG appeared to be all of these things and my two weeks spent there confirmed that this was the case.

Like some other work experiences, I half expected that my time on the vacation scheme would be spent making cups of tea or being chained to the photocopier. However, the reality could not have been further from this.

I spent one week in tax and private capital and the other in the real estate department. My 'buddies', both second seat trainees, were very helpful and took the time to discuss their departments generally and the specific deals that they were working on. Amongst more general duties, including proofreading, bundling and drafting codicils and letters, I was asked to conduct a technical piece of research for one of the partners. My research memo was later used in a case meeting and proved to be a small but key point in the overall deal. Being given such responsibility appears symptomatic of the way that LG treats all of its trainees.

During the fortnight we were given talks from representatives of different departments and were given plenty of opportunities to ask questions about what life is really like as a trainee. We were also treated to lunch at the Law Society, shown some of the sights of London on a City walk and spent a day at an employment tribunal. However, undoubtedly my personal highlight was being invited to drinks in the LG local at the end of the week.

I thoroughly enjoyed the vacation scheme and LG proved to be a challenging yet dynamic and fun place to work. I am now looking forward to starting my training contract and I have every confidence that LG is the right firm for me.

**No of scheme places**
32

**Location of schemes**
London

**Length of schemes**
2 weeks

**Remuneration (per week)**
£250

**Dates of schemes**
One scheme at Easter and three over the summer running through June and July

**Closing date for applications**
31 January 2008

**Application procedure**
Firm's application form (available on website: www.lg-legal.com)

For full contact information and details of Training Contract, see the firm's full entry in the main directory on page 503

# Our training contracts are tailor-made.

## Suit you?

## Lovells

THE TIMES
TOP 100
GRADUATE EMPLOYERS

**Kathryn McArdle**, who is studying BA Jurisprudence Law at Jesus College, Cambridge, attended the Summer 2007 scheme at Lovells LLP.

Lovells is undoubtedly a leading international law firm but what made it stand out for me is that not only does the firm hold its own amongst its 'magic circle' rivals but it does so with a great deal of charm and personality. From my initial application right through to the interview and vacation scheme placement itself, Lovells made it clear that every member of its team is treated as an asset and you will, as a result, be very well looked after.

The graduate recruitment team for me are crucial in my opinion of a firm and Lovells have one of the best that I have come across. They well represent the friendliness of the firm. That paired with the unlimited homemade cookies made it clear from the start that I was going to enjoy myself. The partners right through to the trainees made me feel welcome and everyone went out of their way to involve us all. The work was varied and undoubtedly challenging but it was complimented by a well thought out programme of talks and sessions, which ensured that I never tired of the scheme.

The social events were a high and Lovells really pulled the cat out of the bag. From an unusual Jack the Ripper tour and curry in Brick Lane to a yummy meal on Bond Street we were given plenty of opportunities to relax and enjoy the company of new found friends. There was something for everyone and the atmosphere, throughout the scheme, was pitched at just the right level. In fact, the only problem was my expanding waistline but even that was thought of by the firm and we were given free access to their gym facilities throughout- however watch out for the risk of seeing your assigned partner in a new, rather 'rouge' light.

Like any other bustling city firm you will have to put the hours in but you will be rewarded for your efforts here. The intimacy of the close-knit community in the office meant I never felt like just another cog in the machine. I was given a purpose and a place even in the short time I spent there. The one problem with the firm? It will spoil you and you may find, like I did, that other vacation schemes simply cannot match the exceedingly high benchmark that Lovells sets.

**No of scheme places**
90

**Location of schemes**
London

**Length of schemes**
Christmas and Easter: 2 weeks
Summer: 3 weeks

**Remuneration (per week)**
£300

**Dates of schemes**
Christmas, Easter and Summer 2008

**Closing date for applications**
Christmas:
10 November 2007
Easter/Summer:
31 January 2008

**Application procedure**
Visit our website at www.lovells.com/graduates and complete an application form online

For full contact information and details of Training Contract, see the firm's full entry in the main directory on page 513

# exposure...

## to what **you** want

### to real **work**
We believe the best way to develop your raw talent is to expose you to the rigours and pressures of actually practising law.

### to real **clients**
You'll attend client meetings, make and take calls and play an important part in developing the firm's client relationships.

### to a unique **culture**
Supportive, informal and self-confident, Macfarlanes is an environment that recognises and celebrates individuality.

### to quality **training**
Real work, client contact and first-class education – come qualification, you will know what it's like to be a lawyer.

# MACFARLANES

For more information please contact:
Vicki Dimmick
**Macfarlanes**
10 Norwich Street, London, EC4A 1BD

Tel:   020 7831 9222
Fax:   020 7831 9607
email: gradrec@macfarlanes.com
www.macfarlanes.com

**Paul Doran** is a History and International Politics graduate from the University of Sheffield. He attended a two-week vacation scheme with Macfarlanes in Easter and will commence his training contract with the firm in September 2009.

The kind of firm I chose for a vacation placement was one where I had also hoped to train. It had to be medium-sized with a superb reputation in corporate law, preferably in private equity, which was committed to the future of its trainees. Macfarlanes was a unique fit when ticking these boxes, with the added bonus of an internationally-renowned private client department.

What I didn't find out until I joined the firm was its exceptionally friendly atmosphere. Throughout the scheme, everyone I met, from partners to current trainees, was enthusiastic about getting to know us. This was very refreshing; at Macfarlanes you are seen as the future of the firm, not just a trainee.

The seriousness with which Macfarlanes approaches its graduate recruitment was also shown by Robert Sutton, the Senior Partner, spending time with us and explaining the firm's strategy and answering our many questions. This is unusual for any city firm, and it reflects the involvement trainees have at every level at Macfarlanes. Another advantage of a medium-sized practice is that you actually work closely with the partners, many of whom are leaders in their field.

The kind of work I did on the scheme also reflected the responsibility trainees are given. For example, I was asked to investigate the restrictions involved in becoming a UK charity for a client considering philanthropic activity. I consequently joined in a conference call where the issue was discussed. Exposure to this kind of business-critical work is just what a vacation student is looking for.

The two weeks were not without their socialising and fun, however. I participated in a number of events ranging from a comedy night in Leicester Square to a guided law walk of the famous Inns of London. We also spent considerable time in the pub that the whole of Macfarlanes regularly overruns: The Castle, just a few metres from the entrance to the firm.

I really enjoyed the scheme and, by the end of it, I really felt at home, convinced a legal career was for me and Macfarlanes was the firm at which to begin it.

**No of scheme places**
66

**Location of schemes**
London

**Length of schemes**
2 weeks

**Remuneration (per week)**
£250

**Dates of schemes**
Easter and Summer 2008

**Closing date for applications**
29 February 2008

**Application procedure**
Online application form followed by open day

For full contact information and details of Training Contract, see the firm's full entry in the main directory on page 516

# You want the best
# And so do we

Making the right choice for your future career may take time. You'll need to weigh up the options, and get the real flavour of the firm you want to join.

Mayer, Brown, Rowe & Maw is one of the largest international legal practices in the world and given our ambitious growth plans there's plenty of opportunity for the best to share in our success.

For more information on the opportunities available and to apply on-line, please visit our website: www.mayerbrownrowe.com/london/careers/gradrecruit

Further enquiries should be made to: Maxine Goodlet, Graduate Recruitment Manager. Tel: 020 7248 4282 Email: graduaterecruitment@mayerbrownrowe.com

**www.mayerbrownrowe.com**

**Devora Kirk**, who studies Music at Nottingham University, undertook a two-week vacation placement at Mayer Brown Rowe & Maw LLP. She will join the firm as a trainee in September 2009.

It was Mayer, Brown, Rowe & Maw's ambitious, professional and down-to-earth reputation that led me to apply to the firm for a vacation scheme. These characteristics were obvious from the start of the scheme and I was made to feel welcome right from day one.

The scheme lasted two weeks and my time was split equally between two departments, construction and intellectual property, working directly with a supervisor gaining valuable hands-on experience. This included fulfilling research requests, taking part on conference calls and attending court. I found some of the tasks a little daunting at first, but the firm really encourages you to throw yourself into your tasks and my supervisors were always happy to answer any questions, regardless of how trivial I felt they appeared.

In addition to the important work experience there was also a fantastic social element to the vacation scheme. The trainees organised a number of activities ranging from going out for dinner to a cocktail-making workshop, which was enormous fun and provided an opportunity to speak candidly to the current trainees in an informal environment.

The placement was very well organised and everybody that I met during my time, from trainees to partners to HR, were, without exception, very approachable. In addition, I was very impressed by the firm's recruitment process, particularly because I found the assessment to be very personal with very few people being assessed at one time.

Overall this varied experience really gave me an accurate insight into the day-to-day life of a solicitor in the City and confirmed for me that I did want to pursue such a legal career. My two weeks at Mayer, Brown, Rowe & Maw were hugely insightful and enjoyable and I would strongly recommend applying to the firm.

**No of scheme places**
30 approx

**Location of schemes**
London

**Length of schemes**
3 weeks

**Remuneration (per week)**
£275

**Dates of schemes**
Easter 2008:
31 March - 18 April 2008
Summer 2008:
30 June - 18 July 2008
25 July - 15 August 2008

**Closing date for applications**
Easter: 11 January 2008
Summer: 31 January 2008

**Application procedure**
Online (application form available if required)

For full contact information and details of Training Contract, see the firm's full entry in the main directory on page 526

# McGrigors
## Solicitors

# Challenging?
# Does that mean
# I'll be home late?

Here at McGrigors LLP we're not going to lie – probably, yes, you may be home late from time to time.

But... not every day and it usually means a tight deadline so you will be working closely with the team, getting involved and seeing the work through to the end.

For more information on our honest approach and trainee opportunities go to:

# www.mcgrigors.com
**London | Edinburgh | Glasgow | Aberdeen | Belfast**

**Oliver Bett** completed a three-week placement at the London office of McGrigors in the Summer of 2007.

Insider report

# McGrigors LLP

I chose to apply to McGrigors because they are an ambitious mid-market firm who are continuing to expand within the City. I was also impressed by their refreshingly upfront and honest graduate literature.

The overall structure of the placement was well organised, with a comprehensive introduction to the firm undertaken on the first day and presentations for all departments to cover those which you do not experience whilst on the scheme. The assignment of a 'buddy' and supervisor eased you into your departments and although they were main source of work throughout the placement, I found work from other solicitors, one particular example being to compile a report on a potential client, highlighting recent news in the trade presses to aid in gaining their business, this I found extremely useful and interesting.

During the scheme I spent a week and a half in both corporate and banking partaking in a variety of work giving a real insight into the role of trainee and activities which they would be expected to complete. Within corporate I carried out company secretarial duties for a high street restaurant chain, and also undertook extensive research into private equity firms and the tax systems which aid them.

In banking I worked mainly on supporting my 'buddy' who I was assigned to, I completed charge instruments and registered them at Companies House. I found I was actively involved, I was asked to review the work of other solicitors to give me an insight into what their role was.

Having experienced a number of regional firms, varying in size, this was my first experience in London. It lived up to expectation through the quality of work, the buzz associated with working in the City and from a firm point of view it maintained the intimacy that I am looking for.

The firm was very sociable, there were the obvious summer student specific events including the duck tour (sightseeing in an amphibious vehicle) and an excellent meal on the last day. The atmosphere was very inclusive, students were invited to departmental drinks and I played in a football tournament with teams from one of the firm's clients.

The summer scheme was a truly enjoyable and valuable experience, it reaffirmed my decision to apply to the firm, one which is ambitious and a real alternative from larger City institutions.

**No of scheme places**
London: 15
Edinburgh: 15
Glasgow: 15
Aberdeen: 6
Belfast: 3

**Location of schemes**
London, Edinburgh, Glasgow, Aberdeen, Belfast

**Length of schemes**
3 weeks

**Remuneration (per week)**
£250 - London

**Dates of schemes**
Summer 2008

**Closing date for applications**
31 January 2008

**Application procedure**
Online application form

For full contact information and details of Training Contract, see the firm's full entry in the main directory on page 528

# Excuse me,

are you looking to discover a firm
with a choice of UK locations, a noted
six-seat training contract and a promise
of early responsibility?

A firm recognised nationally for valuing
and respecting its people?

A firm committed to working responsibly
with its clients and neighbours?

If you are, you'll discover a growing firm,
with an enviable record of success and
an even brighter future.

An ambitious and dynamic firm with
huge potential.

A firm where you can reach your goals.

## MILLS & REEVE

DISCOVER HOW FAR YOU CAN GO.
DISCOVER MILLS & REEVE.

www.mills-reeve.com/graduates

**Samantha Finchman**, an Education Studies with History graduate from Homerton College, Cambridge, attended the summer scheme at Mills & Reeve LLP's Cambridge office. She will start her training contract with the firm in September 2009.

# Mills & Reeve LLP

I was delighted to discover that I had been offered a two week summer vacation placement with Mills & Reeve because I was certain that I would be working in a challenging yet friendly environment.

My initial feelings were overwhelmingly confirmed. I was given the opportunity to fully experience the diverse range of corporate and private client services offered by Mills & Reeve as I sat in four extremely different areas: real estate, banking and finance, education, and family and matrimonial. I was always given interesting and thought provoking work to do, such as conducting legal research and drafting and editing legal documents. As a non-law graduate I was reassured that everyone explained new things clearly as well as giving me some useful feedback on my work. Furthermore, I was lucky enough to observe a client meeting, visit court, and attend several engaging talks about life as a solicitor at Mills & Reeve.

As well as gaining some excellent hands-on legal experience, Mills & Reeve ensured that their vacation placement was not all work and no play, and this made them stand out for me in comparison to other firms. I enjoyed meals and a punting trip (a perk of being at the Cambridge office!) with the current trainees, with an invitation to the annual summer party representing a particular highlight. The party had a Hawaiian theme and was a great opportunity to socialise with a brilliant group of people. Everyone I met was very enthusiastic about working for Mills & Reeve, and it was great being assigned a 'buddy', or current trainee, who was available to answer all sorts of questions.

After my vacation scheme I fervently hoped I would receive a training contract with Mills & Reeve, which I am happy to say I did! This placement made me fully realise that being a solicitor is definitely the right career for me. I learnt so much and found the work fascinating, and I enjoyed it even more because I was working with people who made a great deal of effort to make us feel welcome.

**No of scheme places**
30

**Location of schemes**
Cambridge (10), Norwich (10), Birmingham (10)

**Length of schemes**
2 weeks

**Remuneration (per week)**
£200

**Dates of schemes**
Cambridge: 23 June 2008
Norwich: 7 July 2008
Birmingham: 21 July 2008

**Closing date for applications**
31 January 2008

**Application procedure**
Firm's online application form

For full contact information and details of Training Contract, see the firm's full entry in the main directory on page 534

# to you, he's Raj

**To the client, he's the top corporate finance lawyer who advised on a US$8.3 billion merger to create the world's No.1 gold mining company**

As with all top legal practices, you'll find yourself surrounded by highly accomplished lawyers handling complex legal issues relating to high-profile, multimillion-pound negotiations. The major difference is, ours is a much more informal environment, where no one's too caught up in status to listen to your fresh ideas and offer you the individual attention you deserve. Moreover, once you've completed the six-seat training scheme and chosen your preferred specialist area, you'll be given responsibility and continued support to progress to partner level far quicker than you expected.

To experience the unique culture for yourself, contact our graduate recruitment team on +44 (0)20 7283 6000 for details about our placement scheme, training contracts and open days.

NR4052

**Chin Lau**, a law student at the University of Warwick who is spending his third year abroad at the University of Hong Kong, undertook a summer placement with Norton Rose LLP in London and Dubai, and will shortly undertake a winter placement in Hong Kong.

# Norton Rose LLP

I believe "why do you want to work for us?" is one of the hardest questions to answer on an application form for a placement or training contract with an international legal practice. However, once I met the friendly, genuine and down-to-earth people from Norton Rose Group, I found the answer and decided to spend my summer vacation working with the practice.

My first contact with Norton Rose Group was at an open day for ethnic minorities during my first year. At the end of the event, I was invited to be the contact person on campus to run marketing campaigns such as the Chinese open day. Through my further contact with the Norton Rose Group I have been impressed with their industry focus and training contract programme - particularly the City LPC and six-seat system, not to mention the diverse culture (which is what led me to them initially).

I sat alongside a senior associate in the competition, EU and regulatory department for the first two weeks at Norton Rose. Some background knowledge in this practice area enabled me to draft a memorandum which was sent to the EU Commission. I spent the next two weeks working with a senior associate in international corporate finance on a £130 million cross-border acquisition deal.

All placement students were involved in a business project where we were required to submit a report and present our ideas to senior partners. It was great fun working with my team members and we were awarded first prize in both the written report and the presentation. I was also short-listed for the title of best speaker. In addition, the graduate recruitment team arranged a full schedule of social activities for placement students and trainees including softball matches, sailing, a treasure hunt, paintballing, and a day trip in the City.

During my placement, I gained exposure to excellent international transactions, I worked in the inspiring new London office, I enjoyed mouth-watering food in the canteen with a fantastic view overlooking Tower Bridge and all staff were very supportive, which was very different to my previous work experience at a barrister's chambers and a high street law firm. However, what impressed me the most is the smiling faces of everyone in the practice just as the first time I met them in my first year. That was why I decided to spend an extra few weeks in the business development department in London, and in the Dubai and Hong Kong offices.

**No of scheme places**
45

**Location of schemes**
London

**Length of schemes**
Winter: 2 weeks
Summer: 4 weeks

**Remuneration (per week)**
£250

**Dates of schemes**
Winter 2007
Summer 2008

**Closing date for applications**
Winter: 31 October 2007
Summer: 31 January 2008

**Application procedure**
Online application form

For full contact information and details of Training Contract, see the firm's full entry in the main directory on page 544

# Insider report
## Nabarro

**Rebecca Gill**, a Politics graduate from Durham University, attended a three-week vacation scheme placement at Nabarro in summer 2007 and will commence her training contract at the firm in September 2008.

I initially applied for the vacation scheme at Nabarro because I thought it would provide a good opportunity for me to learn more about the firm, and for Nabarro to learn more about me.

Both of these aims were definitely achieved during the scheme. Nabarro offer a three-week scheme, (most firms only offer two weeks), and I definitely found this a bonus as it gave me time to really see what life as a trainee with Nabarro would be like.

One of the reasons I was keen to apply to Nabarro was the high level of support they offer to summer students and trainees. Throughout the scheme I was assigned a buddy, (who was a current trainee), as well as a supervisor within my department. This meant that there was always someone there I could approach with any questions I had.

The scheme itself was well structured with time split between working within a department and working with other summer students on a series of presentations and a written assignment. Within my department I carried out a wide range of tasks from drafting minutes and letters to clients, and to carrying out research for other members of the department. I was also taken along to several client meetings, and attended a hearing at the Royal Courts of Justice.

Additionally Nabarro organised several presentations about the different departments and what being a trainee in different seats involves, these sessions were particularly useful and really helped me to start to understand all the different areas of law I could qualify into.

The vacation scheme was also a lot of fun! There was a busy schedule of events and activities organised giving us a chance to socialise with the other students and trainees; this also provided plenty of opportunity to ask questions about working at Nabarro, or being a trainee generally. Everyone at the firm was so friendly and people were really willing to talk to you and share their experiences.

I would recommend to anyone considering Nabarro that they apply for their vacation scheme. The three weeks I spent with Nabarro were both hard work and really good fun and convinced me that I definitely wanted a training contract with the firm.

**No of scheme places**
55 in London
8 in Sheffield

**Location of schemes**
London and Sheffield

**Length of schemes**
3 weeks

**Remuneration (per week)**
£250 in London
£180 in Sheffield

**Dates of schemes**
London:
16 June - 4 July 2008
7 July - 25 July 2008
28 July - 15 August 2008
Sheffield:
21 July - 8 August 2008

**Closing date for applications**
8 February 2008

**Application procedure**
Online application form at www.nabarro.com

For full contact information and details of Training Contract, see the firm's full entry in the main directory on page 542

**Kathryn Noble**, a History graduate from Royal Holloway University, attended a two-week vacation scheme programme at Olswang in June 2007. She will join the firm as a trainee in 2009.

There is no need to inform applicants for Olswang's work placement scheme about the firm's reputation for media law and the impressive client list to its name; Olswang is known for excelling in this area, and is the choice of budding media lawyers and clients in the media field. However, Olswang also has well-known and growing strongholds in corporate, real estate, finance and litigation that makes it much more than a specialist in media law. In fact, the media, communications and technology department is not the only practice area that draws applicants towards the firm, with the other teams constantly proving to be equally popular among trainees. The firm's departments are growing in terms of size and reputation, and this is reflected in the exciting expansion of the firm in general.

During the work placement scheme interns get an opportunity to spend time in two seats, in which they get a true feel of what it is really like to work there and the day to day experiences of the partners, associates and trainees. Interns are not simply handed a week's worth of photocopying, nor are they left to their own devices, but they are exposed to as much of the varied work in the department as possible and encouraged to contribute to real projects being worked on at the time. Interns do not, however, face this task alone as they are each assigned a 'mentor' who is on hand to assist, offer advice and answer questions on work and life at Olswang. The working day is interspersed with various talks by all the main departments and HR to ensure interns get the most out of their two weeks, and to allow insight into the culture and values of the firm.

Outside working hours interns are invited to social activities to allow them to get to know the people they are working with outside of the office environment. These include drinks nights, a pub quiz and bowling which is entertaining for participants and spectators alike!

There is something about Olswang that cannot be picked up from reading material or websites. The culture, the welcoming atmosphere and the enthusiastic energy that can be detected from the people who work there are things that become evident from spending time at the firm. I would recommend applying for a work placement scheme as the only way to find out what Olswang is really about.

**No of scheme places**
34

**Location of schemes**
London and Reading

**Length of schemes**
2 weeks

**Remuneration (per week)**
£275

**Dates of schemes**
June and July 2008

**Closing date for applications**
31 January 2008

**Application procedure**
Online application at www.olswang.com

For full contact information and details of Training Contract, see the firm's full entry in the main directory on page 546

# Insider report
## Osborne Clarke

**Dave Kerr** studied Law at Bristol University. He attended a vacation scheme at Osborne Clarke in summer 2006 and will be starting with the firm in March 2009.

Having spent two years studying law at Bristol University, I knew when I was applying for vacation placements that I wanted to stay in Bristol. I was therefore fortunate enough to secure a place in the Bristol office of European law firm Osborne Clarke.

My first day consisted of an induction and welcome to the firm. I was then taken to meet the team with whom I'd be spending the week – the private equity team. Everyone in the department made me very welcome and I was immediately impressed with how friendly everyone was.

During my time with the private equity team, I undertook tasks such as drafting a sale purchase agreement and helping with a company search. Although I had no previous experience in corporate law, everyone was more than happy to explain any difficulties I encountered.

The Wednesday evening gave everyone on the vacation scheme a chance to go out for a meal with some of the current trainees. This provided an opportunity to get to know some of the trainees from different departments and get a valuable insight into the type of work they were involved in and a more informal picture of the workings of the office.

During my time at Osborne Clarke, I also attended lunch time solicitor talks. These gave me the chance to ask some of the solicitors about the particular department they were in.

On the Thursday, I had the opportunity to spend the day in an alternative department. I spent the day in the banking department where I learnt about another area of law with which I had had no previous contact. I was also given the chance to sit in on a corporate know-how session, which I found really interesting. It was good to be able to follow some of what was said after only a few days in the department!

All in all, I enjoyed being exposed to interesting work and was very impressed with how supportive and approachable everyone was. It was obvious from the start that Osborne Clarke is a very positive, forward looking firm and I am really pleased that I have been able to secure a training contract with them.

**No of scheme places**
20

**Location of schemes**
Bristol, London, Thames Valley

**Remuneration (per week)**
£250

**Dates of schemes**
April, June and July 2008

**Closing date for applications**
31 January 2008

**Application procedure**
Online application form

For full contact information and details of Training Contract, see the firm's full entry in the main directory on page 550

**Ayse Ince**, a Psychology graduate from Leeds University, attended a one-week vacation placement at Pannone LLP in 2006. She worked at Pannone as a paralegal before leaving to complete the LPC prior to joining the firm as a trainee solicitor in 2008.

I applied for a vacation placement at Pannone because it is a full service firm and I was unsure what area of law would interest me the most. The number of awards Pannone had received, particularly being third best employer of the year, also astounded me.

I honestly believe the only way to gain a genuine understanding of a law firm is to spend time there. During my week at Pannone I visited the corporate, personal injury, clinical negligence and employment departments. Each day a trainee would introduce me to fee earners in their department, explain the type of work they do and their client profile. I found this really interesting as I was studying for the GDL and some of these areas were rather alien to me. All the trainees devoted a great deal of time to answering my questions about the firm. I was also given the opportunity to go for lunch with several trainees and my vacation scheme placement colleagues. Again, this gave us an invaluable insight into the quality of the training at the firm, something you cannot appreciate from a law fair.

The tasks I completed ranged from drafting letters of advice to clients, completing research and costing for an employment tribunal. I was also taken to client meetings. I think this is where I distinguished Pannone from other law firms I had completed vacation schemes with. The level of involvement in the work at Pannone was fantastic; I was really being involved with active files. Everyone seemed happy to answer my questions and talk about their experiences at the firm. I was asked for my opinion on the placement at the end and whether I thought it could be improved.

Right the way through the placement I felt relaxed and happy to be at Pannone, even at the training contract interview which is included for every placement student. It was the friendliness of the firm and obvious enjoyment in their work the trainees portrayed that were the most important factors when I was making my choice. I am thoroughly looking forward to starting my training contract next year.

**No of scheme places**
60

**Location of schemes**
Manchester

**Length of schemes**
1 week

**Dates of schemes**
Easter and Summer

**Closing date for applications**
Easter: 25 January 2008
Summer: 13 July 2008

**Application procedure**
Application opens November 2007. Online application is available on our website where you will also find our graduate recruitment brochure.

For full contact information and details of Training Contract, see the firm's full entry in the main directory on page 554

# Well connected

## At Reed Smith Richards Butler you'll feel part of the wider world

That might be because our 21 offices, located over 3 continents, handle so much international work, or because our departments are structured across our offices so that you are regularly in touch with colleagues and clients in different countries. It could even be because all our trainee solicitors have the option to take international or client secondments.

But we think you'll feel connected mostly because we'll encourage you to get involved from the outset. You'll get access to real work, opportunities to take part in community projects or pro bono work and you'll still have a work/life balance that allows you to get out and do your own thing.

**ReedSmith**
**Richards Butler**

The business of relationships.

www.reedsmith.com

NEW YORK
LONDON
CHICAGO
PARIS
LOS ANGELES
WASHINGTON, D.C
SAN FRANCISCO
PHILADELPHIA
PITTSBURGH
OAKLAND
MUNICH
ABU DHABI
PRINCETON
N. VIRGINIA
WILMINGTON
DUBAI
BIRMINGHAM
CENTURY CITY
RICHMOND
GREECE

**Yousef Hatem**, a Law student at Durham University, attended the Reed Smith Richards Butler LLP work placement scheme in Summer 2007.

# Reed Smith Richards Butler LLP

My summer vacation experience at Reed Smith Richards Butler was a challenging, fulfilling, yet at the same time thoroughly enjoyable experience. The aim of the scheme was to give a genuine and realistic impression of the firm – and the varied programme which had been carefully planned certainly left me with a far clearer idea of life at a City law firm than any brochure or careers guide could give me!

The programme itself was a healthy mix of group-orientated exercises and individual placement in mini-seats as varied as shipping, media, intellectual property and litigation. The group exercises included a mock employment tribunal, (chaired by a former judge of the Employment Appeals Tribunal!) a sales/pitching exercise and a negotiation skills workshop. From these group exercises, we not only developed core skills and competencies, but also got to know one another better and develop new friendships.

We were given the choice of which mini-seats we would like to experience – a positive difference when compared with vacation schemes of some other firms which do not necessarily offer this choice. I chose litigation and shipping, and felt that the associates and partners within these departments effectively treated me as if I were a trainee. I was kept busy all the time - lawyers asked me to do valuable research for them – I was asked by an associate to investigate the Carlos Tevez affair as he was preparing an academic article on it, and was asked by a partner to investigate the law relating to the enforceability of arbitration decisions abroad. The research was challenging, but rewarding – there was a feeling amongst the group that we were genuinely contributing to the work of the department and were made to feel wanted there during our time. We were given an introductory talk on the first day on how to use the library and how to navigate through online legal databases, which proved valuable to me, but even more valuable to non-law students with no prior experience of Westlaw or LexisNexis.

The scheme was not all work and no play however – on no fewer than four occasions during the two weeks, the firm took us out for drinks, and also treated us to a curry on Brick Lane! These social events were also well attended by trainees and even a few associates – yet again showing that the firm went to real lengths to make us feel comfortable as well as challenged. Everyone on the scheme was given a 'buddy' – a current trainee to use as a point of contact for any queries or concerns during the scheme – and it was genuinely reassuring to see how personable, friendly and relaxed the people and atmosphere could be in such a large and busy City firm.

Everyone on our scheme happily accepted an invitation to a training contract interview – testament indeed to the warm welcome which the firm provided us, and the quality of the work that we experienced during our two weeks. In short, I would strongly recommend a vacation scheme at RSRB to anyone. The firm comes across as being down-to-earth and personable at the same time as being ambitious and forward-looking, and this is reflected in the healthy balance of challenging work and enjoyable social events that make up its vacation scheme. It is a genuinely worthwhile and rewarding experience.

**No of scheme places**
30

**Location of schemes**
London and Birmingham

**Length of schemes**
2 weeks

**Remuneration (per week)**
£250

**Dates of schemes**
End of June to end of July

**Closing date for applications**
31 January 2008

**Application procedure**
Online application form via our website, www.reedsmith.com. Details for scholarship entry can also be found on the website.

For full contact information and details of Training Contract, see the firm's full entry in the main directory on page 567

Reynolds
Porter
Chamberlain LLP

presents...

# DECISION IMPOSSIBLE

rpc

**THE TALE OF TWO TRAINEES' JOURNEY INTO THE WORLD OF LAW**

The recruitment process, a seductive world of beautiful brochures, snazzy exhibition platforms and high-spec websites... you read them all and still don't know which firm is right for you.

However, if you're looking to train with a London law firm where you're in touch with what's happening right from the word go; where you can get hands-on experience of important, high profile issues; where you know your contribution is valued – you've found just what you're looking for.

email us at **training@rpc.co.uk**
or visit **www.rpc.co.uk/training**
or call **020 3060 6000**
to request a brochure.

**Laura Clutterbuck**, a History graduate from Warwick University, attended a two-week vacation scheme placement at Reynolds Porter Chamberlain LLP in Summer 2007. She will join the firm as a trainee solicitor in September 2009.

I applied to Reynolds Porter Chamberlain LLP primarily because of its reputation as a leading City law firm. However I also wanted to work at a firm within which I could make a difference and take on real work rather than being part of a large faceless intake. The vacation scheme confirmed these expectations and I had a fantastic time.

Being a non-law student and having only previously done work experience at a small high street firm, I was apprehensive that the work would require an in depth knowledge of commercial law. However although the work was challenging I found that it mostly required common sense rather than technical expertise.

The vacation scheme was well structured allowing me to spend one week in insurance and another in corporate. This gave me a good insight into the wide variety of work available in two very different divisions at RPC. I was involved in real work, including drafting correspondence, writing an article and carrying out research. I even dictated client letters which was somewhat daunting in an open plan office, but very good experience! I was treated as part of the team and taken to client meetings, presentations and the Royal Courts of Justice. We were also given a series of talks on the work at RPC and the opportunities available to us.

The social side was not at all neglected either! Events included a tour of Lloyds of London reflecting the importance of RPC's insurance work; whereas a cruise on the Thames and a trip on the London Eye with the trainees, gave us great opportunities to find out more about life at RPC.

I found that everyone I met, from the partners to the trainees and support staff, were extremely welcoming and friendly. There was no sense of hierarchy that can be found at other City firms, and this is aided by the impressive open plan offices. Above all RPC is an innovative firm with great prospects for continued expansion yet it retains a very supportive and open atmosphere. If the vacation scheme is anything to go by I know I will I have a great future with RPC!

**No of scheme places**
24

**Location of schemes**
London

**Length of schemes**
2 weeks

**Remuneration (per week)**
£275

**Dates of schemes**
Summer 2008

**Closing date for applications**
29 February 2008

**Application procedure**
Firm's online application form available at www.rpc.co.uk/training followed by interview with Human Resources

For full contact information and details of Training Contract, see the firm's full entry in the main directory on page 569

# SHEARMAN & STERLING LLP

"FROM DAY ONE, TRAINEES AT SHEARMAN & STERLING ARE AN INTEGRAL PART OF A DYNAMIC INTERNATIONAL ORGANISATION THAT VALUES THE INDIVIDUAL. SMALLER GROUPS AND HIGH-END DEALS MEAN REAL RESPONSIBIL-ITY, QUALITY WORK, AND EVERY OPPORTUNITY TO SHINE."

**EMMA HARDWICK | TRAINEE**

# Want to be a lawyer, not just a trainee?

At Shearman & Sterling LLP you will get hands on experience of high profile deals and be given responsibility and continued support to achieve your full potential.

Our reputation and worldwide experience means that you will work on major international transactions from day one. Because of our size you will be an integral and valued member of your team, working in the informal yet professional environment of our London office, which has now grown to over 300 people.

In your two-year training contract you will train in our core business practices, including project finance, banking and mergers and acquisitions and may have the opportunity to spend six months in our New York, Abu Dhabi or Singapore offices. We provide a maintenance grant and cover PgDL and LPC fees.

**Rachel Weatherup**, a final-year Law student at Cambridge University, completed a summer placement with Shearman & Sterling LLP's Mergers & Acquisitions group in July 2007. Rachel will join the firm as a trainee in September 2010.

I applied for a vacation placement at Shearman & Sterling as I wanted to gain experience of different types of law firm during my vacation placements. I had heard that American law firms give their trainees a lot of responsibility which appealed greatly to me. Shearman & Sterling's excellent international reputation sealed the deal for me and I was delighted when I was offered a place on their summer vacation scheme.

What impressed me about the vacation scheme was the way the various associates that I sat with went to great lengths to give me 'proper' work to do, rather than just proof reading or photocopying. I was in the M&A department and was asked to assist in the compilation of a virtual data room for potential bidders in a large cross-border takeover. I then sat with a different associate for a few days in the middle of the placement and helped to draft a client note regarding the employment law and tax implications of a US employee moving to the UK. Throughout the placement the work given to me was interesting and provided a real insight into the life of a trainee at the firm.

From the very first day I got on really well with the other students on the scheme. Being a small group of 10 allowed us to get to know one another and whilst there were great social events organised by the firm, we also organised our own nights out; one of which ended up in a karaoke bar! As well as this everyone at the firm from the partners to the administrative staff was really friendly and helpful. We were taken out to lunch by our departments and really made to feel like one of the team. It was a much more inclusive and supportive culture than I had experienced on the other vacation scheme I had attended.

All in all I really enjoyed the placement at Shearman & Sterling; I would definitely recommend it to anyone thinking of applying. You will get the support and camaraderie of a friendly office without compromising on the quality of work available to you, which is by the way, outstanding!

**No of scheme places**
30

**Location of schemes**
London

**Length of schemes**
3 x 2 weeks

**Remuneration (per week)**
£300 (as at Summer 2007)

**Dates of schemes**
16 June - 27 June 2008
30 June - 11 July 2008
14 July - 25 July 2008

**Closing date for applications**
28 February 2008 (open from 1 December 2007)

**Application procedure**
Online at www.shearman.com

For full contact information and details of Training Contract, see the firm's full entry in the main directory on page 582

# Where will you be a leading international business lawyer?

A dynamic and innovative international law firm, Simmons & Simmons has offices in the major business and financial centres of Europe, the Middle East and Asia.

The skills and expertise of our people are key, so we only recruit the best.

Join us, and in return for your commitment, ambition and enthusiasm, we'll give you support, responsibility and the opportunity to become a leading international business lawyer. To find out more visit our website.

www.simmons-simmons.com/traineelawyers

**Simmons & Simmons**

**Anna Burns** participated in a four-week summer placement with Simmons & Simmons in 2007.

# Simmons & Simmons

I chose Simmons & Simmons primarily due to the length of the vacation scheme. I felt a four week placement would provide an honest and realistic picture of what it is like to work for Simmons. Having done a placement elsewhere in the city, I felt that two weeks wasn't really long enough to get a genuine view of life at a firm. Simmons was also appealing in that it has a reputation for being extremely supportive. This was a decisive factor for me. Simmons has the level of clientele and work that you would expect from any top law firm therefore I felt it was important to base my decision on something that would distinguish one leading practice from another. This for me was the working atmosphere which I perceived each firm to have.

When I arrived at Simmons & Simmons I was not disappointed. The first thing I noticed was that the graduate recruitment team had done an excellent job of selecting people who would get along well together. The various social events throughout the scheme allowed both the interns and the trainees to really gel together so that genuine friendships were formed and I know that many people have kept in touch after the scheme.

Whilst on the placement I spent time in both the Corporate & Commercial Projects and IP departments. I was in each department for two weeks and was therefore able to get involved in real work and not just mundane tasks given just for the sake of passing time. Interns are given ample time in their departments which I considered more worthwhile than the endless workshops and group work I had experienced elsewhere. Everyone I met at Simmons was extremely friendly and most importantly approachable. I felt comfortable asking what I considered to be stupid questions and was always met with a helpful and friendly response.

This vacation scheme was overall an excellent experience. I was surprised at how friendly and good humoured everyone was especially as I did not really expect this at a firm of Simmons' size and calibre. I would highly recommend Simmons to anyone who wants to do a vacation placement at a firm where the interns are given real work in a friendly and honest atmosphere.

**No of scheme places**
40

**Location of schemes**
London, Rotterdam, Hong Kong, Tokyo

**Length of schemes**
4 weeks

**Remuneration (per week)**
£250

**Dates of schemes**
Summer 2008

**Closing date for applications**
31 January 2008

**Application procedure**
Online application form

For full contact information and details of Training Contract, see the firm's full entry in the main directory on page 587

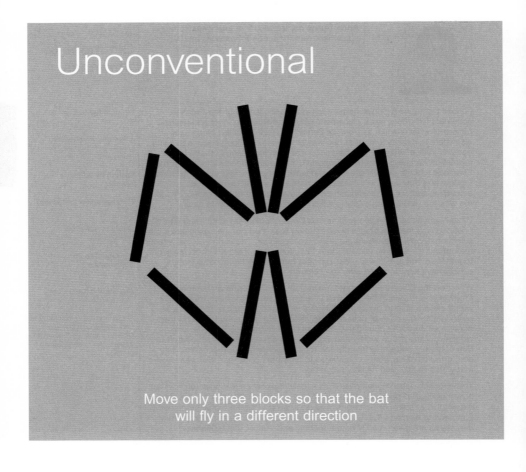

**Unconventional**

Move only three blocks so that the bat
will fly in a different direction

For Open Days, Summer Vacation Schemes
and Training Contracts please apply on-line at
**www.sjberwin.com/gradrecruit**

For enquiries contact:
*E*  graduate.recruitment@sjberwin.com
*T*  Graduate Recruitment Helpdesk 020 7533 2268

**www.sjberwin.com**

sj**berwin**

**Berlin**      **Brussels**      **Frankfurt**      **London**      **Madrid**      **Munich**      **Paris**

SJ Berwin LLP is a limited liability partnership registered in England no OC313176

**Tom Audritt**, a Law graduate from Liverpool University, has recently completed the LPC at the College of Law. He attended a vacation scheme at SJ Berwin in 2007 and joins the firm as a trainee in September 2008

I was delighted to accept an offer to attend SJ Berwin's summer vacation scheme, and as soon as I stepped into the stunning offices at 10 Queen Street Place I had an inkling that the following two weeks were going to be something completely different.

Upon meeting my fellow summer schemers it became apparent that SJ Berwin recruits a diverse and interesting bunch of participants. There was a good mix of law, non-law students and graduates and we bonded quickly as a group.

The first day was mainly filled with introductions, office tours and general administration so that we were fully equipped to master the computer system and outlook (which can quickly organise your life, even in a two week period!).

Over the two weeks the firm organised many different evening entertainments. To break the ice, on the first night, there was a fun pub quiz with trainees. We also had a gourmet dinner at the offices with partners, drinks and BBQ hosted by the corporate department on the roof terrace and dinner with the trainees. A highlight for me was the tour of London on the SJ Berwin open-topped double-decker bus (to mark the firm's 25th anniversary) where we dined on champagne and sushi.

The scheme was well organised and every morning we had talks by different departments which gave us a great overview of the firm and the type of work it undertakes. After the talks we went back to our departments where we were given the opportunity to assist on real transactions. I joined the finance department for the two week scheme and on the first afternoon was immediately invited to attend a conference call where the terms of a loan agreement were being negotiated. I attended further client meetings and conference calls to do with this client and felt I was really included in what was going on.

Most firms claim to be non-hierarchical but in SJ Berwin's case this can be substantiated. This was demonstrated by the somewhat heated and competitive table football games between partners, associates and trainees that took place regularly. Having been invited to play it was apparent that to be a successful lawyer at SJ Berwin I would need to improve my table football skills!

I thoroughly enjoyed my time at SJ Berwin and it is clear that the firm encourages hard work but at the same time recognises the importance of employee morale and endeavours to provide a friendly work environment. I made new friends over the two weeks and would urge anyone of thinking of applying to do so.

**No of scheme places**
60

**Location of schemes**
London

**Length of schemes**
2 weeks

**Remuneration (per week)**
£270

**Dates of schemes**
End of June to mid August

**Closing date for applications**
31 January 2008

**Application procedure**
Online application form at www.sjberwin.com/gradrecruit

For full contact information and details of Training Contract, see the firm's full entry in the main directory on page 589

# Insider report
## Shoosmiths

**Alex Newborough**, a Law student at the University of Northampton, completed a two-week placement in Shoosmiths in Northampton during August 2007.

I had been aware of Shoosmiths by reputation for a number of years and was thrilled to secure a summer placement with this successful and rapidly expanding firm. Shoosmiths run a well organised, engaging and diverse work experience programme. The bulk of my time was split between the insurance litigation & regulatory and the finance litigation departments at The Lakes office in Northampton, although the firm were also able to accommodate my request to spend a day with the private client team based at the Milton Keynes office. My vacation scheme involved court visits, to observe both a judgment and a full trial, in relation to two cases in which Shoosmiths were defending Northamptonshire County Council against personal injury claims. I also accompanied one of the trainees to a local school in order to take a witness statement; was party to a telephone hearing, two client meetings and an interview under caution. Whilst in the office I was asked to write and dictate reports and undertake a variety of research projects.

My experience at Shoosmiths served to dispel any concerns I may have had that the practical, day-to-day application of the law would not be as engaging or inspiring as its academic side. The vacation programme has given me an invaluable insight into both working life in general at a busy firm and the role and responsibilities of a trainee solicitor.

I received a warm reception from all at Shoosmiths and, from day one, was made to feel part of the professional, cohesive and upbeat team, with staff at all levels being approachable and supportive. The trainees in particular are incredibly friendly and are valuable sources of information, having themselves been through all of the rather daunting stages that those seeking to pursue a legal career have ahead of us. The social aspects of the vacation scheme were great fun and provided further opportunity to gain insight into life at the firm. I was treated to lunches, took part in a netball match against another company and went along to support the Shoosmiths cricket team in one of their games (inspired as much by the beautiful game as the promise of food and a pint afterwards!). All in all I would wholeheartedly recommend the Shoosmiths vacation scheme to anyone who has an interest in commercial law.

**No of scheme places**
35

**Location of schemes**
Nottingham, Milton Keynes, Reading, Solent, Birmingham

**Length of schemes**
1-2 weeks

**Remuneration (per week)**
£250

**Dates of schemes**
June, July and August 2008

**Closing date for applications**
28 February 2008

**Application procedure**
Application form available on firm's website
www.shoosmiths.co.uk

For full contact information and details of Training Contract, see the firm's full entry in the main directory on page 584

**Anna Heimbichner**, an International Relations postgraduate student at the University of Oxford, completed a two-week vacation scheme placement at Skadden, Arps, Slate, Meagher & Flom (UK) LLP in Summer 2007. She will commence a training contract with the firm in 2009.

## Skadden, Arps, Slate, Meagher & Flom (UK) LLP

My introduction to Skadden came at an evening recruitment event held in Oxford, where I learned a great deal about the firm and decided to apply for the vacation scheme. My initial impression from that evening was that Skadden had everything I was looking for in a firm and ultimately, in a training contract, and after completing the vacation scheme I can say with confidence that my initial impression was correct. I would add to this that my placement has only scratched at the surface of the range of work and experiences the firm can offer to vacation students and to its trainee solicitors. Skadden offers challenging, multi-dimensional work with clients from across the globe; however, the relatively small size of the office, compared to the size of the firm internationally, promotes a uniquely tight-knit feel. I would encourage those seeking a distinctive and challenging training contract to apply for the vacation scheme and find out first-hand what else Skadden has to offer.

For the duration of my vacation placement I sat with an associate in the M&A department and received my assignments from him and the partners he was working for. Right from the outset I hit the ground running and was asked to draft a share purchase agreement; later that day I undertook a research project relating to a multi-billion pound deal that was reported on the front pages of the FT the next day. By the second week I was asked to complete work for another multi-billion pound acquisition and drafted documents that were sent out to the client. My shock that a vacation student would receive such exposure soon abated: I learned that it is not at all unusual for junior members (and even non-law vacation students like myself!) to participate in a significant manner from day one. In doing so Skadden strongly encourages its trainees and vacation students to think for themselves. I also found the level of support available to be reassuring—people here genuinely take an interest in your education and training and will always endeavour to lend a hand.

I should also note that the vacation scheme was not without a full array of social events in which trainees, associates, and partners alike participated. In addition to lunches, dinners, and drinks parties there was a surprise boat cruise on the Thames, a private tour of Churchill's Cabinet War Rooms, a wine tasting event at a partner's house and a tour of Buckingham Palace followed by champagne afternoon tea at Claridges. In my weeks at the firm I found everyone, regardless of their level of seniority, to be truly welcoming and willing to get involved with those of us on the scheme.

**No of scheme places**
16-20

**Location of schemes**
London

**Length of schemes**
2 weeks

**Remuneration (per week)**
£300

**Dates of schemes**
Easter and Summer 2008

**Closing date for applications**
4 January 2008

**Application procedure**
Apply online at www.skadden.com

For full contact information and details of Training Contract, see the firm's full entry in the main directory on page 590

**Edward Comber**, an English Literature graduate from Bristol University, attended a two-week Easter Work Experience Scheme at Slaughter and May in 2007. Edward will commence his training contract with the firm in March 2010.

Given Slaughter and May's reputation as one of the leading law firms and a member of the magic circle, I was surprised by the straightforwardness of the application procedure. Right from the outset, I had the sense that this was a firm that treats its applicants as individuals and I was pleased to have been given the opportunity of working alongside some of the most talented lawyers in the City.

The Work Experience Scheme was structured such that the mornings were generally dedicated to lectures and workshops from various groups within the firm. As a non-law student, I was worried that I would struggle to understand the legal concepts that would arise during my placement. However, I was relieved to find that legal jargon was kept to a minimum; moreover, everything was explained to us in such a way that I did not find my non-legal background to be a handicap. In the afternoons, I tended to sit with an associate in the firm's commercial real estate group who was happy to involve me in the 'live' deals that she was working on. I carried out research, proof-read documents and helped draft letters to clients. I also worked with one of the trainees and got a feel for the type of work that I could expect to be doing during a training contract. In addition, all the students were given research projects centred on a commercial acquisition – I was certainly kept busy and intellectually stimulated.

There were three things that really impressed me about the firm: (1) the patience and friendliness of everyone I met despite their busy workloads; (2) the sense of pride towards the firm that was felt by all, from the receptionists to the senior-ranking partners, and their obvious commitment to excellence; (3) the culture and importance of knowledge-sharing that exists in the firm as shown by the recording of experiences and advice to a central 'know-how' database. All of these factors helped me to understand how the firm maintains its outstanding reputation.

My internship with Slaughter and May was both challenging and enjoyable as it allowed me to experience work at both a trainee and associate level on real transactions. I felt valued and involved during my time with the firm, and was especially pleased to have been included in several social events with partners, associates and trainees. Above all, I was made to feel very welcome.

Encouraged by my experiences and by the people that I had met, I applied for and was offered a training contract, which I was delighted to accept without hesitation.

**No of scheme places**
100 approx

**Location of schemes**
London

**Length of schemes**
2 weeks

**Remuneration (per week)**
£275

**Dates of schemes**
Christmas, Easter and Summer

**Closing date for applications**
Christmas: 26 October 2007
Easter: 4 January 2008
Summer: 25 January 2008

**Application procedure**
Our preferred method of application is online at www.slaughterandmay.com. You will be asked to fill in a short form and to attach your full CV and covering letter. We will also accept postal applications – please send a CV and covering letter including a full percentage breakdown of all examination results. We do not accept applications by email.

For full contact information and details of Training Contracts, see the firm's full entry in the main directory on page 591

## Got that Speechlys something?

Here at Speechly Bircham, we're as interested in your personal qualities as we are in your qualifications. We're looking for graduates who share our passion for the law and who relish the idea of building relationships with colleagues and clients alike. In return we're offering an environment where you'll be encouraged to make your own mark and you'll be rewarded for the difference you make.

**Think you've got that Speechlys something? Find out more at speechlys.com/trainingcontracts**

Winner
'Best Trainer
Medium City
Firm' Award

**Christopher Bushnell** attended a three-week summer placement at Speechly Bircham.

Monday morning; I sat nervously waiting on cramped commuter trains and enduring seemingly endless 'minor delays' on the tube. Fortunately, this was the worst part of my three weeks at Speechly Bircham. Any doubts I had evaporated the moment I met with the Human Resources Manager and the other summer students. Having had a chance to chat and get to know each other, we heard talks from current trainees who explained each of the main departments before joining them for an informal lunch. The first day concluded with a tour of the building and IT training, in which I felt computer illiterate for the first time in my life. I needn't have worried however, as the training was excellent and I was amazed to find that I could successfully navigate the firm's IT system the following day.

On Tuesday the real work started, with the first of my three seats being in the employment group. My activities ranged from researching conditional fee agreements, attending an employment tribunal and completing a response form for a case that we were defending. By the time I left on the fourth day I actually felt like a lawyer!

My second week was spent in the property department. Having previously studied land law, I had a vague idea of some of the relevant law but found that most of the work was quite different in practice to that of the lecture hall. During the week my tasks included amending a precedent lease to suit a new client's requirements, writing letters to clients, researching an issue relating to a recent change in the law and attending a client meeting and conference call.

My third and final week was spent in the construction group, and involved attending a complex court hearing, helping to prepare witness statements and comparing two contracts. The final week also included the traditional end of placement presentation, which was on issues of current affairs. Whilst sounding daunting, when the time arrived it was quite relaxed, even for those such as myself who had never had any public speaking experience.

I'm certainly glad that the placement was three weeks rather than the more standard two, and by the end of the second, far from being exhausted and wanting to go home, I felt I was at home with the firm and looking forward to the next week. Overall, everyone was very friendly and willing to offer help if anything was unclear. In fact people were so approachable that I had to use the firm's intranet to work out who the partners were! Whilst there we were invited to participate in all activities happening throughout the firm, from departmental training sessions to the firm's summer party at which everyone was happy to chat with the summer students. The summer scheme was a great help in making decisions about my future career plans and I would certainly recommend it.

**No of scheme places**
20

**Location of schemes**
London

**Length of schemes**
3 weeks

**Remuneration (per week)**
£250

**Dates of schemes**
July and August

**Closing date for applications**
15 February 2008

**Application procedure**
Apply online at www.speechlys.com

For full contact information and details of Training Contract, see the firm's full entry in the main directory on page 592

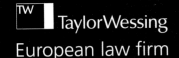

TaylorWessing

European law firm

# WHY WAIT?
# RESPONSIBILITY
# FROM THE WORD GO

Frustrating isn't it? Being held back when you're raring to go. Thankfully that won't be your experience at Taylor Wessing because we have full confidence in the trainees we recruit. Which means when you join, you'll be entrusted with high-quality work from day one. Don't waste your time – find out more about training contracts and vacation placements at www.taylorwessing.com/graduate

**Benjamin Lister**, a Classics student at Bristol University, completed the vacation scheme at Taylor Wessing LLP in Summer 2007. He will commence a training contract with the firm in September 2009.

I was attracted to Taylor Wessing because of its outstanding reputation as a highly respected full-service European law firm. I was particularly drawn to the firm's open and supportive working environment, and to its commitment to giving trainees responsibility from day one. I was keen to gain experience at a firm where I would get a chance to work closely with partners and associates on high quality projects from the outset. The opportunity of a summer vacation placement at Taylor Wessing was therefore extremely attractive.

I chose to spend the first week of my placement with the finance and projects department and the second week in the employment and pensions team. Everyone sits with a partner or associate, but in both departments a number of partners and associates involved me in a broad range of tasks. These included research, document production, and client contact, all of which contributed to live deals and cases. At Taylor Wessing, in contrast to vacation schemes I took with other firms, I was given work that would usually be assigned to a trainee. Everyone I met was very approachable and always took time to explain both the broader context and the intricate complexities of the task in hand. My trainee buddies in each department were very welcoming and very keen to answer questions.

A series of presentations on the firm's key practice areas along with group exercises gave me an excellent insight into the firm's clients and the dynamics of each department. As a non-law student I found the group exercises particularly valuable in furthering my legal and commercial awareness. The chance to work closely over the two weeks with other students to produce a presentation was both stimulating and insightful.

A range social events organised as part of the scheme provided further opportunities to gain a real feel for the firm's dynamics. All the trainees and associates attended the events were keen to get to know the vacation students even better, as was everyone I met during the placement. A particular highlight was attending a major client social event, where I had the invaluable opportunity to meet a number of the firm's key clients.

The vacation scheme was extremely well organised and I strongly recommend it to anyone keen to experience high quality work in the open and collaborative culture of Taylor Wessing.

**No of scheme places**
40

**Location of schemes**
London

**Length of schemes**
2 weeks

**Remuneration (per week)**
£250

**Dates of schemes**
June and July 2008

**Closing date for applications**
31 January 2008

**Application procedure**
Online application form at www.taylorwessing.com/graduate

For full contact information and details of Training Contract, see the firm's full entry in the main directory on page 602

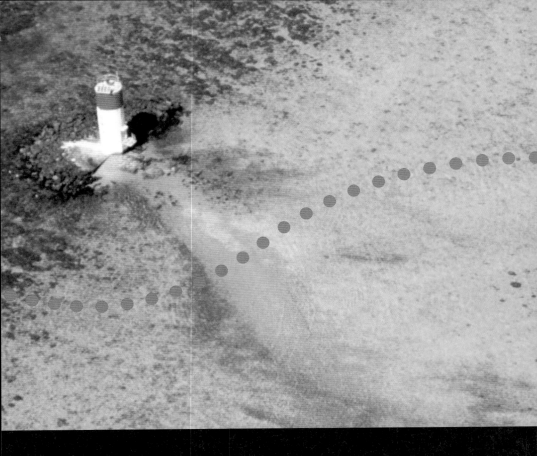

**George Weavil**, a Mathematics and Philosophy graduate from Worcester College, Oxford University, attended a two-week Christmas placement at Travers Smith. He will commence his training contract with the firm in September 2009.

When I returned from a year living in Spain after university having decided that I wished to pursue a career in law but with no legal experience, I found myself faced with the very difficult decision of where to apply. After several careers fairs and many hours trawling through different firms' websites, it became clear that a vacation scheme was the best way to gain the exposure I needed both to confirm my choice of career and to begin the seemingly impossible task of comparing the different firms.

It was an easy decision to accept the offer of a place on the Travers Smith vacation scheme. I already knew of the scheme's excellent reputation and the application process gave me a very good feeling about the culture I could expect to find at the firm. My interview felt more like a relaxed chat and I was particularly impressed at how keen the partner seemed both to get to know me and to tell me anything I wanted to know about the firm. This was my first taste of the friendly and supportive yet professional and intellectually focused atmosphere which, for me, defines Travers Smith.

On the scheme, we were involved in a wide range of different activities designed to give us the best possible insight into the working life of a Travers Smith lawyer. For me, this even included being taken along to a client meeting and helping with real work following on from it, which was a challenging and highly rewarding experience. It wasn't all hard work, though, as there were plenty of opportunities to get to know people at the firm over lunches, evening drinks and at the Christmas Party, to which we were all invited.

The highly effective combination of informative seminars and workshops focussing on key skills such as negotiation interspersed with time spent in the office observing and helping the lawyers go about their daily work left me feeling that I had learnt a great deal about life as a city lawyer and in no doubt as to where I wanted to apply for a training contract.

**No of scheme places**
Christmas - 15 (Non-law)
Summer - 45 (Law)

**Location of schemes**
London

**Length of schemes**
2 weeks

**Remuneration (per week)**
£250

**Dates of schemes**
Christmas:
10 - 21 December 2007
Summer:
23 June - 4 July 2008
7 July - 18 July 2008
21 July - 1 August 2008

**Closing date for applications**
Summer: 31 January 2008

**Application procedure**
CV and covering letter online or by post

For full contact information and details of Training Contract, see the firm's full entry in the main directory on page 613

th trowers & hamlins

MANCHESTER th
EXETER th LONDON

CAIRO th

BAHRAIN th th DUBAI
ABU DHABI th th OMAN

www.trowers.com

For further information about our graduate process please contact
the graduate recruitment team on tel +44 (0)20 7423 8312 or
hking@trowers.com

Trowers & Hamlins is an equal opportunities employer

**Louis Sebastian**, a Politics, Philosophy and Economics graduate from the University of York, participated in a two-week vacation placement with Trowers and Hamlins in the summer of 2007.

# Trowers & Hamlins

Though the sources of information about training contracts are extensive, ranging from websites and books to law fairs, it was clear to me that no number of free pens or evenings on the internet would tell me what it is like to work for a commercial law firm. My unlikely combination of interests – in PFI Projects and Middle Eastern politics – brought Trowers and Hamlins to my attention immediately. Learning that it has the largest presence in the Middle East and is the market leader in Social Housing compelled me to apply for their vacation scheme.

The scheme was well constructed with a thorough induction and orientation on the first day that allowed me to settle in quickly. In addition, the evening excursions, for wine tasting and to the London Eye, gave ample time to talk to current trainees about their experiences at Trowers and Hamlins. A week in each of the Housing and Employment departments gave me a good idea of the variety of work on offer within the firm. Further, I was given work similar to that which current trainees perform. Being asked to conduct research, draft letters, meet clients, proof-read documents and report to solicitors, and even partners, made me feel very much part of the team.

The atmosphere I encountered was one which could only be generated by a firm that is refreshingly comfortable with itself and is therefore able to accommodate a range of personalities. Having said that, it was noticeable that all of the people I met at Trowers had one thing in common; they all conducted their business with a quiet confidence in the work of the firm and in their own abilities. This feeling is engendered by the close working partnerships that I witnessed between partners, associates and trainees, and reinforced by the indubitable quality of the firm's output. No-doubt winning 'Law Firm of the Year' recently has added to their swagger.

My two weeks with the firm seem to have been a microcosm of what a training contract with Trowers and Hamlins would be like. I was welcomed into each department and immediately given work that, though challenging, was never beyond me. Encouragement and praise were forthcoming as was constructive criticism, with experienced hands always available to answer any questions that I had. My non-law background hardly raised an eyebrow and I was given numerous opportunities to learn new skills and demonstrate my abilities.

My vacation scheme has given me the perfect insight into what working for Trowers and Hamlins involves. This experience has energised me and increased my determination to secure a training contract with them.

**No of scheme places**
27 - London
3 - Manchester

**Location of schemes**
London and Manchester

**Length of schemes**
2 weeks

**Remuneration (per week)**
£225

**Dates of schemes**
Mid-June - August 2008

**Closing date for applications**
1 March 2008

**Application procedure**
Please visit our website www.trowers.com and complete an online application.

For full contact information and details of Training Contract, see the firm's full entry in the main directory on page 615

## Teacher
## Stern Selby

**Will Russell**, a Classics graduate from University College London, completed a two-week vacation scheme placement at Teacher Stern Selby in summer 2007.

Teacher Stern Selby's vacation scheme gives students the opportunity to sample life in all three of the firm's departments (property, litigation, corporate and commercial). Over the two weeks of the scheme I was given work on subjects as diverse as jurisdiction issues in a cross-border distribution agreement, landlord and tenant disputes, employees' rights in the sale of a business, and the criteria for council tax banding (more interesting than it sounds). Often these tasks involved writing research memos on relevant points of law, but I also had the opportunity to shadow an assistant and trainee team as they neared completion on an asset transfer, a valuable lesson in the need for good communication in dealing with clients and the inevitable last minute problems. Fee-earners were always ready to answer questions – if they were busy, I wasn't told to come back later, they came and found me – and the feedback they gave me was very useful: putting what I had worked on in the bigger picture, and giving me a real understanding of a solicitor's role in transactional and contentious work.

Seeing the litigation department in action was particularly interesting: TSS has a broad range in contentious expertise, from standard commercial fare to IP and employment, and the firm has carved out a real niche for itself in media and sports cases, with some very high-profile clients. Following one case in the office and then in the newspapers the next day was fascinating, and showed me the need for both quick responses and strategy in this area of law.

The trainees at TSS seem to have the answer to the old chestnut: when it comes to law firms and training contracts, does size matter? Certainly the levels of client contact and responsibility they enjoy surpass those which trainees receive at larger firms I have encountered, and the broadly defined departments give trainees exposure to a very wide range of work in each seat. Moreover, the quality of work, particularly in TSS's specialist areas, is impressive, and belies the firm's comparatively small size. For these and other reasons - friendly, accessible people, and office hours conducive to actually having a life - I think firms like TSS offer an excellent alternative for those willing to look beyond the likes of Goliath LLP.

**No of scheme places**
20

**Location of schemes**
London

**Length of schemes**
1 or 2 weeks

**Remuneration (per week)**
£200

**Dates of schemes**
Mid-June to mid-September

**Closing date for applications**
30 April 2008

**Application procedure**
Completed training contract application form

For full contact information and details of Training Contract, see the firm's full entry in the main directory on page 603

**Tim Varney** is an English Literature graduate from the University of Leeds. He completed a one-week summer vacation placement at Walker Morris in 2007 and will be joining the firm as a trainee solicitor in September 2008.

I undertook Walker Morris's vacation scheme in June 2007 and was delighted to discover that all the literature that I had read about the firm's friendly reputation was not merely a sales pitch to draw people in, but was something that permeates the whole of the Walker Morris institution. Making its 'vac schemers' comfortable was a priority from the moment we entered the building on Monday morning. Efforts were made to integrate all the vac schemers into the firm for the week, providing us with a real taste of what life as a Walker Morris trainee solicitor might be like, with special emphasis placed on us building relationships with each other, as well as with the current group of trainees.

Upon the conclusion of the week, I truly felt like I had a good understanding of the atmosphere and ethos of Walker Morris. I was introduced to each and every one of the current trainees, who were all extremely helpful, honest, and kind, as well as being full of personality. I met paralegals, secretaries, associates and partners and found everyone to be warm, willing to help (even when I thought I had broken the photocopier for the fifth time that day), and also trusting enough to give me some exciting work that I was really able to get my teeth into.

We were taken out on several evenings out with the trainees, allowing us to get to know them in a relaxed and sociable environment, which provided ample opportunity for us to ask those questions that you might not feel comfortable asking in the work place. The work itself was challenging and thus rewarding, and if you ever found yourself struggling there would be a trainee just around the corner to offer some help.

We also undertook two valuable scenario-based exercises as a group to give us a taste of what life as a solicitor might be like. The week was impeccably organised, and at no time did I feel like I was in the way or inconveniencing anybody as we were treated with respect and courtesy at all times. For me, the week was a perfect combination of getting to know the firm and its staff, challenging and rewarding tasks, and real, valuable experiences that gave me a great insight into a genuinely unique law firm.

**No of scheme places**
48

**Location of schemes**
Leeds

**Length of schemes**
1 week

**Remuneration (per week)**
£200

**Dates of schemes**
June and July

**Closing date for applications**
31 January 2008

**Application procedure**
Online application form

For full contact information and details of Training Contract, see the firm's full entry in the main directory on page 620

# Broaden your
# horizons

Many City firms have a string of offices outside the UK. The chances are, as a trainee, you won't be the one to go and work there.

Here at Watson, Farley & Williams we believe in letting you find out how an international firm works by seeing for yourself.

This means that during your training period with us in London, you'll be offered a four month seat in one of our overseas offices.

We look for people who get a buzz out of being part of the commercial world and a valuable member of busy teams specialising in Corporate, Finance, Litigation and Tax.

For more information on vacation placements in 2008 and/or training contracts to commence in 2010, please visit our website at www.wfw.com or email us at graduates@wfw.com

Watson, Farley & Williams
www.wfw.com

**Isidore Caroussis**, a non-law student at Oxford participated in the summer vacation scheme at Watson, Farley & Williams. He will join the firm as a trainee in September 2007.

# Watson, Farley & Williams LLP

Having spent three years reading history at Oxford, I was keen to pursue a career that would make use of the analytical and reasoning skills I had developed. Although law seemed to be the ideal choice I was undecided for a time so I undertook a number of vacation placements. It was not until I had completed the vacation scheme at WFW that I finally decided that I actively wanted to work in the legal profession.

The vacation scheme at WFW was interesting and enjoyable, and, significantly for me, accessible to those who have no previous experience of the law. It was suitably coherent with a good combination of lectures, group discussions and hands-on legal experience. Working side by side with an associate on his projects, my involvement ranged from contract drafting to sitting in on client meetings. The people at WFW came across as very professional but also friendly and approachable, with advice and criticism always helpful and constructive. In general, I was impressed by the amount that WFW managed to fit in a two week scheme and I perceived a healthy and productive working ethos that I had not found in any of the other places that I had worked. Overall, I got the impression that WFW is an established yet dynamic firm that would offer wide-ranging opportunities and is eager for fresh contributions.

It seems that the training programme is similarly well-structured. The offer of six four-month seats was very appealing to me given that I am undecided as to the area of law in which I intend to specialise and wish to experience as much variety as possible. I was also particularly attracted to the guarantee of a seat abroad that would add an international perspective to my legal training.

Please feel free to email me on isidore@caroussis.com should you have any questions about applying for the WFW vacation scheme or simply if you're like I was and somewhat unsure as to the correct road to travel...

**No of scheme places**
40

**Location of schemes**
London

**Length of schemes**
2 weeks

**Remuneration (per week)**
£250

**Dates of schemes**
Please visit our website
www.wfw.com

**Closing date for applications**
24 February 2008

**Application procedure**
Online application only

For full contact information and details of Training Contract, see the firm's full entry in the main directory on page 625

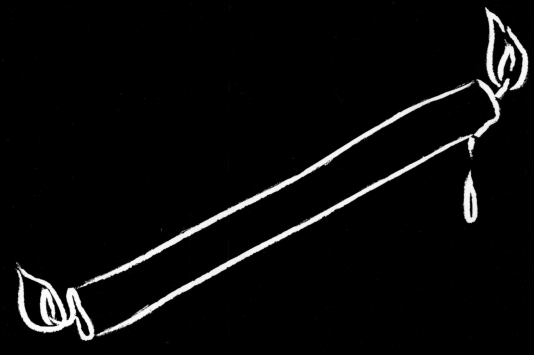

# Intense

**WORKING AT WEIL, GOTSHAL & MANGES IS NOT FOR EVERYONE.**

How do you cope when asked to face your fears? In our experience, it's often a good way to get the best out of people. We encourage our employees to leave their comfort zones and experience the thrill of those butterflies and heart-stopping moments.

Invited to join a set of top private equity investors for a night's entertainment, new trainee David embarked on his evening with eager anticipation but also some trepidation. The only representative of the firm, his desire to maintain professional client relations while in an informal social setting made for an intense assignment. His diplomacy skills were up to the task though, as his supervisor confirmed the following morning.

We're currently looking for people like David to join our vacation scheme. If you want to learn at the sharp end and are ready for a challenge, come and talk to us…

**Do something that scares you** www.weil.com/wgm/recruiting

WEIL, GOTSHAL & MANGES

**James Dodd** is studying in Law with American Law at Nottingham University. James completed a two-week placement at Weil Gotshal & Manges in 2007 and has accepted a training contract with the firm to begin in September 2009.

# Weil Gotshal & Manges

My first contact with Weil, Gotshal & Manges arose more from coincidence than careful planning on my part as I happened to attend a social event at the University of Nottingham that was being sponsored by the firm. The people from Weil Gotshal immediately impressed me, both in terms of the number present and their qualities. They were all from diverse backgrounds but were equally friendly and interested in meeting the students. It was a great introduction to the firm and I was keen to learn more about it. Soon after this I was very happy to gain a place on the firm's vacation scheme.

The vacation scheme was fantastic and confirmed to me that practising law in an international law firm was right for me, and that the firm itself suited me perfectly. From my own experience with other firms, and from talking to others, there is one thing that made the vacation scheme at Weil great, which is the same thing that makes the firm great: size. The small number of vacation scheme students meant that, within the first hour, we all knew each other's names, all met up every lunch time and attended all the social events together. One of the most rewarding parts of my vacation scheme at Weil Gotshal on a more personal level was how much I learnt from talking to others. As a result of the firm's friendly culture it was easy to arrange to speak to anyone (including head of department partners). This meant that, even if you were not in a particular department, partners from the group would make time to talk with you. It also struck me during these conversations how much the partners were interested in you and the amount of time that they were willing to spend with each student.

In addition to this partner contact, each of us were assigned a partner mentor in addition to the usual mentor and supervisor, which I found very useful. It meant that we each received even more contact with people from all levels of the firm. The small size and high quality of work associated with Weil Gotshal filtered through the office and meant that, just as trainees at Weil Gotshal are not just another cog in a huge wheel, as vacation scheme students we were doing meaningful and high calibre work as well. I found it particularly rewarding that when I was asked to do work for a partner, he then phoned the client as soon as I discussed it with him, using my research for their subsequent conversation. For all of these reasons, and many more besides, I had a particularly enjoyable two weeks with Weil Gotshal and I actually looked forward to waking up each morning and going to work! I would encourage anyone who wants a hands-on experience of high-quality City law, whilst being part of a firm where everyone at all levels wants to get to know you, and where you will not be simply another vacation scheme student, to apply to Weil Gotshal.

**No of scheme places**
20

**Location of schemes**
London
New for 2008: 5 students will spend 3 weeks in the New York office

**Length of schemes**
2 weeks

**Remuneration (per week)**
£400

**Dates of schemes**
Easter and Summer 2008

**Closing date for applications**
14 February 2008

**Application procedure**
Application form

For full contact information and details of Training Contract, see the firm's full entry in the main directory on page 628

# Insider report
## White & Case LLP

**Stefan Mrozinski**, a Law graduate from the London School of Economics and Political Science, joined White & Case LLP for a summer vacation placement in 2007. He will start his training contract with the firm in August 2009.

When applying for vacation placements, I was looking for a global firm that provided their lawyers with top quality work, had world-renowned clients, offered opportunities to work overseas and expected their trainees to take on early responsibility. Two weeks with White & Case convinced me that this firm offers all this and more.

After an introduction to the firm, I was taken to meet my supervisor in the banking and capital markets practice group. Having already spent the previous summer doing vacation placements with other top City law firms I was somewhat sceptical about the quality of work that I would be given. But by the second day with White & Case, I was already undertaking research on Polish securities law in order to help construct a cross border database on securities regimes that will be distributed around the firm's offices. Also, I was working on deals that involved some of the biggest names in global finance. During my second week, which was spent in corporate, I went to Birmingham in order to get documents stamped for a multi-million pound deal that was nearing completion.

A standout feature of the firm's training contract is the guaranteed overseas seat, and with the options including six months in places such as Tokyo, Johannesburg, or Almaty, there is certainly something for everyone. Since movement between the firm's 35 offices is so common, the London office is genuinely international. Therefore, I found myself working alongside lawyers who were not only friendly, approachable, and highly intelligent, but who were also from countries as diverse as Australia, China, and the United States. The year-round business-casual dress policy is also a major bonus, especially in the summer!

Apart from the after work drinks that we organised between ourselves and the trainees, there were a range of highly enjoyable social activities that the graduate recruitment team organised for us.

I am excited about starting my training contract with White & Case in August 2009 and am looking forward to seeing the trainees again at the various social events which future trainees are invited to attend. I cannot recommend them highly enough!

If you would like to find out more, please email me at stefan_mrozinski@hotmail.com.

**No of scheme places**
80

**Location of schemes**
London

**Length of schemes**
Easter - 1 week
Summer - 2 weeks

**Remuneration (per week)**
£350

**Dates of schemes**
Easter and Summer

**Closing date for applications**
31 January 2008

**Application procedure**
Apply online at
www.whitecase.com/trainee

For full contact information and details of Training Contract, see the firm's full entry in the main directory on page 630

**Julia Schaefer**, a European Law graduate from Warwick University, attended a two-week vacation scheme placement at Withers LLP. She will join the firm as a trainee in 2008.

Having been attracted to Withers' excellent reputation in private client work, its medium size and international dimension, I was excited to secure a place on the firm's renowned vacation placement at Easter.

During the first week I worked in the family department where I accompanied my supervisor and a client to a meeting with Counsel and attended the subsequent court hearing about child contact. On both occasions I took notes and later wrote a file memo. The parties agreed to mediation and I was asked to research and contact possible mediation services.

I also accompanied a solicitor to a client meeting concerning divorce proceedings, where I took detailed notes outlining the client's financial situation. In addition, I drafted client correspondence, collated a bundle of cases and observed a Court of Appeal hearing at the Royal Courts of Justice in which the parties argued about whether their post-divorce asset distribution should take place in England or Spain.

During the second week I sat in the commercial department, sharing an office with a partner. On my first day I accompanied him to a client meeting in which the possibility of floating the client's company on the Alternative Investment Market (AIM) was discussed. I also drafted a contract for the sale of a sports car, assisted in finalising a company incorporation and conducted research into company tax law in order to establish the most favourable tax regime for a client.

During the vacation scheme, I was invited to departmental meetings and briefings, as well as training sessions for trainees.

I was warmly welcomed by my host departments and my supervisors and trainee 'buddies' went out of their way to expose me to a range of work that was both interesting and intellectually stimulating.

There were a few social events too including a wine tasting evening, where I had the opportunity to talk to trainees and associates from different departments.

I was delighted to be offered a training contract with Withers and will be joining the firm in 2008. In the meantime I am going to study French in Paris and fulfil my dream of sailing across the Atlantic on a Brig!

**No of scheme places**
35

**Location of schemes**
London and Milan

**Length of schemes**
2 weeks

**Remuneration (per week)**
£250

**Dates of schemes**
Easter and Summer 2008

**Closing date for applications**
31 January 2008

**Application procedure**
Online application form

For full contact information and details of Training Contract, see the firm's full entry in the main directory on page 636

# WANTED
## LAW BREAKERS

---

# REWARD
## A GREAT CAREER AT
# WRAGGE & CO

Want a career in a successful firm doing great work for great clients and still have a life?   How about the chance to realise your ambition to make it to the top without compromising your personal beliefs and values?   Where else could you find a firm a firm that has always offered certainty of a job at the end of your training?   And what about being part of a forward-thinking business that celebrates diversity and even wants you to be different?   All that and the opportunity to join  the only law firm listed in the Financial Times Best Workplaces in the UK 2007?

If you want to join a firm that challenges conventions and breaks the rules, visit
**www.wragge.com/graduate**

**Hannah Rees** completed an English degree at Birmingham University and is now studying the two-year programme in Law at Birmingham University. She attended a one-week Easter vacation scheme at Wragge & Co LLP.

I applied for a vacation scheme at Wragge & Co for several reasons: primarily I was eager to see whether it lived up to its reputation as an innovative, individual and friendly firm. I can say with complete confidence that it did.

The people focus of the firm was evident from the beginning: the first day was an induction which enabled placement students to get to know each other. We gelled as a team immediately; this was due to activities throughout the day, culminating in a treasure hunt around Birmingham. We were each allocated a trainee as a 'buddy'; this was a great system as it meant that the trainee's were always at hand to help out and answer any questions. The fun filled first day ensured that we felt welcome and prepared for the following two weeks.

During my first week I sat in real estate; I was given a variety of work which involved drafting and proof reading legal documents, making telephone calls and researching legal issues. In my second week I sat in the outsourcing, technology and trade team, where most of my time was spent reading and drafting a contract. Throughout the two weeks, I felt that the work I was given was always for my benefit; I was given the right level of supervision and gained a real insight into the expectations and responsibilities of a trainee.

Aside from the time spent in our groups, we were given talks by partners, newly qualified solicitors and trainees about various aspects of life at Wragge & Co. We spent a day at the London office where we were given further insight into the single team approach of the firm. The placement also incorporated a trip to the College of Law, where we took part in an interviewing workshop; this, coupled with a mediation exercise and a role play, provided a real insight into the skills required of a solicitor. The flexibility and fantastic organisation of the placement meant that our time was optimised effectively so as to get the most out of our experience.

There were numerous social events throughout the placement: as well as regular drinks with trainees and lunch outings, we were treated to dinners and took part in a fun game of rounders. What struck me most about Wragge & Co were the people and the socials provided a great opportunity to mix with many people at different levels. Everyone was so friendly and approachable, and genuinely seemed to enjoy life at Wragges; it is largely for this reason that I know Wragge & Co are the firm for me. I thoroughly enjoyed the vacation scheme and I highly recommend it to anyone considering applying to a professional and friendly firm, which values individuality.

**No of scheme places**
40-50

**Location of schemes**
Birmingham

**Length of schemes**
Easter: 1 week
Summer: 2 weeks

**Remuneration (per week)**
£220

**Dates of schemes**
Easter and Summer 2008

**Closing date for applications**
31 January 2008

**Application procedure**
Applications are made online at www.wragge.com/graduate (paper application form available on request)

For full contact information and details of Training Contract, see the firm's full entry in the main directory on page 639

# Firms that offer work placement schemes

Firms in **bold** have provided detailed information in the directory section
Firms in purple have provided an Insider Report

Addie & Co
Addison O'Hare
**Addleshaw Goddard**
Advance Legal
Allan Janes
**Allen & Overy LLP**
Alliance Solicitors
Andrew Isaacs Solicitors
Andrew Jackson
Anthony Jacobs & Co
AP Law
Arlingtons Sharmas Solicitors
**Arnold & Porter (UK) LLP**
AS Law Practice
**Ashfords**
Ashton Bell
**Ashton Graham**
Ashurst
Aston Clark Solicitors
Avery Emerson
Backhouse Jones
Baileys
Bains & Co
**Baker & McKenzie LLP**
**Barlow Lyde & Gilbert LLP**
Baron Grey
Bates, Wells & Braithwaite
**Beachcroft LLP**
Beardsells
Bell Lax Solicitors
Berg Legal
Berkeley Solicitors
**Berrymans Lace Mawer**
**Berwin Leighton Paisner LLP**
**Bevan Brittan LLP**
Bhogal Partners
BHW Commercial Solicitors
Bilton Hammond
**Bircham Dyson Bell LLP**
**Bird & Bird**
Bird & Co
Birkett Long
BKM Solicitors
Blackhurst Swainson Goodier
**Blake Lapthorn Tarlo Lyons**
Bolitho Way
**Bond Pearce LLP**
**Boodle Hatfield**
**BP Collins**
**BPE**
**Brabners Chaffe Street LLP**
Brian Camp & Co
**Bristows**
Bryan and Armstrong
Bryan Cave
BS Singh & Co
BTMK Solicitors LLP

Burges Salmon
Cains Advocates Limited
**Capsticks**
Cartmell Shepherd
**Charles Russell LLP**
**Clarion Solicitors**
**Clarkson Wright & Jakes**
Cleary Gottlieb Steen & Hamilton LLP
**Clifford Chance**
Clintons
**Clyde & Co LLP**
**CMS Cameron McKenna LLP**
**Cobbetts LLP**
**Coffin Mew LLP**
Colemans
Colemans-ctts
Collas Day
Covington & Burling LLP
**Crown Prosecution Service**
Cunningtons
Curwens
DAS Legal Expenses Insurance
**Davenport Lyons**
David Phillips & Partners
**Davies Arnold Cooper**
Davies Johnson & Co
Dawson Cornwell
**Dawsons LLP**
**Debevoise & Plimpton LLP**
**Dechert LLP**
Denton Wilde Sapte
Dexter Montague & Partners
Df Legal LLP
**Dickinson Dees LLP**
Dilwyns
**DLA Piper UK LLP**
**DMH Stallard Solicitors**
Dolmans
Donald Race & Newton
Druces & Attlee
Duncan Lewis & Co
**Dundas & Wilson LLP**
**DWF**
Eden & Company
Edmondson Hall
Edward de Silva & Co
Edwin Coe LLP
Elliott Bridgman
Emery Johnson Solicitors
The Endeavour Partnership LLP
Eversheds LLP
Express Solicitors
**Faegre & Benson LLP**
**Farrer & Co LLP**
Fenwick Elliott LLP
**Field Fisher Waterhouse LLP**
Field Seymour Parkes

Follett Stock
**Foot Anstey**
**Forbes Solicitors**
**Foreman Laws**
**Forsters LLP**
Fox Williams
Freeman Johnson
**Freshfields Bruckhaus Deringer**
Garden House Solicitors
**Geldards LLP**
Glaisyers
Goody Burrett LLP
**Government Legal Service**
Graham & Rosen
Gregory Abrams Davidson LLP
**Halliwells LLP**
**Hammonds**
Hansells
Harris Waters & Co
Harrow Solicitors & Advocates
Harrowell Shaftoe
**Harvey Ingram LLP**
Hatton
**Hay & Kilner**
**HBJ Gateley Wareing LLP**
Henry's Solicitors Limited
**Herbert Smith LLP**
Hertfordshire District Council
**Hewitsons**
**Hextalls LLP**
**Hill Dickinson LLP**
Hilton Norbury
HKH Kenwright & Cox
hlw Commercial Lawyers LLP
**Hodge Jones & Allen**
**Holman Fenwick & Willan**
Hooper & Wollen
Howarth Goodman
**Howes Percival LLP**
**Hugh James**
Humphreys & Co
Hunt Kidd
Hunters
Hutchinson Thomas
Huttons
**Ince & Co**
**Irwin Mitchell**
JA Forrest & Co
JA Hughes
Jepson & Co
Jeremy Roberts & Co
**Jones Day**
Jones Mordey Davies Solicitors
JR Jones Solicitors
Kaim Todner
**Kendall Freeman**
Kenneth Elliott & Rowe

Kester Cunningham John
**Kimbells LLP**
**Kirkland & Ellis**
**Kirkpatrick & Lockhart Preston Gates Ellis LLP**
KJD
**Knight & Sons**
Knights
KSB  Law
KSL Solicitors
LA Steel
Landes Hutton LLP
**Langleys**
**Latham & Watkins**
Latimer Lee
**Lawrence Graham LLP**
**Laytons**
**LeBoeuf Lamb Greene & MacRae**
Leigh Day & Co
**Lester Aldridge**
**Lewis Silkin LLP**
**Linklaters LLP**
**Lovells LLP**
Lupton Fawcett
Lyons Davidson
M Olubi Solicitors
**Mace & Jones**
**Macfarlanes**
**Maclay Murray & Spens LLP**
Makin Dixon Solicitors
Malcolm C Foy & Co
Malik & Malik
Malletts
**Manches LLP**
Martin Cray and Co
**Martineau Johnson**
Matrix Solicitors
Maudsley Wright & Pearson
Maxwell Hodge
**Mayer Brown International LLP**
**McGrigors LLP**
Meldrum Young Solicitors
Merriman White
**Michelmores**
Middleweeks
Millan Solicitors
**Mills & Reeve LLP**
**Mishcon de Reya**
MLM
Mohammed & Co
Moosa-Duke Solicitors
**Morgan Cole**
Morrison & Foerster
**Muckle LLP**
Myers Lister Price
**Nabarro**
**Needham & James LLP**
NK Legal Solicitors

# Firms that offer work placement schemes

Firms in **bold** have provided detailed information in the directory section
Firms in purple have provided an Insider Report

Noble
North Yorkshire County Council
**Norton Rose LLP**
Olswang
**O'Melveny & Myers**
Orchard Brayton Graham LLP
**Osborne Clarke**
Osbornes
Osmond & Osmond
Oxley & Coward
Ozannes
**Palmers**
**Pannone LLP**
**Paris Smith & Randall LLP**
**Paul Hastings**
**Penningtons Solicitors LLP**
**Pinsent Masons**
Pitmans
Powell Spencer & Partners
**Prettys**
**PricewaterhouseCoopers Legal LLP**
**Pritchard Englefield**
Punatar & Co
**RadcliffesLeBrasseur**
Rawstorne Heran
**Reed Smith Richards Butler LLP**
Renaissance Solicitors
Reynolds Colman Bradley LLP
**Reynolds Porter Chamberlain LLP**
Richmonds
**Rickerbys**
The Roland Partnership
Rollits
Rosenblatt
Rowlands Solicitors LLP
Royds
Russell & Co
Samuel Phillips Law Firm
SB Solicitors
Schillings
Schofield Sweeney LLP
Scott Rees & Co
The Sethi Partnership Solicitors
SFM Legal Services
**Shadbolt LLP**
**Shearman & Sterling LLP**
Sheikh & Co
**Shoosmiths**
**Shulmans**
**Simmons & Simmons**
Sintons LLP
**SJ Berwin LLP**
**Skadden, Arps, Slate, Meagher & Flom (UK) LLP**
**Slaughter and May**
Smith Llewelyn Partnership
**Speechly Bircham LLP**
Spence & Horne

**Squire, Sanders & Dempsey**
Stamp Jackson and Procter
**Stanley Tee LLP**
steeles
**Stephenson Harwood**
Stephensons
**Stevens & Bolton LLP**
Stone Wilder
Sweetman Burke & Sinker
Sykes Anderson LLP
Talbot & Co
Tassells
**Taylor Vinters**
**Taylor Walton**
Taylor Wessing
**Teacher Stern Selby**
Temple Heelis
**Thomas Cooper**
**Thomas Eggar**
**Thomson Snell & Passmore**
**TLT Solicitors**
TMJ Law Solicitors
TMJ Legal Services LLP
Toller Beattie
Tranters
Tranters Freeclaim Solicitors
**Travers Smith**
Trobridges
**Trowers & Hamlins**
Tucker Turner Kingsley Wood & Co
Veale Wasbrough Lawyers
**Vertex Law LLP**
Vincent Sykes
**Vinson & Elkins RLLP**
Vodafone Group Services
Wainwright & Cummins
**Walker Morris**
Wallace Robinson & Morgan
**Ward Hadaway**
Watkins Solicitors
**Watson Burton LLP**
**Watson, Farley & Williams LLP**
**Wedlake Bell**
**Weil Gotshal & Manges**
West London Law Solicitors
Whetter Duckworth Fowler
**White & Case LLP**
**Wilsons Solicitors LLP**
Winckworth Sherwood
**Withers LLP**
Woodfines LLP
Worthingtons
**Wragge & Co LLP**
Wright Hassall  LLP
Wrigleys Solicitors LLP
Young & Pearce
Zeckler & Co

# Chambers that offer mini-pupillages

Chambers in **bold** have provided detailed information in the directory section

Albany Chambers
Angel Chambers
**Arden Chambers**
**Atkin Chambers**
**Atkinson Bevan Chambers**
Atlantic Chambers
2 Bedford Row
9 Bedford Row
42 Bedford Row
**25 Bedford Row**
36 Bedford Row
29 Bedford Row Chambers
9-12 Bell Yard
Blackstone Chambers
1 Brick Court
**4 Brick Court**
Brick Court Chambers
Broadway House Chambers
18 Carlton Crescent
**Carmelite Chambers**
1 Chancery Lane
Charter Chambers
Chartlands Chambers
Chavasse Court Chambers
Citadel Chambers
Cloisters
College Chambers
12 College Place
Coram Chambers
**Crown Office Chambers**
**One Crown Office Row**
Crown Office Row Chambers
**Crown Prosecution Service**
Deans Court Chambers
Devereux Chambers
Doughty Street Chambers
2 Dr Johnson's Buildings
2 Dyer's Buildings
East Anglian Chambers
Eastbourne Chambers
Ely Place Chambers
Enterprise Chambers
**Erskine Chambers**
One Essex Court
5 Essex Court
Essex Court Chambers
20 Essex Street
**23 Essex Street**
**39 Essex Street**
**Exchange Chambers**
Falcon Chambers
**Farrar's Building**
Fenners Chambers
Field Court Chambers
187 Fleet Street
Fountain Chambers

8 Fountain Court
Fountain Court Chambers
**Francis Taylor Building**
Furnival Chambers
1 Garden Court
Garden Court Chambers
Garden Square
**9 Gough Square**
Gough Square Chambers
1 Gray's Inn Square
**4-5 Gray's Inn Square**
14 Gray's Inn Square
Gray's Inn Tax Chambers
Guildford Chambers
Guildhall Chambers
**Hailsham Chambers**
Harcourt Chambers
**Hardwicke Building**
**1 Hare Court**
2 Hare Court
3 Hare Court
**Henderson Chambers**
**Hogarth Chambers**
Hollis Whiteman Chambers
India Buildings
1 Inner Temple Lane
Iscoed Chambers
**11 KBW**
KCH Chambers
**Keating Chambers**
Kenworthy's Chambers
King Street Chambers
8 King Street Chambers
King's Bench Chambers
**1 King's Bench Walk**
5 King's Bench Walk
**6 King's Bench Walk**
6 King's Bench Walk
**7 King's Bench Walk**
**12 King's Bench Walk**
Kings Chambers
Lamb Building
Lamb Chambers
**Landmark Chambers**
9 Lincoln's Inn Fields
Littleton Chambers
Maidstone Chambers
**Maitland Chambers (incorporating 9 Old Square)**
1 Mitre Court Buildings
Mitre House Chambers
Monckton Chambers
New Bailey Chambers
New Court Chambers
New Court Chambers
3 New Square
**4 New Square**

# Chambers that offer mini-pupillages

Chambers in **bold** have provided detailed information in the directory section

8 New Square
**New Square Chambers**
2 New Street Chambers
New Walk Chambers
Nicholas Street Chambers
**No 5 Chambers**
Northampton Chambers
**24 Old Buildings**
15 Old Square
**10 Old Square**
**Old Square Chambers**
Oriel Chambers
Outer Temple Chambers
Pallant Chambers
2 Paper Buildings
3 Paper Buildings
4 Paper Buildings
5 Paper Buildings
5 Paper Buildings
Paradise Chambers
Park Court Chambers
Park Lane Chambers
9 Park Place
**30 Park Place**
33 Park Place
37 Park Square
1 Pump Court
2 Pump Court
**4 Pump Court**
6 Pump Court
5 Pump Court Chambers
**Pump Court Tax Chambers**
**Quadrant Chambers**
**Queen Elizabeth Building**
**Radcliffe Chambers**
3 Raymond Buildings
5RB
**18 Red Lion Court**
Regency Chambers
Renaissance Chambers
**Ropewalk Chambers**
Rougemont Chambers
**Selborne Chambers**
3 Serjeants' Inn
**Serle Court**
**3-4 South Square**
11 South Square
5 St Andrew's Hill
**3 Stone Buildings**
4 Stone Buildings
**5 Stone Buildings**
9 Stone Buildings
11 Stone Buildings
Stone Chambers
St Ive's Chambers
St James's Chambers

18 St John Street
St John's Buildings
St John's Chambers
St Mary's Family Law Chambers
St Paul's Chambers
**St Philips Chambers**
1 Stanley Place
Stour Chambers
Tanfield Chambers
Temple Chambers
55 Temple Chambers
1 Temple Gardens
2 Temple Gardens
3 Temple Gardens
3 Temple Gardens
3 Temple Gardens
Tooks Chambers
Trinity Chambers
Unity Street Chambers
3 Verulam Buildings
Walnut House
**Westgate Chambers**
**Wilberforce Chambers**
15 Winckley Square
York Chambers
Young Street Chambers

# Postgraduate Training

# Postgraduate training

There has been much discussion over the past couple of years of the ways in which postgraduate training is going to change. The Law Society's Training Framework Review Group announced several root and branch reforms in 2005, suggesting changes to make the current training contract scheme more flexible. The responsibility for the reforms has been taken over by the newly established Solicitors Regulation Authority (SRA), which has delayed the pilot of alternative routes to qualification until 2008. So, at present, this is how things are arranged.

The SRA and the Bar Council are responsible for laying down the training requirements for qualification as a solicitor or barrister in England and Wales. In both cases, training comprises two stages: academic and vocational.

The academic stage can be completed in one of three ways:
- a qualifying law degree;
- the Graduate Diploma in Law (GDL) for non-law graduates; or
- the Institute of Legal Executives (ILEX) exams, which enable people who are already in legal employment to qualify while they are working (see "Alternative careers").

The vocational stage involves the completion of the Legal Practice Course (LPC) or Bar Vocational Course (BVC), plus completion of a two-year training contract or one-year pupillage.

## GDL
The GDL (also known as the Common Professional Examination) is a conversion course that non-law graduates can take to enable them to apply for an LPC or BVC place. It is a one-year, full-time course designed to enable non-law graduates to fulfil the academic stage of legal training.

The course can also be taken over two years, either part time or by distance learning.

Applications should be submitted before 1 February of the year in which you intend to commence the course. Applications for the full-time course must be made online through the Central Applications Board (www.lawcabs.ac.uk). Part-time applications should be made direct to the institution.

To be eligible for the GDL, students must hold a degree from a UK university or be granted a certificate of academic standing by the SRA. Subject to various criteria, the following people may be eligible for such a certificate:
- overseas graduates;
- ILEX fellows and members;
- mature students;
- those with professional qualifications equivalent to a degree; and
- those with a diploma in magisterial law.

### Course content
The GDL is an intensive, demanding programme focusing on the seven foundations of legal knowledge, which are:
- contract;
- tort;
- criminal;
- equity and trusts;
- European Union;
- property; and
- public/constitutional.

Be aware that this stage of training is widely regarded as the most difficult; the BVC and LPC are by all accounts a breeze in comparison! Specific course content is set internally by the individual institution. However, for full-time students, the final examination comprises a three-hour paper in each of the seven core areas. All papers will usually need to be passed on the same occasion. Although you have up to three years to complete the GDL, you will not be allowed to attempt any paper more than three times. Part-time and distance-learning GDL students must attend a recognised course which lasts two years. Exams in four foundation subjects must be passed in the first year, and the remaining three areas in the second year. Part-time and distance-learning students must complete the GDL course within four years.

Note that as an alternative to the GDL, a two-year, senior-status law degree can be studied. After this degree, students go straight on to the appropriate vocational stage of legal training. Universities that offer senior-status degrees include Birmingham, Bristol, Cambridge, Cardiff, City, Coventry, Greenwich, Hertfordshire, Hull, Kent, Leeds, Leicester, London, Queen Mary, Sheffield, Wales and Wolverhampton. For a full list contact the SRA.

Finally, it's worth taking into account the fact that many institutions teaching both the GDL and LPC will automatically offer you a place on the latter if you successfully complete the GDL.

### LPC and BVC
All institutions that offer the full-time LPC are managed by the Central Applications Board. You should contact them for an application form or apply online at www.lawcabs.ac.uk. Similarly, students seeking a place on the BVC must go through the centralised online application process at www.bvconline.co.uk.

Overseas students wishing to apply for a place on the LPC or BVC should check with the jurisdiction in which they wish to practise that the course is recognised there.

### LPC
The LPC is the vocational stage of training to be a solicitor. It is a one-year full-time (or two-year part-time) course designed to bridge the academic degree and training

contract. It aims to provide students with sufficient knowledge and skills to ensure that they are well equipped to undertake the work of a trainee solicitor.

The LPC focuses not on learning by rote but on the mastering of practical skills. Teaching methods are no longer just academic: the emphasis is on workshops, continuous assessment, independent research and group discussions. The course also permits a certain amount of specialisation through a range of optional subjects.

The main areas of study are:
• core/pervasive areas;
• compulsory areas;
• elective areas; and
• skills areas.

The core/pervasive subjects cover professional conduct, accounts, EU law, probate, human rights law and revenue law. The compulsory areas comprise business law and practice, property law and practice, and civil/criminal litigation and advocacy.

Three electives must be studied from a range of subjects in private and corporate client work (eg, commercial law and practice, employment, landlord and tenant, consumer, housing, family and serious crime). Specific skill areas that the course seeks to develop are advocacy, drafting and writing, interviewing and advising, problem solving and legal research.

### BVC
Anyone wanting to become a barrister must pass the BVC, which effectively bridges the gap between the study of law (via either a law degree or conversion course) and work as a pupil.

The three essential areas of knowledge are civil litigation and remedies, criminal litigation and sentencing, and evidence. Professional ethics must also be covered. The following seven skills are integrated so that knowledge can be applied in a practical context:

- advocacy;
- conference;
- drafting;
- fact management;
- legal research;
- negotiation; and
- opinion writing.

Various option subjects are available during the course.

### LLM

A master's degree in law is becoming an increasingly popular option as the profession becomes more competitive and students seek to add an extra edge to their CV. Not only is the LLM valuable in helping you to stand out from the crowd, it's also a sure-fire way of developing your expertise in a niche area of the law.

Barrister Anneli Howard of Monckton Chambers comments: "The law degree is quite narrow so it does no harm to widen your perspective by further study or employment. If students are relatively young, I would strongly advise that they do an LLM to add a string of specialisations to their bow (the Bar and law firms are so competitive). For law firms, study abroad and learn a new language for a year. For the Bar, spend some time working for the European Commission, the European Court of Human Rights, a government department or a non-governmental organisation. It is very important to have a breadth of experience before you start."

In addition, the LLM is a good alternative for those who aren't quite ready for the trials and tribulations of the recruitment process and who could do with a little extra time to decide on their career path.

In marketing your LLM to potential employers, you'll be able to point out that you've not only gained a thorough knowledge of a particular area of law or legal practice, but also improved your communication and research skills no end.

Bear in mind that, while most law firms don't mind where you've studied the GDL as long as you've passed it, this isn't the case with LLMs. The LLM programmes are as much governed by snobbery as undergraduate law degrees and there is no point pretending otherwise. Thus, our advice for LLMs is to use the same principles for selecting a course as you would at undergraduate level.

And a final note of caution: if you see doing a master's as the way around a lower-than-expected first degree result in order to get a training contract/pupillage, beware! Few law firms/chambers will take account of a master's if your first degree result falls below their entry requirement and you have no genuine mitigating circumstances.

### What to look for in an institution

You have a wide range of choice when it comes to the postgraduate law courses. There are nearly 30 institutions – some with more than one site – offering the LPC alone. Whether you're about to do the GDL, LPC or BVC, a number of factors may guide which law schools you apply to.

Those of you with the easiest choice have already secured a training contract or pupillage and your future firm/chambers has specified the provider that you should attend. It's pretty sensible just to do as you're asked.

Quite a few others with training contracts or pupillages will find themselves in a position where the firm/chambers is paying all their fees, and with a bit of luck some maintenance as well. In this case, you don't have to pay too much heed to financial considerations.

The rest (and the majority) of you should pay close attention to each of the factors listed below.

## Course fees

This boils down to how much money you can afford to hand over for the privilege of attending the course. Fees for a one-year course can be as much as £12,000. However, do not make the mistake of thinking that the more expensive a course is, the better it's going to be. That's not necessarily the case.

## Course structure/type

It's essential for you to do an LPC or BVC that reflects the type of law you wish to practise. The LPC at its core remains the same course for everyone, but in recent years institutions have begun to offer versions with different emphases. For example, BPP Law School offers the business-focused City LPC to a five-firm consortium that includes Freshfields Bruckhaus Deringer and Herbert Smith. The College of Law also offers a bespoke LPC course, available to the trainees of a variety of firms that include Baker & McKenzie and Halliwells. Ask potential providers what they have to offer and how this differs from what is available elsewhere.

## Teaching quality

Some courses have better teachers and teaching methods than others. The SRA continually monitors course quality and rates LPC courses. It recently changed the way ratings are given. Rather than simply giving schools a grading from 'excellent' to 'unsatisfactory', the new system focuses on assessing six different areas. They are:
- teaching and learning the curriculum;
- assessment;
- students and their support;
- learning and resources;
- leadership and management; and
- quality assurance and enhancement.

Contact the SRA to find out more (info.services@sra.org.uk or tel: 0870 606 2555).

## Facilities

Not all courses and institutions offer the same level of facilities, resources, support and class sizes. Some institutions include books and materials, while at others these are additional costs. Don't be afraid to ask some searching questions.

## Housing/living costs

London is an expensive city in which to live, while the rest of the country is (mostly) cheaper. This should be factored in when you consider how much you will be paying for the course. Ask the questions, do your research.

## Location

If you study somewhere near home, you can live there and save on costs. Plus you will know people and have a life outside the institution you are joining. If you are keen to move elsewhere, first work out whether you are likely to be happy there. You might like to do a preliminary visit to get a sense of the place. The BVC and LPC are usually completed in a year, which is a manageable amount of time wherever you are, but be sure to consider the factors that are important to you.

## Reputation

This is listed last as it is the most nebulous of considerations. There are plenty of people whose opinion you can elicit (potential employers, tutors, careers advisers, friends, relations, colleagues and fellow students). Just remember to pay more heed to those who actually know what they are talking about!

# Postgraduate careers advice

**What is the right approach to getting a training contract? Your own hard work can be wasted unless you take a structured approach. To help, make use of the careers service at your university and at your Graduate Diploma in Law (GDL) or Legal Practice Course (LPC) provider. Giles Proctor, head of the new Kaplan Law School in London, which offers the 'excellent' graded Nottingham Law School GDL and LPC courses, gives his careers advice.**

There is lots of competition for training contracts. Their availability has been markedly affected by the economic climate and there are many more students seeking training contracts than there are training contracts available. In 2006/2007 there were approximately 11,500 students on the LPC, with only 6,000 training contracts available nationally. It is fair to say that most LPC providers will have many students starting their LPC without a training contract. So if you are in that position, you are not alone!

Given the competition, you must use the time spent on your applications as effectively as possible. It is essential to produce quality applications, showing the best possible match between what your chosen firm is looking for and what you have to offer. You can do this by working with the careers service at your provider and by preparing the ground thoroughly yourself. So here is a suggested, three-step approach to a successful application.

## Step one – what type of lawyer?
Deciding what type of lawyer you want to be is not as easy as it sounds! Your decision will be influenced by the following factors:
- Lifestyle. If you work in a City practice or in the corporate department of a large London or regional practice, you must expect to work evenings and weekends. This will affect your social and home life.

Large regional firms and the legal departments of major industry players require lawyers to work more than nine to five, but the hours tend to depend on the department. High street practices tend to be flexible, but do not necessarily mean shorter hours.
- Geography. Do you want to live in a city or in a rural area such as Devon and Cornwall? Particularly in relation to regional and high street firms, if you can show a geographical connection to the firm's location, your application will be viewed more favourably.
- Work/clients. Do you have a clear idea of what area of law you are interested in? If so, find out what lawyers in that field do, so that when you roll up to an interview to talk about corporate law, you can do so with some authority.
- Qualifications. If your first degree is in a non-law subject or you have a previous career or other relevant interests, you may decide to apply to a firm that reflects these. For example, medical experience may lend itself to a medical negligence practice, while a language degree may be well suited to an international firm. If you did a law degree, are any of your options relevant to your interests? Will your LPC options help? Also, you must be realistic: a 2.2 degree will make it hard to obtain an interview at many large commercial firms, so consider other firms and/or speak directly to the firm in question to see what their view is. It may be that your mix of personal attributes, skills and experience will count in your favour.

If you need to bounce your ideas off a professional careers adviser, contact your provider to see if they can help. At Kaplan, the students can contact our careers service for guidance from the moment they accept a place on one of our courses.

### Step two – what type of firm?

When looking for your perfect match in a firm, there are several things to consider. They include the following:

- What type of practice? Do your homework; look at the firm's literature, its website and the legal press.
- What is the size and location of the practice? Get a feel for the firm. The best preparation is to get a work placement and see it from the inside. If you can't, try to chat with firm representatives at a law or careers fair, or contact someone you know who works there.
- What are the distinctive features of the practice? Why is this the firm for you? Try to highlight these reasons in your application.

At Kaplan, our careers team are familiar with the recruitment strategies of law firms and can help you to clarify which firm(s) may be your perfect match. Also, use your personal tutors on your GDL and LPC courses; staff at most providers, like Kaplan, will have come from private practice, and may be able to help you with links to firms and their own experiences of which students have gone to which firms.

Remember that, in your application, the firm will be looking for evidence that you have the right skills, qualities, experiences and achievements to match what they are looking for. Highlight your law firm experience (eg, work placements) or engagement in pro bono work. If you have not thought about pro bono, you should get involved – find out whether your GDL or LPC provider runs a pro bono programme. We find at Kaplan that our pro bono programme, run with Nottingham Law School, gives students a unique insight into what legal practice is really like, with exposure to real clients and legal problems.

Applications for training contracts can be made as early as two years before being taken up. This is certainly the case for larger London and regional firms. However, economic conditions can change in two years and recently some of the larger firms have sought to top up their complement of trainees closer to the starting date.

Other firms prefer to recruit nearer the beginning of the training contract. This is particularly true of high street practices that will handle general work such as property, family and publicly funded litigation/dispute resolution. Many practices recruit paralegals and then offer a training contract if the person performs well during an agreed period.

Go to the careers service at your provider and arrange to get details of vacancies sent to you. At Kaplan, we find that sending vacancies to students in the summer before they start their GDL or LPC, and discussing their choice of firms with them, can really help them to form a coherent plan. During the summer months, students can lay the groundwork of a successful application when they have time free from the pressures of studying.

### Step three – a quality application

Remember that the essence of an effective application is to sell yourself by showing how well you and the employer match up. Whether you are applying online, by CV or on a firm-specific application form, be prepared to address any academic blips in your application, but keep them in context and highlight your achievements.

The careers service or your careers tutor at your provider should help you. At Kaplan, our careers team is pleased to discuss draft applications, CVs and covering letters, and provide an independent and objective assessment of how well students have marketed themselves.

However you're applying, keep a copy of what you have written – you will need it to prepare for your interview!

Finally, having put your application together, think about the type of questions that firms are likely to ask, such as:

- How would you describe yourself?
- Why would you make a successful lawyer?
- Describe an achievement of importance to you.
- Describe when you have worked in a team and your contribution to it.
- What are your interests and what do you get out of them?

If you can answer these, you are well on the way to a successful interview and the start of your legal career. The best of luck!

*Giles Proctor is head of Kaplan Law School, London.*

# Financing the vocational courses

How do we put this? Training to be a lawyer isn't cheap. The reality is that if you have to pay for all your university tuition fees and vocational courses, you could incur as much debt as £40,000. And it's not just course fees that have to be taken into account – there are also the hidden costs of books, accommodation, food, transport and at least one good suit! This is a huge financial investment with no guarantee of a training contract or pupillage at the end of it.

So with that in mind, how do you go about financing the vocational stage of your study? Thankfully, there are a variety of options. For the lucky students who secure a training contract or pupillage before they begin their vocational training, sponsoring firms or chambers may pay fees and/or a maintenance grant. Phew! However, most students have little choice but to finance their own way through this stage and careful financial planning is therefore essential. Graduate Diploma in Law (GDL) course fees are £5,000 on average. Legal Practice Course (LPC) and Bar Vocational Course (BVC) fees are even higher, with the LPC costing around £10,000 and the BVC as much as £12,000! Clearly, these fees represent a significant financial undertaking, especially given the rising cost of living throughout the country. Sponsorship, local authority grants, bursaries, college access funds and loans are all worth looking into.

## Sponsorship

An increasing number of firms and chambers are offering financial assistance to their future trainees and pupils, from full payment of fees and maintenance for up to two years of postgraduate study to the provision of an interest-free loan towards LPC/BVC course fees. One thing to remember is that the terms of sponsorship may tie you to the firm for a period of time after your training contract. This is something worth checking at the outset. Details of individual policies can be found in the directory section of this book.

## Local authority grants

Such grants are available, but funds are extremely limited. In addition, grants are discretionary for the GDL and LPC, which means that they are difficult to get. As a result, you should contact your local authority as soon as possible to find out the situation and apply immediately. Local authorities will supply a booklet describing the details of their award policies. Most authorities require you to complete an application form with details of your education history, financial circumstances, income and savings. Most authorities have an appeals procedure as a last resort.

## The Law Society

The Law Society has a bursary scheme for the GDL and LPC courses. It is funded by a variety of trusts and scholarships. To be eligible to apply for an award, you must be able to demonstrate, among other things, that your financial position would make it difficult for you to further your legal studies and you are committed to pursuing a career as a solicitor. The Law Society advises that the fund is limited and competition for awards is intense. In 2008 applications will be invited in March, to be returned by the end of April.

The Law Society also runs a Diversity Access Scheme, which provides support to talented people who will have to overcome a specific obstacle in order to qualify. Such obstacles might include social, educational or financial factors. In past years, successful applicants have been people with a wide range of disabilities and single parents who have combined studying with their caring responsibilities.

## The Bar Council

Brian Buck, the Bar Council's chief

# Talk to a bank that knows its Pupils from its Temples.

Our specialist banking managers speak your language, because they only act for members of the Bar. It's their full-time mission to provide the solutions you need to keep your finances running smoothly. With extensive experience of the legal profession, our team of experts are empowered to make fast lending decisions. Additionally, they're available by direct line the moment you need them. For more information, call Nik Patel on 08455 837241. And let's talk business.

accountant, says the aim of the Bar Council Scholarship Trust is to "further the training of young men and women seeking to become practising members of the Bar of England and Wales by paying or helping to pay the expenses of their legal education or allowances to assist them with their living expenses".

Since all pupils are now paid, trustees of the fund have been searching for a new target population. Having such a small admin resource, the trust cannot accept copious numbers of applications for BVC funding. Brian says: "For that matter, while our resources are not insignificant, we need to stretch our means as far as possible (which is why we gave out loans to pupils, rather than grants)." As well as loans, in 2007 the trust sponsored an essay competition and initiated an exchange arrangement between the Bar of England and Wales and the Irish Bar. Further details are available on the Bar Council's website at www.legaleducation.org.

### Inns of Court

Between them, the four Inns managed to dish out over £3.5 million in awards last year. They all seem to use the umbrella term 'award' to describe scholarships, bursaries and grants. Inner Temple even calls them exhibitions. Curiously, most wannabe barristers know little about the awards available, and although the Inns' websites provide some information, it's actually a complex web of requirements, applications procedures and working out exactly what is available for what.

Clare Heaton is the scholarships and recruitment officer at Inner Temple. She says: "All the four Inns are different and it's difficult to get your head round all the different awards. We all have a scholarships fund and we all give money out mostly on merit, using different kinds of means testing to fine tune that. The scholarships

committees think: 'Does this person have a good chance of succeeding at the Bar?' That's the bottom line."

The Inns' websites have application forms for you to complete and send to the relevant person. The forms ask for character details, legal experience, income/funds and references. You can only apply for scholarships at one Inn. If the scholarships committee likes your application, it will invite you to an interview.

Here's a breakdown of what's on offer:

### Lincoln's Inn

Lincoln's Inn offers 32 scholarships for those studying the GDL and 70 for those on the BVC. The total value of the Inn's awards tops £1 million. Individual scholarships range from £2,000 to £15,000. Lincoln's Inn has many other awards and bursaries available, from its £25,000 fund for up to 40 awards of £200 for pupillage through to the Peter Duffy Human Rights Award for young barristers to spend three months at the European Court of Human Rights in Strasbourg. Students are recommended to apply for awards in their third year at university, or the year prior to starting the GDL or BVC. The Inn's website (www.lincolnsinn.org.uk) has clear instructions and a downloadable application form, which you submit to student administrator Judith Fox (judith.fox@lincolnsinn.org.uk).

### Inner Temple

Probably the Inn with the most accessible information, Inner Temple offered a total of £1 million in awards in 2007. The Inn usually offers 80 to 100 scholarships per year for those on the BVC. These vary in value from £2,500 to £20,000. For those on the GDL, 20 to 25 scholarships have values ranging from £5,000 to £10,000. A small number of pupillage awards are available, as well as small entrance awards and disability grants. The Inn has a scholarships and recruitment officer, Clare

Natwest can **help** with the **cost** of your **legal studies**

If you are looking to finance the costs of your legal studies then look no further

♻ **NatWest**                                            another way

The NatWest Professional Trainee Loan scheme allows you to borrow for the GDL, LPC and BVC.

For more information please contact your NatWest Legal Student Services Manager,

Scott Jago on 020 7353 7671 or visit natwest.com/professions.

Textphone users please dial 01189 639 148

Heaton (cheaton@innertemple.org.uk). Its website (www.innertemple.org.uk) has all the info you need and you can apply online.

## Middle Temple

In 2007 Middle Temple made £900,000 worth of awards. The biggest portion (around £800,000) goes to those on the BVC, with the rest awarded to GDL students. Although the exact number of scholarships varies from year to year, the Inn helped over 150 students in 2007, with amounts ranging from £500 to £17,000. The Inn also has a pupillage hardship fund for pupils who come across severe, unforeseen financial difficulties. For those who make it to tenancy, Middle Temple offers a loan scheme of up to £5,000 over two years at a basic rate. Although the website (www.middletemple.org.uk) tells you a lot about the scholarship scheme, it fails to mention the all important figures quoted above. It does, however, have a downloadable application form with clear instructions. Awards are part of the Inn's treasury, and Christa Richmond is the deputy under-treasurer for education.

## Gray's Inn

Although Gray's Inn is the smallest of the four, it managed to dish out over £750,000 in 2007. The Inn spread £130,000 over 15 GDL scholarships, but it has nearly four times as many scholarships available for those on the BVC, worth a total of £570,000. Furthermore, four awards of £5,000 each are available for pupillage. There are awards for overseas students and disabled students. Also, £1,500 is up for grabs as first prize in the Lee essay competition. The Inn's student education officer is Sue Harrop. The website (www.graysinn.org.uk) doesn't tell you the values of most of the Inn's awards but it does summarise the details of the scholarships and provides downloadable application forms.

## College access funds

College access funds are available to postgraduate students at universities and publicly funded colleges, mainly to provide additional assistance to meet living costs. The funds are available at the discretion of your college. Students should contact the student support department of their institution for further details. Note that these funds are intended for students who are experiencing particular difficulties in meeting their living costs.

## Loans

Most high street banks offer some sort of specialised loans for those wishing to study for professional qualifications. We spoke to Tim Evenden, commercial manager at HSBC, about what they can offer: "We have professional studies loans for students embarking on the LPC, BVC, LLM or GDL. More specifically, we have a dedicated unit called the HSBC London Barrister Commercial Centre, which aims to provide flexible financial solutions, recognising the unusual ways that barristers are paid and the timescales involved. It is here that we assess the loans for the BVC. More broadly, we are keen to provide law students with loans and continue to follow their careers at the Bar, offering bespoke services. From BVC to QC, if you like!" Such loans are available to existing and new customers, and up to £25,000 can be taken over the period of study. For more details of rates, and terms and conditions, contact HSBC (www.hsbc.co.uk) for a brochure.

Scott Jago, manager for legal student services at NatWest's specialist Legal Centre, advises students to sort out their finances as early as possible: "Course fees tend to be required well in advance and if you leave things to the last minute, then you are likely to be disappointed. I recommend that my clients arrange finance under our professional trainee loan scheme as soon as they are accepted on a course – certainly before they take a summer break and definitely no later than July."

Career development loans, operated by the Department for Education and Skills, are deferred repayment loans that are available to help pay for vocational courses up to 80% of your course fees and up to 100% of any related expenses, not exceeding a total of £8,000. The government then pays the interest on the loan for the period you're studying and up to one month afterwards. You then pay back the loan to the bank over an agreed period and at an agreed rate. The three banks that are involved are Barclays, The Co-operative Bank and The Royal Bank of Scotland. Applicants must show that: (i) they intend to use the resulting qualification for the purposes of finding employment in the United Kingdom or European Union; and (ii) they are unable to fund the course from other sources.

Worth noting is that the Learning and Skills Council has recently clarified that career development loans should not be used to fund a course that leads to another course rather than employment. This means that banks cannot offer them to help students fund the GDL. More information and an application form may be obtained from the participating banks or at www.lifelonglearning.co.uk/cdl.

### Charities and grant-making trusts
Some grant-making trusts and charities may offer financial assistance to those seeking to qualify as a lawyer. The application criteria for these awards vary enormously, but they are often so specific that eligibility is limited to just a few. Usually, charities and grant-making trusts provide only small amounts of money and so should not be relied on to provide financial support for either tuition or maintenance for a whole year. The best place to find a full list of such organisations

is in the reference section of a local library. Try publications such as *Money to Study*, *The Directory of Grant-Making Trusts*, *The Grants Register*, *The Guide to Grants for Individuals in Need* and *Charities Digest*. Alternatively, you can find information about grants, loans and other funds at www.support4learning.org.uk/money.

# Course directory

# The Legal Practice Course (LPC)
# at Aberystwyth

## The LPC to define your future

- Small class sizes for personal attention
- Professional focus with practical outcomes
- Dedicated computer suite and practitioner support materials
- Wide range of electives from Commercial and Private practice
- Proactive links with the profession
- Lively and vibrant campus environment
- Eligibility for student residential accommodatio
- Staged fees

**The oldest Law Department in Wales now has its own Legal Practice Course.** Join us and benefit from our expertise and long standing links with the profession. Enjoy studying and living in the stunning environment of the west Wales coast. Aberystwyth will provide you with an excellent LPC to launch your career and a lifestyle that is second to none.

**For enquiries, please contact the LPC Administrator Rachel Tod on email: studylpc@aber.ac.uk or phone (01970) 622857.**

# www.aber.ac.uk/lpc

Prifysgol Cymru
Aberystwyth
1872 The University of Wales

# Aberystwyth University

Department of Law and Criminology , Hugh Owen Building, Penglais, Aberystwyth SY23 3DY
**Tel:** 01970 622 857
**Email:** studylpc@aber.ac.uk
**Web:** www.aber.ac.uk/lpc

**College overview** Founded in 1901, the Department of Law and Criminology at Aberystwyth bases itself on a long, reputable and increasingly varied experience of legal education and academic work. Over the years a large number of well-known legal academics have taught in the department and Aberystwyth law graduates have made their mark in a range of subsequent careers. The department is confident in its distinctive identity and reputation for teaching of a high quality, linked to a vigorous research activity and carried out in a stimulating and friendly environment. Our comprehensive range of courses includes undergraduate degrees, postgraduate research degrees, masters' degrees by distance learning and a Legal Practice Course (LPC).

The department is committed to a policy of innovation and development in teaching and research and regularly reviews both the range and content of its degree schemes and its modes of teaching and assessment in order to respond effectively to the needs and expectations of its student body. The department aims to maximise choice in its provision of legal education while ensuring that teaching is informed by up-to-date scholarship at the highest level. All members of academic staff are active in research and publication and a number of staff participate in national and international debate and policy-making in the legal and related fields.

**LPC: Legal Practice Course (full time)** The LPC at Aberystwyth is a young and vibrant course with excellent resources, enthusiastic staff, excellent practice based teaching from qualified solicitors and a strong network of legal contacts. We have a broad range of electives drawing from commercial and private practice and a diversity of experience amongst our teaching staff. Our highly practical course combined with small class numbers ensures that you receive excellent teaching, support, feedback and careers advice that will help you get your career off to a flying start. You will have access to the law department's wealth of high quality legal resources, library, IT facilities and the National Library of Wales. We will give you the utmost assistance in securing a training contract and in moving on to the career that you choose.

At Aberystwyth you have all of the advantages of an established, campus based university with the benefits of a compact town centre and beautiful natural surroundings. In a recent online survey by www.accommodationforstudents.com Aberystwyth was ranked the UK's favourite university town. As a student at Aberystwyth, you are only a short walk from your accommodation to your classes, the sports facilities, and town. Aberystwyth provides an educational and lifestyle experience that is second to none.

**Other postgraduate courses**
Master of Laws (LLM) International Business Law*
Master of Laws (LLM) Information Technology Law
Master of Laws (LLM) Environmental Law and Management **
Master of Philosophy (MPhil)
Doctor of Philosophy (PhD)
Master of Research (MRes)
Master of Laws (LLM)
* Taught on campus or distance learning mode
** Distance learning mode only

| | |
|---|---|
| LPC | 50 |

Apply to

**LPC** Central Applications Board

Contact names

**LPC** Rachel Tod

# BPP Law School
## preparing you for practice

As a leading provider of professional legal education BPP offers:

- legal education highly regarded by the profession and underpinned by a specialist careers service, unrivalled tutor support and an award-winning pro bono centre

- first rate resources including a well equipped library and access to an extensive online law database available 24 hours a day

- more part-time study options than any other leading provider available at four locations nationwide

> *"BPP's Careers Service was instrumental in my successful quest for a training contract."*
> Duncan Firman, Trainee, Brooke North Solicitors

Find out more about how BPP can help you start your career in law:
0845 070 2879  admissions@bpp.com  www.bpplawschool.com

LEEDS
LONDON
MANCHESTER

FULL-TIME
PART-TIME
DISTANCE LEARNING

SCHOLARSHIPS
AVAILABLE

LAW SCHOOL
preparing you for practice

# BPP Law School

68-70 Red Lion Street, London WC1R 4NY
**Tel:** 0845 070 2879
**Email:** admissions@bpp.com
**Web:** www.bpplawschool.com

**College overview** BPP is a leading provider of professional legal education, committed to providing you with an outstanding legal education, whether you study in Leeds, London (Holborn and Waterloo) or Manchester.

BPP provides the skills, resources and individual support needed to prepare you for the realities of legal practice. This is achieved using a unique mix of academic and practitioner lecturers, first-rate facilities, award-winning pro bono projects and a dedicated Careers Service. Our Careers Service comprises specialist careers advisers and tutors, who have worked in practice and participated in the recruitment of trainees, ensuring you are fully equipped with the knowledge and support needed to help you secure a training contract or pupillage.

**GDL: Graduate Diploma in Law (full-time, part-time and distance learning)**
BPP's GDL is taught with a practical approach using a combination of lectures and a focus on small group sessions held each week in each module to maximise your contact time with tutors. Our GDL is the only programme in the country to feature an optional Company Law Programme and 'GDL Extra' - your opportunity to specialise early in areas related to practice.

Although competition is intense, our GDL graduates are guaranteed a place on BPP's LPC and intending barristers can apply to join our BVC.

**LPC: Legal Practice Course (full-time and part-time)**
BPP's LPC is designed to prepare you for a career as a trainee solicitor in a wide variety of practice areas including, City, Commercial High Street and specialist.

Our LPC is taught by experienced solicitors from a variety of practice backgrounds, you will benefit from a programme designed in close collaboration with leading law firms and a wide range of electives to suit your interests and intended areas of practice. With a strong reputation within the legal community, many of the country's leading law firms exclusively send their trainees to BPP. Our LPC reflects the growing role of lawyers as business advisers and contains 'MBA-style' training in business and finance.

**BVC: Bar Vocational Course (full-time and part-time)**
Offered in Leeds and London, our BVC is highly regarded by the profession and is the only programme in London to be validated unconditionally by the Bar Council for the full six-year term.

Studying the BVC at BPP will allow you to develop the essential barristerial skills of drafting, legal research, opinion writing, advocacy, conference and negotiation. These skills will be refined in groups as small as six students alongside practising barristers, who act as your opponents in mock trials and final assessments.

**Summer School (one week 'taster')** If you are unsure whether a career in law is for you, our popular taster programme, the BPP Law Summer School, is available to give you an insight into the study of law and legal careers.

**Scholarship**
Scholarships available.
See www.bpplawschool.com/funding_and_scholarships.

Contact

Admissions

Apply to

**GDL & LPC (full-time)**
Central Applications Board
(www.lawcabs.ac.uk)
**GDL & LPC (part-time and distance learning)**
Directly to BPP Law School
(www.bpplawschool.com/apply_now)
**BVC (full and part-time)**
BVC online
(www.bvconline.co.uk)
**Summer School**
Directly to BPP Law School
(www.bpplawschool.com/apply_now)

Locations
Leeds, London (Holborn and Waterloo), Manchester

LAW SCHOOL
Preparing you for practice

# Bristol Institute of Legal Practice

University of the West of England, Coldharbour Lane, Frenchay, Bristol BS16 1QY
**Tel:** 0117 328 2604
**Fax:** 0117 328 2268
**Email:** law@uwe.ac.uk
**Web:** http://law.uwe.ac.uk

**College overview** Students at the Bristol Institute of Legal Practice benefit from the experience and expertise acquired over nearly 40 years' of providing vocational legal training. We offer an extensive range of professional training courses that have been consistently commended for quality. The LPC has a national reputation for its high quality having been rated as Excellent since 1996 and in 2006, under the new grading system, attained the highest possible rating in all six categories. The learning experience here is enhanced by the extensive use of up to the minute technology including, digital courtrooms and a range of e-learning resources. Students on the LPC and BVC are allocated a base room which contains IT/AV equipment and a mini-library. Additionally there is a well stocked 'Practitioner Library'.

**Graduate Diploma in Law/CPE (full time and distance learning)** This course represents the academic stage of the training of non-law graduates and is also of great value to those considering other careers where an understanding of the legal system and an appreciation of basic 'lawyerly' skills would be helpful. Class contact focuses on highly interactive workshop-style sessions designed to assist each student with the acquisition of legal skills, and small group seminars that consolidate the substantive law and develop legal research techniques.
Places offered: 110 (full time); 40 (distance learning)

**Legal Practice Course (full and part time)** This course caters for those wishing to qualify as a solicitor. Throughout the course emphasis is placed on skills acquisition and real practice experience, with professionally qualified staff conducting workshop activities within each group's study room. A full range of commercial and private client electives are offered: charities/not for profit sector; corporate finance; acquisitions and mergers; banking and capital markets; commercial; commercial property; commercial litigation; employment; family breakdown; housing and public child care; advanced criminal litigation; media entertainment; private client estate planning; local government law; personal injury and clinical negligence.
Places offered: 320 (full-time) 80 (part-time)

**Bar Vocational Course (full and part time)** The BVC provides practical training in all the skills that students require to enter independent practice as a barrister or other forms of legal employment. The course is delivered by practitioners and aims, as far as possible, to replicate the realities of practice. At UWE students undertake a week's placement in Chambers (or a similar form of legal employment), a week of court marshalling, and also have the opportunity to represent real client's through the Legal Representation service.
Places offered: 120 (full-time) 40 (part-time by open learning)

## Other professional courses
Professional Skills Course
Higher Rights Course

LLM in Advanced Legal Practice

## Other postgraduate courses
LLM in Commercial Law
LLM in Employment Law
LLM in European Public Law
LLM in International Law
LLM in International Trade Law

LLM in Criminal Justice
LLM in European Business Law
LLM in Industrial and Commercial Law
LLM in International Human Rights Law
LLM in International Economic Law

---

| | |
|---|---|
| CPE/GDL | 150 |
| LPC | 400 |
| BVC | 160 |

**Apply to**

**CPE/GDL** Central Applications Board
**LPC** Central Applications Board
**BVC** Central Applications Board
**Other professional courses**
Maurice Cook
**Other postgraduate law courses**
Dr Peter Billings

**Contact names**

**CPE/GDL** Alex Geal
**LPC** Gillian Burridge
**BVC** Gabriel Fallon
**Other professional courses**
Maurice Cook
**Other postgraduate law courses**
Nicola Liles

 Faculty of Law

# Cardiff Law School

Cardiff Law School, Cardiff University, Museum Avenue, Cardiff CF10 3AX
**Tel:** 029 2087 4941/4964/6660
**Fax:** 029 2087 4984
**Email:** law-lpc@cf.ac.uk or law-bvc@cf.ac.uk
**Web:** www.law.cardiff.ac.uk/cpls

**College overview** Cardiff Law School is a thriving, high-quality institution committed to excellence in teaching and research. This commitment to excellence is borne out by the Law School receiving a Grade 5 rating in the latest Government Research Assessment Exercise, which placed Cardiff Law School among the premier institutions in the United Kingdom. The Grade 5 rating indicates that research of international quality is being undertaken.

A part of the Law School, the Centre for Professional Legal Studies is the leading provider of legal training in Wales and is validated to offer both the Legal Practice Course and the Bar Vocational Course. You will be taught by experienced solicitors and barristers who have been specifically recruited for this purpose. Both courses have strong links with the legal profession and offer work experience placements during the course.

## Legal Practice Course (full time)

Cardiff has delivered the LPC since it was first introduced in 1993 and has established a national reputation for a demanding and high quality course. The Law Society has rated Cardiff's LPC as 'Excellent' four times in succession. In 2005, Cardiff's LPC once again achieved the highest rating following the Law Society's assessment visit. The Law Society praised the challenging learning environment and stimulating range of activities. Cardiff is renowned for its traditional hands-on approach to teaching delivered in state-of-the-art facilities.

## Bar Vocational Course (full time)

Cardiff has delivered a high quality BVC since it was first introduced by the Bar Council in 1997. The Cardiff BVC offers all the advantages of close and regular contact with staff in a generous programme of small group activity and in a convivial staff/student environment. The course is highly regarded and draws on the wealth of practice and teaching experience available at Cardiff Law School.

We have dedicated accommodation for both the Legal Practice Course and the Bar Vocational Course which houses a practitioner library, courtroom facilities, fixed and moveable audio visual equipment for recording practitioner skills, inter-active teaching equipment and extensive computer facilities. In addition, the main law library contains one of the largest collections of primary and secondary material within the UK.

The Law School is at the heart of the campus, itself located in one of the finest civic centres in Britain only a short walk from the main shopping area. The University has its own postgraduate centre, together with a full range of sports and social activities. Cardiff is a vibrant capital city with excellent cultural, sporting and leisure pursuits.

## Other postgraduate courses

LLM in Canon Law
LLM in Commercial Law
LLM in European Legal Studies
LLM in Legal Aspects of Medical Practice

---

LPC 180
BVC 72

**Apply to**

LPC Byron Jones
BVC Lucy Burns
Other postgraduate
law courses
The Postgraduate Office

**Contact names**

LPC Byron Jones
BVC Lucy Burns
Other postgraduate
law courses
Sharron Alldred/
Helen Calvert

CARDIFF
UNIVERSITY
PRIFYSGOL
CAERDYⱭ

# UCE Birmingham

School of Law, Perry Barr, Birmingham B42 2SU
**Tel:** 0121 331 6600
**Fax:** 0121 331 6622
**Email:** law@uce.ac.uk
**Web:** www.lhds.uce.ac.uk

**College overview** UCE's Birmingham School of Law has been a major centre for legal education and training in the city of Birmingham for over 30 years and is committed to providing a service that meets your needs – whether academic, professional or personal. Our approachable and experienced staff are part of the extensive range of support provision and learning facilities, including a legal practice resource centre, dedicated IT workrooms, a mock courtroom and legal office. And, of course, our students have all the additional benefits that you would expect to find in a large university.

### Graduate Diploma in Law/GDL (full or part time)
The GDL course is designed for non-law graduates wishing to enter the profession as solicitors or barristers. Our GDL provides legal training, which although primarily academic in nature reflects the demands that legal practice will place on that academic knowledge. The GDL emphasises active and student-centred learning. A variety of teaching methods are employed in order to develop the legal skills which will form the basis of a successful career in law. Our commitment to each individual ensures students are given every possible advantage in their chosen career.

### Postgraduate Diploma in Legal Practice/LPC (full or part time)
UCE Birmingham's LPC has been awarded the highest grade of 'commendable practice' in a recent assessment of all six Solicitor Regulation Authority quality criteria. Recognised for the practice skills emphasised in our training, we offer distinctive electives for students who enter general and specialised practice in small and medium sized firms. Training will develop the full range of practice skills, commercial awareness and self-sufficiency that a trainee solicitor needs. With our careers guidance and support, small class sizes and enthusiastic and committed staff, we ensure that individual study needs are met and students receive the support and encouragement to maximise their potential.

### Other postgraduate courses
### LLM/PgCert/PgDip Corporate and Business Law
Explores in-depth contemporary issues in corporate and business law within the UK and Europe. The programme addresses topical issues in employment law, corporate responsibility for the environment, intellectual property rights, trusts and pensions, international commercial law, corporate crime and corporate insolvency.

### LLM/PgDip International Human Rights
This LLM studies the issues of human rights, both in the UK and internationally, and it looks closely at the conflict between national and international standards.

USA pathway: The opportunity exists to undertake an internship in America, assisting on death row trials and related issues. This can potentially count towards a training contract or as a period of pupillage. You will also be involved in the preparation of an 'Amicus' brief, arguing a point of human rights law for submission to a US court.

International pathway: An opportunity for you to take part in a work placement with human rights organisations around the world. A core element of this pathway is an independent project where you will develop a human rights activity in a community setting.

---

**Apply to**

**Full-time GDL and LPC courses**
Central Applications Board
**Part-time GDL and LPC courses**
Direct to university
**Other courses**
Direct to university

**Contact names**

**GDL** Dr Ewan Kirk
**LPC** Keith Gompertz
**Other postgraduate courses**
The Faculty Office

UCE BIRMINGHAM
Faculty of Law, Humanities
Development and Society

# Lancashire Law School

University of Central Lancashire, Preston PR1 2HE
**Tel:** 01772 893062 / 893929
**Fax:** 01772 892972
**Email:** lsmith2@uclan.ac.uk
**Web:** www.uclan.ac.uk

**College overview** Lancashire Law School has developed an excellent reputation for both teaching and research and offers a wide range of undergraduate postgraduate and professional programmes in both full-time and part-time modes. It has over forty highly qualified staff including five professors and the majority of its staff are either professionally qualified or have experience of working with business or public sector organisations.

The School is located within the Faculty of Arts, Humanities and Social Science at University of Central Lancashire (visit www.uclan.ac.uk ), one of the largest modern universities in the country. It is in the heart of Preston, England's newest city. The student population makes the city a vibrant and cosmopolitan place to live. Shops, pubs, clubs and eateries are within easy reach of the campus. There's a lively nightlife and prices are about the best in the country. The big cities of Manchester and Liverpool are nearby, as is the Lake District and the great outdoors. The city itself is surrounded by some beautiful countryside.

We aim to provide the best possible facilities for our students, including a large and widely-stocked library together with its extensive range of IT and support services. Recently a massive extension to our Students' Union has put it on the map as one of the finest in the country (visit www.yourunion.co.uk for more information). Millions have also been invested in teaching buildings for a range of subject areas. A plentiful supply of modern residences right next to the campus means that we can accommodate all students seeking rooms.

## Graduate Diploma in Law/CPE (full and part time)
Academically rigorous education in law that will establish a sound foundation in major areas of law and highlight its wider implications.
Provides a platform from which to further develop legal competencies necessary for a career in legal practice.
Dedicated and well qualified staff with emphasis on small group teaching.
Places offered: 40 (full time); 30 (part time)

## Legal Practice Course (full and part time)
Range of commercial and High Street electives.
Dedicated facilities including resources rooms, moot court room and oral skills practice rooms.
Pro bono Student Law Clinic.
'Very good' rating from Law Society Assessors.
Emphasis on small group teaching.
Professional and supportive staff.
Places offered: 60 (full time); 48 (part time)

## Other postgraduate courses
LLM in International Business Law
LLM in Medical Law & Bioethics
LLM in Employment Law
LLM in Environmental Law
LLM in European Law
LLM in Law, Information and Converging Technologies
LLM by Research
MPhil/PhD Law
Post-Graduate Certificate in Environmental Law (Distance)
Post-Graduate Certificate in Employment Law (Distance)

| | |
|---|---|
| CPE/GDL | 70 |
| LPC | 108 |

Apply to

**CPE full time** CPE Central Applications Board
**CPE part time** LPC Admissions Tutor
**LPC full time** LPC Central Applications Board
**LPC part time** LPC Admissions Tutor

Contact names

**CPE/GDL** Jane Anthony
**LPC** Lynne Livesey
**Other postgraduate courses** Michael Doherty

UNIVERSITY
— OF CENTRAL —
LANCASHIRE

# DISPUTE RESOLUTION?

Sometimes it pays to re-examine the obvious. More lawyers have found a perfect route to practice through The College of Law than with anyone else.

We're at the heart of the legal profession and provide highly professional, top quality, challenging training to propel the lawyers of the future towards successful careers in a competitive world. Perfect for practice.

GDL, LPC and BVC. Full-time and part-time places available.

**0800 328 0153**
**admissions@lawcol.co.uk**
**www.college-of-law.co.uk/perfectforpractice**

Birmingham | Chester | Guildford | London | York

*The College of Law*

# The College of Law

Braboeuf Manor, Portsmouth Road, St Catherines, Guildford GU3 1HA
**Tel:** Freephone 0800 328 0153 **Overseas:** (+44) (0)1483 216500
**Email:** admissions@lawcol.co.uk
**Web:** www.college-of-law.co.uk/perfectforpractice

## College overview
At The College of Law you'll get the best possible start to your legal career. With centres in Birmingham, Chester, Guildford, London (two) and York, we're the UK's leading provider of legal education. Our innovative courses are designed and taught by lawyers, with a clear focus on building the practical skills, commercial awareness and independent thinking you'll need to succeed. This is supported by an award-winning pro bono programme and the largest and best-resourced careers service in UK legal education. You'll benefit from excellent tutor support and access to unrivalled on-line and off-line learning methods and resources.

## Graduate Diploma in Law (full or part time)
Designed to build knowledge and skills that more than match a law degree – with a clear focus on preparing you for life in practice. Academic training is built around real-life examples and case studies, and you'll be given research assignments that directly reflect the way you'll work as a lawyer. A multi-media package will develop your business awareness, and you can tailor your independent research work to reflect the areas of law in which you intend to specialise – enhancing your career prospects. Students who pass our GDL are guaranteed a place on our LPC (as long as they apply within two years), and you'll graduate with a Bachelor of Law degree if you go on to successfully complete your LPC or BVC at the College.

## Legal Practice Course (full or part time)
Our LPC is rigorous and practical – equipping you with the skills you need to succeed. You'll get plenty of opportunities to practice your skills through real cases in a context appropriate to your area of interest. We have the widest selection of elective subjects available and uniquely offer three different LPC routes, allowing you to specialise in your chosen field: corporate, commercial & private and public legal services. The majority of teaching is in small, student-centred groups and the course features extensive use of multi-media learning resources, including interactive i-Tutorials. And from 2008 we'll award a Master of Law degree to those students who successfully study modules in addition to the College LPC.

## Bar Vocational Course (full or part time)
Our BVC has been designed to resemble practice as closely as possible. The course is litigation-based with a heavy emphasis on developing and honing skills. Study follows a logical, realistic process from initial instruction to final appeal, and learning is based around the seven core skills and three knowledge areas stipulated by the Bar Standards Board. Most of your learning will be in small groups, and you'll have plenty of opportunities to put your learning into action through: practitioner evenings, mock trials, court visits, mooting, negotiating and advocacy competitions, and our tailored pro bono programmes. And from 2008 we'll award a Master of Law degree to those students who successfully study modules in addition to the College BVC.

## Information days
Find out more by attending an information day or arranging a centre visit. For further details and to book a place, visit www.college-of-law.co.uk/comeandseeus

**Contact**

Admissions

**Apply to**

**GDL & LPC full time**
Central Applications Board

**GDL & LPC part time**
Direct to the College

**BVC full and part time**
www.bvconline.co.uk

**Locations**
Birmingham, Chester, Guildford, London (two), York

*The College of Law*
of England and Wales

# The City Law School, London

The City University, Northampton Square, London EC1V 0HB
**Tel:** 020 7040 3309
**Email:** law@city.ac.uk
**Web:** www.city.ac.uk/law

**College overview** The City Law School is one of London's major law schools, offering an impressive range of academic and professional programmes. Law has been taught at City since 1977 and we are the first law school in London to educate students and practitioners at all stages of legal education.

Our GDL is one of the largest and most respected in the UK, with a strong reputation with the Bar and amongst City law firms. In addition to professional legal training for both solicitors and barristers, The City Law School offers a well-established CPD programme which includes the PSC for trainee solicitors and Higher Rights training.

Our professional programmes are delivered through the Inns of Court School of Law (ICSL became part of the City University in 2001), which for generations has been the leading educator of barristers in the country and a key provider of the Legal Practice Course (for intending solicitors), one that carries the Law Society's highest rating in all assessment areas.

**Graduate Diploma in Law/CPE (full time)** Our GDL has a strong academic focus, providing a solid foundation in law. It is one of the largest and most respected GDL courses in the UK and benefits from specialist staff with unrivalled experience including visiting academics from Oxford, Cambridge and other universities.

**Legal Practice Course (full time)** The City Law School LPC carries the Law Society's highest rating in all assessment areas and has been devised to meet the needs of students in practice, with a heavy emphasis on the teaching of practitioner skills. Small group teaching is emphasised to give students the most effective environment for learning. A wide range of elective subjects are offered.

**Bar Vocational Course (full or part time)** Our BVC aims to effectively train future barristers and equip them with the key skills needed to be successful in pursuing a career at the Bar. The five core lawyer skills are taught: advocacy, opinion writing, drafting, negotiation and client conference skills, plus legal research and case management, as well as issues of professional conduct and professional ethics. The use of IT is regarded as fundamental to the teaching and learning process.

The City Law School also offers BVC students the opportunity to gain an LLM in Professional Legal Practice, awarded on successful completion of the BVC and a supervised dissertation.

**Graduate entry LLB (two years full time)** Our GE LLB is for non-law graduates who want a broader two-year course leading to a qualifying law degree. It is designed both to provide a general knowledge of the central areas of the law and to allow special interests to be developed.

**LLM programme (full or part time)** The City Law School also offer an impressive range of LLM, including:
LLM International Commercial Law
LLM International Law
LLM Housing & Environmental Law
LLM Media Law
LLM Criminal Litigation

| | |
|---|---|
| CPE | 190 |
| LPC | 200 |
| BVC | 565 |
| LLB | 165 |
| LLM | 125 |

Contacts

**Graduate Diploma in Law/CPE**
020 7040 8301
cpe@city.ac.uk

**LPC**
020 7404 5787
lpc@city.ac.uk

**BVC**
020 7404 5787
bvc@city.ac.uk

**LLB (Graduate Entry)**
020 7040 3309
law@city.ac.uk

**LLM**
020 7040 8167
llm-lawdept@city.ac.uk

**LLM Criminal Litigation**
020 7404 5787
llm-icsl@city.ac.uk

CITY The City Law School
London

# De Montfort University

De Montfort Law School, The Gateway, Leicester LE1 9BH
**Tel:** 0116 257 7177
**Fax:** 0116 257 7186
**Email:** law@dmu.ac.uk
**Web:** dmu.ac.uk/law

**College overview** With over 100 years of history, De Montfort University is particularly experienced in providing first-class professional and vocationally relevant courses. De Montfort Law School has established an excellent academic success rate, achieving a Grade 4 ranking (research of national excellence) in the most recent Research Assessment Exercise, while research in Public Policy achieved a Grade 5 (research of international excellence). All teaching staff in the Department of Professional Legal Studies are professionally qualified with extensive experience of practice. Great emphasis is placed on studying law and procedure in a practical context throughout. The Department has developed a wide range of specialist electives to meet the demands of the practitioner in either commercial or client-based practice.

**CPE/Graduate Diploma in Law (full-time or part-time by distance learning)**
A conversion course for non-law graduates wishing to enter the legal profession. Full-time students complete a three-week induction programme covering the principal features of the English legal system. The induction programme enables students to develop their legal research skills and demonstrates the role of IT in the study of law. The remainder of the course is taught in large group lectures and smaller group tutorials (approximately 10 students) for each foundation subject on the full-time course. Distance learning is ideal for those in work wishing to qualify as a solicitor or barrister. The part-time by distance learning course requires attendance for nine study weekends (Saturday and Sunday save the first weekend which runs from Friday to Sunday) over two years and submission of non-assessed assignments. Both courses cover the English legal system, criminal law, property law, the law of tort, contract law, equity and the law of trusts, public law and European Union law. Additionally, students must submit a 5,000 word project on a legal topic of their choice.
Places offered: 40 (full-time); 60 (part-time by distance learning)

**Legal Practice Course (full-time or part-time by open learning)**
De Montfort Law School's LPC was awarded the highest grade of 'commendable practice' by the Solicitors Regulation Authority in five areas, including teaching, learning and the curriculum and student support. Compulsory subjects are followed by electives which include: commercial law, commercial litigation, commercial property, employment law, personal injury and clinical negligence, law and the elderly client, matrimonial practice, child law, and sports and media law. The open learning course is mainly taught through study weekends (Friday- Sunday inclusive) held on a monthly basis and ideal for those in work wishing to qualify as a solicitor.
Places offered: 100 (full-time); 130 (part-time by open learning)

**Other postgraduate courses**
**LLM in Advanced Legal Practice and LLM in Legal Practice (open learning):** These courses enhance legal research skills and enable students to keep abreast of developments within their field while studying areas directly relevant to practice.
**LLM Business Law (full time) and LLM Business Law, LLM Environmental Law, LLM Food Law, LLM Employment Law in Context and LLM Medical Law and Ethics (distance learning):** A background knowledge of law or an appropriate related discipline is required. A law degree is desirable, although not essential. Relevant professional qualifications are accepted. Each course offers accelerated learning and several exit points, each awarding a postgraduate qualification.

| | |
|---|---|
| GDL/CPE | 40 (full-time) |
| | 60 (part-time) |
| LPC | 100 (full-time) |
| | 130 (part-time) |

Contact names

**GDL full-time**
Vaughan Hall
**GDL distance learning**
Graham Hipwell
**LPC full-time**
Oliver Bennett
**LPC open learning**
Rachel Grimley
**LLM Advanced Legal Practice and LLM Legal Practice**
Amarjit Morrow
**Other postgraduate law courses**
Neil Parpworth

dmu.ac.uk
**DE MONTFORT UNIVERSITY**
LEICESTER

# University of Glamorgan

Enquiry & Admissions Unit, Pontypridd CF37 1DL
**Tel:** 0800 716925
**Web:** www.glam.ac.uk

**College overview** The Law School at Glamorgan was formally established in September 1995 after 25 years' experience of law teaching. It is based in a modern, purpose-built building and boasts excellent lecture theatres and workshop rooms, all equipped with digital projectors. The Law School also has open-access computer laboratories with internet and CD-ROM facilities; a comprehensive law library; a mock court room; two interview suites with full video recording and monitoring facilities; a workshop room with laptop facilities and a recently extended refectory.

The Law School is situated a short walk from the other campus which houses a recreation centre, university creche, play scheme for older children, centre for lifelong learning and careers centre.

**Graduate Diploma in Law/CPE (one year full time or two years part time)**
This is an intensive conversion course for those intending to become solicitors or barristers, designed for non-law graduates of any discipline. The University has over 15 years' experience of providing the CPE course. Students completing the CPE are then able to join the Law School's LPC.

The University also provides a part-time course over a period of two years where students attend two evenings a week.

**Legal Practice Course (one year full time or two years part time)**
This is a one-year vocational course catering for those wishing to qualify as a solicitor. Throughout the course emphasis is placed on skills acquisition and real practical experience, with professionally qualified staff conducting lectures and workshop activities.

Students on the course study three compulsory areas of general practice and choose three electives of specialist study. We offer a range of both commercial and private client electives. The University also provides a part-time LPC where students attend one day a week over a two-year period.

The Law School also runs a very successful work placement scheme. This offers students the opportunity during the elective phase of the LPC to spend one day a week in solicitors' practices and other legal environments. The Law Society's assessors in their report say that "the work placement scheme… continues to provide excellent opportunities for those on both full-time and part-time courses seeking training contracts".

**Other postgraduate courses**
The Law School offers a number of other postgraduate courses. These include LLMs in International Commercial Law, Commercial Law, Intellectual and Industrial Property Law, Dispute Resolution and Public International Law.

| | |
|---|---|
| CPE | 70 |
| LPC | 140 |

**Contact names**

**CPE (full time and part time)**
Brian Dowrick
bmdowric@glam.ac.uk
01443 483048
**LPC (full time)**
Karen Jones
kejones1@glam.ac.uk
01443 483027
**LPC (part time)**
Maria Keyse
mjkeyse@glam.ac.uk
01443 483038

# University of Huddersfield

Queensgate, Huddersfield HD1 3DH
**Tel:** 01484 472192
**Fax:** 01484 472279
**Web:** www.hud.ac.uk

**College overview** The University of Huddersfield School of Law is an integral part of the University's Business School. The School provides a range of undergraduate and postgraduate courses. In law school terms, the department is small with 25 full-time members of staff, but this ensures a warm, friendly learning environment. The School prides itself on its 'open door' policy for students seeking help and assistance.

**Graduate Diploma in Law/CPE (full time, part time or distance learning)**
The CPE at the University of Huddersfield (whether studied full time or part time) is a flexible learning course. Whichever study option chosen, the course commences with face-to-face tuition to introduce students to the course director and subject leaders. Attendance at this induction session is compulsory for all students. The course is then primarily delivered over the Internet. Each subject is divided into self-contained units. A schedule is issued to ensure that students know what work needs to be done during any particular week. Students are required to undertake some directed reading and in addition to submit a written tutorial for marking and feedback or attend a face-to-face tutorial and make contributions to the online discussion board. The CPE is competitively priced and flexible payment arrangements are available. Successful students on the CPE can also go on to study for an additional year and obtain the 'top-up' LLB.
Places offered: 30 (full time); 60 (part time)

**Legal Practice Course (full or part time)**
"The course is delivered by professional, well-prepared and knowledgeable tutors" – the Law Society Monitoring Team March 2006. The LPC at Huddersfield is delivered in both full-time and part-time modes. Both courses start in September. The full-time course is taught over four days each week and the part-time course is taught one afternoon and evening (same day) each week. Both courses have been designed to create close working relationships between members of a supportive teaching team and students. The university has a well-developed IT provision which includes both legal management software and a virtual learning environment which is accessible from home. The elective subjects offered to students on both the full-time and part-time LPC courses are: commercial law; family law; insolvency law; employment law; immigration law; commercial property law and estate planning. The Legal Practice Course is competitively priced and flexible payment arrangements are available. Sponsored prizes are available to the most successful students in certain subject areas.
Places offered: 80 (full time); 35 (part time)

**Other postgraduate courses**
**MA in Health Care Law:** This course is a taught masters programme over one year for full-time students (two half-days a week) and over two years for part-time students (one half-day a week). The course has been designed to develop your understanding of the legal and ethical issues, which are relevant to both the clinical practice in health care and to the administration and management of the National Health Service.
Places offered: 20 (full time); 30 (part time).
**LLM by Distance Learning:** This course lasts for a minimum of one year and builds upon a student's existing qualifications as it is only open to legal practitioners and successful LPC and BVC students. Award of the LLM requires successful completion and presentation of a dissertation on a topic of the student's choice. The Law Society has accredited the course for CPD accreditation.

| | |
|---|---|
| LPC | 105 |
| CPE | 90 |

Apply to

CPE full time
Central Applications Board
CPE part time
Melanie Fellowes
LPC full time
Central Applications Board
LPC part time
James Mendelsohn
MA in Health Care Law
Dr Lynne Foxcroft
LLM
Tina Hart

Contact names

CPE Melanie Fellowes
LPC James Mendelsohn

# University of Hertfordshire

## *School of* **Law**

# Training the lawyers of tomorrow, supporting the lawyers of today

We offer a full range of postgraduate programmes, both professional and academic

- **LPC**
- **Graduate Diploma in Law (CPE) -**
  Study on Campus or on our new 100%
  Distance Learning route

- **LLM** *in:*
  - Commercial Law
  - Telecommunications Law
  - International Law
  - Intellectual Property Law
  - e-Commerce Law
  - Maritime Law
  - m-Commerce Law

*Students benefit from:*

- Excellent teaching facilities - courtroom, law learning resource centre, and IT suites - all on one campus
- The opportunity to gain valuable legal experience working in our pro bono law clinic
- Individual bespoke careers guidance advice from day one
- Small classes taught by experienced legal professionals and academics
- Flexible study patterns

For further information on our programmes contact:

Tel 01707 286212   Email k.rogers@herts.ac.uk   www.herts.ac.uk/law

# Hertfordshire University

School of Law, 7 Hatfield Road, St Albans AL1 3RR
**Tel:** 01707 284800
**Fax:** 01707 284870
**Email:** admissions@herts.ac.uk
**Web:** www.herts.ac.uk/law

**College overview** We are a longstanding provider of excellent postgraduate programmes, to students from the UK and overseas. The School of Law is located in St Albans at the heart of the regional legal community. Of our 45 fulltime academic staff, half are experienced academic lawyers and half have joined the School directly from the legal profession. Our close links with the profession inform our teaching practice, both on our Postgraduate Diplomas and Masters degrees, and on our Continuing Professional Development short courses for the legal profession. We offer superb facilities (IT, library, courtroom, and Law Clinic) and excellent pastoral care. Students benefit from professional careers guidance from day one. All our postgraduate students have the opportunity to train as student advisers in our Pro Bono Law Clinic.

## Graduate Diploma in Law/CPE (full and part time, campus based and distance learning)

Our Graduate Diploma in Law is offered on a full-time (one year) or part-time (two years) basis. The part-time programme is offered one day a week over two years. In addition to our campus based GDL we offer a distance learning model providing our students with even greater flexibility. All formats of the GDL are taught through a combination of lectures and seminars, with considerable emphasis on skills development. Seminar groups are small allowing for close academic support throughout. Successful students are guaranteed a place on our LPC.

## Law Society's Legal Practice Course (part time)

Our stimulating and rigorous LPC is offered on a day-release basis over two years, and is taught primarily through a combination of large group sessions and workshops, utilising real case scenarios, to fully prepare you for life as a solicitor. Skills' training is provided throughout the course, using our courtroom and video facilities for accurate feedback and analysis of student performance. Electives offered include commercial law, employment law, environment law, commercial property, personal injury law and family law. The course offers students the advantage of studying at the same time as being in a study training contract or other employment, and thereby helps to offset the costs of qualification. The LPC enjoys the highest Law Society rating of 'commendable practice' in five out of the six areas.

## Other postgraduate courses
### LLM in Maritime Law, International Law, Commercial Law, E-commerce Law and Telecommunications Law

Our Masters programmes offer students the opportunity to develop expertise in both established and rapidly developing areas of law. All teaching takes the form of small group seminars and seminar tutors are all specialists in their area of teaching. Subjects offered include telecommunications law, shipping law, e-contracts, data protection and e-finance, company law, commercial law, public international law, private international law, international commercial law, intellectual property, cyber piracy and virtual property law, banking law, international financial services law and m-commerce.

| | |
|---|---|
| CPE/GDL | 60 |
| LPC | 64 |
| LLM | 90 |

Apply to

admissions@herts.ac.uk

Contact names

Kevin Rogers
01707 286212
k.rogers@herts.ac.uk

University of
Hertfordshire

## LAY THE RIGHT FOUNDATIONS FOR YOUR FUTURE CAREER

### EXCELLENCE

Kaplan Law School offer you Nottingham Law's excellent LPC and GDL courses in central London

### EXPERTISE

Kaplan have a long-standing reputation for professional training expertise and a global history as a learning provider.

### INNOVATION

Kaplan Law School's state of the art campus has the technology and facilities you need, with innovative pro-bono schemes and dedicated careers support.

**Find out more:**

**email:** admissions@kaplanlawschool.org.uk
**web:** www.nottingham-kaplan.org.uk
**Tel:** 0845 450 8993

SCHOLARSHIPS AVAILABLE

# Kaplan Law School

Palace House, 3 Cathedral Street, London SE1 9DE
**Tel:** 0845 450 8993 / 020 7367 6400
**Email:** info@kaplanlawschool.org.uk
**Web:** www.nottingham-kaplan.org.uk

**College overview** Kaplan Law School have partnered with Nottingham Law School to open a brand new campus offering Nottingham Law's market leading LPC and GDL courses in central London.

Nottingham Law at Kaplan Law School will combine Nottingham's reputation for excellence in legal training with Kaplan's professional qualifications expertise and facilities.

The Kaplan Law School campus has been custom built and offers state of the art facilities with the convenience of a London Bridge location providing excellent transport links and close proximity to the City's legal community.

### GDL: Graduate Diploma in Law (full time)

This is a one year conversion course designed for any non-law graduate who intends to become a solicitor or barrister in the UK. The intensive course effectively covers the seven core subjects of an undergraduate law degree in one go. It is the stepping stone to the LPC or BVC and to a legal career thereafter.
Places: 150

### LPC: Legal Practice Course (full time and part time)

This course has been designed to be challenging and stimulating for students and responsive to the needs of firms, varying from large commercial to smaller high street practices.

Course features: integration of transactions and skills, so that each advances the other; carefully structured interactive group work which develops the ability to handle skills and legal transactions effectively; a rigorous assessment process that nevertheless avoids 'assessment overload', to maintain a teaching and learning emphasis to the course; a professionally qualified team, retaining substantial links with practice; an 'Excellent' rating from the Law Society's Assessment Panel in every year of its operation.
Places: 300

### BVC and other postgraduate courses

At present we do not offer the BVC or other post graduate courses. We will be running the BVC course from September 2009.

Contact
Admissions
admissions@kaplanlaw
school.org.uk

Apply to

GDL
Central Applications Board
LPC (full time)
Central Applications Board
LPC (part time)
Nottingham Law at Kaplan
Law School
admissions@kaplanlaw
school.org.uk

# Graduate Law Courses at Leeds Law School

## Legal Practice Course (LPC) and Graduate Diploma in Law (CPE) Programmes

Based in prestigious new buildings in Leeds City Centre, Leeds Law School at Leeds Metropolitan University provides a friendly and supportive teaching environment for all students.

- Study in the heart of the city's legal quarter
- Flexible courses - study full-time or part-time
- Outstanding facilities including modern lecture theatres and mock courtroom
- Highly experienced tutors with considerable experience in legal practice
- Professional Mentor Scheme with over 100 mentors
- Individual careers advice

For more information, please contact us on
0113 812 6082 or email
admissions.fblpg@leedsmet.ac.uk

www.leedsmet.ac.uk/lbs/law

leeds
metropolitan
university

# Leeds Metropolitan University

Leeds Law School, Cloth Hall Court, 10 Quebec Street, Leeds LS1 2HA
**Tel:** 0113 812 6082
**Email:** admissions.fblpg@leedsmet.ac.uk
**Web:** www.leedsmet.ac.uk/lbs/law

| | |
|---|---|
| CPE/GDL | 52 (full time) |
| | 52 (part time) |
| LPC | 105 (full time) |
| | 90 (part time) |
| LLM | 100 |

**Contact names**

CPE/GDL Vicky Thirlaway
LPC Darren Shaw

**College overview** Leeds Law School at Leeds Metropolitan University provides a friendly and supportive teaching environment for all students. In September 2005, Leeds Law School moved into prestigious new buildings at Cloth Hall Court in Leeds City Centre. The new buildings are only a few minutes' walk from Leeds train station and are very close to all bus routes. Our new buildings have excellent facilities including modern lecture theatres and seminar rooms, a mock courtroom, a careers room and a dedicated LPC resources room including new computers and extensive texts. They also contain a brand new skills suite which can be used by students for video recording oral skills including advocacy, interviews and presentations. The buildings are wireless with the opportunity for students to borrow laptops to work on-site. Students can also use all the facilities in the University's Library which is open 24 hours during the academic year. Our provision was praised by the QAA in 2004 and received the top rating from the Law Society in 2006 for teaching, assessments, student support and quality assurance & enhancement.

**Graduate Diploma in Law/CPE (one year full time or two years part time)**
This course is ideal for graduates wishing to convert from a non-law background to a rewarding career as a solicitor or barrister. The course assumes no prior knowledge of law and covers all the main legal subjects. During the course, comprehensive careers advice is available and all students have the opportunity to participate in the Professional Mentoring Scheme, where students can gain advice and make contacts with current legal professionals. The full-time course is delivered on four days every week, with one day for private study. Students are required to attend one lecture per module every week and one two-hour seminar per module every two weeks. The part-time course comprises a combination of lectures and seminars. All graduate diploma students receive a discount on their LPC fees if they stay at Leeds Met. This was 10% for 2006-2007.

**Legal Practice Course (one year full time or two years part time)**
The Legal Practice Course provides the taught part of the vocational stage of training required by the Law Society for entry to the solicitors' profession. This course will ensure that students, as trainee solicitors, have the necessary skills and knowledge to undertake appropriate tasks under supervision during their training contract. The LPC staff at Leeds Met has considerable experience in legal practice and includes local practitioners. The course as a whole has very strong links with the local legal profession including the Professional Mentor Scheme. All LPC students at Leeds Met are allocated a professional mentor. These are local solicitors who are working in practice in Leeds and West Yorkshire. Many of them are partners in their firms and they represent the full range of firms in the region, from large commercial firms to small high street practices. They also include representatives from the Crown Prosecution Service and in-house legal departments. Leeds Met also provides students with extensive careers support including CV workshops and sessions on applications/interview techniques.

**Other postgraduate courses**
**LLM (one year full time or two years part time)**
The course is intended to equip students with an understanding of specific areas of law as well as providing them with those cutting-edge skills sought after by employers. This is in terms of communication and effective team skills.

 leeds metropolitan university

# Liverpool John Moores University

The School of Law, Josephine Butler House, 1 Myrtle Street, Liverpool L7 4DN
**Tel:** 0151 231 3979
**Email:** j.e.seddon@livjim.ac.uk
**Web:** www.livjim.ac.uk

**College overview** Liverpool John Moores University (JMU) is a contemporary university in one of the most famous cities in the world. We aim to give people the opportunity to maximise their potential in an environment that is stimulating, challenging and exciting, but also caring and supportive.

The School of Law offers a broad portfolio of academic, vocational and professional programmes in both full-time and part-time modes. The School provides undergraduate, postgraduate and professional programmes in law, legal practice and criminal justice. It also offers opportunities to study for an MPhil or PhD by research. School staff are engaged in a wide range of law and criminal justice research, and the School hosts the Centre for Criminal Justice.

The School has invested significantly in staff development, with the emphasis on enhancing the status and quality of teaching and learning, and also in providing excellent information technology facilities.

The School is one of the five making up the Faculty of Business & Law at JMU, set around tranquil gardens with an award-winning resource centre, yet only five minutes' walk from the lively city centre. Liverpool, voted European Capital of Culture for 2008, has a student population of 55,000 and is a vibrant and exciting place to study.

## Legal Practice Course (full or part time)
The LPC has been designed to meet the requirements and needs of the legal profession of the 21st century. The LPC aims to produce a highly skilled, commercially aware and effective trainee solicitor, who is prepared for the rigours and demands of a training contract. Students will join a team of professional lawyers who are highly committed, enthusiastic and skilled teachers.

Liverpool John Moores University offers 72 full-time and 72 part-time places.

## Other postgraduate courses
Graduate Diploma in Law (from 2009)
LLM in Advanced Legal Practice (subject to validation)
LLM in Business & Commercial Law
MA Criminal Justice part time

In addition to the above courses we have a broad range of postgraduate and professional programmes in all areas of management, cororate governance and banking and finance. For further details visit our website www.ljmu.ac.uk or telephone 0151 231 3957.

LPC                144

**Apply to**
Full time: Central Applications Board
Part time: Apply direct

**Admissions contact**
Anita Ellis
a.ellis@livjim.ac.uk
0151 231 3936

**LPC administrators**
Julie Seddon
j.e.seddon@livjim.ac.uk
0151 231 3979
Erika Raffle
e.raffle@livjim.ac.uk
0151 231 3952

# London Metropolitan University

Law Department, 16 Goulston Street, London E1 7TP
**Tel:** 020 7133 4202
**Fax:** 020 7133 2677
**Email:** admissions@londonmet.ac.uk
**Web:** www.londonmet.ac.uk

**College overview** London Metropolitan University is one of Britain's largest universities with over 34,000 students and is committed to the delivery of academic excellence, vocational relevance and personal development. Our law department is one of the largest of its kind and has a strong research culture. We have a close working relationship with the City of London and its practitioners proving beneficial both to course development and to students' employability. Our courses offer a considerable range of content and flexibility in duration and mode of study, most courses being offered on a full and part-time basis. Our facilities include our purpose-built law building in Goulston Street near Aldgate tube housing a mock courtroom for moots and state-of-the-art teaching facilities. Our law materials collection comprises approximately 10,000 volumes and subscriptions are maintained to some 155 print journals and series of law reports. Our students have the benefit of our careers service, which includes the Law Graduates Employability Network (LAGREN) assisting students with the preparation of CVs, providing general advice on traineeships, and organising talks from practitioners and a mentoring scheme.

## Graduate Diploma in Law/CPE (full and part time)

Our intensive postgraduate conversion course will develop your understanding of the English legal system providing a thorough grounding in the foundations of legal knowledge and training students in the professional skills of legal research, analysis and presentation in a friendly and nurturing environment.

## Legal Practice Course (full and part time)

The university was one of the first to be validated to run the Legal Practice Course and has a long-standing reputation for training solicitors. You will be taught by a friendly team of qualified solicitors who have experience from City law firms, high street firms and the not-for-profit sector. The course emulates the nature of the work encountered in practice and teaches skills of practical legal research, interviewing and advising, writing and drafting, and advocacy required for professional training and for practice. You can study on a part-time day or evening basis or on the full-time course. Part-time evening students have the option of studying at Canary Wharf in addition to the City campus. We offer a wide range of electives, currently including corporate finance, intellectual property, immigration, child, and housing law. Whether you want to work in a law centre, as an in-house legal adviser or in a large City law firm we can provide a solid base for your future career.

## Other postgraduate courses

LLM Employment Law
LLM European and International Law
LLM European Law
Postgraduate Diploma Financial Services Law
LLM Human Rights
MA Human Rights and Social Justice
LLM International and Comparative Business Law
LLM International and Comparative Intellectual Property Law
LLM International Banking and Insurance Law
LLM International Economic Law
LLM International Law
LLM International Trade Law
LLM International Transport and Maritime Law
MA Maritime Law

| | |
|---|---|
| CPE/GDL | 60 |
| LPC | 110 |

**Apply to**

Postgraduate Admissions,
London Metropolitan
University,
166-220 Holloway Road,
London N7 8DB,
Tel: 020 7133 4202
Fax: 020 7133 2677
Email: admissions@
londonmet.ac.uk

**Contact names**

CPE/GDL
Barrie Goldstone
Tel: 020 7320 4923
Email: barrie.goldstone@
londonmet.ac.uk
LPC
Mark Blakely
Tel: 020 7320 4960
Email: m.blakely@
londonmet.ac.uk
Sarah Campling
Tel: 020 7320 4928
Email: s.campling@
londonmet.ac.uk

LONDON
metropolitan
university

# Manchester Metropolitan University

School of Law, Sandra Burslem Building, Lower Ormond Street, Manchester M15 6HB
**Tel:** 0161 247 3050
**Fax:** 0161 247 6309
**Email:** law@mmu.ac.uk
**Web:** www.law.mmu.ac.uk

**College overview** The School of Law is one of the largest providers of legal education in the UK, and enjoys an excellent reputation for the quality and range of its courses. The school's courses are well designed and well taught, combining rigorous academic standards with practical application to give you the best possible start for your career. In September 2003 the school moved into a brand new, state-of-the-art building.

## Bar Vocational Course (full or part time)
This course provides the vocational stage of training for intending practising barristers. However, skills learnt on the course such as advocacy and drafting are transferable to other professions. The BVC is skills-based and interactive, with particular emphasis on advocacy which is taught in groups of six. The course adopts a syndicate (mini-chambers) approach. Students are allocated to a particular group which has its own base room which contains extensive practitioner legal resources in both hard copy and online form. Each room has the latest in IT and AV equipment. There is also a BVC court room and a separate BVC resource room. Excellent student support is provided, including careers advice and an additional professional programme that is designed to bridge the gap between student and professional life. A particular feature of the course is the close links it enjoys with the Northern Circuit, whose members are involved in advocacy master classes, the teaching of professional conduct and a student mentoring scheme.

## Legal Practice Course (full or part time)
(Part time requires attendance on Thursdays over two years).
The Legal Practice Course provides the vocational stage of training for those wishing to qualify as a solicitor. Offering a full range of private client and commercial electives, we aim to cater for students who are looking to practise in specialised areas (eg, entertainment law or advanced criminal litigation) as well as students who wish to develop a broad subject base. A mentor scheme operates to put students in touch with local practitioners. Consistently commended for its state-of-the-art resources, student support and careers guidance, and staffed by approachable and knowledgeable teaching staff, the LPC at Manchester Metropolitan University will provide a sound foundation for your legal career.

The LPC at MMU was awarded top marks by the Law Society in their latest assessment visit.

## CPE/Graduate Diploma in Law (full or part time)
An increasing number of graduates enter the legal profession this way, with employers attracted by the applicant's maturity and transferable skills. The course places emphasis on the acquisition of legal research and relevant skills. Students completing the GDipL can go on to join the school's LPC or BVC. This means that in two years (three years if part-time GDipL) graduates can complete their legal professional qualifications and become solicitors or barristers. A place on the school's LPC is guaranteed, provided certain conditions are satisfied. Graduates from the GDipL at MMU who take up a place on MMU's BVC or LPC receive a fee discount.

| LPC | 216 |
| BVC | 100 |
| CPE | 100 |

**Apply to**

**CPE/GDL & LPC** Central Applications Board
**BVC**
BVC online
**Part-time CPE**
Catherine Higgins
**Part-time LPC**
Julia Frew

**Contact**

**CPE/GDL**
gdipl@mmu.ac.uk
**LPC**
lpc@mmu.ac.uk
**BVC**
bvc@mmu.ac.uk

Manchester
Metropolitan
University

# Take the Law into your own hands

**northumbria**
UNIVERSITY
*great **learning** great **experience** great **future***

Located in a brand new state-of-the-art £70m development in the heart of Newcastle, Northumbria's Law School is renowned for its excellence in legal education.

## Graduate Diploma in Law (GDL)

- 1 year full-time programme or 2 years via distance learning
- New e-learning route from September 2008
- Study days on campus for distance learning students
- £1000 discount on our Legal Practice Course or Bar Vocational Course following successful completion of the GDL at Northumbria

## Bar Vocational Course (BVC)

- Practical skills training
- Strong practitioner participation
- Dedicated base room for BVC students
- Student Law Office elective
- Opportunity to study on an LLM/MA programme alongside the BVC
- New part-time route available

## Legal Practice Course (LPC)

- Wide choice of commercial and 'High Street' electives, including student law office
- Practical workshops
- Staff with extensive experience in teaching and practice
- Opportunity to study on the LLM/MA programme alongside the LPC

## Masters Programmes (LLM)

- Extensive range of programmes
- Full-time and distance learning modes of study

**For further information
visit our website:**
**www.northumbria.ac.uk/law**
**telephone:**
# 0191 227 4433
**or email**
**nb.admissions@northumbria.ac.uk**

# Northumbria University

School of Law, Newcastle upon Tyne NE1 8ST
**Tel:** 0191 227 4433
**Fax:** 0191 227 4561
**Email:** nb.admissions@northumbria.ac.uk
**Web:** www.northumbria.ac.uk/law

**College overview** Situated in a brand new, state of the art £70m development in the heart of Newcastle, Northumbria University Law School is known throughout the country for its distinctive and innovative programmes. The School of Law has a large practitioner library, mock courtrooms with dvd facilities and a Student Law Office.

### GDL (full time or distance learning)
The GDL is offered on a one-year full-time basis or two years distance learning, and covers the seven core subjects stipulated by the professional bodies as being the foundations of legal knowledge. Detailed study guides are provided. Students are also required to choose an eighth optional subject from a wide range available. Successful GDL students choosing to continue to study at Northumbria are guaranteed a place on the LPC and are entitled to a discount of £1,000 off course fees. A new e-learning route will be available from September 2008.

### Legal Practice Course (full or part time)
The Solicitors Regulation Authority awarded the School the 'commendable practice' rating across all of its monitoring categories. Students study three compulsory areas of general legal practice (civil and criminal litigation, property law and practice and business law and practice) and three electives from an extensive range. The electives now cover the full range of commercial and private client practice and students may choose a high street or commercial focus. The Student Law Office is an elective on the LPC where students work on real cases.

### Bar Vocational Course (full or part time)
Northumbria University is one of only six institutions outside of London to offer the Bar Vocational Course (BVC). Lectures which focus on key areas of practice are given regularly by senior practitioners and the programme is delivered from modern, purpose-built accommodation. The Student Law Office is an optional module on the BVC where students are able to work with clients on live cases. A part-time, day release mode of study has been launched for the September 2007 intake.

Students studying on the LPC or BVC at Northumbria are able to study on the LLM programme in Advanced Legal Practice at the same time. Both courses can be completed in between 12 and 18 months.

### Other postgraduate courses
LLM in Advanced Commercial Property Law
LLM in Advanced Legal Practice
LLM in Child Law
LLM in Commercial Law
LLM in Employment Law in Practice
LLM Information Rights Law and Practice
LLM in International Commercial Law
LLM in International Trade Law
LLM in Medical Law
LLM in Mental Health Law
LLM in Mental Health Law, Policy and Practice
Postgraduate Certificate in Business Law
MA in Legal Practice and Policy

| | |
|---|---|
| LPC | 150 (full time) |
| | 50 (part time) |
| CPE | 80 (full time) |
| | 60 (distance) |
| BVC | 80 (full time) |
| | 48 (part time) |

Contact

Admissions
0191 227 4433
nb.admissions@unn.ac.uk

great **learning** great **experience** great *future*

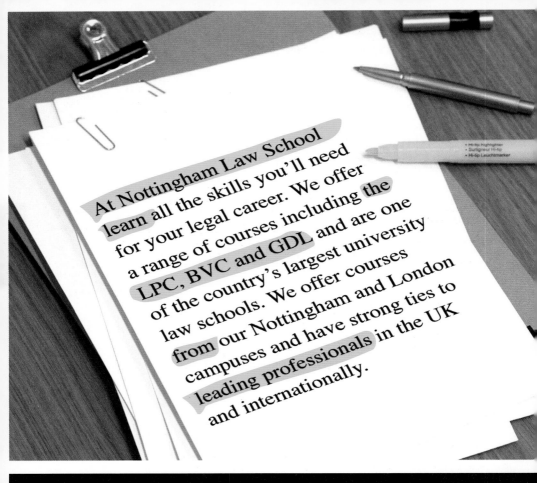

At Nottingham Law School learn all the skills you'll need for your legal career. We offer a range of courses including the LPC, BVC and GDL and are one of the country's largest university law schools. We offer courses from our Nottingham and London campuses and have strong ties to leading professionals in the UK and internationally.

# The evidence is clear

At Nottingham Law School you will be taught by qualified lawyers who work closely with some of the world's leading firms. Our LPC is the only one to have received the highest rating from the Law Society every year since launch. We are one of only eight providers validated by the Bar Council to deliver the BVC and the pass rate for our GDL course is over 90%. We offer a unique academic legal community and we are proud of our professional focus. You can choose to study in Nottingham or at our new London campus, which has been set up in partnership with Kaplan Law School. So you won't get a more authentic learning experience, or a better start to your professional career. Case closed.

## Law for lawyers, by lawyers. Visit **www.ntu.ac.uk/law**

NOTTINGHAM
LAW SCHOOL
Nottingham Trent University

# Nottingham Law School

Belgrave Centre, Chaucer Street, Nottingham NG1 5LP
**Tel:** 0115 848 6882
**Fax:** 0115 848 6878
**Email:** nls.enquiries@ntu.ac.uk
**Web:** www.ntu.ac.uk/nls

**College overview** One of the largest and most diverse law schools in the UK, we are committed to retaining strong links to practice. We seek to ensure that all our clients, from students to experienced practitioners, receive the best practical legal education and training. From September 2007 Nottingham Law School's LPC and GDL will be offered in London, where we have opened a brand new campus in partnership with Kaplan Law School.

**Graduate Diploma in Law (full time or distance learning)** The course is a one-year conversion course designed for any non-law graduate who intends to become a solicitor or barrister in the UK. The intensive course effectively covers the seven core subjects of an undergraduate law degree in one go. It is the stepping stone to the LPC or the BVC and to a legal career thereafter. Students who complete their GDL with us and then embark upon our excellent rated LPC or BVC will be eligible for a full LLB on successful completion of that professional course.
Places offered: 220 (full time); 130 (distance learning)

**Legal Practice Course (full time or block)** This course has been designed to be challenging and stimulating for students and responsive to the needs of firms, varying from large commercial to smaller high street practices. Course features: integration of transactions and skills, so that each advances the other; carefully structured interactive group work which develops an ability to handle skills and legal transactions effectively; a rigorous assessment process that nevertheless avoids 'assessment overload', to maintain a teaching and learning emphasis to the course; a professionally qualified team, retaining substantial links with practice; an 'Excellent' rating from the Law Society's Assessment Panel in every year of its operation.
Places offered: 650 (full time) 70 (block)

**Bar Vocational Course (full time)** Nottingham Law School designed its BVC to develop to a high standard a range of core practical skills, and to equip students to succeed in the fast-changing environment of practice at the Bar. Particular emphasis is placed on the skill of advocacy. The BVC is taught entirely by qualified practitioners, and utilises the same integrated and interactive teaching methods as all of the school's other professional courses. Essentially, students learn by doing. Students are encouraged to realise, through practice and feedback, their full potential.
Places offered: 120

## Other postgraduate courses

Postgraduate Diploma in Legal Practice
MBA in Legal Practice
Postgraduate Diploma in Advanced Litigation and Dispute Resolution
LLM Corporate Law
LLM Health Law
Postgraduate Diploma in Know-How Management
LLM Europe and the Law
LLM Sports Law
Postgraduate Diploma in Commercial Intellectual Property
LLM General Law
LLM International Criminal Justice
LLM International Trade
LLM Competition Law
LLM Employment Law

| | |
|---|---|
| GDL | 220 |
| LPC | 650 |
| BVC | 120 |

**Apply to**

**CPE/GDL** Central Applications Board & Clearing House
**CPE/GDL Distance** Direct to Law School
**LPC** Central Applications Board & Clearing House
**LPC Block** Direct to Law School
**BVC** Central Applications Board & Clearing House
**Other postgraduate law courses** Direct to Law School

**Location**
Nottingham, London

NOTTINGHAM
LAW SCHOOL
Nottingham Trent University

# GDL, LPC, LLB and LLM in
# Oxford

## Oxford Brookes University

The UK's 'top-performing modern university'.
*Sunday Times University Guide*

- Graduate Diploma in Law (GDL)
- LLM in International Law
- LLM in Public International Law
- LLM in International Human Rights Law
- LLM in International Economic Law
- LLM in WTO Law
- LLM in International Trade and Commercial Law
- LLM in International Banking Law
- Pre-sessional English for international law students

Oxford Brookes University
Tel: +44 (0) 1865 484931
Email: pglaw@brookes.ac.uk
Web: http://ssl.brookes.ac.uk/law

## Oxford Institute of Legal Practice

Awarded highest grade of 'commendable practice' across all Law Society assessment areas.

- Full-time Legal Practice Course (LPC)
- Part-time Legal Practice Course (LPC)
- Qualified Lawyers Transfer Test (QLTT)
- CPD accredited training courses

### New!
### Study the GDL at Brookes and the LPC at OXILP and receive an LLB degree

Oxford Institute of Legal Practice
Tel: +44 (0) 1865 260000
Email: lpcadmin@oxilp.ac.uk
Web: www.oxilp.ac.uk

**Oxford Institute**
of
**Legal Practice**

OXFORD
**BROOKES**
UNIVERSITY

# Oxford Institute of Legal Practice

King Charles House, Park End Street, Oxford OX1 1JD
**Tel:** 01865 260000
**Fax:** 01865 260002
**Email:** lpcadmin@oxilp.ac.uk
**Web:** www.oxilp.ac.uk

**College overview** OXILP was established as a joint foundation by Oxford University and Oxford Brookes University to provide vocational legal training and to form links between academic law and the practice of law. OXILP's LPC has an excellent reputation and has received the top SRA grading of 'commendable practice' across all six areas of assessment.

We offer a friendly, collegiate atmosphere with supportive and responsive staff. Students can choose from a range of extracurricular activities: pro bono, advocacy master classes, and a wide variety of sports clubs. Students may join the law societies and other student societies at both our parent universities and can use their sports facilities. Various social events are organised throughout the year.

## Legal Practice Course (full time, 300 places; part time, 50 places)
We aim to prepare students for a successful career as a solicitor. Our LPC is taught by professionally qualified staff with an excellent range of practice experience who offer a practically focused, skills-based approach. We try to provide students with a wider perspective on the practice of law through our series of foundation law lectures given by academic lawyers from our parent universities, and by lectures and workshops given by speakers from practice.

OXILP assists students in mapping career paths, connecting with career opportunities, and preparing them for the job market. We also provide students with career development tools, individual career coaching and events. All OXILP students have access to their own dedicated careers advisor, in addition to use of the career facilities at our parent universities. The Oxford University Careers Service (OUCS) is one of the best resourced career facilities available, and organises an extensive programme of talks and visits from recruiters.

We offer a range of electives, which have been designed with extensive input from solicitors in all areas of practice. These include: private acquisitions; equity finance; debt finance; employment; advanced property; clinical negligence and personal injury litigation; family law; private client; and commercial law and intellectual property.

## Graduate Diploma in Law (CPE) at Oxford Brookes University (one year full time or two years part time)
The CPE at Oxford Brookes University is designed for non-law graduates who wish to qualify as either solicitors or barristers. Oxford Brookes is a leading new university whose Law Department has high ratings in both teaching quality and research. The CPE is an intensive conversion course. The 90 students benefit from an individualised approach, which recognises both the academic and the professional requirements of the qualification. Students will study the following foundation subjects: European Union law, criminal law, public law, property and equity and trusts, civil obligations (contract, tort and restitution), as well as a legal research project. Extracurricular activities such as mooting, client interviewing and pro bono work are popular. Links with OXILP are close and those who pass the CPE are guaranteed a place on the OXILP Legal Practice Course. Students who take the GDL at Brookes and the LPC at OXILP will receive an LLB degree from Oxford Brookes.

| | |
|---|---|
| LPC | 300 (full time) |
| | 50 (part time) |
| CPE | 90 |

Contact
**LPC:** Administration
01865 260000
**CPE:** 01865 484901

  **Oxford Institute** of **Legal Practice**

**LC.N Weekly**

*Get your career online*

*Employer profiles*
*Features*
*Brochures*
*Meet The Recruiter*
*The Oracle*
*The Burning Question*
*Latest news*
*Immediate vacancies*
*Diary*
*And more...*

*To receive LC.N Weekly register*
*at **www.LawCareers.Net***

# Staffordshire University

Law School, Leek Road, Stoke on Trent, Staffordshire ST4 2DF
**Tel:** 01782 294550
**Fax:** 01782 294335
**Web:** www.staffs.ac.uk

**College overview** The Law School at Staffordshire University was established in April 1992 following almost 25 years' experience in law teaching. It is housed in its own state-of-the-art building, which is a short walk from Stoke on Trent railway station. Within the building is the Law Library and the Learning Resources Centre. The school is close to a suite of modern lecture theatres and is surrounded by the university's sports fields and sports facilities.

The university continues to make major investment in staff, accommodation and equipment. This includes professional quality dedicated Legal Practice Course facilities, extensive IT equipment and a well-stocked practitioner library including an extensive range of electronic legal precedents. We have a large and enthusiastic team of professionally qualified staff maintaining strong links with practice.

**The Common Professional Examination/Graduate Diploma in Legal Studies (full and part time)**
This course provides two outcomes. Firstly, it enables graduates (and others with appropriate qualifications) to obtain a valuable graduate law qualification. Secondly, it is a speedy route for non-law graduates to progress to the solicitors' (LPC) or barristers' finals courses.

**Legal Practice Course (full and part time)**
The Legal Practice Course is offered either as a one-year full-time course or by way of part-time study over two years. Either mode fulfils the Solicitors Regulation Authority's requirements for the vocational stage of training for those wishing to qualify as a solicitor. The provision at Staffordshire University Law School has been awarded the highest possible Solicitors Regulation Authority ratings of 'commendable practice' across all six areas of assessment.

**Other postgraduate courses**
LLM with named routes in business, commercial, critical legal studies, employment, environment, family, human rights, intellectual property, international, legal practice and advanced legal practice.
**Postgraduate MPhil/Phd by Dissertation** is also available.

Contact names

**CPE/GDL** Chris Culverwell
**LPC** Julie Gingell
**LLM** Chris Culverwell

# University of Westminster

School of Law, 4-12 Little Titchfield Street, London W1W 7UW
**Tel:** 020 7915 5511
**Email:** course-enquiries@wmin.ac.uk
**Web:** www.wmin.ac.uk/law

**College overview** The School of Law impresses students and visitors alike with the high quality of the building and teaching facilities. It is centrally located near Oxford Circus, which provides excellent access to political, legal and financial institutions and is in the middle of the largest concentration of solicitors' firms and barristers' chambers in the world. With nearly 2,000 students, the School of Law is one of the largest in London and offers a broad academic and professional course portfolio. As well as the diversity of courses offered, the School of Law prides itself on the strong collegial relationships between staff and students. The School of Law is fully equipped with a legal skills suite and mock courtroom, as well as an impressive library.

**Graduate Diploma in Law (CPE) (one year full-time or two year part-time)**
This is an intensive one-year conversion course designed for non-law graduates of any discipline or overseas law graduates who wish to qualify as barristers or solicitors. The University has over 25 years' experience in providing a law conversion course in this area. You are required to study the following foundation subjects: contract, tort, criminal law, public law, land law, equity and trusts, and the law of the European Union. Students are also required to study another different legal subject.

**Legal Practice Course (LPC) (one year full-time or two year part-time)**
The University of Westminster has offered the Legal Practice Course (LPC) since its introduction in 1993 and was awarded the highest possible grade of 'commendable practice' by the Law Society in October 2005. The LPC is the compulsory vocational course for intending solicitors. A distinctive feature of the University's course is the broad range of electives offered, reflecting areas of practice from high street to City firms. The hallmark of the approach is small, interactive group work, which allows individual guidance.

## Other postgraduate courses
**LLM Corporate Finance Law**
This course will appeal to those planning to work in fields including law, investment banking, corporate finance, private equity, securities and investment.
**LLM Dispute Prevention and Resolution**
This course covers the processes of negotiation, litigation and arbitration as well as alternative dispute resolution (ADR) processes, such as mediation and conciliation.
**LLM Entertainment Law**
This course combines academic analysis and commercial practice elements of entertainment law.
**LLM International and Commercial Dispute Resolution**
This course takes a broad approach to the study of disorder, order and justice in the public and private international and commercial spheres.
**LLM International Commercial Law**
With the growth in international trade and commerce, law firms, business enterprises and government organisations place a very high premium on graduates with commercial law skills.
**LLM International Law**
This course develops an innovative focus on contemporary legal and political issues in the international community.

| | |
|---|---|
| GDL | 90 (full-time) |
| | 60 (part-time) |
| LPC | 120 (full-time) |
| | 64 (part-time |

Apply to

**GDL full-time**
Central Applications Board
**GDL part-time**
GDL Admissions,
University of Westminster,
4-12 Little Titchfield Street,
London W1W 7UW
Email:
lpcadmin@wmin.ac.uk
Tel: 020 7911 5000
**LPC full-time**
Central Applications Board
**LPC part-time**
LPC Amissions,
University of Westminster,
4-12 Little Titchfield Street,
London W1W 7UW
Email:
lpcadmin@wmin.ac.uk
Tel: 020 7911 5000
**Other postgraduate
law courses**
Admissions & Marketing
Office
32-38 Wells Street,
London W1T 3UW
Email: regentadmissions@
wmin.ac.uk
Tel: 020 7911 5000

UNIVERSITY OF WESTMINSTER

# School of Legal Studies

## Turning our knowledge into your practice.

The School of Legal Studies has over 30 years' experience of providing relevant, dynamic and forward thinking legal education. We offer a wide range of undergraduate, postgraduate and professional courses.

### Professional courses offered

■ **Common Professional Examination/LLDip**
For non-law graduates wanting to pursue a career in the law.

■ **Legal Practice Course**
Taught in purpose-built accommodation with low staff/ student ratios and excellent support.

### Postgraduate courses offered

■ **LLM**
Designed to give students a wide variety and choice of study.

■ **LLM (top-up degree)**
Top-up your LPC or BVC to an LLM after completing research methods and submitting a dissertation.

■ **LLM International Corporate & Finance Law**
Designed for students interested in international corporate law.

■ **MA Practice Management**
For those involved in professional office management who want to improve their skills.

**For further information contact the Admissions Unit on tel: 01902 321633 or email: sls-enquiries@wlv.ac.uk**

UNIVERSITY OF
WOLVERHAMPTON

**www.wlv.ac.uk/sls**

# University of Wolverhampton

School of Legal Studies, Molineux Street, Wolverhampton WV1 1SB
**Tel:** 01902 321633
**Fax:** 01902 323569
**Email:** sls-enquiries@wlv.ac.uk
**Web:** www.wlv.ac.uk/sls

**College overview** The School of Legal Studies at Wolverhampton is home to one of the largest and most comprehensive law schools in the country, with a reputation for high quality provision of both undergraduate and postgraduate education in law. The School offers a wide range of academic and professional training, as well as providing specialised courses for practising solicitors and other professionals from industry, commerce, banking and financial and government institutions.

The courses benefit from the School's expertise in both national and international law, especially in the fields of corporate and financial law, criminal justice and social welfare.

### CPE/GDL: PG Diploma in Law (full or part time)
Full induction course.
Taught in a professional environment.
Use of ICT to support student learning.

### Legal Practice Course (full or part time)
Full induction course at start.
Small group size – greater individual attention.
High-quality, purpose-built teaching accommodation.

### Other postgraduate courses
### LLM (full or part time)
The LLM is designed to provide a programme of full-time or part-time study aimed primarily, but not exclusively, at law graduates. Graduates from other disciplines are also encouraged to undertake this programme where they can show sufficient legal study at undergraduate level, or equivalent. The course comprises both taught and research elements and includes modules covering:
IT Law
IP Law
International Corporate Finance
Risk Management
International Banking Law
Dispute Resolution and Conflict Management

### LLM in International Corporate and Financial Law (full or part time)
This specialist LLM is designed for people wishing to enhance their expertise and qualifications in the fields of international commerce, banking and business law. The course comprises both taught and research elements, and includes modules covering:
Money Laundering
Commercial Awareness
International Corporate Finance, Governance and Liquidation

### LLM (top-up degree)
The LLM top-up degree is for students who successfully obtain the LPC or BVC at a recognised institution. This 180-credit award is obtained after completing the Research Methods module and the submission of a dissertation, supported by a supervisor and personal tutor.

| | |
|---|---|
| CPE/GDL | 60 |
| LPC | 90 |

Contact names

CPE/GDL Clare Foster
LPC Clare Foster
Other postgraduate
law courses
Clare Foster

# Course providers

Institutions in **bold** have provided detailed information in the course directory section

## Institutions that offer the GDL

Anglia Ruskin University
University of Birmingham
**University of Central England in Birmingham**
Bournemouth University
**BPP Law School**
University of Brighton
**Bristol Institute of Legal Practice, University of the West of England**
Brunel University
**City University**
**The College of Law**
**De Montfort University**
University of East Anglia
University of Exeter
**University of Glamorgan**
**University of Hertfordshire**
Holborn College
University of Hong Kong (franchised by Manchester Met)
**University of Huddersfield**
Keele University
Kingston University
**University of Central Lancashire**
**Leeds Metropolitan University**
University of Lincoln
**London Metropolitan University**
London South Bank University
**Manchester Metropolitan University**
Middlesex University
**Northumbria University**
**Nottingham Law School**
Oxford Institute of Legal Practice
University of Plymouth
Southampton Solent University
**Staffordshire University**
Staffordshire University and Worcester College of Technology at Worcester
University of Sussex
Swansea University
Thames Valley University
University of Wales. Swansea
**University of Westminster**
**University of Wolverhampton**

## Institutions that offer the LPC

**Aberystwyth University**
Anglia Ruskin University
Bournemouth University
**BPP Law School**
**Bristol Institute of Legal Practice, University of the West of England**
**Cardiff Law School**
**University of Central England in Birmingham**
**City University**
**The College of Law**
**De Montfort University**
University of Exeter
**University of Glamorgan**
**University of Hertfordshire**
**University of Huddersfield**
**University of Central Lancashire**
**Leeds Metropolitan University**
**Liverpool John Moores University**
**London Metropolitan University**
**Manchester Metropolitan University**
**Middlesex University**
**Northumbria University**
**Nottingham Law School**
**Oxford Institute of Legal Practice**
University of Plymouth
University of Sheffield
**Staffordshire University**
Swansea University
Thames Valley University
University of Wales, Swansea
**University of Westminster**
**University of Wolverhampton**

## Institutions that offer the BVC

**BPP Law School**
**Bristol Institute of Legal Practice, University of the West of England**
**Cardiff Law School**
**City University**
**The College of Law**
**Manchester Metropolitan University**
**University of Northumbria**
**Nottingham Law School**

# Solicitors

# Introducing the Law Society

## Junior Lawyers Division

An exclusive new membership group for students, trainees and newly qualified solicitors (NQs) is being launched by the Law Society in January 2008. The Junior Lawyers Division (JLD) will be the voice of new solicitors across the country and in every type of practice. Membership is free. Please note that you must be enrolled with the Solicitors Regulation Authority to be eligible for membership. NQs are those who have been in practice for up to five years.

The JLD has been created in partnership with the Trainee Solicitors' Group (TSG) and the Young Solicitors Group (YSG). The YSG ended its operations on 30 June 2007. The TSG will continue to operate until the end of November 2007, holding its final conference on 17 November in Leeds.

The work of the new division is being led by its Interim Executive Committee, chaired by Katherine Gibson, herself a recently qualified solicitor. Katherine is supported by seven other committee members who are students, trainees and NQs, and three members of the Law Society's Council – the society's governing body.

## Membership benefits

The JLD will ensure that your views are heard on important issues before and after qualification. Part of the national Law Society – the number one representative body for solicitors – it takes you straight to the heart of your profession. Specific benefits include:

- an exclusive web area to support you through the early stages of your career – from getting a training contract to taking on supervisory responsibilities;
- a telephone helpline and access to advice via a range of specialist personal support services;
- careers advice and planning services;
- social and networking events held nationally and locally;
- competitively priced and accredited continuing professional development training;
- a quarterly magazine with informative articles, useful tips and discount offers; and
- the opportunity to influence the future of your profession by helping to run the JLD – find out more at www.lawsociety.org.uk/juniorlawyers.

## Local groups

The Interim Executive Committee is supported by the Interim National Committee, which is a wider forum for debating issues that affect students, trainees and NQs. The Interim National Committee comprises local and regional representatives of trainees and/or new solicitors' networks.

Local groups are a great way of getting to know colleagues in your area and having your say. Over time, these local groups might decide to follow the national model by coming together and forming a local Junior Lawyers group. Details of local groups are available on the JLD website.

## Find out more

From January 2008 the Law Society will be holding a series of launch events to tell you more about the JLD. The events will also be a great opportunity to meet other students, trainees and NQs in your region.

Don't miss your chance to be involved, get career support and help shape the future of your profession. Visit the website (www.lawsociety.org.uk/juniorlawyers) to find out more.

## Law Society

The services provided by the JLD are in addition to the full range of services that the Law Society offers to all its members.

The Law Society is the professional body that represents solicitors in England and

Wales. It builds market opportunities and influences the development of effective law. It supports solicitors in their day-to-day work and in their career progression throughout their working lives.

The Law Society activities outlined below may be of special interest to JLD members. Find out more at www.lawsociety.org.uk.

### Diversity Access Scheme

This scheme aims to help exceptionally talented, committed people overcome social, economic or personal barriers to entering the solicitors' profession. It funds places on the Graduate Diploma in Law and Legal Practice Course at a number of teaching institutions. It also offers a small number of scholarships, mentoring support and work placements.

For more on the scheme, see "Financing the vocational courses".

### Careers workshops

The Law Society runs careers workshops for second-year undergraduate students in conjunction with other professional networks.

### Equality and diversity

The Law Society provides guidance and support on a wide range of equality and diversity issues in line with the Solicitors' Code of Conduct to help promote a truly diverse profession. Recent campaigns have covered age regulations, disability and ethnic monitoring. The society also helps firms to network and share information on best practice, recently establishing a City firms' forum to this end.

### Pro bono work

The Law Society encourages solicitors at all stages of their careers to become involved in the community through pro bono activity. Pro bono work is rewarding and can be an opportunity to develop new skills. The society helps to organise the annual National Pro Bono Week and pro bono awards for deserving young lawyers.

*Stephen Ward is director of communications at the Law Society.*

# Training as a solicitor

Solicitors provide legal advice and representation. They work directly with their clients and are usually the first point of contact for anyone looking for legal advice. In general practice, solicitors may be called on to give advice on issues ranging from crime, personal injury, and drawing up contracts and wills to buying houses and taking over a business.

Increasingly, solicitors and firms specialise in certain areas of law. A run-down of various specialisations can be found in "Solicitor practice areas".

## Training contract

The training contract is a two-year employment contract with a law firm or other approved organisation, akin to an apprenticeship. The two years provide an opportunity for trainees to put into practice all the knowledge and skills they have learnt so far, with the firm assessing the trainee's suitability for retention upon completion of the training period.

## Structure

The training contract format varies between firms. Most (although not all) firms operate a 'seat' system in which trainees spend six months in four different departments. This gives trainees exposure to different practice areas so that they can make an informed choice as to their preferred qualification area. As far as possible, firms will try to accommodate the individual wishes of trainees in terms of seats, although they have to consider the overall needs of the firm as well as those of the other trainees. The Solicitors Regulation Authority (which has taken over responsibility for regulatory training from the Law Society) has a number of guidelines that also need to be followed. These include ensuring trainees are exposed to at least three practice areas, and both contentious and non-contentious work. In some firms, trainees may also have the opportunity to spend a seat in an overseas office or on secondment to a client.

Training may be less structured in smaller and high street firms. As many small firms cannot offer detailed training over a wide spread of specialisations, trainees are sometimes permitted to undertake consortium training, fulfilling different training seats in different firms. Certainly, training contracts with smaller and high street firms are less rigid than with the larger commercial firms – an approach that might appeal to those who fear a conveyor belt training mentality in the City firms.

## Content

What trainees learn during the training contract will depend on the type of firm and its solicitors. Clearly, the practice areas you learn about as a solicitor working at a commercial firm in the City are going to differ from those learnt by your peers at provincial high street firms. The smaller firms that mainly concentrate on a single area of work will obviously provide the most limited experience, but conversely can offer the most responsibility.

## Assessment and support

Trainee solicitors are assessed continuously throughout their training contract, a fact from which you should take comfort – it means that problems are likely to be nipped in the bud, not left to snowball. Almost without exception, firms have a three and six-monthly appraisal for each training contract seat. In this way the trainees get good feedback about their performance both during and after a seat, and get to have their say about anything they're not 100% happy with. You ought to be treated sympathetically in all your seats and should never feel as though you're being given more responsibility than you can handle. Nobody will expect you to know everything from day one of your training contract; indeed, some firms dedicate the first few weeks of a training contract with induction lectures and presentations to get you up to speed with the firm, its clients and its different practice areas. Most of your work will involve drafting, writing and researching, with everything being checked by a qualified solicitor and your supervision overseen by a partner (many trainees actually share an office with a partner during their seats).

Legal aid firms shouldn't be overlooked despite the fact that they can't offer the big bucks of magic circle firms. Often, trainees find legal aid work far more rewarding if the bottom line involves more than billing targets and financial gain. The Legal Services Commission, the Legal Aid Practitioners Group and The College of Law produce a booklet entitled *Working for Justice: Legal Aid – A Great Opportunity*. It outlines how to get a job in the sector and should be available free of charge from your university careers service or the bodies mentioned above.

Other training opportunities exist with the Crown Prosecution Service and the Government Legal Service, and with some companies outside private practice in commerce and industry (see "Alternative careers").

### Professional Skills Course

The Professional Skills Course (PSC) was introduced in the summer of 1994 as part of the new training scheme for solicitors – you cannot qualify as a solicitor without passing it. This is a modular course which aims to ensure that you have reached the appropriate level of skills and knowledge during the LPC and the training contract. Firms must pay for their trainees to attend the PSC.

The three core modules are:
• financial and business skills;
• advocacy and communication skills; and
• client care and professional standards

There is a written exam for the financial and business skills module, but no formal assessment of the others. You'll also need to complete 24 hours' worth of elective modules. If it is taken full-time, the PSC will last up to 20 days. However, each module can be taken individually. Many of the larger firms will run the PSC in-house as part of their ongoing training programmes at the beginning of each trainee's contract.

### Non-graduates

Non-graduates can qualify as a solicitor by a lengthy route that involves working in a legal office, joining the Institute of Legal Executives (ILEX) and passing ILEX exams to qualify as a member, then a fellow. A stage of vocational training, including the LPC, must also be completed. For more on ILEX, see "Alternative careers".

# Career timetable: solicitors

## First-year law degree students and second-year non-law degree students

What does it mean to be a solicitor? Am I cut out for the work? Why do I want to be a solicitor rather than a barrister? Do I want to practise in London or the regions? What practice area? These are the questions to be asking around this time. Answers can be gleaned by delving into the law section of your university careers centre and undergoing a healthy dose of self-analysis.

You might like to arrange some summer work experience to begin checking out the different types of firm (note that the formal work placement schemes don't take place for another year, however). Above all, work at achieving and maintaining good grades – when it comes to applying for formal work placement schemes and training contracts, firms will want to know your first and second-year grades, not just what degree you've ended up with.

## Second-year law degree students and final-year non-law degree students
### Autumn term, Christmas vacation and spring term

Decide whether you genuinely believe law is a career which will suit your character and skills through further research into the profession. Go to a careers advice service and discuss the profession generally with a careers adviser. Attend law firm presentations on campus and at firms' offices, and research and apply for work placement schemes for your summer vacation (some firms also offer Christmas and Easter work). It's a good idea to do a few schemes in order to get a feel for the range and types of practice available to you.

Virtually all university law career fairs take place in October and November. Attend and meet some firms – this is your best chance to meet firms face to face. It is sensible to have done some preliminary research so that you can ask intelligent questions. Many firms also organise on-campus presentations during these two terms.

Look into the funding possibilities for your legal training (in particular, local education authority grants) and check closing dates for applications.

Non-law degree students should apply for a place on a conversion course, known as the Graduate Diploma in Law (GDL), before 1 February. Applications for full-time places must be made through the Central Applications Board (www.lawcabs.ac.uk). Although online applications are greatly preferred, you can phone 01483 451080 to request a hard-copy form. Applications for part-time courses must be made direct to the provider.

### Easter vacation

Apply for further work placements for the summer vacation. Thoroughly research the applications procedure for training contracts, especially those at firms you are interested in. By now you should be beginning to shortlist the firms to which you want to apply.

### Summer vacation

Most major law firms have training contract application deadlines during this period (from mid-July onwards). Gain some further work experience, either on a formal work placement scheme or through other means. Check deadlines for Legal Practice Course (LPC) applications at www.lawcabs.ac.uk.

## Final-year law degree students and GDL conversion course students
### Autumn term

Employers can start interviewing candidates for training contracts from 1 September in their final year of a law degree, so you should be busy with interviews now! You must also apply for LPC courses now through the Central Applications Board. The deadline for the initial selection and allocation process is 1 December.

### Spring term
You must enrol at the Law Society as a student member before you start your LPC. However, if you have submitted your application for a full-time LPC place, you will automatically be sent the necessary forms. The closing date for the return of forms is 1 August in the year you hope to start the LPC. For those with suitability issues, such as a police caution, the deadline is 1 April because you have to submit supporting documents. Part-time LPC applicants need to contact the Solicitors Regulation Authority (SRA) to enrol (email info.services@sra.org.uk or call 0870 606 2555).

### Summer term
The deadline for LPC acceptances is during this term. If you haven't succeeded in obtaining a training contract, keep making further applications until you get one. Obtain a certificate for the completion of the academic stage of legal training.

### LPC year
If you have yet to find a training contract, keep making further applications throughout the year until you get one. Attend as many law fairs as possible and check for adverts in the *Law Society Gazette* and on www.LawCareers.Net.

### Autumn term
Introduction course followed by compulsory subject courses.

### Spring term
Compulsory subject courses.

### Summer term
Optional subject courses.

### Training contract
#### Year one
Ensure that your training contract has been registered with the SRA (your firm will usually do this for you). Most firms operate a series of departmental rotations (most often four seats in separate departments, each lasting six months). On-the-job training is provided throughout and is supplemented by courses and lectures throughout the two-year training period.

#### Year two
Around the middle of your second year, most firms will run through their post-training job offer process and you will know whether you are going to be offered a position at your firm at the end of your training. At the end of year two you will finish your training contract and will have qualified as an assistant solicitor.

Approximately six to eight weeks before your training contract is due to end, the SRA will send you the necessary forms so that you can apply to be formally admitted to the roll of solicitors. Provided all necessary training conditions have been satisfied, you will be admitted to the roll. Congratulations – you are a solicitor!

# Law *Careers*.Net

*5750 training contracts*
*500 pupillages*
*8500 users every day*
*One address*
**www.LawCareers.Net**

# Arbitration

Arbitration law falls under the broad umbrella of alternative dispute resolution and, along with mediation, is an increasingly popular way for parties to resolve their commercial disputes. In practice, arbitration is an alternative to drawn-out litigious battles in the courts. Perceived advantages over traditional litigation include privacy, speed and, on occasion, a level of informality which can allow, for example, the parties to avoid the expense of a detailed disclosure exercise.

Mark Everiss is a partner at Kendall Freeman, a City firm that specialises in insurance/reinsurance, litigation and corporate work. He studied law at the University of Liverpool, joining Kendall Freeman (DJ Freeman & Co, as it was then) as a trainee in 1988: "It was a very different firm then from the one it is now. The insurance practice grew and grew, and the insurance and reinsurance group (doing both contentious and non-contentious work) is now at the core of Kendall Freeman."

Mark specialises in large-scale, high-value reinsurance litigation and arbitration – as such, there's no such thing as a typical day! He discusses what drives him: "The aim of every day is getting results for clients on areas of contention. A good result might mean winning a case or achieving a good settlement (very few cases actually reach a full-blown arbitration hearing). You want to keep clients happy so that they come back again."

Mark highlights various aspects of his arbitration work: "The arbitration process is confidential, which means that when an arbitrator makes an award, nobody but the parties is entitled to see it (although people often hear whispers, especially in the insurance market). That makes it difficult to talk publicly about my practice. I can say that I regularly act on large arbitrations that involve key insurance issues. I have actually done relatively few substantive final hearings in 17 years of practice – probably resulting in fewer than 10 awards and judgments – but that reflects the size of the matters and the fact that I'm not doing lots of cases at any one time. And I do have a high success rate!" Of the key reinsurance issues that he handles, Mark says: "In broad terms, they are policy interpretation issues or issues arising in connection with the placing of an insurance contract. Typically, the aim of the litigation or arbitration is to ensure payment for my insurance company client by their reinsurer."

With only glowing things to report about his life as an arbitration specialist, Mark's natural optimism about the job is clear: "I'm very happy in my environment. I guess you don't stay somewhere for 19 years without enjoying what you're doing, who you're doing it for and who you work with. And if I'm not finding something enjoyable, I will try and change things to turn them around. Aside from winning, one thing I particularly enjoy is bringing order and sense to a heap of documents, which is an integral part of the job and leads to the successful outcome that I am seeking to achieve."

Flexibility is a particular asset in arbitration, says Mark: "While you have to know your way around the key piece of legislation (the Arbitration Act 1996), you're not dealing with the same sort of prescriptive set of rules you have in the courts. Arbitrators have a lot of flexibility, and thus you have the latitude to try and find alternative, creative ways of getting an effective resolution. I've just done an arbitration in which we were ordered by the arbitrators to prepare for a full hearing in two months. We got on and did it, and had a successful outcome – that was clearly preferable to the clients, who would have had to wait much longer if it had gone through the courts. But what it doesn't mean is ripping up the rulebook! It's important not to compromise the result. You also have to be flexible about addressing clients' requirements, and that may mean being increasingly available (at least electronically)."

Mark identifies some of the other skills that are useful in arbitration: "You've got to be resilient, firm and able to argue your points convincingly. You need to be able to write a good, solid letter, but you also need to be able to present your arguments orally. Civility in your correspondence is important – while you need to be robust and tenacious, you mustn't resort to being rude or over-aggressive. That gets you nowhere. The letters you send to the other side often also go to the arbitrators, so going over the top won't endear you to them! Don't forget that you want them to embrace your argument."

Mark has some sound advice on how to shine at training contract interviews: "So much is down to first impressions, so dress appropriately and relax – interviewers want to get the best out of you, so try and enjoy the process. Be natural; trying to be something you're not can only lead to a sticky end. If you haven't heard something or you don't understand a question, don't be afraid to ask for it to be repeated or explained. Take your time. Show you are the kind of person who doesn't rush into things. There will be very few one-word answers, so try and see different angles on the same question. It is worth expressing the opposite of the answer that you yourself might support, because it shows you can see both sides of an issue and respect an alternative point of view. Having said all of that, you do still need to be able to express your own opinion."

Finally, Mark has more to say on the benefits of taking a flexible approach – this time, to your career progression. He says: "There is so much fortune in what you do; a different first seat or supervisor might have put me on a different path altogether. Sometimes though, things just fall into place. I'd be surprised to hear someone at interview say that they want to be an insurance litigator on qualification. More believably, you want someone who knows why they're applying to your firm and what they want in broad terms, but is prepared to be guided by what they experience during their training contract."

# Banking and finance

Banking and finance is a global industry that attracts high-fliers dealing in major transactions and disputes covering multi-jurisdictional issues. Increasing internationalisation and a wide variety of financial products mean that modern banking is becoming ever more complex.

One result of this complexity is that the scope for banking litigation is increasing. Disputes may involve insolvency proceedings and the enforcement of rights under financing agreements and money-laundering regulations, as well as criminal prosecutions and Department for Business, Enterprise and Regulatory Reform inquiries.

Liam Terry is a solicitor at Pinsent Masons, a full-service international law firm. Liam studied law at the University of Nottingham, followed by a year out coaching football. Then it was back to the legal coalface and the LPC at Nottingham Law School.

Liam describes his training contract experience at Pinsents: "It was my first proper office job, and it was interesting trying to adjust to the rigours of what can't be described as a nine-to-five job! There are ups and downs, as any trainee will tell you, but it's generally very exciting to be doing transactional law. My first seat was in corporate (private equity), followed by general litigation, banking and finance, and projects. I was interested in the mechanics of how debt finance works, how banks raise money, how it's controlled and the different types of finance. I was exposed to a broad mix of transactions, most of which involved acquisitions and leveraged finance. You only really get a flavour as a trainee, but I definitely got a sense that it was something I was interested in."

Qualifying into the banking and finance department, Liam discusses the work he does now: "I now work on leveraged and acquisition finance deals at a mid-market level. I have also worked on several property finance deals and recently was involved in a corporate jet financing. I act for a mix of both bank and borrower clients. Each day includes liaison with clients, which might mean getting the initial instructions on a transaction and producing (or commenting on) the finance or security documents. There will also be other non-banking aspects of a deal that crop up when corporates borrow money (for example, corporate, IP issues) that need input from my colleagues. There can be quite a lot of cross-departmental coordination and, as a junior lawyer, you're often the one doing the coordinating."

Private equity is an aspect of Liam's work that he finds particularly interesting: "With it being such a hot topic, I've probably most enjoyed working on private equity backed transactions. It's often very exciting, usually with a short time period and interesting parties involved. It's interesting looking at how these companies operate – they're possibly not as bad as the press would have you believe!"

Liam is currently on secondment to a major clearing bank, sitting with its corporate leveraged finance team and working on mid-market transactions. He discusses his experiences so far: "The advantage is that this is a business secondment, so I'm really getting under the skin of what the finance team does. A lot of transactions begin well before lawyers start documenting them, so it's interesting to get to see how these deals originate, the credit process, and the ways that banks make decisions on what they can lend and what structure to use. Undoubtedly, this will be helpful when I go back to the firm. Lawyers can get very bogged down in the legal details, but sometimes there are important commercial drivers and it's crucial to find those out and give them due consideration in conjunction with the legal details."

Liam enjoys the fact that clients rely on his professional knowledge: "People often come to you with the idea of what they want to achieve and you have to think about how to put that into practice – it's a challenge, but it's very satisfying. There is a lot of effort in working out how to do things, but it's exciting to be adding value, seeing it all come to fruition and using your brain to get there." The long hours are less enjoyable, says Liam, but no surprise if you've gone into the job with your eyes open. Equally, it can be difficult when "parties are pulling in different directions and you're trying to get everyone on the same page".

As ever, the importance of commercial awareness looms large. Liam explains why this, and other skills, are so important: "I know all the brochures say the same thing, but commercial awareness really is vital! It's crucial to have an understanding of the business markets and not just focus on the law. You also have to be adaptable, so that you're confident in what you think is right but can also listen to the thoughts of others. In a big firm, there are lots of different personalities and ways of working, so you need to be able to work within that. You have to have a willingness to learn and not get too stressed under pressure. And don't forget to have something outside of work – you will hear a lot about a work-life balance!"

Finally, Liam suggests the best approach to securing a training contract. He says: "Summer work placements are a chance to get to know the firm, and for both you and the firm to take a more measured decision than one based solely on an interview. General work experience is good too – for example, banks offer internships which can give a flavour of how international finance organisations work. You should talk to lawyers to get an idea of what it's actually like – it's not a John Grisham novel! But you don't have to decide exactly what you want to be early on. It's better to have an inkling of an idea. For example, you're not going to apply to a corporate focused City firm if it's a discipline such as criminal law that they may not do you're interested in. It is important to do your research, go to law fairs and talk to trainees. The more information you have, the better your decision-making will be!"

# Commercial litigation

**Commercial litigation involves the resolution of disputes arising in the corporate and commercial sectors, such as asset and venture capital projects, banking transactions, civil fraud, corporate governance, European Union/competition, financial services regulation, mergers and acquisitions, share capital reorganisations and professional negligence.**

**The 1999 Woolf reforms aimed to produce a fairer, quicker and less expensive system that encourages the early settlement of disputes through mechanisms such as alternative dispute resolution. As a result, fewer cases now reach the courts and larger cases are being concluded more swiftly.**

Joel Heap is a partner in the dispute resolution department of Cobbetts, a leading national law firm. Bucking his family trend of becoming an accountant ("the last thing I wanted to be!"), Joel studied law at Leeds Metropolitan University, followed by the LPC at The College of Law in York. In hindsight, he isn't convinced that doing a law degree is essential: "I much preferred the practical side of law school, so I wish I'd studied history or economics at university. Not having done a law degree is no barrier to success – in fact, those people I knew on the LPC who had converted had an advantage because the law was fresh in their minds, whereas for me, I'd done it three years prior."

After the LPC, Joel secured a year's paralegal work at Hammonds in Leeds, working in the litigation department with the now managing partner. However, timely news from a friend at Cobbetts alerted Joel to some last-minute trainee recruitment. He applied, was successful and started a couple of days later. He describes the training experience: "It was brilliant. I knew from my work at Hammonds that I loved litigating –

the arguments, the tactics, the winning and losing (hopefully not too much losing!) – and I was lucky to be able to do three contentious seats during my training contract. However, it suddenly dawns on you that the training contract is not an extension of university with a bit of work experience thrown in – you're there to work hard." Joel comments that it is usually easy to spot the difference between those who have spent time working in an office environment and those who haven't (an inability to use the photocopier is usually a key indicator).

Qualifying into the dispute resolution department, Joel found that "having so much contentious experience meant I hit the ground running, but on qualification you're still wet behind the ears". Nevertheless, he received lots of support and now, he's the one doing the supporting, as a partner in the department and a trainee supervisor. He discusses his work: "A large part of the job is winning work, building client relationships and managing my team. When I receive instructions from a client, I will either delegate or get to work on it myself with an assistant and possibly my trainee. I have just finished a case that involved a local company. One of the directors and four employees handed in their notice, walked out and set up in competition next door, having taken confidential information, customer contacts and technical data. We spent an intense fortnight working very long hours, preparing to apply for an urgent injunction without notice to the other side to seize computers and documents. We were gathering witness statements, working with IT experts, instructing leading counsel, and getting information to the mercantile judge. The team on it successfully obtained an interim injunction and subsequently the parties settled, but it was a massive job. Because of its reactive nature, litigation is not for those people that want a structured lifestyle. I can have a 'to do' list, but then a fax comes in that turns everything upside-down. Managing clients and juggling your caseload is an important skill. There is a real ebb and flow of cases; you just have to hope they don't all ebb at once!"

Joel specialises in the cut and thrust of emergency relief (eg, injunctions, and search and seizure), particularly in relation to disputes arising out of the sale and purchase of companies, and between shareholders and partners. He comments: "I work very closely with our corporate finance team – they do the deals, but I get involved when disputes arise. I'm lucky to have found a niche that suits me down to the ground."

In recognition of his making partner at 29 years old, Joel was named Young Lawyer of the Year by *North West Business Insider* magazine. He elaborates: "The award helped raise my profile and get new business, which is a fundamental part of being a lawyer. This is a "relationship business", and one way of differentiating yourself from the competition is to make a client a friend and not just a colleague. That way, you'll have them for life."

Variety is the spice of a litigator's life, according to Joel: "I've never advised on one dispute that is the same as another. While the process and some of the legal principles may be the same, the subject matter could be anything. I've been involved with one matter to do with a collapsing slate mine in Wales, and another to do with a collapsing biscuit manufacturing process."

And the way to enjoy that spicy variety is to hone your ability to prioritise: "It's a key skill because of the pace with which things move. Compared to other areas, where you may have to get a letter done in a couple of days, we have to do things now! Another fundamental skill is commerciality – understanding what a client wants to achieve

– and the sooner you can develop that, the better. Attention to detail is also essential. We are paid a lot of money by our clients, and we should know every detail, from every angle."

Joel expands on some of the other things that will make you an attractive trainee candidate: "Make sure you understand where the market is going in your area of interest. The way things are done now is unlikely to be the way things will be done in 10 years' time. In terms of a successful interview, I refer back to what I did wrong! I remember saying what I thought they wanted to hear, about being a corporate lawyer, and buying and selling companies. In hindsight, I think interview success comes from being interesting about whatever it is, be that trekking through Peru, being an extra on *Coronation Street*, or running a small business while at school. You've got to have an angle! Then there's the same old stuff – do your research and understand the firm, but make sure you're up-to-date. We had one person on our vacation scheme who asked me whether I thought the firm would ever move to London – we'd published the opening of our London office some months earlier!"

Finally, Joel advises against early specialisation: "Just because you enjoyed studying a particular area of law doesn't mean you'll be good at, or enjoy, working in it. I'm testament to that! I never thought I'd be a litigator, but I really enjoy it. So don't pigeonhole yourself too early. I think it's better to get as wide an experience as possible. You'll be doing this job from early morning until late at night until you're at least 55 years old, so you need to love it!"

# Commercial property

**Commercial property (or real estate) lawyers advise on transactions and act for a variety of domestic and international clients – including property investors and developers, governments, landowners and public sector bodies – on a wide range of property-related transactions, involving anything from offices and houses to retail developments and industrial units.**

**In general, the legal issues on which firms offer expertise include acquisitions and disposals of commercial properties, investments, landlord and tenant matters, lettings, sales, developments and contracts, insolvency planning applications, and environment laws and liabilities. A great deal of the work involves new ways of transacting, whether through financing, developing or co-investing.**

Richard Larking is an associate solicitor at commercial Leeds firm Walker Morris, advising national and international clients. He recalls his path to law: "I left school when I was 16 without any educational qualifications to speak of. I spent seven years in the Royal Navy and while I was there I did an A-level in law and found it really interesting. It was something different to what I was used to." He went on to read law at the University of Sheffield and managed to bag a scholarship to spend his second year in New York.

Richard did his training contract at Eversheds, during which he "did a seat in the recoveries unit which was effectively bulk litigation. Then I had seats in private client, commercial property and banking". He enjoyed his commercial property seat because he got involved in some large, high-value transactions. "I remember being involved in a very big job for DuPont," he recalls, "and the deal was big numbers." But

he did do some smaller jobs as well – like a residential conveyance for the friend of a property partner!

Richard actually qualified as a commercial contracts lawyer and did a secondment with Oftel, the former telecommunications regulatory body. But now he's back into commercial property and enjoys the fact that "I'm a lot more autonomous now". Thankfully though, "the support network is there if I need it, but I'm really left to my own devices".

Richard's workload usually centres on a dozen or so ongoing deals including property finance transactions and acquisitions, and sales of large commercial developments. He describes his typical day: "I get in around 8:00am and catch up with the jobs I was finishing off the previous afternoon or evening. The post comes in about 8:45am, so I look at that and deal with any urgent queries straight away. Otherwise, I just crack on with the ongoing jobs which will take me up to about 12:30pm depending on any meetings I have scheduled. During the day, calls are coming in, which may be queries from existing clients or new jobs. And then in the afternoon, I'll continue to work on the ongoing jobs. Depending on how busy things are, I'll be here until about 6:30pm."

Richard's client base is very varied. He explains: "I've got one particularly large client that is US-based but which has a large UK presence. I deal with their in-house legal team and they, in turn, deal with the company's directors and senior managers, so I'm instructed by them too. Often it's just making sure you're asking the right questions to the right people and keeping everybody informed. At the other end of the scale I'm dealing with individuals who are constantly on the phone, making sure they know everything that's going on in respect of their transaction. Often they'll be developing a small number of industrial or retail units. We'll get involved in the purchasing, building phase and construction aspects, as well as eventually selling the site or new development." And although, as Richard notes, lawyers have a bad reputation for dealing with sites and buildings and not ever seeing them, "we often go on-site or view the buildings and the client tends to be very positive about that".

Richard says commercial property is consistently busy, far more so than other practice areas which tend to be very busy one week and quieter the next. Also, commercial property people seem to be a select breed: "I usually find property people to be fairly balanced. They're dealing with transactions that don't happen very quickly, but they're often working to very tight deadlines. It's well understood what commercial property transactions entail and it's quite a close-knit community."

Richard admits that although a career in law has both ups and downs, "you remember the ups a lot more. The thing that I most enjoy about being a solicitor is the other people I deal with – not just the fellow professionals in my firm – who are genuinely excited about a job". He explains that some individual clients rely on him a great deal: "You're going to be working on transactions with people that are once in a lifetime opportunities so you've got to learn not to panic. You're often dealing with tens of millions of pounds. You've got to rely on your experience and colleagues. If I stopped to think about the responsibility, it'd be quite worrying, but given that it happens every day, you become a bit more relaxed about it."

That said, you can't be too laid-back. Richard notes: "You need to be organised because you're dealing with a large quantity of information and paper. And also, of course, you need to have good interpersonal skills."

Richard remembers applying for training contracts a decade ago. One of the most important lessons he learnt then was to be commercially minded: "You need to have a real think about the commercial aspects of your experience and of the firm you're applying to. Everyone's got experience in some way. Even a job delivering newspapers has commercial aspects!"

In commercial property, comments Richard, you're going to be busy: "You wouldn't go into it to put your feet up. There's great job satisfaction in that there's loads of transactions to get involved in at different levels. And I think in commercial property you're given a great degree of responsibility early on and, in the right support environment, that's great."

Richard's final piece of advice is this: "Nothing can prepare you for what you do on a day-to-day basis (other than to a small degree the LPC and previous work experience). Being a solicitor is what you make of it. You'll get out what you put in."

# Company/commercial and corporate

**Company/commercial and corporate lawyers advise on complex transactions and work closely with other specialist departments in acting for businesses of all sizes. General company law work involves advising on company directors' rights, duties and responsibilities, company board meetings, memoranda and articles of association, company secretarial matters and shareholders' rights.**

**Corporate transactional work concerns mergers and acquisitions, demergers and restructurings, joint ventures, takeovers, equity financings, privatisations, initial public offerings and new issues of shares and other securities on the international markets.**

Jonathan Wood is a partner in the London office of Weil, Gotshal & Manges, a US firm with international reach. He went to the University of Dundee, after his dreams of becoming a pilot were dashed because of "an allergy to house-dust!". Dundee offers a combined English and Scottish Law degree, something which appealed to Jonathan's new life plan: "Law seemed like a good general professional degree, so I toddled off to Dundee to get maximum flexibility. The first two years were very academic and they didn't really set me on fire, so I took a year out to work for a high street firm in my hometown. It was an amazing year because it clarified two things; first, that I definitely wanted to be a lawyer and second, that I didn't want to do private client work ever again!" Jonathan returned to university, full of enthusiasm and a desire to pursue corporate law as a career. He chose business and English law subjects to strengthen his position when applying for a training contract in London.

Happily, the training contract dream became a reality and Jonathan was taken on at Lovells. After doing the LPC at The College of Law, Jonathan began his training contact

and qualified into the private equity team. Famously, the entire private equity team (bar a partner and a couple of associates) moved across from Lovells to Weil Gotshal in April 2006.

Jonathan discusses his current position as partner in the corporate (private equity) team: "My work usually involves acting for private equity houses in conjunction with the acquisition or disposal of, or investment in, private or public companies. I am involved right from the early stages of the decision-making process, which is one of the great joys of the job – you become an integral part of the team and a trusted adviser. So although the remit is legal, it extends beyond that into commercial execution and strategy."

One of Jonathan's recent deals centred on the sale of clothing brand Fat Face to Advent International: "It was a watershed transaction, because of the competitive environment and the speed with which it happened. Typically, when a business is sold by way of auction, a list of potential purchasers are given an information memorandum and are asked to give an indication of how much they might pay for the business, what the terms might be, and how quickly they could proceed. Any attractive bids would then be invited to a second stage which would involve access to more detailed information about the company. They would then submit a more final offer. We'd also send out a draft sale and purchase agreement, asking them to make changes so that we'd be able to compare prices and terms. With Fat Face, at the first round we had six or seven credible bids! Two of which were ready to enter a binding agreement in 48 hours, and one of which was offering a significant non-refundable deposit to be given preferred access to the management team. The seller deliberated for one day and then it took less than 48 hours to sign a deal. The sellers were very pleased with the terms and the deal was a high watermark in terms of what sellers can hope to achieve."

Jonathan's personal career highlights have been making partner and moving across from Lovells, bringing his clients with him: "It meant they were comfortable enough to trust that we were moving to a better home and that their interests were going to be looked after. Private equity is very much about individual, personal relationships because as clients, they are the most sophisticated users of legal services, always speaking to lawyers about transactions and doing deals every few months. What that means is that you have to wear the T-shirt and be their guy!"

In addition to client development, Jonathan thinks there are other key skills in this field: "Business acumen, common sense, and a desire and ability to be as technically skilled as possible. There are new developments every day and it's important to stay on top of that."

Jonathan stresses the importance of examining the reasons why you've chosen law as a career. He looks back at his own path as an example (albeit not necessarily an example to be followed!). He says: "With my CV and patchy decision-making at the time, I was pretty lucky to get in front of a City firm for an interview! So, with hindsight, I think the most important thing is to think about what turns you on and why that is. I interview a lot of people for training contracts and I hear a lot of contrived answers. They say what they think we want to hear, rather than what really gets them going and why. For example, if you say you have an interest in M&A, you ought to have enough of an interest to read some of the business papers. You need to demonstrate an interest and show that it's genuine. The other thing is to spend time being honest with yourself about what you enjoy and what it is that attracts you to being a lawyer. We're looking for people with backbone and character and their own ideas."

And while a gap year is no bad thing, Jonathan has some stern words about people who think having done one will necessarily endear them to an interview panel: "I wouldn't advocate gap years for everybody, but I think what people *should* do is take time to think about what they want to do. Just taking a year out to mess around is fine, but it doesn't necessarily enhance your chances of getting a training contract! And if the reason you're doing it is because you think you're going to have to buckle down to a really boring life as a lawyer, then maybe you're thinking about doing the wrong job!"

If you want to survive as a young corporate lawyer, Jonathan suggests invoking a moment of calm each day: "There's lots of jargon and moving parts in this environment, and it's very easy not to be able to see the wood for the trees. Instead, you should take five minutes at the beginning and end of each day to look at the big picture. What are you trying to achieve? It's important to put things into context – without direction, you don't get the same sense of reward and you sometimes miss important features because you've forgotten why you're doing it."

And if you needed an excuse, Jonathan offers more good reasons to spend time socialising with friends and spending hours networking on Facebook. He says: "Without wanting to seem too Machiavellian, it's good to maintain contacts you've made through school and university from the outset of your career. You may find out that as you've been developing, your contemporaries have been becoming influential too! And there is the reward of give and take: you might be able to help someone and they might be able to help you. Don't forget that this is a business like any other – it's no good just being a skilled tactician if nobody knows you!"

# Competition

Typically, competition and regulatory work includes merger control under the Enterprise Act 2002 or the EC Merger Regulation, proceedings under the Competition Act 1998, issues arising from sector specific regulation, state aid, public sector and utility procurement issues.

In addition to the main UK legislation, UK companies must also comply with the relevant EU rules which apply directly to their conduct. There has been significant reform of both UK and EU competition law and practice in recent years and further reform proposals are currently being considered. An interesting recent development in the United Kingdom has been the introduction of a cartel offence giving rise to liability for individuals, rather than just businesses; this adds an important new criminal dimension to competition law work. Private competition law actions are a particular area to watch, with both the UK and EU authorities keen to foster such actions.

Katie Herald is a senior assistant at Travers Smith, a mid-tier City firm. She read modern history at the University of Oxford, and the GDL and LPC at BPP in London. She explains: "It was on the LPC as part of one of my electives that I had my first taste of competition law. There wasn't that much scope for doing extensive amounts of competition law but it was sufficient to flag it as an area of law I definitely wanted to come back to."

Katie went on to do her training contract at Travers Smith. Her seats comprised litigation, corporate, property and also, of course, competition. In addition to picking up experience in these practice areas, Katie learnt that she needed "a great eye for detail" and the ability to communicate "in a client-friendly way".

These are the things it can be difficult to pick up at law school, comments Katie: "I think when you come from the legal hothouse of law school you can forget the practicalities of having to be commercial. You can know the letter of the law backwards but unless you can communicate that effectively to clients in a way that's going to help them with their business or transaction, it's of very limited use to them."

Katie recalls what it was like to do a seat in competition: "I was fully involved in many aspects of the work from the outset. For example, I worked closely on a UK merger of two franking machine businesses in the run-up to it being referred to the Competition Commission. As you can imagine, there was a lot of complex work to do within a pressured timetable and I learnt a great deal by being part of the team preparing the merger control filing." Katie notes that generally the type of work she does as a qualified competition lawyer has not changed that much from when she was a trainee: "Clearly I have a higher level of responsibility and independence, but the types of work are broadly the same."

Indeed, Katie has a lot of work on her plate: "As part of my work relates to M&A deals, a typical day might include hearing about a new corporate deal and analysing whether merger control filings are required; drafting a filing to the European Commission or the Office of Fair Trading; and, as we often act on cross-border transactions, coordinating multi-jurisdictional filings by liaising with foreign lawyers. Another key area of work is behavioural competition law – for example, we draft submissions to authorities that are investigating clients for alleged breaches of competition law and review draft commercial agreements for compliance with competition law."

Skills from Katie's history degree often come

into play during her daily work. Drafting submissions to merger control/competition authorities is a bit like writing a history essay, she notes: "You're setting out the facts and legal and economic principles on which you then base your arguments – in essence, it's being persuasive on paper."

Competition is a dynamic area of law. Katie explains: "In recent years, there has been a significant amount of new legislation and guidance from the European Commission and UK authorities, including of course the Enterprise Act in the United Kingdom. And there is certainly a great deal of scope for ongoing discussion within competition circles about the best way to develop the legal and practical framework for competition law – it is fascinating to be a part of this."

With competition being such a growing area of law, Katie gets to see a number of exciting cases: "Recently, I've been acting for Red Bee Media in relation to Ofcom's investigation into its access service contracts with Channel 4 and the BBC. After a long-running investigation that started almost two years ago, Ofcom has just announced its non-infringement and case closure decisions in favour of my client."

Katie explains what she enjoys most about being a solicitor: "Appreciative clients! Particular to competition law, there's also the satisfaction of successfully achieving clearance or the desired outcome at the end of a long investigation." The insight gained into clients' businesses is also rewarding: "Competition lawyers often need very detailed market information. We work closely with the client and get to know its business, whether it's radio, gas, carpets or ports. It's interesting to apply the same legal framework to a wide variety of market sectors and also valuable to come to understand a client's business that well."

Sometimes it's easier said than done, as Katie explains: "It can prove difficult convincing a client that you really do need that in-depth information – you can be met with initial consternation at the other end of the phone! That said, with the growing profile of competition law, I do think that clients are increasingly aware of its importance, and also the risks of non-compliance. The possibility of a fine of up to 10% of worldwide turnover is usually enough for clients to take it seriously!"

Law students interested in competition should try to do a competition module, advises Katie. If that's not possible, "make sure you choose an elective on the LPC that covers competition, just to give you a taste. If you have the opportunity and the language skills, another possibility would be to do a *stage* with the European Commission".

Katie looks back over her path to competition law and mentions that she deliberated for a long time before taking the plunge into a legal career: "I'd like to have been saved the angst, and known that this many years on I'd still be practising law and enjoying it."

# Construction

Contentious construction work involves dispute resolution and encouraging the early settlement of disputes through mediation, other forms of alternative dispute resolution, adjudication, or litigation or arbitration. Non-contentious work involves drafting and negotiating contracts, and advising on projects, insurance, health and safety, environmental matters and insolvency. Clients range from industry associations, insurers, contractors, architects, engineers, public authorities, and governmental bodies to major companies and partnerships.

Sally Davies is a partner at City firm Mayer Brown International LLP. Having studied law at University College London, she began her career at what was then Rowe & Maw and qualified in 1994. She says: "I always had an interest in construction because my father was an engineer. I knew about it, but I never knew that there was a specialist area called construction law."

Due to the document intensive, complicated, multi-party nature of construction cases, Sally could not get heavily involved in major pieces of litigation as a trainee, but she did have some really interesting cases involving well-known contractors. She remembers: "I worked on the shopping centre in Broadmead in Bristol and that was an enormous dispute involving several parties. The person I sat with, who's still the head of department, was involved in coordinating the defendants. I went along to case management conferences at court and found it incredibly interesting." Now, with 13 years post-qualification experience, Sally enjoys coordinating the cases herself and leading teams of junior solicitors, although notes that she's "done a lot of learning along the way".

Sally says that her caseload normally consists of eight or nine large and contentious cases, all in various stages of progress. She elaborates: "This afternoon I've got a meeting on a case which is in the pre-action protocol stage, so that's finding out what the claim is actually about, considering the letter of claim from the other side, formulating a response with the client, researching and finding a suitable expert witness, establishing who the key factual witnesses are, and finding out about the background and the facts." Going to the Technology and Construction Court, a division of the High Court, is a real bonus for Sally: "I might be in court on a case management conference, talking about a timetable for the trial, the number of witnesses and experts, and how the trial's going to be managed."

Currently she's involved in disputes relating to the construction of Wembley Stadium. The huge project involves many subcontractors and Sally is investigating the reasons for its various delays.

As a partner in a busy construction department, Sally deals with a lot of "outward-looking work", such as pitching to clients and client development. Dealing with clients is definitely one of her favourite things about the job: "I enjoy the variety of people that I meet. One of the benefits of doing construction work is that you get to work with a massive range of people from commercial directors of construction companies to insurers and barristers – I've been lucky enough to work with some eminent QCs – and technical experts such as structural engineers, roofing specialists and foundation designers." It's the face-to-face contact that Sally relishes. "The construction industry is very hands-on," she says.

If Sally spends a lot of time advising and assisting clients, her more junior assistants do what she calls "the hands-on work". Sally explains: "A mediation submission will be done by one of my assistants and then I'll go through it with them, so I have a lot of supervisory work." But the real buzz is still the litigious side of her job: "The highlight of my career to date was when I got a case struck out of the High Court – it was a £4 million valuation negligence case. We got it dismissed because of a procedural irregularity: the claimant hadn't filed a complete list of documents by the deadline. That was just absolutely fantastic. The low point was when it went to the Court of Appeal and was reinstated!"

Construction solicitors work on intensive cases with hefty files. Sally's advice is to "roll your sleeves up and don't be put off by the vast quantity of documents". She says that "to be a top solicitor in construction you need to be unflappable and take everything in your stride. You need a thick skin. You deal with a lot of people who call a spade a spade. You've got to be down to earth and gritty". As with all areas of law, something else you'll need is attention to detail. Sally explains why, in construction, this skill is especially important: "Construction is an area of law which is always changing. All the main cases that change the law – in tort particularly – tend to be construction cases. You need to have a good understanding of the legal issues and the law, and be quite practical and, most importantly, commercial."

For those thinking about construction as a potential practice area, Sally recommends finding out as much as possible about what the work involves, especially by doing a work placement in a construction department. Be prepared to do some unpaid work experience, she says, even just shadowing someone for a week. "And don't be snobby about location," she warns. "If you can't get a training contract in London, go to the regions, but pick a good firm that will give you really good experience and you can always move into London afterwards."

Sally knows that lots of students worry about specialising too early but she says you don't need to do this: "I knew I was interested in litigation and I wanted to go to court, but I didn't even know there was a discipline in construction at that stage."

In this area you have to work very hard. Sally weighs things up: "You are paid a lot of money but it requires a huge commitment. I don't think you appreciate that until you're in the thick of it. When you're coming up to trial you'll be under great pressure working 12 to 18-hour days but only for three or four days. Then, when the case is finished or settled, everyone is in the pub and normal life resumes."

# Corporate tax

**Virtually all commercial transactions have tax implications. Accordingly, corporate tax is one of the most important practice areas for any major law firm. Working in corporate tax involves giving advice on the most tax-efficient means of acquiring, divesting or restructuring assets, negotiating and documenting the transaction, and ensuring the smooth running of the resulting deal. On the contentious side, corporate tax lawyers advise on all aspects of tax litigation and investigations, negotiate with tax authorities, and conduct litigation in the civil and criminal courts.**

David Gubbay is a partner at international firm Dechert. He says: "I originally did a history degree at Rhodes University in South Africa. My father had been a lawyer so I knew something about it and was keen to study it." David came to England to do a law degree at the University of Oxford and has stayed ever since. Now he specialises in corporate tax and enjoys "helping clients on deals and seeing things come together as you planned them".

David knows that tax is a practice area that it can be hard to get a hold on. He says: "It's quite difficult as a law student to have a real idea about which areas of law you want to practise. At that stage I certainly didn't think I'd be working in tax and didn't even study it. Not many law degrees include that as an option." And anyway, as David notes wisely, "the actual practice of law is really quite different from studying it".

David's training contract was at a big City firm and he favoured his tax seat: "I liked the fact that you were dealing with many of the other practice areas within the firm, so you'd be working on corporate transactions, property transactions and fund transactions. Actually you needed to apply quite a bit of general law knowledge as well as having the specific tax knowledge. I liked the idea of being a bit of a specialist but still keeping in touch with all the other things that were going on in the firm."

David stresses that tax lawyers need to understand other practice areas in their firm. He explains: "One obviously needs a good knowledge of tax law but it's also important to have a decent understanding of the other areas that you'll be interacting with. Typically, as a tax lawyer, you are primarily a service function to the other groups in your firm. So you need to understand how the deals work to make sure your advice fits into the deal structure and its commercial drivers."

David has several large transactions on at any one time. He describes a memorable day: "A couple of weeks ago I was working on an interesting deal that had been in the press a lot, acting for the sellers of internet radio company Last FM to CBS, the big US broadcaster. On that particular day we had a meeting with our clients to go through certain elements of the transaction. The tax issues on that were quite important because we had a number of sellers with different tax requirements. There was then drafting to do on the sale contract and also a negotiation to be had with the lawyers acting for the buyer. A colleague from our financial services group and I then had a lunch meeting with a potential client who wanted to set up a hedge fund, so we met with two people from that company. Then in the afternoon I had a meeting with people from a Canadian real estate company who were looking to sell their UK property portfolio, so I went with a colleague from our real estate group and we met to go through things relating to the sale of the properties. And then late afternoon, into the evening, it was back on to the Last FM deal. We had a number of phone calls with our clients and the other side to try and agree on the deal and get it towards closing. That was a busy day!"

Being a corporate tax lawyer is very demanding, not least because of the volume of work. Having the ability to get to know clients and understand their business needs can also take a lot of effort. David explains that "being a tax lawyer, you're asked to structure transactions in particular ways that enable the client to achieve their goals in a tax-efficient manner". All the hard graft does pay off though. He says: "I enjoy it when you get involved with a client's transactions early on and are able to add value to what they're doing. I find that really satisfying."

But still, tax is a complicated area of law. "You need to be an analytical lawyer who quite likes researching and thinking about difficult areas of law," notes David. "You also need to have the ability to absorb very detailed factual situations and to break them down to their essence. That's because if you're trying to understand how something is going to be taxed, you need to get to grips with that and have the ability to work through complex factors."

David has some concrete advice for budding tax lawyers: "You don't need a detailed knowledge of accounting, but it helps to be able to look at a set of accounts and understand what the main numbers mean. That's a useful skill to have." And with firms increasingly wanting to see more than good grades, David advises that at interview it helps to "show you have a sense of humour and a point of view on things. Firms are looking for rounded people. It's important to show your personality".

# Crime

Criminal law solicitors advise and appear in court on behalf of accused persons, dealing with the complete range of offences from minor motoring misdemeanours to more serious crimes, including murder. They deal with the full spectrum of the criminal justice system, from the initial police station interview to the final contested hearing before the court.

Alison Muir is a partner at regional firm Metcalfe Copeman & Pettefar. She read geography at the University of London, and then undertook the CPE and Law Society Finals at The College of Law in Guildford.

Alison discusses her training contract experience at Metcalfe Copeman & Pettefar: "I was involved mainly in conveyancing and property work, and to a lesser degree I helped out in the commercial and family departments. As the office trainee, I also assisted all the fee earners when required. I now specialise solely in criminal law, which I never studied as a trainee. I think it's not until you start your training contract that you see the reality of being a lawyer. However good your lecturers are, they can't bring it life to the same extent. I never imagined that I'd end up as an advocate, but that's just where I found my strengths to be."

Alison has an impressive number of strings to her bow – head of the criminal department, managing partner of the firm's King's Lynn office and vice-chair of the Regional Duty Solicitor Committee. She talks us through a typical day: "As my career has progressed, I have found that I am increasingly undertaking more administration and less legal work. I get to the office between 7:15am and 7:30am. I open the post and check it through before allocating it to each individual fee earner, check my emails, prepare my files for the day's court and have diary meetings with members of my department. I then attend court and the police station, or appointments as the case may be, hopefully returning to the office in time to say goodbye to everybody else. I then prepare cases for the next day, am often on call for the police station through the night, deal with emails, and dictate the day's work and post. Occasionally, I might even get some sleep!"

As for recent work, Alison gives us a flavour of the issues she deals with: "I've just come back from Huntingdon in relation to a case of possession with intent to supply cocaine and ecstasy. I have several rape cases on and I have a murder response this afternoon. Those are the main offences I deal with: drugs, rape and assault. I'm in court this afternoon for a client who was chasing people down the road with a machete – he's one of my regulars! I also do some white collar fraud work, and Environment Agency and Department for Work and Pensions prosecutions as well. There's a fair mix of things; if it comes through the door and it's a magistrates' court matter, we deal with it."

Regional lawyering suits Alison well for a number of reasons: "You may sacrifice some of the financial rewards of a career in the City, but there is a quality of life that you can't beat. Also, because you're local you know the police officers, the prosecutors and most of the clients! Often, everybody is heading in the same direction, which is much more pleasant than I imagine it is in a big city. You just wouldn't get the same personal approach. And you do get to have a bit of a life (and doing crime, it really is only a bit of a life!)."

Alison discusses the high points of her career so far: "I was delighted to have been promoted to partnership aged 29 and, at the age of 36, was the first female equity partner in the firm's history. I have recruited a number of quality criminal lawyers to my department and am proud to run one of the biggest criminal law departments in the region. I would not have been able to do that without the support of my colleagues."

Ups and downs are all part of the job, explains Alison: "Probably the most enjoyable part of my career is that I have been able to develop my skills to the extent that I feel confident in my job, that I can deal with a high volume of cases with a great deal of aplomb and that I have gained the respect of a large number of professionals with whom I have regular contact. The least enjoyable part of my career has to be the late nights, holidays and weekends spent at the police station. I also feel that solicitors get very bad publicity and everyone assumes that we are all fat cat lawyers, when the vast majority of my peers are hardworking professionals who put their clients first and do not receive the recognition or the salary that they deserve."

The reality of the legal aid landscape is that you have to be "devoted to your work, rather than motivated by money. So many people are resigning or firms are giving up on crime altogether. However, those that remain are standing firm – it's not just about your career, it's about the fact that the most vulnerable people in society will be further disadvantaged by there being no free access to legal representation". As a result, Alison recommends taking a long hard look at whether a career in criminal law is the thing for you. She tells it like it is: "We are poorly paid for long hours and the job can be antisocial in terms of being away from home a lot. Unless you are prepared to tolerate criticism in the press, then it is not an area of law that I would encourage any young lawyer to enter. Saying that, I have the opportunity of mixing with some very personable people, I have a great deal of job satisfaction and my life is never dull."

Alison receives many applications for training contracts and she assures us that she reads them all. Her top tips include the following: "What is sadly apparent from a lot is that they have not taken the time to spell my name or the firm's name correctly and those applications which do not have the basic information accurate are not considered. Also, check the firm's website. Our website has a lot of helpful information for trainees about the recruitment process and it is good to know that an applicant has taken the trouble to read information about the firm beforehand. For those applicants who are selected for interview, one or two have taken the trouble to contact our current trainees to find out a little bit more about the training contract and working for the firm, which goes in their favour. Also, do not be deterred by lack of interviews, be persistent. Always ask for feedback on your performance at interview as it will be invaluable in future applications."

Alison finishes with some advice on how to be a successful criminal lawyer: "You need to be extremely hard working and conscientious, not afraid to stand up for your client's rights and be able to withstand pressure. You need to be fast thinking, particularly on your feet in court. However, you must also be compassionate and learn to be able to deal with every stratum of society, from your clients who may not be able to read and write, to some of the finest barristers in the country. You must always be fair and open in order to gain respect from your peers."

# Employment

A popular misconception is that this area of law is just about employment contracts. In fact, employment lawyers can be expected to handle all areas of employment law, including discrimination, flexible working, workplace monitoring and restructuring, and employee representation. They work on everything from drafting policies to dealing with inappropriate use of the Internet in the workplace.

At trainee level, lawyers assist with the employment aspects of corporate transactions and with preparations for tribunal claims, as well as attending hearings and meetings with clients and helping to draft employment documents.

Eleanor Winslet is a newly qualified lawyer at DLA Piper UK LLP, one of the world's largest law firms. She studied English at the University of Southampton, taking the view that the conversion course offered "a great opportunity to take English at university level but still convert to law afterwards". Going to the Bar was an option, but Eleanor decided that she preferred the life of a solicitor, "seeing matters through from beginning to end, having close contact with clients and working in a large organisation".

Eleanor did her training contract at DLA Piper: "It was a great training contract; really broad and varied. I sat in employment, insolvency and restructuring, corporate, litigation and also had a secondment to ITV. I enjoyed the study of employment law at law school and enjoyed working in the department from the outset. It's very legislative, topical, wide ranging and can be high profile. I also think it's good if you're interested in the academic side of things and want to work in a fast moving area."

Eleanor qualified into the employment department in September 2006. She describes what her day might involve: "You never know what each day will throw up – it's very varied. You can be dealing with matters including tribunal, county court or High Court claims, while at the same time, you may be advising on corporate deals and handling client queries that come in on a daily basis. Non-contentious issues might include contract and policy reviews, sometimes involving companies with offices in different jurisdictions, which requires us to liaise with our international offices. Small issues can have the potential to become much bigger, so you may need to hold your client's hand through a developing process." Right now, Eleanor is involved in a variety of ongoing matters: "I've been working on a breach of contract claim in relation to a redundancy policy, a few tribunal matters involving sex, race, disability and age discrimination, and two large-scale High Court injunction cases involving restrictive covenants."

Compared to her time as a trainee, Eleanor feels that she exerts greater control over the progress of the matters she is working on, "although there's still a lot of support. But more often now, I'm the one that has to move things forward. There's also a lot more continuity – when you're a trainee, you find yourself pulled in a lot of different directions, doing a discrete task on one matter and then moving on to the next".

Eleanor's view is that employment is a dynamic, challenging and ever-changing field of law: "You might hear something announced on the news one evening that has an impact on what you're doing the next day. I also enjoy the problem-solving component; you have to take a different approach to each matter that falls on your desk." The downside to any legal career, says Eleanor, "is that it can be quite stressful. You can be just about out the door and then get called up about something that needs an answer there and then. But a more positive way to look at it is that it's good not to have too predictable a job!"

Eleanor discusses some of the skills that are key to her job: "The issues that we deal with can become highly emotional, especially for the HR manager and the individual directly involved, so client handling skills, as for most areas of law, are very important. You also really have to multitask – you're never working exclusively on a single big deal. Instead, it's a question of handling lots of smaller matters all at once. You have to be able to manage client and colleague expectations, so organisation is important. Furthermore, you need to think creatively around problems and keep in touch with what's going on legally – a case could come up that completely changes something you're working on."

You also need to have a genuine interest in both the field and the firm, she says: "When I was applying, I was most successful with those firms that I genuinely wanted to work for and whose work I was interested in. If you can keep an eye on, and be able to talk about, recent employment cases or legal developments, then that's all the better." Eleanor also advises getting as much experience in as many areas as possible and taking an informed view when applying for training contracts: "Try and see what goes on in different firms and different departments."

And if you want to win the training contract prize, it helps to show that you really want to be a solicitor! Eleanor explains: "Lawyers tend to be quite driven, so those people that will stand out are those that can show commitment and determination, can keep up-to-date with changes to the law, and who are prepared to make a number of applications. It is such a competitive environment that it helps to be focused."

Finally, Eleanor explodes the myth that on entering the office as a trainee you are expected to be an expert in the field immediately. She advises: "When you enter the workplace, you think everyone else knows everything and you know nothing. That's not necessarily the case and you will get a lot of support and shouldn't be worried about asking questions. You never stop learning and it's always good to keep bouncing ideas off other colleagues."

# Environment

Environment law is a growth area, especially given the increasing global awareness of issues such as climate change and the need for alternative sources of energy. It seeks to protect both humans and the physical environment against pollution and the impact of human activity on the natural world.

Given this broad aim, environment lawyers will find themselves involved in a wide range of matters, as diverse as health and safety, risk management, contaminated land, waste, renewable energy, environmental finance, commercial and property transactions, nuclear law and litigation. Clients may include individuals, community groups, organisations, local authorities and the government.

Ian Salter is a partner in one of the largest environment departments in the country, at national firm Burges Salmon. He remembers encountering a fork in the road after graduating from the University of Bristol in 1989, when environmental law was not really on the agenda of most major law firms. All his friends went to work in the City but, at the suggestion of a professor, Ian decided to stay in Bristol and work for Burges Salmon. Ian says: "I'd like to say I planned my career from A to Z perfectly, but environment law was just a concept when I was at university. While it has arguably been around for over 300 years, it's generally been called different things – usually a nuisance. The main development in environmental legislation came with the Environmental Protection Act in 1990 which post-dated my degree." Now, of course, "the environment isn't out of the news – it's extremely busy".

It was the end of the Eighties boom and Ian remembers how "firms in the City were just getting into recruitment in a big way and offering lucrative packages. I thought long and hard about what I wanted, which was not to make sacrifices on the quality of work I did. But I wanted to stay in Bristol. My university tutor told me Burges Salmon was the obvious choice".

So, Ian stayed in Bristol and qualified in planning. He notes: "I was lucky to hit a firm that survived the early Nineties recession reasonably unaffected. I stayed in planning for the next five years. We did any environmental work that came in, having set up an environmental law unit around the time I qualified. No one specialised full time in it then. A lot of the London firms went for it as the next big thing but it didn't really happen as a practice area to start with. There wasn't the work they were anticipating and as a result the London firms may have become a little disenchanted with it." Indeed, by 1995 many of them reduced their investment in the area. It was about that time that Burges Salmon set up an environment department with full-time specialists and since then the team has grown to 14 lawyers, separate from the successful planning team at the firm.

Ian's group forms a dedicated environment department recognised nationwide for advising major clients, both public and private sector. "What's happened is that from humble beginnings we now tend to specialise quite carefully," says Ian. Specialisation was key in developing the department so that individuals could get to grips with the details of certain areas. With Ian's central specialisation being nuclear, his colleagues work on areas from renewable energy to emissions trading.

Ian explains how it works: "My own caseload is dominated by three sectors: nuclear, waste and transport. The biggest of those for me is nuclear. There are three things happening: first is the potential for new nuclear power stations, second is cleaning up our old nuclear industry – a £70 billion industry – and third is nuclear waste. It's an environmental job because it's about cleaning up something which exists at the moment. It's a big moral and ethical issue about how you clean up our legacy for future generations, where do you put the waste, who pays for it and what are the impacts."

With all that in mind, it's the variety of his work that Ian enjoys the most: "The skills you employ go across the whole range. You can do commercial drafting, project work, a regulatory issue that might involve a criminal prosecution, a corporate finance deal, civil litigation and tax advice (for instance there is a tax relief on cleaning contaminated land), then you might be doing advocacy at a public inquiry. You need to develop this incredibly diverse range of skills emanating from one sector."

Added to that is the unprecedented nature of his work. Ian says: "If you pick up a textbook on environmental law, most of the subjects on which we advise won't be in there. You can't buy a textbook on carbon law or areas like waste electronics. It's right at the cutting edge."

Such a dynamic practice area requires specific skills. The central one is flexibility, says Ian: "You can have a number of things on the go involving different legal skills and areas. You have to be able to manage that, which can be quite difficult. You have to be able, even with all the electronic tools we've got, to keep on top of such a rapidly evolving subject."

Even though the environment is on everyone's lips, Ian recommends that moral implications have to be separated from professionalism. "While I personally do have environmental views," he says "I think that when you're acting for clients, you've got to act in their best interests. Sometimes we're defending clients charged with environment crimes, but usually there's a positive role to

play there. If they're found guilty, you'll be helping them learn the lessons. It goes without saying that none of them usually want a repeat experience."

For those just about to start out on a legal career, Ian advises keeping your options open for as long as possible. He says: "Until you get into the firm and do your work it's too early to say, so don't make any judgements about what you want to do until you've tried it to see if you enjoy it. Keep an open mind about where you want to be on qualification. Try your best in every seat."

And when it comes to environmental law, there are now three roads. "If you want to do standalone, regulatory environmental work," says Ian, "then a firm like Burges Salmon would, in my view, be better than a City M&A firm where the vast amount of environmental work will be on corporate transaction support. The third option of course is if you want to work for a green NGO, then you want to be working for a different firm again."

As for the future Ian is optimistic for the legal profession's role in the environment sector. The times are a-changing and, as Ian says: "I think there are a lot of exciting developments soon to happen."

# Family

Family lawyers deal with all legal matters relating to marriage, separation, divorce, cohabitation and all issues relating to children (eg, maintenance and access arrangements, and adoption both in England and internationally). Family law also encompasses financial negotiations, inheritance issues and prenuptial contracts. Some family law cases involve substantial assets and complex financial arrangements, or high-profile cases with well-known personalities.

Family law developments are very much driven by changes in society, and although the role of a family law solicitor calls for an astute legal mind, you also need 'softer' skills such as tact and sympathy.

Rachel Cantwell is a second-year trainee at Penleys LLP, a private client firm in Gloucestershire. Rachel studied law at Leeds Metropolitan University, following some work experience while at school and consultation with family friends.

Rachel took a couple of years out after university to go travelling and get some hands-on experience in the legal world, first in the admin department of an Australian law firm and then as a paralegal back in Bristol at national firm Lyons Davidson. She explains: "I worked in the insurance litigation department, small claims unit, on a recovery project. This gave me the opportunity to effectively manage a high volume of my own files – under supervision, of course! Conduct of claims covered all aspects of the small claims procedure, from initial investigations and issuing a claim, through to preparation of the trial bundle and instructing counsel. It was necessary to liaise and communicate with all parties to the claim, to discuss and negotiate, in order to reach a realistic settlement in the interest of my clients. Overall, working at Lyons Davidson was good general litigation experience, which

was especially helpful when I did the LPC." And even better, three months has been taken off Rachel's training contract because of her time as a paralegal, as 'time to count'.

Rachel studied the LPC at the University of the West of England, Bristol, which she says "was well organised, well structured and well taught – I really enjoyed it. It was a hard and intense nine months, but the tutors were very helpful if you had any difficulties. My paralegal experience also helped, particularly with the civil litigation and the skills modules".

With her LPC and paralegal experiences behind her, Rachel has now embarked on the next stage of her journey – a training contract with Penleys, a small firm based in Dursley. She is currently in the litigation department and undertakes family work as part of that seat. She explains the type of family work that she's been exposed to thus far and what she can expect a bit further down the line: "I have been doing work in relation to divorce and ancillary relief proceedings, which includes drafting divorce petitions and statement of arrangements for children, as well as preparing financial statements, questionnaires and briefs to counsel. I do a lot of liaising with clients and also observe meetings between my supervisor and clients, and attend conferences and court with clients and counsel. In due course, I will be getting more involved with disputes relating to children – for example, Section 8 orders concerning contact or residence, and some domestic violence cases."

Rachel talks about the broad nature of her traineeship: "My present seat is in the litigation department, so in addition to family matters, I am involved in personal injury and general civil litigation cases. I also help out other departments occasionally by carrying out research or if something is urgent. To *try* and organise my workload, I write a 'to do' list every day, which I find helps me to focus. Today, for example, I am working on a reply to a questionnaire and a narrative statement for ancillary relief proceedings, which will probably take most of the day. Other days, I might observe a meeting with a client, draft a divorce petition and assist with a personal injury or civil litigation case. Every day is different!"

Client contact and care is paramount in family law, explains Rachel, and one of the most rewarding parts of the job. She says: "With family law you have a lot of client contact throughout the case, whether face-to-face or on the telephone, which is great. I also enjoy going to court and observing counsel. It's nice when matters are settled with an outcome that the client is pleased with – you can tell that the weight has been lifted off their mind." Obviously, part and parcel of the job is the more mundane task of form filling; for example legal aid forms or the Form E, Financial Statement – "this is 26-pages long and seems to be never-ending at times!".

There are particular attributes that make a good family lawyer. Rachel elaborates: "You need to have good listening and people skills. It's important that you address your clients' concerns with diplomacy and professionalism, as you are often dealing with people at an emotional and vulnerable stage in their lives. You also need to be honest with clients and take a pragmatic approach. These are very sensitive issues, so you have to be approachable. More generally, you have to be organised, diligent and able to work efficiently within limited timescales. For example, if you have an emergency injunction in relation to domestic violence, you need to drop everything and do it."

Work experience is essential for getting ahead and impressing prospective employers. Rachel's background is testament to this, as she explains: "For any type of law, it is highly beneficial to have had some work experience (or even paid employment) in a legal environment – if you can get paralegal work, that's even better. Firms have such high expectations of their potential trainees and the competitive nature of the sector means that you need to stand out. It's also essential for working out whether it's something you really want to do – there's an awful lot of time and money invested in training, so make sure it's really what you want to do! I took three years out, travelling and working, to make sure that the hard work and six years of training and expense was the right decision."

Looking ahead, Rachel is keen to keep developing: "Once you start working, it's a lot more enjoyable and you learn so much, actually practising the law, rather than studying it. I'm sure that when I qualify it will be another steep learning curve, but one of the best parts of this profession is that you're forever learning anyway – it would be hard to get bored!"

# Human rights

In recent years human rights law has become an increasingly popular choice for both students and practitioners. University law faculties are increasingly offering human rights modules as part of their law degrees and more firms boast specialisms in the field. The introduction of the Human Rights Act 1998 has incorporated human rights law, public law and EU law into English law, and made the European Convention on Human Rights directly enforceable in the national courts.

Susie Labinjoh is a partner at Hodge Jones & Allen, one of the leading predominantly publicly funded law practices in the country. She studied philosophy at the University of Hull and, while her mind was on the big questions, she didn't think about a career, least of all in law. "It didn't even cross my mind!" she says. It wasn't until she left university and started working in a law firm that she found the law interesting. Susie continued to work, studying the GDL in the evenings, before moving to The College of Law in Guildford for her LPC. She won a training contract at Hodge Jones & Allen and has stayed there since qualifying in 1999.

Susie's seats ranged from crime to employment to personal injury and actions against the police. In this final seat she was involved in specific human rights work: "I did compensation claims for miscarriages of justice, judicial reviews, death in custody inquests and civil actions against the police. One of my first cases was a false imprisonment claim. My client had been arrested and detained in the police station for three days and it turned out the police had the wrong person. My client unfortunately had the same surname as the real suspect." Another memorable case involved an Article 2 inquest after the police shot someone carrying an air rifle.

Susie notes that the Hodge Jones & Allen training contract was very hands-on. She says: "You get to do a lot more than you would in other firms. I worked with my supervisor and would be given specific tasks to do, such as drafting pleadings, taking instructions from clients and taking statements on my supervisor's files. However, in most of the seats, I also had a small caseload of my own to work on."

As a partner, Susie works on more complex cases, as well as supervising her own trainee and three other solicitors. Her total caseload tops 100: "I have inquest cases involving deaths in police or prison custody. I have Human Rights Act cases where people have been wrongly detained in immigration custody with the threat of being deported to war zones. Then there are false imprisonment, assault, and malicious prosecution and misfeasance cases, generally against the police."

Susie also works on "more complex claims for compensation arising from miscarriages of justice. Claims against the police or Customs and Excise can also arise out of these cases". She spends most days "interviewing clients and witnesses, taking statements, writing letters to the other side, preparing documents for court and supervising other solicitors".

Although it's rare that Susie goes to court, this year she did end up in the House of Lords. She says: "The case arose from a miscarriage of justice compensation claim. We judicially reviewed the clients' awards of compensation because there had been a deduction for their so-called 'saved living expenses' while they were incarcerated. I considered that it was palpably unfair that someone could be sent to prison for 18 years for a crime they didn't commit and then have their award of compensation reduced by the money they were supposed to have saved by being in prison. So we challenged the decision by way of judicial review in the High Court, winning some of the issues and losing others. We appealed to the Court of Appeal and again, won some, lost some. Finally we appealed to the House of Lords."

Although Susie's team lost the appeal, the experience was the highlight of her career thus far. She comments: "It was an amazing experience to listen to five judges considering and discussing a case you have brought. I remember being a student, reading countless House of Lords decisions. I never ever imagined that one day one of my cases would be in the Lords."

As human rights is a practice area that frequently raises moral issues, Susie says that you must have "a strong sense of fairness and be able to appreciate when something isn't right. For me, it's always been about acting for people, helping them improve their lives or right wrongs done to them – not being a faceless corporate bod who's perusing shipping contracts".

Another interesting side to the area is the media interest. Susie shrugs it off but stresses the importance of getting it right. She says: "It's very important to explain your cases in an interesting and accessible way as there can be a lot of negativity towards human rights and civil liberties, especially in the tabloid press. People perhaps have the impression that it's gone too far but that's generally because cases aren't reported correctly."

Because human rights cases often make the news, Susie says it's essential to have an awareness of current affairs. Also, you need to be "tenacious, able to deal with people who are in vulnerable situations, and generally patient and empathetic". Sometimes it won't be obvious what the problem is. "A client's not going to turn up at the office and say, 'I think I have a Human Rights Act claim'," says Susie, so you need a complete legal knowledge.

If Susie regrets anything, it's not having much experience when she started her career. She advises students to volunteer at the Citizens Advice Bureau or law centres: "It's a very good thing to do because it is rewarding in itself, gives you invaluable experience and will make your application form and CV stand out. Don't be afraid to write to firms who do those areas of work and ask if it would be possible to do some work experience."

If legal knowledge and work experience are technical prerequisites for working in human rights, Susie emphasises the magic ingredient you'll need. "I wanted to make a difference to people's lives," she says. "You have to be very passionate about it – it would be too difficult if you weren't."

# Insurance

Insurance (and reinsurance) is an integral part of commercial activity throughout the world. The insurance practices of top-end firms offer advice on a range of areas, including disputes as to insurance coverage, investment management, insurance documentation (covering the drafting of policy documents and agreements), mergers and acquisitions of insurance companies, and transferring books of business between insurance companies.

Regulatory law concerns matters such as the establishment and regulation of insurance/reinsurance companies throughout the world. In addition, most firms offer reinsurance (insurance of insurers) and general advisory services concerning compliance with relevant codes of practice. Clients include insurers, reinsurers and UK insurance institutions, as well as major insured companies and their captive insurers.

Sam Tacey is a second-year trainee at Kendall Freeman, a City firm practising litigation and non-contentious insurance industry work, as well as general litigation, insolvency and public international law. Sam studied law at the University of Bristol and completed his LPC at BPP in London. Since then he's been busy working his way through his training contract at Kendall Freeman and will be qualifying into the insurance litigation group in September 2007.

Sam has had experience in three insurance related seats: insurance litigation, insurance corporate and insurance insolvency. He says: "I started in insurance litigation. but really I was doing reinsurance arbitration, working on big disputes that had been going on for a few years. As a trainee, they were pretty difficult to get your head around at first, but I found the work both challenging and rewarding. I did things like writing formal arbitration documents such as pleadings, and lots of general research. I also did the first draft of a commutation agreement which was the basis of a settlement."

Sam's work still involves a lot of research, which means that the documents he's drafting are very labour intensive. "Yesterday," he explains, "I drafted some affidavits and did some research on that to make sure they were drafted according to Canadian court rules. In the same matter I drafted a request for assistance from a Canadian court to the English court, which was really great work for a trainee."

It all sounds like a lot of deskwork, but Sam says he does get to spend time with clients too: "I think that, as a trainee, you love being able to build up a working relationship with clients, calling them on the phone and so on. It's great to have any kind of client contact."

Sam found the interpersonal element of the job most important when he did a seat in corporate insurance. He says: "You have to really get to know your clients and their business, so you're more like a business adviser. One highlight was working on the third attempt to get a solvent scheme of arrangement approved by the members of a mutual insurer. I'd seen it from start to finish and I got to go to client meetings on my own which, for a first-year trainee, was a pretty good experience."

Sam was also involved in the sale of an insurance company. "I had responsibility for drafting the disclosure letter and getting the disclosure bundles together." In corporate insurance, Sam's hours were rather unstable. "It was often hard to predict whether I'd be leaving the office at 6:30pm or 12:30am," he remembers. "We have a lot of overseas clients, so things tend to happen later on in the day. If the client wants something done, you've got to do it."

It's not really the hours that bother Sam. If there's something that he has a hard time with, it's the Financial Services Authority handbook, which details all the regulations those who work in financial services have to obey. "It's really hard to navigate," he notes of the handbook. Sam says that a lot of regulatory work can be quite dry, but he does acknowledge how important it is for a trainee to have a good grasp of this aspect of insurance, because it really helps in practice. "It's important to have an eye for detail when you are interpreting the rules and a practical approach is essential for applying the rules to your client's business." Sam remembers: "Once I had a client's business proposal and I had to evaluate it against the regulations to see whether or not they could do it without getting authorised. That was quite fun because it brought it to life."

Law firms always want prospective trainees to have plenty of work experience and bags of commercial awareness. Sam says that in insurance, this is even more important. He notes: "Some people come into this area because they already have industry experience. If you want to work for an insurance law firm, experience at an insurance company is a real plus, while an understanding of the market is a big advantage it is something that all trainees are expected to develop." Sam points out that as a trainee, even with some work experience, you still haven't had much exposure to the workplace. This means that "you spend a good deal of time working to understand the complexities of the insurance industry, particularly Lloyd's, and how everything fits together".

For those thinking about what kind of practice area they will suit, Sam advises simply getting as much experience as possible. "You probably have a feeling about the kind of work you want, and then it's just about getting as much experience in the area as possible."

Sam knows that a lot of people see insurance as a little dull but, as he says, "it's actually a lot more interesting than you think! You only need to think about all the things that need insuring to understand the breadth of your work". He adds: "Something I really enjoyed working on was a catastrophe bond issue, which involved shifting the risk of catastrophes such as hurricanes or earthquakes from insurers to the capital markets by a bond issue. That was fun, going through all the trigger events and categories of storms and how they're measured. The insurers and reinsurers know they'll go bust if there are lots of natural disasters and they haven't got adequate assets through reserves, reinsurance or other types of protection. Insurance doesn't sound very sexy, but it can be interesting!"

# Intellectual property

**IP work can be divided into two main areas: hard and soft intellectual property. 'Hard' intellectual property relates to patents, while 'soft' intellectual property covers trademarks, copyright, design rights and passing-off. IP lawyers will advise on issues that range from commercial exploitation to infringement disputes, and agreements that deal either exclusively with IP rights or with IP rights in the wider context of larger commercial transactions. Many lawyers will specialise in either contentious or non-contentious IP work.**

Dominic Hornblow is an associate in the London office of international firm Jones Day. He did his training contract at Gouldens and qualified in real estate. After the firm merged with Jones Day in 2003, Dominic transferred to the IP department.

During his studies, intellectual property was always something Dominic was interested in but didn't have an opportunity to study academically. He says: "In terms of formal training, I didn't do any until I did the IP diploma in Bristol. Quite a lot of IP departments put people onto one of the postgraduate diploma in IP courses – especially if someone has not studied it previously. The Bristol course lasts one year with a two-week residential element. Every six weeks you have an all-day class. You have coursework every six weeks, an exam in May or June and, hopefully, at the end you have a diploma in IP practice."

Dominic reflects that the diploma was a great way for him to make a detailed study of the different areas of IP law so that he had a good grounding. "It starts with a two-week crash course and ensures that you cover all areas of intellectual property," he remembers. "For example, I did a lot of work on registered designs. They're not something that I tend to come across very often in what

I do now but when I do, it's useful to have that knowledge as a back up. Some firms that specialise in intellectual property send their trainees to do the course in the final year of their training contract. Others send them after they qualify."

Now, Dominic works mostly on non-contentious IP matters: "I tend to negotiate commercial contracts or coordinate due diligence on companies. At the moment I've got four major due diligence exercises on and another half a dozen or so commercial contracts." His caseload varies quite a lot, and often fluctuates in proportion to the corporate department's level of work. He says: "If the corporate department is dealing with 30 M&A deals, each person there is probably dealing with one or two, but our IP department is relatively small so we'll each be working on five or six cases."

Dominic acknowledges that it's very important to be able to plan your time. "The first thing I do in the day is deal with all the smaller things," he says. "I've learnt that you try and take the small things first. So if an email has come in with a client's query and it's just a case of looking something up, I'll deal with that first. Also, the client perceives that they are getting a good level of service because they've received a response straightaway. Then I'll get into all the more in-depth things. It could be that I've got an agreement to draft. Sometimes there's a precedent that you can work from, but often it's not particularly similar to anything that you, or the firm, have worked on before so you need to sit down and draft things almost from first principles. You need to think about the transaction in detail and work out what the implications are, and what happens if something goes wrong that the parties themselves may not have considered."

As a Formula One fan, Dominic enjoyed dealing with the acquisition of a team. He says: "It's probably the most high-profile thing I've worked on. Formula One is a global business so they have a large portfolio of trademarks. Although there's a lot of research and development, because the cars are different every year, you'd normally think they'd protect those with patents. But they don't tend to do that in Formula One because the pace of development is so quick. If something changes, they don't worry about it because next year they'll have to come up with something else. The main way they do it is to keep it confidential."

Dominic's also managed to bag work from leading computer game publisher Eidos. "The main thing about computer games is that they're protected by copyright," Dominic explains, "which is just a right to stop someone copying something you created. In the computer industry, it's about digital rights management, which is what they put on the game to try and stop you making copies. Someone like Eidos, with recognisable brands like Lara Croft, has a big task to make sure that they're not being ripped off in the Far East or somewhere."

From fast cars to tomb raiders, it sounds like Dominic's client base is rather varied. "I never get bored! Intellectual property comes up in a lot of different areas. I've been doing quite a lot for clothing companies and pharmaceutical companies at the moment. Quite often you're dealing with new sciences and different technologies. I've even started reading *New Scientist*. The actual types of intellectual property vary a lot – a trademark is different from a copyright and patents are in a weird world of their own."

The varied work requires a flexible mind. "One day you might be dealing with patents for pharmaceuticals and the next day you might be working on patents for some technological device," notes Dominic. "You need to be able to understand the science behind it. That doesn't mean you need a science or engineering degree but you need to be able to grasp what's novel or inventive about what's going on, or what the important markets are for a trademark." As well as an open mind, "you need to be pretty good at drafting – and drafting from scratch, because quite often there isn't a precedent clause that you can dig up".

If Dominic has any advice for those seeking a training contract, it's to chill out about training contract applications. "Don't pin your hopes on any one firm," he says. "If you're good enough, you'll find somewhere to do your training contract and you'll have a good time. If you don't get your first choice, you can always end up working for them later on. It's a bit like university: when you're applying you think it's the be all and end all to get your first choice and that if you don't you'll have a dire time. But hardly anyone has a bad time at university!"

# Personal injury

**Personal injury (PI) law deals with compensation for accidents and diseases. This area of law is flourishing in light of the recognition of new types of physical and mental illness. The subject matter varies considerably and can range from controversial, high-profile disaster cases to road traffic accidents to health and safety cases involving what one lawyer describes as "trippers, slippers and whiplash". A related, specialised practice area of PI law is clinical negligence, which involves injuries suffered during medical procedures.**

Shabana Ali is a solicitor at Atherton Godfrey, a Doncaster firm founded in 1979. She completed a law degree at the University of Leicester, followed by the LPC at the University of Birmingham. It was during law school that she found herself drawn to PI. She says: "The whole history of negligence and PI interested me – how over the last 50 to 60 years PI has changed and developed." She then chose to work as a paralegal for a couple of years. She explains why: "I found it quite difficult to secure a training contract at first. I also thought I'd gain as much practical experience as I could, which would help me in the long run. I joined Atherton Godfrey in 2002 and started working in the PI department as a fee earner. A year later I secured a training contract."

Shabana says: "The route I took worked for me, as during university I had not gained a lot of practical work experience. Upon leaving university I didn't really know what to expect from working in a law firm and was quite nervous. After starting work as a paralegal, I gained in confidence and learnt a lot, which set me up for my training contract."

At university, Shabana did not feel encouraged to start applying for training contracts early, and stresses that it is hard to do so "because you haven't seen or experienced much of life. So, it is important to try and gain all the work experience you can get; it shows you are keen and willing, and will introduce you to the working environment". She adds: "If you don't start early, you may struggle and have difficulty securing a training contract. This can become quite disheartening and you start to wonder 'is this the career for me?'. My advice is to keep trying and never give up." With this in mind, the highlight of Shabana's career was qualifying as a solicitor. "I made it in the end!" she says happily.

And now that she's fully qualified, Shabana has taken on much more responsibility. She handles over 90 cases, including several that are high value and complex: "At the beginning of my career, as I didn't have the experience in handling high-value cases, I didn't undertake this kind of work. As I have gained experience and confidence, I have taken on more complex issues and now deal with cases without constant supervision."

Dealing with 90 cases sounds awfully intensive. Shabana agrees: "You do have to use your own initiative. You have to be organised and prioritise work, as in a typical day you will find yourself drafting, writing letters, reviewing files, preparing court applications and preparing court documents, all with strict time constraints. In among all this you will be taking initial instructions from new clients and researching areas of law. Even though I am qualified, I am always learning and always being challenged with each task I undertake. PI is a constantly changing area; there are so many new cases every day."

Despite the heavy workload, Shabana's passion for PI sees her through. She explains: "I feel strongly about the area. It's not just about the money – it's also about helping people and trying to find solutions for them. You get serious cases where people have had medical problems which have had a huge impact on their lives. I find it stimulating to help clients work through that and find solutions. Each individual case is different and you apply different areas of law to each. You have to enjoy talking to people and be positive."

Shabana advises that passion is very important if you want to work in PI. "You have to enjoy client contact," she adds, "because there is a lot of it. Often it's in difficult situations – if the client's irate, you have to be able to placate them. If the client's had serious injuries, you have to be sensitive. You need to be confident and be good at communicating."

Shabana looks back on her career path to PI: "If I did it again, I'd start earlier. I'd find out what firms interested me, whether it's large City, medium-sized or small niche, and I'd target them specifically by researching them, contacting them and trying to get some work experience – it's all useful. You'd be surprised how many firms do want to help people get into the law. I'd go to more open days. I'd also try and get paralegal work, maybe in the holidays. I found doing the LPC was completely different to practising law."

Proud she qualified and made it into the area she has lots of passion for, Shabana enjoys keeping up to date with a constantly changing industry. She says: "It's become more media focused in the last few years. Because of the so-called compensation culture, things are changing with regards to how cases are being handled. I'm now secretary of the regional group of the Association of Personal Injury Lawyers, and am actively involved in bringing together PI lawyers to update them with information on PI law and practice."

# Private client

A private client solicitor looks after the affairs of individual clients and trustees, planning and managing all aspects of their finances including wills and probate, onshore and offshore trusts, and tax matters. Private client lawyers also handle a wide range of charity work, advising on specific charity law issues as well as on commercial and property matters that affect charitable organisations and the establishment of charities.

Private client work is booming and, increasingly, multi-jurisdictional issues are becoming more important for the private client lawyer as a result of acting for clients who are based outside the United Kingdom or who own assets in various countries throughout the world.

Jessica Jamieson is an associate at Cripps Harries Hall LLP, a leading southeast law firm. She studied law at the University of Nottingham, motivated by the "glamorous" lives of televisual lawyers (*Kavanagh QC*, anyone?). An enjoyable year doing the LPC at Nottingham Law School was made even more so by the knowledge that she had a training contract with Cripps safely tucked under her belt: "It meant I could do the private client module and a couple of others that were interesting and related to what I do now, rather than having to do the hardcore corporate subjects."

The training contract experience at Cripps was a good one, due in large part to the flexible seat system: "It is geared towards both the needs of trainees and departments, and I was fortunate to work in departments that I was interested in. I had a long six-month seat in private client, with shorter periods spent in other departments – for example, three months of conveyancing was quite enough!"

Jessica qualified into the private client department in 2003. Her day begins with the all-important cup of tea, she says: "After that, I might be drafting a will, chasing people to return powers of attorney, supervising the work of one of our trainees or newly qualified solicitors, or attending an internal meeting. I spend quite a lot of time managing client expectations – they generally will have no idea of the steps involved and may have an unrealistic view of how things work. I usually have one or two client meetings a week, possibly about a discretionary trust or probate matter. At the end of the working day, there's often a seminar, which may in turn be followed by drinks!"

Jessica enjoys the benefits of working in a regional firm: "There are definite advantages to being in Tunbridge Wells rather than London, especially as a trainee. You're given a lot more responsibility and client contact – I took my own client meeting when I was still a first year. There is also a really good social scene already set up. I specifically didn't want to work in London; the commute and the hours deterred me. However, I would stress that private client isn't nine 'til five – there's always at least a week's worth of work to do and you spend a lot of time keeping on top of the law."

A recent turning point in Jessica's career was the publication in the *New Law Journal* of an article she had written on radical changes to the taxation of trusts contained in the Finance Act 2006. She explains: "People started to think of me as having a head for the tax side of things. It felt like I'd made the transition from trainee to someone with a developing career. Also, I've just been made an associate, which I think related in part to the article." She also mentions a recent receivership case as having been particularly enjoyable to be involved with: "It centres on two mentally disabled children and an estate of £14 million on the Isle of Man. We've been trying to work out the tax and domicile issues. There are six different firms involved and lots to be done, especially keeping all the different personalities in the family happy. We've had some very tight deadlines, including one where we ended up with just days to spare but which saved the client about £5 million in tax. It's been really interesting."

Jessica discusses what she most and least enjoys about being a private client lawyer; the good, the bad and the paperwork, if you will: "I like the client contact and the detailed analysis – I enjoy looking at the law. What I wasn't prepared for is the amount of admin involved. There's time recording, billing, being chased about having too much work in progress, being chased when bills haven't been paid, checklists on files – it goes on! There is an awful lot to be done that isn't law. Then there's the internal side of things as well: marketing, drafting client notes and working on precedents (which seems to involve an inordinate amount of arguing about commas!). But it's all a necessary part of the job and would be the same in any law firm. It helps you to understand that this is a business, and we have to make money and get bills paid. The more you understand that, the easier it is to understand your role."

As Jessica has mentioned, the ability to manage client relations well is a key skill: "Every client is different, so you need to work out what each client needs and try to provide it. For example, someone may have been recently bereaved and emotionally distressed, so you have to understand his/her needs and be aware of the underlying issues. You also need to manage their expectations about cost and timescales. Cost can be a big issue – people want the work done and they know the hourly rate, but they still contest it. Clear explanations are required; it's all very well knowing the law, but you have to translate that into what the client needs to know and can understand."

Other key skills include "the ability to analyse legislation. I often refer back to it, particularly in relation to tax. Good drafting skills are also important, as is an eye for detail. Mental arithmetic is important too. We have a lot of high net worth clients here, so tax issues come up a lot".

Jessica has some nuggets of advice to offer as to improving your chances of training contract success: "Any work exposure is good, although it's difficult to get meaningful experience before university. It's also important to get a feel for the area and begin to see what kind of things people are working on and whether it's of interest. Starting early on applications is always good, although I did it late! And take a focused, rather than scattergun, approach – make sure you know about the firm and what they do, and target your covering letter accordingly so that they know you've done your homework. Confidence is essential as well – I swotted up on legal changes and financial news, but in the end it is as much about whether I was confident and whether the firm would be happy putting me in front of a client. It's also worth thinking about where you want to work – for example, London or not?"

Ultimately, says Jessica, it's not just about the law: "You may love the study of the law, but the job is much more than that. You need to practise applying what you learn, and you have to have common sense and business skills. And, of course, an ability to keep up with the admin!"

# Shipping

**Shipping law is one of the most specialised areas of law, so its practitioners are always in demand. It falls into two areas: 'dry' shipping includes contractual issues, bill of lading and charterparty disputes, and disputes about damage to cargo, whereas 'wet' shipping usually involves casualties (eg, where a ship has sunk or collided with another vessel). The work can be contentious or non-contentious. Even when the world economy is slow, shipping litigation remains buoyant and generally fares well because of its counter-cyclical nature. Non-contentious work, on the other hand, tends to follow the economic trends.**

Pawel Wysocki is an assistant solicitor at Hill Dickinson, which is noted for its large marine practice, incorporating cargo and freight, marine regulatory, and shipping and yachts, among other niche areas. He was raised in Finland around ships and seafarers. "My father worked for a Polish-Finnish joint venture shipping company," he says, "and other members of my family are involved in the marine business as well." Pawel grew up listening to discussions about legal issues and shipping. He says: "It was something that appealed to me from a very young age."

Pawel went on to study law at the University of East Anglia, which included a year at the University of Maastricht in the Netherlands as part of the ERASMUS exchange programme. Following his degree, he went to Guildford to do the LPC at The College of Law.

A home grown Hill Dickinson lawyer, Pawel describes his training contract at the firm: "I did a seat in the professional risks team, involved predominantly in defence work for medical and legal professionals, which was quite exciting. I did another seat in a similar area, but more on the side of construction professionals. Then I trained with the yacht team, focusing on insurance litigation and personal injury, all to do with yachts. Finally, I did a non-contentious seat in the yacht team, doing what I do now."

Pawel works mainly on transactional yacht work: "This includes drafting or negotiating yacht construction contracts, and ancillary agreements for project managers, designers and so on. As we approach delivery of a yacht, I might be involved in drafting crew management agreements, looking at insurance coverage and dealing with the myriad issues arising on handover of these multi-million pound assets."

Pawel continues: "I also do a fair bit of sale and purchase work. Some days are taken up entirely by negotiation and then, in due course, completion of a transaction. Completions are often stressful but exciting, especially when you're dealing with different parties across the globe. You communicate with the crew via Iridium phones and you have to review a plethora of documentation and maintain close contact with brokers, bankers, ship registries, classification societies, clients and their various advisers. I'd have to say that the completion of a transaction or the signing of any agreement you've been involved in is particularly rewarding because you get to see the value of something you've been working towards."

Although marine work is a specialist area, the breadth of work involved is surprising. Some solicitors work on high-profile international cases to do with oil and gas rigs, others present seminars in exotic locations and visit shipyards around the world. Pawel explains his own niche area, buying and selling yachts: "Things begin with an approach by a buyer or seller to represent their interests. Once you've got the draft memorandum in place you negotiate a list of documents that are to be provided on completion. Sometimes you'll be asked to hold funds pending completion. Following execution of the memorandum there will usually be a survey and sea trial, and we might be asked to comment on the outcome and to document any necessary variations. We'll draft a completion agenda as a guide to how the process will be achieved on the day. Then we'll provide an opinion on the corporate documents and liaise with the various registration authorities. Once we and the client are both happy, completion will take place, often with the yacht in international waters. Lawyers and brokers in London or the south of France are on hand by telephone and email."

While Pawel's clients are usually individuals, many solicitors in shipping work for large international shipping and freight companies. For example, a case might involve a charterer giving a wrongful voyage order, sending cargo to the wrong destination and potentially causing major problems.

The quality of work at Hill Dickinson attracted Pawel to the firm. "I applied here because of the firm's marine expertise," he remembers, "and it just so happened that I was lucky enough to end up in the yacht team. The market is on the up and the interest is phenomenal. The build slots in shipyards are filled for years ahead and there are many wealthy people who wish to invest in these sorts of yacht. For me, it's the place to be."

The legal issues themselves are as diverse as the oceans. Pawel does some work on contentious cases involving "complex legal points and multi-jurisdictional aspects which are always challenging". Although the shipping industry is old, its laws have become extremely refined and remain dynamic.

Pawel's very proud of the work he does. He describes the highlight of his career so far as "becoming an assistant solicitor in the Hill Dickinson yacht team. I enjoy working with my clients and my colleagues. We're very privileged to be able to work for some very senior clients and the people I work with are truly amazing".

The nature of Pawel's work calls for a key skill: flexibility. It's a strength necessary in most areas of marine law, where you may be required to travel a lot, work late, acquire new skills at a moment's notice and investigate relatively uncharted legal waters. If you represent a ship-owner client, you might, for example, be called on if one of their vessels is stranded in the Pacific amid a variety a range of multi-jurisdictional problems. Other skills necessary, especially for working in a yacht team, include "good commercial acumen and proactive business development," explains Pawel. "Because of the nature of the work and the calibre of the clients, we strive to provide a first-class service. Responding to the clients' needs is key."

To wannabe lawyers, Pawel says: "Get as much experience as you can. Try big firms, try small firms. Get a feel for what office life is like. Make sure your CV is correct and up-to-date, emphasising your strengths. Draft a covering letter that stands out from the crowd."

More importantly, because of the many niche practice areas within shipping, Pawel advises doing your research: "I remember when I trained, the yacht team was an enigma. I wasn't quite sure what they did but it sounded rather exciting. While a lot of the time it isn't, there is an element of glamour, so I feel privileged to be able to do something that I truly enjoy and I do take pleasure in working in this unique market, surrounded – in spirit at least – with some wonderful feats of design and engineering."

# TMT

Technology, media and telecommunications (TMT) is one of the fastest-developing sectors in the legal market. The continual introduction of new technology pushes legal boundaries and practically begs for the development of precedents. TMT lawyers advise on market developments, regulatory changes, legislation, and commercial and technical issues. Outsourcing continues to be a particularly hot topic.

Laura Berton is an associate solicitor at medium-sized City firm Field Fisher Waterhouse LLP (FFW). She studied English and French law at the University of Kent: "I really enjoyed it and had brilliant lecturers, including one who even made me like property law!" After a year in Paris as part of her degree (where French-born Laura was complimented on her "quite good" French!), her initial idea of defending "widow and orphan" was replaced by a more commercial motivation – the need to make some money: "Although I initially wanted to do both contentious and non-contentious work, I decided that if I was going to do commercial law, it would be more interesting to work on negotiations and deals, rather than just problems."

After a year of travelling and then the LPC at The College of Law in Guildford, Laura did her training contract at niche media firm, the Simkins Partnership. Part of her role involved watching reality TV and going to screenings – nice work if you can get it! On qualification, Laura worked in-house at a software company, after which it was off to FFW, where she's been now for just over a year.

As part of the firm's technology group, Laura enjoys the variety and commercial focus of her work: "A typical day would be drafting, reviewing and analysing IT-related agreements, such as website terms of use, privacy policies and software licences. I also give advice on data protection, e-commerce and new media issues. We also work a lot at an international level, dealing with our European offices and other firms in China, the Middle East and the United States, and some very high-profile UK government projects." True to its high-tech reputation, FFW is involved with virtual world Second Life. Laura explains: "It is a parallel, online life. We were the first serious law firm to open offices there, which is exciting. Part of my job is for my avatar to be online and talk to clients in our virtual offices. It's a great marketing and recruitment tool."

The opportunity to go on secondment is one that FFW is keen to promote, which meant that Laura found herself in Saudi Arabia practising her Arabic: "FFW has a great range of clients – telecom, media, government – so there are some really interesting secondment opportunities. I had a great seven months running the legal department of a Saudi aviation company; everyone else was male and twice my age, which was a challenge! But what's nice on secondments is that you have the security of the firm's support, but you're exposed to issues from the client's point of view having to offer them real-time solutions."

Laura considers the best and worst aspects of the job as two sides of the same coin: "Having chargeable hours means the figures speak for themselves – there's no-one looking over your shoulder. On the other hand, you have to work intensely all the time you are in the office. On those days when you're tired or not in the mood for work, you can't take things easy. You cannot charge clients for work you haven't done!" We suppose that curbs the time spent on Facebook somewhat.

Laura explains the sort of skills that are useful in TMT: "As in most practice areas, you have to be very commercially oriented as well as having a full range of legal skills. However, specific to IT, I think that clients need an extra level of support and guidance because the industry has developed so quickly. Clients don't always know what they should be asking for, so it's your job to understand what they need. A lot of smaller businesses are really enthusiastic and doing fantastic jobs, but you have to be commercially minded – it's no good just giving them a legal memo!"

In terms of securing a training contract, Laura suggests that "work experience is always good because you get to see what people actually do", but good grades are essential: "You won't be recruited because of them, but they will stop you from being eliminated from the process. Paralegal experience is also useful for making contacts and trying your hand at drafting. But at the end of the day, it's about creating the magic on paper that gets people interested." She also has a warning about what not to do: "I was once showing around some prospective trainees, all of whom had brilliant CVs. I was talking to one of the guys, who ended up insulting me! So I'd suggest being confident but not arrogant."

Finally, Laura has some sage advice on knuckling down while at university: "Doing the work when you're younger means you get the freedom to do what you want when you're older. And law is good training in being highly efficient, detailed and extremely client oriented, which are great skills and training for any job."

# *LawCareers.Net*
# *Basic Training*
# **Are you ready?**

*It's never too early to start
planning your career in the law.
Don't risk missing out! The
LawCareers.Net Basic Training
events will be coming to a
campus near you in early 2008.
Keep checking www.LawCareers.Net
for further information.*

# Training Contract Directory

# How to use the solicitors' regional indexes and directory

**Solicitors' regional indexes**

These tables are designed to allow you to shortlist firms by particular criteria. Further information about each firm is contained within the training contract directory.

The tables detail:
- the number of annual vacancies at the firm (unless a particular year has been specified);
- the number of partners (which generally includes equity and salaried partners) and total staff;
- whether work placement schemes are available; and
- up to five general practice and 19 specialisation work areas.

Firms that claim to have an office in a particular region are listed from A to Z in the appropriate regional table.

For the purposes of the indexes we have used the 10 standard economic planning regions of Great Britain (not including Scotland), and London is dealt with separately. There is also a table for the Channel Islands and the Isle of Man, and an international table.

Please note, the following abbreviations have been used for the specialisation work areas:
- 'Banking' refers to Banking and finance;
- 'Litigation' refers to Commercial litigation;
- 'Property' refers to Commercial property; and
- 'Comp/comm' refers to Company/commercial.

It should be noted that the information has been provided by the firms themselves and has generally not been verified by us. We do not, therefore, claim that the information is fully accurate and comprehensive, only that it can be used as a starting point for shortlisting appropriate firms. Furthermore, although we have attempted to contact every firm on the Solicitors Regulation Authority's (SRA) list of firms that are authorised to provide training contracts, not all firms that take trainees have supplied their details.

**Training contract directory**

The directory contains contact information and a brief practice description for all firms that are authorised to offer training contracts by the SRA and have supplied us with their details. It is therefore an essential reference guide to firms that offer work placement schemes, training contracts and funding.

The basic entry includes the firm's application address (not necessarily its main office), telephone and fax numbers, email address (if available), the applications contact and a brief description of the firm, together with the number of vacancies per year (unless a particular year is specified), the number of current trainees, partners and total staff, and whether the firm offers work placement schemes. Firms with a more detailed directory entry appear in bold in the regional indexes.

Every effort has been made to collate accurate information from all firms that are authorised to provide training contracts and we are confident that the directory is the most comprehensive of its kind.

These resources should be used in conjunction with the section on law firm practice areas, which features in-depth interviews with numerous solicitors who are keen to pass on their advice about making it in the legal profession.

# Regional indexes

# Channel Islands

| | Vacancies | Partners | Total staff | Work placement | Corporate/commercial | General commercial | Niche | General practice | High street/legal aid |
|---|---|---|---|---|---|---|---|---|---|
| Cains Advocates Limited | 2 | 6 | 70 | ✔ | • | • | • | • | |
| Collas Day | 0 | 7 | 65 | ✔ | | | | • | |
| Ozannes | 1 | 13 | 95 | ✔ | • | • | | | |
| **Wedlake Bell** | 7 | 41 | 200 | ✔ | • | • | | | |

# East Anglia

| | Vacancies | Partners | Total staff | Work placement | Corporate/commercial | General commercial | Niche | General practice | High street/legal aid |
|---|---|---|---|---|---|---|---|---|---|
| Adlams | 0 | 4 | 23 | | | | | | • |
| **Ashton Graham** | 2 | 22 | 150 | ✔ | • | • | | • | • |
| Bates, Wells & Braithwaite | 5 | 21 | 130 | ✔ | | • | • | | |
| Birkett Long | 3 | 18 | 150 | ✔ | • | • | | • | |
| Birketts LLP | 5 | 36 | 225 | | • | | | | |
| Buckles Solicitors LLP | 0 | 14 | 96 | | • | • | | | |
| Chamberlins | 0 | 5 | 32 | | | | | • | • |
| Chelmsford Borough Council | 0 | | 16 | | | | • | | |
| Cozens-Hardy LLP | 1[09] | 9 | 75 | | | • | | • | • |
| Crossmans | 0 | 3 | 22 | | • | • | | • | |
| **Crown Prosecution Service** | 25 | | 9000 | ✔ | | | • | | |
| Cunningtons | Varies[09] | 10 | 180 | ✔ | | | | • | • |
| Edmondson Hall | 0 | 2 | 17 | ✔ | | • | • | | |
| **Eversheds LLP** | 80+ | 340 | 4000 | ✔ | • | • | | | |
| Fosters | 4 | 11 | 100 | | | | | • | • |
| Goody Burrett LLP | 1[08] | 5 | 42 | ✔ | | | | • | |
| Gotelee & Goldsmith | 1[09] | 13 | 92 | | • | | | • | • |
| **Government Legal Service** | 22-30 | | 1950 | ✔ | • | • | | • | |
| Greenwoods | 2-3 | 11 | 76 | | • | • | | | |
| Hansells | 1-2 | 15 | 130 | ✔ | | | | | |
| Hayes + Storr | 0 | 8 | 60 | | • | • | | • | |
| HC Solicitors LLP | 0 | 14 | 97 | | | • | | • | • |
| Heald Solicitors | 2 | 6 | 30 | | • | • | | | |
| **Hewitsons** | 15 | 44 | 288 | ✔ | • | • | • | • | |
| Hilliers HRW | 2[08] | 5 | 55 | | • | • | | | • |
| Hood Vores & Allwood | 1[09] | 6 | 35 | | | | | • | • |
| **Howes Percival LLP** | 10 | 31 | 300 | ✔ | • | • | | | |
| Irena Spence & Co | 0 | 5 | 30 | | | | | • | • |
| Jeremy Roberts & Co | 1[09] | 1 | 8 | ✔ | | | | | |
| John A White & Co | 1 | 1 | 16 | | | | | • | • |

| Arbitration | Banking | Comp/comm | Competition | Construction | Corporate tax | Crime | Employment | Environment | Family | Human rights | Insurance | IP | Litigation | Personal injury | Private client | Property | Shipping | TMT |
|---|---|---|---|---|---|---|---|---|---|---|---|---|---|---|---|---|---|---|
|  | • | • |  |  |  |  | • |  |  |  | • | • | • |  | • | • | • | • |
|  | • | • |  |  | • |  | • |  | • |  | • | • | • | • | • | • |  | • |
| • | • | • |  |  | • | • | • |  | • |  | • |  | • | • | • | • |  | • |
|  | • | • | • | • | • |  | • |  |  |  |  |  | • | • |  | • |  | • |
|  |  | • |  |  |  |  | • |  | • |  |  |  |  | • | • | • |  |  |
| • |  | • |  |  |  |  | • |  | • |  |  |  | • | • | • | • |  |  |
| • |  | • | • | • | • |  | • | • |  | • |  | • | • | • | • | • |  | • |
| • | • | • | • | • | • |  | • | • |  | • |  | • | • | • | • | • |  | • |
| • | • | • | • |  | • |  | • |  | • |  |  | • | • | • | • | • | • | • |
| • |  | • |  |  | • |  | • |  | • |  |  | • | • | • | • | • |  | • |
|  |  | • |  |  |  |  | • |  | • |  |  |  | • | • | • | • |  |  |
|  |  | • |  |  |  |  | • |  | • |  |  |  | • | • | • | • |  |  |
|  |  | • |  | • |  |  | • |  | • |  |  |  | • | • | • |  |  |  |
|  |  |  |  |  | • |  | • |  | • |  |  |  |  |  |  |  |  |  |
|  |  | • |  |  |  |  | • |  | • |  |  |  | • |  | • |  |  |  |
|  |  | • |  |  |  |  | • |  | • |  | • |  | • | • | • |  |  | • |
| • | • | • | • | • | • |  | • | • |  | • | • | • | • |  |  | • | • | • |
|  |  | • |  |  | • |  | • |  | • |  |  |  | • | • | • | • |  |  |
|  |  |  |  |  |  |  | • |  | • |  |  |  | • |  | • |  |  |  |
|  |  | • |  | • | • |  | • | • | • |  |  |  | • | • | • | • |  | • |
| • | • | • | • | • | • | • | • | • | • | • | • |  | • | • | • | • | • | • |
| • |  | • | • | • |  |  | • | • |  |  |  |  | • |  | • | • |  | • |
|  |  | • |  |  |  |  | • |  | • |  |  |  | • | • | • | • |  |  |
|  |  | • |  |  |  |  | • |  | • |  |  |  | • | • | • | • |  | • |
|  |  | • | • |  |  | • | • | • | • | • |  |  | • | • | • | • |  | • |
|  |  | • |  | • | • |  | • |  | • |  |  | • | • | • | • | • |  | • |
|  | • | • | • | • | • |  | • | • |  |  |  |  | • | • | • | • |  | • |
|  |  | • |  |  | • | • | • |  | • |  |  | • | • | • | • | • |  |  |
|  |  | • |  |  |  |  | • |  | • |  |  |  | • | • | • | • |  |  |
| • | • | • |  |  | • |  | • | • |  |  |  |  | • | • | • | • |  | • |
|  |  |  |  |  |  |  | • |  | • |  |  |  | • | • | • | • |  |  |
|  |  |  |  |  |  | • | • |  | • |  |  |  |  | • |  |  |  |  |
|  |  | • |  |  |  |  | • |  | • |  |  |  | • |  | • | • |  |  |

| | Vacancies | Partners | Total staff | Work placement | Corporate/ commercial | General commercial | Niche | General practice | High street/ legal aid |
|---|---|---|---|---|---|---|---|---|---|
| **Kennedys** | 10[08] | 90 | 530 | | • | • | • | | |
| Kester Cunningham John | 6[09] | 26 | 200 | ✔ | • | • | | • | |
| Leathes Prior | 1-3 | 11 | 55 | | • | • | • | • | |
| Malletts | 1-2[08] | 6 | 34 | ✔ | • | | | • | • |
| Maudsley Wright & Pearson | 1[08] | 3 | 19 | ✔ | | | | | • |
| Metcalfe Copeman & Pettefar | 1[08] | 15 | 120 | | | • | | • | |
| **Mills & Reeve LLP** | 22 | 79 | 760 | ✔ | • | • | • | | |
| Morgan Jones & Pett | 0 | 3 | 23 | | | | | • | |
| Norton Peskett | 1 | 11 | 133 | | | | | • | • |
| Paul Norton & Co | Poss | 1 | 10 | | | | | • | |
| Paul Robinson Solicitors | 1[08] | 7 | 70 | | | | | • | • |
| Pothecary Witham Weld | 2[08] | 8 | 48 | | | | • | | |
| **Prettys** | 6 | 15 | 140 | ✔ | • | • | | • | |
| Ronaldsons | 1 | 1 | 10 | | | | • | | • |
| Ross Coates Solicitors | 1-2 | 5 | 45 | | | | | • | |
| Roythorne & Co | 3-4[09] | 20 | 180 | | • | • | | | |
| The Sethi Partnership Solicitors | 0 | 2 | 25 | ✔ | | • | | | |
| **Shoosmiths** | 17 | 105 | 1450 | ✔ | • | • | • | • | |
| **Stanley Tee LLP** | 4 | 17 | 175 | ✔ | • | • | | • | • |
| steeles | 6[09] | 19 | 180 | ✔ | • | • | | • | |
| **Taylor Vinters** | 7 | 30 | 200 | ✔ | • | • | • | • | |
| **Taylor Wessing** | 24 | 264 | 1000 | ✔ | • | • | | | |
| Ward Gethin | 1 | 13 | 96 | | | | | • | |
| Wilkinson & Butler | 0 | 4 | 20 | | | | | • | • |
| Winckworth Sherwood | 4[09] | 24 | 185 | ✔ | | • | • | | |
| **Wollastons** | 2 | 13 | 103 | | • | • | | | |
| Woodfines LLP | 3[09] | 22 | 152 | ✔ | | | | • | |

| Arbitration | Banking | Comp/comm | Competition | Construction | Corporate tax | Crime | Employment | Environment | Family | Human rights | Insurance | IP | Litigation | Personal injury | Private client | Property | Shipping | TMT |
|---|---|---|---|---|---|---|---|---|---|---|---|---|---|---|---|---|---|---|
| • | • | • |  | • |  |  | • | • |  |  | • | • | • | • | • | • | • |  |
| • |  | • |  | • | • |  | • | • | • |  |  |  | • | • | • | • |  | • |
| • | • | • |  |  |  | • | • |  | • | • |  |  | • | • | • | • |  |  |
|  |  | • |  |  |  | • |  |  | • |  |  |  | • |  |  |  |  |  |
|  |  |  |  |  |  | • | • |  | • |  |  |  |  | • |  |  |  |  |
|  |  | • |  |  |  | • | • |  | • |  |  |  | • | • | • | • |  |  |
| • | • | • | • | • | • |  | • | • | • |  | • | • | • | • | • | • |  | • |
|  |  |  |  |  |  |  |  |  | • |  |  |  |  |  |  |  |  |  |
|  |  | • |  |  |  |  | • |  | • |  |  |  | • | • | • | • |  |  |
|  |  | • |  |  |  |  |  |  | • |  |  |  |  | • |  |  |  |  |
| • |  | • | • | • | • |  | • | • | • |  | • | • | • | • | • | • | • | • |
|  |  | • |  |  |  |  |  |  | • |  |  |  |  |  |  |  |  |  |
| • |  | • |  | • | • |  | • | • | • |  |  |  | • | • | • | • |  |  |
|  |  | • |  |  |  | • |  |  | • |  |  |  | • | • | • | • |  | • |
| • | • | • | • | • | • |  | • | • | • |  | • | • | • | • | • | • |  | • |
|  |  | • |  | • |  | • | • | • | • |  | • |  | • | • | • | • |  | • |
| • | • | • | • | • | • |  | • | • | • |  | • | • | • | • | • | • | • | • |
| • | • | • | • | • | • |  | • | • | • |  | • | • | • | • | • | • | • | • |
|  |  | • |  |  |  |  | • | • | • |  |  |  | • | • | • | • |  |  |
|  |  |  |  |  | • |  |  |  |  |  |  |  |  |  |  |  |  |  |
| • |  | • |  | • |  |  | • |  | • |  |  |  | • |  | • | • |  |  |
|  |  | • |  | • |  |  | • |  | • |  |  | • | • |  | • | • |  | • |
| • |  | • | • | • |  | • | • | • | • |  |  | • | • | • | • | • |  | • |

# East Midlands

| | Vacancies | Partners | Total staff | Work placement | Corporate/commercial | General commercial | Niche | General practice | High street/legal aid |
|---|---|---|---|---|---|---|---|---|---|
| Actons | 1 | 14 | 85 | | • | • | | • | |
| Advance Legal | 8 | 2 | 45 | ✔ | | | • | | |
| Bakewells | 0 | 3 | 48 | | | • | | | |
| Banner Jones Solicitors | Poss(09) | 17 | 80 | | | | | • | • |
| Barlow Poyner Foxon | 1 | 3 | 22 | | | | | • | |
| Berryman | 4 | 15 | 125 | | • | • | | • | • |
| Bhatia Best | 2-4 | 13 | 113 | | | | | • | • |
| BHW Commercial Solicitors | 1 | 2 | 12 | ✔ | | | | | |
| Bilton Hammond | 0 | 6 | 35 | ✔ | | | | • | • |
| Bird & Co | 0 | 3 | 47 | ✔ | | | | | • |
| Bridge McFarland | 0 | 20 | 170 | | | • | | | |
| **Browne Jacobson LLP** | 12 | 60 | 517 | | • | • | • | | |
| Bryan and Armstrong | 0 | 7 | 35 | ✔ | | | | • | • |
| Burton & Burton | 0-1 | 2 | 14 | | | | | | • |
| Burton & Co | 0 | 8 | 60 | | • | • | | • | • |
| **Crown Prosecution Service** | 25(09) | | 9000 | ✔ | | | • | | |
| DFA Law | 0-2(08) | 10 | 56 | | | • | | | |
| Eden & Company | 1 | 2 | 12 | ✔ | | | | • | |
| Emery Johnson Solicitors | 2 | 2 | 24 | ✔ | | | • | | • |
| **Eversheds LLP** | 80+ | 340 | 4000 | ✔ | • | • | | | |
| Fishers | 0-1 | 6 | 58 | | • | • | • | • | • |
| Flint Bishop | 4(09) | 22 | 250 | | • | • | | • | |
| Franklins Solicitors LLP | 0 | 9 | 125 | | • | • | | | |
| Frearsons | 0-1 | 4 | 28 | | | | | • | • |
| **Freeth Cartwright LLP** | 7 | 70 | 509 | | • | • | | • | |
| **Geldards LLP** | 8 | 53 | 400 | ✔ | • | • | • | | |
| **Government Legal Service** | 22-30 | | 1950 | ✔ | • | • | | • | |
| Greenwoods | 2-3 | 11 | 76 | | • | • | | | |
| **Harvey Ingram LLP** | 4-5 | 33 | 200 | ✔ | • | • | | | |
| Hatton | 1-2 | 1 | 6 | ✔ | | | • | | |
| **HBJ Gateley Wareing LLP** | 11 | 75 | 488 | ✔ | • | • | | | |
| Heald Solicitors | 2 | 6 | 30 | | • | • | | • | |
| **Hewitsons** | 15 | 44 | 288 | ✔ | • | • | • | • | |
| Hopkins Solicitors | 0 | 8 | 50 | | • | • | | • | • |
| **Howes Percival LLP** | 10 | 31 | 300 | ✔ | • | • | | | |
| HSR Law | 0-1(08) | 6 | 42 | | • | • | | • | • |
| Jeremy Roberts & Co | 1(09) | 1 | 8 | ✔ | | | | | |
| JH Powell & Co | 1(09) | 6 | 20 | | • | • | | • | |
| Johar & Co | 1 | 2 | 25 | | | | | • | • |
| John A White & Co | 1 | 1 | 16 | | | | | • | • |
| The Johnson Partnership | 1-2 | 13 | 80 | | | | | | • |

| Arbitration | Banking | Comp/comm | Competition | Construction | Corporate tax | Crime | Employment | Environment | Family | Human rights | Insurance | IP | Litigation | Personal injury | Private client | Property | Shipping | TMT |
|---|---|---|---|---|---|---|---|---|---|---|---|---|---|---|---|---|---|---|
|  |  | • |  | • |  |  | • |  | • |  |  |  | • | • | • | • |  |  |
|  |  |  |  |  |  |  | • |  |  |  |  |  | • | • | • |  |  |  |
|  |  | • |  |  |  |  | • |  | • |  | • |  | • | • | • | • |  |  |
|  |  | • |  |  |  | • | • |  | • |  |  |  | • | • | • | • |  |  |
|  |  |  |  |  |  |  | • |  | • |  |  |  |  | • | • | • |  |  |
| • | • | • | • | • | • |  | • | • | • |  | • | • | • | • | • | • |  | • |
|  |  |  |  |  |  | • |  |  | • | • |  |  |  | • | • | • |  |  |
|  |  | • | • | • | • |  |  |  |  |  |  | • | • |  |  |  |  | • |
|  |  |  |  |  |  |  | • |  | • |  |  |  | • | • | • | • |  |  |
|  |  | • |  |  |  |  | • |  | • |  |  |  | • | • | • | • |  |  |
| • |  | • |  | • |  |  | • |  | • |  | • |  | • | • | • | • | • |  |
| • | • | • |  | • | • |  | • | • |  |  | • |  | • | • | • | • |  | • |
|  |  |  |  |  |  |  | • | • |  |  |  |  | • | • | • | • |  |  |
|  |  |  |  |  |  |  |  |  | • |  |  |  |  | • | • | • |  |  |
|  |  | • |  |  |  |  | • | • | • | • |  |  | • | • | • | • |  |  |
|  |  |  |  |  |  | • |  |  | • |  |  |  |  |  |  |  |  |  |
| • |  | • |  |  |  |  | • |  | • |  | • |  | • | • | • | • |  | • |
|  |  | • |  |  |  |  |  |  | • |  |  |  |  | • | • | • |  |  |
|  |  |  |  |  |  | • |  |  | • |  |  |  |  |  |  |  |  |  |
| • | • | • | • | • | • |  | • | • |  | • | • | • | • |  |  | • | • | • |
|  |  | • |  | • | • |  | • | • |  |  |  | • | • | • | • | • |  |  |
|  |  | • |  | • | • |  | • |  | • |  |  | • |  | • | • | • |  |  |
|  |  | • |  |  |  |  | • |  | • |  |  | • |  | • | • | • |  |  |
|  |  |  |  |  |  |  |  |  | • |  |  |  |  | • | • | • |  |  |
| • | • | • | • | • | • |  | • | • | • | • | • | • | • | • | • | • |  | • |
| • | • | • | • | • | • |  | • | • |  |  | • | • | • | • | • | • |  | • |
| • | • | • | • | • | • |  | • | • | • | • | • | • | • | • | • | • | • | • |
| • |  | • |  | • | • |  | • |  |  |  |  |  | • | • | • | • |  |  |
| • | • | • | • | • | • | • | • |  | • |  | • | • | • | • | • | • |  |  |
|  | • | • |  | • | • | • | • |  | • | • | • |  | • | • | • | • |  |  |
| • | • | • | • | • |  |  | • | • |  |  |  |  | • | • | • | • | • | • |
|  |  | • |  | • | • |  | • |  | • |  |  |  | • | • | • | • |  | • |
|  | • | • | • | • | • |  | • | • |  |  |  |  | • | • | • | • |  | • |
|  |  | • |  |  |  |  | • |  | • |  |  | • | • | • | • | • |  |  |
| • | • | • |  |  | • |  | • | • |  |  |  |  | • | • | • | • |  | • |
|  |  | • |  |  |  | • | • |  | • |  |  |  | • | • | • | • |  |  |
|  |  |  |  |  |  | • | • |  | • |  |  |  |  | • |  |  |  |  |
| • |  | • |  | • |  |  | • |  | • |  |  | • | • |  | • | • |  | • |
|  |  |  |  |  |  | • | • |  | • | • |  |  | • | • | • | • |  |  |
|  |  | • |  |  |  |  | • |  | • |  |  |  | • |  | • | • |  |  |
|  |  |  |  |  |  | • |  |  |  |  |  |  |  |  |  |  |  |  |

| | Vacancies | Partners | Total staff | Work placement | Corporate/ commercial | General commercial | Niche | General practice | High street/ legal aid |
|---|---|---|---|---|---|---|---|---|---|
| **Langleys** | 6 | 38 | 325 | ✔ | • | • | | • | • |
| Marrons | 2 | 7 | 32 | | | | • | | |
| Martin & Haigh | 0 | 4 | 37 | | | | | • | • |
| Mason Bullock | 0 | 2 | 9 | | | • | | • | |
| Matrix Solicitors | 0 | 1 | 7 | ✔ | • | | • | | |
| Moosa-Duke Solicitors | 1[09] | 1 | 5 | ✔ | | | • | | |
| **Morgan Cole** | 12 | 47 | 410 | ✔ | • | • | | | |
| Nelsons | 0 | 34 | 241 | | • | • | | • | • |
| Oldham Marsh Page Flavell | Poss | 3 | 30 | | | | | • | • |
| Phillips | 0-1 | 2 | 9 | | | | | | • |
| Richmonds | 2[09] | 3 | 48 | ✔ | • | | | | • |
| Robinsons | Poss | 7 | 68 | | • | • | | • | |
| Roythorne & Co | 3-4[09] | 20 | 180 | | • | • | | • | |
| Sharp & Partners | 0-1 | 10 | 60 | | | | | • | |
| **Shoosmiths** | 17 | 105 | 1450 | ✔ | • | • | • | • | |
| Sills & Betteridge | 2 | 18 | 120 | | • | • | | • | • |
| Smith Partnership | 1[09] | 20 | 200 | | • | • | | | • |
| Spearing Waite | 3-4[08] | 12 | 70 | | • | | | • | |
| Talbot & Co | 1[08] | 1 | 20 | ✔ | • | • | • | • | |
| Tallents Solicitors | 0 | 7 | 51 | | | | | • | • |
| Thompsons | Poss[09] | 38 | 800 | | | | | • | |
| Tinn Criddle & Co | 0 | 4 | 10 | | | | | • | |
| **Tollers** | 6 | 21 | 237 | | • | • | | • | |
| Vincent Sykes | 0 | 2 | 10 | ✔ | | | | • | |
| **Weightmans** | Up to 14 | 90 | 750 | | | • | | • | |
| **Wilkin Chapman** | 2 | 33 | 265 | | • | • | | • | • |
| Woodfines LLP | 3[09] | 22 | 152 | ✔ | | | | • | |
| Young & Pearce | 1 | 8 | 33 | ✔ | | • | • | • | • |

| Arbitration | Banking | Comp/comm | Competition | Construction | Corporate tax | Crime | Employment | Environment | Family | Human rights | Insurance | IP | Litigation | Personal injury | Private client | Property | Shipping | TMT |
|---|---|---|---|---|---|---|---|---|---|---|---|---|---|---|---|---|---|---|
| | | • | | • | | • | • | | • | | | | • | • | • | • | | |
| | | • | | | | | | • | | | | | | | | • | | |
| | | | | | | | | | • | | | | | | • | | | |
| | | • | | | | | • | | | • | | • | • | • | • | • | | • |
| | | • | | | | | | • | | | | • | • | • | • | • | | • |
| | | | | | | | | | | | | | | • | | | | |
| • | • | • | • | • | • | • | • | | • | | • | • | • | • | • | • | • | |
| • | • | • | • | • | • | • | • | | • | • | • | | • | • | • | • | | |
| | | | | | • | • | | | • | | | | | • | | • | | |
| | | | | | | • | | | • | | | | | | | | | |
| • | | • | | | | | • | | | | | | • | • | • | • | | |
| • | | • | • | | | | • | | | | | • | • | • | • | • | | • |
| • | | • | | • | • | • | • | | • | | | | • | • | • | • | | • |
| | | • | | | | | • | • | | | | | • | • | • | • | | • |
| • | • | • | • | • | • | | • | • | | | • | • | • | • | • | • | | • |
| | | • | | | | | • | | • | | | | • | • | • | • | | |
| | | • | | | | | • | | • | | | • | • | • | • | • | | |
| | | • | | | | | • | | • | | | | • | • | • | • | | |
| | | | | • | | | • | • | | • | | | | • | • | • | | |
| | | | | | | | • | • | | | | | | | • | | | |
| | | | | | | | | | | | | | | | • | | | |
| | | • | • | • | | | • | | • | | | • | • | • | • | • | | |
| | | • | | | | | • | | • | | | | • | • | • | | | |
| • | • | • | | • | • | | • | | | • | | • | • | • | • | | • | |
| | | • | • | | • | | • | | • | | | | • | • | • | • | | |
| • | | • | • | • | | • | • | • | • | | | | • | • | • | • | | • |
| | | • | | | | | • | • | | • | | | • | • | • | • | | • |

# International

| | Vacancies | Partners | Total staff | Work placement | Corporate/ commercial | General commercial | Niche | General practice | High street/ legal aid |
|---|---|---|---|---|---|---|---|---|---|
| **Allen & Overy LLP** | 120 | 470 | 4800 | ✔ | • | | | | |
| **Arnold & Porter (UK) LLP** | 2 | 14 | 64 | ✔ | • | • | • | | |
| **Ashurst** | 55 | 195 | 1650 | ✔ | • | | | | |
| **Baker & McKenzie LLP** | 38 | 88 | 722 | ✔ | • | | | | |
| **Barlow Lyde & Gilbert LLP** | 18-20 | 82 | 671 | ✔ | • | • | | • | |
| **Berrymans Lace Mawer** | 17 | 115 | 792 | ✔ | | • | | | |
| **Bird & Bird** | 18 | 148 | 900 | ✔ | • | | | | |
| **Cadwalader Wickersham & Taft LLP** | 6-8 | 11 | 160 | | • | | | | |
| **Cleary Gottlieb Steen & Hamilton LLP** | 10 | 18 | 189 | ✔ | • | | | | |
| **Clifford Chance** | 130 | 236 | 2815 | ✔ | • | • | | | |
| **Clyde & Co LLP** | 24 | 140 | 1080 | ✔ | • | • | | | |
| **CMS Cameron McKenna LLP** | 60 | 131 | 1500 | ✔ | • | • | | | |
| **Collyer Bristow LLP** | 3 | 30 | 136 | | • | • | | • | |
| Constant & Constant | 0 | 16 | 64 | | • | • | | | |
| **Covington & Burling LLP** | 6 | 190 | 1300 | ✔ | • | • | | | |
| Curtis Mallet-Prevost Colt & Mosle LLP | 0 | 3 | 12 | | • | | | | |
| **Davies Arnold Cooper** | 5 | 68 | 308 | ✔ | • | • | • | | |
| **Debevoise & Plimpton LLP** | 6 | 16 | 165 | ✔ | | | | • | |
| **Dechert LLP** | 15 | 37 | 300 | ✔ | • | | | | |
| **Denton Wilde Sapte** | 35 | 165 | 1400 | ✔ | • | • | • | | |
| **DLA Piper UK LLP** | 95+ | 1200 | 7000 | ✔ | • | | | | |
| **Dorsey & Whitney** | 4 | 14 | 75 | | • | | | | |
| **Eversheds LLP** | 80+ | 340 | 4000 | ✔ | • | • | | | |
| **Faegre & Benson LLP** | 2 | 12 | 55 | ✔ | • | • | | | |
| **Field Fisher Waterhouse LLP** | 20 | 101 | 640 | ✔ | • | • | • | | |
| **Freshfields Bruckhaus Deringer** | 100 | 474 | 5517 | ✔ | • | | | | |
| **Hammonds** | 40 | 189 | 1300 | ✔ | • | | | | |
| **Herbert Smith LLP** | Up to 100 | 233 | 2200 | ✔ | • | | | | |
| Hogan & Hartson | 2-3 | 20 | 115 | | • | • | | | |
| **Holman Fenwick & Willan** | 10 | 88 | 500 | ✔ | • | • | • | | |
| **Ince & Co** | 12 | 79 | 462 | ✔ | | | • | | |
| **Jones Day** | 15-20 | 45 | 371 | ✔ | • | | | | |
| **Kennedys** | 10(08) | 90 | 530 | | • | • | • | | |
| **Kirkland & Ellis** | 4 | 523 | 3000 | ✔ | • | | | | |
| **Kirkpatrick & Lockhart Preston Gates Ellis LLP** | Up to 15 | 54 | 301 | ✔ | • | • | | | |
| **Latham & Watkins** | 10-15 | 38 | 265 | ✔ | • | | | | |
| **LeBoeuf Lamb Greene & MacRae** | 15 | 35 | 220 | ✔ | • | • | | | |
| **Linklaters LLP** | 130 | 500 | 5000 | ✔ | • | | | | |
| **Lovells LLP** | 90 | 319 | 3000 | ✔ | • | | | | |
| **Mayer Brown International LLP** | 25-30 | 101 | 625 | ✔ | • | • | | | |

| Arbitration | Banking | Comp/comm | Competition | Construction | Corporate tax | Crime | Employment | Environment | Family | Human rights | Insurance | IP | Litigation | Personal injury | Private client | Property | Shipping | TMT |
|---|---|---|---|---|---|---|---|---|---|---|---|---|---|---|---|---|---|---|
| • | • | • | • | • | • |  | • | • |  |  | • | • | • |  | • | • |  | • |
| • | • | • | • |  | • |  |  |  |  |  |  |  | • | • | • | • |  | • |
| • | • | • | • | • | • |  | • | • |  |  | • | • | • |  |  | • |  | • |
| • | • | • | • | • | • |  | • | • |  |  | • | • | • |  | • | • |  | • |
| • | • | • | • | • | • |  | • | • |  |  | • | • | • | • |  | • | • | • |
|  |  |  | • |  |  |  | • | • |  |  | • |  | • | • |  |  | • |  |
| • | • | • | • |  | • |  | • |  |  |  |  | • | • |  |  | • |  | • |
|  | • |  |  |  |  |  |  |  |  |  | • |  |  |  |  | • |  |  |
| • | • | • | • |  | • |  | • |  |  |  |  | • | • |  |  | • |  | • |
| • | • | • | • | • | • |  | • | • |  |  | • | • | • |  |  | • | • | • |
|  | • | • | • | • | • |  | • | • |  |  | • | • | • | • | • | • |  | • |
| • | • | • | • | • | • |  | • | • |  |  | • | • | • |  |  | • |  | • |
| • | • | • | • | • | • | • | • | • |  |  | • | • | • | • |  | • | • | • |
| • | • | • | • |  |  |  | • |  |  |  | • |  | • |  |  | • | • | • |
| • | • | • | • |  | • |  | • |  |  | • | • | • | • |  |  | • | • | • |
|  | • | • |  |  |  |  | • |  |  |  |  | • |  |  |  | • |  |  |
| • | • | • | • | • |  |  | • | • |  |  | • |  | • | • |  | • | • | • |
| • | • |  |  |  | • |  | • |  |  |  | • |  | • |  |  | • |  | • |
| • | • | • | • | • | • |  | • |  |  |  | • | • | • |  |  | • | • | • |
| • | • | • | • | • | • |  | • | • |  |  | • | • | • |  |  | • | • | • |
| • | • | • | • | • | • |  | • | • |  |  | • | • | • |  |  | • | • | • |
| • | • | • | • | • |  |  | • | • | • |  | • | • | • |  |  | • | • | • |
| • | • | • | • | • |  |  | • |  |  |  |  | • | • |  |  | • |  | • |
| • | • | • | • | • | • |  | • | • |  |  | • | • | • | • | • | • | • | • |
| • | • | • | • | • | • |  | • | • |  |  | • | • | • |  |  | • |  | • |
| • | • | • | • | • | • |  | • | • |  |  |  | • | • |  |  | • |  | • |
| • | • | • | • |  | • |  | • |  |  |  |  | • | • |  |  | • |  | • |
|  | • | • | • | • |  |  | • | • |  |  | • |  | • |  |  | • | • |  |
|  | • | • |  |  |  |  |  |  |  |  | • |  | • | • |  | • | • |  |
| • | • | • | • | • | • |  | • | • |  |  |  | • | • |  |  | • |  | • |
| • | • | • |  | • | • |  | • | • |  |  | • | • | • |  | • | • | • |  |
| • | • | • | • |  | • |  | • |  |  |  | • | • | • | • | • | • | • |  |
| • | • | • | • |  |  |  | • |  |  |  | • | • | • |  |  | • |  |  |
| • | • | • | • | • | • |  | • | • |  |  | • | • | • |  |  | • |  | • |

| | Vacancies | Partners | Total staff | Work placement | Corporate/commercial | General commercial | Niche | General practice | High street/legal aid |
|---|---|---|---|---|---|---|---|---|---|
| McDermott Will & Emery UK LLP | 4 | 605 | 2171 | | • | • | | | |
| Nabarro | 30 | 126 | 945 | ✔ | • | | | | |
| Norton Rose LLP | 55 | 245 | | ✔ | • | | | | |
| Olswang | Up to 24 | 83 | 585 | ✔ | • | | • | | |
| Orrick, Herrington & Sutcliffe | 8 | 14 | 105 | | • | | | | |
| Osborne Clarke | 20 | 109 | 677 | ✔ | • | • | • | | |
| Paul Hastings | 4(09) | 10 | 70 | ✔ | • | | | | |
| Pinsent Masons | 55 | 260 | 1500 | ✔ | • | • | | | |
| Reed Smith Richards Butler LLP | 32 | 108 | 664 | ✔ | • | | | | |
| Royds | 2(09) | 19 | 85 | ✔ | | • | | | |
| Salans | 3-4 | 154 | 1300 | | • | • | | | |
| Shadbolt LLP | 4 | 24 | 104 | ✔ | • | • | • | | |
| Shearman & Sterling LLP | 15 | 29 | 300 | ✔ | • | | | | |
| Sidley Austin | 15 | 38 | 260 | | • | | | | |
| Simmons & Simmons | 50 | 227 | 1980 | ✔ | • | | | | |
| SJ Berwin LLP | 50 | 170 | 1200 | ✔ | • | | | | |
| Skadden, Arps, Slate, Meagher & Flom (UK) LLP | 10 | 23 | 240 | ✔ | • | | | | |
| Slaughter and May | 95 approx | 133 | 1300 | ✔ | • | • | | | |
| Squire, Sanders & Dempsey | 3-4 | 282 | 1720 | ✔ | • | | | | |
| Stephenson Harwood | 12 | 75 | 545 | ✔ | • | | | | |
| Taylor Wessing | 24 | 264 | 1000 | ✔ | • | • | | | |
| Thomas Cooper | 2(09) | 25 | 80 | ✔ | | | • | | |
| Travers Smith | 25 | 66 | | ✔ | • | | | | |
| Trowers & Hamlins | 22 | 106 | 652 | ✔ | • | • | | | |
| Vinson & Elkins RLLP | 2 | 8 | 49 | ✔ | • | | | | |
| Watson, Farley & Williams LLP | 12 | 68 | 450 | ✔ | • | • | | | |
| Weil Gotshal & Manges | 12 | 24 | 242 | ✔ | • | | | | |
| White & Case LLP | 30-35 | 68 | 567 | ✔ | • | | | | |
| Wiggin LLP | 4 | 14 | 83 | | • | | | • | |
| Wilmer Cutler Pickering Hale & Dorr | 2-4(08) | 10 | 90 | | • | | | | |
| Withers LLP | 18 | 100 | 600 | ✔ | • | | | | |

| Arbitration | Banking | Comp/comm | Competition | Construction | Corporate tax | Crime | Employment | Environment | Family | Human rights | Insurance | IP | Litigation | Personal injury | Private client | Property | Shipping | TMT |
|---|---|---|---|---|---|---|---|---|---|---|---|---|---|---|---|---|---|---|
| • | • | • | • |  | • |  | • | • |  |  |  | • | • |  |  |  |  | • |
| • | • | • | • | • | • |  | • | • |  |  |  | • | • | • |  | • |  | • |
| • | • | • | • | • | • |  | • | • |  |  | • | • | • |  |  | • | • | • |
|  | • | • | • | • | • |  | • | • |  |  |  | • | • |  |  | • |  | • |
| • | • | • | • |  | • |  | • |  |  |  |  | • | • |  |  | • |  |  |
| • | • | • | • | • | • |  | • | • |  |  |  | • | • |  | • | • |  | • |
|  | • |  |  |  | • |  |  |  |  |  |  |  |  |  |  | • |  |  |
| • | • | • | • | • | • |  | • | • |  |  | • | • | • |  |  | • |  | • |
| • | • | • | • | • | • |  | • | • |  |  | • | • | • |  |  | • | • | • |
|  |  | • |  |  |  |  | • | • | • | • |  | • | • | • | • | • |  | • |
| • | • | • | • | • |  |  | • | • |  |  |  | • | • |  |  | • | • | • |
| • |  | • | • | • |  |  | • | • |  |  | • | • | • |  |  | • |  | • |
| • | • |  |  |  | • |  | • |  |  |  |  | • | • |  |  | • |  | • |
|  | • |  |  | • | • |  | • |  |  |  | • | • | • |  |  | • |  | • |
| • | • | • | • | • | • |  | • | • |  |  | • | • | • |  |  | • |  | • |
| • | • | • | • | • | • |  | • | • |  |  |  | • | • |  |  | • |  | • |
| • | • | • | • |  | • |  |  |  |  |  |  |  | • |  |  |  |  |  |
| • | • | • | • | • | • |  | • | • |  |  | • | • | • |  |  | • |  | • |
| • | • | • | • |  | • |  | • |  |  |  |  | • | • |  | • | • |  | • |
| • | • | • | • | • | • |  | • | • |  |  | • | • | • |  |  | • | • | • |
| • | • | • | • | • | • |  | • | • | • |  | • | • | • |  | • | • | • | • |
| • | • | • | • | • | • |  | • |  |  |  | • |  | • | • |  |  | • |  |
| • | • | • | • | • | • |  | • | • |  |  | • | • | • |  |  | • |  | • |
|  | • | • | • | • | • |  | • | • |  |  |  | • | • | • | • | • |  |  |
| • | • |  |  | • | • |  | • |  |  |  |  | • | • |  |  | • |  | • |
|  | • | • | • |  | • |  | • |  |  |  |  | • | • |  |  | • | • | • |
|  | • | • | • |  | • |  | • | • |  |  |  | • | • |  | • | • |  | • |
| • | • |  |  | • | • |  | • |  |  |  |  | • | • |  |  | • |  | • |
|  |  | • |  |  |  |  |  |  |  |  |  | • | • |  |  | • |  | • |
|  | • | • |  |  | • |  | • |  |  |  |  | • |  |  |  |  |  | • |
|  | • | • | • |  | • |  | • | • | • |  |  | • | • |  | • | • |  | • |

| | Vacancies | Partners | Total staff | Work placement | Corporate/ commercial | General commercial | Niche | General practice | High street/ legal aid |
|---|---|---|---|---|---|---|---|---|---|
| Abrahams Dresden | 2[08] | 4 | 19 | | • | • | | • | |
| Addie & Co | 0 | 2 | 8 | ✔ | | • | • | • | |
| **Addleshaw Goddard** | 50 | 182 | 1300 | ✔ | • | | | | |
| Ahmed & Co | 0 | 2 | 15 | | | | | | • |
| Alan Edwards & Co | 0 | 5 | 22 | | | | • | | • |
| **Allen & Overy LLP** | 120 | 470 | 4800 | ✔ | • | | | | |
| Alliance Solicitors | 0 | | 5 | ✔ | | | | • | |
| Anthony Gold Solicitors | 4 | 15 | 85 | | | • | | | |
| AP Law | 4 | 2 | 60 | ✔ | • | | • | • | |
| Archon Solicitors | 0 | 4 | 14 | | | | • | | |
| Arlingtons Sharmas Solicitors | Poss[09] | 3 | 14 | ✔ | • | • | | | |
| **Arnold & Porter (UK) LLP** | 2 | 14 | 64 | ✔ | • | • | • | | |
| AS Law Practice | 1[08] | 1 | 4 | ✔ | | | | • | |
| **Ashfords** | 15 | 51 | 450 | ✔ | | | | | |
| **Ashurst** | 55 | 195 | 1650 | ✔ | • | | | | |
| Aston Clark Solicitors | 2 | 3 | 26 | ✔ | | | | • | • |
| Atkins Hope | 0 | 5 | 38 | | | | | • | • |
| Avery Emerson | 1-2[08] | 1 | 6 | ✔ | | | | • | |
| Bains & Co | 0 | 2 | 13 | ✔ | | | • | | |
| **Baker & McKenzie LLP** | 38 | 88 | 722 | ✔ | • | | | | |
| **Barlow Lyde & Gilbert LLP** | 18-20 | 82 | 671 | ✔ | • | • | | | |
| Baron Grey | 0 | 1 | 9 | ✔ | | • | | | |
| Bart-Williams & Co | Poss | 1 | 6 | | | | | • | • |
| Bates, Wells & Braithwaite | 5 | 21 | 130 | ✔ | | • | • | | |
| **Beachcroft LLP** | 30[09] | 147 | 1400 | ✔ | • | • | | • | |
| Beale and Company Solicitors LLP | 2-3 | 11 | 75 | | • | • | • | | |
| **Berrymans Lace Mawer** | 17 | 115 | 792 | ✔ | | • | | | |
| **Berwin Leighton Paisner LLP** | 50 | 180 | 1200 | ✔ | • | • | | | |
| **Bevan Brittan LLP** | 12 | 62 | 520 | ✔ | • | • | | | |
| Bhatt Murphy | 0 | 4 | 16 | | | | • | | |
| Bhogal Partners | 2[09] | 2 | 20 | ✔ | | | | • | • |
| Bindman & Partners | 0 | 14 | 90 | | | | | • | • |
| Bingham McCutchen (London) LLP | 2 | 12 | 80 | | • | | | | |
| **Bircham Dyson Bell LLP** | 8 | 52 | 300 | ✔ | | | | • | |
| **Bird & Bird** | 18 | 148 | 900 | ✔ | • | | | | |
| Birnberg Peirce & Partners | 1[08] | 2 | 29 | | | | | | • |
| Bishop & Sewell LLP | 2[09] | 8 | 52 | | • | • | | • | |
| Blackfords LLP | Poss | 5 | 60 | | | | • | | • |
| **Blake Lapthorn Tarlo Lyons** | 17 | 104 | 700 | ✔ | • | • | | • | |
| Blaser Mills | 2-4[09] | 12 | 100 | | • | • | | • | • |
| **Bond Pearce LLP** | 15 | 74 | 700 | ✔ | • | • | | | |

| Arbitration | Banking | Comp/comm | Competition | Construction | Corporate tax | Crime | Employment | Environment | Family | Human rights | Insurance | IP | Litigation | Personal injury | Private client | Property | Shipping | TMT |
|---|---|---|---|---|---|---|---|---|---|---|---|---|---|---|---|---|---|---|
|  |  | • |  | • |  |  | • |  | • |  |  |  | • |  | • | • |  |  |
|  |  | • |  |  |  |  | • |  |  |  |  | • | • |  | • | • |  |  |
| • | • | • | • | • | • |  | • | • | • |  |  | • | • |  | • | • |  | • |
|  |  |  |  |  | • |  |  |  |  |  |  |  |  |  |  |  |  |  |
|  |  |  |  |  | • |  |  |  |  | • |  |  | • |  | • | • |  |  |
| • | • | • | • | • | • |  | • | • |  |  | • | • | • |  | • | • |  | • |
|  |  |  |  |  |  |  |  |  | • |  |  |  |  | • | • | • |  |  |
| • |  | • |  | • |  |  |  |  | • | • |  |  | • |  | • | • |  | • |
|  |  | • |  |  |  | • | • |  |  |  |  |  | • |  | • | • |  |  |
|  |  |  |  |  |  |  | • |  |  |  |  |  |  |  |  |  |  |  |
| • | • | • |  | • |  |  | • |  |  |  |  | • | • |  | • | • | • | • |
| • | • | • |  | • |  | • |  |  |  |  |  | • | • |  | • | • |  | • |
|  |  | • |  |  |  |  | • |  | • |  |  |  | • |  | • | • |  | • |
| • | • | • | • | • | • | • | • | • |  |  | • | • | • |  | • | • | • | • |
| • | • | • | • | • | • |  | • | • |  |  | • | • | • |  | • | • |  | • |
|  |  | • |  |  |  | • |  |  | • |  |  |  | • | • | • | • |  |  |
|  |  |  |  |  |  | • |  |  |  |  |  |  |  |  | • | • |  |  |
|  |  | • |  |  |  |  | • |  | • |  |  |  | • |  | • | • |  |  |
| • | • | • | • | • | • |  | • | • |  |  | • | • | • |  | • | • |  | • |
| • | • | • | • | • | • |  | • | • |  |  | • | • | • | • | • | • |  | • |
| • | • | • | • | • | • |  | • | • |  |  |  | • | • |  | • | • |  | • |
|  |  | • |  |  |  |  | • | • | • |  |  |  | • | • | • | • |  |  |
| • | • | • | • | • | • |  | • | • |  |  | • | • | • | • | • | • |  | • |
| • | • | • | • | • | • |  | • | • |  |  | • | • | • |  | • | • |  | • |
|  |  |  |  |  |  |  |  |  |  | • |  |  |  |  |  |  |  |  |
|  |  | • |  |  |  |  | • | • |  | • | • |  | • |  | • | • |  |  |
|  |  |  |  |  |  | • | • | • | • | • |  |  | • | • |  | • |  | • |
|  | • |  |  |  |  |  |  |  |  |  |  |  | • |  |  |  |  |  |
|  |  | • | • | • |  |  | • | • | • |  |  | • | • | • | • | • |  |  |
| • | • | • | • |  |  | • | • |  |  |  |  | • | • |  |  | • |  | • |
|  |  |  |  |  |  | • |  |  |  | • |  |  |  |  |  |  |  |  |
|  | • | • |  | • |  |  | • |  | • |  |  | • | • |  | • | • |  | • |
|  |  |  |  |  |  | • |  |  | • |  |  |  |  |  |  |  |  |  |
| • | • | • | • | • | • |  | • | • | • |  | • | • | • | • | • | • | • | • |
|  |  | • |  |  |  | • | • |  | • |  |  |  | • | • | • | • |  |  |
| • | • | • | • | • | • |  | • | • |  |  | • | • | • | • | • | • | • | • |

| | Vacancies | Partners | Total staff | Work placement | Corporate/ commercial | General commercial | Niche | General practice | High street/ legal aid |
|---|---|---|---|---|---|---|---|---|---|
| **Boodle Hatfield** | 8 | 31 | 200 | ✔ | • | • | • | | |
| **BPE** | 1 | 25 | 135 | ✔ | • | | | | |
| Brachers | 2 | 21 | 200 | | • | | | • | |
| Brecher Abram | 1[09] | 12 | 48 | | • | | • | | |
| **Bristows** | Up to 10 | 21 | 180 | ✔ | • | | | | |
| Bross Bennett | 0 | 4 | 16 | | | | • | | |
| Brown Cooper Monier-Williams | 0 | 8 | 20 | | • | • | • | • | |
| **Browne Jacobson LLP** | 12 | 60 | 517 | | • | • | • | | |
| Bryan Cave | 0 | 10 | 82 | ✔ | • | | | | |
| BWF Solicitors | 2 | 2 | 5 | | | | | • | |
| **Cadwalader Wickersham & Taft LLP** | 6-8 | 11 | 160 | | • | | | | |
| Cains Advocates Limited | 2 | 6 | 70 | ✔ | • | • | • | | |
| Caldicotts | 0 | 2 | 14 | | | | | | • |
| Campbell Chambers | 0 | 2 | 10 | | | | • | | • |
| **Campbell Hooper Solicitors LLP** | 5 | 23 | 124 | | • | • | | • | |
| Cannings Connolly | 2[09] | 7 | 28 | | | | • | | |
| **Capsticks** | 4-5 | 32 | 170 | ✔ | | | • | | |
| **Charles Russell LLP** | 20 | 93 | 626 | ✔ | • | • | | | |
| Chhokar & Co | 1[08] | 2 | 13 | | | | | • | |
| **Clarkson Wright & Jakes** | 3 | 14 | 100 | ✔ | • | • | | • | • |
| Claude Hornby & Cox | 1[08] | 2 | 15 | | | | | | • |
| **Cleary Gottlieb Steen & Hamilton LLP** | 10 | 18 | 189 | ✔ | • | | | | |
| **Clifford Chance** | 130 | 236 | 2815 | ✔ | • | • | | | |
| Clifford Harris & Co | 1[09] | 4 | 20 | | • | • | | | |
| Clintons | 3 | 20 | 75 | ✔ | | • | • | | |
| **Clyde & Co LLP** | 24 | 140 | 1080 | ✔ | • | • | | | |
| **CMS Cameron McKenna LLP** | 60 | 131 | 1500 | ✔ | • | • | | | |
| **Cobbetts LLP** | 20 | 136 | 815 | ✔ | • | • | | | |
| **Collyer Bristow LLP** | 3 | 30 | 136 | | • | • | | • | |
| Community Law Clinic Solicitors | 0 | 1 | 12 | | | | | • | • |
| Constant & Constant | 0 | 16 | 64 | | • | • | | | |
| **Covington & Burling LLP** | 6 | 190 | 1300 | ✔ | • | • | • | | |
| **Cripps Harries Hall LLP** | 7 | 41 | 270 | | • | • | | • | |
| Crossmans | 0 | 3 | 22 | | • | • | | • | |
| **Crown Prosecution Service** | 25 | | 9000 | ✔ | | | • | | |
| Cunningtons | Varies[09] | 10 | 180 | ✔ | | | | • | • |
| Curtis Mallet-Prevost Colt & Mosle LLP | 0 | 3 | 12 | | • | | | | |
| Curwens | 2[08] | 15 | 120 | ✔ | | | | • | |
| Darlingtons | 2[08] | 3 | 30 | | | | | • | |
| **Davenport Lyons** | 8 | 37 | 197 | ✔ | | | | | |
| David Phillips & Partners | 2 | 11 | 60 | ✔ | | | | • | • |

| Arbitration | Banking | Comp/comm | Competition | Construction | Corporate tax | Crime | Employment | Environment | Family | Human rights | Insurance | IP | Litigation | Personal injury | Private client | Property | Shipping | TMT |
|---|---|---|---|---|---|---|---|---|---|---|---|---|---|---|---|---|---|---|
|  |  | • |  | • | • |  | • |  | • |  |  |  | • |  | • | • |  |  |
|  |  | • |  | • |  |  | • |  |  |  | • |  | • | • | • | • |  |  |
|  |  | • |  |  |  |  | • | • | • |  |  |  | • | • | • | • |  |  |
| • |  | • |  |  | • |  | • | • |  |  |  |  | • |  | • | • |  |  |
| • |  | • | • |  | • |  | • | • |  |  |  | • | • |  | • | • |  | • |
|  |  |  |  |  |  |  |  |  | • |  |  |  |  |  |  |  |  |  |
|  |  | • | • |  |  |  | • |  |  |  |  |  | • |  | • | • |  |  |
| • | • | • |  | • | • |  | • | • |  |  | • |  | • | • | • | • |  | • |
|  | • | • | • |  | • |  | • |  |  |  | • | • | • | • | • | • |  |  |
|  |  |  |  |  |  |  |  |  | • |  |  |  |  |  | • | • |  |  |
|  | • |  |  |  |  |  |  |  |  |  | • |  |  |  |  | • |  | • |
|  | • | • |  |  |  |  | • |  |  |  | • | • | • |  | • | • | • | • |
|  |  |  |  |  | • | • | • |  | • |  |  |  |  |  | • |  |  |  |
|  |  |  |  |  |  | • | • |  | • |  |  |  |  |  |  |  |  |  |
| • |  | • | • |  | • | • | • | • | • |  | • | • | • |  | • | • |  |  |
|  |  | • |  | • |  |  | • |  |  |  |  |  | • |  |  | • |  |  |
| • |  | • | • | • |  |  | • | • |  |  |  | • | • | • | • | • |  | • |
| • | • | • | • | • | • |  | • | • | • |  | • | • | • | • | • | • |  | • |
|  |  | • |  |  |  |  | • |  | • | • |  |  | • |  | • | • |  | • |
| • |  | • |  | • |  |  | • |  | • |  |  |  | • | • | • | • |  |  |
| • |  | • |  |  |  | • | • |  |  |  | • |  | • |  |  |  |  | • |
| • | • | • | • | • |  | • | • | • |  |  |  | • | • |  |  | • | • | • |
|  | • | • |  |  |  |  | • |  | • |  |  |  | • |  | • | • |  |  |
| • |  | • |  |  |  |  | • |  | • |  |  | • | • | • | • | • |  | • |
|  | • | • | • | • | • |  | • | • |  |  | • | • | • | • | • | • | • | • |
| • | • | • | • | • | • |  | • | • |  |  | • | • | • | • | • | • | • | • |
| • | • | • | • | • |  |  | • | • |  |  |  | • | • |  | • |  |  | • |
| • | • | • | • |  |  |  | • | • | • |  | • | • | • | • | • | • |  | • |
|  |  |  |  |  |  |  | • | • |  |  |  |  |  |  |  |  |  |  |
| • | • | • | • |  |  |  | • |  |  |  | • |  | • |  |  | • | • | • |
| • | • | • |  |  | • |  | • |  |  | • | • | • | • |  |  |  |  | • |
| • |  | • |  | • | • |  | • | • | • |  | • | • | • |  | • | • |  | • |
|  |  | • |  | • |  |  | • |  | • |  |  |  |  | • | • | • |  |  |
|  |  |  |  |  | • |  |  |  |  |  |  |  |  |  |  |  |  |  |
|  |  | • |  |  |  |  | • |  | • |  |  |  |  | • |  | • |  |  |
|  | • | • |  |  |  |  | • |  |  |  |  | • |  |  |  |  |  |  |
|  |  | • | • |  |  |  | • |  | • |  |  |  | • | • | • | • |  |  |
|  |  | • |  |  |  |  | • |  | • |  |  |  | • |  |  |  |  |  |
|  | • | • |  |  | • |  | • |  | • |  |  |  | • |  | • | • |  | • |
|  |  |  |  |  | • |  | • |  |  |  |  |  |  | • | • |  |  |  |

| | Vacancies | Partners | Total staff | Work placement | Corporate/ commercial | General commercial | Niche | General practice | High street/ legal aid |
|---|---|---|---|---|---|---|---|---|---|
| **Davies Arnold Cooper** | 5 | 68 | 308 | ✔ | • | • | • | | |
| Davis & Co | 1-2 | 1 | 8 | | | | • | | |
| Dawson Cornwell | 1(09) | 9 | 27 | ✔ | | | • | | |
| **Dawsons LLP** | 4 | 21 | 80 | ✔ | | | | • | |
| **Debevoise & Plimpton LLP** | 6 | 16 | 165 | ✔ | | | | • | |
| **Dechert LLP** | 15 | 37 | 300 | ✔ | • | | | | |
| **Denton Wilde Sapte** | 35 | 165 | 1400 | ✔ | • | • | • | | |
| Devonshires | 4-5(09) | 25 | 170 | | • | | | | |
| Dewar Hogan | 0 | 2 | 6 | | | | • | | |
| **Dickinson Dees LLP** | 15 | 78 | 920 | ✔ | • | • | • | | |
| **DLA Piper UK LLP** | 95+ | 1200 | 7000 | ✔ | • | | | | |
| DMA Legal LLP | 1 | 4 | 15 | | • | • | • | | |
| **DMH Stallard Solicitors** | 10 | 52 | 350 | ✔ | • | • | | | |
| Donald Galbraith & Co | 0 | | 14 | | | | | | • |
| **Dorsey & Whitney** | 4 | 14 | 75 | | • | | | | |
| Druces & Attlee | 1 | 16 | 68 | ✔ | • | • | | | |
| Duncan Lewis & Co | 8 | 15 | 200 | ✔ | | • | | • | • |
| **Dundas & Wilson LLP** | 30 | 83 | 599 | ✔ | • | | | | |
| **EDF Energy** | 0 | | 43 | | • | | | | |
| Edwards Duthie | 6(09) | 20 | 200 | | • | • | | | |
| Edwin Coe LLP | 5 | 25 | 100 | ✔ | • | • | | | |
| **Elborne Mitchell** | 2 | 12 | 41 | | | | • | | |
| Everatts Solicitors | 1 | 2 | 10 | | | | | • | |
| **Eversheds LLP** | 80+ | 340 | 4000 | ✔ | • | • | | | |
| Eversleys | 2 | 2 | 6 | | | • | | | |
| Ewings & Co | Varies(08) | 3 | 25 | | | | | • | • |
| **Faegre & Benson LLP** | 2 | 12 | 55 | ✔ | • | • | | | |
| Fancy & Jackson | 1 | 4 | 21 | | | • | | • | • |
| Faradays Solicitors | 0 | 4 | 17 | | | | | • | • |
| **Farrer & Co LLP** | 10 | 61 | 316 | ✔ | • | • | • | | |
| Fasken Martineau Stringer Saul LLP | 2 | 25 | 95 | | • | • | | | |
| Fellowes | 2 | 3 | 28 | | | | | • | • |
| Fenwick Elliott LLP | 1(08) | | | ✔ | | | • | | |
| **Field Fisher Waterhouse LLP** | 20 | 101 | 640 | ✔ | • | • | | | |
| **Finers Stephens Innocent** | 6 | 36 | 180 | | • | | | | |
| Fisher Meredith | 5+(09) | 9 | 110 | | | | • | | • |
| **Fladgate Fielder** | 6-8 | 42 | 197 | | • | • | | | |
| Fletcher Dervish | 0 | 1 | 20 | | | | | • | • |
| **Forsters LLP** | 5-6 | 29 | 190 | ✔ | | | • | | |
| Fox Williams | 5(08) | 17 | 100 | ✔ | • | • | • | | |
| **Freshfields Bruckhaus Deringer** | 100 | 474 | 5517 | ✔ | • | | | | |

| Arbitration | Banking | Comp/comm | Competition | Construction | Corporate tax | Crime | Employment | Environment | Family | Human rights | Insurance | IP | Litigation | Personal injury | Private client | Property | Shipping | TMT |
|---|---|---|---|---|---|---|---|---|---|---|---|---|---|---|---|---|---|---|
| • | • | • | • | • |  |  | • | • |  |  | • |  | • | • |  | • | • | • |
|  |  |  |  |  |  |  |  |  |  |  | • |  | • |  |  |  | • | • |
|  |  |  |  |  |  |  |  |  | • |  |  |  |  |  | • |  |  |  |
|  |  | • |  | • | • |  | • | • | • |  |  |  | • |  | • | • |  |  |
| • | • |  |  |  | • |  | • |  |  |  | • |  | • |  |  |  |  | • |
| • | • | • | • | • | • |  | • |  |  |  | • | • | • |  |  | • |  | • |
| • | • | • | • | • | • |  | • | • |  |  | • | • | • |  |  | • | • | • |
|  | • | • |  | • |  |  | • |  |  |  |  |  | • | • | • | • |  |  |
|  |  |  |  |  |  |  |  |  |  |  |  |  |  |  |  |  |  |  |
| • | • | • | • | • | • |  | • | • | • |  | • | • | • | • | • |  |  | • |
| • | • | • | • | • | • |  | • | • |  |  | • | • | • |  |  | • | • | • |
|  |  | • | • |  |  |  | • |  |  |  |  | • | • |  |  | • |  | • |
| • | • | • |  | • |  |  | • |  |  |  |  | • | • | • | • | • |  | • |
|  |  |  |  |  |  |  |  |  | • |  |  |  |  |  |  |  |  |  |
| • | • | • | • | • | • |  | • |  |  |  |  |  | • | • | • | • |  | • |
|  | • | • |  | • | • |  | • |  |  |  | • | • | • |  | • | • |  | • |
|  |  |  |  |  |  | • | • |  | • | • |  | • | • |  | • | • |  |  |
| • | • |  | • | • | • |  | • | • |  | • | • | • | • | • |  | • | • | • |
|  |  |  |  |  |  |  |  |  |  |  |  |  |  |  |  |  |  |  |
|  |  |  |  |  |  | • | • |  | • |  |  |  | • | • | • | • |  |  |
| • | • | • | • | • |  |  | • |  |  |  | • | • | • |  | • | • |  | • |
| • |  | • |  |  |  |  | • | • |  |  | • |  | • | • | • | • |  |  |
|  |  |  |  |  |  |  | • | • | • |  |  | • | • |  | • |  |  |  |
| • | • | • | • | • | • |  | • | • |  | • | • | • | • |  |  | • | • | • |
|  |  |  |  |  |  | • |  |  | • |  |  |  |  |  |  | • | • |  |
| • | • | • | • | • |  |  | • |  |  |  |  | • | • |  | • | • |  | • |
| • |  |  |  |  |  |  | • | • |  |  |  |  | • | • | • | • |  |  |
|  |  |  |  |  |  | • | • |  | • |  |  |  |  | • | • | • |  |  |
| • | • | • | • | • | • |  | • | • |  |  | • | • | • |  | • | • |  | • |
| • | • | • | • |  | • |  | • |  |  |  |  | • | • | • | • | • | • | • |
|  |  |  |  |  |  | • |  |  | • |  |  |  | • |  | • | • |  |  |
| • |  |  | • |  |  |  | • |  |  |  |  |  | • |  |  |  |  |  |
| • | • | • | • | • | • |  | • | • |  |  | • | • | • | • | • | • |  | • |
| • | • | • | • |  | • |  | • |  |  |  |  | • | • | • | • | • |  | • |
|  |  |  |  |  |  | • | • |  | • | • |  |  | • |  | • |  |  |  |
| • | • | • | • | • | • |  | • | • |  |  | • | • | • |  | • | • |  | • |
|  |  |  |  |  |  | • |  |  | • |  |  |  | • | • | • | • |  |  |
|  |  | • |  |  | • |  | • |  | • |  |  |  | • |  | • | • |  |  |
| • |  | • | • |  | • |  | • |  |  |  |  | • | • |  | • | • |  | • |
| • | • | • | • | • | • |  | • | • |  |  | • | • | • |  | • | • |  | • |

| | Vacancies | Partners | Total staff | Work placement | Corporate/ commercial | General commercial | Niche | General practice | High street/ legal aid |
|---|---|---|---|---|---|---|---|---|---|
| Gersten & Nixon | 0 | 3 | 15 | | | • | | | |
| Gill & Co | 1[08] | 2 | 14 | | | | | • | • |
| Glovers | 2 | 14 | 46 | | | • | | | |
| **Goodman Derrick LLP** | 3 | 21 | 90 | | • | • | • | • | |
| Goodman Ray | 0 | 4 | 17 | | | | • | | • |
| Gordon Dadds | 2 | 10 | 45 | | • | • | | • | |
| **Government Legal Service** | 22-30 | | 1950 | ✔ | • | • | | • | |
| Greenwich Community Law Centre | 0 | | 12 | | | | | | • |
| Gregory Rowcliffe Milners | 1[09] | 13 | 55 | | | | | • | |
| GSC Solicitors | 2[08] | 8 | 38 | | • | • | | • | |
| GT Stewart Solicitors | 1-2[09] | 1 | 21 | | | | • | | • |
| **Halliwells LLP** | 38 | 165 | 1300 | ✔ | • | • | | | |
| **Hammonds** | 40 | 189 | 1300 | ✔ | • | | | | |
| Harbottle & Lewis LLP | 4 | 24 | 170 | | • | • | • | | |
| Harper & Odell | 0 | 2 | 5 | | | • | | | |
| Harris Cartier LLP | 2[08] | 9 | 100 | | • | • | • | • | |
| Harris Waters & Co | 1[08] | 2 | 11 | ✔ | • | • | | • | • |
| Harrow Solicitors & Advocates | 0 | 4 | 33 | ✔ | | • | | | |
| **HBJ Gateley Wareing LLP** | 11 | 75 | 488 | ✔ | • | • | | | |
| HCL Hanne & Co | 1-2[08] | 7 | 50 | | | | | • | • |
| Hempsons | 6 | 30 | 300 | | | | • | | |
| **Herbert Smith LLP** | Up to 100 | 233 | 2200 | ✔ | • | | | | |
| **Hextalls LLP** | 2 | 20 | 100 | ✔ | | | • | | |
| **Hill Dickinson LLP** | 17 | 152 | 1000 | ✔ | • | • | • | | |
| Hilliers HRW | 2[08] | 5 | 55 | | • | • | | • | • |
| HKH Kenwright & Cox | 0 | 2 | 19 | ✔ | • | | | • | • |
| Hodders | 0 | 4 | 65 | | • | • | | • | • |
| **Hodge Jones & Allen** | 7 | 18 | 180 | ✔ | | | • | • | |
| Hogan & Hartson | 2-3 | 20 | 115 | | • | • | | | |
| **Holman Fenwick & Willan** | 10 | 88 | 500 | ✔ | • | • | • | | |
| **Howard Kennedy** | 4 | 75 | 335 | | • | • | | | |
| Hunters | 2 | 21 | 81 | ✔ | | | | • | |
| Hunton & Williams | 2 | 9 | 51 | | • | | | | |
| Ikie Solicitors | 0 | 2 | 5 | | | | | | • |
| **Ince & Co** | 12 | 79 | 462 | ✔ | | | • | | |
| **Irwin Mitchell** | 20-25 | 137 | 2000 | ✔ | • | • | | • | |
| JA Forrest & Co | 0 | 1 | 3 | ✔ | | • | • | • | |
| Jay Vadher & Co | 1[09] | 3 | 8 | | | • | | • | • |
| **Jeffrey Green Russell** | 1-2 | 18 | 120 | | • | | | • | |
| Joachim G Remde Solicitors | 0 | | 2 | | | | • | | |
| Joelson Wilson & Co | 2[08] | 7 | 45 | | • | • | • | | |

| Arbitration | Banking | Comp/comm | Competition | Construction | Corporate tax | Crime | Employment | Environment | Family | Human rights | Insurance | IP | Litigation | Personal injury | Private client | Property | Shipping | TMT |
|---|---|---|---|---|---|---|---|---|---|---|---|---|---|---|---|---|---|---|
|  |  | • |  |  |  |  | • | • | • |  |  | • | • |  | • | • |  | • |
|  |  |  |  |  |  | • |  |  | • |  |  |  | • |  | • | • |  |  |
| • | • | • |  | • |  |  | • |  |  |  |  |  | • |  | • | • |  |  |
| • | • | • | • | • | • |  | • |  |  |  |  | • | • | • | • | • |  | • |
|  |  |  |  |  |  |  | • |  |  |  |  |  |  |  |  |  |  |  |
|  |  | • |  | • |  |  | • |  | • |  |  | • | • |  | • | • |  |  |
| • | • | • | • | • | • | • | • | • | • | • | • | • | • | • | • | • | • | • |
|  |  |  |  |  |  |  | • |  |  |  |  |  |  |  |  |  |  |  |
|  |  | • | • |  |  |  | • |  | • |  |  | • | • |  | • | • |  | • |
| • | • | • |  |  |  |  | • |  |  |  |  | • | • |  | • | • |  | • |
|  |  |  |  |  |  | • |  |  |  | • |  |  |  |  |  |  |  |  |
|  | • | • | • | • | • |  | • | • | • |  | • | • | • |  | • | • | • | • |
| • | • | • | • | • | • |  | • | • |  |  |  | • | • |  | • | • |  |  |
|  |  | • | • |  |  |  | • |  | • |  |  | • | • |  |  | • |  | • |
|  |  |  |  |  |  |  |  |  |  |  |  |  | • | • |  | • |  |  |
|  |  | • |  |  |  |  | • |  | • |  |  |  | • | • | • | • |  |  |
|  |  | • |  |  |  |  | • |  | • |  |  |  | • |  | • | • |  |  |
|  |  |  |  |  |  | • | • |  |  |  |  |  |  |  | • |  |  |  |
| • | • | • | • | • | • |  | • | • |  |  |  | • | • |  | • | • | • | • |
|  |  |  |  |  |  | • | • | • | • |  |  |  |  | • | • |  |  |  |
|  |  | • |  | • |  |  | • |  |  |  |  | • | • | • | • | • |  |  |
| • | • | • | • | • | • |  | • | • |  |  | • | • | • | • | • | • |  | • |
| • | • | • | • | • |  |  | • |  |  |  | • | • | • | • | • | • | • | • |
| • | • | • | • | • | • | • | • |  | • |  |  | • | • |  | • | • | • | • |
|  |  | • |  | • | • |  | • |  | • |  |  | • | • | • | • | • |  |  |
|  |  |  |  |  |  | • | • |  | • |  |  | • | • |  | • | • |  | • |
|  |  | • |  |  |  |  | • |  | • |  |  |  | • |  | • | • |  |  |
| • |  |  |  |  |  | • |  |  | • | • |  |  | • | • |  | • |  |  |
| • | • | • | • |  | • |  | • |  |  |  |  |  | • |  |  | • |  | • |
| • |  | • | • | • |  |  | • | • |  |  | • |  | • |  |  | • | • |  |
| • | • | • |  | • | • |  | • |  | • |  | • |  | • |  | • | • |  | • |
|  |  | • |  |  |  |  | • |  | • |  |  |  | • | • | • | • |  |  |
|  | • | • | • | • | • |  | • | • |  |  |  |  | • |  |  |  |  | • |
|  |  |  |  |  |  | • | • |  | • |  |  |  |  |  | • | • |  |  |
| • |  | • | • |  |  |  |  |  |  |  |  | • |  | • | • |  | • |  |
| • |  | • | • | • |  |  | • | • | • | • | • | • | • | • | • | • |  | • |
| • |  | • | • |  |  |  | • |  | • |  |  | • | • | • | • | • |  | • |
|  |  | • |  |  |  |  |  |  | • |  |  |  | • | • | • | • |  |  |
| • | • | • |  | • |  |  | • |  | • |  |  | • | • |  | • | • |  | • |
|  | • |  | • |  |  |  |  |  |  |  |  |  |  |  | • |  |  |  |
|  |  | • | • |  |  | • |  |  | • |  |  |  | • | • |  | • |  | • |

| | Vacancies | Partners | Total staff | Work placement | Corporate/commercial | General commercial | Niche | General practice | High street/legal aid |
|---|---|---|---|---|---|---|---|---|---|
| John Chapman and Co | 0 | 4 | 22 | | | | | • | • |
| **Jones Day** | 15-20 | 45 | 371 | ✔ | • | | | | |
| JR Jones Solicitors | 2 | 3 | 39 | ✔ | | | | • | • |
| Kaim Todner | 2(09) | 7 | 80 | ✔ | | | | • | • |
| KCP Law | 0-2 | 1 | 3 | | | • | | • | • |
| **Kendall Freeman** | 7 | 19 | 145 | ✔ | • | • | | | |
| **Kennedys** | 10(08) | 90 | 530 | | • | • | • | | |
| Kenneth Elliott & Rowe | Poss(09) | 10 | 65 | ✔ | • | • | | | |
| Kingsley Napley | 0 | 36 | 160 | | • | | | • | • |
| **Kirkland & Ellis** | 4 | 523 | 3000 | ✔ | • | | | | |
| **Kirkpatrick & Lockhart Preston Gates Ellis LLP** | Up to 15 | 54 | 301 | ✔ | • | • | | | |
| Kotecha & Co | 1 | 2 | 5 | | | • | | | |
| KSB Law | 2 | 22 | 111 | ✔ | | • | | • | |
| KSL Solicitors | 0 | | | ✔ | | | | • | |
| Laderman and Co | Poss | 2 | 13 | | • | • | | • | |
| Lane & Partners | 2 | 19 | 70 | | • | • | • | | |
| **Latham & Watkins** | 10-15 | 38 | 265 | ✔ | • | | | | |
| **Lawrence Graham LLP** | 20-25 | 85 | 500 | ✔ | • | • | | | |
| **Laytons** | 6 | 34 | 170 | ✔ | • | • | | | |
| **LeBoeuf Lamb Greene & MacRae** | 15 | 35 | 220 | ✔ | • | • | | | |
| **Lee Bolton & Lee** | 3 | 13 | 85 | | | • | • | • | |
| Leigh Day & Co | 0 | 18 | 90 | ✔ | | | | • | |
| **Lester Aldridge** | 6 | 31 | 300 | ✔ | • | • | | | |
| **Lewis Silkin LLP** | 5 | 45 | 245 | ✔ | • | • | | | |
| **Linklaters LLP** | 130 | 500 | 5000 | ✔ | • | | | | |
| **Lovells LLP** | 90 | 319 | 3000 | ✔ | • | | | | |
| Luqmani Thompson & Partners | 0-1 | 3 | 5 | | | | | | • |
| Lyons Davidson | 5-7 | 31 | 750 | ✔ | • | • | | • | • |
| M Olubi Solicitors | 2 | | | ✔ | | | | | |
| **Macfarlanes** | 30 | 72 | 528 | ✔ | • | | | | |
| Mackrell Turner Garrett | 2 | 13 | 60 | | • | | | | |
| **Maclay Murray & Spens LLP** | 30 | 2 | 550 | ✔ | • | | | | |
| Macleish Littlestone Cowan | 1(08) | 6 | 34 | | • | • | | | |
| MacRae & Co | Poss | 3 | 7 | | | | • | | |
| **Magrath & Co** | 2(09) | 11 | 60 | | | • | • | | |
| Malik & Malik | 2(08) | 2 | 15 | ✔ | | | | • | • |
| Malletts | 1-2(08) | 6 | 34 | ✔ | • | | • | | • |
| **Manches LLP** | 10 | 60 | 290 | ✔ | • | • | • | | |
| Maples Teesdale | 2 | 9 | 47 | | | | • | | |
| Marriott Harrison | 1-2(09) | 13 | 54 | | • | • | • | | |

| Arbitration | Banking | Comp/comm | Competition | Construction | Corporate tax | Crime | Employment | Environment | Family | Human rights | Insurance | IP | Litigation | Personal injury | Private client | Property | Shipping | TMT |
|---|---|---|---|---|---|---|---|---|---|---|---|---|---|---|---|---|---|---|
| • | • | • | • | • | • |  | • | • | • |  | • | • | • | • |  | • |  | • |
|  |  |  |  |  |  | • | • |  | • |  |  |  |  | • | • | • |  |  |
|  |  |  |  |  |  | • |  |  | • |  |  |  |  |  |  |  |  |  |
|  |  | • |  |  |  | • |  |  |  |  |  |  | • |  | • | • |  | • |
| • | • | • |  |  |  |  | • | • |  |  | • |  | • |  |  |  |  |  |
| • | • | • |  | • |  |  | • | • |  |  | • | • | • | • | • | • | • |  |
|  |  | • |  |  |  |  | • | • | • |  |  | • | • | • | • | • | • |  |
|  |  | • |  | • |  | • | • | • | • |  |  | • | • | • | • | • |  | • |
| • | • | • | • |  | • |  | • |  |  |  |  | • | • |  |  |  |  |  |
| • | • | • | • | • | • |  | • | • |  |  | • | • | • |  |  | • |  | • |
|  |  |  |  |  |  |  |  |  | • |  |  |  |  | • |  | • |  |  |
| • |  | • |  |  |  |  | • |  | • |  | • | • | • |  | • | • | • |  |
|  |  |  |  |  |  |  | • |  | • |  |  |  |  |  | • | • |  |  |
|  |  | • |  |  |  |  | • |  | • |  |  |  | • |  | • | • |  |  |
| • |  | • | • | • |  |  | • |  |  |  | • | • | • |  |  | • |  | • |
| • | • | • | • |  | • |  | • |  |  |  |  | • | • |  |  | • |  | • |
| • | • | • | • | • | • |  | • | • |  |  | • | • | • |  |  | • | • | • |
| • | • | • | • | • | • |  | • | • | • |  | • | • | • |  |  | • | • | • |
| • | • | • | • | • | • |  | • | • |  |  | • | • | • |  |  | • | • | • |
|  |  | • |  |  |  |  | • | • |  |  |  | • | • | • | • | • |  |  |
|  |  |  |  |  |  |  |  | • |  | • |  |  |  | • |  |  |  |  |
| • | • | • | • | • | • |  | • | • | • |  | • | • | • | • |  | • |  | • |
| • |  | • |  | • |  |  | • |  |  |  |  |  | • | • |  | • |  | • |
| • | • | • | • | • |  |  | • | • |  |  | • | • | • |  |  | • |  | • |
| • | • | • | • | • | • |  | • | • |  |  |  | • | • |  |  | • |  | • |
| • | • | • | • | • |  |  | • | • | • |  | • | • | • | • | • | • |  | • |
|  |  |  |  |  |  | • | • |  | • |  |  |  | • | • | • |  |  |  |
| • |  | • | • | • | • |  | • | • |  |  | • | • | • |  | • | • |  | • |
|  |  | • |  |  |  |  | • |  | • |  |  | • | • |  | • | • |  | • |
|  | • | • | • | • | • |  | • |  |  |  |  | • | • |  | • | • |  | • |
| • | • | • |  | • | • |  | • |  | • |  | • | • | • | • | • | • |  |  |
|  | • | • | • | • |  |  | • |  |  |  |  |  | • | • |  | • |  | • |
|  | • |  |  |  |  |  | • |  |  |  |  |  | • |  |  | • |  | • |
|  |  |  |  |  |  | • |  |  |  |  |  |  |  | • |  |  |  |  |
|  | • | • |  |  |  | • |  |  | • |  |  |  | • |  |  |  |  |  |
|  | • | • | • | • | • |  | • | • | • |  | • | • | • |  | • | • |  | • |
|  |  | • |  | • |  |  | • |  |  |  |  |  |  |  |  | • |  |  |
|  |  | • |  |  |  |  | • |  |  |  |  |  | • | • |  | • | • | • |

# London continued

| | Vacancies | Partners | Total staff | Work placement | Corporate/ commercial | General commercial | Niche | General practice | High street/ legal aid |
|---|---|---|---|---|---|---|---|---|---|
| Martin Murray & Associates | 0 | 6 | 70 | | | | | • | • |
| Martin Shepherd & Co | 1(08) | 6 | 35 | | | | | • | |
| **Martineau Johnson** | 10-12 | 42 | 270 | ✔ | • | | | | |
| **Matthew Arnold & Baldwin** | 4(09) | 32 | 265 | | • | • | | | |
| Max Bitel Greene | 1 | 7 | 19 | | • | • | • | • | |
| **Maxwell Winward LLP** | 4(09) | 21 | 100 | | | | • | | |
| **Mayer Brown International LLP** | 25-30 | 101 | 625 | ✔ | • | • | | | |
| **McDermott Will & Emery UK LLP** | 4 | 605 | 2171 | | • | • | | | |
| **McGrigors LLP** | 35-40 | 78 | 639 | ✔ | • | | | | |
| Meldrum Young Solicitors | 4 | 4 | 106 | ✔ | | | | | • |
| **Memery Crystal LLP** | 5-6 | 21 | 107 | | • | • | • | | |
| Merriman White | 0 | 2 | 40 | ✔ | • | • | | • | |
| Meyrick Mills | Poss | 5 | 7 | | | | | | |
| **Michelmores** | 10 | 32 | 286 | ✔ | | • | | | |
| Middleton Potts | 1 | 12 | 45 | | • | • | • | | |
| **Mills & Reeve LLP** | 22 | 79 | 760 | ✔ | • | • | • | | |
| **Mishcon de Reya** | 10-12 | 55 | 267 | ✔ | • | • | | • | |
| Monro Fisher Wasbrough | 1(09) | 7 | 40 | | | | • | | |
| Morrison & Foerster | 3 | 16 | 95 | ✔ | • | | | | |
| **Nabarro** | 30 | 126 | 945 | ✔ | • | | | | |
| Nandy & Co | 0 | | | | | | | • | |
| **Norton Rose LLP** | 55 | 245 | | ✔ | • | | | | |
| **Olswang** | Up to 24 | 83 | 585 | ✔ | • | | • | | |
| Orchard Brayton Graham LLP | 4 | 10 | 49 | ✔ | • | • | | | |
| **Orrick, Herrington & Sutcliffe** | 8 | 14 | 105 | | • | | | | |
| **Osborne Clarke** | 20 | 109 | 677 | ✔ | • | • | | | |
| Osbornes | 3 | 7 | 57 | ✔ | | | | • | • |
| Osmond & Osmond | 0 | 2 | 8 | ✔ | • | • | | | |
| Ozoran Turkan | 2 | 3 | 20 | | | | | • | • |
| Parabis Law LLP | 3(09) | 21 | 263 | | | | • | | |
| **Paul Hastings** | 4(09) | 10 | 70 | ✔ | • | | | | |
| Payne Hicks Beach | 3 | 29 | 140 | | | | | • | |
| Pemberton Greenish | 2 | 14 | 65 | | | | • | | |
| **Penningtons Solicitors LLP** | 14 | 70 | 420 | ✔ | • | • | | | |
| Peter Brown & Co | 0 | 3 | 15 | | • | • | | • | |
| Peters & Peters | 2 | 12 | 70 | | | | • | | |
| **Pinsent Masons** | 55 | 260 | 1500 | ✔ | • | • | | | |
| **Piper Smith Watton LLP** | 2 | 8 | 50 | | • | • | • | | |
| Pitmans | 6 | 28 | 210 | ✔ | • | • | • | | |
| Pothecary Witham Weld | 2(08) | 8 | 48 | | | | • | | |
| Portner and Jaskel LLP | 1 | 7 | 80 | | | • | • | • | |

| | Arbitration | Banking | Comp/comm | Competition | Construction | Corporate tax | Crime | Employment | Environment | Family | Human rights | Insurance | IP | Litigation | Personal injury | Private client | Property | Shipping | TMT |
|---|---|---|---|---|---|---|---|---|---|---|---|---|---|---|---|---|---|---|---|
| | | | | | | | • | | | • | | | | | | | | | |
| | | | • | | | | | • | | • | | | | • | • | • | • | | |
| | • | • | • | • | • | • | | • | • | • | | | • | • | • | | • | | • |
| | • | • | • | • | • | • | | • | | • | | • | • | • | • | | • | | • |
| | | | • | | | | | • | | • | | | • | • | | | • | | • |
| | • | • | • | | • | | | • | | • | | | | • | | | • | | |
| | • | • | • | • | • | • | | • | | • | | • | • | • | • | | • | | • |
| | • | • | • | | • | • | | • | | • | | | | • | | | • | | • |
| | | | • | • | | | • | | | | | | | • | • | • | • | | |
| | • | | • | | • | • | | • | | • | | | • | • | | | • | | • |
| | | | • | | • | | | • | | | • | | • | • | • | • | • | | |
| | • | | • | | • | | | • | • | • | | | • | • | | • | • | | |
| | • | • | • | • | • | | | • | | | | • | • | • | • | | • | | • |
| | • | • | • | • | | | | • | • | • | | • | • | • | • | | • | | • |
| | • | • | • | | • | | | • | | • | | | • | • | • | • | • | | • |
| | | | | | | | | | | • | | | | | • | • | • | | |
| | | • | • | | | | | • | | | | | • | • | | | • | | • |
| | • | • | • | • | • | • | | • | • | | | | • | • | • | | • | | • |
| | | | | | | | | | | • | • | | | | | | | | |
| | • | • | • | • | • | | | • | | | | • | • | • | | | • | • | • |
| | • | • | • | • | • | | | • | | • | | | • | • | | | • | | • |
| | • | • | • | • | | | • | • | | | | • | • | • | | | • | | • |
| | • | • | • | • | | | | • | | | | | | • | | | • | | |
| | • | • | • | • | • | • | | • | • | | | | • | • | | • | • | | • |
| | | | | | | | | | | • | | | | • | • | • | • | | |
| | • | • | • | | | | | • | | | | | • | • | • | • | • | | |
| | | | | | | | | | | • | | | | | • | • | • | | |
| | | | | | | | | | | • | | | | | | • | • | | |
| | | | • | | | • | | • | | | | | | | | | • | | |
| | | | • | | | | | • | | • | | | • | • | | • | • | | • |
| | | | • | | | | | | | | | | | | | • | • | | |
| | | • | • | • | • | • | | • | • | • | | | • | • | • | • | • | | • |
| | | | • | | | | | | | | | | | | | • | • | | • |
| | | | | | • | | • | | | | | | | • | | | • | | |
| | • | • | • | • | • | • | | • | • | | | • | • | • | | | • | | • |
| | | • | | | | | | • | | • | | | • | • | • | | • | | |
| | • | | • | | • | | | • | | | | | | • | • | | • | | |
| | | • | | | | | | • | | • | | | | | | • | • | | |
| | | | • | | | | | • | | | | | | • | • | • | • | | |

| | Vacancies | Partners | Total staff | Work placement | Corporate/commercial | General commercial | Niche | General practice | High street/legal aid |
|---|---|---|---|---|---|---|---|---|---|
| Powell Spencer & Partners | Poss 2 | 7 | 75 | ✔ | | | | | • |
| **PricewaterhouseCoopers Legal LLP** | 9 | 13 | 135 | ✔ | • | | | | |
| **Pritchard Englefield** | 3-4 | 23 | 83 | ✔ | • | • | • | • | |
| The Projects Partnership Limited | Poss | 3 | 15 | | | | • | | |
| Punatar & Co | Varies | 5 | 24 | ✔ | | | | | • |
| **RadcliffesLeBrasseur** | 5 | 42 | 210 | ✔ | • | • | | • | |
| Ratna & Co | Poss | 2 | 7 | | | | | • | • |
| Rawal & Co | 0 | 1 | 7 | | | | | • | • |
| **Reed Smith Richards Butler LLP** | 32 | 108 | 664 | ✔ | • | | | | |
| Renaissance Solicitors | 1 | 2 | | ✔ | | | | • | |
| Reynolds Colman Bradley LLP | 1 | 3 | 7 | ✔ | | | • | | |
| **Reynolds Porter Chamberlain LLP** | 15 | 65 | 500 | ✔ | • | • | | | |
| Robin Simon LLP | 2[08] | 10 | 50 | | | | • | | |
| Rochman Landau | 1[08] | 11 | 50 | | • | • | | • | |
| **Rooks Rider** | 0[09] | 17 | 85 | | • | • | • | | |
| Rosenblatt | 4 | 13 | 90 | ✔ | • | | | | |
| Rosling King Solicitors | 3 | 9 | 75 | | | | • | | |
| Royds | 2[09] | 19 | 85 | ✔ | | • | | | |
| Russell & Co | 1 | 2 | 10 | ✔ | | • | • | | |
| Russell Jones & Walker | 10 | 49 | 630 | | | • | • | • | • |
| **Russell-Cooke** | 8 | 42 | 310 | | • | • | • | | |
| **Salans** | 3-4 | 154 | 1300 | | • | • | | | |
| Samy & Co Solicitors | 0 | | | | | | | • | • |
| SB Solicitors | 0 | 2 | 4 | ✔ | | | | • | |
| Schillings | 2 | 6 | 34 | ✔ | • | • | • | | |
| Seddons | 2[08] | 16 | 62 | | • | • | | | |
| The Sethi Partnership Solicitors | 0 | 2 | 25 | ✔ | | • | | | |
| **Shadbolt LLP** | 4 | 24 | 104 | ✔ | • | • | • | | |
| **Sharpe Pritchard** | 3 | 18 | 65 | | | | • | | |
| **Shearman & Sterling LLP** | 15 | 29 | 300 | ✔ | • | | | | |
| Sheikh & Co | 2 | 3 | 28 | ✔ | | | • | • | |
| Shepherd Harris & Co | 1 | 2 | 30 | | | • | • | • | |
| Shranks | 0 | 2 | 9 | | | • | • | | |
| **Sidley Austin** | 15 | 38 | 260 | | • | | | | |
| Silverman Sherliker LLP | 3[08] | 9 | 28 | | • | • | | | |
| **Simmons & Simmons** | 50 | 227 | 1980 | ✔ | • | | | | |
| **SJ Berwin LLP** | 50 | 170 | 1200 | ✔ | • | | | | |
| **Skadden, Arps, Slate, Meagher & Flom (UK) LLP** | 10 | 23 | 240 | ✔ | • | | | | |
| **Slaughter and May** | 95 approx | 133 | 1300 | ✔ | • | • | | | |
| Sonn Macmillan | 2[08] | 2 | 12 | | | | | | • |

| Arbitration | Banking | Comp/comm | Competition | Construction | Corporate tax | Crime | Employment | Environment | Family | Human rights | Insurance | IP | Litigation | Personal injury | Private client | Property | Shipping | TMT |
|---|---|---|---|---|---|---|---|---|---|---|---|---|---|---|---|---|---|---|
|  |  |  |  |  |  | • |  |  | • | • |  |  |  | • |  |  |  |  |
|  |  | • |  |  | • |  | • |  |  |  |  | • | • |  | • | • |  |  |
| • | • | • |  | • |  |  | • | • | • |  | • | • | • |  | • | • |  | • |
|  |  | • |  | • |  |  |  |  | • | • |  |  |  |  |  | • |  |  |
| • | • | • | • | • | • | • | • | • | • |  | • | • | • | • | • | • |  | • |
|  |  |  |  |  |  |  | • |  | • |  |  |  |  |  |  | • |  |  |
|  |  |  |  |  |  |  | • |  | • |  |  |  |  |  |  | • |  |  |
| • | • | • | • | • | • |  | • | • |  |  | • | • | • |  | • | • | • | • |
|  |  |  |  |  |  |  |  |  | • |  |  |  |  |  |  | • |  |  |
| • |  |  |  | • |  |  |  |  |  |  | • |  | • |  |  |  |  | • |
|  |  | • |  | • | • |  | • |  | • |  | • | • | • | • | • | • |  | • |
|  |  |  |  |  |  |  |  |  |  |  | • |  |  |  |  |  |  |  |
| • |  | • |  | • |  |  | • |  | • |  |  | • | • | • | • | • |  | • |
|  | • | • | • | • | • |  | • | • | • |  |  | • | • |  | • | • |  | • |
|  |  | • |  |  |  |  | • |  |  |  |  | • | • | • | • | • |  | • |
| • | • | • |  | • |  |  | • | • |  |  | • | • | • | • | • | • |  | • |
|  |  | • |  |  |  |  | • |  | • | • |  | • | • | • | • | • |  | • |
|  |  |  |  |  |  |  | • |  |  |  |  | • | • | • | • | • |  | • |
|  |  | • |  |  | • | • | • | • | • | • |  | • | • | • | • | • |  | • |
| • |  | • |  | • | • | • | • |  | • |  |  | • | • | • | • | • |  | • |
| • | • | • | • | • |  |  | • | • |  |  |  | • | • |  |  | • | • | • |
|  |  |  |  |  |  | • |  |  |  |  |  |  | • |  | • |  |  |  |
| • |  |  |  | • |  |  |  |  |  |  |  |  |  |  |  |  |  |  |
|  |  |  |  |  |  |  |  |  |  |  |  | • | • |  |  |  |  | • |
| • |  | • |  |  |  |  | • |  |  |  |  | • | • | • | • | • | • | • |
|  |  | • |  |  |  |  | • | • |  | • |  | • | • |  |  | • |  | • |
| • |  | • | • | • | • |  | • | • |  |  | • | • | • |  |  | • |  | • |
| • |  |  |  | • |  |  | • | • |  |  |  | • | • |  | • | • |  | • |
| • | • |  | • |  |  |  | • |  |  |  |  | • | • |  |  | • |  | • |
|  |  |  |  |  |  | • |  |  | • |  |  |  | • |  |  | • |  |  |
|  |  | • |  |  |  | • | • |  | • |  |  |  |  | • | • | • |  |  |
|  |  | • |  |  |  |  |  |  | • |  |  | • | • | • | • | • |  |  |
|  | • | • | • |  | • |  | • |  |  |  | • | • | • |  |  | • |  | • |
| • |  | • | • | • |  |  | • |  | • |  |  | • | • |  | • | • |  | • |
| • | • | • | • | • | • |  | • | • |  |  | • | • | • |  |  | • |  | • |
| • | • | • | • | • | • |  | • | • |  |  |  | • | • |  |  | • |  | • |
| • | • | • | • |  | • |  |  |  |  |  |  |  | • |  |  |  |  |  |
| • | • | • | • | • | • |  | • | • |  |  | • | • | • |  |  | • |  | • |
|  |  |  |  |  |  | • |  |  |  |  |  |  |  |  |  |  |  |  |

| | Vacancies | Partners | Total staff | Work placement | Corporate/ commercial | General commercial | Niche | General practice | High street/ legal aid |
|---|---|---|---|---|---|---|---|---|---|
| Sookias & Sookias | 0 | 4 | 20 | | | • | | | |
| **Speechly Bircham LLP** | 10 | 62 | 278 | ✔ | | | | • | |
| Spence & Horne | 0-2 | 2 | 8 | ✔ | | | | • | • |
| **Squire, Sanders & Dempsey** | 3-4 | 282 | 1720 | ✔ | • | | | | |
| steeles | 6[09] | 19 | 180 | ✔ | • | • | | | |
| **Stephenson Harwood** | 12 | 75 | 545 | ✔ | • | | | | |
| Stone King | 0 | 17 | 130 | | • | • | • | • | |
| Stone Rowe Brewer | 1-2 | 5 | 50 | | • | • | | | |
| Stringfellow & Gowthorpe | 1[08] | 2 | 15 | | | | • | | • |
| Sweetman Burke & Sinker | Poss[09] | 4 | 16 | ✔ | | | | • | • |
| Sykes Anderson LLP | 1[09] | 5 | 25 | ✔ | | | • | | |
| Talfourds | 1-2[08] | 5 | 35 | | | • | | | |
| **Taylor Wessing** | 24 | 264 | 1000 | ✔ | • | • | | | |
| **Teacher Stern Selby** | 3 | 21 | 99 | ✔ | • | • | • | | • |
| **Thomas Cooper** | 2[09] | 25 | 80 | ✔ | | | | | |
| **Thomas Eggar** | 6 | 60 | 429 | ✔ | • | • | • | | |
| Thompsons | Poss[09] | 38 | 800 | | | | • | | |
| **Thring Townsend Lee & Pembertons Solicitors** | 9 | 46 | 311 | | • | • | • | • | |
| Tinklin Springall | 1[08] | 6 | 40 | | | | | • | |
| **TLT Solicitors** | 10 | 60 | 600 | ✔ | • | • | • | • | |
| **Travers Smith** | 25 | 66 | | ✔ | • | | | | |
| **Trowers & Hamlins** | 22 | 106 | 652 | ✔ | • | • | | | |
| Tucker Turner Kingsley Wood & Co | 1-2 | 9 | 33 | ✔ | • | • | • | • | |
| Turbervilles | 1-2[09] | 11 | 67 | | • | • | • | • | |
| TV Edwards Solicitors | 0 | 6 | 64 | | | | | | • |
| Vahib & Co | 0-3 | 1 | 22 | | | | | • | • |
| **Vinson & Elkins RLLP** | 2 | 8 | 49 | ✔ | • | | | | |
| Vizards Tweedie | 0 | 20 | 51 | | • | • | | • | |
| Vizards Wyeth | 2 | 22 | | | • | • | • | • | |
| Wainwright & Cummins | 0 | 2 | 25 | ✔ | | | | | • |
| **Wallace LLP** | 2[09] | 10 | 60 | | • | • | | | |
| **Watson Burton LLP** | 6 | 40 | 300 | ✔ | | • | | | |
| **Watson, Farley & Williams LLP** | 12 | 68 | 450 | ✔ | • | • | | | |
| **Wedlake Bell** | 7 | 41 | 200 | ✔ | • | • | | | |
| **Weightmans** | Up to 14 | 90 | 750 | | • | | • | | |
| **Weil Gotshal & Manges** | 12 | 24 | 242 | ✔ | • | | | | |
| Wellers | 1-2[09] | 4 | 37 | | • | • | | • | |
| West London Law Solicitors | 2 | 1 | 7 | ✔ | | | • | | |
| WH Matthews & Co | 3[09] | 10 | 60 | | | | | • | |
| **White & Case LLP** | 30-35 | 68 | 567 | ✔ | • | | | | |

| Arbitration | Banking | Comp/comm | Competition | Construction | Corporate tax | Crime | Employment | Environment | Family | Human rights | Insurance | IP | Litigation | Personal injury | Private client | Property | Shipping | TMT |
|---|---|---|---|---|---|---|---|---|---|---|---|---|---|---|---|---|---|---|
|  |  | • |  |  |  |  |  |  |  |  |  |  | • |  |  | • |  |  |
| • | • | • |  | • | • |  | • | • | • |  | • | • | • |  | • | • |  | • |
|  |  |  |  |  |  |  | • |  | • |  |  |  |  |  | • | • |  |  |
| • | • | • | • |  | • |  | • |  |  |  |  | • | • |  | • | • |  | • |
| • |  | • | • | • |  | • | • | • | • |  |  | • | • | • | • | • |  | • |
| • | • | • | • | • | • |  | • | • |  |  | • | • | • |  |  | • | • | • |
|  |  | • |  |  |  | • | • |  | • |  |  |  | • | • | • | • |  |  |
|  |  | • |  |  |  | • | • |  | • |  |  |  | • | • | • | • |  |  |
|  |  |  |  |  |  | • |  |  |  |  |  |  |  |  |  |  |  |  |
|  |  |  |  |  |  | • |  |  | • |  |  |  |  | • | • | • |  |  |
|  |  | • |  | • | • |  | • |  |  |  |  |  | • |  | • | • |  |  |
|  |  | • |  | • |  |  |  |  | • |  |  |  | • | • | • | • |  |  |
| • | • | • | • | • | • |  | • | • | • |  | • | • | • |  | • | • | • | • |
| • | • | • | • | • | • |  | • | • |  |  | • | • | • | • | • | • |  | • |
| • | • | • | • |  |  |  | • | • |  |  | • | • | • |  |  | • | • | • |
| • | • | • | • | • | • | • | • | • | • |  |  | • | • | • | • | • |  | • |
|  |  |  |  |  |  | • | • |  |  |  |  |  |  | • |  |  |  |  |
|  | • | • | • | • |  |  | • | • | • |  |  | • | • | • | • | • |  | • |
|  |  | • |  |  |  |  | • |  | • |  |  |  | • |  | • | • |  |  |
| • | • | • | • | • | • |  | • | • | • |  | • | • | • |  | • | • | • | • |
| • | • | • | • | • | • |  | • | • |  |  | • | • | • |  |  | • |  | • |
|  |  | • | • | • | • |  | • | • |  |  |  | • | • | • | • | • |  |  |
|  |  | • |  |  |  |  | • |  |  |  |  |  | • |  |  | • |  |  |
|  |  | • |  | • | • | • | • | • | • |  |  | • | • |  | • | • |  | • |
|  |  |  |  |  |  | • | • |  | • |  |  |  | • | • |  |  |  |  |
|  |  |  |  |  |  |  | • |  | • |  |  |  |  |  |  |  |  |  |
| • | • | • |  | • |  |  | • |  | • |  |  |  | • |  |  | • |  | • |
| • | • | • | • |  | • |  | • |  | • |  |  | • | • | • | • | • |  | • |
|  |  | • |  | • |  |  | • |  | • |  | • |  | • | • | • | • |  |  |
|  |  |  |  |  |  | • |  |  | • |  |  |  |  |  |  |  |  |  |
|  |  | • |  |  |  |  | • |  | • |  |  | • | • |  | • | • |  | • |
| • | • | • | • | • | • |  | • | • |  |  | • | • | • | • | • | • |  | • |
|  | • | • | • |  | • |  | • |  |  |  |  |  | • | • |  | • | • | • |
|  | • | • |  | • | • |  | • |  |  |  |  |  | • | • |  | • |  | • |
| • | • | • |  | • | • |  | • |  |  |  | • | • | • | • |  | • | • |  |
|  | • | • | • |  | • |  | • | • |  |  |  |  | • | • |  | • |  | • |
|  |  | • |  |  |  |  | • | • | • |  |  |  | • | • | • | • |  |  |
| • | • |  |  |  |  |  |  |  | • |  |  |  | • |  |  |  |  |  |
|  |  | • |  | • |  | • | • |  | • |  |  |  | • | • | • | • |  |  |
| • | • |  |  | • | • |  | • |  |  |  |  |  | • |  |  | • |  | • |

| | Vacancies | Partners | Total staff | Work placement | Corporate/ commercial | General commercial | Niche | General practice | High street/ legal aid |
|---|---|---|---|---|---|---|---|---|---|
| **Wiggin LLP** | 4 | 14 | 83 | | • | | • | | |
| Wilmer Cutler Pickering Hale & Dorr | 2-4[08] | 10 | 90 | | • | | | | |
| Wilson & Co | 0 | 8 | 69 | | | | | | • |
| Winckworth Sherwood | 4[09] | 24 | 185 | ✔ | | • | • | | |
| **Withers LLP** | 18 | 100 | 600 | ✔ | • | | | | |
| Woodhouse Davies & Martin | 1 | 2 | 17 | | | | | • | |
| **Wragge & Co LLP** | 30 | 110 | 1017 | ✔ | • | • | • | | |
| Zeckler & Co | 2 | 4 | 12 | ✔ | • | • | | • | • |

# North

| | Vacancies | Partners | Total staff | Work placement | Corporate/ commercial | General commercial | Niche | General practice | High street/ legal aid |
|---|---|---|---|---|---|---|---|---|---|
| Beecham Peacock | 0 | 6 | 60 | | | | | • | • |
| Ben Hoare Bell | 3[09] | 7 | 80 | | | | | • | • |
| **Berrymans Lace Mawer** | 17 | 115 | 792 | ✔ | | • | | | |
| Cartmell Shepherd | 3 | 17 | 95 | ✔ | | | | • | |
| **Crown Prosecution Service** | 25 | | 9000 | ✔ | | | • | | |
| Crutes | 2[09] | 18 | | | | | | • | |
| Darlington Borough Council | 0 | 7 | 15 | | | | | • | |
| David Gray Solicitors | 1[09] | 9 | 54 | | | | | • | • |
| **Dickinson Dees LLP** | 15 | 78 | 920 | ✔ | • | • | • | | |
| Donnelly Adamson | 0 | 5 | 34 | | | | | • | |
| The Endeavour Partnership LLP | 2 | 9 | 43 | ✔ | • | | | | |
| **Eversheds LLP** | 80+ | 340 | 4000 | ✔ | • | • | | | |
| Freeman Johnson | 1 | 8 | 45 | ✔ | | | | • | • |
| Goodswens | Poss | 3 | 18 | | | • | | • | |
| **Government Legal Service** | 22-30 | | 1950 | ✔ | • | • | | • | |
| **Hay & Kilner** | 2 | 22 | 150 | ✔ | • | • | | • | |
| **HBJ Gateley Wareing LLP** | 11 | 75 | 488 | ✔ | • | • | | | |
| Hethertons LLP Solicitors | 0 | 3 | 17 | | | | | • | • |
| Hewitts | Poss[08] | 16 | 103 | | | | | • | |
| Hunt Kidd | 1-2[09] | 4 | 26 | ✔ | • | • | • | | |
| **Irwin Mitchell** | 20-25 | 137 | 2000 | ✔ | • | • | | • | |
| Jacksons | 0 | 11 | 73 | | • | • | | • | • |
| Kevin J Commons & Co | Poss | 2 | 55 | | | | | • | • |
| Latimer Hinks | Poss | 7 | 56 | | | | | • | |
| Lawson & Thompson | 1 | 6 | 30 | | | | | • | • |
| McKeags | 6[09] | 12 | 300 | | | | | • | |
| Mortons | 0 | 6 | 48 | | | | | • | |

| Arbitration | Banking | Comp/comm | Competition | Construction | Corporate tax | Crime | Employment | Environment | Family | Human rights | Insurance | IP | Litigation | Personal injury | Private client | Property | Shipping | TMT |
|---|---|---|---|---|---|---|---|---|---|---|---|---|---|---|---|---|---|---|
| | | • | | | | | | | | | | • | • | | | • | | • |
| | | • | | | • | | • | | | | | • | | | | | | • |
| | | | | | • | | | | • | | | | | | | | | |
| • | | • | | • | | | • | | • | | | | | • | | • | • | |
| | • | • | • | | • | | • | • | • | | | • | • | | • | • | | • |
| | | | | | | | • | | • | | | | | | • | • | | |
| • | • | • | | • | • | | • | • | • | | • | • | • | • | • | • | | • |
| | | • | | • | • | | • | • | • | • | | | • | • | • | • | | • |

| Arbitration | Banking | Comp/comm | Competition | Construction | Corporate tax | Crime | Employment | Environment | Family | Human rights | Insurance | IP | Litigation | Personal injury | Private client | Property | Shipping | TMT |
|---|---|---|---|---|---|---|---|---|---|---|---|---|---|---|---|---|---|---|
| | | | | | | • | • | | • | | | | | | • | • | | |
| | | | | | | • | | | • | • | | | | • | | | | |
| | | | | • | | | • | • | | | • | | • | • | | | • | |
| | | • | | | | | • | | • | | | | • | • | • | • | | |
| | | | | | | • | | | • | | | | | | | | | |
| • | | • | | | | | • | | • | | | | • | • | • | • | | |
| | | | | | | • | | | • | • | | | | • | • | | | |
| • | • | • | • | • | • | • | • | • | • | | • | • | • | • | • | • | | • |
| | | | | | | • | | | • | | | | | | • | | | |
| | | • | | | | | • | | • | | | | • | • | | • | | • |
| • | • | • | • | • | • | | • | • | • | • | • | • | • | • | • | • | • | • |
| | | • | | | | • | • | | • | | | | | • | • | • | | |
| | | • | | | | | • | | • | | | | | • | • | • | | |
| • | • | • | • | • | • | • | • | • | • | • | • | • | • | • | • | • | • | • |
| • | • | • | | • | • | • | • | • | • | | • | • | • | • | • | • | | • |
| • | • | • | • | • | • | | • | • | • | | | • | • | • | • | • | • | • |
| | | | | | | | | | • | | | | | • | • | | | |
| • | | • | | • | | | • | | • | | | | • | • | • | • | | |
| | | • | | • | | | | | • | | | | | | • | • | | |
| • | | • | • | • | | | • | • | • | • | • | • | • | • | • | • | | • |
| • | | • | • | | | | • | • | • | | | • | • | • | • | • | | • |
| | | | | | | • | | | • | | | | | • | • | • | | |
| | | • | | | | | • | • | • | | | | • | • | • | • | | • |
| | | | | | | • | • | | • | | | | | • | • | | | |
| • | • | | | | | • | • | | • | | | | • | • | • | • | | |
| | | | | | | | | | • | | | | | • | | | | |

| | Vacancies | Partners | Total staff | Work placement | Corporate/ commercial | General commercial | Niche | General practice | High street/ legal aid |
|---|---|---|---|---|---|---|---|---|---|
| **Muckle LLP** | 4 | 19 | 132 | ✔ | • | • | | | |
| **Pinsent Masons** | 55 | 260 | 1500 | ✔ | • | • | | | |
| Punch Robson | 1-2[09] | 10 | 50 | | | • | • | • | • |
| Russell Jones & Walker | 10 | 49 | 630 | | | • | • | • | |
| Samuel Phillips Law Firm | 1 | 5 | 44 | ✔ | | • | • | • | |
| SFM Legal Services | 1[09] | 2 | 60 | ✔ | | | • | | |
| **Shulmans** | 2-3 | 11 | 140 | ✔ | • | • | • | • | |
| Sintons LLP | 0 | 20 | 140 | ✔ | • | • | | | |
| Taylor & Emmet | 3 | 7 | 145 | | • | • | | • | • |
| Thompsons | Poss[09] | 38 | 800 | | | | • | | |
| Tilly Bailey & Irvine | 2-3[08] | 16 | 146 | | • | • | | • | • |
| TMJ Legal Services LLP | Poss | 3 | 39 | ✔ | | | | • | • |
| **Ward Hadaway** | 10 | 57 | 395 | ✔ | • | • | | | |
| **Watson Burton LLP** | 6 | 40 | 300 | ✔ | | • | | | |
| Whittles | 2[08] | 10 | 165 | | | | • | | |

# Northwest

| | Vacancies | Partners | Total staff | Work placement | Corporate/ commercial | General commercial | Niche | General practice | High street/ legal aid |
|---|---|---|---|---|---|---|---|---|---|
| Aaron and Partners | 2[09] | 20 | 86 | | • | • | • | | |
| Abney Garsden McDonald | 0 | 1 | 45 | | | | • | • | • |
| **Addleshaw Goddard** | 50 | 182 | 1300 | ✔ | • | | | | |
| Antony Hodari & Co | Varies | 6 | 140 | | | | | • | |
| Backhouse Jones | 0 | 4 | 26 | ✔ | | | | • | |
| Baileys | 0 | 1 | 6 | ✔ | | | | • | |
| Barnetts | 2 | 4 | 250 | | | | • | | |
| **Beachcroft LLP** | 30 | 147 | 1400 | ✔ | • | • | | | |
| Beardsells | 2-3[08] | 12 | 65 | ✔ | | | | | |
| Berg Legal | 3[08] | 10 | 57 | ✔ | • | • | | | |
| Berkeley Solicitors | 1[09] | 1 | 7 | ✔ | | | | • | • |
| Bermans | 2[09] | 11 | 100 | | • | | • | | |
| Berry & Berry | 1 | 8 | 52 | | • | • | | • | • |
| **Berrymans Lace Mawer** | 17 | 115 | 792 | ✔ | | • | | | |
| Birch Cullimore | 1[09] | 7 | 44 | | | | | • | |
| Birchall Blackburn | 0 | 15 | 160 | | • | | | | • |
| Blackhurst Swainson Goodier | 2 | 9 | 53 | ✔ | • | • | | • | • |
| Bowcock Cuerden LLP | 1 | 4 | 40 | | | • | • | | |
| **Brabners Chaffe Street LLP** | 14 | 56 | 341 | ✔ | • | • | | | |
| Bremners | 0 | 9 | 35 | | • | • | • | | |

| Arbitration | Banking | Comp/comm | Competition | Construction | Corporate tax | Crime | Employment | Environment | Family | Human rights | Insurance | IP | Litigation | Personal injury | Private client | Property | Shipping | TMT |
|---|---|---|---|---|---|---|---|---|---|---|---|---|---|---|---|---|---|---|
| ● | ● | ● | ● | ● |  |  | ● | ● |  |  |  | ● | ● |  | ● | ● |  | ● |
| ● | ● | ● | ● | ● | ● |  | ● | ● |  |  | ● | ● | ● |  |  | ● |  | ● |
|  |  | ● |  |  |  |  | ● | ● |  |  |  |  | ● | ● | ● | ● |  |  |
|  |  |  | ● |  |  | ● | ● | ● | ● | ● |  |  | ● | ● | ● | ● |  | ● |
|  |  | ● |  |  |  | ● | ● |  | ● |  |  |  | ● | ● | ● | ● |  |  |
|  |  |  |  |  |  |  |  |  |  |  |  |  |  |  | ● |  |  |  |
|  | ● | ● | ● | ● | ● |  | ● | ● | ● | ● |  | ● | ● |  | ● | ● |  | ● |
|  | ● | ● |  |  |  |  | ● | ● |  |  |  | ● | ● | ● | ● | ● |  |  |
|  |  | ● |  | ● |  |  | ● | ● |  |  |  | ● | ● | ● | ● | ● |  |  |
|  |  |  |  |  |  | ● | ● |  |  |  |  |  |  | ● |  |  |  |  |
| ● |  | ● |  |  |  |  | ● | ● | ● |  |  | ● | ● | ● | ● | ● |  |  |
|  |  |  |  |  |  | ● | ● |  |  |  |  |  |  | ● |  |  |  |  |
|  | ● | ● | ● | ● | ● |  | ● | ● | ● |  |  | ● | ● | ● | ● | ● |  | ● |
| ● | ● | ● | ● | ● | ● |  | ● | ● | ● |  | ● | ● | ● | ● | ● | ● |  | ● |
|  |  |  |  |  |  |  | ● |  |  |  |  |  |  | ● | ● |  |  |  |

| Arbitration | Banking | Comp/comm | Competition | Construction | Corporate tax | Crime | Employment | Environment | Family | Human rights | Insurance | IP | Litigation | Personal injury | Private client | Property | Shipping | TMT |
|---|---|---|---|---|---|---|---|---|---|---|---|---|---|---|---|---|---|---|
|  | ● | ● | ● | ● |  |  | ● | ● | ● |  |  | ● | ● |  | ● | ● |  | ● |
|  |  |  |  |  |  |  |  | ● |  |  |  |  |  | ● |  |  |  |  |
| ● | ● | ● | ● | ● | ● |  | ● | ● | ● |  | ● | ● | ● |  | ● | ● |  | ● |
|  |  |  |  |  |  |  |  |  |  |  |  |  |  | ● |  |  |  |  |
|  |  |  |  |  |  | ● | ● |  |  |  |  | ● | ● | ● |  |  |  |  |
|  |  | ● |  |  |  |  |  |  |  |  |  | ● | ● | ● |  | ● |  |  |
| ● |  | ● | ● | ● | ● |  | ● | ● |  |  | ● | ● | ● |  | ● |  |  | ● |
|  | ● | ● |  | ● |  |  | ● | ● |  |  |  | ● | ● |  | ● |  |  | ● |
|  |  | ● |  |  |  |  | ● | ● |  |  |  |  | ● | ● |  | ● |  |  |
|  |  | ● |  |  |  |  | ● |  |  |  |  |  | ● |  |  | ● |  |  |
| ● |  | ● |  | ● |  | ● | ● |  |  |  |  | ● | ● | ● | ● | ● |  |  |
|  |  | ● |  |  |  |  | ● | ● |  |  | ● |  | ● | ● |  |  | ● |  |
|  | ● | ● |  |  |  |  | ● | ● | ● |  |  |  | ● | ● | ● | ● |  |  |
|  |  | ● |  |  |  | ● | ● |  | ● | ● |  |  | ● |  | ● | ● |  |  |
|  |  | ● |  |  |  |  | ● | ● | ● |  |  |  | ● | ● | ● | ● |  |  |
| ● |  | ● |  |  |  |  | ● | ● | ● |  |  |  | ● |  | ● | ● |  |  |
| ● | ● | ● | ● | ● | ● |  | ● | ● | ● |  |  | ● | ● | ● | ● | ● |  | ● |
|  |  | ● |  | ● |  |  | ● |  |  |  |  | ● | ● |  | ● | ● |  |  |

| | Vacancies | Partners | Total staff | Work placement | Corporate/commercial | General commercial | Niche | General practice | High street/legal aid |
|---|---|---|---|---|---|---|---|---|---|
| Brian Camp & Co | 0 | 4 | 62 | ✔ | | | • | | |
| Brighouse Wolff | 1 | 10 | 80 | | | | | • | |
| Burnetts | 2[09] | 19 | 111 | | | | | • | |
| Butcher & Barlow | 2[09] | 15 | 77 | | | | | • | |
| C Turner | 0 | | 43 | | | | | • | |
| Canter Levin & Berg | 1-2 | 15 | 220 | | | | | • | • |
| Cartmell Shepherd | 3 | 17 | 95 | ✔ | | | | • | |
| Chenery Maher | 0 | 2 | 9 | | | | • | | |
| **Cobbetts LLP** | 20 | 136 | 815 | ✔ | • | • | | | |
| Colemans-ctts | 2 | 12 | 250 | ✔ | | | | • | |
| Cottrill Stone Lawless | 1 | 6 | 30 | | | | | • | |
| **Crown Prosecution Service** | 25 | | 9000 | ✔ | | | • | | |
| David Phillips & Partners | 2 | 11 | 60 | ✔ | | | | • | • |
| **Davies Arnold Cooper** | 5 | 68 | 308 | ✔ | • | • | • | | |
| Davis Blank Furniss | 1-2 | 14 | 77 | | • | • | | • | |
| Denby & Co | 1 | 5 | 28 | | | • | | • | • |
| Derek B Forrest Solicitors | 1[09] | 1 | 7 | | | | | | |
| **DLA Piper UK LLP** | 95+ | 1200 | 7000 | ✔ | • | | | | |
| Donald Race & Newton | 0 | 6 | 47 | ✔ | | | | • | • |
| Drummonds | 1[09] | 3 | 38 | | | | | • | |
| **DWF** | 20 | 119 | 804 | ✔ | • | • | • | | |
| **Eversheds LLP** | 80+ | 340 | 4000 | ✔ | • | • | | | |
| Express Solicitors | 2 | 2 | 30 | ✔ | | | • | | |
| Fentons | 0 | 5 | 110 | | | | | • | • |
| Field Cunningham & Co | 1 | 4 | 30 | | | | • | | |
| Fieldings Porter | 3-4 | 12 | 76 | | • | • | | • | • |
| Fletchers Solicitors | 2[09] | 4 | 85 | | • | • | | • | • |
| **Forbes Solicitors** | 4 | 29 | 350 | ✔ | • | • | • | • | |
| **George Davies Solicitors LLP** | 5[09] | 15 | 85 | | • | | | | |
| Glaisyers | 1-2 | 15 | 90 | ✔ | | • | | • | • |
| GLP Solicitors | 0-1 | 3 | 9 | | | | | • | • |
| Goodmans | 2[09] | 7 | 80 | | | | | • | |
| **Government Legal Service** | 22-30 | | 1950 | ✔ | • | • | | • | |
| Gregory Abrams Davidson LLP | 2[09] | 4 | 58 | ✔ | | • | | • | |
| **Halliwells LLP** | 38 | 165 | 1300 | ✔ | • | • | | | |
| **Hammonds** | 40 | 189 | 1300 | ✔ | • | | | | |
| The Hardman Partnership | 1-2[09] | 3 | 15 | | • | • | • | | |
| Hempsons | 6 | 30 | 300 | | | | • | | |
| Henry's Solicitors Limited | 1[09] | | 25 | ✔ | | | | • | |
| Hibbert Durrad Moxon LLP | 1 | 7 | 63 | | | • | | • | • |
| **Hill Dickinson LLP** | 17 | 152 | 1000 | ✔ | • | • | • | | |

| Arbitration | Banking | Comp/comm | Competition | Construction | Corporate tax | Crime | Employment | Environment | Family | Human rights | Insurance | IP | Litigation | Personal injury | Private client | Property | Shipping | TMT |
|---|---|---|---|---|---|---|---|---|---|---|---|---|---|---|---|---|---|---|
|  |  |  |  |  |  |  |  |  |  |  |  |  | • | • | • |  |  |  |
|  |  |  |  |  |  | • |  |  | • |  |  |  | • | • | • | • |  |  |
|  |  | • |  | • |  |  | • |  | • |  |  |  | • | • | • | • |  | • |
|  |  | • |  | • |  |  | • |  | • |  |  |  | • |  |  | • |  |  |
|  |  |  |  |  |  | • | • |  | • |  |  |  |  | • | • |  |  |  |
|  |  |  |  |  |  | • | • |  | • |  |  |  |  | • | • |  |  |  |
|  |  | • |  |  |  |  | • |  | • |  |  |  | • | • | • | • |  |  |
|  |  | • |  |  |  |  | • |  | • |  |  |  | • | • | • | • |  |  |
|  |  |  |  |  |  | • |  |  |  |  |  |  |  |  |  |  |  |  |
|  |  |  |  |  |  | • |  |  | • |  |  |  | • | • |  |  |  |  |
| • | • | • | • | • | • |  | • | • |  |  |  | • | • |  |  | • | • | • |
|  |  | • |  |  |  |  | • |  | • |  |  |  | • | • | • | • |  |  |
|  |  | • |  |  |  |  | • |  | • |  |  |  | • | • | • | • |  |  |
| • | • | • | • | • |  |  | • | • |  |  | • |  | • |  |  | • | • | • |
| • | • | • | • | • |  |  | • |  | • |  | • | • | • | • | • | • |  | • |
|  |  | • |  |  |  |  | • | • | • |  |  |  | • | • | • | • |  |  |
|  |  |  |  |  |  | • | • |  | • |  |  |  | • | • |  |  |  |  |
| • | • | • | • | • | • |  | • | • | • |  | • | • | • |  |  | • | • | • |
|  |  |  |  |  |  |  | • | • |  |  |  |  | • | • | • |  |  |  |
|  |  |  |  |  |  |  |  |  | • |  |  |  | • | • | • |  |  |  |
| • | • | • |  | • |  |  | • |  | • |  | • | • | • | • |  | • |  |  |
| • | • | • | • | • |  |  | • | • |  |  | • | • | • | • | • | • |  | • |
|  |  | • |  |  |  |  | • | • | • |  |  |  | • | • | • | • |  |  |
|  |  |  |  |  |  |  | • |  | • |  |  |  |  |  |  |  |  |  |
|  |  | • |  |  |  |  |  |  | • |  |  |  | • | • | • | • |  |  |
| • | • | • | • | • | • | • | • |  | • | • |  | • | • | • | • | • | • | • |
|  |  | • |  |  |  |  | • |  | • |  |  |  | • | • | • | • |  |  |
|  | • | • | • | • | • |  | • | • | • |  |  | • | • | • | • | • | • | • |
| • | • | • | • | • | • |  | • | • |  |  |  |  | • | • |  | • |  | • |
|  |  | • |  |  |  |  | • |  | • |  |  |  | • | • | • | • |  |  |
|  |  | • |  | • |  | • | • |  | • |  |  |  | • | • | • | • |  |  |
|  |  | • |  |  |  | • | • |  | • |  |  |  |  | • |  |  |  |  |
|  |  | • |  |  |  |  | • | • |  |  |  |  | • |  | • | • |  | • |
| • | • | • | • | • | • | • | • | • | • |  | • | • | • | • | • | • | • | • |

| | Vacancies | Partners | Total staff | Work placement | Corporate/commercial | General commercial | Niche | General practice | High street/legal aid |
|---|---|---|---|---|---|---|---|---|---|
| Hillyer McKeown | 2 | 9 | 60 | | • | • | | • | • |
| Hilton Norbury | 1 | 2 | 10 | ✔ | | | | • | • |
| Horwich Farrelly | 0 | 10 | 300 | | | • | • | | |
| Hough Halton & Soal | 1-2 | 3 | 20 | | | | | • | • |
| Howarth Goodman | Poss[09] | 4 | 50 | ✔ | • | • | | | |
| Inghams | Poss | 11 | 100 | | • | • | | • | • |
| **Irwin Mitchell** | 20-25 | 137 | 2000 | ✔ | • | • | | | |
| James Murray Solicitors | 0 | 5 | 58 | | | | | • | • |
| Jobling & Knape | Poss | 5 | 34 | | | | | • | • |
| **Keoghs LLP** | 4 | 30 | 506 | | | | • | | |
| Kirwans | 2[09] | 7 | 79 | | • | • | | • | • |
| Kuit Steinart Levy | 3 | 19 | 105 | | • | • | • | • | |
| Latimer Lee | 0 | | | ✔ | | • | | | |
| **Laytons** | 6 | 34 | 170 | ✔ | • | • | | | |
| Leech & Co | Poss 2 | 7 | 45 | | | | | • | |
| Lees & Partners | 1-2[09] | 14 | 100 | | | | | • | |
| **Mace & Jones** | 6 | 38 | 240 | ✔ | • | • | | • | |
| Maidments | Poss | 6 | 100 | | | | • | | • |
| Maxwell Hodge | 0 | 19 | 130 | ✔ | | | | • | • |
| McHale & Company | 2 | 2 | 21 | | • | • | | • | • |
| Meldrum Young Solicitors | 4 | 4 | 106 | ✔ | | | | | • |
| Middleweeks | 0 | 2 | 19 | ✔ | | | • | | • |
| Milburns | Poss[08] | 8 | 43 | | | | | • | • |
| Milne Moser | 0 | 5 | 30 | | | | | • | • |
| Mohammed & Co | 0 | 1 | 13 | ✔ | | | | • | • |
| Molesworths Bright Clegg | Varies[09] | 7 | 69 | | • | • | | | |
| Myers Lister Price | 2[09] | 7 | 53 | ✔ | • | • | • | • | • |
| Napthens | 2-3[09] | 12 | 70 | | | | | • | |
| Neil Myerson Solicitors | 2[09] | 6 | 50 | | • | • | • | | |
| Nexus Solicitors | 2[09] | 9 | 40 | | • | • | | | |
| NK Legal Solicitors | 0 | 2 | 8 | ✔ | | | | | • |
| Oglethorpe & Broatch | 0 | 3 | 10 | | | | | • | • |
| Oglethorpe Sturton & Gillibrand | 1-2 | 7 | 46 | | | • | | • | |
| O'Neill Patient Solicitors | 0 | 4 | 180 | | | | | • | |
| **Pannone LLP** | 14 | 99 | 707 | ✔ | • | • | | • | • |
| Pearson Hinchliffe | 2[08] | 10 | 63 | | • | • | | • | |
| **Pinsent Masons** | 55 | 260 | 1500 | ✔ | • | • | | | |
| Robert Lizar | Poss | 6 | 22 | | | | | | • |
| Robin Simon LLP | 2[08] | 10 | 50 | | | | • | | |
| The Roland Partnership | 0 | 2 | 21 | ✔ | | | • | • | • |
| Rowlands Solicitors LLP | 5 | 26 | 150 | ✔ | | | | • | |

| Arbitration | Banking | Comp/comm | Competition | Construction | Corporate tax | Crime | Employment | Environment | Family | Human rights | Insurance | IP | Litigation | Personal injury | Private client | Property | Shipping | TMT |
|---|---|---|---|---|---|---|---|---|---|---|---|---|---|---|---|---|---|---|
| • | | • | | • | | | • | | • | | | • | • | • | • | • | | • |
| | | | | | | | | | • | | | | | • | | | | |
| | | • | | | | | | | | | | | • | • | • | | | |
| | | • | | | | • | | | • | | | | • | • | • | • | | |
| | | • | | | | | | | • | | | | • | • | • | • | | |
| • | | • | • | • | | | • | • | • | • | • | • | • | • | • | • | | • |
| | | | | | | • | | | • | | | | | • | | | | |
| | | | | | | | | | | | | | | | | | | |
| | | | | | | • | • | | | | • | | • | • | | | | |
| | | • | | | | • | • | | | | | • | • | • | • | • | | • |
| • | • | | • | | • | | • | | | | | • | • | • | • | • | | • |
| | | • | | | | | • | | • | • | | • | • | • | • | • | | |
| • | • | • | • | • | • | | • | • | • | | | • | • | • | • | • | • | • |
| | | • | | | | | • | | | | | | • | • | | • | | |
| | | • | | • | | | • | | • | | | | • | • | • | • | | |
| • | • | • | • | • | • | | • | • | • | | | • | • | • | • | • | | • |
| | | | | | | • | • | | • | | | | • | • | • | • | | |
| | | • | | | | | • | | • | | | | • | • | • | • | | |
| | | | • | | | | | | | | | | • | • | • | • | | |
| | | | | | | • | | | | | | | | | | | | |
| | | | | | | • | | | | | | | | | | | • |
| | | | | | | | • | | • | | | | | • | | • | | |
| | | | | | | | • | • | • | | | | | • | • | • | | |
| | | | | | | | • | • | • | | | | • | • | • | • | | |
| | | • | | | | | • | | • | | | | • | • | • | • | | |
| | | • | | | | | • | | • | | | | • | • | • | • | | |
| | | • | | | | | • | • | • | | | | • | • | • | • | | |
| • | • | • | • | | | • | • | • | • | | | | • | • | | • | | • |
| • | | • | | | | | • | | • | | • | • | • | • | | • | | • |
| | | | | | | • | • | | • | | | | | • | | | | |
| | | | | | | | | | • | | | | | • | | • | | |
| | | • | | | | | • | • | • | | | | • | • | • | • | | |
| | • | • | | | | | • | | • | | | | | • | • | • | | |
| • | • | • | • | • | • | • | • | • | • | | | | • | • | • | • | | • |
| | | • | | | | | • | • | • | | | | • | • | • | • | | |
| • | • | • | • | • | • | | • | • | | | • | • | • | • | | • | | • |
| | | | | | | • | | | | • | • | | | | | | | |
| | | | | | | | | | | | | • | | | | | | |
| | | | | | | | | | | | | | | • | | | | |
| | | • | | | | | • | • | • | • | | | • | • | • | • | | • |

| | Vacancies | Partners | Total staff | Work placement | Corporate/ commercial | General commercial | Niche | General practice | High street/ legal aid |
|---|---|---|---|---|---|---|---|---|---|
| Russell & Russell | 0 | 14 | 165 | | | | | • | • |
| SAS Daniels | 0 | 19 | 130 | | | | | • | |
| Scott Rees & Co | 2(08) | 7 | 170 | ✔ | | | • | | |
| Sherrington Law, The Accident Solicitors | Poss | 4 | 90 | | | | • | | |
| Silverbeck Rymer | 0-3(09) | 7 | 218 | | | | • | | |
| Southerns | 1(08) | 9 | 60 | | | | | • | • |
| Stephensons | 10 | 25 | 400 | ✔ | • | • | | • | • |
| Storrar Cowdry | 0 | 7 | 24 | | | | | | |
| Temple Heelis | 0 | | | ✔ | | | | | |
| Thompsons | Poss(09) | 38 | 800 | | | | • | | |
| Tickle Hall Cross | 1 | 6 | 40 | | | | | • | |
| TMJ Law Solicitors | 2 | 2 | 12 | ✔ | | • | | | |
| Tranters | 4 | 6 | 100 | ✔ | | | | | • |
| Tranters Freeclaim Solicitors | 4 | 3 | 47 | ✔ | | | | | |
| **Trowers & Hamlins** | 22 | 106 | 652 | ✔ | • | • | | | |
| Walker Smith Way Solicitors | 3-4 | 31 | 165 | | • | • | | | |
| **Weightmans** | Up to 14 | 90 | 750 | | • | | | | |
| WH Darbyshire & Son | 0 | 5 | 13 | | | • | | • | • |
| Whiteheads Solicitors Limited | 0 | 2 | 23 | | | | • | | |
| Whittles | 2(08) | 10 | 165 | | | | • | | |
| Wrigley Claydon | 1 | 6 | 32 | | | | | • | • |

# Southeast

| | Vacancies | Partners | Total staff | Work placement | Corporate/ commercial | General commercial | Niche | General practice | High street/ legal aid |
|---|---|---|---|---|---|---|---|---|---|
| Alan Edwards & Co | 0 | 5 | 22 | | | | • | | • |
| Alan Simpson & Co | 0-1 | 1 | 12 | | | | | • | |
| Allan Janes | 1 | 4 | 30 | ✔ | • | | | | |
| **asb law** | 5 | 37 | 260 | | • | • | | • | |
| Atkins Hope | 0 | 5 | 38 | | | | | • | • |
| AWB Partnership | 1(09) | 11 | 55 | | • | • | | • | |
| **Barlow Robbins LLP** | 4 | 23 | 225 | | • | | | • | |
| Barrea & Co | 0 | 3 | 16 | | | • | | • | • |
| Barrett & Co | 0 | 5 | 30 | | • | | | • | |
| Basingstoke & Deane Borough Council | 2 or 3 | 1 | 18 | | | | • | | |
| **Beachcroft LLP** | 30(09) | 147 | 1400 | ✔ | • | • | | • | |
| Beardsells | 2-3(08) | 12 | 65 | ✔ | | | • | • | |
| Berry & Berry | 2(09) | 10 | 69 | | | | | • | • |
| BG Energy Holdings | 0 | | 40 | | | | • | | |

| Arbitration | Banking | Comp/comm | Competition | Construction | Corporate tax | Crime | Employment | Environment | Family | Human rights | Insurance | IP | Litigation | Personal injury | Private client | Property | Shipping | TMT |
|---|---|---|---|---|---|---|---|---|---|---|---|---|---|---|---|---|---|---|
| | | | | | | • | | | • | | | | | • | • | • | | |
| | | • | | | | | • | | • | | | | • | • | • | • | | |
| | | | | | | | | | | | | | | • | | | | |
| | | | | | | | | | | | | | | • | • | | | |
| | | • | | | | • | • | | • | | | | | • | • | • | | |
| • | | • | | • | | • | • | • | • | | | • | • | • | • | • | | |
| | | • | | | | | • | | • | | | | | • | • | • | | |
| | | | | | | | • | | • | | | | | • | • | • | | |
| | | | | | | • | • | | | | | | | • | | | | |
| | | • | | | | | • | | • | | | | • | • | • | • | | |
| | | • | | | | | • | | | | | | • | | • | • | | • |
| | | | | | | • | | | | | | | | • | • | • | | |
| | • | • | • | • | • | | • | • | | | | | • | • | • | • | | |
| • | | • | | • | • | • | • | • | • | | | | • | • | • | • | | |
| • | • | • | | • | • | | • | | | | • | • | • | • | | • | • | |
| | | | | | | • | | | | | | | | • | • | • | | |
| | | | | | | | • | | • | | | | | • | • | | | |
| | | • | | | | | • | | • | | | | • | • | • | • | | • |

| Arbitration | Banking | Comp/comm | Competition | Construction | Corporate tax | Crime | Employment | Environment | Family | Human rights | Insurance | IP | Litigation | Personal injury | Private client | Property | Shipping | TMT |
|---|---|---|---|---|---|---|---|---|---|---|---|---|---|---|---|---|---|---|
| | | | | | | • | | | • | | | | | • | | • | | |
| | | • | | | | | • | | • | | | | | • | | • | | |
| | | • | | • | | | • | | | | | | • | • | • | • | | • |
| • | • | • | • | • | • | | • | • | • | | • | • | • | • | • | • | • | • |
| | | | | • | | | | | • | | | | | • | • | • | | |
| | | • | | | | | • | | • | | | • | • | • | • | • | | |
| • | | • | | | | | • | | • | | | • | • | • | • | • | | • |
| | | • | | • | | | • | | • | | | | • | • | • | • | | |
| | | • | | • | | | • | | • | | | | • | • | • | • | | |
| | | • | • | | • | | • | • | | | | • | • | • | | • | | • |
| • | | • | • | • | • | | • | • | | | • | • | • | • | | • | | • |
| | | | | | | | | | • | | | | | • | • | • | | |
| • | | • | | • | | | • | | • | • | | | • | • | • | • | | • |
| | | • | | | | | • | | | | | | | | | | | |

| | Vacancies | Partners | Total staff | Work placement | Corporate/commercial | General commercial | Niche | General practice | High street/legal aid |
|---|---|---|---|---|---|---|---|---|---|
| Birkett Long | 3 | 18 | 150 | ✔ | • | • | | • | |
| Blackfords LLP | Poss | 5 | 60 | | | | • | | • |
| **Blake Lapthorn Tarlo Lyons** | 17 | 104 | 700 | ✔ | • | • | | • | |
| **Blandy & Blandy** | 3 | 18 | 94 | | • | • | | • | |
| Blaser Mills | 2-4(09) | 12 | 100 | | • | • | | • | • |
| Bolitho Way | 0 | 7 | 22 | ✔ | • | • | • | • | • |
| **Bond Pearce LLP** | 15 | 74 | 700 | ✔ | • | • | | | |
| **Boodle Hatfield** | 8 | 31 | 200 | ✔ | • | • | • | | |
| **Borneo Linnells** | 2(09) | 21 | 130 | | • | • | | • | • |
| Bosley & Co | 2 | 2 | 13 | | | | | • | • |
| **Boyes Turner** | 4 | 26 | 150 | | • | • | • | • | |
| **BP Collins** | 4(09) | 20 | 140 | ✔ | • | • | | • | |
| Brachers | 2 | 21 | 200 | | • | | | • | |
| Bramsdon & Childs | 1(09) | 5 | 34 | | | • | | • | • |
| Breeze & Wyles | 2(09) | 11 | 160 | | | • | | • | • |
| Brignalls Balderston Warren | 0 | 13 | 61 | | | | | • | |
| Brooks & Partners | 0 | 1 | 26 | | • | • | | • | |
| BTMK Solicitors LLP | Up to 5(08) | 15 | 160 | ✔ | | | | • | |
| Buss Murton LLP | 1(09) | 5 | 90 | | | | | • | |
| CGM Solicitors | 0-2 | 9 | 35 | | | • | | • | • |
| **Charles Russell LLP** | 20 | 93 | 626 | ✔ | • | • | | • | |
| Christopher Wright & Co | 0 | 1 | 5 | | | | • | | |
| Clarke Kiernan | 1-2(09) | 2 | 31 | | | | | | • |
| **Clarkson Wright & Jakes** | 3 | 14 | 100 | ✔ | • | • | | • | • |
| Clifton Ingram | 1 | 10 | 64 | | | | | • | |
| **Clyde & Co LLP** | 24 | 140 | 1080 | ✔ | • | • | | | |
| **Coffin Mew LLP** | 6 | 21 | 247 | ✔ | • | • | • | | |
| Colemans | Poss(08) | 14 | 180 | ✔ | | | | • | • |
| Colemans-ctts | 2 | 12 | 250 | ✔ | | | | • | |
| Collins | 0 | 3 | 25 | | | | • | | • |
| **Cripps Harries Hall LLP** | 7 | 41 | 270 | | • | • | | • | |
| **Crown Prosecution Service** | 25 | | 9000 | ✔ | | | • | | |
| Cunningtons | Varies(09) | 10 | 180 | ✔ | | | | • | • |
| Curwens | 2(08) | 15 | 120 | ✔ | | | | • | |
| Darbys | 3 | 25 | 145 | | • | • | • | • | • |
| David Cowan Solicitors | 0 | 1 | 19 | | | | | • | • |
| Dean Wilson Laing | 1(09) | 8 | 46 | | • | • | • | • | |
| Dexter Montague & Partners | 1-2(08) | 4 | | ✔ | | | | | • |
| **DMH Stallard Solicitors** | 10 | 52 | 350 | ✔ | • | • | | • | |
| Dollman and Pritchard | Poss | 3 | 38 | | | | | • | • |
| **Dorsey & Whitney** | 4 | 14 | 75 | | • | | | | |

| Arbitration | Banking | Comp/comm | Competition | Construction | Corporate tax | Crime | Employment | Environment | Family | Human rights | Insurance | IP | Litigation | Personal injury | Private client | Property | Shipping | TMT |
|---|---|---|---|---|---|---|---|---|---|---|---|---|---|---|---|---|---|---|
| • | • | • | • | • | • |  | • | • | • | • |  | • | • | • | • | • |  | • |
|  |  |  |  |  |  | • |  |  | • |  |  |  |  |  |  |  |  |  |
| • | • | • | • | • | • |  | • | • | • |  | • |  | • | • | • | • | • | • |
|  |  | • | • |  | • |  | • | • | • |  |  |  | • | • | • | • |  | • |
|  |  | • |  |  |  | • | • |  | • |  |  | • | • | • | • | • |  | • |
|  |  | • |  | • | • |  | • |  | • |  |  | • | • | • | • | • |  | • |
|  |  | • |  |  |  |  | • | • | • |  |  | • | • | • | • | • |  |  |
| • |  |  |  |  |  |  | • | • | • |  |  |  | • | • | • |  |  |  |
|  |  | • |  |  | • |  | • | • | • |  |  | • | • | • | • | • |  | • |
| • |  | • |  |  | • |  | • | • | • |  |  | • | • | • | • | • |  | • |
|  |  | • |  |  |  |  | • | • | • |  |  |  | • | • | • |  |  |  |
|  |  |  |  |  |  | • | • | • | • |  |  |  | • | • | • | • |  |  |
|  |  | • |  |  |  |  | • | • | • |  |  | • | • | • | • | • |  |  |
|  |  | • |  |  |  |  | • | • | • |  |  |  | • | • | • | • |  |  |
|  |  | • |  | • |  |  | • | • | • |  |  |  | • | • | • | • |  |  |
|  |  | • |  |  |  |  | • | • | • |  |  |  | • | • | • | • |  |  |
|  |  | • | • | • | • |  | • | • | • | • |  |  | • | • | • | • |  |  |
|  |  |  |  |  |  |  | • | • | • |  |  |  |  | • | • | • |  |  |
| • | • | • | • | • | • |  | • | • | • |  | • | • | • | • | • | • |  | • |
| • |  |  |  | • |  |  | • | • | • |  |  |  |  |  | • |  |  |  |
|  |  |  |  |  |  |  | • | • | • | • |  |  | • |  |  |  |  |  |
| • |  | • |  | • |  |  | • |  | • |  |  |  | • | • | • | • |  |  |
|  |  | • |  |  |  |  | • |  | • |  |  |  | • | • | • | • |  |  |
|  | • | • | • | • | • |  | • | • | • |  | • | • | • | • | • | • | • | • |
| • | • | • | • | • |  |  | • |  | • |  | • | • | • | • | • | • |  | • |
|  |  | • |  |  |  |  | • |  | • |  |  |  |  | • |  |  |  |  |
|  |  |  |  |  |  |  | • |  | • |  |  |  | • | • | • | • |  |  |
| • |  | • |  | • | • |  | • | • | • |  |  | • | • | • | • | • |  | • |
|  |  |  |  |  |  | • |  |  |  |  |  |  |  |  |  |  |  |  |
|  |  | • |  |  |  |  | • |  | • |  |  |  | • |  | • |  |  |  |
|  |  | • | • |  |  |  | • |  | • |  |  |  | • | • | • | • |  |  |
|  |  | • |  |  |  |  | • | • | • |  |  | • | • | • | • | • |  | • |
|  |  |  |  |  |  |  | • |  | • |  |  |  |  |  | • |  |  |  |
| • |  | • |  | • |  |  | • |  | • |  |  |  | • | • | • | • |  |  |
|  |  |  |  |  |  |  | • | • |  | • | • |  | • | • | • | • |  |  |
| • | • | • |  | • |  |  | • | • | • |  |  |  | • | • |  | • |  | • |
|  |  |  |  |  |  | • | • |  | • |  |  |  |  |  | • | • |  |  |
| • | • | • | • | • | • |  | • |  |  |  |  |  | • | • |  | • |  | • |

| | Vacancies | Partners | Total staff | Work placement | Corporate/commercial | General commercial | Niche | General practice | High street/legal aid |
|---|---|---|---|---|---|---|---|---|---|
| Dover District Council | 0 | | 9 | | • | | | | |
| Drysdales | 1(09) | 2 | 18 | | | | | • | |
| East Hampshire District Council | 0 | | 7 | | | | | | |
| **EDF Energy** | 0 | | 43 | | • | | | | |
| Edward de Silva & Co | 1 | 1 | 10 | ✔ | | • | • | • | |
| Edwards Duthie | 6(09) | 20 | 200 | | • | • | | • | • |
| **emw law LLP** | 3(09) | 19 | 130 | | • | • | | • | |
| Eric Robinson Solicitors | 1(09) | 8 | 140 | | | | | • | |
| Essex County Council | 0 | 0 | 105 | | | | | • | |
| Fancy & Jackson | 1 | 4 | 21 | | | • | • | • | • |
| Fearon & Co | 1(08) | 2 | 8 | | | | | • | |
| Field Seymour Parkes | 3 | 13 | 105 | ✔ | • | • | | • | • |
| **Foreman Laws** | 2(08) | 12 | 55 | ✔ | | • | | | |
| Frances Lindsay & Co | 0-1 | 1 | 5 | | | | • | | |
| Franklins Solicitors LLP | 0 | 9 | 125 | | • | • | | • | • |
| **Furley Page LLP** | 2 | 20 | 100 | | • | | | | |
| **Gaby Hardwicke** | 1(09) | 17 | 180 | | • | • | | • | |
| Garden House Solicitors | 0 | 1 | 4 | ✔ | | | | | |
| Gill Turner Tucker | 1 | 6 | 25 | | | • | | | |
| Glanvilles | 1 | 12 | 120 | | • | • | | • | • |
| **Government Legal Service** | 22-30 | | 1950 | ✔ | • | • | | | |
| Gregory Rowcliffe Milners | 1(09) | 13 | 55 | | | | | | |
| Guildford Borough Council | 0 | | 17 | | | | | | |
| Gurney-Champion & Co | 0 | 2 | 8 | | | | | • | |
| Harris Cartier LLP | 2(08) | 9 | 100 | | • | • | • | • | |
| Hart Brown | 2 | 14 | 110 | | • | | | • | |
| Hart Reade | 0 | 8 | 72 | | | • | | • | • |
| Hawkes Hill | 0 | | | | | | | • | |
| Hawkins Russell Jones | 0 | 14 | 72 | | | | | • | |
| Heath Buckeridge | 0-1 | 2 | 15 | | • | • | | | |
| **Henmans LLP** | 3 | 23 | 140 | | • | • | • | | |
| Herrington & Carmichael | 1-2(09) | 10 | 80 | | • | • | | • | • |
| Hill & Abbott | 0(09) | 7 | 60 | | | | | • | • |
| HKH Kenwright & Cox | 0 | 2 | 19 | ✔ | • | | | • | • |
| Hodders | 0 | 4 | 65 | | • | • | | • | • |
| Holden & Co | 1 | 1 | 36 | | | | | • | • |
| Holmes & Hills Incorporating Young & Co | 0 | 12 | 100 | | | | | • | |
| Horwood & James | 1 | 5 | 32 | | | | | • | |
| Howell-Jones LLP | 2+(09) | 11 | 45 | | | | | • | |
| Howlett Clarke | 2 | 9 | 70 | | | | | • | |
| **IBB Solicitors** | 6(08) | 32 | 200 | | • | • | | • | • |

| Arbitration | Banking | Comp/comm | Competition | Construction | Corporate tax | Crime | Employment | Environment | Family | Human rights | Insurance | IP | Litigation | Personal injury | Private client | Property | Shipping | TMT |
|---|---|---|---|---|---|---|---|---|---|---|---|---|---|---|---|---|---|---|
| | | | • | | | • | • | • | | | | | | | | • | | |
| | | • | | | | | • | | | | | • | • | • | • | • | | |
| | | | | | | • | | • | | | | | | | | | | |
| | | | | | | | | | | | | | | | | | | |
| | | | | | | • | | | • | | | | | | | • | | |
| | | | | | | • | • | | • | | | | • | • | • | • | | |
| | • | • | | • | | | • | | | | | • | • | | | • | | • |
| | | • | | • | | | • | | • | | | | | | | • | | |
| | | • | | | | • | • | • | • | | • | | | | | • | | |
| • | | • | | | | • | • | | • | | | | • | • | • | • | | |
| | • | • | • | • | | | • | • | • | | | • | • | • | • | • | | • |
| | | • | • | | | | • | • | • | | | • | • | • | • | • | | • |
| | | | | | | | | | • | | | | | | | | | |
| | | • | | | | | • | | • | | | • | | | • | • | | |
| • | | • | | | | | • | • | • | | | • | • | • | • | • | | • |
| | | • | | | | | • | | • | | | • | • | • | • | • | | |
| | | | | | | | | | | | | | | • | | | | |
| | | • | | | | | • | | • | | | | | | • | • | | |
| | | • | | | | | • | | • | | | | • | • | • | • | | • |
| • | • | • | • | • | • | • | • | • | • | • | • | • | • | • | • | • | • | • |
| | | • | • | | | | • | | • | | | | • | • | • | • | | • |
| | | • | | | | | • | | • | | | | • | • | • | • | | |
| | | • | | | | | • | | • | | | | • | • | • | • | | |
| | • | • | | • | | | • | | • | • | • | | • | • | • | • | | • |
| • | | • | | | | | • | | • | | | | • | • | • | • | | |
| | | | | | | | • | | • | | | | | | | • | | |
| | | • | | | | | • | | • | | | | • | • | • | • | | |
| | | • | | | • | | • | | • | | | | • | • | • | • | | |
| | | • | | • | • | | • | | • | | | • | • | • | • | • | | • |
| | | • | | | | | • | | • | | | • | • | • | • | • | | • |
| | | • | | | | | • | | • | | | | • | • | • | • | | |
| | | | | | | • | • | | • | | | | • | • | • | • | | • |
| | | • | | | | | • | | • | | | | • | • | • | • | | |
| | | | | | | • | • | | • | | | | | • | | | | |
| | | • | | | | | • | | • | | | | • | • | • | • | | |
| | | • | | | | | • | | • | | | • | • | • | • | • | | |
| | | • | | | | | • | | • | | | • | • | • | • | • | | |
| | | • | | | | | • | | • | | | | | • | • | • | | |
| | | • | | • | | • | • | | • | | • | | • | • | • | • | | |

| | Vacancies | Partners | Total staff | Work placement | Corporate/ commercial | General commercial | Niche | General practice | High street/ legal aid |
|---|---|---|---|---|---|---|---|---|---|
| Jarmans Solicitors | 0[08] | 2 | 21 | | | | | • | • |
| John Chapman and Co | 0 | 4 | 22 | | | | | • | • |
| **Kennedys** | 10[08] | 90 | 530 | | • | • | • | | |
| Kenneth Elliott & Rowe | Poss[09] | 10 | 65 | ✔ | • | • | | • | |
| **Kimbells LLP** | 6[09] | 12 | 85 | ✔ | • | • | • | • | |
| Kingsley Smith Solicitors LLP | 0 | 4 | 20 | | • | • | | | |
| Knights | 0 | 5 | 14 | ✔ | | • | | | |
| Kpfd Solicitors | 1 | 3 | 8 | | | | | | • |
| KSB Law | 2 | 22 | 111 | ✔ | | • | | | |
| Lamport Bassitt | 3 | 10 | 80 | | • | • | • | | |
| Landes Hutton LLP | 1[08] | 2 | 14 | ✔ | | | | • | |
| Larcomes LLP | 1 | 4 | 53 | | | • | • | • | • |
| Lawson Lewis & Co | 2[09] | 3 | 60 | | | | | • | |
| Layard Horsfall | 0 | 1 | 3 | | | | • | | |
| **Laytons** | 6 | 34 | 170 | ✔ | • | • | | | |
| Lennon & Co | 0 | 6 | 31 | | | | | • | |
| Leonard & Co | 1 | 3 | 20 | | | | | | • |
| **Lewis Silkin LLP** | 5 | 45 | 245 | ✔ | • | • | | | |
| Lightfoots | 0 | 3 | 106 | | | • | • | • | |
| M S Solicitors Limited | 0 | 3 | 8 | | | | • | | |
| Machins | 0 | 9 | 80 | | • | • | • | • | • |
| Mackarness & Lunt | 0 | 6 | 35 | | | | | • | |
| Mackrell Turner Garrett | 2 | 13 | 60 | | • | | | | |
| **Manches LLP** | 10 | 60 | 290 | ✔ | • | • | • | | |
| Martin Cray and Co | 1 | 2 | 22 | ✔ | | | | • | |
| Martin Murray & Associates | 0 | 6 | 70 | | | | | • | • |
| **Matthew Arnold & Baldwin** | 4[09] | 32 | 265 | | • | • | | | |
| Mayo Wynne Baxter | 4[09] | 32 | 240 | | | | | • | • |
| Meldrum Young | 2 | 3 | 30 | | | | • | | |
| Meldrum Young Solicitors | 4 | 4 | 106 | ✔ | | | | | • |
| Merriman White | 0 | 2 | 40 | ✔ | • | • | | • | |
| Monarch Airlines Limited | 0 | | 5 | | | | | | |
| **Morgan Cole** | 12 | 47 | 410 | ✔ | • | • | | | |
| Mowll & Mowll | 0 | 4 | 26 | | • | • | | • | |
| Mullis & Peake | Poss[08] | 9 | 70 | | | | | • | |
| **Mundays LLP** | 3 | 26 | 155 | | • | • | • | | |
| Noble | 0 | 3 | 40 | ✔ | | | | | • |
| Nockolds | 3[09] | 8 | 85 | | • | • | | • | • |
| Oldhams Solicitors | 2 | 4 | 16 | | | | | • | • |
| **Olswang** | Up to 24 | 83 | 585 | ✔ | • | | • | | |
| Ormerods | 2[09] | 8 | 120 | | | | | • | • |

| Arbitration | Banking | Comp/comm | Competition | Construction | Corporate tax | Crime | Employment | Environment | Family | Human rights | Insurance | IP | Litigation | Personal injury | Private client | Property | Shipping | TMT |
|---|---|---|---|---|---|---|---|---|---|---|---|---|---|---|---|---|---|---|
|  |  | • |  |  |  |  | • | • | • |  |  |  | • |  | • | • |  |  |
|  |  |  |  |  |  |  |  |  | • |  |  |  |  | • |  |  |  |  |
| • | • | • |  | • |  |  | • | • |  |  | • | • | • | • | • | • | • |  |
|  |  | • |  |  |  |  | • |  | • |  |  | • | • | • | • | • | • |  |
|  | • | • | • | • |  |  | • |  |  |  |  | • | • |  |  | • |  | • |
|  |  | • | • | • |  |  | • | • |  | • |  |  | • |  |  | • |  | • |
|  |  |  |  |  | • |  | • | • |  |  |  |  | • | • | • | • |  | • |
|  |  |  |  |  | • |  | • |  |  |  |  |  |  | • | • |  |  |  |
| • |  | • |  |  |  |  | • |  | • |  | • | • | • |  | • | • | • |  |
|  |  | • |  |  |  |  | • |  | • |  |  |  | • |  | • | • |  |  |
|  |  |  |  |  | • |  | • |  | • |  |  |  |  |  | • | • |  |  |
|  |  | • |  |  | • |  | • |  | • |  |  |  | • | • | • | • |  |  |
|  |  |  |  |  |  |  | • |  | • |  |  |  | • |  |  | • |  |  |
|  |  |  |  |  |  |  |  |  |  |  |  |  | • |  |  | • |  |  |
| • | • | • | • | • | • |  | • | • | • |  |  | • | • | • | • | • | • | • |
|  | • | • |  |  |  |  | • | • | • |  |  |  |  | • | • | • | • |  |
|  |  |  |  |  |  | • | • |  | • | • |  |  |  |  |  |  |  |  |
| • |  | • |  | • |  |  | • |  |  |  |  |  | • | • |  | • |  | • |
|  |  | • |  |  |  |  | • |  | • |  | • |  | • |  | • | • |  |  |
|  |  |  |  |  |  |  | • |  |  |  |  |  |  |  |  |  |  |  |
|  |  | • |  | • |  |  | • | • | • |  |  |  | • | • | • | • |  | • |
|  |  | • |  |  |  |  | • |  | • |  |  |  |  | • | • | • |  |  |
|  |  |  |  |  |  |  | • |  | • |  |  |  | • |  |  | • |  |  |
|  | • | • | • | • | • |  | • |  | • |  | • | • | • | • | • | • |  | • |
|  |  | • |  |  |  | • | • |  | • |  |  |  |  | • | • | • | • |  |
|  |  |  |  |  |  | • |  |  | • |  |  |  |  |  |  |  |  |  |
| • | • | • | • | • | • |  | • |  | • |  | • | • | • | • | • | • |  | • |
|  |  | • |  |  |  |  | • | • |  | • |  |  | • | • | • | • |  |  |
|  |  |  |  |  |  |  | • |  |  |  |  |  |  |  |  |  |  |  |
|  |  | • |  | • |  | • | • |  | • |  |  |  | • | • | • | • |  |  |
|  |  | • | • |  |  |  | • |  |  |  |  |  | • | • | • |  |  |  |
| • | • | • | • | • | • |  | • | • | • |  | • | • | • | • | • | • |  | • |
|  |  | • |  |  |  |  |  |  | • |  |  |  | • | • | • | • |  |  |
| • | • | • |  |  | • |  | • |  | • |  |  |  | • | • |  | • | • | • |
|  |  |  |  |  |  | • |  |  |  |  |  |  |  |  |  |  |  |  |
|  |  | • |  |  |  |  | • |  | • |  |  |  |  | • | • | • | • |  |
|  |  |  |  |  |  | • | • |  | • |  |  |  |  | • |  |  |  |  |
|  | • | • | • | • | • |  | • | • |  |  |  |  | • | • |  | • |  | • |
|  |  | • |  |  |  |  | • | • |  | • |  |  |  | • | • | • |  |  |

| | Vacancies | Partners | Total staff | Work placement | Corporate/ commercial | General commercial | Niche | General practice | High street/ legal aid |
|---|---|---|---|---|---|---|---|---|---|
| **Osborne Clarke** | 20 | 109 | 677 | ✔ | • | • | • | | |
| **Owen White** | 2 | 7 | 45 | | • | • | • | | |
| Owen White and Catlin | 4 | 7 | 90 | | | • | | • | • |
| **Palmers** | 3 | 10 | 116 | ✔ | • | • | | • | • |
| Parabis Law LLP | 3[09] | 21 | 263 | | | | • | | |
| **Paris Smith & Randall LLP** | 3 | 24 | 180 | ✔ | | • | | | |
| Parker Bullen | 0 | 9 | 66 | | • | • | | • | |
| Paul Robinson Solicitors | 1[08] | 7 | 70 | | | | | • | • |
| Pearson Maddin | 1 | 5 | 49 | | | • | | | |
| **Penningtons Solicitors LLP** | 14 | 70 | 420 | ✔ | • | • | | | |
| Pictons | 6 | 15 | 160 | | | • | | • | • |
| Pitmans | 6 | 28 | 210 | ✔ | • | • | • | | |
| Premier Solicitors LLP | 2 | 3 | 7 | | | | | • | |
| Pryce & Co | 0-1[09] | 1 | 18 | | | | | • | |
| Ratcliffe Duce & Gammer | 2[09] | 7 | 44 | | | • | | • | • |
| Reena Ghai Solicitors | 0-1 | 1 | 6 | | | | | | • |
| Reynolds Johns Partnership | 0 | 2 | 15 | | | | | • | |
| Reynolds Parry-Jones | 1 | 6 | 38 | | | | | • | |
| Robinson Jarvis & Rolf (RJR Solicitors) | 1 | 7 | 50 | | | | | • | • |
| Robson & Co | 0 | | | | | | | • | • |
| Russell & Co | 1 | 2 | 10 | ✔ | | • | • | | • |
| SA Law | 2[09] | 7 | 70 | | | • | | | |
| Scott Bailey | 1[09] | 4 | 18 | | | | | • | |
| The Sethi Partnership Solicitors | 0 | 2 | 25 | ✔ | | • | | • | • |
| **Shadbolt LLP** | 4 | 24 | 104 | ✔ | • | • | • | | |
| Shepherd Harris & Co | 1 | 2 | 30 | | | • | | | • |
| Sherrards | Poss[09] | 13 | 49 | | • | • | | • | |
| **Shoosmiths** | 17 | 105 | 1450 | ✔ | • | • | • | | |
| Silverbeck Rymer | 0-3[09] | 7 | 218 | | | | • | | |
| South Bedfordshire District Council | 0 | | 8 | | | | • | | |
| Southampton City Council | 0-1 | | 50 | | | | | | |
| Staffurth & Bray | 0 | 5 | 45 | | | | | • | • |
| **Stanley Tee LLP** | 4 | 17 | 175 | ✔ | • | • | | | |
| Stephens & Son LLP | 21[09] | 7 | 47 | | | • | | • | • |
| **Stevens & Bolton LLP** | 4 | 31 | 150 | ✔ | • | • | | | |
| stevensdrake | 2[09] | 9 | 65 | | • | • | • | | |
| Stone Wilder | 1 | 1 | 9 | ✔ | | | • | | |
| Talbot Walker LLP | Poss[09] | 2 | 35 | | • | • | | • | |
| Tassells | 1[09] | 3 | 24 | ✔ | | • | | • | • |
| **Taylor Walton** | 5 | 23 | 200 | ✔ | • | | | | |
| Thackray Williams | 2[09] | 20 | 145 | | • | • | | • | • |

| Arbitration | Banking | Comp/comm | Competition | Construction | Corporate tax | Crime | Employment | Environment | Family | Human rights | Insurance | IP | Litigation | Personal injury | Private client | Property | Shipping | TMT |
|---|---|---|---|---|---|---|---|---|---|---|---|---|---|---|---|---|---|---|
| • | • | • | • | • | • |  | • | • |  |  |  | • | • |  | • | • |  | • |
| • |  | • | • |  |  |  | • |  |  |  |  | • | • | • |  | • |  | • |
|  |  |  |  |  | • |  | • |  | • |  |  |  |  | • | • |  |  |  |
| • |  | • |  | • | • | • | • |  | • |  |  | • | • |  | • | • |  | • |
|  |  |  |  |  |  |  |  |  |  |  |  |  |  | • |  |  |  |  |
|  |  | • |  | • |  |  | • | • | • |  |  |  | • | • | • | • |  | • |
| • | • | • | • | • |  |  | • | • | • |  |  | • | • | • | • | • |  | • |
|  |  | • |  |  |  | • | • |  | • |  |  |  | • | • | • | • |  |  |
|  |  | • |  |  |  |  | • |  | • |  |  |  | • | • | • | • |  |  |
|  | • | • | • | • | • | • | • | • | • |  |  | • | • | • | • | • |  | • |
|  |  | • |  |  |  |  | • |  | • |  |  |  | • | • | • | • |  |  |
| • |  | • |  | • |  |  | • |  |  |  |  | • | • |  | • |  |  |  |
|  |  |  |  |  |  |  |  |  |  |  |  |  |  |  | • | • |  |  |
|  |  |  |  |  |  |  |  |  | • |  |  |  |  |  | • | • |  |  |
|  |  | • |  |  |  |  | • |  | • |  |  |  | • | • | • | • |  |  |
|  |  |  |  |  |  | • |  |  | • |  |  |  |  |  |  |  |  |  |
|  |  | • |  |  |  |  | • | • | • |  |  |  | • | • | • | • |  | • |
|  |  | • |  |  | • | • |  |  | • |  |  |  | • | • | • | • |  |  |
|  |  |  |  |  |  |  |  |  | • |  |  |  |  |  | • | • |  |  |
|  |  |  |  |  |  |  | • |  | • |  |  | • | • | • | • | • |  | • |
| • | • | • |  |  |  |  | • |  | • |  |  | • | • |  | • | • |  | • |
|  |  | • |  |  |  | • | • |  | • |  |  |  | • |  |  | • |  |  |
| • |  | • | • | • | • |  | • | • | • |  | • | • | • |  |  | • |  | • |
|  |  | • |  |  |  | • | • |  | • |  |  |  |  | • | • | • |  |  |
| • | • | • |  |  |  |  | • |  | • |  |  | • | • |  | • | • |  |  |
| • | • | • | • | • | • |  | • | • | • |  | • |  |  |  | • | • |  | • |
|  |  |  |  |  |  |  |  |  |  |  |  |  |  | • | • |  |  |  |
|  |  | • |  | • |  |  | • |  | • |  |  |  |  |  |  | • |  | • |
|  |  | • |  |  |  |  | • | • | • | • |  |  | • | • | • | • |  |  |
|  |  | • | • |  | • |  | • | • | • |  | • |  | • | • | • | • |  |  |
|  |  | • |  |  |  |  | • |  | • |  |  |  | • | • | • |  |  |  |
| • | • | • | • | • |  |  | • | • | • |  |  | • | • |  | • | • |  | • |
|  |  | • | • | • | • |  | • |  | • |  |  | • | • | • | • | • |  | • |
|  |  | • |  |  |  |  | • |  |  |  |  |  | • |  |  |  |  |  |
|  |  | • |  |  |  | • |  |  |  |  |  |  | • | • |  |  |  |  |
|  |  |  |  | • |  |  | • |  | • | • |  |  | • | • | • | • |  |  |
|  |  | • |  |  |  |  | • |  | • |  |  | • | • |  | • | • |  | • |
|  |  | • |  | • |  |  | • |  | • |  |  | • | • | • | • | • |  |  |

| | Vacancies | Partners | Total staff | Work placement | Corporate/ commercial | General commercial | Niche | General practice | High street/ legal aid |
|---|---|---|---|---|---|---|---|---|---|
| Thales Corporate Services Limited | 0 | | 10000 | | • | | | | |
| **Thomas Eggar** | 6 | 60 | 429 | ✔ | • | • | • | | |
| Thompsons | Poss(09) | 38 | 800 | | | | • | | |
| **Thomson Snell & Passmore** | 5 | 34 | 200 | ✔ | • | • | | • | |
| Thomson Webb & Corfield | 1 | 9 | 39 | | | | | • | |
| **Trethowans** | 4 | 24 | 160 | | • | • | | • | • |
| Truemans | 0 | 2 | 18 | | | | | • | • |
| Turbervilles | 1-2(09) | 11 | 67 | | • | • | • | • | |
| Underwoods | 1-2(09) | 3 | 15 | | | | • | • | |
| **Vertex Law LLP** | 0(09) | 8 | 42 | ✔ | • | | | | |
| Vizards Tweedie | 0 | 20 | 51 | | • | • | | • | |
| Vizards Wyeth | 2 | 22 | | | • | • | • | | |
| Vodafone Group Services | 1 | | 70 | ✔ | • | • | | | |
| Wannop & Fox | 1-2(09) | 6 | 52 | | | | | • | • |
| Warner Goodman LLP | 3 | 17 | 240 | | | • | | • | • |
| Warners | 2(09) | 13 | 125 | | | | | • | |
| Watkins Solicitors | 0 | 2 | 7 | ✔ | | | • | | |
| Wellers | 1-2(09) | 4 | 37 | | • | • | | • | |
| WH Matthews & Co | 3(09) | 10 | 60 | | | | | • | |
| White & Co | 1 | 1 | 7 | | | | • | | • |
| Whitehead Monckton | Varies(09) | 12 | 68 | | | | | • | |
| Wills Chandler | 1(09) | 4 | 22 | | | | | • | • |
| Wilmer Cutler Pickering Hale & Dorr | 2-4(08) | 10 | 90 | | • | | | | |
| Wilson & Bird | 1(08) | 1 | 9 | | | | | • | • |
| Winckworth Sherwood | 4(09) | 24 | 185 | ✔ | | • | • | | |
| Windsor Bronzite | 0 | 3 | 11 | | | | | • | |
| **Wollastons** | 2 | 13 | 103 | | • | • | | | |
| Woodfines LLP | 3(09) | 22 | 152 | ✔ | | | | • | |
| Woodhouse Davies & Martin | 1 | 2 | 17 | | | | | • | |
| Worthingtons | 0 | 3 | 20 | ✔ | | | | • | • |
| Wortley Byers LLP | 2(09) | 9 | 65 | | • | • | | • | |

| Arbitration | Banking | Comp/comm | Competition | Construction | Corporate tax | Crime | Employment | Environment | Family | Human rights | Insurance | IP | Litigation | Personal injury | Private client | Property | Shipping | TMT |
|---|---|---|---|---|---|---|---|---|---|---|---|---|---|---|---|---|---|---|
|  |  |  |  |  |  |  |  |  |  |  |  | • | • |  |  | • |  |  |
| • | • | • | • | • | • | • | • | • | • |  |  | • | • | • | • | • |  | • |
|  |  |  |  |  | • |  | • |  |  |  |  |  |  | • |  |  |  |  |
| • |  | • | • | • | • |  | • | • | • | • | • | • | • | • | • | • |  | • |
|  |  | • |  |  | • |  | • |  | • |  |  |  | • |  | • | • |  |  |
|  |  | • |  |  |  |  | • |  | • |  |  | • | • | • | • | • |  |  |
|  |  | • |  |  | • |  | • |  | • |  |  |  | • | • | • | • |  |  |
| • |  | • |  | • | • | • | • | • | • |  |  | • | • | • | • | • |  | • |
|  |  | • |  |  |  |  | • |  | • |  |  | • | • | • | • | • |  | • |
|  | • | • |  |  | • | • |  | • |  |  |  | • | • | • | • | • |  | • |
| • | • | • | • |  |  | • |  | • |  |  |  | • | • | • | • | • |  | • |
|  |  | • |  | • |  |  | • |  | • |  | • | • | • | • | • | • |  |  |
|  | • | • | • |  |  |  | • |  | • |  |  | • | • |  |  |  |  | • |
|  |  | • |  |  | • |  | • |  | • |  |  | • | • | • | • | • |  |  |
|  |  | • |  |  | • | • | • |  | • | • |  | • | • | • | • | • |  |  |
|  |  | • |  | • |  |  | • |  | • |  |  | • | • | • | • | • |  |  |
|  |  | • |  |  |  |  |  |  | • |  |  |  |  |  |  |  |  |  |
|  |  | • |  |  |  | • | • | • | • |  |  | • | • | • | • | • |  |  |
|  |  | • |  | • |  | • | • |  | • |  |  | • | • | • | • | • |  |  |
|  |  |  |  |  |  | • |  |  | • |  |  | • |  |  |  |  |  |  |
|  | • | • |  |  | • |  | • |  | • |  |  | • | • | • | • | • |  |  |
|  |  | • |  |  |  |  | • | • | • |  |  |  |  |  | • | • |  |  |
|  |  | • |  |  | • |  | • |  | • |  |  | • |  |  |  |  |  | • |
|  |  |  |  |  | • |  |  |  | • |  |  |  | • | • | • | • |  |  |
| • |  | • |  | • |  |  | • |  | • |  |  |  | • |  | • | • |  |  |
|  |  |  |  |  |  |  |  |  | • |  |  |  |  | • | • | • |  |  |
|  |  | • |  | • |  |  | • |  | • |  |  | • | • | • | • | • |  | • |
| • |  | • | • | • |  | • | • | • | • |  |  | • | • | • | • | • |  | • |
|  |  |  |  |  |  |  | • |  | • |  |  |  |  | • | • | • |  |  |
|  |  |  |  |  | • |  | • |  | • |  |  |  |  | • | • |  |  |  |
| • |  | • |  | • | • |  | • | • | • |  |  | • | • |  | • | • |  | • |

# Southwest

| | Vacancies | Partners | Total staff | Work placement | Corporate/ commercial | General commercial | Niche | General practice | High street/ legal aid |
|---|---|---|---|---|---|---|---|---|---|
| AMD Solicitors Limited | 1(08) | 2 | 30 | | | • | | • | • |
| Andrew Isaacs Solicitors | 0 | 2 | 14 | ✔ | | | | • | |
| **Ashfords** | 15 | 51 | 450 | ✔ | | | | | |
| Awdry Bailey & Douglas | 0 | 6 | 132 | | • | • | • | • | • |
| Battens Solicitors Limited | 0 | 15 | 144 | | | | | • | • |
| **Beachcroft LLP** | 30 | 147 | 1400 | ✔ | • | • | | | |
| Beale and Company Solicitors LLP | 2-3 | 11 | 75 | | • | • | • | | |
| Bennetts Solicitors & Attorneys | 1 | 4 | 15 | | • | • | • | | |
| **Berrymans Lace Mawer** | 17 | 115 | 792 | ✔ | | • | | | |
| **Bevan Brittan LLP** | 12 | 62 | 520 | ✔ | • | • | | | |
| Bevirs | 1 | 7 | 56 | | | | | • | • |
| Beviss & Beckingsale | 1(09) | 9 | 60 | | | | | • | |
| Blanchards | 1(09) | 3 | 45 | | | | | • | |
| **Bond Pearce LLP** | 15 | 74 | 700 | ✔ | • | • | | | |
| **BPE** | 1 | 25 | 135 | ✔ | • | | | | |
| Brain Sinnott & Co | 0-1 | 3 | 25 | | | | | • | • |
| BS Singh & Co | Poss 2 | 2 | 3 | ✔ | | | | • | |
| **Burges Salmon** | 22 | 64 | 614 | ✔ | • | • | • | | |
| Burroughs Day | 2 | 13 | 131 | | • | • | | • | |
| Capital Law | 3(09) | 12 | 57 | | • | • | | | |
| Chanter Ferguson | 0 | 3 | 20 | | | | | • | • |
| **Charles Russell LLP** | 20 | 93 | 626 | ✔ | • | • | | | |
| Charlesworth Nicholl & Co | 1 | 2 | 20 | | | | | | • |
| Clarke & Son LLP | 0 | 5 | 30 | | • | • | | • | • |
| **Clarke Willmott** | 10 | 84 | 625 | | • | • | | | |
| **CMS Cameron McKenna LLP** | 60 | 131 | 1500 | ✔ | • | • | | | |
| Coles Miller | 2(09) | 11 | 110 | | • | • | | • | |
| Crosse & Crosse | 0 | 8 | 56 | | • | • | | | |
| **Crown Prosecution Service** | 25 | | 9000 | ✔ | | | • | | |
| Davies and Partners | 5(09) | 25 | 203 | | • | • | | • | |
| Davies Johnson & Co | 1(09) | 4 | 12 | ✔ | | | • | | |
| Devon & Cornwall Constabulary | 0 | 1 | 7 | | | | • | | |
| Dickinson Manser | 2(09) | 7 | 80 | | | • | | • | • |
| Douglas & Partners | 0-2(09) | 4 | 26 | | | | • | • | • |
| Douglas Pidsley & Roberts | 1 | 2 | 15 | | | | | • | |
| Ellis Jones | 2(09) | 11 | 125 | | • | • | | • | • |
| Everys | 0 | 23 | 170 | | • | • | | • | • |
| Farnfield & Nicholls | 0 | 4 | 65 | | | | | • | • |
| Follett Stock | 2(09) | 5 | 45 | ✔ | • | | • | | |
| **Foot Anstey** | 12 | 30 | 300 | ✔ | • | • | • | • | |
| Ford Simey | 2 | 14 | 92 | | | | | • | |

| Arbitration | Banking | Comp/comm | Competition | Construction | Corporate tax | Crime | Employment | Environment | Family | Human rights | Insurance | IP | Litigation | Personal injury | Private client | Property | Shipping | TMT |
|---|---|---|---|---|---|---|---|---|---|---|---|---|---|---|---|---|---|---|
|  |  |  |  |  |  |  |  |  | • |  |  |  |  |  | • | • |  |  |
|  |  |  |  |  |  |  |  |  | • |  |  |  | • | • |  |  |  |  |
| • | • | • | • | • | • | • | • | • | • |  | • | • | • | • | • | • | • | • |
|  |  | • |  | • |  | • | • |  | • |  |  |  |  | • | • | • |  |  |
| • | • | • | • | • | • |  | • | • | • |  |  | • | • | • | • | • |  | • |
| • |  | • | • | • | • |  | • | • |  |  | • | • | • | • | • | • |  | • |
| • | • | • | • |  | • |  | • | • |  |  | • | • | • | • | • | • |  | • |
| • |  | • | • | • |  |  | • |  |  |  | • | • | • | • | • | • | • | • |
|  |  | • |  | • |  |  | • | • |  |  | • | • | • | • |  | • |  |  |
| • | • | • | • | • | • |  | • | • |  |  | • | • | • | • | • | • |  | • |
|  |  | • |  |  |  |  | • |  | • |  |  |  | • | • | • | • |  |  |
|  |  | • |  |  |  |  | • | • | • |  |  |  | • | • | • | • |  |  |
| • | • | • | • | • | • |  | • | • | • |  | • | • | • | • | • | • | • | • |
| • |  | • |  | • |  |  | • |  | • |  |  |  | • | • | • | • |  | • |
|  |  | • |  |  |  |  | • | • |  |  |  |  | • | • |  | • |  | • |
| • | • | • | • | • | • |  | • | • | • |  | • | • | • | • | • | • |  | • |
|  |  | • |  |  |  |  | • |  | • |  |  |  | • | • | • | • |  |  |
|  |  | • |  |  |  |  | • |  | • |  |  |  | • | • | • | • |  |  |
| • | • | • | • | • | • |  | • | • | • |  | • | • | • | • | • | • |  | • |
| • | • | • |  | • | • |  | • | • | • |  | • | • | • | • | • | • | • | • |
|  |  | • |  | • |  |  | • | • | • |  |  |  | • | • | • | • |  |  |
|  |  | • |  |  |  |  | • | • | • |  |  |  | • | • | • | • |  |  |
|  |  |  |  |  |  | • |  |  |  |  |  |  |  |  |  |  |  |  |
| • |  | • |  |  |  |  | • | • |  |  |  |  | • | • | • | • |  | • |
| • |  |  |  |  |  |  | • |  |  |  |  | • | • | • |  |  | • |  |
|  |  |  |  |  |  |  | • | • |  | • |  |  |  | • |  |  |  |  |
|  |  | • |  |  |  |  | • |  | • |  |  |  | • | • | • | • |  |  |
|  |  |  |  |  |  | • |  |  |  |  |  |  |  |  |  |  |  |  |
|  |  |  |  |  |  |  |  |  | • |  |  |  |  |  | • | • |  |  |
|  |  | • |  |  | • |  | • |  | • |  |  |  | • | • | • | • |  |  |
|  |  | • |  |  |  | • | • |  | • | • |  | • | • | • | • | • |  |  |
|  |  | • |  |  |  |  | • |  | • |  |  |  | • | • | • | • |  |  |
|  |  | • |  |  |  |  | • |  | • |  |  |  | • | • | • | • |  |  |
| • |  | • |  | • |  |  | • |  |  |  |  |  | • | • |  | • |  | • |
| • | • | • | • | • | • | • | • | • | • |  | • |  | • | • | • | • | • | • |
|  |  | • |  |  |  |  | • |  | • |  |  |  | • | • | • | • |  |  |

| | Vacancies | Partners | Total staff | Work placement | Corporate/ commercial | General commercial | Niche | General practice | High street/ legal aid |
|---|---|---|---|---|---|---|---|---|---|
| Gammon Bell & Co | 1 | 2 | 25 | | | | | • | |
| Gilbert Stephens | 0 | 9 | 60 | | | | | • | • |
| Gill Akaster | 1-2(09) | 13 | 100 | | | • | • | • | • |
| **Government Legal Service** | 22-30 | | 1950 | ✔ | • | • | | • | |
| Gregg Latchams WRH | 0 | 9 | 75 | | | • | | | |
| Hooper & Wollen | 1(08) | 13 | 92 | ✔ | | | | • | • |
| Howard & Over | 0 | 3 | 32 | | | | | • | • |
| Hughes Paddison | 0 | 7 | 32 | | | | | • | • |
| Humphreys & Co | 1-2 | 4 | 30 | ✔ | • | • | • | | |
| Humphries Kirk | 1(09) | 15 | 150 | | | | | • | |
| Jacobs & Reeves | 0-1(09) | 7 | 50 | | | • | | • | |
| Jeremy Wood & Co Solicitors | 0 | 3 | 10 | | • | • | | | |
| Kirby Simcox | 0 | 7 | 65 | | | • | | • | |
| Kitson Hutchings | Poss | 16 | 90 | | • | • | | • | • |
| Laceys | 0 | 8 | 60 | | | | | • | |
| Large & Gibson | 0 | 2 | 20 | | • | • | | • | • |
| **Lester Aldridge** | 6 | 31 | 300 | ✔ | • | • | • | • | |
| Leung & Co | 1(08) | 1 | 8 | | | | | • | |
| Lyons Davidson | 5-7 | 31 | 750 | ✔ | • | • | | • | • |
| McEwens Solicitors | 0-1 | | 40 | | | | | • | |
| Metcalfes Solicitors | 1 | 9 | 55 | | | • | • | | |
| **Michelmores** | 10 | 32 | 286 | ✔ | | • | | | |
| Mogers | 2(09) | 7 | 51 | | | | | • | |
| Mustoe Shorter | 0 | 7 | 50 | | | | | • | • |
| Nalders | 1(09) | 9 | 115 | | | • | | • | |
| Nash & Co | 1 | 7 | 70 | | | • | | • | |
| **Osborne Clarke** | 20 | 109 | 677 | ✔ | • | • | • | • | |
| Pardoes | 2 | 12 | 100 | | • | • | | • | • |
| Parker Bullen | 0 | 9 | 66 | | • | • | | • | |
| Penleys LLP | 0 | 4 | 23 | | | | | • | • |
| **Pinsent Masons** | 55 | 260 | 1500 | ✔ | • | • | | | |
| Porter Dodson | Poss(09) | 25 | 170 | | • | • | | • | • |
| Rawlins Davy | 0 | 8 | 45 | | • | • | | • | |
| **Reynolds Porter Chamberlain LLP** | 15 | 65 | 500 | ✔ | • | • | | | |
| **Rickerbys** | 3-4 | 20 | 188 | ✔ | • | • | | | |
| Ross Solicitor | 0 | 1 | 11 | | | | | | • |
| Samuels | 1(09) | 3 | 21 | | | | | • | |
| Scott Rowe Solicitors | 1 | 3 | 25 | | | | | • | |
| **Sewell Mullings & Logie** | 1(09) | 5 | 45 | | | | | • | |
| **Shoosmiths** | 17 | 105 | 1450 | ✔ | • | • | • | • | |
| Slee Blackwell | 0 | 13 | 85 | | | | | • | |

| Arbitration | Banking | Comp/comm | Competition | Construction | Corporate tax | Crime | Employment | Environment | Family | Human rights | Insurance | IP | Litigation | Personal injury | Private client | Property | Shipping | TMT |
|---|---|---|---|---|---|---|---|---|---|---|---|---|---|---|---|---|---|---|
|  |  |  |  |  |  |  |  |  | • |  |  |  |  | • | • | • |  |  |
|  |  | • |  |  |  |  | • |  | • |  |  |  | • | • | • | • |  |  |
| • | • | • | • | • | • | • | • | • | • | • | • | • | • | • | • | • | • | • |
|  |  | • |  |  |  | • | • | • | • |  |  | • | • | • | • | • | • | • |
|  |  | • |  |  |  |  | • | • | • |  |  | • | • | • | • | • | • | • |
|  |  |  |  |  |  | • | • |  | • |  |  |  |  | • | • | • |  |  |
|  |  |  |  |  |  |  | • |  | • |  |  |  |  | • | • | • |  |  |
| • |  | • | • |  | • |  | • |  | • |  | • | • | • | • | • | • |  | • |
|  |  | • |  | • |  |  | • |  | • |  |  | • | • | • | • | • |  |  |
|  |  | • |  |  |  | • | • |  | • |  |  |  | • | • | • | • |  |  |
|  |  | • |  |  |  |  | • |  | • |  |  |  | • | • | • | • |  |  |
|  |  | • |  |  |  |  | • |  | • |  |  |  | • | • | • | • |  |  |
|  |  | • |  |  | • |  | • | • | • |  |  | • | • | • | • | • |  |  |
| • |  | • |  |  |  |  | • |  | • |  |  | • | • | • | • | • |  | • |
|  |  | • |  |  |  | • | • |  | • |  |  |  | • | • | • | • |  |  |
| • | • | • | • | • | • |  | • |  | • |  | • | • | • | • | • | • | • | • |
|  |  |  |  |  |  |  | • |  | • |  |  |  |  | • | • | • |  |  |
| • | • | • | • |  |  |  | • |  | • |  | • | • | • | • | • | • |  | • |
|  |  |  |  |  |  |  |  |  |  |  |  |  |  | • |  |  |  |  |
|  | • | • |  | • |  |  | • |  | • |  |  |  | • | • | • | • |  | • |
| • |  | • |  | • |  |  | • | • | • |  |  |  | • | • | • | • |  | • |
|  |  | • |  |  |  |  | • |  | • |  |  |  | • | • | • | • |  | • |
|  |  |  |  |  | • |  | • |  | • |  |  |  |  | • |  |  |  |  |
| • |  | • |  | • |  |  | • |  | • |  |  |  | • | • | • | • |  | • |
|  |  | • |  |  |  |  | • |  | • |  |  | • | • | • | • | • | • |  |
| • | • | • | • | • | • |  | • | • |  |  |  |  | • | • | • | • |  | • |
| • |  | • | • | • |  | • | • | • | • | • |  |  | • | • | • | • |  | • |
| • | • | • | • | • |  | • | • |  | • |  |  |  | • | • | • | • |  | • |
|  |  |  |  |  |  |  | • |  | • |  |  |  |  | • | • | • |  |  |
| • | • | • |  | • | • |  | • | • |  |  | • | • | • |  |  | • |  | • |
| • |  | • |  | • | • | • | • |  |  |  |  | • | • | • |  | • |  | • |
|  |  | • |  |  |  |  | • |  | • |  |  |  | • |  | • | • |  | • |
|  |  | • |  | • | • |  | • |  | • |  | • | • | • | • | • | • |  | • |
|  |  | • | • | • | • |  | • |  | • |  |  | • | • |  | • | • |  | • |
|  |  |  |  |  |  | • |  |  |  |  |  |  |  |  |  |  |  |  |
|  |  |  |  |  |  |  | • |  | • |  |  |  |  | • | • | • | • |  |
|  |  |  |  |  |  |  | • |  | • |  |  |  |  | • | • | • |  |  |
|  |  | • |  |  |  |  | • |  | • |  |  |  | • | • | • | • |  |  |
| • | • | • | • | • | • |  | • | • |  |  | • | • | • | • | • | • |  | • |
|  |  |  |  |  |  | • | • |  | • |  |  |  |  | • | • | • | • |  |

| | Vacancies | Partners | Total staff | Work placement | Corporate/ commercial | General commercial | Niche | General practice | High street/ legal aid |
|---|---|---|---|---|---|---|---|---|---|
| Stephens & Scown | 2[08] | 33 | 230 | | | | | • | |
| Stone King | 0 | 17 | 130 | | • | • | • | • | • |
| Stones | 2[09] | 23 | 150 | | • | • | • | • | |
| Talbot Walker LLP | Poss[09] | 2 | 35 | | • | • | • | | |
| Thompsons | Poss[09] | 38 | 800 | | | | • | | |
| **Thring Townsend Lee & Pembertons Solicitors** | 9 | 46 | 311 | | • | • | • | • | |
| **TLT Solicitors** | 10 | 60 | 600 | ✔ | • | • | • | • | |
| Toller Beattie | 1[09] | 3 | 40 | ✔ | • | • | | • | • |
| **Trethowans** | 4 | 24 | 160 | | • | • | | • | • |
| Triggs Read & Dart | 0-1 | 2 | 49 | | | | • | • | • |
| Trobridges | 2 | 3 | 25 | ✔ | | | | • | |
| **Trowers & Hamlins** | 22 | 106 | 652 | ✔ | • | • | | | |
| Veale Wasbrough Lawyers | 9 | 36 | 260 | ✔ | • | • | • | | |
| Wansbroughs | 1[09] | 7 | 102 | | | | | • | |
| WBW Solicitors | 0-3[09] | 22 | 140 | | | | | • | • |
| **Wiggin LLP** | 4 | 14 | 83 | | • | | • | | |
| Willans | 1 | 12 | 70 | | • | • | | • | |
| **Wilsons Solicitors LLP** | 4[09] | 30 | 152 | ✔ | • | • | • | • | |
| Withy King | 4-5 | 29 | 200 | | • | • | | • | • |
| Wood Awdry & Ford | 0 | 14 | 80 | | | | | • | |

| Arbitration | Banking | Comp/comm | Competition | Construction | Corporate tax | Crime | Employment | Environment | Family | Human rights | Insurance | IP | Litigation | Personal injury | Private client | Property | Shipping | TMT |
|---|---|---|---|---|---|---|---|---|---|---|---|---|---|---|---|---|---|---|
| • | • | • | • | • | • | • | • | • | • | • |  | • | • | • | • | • |  | • |
|  | • |  |  |  |  | • | • |  | • |  |  |  | • | • | • | • |  |  |
| • |  | • | • | • | • | • | • |  |  |  | • | • | • |  | • | • |  | • |
|  |  | • |  |  |  | • |  |  |  |  |  |  | • | • | • |  |  |  |
|  |  |  |  |  |  | • | • |  |  |  |  |  |  |  | • |  |  |  |
|  | • | • | • | • |  |  | • | • | • |  |  | • | • | • | • | • |  | • |
| • | • | • | • | • | • |  | • |  | • |  | • | • | • | • | • | • | • | • |
|  |  | • |  |  |  | • | • | • | • |  |  |  | • | • | • | • |  | • |
|  |  | • |  |  |  |  | • |  | • |  |  | • | • | • | • | • |  |  |
|  |  |  |  |  |  | • | • |  | • |  |  |  |  | • | • | • |  |  |
|  |  |  |  |  |  |  |  |  |  |  |  |  |  |  | • |  |  |  |
|  | • | • | • | • | • | • | • |  | • |  |  | • | • | • | • | • |  | • |
| • | • | • | • | • | • |  | • |  | • |  | • | • | • | • | • | • |  | • |
|  |  | • |  | • |  | • | • | • | • |  |  |  | • | • | • | • |  |  |
|  |  | • |  |  |  |  | • |  | • |  |  | • | • |  | • | • |  | • |
| • | • | • | • |  |  |  | • |  | • |  |  | • | • | • | • | • |  | • |
| • |  | • | • |  | • |  | • |  | • |  |  |  | • |  | • | • |  |  |
| • | • | • | • | • | • | • | • |  | • |  |  | • | • | • | • | • |  | • |
|  |  |  |  |  |  |  | • |  | • |  |  |  |  | • | • | • |  |  |

# Wales

| | Vacancies | Partners | Total staff | Work placement | Corporate/commercial | General commercial | Niche | General practice | High street/legal aid |
|---|---|---|---|---|---|---|---|---|---|
| Anthony Jacobs & Co | 2[08] | 1 | 5 | ✔ | | | | • | |
| Cameron Jones Hussell & Howe | 0 | 6 | 24 | | | | | • | |
| Capital Law | 3[09] | 12 | 57 | | • | • | | | |
| Carmarthenshire County Council | 1 | 6 | 16 | | • | | | | |
| Charles Crookes | 1[08] | 4 | 19 | | • | • | • | | |
| City and County of Swansea | 0 | | 60 | | | | | | |
| **Clyde & Co LLP** | 24 | 140 | 1080 | ✔ | • | • | | | |
| **Crown Prosecution Service** | 25 | | 9000 | ✔ | | | • | | |
| Cyril Jones & Co | 0 | 4 | 15 | | | | | • | |
| Darwin Gray | 0 | 5 | 17 | | | • | | | |
| DAS Legal Expenses Insurance | 1-2 | | 500 | ✔ | • | | | • | |
| David & Snape | 0 | 4 | 30 | | | • | | • | • |
| Dilwyns | 1 | 3 | 20 | ✔ | | | | • | |
| Dolmans | 4 | 14 | 106 | ✔ | • | • | • | | |
| Douglas-Jones Mercer | 2[09] | 12 | 83 | | • | • | | • | • |
| **Eversheds LLP** | 80+ | 340 | 4000 | ✔ | • | • | | | |
| Gamlins | Varies | 6 | 50 | | | • | | • | • |
| **Geldards LLP** | 8 | 53 | 400 | ✔ | • | • | • | | |
| **Government Legal Service** | 22-30 | | 1950 | ✔ | • | • | | | |
| Gwilym Hughes & Partners | 1[09] | 10 | 98 | | | | | • | • |
| Gwynne Hughes | 1 | 2 | 12 | | | | | • | • |
| Hains & Lewis | 0 | 2 | 42 | | | | | • | • |
| Harding Evans LLP | 4 | 11 | 124 | | | | | | • |
| **Hugh James** | 8 | 50 | 550 | ✔ | • | • | | • | |
| Hutchinson Thomas | 0 | 9 | 50 | ✔ | | | | • | • |
| Huttons | 1 | 5 | 35 | ✔ | | | | • | • |
| JA Hughes | 0 | 6 | 40 | ✔ | | | | • | • |
| Jones Mordey Davies Solicitors | 1[09] | 3 | 15 | ✔ | | | | • | |
| JW Hughes & Co | 1[08] | 6 | 34 | | | | | • | • |
| Kirwans | 2[09] | 7 | 79 | | • | • | | • | • |
| Leo Abse & Cohen | 0 | 13 | 140 | | • | • | | • | • |
| M & A Solicitors LLP | 3[08] | 9 | 40 | | • | | • | | |
| MLM | Varies[08] | 7 | 36 | ✔ | | • | • | | |
| **Morgan Cole** | 12 | 47 | 410 | ✔ | • | • | | | |
| PJE Solicitors | 0-1 | 2 | 10 | | | | | • | |
| R L Edwards Solicitors Ltd | 1 | 6 | 65 | | | | | • | • |
| **RadcliffesLeBrasseur** | 5 | 42 | 210 | ✔ | • | • | | | |
| Russell Jones & Walker | 10 | 49 | 630 | | | • | • | | |
| Smith Llewelyn Partnership | 1 | 4 | 40 | ✔ | | | | • | • |
| Speakeasy Advice Centre | 0 | | 15 | | | | • | | • |
| Thompsons | Poss[09] | 38 | 800 | | | | • | | |

| Arbitration | Banking | Comp/comm | Competition | Construction | Corporate tax | Crime | Employment | Environment | Family | Human rights | Insurance | IP | Litigation | Personal injury | Private client | Property | Shipping | TMT |
|---|---|---|---|---|---|---|---|---|---|---|---|---|---|---|---|---|---|---|
|  |  |  |  |  |  |  | • |  | • |  |  |  |  | • |  | • |  |  |
| • |  |  |  |  |  |  |  |  | • |  |  |  |  | • | • |  |  |  |
|  |  | • |  |  |  |  | • | • |  |  |  | • |  | • |  | • |  | • |
|  |  |  |  | • |  | • | • | • | • |  |  |  |  | • |  | • |  |  |
|  |  | • |  |  |  |  | • | • |  |  |  | • | • | • | • | • |  |  |
|  |  | • | • | • | • | • |  | • |  |  |  | • | • | • | • | • | • | • |
|  |  |  |  |  | • |  |  |  |  |  |  |  |  |  |  |  |  |  |
|  |  | • |  |  |  | • | • |  | • |  |  |  |  | • | • | • |  |  |
| • |  | • |  | • |  |  | • |  |  |  |  |  | • |  |  | • |  |  |
|  |  |  |  |  |  |  | • |  |  |  | • |  | • |  |  |  |  |  |
|  |  | • |  |  |  | • | • |  | • |  |  |  | • | • | • | • |  |  |
|  |  | • |  |  |  | • | • | • | • |  |  | • | • | • | • | • |  |  |
| • |  | • |  |  |  | • | • |  |  |  |  |  | • | • | • | • |  | • |
| • | • | • |  | • |  | • | • |  | • |  | • |  | • | • | • | • |  |  |
| • | • | • | • | • | • | • | • | • | • | • | • |  | • | • |  | • | • | • |
|  |  | • |  |  |  | • | • |  | • |  |  | • | • | • | • | • |  |  |
| • | • | • | • | • | • | • | • | • | • |  | • |  | • | • | • | • |  | • |
| • | • | • | • | • | • | • | • | • | • | • | • |  | • | • | • | • | • | • |
|  |  | • |  |  |  |  | • | • | • |  |  |  | • | • |  | • |  |  |
|  |  |  |  |  |  |  | • |  | • |  |  |  | • | • | • | • |  |  |
|  |  |  |  |  |  | • |  |  | • |  |  |  | • | • | • | • |  |  |
|  |  |  |  |  |  |  | • |  | • |  |  |  | • | • | • | • |  |  |
| • | • | • |  | • |  |  | • | • | • |  | • |  | • | • | • | • |  | • |
|  |  | • |  |  | • |  | • | • | • |  |  |  | • | • | • | • |  |  |
|  |  | • |  |  |  |  | • | • | • | • |  |  | • | • | • | • |  | • |
|  |  | • |  |  |  | • | • |  | • |  |  |  | • | • | • | • |  |  |
|  |  |  |  |  |  |  | • |  |  |  |  |  | • | • | • | • |  |  |
|  |  | • |  |  |  | • |  |  | • |  |  |  | • | • | • | • |  |  |
|  |  | • |  |  |  |  | • |  | • |  | • |  | • | • | • | • |  | • |
|  | • | • |  |  |  |  | • |  | • |  |  |  | • |  |  | • |  | • |
| • | • | • | • | • | • |  | • | • | • |  | • |  | • | • | • | • |  | • |
|  |  | • |  |  |  |  | • |  | • |  |  |  | • | • | • | • |  |  |
| • |  | • |  | • |  |  | • |  | • |  |  |  | • | • | • | • |  |  |
| • | • | • | • | • | • | • | • | • | • |  | • | • | • | • | • | • |  | • |
|  |  | • |  |  |  | • | • | • | • | • |  |  | • | • | • | • |  | • |
| • |  |  |  |  |  |  | • |  | • | • |  |  |  | • | • | • |  |  |
|  |  |  |  |  |  | • | • |  |  |  |  |  |  | • |  |  |  |  |

| | Vacancies | Partners | Total staff | Work placement | Corporate/ commercial | General commercial | Niche | General practice | High street/ legal aid |
|---|---|---|---|---|---|---|---|---|---|
| Walker Smith Way Solicitors | 3-4 | 31 | 165 | | • | • | | • | • |
| Wendy Hopkins Family Law Practice | 2[08] | 3 | 26 | | | | • | | • |

# West Midlands

| | Vacancies | Partners | Total staff | Work placement | Corporate/ commercial | General commercial | Niche | General practice | High street/ legal aid |
|---|---|---|---|---|---|---|---|---|---|
| Addison O'Hare | 0 | 5 | 38 | ✔ | | | | | • |
| Alsters Kelley | 2-3[09] | 14 | 140 | | | • | | • | • |
| Anthony Collins Solicitors | 6 | 20 | 200 | | • | • | • | • | • |
| Argyles | Poss | 3 | 13 | | | | | • | |
| Atter Mackenzie & Co | 1[08] | 5 | 26 | | | | | • | • |
| **Beachcroft LLP** | 30[09] | 147 | 1400 | ✔ | • | • | | | |
| **Bell Lax Solicitors** | 2-3[09] | 4 | 25 | ✔ | | | • | | |
| **Berrymans Lace Mawer** | 17 | 115 | 792 | ✔ | | • | | | |
| **Bevan Brittan LLP** | 12 | 62 | 520 | ✔ | • | • | | | |
| BKM Solicitors | 1[09] | 2 | 8 | ✔ | | | | | • |
| **BPE** | 1 | 25 | 135 | ✔ | • | | | | |
| Brethertons | 2 | 10 | 127 | | | | | • | |
| **Browne Jacobson LLP** | 12 | 60 | 517 | | • | • | • | | |
| Brownings | 0 | 3 | 55 | | | | | • | • |
| Buller Jeffries | 0 | | 55 | | | | • | | |
| Caldicotts | 0 | 2 | 14 | | | | | | • |
| Capital Law | 3[09] | 12 | 57 | | • | • | | | |
| Carvers | 1 | 4 | 50 | | | | | • | |
| Challinors | 4[09] | 31 | 240 | | | | | • | • |
| **Clarke Willmott** | 10 | 84 | 625 | | • | • | | • | |
| **Cobbetts LLP** | 20 | 136 | 815 | ✔ | • | • | | | |
| Cotterhill Hitchman LLP | 0 | 2 | 8 | | | • | | | |
| Coventry City Council | 0 | | 170 | | | | | | |
| Cowlishaw & Mountford | 0 | 2 | 10 | | | | | • | |
| **Crown Prosecution Service** | 25 | | 9000 | ✔ | | | • | | |
| Cunningtons | Varies[09] | 10 | 180 | ✔ | | | | • | • |
| Davies and Partners | 5[09] | 25 | 203 | | • | • | | • | |
| Df Legal LLP | 2 | 3 | 24 | ✔ | | | | • | |
| **DLA Piper UK LLP** | 95+ | 1200 | 7000 | ✔ | • | | | | |
| Elliott Bridgman | Poss 1[09] | 1 | 20 | ✔ | | | | • | • |
| Enoch Evans | 0 | 10 | 70 | | • | • | | • | • |
| **Eversheds LLP** | 80+ | 340 | 4000 | ✔ | • | • | | | |

| | Arbitration | Banking | Comp/comm | Competition | Construction | Corporate tax | Crime | Employment | Environment | Family | Human rights | Insurance | IP | Litigation | Personal injury | Private client | Property | Shipping | TMT |
|---|---|---|---|---|---|---|---|---|---|---|---|---|---|---|---|---|---|---|---|
| | • | | • | | • | • | • | • | • | • | | | • | • | • | • | • | | |
| | | | | | | | | | | • | | | | | | • | | | |

| | Arbitration | Banking | Comp/comm | Competition | Construction | Corporate tax | Crime | Employment | Environment | Family | Human rights | Insurance | IP | Litigation | Personal injury | Private client | Property | Shipping | TMT |
|---|---|---|---|---|---|---|---|---|---|---|---|---|---|---|---|---|---|---|---|
| | | | | | | | • | | | • | | | | | • | • | • | | |
| | | | • | | | | • | | | • | | | | | • | • | • | | • |
| | • | | • | | | | • | | | • | | | | • | • | • | • | | |
| | | | • | | | • | • | | | • | | | | • | • | • | • | | |
| | • | | • | • | • | • | | | • | • | | | • | • | • | | • | | • |
| | • | • | | | | | • | | | • | | | | • | • | • | | | |
| | | | | | | | • | | | • | • | | | • | • | | | • | |
| | • | • | • | • | • | • | | | • | • | | | • | • | • | | • | | • |
| | | | | | | | • | | | | | | | | | | | | |
| | | | • | | | • | | | | • | | | | • | • | • | • | | |
| | | | • | | | | | | | • | | | | • | • | • | • | | • |
| | • | • | • | | | • | | | • | • | | | • | • | • | • | • | | • |
| | | | • | | | | | | | • | | | | | • | | • | | |
| | | | | | | | | | | | | • | | | | | • | | |
| | | | | | | • | • | | | • | | | | | | • | | | |
| | | | • | | | | | | | • | • | | | • | • | | • | | • |
| | | | | | | | • | | | • | | | | | • | • | | | |
| | • | | • | | • | | • | | | • | | | | • | • | • | • | | |
| | • | • | • | • | • | • | | | • | • | • | | • | • | • | • | • | | • |
| | • | • | • | • | • | • | | | • | • | | | | • | • | • | • | | • |
| | • | | • | | • | | | | | • | | | | • | • | • | • | | |
| | | | | | | | | | | | | | | | | | | | |
| | | | • | | | • | | | | | | | | | • | | • | | |
| | • | | • | | • | | | | • | • | | | | • | • | • | • | | • |
| | | | • | | | | | | | • | | | | • | | • | • | | |
| | • | • | • | • | • | • | | | • | • | | • | • | • | | | • | • | • |
| | | | | | | • | | | | • | | | | | | • | | | |
| | • | | • | • | • | • | • | | • | • | | • | • | • | | • | • | | • |
| | • | • | • | • | • | • | | | • | • | • | • | • | • | | | • | • | • |

| | Vacancies | Partners | Total staff | Work placement | Corporate/ commercial | General commercial | Niche | General practice | High street/ legal aid |
|---|---|---|---|---|---|---|---|---|---|
| FBC Solicitors | 3(09) | 18 | 140 | | | • | | | |
| Ferdinand Kelly | 0 | 2 | 5 | | | • | • | | • |
| George Green | 2(09) | 10 | 71 | | • | • | | | |
| Gorrara Haden Solicitors | 0 | 2 | 12 | | | | • | | |
| Gough-Thomas & Scott | 1(08) | 4 | 18 | | | | | • | |
| **Government Legal Service** | 22-30 | | 1950 | ✔ | • | • | | • | |
| Gwilym Hughes & Partners | 1(09) | 10 | 98 | | | | | • | • |
| Hacking Ashton LLP | Poss 1 | 10 | 38 | | • | • | | • | |
| Hadens | 2(09) | 9 | 70 | | • | • | | • | |
| Hamilton Pratt | 1 | 3 | 10 | | | | • | | |
| **Hammonds** | 40 | 189 | 1300 | ✔ | • | | | | |
| Harrison Clark | 0 | 19 | 130 | | | • | | • | • |
| **Harvey Ingram LLP** | 4-5 | 33 | 200 | ✔ | • | • | | | |
| Hatchers | 0 | 12 | 80 | | • | • | • | • | • |
| **HBJ Gateley Wareing LLP** | 11 | 75 | 488 | ✔ | • | • | | | |
| Herefordshire District Council | 0 | 1 | 25 | | | | • | | |
| Hertfordshire District Council | 0 | | 31 | ✔ | | | • | | |
| **Higgs & Sons** | 4 | 26 | 269 | | • | • | | • | • |
| HMCS West Mercia | 0 | 0 | 43 | | | | | | |
| **Irwin Mitchell** | 20-25 | 137 | 2000 | ✔ | • | • | | • | |
| Kangs Solicitors | 1-2(09) | 1 | 10 | | | | • | | |
| **Keoghs LLP** | 4 | 30 | 506 | | | | • | | |
| KJD | 1-2(09) | 17 | 54 | ✔ | • | • | | • | |
| **Knight & Sons** | 3 | 16 | 150 | ✔ | • | • | | • | |
| Kundert & Co | 0 | 5 | 30 | | | | | • | • |
| Lanyon Bowdler | 2-3(09) | 13 | 155 | | • | | | | • |
| **Lodders Solicitors LLP** | 2(09) | 15 | 130 | | | | | • | |
| Lyons Davidson | 5-7 | 31 | 750 | ✔ | • | • | | | • |
| Maidments | Poss | 6 | 100 | | | | • | • | |
| Manby Steward Bowdler LLP | 2(09) | 20 | 145 | | | | | • | |
| Mander Hadley & Co | 0 | 9 | 46 | | • | • | | • | • |
| March & Edwards | 1(08) | 6 | 40 | | | | | • | |
| **Martineau Johnson** | 10-12 | 42 | 270 | ✔ | • | | | | |
| Martin-Kaye Solicitors | Poss | 9 | 100 | | • | • | • | • | • |
| **MFG Solicitors LLP** | 4(09) | 29 | 201 | | • | • | • | • | • |
| Mian & Co | 0 | 2 | 9 | | | | | | • |
| **Mills & Reeve LLP** | 22 | 79 | 760 | ✔ | • | | • | • | |
| **Needham & James LLP** | 5 | 25 | 180 | ✔ | | • | | | |
| Newcastle Under Lyme Borough Council | 0 | | 4 | | | | | | |
| Nijjar Solicitors | 1(09) | 2 | 10 | | | | | | • |
| Peter Scaiff LLP | 1 | 5 | 17 | | | | | • | |

| Arbitration | Banking | Comp/comm | Competition | Construction | Corporate tax | Crime | Employment | Environment | Family | Human rights | Insurance | IP | Litigation | Personal injury | Private client | Property | Shipping | TMT |
|---|---|---|---|---|---|---|---|---|---|---|---|---|---|---|---|---|---|---|
|  |  | • |  |  |  |  | • |  | • |  |  |  | • | • | • | • |  |  |
| • |  | • | • |  |  |  | • |  |  |  | • | • | • |  |  |  |  | • |
| • | • | • |  |  |  |  | • | • | • |  |  | • | • |  | • | • |  | • |
|  |  |  |  |  |  |  |  |  |  |  |  |  | • |  |  |  |  |  |
|  |  |  |  |  |  |  | • |  | • |  |  |  | • | • |  | • |  |  |
| • | • | • | • | • | • | • | • | • | • | • | • | • | • | • | • | • | • | • |
|  |  | • |  |  | • | • | • | • | • |  |  |  | • | • | • | • |  |  |
| • |  | • |  | • |  |  | • |  |  |  |  |  | • | • | • | • |  |  |
|  |  | • |  |  |  |  | • | • | • |  |  |  | • | • | • | • |  |  |
|  |  | • | • |  |  |  |  |  |  |  |  | • | • |  |  |  |  |  |
| • | • | • | • | • | • |  | • | • |  |  |  |  | • | • |  | • |  | • |
| • |  | • |  | • | • |  | • | • | • |  |  |  | • | • | • | • |  | • |
| • | • | • | • | • | • |  | • | • | • | • |  | • | • | • | • | • |  | • |
|  |  | • |  | • |  | • | • | • |  |  |  |  | • | • | • | • |  |  |
| • | • | • | • | • | • |  | • | • |  |  |  |  | • | • |  | • | • | • |
|  |  | • |  |  |  |  | • | • |  |  |  |  | • | • |  | • |  | • |
| • |  | • | • | • | • |  | • | • | • |  |  |  | • | • | • | • | • | • |
|  |  |  |  |  |  | • |  |  | • |  |  |  |  |  |  |  |  |  |
| • |  | • | • | • |  |  | • | • | • | • |  | • | • | • | • | • |  | • |
|  |  |  |  |  |  | • |  |  |  |  |  |  |  |  |  |  |  |  |
|  |  |  |  |  |  | • | • |  |  |  | • |  | • | • |  |  |  |  |
| • | • | • | • | • | • |  | • | • |  |  |  | • | • |  | • | • |  | • |
| • | • | • | • | • |  |  | • |  | • |  |  | • | • | • | • | • |  | • |
|  |  | • |  |  |  | • | • |  | • |  |  |  |  | • | • |  |  | • |
|  |  | • | • |  |  | • | • |  | • |  |  |  | • | • |  | • |  |  |
|  |  | • |  |  |  |  | • |  |  |  |  |  |  |  | • | • |  |  |
| • | • | • | • | • |  |  | • | • | • |  | • |  | • | • | • | • |  |  |
|  |  |  |  |  |  |  | • | • | • |  |  |  |  |  | • |  |  |  |
|  |  | • |  |  |  | • | • | • | • |  |  |  | • | • | • | • |  |  |
|  |  | • |  |  | • | • | • | • |  |  |  |  | • | • | • | • |  |  |
| • | • | • | • | • | • |  | • |  | • |  |  |  | • | • | • | • |  | • |
|  |  | • |  |  |  |  | • |  | • |  |  |  | • | • | • | • |  |  |
| • |  | • |  |  | • | • | • |  | • |  |  |  | • | • | • | • |  |  |
|  |  |  |  |  |  | • |  |  |  |  |  |  |  |  |  |  |  |  |
| • | • | • | • | • | • |  | • | • | • |  | • | • | • | • | • | • |  | • |
|  | • | • |  |  |  |  | • | • | • |  |  |  | • |  | • | • |  |  |
|  |  |  |  |  |  | • |  |  |  |  |  |  |  |  |  |  |  |  |
|  |  | • |  |  |  |  |  |  | • |  |  |  | • | • |  | • |  |  |

| | Vacancies | Partners | Total staff | Work placement | Corporate/ commercial | General commercial | Niche | General practice | High street/ legal aid |
|---|---|---|---|---|---|---|---|---|---|
| Pickerings Solicitors LLP | 1 | 4 | 33 | | • | • | • | • | • |
| **Pinsent Masons** | 55 | 260 | 1500 | ✔ | • | • | | | |
| Rawstorne Heran | 0-1 | 2 | 7 | ✔ | | | | • | • |
| **Reed Smith Richards Butler LLP** | 32 | 108 | 664 | ✔ | • | | | | |
| Rees Page | 0 | 8 | 46 | | | | | • | • |
| RN Williams & Co | 0 | 3 | 17 | | | • | | • | • |
| Robin Simon LLP | 2[08] | 10 | 50 | | | | • | | |
| Russell Jones & Walker | 10 | 49 | 630 | | | • | • | • | |
| Shakespeare Putsman | 6[09] | 44 | 264 | | | • | | | |
| **Shoosmiths** | 17 | 105 | 1450 | ✔ | • | • | • | • | |
| Terry Jones Solicitors & Advocates | Poss | 2 | 90 | | | | | • | |
| Thompsons | Poss[09] | 38 | 800 | | | | • | | |
| Thursfields | 0 | 16 | 110 | | | | | • | • |
| Tinsdills | Poss | 13 | 85 | | | | | • | |
| TMJ Law Solicitors | 2 | 2 | 12 | ✔ | | • | | | |
| Toussaints | 0 | 1 | 3 | | | | | • | • |
| Wallace Robinson & Morgan | 1-2[09] | 6 | 40 | ✔ | • | • | | • | |
| Walters & Plaskitt | Poss | 5 | 50 | | | | | • | • |
| **Weightmans** | Up to 14 | 90 | 750 | | • | | | | |
| Whetter Duckworth Fowler | 1 | 3 | 25 | ✔ | | | | • | • |
| Whittles | 2[08] | 10 | 165 | | | | • | | |
| Worcestershire County Council | 0 | | 28 | | | | | | |
| **Wragge & Co LLP** | 30 | 110 | 1017 | ✔ | • | • | • | | |
| Wright Hassall  LLP | 4[10] | 26 | 186 | ✔ | • | • | • | | |

# Yorkshire

| | Vacancies | Partners | Total staff | Work placement | Corporate/ commercial | General commercial | Niche | General practice | High street/ legal aid |
|---|---|---|---|---|---|---|---|---|---|
| **Addleshaw Goddard** | 50 | 182 | 1300 | ✔ | • | | | | |
| Addlestone Keane | 1[08] | 3 | 18 | | • | • | • | | |
| Andrew Jackson | 6 | 33 | 195 | ✔ | • | • | | • | |
| Atherton Godfrey | 2[09] | 6 | 80 | | | | | • | |
| Ashington Denton | 1 | 2 | 28 | | | | | • | |
| Ashton Bell | 1[08] | 1 | 6 | ✔ | • | • | • | • | |
| Ashton Morton Slack LLP | 2[09] | 16 | 160 | | • | • | | • | • |
| Bassra Solicitors (Incorporating John Kelly & Co) | 0 | 2 | 8 | | | | | | • |
| **Beachcroft LLP** | 30[09] | 147 | 1400 | ✔ | • | • | | • | |

| Arbitration | Banking | Comp/comm | Competition | Construction | Corporate tax | Crime | Employment | Environment | Family | Human rights | Insurance | IP | Litigation | Personal injury | Private client | Property | Shipping | TMT |
|---|---|---|---|---|---|---|---|---|---|---|---|---|---|---|---|---|---|---|
|  |  | • |  |  |  |  | • |  | • |  |  | • | • |  | • | • |  |  |
| • | • | • | • | • | • |  | • | • |  |  | • | • | • |  |  | • |  | • |
|  |  |  |  |  |  | • |  |  | • |  |  |  |  |  |  |  |  |  |
| • | • | • | • | • | • |  | • | • |  |  | • | • | • |  |  | • | • | • |
|  |  | • |  |  |  |  | • | • | • |  |  |  | • | • | • | • |  |  |
|  |  |  |  |  |  |  | • | • | • |  |  |  | • | • | • |  |  |  |
|  |  |  |  |  |  |  |  |  |  | • |  |  |  |  |  |  |  |  |
|  |  |  |  |  | • |  | • |  | • | • |  | • | • | • | • | • |  | • |
| • |  | • | • | • | • |  | • | • | • |  | • | • | • | • | • | • |  | • |
| • | • | • | • | • | • |  | • | • | • |  | • | • | • | • | • | • |  | • |
|  |  | • |  |  |  | • |  |  | • |  |  | • | • | • | • | • |  |  |
|  |  |  |  |  |  | • |  | • |  |  |  |  | • |  |  |  |  |  |
|  |  | • |  |  |  | • |  |  | • |  |  | • | • | • | • | • |  |  |
|  |  | • |  |  | • |  | • |  |  |  |  | • | • | • | • | • |  |  |
|  |  | • |  |  |  |  | • |  | • |  |  | • | • | • | • | • |  | • |
|  |  |  |  |  |  |  |  |  | • |  |  |  | • |  |  |  |  |  |
| • |  | • |  |  |  |  | • |  | • |  |  | • | • |  | • | • |  |  |
|  |  |  |  |  |  | • |  |  | • | • |  |  |  | • | • |  |  |  |
| • | • | • |  |  | • | • |  | • |  |  |  | • | • |  | • |  | • |  |
|  |  |  |  |  |  |  |  |  | • |  |  |  |  |  |  |  |  |  |
|  |  |  |  |  |  |  | • | • | • |  |  |  |  |  |  | • |  |  |
| • | • | • |  |  | • | • |  | • | • |  | • | • | • | • |  | • |  | • |
| • | • | • | • | • | • |  | • | • | • |  | • | • | • |  |  | • |  | • |

| Arbitration | Banking | Comp/comm | Competition | Construction | Corporate tax | Crime | Employment | Environment | Family | Human rights | Insurance | IP | Litigation | Personal injury | Private client | Property | Shipping | TMT |
|---|---|---|---|---|---|---|---|---|---|---|---|---|---|---|---|---|---|---|
| • |  | • | • | • | • |  | • | • | • |  | • | • | • |  | • | • |  | • |
|  |  | • |  |  |  |  | • |  |  |  |  |  | • |  |  | • |  |  |
| • |  | • |  | • |  |  | • |  | • |  |  | • | • | • | • | • | • |  |
| • |  | • |  |  |  |  | • |  | • |  |  |  | • | • | • | • |  |  |
|  |  |  |  |  |  |  |  |  | • |  |  |  |  | • | • |  |  |  |
|  |  | • |  |  |  |  | • |  | • |  |  | • | • | • | • | • |  | • |
|  |  | • | • | • | • | • | • | • | • |  |  | • | • | • | • | • |  | • |
|  |  |  |  |  |  | • |  |  | • |  |  |  |  |  |  |  |  |  |
| • |  | • | • | • | • |  | • | • |  |  | • | • | • | • |  | • |  | • |

| | Vacancies | Partners | Total staff | Work placement | Corporate/commercial | General commercial | Niche | General practice | High street/legal aid |
|---|---|---|---|---|---|---|---|---|---|
| Blacks | 3[09] | 12 | 100 | | | • | | | |
| Bradbury Roberts & Raby | 1[08] | 6 | 30 | | | | | • | • |
| Bridge McFarland | 0 | 20 | 170 | | | • | | • | • |
| Bridge Sanderson Munro | 0 | 6 | 40 | | | | | • | |
| Burn & Company | 0 | 6 | 17 | | | | | • | • |
| Bury & Walkers | 1 | 11 | 60 | | • | • | | | • |
| **Clarion Solicitors** | 4 | 13 | 101 | ✔ | • | • | • | | |
| **Cobbetts LLP** | 20 | 136 | 815 | ✔ | • | • | | | |
| Corries Solicitors Ltd | Poss 2 | 2 | 60 | | | | | • | |
| Crockett & Co | 0 | 2 | 12 | | | | | | • |
| **Crown Prosecution Service** | 25 | | 9000 | ✔ | | | • | | |
| Cunningtons | Varies[09] | 10 | 180 | ✔ | | | | • | • |
| **Dickinson Dees LLP** | 15 | 78 | 920 | ✔ | • | • | | • | |
| **DLA Piper UK LLP** | 95+ | 1200 | 7000 | ✔ | • | | | | |
| **DWF** | 20 | 119 | 804 | ✔ | • | • | | • | |
| Eaton Smith LLP | 0 | 14 | 100 | | • | • | | • | • |
| Emsleys | 2[09] | 7 | 145 | | | | | • | |
| **Eversheds LLP** | 80+ | 340 | 4000 | ✔ | • | • | | | |
| Finn Gledhill | 0 | 8 | 60 | | | | | • | |
| **Forbes Solicitors** | 4 | 29 | 350 | ✔ | • | • | | • | • |
| Ford & Warren | 4 | 21 | 200 | | • | • | | | |
| Fox Hayes LLP | 2[08] | 22 | 200 | | • | • | | • | • |
| **Gordons LLP** | 6 | 38 | 314 | | | | | • | |
| Gosschalks | 3 | 33 | 120 | | • | • | • | | |
| **Government Legal Service** | 22-30 | | 1950 | ✔ | • | • | | • | |
| Graham & Rosen | 1-2 | 10 | 60 | ✔ | | | | • | • |
| Grays | 0 | 4 | 30 | | | | • | | |
| **Halliwells LLP** | 38 | 165 | 1300 | ✔ | • | • | | | |
| **Hammonds** | 40 | 189 | 1300 | ✔ | • | | | | |
| Harrowell Shaftoe | 3[08] | 20 | 175 | ✔ | | | | • | |
| The Hawkswell Kilvington Partnership | 0 | 3 | 12 | | | | • | | |
| Hempsons | 6 | 30 | 300 | | | | • | | |
| Heptonstalls | 1-2 | 6 | 98 | | | | | • | • |
| Hethertons LLP Solicitors | 0 | 3 | 17 | | | | | • | • |
| hlw Commercial Lawyers LLP | 2-3 | 19 | 100 | ✔ | • | • | | | |
| Howells LLP | 2 | 16 | 120 | | | | | • | • |
| HSR Law | 0-1[08] | 6 | 42 | | • | • | | • | • |
| **Irwin Mitchell** | 20-25 | 137 | 2000 | ✔ | • | • | | • | |
| Jacksons | 0 | 11 | 73 | | • | • | | • | • |
| Jepson & Co | 0 | 2 | 5 | ✔ | | | | • | • |
| Kamrans Solicitors | 1[08] | 2 | 7 | | | | | • | • |

| | Arbitration | Banking | Comp/comm | Competition | Construction | Corporate tax | Crime | Employment | Environment | Family | Human rights | Insurance | IP | Litigation | Personal injury | Private client | Property | Shipping | TMT |
|---|---|---|---|---|---|---|---|---|---|---|---|---|---|---|---|---|---|---|---|
| | | | • | | | | | • | | • | | | | • | • | • | • | | |
| | | | • | | | | | • | | • | | | | | • | • | • | | |
| | • | | • | | • | | • | • | | • | | | • | • | • | • | • | • | |
| | | | | | | | | | | | | | | | | | | | |
| | | | • | | | | | • | | • | | | | | • | • | • | | |
| | • | • | • | • | • | • | • | • | • | • | • | | • | • | • | • | • | | • |
| | • | • | • | • | • | • | • | • | | • | | | • | • | | • | • | | • |
| | • | • | • | • | • | | • | • | | | | | • | • | | • | • | | |
| | | | | | | | | | | | | • | | • | • | • | | | |
| | | | | | | | | | | • | | | | | | | | | |
| | | | | | | | • | | | | | | | | | | | | |
| | | | • | | | | | • | | • | | | | • | | • | | | |
| | • | • | • | • | • | • | | • | • | • | | • | • | • | • | | • | | • |
| | • | • | • | • | • | • | | • | • | | | • | | • | | | • | • | • |
| | • | • | • | • | • | | | • | | • | | | • | • | • | • | • | | |
| | | | • | | • | • | • | • | • | • | | | • | • | • | • | • | | • |
| | | | | | | | | • | | • | | | | • | • | • | • | | |
| | • | • | • | • | • | • | | • | | • | • | • | • | • | • | • | • | • | • |
| | | | • | • | • | • | • | • | | • | | | | • | • | • | • | | |
| | • | | • | • | • | • | | • | | • | • | • | • | • | • | • | • | | • |
| | | | • | | • | • | • | • | | • | | | • | • | • | • | • | | • |
| | • | • | • | | • | • | | • | | • | | | • | • | • | • | • | | • |
| | | | | | | | | • | | • | | | | • | • | • | • | | |
| | | | | | | | | • | | • | | | | • | • | • | • | | |
| | | • | • | • | • | • | | • | • | • | | • | | • | • | • | • | • | • |
| | • | • | • | • | • | • | | • | • | | | | | • | | | • | | • |
| | • | | | | • | | | | | | | | | • | | | | | |
| | | | • | | • | | • | • | | | | | • | • | • | • | • | | |
| | | | | | | | | | | | | | | • | • | | | | |
| | | | | | | | | | | • | | | | | • | • | | | |
| | | • | • | | | | | • | | | | | • | • | | | • | | • |
| | | | | | | | • | • | • | • | • | | | | • | • | | | |
| | | | • | | | | • | • | | • | | | • | • | • | • | • | | |
| | • | | • | • | • | | | • | • | • | • | • | • | • | • | • | | | • |
| | • | | • | • | | | | • | • | • | • | | • | • | • | • | • | | • |
| | | | • | | | | | • | • | | • | | | • | • | | • | | |
| | | | | | | | | • | • | | | | | | • | | | | |

| | Vacancies | Partners | Total staff | Work placement | Corporate/commercial | General commercial | Niche | General practice | High street/legal aid |
|---|---|---|---|---|---|---|---|---|---|
| Kingsley Brookes | 0 | 2 | 8 | | | | • | | • |
| LA Steel | 0 | 0 | 8 | ✔ | | | • | | |
| **Langleys** | 6 | 38 | 325 | ✔ | • | • | | • | • |
| Last Cawthra Feather LLP | 1 | 12 | 140 | | • | | | | |
| Lee & Priestley | 2(09) | 12 | 100 | | | | • | | |
| Lester Morrill | 1 | 5 | 31 | | | | • | | • |
| Lupton Fawcett | 3 | 29 | 190 | ✔ | • | • | | | |
| Makin Dixon Solicitors | 0 | 2 | 20 | ✔ | | | | | • |
| Malcolm C Foy & Co | 0 | 3 | 65 | ✔ | | | | • | • |
| Malcolm Cooke & Co | Poss | 2 | 8 | | • | • | • | • | |
| Millan Solicitors | 0 | 2 | 5 | ✔ | | | | • | |
| Morrish & Co | 0 | 12 | 90 | | | | | • | • |
| Musa A Patel & Co | 0 | 3 | 22 | | | | | • | • |
| **Nabarro** | 30 | 126 | 945 | ✔ | • | | | | |
| Nicholas Smith | 1 | 2 | 20 | | | | | • | |
| North Yorkshire County Council | 1 | | 43 | ✔ | | | • | | |
| Oxley & Coward | 0 | 8 | 80 | ✔ | • | • | | • | • |
| Parker Rhodes | 0 | 5 | 49 | | | | | • | • |
| **Pinsent Masons** | 55 | 260 | 1500 | ✔ | • | • | | | |
| **RadcliffesLeBrasseur** | 5 | 42 | 210 | ✔ | • | • | | • | |
| Read Dunn Connell | 0 | 5 | 29 | | • | • | | • | |
| Richmonds | 2(09) | 3 | 48 | ✔ | • | | | | • |
| Robin Simon LLP | 2(08) | 10 | 50 | | | | • | | |
| Rollits | 3 | 21 | 118 | ✔ | • | • | | | |
| Runhams | 0-1 | 4 | 32 | | | | | • | |
| Russell Jones & Walker | 10 | 49 | 630 | | | • | • | • | • |
| Schofield Sweeney LLP | 2-3(08) | 14 | 80 | ✔ | • | • | | | |
| Sergeant & Collins | 0 | 2 | 15 | | | | | • | • |
| **Shulmans** | 2-3 | 11 | 140 | ✔ | • | • | • | • | |
| Stamp Jackson and Procter | 2 | 8 | 65 | ✔ | • | • | | | |
| Taylor & Emmet | 3 | 7 | 145 | | • | • | | • | • |
| Thompsons | Poss(09) | 38 | 800 | | | | • | | |
| Thorpe & Co | 1 | 12 | 55 | | | | | • | • |
| Tofields | 0 | 7 | 42 | | | | | • | |
| W Brook & Co | 1(08) | 2 | 20 | | | | | | • |
| Wake Smith | 2 | 15 | 145 | | • | • | | • | • |
| **Walker Morris** | 20 | 52 | 580 | ✔ | • | • | | | |
| Ware & Kay | 2 | 6 | 60 | | | | | • | |
| **Watson Burton LLP** | 6 | 40 | 300 | ✔ | | • | | | |
| Whittles | 2(08) | 10 | 165 | | | | • | | |
| **Wilkin Chapman** | 2 | 33 | 265 | | • | • | | • | • |

| Arbitration | Banking | Comp/comm | Competition | Construction | Corporate tax | Crime | Employment | Environment | Family | Human rights | Insurance | IP | Litigation | Personal injury | Private client | Property | Shipping | TMT |
|---|---|---|---|---|---|---|---|---|---|---|---|---|---|---|---|---|---|---|
| | | | | | | • | | | | | | | | | | | | |
| | | | | | | | • | | | | | | • | • | | | | |
| | | • | | • | | • | • | | • | | | | • | • | • | • | | |
| | | • | | • | | | • | | • | | | • | • | • | • | • | | • |
| | • | • | | | • | | • | | • | | | • | • | | • | • | | |
| | | | | | | • | • | | • | | | | | • | | | | |
| • | • | • | • | • | • | | • | • | • | | • | | • | • | • | • | • | • |
| | | | | | | | • | | • | | | | • | • | • | • | | |
| | • | • | | • | | | • | | • | | | • | • | • | • | • | | |
| | | | | | | | | | | | | | | | • | | | |
| | | | | | | | • | | • | | | • | | • | • | • | | |
| • | | | | | | • | • | | • | | | | • | • | • | • | | |
| • | • | • | • | • | • | | • | • | | | | • | • | | • | | | • |
| | | • | | | | | • | • | • | | | • | • | | • | • | | |
| • | | • | | • | | • | • | | • | | | | • | • | • | | | |
| | | | | | | | • | | • | | | • | • | • | • | • | | |
| • | | • | | | | | • | | | | | | • | • | • | • | | |
| | | | | | | | | | | | • | | | | | | | |
| • | • | • | | • | | | • | | | | | • | • | • | • | • | | • |
| | | • | | | | | • | | | | | | • | • | • | • | | |
| | | | • | | | • | • | | • | • | | • | • | • | • | • | | • |
| | | • | • | | | | • | | | | | | • | | | • | | |
| | • | • | • | • | • | | • | • | • | • | | • | • | | • | • | | • |
| | | • | | | | | • | • | | | | • | | • | • | • | | • |
| | | • | | • | | | • | | | | | • | • | • | • | • | | |
| | | | | | | • | • | | | | | | | • | | | | |
| | | | | | | | • | | • | | | | | • | • | | | |
| | | • | | | | | • | | • | | | | • | • | | • | | |
| | | | | | | • | • | | • | | | | | • | | | | |
| • | | • | | | • | | • | | • | | | • | • | • | • | • | | • |
| • | • | • | • | • | • | | • | • | | | • | • | • | • | • | • | | • |
| | | • | | | | | • | | • | | | | • | • | • | • | | |
| • | • | • | • | • | • | | • | • | • | | • | • | • | • | • | • | | • |
| | | | | | | | • | | • | | | | | • | • | | | |
| | | • | • | | | • | • | | • | | | | • | • | • | • | | |

| | Vacancies | Partners | Total staff | Work placement | Corporate/commercial | General commercial | Niche | General practice | High street/legal aid |
|---|---|---|---|---|---|---|---|---|---|
| Wilkinson Woodward inc Boococks | 1-2 | 9 | 85 | | | | | • | • |
| Wrigley Claydon | 1 | 6 | 32 | | | | | • | • |
| Wrigleys Solicitors LLP | 1-2 | 17 | 111 | ✔ | | | • | | |

| Arbitration | Banking | Comp/comm | Competition | Construction | Corporate tax | Crime | Employment | Environment | Family | Human rights | Insurance | IP | Litigation | Personal injury | Private client | Property | Shipping | TMT |
|---|---|---|---|---|---|---|---|---|---|---|---|---|---|---|---|---|---|---|
|  |  | • |  |  |  | • | • |  | • |  |  | • | • | • | • | • |  |  |
|  |  | • |  |  |  |  | • |  | • |  |  |  | • | • | • | • |  | • |
|  |  | • |  |  |  |  | • |  |  |  |  | • |  |  | • | • |  |  |

# Training contract directory

## AARON AND PARTNERS
Grosvenor Court, Foregate Street,
Chester CH1 1HG
**Tel:** 01244 405555
**Fax:** 01244 405566
**Apply to:** Mr Tim Culpin

Working principally for business clients providing general commercial services (property, litigation and company/commercial) plus specialist areas - planning, minerals, environmental, transport, construction and insolvency.

| | |
|---|---|
| V | 2[09] |
| T | 4 |
| P | 20 |
| TS | 86 |
| WP | no |

## ABNEY GARSDEN MCDONALD
37 Station Road, Cheadle Hume, Cheadle,
Cheshire SK8 5AF
**Tel:** 0161 482 8822
**Fax:** 0870 990 9350
**Email:** peter@abneys.co.uk
**Apply to:** Mr Peter WA Garsden

The firm handles personal injury and family and has one of the largest UK specialist child abuse compensation departments acting for victims of abuse.

| | |
|---|---|
| V | 0 |
| T | 3 |
| P | 1 |
| TS | 45 |
| WP | no |

## ABRAHAMS DRESDEN
111 Charterhouse Street, London EC1M 6AW
**Tel:** 020 7251 3663
**Fax:** 020 7251 3773
**Apply to:** Mrs Lara Myers

Small progressive commercial firm committed to providing a superior service and excellent client care. Impressive range of legal services provided. Happy office. Apply between 01/12/07 and 31/01/08. Email applications not accepted.

| | |
|---|---|
| V | 2[08] |
| T | 4 |
| P | 4 |
| TS | 19 |
| WP | no |

## ACTONS
20 Regent Street, Nottingham NG1 5BQ
**Tel:** 0115 910 0200
**Fax:** 0115 844 8333
**Email:** ceb@actons.co.uk
**Apply to:** Claire Bell

Full range of services to businesses and private clients. Particularly strong reputation in insolvency, personal injury and commercial work. Apply in Aug 2008 for Sept 2010.

| | |
|---|---|
| V | 1 |
| T | 3 |
| P | 14 |
| TS | 85 |
| WP | no |

## ADDIE & CO
9 Masons Yard, Duke Street, St James's,
London SW1Y 6BU
**Tel:** 020 7930 7773
**Fax:** 020 7930 7774
**Email:** info@addielaw.com
**Apply to:** Ms Kenny Gbaja

We are a small but very busy practice specialising in property, commercial and private client advice, located in central London.

| | |
|---|---|
| V | 0 |
| T | 2 |
| P | 2 |
| TS | 8 |
| WP | yes |

## ADDISON O'HARE
Kelvin House, 23 Lichfield Street, Walsall WS1 1UL
**Tel:** 01922 725515
**Fax:** 01922 722004
**Email:** mail@addisonohare.co.uk
**Apply to:** Mr DR Wilton

Long etsbalished firm, town centre practice, offering wide range of work including crime, family, probate, litigation, property, legal aid franchise.

| | |
|---|---|
| V | 0 |
| T | 0 |
| P | 5 |
| TS | 38 |
| WP | yes |

## ADDLESTONE KEANE
Carlton Tower, 34 St Pauls Street, Leeds LS1 2QB
**Tel:** 0113 244 6700
**Fax:** 0113 244 6680
**Email:** markkeane@aklaw.co.uk
**Apply to:** Mr Mark Keane

Niche commercial practice advising PLCs, substantial private clients and companies across a broad range including sport, merger and acquisition, and employment.

| | |
|---|---|
| V | 1[08] |
| T | 1 |
| P | 3 |
| TS | 18 |
| WP | no |

## ADLAMS
37b Market Square, St Neots,
Cambridgeshire PE19 2AR
**Tel:** 01480 474061
**Fax:** 01480 474959
**Email:** adlams@adlams.co.uk
**Apply to:** Mrs LJ Eaton

Long established small high street practice specialising in conveyancing, family, probate and some commercial work. Good IT skils an advantage for candidates.

| | |
|---|---|
| V | 0 |
| T | 2 |
| P | 4 |
| TS | 23 |
| WP | no |

**V** = Vacancies / **T** = Trainees / **P** = Partners / **TS** = Total Staff / **WP** = Work Placement

# Addleshaw Goddard

150 Aldersgate Street, London EC1A 4EJ
**Tel:** 020 7606 8855
**Fax:** 020 7606 4390
**Email:** grad@addleshawgoddard.com
**Web:** www.addleshawgoddard.com

**The firm** Addleshaw Goddard is a major force on the UK legal landscape with the capability to provide excellent service to a global client base from our three high-calibre UK locations. Ranked 15th largest law firm in the UK, with a fee income in 2006/7 of over £176 million, we were ranked in the *Sunday Times* 2007 '100 Best Companies to Work For' survey and in the *Times* Top 100 Graduate Employers survey 2007.

**Types of work** We have four main business divisions: finance & projects, contentious & commercial, corporate and real estate. Within these divisions also operate some of our specialist areas, including sport, intellectual property, employment and private client.

**Who should apply** We would like to hear from graduates or undergraduates of any discipline who possess the motivation, energy, commitment and communication skills necessary to join a top 20 law firm and are capable of achieving, or who have achieved, at least a 2.1 degree in addition to three Bs at A level, excluding General Studies. We also have a diversity access programme for applicants on GDL or LPC with less conventional academic backgrounds. Further details can be found on our website.

**Training programme** From induction to qualification, your bespoke training programme is designed to give you the opportunity to experience a broad range of commercial and corporate work, and to do so in depth. Working as a key member of our team, you will develop the professional skills necessary to deal with the demanding and challenging work we carry out for our clients.

Your on-the-job training is complemented by a series of high-quality training courses provided by our in-house team and external experts.

As a firm, we have a strong commitment to our Corporate Social Responsibilities (CSR). One of our projects has been to offer all our new graduates the opportunity to spend a week in Romania working on a community based house building project. We will be working with a charity called Habitat for Humanity and hope that this project will enable the trainees to make an active contribution to the community whilst also helping to engender a great team working spirit with fellow trainees. We encourage all of our employees to take an active role in CSR issues, and you can find out more about some of the things we have taken part in by visiting www.addleshawgoddard.com/csr.

**When and how to apply** Candidates must complete our online application form by 31 July 2008 to begin training contracts in September 2010/March 2011.

**Work placements** We run placement schemes in each of our offices in Leeds, London and Manchester. These last for one, two or three weeks and take place over Easter and in June, July and August. Applications should be made online by 31 January 2008.

**Sponsorship** Tuition fees are paid for both GDL and LPC courses, along with an annual maintenance grant, currently £7,000 per course studied in London and £4,500 per course studied elsewhere in the UK.

| | |
|---|---|
| Vacancies | 50 |
| Trainees | 89 |
| Partners | 182 |
| Total staff | 1300 |

**Work placement**   yes
*(see Insider Report on p65)*

**Apply**
Online

**Starting salary**
London:
1st year - £36,000
2nd year - £39,500
Leeds and Manchester:
1st year - £24,750
2nd year - £27,500

**Minimum qualifications**
3 Bs at A level (excluding General Studies)
2.1 degree

**Sponsorship**
GDL/LPC

**Offices**
Leeds, London, Manchester

ADDLESHAW GODDARD

**ADVANCE LEGAL**
Suites 1-9 Imex Business Park, Shobnall Road,
Burton-on-Trent, Staffs DE14 2AZ
**Tel:** 01283 544492
**Fax:** 01283 545584
**Email:** pauline.spence@advancelegal.co.uk
**Apply to:** Pauline Spence

A modern and rapidly growing firm which primarily specialises in PI and employment law, but also other services including conveyancing and probate. Recruitment ongoing.

| | |
|---|---|
| V | 8 |
| T | 5 |
| P | 2 |
| TS | 45 |
| WP | yes |

---

**AHMED & CO**
67a Camden High Street, London NW1 7JL
**Tel:** 020 7383 2243
**Fax:** 020 7383 2166
**Email:** mail@ahmedco.com
**Apply to:** Ms Nosheen Saleem

Specialist services provided in crime, housing, immigration/nationality and welfare benefits law for individuals who are disadvantaged in some way to enable them to seek justice.

| | |
|---|---|
| V | 0 |
| T | 4 |
| P | 2 |
| TS | 15 |
| WP | no |

---

**ALAN EDWARDS & CO**
192-196 Campden Hill Road, London W8 7TH
**Tel:** 020 7221 7644
**Fax:** 020 7243 1076
**Apply to:** Mr GA French

Small to medium firm. Strong emphasis on landlord & tenant/housing/enfranchisement and related work, also residential and commercial conveyancing, crime and civil litigation.

| | |
|---|---|
| V | 0 |
| T | 3 |
| P | 5 |
| TS | 22 |
| WP | no |

---

**ALAN SIMPSON & CO**
Mill Court, 19 London Hill, Rayleigh SS6 7HW
**Tel:** 01268 745406
**Fax:** 01268 742299
**Email:** ajs@alansimpson.com
**Apply to:** Mr AJ Simpson

General High Street practice serving private and commercial clients.

| | |
|---|---|
| V | 0-1 |
| T | 1 |
| P | 1 |
| TS | 12 |
| WP | no |

---

**ALLAN JANES**
21-23 Easton Street, High Wycombe HP11 1NU
**Tel:** 01494 521301
**Fax:** 01494 442315
**Email:** enquiries@allanjanes.com
**Apply to:** Mr CJG Hitchen

Niche commercial practice focusing on the South Bucks geographical area with a private client department servicing high net worth clients.

| | |
|---|---|
| V | 1 |
| T | 1 |
| P | 4 |
| TS | 30 |
| WP | yes |

---

**ALLIANCE SOLICITORS**
595 Kenton Road, Harrow, Middlesex HA3 9RT
**Tel:** 020 8206 3530
**Fax:** 020 8204 4972
**Email:** pp@alliance-solicitors.com
**Apply to:** Mr P N Patel

Friendly practice with well established clients, specialising in various areas of law including personal injury, civil litigation, family, licensing and landlord & tenant.

| | |
|---|---|
| V | 0 |
| T | 2 |
| P | - |
| TS | 5 |
| WP | yes |

---

**ALSTERS KELLEY**
Hamilton House, 20-26 Hamilton Terrace,
Leamington Spa CV32 4LY
**Tel:** 0870 774 5400
**Fax:** 0870 774 9100
**Email:** gemma.raisbeck@alsters.com
**Apply to:** Mrs Gemma Raisbeck

Fourteen-partner, three-office practice in Coventry and Warwickshire undertaking private client and commercial work.

| | |
|---|---|
| V | 2-3 [09] |
| T | 4 |
| P | 14 |
| TS | 140 |
| WP | no |

---

**AMD SOLICITORS LIMITED**
43 North View, Westbury Park, Bristol BS6 7PY
**Tel:** 01179 621205
**Fax:** 01179 467539
**Email:** admin@amdsolicitors.com
**Apply to:** Mrs MK Davies

High Street firm undertaking residential conveyancing, commercial property, probate, trusts, family (both private and legal aid) and mental health work.

| | |
|---|---|
| V | 1 [08] |
| T | 0 |
| P | 2 |
| TS | 30 |
| WP | no |

---

V = Vacancies / T = Trainees / P = Partners / TS = Total Staff / WP = Work Placement

# Allen & Overy LLP

One Bishops Square, London E1 6AO
**Tel:** 020 3088 0000
**Fax:** 020 3088 0088
**Email:** graduate.recruitment@allenovery.com
**Web:** www.allenovery.com/careeruk

**The firm** Allen & Overy is an international legal practice with 5,100 people in 24 major centres worldwide. Our client list includes many of the world's leading businesses, financial institutions, governments and private individuals and, naturally, we are committed to providing innovative advice of the highest quality to them. By developing tailored solutions to a wide range of business issues, our partners are recognised as leaders in their areas of expertise and we have earned an enviable reputation and outstanding success in high-profile deals.

**Types of work** We are renowned for the high quality of our corporate, banking and international capital markets advice, but also have major strengths in areas such as dispute resolution, tax, employment and employee benefits, real estate and private client.

**Who should apply** We expect to see a strong, consistent academic performance with at least a 2.1 (or equivalent) predicted or achieved. At Allen & Overy you will be working in a team where you will use your initiative and manage your own time and workload, so we also look for evidence of teamwork, leadership and problem-solving skills.

**Training programme** A training contract with Allen & Overy is just the beginning of a stimulating and rewarding legal career. We work closely with you to ensure you have the right support and training to develop into a successful commercial solicitor. Indeed, our training is widely regarded as the best in the City. The seat structure ensures that you get to see as many parts of the practice as possible and that your learning is hands-on, guided closely by an experienced associate or partner. A series of evening presentations by departments facilitates your choice of a priority seat and other areas you may like to experience. Given the strength of our international finance practice, we require our trainees to spend a minimum of 12 months in our core areas of banking, corporate and international capital markets, with a contentious seat in either dispute resolution or employment. There are also opportunities for trainees to undertake an international seat or a client secondment.

**When and how to apply** We offer 120 training contracts each year across two intakes (March and September). For the September 2010/March 2011 intakes, non-law finalists and graduates should apply from 1 October 2007 – 18 January 2008. Law undergraduates should apply from 1 June 2008 – 31 July 2008, following confirmation of their penultimate year results.
All applications should be made online at www.allenovery.com/careeruk.

**Work placements** We recruit approximately 120 vacation students across the year. For winter, please apply from 1 October – 31 October 2007. For spring and summer, please apply from 1 October 2007 – 18 January 2008. The winter placement is for final year non-law students or graduates. Applications are welcomed from both law and non-law students for the spring and summer placements, for undergraduates at the end of their penultimate year of study, or at the end of the second year (if the third year is spent abroad).

**Sponsorship** We pay your GDL and LPC course fees and contribute to your maintenance costs. We pay a £7,000 maintenance grant for the Allen & Overy LPC in London. For the GDL we pay £6,000 in London and £5,000 elsewhere.

| | |
|---|---|
| Vacancies | 120 |
| Trainees | 240 |
| Partners | 470* |
| Total staff | 5100* |

*denotes worldwide figures

**Work placement** yes
(see Insider Report on p67)

**Apply**
Online at
www.allenovery.com/careeruk

**Starting salary**
Year 1: £36,200
Year 2: £40,300

**Minimum qualifications**
2.1 degree (or equivalent)

**Sponsorship**
GDL/LPC

**Offices**
Amsterdam, Antwerp, Bangkok, Beijing, Bratislava, Brussels, Budapest, Dubai, Frankfurt, Hamburg, Hong Kong, London, Luxembourg, Madrid, Milan, Moscow, New York, Paris, Prague, Rome, Shanghai, Singapore, Tokyo, Warsaw

ALLEN & OVERY

# Arnold & Porter (UK) LLP

Tower 42, 25 Old Broad Street, London EC2N 1HQ
**Tel:** 020 7786 6100
**Fax:** 020 7786 6299
**Email:** graduates@aporter.com
**Web:** www.aporter.com

**The firm** Arnold & Porter is a US-based firm with a deserved reputation for its quality of service and expertise in handling the most complex legal and business problems, which require innovative and practical solutions.

**Types of work** Our London lawyers advise on a full range of regulatory, transactional and litigation matters, and focus especially on intellectual property and technology transactions and litigation, pharmaceuticals and medical device regulation and litigation, telecommunications, competition, corporate transactions and product liability advice and litigation. Arnold & Porter is committed to strategic growth in London in these and other areas with the same emphasis on quality of service and in-depth expertise as it provides in the Unites States. Providing our clients with an excellent service is our number one priority, and our lawyers need to be commercially minded, approachable and able to work with our clients as part of a team on complex and often high profile legal issues.

**Who should apply** We welcome applications from both law and non-law graduates. We are looking for talented individuals from all backgrounds and cultures who share our commitment to excellence, and who want to be part of the continued growth of our London office and become part of our next generation of partners and lawyers. Candidates applying to Arnold & Porter need to demonstrate a consistently high academic background. We expect candidates to have at least a 2.1 degree, AAB at A-level or equivalent, and look for well-rounded individuals who can demonstrate their participation in a range of extra curricular activities and achievements.

**Training programme** Trainees will have the opportunity to spend six months working within four of our practice groups: life sciences, intellectual property, corporate and securities and commercial. Arnold & Porter encourages individuals to work across specialisms, so trainees may find that whilst they are working in one practice group, they undertake work in a variety of different areas, and for a variety of partners and fee-earners throughout the firm. Trainees will be expected to work on several matters at once, and to assume responsibility at an early stage. We emphasise teamwork, and trainees will be exposed to working for a variety of partners and fee earners throughout the office and the firm. Trainees may also have an opportunity to work in our Brussels office.

**When and how to apply** For our 2008 summer vacation scheme, details are available from our graduate recruitment team. For training contracts commencing in September 2010, by 26 July 2008. Apply on our application form, available by emailing us or downloadable from the London Trainees page of our website.

**Work placements** We take up to eight summer vacation students. Students will spend two weeks working on a variety of projects with partners and associates throughout the London office. Students will also attend a practice workshop each day, and will be asked to prepare a team-based assignment, presenting this to partners and associates at the end of the vacation scheme. In addition to this, a number of social events are organised for our summer vacation students to enable them to meet the partners, associates and trainees working in our London office.

**Sponsorship** Arnold & Porter will pay your fees for the LPC and the CPE. In addition we will pay a maintenance grant for each course.

| | |
|---|---|
| Vacancies | 1-2 |
| Trainees | 0 |
| Partners | 13 |
| Total staff | 65 |

**Work placement**  yes

**Apply to**
Graduate Recruitment

**Starting salary**
TBC (US firm market rate)

**Minimum qualifications**
2.1 degree

**Sponsorship**
GDL/LPC

**Offices**
London, Washington DC, New York, Los Angeles, Denver, Northern Virginia, San Francisco, Brussels

ARNOLD & PORTER (UK) LLP

## ANDREW ISAACS SOLICITORS
7 Stephens Court, 15-17 St Stephens Road,
Bournemouth BH2 6LA
**Tel:** 01202 299992
**Fax:** 01202 297329
**Apply to:** Mr AG Isaacs

Solicitors' providing a quality assured legal service for personal injury, family and civil litigation.

| | |
|---|---|
| V | 0 |
| T | 0 |
| P | 2 |
| TS | 14 |
| WP | yes |

---

## ANDREW JACKSON
Essex House, Manor Street, Hull HU1 1XH
**Tel:** 01482 325242
**Fax:** 01482 212974
**Email:** lawyers@andrewjackson.co.uk
**Apply to:** Ms Louise Dawson

| | |
|---|---|
| V | 6 |
| T | 12 |
| P | 33 |
| TS | 195 |
| WP | yes |

---

## ANTHONY COLLINS SOLICITORS
134 Edmund Street, Birmingham B3 2ES
**Tel:** 0121 200 3242
**Fax:** 0121 212 7442
**Email:** laura.hinson@anthonycollinssolicitors.com
**Apply to:** Mrs Laura Hinson

Fast-growing niche commercial and private client practice with national client base boasting the largest social housing, charities and community regeneration operations outside London.

| | |
|---|---|
| V | 6 |
| T | 12 |
| P | 20 |
| TS | 200 |
| WP | no |

---

## ANTHONY GOLD SOLICITORS
New London Bridge House, 25 London Bridge Street, London SE1 9TW
**Tel:** 020 7940 4000
**Fax:** 020 7378 8025
**Email:** corinne.simpson@anthonygold.co.uk
**Apply to:** Ms Kim Beatson

General practice with excellent reputation for family work, plaintiff personal injury/medical negligence and housing. Offices in London Bridge, Streatham and Walworth.

| | |
|---|---|
| V | 4 |
| T | 7 |
| P | 15 |
| TS | 85 |
| WP | no |

---

## ANTHONY JACOBS & CO
91 Albany Road, Cardiff CF24 3LP
**Tel:** 029 2048 3509
**Fax:** 029 2046 5512
**Email:** anthonyjacobs@btconnect.com
**Apply to:** Mr Anthony Jacobs

General practice with emphasis on property law and family law. No criminal law or legal aid.

| | |
|---|---|
| V | 2[08] |
| T | 2 |
| P | 1 |
| TS | 5 |
| WP | yes |

---

## ANTONY HODARI & CO
34 High Street, Manchester M4 1AH
**Tel:** 0161 832 4781
**Fax:** 0161 832 3319
**Apply to:** Ms Jennie Wright

Establsihed in 1984, specialists in RTA personal injury claims.

| | |
|---|---|
| V | Varies |
| T | 7 |
| P | 6 |
| TS | 140 |
| WP | no |

---

## AP LAW
257 Balham High Road, London SW17 7BD
**Tel:** 020 8672 2488
**Fax:** 020 8767 8533
**Email:** ap@aplaw.co.uk
**Apply to:** Mr Mike Rainsbury

High quality of work in specialist areas. Fast expanding, highly motivated young firm. Strong team spirit and excellent opportunities.

| | |
|---|---|
| V | 4 |
| T | 2 |
| P | 2 |
| TS | 60 |
| WP | yes |

---

## ARCHON SOLICITORS
Martin House, 5 Martin Lane, London EC4R ODP
**Tel:** 020 7397 9650
**Fax:** 020 7929 6316
**Email:** reception@archonlaw.co.uk
**Apply to:** Ms Corinne Aldridge

Niche employment law practice offering advice in relation to all aspects of employment law to both employers and senior employees.

| | |
|---|---|
| V | 0 |
| T | 1 |
| P | 4 |
| TS | 14 |
| WP | no |

# asb *law*

Innovis House, 108 High Street, Crawley, West Sussex RH10 1AS
**Tel:** 01293 861218
**Fax:** 01293 861250
**Email:** donna.flack@asb-law.com
**Web:** www.asb-law.com

**The firm** A rising-50 firm, asb law has clear strategic plans and both the capacity and determination to earn our place as the leading full service firm in the south east. From offices in Brighton, Crawley, Croydon, Horsham and Maidstone we offer unrivalled coverage throughout Surrey, Sussex and Kent, with the skills and experience to service national as well as regional clients. This is a vibrant partnership intent on capitalising on our position within two of the most dynamic development areas in the country – the Gatwick Diamond and Thames Gateway. Business development is a clearly defined element of every partner's role.

Our diverse client range includes businesses, financial institutions and public sector bodies of all shapes and sizes. We also have significant private client capability with full service offerings for mid- and high net worth individuals from our family, residential property and tax, trusts and probate teams. The convergence of commercial and private client services is at the heart of our approach as we bring together multi-disciplinary teams to deliver practical solutions to our clients. Intensive, ongoing training of both partners and staff ensure that we continue to win new clients and work. Our prestigious clients and the range of services we provide demonstrate effectively that it is more than possible to enjoy a challenging and rewarding career without the grind of a daily commute to the City.

**Types of work** We have a strong team culture built through the development of current expertise, quality recruitment and extensive training. Principal areas of work include corporate finance, commercial (contracts), employment, recovery and insolvency, commercial litigation, commercial property and defendant. We have clients across many industry sectors and have developed particular expertise in a number including banking, travel, aviation, technology and property litigation. Several partners are acknowledged in *Legal 500* as experts in their respective fields. Our private client sector teams are amongst the largest in the region and include members of STEP, Resolution and the Law Society Children Panel. We also have partners qualified in collaborative law.

**Who should apply** As you would expect we're looking for strong intellectual ability. That ability must combine with drive, initiative, a clear client focus and a commercial approach. You should also be articulate and have demonstrable interpersonal skills. You should relish the prospect of early responsibility and contact with clients in a supportive environment.

**Training programme** Our two year programme divides into four six-month seats tailored to your strengths and particular interests. Training is structured to empower you to learn, take responsibility and interact with clients from an early stage and is supplemented with a series of workshops and seminars delivered as part of our professional development programme. The seats can be in any of our five offices, so a degree of flexibility is required. A structured career path from trainee to partner is in place for the right candidates. We are proud of our history of retaining our trainees on qualification – and on the number who go on to become associates and partners themselves.

**When and how to apply** Before 31 July for entry in September 2010. Applications can be downloaded from www.asb-law.com and must be submitted online.

**Sponsorship** An interest-free loan is available for the LPC which is repayable over the period of the training contract.

| Vacancies | 5 |
| Trainees | 10 |
| Partners | 37 |
| Total staff | 260 |

**Apply to**
Donna Flack

**Starting salary**
£19,000

**Minimum qualifications**
2.1 degree preferred

**Offices**
Brighton, Crawley, Horsham, Croydon, Maidstone

# Ashfords

Ashford House, Grenadier Road, Exeter EX1 3LH
**Tel:** 0870 427 7000
**Fax:** 0870 427 7001
**Email:** j.brierley@ashfords.co.uk
**Web:** www.ashfords.co.uk

**The firm** Ashfords is one of the UK's leading full-service law firms, which continues to expand and consolidate its reputation for delivering high-quality legal advice and is committed to understanding and building long-term relationships with its clients. We pride ourselves on our ability to deliver City-quality advice, often at half the hourly rates charged by City firms. This is increasingly recognised by large multi-national and national companies and organisations in the public and private sectors as a reason for using Ashfords.

Our new Bristol office continues to expand its corporate practice with ancillary skills such as IP/IT, corporate recovery, employment, construction and property.

Principal areas of work include a highly-regarded corporate and commercial department, which contains experienced teams of banking, corporate, commercial, IP/IT and tax experts; a heavyweight litigation department with specialist teams in insolvency, employment, construction, property litigation, debt recovery and sport; and commercial property including planning/environment, local government and projects/procurement which advise first and second-tier local authorities, regional development agencies, further and higher education establishments and advising on PFI projects. We also provide a full range of services to the individual, including personal injury, residential property, remortgage, crime, family and tax, wills, trusts & probate advice.

Internationally we have associations with commercial law firms in over 50 cities worldwide through our membership of ADVOC.

If you are interested in a career with Ashfords or just want to know more about us, our website (www.ashfords.co.uk) will help you find what you need.

**Who should apply** Our lawyers are recognised as being pragmatic, approachable, commercially aware and results-focused. We welcome applications from talented commercial thinkers (both law and non-law graduates) who are flexible and committed to working in a friendly team-based environment. We are an equal opportunities employer.

**Training programme** You will gain a thorough grounding in what clients expect from a busy, full-service commercial law firm. You will be given the best theoretical and practical training with us on substantive law, client relations, drafting, public speaking, IT skills, time management, leadership and other practical skills. We provide our trainees with the widest range of training.

Training is delivered during your training contract in a variety of ways, including induction training in the first weeks at the firm, departmental training as you move round the firm, in-house seminars, external courses and video training.

**When and how to apply** You should apply by using our own form which you will find, with our brochure, on our website. Your completed form must arrive no later than the end of March 2008 for work experience and end of July 2008 for a training contract in 2010.

**Sponsorship** LPC fees and maintenance bursary for the LPC year.

| | |
|---|---|
| Vacancies | 15 |
| Trainees | 24 |
| Partners | 51 |
| Total staff | 450 |

**Work placement** yes

**Apply to**
See website

**Starting salary**
Currently £19,250

**Minimum qualifications**
Generally a 2.1 degree although we do consider exceptional circumstances

**Sponsorship**
LPC plus bursary

**Offices**
Exeter, Bristol, Plymouth, Taunton, Tiverton, London (no training contracts in London).

Associations with over 40 independent firms worldwide.

Ashfords
Solicitors

## ARGYLES
43 Albert Road, Tamworth, Staffordshire B79 7JZ
**Tel:** 01827 56276
**Fax:** 01827 66628
**Email:** lesleysouthall@argylessolicitors.co.uk
**Apply to:** Mrs Lesley Southall

Tamworth's longest established law firm founded in 1749 (market town practice), offering a fully comprehensive range of legal services for both private and business clients.

| | |
|---|---|
| V | Poss |
| T | 2 |
| P | 3 |
| TS | 13 |
| WP | no |

## ARLINGTONS SHARMAS SOLICITORS
6 Arlington Street, St James's, London SW1A 1RE
**Tel:** 020 7299 8999
**Fax:** 020 7299 8900
**Email:** law@arlingtons.co.uk
**Apply to:** Mrs Awal

A well-established firm with a strong client base covering commercial work, litigation, property (commercial and residential), employment, trusts, probate and private client work.

| | |
|---|---|
| V | Poss[09] |
| T | 1 |
| P | 3 |
| TS | 14 |
| WP | yes |

## AS LAW PRACTICE
119 Kenton Road, Kenton, Harrow, Middlesex HA3 0AZ
**Tel:** 020 8907 1616
**Fax:** 020 8909 1377
**Apply to:** The Practice Manager

Specialities include civil litigation, family, personal injury, wills and probate, conveyancing and employment. Current year applications only considered. Require LPC distinction/commendation and 2.1 honours degree.

| | |
|---|---|
| V | 1[08] |
| T | 1 |
| P | 1 |
| TS | 4 |
| WP | yes |

## ASHINGTON DENTON
18/20 Norfolk Row, Sheffield S1 1SP
**Tel:** 0114 276 8987
**Fax:** 0114 276 8582
**Apply to:** Mr Avayard

Sheffield city centre firm undertaking all aspects of legal work.

| | |
|---|---|
| V | 1 |
| T | 1 |
| P | 2 |
| TS | 28 |
| WP | no |

## ASHTON BELL
19 Hanover Square, Leeds LS3 1AP
**Tel:** 0113 2438688
**Fax:** 0113 2428379
**Apply to:** Ms Maxine Brown

Predominantly private client practice. Most high street work undertaken except crime. Significant personal injury and divorce work. Apply in writing with CV and handwritten letter.

| | |
|---|---|
| V | 1[08] |
| T | 0 |
| P | 1 |
| TS | 6 |
| WP | yes |

## ASHTON MORTON SLACK LLP
35-47 North Church Street, Sheffield S1 2DH
**Tel:** 0870 609 3627
**Fax:** 0114 228 9813
**Email:** recruitment@ashtonmortonslack.co.uk
**Apply to:** The HR Department

Ashton Morton Slack LLP boasts a good reputation, friendly environment and strategic focus. Our people are committed to achieving the best results but will demonstrate passion, integrity and are an inspiration of success.

| | |
|---|---|
| V | 2[09] |
| T | 6 |
| P | 16 |
| TS | 160 |
| WP | no |

## ASTON CLARK SOLICITORS
225-227 High Street, Acton, London W3 9BY
**Tel:** 020 8752 1122
**Fax:** 020 8752 1128
**Apply to:** Mr MT Aslam

Busy High Street practice offers a professional, efficient, friendly, cost-effective service from pleasant West London offices.

| | |
|---|---|
| V | 2 |
| T | 4 |
| P | 3 |
| TS | 26 |
| WP | yes |

## ATHERTON GODFREY
8 Hall Gate, Doncaster, South Yorkshire DN1 3LU
**Tel:** 01302 320 621
**Fax:** 01302 340 692
**Email:** d.parker@athertongodfrey.co.uk
**Apply to:** Ms Diane Parker

A High Street firm doing claimant personal injury work, clinical negligence, family, company and commercial, domestic conveyancing, will and probate and general litigation.

| | |
|---|---|
| V | 2[09] |
| T | 2 |
| P | 6 |
| TS | 80 |
| WP | no |

---

**V** = Vacancies / **T** = Trainees / **P** = Partners / **TS** = Total Staff / **WP** = Work Placement

# Ashton Graham

Waterfront House, Wherry Quay, Ipswich, Suffolk IP4 1AS
**Tel:** 01473 232425
**Fax:** 01473 230505
**Email:** lawyers@ashtongraham.co.uk
**Web:** www.ashtongraham.co.uk

**The firm** Ashton Graham is a leading firm in East Anglia with offices in Ipswich, Bury St Edmunds and Felixstowe, spanning the A14 corridor. We deliver client focused service excellence through our teams of dedicated specialist lawyers. We strive to provide commercial, practical solutions and value to our clients who are based predominantly in the southeastern region. We are a progressive and expanding firm. Trainees are regarded as potential partners of the future and we pride ourselves on our excellent training record.

We are accredited with the ISO 9001 Kitemark and Investors in People standard, and have been awarded the National Community Mark.

**Types of work** Ashton Graham's main services are company/commercial and commercial property, employment, private client and agriculture, dispute resolution, personal injury litigation and family.

**Who should apply** We welcome applications from all law and non-law graduates or from other eligible qualification routes. We are looking to recruit candidates with good interpersonal skills, a natural ability in dealing with people, commercial awareness, and with the ability, desire and drive to help grow our business. We value diverse interests and additional skills such as languages or commercial experience.

**Training programme** We aim to provide excellent quality of training and offer a unique set-up where trainees complete four seats, of five months each, leaving a final four months for a continuation of training in one of the disciplines. We give trainees the opportunity to obtain a breadth of experience before specialisation and most of our training programmes include a property seat (residential, commercial or agricultural), a private client seat (will drafting, probate, trusts and tax), a commercial seat (company commercial/commercial property or employment) and a litigation seat (civil/commercial, personal injury or family). Trainees will work closely with partners and solicitors in a supportive environment, and will have regular reviews and feedback.

**When and how to apply** The closing date for applications for entry in 2010 is 31 July 2008. Please apply by letter and CV to Mr J A Outen, Training Contracts Partner, at Ashton Graham's Ipswich office.

**Work placements** We have two one-week summer placement schemes for each of which we accept eight applicants. Please see application details on our website.

**Sponsorship** We offer a bursary scheme for assistance with the GDL and LPC.

| | |
|---|---|
| Vacancies | 2 |
| Trainees | 4 |
| Partners | 22 |
| Total staff | 150 |

**Apply to**
Julian Outen

**Starting salary**
Law Society recommended

**Sponsorship**
Bursary scheme

**Offices**
Ipswich, Bury St Edmunds, Felixstowe

ashton graham

# Ashurst

Broadwalk House, 5 Appold Street, London EC2A 2HA
**Tel:** 020 7638 1111
**Fax:** 020 7859 1800
**Email:** gradrec@ashurst.com
**Web:** www.ashurst.com

**The firm** Ashurst is a leading international law firm advising corporates and financial institutions, with core businesses in mergers and acquisitions, corporate and structured finance. Our strong and growing presence around the world is built on extensive experience in working with our clients on the complex international and regulatory issues relating to cross-border transactions. It is only by selective recruitment that we can maintain the Ashurst culture and the high quality and consistency of our service. And our vision? To be the legal adviser of choice to the world's most ambitious organisations.

**Types of work** Our main areas of practice are in corporate; employment, incentives and pensions; energy, transport and infrastructure; EU and competition; international finance; litigation; real estate; tax; and technology and commercial.

**Who should apply** At Ashurst, we hire the brightest and the best. We look for talented people who like to break new ground. If you have the ambition to reach the very top in your law career, we can help you achieve it. To become an Ashurst trainee, you will need to show common sense and good judgement. We need to know that you can handle responsibility, because you will be involved in some of the highest quality international work on offer anywhere. The transactions and cases you will be involved in will be intellectually demanding, so we are looking for high academic achievers who are able to think laterally. But it's not just academic results that matter. We want people who have a range of interests outside of their studies. And we want outgoing people with a sense of humour who know how to laugh at themselves.

**Training programme** Your training contract will consist of four seats. For each, you will sit with a partner or senior solicitor who will be the main source of your work and your principal supervisor during that seat. You will, however, be encouraged to work for a variety of solicitors during the course of your training. Seats are generally for six months. Anything less than that will not give you sufficient depth of experience for the responsibility we expect you to take on. We ask trainees to spend one seat in our corporate department and one seat in our international finance department. Trainees spend their remaining two seats in our other areas of practice or on secondment.

We also provide a comprehensive training programme to support the practical experience that you will gain on your training contract. You will attend courses, lectures and workshops, and undertake a number of practical exercises. You will also be encouraged to attend regular departmental meetings, where topical developments in the law are discussed by solicitors at all levels.

**When and how to apply** Before 31 July 2008 to begin in September 2010/March 2011. Apply online via our website.

**Work placements** A two-week Easter placement scheme and two three-week summer placement schemes. Apply online before 31 January 2008.

**Sponsorship** Full fees for the GDL and LPC, plus maintenance allowances of £7,500.

| | |
|---|---|
| Vacancies | 55 |
| Trainees | 100 |
| Partners | 195 |
| Total staff | 1650 |

**Work placement** yes
*(see Insider Report on p69)*

**Apply to**
Mr Stephen Trowbridge

**Starting salary**
£36,000 (May 2007)

**Minimum qualifications**
2.1 degree and 28 UCAS points

**Sponsorship**
GDL/LPC

**Offices**
Brussels, Dubai, Frankfurt, London, Madrid, Milan, Munich, New Delhi, New York, Paris, Singapore, Stockholm, Tokyo

## ATKINS HOPE
74-78 North End, Croydon, Surrey CR9 1SD
**Tel:** 020 8680 5018
**Fax:** 020 8688 8347
**Apply to:** Ms Charlotte Collier

High street practice with five partners and two offices, commitment to publicly funded litigation and non contentious work. Privately funded litigation also.

| | |
|---|---|
| V | 0 |
| T | 1 |
| P | 5 |
| TS | 38 |
| WP | no |

## ATTER MACKENZIE & CO
64 Bridge Street, Evesham WR11 4RY
**Tel:** 01386 425300
**Fax:** 01386 765170
**Email:** am@attermackenzie.co.uk
**Apply to:** Ms Julia Cooper

Legal aid franchised high street general practice. Litigation orientated.

| | |
|---|---|
| V | 1[08] |
| T | 3 |
| P | 5 |
| TS | 26 |
| WP | no |

## AVERY EMERSON
Gloucester House, 335 Green lane, Ilford, Essex IG3 9TH
**Tel:** 020 8215 0884
**Fax:** 020 8599 9442

Proactive and innovative law firm which undertakes a wide variety of work; employment, immigration, conveyancing, family, landlord and tenancy, litigation and business.

| | |
|---|---|
| V | 1-2[08] |
| T | 2 |
| P | 1 |
| TS | 6 |
| WP | yes |

## AWB PARTNERSHIP
3 + 5 Jenner Road, Guildford GU1 3AQ
**Tel:** 01483 302345
**Fax:** 01483 301339
**Email:** info@awb.co.uk
**Apply to:** Ms Debbie Howard-Moore

Two offices specialising in civil litigation, personal injury, employment and matrimonial company and commercial property, residential conveyancing and probate and trust.

| | |
|---|---|
| V | 1[09] |
| T | 1 |
| P | 11 |
| TS | 55 |
| WP | no |

## AWDRY BAILEY & DOUGLAS
33 St John's Street, Devizes SN10 1BW
**Tel:** 01380 722311
**Fax:** 01380 721113
**Email:** ishr@awdrys.co.uk
**Apply to:** Mr Ian Richards

General high street practice.

| | |
|---|---|
| V | 0 |
| T | 4 |
| P | 6 |
| TS | 132 |
| WP | no |

## BACKHOUSE JONES
The Printworks, Heys Road, Ribble Valley, Enterprise Park, Clitheroe BB7 9WD
**Tel:** 01254 828 300
**Fax:** 01254 828 301
**Email:** ian@backhousejones.co.uk
**Apply to:** Mr Ian K Jones

| | |
|---|---|
| V | 0 |
| T | 1 |
| P | 4 |
| TS | 26 |
| WP | yes |

## BAILEYS
44 Henrietta Street, Ashton-Under-Lyne, Lancashire OL6 6HW
**Tel:** 0161 343 4182
**Fax:** 0161 343 7057
**Email:** infoashton@baileyssolicitors.co.uk
**Apply to:** Mr DG Bailey

| | |
|---|---|
| V | 0 |
| T | 1 |
| P | 1 |
| TS | 6 |
| WP | yes |

## BAINS & CO
14 Station Road, Watford, Herts WD17 1EN
**Tel:** 01923 288488
**Fax:** 01923 249933
**Email:** abains@bainsandco.com
**Apply to:** Mrs A Bains

Commercial property firm.

| | |
|---|---|
| V | 0 |
| T | 2 |
| P | 2 |
| TS | 13 |
| WP | yes |

# Baker & McKenzie LLP

100 New Bridge Street, London EC4V 6JA
**Tel:** 020 7919 1000
**Fax:** 020 7919 1999
**Email:** london.graduate.recruit@bakernet.com
**Web:** www.ukgraduates.bakernet.com

**The firm** Baker & McKenzie is a leading global law firm based in 70 locations across 38 countries. With a presence in virtually every important financial and commercial centre in the world, our strategy is to provide the best combination of local legal and commercial knowledge, international expertise and resources. Our trainee solicitors are a vital part of that strategy, exposed to the international scope of the firm from the moment they start. There is also the possibility of an overseas secondment, recent secondees have spent time in Sydney, Brussels, Madrid, Moscow, Chicago and Washington.

**Types of work** Baker & McKenzie, London is an established City firm of solicitors with a strong domestic and foreign client base providing legal services to multinational and domestic corporations, financial institutions, governments and entrepreneurs. At the heart of the firm is the corporate department which has acknowledged expertise in international securities work, strong links with venture capital houses and has acted in relation to several privatisations. We also have a strong local reputation in specialist areas including intellectual property, information technology, telecoms, employment, pensions, banking and structured capital markets. As may be expected of a firm with a very strong international client base, we have considerable expertise in acting on, and co-ordinating, cross-border transactions and disputes.

**Who should apply** The firm is looking for trainees who are stimulated by intellectual challenge and want to be 'the best' at what they do. Effective communication skills, together with the ability to be creative and practical problem solvers, team players and to have a sense of humour, are qualities which will help them stand out from the crowd.

**Training programme** The two-year training contract comprises of four six-month seats which include a corporate and a contentious seat, usually within our highly regarded dispute resolution department, together with the possibility of a secondment abroad or with a client. During each seat you will have formal and informal reviews to discuss your progress as well as subsequent seat preferences. Your training contract commences with a highly interactive and practical induction programme which focuses on key skills including practical problem solving, interviewing, presenting and the application of information technology. The firm's training programmes include important components on management and other business skills, as well as seminars and workshops on key legal topics for each practice area. There is a Trainee Solicitor Liaison Committee which acts as a forum for any new ideas or problems which may occur during the training contract.

**When and how to apply** The firm is aiming to recruit 38 individuals looking to commence their training contracts in either September 2010 or March 2011. The closing date for non-law students (ie, those who have to undertake, are currently undertaking or have completed the CPE/GDL) is 18 February 2008. The closing date for law students is 31 July 2008. Application is by way of an online application form which can be found on our website.

**Work placements** London Summer Placement - three weeks' duration. International Summer Placement - six to twelve weeks spent in London and one of our overseas offices.

**Sponsorship** Payment of full fees and maintenance grant of £8,000 for LPC and £6,000 for CPE/GDL.

| | |
|---|---|
| Vacancies | 38 |
| Trainees | 61 |
| Partners | 88 |
| Total staff | 722 |

**Work placement**   yes
*(see Insider Report on p71)*

**Apply to**
Suzanne Dare, Graduate Recruitment & Development Manager

**Starting salary**
£36,500

**Minimum qualifications**
2.1 degree

**Sponsorship**
CPE/GDL and LPC

**Offices**
70 locations across 38 countries

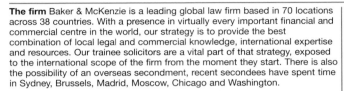

# Barlow Lyde & Gilbert LLP

Beaufort House, 15 St Botolph Street, London EC3A 7NJ
**Tel:** 020 7247 2277
**Fax:** 020 7643 8500
**Email:** grad.recruit@blg.co.uk
**Web:** www.blg.co.uk

**The firm** Barlow Lyde & Gilbert LLP is a leading international legal practice with more than 80 partners and over 300 lawyers. The firm has offices in the City of London and Singapore, and affiliated undertakings in Hong Kong and Shanghai. We provide an extensive range of legal services to clients from many industries across the world, and are renowned for our litigation and insurance expertise. Our dispute resolution practice is one of the UK's largest and highest rated. Our experience is wide-ranging, from complex boardroom or IT disputes to professional negligence actions and major reinsurance arbitrations. The firm scooped "Litigation Team of the Year" at the *Legal Week* Awards in 2005, and again at both *The Lawyer* Awards and the *Legal Business Awards* in 2006. Our top-ranked insurance and reinsurance practice is one of the largest in the world, providing services of unparalleled breadth across the sector. The firm was ranked 'best in Europe' in the 'Reactions' 2007 annual legal survey of over 100 in-house counsel, top executives and claim handlers at insurers, reinsurers and brokers. Our lawyers are also leaders in international transport and trade sectors. The firm has significant experience representing and advising some of the world's major players in the aerospace and marine, energy and trade fields, including airlines, ship owners, charterers, manufacturers, airports, insurers, regulatory agencies and international trade associations. Our non-contentious department handles the full spectrum of corporate, financial, commercial and employment and pensions work for public and private companies from a wide range of sectors as well as financial institutions.

**Who should apply** We recruit 18 to 20 trainees a year. We look for intelligent and motivated graduates with good academic qualifications and excellent communication skills. Trainees must be able to work independently or in a team, and are expected to display common sense and initiative. An appreciation of the client's commercial interests is essential.

**Training programme** During your training contract you will have six-month seats in four different practice areas. We always try to accommodate a trainee's preference for a particular type of work. There may be opportunities to spend time in our other offices, on secondment with clients or on exchange programmes with overseas law firms. A capable trainee will deal regularly with clients from an early stage in his or her training, subject to supervision. All trainees are expected to undertake and assist in practice development and client care. Successful candidates will enjoy a wide variety of social and sporting events at Barlow Lyde & Gilbert LLP, ensuring that trainees have the chance to meet and stay in contact with employees from across the firm.

**When and how to apply** Whether you wish to apply for an interview day or a vacation scheme, apply via our website at www.blg.co.uk. The closing date for our interview days is 31 July 2008.

**Work placements** An increasing number of our trainees come to us through our vacation schemes. Whether you are a law or non-law student we will introduce you to life in a City law firm. You can even choose which department you want to spend time in. The closing date for applications is 31 January 2008. We also run open days and drop-in days throughout the year.

**Sponsorship** A maintenance grant is provided and fees are paid in full.

| | |
|---|---|
| Vacancies | 18-20 |
| Trainees | 38 |
| Partners | 82 |
| Total staff | 650 |

**Work placement**  yes
*(see Insider Report on p73)*

**Apply to**
Ms Caroline Walsh, Head of Graduate Recruitment and Trainee Development

**Starting salary**
1st year: £32,000
2nd year: £35,000

**Minimum qualifications**
2.1 degree

**Sponsorship**
GDL/LPC

**Offices**
London, Hong Kong, Shanghai, Singapore

BARLOW LYDE & GILBERT

| | | | |
|---|---|---|---|
| **BAKEWELLS**<br>64 Friar Gate, Derby DE1 1DJ<br>**Tel:** 01332 348791<br>**Fax:** 01332 746130<br>**Email:** enquiries@bakewells.co.uk<br>**Apply to:** Ms Edie Jacobson | Single office. Medium practice specialising in private client and business services including residential conveyancing, matrimonial, personal injury, wills, company and commercial law and litigation. | V<br>T<br>P<br>TS<br>WP | 0<br>3<br>3<br>48<br>no |
| **BANNER JONES SOLICITORS**<br>Marsden Chambers, 2/4 Marsden Street,<br>Chesterfield S40 1JY<br>**Tel:** 01246 560560<br>**Fax:** 01246 231188<br>**Email:** info@bannerjones.co.uk<br>**Apply to:** The Training Partner | A general practice with particular specialisation in property, company/commercial, crime, family and personal injury work. Six office sites in North Derbyshire. Main offices in Chesterfield. | V<br>T<br>P<br>TS<br>WP | Poss(09)<br>3<br>17<br>80<br>no |
| **BARLOW POYNER FOXON**<br>1 Berridge Street, Leicester LE1 5JT<br>**Tel:** 0116 251 8295<br>**Fax:** 0116 253 7850<br>**Email:** richard.poyner@barlowpoynerfoxon.co.uk<br>**Apply to:** Mr Richard J Poyner | High street specialist firm involved in residential and commercial conveyancing, wills, probate and trusts, family and general litigation. | V<br>T<br>P<br>TS<br>WP | 1<br>1<br>3<br>22<br>no |
| **BARNETTS**<br>Southport Buiness Park, Wight Moss Way, Kew,<br>Southport PR8 4HQ<br>**Tel:** 01704 511 378<br>**Fax:** 0870 787 3601<br>**Email:** opportunity@barnetts-solicitors.co.uk<br>**Apply to:** Ms Andrea Parry | Niche property and personal injury practice. Applicants must have completed both LLB (or equivalent) and LPC and work as an assistant for 12 months. | V<br>T<br>P<br>TS<br>WP | 2<br>12<br>4<br>250<br>no |
| **BARON GREY**<br>Langtry House, 441 Richmond Road,<br>Middlesex TW1 2EF<br>**Tel:** 020 8891 4311<br>**Fax:** 020 8891 2058<br>**Email:** info@barongrey.co.uk<br>**Apply to:** Mr Hambleton-Grey | Multi discipline practice with general commercial and family clientele, specialising in litigation, conveyancing and probate. | V<br>T<br>P<br>TS<br>WP | 0<br>1<br>1<br>9<br>yes |
| **BARREA & CO**<br>51 Castle Street, High Wycombe,<br>Buckinghamshire HP13 3RN<br>**Tel:** 01494 537699<br>**Fax:** 01494 438612<br>**Email:** admin@barrea.co.uk<br>**Apply to:** Mr A Barrea | Modern high street practice with friendly environment. Exciting prospects for suitable candidates. | V<br>T<br>P<br>TS<br>WP | 0<br>1<br>3<br>16<br>no |
| **BARRETT & CO**<br>54 Queens Road, Reading RG1 4AZ<br>**Tel:** 0118 9589711<br>**Fax:** 0118 9504836<br>**Apply to:** Mr SA Barrett | Based in Reading and South Oxfordshire, the firm specialises in personal injury, conveyancing, civil litigation, commercial, company, employment, family law, wills, probate and inheritance tax planning. | V<br>T<br>P<br>TS<br>WP | 0<br>0<br>5<br>30<br>no |
| **BART-WILLIAMS & CO**<br>Second Floor, 34-36 High Street, Ilford,<br>Essex IG6 2DQ<br>**Tel:** 020 8551 4747<br>**Fax:** 020 8551 5777<br>**Email:** bwcsolicitors@yahoo.co.uk<br>**Apply to:** Mr A Bart-Williams | Small friendly practice specialising in employment and immigration. Additionally firm undertakes general civil work. | V<br>T<br>P<br>TS<br>WP | Poss<br>1<br>1<br>6<br>no |

**V** = Vacancies / **T** = Trainees / **P** = Partners / **TS** = Total Staff / **WP** = Work Placement

# Barlow Robbins LLP

Concord House, 165 Church Street East, Woking, Surrey GU21 6HJ
**Tel:** 01483 748500
**Fax:** 01483 729933
**Email:** sheilanewey@barlowrobbins.com
**Web:** www.barlowrobbins.com

**The firm** Barlow Robbins LLP with offices in Guildford, Woking and Godalming is a leading and expanding Surrey practice with 225 staff and 23 partners. Our office locations allow easy access to London and airports, to enable the provision of legal services to local, South East, London, national and some international clients. We provide clients with expert advice on commercial and private client matters adopting an integrated approach across departments to ensure the best solutions are found.

Barlow Robbins LLP recognises the importance of a work/life balance.

**Types of work** Barlow Robbins LLP provides a full range of specialist work areas including corporate, commercial property, commercial litigation, dispute resolution, employment, intellectual property, computer and IT, mortgage repossession, private client, charities, residential property, family, clinical negligence and personal Injury.

**Who should apply** We aim to recruit high calibre graduates with a 2.1 degree preferably in law and three A levels at grade A-B. The practice looks for individuals who are articulate, ambitious, client orientated, react positively to pressure and have preferably gained commercial and legal work experience.

**Training programme** Trainees spend six months in four departments across our offices, sharing an office with a partner to ensure involvement with a wide range of cases and clients. Training is highly personalised and trainees are given a large degree of responsibility and client involvement from an early stage. Once considered competent and sufficiently confident, trainees are allowed to handle their own cases. Trainees also get involved with marketing and business development.

Mentoring scheme: Barlow Robbins LLP provides a mentoring scheme for trainees. This scheme aims to support and encourage trainees to manage their own learning in order to maximise their potential, develop their skills and improve their performance. Each trainee is assigned to a mentor throughout their training period. The mentor acts as a confidential point of contact and support.

Career prospects: The Training Principal and HR Manager take joint responsibility for regularly monitoring trainees' progress. Trainees are seen as an investment for the future growth and development of the practice and are treated in every respect as a full member of the team. Those who prove themselves can expect excellent long term prospects. We aim to retain as many trainees as possible provided there are relevant opportunities at the time of qualification.

**When and how to apply** Full details of our training contract application procedure and more information about the practice can be found on our website www.barlowrobbins.com. The closing date for applications is 31st July 2008 for a start date in September 2010.

**Sponsorship** The practice will make a £5000 contribution towards the cost of the LPC, plus an interest free loan for the balance of the fees, re-payable over the 2 years of the training contract.

| | |
|---|---|
| Vacancies | 4 |
| Trainees | 8 |
| Partners | 23 |
| Total staff | 225 |

**Work placement** no

**Apply to**
Sheila Newey

**Starting salary**
Market rate

**Minimum qualifications**
2.1 degree and A levels at grades A-B

**Sponsorship**
LPC

**Offices**
Guildford, Woking, Godalming

BARLOW ROBBINS LLP
Solicitors

| BASINGSTOKE & DEANE BOROUGH COUNCIL<br>Civic Offices, London Road, Basingstoke,<br>Hampshire RG21 4AH<br>**Tel:** 01256 845402<br>**Fax:** 01256 845200<br>**Email:** chris.guy@basingstoke.gov.uk<br>**Apply to:** Mr Chris Guy | Leading e-enabled local government practice involved with high value development, regeneration and commercial property projects. Trainees have own caseloads with opportunities for advocacy. Applications continually sought via website. | V 2-3<br>T 3<br>P 1<br>TS 18<br>WP no |
|---|---|---|
| BASSRA SOLICITORS (INCORPORATING JOHN KELLY & CO)<br>89/93 Manningham Lane, Bradford,<br>West Yorkshire BD1 3DN<br>**Tel:** 01274 307060<br>**Fax:** 01274 769651<br>**Apply to:** Mr John Kelly | Small North West Yorkshire firm specialising in crime. Legal aid franchise. | V 0<br>T 2<br>P 2<br>TS 8<br>WP no |
| BATES, WELLS & BRAITHWAITE<br>2-6 Cannon Street, London EC4M 6YH<br>**Tel:** 020 7551 7777<br>**Fax:** 020 7551 7800<br>**Email:** training@bwbllp.com<br>**Apply to:** Mr Peter Bennett FCCA MCIM<br>Partnership Executive Officer | Formed 1970; practice areas: charity, commercial, general litigation, administrative, media and sports law, employment, immigration and asylum, property. Diversity within the office. Time for life outside it. | V 5<br>T 10<br>P 21<br>TS 130<br>WP yes |
| BATTENS SOLICITORS LIMITED<br>Mansion House, Princes Street, Yeovil BA20 1EP<br>**Tel:** 01935 846000<br>**Fax:** 01935 846001<br>**Email:** h.green@battens.co.uk<br>**Apply to:** Miss Hannah Green | Battens is a long established but progressive firm with four offices in Somerset and Dorset. Extremely strong presence in all practice areas, except criminal law. | V 0<br>T 5<br>P 15<br>TS 144<br>WP no |
| BEALE AND COMPANY SOLICITORS LLP<br>Garrick House, 27-32 King Street,<br>London WC2E 8JB<br>**Tel:** 020 7240 3474<br>**Fax:** 020 7240 9111<br>**Email:** l.richards@beale-law.com<br>**Apply to:** Mr Lyndon Richards | A commercial practice which specialises in construction, insurance, IT, corporate and commercial, employment and international business. Some private client and property also carried out. | V 2-3<br>T 3<br>P 11<br>TS 75<br>WP no |
| BEARDSELLS<br>Vienna House, Eden place, Cheadle,<br>Cheshire SK8 1AT<br>**Tel:** 0161 477 2288<br>**Fax:** 0161 474 7268<br>**Email:** contact@beardsells.co.uk<br>**Apply to:** Mr CJ Worthy | Applications to be made in February of year contract sought. Specialise in road traffic litigation, also commercial litigation, matrimonial, conveyancing, probate and personal injury litigation. | V 2-3(08)<br>T 2<br>P 12<br>TS 65<br>WP yes |
| BEECHAM PEACOCK<br>7 Collingwood Street, Newcastle upon Tyne NE1 1JE<br>**Tel:** 0191 232 3048<br>**Fax:** 0191 261 7255<br>**Email:** genenquiry@beechampeacock.co.uk<br>**Apply to:** The Practice Manager | We are a city firm. Our practice deals primarily with personal injury work. In addition we have criminal, family, employment and conveyancing departments. | V 0<br>T 2<br>P 6<br>TS 60<br>WP no |
| BELL LAX SOLICITORS<br>New Bank House, 21 Maney Corner,<br>Sutton Coldfield B72 1QL<br>**Tel:** 0121 355 0011<br>**Fax:** 0121 355 0099<br>**Email:** trainees@belllax.com<br>**Apply to:** Miss Angela Davis | Specialist litigation practice - 70% commercial litigation, 30% personal injury. Trainees are given considerable responsibility, but benefit from close supervision on all matters. | V 2-3(09)<br>T 5<br>P 4<br>TS 25<br>WP yes |

**V** = Vacancies / **T** = Trainees / **P** = Partners / **TS** = Total Staff / **WP** = Work Placement

# Beachcroft LLP

100 Fetter Lane, London EC4A 1BN
**Tel:** 020 7242 1011
**Fax:** 020 7831 6630
**Email:** trainee@beachcroft.co.uk
**Web:** www.bemore.beachcroft.co.uk

**The firm** Beachcroft LLP (formerly Beachcroft Wansbroughs) is one of the largest commercial law firms in the UK, with a turnover of over £111m, a 12% increase on 2005/2006. An enviable client base and over 1,400 people working out of eight offices means we can provide truly exceptional career opportunities, whatever your aspirations.

Our national teams allow clients to benefit from some of the best specialists in the UK with expert local knowledge and a consistent commercial view wherever they are. For our fee earners and support staff it's a chance to work alongside nationally respected lawyers as part of progressive multi-disciplinary teams.

*Chambers UK*, A Client's Guide to the Legal Profession 2007, will recognise 65 Beachcroft partners as leading lawyers, ranking the firm at number 16 in the UK, up from 19 last year. In *Legal 500*, a guide to the top 500 UK lawyers, the firm received a tier one ranking for 17 of its practice areas across the UK. In *Legal Week*'s client satisfaction survey, the firm came second amongst all law firms in the UK. Beachcroft is one of the largest law firms in the country to obtain the 'Investors in People' award across all of its offices.

The key to our continued success is, of course, our people. In our most recent internal attitude survey, conducted once every two years, we scored the highest response for being a friendly place to work.

**Types of work** We operate through specialist practice area teams to deliver an integrated service to clients in six main industry groups: financial institutions (including the insurance industry), health and public sector, real estate, technology and telecommunications, industrial manufacturing & transportation and consumer goods & services. Key clients include Guy's and St Thomas's NHS Foundation Trust, Balfour Beatty, Westfield Shoppingtowns, Zurich, Allianz Insurance, BAE Systems, L'Oreal, Unilever, Waitrose, Freescale Semiconductor and Getronics. We're helping them get more from their businesses, and we can help you get more from your career.

**Who should apply** We look for outgoing, commercially minded people with a 2.1 honours degree in any subject. You'll need to be an excellent team player and possess a mind capable of analysing, interpreting and applying complex points of law.

**Training programme** Training takes place over a two-year period in London, Bristol, Manchester or Leeds, during which time you'll pursue a demanding study programme, while occupying four six-month seats in some of the key areas of commercial law. Responsibility will come early and we provide the supervision and support to enable you to develop and grow.

**When and how to apply** Please visit www.bemore.beachcroft.co.uk for our online brochure and an application form. The deadline for training contract applications is 1 August each year.

**Work placements** Beachcroft runs a paid placement scheme each summer. Please visit our website for more information.

**Sponsorship** The firm operates a flexible benefits scheme, allowing you to buy and sell certain aspects of your benefits package, including holiday, pension and private healthcare. This gives you individual choice, depending on your current needs and circumstances. Beachcroft provides payment for the GDL and LPC, and a £5,000 bursary.

| | |
|---|---|
| Vacancies | 30 |
| Trainees | 77 |
| Partners | 147 |
| Total staff | 1400 |

**Work placement** yes
*(see Insider Report on p75)*

**Apply to**
Carrie Daniels, Graduate
Recruitment Officer

**Starting salary**
1st year, regions - £22,000
2nd year, regions - £24,000
1st year, London - £30,000
2nd year, London - £33,000

**Sponsorship**
LPC/GDL

**Offices**
Birmingham, Bristol,
Brussels, Leeds, London,
Manchester, Winchester

**beachcroft**

# Berrymans Lace Mawer

Salisbury House, London Wall, London EC2M 5QN
**Tel:** 020 7638 2811
**Fax:** 020 7920 0361
**Email:** graduate.recruitment@blm-law.com
**Web:** www.blm-law.com

**The firm** Berrymans Lace Mawer is a national and international legal firm that specialises in dispute resolution and litigation. Our client base is spread across commercial, FTSE-100 companies, local authorities, police authorities, professional service organisations and other public sector bodies, which rely on us to provide a stream-lined process that keeps costs down to a minimum through the use of IT, MI, standard documents and strict adherence to quality standards. For many we are the preferred or nominated solicitors.

The firm handles more than 25,000 live cases at any time covering a broad range of disputes. We work to more than 250 client protocols which form the basis of unique Service Level Agreements.

**Types of work** The firm is a defendant practice that deals with predominantly contentious matters in more than thirty different areas, in eight main groups: commercial, dispute resolution, human resources, insurance, public sector, property, media and technology and transport.

BLM has teams led by partners with established reputations as some of the very best in the field: catastrophic injury, abuse, clinical negligence, construction, education, employers' liability, employment, environmental, mediation, motor, occupational disease, personal injury, police and emergency services, professional indemnity, property insurance and recovery, public liability and stress.

**Who should apply** Undergraduates and graduates in all disciplines seeking a training contract in 2010. We also welcome applications from those who have taken the legal executive or paralegal route.

**Training programme** We recruit a small number of high-quality trainees each year to ensure that we can provide the best possible training and development opportunities.

The training contract is divided into four seats, with exposure to both contentious and to a lesser extent non-contentious work. You are encouraged to practise and develop the skills set down by the Law Society, including negotiation, drafting, interviewing, research, dispute resolution and case management.

You will be provided with a training programme to help you be an asset to your team from the start. You are encouraged to take responsibility for your own continuing professional development and identify your own training needs in addition to attendance at in-house courses.

**When and how to apply** A brochure, application and equal opportunities form will be available from November 2007 and can be downloaded from our website. Return your completed documents and cover letter to the Graduate Recruitment Department at our London office. The closing date for receipt of completed applications is 31 July 2008.

**Work placements** The firm's London and Birmingham branches will be offering vacation placements over the Easter period and in the summer months covering June/July/August. Our training contract application form has the dual purpose of a vacation placement application. Your application, equal opportunities form and cover letter should be returned to the Graduate Recruitment Department by 31 January 2008 for Easter placements and by 30 April 2008 for summer placements.

| | |
|---|---|
| Vacancies | 17* |
| Trainees | 41 |
| Partners | 115 |
| Total staff | 792 |

*in London (6), Birmingham (1), Manchester (6), Leeds (2), Liverpool (2)

**Work placement** yes
(London and Birmingham only)

**Apply to**
Graduate Recruitment Department

**Starting salary**
London: £23,000
Birmingham: £18,000
Northern offices: £18,000

**Minimum qualifications**
2.1 degree

**Sponsorship**
LPC

**Offices**
Birmingham, Leeds, Liverpool, London, Manchester, Southampton, Stockton-on-Tees, Dubai

Berrymans Lace Mawer

| | | | |
|---|---|---|---|
| **BEN HOARE BELL**<br>47 John Street, Sunderland SR1 1QU<br>**Tel:** 0191 565 3112<br>**Fax:** 0191 510 9122<br>**Email:** advice@benhoarebell.co.uk<br>**Apply to:** Mr Jeff Dean | Clinical negligence, crime, housing, family, public law, community care, immigration, mental health, personal injury. Strong links to universities and other key agencies. | V<br>T<br>P<br>TS<br>WP | 3[09]<br>6<br>7<br>80<br>no |
| **BENNETTS SOLICITORS & ATTORNEYS**<br>High Street, Wrington, Bristol BS40 5QB<br>**Tel:** 01934 862786<br>**Fax:** 01934 862404<br>**Apply to:** Mrs Alison Reed | Training at Bennetts (see Legal 500) is practical, gives broad but specialist commercial and private client experience, develops problem solving, client care and high professional standards. | V<br>T<br>P<br>TS<br>WP | 1<br>2<br>4<br>15<br>no |
| **BERG LEGAL**<br>35 Peter Street, Manchester M2 5BG<br>**Tel:** 0161 833 9211<br>**Fax:** 0161 834 5566<br>**Email:** recruitment@berg.co.uk<br>**Apply to:** Mr Jonathan Dover | The firm undertakes all aspects of commercial work for business clients. The firm's mission is to be recognised as the clever choice, giving imaginative advice and value for money. | V<br>T<br>P<br>TS<br>WP | 3[08]<br>5<br>10<br>57<br>yes |
| **BERKELEY SOLICITORS**<br>100-102 Market Street, Droylsden,<br>Manchester M43 6DE<br>**Tel:** 0161 371 0011<br>**Fax:** 0161 371 0022<br>**Email:** personnel@claim.co.uk<br>**Apply to:** Mrs Berkeley | A high street practice where every person plays a vital role as part of a team. Please apply with CV and a covering letter. | V<br>T<br>P<br>TS<br>WP | 1[09]<br>2<br>1<br>7<br>yes |
| **BERMANS**<br>Lancaster House, Mercury Court, Tithebarn Street,<br>Liverpool L2 2QP<br>**Tel:** 0151 224 0500<br>**Fax:** 0151 236 2107<br>**Email:** trainees@bermans.co.uk<br>**Apply to:** Miss Julie Hunter | Manchester and Liverpool. No nonsense business lawyers. Niches in factoring/leasing and leisure/creative. | V<br>T<br>P<br>TS<br>WP | 2[09]<br>2<br>11<br>100<br>no |
| **BERRY & BERRY**<br>11 Church Road, Tunbridge Wells TN1 1JA<br>**Tel:** 01892 526344<br>**Fax:** 01892 511223<br>**Email:** schapman@the-solicitors.co.uk<br>**Apply to:** Miss S Chapman | General high street practice including criminal work. Emphasis on litigation. | V<br>T<br>P<br>TS<br>WP | 2[09]<br>4<br>10<br>69<br>no |
| **BERRY & BERRY**<br>1-5 Longley Road, Worsley, Manchester M28 3JB<br>**Tel:** 0161 790 1411<br>**Fax:** 0161 790 1971<br>**Apply to:** Ms Margaret McCormack | A well-established general practice with four offices in Greater Manchester covering matrimonial, crime, personal injury, commercial conveyancing and litigation. Legal aid franchise. | V<br>T<br>P<br>TS<br>WP | 1<br>3<br>8<br>52<br>no |
| **BERRYMAN**<br>Park House, Friar Lane, Nottingham NG1 6DN<br>**Tel:** 0115 945 3700<br>**Fax:** 0115 948 0234<br>**Email:** cheryl.peto@berryman.co.uk<br>**Apply to:** Ms Cheryl Peto | 18 partner firm. Main areas of work: company/commercial, litigation, employment, (defended) insurance and private client work (including domestic conveyancing, trusts and tax, and family). | V<br>T<br>P<br>TS<br>WP | 4<br>6<br>15<br>125<br>no |

# Berwin Leighton Paisner LLP

Adelaide House, London Bridge, London EC4R 9HA
**Tel:** 020 7760 1000
**Fax:** 020 7760 1111
**Email:** traineerecruit@blplaw.com
**Web:** www.blplaw.com

**The firm** Berwin Leighton Paisner LLP is a premier, full service City law firm, with particular strengths in real estate, corporate, finance and a strong litigation and dispute resolution capability. We have over 600 lawyers and over 180 Partners. In addition to our London office, we have an office in Brussels, incorporating our fast expanding EU and competition practice, and offices in Paris and Singapore. We actively manage relationships with two or more preferred firms in over 50 countries. This approach enables us to maintain the flexibility and quality service for our clients. Our open and friendly culture, combined with a strong commitment to career development and internal communication means that we have become a magnet for quality staff.

**Types of work** The full range of real estate work including investment, development, planning, construction, real estate finance, litigation and funds. Traditional corporate finance areas of M&A, equity capital markets and investment funds, as well as outsourcing, EU, competition, IT, telecoms and employment. An active banking and capital markets team with a growing securitisation capability, a project finance team that is expanding internationally, and an asset finance team. Strong and growing corporate tax team, intellectual property, commercial litigation, and reinsurance and insurance. We are widely recognised for our expertise in a number of industry sectors, including real estate, hotels, leisure and gaming, defence, energy, utilities and retail.

**Who should apply** The firm is looking for intelligent, energetic, positive and hard-working team players who have an interest in business and gain a sense of achievement from finding solutions.

**Training programme** When recruiting trainees, our focus is on quality rather than quantity. As a result, our trainees are rewarded with a high degree of responsibility and involvement underpinned by an exceptional standard of training and support. BLP has always prided itself on providing the right environment for people to grow. Trainees spend six months in four seats and progress is reviewed every three months. All our people believe that BLP is a genuinely innovative and friendly firm with a refreshing lack of hierarchy, our open-door policy is something that our trainees value tremendously.

**LPC+** The firm runs the UK's first tailor-made LPC Course, called the LPC+. All trainees will study at the College of Law, where tutors are joined by BLP lawyers and trainers who help to deliver some of the sessions, using BLP precedents and documents, discussing how theory is applied to real cases and transactions.

**When and how to apply** Apply for a training contract for September 2010 or March 2011 online via our website by 31 July 2008.

**Work placements** Places for 2008: Assessment centres held during December, January and February at the firm's London office, applications accepted online before 31 January 2008 (at www.blplaw.com).
Summer vacation scheme, two weeks - aimed at those in their penultimate year and above (law and non-law).
Easter vacation scheme, one week - aimed at final year law students and those at a later stage of legal education/employment.

**Sponsorship** CPE/GDL and LPC+ fees paid and £7,200 maintenance p.a.

| | |
|---|---|
| Vacancies | 40 |
| Trainees | 80 |
| Partners | 180 |
| Total staff | 1200 |

**Work placement** yes
*(see Insider Report on p77)*

**Apply to**
Jennie Moore

**Starting salary**
£33,000 with £2,500 golden hello

**Minimum qualifications**
320 UCAS points and a 2.1 degree

**Sponsorship**
GDL and LPC+

**Offices**
Brussels, London, Paris, Singapore and a best friend network in over 50 countries

*berwin leighton paisner

# Bevan Brittan LLP

Kings Orchard, 1 Queen Street, Bristol BS2 0HQ
**Tel:** 0870 194 3050
**Fax:** 0870 194 8954
**Email:** HR.Training@bevanbrittan.com
**Web:** www.bevanbrittan.com

**The firm** Bevan Brittan LLP has firmly established itself as a truly national law firm and continues to attract high-profile national and international clients and challenging, groundbreaking work. The firm is recognised for its expertise in providing legal advice to clients in both the public and private sectors, and is noted for being one of the very few practices whose work is equally strong in both sectors.

**Types of work** To meet the demands of today's clients the firm is structured around four primary areas of the UK economy: built environment, health, government and education, and commerce, industry and services. The firm operates in cross-departmental teams across these markets, harnessing the full range of skills and experience needed to provide top-quality legal advice. Teams are established in practice areas such as employment, corporate and commercial, real estate, planning, construction and IT/IP covering both private and public sectors. The range of litigation work – insurance, banking, property, construction, IT/IP, professional indemnity and medical – confirms this cross–department practice area as one of the most talented teams outside London. The PFI and projects team is recognised as one of the leading teams in the country, and the firm is renowned for its specialist health and social care advisory work and medical litigation practice.

**Who should apply** We recognise that the most important prerequisite of quality service is a team of lawyers dedicated to service excellence. Our success is maintained by attracting and keeping talented legal minds. We are looking for bright people with sound common sense and plenty of energy, who can think logically and clearly. You need drive, commitment, willingness to take responsibility and the ability to adapt to the ever-changing demands of the legal world.

**Training programme** We have a widely respected training programme and with our Investors in People accreditation, we are committed to ongoing training and development. Your training will consist of practical work experience in conjunction with an extensive educational programme. The training is aimed at developing attitudes, skills, and legal and commercial knowledge which is essential for your career success. You are encouraged to take on as much work and responsibility as you are able to handle, which will be reviewed on a regular basis with your supervising partner. We are committed to retaining trainees as qualified solicitors and progression can be rapid, based on individual performance and merit.

**When and how to apply** Applications for training contracts commencing in 2010 must be received by 31 July 2008. Bevan Brittan only accepts online application forms which can be found, along with other information, on the website. For more information contact the HR and Training Department on 0870 194 3050.

**Work placements** We run summer vacation schemes in London, Bristol and Birmingham. They last for two weeks and take place during June and July 2008. Applications must be made via the online application form by 31 March 2008.

**Sponsorship** Bursary and funding for the GDL and LPC available.

| | |
|---|---|
| Vacancies | 22 |
| Trainees | 33 |
| Partners | 62 |
| Total staff | 620 |

**Work placement**   yes

**Apply**
Online

**Starting salary**
Above local rate

**Minimum qualifications**
2.1 degree and 300 UCAS points or 3 years' commercial experience

**Sponsorship**
GDL/LPC

**Offices**
London, Bristol, Birmingham

| **BEVIRS**<br>36 Regent Circus, Swindon SN1 1UQ<br>**Tel:** 01793 532363<br>**Fax:** 01793 619585<br>**Apply to:** Mr Stuart McNeil | Broadly based general practice in expanding area of South West. Mix of private client, commercial, family and civil litigation. | V 1<br>T 1<br>P 7<br>TS 56<br>WP no |
|---|---|---|
| **BEVISS & BECKINGSALE**<br>Law Chambers, Silver Street, Axminster, Devon EX13 5AH<br>**Tel:** 01297 630700<br>**Fax:** 01297 630701<br>**Email:** enquiries@bevissandbeckingsale.co.uk<br>**Apply to:** Mr Anthony Osborne | A general practice with four offices with an emphasis on private client work, residential and commercial property, and with a niche agricultural practice and family law department. | V 1(09)<br>T 2<br>P 9<br>TS 60<br>WP no |
| **BG ENERGY HOLDINGS**<br>100 Thames Valley Park Drive, Reading RG6 1PT<br>**Tel:** 0118 935 3222<br>**Fax:** 0118 935 3484<br>**Email:** lisa.baker@bg-group.com<br>**Apply to:** Mrs HR Pearson | BG Group will usually recruit (by advertisement) for paralegals and may then offer a training contract at the end of a 1 or 2 year placement. | V 0<br>T 2<br>P -<br>TS 40<br>WP no |
| **BHATIA BEST**<br>12 Carrington Street, Nottingham NG1 7FF<br>**Tel:** 0115 950 3231<br>**Fax:** 0115 941 3169<br>**Email:** nottingham@bhatiabest.co.uk<br>**Apply to:** Ms Jayne Sheehan | An 13 partner, city centre, legal aid franchise practice with a dynamic, progressive approach. Specialising in crime, matrimonial, general civil litigation, PI and conveyancing. | V 2-4<br>T 10<br>P 13<br>TS 113<br>WP no |
| **BHATT MURPHY**<br>27 Hoxton Square, London N1 6NN<br>**Tel:** 020 7729 1115<br>**Fax:** 020 7729 1117<br>**Email:** m.kelly@bhattmurphy.co.uk<br>**Apply to:** Ms M Kelly | Bhatt Murphy is a human rights practice specialising in the protection of civil liberties, dealing particularly with actions against the police, public and prison law. | V 0<br>T 1<br>P 4<br>TS 16<br>WP no |
| **BHOGAL PARTNERS**<br>51-53 High Street, Hounslow, London TW3 1RB<br>**Tel:** 020 8572 9867<br>**Fax:** 020 8572 9228<br>**Apply to:** Mr Bhogal | Young, dynamic, forward-thinking high street practice, with emphasis on human rights work with most other areas undertaken. | V 2(09)<br>T 3<br>P 2<br>TS 20<br>WP yes |
| **BHW COMMERCIAL SOLICITORS**<br>5 Grove Court, Grove Park, Enderby, Leicester LE19 1SA<br>**Tel:** 0116289 7000<br>**Fax:** 0116281 6229<br>**Email:** julie@bhwlaw.co.uk<br>**Apply to:** Mrs Julie White | A boutique firm providing a high quality personal service to business clients ranging from national PLCs to local entrepreneurs. | V 1<br>T 2<br>P 2<br>TS 12<br>WP yes |
| **BILTON HAMMOND**<br>The Corner House, Union Street, Mansfield, Nottinghamshire NG18 1RP<br>**Tel:** 01623 675 800<br>**Fax:** 01623 675 863<br>**Email:** markbilton@biltonhammond.co.uk<br>**Apply to:** Mr Mark Bilton | Progressive firm specialising in family, crime and property. Only applicants living within ten miles of Chesterfield will be considered for the vacation scheme. | V 0<br>T 2<br>P 6<br>TS 35<br>WP yes |

**V** = Vacancies / **T** = Trainees / **P** = Partners / **TS** = Total Staff / **WP** = Work Placement

# Bircham Dyson Bell LLP

50 Broadway, London SW1H 0BL
**Tel:** 020 7227 7000
**Fax:** 020 7227 7206
**Web:** www.bdb-law.co.uk

**The firm** Bircham Dyson Bell is one of the UK's most progressive and top 10 fastest growing law firms. Employing 300 people, (with 52 partners), the firm has doubled its turnover within the last five years and has been shortlisted for *The Lawyer's* 'Law Firm of the Year' award and real estate and employment teams of the year awards. The firm acts for many high-profile clients from a wide-variety of sectors, including real estate, public and private companies, charities, private clients, and public sector organisations. The firm enjoys a market-wide reputation for the quality of its people, their knowledge, and their pro-active approach to clients.

**Types of work** Located in central London, Bircham Dyson Bell is recognised as having leading departments in the charity, private client, parliamentary, planning and public law fields. The firm also has strong corporate commercial, real estate and litigation teams.

**Who should apply** Applications are welcome from both law and non-law students who can demonstrate a consistently high academic record. The firm is looking for creative thinkers with a confident and practical outlook who will thrive in a friendly, hard-working environment. Many of BDB's current trainees have diverse interests outside law.

**Training programme** The firm's training is designed to produce its future partners. To achieve this they aim to provide a balance of both formal and practical training and will give early responsibility to those who show promise.

The two-year training contract consists of four six-month seats during which you will work alongside partners and other senior lawyers, some of whom are leaders in their field. As the firm practises in a wide variety of legal disciplines, trainees benefit from a diverse experience. Trainees undergo specific technical training in each seat in addition to the mandatory Professional Skills Course (PSC). Great emphasis is now placed on soft skills training and development.

**When and how to apply** Apply via our website www.bdb-law.co.uk in the graduate area. The closing date is 31 July 2008 for 2010.

**Work placements** The closing date for the summer 2008 scheme is 31 January 2008. Apply via the website.

**Sponsorship** Bircham Dyson Bell provides funding for GDL and LPC fees.

| Vacancies | 8 |
|---|---|
| Trainees | 16 |
| Partners | 52 |
| Total staff | 300 |

**Work placement** yes

**Apply to**
Mr David Mundy

**Starting salary**
1st year - £30,000 (2007)
2nd year - £31,000 (2007)

**Minimum qualifications**
2.1 degree preferred

**Sponsorship**
GDL/LPC

**Offices**
London

Bircham Dyson Bell

# Bird & Bird

15 Fetter Lane, London EC4A 1JP
**Tel:** 020 7415 6000
**Fax:** 020 7415 6111
**Email:** info@twobirds.com
**Web:** www.twobirds.com

**The firm** Bird & Bird is a sector-focused, full-service international law firm. We have 148 partners and over 900 staff across offices in Beijing, Brussels, Düsseldorf, Frankfurt, The Hague, Hong Kong, London, Lyon, Madrid, Milan, Munich, Paris, Rome and Stockholm. The firm is proud of its friendly, stimulating environment where individuals are able to develop first class legal business and interpersonal skills.

The firm's international reach and focus on sectors will enable you to work across borders and for a variety of companies, many of which operate at the cutting edge of the industries in which they operate.

**Types of work** The firm has a leading reputation for many of the sectors on which it focuses: aviation & aerospace, banking & financial services, communications, electronics, information technology, life sciences, media and sport.

From each of its offices, it provides a full range of legal services to these sectors: commercial, corporate, corporate restructuring and insolvency, dispute resolution, employment, EU & competition law, finance, intellectual property, outsourcing, public procurement, real estate, regulatory and administrative, tax.

**Who should apply** The firm looks for high-calibre recruits - confident individuals capable of developing expert legal skills and commercial sense.

**Training programme** Following an induction course, you will undertake four six-month seats. Some seats may be spent in our international ofices. Our trainees take on responsibility from day one and enjoy varied and challenging work for industry-shaping clients. If you become a trainee with us, you will be given the chance to excel.

We run a business skills development programme to provide you with the basic building blocks for your future development within the business of law. The firm is still personal enough for our trainees to make their mark in our friendly stimulating work place.

Trainees are encouraged to join the number of sports teams at the firm and to attend various social events.

**When and how to apply** The firm will hold insight and selection days in July and August. Successful applicants from the insight and selection days will be invited to join a panel during the week commencing 1 September 2008. The deadline for applications is 31 July 2008. Please apply online via our website at www.twobirds.com.

We attend many of the university law fairs, where students can meet representatives from the firm.

**Work placements** The firm offers 20 vacation scheme places each year, each for a three-week period. Remuneration is £275 per week and the closing date for the 2008 scheme is 31 January 2008.

**Sponsorship** Bird & Bird pays LPC and GDL fees and offers a yearly maintenance grant of £5,500.

| | |
|---|---|
| Vacancies | 18 |
| Trainees | 31 |
| Partners | 148 |
| Total staff | Over 900 |

**Work placement**  yes
*(see Insider Report on p79)*

**Apply to**
Ms Lynne Walters,
Graduate Recruitment
Manager

**Starting salary**
£31,000

**Minimum qualifications**
2.1 degree

**Sponsorship**
GDL/CPE/LPC

**Offices**
Beijing, Brussels,
Düsseldorf, Frankfurt,
The Hague, Hong Kong,
London, Lyon, Madrid,
Milan, Munich, Paris, Rome,
Stockholm

BIRD & BIRD

## BINDMAN & PARTNERS
275 Gray's Inn Road, London WC1X 8QB
**Tel:** 020 7833 4433
**Fax:** 020 7837 9792
**Email:** info@bindmans.com
**Apply to:** Ms Charlotte Miles

| | |
|---|---|
| V | 0 |
| T | 6 |
| P | 14 |
| TS | 90 |
| WP | no |

## BINGHAM MCCUTCHEN (LONDON) LLP
41 Lothbury, London EC2R 7HF
**Tel:** 020 7661 5300
**Fax:** 020 7661 5400
**Email:** graduaterecruitment@bingham.com
**Apply to:** Ms Lisa Poulley

Bingham's London office represents financial institutions including hedge funds, insurance companies, investment funds and banks.

| | |
|---|---|
| V | 2 |
| T | 4 |
| P | 12 |
| TS | 80 |
| WP | no |

## BIRCH CULLIMORE
20 White Friars, Chester CH1 1XS
**Tel:** 01244 321066
**Fax:** 01244 312582
**Email:** info@bclaw.co.uk
**Apply to:** Mr N Cummings

A friendly city practice offering quality service to commercial, agricultural and private clients.

| | |
|---|---|
| V | 1[09] |
| T | 1 |
| P | 7 |
| TS | 44 |
| WP | no |

## BIRCHALL BLACKBURN
36-48 Avenham Street, Preston PR1 3BN
**Tel:** 01772 561663
**Fax:** 01772 202438
**Email:** cjharris@birchallblackburn.co.uk
**Apply to:** Mrs Christine Harris

Well-established and progressive firm with 6 offices, offering services to business and private clients. Also cover immigration and are specialists in family law, particularly childcare. Recruitment ongoing.

| | |
|---|---|
| V | 0 |
| T | 4 |
| P | 15 |
| TS | 160 |
| WP | no |

## BIRD & CO
15 Castlegate, Grantham, Lincolnshire NG31 6SE
**Tel:** 01476 591711
**Fax:** 01476 593235
**Apply to:** Mrs E Conron

3 partner firm, offices in Grantham and Newark. Young and progressive high street/legal aid practice. Core areas criminal, family, civil litigation, PI, conveyancing, wills & probate.

| | |
|---|---|
| V | 0 |
| T | 1 |
| P | 3 |
| TS | 47 |
| WP | yes |

## BIRKETT LONG
Essex House, 42 Crouch Street, Colchester CO3 3HH
**Tel:** 01206 217300
**Fax:** 01206 711385
**Email:** shirley.tarbin@birkettlong.co.uk
**Apply to:** Mrs Shirley Tarbin

A pre-eminent firm in Essex providing general provincial services with specialisms in commercial, environmental, agricultural, education, employment, computer law, family and private client. Other offices: Chelmsford.

| | |
|---|---|
| V | 3 |
| T | 6 |
| P | 18 |
| TS | 150 |
| WP | yes |

## BIRKETTS LLP
24-26 Museum Street, Ipswich IP1 1HZ
**Tel:** 01473 232300
**Fax:** 01473 230524
**Email:** tracey-hammett@birketts.co.uk
**Apply to:** Mrs Tracey Hammett

Regional firm with commercial and litigation bias, acting for a wide range of clients locally, nationally and internationally.

| | |
|---|---|
| V | 5 |
| T | 10 |
| P | 36 |
| TS | 225 |
| WP | no |

## BIRNBERG PEIRCE & PARTNERS
14 Inverness Street, London NW1 7HJ
**Tel:** 020 7911 0166
**Fax:** 020 7911 0170
**Email:** sueupton@birnbergpeirce.co.uk
**Apply to:** Mrs Sue Upton

Leading criminal defence, immigration & civil liberties firm. Please do not send applications earlier than 1 May 2008 to commence in September 2009/10.

| | |
|---|---|
| V | 1[08] |
| T | 1 |
| P | 2 |
| TS | 29 |
| WP | no |

# Blake Lapthorn Tarlo Lyons

New Court, 1 Barnes Wallis Road, Segensworth, Fareham, Hampshire PO15 5UA
**Tel:** 01489 579990
**Fax:** 01489 579126
**Email:** graduateinfo@bllaw.co.uk
**Web:** www.bllaw.co.uk

**The firm** Blake Lapthorn Tarlo Lyons is one of the largest regional law firms in the UK, with six offices in the south of England including a strong London presence. Our clients include a wide range of UK and multinational companies, from well-known retailers, banks, local authorities and property developers to major charities. We also act for private clients offering specialist services such as French property, tax planning and clinical negligence. Although a large practice we have retained a sense of community. We value diversity, which adds breadth to our expertise. Our professionals have very different backgrounds and skills, many having worked in city firms and in-house. Our advice is practical, providing clients with tailored solutions. We encourage innovation and imagination in order to enhance our client services.

**Who should apply** Fitting in at Blake Lapthorn Tarlo Lyons is about ability, enthusiasm and contribution. In order to maintain our standards of excellence, we need high-calibre people. To be successful you need to demonstrate significant personal achievement and strong interpersonal skills as well as an excellent academic record.

Our selection process consists of four stages:

Stage 1 – Initial review of applications and selection of around 90 candidates to attend stage 2; those candidates demonstrating thorough research, awareness of the firm and outstanding achievement are most likely to succeed.

Stage 2 – Attendance at an assessment day, which includes a series of psychometric tests, group exercises and an interview with a partner. A shortlist of around 30 candidates is drawn up, taking into consideration previous commercial work experience, quality of application, the interview and test results.

Stage 3 – Second interview for short listed candidates, with a panel comprising the trainee principal, a partner and senior manager. This also involves a short presentation.

Stage 4 – Offers and reserves. Candidates are notified the week following the second interviews. If the number of successful candidates exceeds the number of places available, some may be put on a reserve list and offered a place if one becomes available later.

**Training programme** Training is carefully structured and designed to provide variety, responsibility and intellectual challenge. You will have a series of six-month placements in a range of departments. Working with a partner or senior solicitor, you will be exposed to a wide range of clients and work, in private and commercial practice areas. During each placement your supervisor will involve you directly in work so you learn from hands-on experience, as well as observation and instruction. The greater competence you demonstrate, the more responsibility you will be given.

**When and how to apply** Apply for a training contract 2010 online via our website, by 14 July 2008.

| Vacancies | 17 |
|---|---|
| Trainees | 26 |
| Partners | 104 |
| Total staff | 700+ |

**Apply to**
Mrs Lynn Ford

**Starting salary**
Regions:
1st year - £19,000 (2006)
2nd year - £20,500 (2006)
London:
1st year - £27,000 (2006)
2nd year - £30,000 (2006)

**Minimum qualifications**
2.1 degree

**Sponsorship**
LPC

**Offices**
Southampton, Portsmouth, Oxford, London, Fareham, Winchester

Blake Lapthorn Tarlo Lyons

# Blandy & Blandy

One Friar Street, Reading, Berkshire RG1 1DA
**Tel:** 0118 951 6800
**Fax:** 0118 951 6813
**Email:** fiona_baxter@blandy.co.uk
**Web:** www.blandy.co.uk

**The firm** Blandy & Blandy is the longest-established firm of solicitors in Reading and the 25th-oldest firm in the country. However, the firm balances its established reputation and wealth of experience with a very modern outlook - a unique combination which benefits both clients and employees alike.

We attach a great deal of importance to recruiting trainee solicitors as they help to foster our contemporary approach and are an investment for the future. In return, we offer a stimulating and progressive atmosphere with outstanding career opportunities.

The breadth of services that Blandy & Blandy provides enables our trainees to experience working with clients from a wide variety of backgrounds. The firm's clients range from large commercial organisations to private individuals who need assistance with their personal matters.

All of this experience helps our trainees to develop a good base of skills and knowledge on which to base their future legal careers.

**Who should apply** Our minimum requirements are graduates with a 2.1 degree (or above), who are computer literate and who are enthusiastic and resourceful in their outlook, with excellent communication skills.

**Training programme** Each trainee spends six months in four of the eight departments - wherever possible, individual preferences are catered for. Most trainees share an office space with their assigned partner or solicitor, as this normally gives the best opportunity for continuous professional supervision and for the trainee to experience the day-to-day challenges of a qualified solicitor.

Blandy & Blandy also participates in a Professional Skills Course which is compulsory training. There are three core areas covered - business skills, advocacy and client care - and then trainees can choose electives in areas of law they are interested in.

There are regular informal reviews and an official appraisal is held every six months to discuss the trainee's progress and identify areas for development. Trainees are encouraged to attend lectures and seminars to widen the scope of their training.

**When and how to apply** Students should apply by 31 July 2008 for September 2010 entry. If you are interested in applying for a training contract, please write (preferably in your own handwriting) enclosing a CV (which can be typed) to Fiona Baxter at the address above.

| | |
|---|---|
| Vacancies | 3 |
| Trainees | 6 |
| Partners | 18 |
| Total staff | 94 |

**Apply to**
Fiona Baxter

**Minimum qualifications**
2.1 degree

**Offices**
Reading

BLANDY & BLANDY
SOLICITORS

| Firm | Description | V | T | P | TS | WP |
|---|---|---|---|---|---|---|
| **BISHOP & SEWELL LLP**<br>46 Bedford Square, London WC1B 3DP<br>**Tel:** 020 7631 4141<br>**Fax:** 020 7636 5369<br>**Email:** mail@bishopandsewell.co.uk<br>**Apply to:** Mr Michael Gillman | Bishop & Sewell is a firm offering comprehensive range of legal services to both private and commercial clients who range from Plcs, private companies and individuals. | 2[09] | 4 | 8 | 52 | no |
| **BKM SOLICITORS**<br>64 Alum Rock Road, Birmingham B8 1JA<br>**Tel:** 0121 327 2105<br>**Fax:** 0121 328 7409<br>**Email:** bkmsolicitors@yahoo.co.uk<br>**Apply to:** Mr NA Khatlak | Specialist criminal firm that deals with offences from criminal damage to murder, rape, armed robbery etc. Mainly legal aid work health and safety/food hygiene. | 1[09] | 0 | 2 | 8 | yes |
| **BLACKFORDS LLP**<br>Cleary Court, 169 Church Street East, Woking, Surrey GU21 6HJ<br>**Tel:** 01483 723331<br>**Fax:** 01483 724441<br>**Email:** mail@francislovett.co.uk<br>**Apply to:** Mr Trevor Francis | Specialist criminal firm who prosecute and defend. Niche family and child care practice. | Poss | 4 | 5 | 60 | no |
| **BLACKHURST SWAINSON GOODIER**<br>10 Chapel Street, Preston PR1 8AY<br>**Tel:** 01772 253841<br>**Fax:** 01772 201713<br>**Email:** kgp@bsglaw.co.uk<br>**Apply to:** Mr Keith G Parr | General practice. Holder of legal aid franchise. Applications for training contracts and vacation placements accepted anytime. | 2 | 4 | 9 | 53 | yes |
| **BLACKS**<br>Hanover House, 22 Clarendon Road, Leeds LS2 9NZ<br>**Tel:** 0113 207 0000<br>**Fax:** 0113 242 1703<br>**Email:** cdunnill@lawblacks.com<br>**Apply to:** Mr Chris Allen | General commercial practice with increasing emphasis on company commercial and commercial property areas of work. | 3[09] | 6 | 12 | 100 | no |
| **BLANCHARDS**<br>Bunbury House, Stour Park, Blandford St. Mary, Dorset DT11 9LQ<br>**Tel:** 01258 459361<br>**Fax:** 01258 483610<br>**Email:** hazel.hill@blanchards.co.uk<br>**Apply to:** Miss Hazel Hill | Blanchards is a three partner firm with approximately 50 staff split between two offices dealing with a wide range of legal work. | 1[09] | 1 | 3 | 45 | no |
| **BLASER MILLS**<br>Park House, 31 London Road, High Wycombe, Buckinghamshire HP11 1BZ<br>**Tel:** 01494 450171<br>**Fax:** 01494 443183<br>**Email:** legal@blasermills.co.uk<br>**Apply to:** Mr C Donovan | Large modern provincial firm: 15 partners, 39 fee earners, fifty support staff. Offices: Aylesbury, High Wycombe, Chesham, Harrow, Rickmansworth. Departments: crime, litigation, conveyancing, probate, family, commercial. | 2-4[09] | 8 | 12 | 100 | no |
| **BOLITHO WAY**<br>13-18 Kings Terrace, Portsmouth PO5 3AL<br>**Tel:** 023 92820747<br>**Fax:** 023 92862831<br>**Apply to:** Mr DJ Grinstead | General practice with specialism in commercial work (particularly software licensing). Applications by post. | 0 | 2 | 7 | 22 | yes |

**V** = Vacancies / **T** = Trainees / **P** = Partners / **TS** = Total Staff / **WP** = Work Placement

# Bond Pearce LLP

3 Temple Quay, Temple Back East, Bristol BS1 6DZ
**Tel:** 0845 415 0000
**Fax:** 0845 415 7900
**Email:** sam.lee@bondpearce.com
**Web:** www.bondpearce.com

**The firm** Bond Pearce is a major client-focused law firm accustomed to working for organisations based throughout the UK, in both the public and private sectors.

We deliver service excellence through specialist teams of dedicated lawyers who focus on understanding the needs of their clients, delivering solutions and value.

We have 74 partners, 300 other lawyers and a total staff of 700. Bond Pearce has the resources to deal with time-critical projects and to manage the unexpected. Our lawyers work from whichever location is appropriate to meet client needs, enabling us to avoid replicating specialist expertise in each of our offices. We strive to provide clients with confidence that they shall never be short of resources.

**Types of work** Bond Pearce provides the full range of services you would expect from a firm of our size, and much of our work lies at the cutting edge of developments in key sectors such as banking, insurance, technology, energy, education, retail, transport and logistics.

Bond Pearce acts for an increasing institutional/plc client base which includes for example: Associated British Ports Plc, Barclays Bank Plc, BBC, B&Q Plc, Chemring Group Plc, Chubb, Church Commissioners, Computer Associates UK Ltd, Health & Safety Executive, Lloyds TSB Bank Plc, Npower, Royal Mail Group Plc, Sainsburys and Virgin.

In addition, we have a significant public sector practice, acting for numerous government departments/agencies, local authorities, HE and FE colleges, health trusts and other public sector organisations.

**Who should apply** We welcome applications from a diverse range of backgrounds, skills and experience. Candidates should have a genuine desire to work as a commercial lawyer and be able to provide practical business solutions to our clients. They should also have a natural ability in dealing with people and the drive to want to grow our business.

**Training programme** Our training focuses on developing the legal knowledge and skills required of a commercial lawyer. The training programme is structured over four training seats in a broad range of practice areas. Prospects on qualification are good. Training does not end on qualification, however, as throughout your career with us you will be encouraged to develop the broader business and personal skills you need to progress further.

**When and how to apply** Applications for a training contract should be made by 31 July 2008. Apply using the firm's application form on our website.

**Sponsorship** Full GDL and LPC funding and maintenance grant throughout both. Profit-related bonus scheme, 25 days holiday, childcare vouchers, trainee loan at preferential interest rates, pension, BUPA, life assurance and permanent health insurance.

| | |
|---|---|
| Vacancies | 15 |
| Trainees | 37 |
| Partners | 74 |
| Total staff | 700 |

**Apply to**
Samantha Lee

**Starting salary**
£22,000

**Minimum qualifications**
2.1 degree

**Sponsorship**
LPC/CPE

**Offices**
Bristol, Exeter, London, Plymouth, Southampton

*Bond Pearce*

# Boodle Hatfield

89 New Bond Street, London W1S 1DA
**Tel:** 020 7629 7411
**Fax:** 020 7629 2621
**Email:** traineesolicitors@boodlehatfield.com
**Web:** www.boodlehatfield.com

**The firm** Boodle Hatfield is a highly successful medium-sized firm serving property, corporate and private clients throughout the world.

The ethos of facilitating private capital activity underpins the work of the whole firm, and the interplay of skills between four major areas – private client and tax, property, corporate and litigation – makes Boodle Hatfield particularly well placed to serve these individuals and businesses. Boodle Hatfield is based in Mayfair, London, with a smaller office in Oxford.

**Types of work** The highly rated property department is involved in major town centre and out-of-town office, retail and leisure developments, and in large urban estate transactions and associated landlord and tenant matters. It acts for developers, owners, occupiers, funders, and UK-based and international corporate and private investors.

The private client and tax department is a leader in its field domestically and internationally, and handles tax planning for large, complex estates, private companies, high net-worth individuals and families, trustees, executors and charities.

The litigation department is active in a broad range of commercial disputes and has substantial, well-regarded expertise in property and commercial litigation, construction, employment and agrochemicals.

The corporate department focuses on mid-size corporate clients and private capital. It acts for an international mix of private businesses, smaller quoted companies, entrepreneurs, funds, and both corporate and private investors and financiers.

**Who should apply** Students with 2.1 or above and high A levels.

**Training programme** Four trainee seats.

**When and how to apply** Applicants should apply to begin 2010 via the application form on the website at www.boodlehatfield.com.

**Work placements** Two-week placement between June and September, for which we accept 10 students each year. Applicants should apply via the application form on the website at www.boodlehatfield.com.

**Sponsorship** LPC and GDL/CPE plus maintenance grant.

| | |
|---|---|
| Vacancies | 6 |
| Trainees | 10 |
| Partners | 31 |
| Total staff | 200 |

**Work placement** yes

**Apply to**
Justine Fowler

**Starting salary**
£30,000

**Minimum qualifications**
2.1 degree essential

**Sponsorship**
GDL/LPC

**Offices**
London, Oxford

BOODLE
HATFIELD

BESPOKE LEGAL SERVICES

# Borneo Linnells

Chancery House, 199 Silbury Boulevard, Central Milton Keynes MK9 1JL
**Tel:** 01908 696002
**Fax:** 01908 677640
**Email:** mail@borneolinnells.co.uk
**Web:** www.borneolinnells.co.uk

**The firm** With roots going back to 1869 Borneo Linnells has grown dramatically over the last 10 years to become one of the leading firms in the Eastern region with offices in Milton Keynes, Bedford and Newport Pagnell. The firm has concentrated its expansion into Milton Keynes, England's fastest growing city. Its Milton Keynes office opened in 1998 and has recently benefited from the addition of several renowned and experienced commercial, employment and property lawyers. Growth, both numerically and in reputation, has been achieved in part by several mergers and acquisitions, most notably joining with the Newport Pagnell and Milton Keynes offices of Linnells in 2000.

In April 2005 the partnership converted to a LLP, believing that an LLP provides it with the best management structure with which to attract, retain and develop talented professionals who are core to its business and key to providing its clients with a high quality service.

We pride ourselves on retaining highly motivated and gifted young lawyers by providing a positive working environment and competitive salary and benefits on qualification. Many of our current members (formerly partners) joined the firm as trainees and talented and committed fee earners can progress quickly to associate and member status.

**Types of work** The firm's specialist departments include corporate, commercial, employment, Intellectual Property, commercial property, residential property, litigation, crime, private client, family law and child care (the family department's strength being recognised by the Legal 500).

**Training programme** One member has overall responsibility for our trainees' programme, with each trainee's progress monitored by their allocated supervisor. Trainees are encouraged to use their initiative from the outset and given tasks and responsibilities to expand their experience and knowledge base but with all work being closely supervised to enable trainees to develop their skills confidently.

With departments covering all main areas of the law, Borneo Linnells is able to offer trainees a wide breadth of experience throughout their training contract. Trainees undertake seats in at least three different departments including contentious and non contentious, and are encouraged to spend time in more than one office during their training contract where practicable. Progress is regularly reviewed, both with their allocated supervisor and department head so that aptitudes are recognised and developed at an early stage. Trainees are encouraged to spend their last six months in the seat they hope to practice in on qualification. Trainees attend our high quality in-house training events to supplement their on the job training.

The offices are very friendly with all staff being valued and good, strong relationships between colleagues are developed by regular departmental and firm wide social events organised by a social committee. The firm also participates in local football, touch rugby and cricket leagues and organises regular other informal sporting activities which trainees are encouraged to participate in.

**When and how to apply** Apply by CV and handwritten covering letter by 31 July 2008 for training contracts commencing in 2009.

| | |
|---|---|
| Vacancies | 2 |
| Trainees | 4 |
| Partners | 21 |
| Total staff | 130 |

**Work placement** no

**Apply to**
Niky Jeffries

**Starting salary**
Law Society minimum

**Minimum qualifications**
2.1 degree

**Offices**
Milton Keynes, Bedford, and Newport Pagnell

**Borneo Linnells**
Solicitors

| Firm | Description | V | T | P | TS | WP |
|---|---|---|---|---|---|---|
| **BOSLEY & CO**<br>5 Marlborough Place, Brighton BN1 1UB<br>**Tel:** 01273 608181<br>**Fax:** 01273 683913<br>**Apply to:** Mrs Maureen Jaquemai | Offering legal help on residential and commercial conveyancing, consumer and general contract, debt, education, employment, housing, personal injury, action against police and welfare benefits. | 2 | 0 | 2 | 13 | no |
| **BOWCOCK CUERDEN LLP**<br>South Cheshire House, Manor Road, Nantwich, Cheshire CW5 5LX<br>**Tel:** 01270 611106<br>**Fax:** 01270 610515<br>**Email:** jpc@bowcockcuerden.co.uk<br>**Apply to:** Mr JP Cuerden | Four partner LLP; LEXCEL; progressive; quality oriented. Commercial and agricultural property; commercial/general litigation; general commercial/corporate work; minerals, environmental, planning;employment; private client & family. | 1 | 2 | 4 | 40 | no |
| **BRACHERS**<br>Somerfield House, 59 London Road, Maidstone MEI6 8JH<br>**Tel:** 01622 690691<br>**Fax:** 01622 681430<br>**Apply to:** Ms Michelle Perry | Providing extensive legal services to corporate and private clients throughout the South East. Further specialist services located in London office. Application deadline 31 July. | 2 | 7 | 21 | 200 | no |
| **BRADBURY ROBERTS & RABY**<br>Wadsworth House, Laneham Street, Scunthorpe, North Lincolnshire DN15 6PB<br>**Tel:** 01724 854000<br>**Fax:** 01724 856213<br>**Email:** reception@brrlaw.co.uk<br>**Apply to:** Mr Patrick King | Medium-sized firm in town centre, handling personal injury, commercial, employment, conveyancing, probate, matrimonial and family. Legal aid franchise. LEXCEL accredited. | 1(08) | 2 | 6 | 30 | no |
| **BRAIN SINNOTT & CO**<br>1 Moravian Road, Kingswood, Bristol BS15 8LY<br>**Tel:** 0117 960 6880<br>**Fax:** 0117 935 2523<br>**Apply to:** Mrs Claire Haycroft | A general local practice dealing principally in criminal and matrimonial legal aid matters with a small civil litigation client base together with a non-contentious department. | 0-1 | 1 | 3 | 25 | no |
| **BRAMSDON & CHILDS**<br>141 Elm Grove, Southsea, Portsmouth PO5 1HR<br>**Tel:** 023 92821251<br>**Fax:** 023 9289 3777<br>**Apply to:** Mr Andrew White | Well established firm with offices in Southsea, Portsmouth and Fareham with a general practice. | 1(09) | 1 | 5 | 34 | no |
| **BRECHER ABRAM**<br>Heron Place, 3 George Street, London W1U 3QG<br>**Tel:** 020 7563 1000<br>**Fax:** 020 7486 7796<br>**Email:** admin@brecherabram.co.uk<br>**Apply to:** Mr Martin Bennett | Niche property practice, in particular development, secured lending, investment and public sector/local authority work plus dedicated litigation and company/commercial services. | 1(09) | 1 | 12 | 48 | no |
| **BREEZE & WYLES**<br>114 Fore Street, Hertford SG14 1AG<br>**Tel:** 01992 558411<br>**Fax:** 01992 582834<br>**Apply to:** Mr Stephen Blake | Established for over 90 years, progressive and forward thinking. Covers domestic conveyancing/ commercial conveyancing and litigation, matrimonial, probate and private client. | 2(09) | 4 | 11 | 160 | no |

# Boyes Turner

Abbots House, Abbey Street, Reading RG1 3BD
**Tel:** 0118 959 7711
**Fax:** 0118 957 3257
**Email:** recruitment@boyesturner.com
**Web:** www.boyesturner.com

**The firm** Boyes Turner is continuing to flourish in the Thames Valley legal market. The strategy for 2008 and onwards is to continue the growth and development of the firm, its employees and its work.

The firm demands a high standard of quality work from its partners, associates, assistants and trainee solicitors, together with those employees providing support services and facilities. However, the firm also recognises its employees' desire to enjoy their time out of work (social activities/home life), which results in highly motivated employees.

The firm's values fall into the following categories: accessible, close to clients, commercially aware, approachable, honest, enthusiastic, respecting of others, offering creative solutions to clients, modern but professional.

**Who should apply** If you are an enthusiastic, practical and pragmatic individual, take pride in your work, and are prepared to go that extra mile to provide high-quality services to clients, colleagues and the firm as a whole, then apply to Boyes Turner for a 2010 training contract.

**Training programme** The training principal, Andrew Chalkley, and the Human Resources Manager, Helen Barnett, oversee the training of all trainee solicitors. Each trainee has a tutor who is one of the firm's partners. The tutor meets the trainee on a monthly basis throughout the training contract to review the trainee's progress on two levels: (a) how the trainee is developing as a lawyer and (b) how the trainee is developing as an individual.

Training seats are currently organised into a period of six months in each of four areas of work, gaining experience in both commercial and private client areas of law. For each area, a supervisor form the relevant practice group will oversee day-to-day training and work. Boyes Turner seeks to give as much client contact to trainees as possible.

**When and how to apply** If you are interested in applying please apply via our online application form at www.boyesturner.com. We do not have a closing date for the receipt of applications for training contracts, and we make no distinction between law and non-law graduates in the timing of our recruitment. We aim to make our appointments two years prior to the start of the training contract.

**Sponsorship** Candidates who receive and accept our offer of a training contract are eligible for an LPC loan of £4,000 (one loan per applicant). This loan is interest free and is repaid over the period of the training contract.

| | |
|---|---|
| Vacancies | 4 |
| Trainees | 8 |
| Partners | 26 |
| Total staff | 150 |

**Apply to**
The Graduate Recruitment Team

**Minimum qualifications**
2.1 degree

**Sponsorship**
LPC

**Offices**
Reading

# B P Collins

Collins House, 32-38 Station Road, Gerrards Cross SL9 8EL
**Tel:** 01753 889995
**Fax:** 01753 889851
**Email:** jacqui.symons@bpcollins.co.uk
**Web:** www.bpcollins.co.uk

**The firm** B P Collins was established in 1966 and has expanded significantly to become one of the largest and best-known legal practices at the London end of the M4/M40 corridors. At its main office in Gerrards Cross, the emphasis is on commercial work, including corporate/commercial work of all types, commercial conveyancing and general commercial litigation. We also have a successful family law practice and a highly respected private client department who specialise in tax planning, trusts estate planning, wills and probate as well as charities and elder law issues.

**Types of work** Corporate/commercial, employment, IT/IP, civil and commercial litigation, commercial conveyancing, property development, private client and family law.

**Who should apply** Most of the partners and other fee-earners have worked in London at one time or another but, tired of commuting, have opted to work in more congenial surroundings and enjoy a higher-quality lifestyle. Gerrards Cross is not only a very pleasant town with a large number of high net-worth private clients, but is also a convenient location for serving the extremely active business community at the eastern end of the Thames Valley including West London, Heathrow, Uxbridge, Slough and Windsor. The firm therefore looks for trainees who are likely to respond to this challenging environment.

**Training programme** The firm aims to have six trainee solicitors at different stages of their training contracts at all times. Trainees serve five months in four different departments of their choice. The final four months is spent in the department in which the trainee intends to specialise. The firm has a training partner with overall responsibility for all trainees and each department has its own training principal who is responsible for day-to-day supervision. There are regular meetings between the training principal and the trainee to monitor progress and a review meeting with the training partner midway through and at the end of each departmental seat. The firm also involves its trainees in social and marketing events including golf and cricket matches and other sporting and non-sporting activities.

**When and how to apply** CV and handwritten letter from 1 March through to 31 May.

| | |
|---|---|
| Vacancies | 4 |
| Trainees | 6 |
| Partners | 20 |
| Total staff | 140 |

**Work placement** yes

**Apply to**
Jacqui Symons,
HR Manager

**Starting salary**
£20,000

**Minimum qualifications**
2.1 degree

**Offices**
Gerrards Cross,
Beaconsfield

# BPE

St James' House, St James' Square, Cheltenham GL50 3PR
**Tel:** 01242 224433
**Fax:** 01242 574285
**Email:** julia.jones@bpe.co.uk
**Web:** www.bpe.co.uk

**The firm** Hard working, straight talking, fast thinking lawyers.

BPE Solicitors is a predominantly commercial firm that continues to make a name for itself in the South West and West Midlands. Expansion into new offices, multiple lateral hires, national awards and major client wins are some of our recent developments.

We are proud to be different to many other law firms. We are prepared to pioneer new approaches to providing a better service for our clients. We invest time and resources in new teams where we see potential for growth. Our partners do not hide behind closed doors but instead work side-by-side their assistants and trainees so you have an opportunity to learn form their experience every step of the way. Each team provides an exciting and stimulating training environment. You could find yourself getting involved in conference calls, networking at a seminar, attending an employment tribunal or helping to research a target client. We guarantee your training will be wide ranging, intensive and well balanced.

With a presence in Birmingham and Cheltenham you can enjoy the challenge of working in two different legal marketplaces. You will be encouraged to meet clients and take on your own caseload and you will be given the opportunity to enjoy a 'hands-on' approach from a very early stage.

**Types of work** Commercial (including intellectual property and IT and e-commerce), commercial property, construction and engineering, corporate, corporate recovery and insolvency, credit and asset finance, dispute resolution, employment, personal injury and private client.

**Who should apply** Although our current trainees have different backgrounds, they all have considerable commercial acumen and a strong desire to provide the best possible service to our clients. We are looking for law or non-law graduates who are first class team players and problem-solvers, with excellent communication and IT skills.

**Training programme** Although our training is hands-on, we don't throw you in at the deep end. We have a comprehensive induction programme to help you become familiar with the firm's style of working, its culture and everyday policies and procedures. We have created a special training passport to help you keep an accurate record of your work, as well as outlining what experience you need to gain in each department. During each seat you will be allocated a supervisor, experienced in coaching and mentoring trainees. You will begin by shadowing their work and gradually take on more responsibilities as you grow in confidence and ability. You will receive detailed feedback at the end of each of your seats.

Benefits: contributory pension scheme, gym membership at corporate rates, income protection to cover long-term illness, life assurance and 25 days holiday.

**When and how to apply** By 31 July 2008 to begin March 2010. Apply by application form at www.bpe.co.uk.

**Work placements** Summer vacation schemes available. Apply via application form.

| Vacancies | 4 |
| Trainees | 7 |
| Partners | 25 |
| Total staff | 135 |

**Work placement** yes

**Apply to**
Julia Jones

**Starting salary**
1st year: £16,000
2nd year: £17,000

**Minimum qualifications**
2.1 degree, law or non-law

**Offices**
Cheltenham, Birmingham

| **BREMNERS** | Broad based commercial practice | V | 0 |
|---|---|---|---|
| Sixth Floor, Silkhouse Court, Liverpool, | serving corporate and private clients, | T | 2 |
| Merseyside L2 2LZ | housing associations, charities, | P | 9 |
| **Tel:** 0151 227 1301 | friendly societies and landed estate | TS | 35 |
| **Fax:** 0151 227 1300 | owners. | WP | no |
| **Apply to:** Mr Ian Alderson | | | |

| **BRETHERTONS** | Commercial and private client | V | 2 |
|---|---|---|---|
| 16 Church Street, Rugby CV21 3PW | practice with offices in Rugby and | T | 2 |
| **Tel:** 01788 579579 | Banbury. Legal aid franchise in | P | 10 |
| **Fax:** 01788 570949 | family. | TS | 127 |
| **Email:** siansweeney@brethertons.co.uk | | WP | no |
| **Apply to:** Ms Sian Sweeney | | | |

| **BRIAN CAMP & CO** | Specialist plaintiff litigation using | V | 0 |
|---|---|---|---|
| 1 Europa House, Conway Street, | dedicated software. | T | 0 |
| Birkenhead CH 41 4FT | | P | 4 |
| **Tel:** 0151 201 8080 | | TS | 62 |
| **Fax:** 0151 201 4015 | | WP | yes |
| **Email:** brc@camplaw.co.uk | | | |
| **Apply to:** Mr Colin Billing | | | |

| **BRIDGE MCFARLAND** | Expanding firm with main offices in | V | 0 |
|---|---|---|---|
| 9 Cornmarket, Louth, Lincolnshire LN11 9PY | Grimsby, Lincoln and Louth. | T | 4 |
| **Tel:** 01507 605883 | Particular expertise in PI, crime, | P | 20 |
| **Fax:** 01522 534728 | employment, commercial litigation, | TS | 170 |
| **Apply to:** Ms Tina Burton | clinical negligence, family law and | WP | no |
| | commercial property transactions. | | |

| **BRIDGE SANDERSON MUNRO** | Long-established franchised general | V | 0 |
|---|---|---|---|
| 55 Hallgate, Doncaster DN1 3PD | practice with six partners in three | T | 1 |
| **Tel:** 01302 321621 | offices. | P | 6 |
| **Fax:** 01302 367903 | | TS | 40 |
| **Email:** info@bsmlaw.co.uk | | WP | no |
| **Apply to:** Mr PD Davies | | | |

| **BRIGHOUSE WOLFF** | Large general practice specialising in | V | 1 |
|---|---|---|---|
| Whelmar House, Southway, | conveyancing probate litigation, | T | 1 |
| Skelmersdale WN8 6NX | crime, mental health and family law. | P | 10 |
| **Tel:** 01695 722577 | Legal aid franchise and estate | TS | 80 |
| **Fax:** 01695 727501 | agency. | WP | no |
| **Email:** mgh@brighouse-wolff.co.uk | | | |
| **Apply to:** Mr MG Hagerty | | | |

| **BRIGNALLS BALDERSTON WARREN** | General high street practice dealing | V | 0 |
|---|---|---|---|
| Forum Chambers, The Forum, Stevenage, | with conveyancing, probate, wills and | T | 2 |
| Hertfordshire SG1 1EL | trusts, family, crime, corporate and | P | 13 |
| **Tel:** 01438 359311 | commercial matters, employment | TS | 61 |
| **Fax:** 01438 740127 | and general civil litigation. | WP | no |
| **Apply to:** Mr B C Lendrum | | | |

| **BROOKS & PARTNERS** | A progressive law firm based in | V | 0 |
|---|---|---|---|
| Lyons House, 2 Station Road, Camberley, | Surrey handling a wide range of | T | 2 |
| Surrey GU16 7JA | private client and business work. Our | P | 1 |
| **Tel:** 01276 681217 | strength is the qualityof our people. | TS | 26 |
| **Fax:** 01276691290 | | WP | no |
| **Email:** law@brooks-partners.co.uk | | | |
| **Apply to:** Mrs V Lennard | | | |

**V** = Vacancies / **T** = Trainees / **P** = Partners / **TS** = Total Staff / **WP** = Work Placement

# Brabners Chaffe Street LLP

Horton House, Exchange Flags, Liverpool L2 3YL
**Tel:** 0151 600 3000
**Fax:** 0151 227 3185
**Email:** trainees@brabnerscs.com
**Web:** www.BrabnersChaffeStreet.com

**The firm** One of the top Northwest commercial firms, Brabners Chaffe Street, in Liverpool, Manchester and Preston, has the experience, talent and prestige of a firm with a 200-plus year history. Brabners Chaffe Street is a dynamic, client-led specialist in the provision of excellent legal services to clients ranging from large plcs to private individuals.

**Types of work** The firm carries out a wide range of specialist legal services and its client base includes plcs, public sector bodies, banks and other commercial, corporate and professional businesses. Brabners Chaffe Street is organised into client-focused departments: banking, corporate, commercial (including sports law), employment, litigation (including media and sports law), property (including housing association and construction) and private client.

**Who should apply** Graduates and those undertaking the CPE or LPC, who can demonstrate intelligence, intuition, humour, approachability and commitment.

**Training programme** The LLP is one of the few law firms that holds Investor in People status and has a comprehensive training and development programme. The LLP is listed in the *Sunday Times* Best 100 Employers to work for in both 2006 and 2007. Trainees are given a high degree of responsibility and are an integral part of the culture of the firm. Each trainee will have partner-level supervision. Personal development appraisals are conducted at six-monthly intervals to ensure that trainee progress is valuable and informed. The training programme is overseen by the firm's director of training, Dr Tony Harvey, and each centre has a designated trainee partner.

It is not all hard work and the firm has an excellent social programme.

**When and how to apply** Apply online by 31 July 2008 for training contracts commencing in September 2010.

**Sponsorship** Available for the LPC.

| | |
|---|---|
| Vacancies | 14 |
| Trainees | 19 |
| Partners | 56 |
| Total staff | 341 |

**Apply to**
Dr Tony Harvey, Director of Training and Risk Management

**Starting salary**
Not less than £21,000

**Minimum qualifications**
2.1 degree or postgraduate degree

**Offices**
Liverpool, Manchester, Preston

brabners chaffe street

# Bristows

Until Dec 07: 3 Lincoln's Inn Fields, London WC2A 3AA
From Jan 08: 100 Victoria Embankment, London EC4Y 0DH
**Email:** sophia.fitzpatrick@bristows.com
**Web:** www.bristows.com

**The firm** Bristows is a long-established firm committed to excellence. With the continuing recruitment of lawyers and scientists of the highest quality, Bristows aims to stay at the forefront of firms advising businesses in sectors including pharmaceuticals, media and telecommunications, electronics and IT, real estate, consumer goods, learned institutions and charities, and financial institutions. The firm is a market leader in many of these sectors and acts for numerous FTSE 100, Fortune 500 and other multinational companies. Bristows has earned an enviable international reputation and developed one of the largest intellectual property practices in Europe; yet remains an approachable firm, dedicated to serving new entrants as well as established companies, across a full range of legal disciplines.

**Types of work** The firm has a substantial number of lawyers who first trained as scientists and who are readily able to understand sophisticated technology. This factor sets it apart from its competitors and has generated unparalleled expertise in litigation and corporate/commercial transactions in which intellectual property or an understanding of technology plays a significant part. The firm's expertise in dispute resolution extends to commercial conflicts of all kinds.

Many Bristows lawyers are experienced in corporate and commercial law and in all forms of transaction from IPOs, take-overs and mergers to private equity financings, outsourcing, joint ventures and university technology spin-offs. Bristows has highly regarded practices in all the main commercial law disciplines. These include competition, healthcare regulatory, employment, data protection, real estate and real estate finance, publishing, media, advertising and marketing, tax, computer games, charities and partnership.

**Who should apply** Bristows recruits outstanding trainee solicitors each year. The long-term prospects are excellent; many of the firm's present partners trained with the firm. Applicants from all academic disciplines are encouraged to apply and scientific degrees are particularly relavent for certain areas of intellectual property.

**Training programme** Our training programme gives you the knowledge and skills to build on the extensive hands-on experience in each of our main departments, and you'll be working closely with partners, which will accelerate your training. Part of this training may also involve secondment to one of a number of leading clients.

**When and how to apply** Training contract interviews are conducted in February and August. To be sure of being considered, the deadlines are 31 January and 31 July. Please complete the online application form.

**Work placements** Vacation schemes are run for one week during Christmas and Easter breaks, and two weeks during the summer break. We pay a weekly salary of £200.

**Sponsorship** All trainees receive sponsorship through the LPC and, where applicable, the CPE. Sponsorship includes tuition fees as well a £7,000 maintenance grant for each year of study.

| | |
|---|---|
| Vacancies | 6-8 |
| Trainees | 14 |
| Partners | 21 |
| Total staff | 180 |

**Work placement** yes
*(see Insider Report on p81)*

**Apply to**
Trainee Recruitment &
Training Officer

**Starting salary**
£33,000

**Minimum qualifications**
2.1 degree preferred

**Sponsorship**
GDL/LPC

**Offices**
London

BRISTOWS

## BROSS BENNETT
Stable House, 64A Highgate High Street,
London N6 5HX
**Tel:** 020 8340 0444
**Fax:** 020 8341 9100
**Email:** gen@brossbennett.co.uk
**Apply to:** Mrs Sharon Bennett

The firm specialises in family law and is one of the largest niche practices outside of central London.

| | |
|---|---|
| V | 0 |
| T | 1 |
| P | 4 |
| TS | 16 |
| WP | no |

## BROWN COOPER MONIER-WILLIAMS
71 Lincolns Inn Fields, London WC2A 3JF
**Tel:** 020 7405 6195
**Fax:** 020 7831 9856
**Apply to:** Mr MJ Coyne

Private client, general commercial, employment and litigation with niche intellectual property specialism. Committed to high-quality service mainly for established clientele. Traditional, friendly firm.

| | |
|---|---|
| V | 0 |
| T | 1 |
| P | 8 |
| TS | 20 |
| WP | no |

## BROWNINGS
10 Market Place, Redditch B98 8AA
**Tel:** 01527 65595 ext 224
**Fax:** 01527 596613
**Email:** stephenparker@brownings.co.uk
**Apply to:** Mr SJT Parker

High street practice, but with specialist departments. Lexcel, IIP & LSC approved.

| | |
|---|---|
| V | 0 |
| T | 0 |
| P | 3 |
| TS | 55 |
| WP | no |

## BRYAN AND ARMSTRONG
The Old Meeting House, Stockwell Gate,
Mansfield NG18 1LG
**Tel:** 01623 626039
**Fax:** 01623 635077
**Email:** enquiries@bryanandarmstrong.co.uk
**Apply to:** Mr N Croston

Legal aid franchised practice. Heavy emphasis on crime, matrimonial, personal injury and litigation. Two offices in Mansfield.

| | |
|---|---|
| V | 0 |
| T | 0 |
| P | 7 |
| TS | 35 |
| WP | yes |

## BRYAN CAVE
Watling House, 33 Cannon Street,
London EC4M 5TE
**Tel:** 020 7246 5800
**Fax:** 020 7246 5858
**Email:** bjroberts@bryancave.com
**Apply to:** Ms Brenda Roberts

Extensive private client, corporate and commercial practice with offices worldwide. Bryan Cave is one of the leading firms in the U.S. and offers clients a comprehensive service.

| | |
|---|---|
| V | 0 |
| T | 4 |
| P | 10 |
| TS | 82 |
| WP | yes |

## BS SINGH & CO
182 Stapleton Road, Easton, Bristol BS5 0NZ
**Tel:** 0117 935 4500
**Fax:** 0117 951 8699
**Email:** bsinghsolicitors@hotmail.com
**Apply to:** Mr B Singh

Bristol based general small practice. Specialising in immigration and family matters.

| | |
|---|---|
| V | Poss 2 |
| T | 0 |
| P | 2 |
| TS | 3 |
| WP | yes |

## BTMK SOLICITORS LLP
Baryta House, 29 Victoria Avenue,
Southend on Sea SS2 6AR
**Tel:** 01702 349494
**Fax:** 01702 332437
**Email:** mike.warren@btmk.co.uk
**Apply to:** Mr MR Warren

Full service law firm, following the merger of TMK solicitors and Bates Travell Solicitors. Long history of trainee recruitment and retention.

| | |
|---|---|
| V | Up to 5[08] |
| T | 6 |
| P | 15 |
| TS | 160 |
| WP | yes |

## BUCKLES SOLICITORS LLP
Grant House, 101 Bourges Boulevard,
Peterborough PE1 1NG
**Tel:** 01733 888888
**Fax:** 01733 888999
**Apply to:** Christine Walker

Peterborough-based BucklesSolicitors LLP are a regional law Firm dedicated to the provision of quality legal services to both individual and commercial clients.

| | |
|---|---|
| V | 0 |
| T | 4 |
| P | 14 |
| TS | 96 |
| WP | no |

# Browne Jacobson

44 Castle Gate, Nottingham NG1 7BJ
**Tel:** 0115 976 6000
**Fax:** 0115 947 5246
**Email:** traineeapplications@brownejacobson.com
**Web:** www.brownejacobson.com/trainees.aspx

**The firm** We're one of the largest full service commercial law firms in the Midlands with regional and national reach through our offices in Nottingham, Birmingham and London, and we're growing fast. One of the most successful firms in the Midlands, we have more than trebled our turnover since 1996 and continue to drive double-digit annual growth.

Our people are the key to our success and we have a track record of attracting and retaining outstanding individuals. With over 500 people, we're large enough to attract some of the best talent in the country, but small enough to foster a supportive and flexible working environment.

We focus on long-term relationships that are friendly, flexible and straightforward, both with our people and our clients. Our modern, progressive working environment and our friendly and open culture mean that our people enjoy working here so they stay. This allows good working relationships to develop and provides consistency for our clients. It's a simple tactic yet one that works; a large proportion of our client base has been with the firm for a number of years.

**Types of work** We specialise in insurance, corporate and commercial work and have a national reputation for our work in the health, retail and environmental sectors. We are recognised as regional heavyweights for corporate, property, public enquiry, litigation and professional risk work.

**Who should apply** We believe in being open and straightforward and that's exactly what we're looking for, open-minded individuals to join our team. We welcome talented law and non-law graduates who can bring enthusiasm and commitment to build upon our flexible and friendly reputation.

**Training programme** You'll start with a comprehensive induction programme and a fast track professional skills course. Our flexible approach gives trainees the opportunity to do six-month seats in any of our three offices; all based in vibrant city centres. That not only offers variety, but a great social life too!

You'll get great training, a friendly and supportive working environment, and real career opportunities. Our trainees are given quality work and exposure to clients from early on, but are supported in achieving results and recognised for their contribution.

**When and how to apply** Our application deadline is 31 July 2008 for training contracts beginning in September 2010. Apply online at www.brownejacobson.com/trainees.aspx.

**Open days** Open days run in Spring.

**Sponsorship** LPC/GDL tuition fees paid, plus a maintenance grant for LPC/GDL of £5,000.

| | |
|---|---|
| Vacancies | 12 |
| Trainees | 20 |
| Partners | 58 |
| Total staff | 509 |

Work placement  n/a
*(see Insider Report on p83)*

Apply
Online

Starting salary
No less than £24,000

Minimum qualifications
2.1 degree

Sponsorship
LPC/GDL

Offices
Birmingham, London, Nottingham

brownejacobson

| | | | |
|---|---|---|---|
| **BULLER JEFFRIES**<br>36 Bennetts Hill, Birmingham B2 5SN<br>**Tel:** 0121 212 2620<br>**Fax:** 0121 212 2210<br>**Apply to:** Mr Geoffrey Lewis | A niche practice undertaking high volumes of insurance related defendant injury and other more specialist claims, with offices in Birmingham and Coventry. Also private client department. | V<br>T<br>P<br>TS<br>WP | 0<br>2<br>-<br>55<br>no |
| **BURN & COMPANY**<br>Lendal House, 11 Lendal, York YO1 2AQ<br>**Tel:** 01904 655442<br>**Fax:** 01904 627107<br>**Email:** enquiries@burn-company.co.uk | City centre based general practice with strong client base. Franchised (matrimonial) with local branch office. Awarded 'Investors in People' for staff development and improvement. | V<br>T<br>P<br>TS<br>WP | 0<br>0<br>6<br>17<br>no |
| **BURNETTS**<br>6 Victoria Place, Carlisle CA1 1ES<br>**Tel:** 01228 552222<br>**Fax:** 01228 522399<br>**Email:** tsl@burnetts.co.uk<br>**Apply to:** Mr TS Leach | Largest firm in Cumbria. Large commercial department including employment with specialist departments in litigation, personal injury, family and private client. | V<br>T<br>P<br>TS<br>WP | 2[09]<br>3<br>19<br>111<br>no |
| **BURROUGHS DAY**<br>14 Charlotte Street, Bristol BS1 5PT<br>**Tel:** 0117 929 0333<br>**Fax:** 0117 929 0335<br>**Email:** shirley.kent@bd4law.com<br>**Apply to:** Ms Shirley Kent | Specialist teams covering injury claims, employment law, corporate and commercial, commercial property, commercial and private client litigation, home moving, wills and probate and family. | V<br>T<br>P<br>TS<br>WP | 2<br>4<br>13<br>131<br>no |
| **BURTON & BURTON**<br>19/21 Market Place, Mansfield, Nottinghamshire NG18 1HR<br>**Tel:** 0845 034 4050<br>**Fax:** 0845 241 8499<br>**Email:** enquiries@burtonslaw.com<br>**Apply to:** Mrs L Giblin | High street firm which also deals with wide range of internet clients and immigration matters. | V<br>T<br>P<br>TS<br>WP | 0-1<br>1<br>2<br>14<br>no |
| **BURTON & CO**<br>Stonebow, Lincoln LN2 1DA<br>**Tel:** 01522 523215<br>**Fax:** 01522 536902<br>**Email:** inmail@burtonlaw.co.uk<br>**Apply to:** Ms Judith E Brennan | A very well established, well known firm located in the centre of Lincoln, undertaking all types of work for a small city and country clientele. | V<br>T<br>P<br>TS<br>WP | 0<br>1<br>8<br>60<br>no |
| **BURY & WALKERS**<br>Britannic House, Regent Street, Barnsley S70 2EQ<br>**Tel:** 01226 733 533<br>**Fax:** 01226 283 611<br>**Email:** n.smith@burywalkers.com<br>**Apply to:** Mr John Clark | Everything from heavyweight commercial and international work to the full range of high street work for the private client. Franchised legal aid firm. | V<br>T<br>P<br>TS<br>WP | 1<br>1<br>11<br>60<br>no |
| **BUSS MURTON LLP**<br>Wellington Gate, 7-9 Church Road, Tunbridge Wells, Kent TN1 1HT<br>**Tel:** 01892 502330<br>**Fax:** 01892 510333<br>**Email:** psimpson@bussmurton.co.uk<br>**Apply to:** Ms Pat Simpson | Large regional law firm covering most aspects of the law in both commercial and private client areas. Four operating divisions broken down into specialist areas. | V<br>T<br>P<br>TS<br>WP | 1[09]<br>2<br>5<br>90<br>no |

# Burges Salmon

Narrow Quay House, Narrow Quay, Bristol BS1 4AH
**Tel:** 0117 902 2766
**Fax:** 0117 902 4400
**Email:** katy.edge@burges-salmon.com
**Web:** www.burges-salmon.com

**The firm** Burges Salmon is proof that law doesn't have to mean London.

Based in Bristol, our turnover has more than tripled in recent years as we continue to win prestigious clients out of the hands of our City rivals. Clients such as EMI Group, Reuters, Orange and Coca Cola HBC rely on our legal expertise and in doing so have helped cement our reputation as creative, lateral thinkers. But the quality of work we regularly attract would not have come to us were it not for our primary asset – our people. Our trainees benefit from supervision by lawyers who are leaders in their field with a formidable depth of experience. All this against the backdrop of Bristol: a city with a quality of life you would be hard pressed to find anywhere else in the UK.

**Types of work** Burges Salmon provides national and international clients with a full commercial service through six main departments: corporate & financial institutions (CFI); commercial; property; tax & trusts; commercial disputes & construction (CDC); and agriculture, property litigation & environment (APLE). Specialist areas include: banking; EU & competition; planning; corporate finance; employment; IP & IT; and transport. The firm is ranked top tier by *Chambers and Partners* for 18 of its practice areas.

**Training programme** Trainees play a vital role in shaping the future of our firm and we invest a great deal of time and resource into training and development. We are justifiably proud of our reputation for offering one of the best training programmes in the profession: the Law Society accredited the firm's training programme with seven points of good practice, where in previous years the maximum awarded to any firm was two points. Training is personalised to suit each individual, and our six seat structure allows trainees to experience a wider range of practice areas before making a decision on qualification. Our dedication to trainees is demonstrated by a high retention rate, which is well above the industry average.

**When and how to apply** Applications should be made online via our website. Closing date for vacation placement applications: 31 January 2008; training contract applications: 31 July 2008.

**Work placements** Burges Salmon runs two open days in February, and offers 40 two-week vacation placements during the summer. Individuals visit two departments of their choice supervised by a partner or senior solicitor, and attend court visits and client meetings. Current trainees run skills training sessions, sports and social events. Remuneration: £250 per week.

**Sponsorship** The firm pays GDL and LPC fees at the institution of your choice. Maintenance grants of £6,000 are paid to LPC students, and £12,000 to students studying for both the GDL and LPC (£6,000 pa).

| | |
|---|---|
| Vacancies | 22 |
| Trainees | 40 |
| Partners | 64 |
| Total staff | 614 |

**Work placement**   yes
*(see Insider Report on p85)*

**Apply to**
Miss Katy Edge,
Recruitment Manager

**Starting salary**
1st year - £28,000
2nd year - £29,000

**Minimum qualifications**
24/300 UCAS points and
2.1 degree, any discipline

**Sponsorship**
GDL/LPC

**Offices**
Bristol

| Firm | Description | V | T | P | TS | WP |
|---|---|---|---|---|---|---|
| **BUTCHER & BARLOW**<br>2 Bank Street, Bury BL9 0DL<br>**Tel:** 0161 764 4062<br>**Fax:** 0161 797 2912<br>**Email:** cb@butcher-barlow.co.uk<br>**Apply to:** Mr Charles Barlow | We prefer candidates who can develop their careers in any of our offices in Greater Manchester, Cheshire. | 2[09] | 4 | 15 | 77 | no |
| **BWF SOLICITORS**<br>529 Kingsland Road, Dalston, London E8 4AR<br>**Tel:** 0207 241 7180<br>**Fax:** 0207 241 7181<br>**Email:** bowusu@bwfsolicitors.co.uk<br>**Apply to:** Mr B Owusu | Small highly professional solicitors, specialising in family, immigration, civil litigation,, conveyancing, personal injury, wills and probate. | 2 | - | 2 | 5 | no |
| **C TURNER**<br>Oakfield House, 93 Preston New Road, Blackburn BB2 GA6<br>**Tel:** 01254 688400<br>**Fax:** 01254 688417<br>**Email:** law@turnerlaw.co.uk<br>**Apply to:** Mr P Garner | General practice including personal injury, family, commercial and crime. Legal aid franchise in crime and family. | 0 | 1 | - | 43 | no |
| **CAINS ADVOCATES LIMITED**<br>15-19 Athol Street, Douglas, Isle of Man IM1 1LB<br>**Tel:** 01624 638300<br>**Fax:** 01624 638333<br>**Email:** richard.vanderplank@cains.com<br>**Apply to:** Mr Richard Vanderplank | Cains advises many of the world's largest financial and commercial institutions in areas including project finance, corporate law, financial services, commercial litigation and commercial property. | 2 | 4 | 6 | 70 | yes |
| **CALDICOTTS**<br>21 Burgess Street, Leominster, Herefordshire HR6 8DE<br>**Tel:** 01568 614168<br>**Fax:** 01568 611437<br>**Apply to:** Mrs RM Caldicott | Please note that we do not currently have any vacancies. | 0 | 1 | 2 | 14 | no |
| **CAMERON JONES HUSSELL & HOWE**<br>1/3 Grove Place, Port Talbot, West Glamorgan SA13 1HX<br>**Tel:** 01639 885261<br>**Fax:** 01639 887138<br>**Apply to:** Mr JG Hussell | Sound base in conveyancing and probate. Experienced in civil litigation, franchise for matrimonial and family work including child care. | 0 | 1 | 6 | 24 | no |
| **CAMPBELL CHAMBERS**<br>25 Hatton Garden, London EC1N 8BQ<br>**Tel:** 020 7691 8777<br>**Fax:** 020 7691 8778<br>**Apply to:** Ms A Campbell | The firm is progressive and forward thinking, valuing the diversity of its client base. We aim to recruit a workforce that reflects this. No vacancies at present. | 0 | 4 | 2 | 10 | no |
| **CANNINGS CONNOLLY**<br>52 St John Street, London EC1M 4DT<br>**Tel:** 020 7329 9000<br>**Fax:** 020 7329 5000<br>**Apply to:** Mr DM Golten | Cannings Connolly is a niche commercial property, litigation and commercial firm based in the heart of the city of London. | 2[09] | 4 | 7 | 28 | no |

# Cadwalader, Wickersham & Taft LLP

265 Strand, London WC2R 1BH
**Tel:** 020 7170 8700
**Fax:** 020 7170 8610
**Email:** hrdept@cwt-uk.com
**Web:** www.cadwalader.com

**The firm** Cadwalader, Wickersham & Taft LLP is an international law firm with over 1000 staff across five offices in London, New York, Washington DC, Charlotte (North Carolina) and Beijing. Established in New York in 1792, Cadwalader offers legal services to internationally-based clients. The firm has a diverse practice that can dispatch the most demanding, time-critical and resource-intensive transactions across a range of complementary practice areas. Cadwalader's sophisticated real world knowledge of financing is more valuable than ever to clients seeking legal and business advice in today's volatile markets. Whatever the business or industry, we offer clients the ability to analyse broadly their market position and their financing needs with respect to both their short and long-term goals. We then fashion the right solution to achieve their objectives and close transactions with the creativity, flexibility and timeliness required in today's competitive marketplace.

**Types of work** Fully integrated into the firm's wall street practice, Cadwalader's London office provides a powerful presence in Europe. We offer legal advice in capital markets, corporate finance, derivatives, funds, financial restructuring, insolvency, insurance and reinsurance, litigation, mergers and acquisitions, real estate finance, securitisation, structured finance, regulatory and tax matters. These areas of legal advice serve a wide range of clients including investment banks, hedge funds, asset managers, monoline insurers and various other types of financial institutions.

**Who should apply** Successful candidates will have a strong academic background with a minimum A, A, B at A level or equivalent along with an obtained or predicted 1st or 2.1 class degree. Cadwalader seek individuals who are technically sound and can demonstrate commercial acumen together with excellent communication skills.

**Training programme** Our trainees receive thorough and comprehensive training and we are committed to developing professional business skills as well as core technical expertise. All our trainees are seated with partners and are encouraged to make a valuable contribution to the firm's success. Due to the limited intake number, trainees can expect early responsibility and exposure to large transactional matters in a supportive and inclusive environment. Cadwalader offer a four seat rotation programme that takes into account trainees' preferences.

**When and how to apply** To apply for a training contract commencing in 2010, please submit a CV and covering letter to Emma Turner by 31 July 2008. Your CV should provide a breakdown of degree module results.

**Sponsorship** GDL and LPC fees are paid in addition to a maintenance grant of £7,500.

| Vacancies | 6-8 |
| --- | --- |
| Trainees | 7 |
| Partners | 12 |
| Total staff | 160 |

**Work placement**   no

**Apply to**
Emma Turner

**Starting salary**
1st year: £37,000
2nd year - £40,000

**Minimum qualifications**
2.1 degree

**Sponsorship**
GDL/LPC

**Offices**
London, New York, Washington DC, Charlotte, Beijing

CADWALADER

# Campbell Hooper

35 Old Queen Street, London SW1H 9JD
**Tel:** 020 7222 9070
**Fax:** 0870 191 6722
**Email:** humanresources@campbellhooper.com
**Web:** www.campbellhooper.com

**The firm** Campbell Hooper is a medium-sized firm with an established base of commercial and individual clients. With over 200 years' experience, the firm is well equipped to face the requirements of today's ever-changing market, and adopts a modern and dynamic management style with high investment in IT, knowledge management and development.

Membership of Proteus, a European network of independent European law firms committed to providing an integrated service, provides an invaluable international aspect to the firm.

**Types of work** High standards of client service are delivered through four departments: company/commercial, commercial property, construction and private client. The principal areas of work are charities, company, construction, defamation, domestic conveyancing, employment, environmental, European, family, health and safety, immigration, insurance, litigation, media, planning, property, rating, tax, trust and estate planning, and wills and probate.

Multi-disciplinary teams provide a comprehensive service to clients, ranging from small owner-managed companies to multinationals and entrepreneurial businesses, as well as high-profile individuals. Our clients are involved in a wide variety of industries including information technology, telecoms, banking, advertising, construction, property investment and development, media, manufacturing, a number of service industries, and local government and government departments.

**Who should apply** Applications are welcomed from those with a keen commercial focus, complemented by a solid academic history. Motivation, enthusiasm and professional commitment are equally important.

**Training programme** During the training contract you will develop your commercial acumen and legal flair through exposure in each of the four departments. Equal emphasis is placed on providing you with professional and personal career support. This is facilitated through day-to-day coaching from either a partner or solicitor, constructive feedback through mid and end-of-seat reviews, and mentoring from the trainee partner, who will take a personal interest in your professional develoment.

In addition, the firm is committed to continuous development and you will be encouraged to attend client seminars, be actively involved in practice development initiatives and participate in other training and development activities, including the compulsory Professional Skills Course.

Benefits include 25 days' holiday, personal pension plan, life assurance, private medical insurance, permanent health insurance and season ticket loan.

**When and how to apply** Apply between 1 April and 31 July 2008 to commence autumn 2010. Applicants should complete the online application form available at www.campbellhooper.com.

| | |
|---|---|
| Vacancies | 5 |
| Trainees | 9 |
| Partners | 23 |
| Total staff | 124 |

**Apply**
Online

**Starting salary**
£28,000 (2007)

**Minimum qualifications**
2.1 degree, any discipline

**Sponsorship**
CPE/LPC may be available

**Offices**
London

Campbell Hooper

# Capsticks

77-83 Upper Richmond Road, London SW15 2TT
**Tel:** 020 8780 2211
**Fax:** 020 8780 4811
**Email:** career@capsticks.co.uk
**Web:** www.capsticks.com

**The firm** Capsticks is widely regarded as the leading provider of legal services to the healthcare sector. The firm has grown substantially in the last few years and has ambitious plans for further expansion, both in its core market and by promoting its broader capability and expanding private sector client base.

**Types of work** The firm's client base is largely NHS, but with an increasing focus on healthcare regulatory bodies, private sector healthcare and PFI/PPP work. The firm has over 90 fee earners working for over 200 NHS and other healthcare related and regulatory clients.

**Who should apply** We are a diverse firm and encourage applications from all walks of life. The firm recruits four to five trainee solicitors each year and we welcome applications from candidates who are either on course for or have achieved at least a 2.1 (or equivalent) in their undergraduate degree. We also expect candidates to be able to demonstrate they are committed to a career in healthcare law and are highly driven, but well rounded, team players, with good problem solving and communication skills.

Capsticks is committed to providing equal opportunities and encouraging diversity in employment. All job applicants will receive equal treatment regardless of sex, marital status, race, colour, nationality or national or ethnic origins, age, disability, sexual orientation, religion or belief.

**Training programme** Capsticks' broad range of practices and healthcare clients enables us to give our trainees an opportunity to experience a wide variety of legal work. Our trainees are therefore able to acquire an in-depth knowledge of both healthcare law and the healthcare industry, in addition to developing the skills that any good lawyer needs.

Our training contract is designed to give you maximum exposure to the work of the firm and trainees undertake seats in all of our practice areas, including clinical law, commercial, dispute resolution, employment and property.

**When and how to apply** We encourage all prospective trainee solicitors to participate in our vacation scheme (see below) as this is our primary means for selecting our future trainee solicitors. We welcome applications for a training contract commencing in September 2010 between 01 July 2008 and 31 August 2008. Further details are available on our website.

**Work placments** Our vacation scheme runs from the end of June through to the middle of August and placements last for two weeks each. In order to be eligible for our 2008 vacation scheme, you should be looking to secure a training contract with us in September 2010. We welcome applications for a place on our 2008 vacation scheme between 19 November 2007 and 28 February 2008. Further details are available on our website.

**Sponsorship** The firm offers its future trainees financial support for both the Graduate Diploma in Law and the Legal Practice Course.

| | |
|---|---|
| Vacancies | 4-5 |
| Trainees | 10 |
| Partners | 32 |
| Total staff | 170 |

Work placement yes

Apply to
See website

Minimum qualifications
2.1 degree

Sponsorship
GDL/LPC

Offices
London

# Capsticks

| | | | |
|---|---|---|---|
| **CANTER LEVIN & BERG**<br>The Temple, 1 Temple Square, 24 Dale Street,<br>Liverpool L2 5RU<br>**Tel:** 0151 239 1000<br>**Fax:** 0151 239 1001<br>**Email:** nicolarowe@canter-law.co.uk<br>**Apply to:** Ms Nicola Rowe | Offices in Liverpool, St Helens,<br>Skelmersdale and Kirkby. | V<br>T<br>P<br>TS<br>WP | 1-2<br>7<br>15<br>220<br>no |
| **CAPITAL LAW**<br>1 Caspian Point, Caspian Way, Cardiff CF10 4DQ<br>**Tel:** 0870 224 1819<br>**Fax:** 0870 224 9091<br>**Email:** k.philips@capitallaw.co.uk<br>**Apply to:** Ms Hannah Wakefield | Specialising in commercial litigation,<br>employment, non-contentious<br>corporate/commercial matters,<br>insolvency and commercial property. | V<br>T<br>P<br>TS<br>WP | 3[09]<br>3<br>12<br>57<br>no |
| **CARMARTHENSHIRE COUNTY COUNCIL**<br>County Hall, Carmarthen,<br>Carmarthenshire SA31 1JP<br>**Tel:** 01267 224012<br>**Fax:** 01267 230848<br>**Email:** dlthomas@carmarthenshire.gov.uk<br>**Apply to:** Mr Lyn Thomas | Local government legal service | V<br>T<br>P<br>TS<br>WP | 1<br>2<br>6<br>16<br>no |
| **CARTMELL SHEPHERD**<br>Viaduct House, Carlisle CA3 8EZ<br>**Tel:** 01228 516666<br>**Fax:** 01228 401490<br>**Email:** mmh@cartmells.co.uk<br>**Apply to:** Mrs MM Hendry | Cartmell Shepherd is a large, broadly<br>based general practice with five<br>offices throughout the region. A<br>separate branch services agricultural<br>clients. | V<br>T<br>P<br>TS<br>WP | 3<br>6<br>17<br>95<br>yes |
| **CARVERS**<br>10 Coleshill Road, Hodge Hill,<br>Birmingham B36 8AA<br>**Tel:** 0121 784 8484<br>**Fax:** 0121 783 4935<br>**Email:** law@carverslaw.co.uk<br>**Apply to:** Mr Aaron Keene | Progressive, forward-looking firm.<br>Crime, childcare, family work,<br>employment law and housing.<br>Carvers hold franchises in these and<br>continues to enjoy expansion. | V<br>T<br>P<br>TS<br>WP | 1<br>1<br>4<br>50<br>no |
| **CGM SOLICITORS**<br>2-5 College Place, Southampton SO15 2UT<br>**Tel:** 023 8063 2733<br>**Fax:** 023 8033 0954<br>**Email:** enquiries@c-g-m.co.uk<br>**Apply to:** Mr Paul Waring | City centre, opposite courts,<br>commercial anddomestic property<br>and general litigation, matrimonial,<br>childcare, mental health, crime. CLS<br>contracts civil and criminal. | V<br>T<br>P<br>TS<br>WP | 0-2<br>1<br>9<br>35<br>no |
| **CHALLINORS**<br>Guardian House, Cronehills Linkway,<br>West Bromwich B70 8SW<br>**Tel:** 0121 553 3211<br>**Fax:** 0121 553 2079<br>**Apply to:** Chief Executive | General practice with four offices in<br>Birmingham and the West Midlands.<br>Legal aid franchises in some<br>categories. | V<br>T<br>P<br>TS<br>WP | 4[09]<br>8<br>31<br>240<br>no |
| **CHAMBERLINS**<br>4, 5 & 6 Crown Road, Great Yarmouth,<br>Norfolk NR30 2JP<br>**Tel:** 01493 857621<br>**Fax:** 01493 330026<br>**Apply to:** Mr JB Thackray | General practice with five branches.<br>The firm has been established for<br>over 100 years. The first firm in Great<br>Yarmouth to be recommended for a<br>legal aid franchise. | V<br>T<br>P<br>TS<br>WP | 0<br>2<br>5<br>32<br>no |

# Charles Russell LLP

8-10 New Fetter Lane, London EC4A 1RS
**Tel:** 020 7203 5353
**Fax:** 020 7203 5307
**Web:** www.charlesrussell.co.uk

**The firm** Charles Russell LLP is a leading legal practice, providing a full range of services to UK and international businesses, governments, not-for-profit bodies and individuals. It has eight offices: two in London, Guildford, Cambridge, Cheltenham, Oxford, Geneva and Bahrain.

The practice is known for its client care, high quality, expertise and friendly approach. The strategy is simple – to help clients achieve their goals through excellent service.

Experienced in carrying out cross-border corporate and commercial work, the practice also provides clients with access to 150 recommended law firms across the world as part of the two major legal networks; ALFA International and the Association of European Lawyers.

The practice's lawyers and staff are highly motivated and talented people. Many lawyers are ranked as leaders in their field. The practice's commitment to training and development and a strong team spirit are key ingredients to being known as a friendly practice to work with and work at. A social committee organises a wide range of activities.

**Types of work** Seventy five percent of the practice's work is commercial. The principal areas of work include corporate/commercial, media, technology, communications and sport, employment and pensions, charities, private client, family, intellectual property, litigation and dispute resolution, and real estate.

**Who should apply** Trainees should be balanced, rounded achievers with an excellent academic background and outside interests.

**Training programme** For a practice of its size, a small number of trainees are recruited each year. This allows trainees to undergo the best possible training. Trainees spend six months in four of the following training seats: litigation and dispute resolution, corporate/commercial, real estate, private client, family and employment/pensions or on secondment to clients. Wherever possible the practice will try to accommodate individual preferences. You will be seated with a partner/senior solicitor. Regular appraisals are held to discuss progress and direction. Trainees are encouraged to attend extensive in-house training courses. The Professional Skills Course is taught both internally and externally. Trainees are encouraged to take on as much responsibility as possible. For a real insight into life as a trainee take a look at the reviews by current and qualified trainees on our website.

Benefits include: BUPA; PHI and life assurance; pension; season ticket loans; 25 days' holiday plus an additional day's holiday or pay for house moves.

**When and how to apply** Applications should be via our online facility at www.charlesrussell.co.uk submitted by 31 July 2008 to start in September 2010.

**Sponsorship** We undertake to pay your course fees while you are at law school. In addition, we make available a grant of £6,000 per annum (London) or £4,500 per annum (Guildford) or £3,500 per annum (Cheltenham) while you are at law school.

| Vacancies | 20 |
| Trainees | 31 |
| Partners | 93 |
| Total staff | 626 |

**Apply**
Online

**Starting salary**
London:
1st year - £31,000
2nd year - £35,000
Guildford:
1st year - £25,000
2nd year - £27,000
Cheltenham:
1st year - £24,000
2nd year - £25,000

**Sponsorship**
GDL & LPC

**Offices**
Two in London, Guildford, Cheltenham, Cambridge, Oxford, Geneva, Bahrain

CHARLES RUSSELL

| | | | |
|---|---|---|---|
| **CHANTER FERGUSON**<br>17 The Quay, Bideford, Devon EX39 2EN<br>**Tel:** 01237 478751<br>**Fax:** 01237 470893<br>**Apply to:** Mr PR Mole | Two office North Devon firm undertaking a wide range of general practice work for private clients. | V<br>T<br>P<br>TS<br>WP | 0<br>0<br>3<br>20<br>no |
| **CHARLES CROOKES**<br>51 The Parade, Cardiff CF24 3AY<br>**Tel:** 029 2049 1271<br>**Fax:** 029 2047 1211<br>**Email:** jarter@ccj-law.co.uk<br>**Apply to:** Mr Jonathan Arter | General commercial/corporate/ general practice. | V<br>T<br>P<br>TS<br>WP | 1[08]<br>1<br>4<br>19<br>no |
| **CHARLESWORTH NICHOLL & CO**<br>31 High Street, Crediton, Devon EX17 3AJ<br>**Tel:** 01363 774706<br>**Fax:** 01363 775604<br>**Email:** sp@charlesworthnicholl.co.uk<br>**Apply to:** Miss CS Nicholl | A high street practice specialising in residential, agricultural and commercial property work, wills and probate and family work. We have Lexcel and Investors in People. | V<br>T<br>P<br>TS<br>WP | 1<br>1<br>2<br>20<br>no |
| **CHELMSFORD BOROUGH COUNCIL**<br>Legal Services, Civic Centre, Duke Street, Chelmsford CM1 1JE<br>**Tel:** 01245 606606<br>**Fax:** 01245 606693<br>**Email:** susan.deval@chelmsfordbc.gov.uk<br>**Apply to:** Mrs Susan De Val | An in-house service providing a comprehensive range of legal services to the council and other public bodies including advice, litigation, advocacy and mediation services. | V<br>T<br>P<br>TS<br>WP | 0<br>0<br>-<br>16<br>no |
| **CHENERY MAHER**<br>21 Church Street, Clithero, Lancs BB7 2DF<br>**Tel:** 01200 422264<br>**Fax:** 01200 428986<br>**Email:** mail@irenecherymaher.co.uk<br>**Apply to:** Mr Turner | Small semi-niche firm committed to provision of quality professional services in conveyancing, wills and probate, and family specialisation. | V<br>T<br>P<br>TS<br>WP | 0<br>0<br>2<br>9<br>no |
| **CHHOKAR & CO**<br>29a The Broadway, Southall, Middlesex UB1 1JY<br>**Tel:** 020 8574 2488<br>**Fax:** 020 8574 2752<br>**Email:** law@chhokar.com<br>**Apply to:** Mr SS Chhokar | Dynamic and forward looking IT-enhanced West London practice committed to delivering a quality service in family, immigration, property (residential and commercial) and litigation (including personal injury). | V<br>T<br>P<br>TS<br>WP | 1[08]<br>1<br>2<br>13<br>no |
| **CHRISTOPHER WRIGHT & CO**<br>6th Floor, Regal House, 70 London Road, Twickenham TW1 3QS<br>**Tel:** 020 8892 4902<br>**Fax:** 020 8892 4955<br>**Email:** info@cwrightandco.co.uk<br>**Apply to:** Mr Chris Wright | The firm was founded in 1995 and deals with construction, planning, commercial, employment law. We mainly serve small/medium-sized businesses. | V<br>T<br>P<br>TS<br>WP | 0<br>1<br>1<br>5<br>no |
| **CITY AND COUNTY OF SWANSEA**<br>County Hall, Oystermouth Road, Swansea SA1 3SN<br>**Tel:** 01792 636000<br>**Fax:** 01792 636340<br>**Apply to:** Legal Department | Large, busy local government legal department dealing with litigation, commercial property, planning, contracts, employment, housing, social services and education matters. LEXCEL and IIP accredited. | V<br>T<br>P<br>TS<br>WP | 0<br>1<br>-<br>60<br>no |

# Clarion Solicitors

Britannia Chambers, 4 Oxford Place, Leeds LS1 3AX
**Tel:** 0113 246 0622
**Fax:** 0113 246 7488
**Email:** l.jackson@clarionsolicitors.com
**Web:** www.clarionsolicitors.com

**The firm** Clarion Solicitors are a major presence in Leeds, handling legal services for a growing number of leading businesses and individuals both locally and nationwide. We believe that legal services can and should offer genuine benefits and add real value to the lives of the businesses and individuals who use them. To accomplish that, we draw on all the intellectual capability and ability to innovate of all our people, as well as on their human values of humour, communication and engagement with the community.

Clarion Solicitors looks to appoint four trainee solicitors, commencing their training in September, each year. We select trainees from the applications made to us by way of our summer placement scheme. All applications should be made on the form which can be downloaded from our website. We have an excellent retention rate and a high percentage of our trainees go on to have a long term future in the firm.

**Types of work** Corporate and commercial; property; dispute resolution; private client (including family); business crime and regulatory; corporate recovery.

**Who should apply** We expect our candidates to have as a minimum a 2.1 degree from university.

**Training programme** At Clarion Solicitors trainees are considered to be part of the team from the very outset. Each of our six departments listed above offers the opportunity to the firm's trainees to spend one of their four six month seats as part of the department. The training given is hands-on, and driven by an ethos of openness, innovation, ambition and intellectual enquiry. We believe Clarion Solicitors offers a magnificent opportunity to trainee solicitors in a friendly, team-based environment. We are particularly proud that in 2006 the Lex 100 placed us as Lex 100 winners in no less than six categories.

**When and how to apply** Apply before 28 February 2008 to begin September 2010. Please visit our website for full details and appropriate forms for downloading - www.clarionsolicitors.com.

**Work placements** Our summer placement scheme now plays the central role in selecting candidates for training contracts. If you are selected for one of these placements you will be given the opportunity to work for a week in one of our six departments listed above. On the final day you will have assessments and an interview.

For full details please go to www.clarionsolicitors.com.

**Sponsorship** Successful candidates will be sponsored through the Legal Practice Course by payment of their course fee.

| | |
|---|---|
| Vacancies | 4 |
| Trainees | 10 |
| Partners | 13 |
| Total staff | 101 |

**Work placement** yes

**Apply to**
Linda Jackson

**Starting salary**
Competitive

**Minimum qualifications**
2.1 degree

**Offices**
Leeds

**Clarion**Solicitors

# Clarke Willmott

138 Edmund Street, Birmingham B3 2ES
**Tel:** 0121 234 9400
**Fax:** 0121 234 9540
**Email:** careers@clarkewillmott.com
**Web:** www.clarkewillmott.com

**The firm** Clarke Willmott is a UK law firm with a national reputation in key commercial and private client services. With 84 partners and over 620 people in total, we operate from four locations: Bristol, Birmingham, Taunton and Southampton.

Our lawyers are, first and foremost, business advisers with a simple objective: to help our clients achieve their goals and to enhance the value of their opportunities. We take a straightforward, proactive approach, and have helped enterprises of all sizes and at all stages of the business lifecycle to navigate a range of complex legal issues with positive results. Above all, we understand that our clients are not looking for more legal advice, they are looking for more business. We see it as our role to help them achieve it.

**Types of work** Our mission is simple: it's our aim to develop successful, long-term relationships with our clients built on mutual trust and understanding. We also understand that the keyword is 'service'. It's our firm's aim to add more value to our clients' business over the long term. We invest time in understanding our clients and the commercial realities of the markets in which they operate. We also share that knowledge across the firm. This allows us to look for opportunities for our clients – to help their businesses to develop, as well as simply responding to the challenges presented to us.

Our services include corporate, commercial, real estate and construction, business recovery, dispute resolution, employment, health and safety, intellectual property and private capital, as well as a range of services to private clients. We have specialist industry expertise in real estate (development, investment, residential and urban regeneration), banking & financial services, sport and food & drink.

**Who should apply** We like our lawyers to be technically sound but above all commercially smart. We reward ambitious business developers who understand that the business of law is all about clients. Put simply, we want good people and we want them to succeed. We aim to retain all trainees on qualification so we are interested in applications from people who also have local links.

**Training programme** Trainees complete four six-month seats, providing a wide range of practical experience and skills in contentious and non-contentious work. Our trainees work closely with partners and solicitors in a supportive team structure, and have regular reviews to ensure they are reaching their potential.

Training in both legal and non-legal areas is provided to meet the needs of the individual trainee and the Professional Skills Course is undertaken in-house.

**When and how to apply** The closing date for applications for 2010 is 31 July 2008. Please apply using the firm's application form. Further information and an application form are available from our recruitment website at www.futurepilots.co.uk.

| | |
|---|---|
| Vacancies | 10 |
| Trainees | 24 |
| Partners | 84 |
| Total staff | 625 |

**Apply to**
Clare Gibson, Assistant HR Adviser

**Starting salary**
£22,500 (2007)

**Minimum qualifications**
2.1 degree

**Offices**
Bristol, Birmingham, Southampton, Taunton

# Clarkson Wright & Jakes

Valiant House, Knoll Rise, Orpington BR6 0PG
**Tel:** 01689 887887
**Fax:** 01689 887888
**Email:** cwj@cwj.co.uk
**Web:** www.cwj.co.uk

**The firm** We are an ambitious, forward thinking regional legal practice with 100 people operating from one location in Kent. We offer talented graduates the opportunity to fulfil their career aspirations in a relaxed and supportive environment. Please visit our website for a better idea of who we are and what you can expect from a career with us.

**Who should apply** Highly motivated individuals with the drive to take the opportunity to stand out and really influence the future of our business, from the outset of their careers. We see the imminent legal services reforms very much as an opportunity rather than a threat, and seek people who share our appetite for the challenges ahead.

Whilst we expect applicants to already be high achievers in their academic careers, we also place great importance on practical skills. We welcome applications from non-law graduates and those embarking on a career change.

**Training programme** On joining, you will undergo induction training and will be introduced to your first seat. The areas in which you train will be agreed according to your preference and to the needs of the business. You will normally spend a period of six months in each seat, but there may be scope for flexibility. The emphasis here is on providing trainees with the most effective training possible with a view to producing talented self-starters. Our trainees are involved in client work from the outset and are given as much responsibility as they are comfortable with.

Our trainees attend internal and external training sessions and get involved in the delivery of regular seminars held at our office. They are encouraged to contribute to business development and to express their ideas and opinions. There are formal and informal reviews of how things are going, and there is a genuine 'open door' policy throughout the firm.

There is ample opportunity to engage in pro bono and voluntary work in line with our social responsibility policy.

We want you to have fun both at work and after, so we have a social committee who organise regular events.

**When and how to apply** The deadline for the October 2009 intake is 31 August 2007. Please use the online application form which can be accessed on our website.

**Work placements** Our vacation scheme runs throughout the summer. You will spend time in both legal and support departments, to gain an understanding of what is involved in running a law firm. In terms of legal work, you will be assigned to various departments throughout your time with us and will be involved in aspects of client work. The deadline for applications for the summer 2009 scheme is 31 January 2008.

| | |
|---|---|
| Vacancies | 3 |
| Trainees | 5 |
| Partners | 14 |
| Total staff | 100 |

**Work placement** yes

**Apply**
Online

**Starting salary**
£20,000

**Offices**
Orpington, Kent

Clarkson Wright & Jakes
Solicitors and Notaries

# Cleary Gottlieb Steen & Hamilton LLP

City Place House, 55 Basinghall Street, London EC2V 5EH
**Tel:** 020 7614 2200
**Fax:** 020 7600 1698
**Email:** longraduaterecruit@cgsh.com
**Web:** www.clearygottlieb.com

**The firm** Cleary Gottlieb is one of the leading international law firms, with 12 closely integrated offices located in major financial and political centres around the world. In recognition of the strength of the firm's global practice, its effectiveness in dealing with the different business cultures of the countries in which it operates and its success in multiple jurisdictions, Cleary received *Chambers & Partners*' inaugural International Law Firm of the Year award.

**Types of work** Our four core practice groups in London are mergers and acquisitions, private equity, financing, and debt and equity capital markets (IPOs). In addition, we have successful self-standing practices in competition, tax, financial regulation, intellectual property and information technology.

**Who should apply** We seek individuals, both law and non-law graduates, who are confident in their abilities, creative in their thinking, and who display a strong measure of common sense and commercial awareness. To succeed, candidates need to demonstrate exceptional academic ability. We normally expect candidates to attain at least a 2:1 degree from a leading university and AAB at A-level or the equivalent. Alongside academic ability, we value evidence of extra-curricular achievement.

**Training programme** By limiting our graduate intake to ten trainees a year, we are able to offer bespoke training that is individually tailored to the interests, experience and aptitudes of the individuals that join us. We do not believe that the transition from trainee solicitor to associate occurs overnight on qualification, but rather that the transition should be a smooth and gradual one. We therefore encourage our trainee solicitors to accept increased responsibility as soon as they are ready to do so. With appropriate levels of supervision, our trainees operate as lawyers of the firm from the day that they join us.

**When and how to apply** Candidates for trainee solicitor positions should apply before July 31, two years in advance of the year in which the training contract is due to commence. All candidates should submit a cover letter and full curriculum vitae, including a breakdown by subject of all A-level (or equivalent) results and degree results where known.

**Work placements** We offer 30 vacation places each year (10 at Easter and 10 in each of two summer schemes). The vacation scheme aims to provide potential trainee applicants with a practical insight into life as a Cleary lawyer, and our aim throughout the scheme is to involve participants directly in client work. In addition to this hands-on experience, the scheme incorporates a series of practice overview sessions designed to ensure exposure to the full range of work that we undertake in London. There are also a number of organised social events each week so that participants can get to know the current partners, associates and trainees of the firm outside the office. We actively encourage all candidates that are considering applying for a trainee solicitor position with the firm to undertake a vacation placement with us. Applications for Easter and summer placements should be received by January 28 in the year of the scheme.

**Sponsorship** We fund the Legal Practice Course (LPC) for all our future trainee solicitors. For non-law graduates, we also fund the Common Professional Examination (CPE) or the Postgraduate Diploma in Law (GDL). For each year of professional study, we pay a maintenance grant of £8,000.

| | |
|---|---|
| **Vacancies** | 10 |
| **Trainees** | 12 |
| **Partners** | 192 |
| (18 in London) | |
| **Total staff** | 2384 |
| (189 in London) | |

**Work placement** yes
*(see Insider Report on p92)*

**Apply to**
Shaun Goodman,
Graduate Recruitment
Partner

**Starting salary**
1st year - £40,000
2nd year - £45,000

**Minimum qualifications**
High 2.1 degree

**Sponsorship**
GDL/LPC

**Offices**
London, New York,
Washington DC, Paris,
Brussels, Frankfurt,
Cologne, Rome, Milan,
Moscow, Hong Kong,
Beijing

CLEARY
GOTTLIEB

# Clifford Chance

10 Upper Bank Street, Canary Wharf, London E14 5JJ
**Tel:** 020 7006 6006
**Fax:** 020 7006 5555
**Email:** contacthr@cliffordchance.com
**Web:** www.cliffordchance.com/gradsuk

**The firm** Clifford Chance is a truly global law firm, which operates as one organisation throughout the world. Our aim is to provide the highest-quality professional advice by combining technical expertise with an appreciation of the commercial environment in which our clients work. As a trainee this means you will gain breadth and depth in your experiences. We offer a uniquely global perspective and we actively encourage our lawyers to develop international experience. Most trainees interested in an international secondment spend six months abroad.

**Types of work** The range of work performed by the firm worldwide can be divided into six main areas of business: banking and finance, capital markets, corporate, litigation and dispute resolution, real estate and tax, pensions and employment. Our working style is characterised by a real sense of energy, enthusiasm and determination to provide the best possible service to our clients.

**Who should apply** We commit to building the futures of all our trainees. The firm plans to take on 130 trainee solicitors for the August 2010/February 2011 intakes. Applications are welcome from students with law or non-law degrees. We look to recruit trainees who combine a strong academic record with a wide range of skills and experiences.

**Training programme** The Clifford Chance training contract has been devised to provide you with the professional skills and experience you need to contribute to our success on a day-to-day basis, to qualify as a lawyer and to progress to a rewarding career. Our programme offers a good balance of formal and practical on-the-job training and complements the new Legal Practice Course which we are designing in conjunction with The College of Law, specifically for Clifford Chance trainees. Your two-year training contract consists of four six-month seats. Each seat will bring you into contact with new clients and colleagues, and you can expect to work on a variety of deals and projects, both large and small, as you build up your portfolio of skills. In each seat you will work in teams alongside senior lawyers, who will ensure that you are involved in a variety of high-quality, challenging work which reflects our international client base.

**When and how to apply** We are currently recruiting for graduates to start their training contracts in August 2010/February 2011. Law students/graduates should by 31 July 2008 for assessment in September 2008. We would encourage non-law students/graduates to apply by 31 January 2008 for assessment in February and March 2008, but please note that we do accept applications throughout the year. Please apply online at www.cliffordchance.com/gradsuk

**Work placements** We run two-day workshops in winter, which are based in our London office, and longer schemes during the spring or summer. Your placement will expose you to real and interesting 'live' projects within a close-knit team environment. There is a strong social element and you will enjoy a range of informal events with trainee solicitors, lawyers and partners. A number of international placements will also be available during the summer. Selected candidates will have the opportunity to spend two weeks in London, followed by two weeks in one of our European offices.

**Sponsorship** Fees for GDL and LPC covered. Maintenance is also provided – please refer to website for details.

| Vacancies | 130 |
|---|---|
| Trainees | 250 |
| Partners | 236 |
| Total staff | 2815 |

**Work placement**   yes
*(see Insider Report on p87)*

**Apply**
Online

**Starting salary**
£35,700

**Minimum qualifications**
2.1 degree

**Sponsorship**
GDL/LPC

**Offices**
Amsterdam, Bangkok, Barcelona, Beijing, Brussels, Bucharest, Budapest, Dubai, Düsseldorf, Frankfurt, Hong Kong, London, Luxembourg, Madrid, Milan, Moscow, Munich, New York, Paris, Prague, Rome, São Paulo, Shanghai, Singapore, Tokyo, Warsaw, Washington DC

**C L I F F O R D**

**C H A N C E**

# Clyde & Co LLP

51 Eastcheap, London EC3M 1JP
**Tel:** 020 7623 1244
**Fax:** 020 7623 5427
**Email:** theanswers@clydeco.com
**Web:** www.clydeco.com/graduate

**The firm** With roots in international trade, Clyde & Co LLP's main objective is to help clients do business in over 120 countries around the globe. The firm values entrepreneurialism, commercial problem solving, excellence and the freedom to be an individual. Clients value the firm's hands on innovative approach. The firm's lawyers know their industries, they know their clients, and most importantly they understand the commercial realities of business. Availability and responsiveness are key in the firm's core industries and these characteristics have become part of the mindset of a Clyde & Co lawyer.

The firm has expanded rapidly in recent years and is a dominant player in the insurance, reinsurance, international litigation, shipping, aviation, transport, international trade and energy, and commodities sectors. Clyde & Co has one of the largest litigation practices in the UK.

**Types of work** Aviation and aerospace, corporate/commercial, dispute resolution, EC/competition, energy, trade & commodities, insurance & re-insurance, real estate, shipping, transport & logistics.

**Who should apply** The firm is looking for graduates with excellent academic records, outgoing personalities and keen interests. Trainees need to have the social skills that will enable them to communicate effectively and build relationships with clients and colleagues. The ability to analyse problems, apply common sense and provide solutions to situations are all qualities the firm seeks. Ultimately Clyde & Co recruits to retain and they are seeking candidates who will remain with the firm beyond qualification.

**Training programme** You will gain early responsibility and be supported through close personal supervision and day-to-day coaching complemented by a wide range of training courses. You will undertake four six-month seats in London and Guildford, which will cover both transactional and contentious work. You may also choose to be seconded to one of our overseas offices or have the opportunity for a client secondment.

**When and how to apply** For training contracts starting in September 2010 please apply between 1 November 2007 and 31 July 2008. Applications should be made using the online application form via the website. The interview process includes an assessment session with graduate recruitment followed by an interview with two partners. To access the application form and view a copy of our brochure please visit our website at wwww.clydeco.com/graduate.

**Work placements** The firm runs two-week summer vacation schemes for 20 students. The dates for the 2008 schemes are 23 June to 4 July and 21 July to 1 August. Applications are made online and the closing date is 31 January 2008. For more details please visit our website at www.clydeco.com/graduate.

**Sponsorship** GDL and LPC fees paid plus a maintenance grant of £7,000 in London/Guildford and £6,000 elsewhere.

| Vacancies | 24 |
| Trainees | 46 |
| Partners | 140 |
| Total staff | 1080 |

**Work placement** yes
*(see Insider Report on p89)*

**Apply**
Online via website

**Starting salary**
£31,000, reviewed during training contract

**Minimum qualifications**
AAB at A-level and 2.1 degree

**Sponsorship**
GDL/CPE/LPC

**Offices**
Abu Dhabi, Caracas, Doha, Dubai, Guildford, Hong Kong, London, Los Angeles, Moscow, Nantes, New York, Paris, Piraeus, Rio de Janeiro, Shanghai, Singapore
Associate offices in Belgrade, St Petersburg

| **CLARKE & SON LLP**<br>Manor House, 8 Winchester Road,<br>Basingstoke RG21 8UG<br>**Tel:** 01256 320555<br>**Fax:** 01256 843150<br>**Email:** jmckinney@clarkeandson.co.uk<br>**Apply to:** Mrs Julie McKinney | Established in 1862, Clarke & Son is a general high street practice providing a wide range of commercial and private client services. | **V** 0<br>**T** 1<br>**P** 5<br>**TS** 30<br>**WP** no |
|---|---|---|
| **CLARKE KIERNAN**<br>2-4 Bradford Street, Tonbridge TN1 1DU<br>**Tel:** 01732 360 999<br>**Fax:** 01732 773 355<br>**Email:** cmc@clarkekiernan.com<br>**Apply to:** Ms Catherine McCarthy | Two offices. High street practice offering specialist deparment in family and criminal work, growing litigation and prison law departments, principally legal aid work. | **V** 1-2[09]<br>**T** 2<br>**P** 2<br>**TS** 31<br>**WP** no |
| **CLAUDE HORNBY & COX**<br>35-36 Gt Marlborough St, London W1F 7JE<br>**Tel:** 020 7437 8873<br>**Fax:** 020 7494 3070<br>**Email:** law@claudehornbycox.fsnet.co.uk<br>**Apply to:** Mr Andrew Moxon | Long established specialist law firm undertaking work in all aspects of criminal litigation as well as courts martial, extradition and prison law. | **V** 1[08]<br>**T** 2<br>**P** 2<br>**TS** 15<br>**WP** no |
| **CLIFFORD HARRIS & CO**<br>51 Welbeck Street, London W1A 4UA<br>**Tel:** 020 7486 0031<br>**Fax:** 020 7486 3333<br>**Apply to:** Mr Sunil Varma | Small West End commercial practice dealing with general litigation, insolvency, conveyancing, and company/commercial work for established corporate and private clients. | **V** 1[09]<br>**T** 0<br>**P** 4<br>**TS** 20<br>**WP** no |
| **CLIFTON INGRAM**<br>22/24 Broad Street, Wokingham,<br>Berkshire RG40 1BA<br>**Tel:** 01189 780099<br>**Fax:** 01189 771122<br>**Email:** johnhousden@cliftoningram.co.uk<br>**Apply to:** Mr John Housden | A broadly based practice with an emphasis on commercial work and litigation. | **V** 1<br>**T** 3<br>**P** 10<br>**TS** 64<br>**WP** no |
| **CLINTONS**<br>55 Drury Lane, London WC2B 5RZ<br>**Tel:** 020 7379 6080<br>**Fax:** 020 7240 9310<br>**Email:** info@clintons.co.uk<br>**Apply to:** Mr Peter Button | One of the foremost law practices in entertainment, sport and media, with an extensive general practice covering contentious and non-contentious commercial work, family and property. | **V** 3<br>**T** 6<br>**P** 20<br>**TS** 75<br>**WP** yes |
| **COLEMANS**<br>141 New London Road, Chelmsford CM2 0QT<br>**Tel:** 01245 264494<br>**Fax:** 01245 494537<br>**Email:** info@colemans-solicitors.co.uk<br>**Apply to:** Mr Aaron Coombs | A well-established firm of family solicitors and mediators with a private and legal aid client base. Other areas of work include residential conveyancing and probate. | **V** Poss[08]<br>**T** 2<br>**P** 14<br>**TS** 180<br>**WP** yes |
| **COLEMANS-CTTS**<br>1-3 Union Street, Kingston Upon Thames KT1 1RP<br>**Tel:** 020 8296 9966<br>**Fax:** 020 8546 1400<br>**Email:** hr@colemans-ctts.co.uk<br>**Apply to:** Ms Suzanne Kelly | Colemans-ctts is a progressive and dynamic national law firm. Client relationships and the delivery of high levels of service are the hallmarks of its reputation. | **V** 2<br>**T** 5<br>**P** 12<br>**TS** 250<br>**WP** yes |

# CMS Cameron McKenna LLP

Mitre House, 160 Aldersgate Street, London EC1A 4DD
**Tel:** 020 7367 8000
**Fax:** 020 7367 2000
**Email:** gradrec@cms-cmck.com
**Web:** www.law-now.com/graduate

**The firm** CMS Cameron McKenna LLP is a leading international law firm and an integral part of CMS, the alliance of European law firms. We've earned a reputation for outstanding client service, acute business awareness and for being passionate about client relationships. We work for some of the world's leading companies, helping them to solve their problems so they can run their businesses more efficiently. CMS Cameron McKenna focuses upon helping its clients find the right legal solutions for their business uses. The firm believes that to give the best advice, lawyers must clearly understand the industry, marketplace and concerns of their clients. Clients want advice to be delivered clearly, concisely and in a manner that fully reflects their needs. This approach has helped CMS Cameron McKenna build a strong reputation across a range of legal disciplines and industries, and foster strong client relationships, recognised in a number of prestigious awards: Client Relationship Management Development of the Year 2007, Private Equity Law Firm of the Year 2007, CEG Legal & Consulting Firm of the Year 2006, Best Education Project (above £20m), Best Accommodation/Property Project (below £20m), Best PPP Project, Pensions Team of the Year, Construction Team of the Year and Best Trainee Working at a City (London) Firm.

**Types of work** The firm's clients benefit from an extensive range of tailored services, delivered through offices in the UK, Central Europe, North America and Asia. CMS Cameron McKenna's membership of CMS, an alliance of independent law firms in Europe, provides clients with access to like-minded lawyers in over 24 jurisdictions. Our services include banking and international finance, corporate, real estate, commercial, commercial litigation, energy, projects and construction, insurance and reinsurance.

**Who should apply** Law students in their penultimate year. Non-law students in their final year. All students must have 320 UCAS points or equivalent and be on course for a 2.1 degree or above.

**Training programme** Training contracts last for two years. During this time you will have four six-month seats or placements, gaining experience in different practice areas. You will be awarded a priority seat when you start your training contract and will undertake a compulsory seat in the areas corporate or banking, and a contentious seat. To develop you and your legal skills even further, you can expect to be seconded to a client or spend time in one of our international or regional offices. Regular appraisals will be held with your seat supervisor to assess your progress, skills and development needs. The three compulsory modules of the Professional Skills Course will be completed before joining, allowing trainees to become effective and participate on a practical level as soon as possible. The Professional Skills Course is completed by a comprehensive in-house training programme that continues up to qualification and beyond.

**When and how to apply** By 31 July 2008 to begin September 2010/March 2011. Candidates must apply online at www.law-now.com/gradrec.

**Work placements** Up to 80 places for 2007/08 vacation scheme. Two weeks' duration. Easter, summer and Christmas schemes available. Please visit www.law-now.com/gradrec for details about the dates of these schemes.

**Sponsorship** GDL and LPC funding provided. The firm will cover the cost of all law school fees and provide you with a maintenance grant of up to £7,500. Please see our website for further details.

| | |
|---|---|
| Vacancies | 60 |
| Trainees | 120 |
| Partners | 131 |
| Total staff | 1500 |

**Work placement** yes
*(see Insider Report on p91)*

**Apply to**
Vivienne Ball, Graduate Recruitment Manager

**Starting salary**
£36,000

**Minimum qualifications**
2.1 degree

**Sponsorship**
GDL/CPE & LPC

**Offices**
Visit www.law-now.com for details regarding the firm's network of offices

CMS Cameron McKenna

# Cobbetts LLP

58 Mosley Street, Manchester M2 3HZ
**Tel:** 0845 404 2404
**Fax:** 0845 404 2414
**Email:** lawtraining@cobbetts.com
**Web:** www.cobbetts.com

**The firm** Cobbetts LLP is firmly established as one of the UK's leading law firms serving key plc and institutional clients and regional mid-market owner-managed businesses. Cobbetts this year opened a corporate finance practice in London to focus on public markets, M&A and private equity work. The firm continues to place high-quality and long-term relationship building with clients at the forefront of its strategy for success – a strategy which has resulted in controlled, sustained growth. This has been achieved through good management and an emphasis on the needs of clients, intermediaries and the firm's own personnel. Cobbetts believes in relationships, quality of environment and job satisfaction for all.

**Types of work** Cobbetts operates through a number of flexible service teams based on work type and managed across eight distinct areas of practice: corporate, banking, commercial, dispute resolution, employment, private client, real estate and social housing. There is legal expertise across many industry sectors, especially banking and finance, leisure, retail, public transport and information technology.

**Who should apply** We look for high academic achievers with a variety of outside interests. Individuals must demonstrate the confidence and commitment to thrive in a strong client-centred commercial environment, and have a desire for involvement and responsibility early in their training. The firm welcomes applications from students of any discipline.

**Training programme** Four six-month seats are available. Typically these include one property, one litigation and one commercial/corporate seat. There is an opportunity for one trainee each year to spend three months in Brussels.

Benefits include social club and LA Fitness pool and gym.

Comments from previous trainees:

"I would highly recommend Cobbetts as a firm to train with if you are looking for a challenging but enjoyable work environment together with a fun social life."

"Large enough and commercial enough to be one of the big players in the business, but relaxed enough and personal enough to make that difference to your training contract."

"I loved the firm on interview and was desperate to get in."

**When and how to apply** Apply by 14 July 2008 to begin September 2010. Apply online.

**Work placements** 24 placements available in July and August in Manchester; 12 placements in July in Birmingham; and 6 placements in Leeds in August.

**Sponsorship** GDL and LPC fees paid and maintenance grant of £4,000.

| | |
|---|---|
| Vacancies | 20 |
| Trainees | 52 |
| Partners | 136 |
| Total staff | 815 |

**Work placement** yes

**Apply**
Online

**Starting salary**
1st year - £22,000
2nd year - £23,000

**Minimum qualifications**
2.1 degree

**Sponsorship**
GDL/LPC

**Offices**
Manchester, Leeds, London, Birmingham

cobbetts

# Coffin Mew LLP

Fareham Point, Wickham Road, Fareham, Hampshire PO16 7AU
**Tel:** 01329 825617
**Fax:** 01329 825619
**Email:** sarajlloyd@coffinmew.co.uk
**Web:** www.coffinmew.co.uk

**The firm** Coffin Mew LLP offer an exceptional training opportunity. The firm is rapidly expanding to become one of the larger southern regional firms with major offices located in the cities of Portsmouth and Southampton and just off the M27 Motorway at Fareham. The firm is in the enviable position of operating a balanced practice offering top quality commercial and private client services in approximately equal volume and is particularly noted for a number of niche practices with national reputations.

**Types of work** The firm is structured through nine core departments: corporate & corporate finance; commercial services; employment, commercial litigation; property litigation; personal injury; property; family & childcare; and trust/probate. Niche practices (in which training is available) include intellectual property; finance and business regulation; social housing; insolvency; and medical negligence.

**Who should apply** The firm encourages applications from candidates with very good academic ability who seek a broad-based training contract in a highly progressive and demanding, but friendly and pleasant, environment.

**Training programme** The training contract is divided into six seats of four months each which will include a property department, a litigation department and a commercial department. The remainder of the training contract will be allocated after discussion with the trainee concerned. We aim to ensure that the trainee spends the final four months of his or her training contract in the department in which he or she hopes to work after qualification.

**When and how to apply** Applications for training contracts to begin in September 2010 (and possibly September 2009) are accepted between 1 January 2008 and 31 July 2008. The firm's website gives full details of how to apply for both training contracts and the vacation scheme.

**Work placements** Open Week in July each year; applications for the 2008 Open Week are accepted between 1 November 2007 and 31 March 2008.

**Sponsorship** LPC funding available by discussion with candidates.

| | |
|---|---|
| Vacancies | 6 |
| Trainees | 13 |
| Partners | 21 |
| Total staff | 247 |

**Work placement** yes

**Apply to**
Mrs Sara Lloyd,
Practice Manager

**Starting salary**
Competitive market rate for a South East regional firm

**Minimum qualifications**
2.1 degree (save in exceptional circumstances)

**Offices**
Fareham, Gosport, Portsmouth, Southampton

# Collyer Bristow LLP

4 Bedford Row, London WC1R 4DF
**Tel:** 020 7242 7363
**Fax:** 020 7405 0555
**Email:** cblaw@collyerbristow.com
**Web:** www.collyerbristow.com

**The firm** Collyer Bristow LLP is a distinctly unstuffy firm offering a refreshing alternative to those who do not believe that biggest necessarily means best. We have developed a large commercial practice while maintaining our long-standing client base of private individuals and families. Our commercial clients range from popstars to property developers, airlines to arts organisations, e-commerce companies to engineering firms, and we provide the wide range of business-related legal services that you would expect. The typical Collyer Bristow client does not exist - so neither does the typical Collyer Bristow lawyer. We are also unique in that our bright, modern offices in Holborn, Central London, house a professionally run contemporary art gallery.

**Types of work** We cover a wide spread of commercial and private client work, including: residential and commercial property work, particularly major property development; corporate and commercial work for national and international companies; advice to organisations and individuals involved in the sports, media, music, entertainment and technology industries; contentious and non-contentious intellectual property work; employment; general and civil litigation, in particular construction and property disputes, insolvency and defamation; family work, including divorce, financial settlements for married and unmarried couples, child abduction and other related issues; and private client work including tax and estate planning, creation and administration of trusts, wills, probate, resolution of trust and estate disputes.

**Who should apply** We are looking for self-starting graduates with a 2.1 in any discipline, who wish to gain a thorough grounding in a wide range of legal subjects. We positively encourage those embarking on their second career. Common sense and an ability to understand the client's business are essential attributes. We encourage trainees to take responsibility for their own files and to participate in managing the client's work – under close supervision, of course!

**Training programme** Trainees will spend six months in each training seat in up to four different departments and will work with a range of people from senior partners to more recently qualified solicitors. Trainees will also, under supervision, have contact with clients and so develop interpersonal skills as well as technical expertise.

**When and how to apply** Between January and July 2008 to begin September 2010. To apply contact our Human Resources or visit our website for an application form and further information.

**Sponsorship** Tuition fees for LPC plus maintenance of up to £4,000.

| | |
|---|---|
| Vacancies | 3 |
| Trainees | 6 |
| Partners | 30 |
| Total Staff | 136 |

**Work placement** no

**Apply to**
Human Resources

**Starting salary**
Currently £25,500

**Minimum qualifications**
2.1 degree

**Sponsorship**
LPC

**Offices**
London and Geneva.

| | | |
|---|---|---|
| **COLES MILLER**<br>44-46 Parkstone Road, Poole BH15 2PG<br>**Tel:** 01202 673011<br>**Fax:** 01202 675868<br>**Apply to:** Mr David Parfitt | The firm has four offices covering the Bournemouth/Poole conurbation and seeks to provide a wide range of services to both private and commercial clients. | V 2[09]<br>T 4<br>P 11<br>TS 110<br>WP no |
| **COLLAS DAY**<br>PO Box 140, Manor Place, St Peter Port, Guernsey GY1 4EW<br>**Tel:** 01481 723191<br>**Fax:** 01481 711880<br>**Email:** jcottell@collasday.com<br>**Apply to:** Joanne Cottell | Collas Day is a leading and long established firm practicing Guernsey law. The firm provides a comprehensive range of legal services to the international finance and local business communities, and to private individuals. | V 0<br>T 2<br>P 7<br>TS 65<br>WP yes |
| **COLLINS**<br>20 Station Road, Watford WD17 1AR<br>**Tel:** 01923 223324<br>**Fax:** 01923 211399<br>**Email:** collins@collinslaw.co.uk<br>**Apply to:** Ms Lesley Collins | Niche practice specialising in personal injury plus full range of legal services. Situated opposite County Court building. Adjacent to Watford Junction station, 20 mins Euston. | V 0<br>T 3<br>P 3<br>TS 25<br>WP no |
| **COMMUNITY LAW CLINIC SOLICITORS**<br>71 Chamberlayne Road, London NW10 3ND<br>**Tel:** 020 8964 4222<br>**Fax:** 020 8964 4224<br>**Email:** law@clcsolicitors.co.uk<br>**Apply to:** Ms Amrik Bains | Specialists in social welfare law: committed to legal aid work. Areas of work include immigration, housing, debt, welfare benefits, employment, consumer, family, community care, public law. | V 0<br>T 2<br>P 1<br>TS 12<br>WP no |
| **CONSTANT & CONSTANT**<br>Sea Containers House, 20 Upper Ground, London SE1 9QT<br>**Tel:** 020 7261 0006<br>**Fax:** 020 7401 2161<br>**Email:** twoconstants@dial.pipex.com<br>**Apply to:** Mr John Dickinson | International commercial law firm with offices in London and Greece, specialising in the contentious and non-contentious aspects of shipping and overseas trade. | V 0<br>T 4<br>P 16<br>TS 64<br>WP no |
| **CORRIES SOLICITORS LTD**<br>1st Floor, Rowntree Wharf, Navigation Road, York YO1 9WE<br>**Tel:** 0845 241 5566<br>**Fax:** 01904 527431<br>**Email:** sarah.haskins@corries.co.uk<br>**Apply to:** Ms Sarah Haskins | Corries is a modern and progressive law firm, specialising in personal injury claims, conveyancing and wills & probate. | V Poss 2<br>T 2<br>P 2<br>TS 60<br>WP no |
| **COTTERHILL HITCHMAN LLP**<br>Arthur House, 21 Mere Green Road, Sutton Coldfield B75 5BL<br>**Tel:** 0121 323 1860<br>**Fax:** 0121 323 1865<br>**Email:** mail@cotterhillhitchman.co.uk<br>**Apply to:** Mr Michael Cotterhill | Small relatively new firm. Mainly commercial work with some union referred personal injury cases. | V 0<br>T 3<br>P 2<br>TS 8<br>WP no |
| **COTTRILL STONE LAWLESS**<br>Centurion House, 129 Deansgate, Manchester M3 3ST<br>**Tel:** 0161 835 3681<br>**Fax:** 0161 833 0556<br>**Email:** anne.irwin@cottrills.co.uk<br>**Apply to:** Miss AT Irwin | City centre practice specialising in commercial and private client work. Good long-term prospects for the right candidates. | V 1<br>T 1<br>P 6<br>TS 30<br>WP no |

# Covington & Burling LLP

265 Strand, London WC2R 1BH
**Tel:** 020 7067 2000
**Fax:** 020 7067 2222
**Email:** graduate@cov.com
**Web:** www.cov.com

**The firm** Covington & Burling LLP is a leading US law firm, founded in Washington DC, with offices in Brussels, London, New York and San Francisco. The London office was established in 1988 and has grown progressively since then. We have many accomplished lawyers dealing with complex and fascinating legal issues.

**Types of work** In London, the main areas of work are corporate & commercial, employment, insurance, tax, life sciences, litigation & arbitration and IP/IT. There is no formal demarcation between practice areas and much of the work is of a multi-jurisdictional nature, spreading across offices. The firm is known worldwide for its remarkable understanding of regulatory issues as well as its depth and expertise in areas including IT, e-commerce and life sciences. We represent many blue-chip clients including Microsoft, Johnson & Johnson, Bacardi, Krispy Kreme, Qualcomm, Pfizer, Proctor & Gamble and Business Software Alliance.

**Who should apply** The firm is looking to build a strong team of lawyers who have genuine drive and commitment to the legal profession. We seek students who have not only excellent academic ability, but also the imagination and practical social skills required to respond to the evolving needs of our clients. In return, the firm believes it can offer innovative and captivating work in a stimulating and supportive environment. Covington recruits law and non-law students who expect to achieve a 2.1 or above in their degree.

**Training programme** Covington offers a unique and personal training programme to suit the individual needs of each trainee. As a firm, Covington places great importance on training, which is viewed as key to the firm's ability to offer its clients high-quality legal services. The programme offered by Covington is a mixture of structured sessions and on-the-job training. In 2005, the London office won a Best Trainer award at the LCN/TSG Training & Recruitment Awards, which is a reflection of the emphasis it places on training. Trainees joining Covington participate in a comprehensive induction programme, following which they spend six months in each of corporate and dispute resolution departments. The third and fourth seats are spent within the life sciences, IP/IT, employment or tax practice areas. The firm encourages trainees to take early responsibility and we believe they benefit from the lack of demarcation between practice areas. Trainees work closely with senior lawyers and partners to gain practical experience and to achieve their professional goals in a supportive environment. They also have the opportunity to work on pro bono projects which enhance their individual legal skills. Trainees receive regular feedback. This encourages continuous development to ultimately assist them to become well-rounded lawyers.

**When and how to apply** The deadline for our summer placement scheme is 28 February 2008 and for training contracts commencing 2010 the deadline is 31 July 2008. The application form can be accessed via our website at www.cov.com. Please direct any enquiries to graduate@cov.com.

**Work placements** Each year, we have 16 places for applicants on our one-week summer placement schemes. These give students a fantastic opportunity to experience the culture of our firm and the type of work we do.

**Sponsorship** We will pay tuition and examination fees for the GDL and the LPC. Maintenance will be paid at the current rate of £7,250 per annum.

| | |
|---|---|
| Vacancies | 6 |
| Trainees | 8 |
| Partners | 190 |
| Total staff | 1300 |

**Work placement** yes
*(see Insider Report on p93)*

**Apply to**
Graduate Recruitment Manager

**Starting salary**
1st year: £36,500
2nd year: £40,000

**Minimum qualifications**
2.1 degree

**Sponsorship**
GDL/LPC

**Offices**
Brussels, London, New York, San Francisco, Washington DC

COVINGTON & BURLING LLP

# Cripps Harries Hall LLP

Wallside House, 12 Mount Ephraim Road, Tunbridge Wells, Kent TN1 1EG
**Tel:** 01892 506006
**Fax:** 01892 506360
**Email:** graduates@crippslaw.com
**Web:** www.crippslaw.com

**The firm** A leading regional law firm and one of the largest in the South East, we are recognised as being among the most progressive and innovative regional practices.

Our organisation into client-focused, industry sector groups promotes our strong ethos of client service and ensures our solicitors are not only excellent legal practitioners but also experts in specialist business sectors. We are regarded by many businesses, institutions and wealthy individuals as the natural first choice among regional law firms. Although long-established, our profile is young, professional, forward-thinking, friendly and informal.

We achieved the Lexcel quality mark in January 1999, the first 'Top 100' firm to do so.

**Types of work** Commercial 17%; dispute resolution 18%; private client 26%; property 39%.

**Who should apply** Individuals who are confident and capable, with lively but well-organised minds and a genuine interest in delivering client solutions through effective and pragmatic use of the law; keen to make a meaningful contribution during both their contract and long-term career with us.

**Training programme** We offer a comprehensive induction course, a well-structured training programme, frequent one-to-one reviews, regular in-house courses and seminars, good levels of support and real responsibility.

Our training programme is broader than most other firms and typically includes six seats in both commercial and private client areas. Trainees usually share a room with a partner or an associate and gain varied and challenging first-hand experience.

**When and how to apply** 31 July 2008 is the deadline for applications for 2010. Preferred method of application is via our website.

**Sponsorship** Discretionary LPC funding: Fees - 50% interest-free loan, 50% bursary.

| | |
|---|---|
| Vacancies | 7 |
| Trainees | 14 |
| Partners | 41 |
| Total staff | 270 |

**Apply to**
Ms Annabelle Lawrence

**Starting salary**
1st year (2007) £20,000
2nd year (2007) £22,000

**Minimum qualifications**
2.1 in law or another subject and a first-time pass on the Legal Practice Course

**Offices**
Tunbridge Wells, London

CRIPPS HARRIES HALL LLP

| | | V | |
|---|---|---|---|
| **COVENTRY CITY COUNCIL**<br>Legal and Democratic Services Directorate,<br>Council House, Coventry CV1 5RR<br>**Tel:** 024 76833020<br>**Fax:** 024 76833070<br>**Apply to:** Director of Legal and Democratic<br>Services | Legal and Democratic Services<br>Directorate of Coventry City Council<br>dealing with all areas of local<br>government legal work and political<br>management and administrative<br>services. | V 0<br>T 1<br>P -<br>TS 170<br>WP no | |
| **COWLISHAW & MOUNTFORD**<br>90 High Street, Uttoxeter ST14 7JD<br>**Tel:** 01889 565211<br>**Fax:** 01889 565212<br>**Apply to:** Mr AJ Mountford | General practice in a country town<br>with a mix of private and franchised<br>legal aid work. | V 0<br>T 0<br>P 2<br>TS 10<br>WP no | |
| **COZENS-HARDY LLP**<br>Castle Chambers, Opie Street, Norwich NR1 3DP<br>**Tel:** 01603 625231<br>**Fax:** 01603 627160<br>**Email:** pgrudd@cozens-hardy.com<br>**Apply to:** Ms PG Rudd | Recruiting trainees to work in either<br>our Litigation Department or Private<br>Client Department. Up to 18 months<br>specialised training in each<br>department. | V 1[09]<br>T 3<br>P 9<br>TS 75<br>WP no | |
| **CROCKETT & CO**<br>260 Harehills Lane, Leeds LS9 7BD<br>**Tel:** 0113 226 0111<br>**Fax:** 0113 226 0110<br>**Email:** crockettsols@aol.com<br>**Apply to:** Miss H Crockett | Small family and child care practice<br>in outskirts of Leeds. | V 0<br>T 2<br>P 2<br>TS 12<br>WP no | |
| **CROSSE & CROSSE**<br>14 Southernhay West, Exeter EX1 1PL<br>**Tel:** 01392 258451<br>**Fax:** 01392 278938<br>**Apply to:** Mr TP Selley | Well established (1915) firm dealing<br>with all main areas of work. Legal aid<br>franchise. Specialises in personal<br>injury, civil and family. | V 0<br>T 2<br>P 8<br>TS 56<br>WP no | |
| **CROSSMANS**<br>5 St Andrews Street, Cambridge CB2 3AZ<br>**Tel:** 01223 362 414<br>**Fax:** 01223 322 475<br>**Email:** jb@crossmans.co.uk<br>**Apply to:** Mrs JE Ballard | Our philosophy is to use our<br>experience to create a systematic<br>approach to every day requirements<br>enabling us to deal with them quickly<br>and effectively. | V 0<br>T 0<br>P 3<br>TS 22<br>WP no | |
| **CRUTES**<br>Great North House, Sandyford Road, Newcastle<br>upon Tyne NE1 8ND<br>**Tel:** 0191 233 9700<br>**Fax:** 0191 233 9701<br>**Apply to:** Ms Cynthia Leadbitter | Civil litigation mostly for defendants<br>and insurers including medical<br>negligence and personal injury<br>indemnity, commercial property and<br>employment. | V 2[09]<br>T 3<br>P 18<br>TS -<br>WP no | |
| **CUNNINGTONS**<br>Great Square, Braintree CM7 1UD<br>**Tel:** 01376 326868<br>**Fax:** 01376 550003<br>**Apply to:** Mr SE Kew | Cunningtons have over 250 years<br>legal experience, nine branches<br>nationwide and offer a complete<br>range of legal services. Specialist<br>areas: large volume residential<br>conveyancing. | V Varies[09]<br>T 12<br>P 10<br>TS 180<br>WP yes | |

**V** = Vacancies / **T** = Trainees / **P** = Partners / **TS** = Total Staff / **WP** = Work Placement

# Crown Prosecution Service

Enquiries: legal.trainees@cps.gsi.gov.uk
**Tel:** 01904 545621
**Fax:** 01904 545560
**Web:** www.cps.gov.uk

**The organisation** The Crown Prosecution Service is the Government Department responsible for prosecuting people in England and Wales who have been charged with a criminal offence. We employ approximately 9,000 staff throughout the country including caseworkers and administrators and around 3,000 lawyers, of which 2,400 are solicitors.

**Types of work** As the principal prosecuting authority in England and Wales, we are responsible for advising the police on cases for prosecution, making the charging decision, preparing cases for court and presenting them in court. We handle over 1.3 million magistrates' court cases and 115,000 Crown court cases every year. Our work includes advice to the police, legal research, attendance at hearings in the Magistrates' and Crown Courts, case preparation and management and liaison with victims and witnesses.

**Who should apply** The CPS is an equal opportunities employer. Our policies including the need to guard against false assumptions based on sex or marital status, gender reassignment, sexual orientation, colour, race, religion, ethnic or national origin, work pattern, age or disability, are followed at all stages of the recruitment and selection procedure. We are also a Disability Symbol user – all those with a disability who satisfy the minimum criteria for advertised vacancies will be invited for interview.

Many of our trainees do not come through the 'traditional' route but have worked and studied part-time over many years – often after having left school with minimal qualifications. We do not take account of academic qualifications. Minimum entry criteria will be specified for each advertised post.

**Training programme** Trainees are assigned to an individual trained supervisor who is an experienced crown prosecutor and is responsible for the trainee's daily work and personal development. Induction is tailored to the needs of the individual and includes the Solicitors Regulation Authority requirements, what to expect from the CPS and a talk from a current trainee. Further learning and development opportunities are provided as required.

Training is provided in criminal litigation. Trainees work under supervision, handling all cases, from straightforward summary pleas to trials and appeals. Trainee solicitors undertake one or more secondments in order to gain the breadth of experience required by the Solicitors Regulation Authority. There is a broad choice of secondments – many go to private practice but there are opportunities for London-based trainees to undertake secondments in GLS departments. There may also be the opportunity for trainee solicitors to gain rights of audience in the Magistrates' courts and to prosecute straightforward cases. Trainees are appraised every six months and after each formal secondment.

**When and how to apply** Opportunities in local offices are advertised when available. These will generally be for immediate start and applicants will need to have LPC results. We also advertise national trainee recruitment in October. The application procedure is set out in the advertisements and will usually comprise an online application, reasoning tests, a legal case study, an oral presentation and an interview.

**Sponsorship** At present the Law Scholarship Scheme, which provides sponsorship for the academic stages including law degree, GDL & LPC is available to internal applicants only.

| | |
|---|---|
| Vacancies | Varies |
| Trainees | 50 (varies) |
| Total staff | 9000 |

**Work placement** yes

**Apply to**
See details in advertisements

**Starting salary**
£18,425 national
£19,441 London
Pay award pending

**Minimum qualifications**
LPC

**Offices**
Nationwide

| Firm | Description | | |
|------|-------------|---|---|
| **CURTIS MALLET-PREVOST COLT & MOSLE LLP**<br>53 New Broad Street, London EC2M 1BB<br>**Tel:** 020 7011 9500<br>**Fax:** 020 7011 9501<br>**Email:** tdavis@curtis.com<br>**Apply to:** T Davis | | **V** 0<br>**T** 3<br>**P** 3<br>**TS** 12<br>**WP** no |
| **CURWENS**<br>Crossfield House, Gladbeck Way, Enfield EN2 7HT<br>**Tel:** 020 8363 4444<br>**Fax:** 020 8884 7227<br>**Email:** lisa.dearman@curwens.co.uk<br>**Apply to:** Mrs Lisa Hughes | 'Mini-regional' firm covering Hertfordshire and North London. A general practice also having particular strengths in litigation, employment, and company/commercial work. | **V** 2(08)<br>**T** 2<br>**P** 15<br>**TS** 120<br>**WP** yes |
| **CYRIL JONES & CO**<br>17 Egerton Street, Wrexham LL11 1NB<br>**Tel:** 01978 263131<br>**Fax:** 01978 290530<br>**Apply to:** Mr Gareth Jones | Small general practice in North Wales, varied workload covering most areas of law, mainly conveyancing, family & probate and PI. Legal aid franchise. | **V** 0<br>**T** 1<br>**P** 4<br>**TS** 15<br>**WP** no |
| **DARBYS**<br>52 New Inn Hall Street, Oxford OX1 2DN<br>**Tel:** 01865 811700<br>**Fax:** 01865 811787<br>**Email:** info@darbys.co.uk<br>**Apply to:** Mr Paul Lowe | A regional practice with specialist team providing a wide range of legal services to both business and private clients. | **V** 3<br>**T** 6<br>**P** 25<br>**TS** 145<br>**WP** no |
| **DARLINGTON BOROUGH COUNCIL**<br>Feethams, Darlington, County Durham DL1 5QT<br>**Tel:** 01325 380651<br>**Fax:** 01325 388318<br>**Apply to:** Luke Swinhoe | Local authority. | **V** 0<br>**T** 0<br>**P** 7<br>**TS** 15<br>**WP** no |
| **DARLINGTONS**<br>48 High Street, Edgware, Middlesex HA8 7EQ<br>**Tel:** 020 8951 6666<br>**Fax:** 020 8951 6665<br>**Email:** enquiry@darlingtons.com<br>**Apply to:** Mr P Patashnik | | **V** 2(08)<br>**T** 4<br>**P** 3<br>**TS** 30<br>**WP** no |
| **DARWIN GRAY**<br>15 Windsor Place, Cardiff CF10 3BY<br>**Tel:** 029 2082 9100<br>**Fax:** 029 2082 9101<br>**Apply to:** Mr JR Smith | Darwin Gray is a niche commercial practice specialising in commercial property, litigation, employment and commercial law. | **V** 0<br>**T** 1<br>**P** 5<br>**TS** 17<br>**WP** no |
| **DAS LEGAL EXPENSES INSURANCE**<br>DAS House, Quay Side, Temple Back, Bristol BS1 6NH<br>**Tel:** 0117 9342000<br>**Fax:** 0117 934 0251<br>**Email:** hr@das.co.uk<br>**Apply to:** Ms Sasha Davies | DAS Legal Expenses Insurance protect against the cost of potential legal disputes affecting policyholders' motoring, family or business. This includes a 24 hour legal advice service. | **V** 1-2<br>**T** 3<br>**P** -<br>**TS** 500<br>**WP** yes |

**V** = Vacancies / **T** = Trainees / **P** = Partners / **TS** = Total Staff / **WP** = Work Placement

# Davenport Lyons

30 Old Burlington Street, London W1S 3NL
**Tel:** 020 7468 2600
**Fax:** 020 7437 8216
**Email:** dl@davenportlyons.com
**Web:** www.davenportlyons.com

**The firm** Davenport Lyons provides comprehensive legal services across a broad spectrum of market sectors including media (film, TV, radio, music, theatre, publishing and newspapers), retail, advertising, restaurants, hotels, sport, leisure, travel, IT, e-commerce and new media. The firm has close involvement with many US and EU businesses and lawyers and is the only English member of the international law firm association, Globalaw. With a 37 partner strong practice, over 66 fee earners and supporting operational function, we are a commercially focused law firm based in the luxurious surroundings of Mayfair. Coupled with the firm's desire to retain our warm and friendly environment, Davenport Lyons is the ideal place to start your career as a successful solicitor.

**Types of work** The firm provides a full range of services through its five departments, corporate, contentious rights & dispute resolution, property, employment and private client. Areas of expertise include: corporate, commercial, corporate tax, film and tv, music, defamation, contentious and non-contentious IP/IT, commercial dispute resolution, insolvency, liquor and entertainment licensing, property, property dispute resolution, tax & trust, matrimonial and employment.

**Who should apply** We are looking for candidates with excellent academic qualifications (2.1 and above, good A level results) and an interesting background, who are practical and can demonstrate good business acumen. Candidates should have a breadth of interests and foreign language skills are an advantage. In short, we are looking for well-rounded individuals!

**Training programme** Our training programme consists of four six-month seats. During each seat trainees receive mid and end of the seat reviews, and each seat has a dedicated trainee supervisor. We have an on-going in-house training and lecture programme. We pride ourselves on offering interesting, hands-on training with trainees being encouraged to develop their own client relationships and to handle their own files under appropriate supervision, therefore being treated as junior fee earners. We aim to make our training contracts informative, educational, practical, supportive and, let us not forget, as enjoyable as possible.

**When and how to apply** Applications by 31 July 2008 to commence September 2010. Apply online at www.davenportlyons.com.

**Work placements** A limited number of places are available on our summer vacation scheme, which runs during July and August. Remuneration is £200 per week.

**Sponsorship** The firm does not offer financial assistance.

| Vacancies | 8 |
| Trainees | 16 |
| Partners | 37 |
| Total staff | 197 |

**Work placement** yes

**Apply**
Online

**Minimum qualifications**
2.1 degree, AAB at A level
(320+ UCAS points)

**Offices**
London

Davenport Lyons

# Davies Arnold Cooper

6-8 Bouverie Street, London EC4Y 8DD
**Tel:** 020 7936 2222
**Fax:** 020 7936 2020
**Email:** recruitment@dac.co.uk
**Web:** www.recruit.dac.co.uk

**The firm** Davies Arnold Cooper is an international law firm particularly known for its dispute resolution and real estate expertise. It advises in relation to specialist areas of law including insurance, real estate, construction and product liability, and has a leading Hispanic practice. The firm has offices in London, Manchester, Madrid and Mexico City.

**Types of work** We act for some of the leading public and private companies, both in the UK and abroad. Our impressive client list includes many large UK and international companies across a broad range of industry sectors, from insurance and financial institutions (including Lloyds), to real estate, retail, pharmaceuticals, energy, mining and construction.

We advise in relation to insurance and reinsurance (including fraud, professional indemnity, directors' and officers' liability, and property and construction insurance); real estate; property finance; planning; product liability; construction and energy; health and safety; insolvency and business recovery services; corporate; sports law; employment law and travel.

**Who should apply** We look for intellect (a UCAS tariff of 300, excluding General Studies, and a 2.1 degree is usual). We also look for common sense and a mature outlook.

**Training programme** Here at Davies Arnold Cooper our culture appeals to those who enjoy life. The atmosphere lacks the formality and stuffiness of some more 'traditional' practices, yet still maintains the professionalism and dedication our clients expect.

Our induction and training schemes are widely admired, and trainees receive a comprehensive grounding in core legal skills. As a medium-sized firm we offer a flexible training programme, with the opportunity for early responsibility within a supportive environment. During your two-year training contract you will spend six months in each of three different groups within the firm before deciding where to spend your final six months. You will be continually assessed both formally and informally to maximise the opportunities to develop your legal and business skills.

As we view our trainees as the future of our business, we offer a career, not just a training contract. Training and support start from day one of your training contract and continue throughout your career with us. Our well-structured, comprehensive training environment provides the ideal preparation for a career in a modern progressive law firm. Our philosophy is to 'recruit to retain', and therefore we invest a great deal in your training. If you are the candidate we are searching for, you can learn more about what Davies Arnold Cooper has to offer prospective trainees by visiting our website at www.recruit.dac.co.uk and forwarding your application in writing to our Graduate Recruitment Department.

**When and how to apply** Apply by 25 July 2008 to begin 2010 (please refer to website as this date may change). To request an application form please write to Charlotte Stanbridge at the address above. Alternatively a form can be downloaded from our website. Please note that applications will only be considered where the firm's application form has been used.

| | |
|---|---|
| Vacancies | 5 |
| Trainees | 12 |
| Partners | 68 |
| Total staff | 317 |

**Apply to**
Charlotte Stanbridge

**Starting salary**
£29,000

**Minimum qualifications**
2.1 degree

**Sponsorship**
CPE/LPC

**Offices**
London, Manchester,
Madrid, Mexico

DAVIES ARNOLD COOPER

## DAVID & SNAPE
Wyndham House, Wyndham Street,
Bridgend CF31 1EP
**Tel:** 01656 661115
**Fax:** 01656 660545
**Apply to:** Ms Susan Smith

A busy, friendly and progressive high street firm with membership of several law society panels and a legal services commission franchise.

| | |
|---|---|
| V | 0 |
| T | 1 |
| P | 4 |
| TS | 30 |
| WP | no |

## DAVID COWAN SOLICITORS
114 South Street, Dorking RH4 2EW
**Tel:** 01306 886622
**Fax:** 01306 740183
**Email:** enquiries@cowansdorking.co.uk
**Apply to:** Mr David Cowan

General practice including litigation, family and matrimonial, crime, conveyancing, wills and probate. Legal aid franchise and contracts. No vacancies at present.

| | |
|---|---|
| V | 0 |
| T | 1 |
| P | 1 |
| TS | 19 |
| WP | no |

## DAVID GRAY SOLICITORS
Old County Court, 56 Westgate Road,
Newcastle Upon Tyne NE1 5XU
**Tel:** 0191 232 9547
**Fax:** 0191 230 4149
**Email:** lawyers@davidgray.co.uk
**Apply to:** Mr Tony Baldock

LSC contracted firm undertaking crime, family, immigration, housing, conveyancing, wills/probate, personal injury, actions against the police and mental health.

| | |
|---|---|
| V | 1(09) |
| T | 4 |
| P | 9 |
| TS | 54 |
| WP | no |

## DAVID PHILLIPS & PARTNERS
202 Stanley Road, Bootle L20 3EP
**Tel:** 0151 922 5525
**Fax:** 0151 922 8298
**Apply to:** Mr David Phillips

London office deals with high profile criminal cases. Bootle office is a general practice with an emphasis on legal aid work both criminal and civil.

| | |
|---|---|
| V | 2 |
| T | 3 |
| P | 11 |
| TS | 60 |
| WP | yes |

## DAVIES AND PARTNERS
Rowan House, Barnett Way, Barnwood,
Gloucester GL4 3RT
**Tel:** 01452 612345
**Fax:** 01452 611922
**Email:** david.stokes@daviesandpartners.com
**Apply to:** Mr DC Stokes

Regional commercial practice with an emphasis on heavyweight property law, clinical negligence, personal injury and commercial litigation land services. Integrated offices in Bristol, Gloucester and Solihull.

| | |
|---|---|
| V | 5(09) |
| T | 7 |
| P | 25 |
| TS | 203 |
| WP | no |

## DAVIES JOHNSON & CO
Old Harbour Office, Guy's Quay, Sutton Harbour,
Plymouth PL4 0ES
**Tel:** 01752 226020
**Fax:** 01752 225882
**Apply to:** Mr J Johnson

Shipping and commercial.

| | |
|---|---|
| V | 1(09) |
| T | 1 |
| P | 4 |
| TS | 12 |
| WP | yes |

## DAVIS & CO
St Michaels Rectory, St Michaels Alley, Cornhill,
London EC3V 9DS
**Tel:** 020 7621 1091
**Fax:** 020 7621 1050
**Email:** trevor.davis@davis-solicitors.com
**Apply to:** Mr Trevor Davis

Niche City firm specialising in utilities litigation with blue chip client base. Candidates should have a good academic background and have an interest in advocacy.

| | |
|---|---|
| V | 1-2 |
| T | 0 |
| P | 1 |
| TS | 8 |
| WP | no |

## DAVIS BLANK FURNISS
90 Deansgate, Manchester M3 2QJ
**Tel:** 0161 832 3304
**Fax:** 0161 834 3568
**Email:** peter.heginbotham@dbf-law.co.uk
**Apply to:** Mr Peter Heginbotham

Whilst having a successful corporate and business department, the firm is firmly committed to retaining private client work. Training in a wide range of work.

| | |
|---|---|
| V | 1-2 |
| T | 4 |
| P | 14 |
| TS | 77 |
| WP | no |

# Dawsons

2 New Square, Lincoln's Inn, London WC2A 3RZ
**Tel:** 020 7421 4800
**Fax:** 020 7421 4848
**Email:** j.okuns@dawsonsllp.com
**Web:** www.dawsonsllp.com

**The firm** A partnership of lawyers set in the heart of legal London with a solid reputation for high professional standards and a personal, partner-led service. It is our aim to combine the most effective and efficient service with the quality of advice and personal approach which has been the hallmark of the firm since its foundation in the early 18th century.

At Dawsons you will find no cliques or reluctance to delegate or cross-refer work - just a happy, enthusiastic and friendly atmosphere, with an open-door policy and a willingness to discuss ideas and problems. We believe this is the best way to maximise our potential as lawyers and provide the best service for our clients.

**Types of work** The firm is organised into five departments: corporate commercial, family, litigation private client and property.

**Who should apply** Second-year law students and final-year non-law students with excellent A level grades and who are expecting to achieve at least a 2.1 degree. Applications are also welcomed from candidates who are currently on, or have recently completed, the GDL or LPC course.

Candidates need to show excellent intellectual capabilities, a keen interesting the firm's areas of expertise and a practical and commercial approach to problem solving. Trainees are the future of our firm and an important part of building on its success. An open door policy applies and trainees are an integral part of the team they are allocated to. As a result a large number of our current partners and solicitors trained with us.

**Training programme** We have a very good reputation at Dawsons for providing extremely high-quality training, with all trainees assigned to a partner, conducting matters on their own under that partner's supervision and assisting the partner with his or her other work. This allows the trainees to learn and develop under expert guidance and supervision, and at the same time provide a valuable contribution to the busy practitioner. There is also a good programme of internal and external training courses available to the trainees which continues throughout their career.

The training consists of four six-month seats in at least three of the following departments: property, private client, corporate and commercial, litigation and family. You will share an office with a partner to assist your learning and development and provide easy access for support and guidance and three monthly reviews. You will have client contact and assume responsibility from an early stage. Trainees are involved in all social and market events.

**When and how to apply** The deadline for our Easter and Summer vacation scheme is 1 March 2008. The deadline for 2010 training contracts is 31 July 2009. The application form is online.

**Work placements** We offer a number of one-week placements every year, during Easter and Summer vacations. These placements are designed to give you a flavour of what it would be like to train at Dawsons.

**Sponsorship** CPE and LPC fees plus a maintenance allowance of £3,000.

| | |
|---|---|
| Vacancies | 4 |
| Trainees | 8 |
| Partners | 21 |
| Total staff | 101 |

**Work placement** yes

**Apply**
Online

**Starting salary**
Competitive

**Minimum qualifications**
2.1 degree, As and Bs at A level

**Sponsorship**
CPE/LPC

**Offices**
London

DAWSONS
SOLICITORS

# Debevoise & Plimpton LLP

Tower 42, Old Broad Street, London EC2N 1HQ
**Tel:** 020 7786 9000
**Fax:** 020 7588 4180
**Email:** graduaterecruitment@debevoise.com
**Web:** www.debevoise.com

**The firm** Debevoise & Plimpton LLP is a leading international law firm with offices in London, Paris, Hong Kong, Moscow, Frankfurt, New York, Shanghai and Washington DC. The London office works on many of the highest profile and most complex transactions in Europe and worldwide. We do this by virtue of our English and New York law expertise and our close integration with our other offices.

**Types of work** In developing our practice in London, we have sought to replicate the core strengths of our practice worldwide. Our focus is on cross-border M&A, private equity, insurance, capital markets, finance and restructurings, tax planning and dispute resolution.

Clients include: ABN AMRO, Aeroflot, AIG, AXA Private Equity, The Carlyle Group, Catlin Group Limited, Clayton, Dubilier & Rice, Deutsche Bank, Eircom, HarbourVest Partners, Hertz, ING, Italtel, Merrill Lynch Global Private Equity, Providence Equity Partners and Rexel.

**Who should apply** We look for students whose personal qualities, academic records and other achievements demonstrate exceptional ability, motivation and potential growth. We look for applicants who will make a significant contribution to our firm and thrive in our unique culture. We look for an ability to listen actively, think creatively, interact successfully with other people and effectively convey and advocate a point of view. In addition to high academic standards, we look for maturity and leadership qualities.

**Training programme** One of Debevoise's basic principles is that each of our associates should become a 'well rounded' lawyer – an effective counsellor, advisor, and advocate – who can combine specific legal knowledge with the ability to deal with a broad range of situations. We believe that lawyers best develop their skills through a combination of formal training and on-the-job experience, in a respectful and collegial working environment. The two years are split into four six-month seats and trainees have the opportunity to gain experience in at least three distinct areas of law.

**When and how to apply** Our application form is available online on our website or by calling our graduate recruitment team. Applications for September 2010 training contracts should be received between 1 May and 31 July 2008.

**Work placements** Debevoise offers a summer vacation scheme, which runs between June and August each year. Our application form is available online on our website or by calling our graduate recruitment team. Applications for summer 2008 should be made between 1 February and 28 February 2008.

**Sponsorship** Full tuition fees are paid for GDL and LPC, together with a maintenance grant of £7,000 per year.

**Vacancies** 6
**Trainees** 8
**Partners** 16 (London)
144 (Worldwide)
**Total staff** 165 (London)
1667 (Worldwide)

**Work placement** yes

**Apply to**
Michelle Kirkland, HR & Administration Manager

**Starting salary**
1st year - £40,000
2nd year - £45,000

**Minimum qualifications**
2.1 degree

**Sponsorship**
GDL/LPC

**Offices**
London, Paris, Hong Kong, Moscow, Frankfurt, New York, Shanghai, Washington DC

DEBEVOISE & PLIMPTON LLP

# Dechert LLP

160 Queen Victoria Street, London EC4V 4QQ
**Tel:** 020 7184 7000
**Fax:** 020 7184 7001
**Email:** application@dechert.com
**Web:** www.dechert.com

**The firm** Dechert LLP is a dynamic international law firm, with over 1,000 lawyers across the USA and Europe. Our largest offices are in Philadelphia, New York and London.

**Types of work** Our largest practice areas in London are corporate and securities, hedge funds and other investment funds, and finance and real estate. We also have smaller teams practising in areas such as litigation, intellectual property, employment and tax.

**Who should apply** Dechert looks for enthusiasm, intelligence, an ability to find practical solutions, and for powers of expression and persuasion. Graduates from any discipline are welcome to apply.

**Training programme** Your training contract will start with a visit to Philadelphia, to take part in our firm-wide induction, and to learn about our international practice. After that you will do six seats of four months. We believe the six seat system gives the best possible opportunity to experience a wide range of practice areas, and to learn quickly. Every new seat is discussed with you, and will reflect your interests and ambitions, so no two trainees have the same training contract. Your choice of seats, and professional development, is guided by both our Director of Training and your own trainee partner, who meet with you regularly. The firm has a lively training programme covering a wide range of law and skills topics, with many sessions aimed specifically at trainees.

For those who wish to travel, we offer secondments to our Brussels office, and sometimes to our offices in Munich and the USA. There are also opportunities for client secondments and judicial secondments.

Trainees are encouraged to take part in our Pro Bono programme. Not only does this reflect our commitment to Pro Bono, but we believe it helps our young lawyers to develop their skills, particularly in case analysis and in interviewing and counselling clients.

**When and how to apply** Apply online, via our website. Applications for training contracts in September 2010 should be received by 31 July 2008.

**Work placements** We run schemes at Easter, and in the Summer. These give you a chance to experience the sort of work a trainee will do, and to take part in a variety of seminars, exercises and social events. Our vacation schemes are aimed at penultimate year law students. The closing date for applications is 29 February 2008.

**Sponsorship** We pay LPC fees and a maintenance grant of £10,000 (from September 2008).

| Vacancies | Up to 15* |
|---|---|
| Trainees | 25* |
| Partners | 37* |
| Total staff | approx 300* |

*denotes London figure

**Work placement** yes

**Apply**
Online

**Starting salary**
£38,000 (from 2008)

**Minimum qualifications**
2.1 degree

**Sponsorship**
LPC

**Offices**
Austin, Boston, Brussels, Charlotte, Hartford, London, Luxembourg, Munich, Newport Beach, New York, Palo Alto, Paris, Philadelphia, Princeton, San Francisco, Washington

Dechert
LLP

# Denton Wilde Sapte

1 Fleet Place, London EC4M 7WS
**Tel:** 020 7242 1212
**Fax:** 020 7320 6555
**Email:** laura.goode@dentonwildesapte.com
**Web:** www.dentonwildesapte.com

**The firm** Denton Wilde Sapte is an international law firm with over 700 lawyers and a network of offices spanning the UK, Europe, Middle East, Africa and CIS. We advise leading organisations across four core sectors: financial institutions; energy, transport & infrastructure; real estate & retail; and technology, media & telecoms.

**Types of work** We offer a full range of commercial legal services and have leading experts in each of our nine departments: banking & finance; corporate/M&A; dispute resolution; employment & pensions; energy & infrastructure; EU & competition; real estate; tax and technology; media & telecoms.

**Who should apply** We're looking for people with talent, personality and ambition. We accept candidates from any degree discipline, but you must have a strong academic and extracurricular record of achievement. Denton Wilde Sapte lawyers are also good team players with excellent interpersonal skills and the flexibility to grow with the firm.

**Training programme** As a trainee you will undertake four six-month seats. This will include a contentious seat, plus experience in our transaction based departments such as banking, real estate, corporate etc. This may also include the opportunity to work in one of our international offices or with one of our clients.

Whatever your seat you will be expected to rise to the challenge. Our approach will be to give you as much responsibility as you can handle. After all, this is where the real learning starts - on the job – and you will be working with the law and with clients in real business situations.

As part of your training contract, we will cover your law school tuition fees and provide a maintenance grant of £6,000 (£7,000 in London).

**When and how to apply** Our application form is available online on our website or by calling our graduate recruitment team. Applications for March and September 2010 training contracts should be received no later than 31 July 2008.

**Work placements** Denton Wilde Sapte hosts open days in December and summer schemes in July – both designed to help you decide whether ours is the right firm for you. These schemes consist of business games, department visits and social events, giving potential trainees an insight into commercial law and our way of life at Denton Wilde Sapte.

The open days are designed for non-law students who are in their final year or who have already graduated. The closing date for applications is 23 November 2007.

Law graduates or law students who are in their final or penultimate year are invited to apply for our summer schemes. Applications close on 8 February 2008, with interviews held during February and March.

| | |
|---|---|
| **Vacancies** | 10 (March) |
| | 25 (September) |
| **Trainees** | 72 |
| **Partners** | 165 |
| **Total staff** | 1400 |

**Work placement**   yes
*(see Insider Report on p95)*

**Apply to**
Miss Laura Goode

**Starting salary**
£36,000

**Minimum qualifications**
2.1 degree, law or non-law

**Sponsorship**
GDL/LPC

**Offices**
London, Abu Dhabi, Almaty, Cairo, Dubai, Dubai Internet City, Istanbul, Milton Keynes, Moscow, Muscat, Paris, Riyadh (associate office), Tashkent

DentonWildeSapte...

| | | |
|---|---|---|
| **DAWSON CORNWELL**<br>15 Red Lion Square, London WC1R 4QT<br>**Tel:** 020 7242 2556<br>**Fax:** 020 7831 0478<br>**Email:** allenk@dawsoncornwell.co.uk<br>**Apply to:** Ms Kate Allen | A specialist family law firm consistently rated by Chambers and The Legal 500. | V 1[09]<br>T 2<br>P 9<br>TS 27<br>WP yes |
| **DEAN WILSON LAING**<br>96 Church Street, Brighton BN1 1UJ<br>**Tel:** 01273 327241<br>**Fax:** 01273 299699<br>**Apply to:** Mr NJ Perkins | A modern firm with a national reputation for property, landlord and tenant and employment law; solicitors to various national associations; family, probate. | V 1[09]<br>T 2<br>P 8<br>TS 46<br>WP no |
| **DENBY & CO**<br>119 Duke Street, Barrow-In-Furness LA14 1XE<br>**Tel:** 01229 822366<br>**Fax:** 01229 870109<br>**Apply to:** Mr John H Denby | Franchised high street general practice. Offices in Barrow and Ulverston. Personal injury, children panel, family panel, family mediation, duty solicitors rota, large conveyancing and probate departments. | V 1<br>T 1<br>P 5<br>TS 28<br>WP no |
| **DEREK B FORREST SOLICITORS**<br>1/2 Leyland House, Lancashire Enterprise Business, Leyland, Preston PR5 1TZ<br>**Tel:** 01772 424999<br>**Fax:** 01772 433230<br>**Email:** derek@solicitordirect.com<br>**Apply to:** Mr Derek Forrest | A high street solicitor working nationwide over phone and Internet. Heavily computerised without secretaries. | V 1[09]<br>T 1<br>P 1<br>TS 7<br>WP no |
| **DEVON & CORNWALL CONSTABULARY**<br>Middlemoor, Exeter EX2 7HQ<br>**Tel:** 0139 245 2863<br>**Fax:** 0139 245 2183<br>**Apply to:** Mr MDP Stamp | The force's legal advisors officers provides legal support for the chief constable of devon and cornwall across a number of disciplines. Mainly litigious work. | V 0<br>T 0<br>P 1<br>TS 7<br>WP no |
| **DEVONSHIRES**<br>Salisbury House, London Wall, London EC2M 5QY<br>**Tel:** 020 7628 7576<br>**Fax:** 020 7256 7318<br>**Apply to:** The Human Resources Manager | Leading City firm with an established reputation for delivering a personal and bespoke service to private & public sector organisations and private clients. | V 4-5[09]<br>T 10<br>P 25<br>TS 170<br>WP no |
| **DEWAR HOGAN**<br>4 Creed Court, 5 Ludgate Hill, London EC4M 7AA<br>**Tel:** 020 7634 9550<br>**Fax:** 020 7634 9551<br>**Email:** info@dewarhogan.co.uk<br>**Apply to:** Mr RD Hogan | Niche practice specialising in property litigation. | V 0<br>T 1<br>P 2<br>TS 6<br>WP no |
| **DEXTER MONTAGUE & PARTNERS**<br>105 Oxford Road, Reading RG1 7UD<br>**Tel:** 0118 939 3999<br>**Fax:** 0118 959 4072<br>**Email:** info@dextermontague.co.uk<br>**Apply to:** Ms Debby Lancefield | Formed in 1987, we are a progressive leading Thames valley practice specialising in property, contract, family, wills, crime, litigation, employment, housing immigration and mental health. | V 1-2[08]<br>T 3<br>P 4<br>TS -<br>WP yes |

**V** = Vacancies / **T** = Trainees / **P** = Partners / **TS** = Total Staff / **WP** = Work Placement

# Dickinson Dees

St Ann's Wharf, 112 Quayside, Newcastle upon Tyne NE99 1SB
**Tel:** 0191 279 9046
**Fax:** 0191 279 9716
**Email:** graduate.recruitment@dickinson-dees.com
**Web:** www.trainingcontract.com

**The firm** Dickinson Dees enjoys an excellent reputation as one of the country's leading commercial law firms. Based in Newcastle upon Tyne, Tees Valley and Yorkshire, we pride ourselves on the breadth of experience and expertise within the firm which enables us to offer services of the highest standards to our clients. While many of our clients are based in the North, we work on a national basis for national and internationally based businesses and organisations.

**Types of work** The firm has over 900 employees and is organised into four key departments with 38 cross-departmental units advising on specific areas. We also handle large volumes of high-quality work for a diverse client base.

**Who should apply** We are looking for intellectually able, motivated and enthusiastic graduates from any discipline with good communication skills. Successful applicants will understand the need to provide practical, commercial advice to clients. They will share our commitment to self-development and teamwork and our desire to provide our clients with services which match their highest expectations.

**Training programme** Our trainees spend six months in four different seats gaining experience in a wide range of work. Trainees sit with their supervisors and have the opportunity to take responsibility and to gain varied 'hands-on' experience within a supportive and well-structured framework.

**When and how to apply** Apply by 31 July 2008 to begin in September 2010. Apply online at www.trainingcontract.com.

**Work placements** Our work placement weeks are part of the recruitment process and all applicants should apply online at www.trainingcontract.com.

Apply by 31 January 2008 for both Easter and Summer placements.

**Sponsorship** Fees for GDL and LPC plus financial assistance.

**Vacancies** 15 (Newcastle)
3 (Tees Valley)
3 (York)

| | |
|---|---|
| Trainees | 30 |
| Partners | 78 |
| Total staff | 920 |

**Work placement** yes

**Apply to**
Sally Brewis, Graduate
Recruitment Adviser

**Starting salary**
£19,500 (2006)

**Minimum qualifications**
2.1 degree

**Sponsorship**
GDL/LPC

**Offices**
Newcastle upon Tyne,
Tees Valley, York, London,
Brussels (associated office)

**DICKINSON DEES**

# DLA Piper UK LLP

Victoria Square House, Victoria Square, Birmingham B2 4DL
**Tel:** 020 7796 6677
**Fax:** 0121 262 5793
**Email:** recruitment.graduate@dlapiper.com
**Web:** www.dlapiper.com

**The firm** DLA Piper is one of the world's largest full service commercial law firms with offices in Birmingham, Edinburgh, Glasgow, Leeds, Liverpool, London, Manchester and Sheffield. We now have more than 7,000 employees working from over 60 offices across Europe, Asia, the Middle East and the US. Our current vision is to be the leading global business law firm. In 2006 *The Lawyer* awarded us 'Global Law Firm of the Year', proving we are moving closer to that vision. Our clients include some of the world's leading businesses, governments, banks and financial institutions. An emphasis on providing high quality service and teamwork, offers a challenging fast paced working environment. DLA Piper offers trainees the opportunity to apply for international secondments to our Dubai, Hong Kong, Moscow and Singapore offices and we also offer a number of client secondments. We also hold the 'Investors in People' accreditation, demonstrating commitment to our employees and their ongoing development.

**Types of work** DLA Piper has the following main areas of work: corporate; employment, pensions & benefits; finance & projects; litigation & regulatory; real estate; and technology, media & commercial.

**Who should apply** DLA Piper will have approximately 95 vacancies for training contracts commencing in 2010. We welcome applications from students with either a law or non-law background who have a minimum of three Bs at A Level (or equivalent) and expect, or have achieved a 2.1 degree classification. As well as a strong academic background, we look for good communicators and team players who, in line with the firm's main focus of work, have a keen interest in the corporate world, and also an appetite for life!

**Training programme** From induction to qualification and beyond, DLA Piper ensures that its employees develop the necessary skills and knowledge to survive in a busy client-driven environment. Trainees complete four six-month seats during the course of their training contract. If you want responsibility, we will give you as much as you can handle and your progress will be monitored through regular reviews and feedback. The compulsory Professional Skills Course is run in-house and is tailored to meet the needs of our trainees. This combined with on-the-job experience, provides trainees with an excellent grounding on which to build their professional careers. We aim to retain as many trainees as possible after qualification, indeed in September 2006 DLA Piper retained the largest number of trainees of any UK law firm.

**When and how to apply** The deadline for receipt of applications for training contracts commencing in September 2010 is 31 July 2008. All applicants should complete the firm's online application form which can be found at www.dlapiper.com. More details and further recruitment information can also be accessed via the website.

**Work placements** The firm operates a formal summer scheme, which runs between June and August each year. The schemes run for two weeks and allow a thorough insight into DLA Piper. There are approximately 200 places available nationwide. Applications should be made via the firm's online application form and the closing date for summer 2008 is 31 January 2008.

**Sponsorship** Full fees plus a maintenance grant of up to £7,000 pa for the GDL and the LPC.

| Vacancies | 95+ |
| Trainees | 184 |
| Partners | 1200 |
| Total staff | 7000+ |

**Work placement** yes
*(see Insider Report on p97)*

**Apply to**
Sally Carthy, Head of Graduate Recruitment

**Starting salary**
London
1st year: £36,000
2nd year: £39,000
English regions
1st year: £25,000
2nd year: £28,000
Scotland
1st year: £22,000
2nd year: £25,000

**Minimum qualifications**
BBB at A level (or equivalent)
2.1 degree, any discipline

**Sponsorship**
GDL/LPC

**Offices**
UK: Birmingham, Edinburgh, Glasgow, Leeds, Liverpool, London, Manchester, Sheffield, International: Austria, Belgium, Bosnia-Herzegovina, Bulgaria, China, Croatia, Czech Republic, France, Georgia, Germany, Hong Kong, Hungary, Italy, Japan, Netherlands, Norway, Russia, Singapore, Slovak Republic, Spain, Thailand, Ukraine, UAE, USA

## DF LEGAL LLP
62/63 High Street, Tewksbury,
Gloucestershire GL20 5BJ
**Tel:** 01684 850 750
**Fax:** 01684 297 717
**Apply to:** Mr JG Daniels

Expanding forward looking private practice with specialisms in interesting areas of work.

| | |
|---|---|
| V | 2 |
| T | 4 |
| P | 3 |
| TS | 24 |
| WP | yes |

## DFA LAW
Beethoven House, 32 Market Square,
Northampton NN1 2DQ
**Tel:** 01604 230700
**Fax:** 01604 230178
**Apply to:** Mr Philip Humphrys

Northampton based general practice. We are a well established firm with a strong client base.

| | |
|---|---|
| V | 0-2[08] |
| T | 1 |
| P | 10 |
| TS | 56 |
| WP | no |

## DICKINSON MANSER
5 Parkstone Road, Poole BH15 2NL
**Tel:** 01202 673071
**Fax:** 01202 680470
**Email:** garycox@dickinsonmanser.co.uk
**Apply to:** Mr Gary Cox

Dickinson Manser is a seven Partner firm with a total headcount of about 80. The firm's focus is on sound private client and commercial work with emphasis on local businesses.

| | |
|---|---|
| V | 2[09] |
| T | 2 |
| P | 7 |
| TS | 80 |
| WP | no |

## DILWYNS
Temple Chambers, South Crescent,
Llandrindod Wells LD1 5DH
**Tel:** 01597 822707
**Fax:** 01597 824085
**Apply to:** Mr Philip Bridger

Dilwyns is based at Llandrindod Wells, Powys with branches in Aberstwyth, Brecon and Liandovery. Predominantly high street/general work as well as rural/agricultural.

| | |
|---|---|
| V | 1 |
| T | 1 |
| P | 3 |
| TS | 20 |
| WP | yes |

## DMA LEGAL LLP
Fourth Floor, 15-16 New Burlington Street,
London W1S 3BJ
**Tel:** 020 7534 5850
**Fax:** 020 7534 5858
**Email:** deborahm@dmalegal.com
**Apply to:** Ms Deborah Mills

A niche commercial firm.

| | |
|---|---|
| V | 1 |
| T | 2 |
| P | 4 |
| TS | 15 |
| WP | no |

## DOLLMAN AND PRITCHARD
8 The Square, Caterham CR3 6XS
**Tel:** 01883 347823
**Fax:** 01883 340628
**Email:** jb@dollman.co.uk
**Apply to:** Mr JAL Burton

General high street practice with LSC franchise in family and crime.

| | |
|---|---|
| V | Poss |
| T | 2 |
| P | 3 |
| TS | 38 |
| WP | no |

## DOLMANS
17-21 Windsor Place, Cardiff CF10 3DS
**Tel:** 029 2034 5531
**Fax:** 029 2039 8206
**Email:** elizabethp@dolmans.co.uk
**Apply to:** Ms Elizabeth Phipps

Specialist public sector and insurance litigation practice. Dynamic growth in business services including corporate finance, commercial, property and employment. Established dispute resolution and private client departments. Applications by CV and covering letter.

| | |
|---|---|
| V | 4 |
| T | 8 |
| P | 14 |
| TS | 106 |
| WP | yes |

## DONALD GALBRAITH & CO
No.3 Archgate Business Centre,
823-825 High Road, North Finchley,
London N12 8UB
**Tel:** 020 8492 2700
**Fax:** 020 8446 2904
**Email:** mtc@dgsols.co.uk
**Apply to:** Ms M T Charles

We are a specialist family and housing firm covering a wide range of private and publicly funded work in both areas.

| | |
|---|---|
| V | 0 |
| T | 0 |
| P | - |
| TS | 14 |
| WP | no |

# DMH Stallard

100 Queen's Road, Brighton BN1 3YB
**Tel:** 01273 744270
**Fax:** 01273 744290
**Email:** recruitment@dmhstallard.com
**Web:** www.dmhstallard.com

**The firm** DMH Stallard is an approachable and innovative top 100 law firm with an open culture which encourages personal development and provides its personnel with a high level of support in order to achieve this. The firm offers expertise to a range of commercial organisations, non-profit institutions and individual clients. By focusing on the client's needs, DMH Stallard provides practical and creative solutions. DMH Stallard operates from offices in Brighton, Gatwick and London.

**Types of work** Corporate/commercial; commercial property; construction; planning and environmental; employment; intellectual property/IT; dispute resolution; real estate asset management; personal injury; private client.

**Who should apply** We welcome applications from motivated graduates from all backgrounds and age groups. Enthusiasm and commercial awareness are as prized as academic ability, and good communication skills are a must. Ideal applicants are those with the potential to become effective managers or strong marketeers.

**Training programme** Usually four six-month seats taken from the following areas: employment; corporate/commercial; dispute resolution; technology and media; construction; public law; real estate dispute resolution; real estate asset management; environmental; commercial property; personal injury and private client. Trainees are closely supervised but have every opportunity to work as part of a team and deal directly with clients.

**When and how to apply** Apply by 31 July 2008 to begin in 2010 by online application form.

**Work placements** One-week unpaid summer placements.

**Sponsorship** LPC: 50% funded; 50% loan. Bonus payment for those who have already paid for their LPC.

| | |
|---|---|
| Vacancies | 10 |
| Trainees | 19 |
| Partners | 52 |
| Total staff | 350 |

**Work placement**  yes

**Apply to**
Miss Jessica Leigh-Davis

**Starting salary**
Brighton, Gatwick - £22,000
London - £27,000
(2007)

**Minimum qualifications**
2.1 degree preferred

**Sponsorship**
LPC

**Offices**
Brighton, Gatwick, London

■ DMH Stallard

# Dorsey & Whitney

21 Wilson Street, London EC2M 2TD
**Tel:** 020 7588 0800
**Fax:** 020 7588 0555
**Web:** www.dorsey.com

**The firm** Dorsey & Whitney is among the largest law firms in the world. With 21 offices strategically located over three continents and over 640 lawyers and 700 support staff worldwide, Dorsey & Whitney is continuing to build on its traditional core strengths in corporate, M&A, intellectual property and litigation through its wide range of practice groups.

Dorsey & Whitney understands that clients' needs are seldom confined to strict categories and that major transactions and disputes often require advice that spans practices. Focusing on clients' many needs is one of the reasons Dorsey is among the best in the business.

**Types of work** The London office offers the full range of legal services including corporate finance, international capital markets, domestic and cross border M&A, private equity, commercial litigation, tax, employment, real estate and intellectual property.

**Who should apply** Dorsey & Whitney is looking for 'self starters', capable of meeting the intellectual and business challenges of a successful global practice. Candidates should be committed team players, who enjoy significant 'first chair' experience and rewarding client work. An honours degree at 2.1 level or above is required and some relevant experience is highly encouraged.

**Training programme** The training contract is split into four individual 'seats' of six months each. Each trainee will be required to complete litigation and corporate seats. Secondments to major clients are also available. All trainees are provided with the encouragement and support necessary to maximize their potential. Trainees will receive significant 'first chair' experience. Through the mentoring and professional development and evaluation programmes, the firm strives to develop and retain the highest calibre lawyers. Dorsey & Whitney deliberately takes a small number of candidates each year, so that they receive the very best training.

**When and how to apply** Closing date is 31 July 2008 to begin 2010. Applications should be by letter plus current curriculum vitae addressed to Mitchell Moss.

**Sponsorship** £7,000 'sign on' bonus payable on commencement of training contract, as a contribution towards LPC fees.

| | |
|---|---|
| Vacancies | 4 |
| Trainees | 8 |
| Partners | 14 |
| Total staff | 75 |

**Work placement** no

**Apply to**
Mitchell Moss

**Starting salary**
1st year - £35,000
2nd year - £39,000

**Minimum qualifications**
2.1 degree

**Sponsorship**
LPC

**Offices**

**USA:** Anchorage, Denver, Des Moines, Fargo, Great Falls, Minneapolis, Missoula, New York, Palo Alto, Salt Lake City, San Francisco, Seattle, Southern California, Washington DC, Delaware

**Canada:** Toronto, Vancouver

**Europe:** London, Cambridge

**Asia:** Hong Kong, Shanghai

( )) DORSEY
DORSEY & WHITNEY
A Multinational Partnership

| | | |
|---|---|---|
| **DONALD RACE & NEWTON**<br>4 Nicholas Street, Burnley BB11 2AG<br>**Tel:** 01282 864500<br>**Fax:** 01282 831720<br>**Apply to:** Mr Paul Mayson | Burnley based – three office general practice specialising in crime, family and personal injury with commercial and domestic conveyancing. LSC contract. Please note that we do not currently have any vacancies. | V  0<br>T  2<br>P  6<br>TS  47<br>WP yes |
| **DONNELLY ADAMSON**<br>155-157 York Road, Hartlepool TS26 9EQ<br>**Tel:** 01429 274732<br>**Fax:** 01429 260199<br>**Apply to:** Mr Malcolm Donnelly | The firm offers a friendly yet challenging environment. Career development is taken seriously. Donnelly Adamson sets high standards wihin the profession and expects nothing less. | V  0<br>T  0<br>P  5<br>TS  34<br>WP no |
| **DOUGLAS & PARTNERS**<br>116 Grosvenor Road, St Pauls, Bristol BS2 8YA<br>**Tel:** 0117 955 2663<br>**Fax:** 0117 954 0527<br>**Apply to:** Mr David Fanson | Long established firm specialising in mental health and criminal defence work. | V  0-2[09]<br>T  3<br>P  4<br>TS  26<br>WP no |
| **DOUGLAS PIDSLEY & ROBERTS**<br>22 Union Street, Newton Abbot, Devon TQ12 2JT<br>**Tel:** 01626 334 455<br>**Fax:** 01626 362 588<br>**Apply to:** Mr WM Douglas | General High Street practice undertaking wills, trusts, probate, family work, civil litigation, residential and commercial property. | V  1<br>T  1<br>P  2<br>TS  15<br>WP no |
| **DOUGLAS-JONES MERCER**<br>147 St Helens Road, Swansea SA1 4DB<br>**Tel:** 01792 650000<br>**Fax:** 01792 656500<br>**Apply to:** Mr Del Cudd | South Wales general practice dealing with private client, legal aid work and growing commercial department. Offices in Swansea. Clients vary from large companies to private individuals. | V  2[09]<br>T  5<br>P  12<br>TS  83<br>WP no |
| **DOVER DISTRICT COUNCIL**<br>White Cliffs Business Park, Dover, Kent. CT16 3PJ<br>**Tel:** 01304 872321<br>**Fax:** 01304 872325<br>**Email:** legal@dover.gov.uk<br>**Apply to:** Mr Harvey Rudd | Dover District Council, Legal Division. | V  0<br>T  0<br>P  -<br>TS  9<br>WP no |
| **DRUCES & ATTLEE**<br>Salisbury House, London Wall, London EC2M 5PS<br>**Tel:** 020 7638 9271<br>**Fax:** 020 7628 7525<br>**Email:** info@druces.com<br>**Apply to:** Mr Richard E Monkcom | Broadly based City practice dealing principally in institutional property, financial services, general corporate, employment, pubs and hotels, charities and private capital. | V  1<br>T  4<br>P  16<br>TS  68<br>WP yes |
| **DRUMMONDS**<br>Windsor House, Pepper Street, Chester CH1 1DF<br>**Tel:** 01244 408300<br>**Fax:** 01244 408310<br>**Email:** enquiries@drummonds-solicitors.co.uk<br>**Apply to:** Ms Elisabeth Bellamy | A forward-thinking solicitors firm specialising in conveyancing but also covering other areas. | V  1[09]<br>T  1<br>P  3<br>TS  38<br>WP no |

**V** = Vacancies / **T** = Trainees / **P** = Partners / **TS** = Total Staff / **WP** = Work Placement

# Dundas & Wilson LLP

Northwest Wing, Bush House, Aldwych, London WC2B 4EZ
**Tel:** 020 7240 2401
**Fax:** 020 7240 2448
**Email:** lorraine.bale@dundas-wilson.com
**Web:** www.dundas-wilson.com

**The firm** Dundas & Wilson (D&W) is a leading UK commercial law firm with offices in London, Edinburgh and Glasgow. Our strategy is to offer clients an integrated UK capability across our key practice areas and we are continually expanding our London capabilities to further support this.

**Types of work** Banking & financial services, construction & engineering, corporate, corporate recovery, dispute resolution, environment, employment, EU & competition, IP/IT, pensions, planning & transportation, projects, property and tax.

The firm services a wide range of prestigious clients, including major commercial companies and public sector organisations, throughout the UK and abroad.

**Who should apply** D&W wants applicants with enthusiasm, commitment, adaptability, strong written and oral communication skills, excellent interpersonal skills and an aptitude for problem solving and analysis.

**Training programme** The two year traineeship is split into four six month seats. The firm aims to accommodate trainees' preferences when allocating seats as we want to encourage them to take an active part in managing their career development.

During the traineeship trainees receive on-the-job training, two day seat training at the beginning of each seat and training in core skills such as drafting and effective legal writing. Trainees receive a formal performance review every three months and are allocated a mentor for each seat.

The firm's open plan environment means that trainees sit amongst assistants, associates and partners – this provides daily opportunities to observe how lawyers communicate both with clients and each other. This type of learning is invaluable and great preparation for life as a fully fledged lawyer.

**When and how to apply** Apply between February 2008 and July 2008 to begin in 2009 by completing our online application form

**Work placement** We offer four-week summer placements. To apply, please visit our website and complete our online application form. The closing date is 26 January 2008.

**Sponsorship** Full fees for the GDL/CPE and the LPC plus a maintenance grant.

| | |
|---|---|
| Vacancies | 30 |
| Trainees | 50 |
| Partners | 83 |
| Total staff | 599 |

Work placement    yes

Apply to
Ms Lorraine Bale

Starting salary
£30,000

Sponsorship
GDL/LPC

Offices
London, Edinburgh,
Glasgow

# D&W

## DUNDAS & WILSON

# DWF

Centurion House, 129 Deansgate, Manchester M3 3AA
**Tel:** 0161 603 5000
**Fax:** 0161 603 5050
**Email:** trainees@dwf.co.uk
**Web:** www.dwf.co.uk

**The firm** DWF is a leading regional firm with national and international reach. We provide a full range of legal services to businesses and individuals in the corporate market and our client base ranges from privately owned entrepreneurial companies to large multi-national organizations. Following our merger with Ricksons in January 2007, we employ around 800 people, including over 100 Partners across the North of England.

We are able to serve clients across the UK from our offices in Leeds, Liverpool, Manchester and Preston and through our network of relationships with law firms around the world, we are able to extend this service internationally. Our business continues to expand, through a combination of organic growth, lateral hires and other consolidation activity.

**Types of work** DWF provide a full range of legal services covering: corporate, real estate, banking & finance, litigation, insurance, business recovery, people and private client. A full list of services available within these areas can be found on our website at www.dwf.co.uk.

DWF also provides legal services across a range of different industries and sectors, and has developed particular expertise in a number of specific areas. To enable our clients to benefit from this expertise, we have developed a series of sector-focussed teams – Automotive, Education, Food and Resourcing.

**Who should apply** Our future depends on recruiting and retaining the right people. At DWF we only recruit people of the highest quality whether they be lawyers or non-lawyers. DWF is always on the look out for ambitious and driven professionals who are able to add value to our developing team. DWF wants its trainee solicitors to play a part in building on its success. The firm is looking for trainees who enjoy working as part of a busy team, respond positively to a challenge and have what it takes to deliver results for clients. The firm is looking for its partners of the future and in recent years virtually all of its qualifying trainees have been offered jobs. DWF is an equal opportunities employer and is committed to diversity in all aspects.

**Training programme** DWF provides a well structured training programme for all new trainee solicitors which combines the day to day practical experience of working with a partner, associate or senior solicitor, backed by a comprehensive in-house lecture and workshop programme and the PSC course. You will very quickly become a vital member of our team, being delegated the appropriate level of responsibility from an early stage in your training. Full supervision is provided and it is our policy for each trainee to sit with a partner or associate, whilst working for a legal team as a whole. The two year training contract is divided into "seats". These will be spent in the firm's main departments (corporate, insurance litigation, commercial property, commercial litigation and HRhorizons) which gives opportunities to look at specialist areas of work within each department.

**When and how to apply** Applications via our online system www.dwf.co.uk Closing date 31st July 2008 to begin 2009/2010.

**Work placements** Paid summer vacation placement lasting one week.

**Sponsorship** Funding for LPC tuition fees.

| | |
|---|---|
| Vacancies | 20 |
| Trainees | 30 |
| Partners | 119 |
| Total staff | 800+ |

**Work placement** yes

**Apply**
Online

**Starting salary**
£23,000 (2007)

**Minimum qualifications**
2.1 degree in any subject preferred

**Sponsorship**
LPC

**Offices**
Leeds, Liverpool, Manchester, Preston

| | | | |
|---|---|---|---|
| **DRYSDALES**<br>Cumberland House, 24-28 Baxter Avenue,<br>Southend-on-Sea SS2 6HZ<br>**Tel:** 01702 423 400<br>**Fax:** 01702 423 409<br>**Apply to:** Mr AD Murrell | | V<br>T<br>P<br>TS<br>WP | 1[09]<br>1<br>2<br>18<br>no |
| **DUNCAN LEWIS & CO**<br>1 Kingsland High Street, London E8 2JS<br>**Tel:** 020 7923 4020<br>**Fax:** 020 7923 3320<br>**Email:** recruitment@duncanlewis.com<br>**Apply to:** Noemi Ares-Birch | Specialises in community care, conveyancing, crime, debt, employment, family/child care, housing, immigration, mental health, public law, welfare benefits and wills/probate. Only internal candidates considered. | V<br>T<br>P<br>TS<br>WP | 8<br>22<br>15<br>200<br>yes |
| **EAST HAMPSHIRE DISTRICT COUNCIL**<br>Council Offices, Penns Place, Petersfield,<br>Hampshire GU31 4EX<br>**Tel:** 01730 234 069<br>**Fax:** 01730 233935<br>**Email:** tracy.beavis@easthamp.gov.uk<br>**Apply to:** Mr Nick Leach | Legal services department within a local authority providing a wide range of services to the council, councillors and officers. | V<br>T<br>P<br>TS<br>WP | 0<br>1<br>-<br>7<br>no |
| **EATON SMITH LLP**<br>14 High Street, Huddersfield HD1 2HA<br>**Tel:** 01484 821300<br>**Fax:** 01484 821333<br>**Email:** mail@eatonsmith.co.uk<br>**Apply to:** Mrs Janet Hogg | Office at 14 High Street, Huddersfield. We provide a complete service to both the commercial and private client. | V<br>T<br>P<br>TS<br>WP | 0<br>2<br>14<br>100<br>no |
| **EDEN & COMPANY**<br>38 Trafalgar Road, Kettering,<br>Northamptonshire NN16 8DA<br>**Tel:** 01536 311690<br>**Fax:** 01536 511336<br>**Apply to:** Mr Robert Eden | A small friendly firm. We are a general practice with the emphasis on private and commercial conveyancing, civil litigation and matrimonial work. Local applicant preferred. | V<br>T<br>P<br>TS<br>WP | 1<br>1<br>2<br>12<br>yes |
| **EDMONDSON HALL**<br>25 Exeter Road, Newmarket CB8 8AR<br>**Tel:** 01638 560556<br>**Fax:** 01638 561656<br>**Email:** solicitors@edmondsonhall.com<br>**Apply to:** Mr Mark Edmondson | Leading niche bloodstock practice. Equine litigation. Vet negligence, sale and purchase disputes etc. Award winning sports lawyers. Friendly but forward thinking. Smart offices. Partners recognised specialists. | V<br>T<br>P<br>TS<br>WP | 0<br>0<br>2<br>17<br>yes |
| **EDWARD DE SILVA & CO**<br>First Floor 54 The Broadway, Southall,<br>Middlesex UB1 1QB<br>**Tel:** 020 8571 2299<br>**Fax:** 020 8893 6287<br>**Email:** edslawyer@tiscali.co.uk<br>**Apply to:** Ms Nancy de Silva | General practice dealing with private and legal aid work. Long established in Southall. | V<br>T<br>P<br>TS<br>WP | 1<br>2<br>1<br>10<br>yes |
| **EDWARDS DUTHIE**<br>9-15 York Road, Ilford IG1 3AD<br>**Tel:** 020 8514 9000<br>**Fax:** 020 8514 9009<br>**Email:** allinfo@edwardsduthie.com<br>**Apply to:** HR Department | A substantial, diverse practice with particular expertise in personal injury, crime and property. Six offices across East London and Essex. Legal aid franchises in all areas. | V<br>T<br>P<br>TS<br>WP | 6[09]<br>15<br>20<br>200<br>no |

# EDF Energy

40 Grosvenor Place, Victoria, London SW1X 7AW
**Tel:** 020 7242 9050
**Email:** graduateenquiries@edfenergy.com
**Web:** www.edfenergy.com/graduates

**The firm** EDF Energy is one of the UK's largest energy companies. We're involved in every part of the energy cycle – from the moment it's harnessed through to the second our customers use it. As part of EDF Group, one of the two biggest energy groups in Europe, we have links with other key businesses in France, Germany and Italy.

EDF Energy is involved in important, bigger picture issues. This is a complicated and ever-evolving industry, and a specialised regulatory environment. And, in the future, there will be many challenges to face – not least of which are the unpredictable effects of climate change.

As a trainee solicitor here, your insightful advice and creative thinking will be crucial in developing our solutions. We won't see you as a 'support function' as many law firms do: we will have the confidence in you to put you in front of clients, and challenge you with big issues. Being involved in the thick of a major business will give you a commercial insight few other trainees will benefit from. What's more, you'll also enjoy an excellent work/life balance.

**Types of work** With the exception of very specialist areas such as tax and pensions, our legal teams offer advice on all areas of law. Your training, therefore, will take the form of four or five rotations around various business areas – customers, networks, energy, litigation and corporate – during which you'll gain practical experience in at least three distinct areas of law, covering both contentious and non-contentious work.

Day-to-day, you'll work on a mixture of projects and cases, from employment, acquisitions, litigation, contracts and restructuring through to large projects – such as sponsorship of Rugby or the 2012 Olympic Games – and major contracts with customers such as Canary Wharf, international airports and the Channel Tunnel. You'll also work with clients and attend high-level meetings very early on in your career.

Because you'll rotate throughout our various departments, you can expect to be based in London, Hove, and Crawley.

**Who should apply** You'll need a 2.1 degree in any discipline (if you're outstanding, we'll consider a 2.2), and to have successfully completed the Legal Practice Course by September 2009 or 2010. Beyond that, we're after bright, enthusiastic and well-rounded people.

**Training programme** You will receive the variety and quality of training you need to become a fully qualified solicitor. You'll be supervised and supported by your Training Principal and other qualified solicitors and receive continuous feedback throughout the two years of your training contract. We'll also support your Professional Skills Course studies. Alongside your legal training, you'll additionally benefit from our eighteen-month graduate development programme, which will boost your business, presentation, team building and management skills. Training you are unlikely to receive elsewhere.

**When and how to apply** We're looking for people to begin in September 2009 and 2010: applications will close 31 December 2007. You can find more information and an online application form at www.edfenergy.com/graduates.

| | |
|---|---|
| Vacancies | 2 (2009) |
| | 2 (2010) |
| Trainees | 2 |
| Total staff | 43 |
| Work placement | no |
| Apply | Online |
| Starting salary | £29,500 (2007) |
| Minimum qualifications | 2.1 degree |
| Offices | London, Hove, Crawley |

# Elborne Mitchell

One America Square, Crosswall, London EC3N 2PR
**Tel:** 020 7320 9000
**Fax:** 020 7320 9111
**Email:** lawyers@elbornes.com
**Web:** www.elbornes.com

**The firm** Elborne Mitchell was established in 1968 and is recognised as a high-profile law firm in the insurance, marine and commercial sectors. The firm regards itself as a small firm doing big firm work, and has always positively structured itself as the antithesis of the 'factory' environment of many of the larger City firms. The firm adopts an eclectic approach to its practice and similarly to its recruitment philosophy. The firm takes on cases of the highest quality and complexity while offering exceptional standards of care tailored to the needs of each client.

**Types of work** We have played a key role in many of the cases which have made headlines within the insurance and marine sectors. Principal areas of work are insurance, reinsurance, marine, corporate, employment, regulatory, insolvency and commercial litigation.

**Who should apply** We aim to recruit motivated, imaginative, personable and adaptable trainees of different backgrounds and experience. Excellent communication skills are essential and previous commercial involvement is welcomed.

**Training programme** A brief induction course acquaints trainees with the firm's IT network, library and administration procedures. Trainees generally spend eight months in three different practice groups within the firm, although individual preferences and talents are accommodated wherever possible. Trainees are encouraged to take an active role in the work of their practice group and work with partners, and will quickly become closely involved with all aspects of the work undertaken by their particular group. Practical training will be complemented by a programme of in-house lectures and external seminars.

**When and how to apply** To apply, contact our HR department or visit our website for an application form and further information.

| | |
|---|---|
| Vacancies | 2 |
| Trainees | 4 |
| Partners | 12 |
| Total staff | 41 |

**Apply to**
Ms Victoria Hinds,
HR Officer

**Minimum qualifications**
2.1 degree preferred

**Offices**
London

## Elborne Mitchell
### SOLICITORS

# emw law LLP

Seebeck House, One Seebeck Place, Knowlhill, Milton Keynes MK5 8FR
**Tel:** 0845 070 6000
**Fax:** 0845 074 2420
**Email:** emw@emwlaw.com
**Web:** www.emwlaw.com

**The firm** emw law is a progressive and well-established commercial firm. We have rapidly gained recognition as one of the leading law firms in our region offering niche legal services not only regionally but beyond. Our philosophy is to deliver the best possible results for our clients in an informal, no-nonsense manner.

We work with our clients to provide solutions, which often involves drawing on expertise from a number of specialist areas within the firm. From these we put together a tailor-made team that will ensure we achieve the best possible results.

We are also very conscious about the future and are constantly responding to the changing needs of the commercial world by renewing and developing our services. This not only benefits our clients but creates opportunities for our existing staff and new recruits. We are not a firm that stands still.

**Types of work** Corporate finance, technology and commerce, employment, property planning and construction, property finance and dispute resolution.

**Who should apply** Candidates with a thirst for knowledge and strong academic qualifications, having achieved a minimum 2.1 degree, should apply. We recruit both law and non-law graduates from a wide range of universities.

**Training programme** We actively promote a friendly, informal, supportive, practical, efficient and businesslike approach to your training by offering a comprehensive induction training programme, quarterly trainee seminars and a detailed appraisal at the end of each six-month seat.

We aim to give all trainees the best commercial grounding by giving them the opportunity to complete their training contract by way of six-month seats within corporate finance and property planning and construction, with the third and fourth seat allocations to be decided during the training contract in two of our remaining practice areas. Trainees are given the opportunity to take on responsibility and be involved in a wide range of legal work. We pride ourselves on our 'open door' policy and encourage coaching and mentoring throughout the training contract.

**When and how to apply** To apply, please visit www.emwlaw.com and follow the recruitment process.

**Work placements** Not currently offered.

| Vacancies | 3 |
| Trainees | 6 |
| Partners | 19 |
| Total staff | 130 |

**Apply to**
Mrs Cynthia Sullivan

**Starting salary**
At least £20,000

**Minimum qualifications**
2.1 degree

**Offices**
Milton Keynes

*an original law firm*

# emw law

emw law llp is a limited liability partnership

| | | | |
|---|---|---|---|
| **EDWIN COE LLP**<br>2 Stone Buildings, Lincoln's Inn,<br>London WC2A 3TH<br>**Tel:** 020 7691 4000<br>**Fax:** 020 7691 4111<br>**Email:** recruitment@edwincoe.com<br>**Apply to:** Mrs Dannii Portsmouth by CV and covering letter | Edwin Coe LLP has expertise in all mainstream areas of commercial legal practice, acting for a worldwide client-base involved in a broad spectrum of business activity. | V 5<br>T 8<br>P 25<br>TS 100<br>WP yes |
| **ELLIOTT BRIDGMAN**<br>10 Court Street, Madeley, Telford TF7 5EB<br>**Tel:** 01952 684544<br>**Fax:** 01952 684559<br>**Email:** info@elliottbridgman.com<br>**Apply to:** Mrs J C Foulkes | Franchised legal aid firm principally concentrating on family, crime and mental health law. | V Poss 1[09]<br>T 1<br>P 1<br>TS 20<br>WP yes |
| **ELLIS JONES**<br>Sandbourne House, 302 Charminster Road,<br>Bournemouth BH8 9RU<br>**Tel:** 01202 525333<br>**Fax:** 01202 535935<br>**Apply to:** Mr Nigel Smith | Progressive and expanding partnership in the south of England. Specialisms include residential and commercial property, company commercial, personal injury, private client, family and civil litigation. | V 2[09]<br>T 3<br>P 11<br>TS 125<br>WP no |
| **EMERY JOHNSON SOLICITORS**<br>3 & 5 Welford Road, Leicester LE2 7AD<br>**Tel:** 0116 2554855<br>**Fax:** 0116 255 5044<br>**Email:** legal@emeryjohnson.com<br>**Apply to:** Miss Jacqui Callan | Niche practice with in Leicester specialising in criminal, family and childcare law. Young, dynamic team committed to providing a quality service to clients. | V 2<br>T 2<br>P 2<br>TS 24<br>WP yes |
| **EMSLEYS**<br>Viscount Court, Leeds Road, Rothwell,<br>Leeds LS26 0GR<br>**Tel:** 0113 201 4900<br>**Fax:** 0113 201 4901<br>**Apply to:** Mrs Corinne Pujara | A seven partner general practice firm with specialised claimant personal injury and commercial property departments and with an estate agency in6 high street locations. | V 2[09]<br>T 4<br>P 7<br>TS 145<br>WP no |
| **THE ENDEAVOUR PARTNERSHIP LLP**<br>Westminster, St Mark's Court, Teesdale Business Park, Stockton on Tees TS17 6QP<br>**Tel:** 01642 610300<br>**Fax:** 01642 610348<br>**Email:** s.wake@endeavourpartnership.com<br>**Apply to:** Simon Wake | Niche commercial firm based on Teesside with a wide variety of commercial clients. Nominated LawCareers.Net for Best Recruiter 2006 and 2007. | V 2<br>T 4<br>P 9<br>TS 43<br>WP yes |
| **ENOCH EVANS**<br>St Pauls Chambers, 6-9 Hatherton Road,<br>Walsall WS1 1XS<br>**Tel:** 01922 720333<br>**Fax:** 01922 720623<br>**Apply to:** Mrs Susan Comrie | A modern practice serving an extensive cross section of both commercial and private clients, Enoch Evans has specialist departments covering a wide range of legal services. | V 0<br>T 2<br>P 10<br>TS 70<br>WP no |
| **ENVIRONMENT AGENCY**<br>Block 1 Government Buildings, Burghill Road,<br>Westbury-on-Trym, Bristol BS10 6BF<br>**Tel:** 0117 915 6203/6204<br>**Fax:** 0117 915 6220<br>**Email:** anne.silvester@environment-agency.gov.uk<br>**Apply to:** Mrs Anne Silvester | Public body and main environmental regulator. HO in Bristol, 7 regions in England and EA Wales. Regional legal departments deal with prosecution and advisory work. | V 0<br>T 1<br>P 1<br>TS 150<br>WP no |

# Eversheds LLP

Senator House, 85 Queen Victoria Street, London EC4V 4JL
**Tel:** 0845 497 9797
**Fax:** 0845 497 4919
**Email:** gradrec@eversheds.com
**Web:** www.eversheds.com

**The firm** Eversheds LLP is one of the largest full service international law firms in the world with over 4,000 people and 32 offices in major cities across the UK, Europe and Asia. We work for some of the world's most prestigious organisations in both the public and private sector, offering them a compelling mixture of straightforward advice, clear direction, predictable costs and outstanding service. It's a winning combination that has meant we are now expanding quicker than any of our closest competitors. We act for 111 listed companies including 43 FTSE 250 companies, 30 of the 37 British based Fortune 500 companies and now have one of the fastest growing corporate teams in the City. In 2006 we laid out strategic plan that will see us build on these achievements and grow over the next few years into a major player on the legal stage around the World. We are looking for highly ambitious and focussed trainees to help us achieve our goals.

**Types of work** Corporate, commercial, litigation, real estate, human resources (employment and pensions) and legal systems group.
Sectors: central government, local government, education, energy, financial services, food, health, retail and telecoms.

In addition to these core and sector areas each office provides further expertise in the following areas: corporate tax, finance, intellectual property, information technology, media, risk management, environment/health and safety, EU/competition and trade, franchising, insolvency, claims management, construction, insurance, regulatory, shipping, licensing, PFI, planning and more.

**Who should apply** Eversheds people are valued for their drive and legal expertise but also for their business advice too. We develop the same qualities in our trainees. As a trainee you'll be given as much responsibility as you can handle and will benefit from our hands on philosophy. We take learning and development very seriously and will look to help you build the career you want.

**Training programme** We offer a full, well-rounded training programme with the opportunity to focus your technical skills in each of the various practice groups as you rotate through four six-month seats. You will also take part in a full programme of personal and commercial development skills training, including finance and business, communication, presenting, business writing, client care, professional standards and advocacy.

**When and how to apply** For training contracts beginning in September 2010, you'll need to apply by the end of July 2008. Apply online at www.eversheds.com.

**Work placements** Places for Summer and Easter 2008: 150. Duration: one-two weeks. Remuneration: London £240, regions £175. The deadline for applications is 31 January 2008. Apply online at www.eversheds.com.

**Sponsorship** GDL and LPC fees and maintenance granted in accordance with our policy.

| | |
|---|---|
| **Vacancies** | 80+ |
| **Trainees** | 160+ |
| **Partners** | 340+ |
| **Total staff** | 4000+ |

**Work placement** yes
*(see Insider Report on p99)*

**Apply**
Online at
www.eversheds.com

**Starting salary**
1st year: £35,000
2nd year: £37,000
(London 2007)

**Minimum qualifications**
2.1 degree

**Sponsorship**
GDL/LPC

**Offices**
Barcelona*, Birmingham, Brussels, Budapest*, Cambridge, Cardiff, Copenhagen, Doha**, Dublin*, Ipswich, Kuala Lumpur*, Leeds, London, Madrid*, Manchester, Milan*, Munich*, Newcastle, Norwich, Nottingham, Paris, Riga, Rome*, Shanghai, Sofia*, Stockholm*, Tallinn*, Valladolid*, Vienna*, Vilnius*, Warsaw*, Wroclaw*
*Associated office
**In cooperation

 EVERSHEDS

# Faegre & Benson LLP

7 Pilgrim Street, London EC4V 6LB
**Tel:** 020 7450 4500
**Fax:** 020 7450 4545
**Email:** recruitment@faegre.com
**Web:** www.faegre.co.uk

**The firm** Faegre & Benson LLP is an international law firm which offers an integrated team of 500 lawyers in the USA, Europe and Asia. We have been well known in the UK business community for two decades, serving the full range of English business law needs for domestic and multinational clients. In London, we have 30 lawyers and a total staff of 55.

**Types of work** Our focus in London is on legal solutions for business clients.

Corporate: includes mergers and acquisitions, takeovers, management buy-outs, joint ventures, private equity, flotations (IPOs), fundraisings and corporate reconstructions. We have particular expertise in advising on AIM listings.

Business litigation: general commercial litigation with a growing emphasis on mediation and arbitration (much of which is international).

IP and commercial: a wide range of contentious and non-contentious commercial and IP matters for a diverse client base in the high technology, computing, multimedia, publishing, telecommunications and e-commerce fields. Our expertise also covers franchising and outsourcing.

Employment: advice on a broad range of employment issues from recruitment to dismissal and also on employers' duties on business sales and reorganisations, share option and incentive plans, and termination issues such as redundancy, unfair and wrongful dismissal and restrictive covenants.

Real estate: advice on all aspects of property investments and management, development and finance, as well as corporate real estate issues. The group is supported by a specialist property litigation unit.

**Who should apply** We are looking for motivated people not only with strong academics, but who are also team players with good all-round ability, common sense and ambition. In addition, strong communication skills and an appreciation of our clients' commercial interests are essential.

**Training programme** The London office is split into five main practice groups. We offer training in at least four of those groups, with trainees spending a minimum of three and a maximum of nine months in a particular group. Every effort is made to accommodate a trainee's preference for a particular type of work. Trainees are assigned to a partner or senior associate in each group, although you will assist a number of partners or solicitors within any group. This provides a good breadth of experience and you will quickly become integrated within the firm. Our aim is for trainees to be one of the team and to have responsibility (subject to appropriate supervision) at an early stage. We provide in-house lectures and training, and trainees are encouraged to attend outside lectures and courses where appropriate. Appraisals are undertaken every three months.

**When and how to apply** Online application form available at www.faegre.com. Your application should be received by 31 July two years before the commencement of the training contract. Interviews take place during September each year.

**Work placements** There are a limited number of places available each year. You should apply using our online application form by 31 March 2008.

**Sponsorship** LPC/GDL fees and a maintenance grant.

| | |
|---|---|
| Vacancies | 2 |
| Trainees | 4 |
| Partners | 12 |
| Total staff | 55 |

**Apply to**
Online

**Starting salary**
£29,500 (September 2007)

**Minimum qualifications**
2.1 degree

**Sponsorship**
GDL/LPC

**Offices**
London, USA, Germany, China

FAEGRE
&
BENSON
LLP

| **ERIC ROBINSON SOLICITORS**<br>Queens Keep, 1-4 Cumberland Place,<br>Southampton SO15 2YB<br>**Tel:** 02380 226891<br>**Fax:** 02380 220699<br>**Apply to:** Mrs Allison Hampshire | Six offices in Southampton region.<br>General practice including legal aid,<br>probate, large matrimonial, crime,<br>personal injury and property.<br>Developing commercial department. | V 1[09]<br>T 4<br>P 8<br>TS 140<br>WP no |
|---|---|---|
| **ESSEX COUNTY COUNCIL**<br>Legal Services Division, County Hall, PO Box 11,<br>Market Road, Chelmsford CM1 1LX<br>**Tel:** 0207 759 00 00<br>**Fax:** 01245 346 994<br>**Apply to:** The Recruitment Contact | Local Authority wide-ranging practice<br>including child care, employment,<br>prosecutions, land, commercial,<br>insurance and civil litigation. 'The<br>Lawyer' Public Sector Team of the<br>Year, 2002. | V 0<br>T 0<br>P 0<br>TS 105<br>WP no |
| **EVERATTS SOLICITORS**<br>6 Churchill Court, 58 Station Road, North Harrow,<br>Middlesex HA2 7SA<br>**Tel:** 020 8424 0088<br>**Fax:** 020 8424 0454<br>**Email:** mail@everatts.co.uk<br>**Apply to:** Mr Shilan N Shah | Small well established general<br>practice with commercial and<br>litigation bias, no legal aid work. | V 1<br>T 1<br>P 2<br>TS 10<br>WP no |
| **EVERSLEYS**<br>363 Liverpool Road, London N1 1NL<br>**Tel:** 020 7607 0001<br>**Fax:** 020 7700 5999<br>**Apply to:** Mr Stuart Appleman | Commercial property, general<br>commercial and commercial<br>litigation. | V 2<br>T 1<br>P 2<br>TS 6<br>WP no |
| **EVERYS**<br>The Laurels, 46 New Street, Honiton EX14 1BY<br>**Tel:** 01404 43431<br>**Fax:** 01404 45493<br>**Email:** law@everys.co.uk<br>**Apply to:** Miss Kerry Stanmore | Progressive, well established practice<br>with offices in Exeter, Honiton,<br>Exmouth, Ottery St Mary, Sidmouth,<br>Seaton, Budleigh Salterton, Taunton. | V 0<br>T 3<br>P 23<br>TS 170<br>WP no |
| **EWINGS & CO**<br>148 High Street, London SE20 7EU<br>**Tel:** 020 8778 1126<br>**Fax:** 020 8676 9662<br>**Email:** enquiry@ewings.uk.com<br>**Apply to:** Mr PI Ewings | General high street practice centrally<br>located. Committed to expansion of<br>its private and publicly funded work.<br>Franchise holders in crime and<br>family. | V Varies[08]<br>T 1<br>P 3<br>TS 25<br>WP no |
| **EXPRESS SOLICITORS**<br>Resolution House, 319 Palatine Road, Northenden,<br>Manchester M22 4HH<br>**Tel:** 0845 4564007<br>**Fax:** 0161 945 2266<br>**Email:** advice@expresssolicitors.com<br>**Apply to:** Mr James Maxey | Young and expanding quality. Mainly<br>personal injury practice. PI panel<br>members and APIL Corporate<br>Accreditation | V 2<br>T 4<br>P 2<br>TS 30<br>WP yes |
| **FANCY & JACKSON**<br>Midland Bank Chambers, 19 High Street, Staines,<br>Middlesex TW18 4QH<br>**Tel:** 01784 462511<br>**Fax:** 01784 456592<br>**Email:** apj@fancyandjackson.co.uk<br>**Apply to:** Mr APC Jackson | | V 1<br>T 2<br>P 4<br>TS 21<br>WP no |

**V** = Vacancies / **T** = Trainees / **P** = Partners / **TS** = Total Staff / **WP** = Work Placement

# Farrer & Co LLP

66 Lincoln's Inn Fields, London WC2A 3LH
**Tel:** 020 7917 7517
**Fax:** 020 7242 9899
**Email:** graduates@farrer.co.uk
**Web:** www.farrer.co.uk

**The firm** Farrer & Co is a successful law firm with a distinguished history and an excellent reputation built up over many years.

The firm provides a full service to clients as well as having outstanding expertise in a number of niche sectors. This is coupled with careful attention to personal service and quality, and a strong emphasis on the human touch based on the goodwill of numerous close client relationships.

We have around 316 staff, including 150 lawyers, many of whom are leaders in their fields and some 61 of whom are partners.

**Types of work** Farrer & Co has a dynamic team structure with twelve teams advising across diverse fields including intellectual property law, sports, media, matrimonial, heritage, employment, estates work, charity law and financial services. Clients range form national institutions, museums, galleries, schools and universities to high profile individuals and companies such as banks and media organisations.

**Who should apply** Those applicants who appear eager to break the mould – as shown by their initiative for organisation, leadership, exploration or enterprise – are far more likely to get an interview than the erudite, but otherwise unimpressive student. Trainees are expected to be highly motivated individuals with keen intellects and engaging and interesting personalities.

**Training programme** The training programme involves each trainee in the widest range of cases, clients and issues possible in a single law firm. This provides a broad foundation of knowledge and experience and the opportunity to make an informed choice about the area of law in which to specialise. A high degree of involvement is encouraged under the direct supervision of solicitors and partners. Trainees attend regular internal and external seminars. The training principal reviews trainees' progress at the end of each seat and extensive feedback is given. The firm has a friendly atmosphere and holds regular sporting and social events.

**When and how to apply** You can apply at any time. The closing date for training contract applications is 31 July 2008. Applications are dealt with online via the firm's website. A well-constructed covering letter forms part of the online application.

**Work placements** Farrer & Co runs Easter and summer vacation schemes for undergraduates considering a career in law. Students receive an allowance of £250 per week. The dates for the 2008 scheme applications will be available from the autumn of this year. The deadline is 31 January 2008 for all schemes. Approximately 100 applicants for summer vacation schemes will be invited to one of three open days held at the firm's offices in March 2008 which present a good opportunity to get to know the firm. Assessment mornings are likely to be held for both Easter and summer vacation schemes to help us make the final selection of successful candidates.

**Sponsorship** Fees for GDL and LPC and £5,000 grant per year.

| | |
|---|---|
| Vacancies | 10 |
| Trainees | 18 |
| Partners | 61 |
| Total staff | 316 |

**Work placement**  yes

**Apply to**
Trainee Recruitment Manager

**Starting salary**
£29,500 (Sept 2007)

**Minimum qualifications**
2.1 degree

**Sponsorship**
GDL/LPC

**Offices**
London

FARRER&Co

| | | |
|---|---|---|
| **FARADAYS SOLICITORS**<br>117-119 Seven Sisters Road, London N7 7QG<br>**Tel:** 020 72811001<br>**Fax:** 0207 281 1021<br>**Email:** faradaysolicitor@aol.com<br>**Apply to:** Mr P Symeou | Four partner firm that specialises in criminal law and family law and personal injury with partner on both family law and personal injury panel. | V 0<br>T 4<br>P 4<br>TS 17<br>WP no |
| **FARNFIELD & NICHOLLS**<br>The Square, Gillingham SP8 4AX<br>**Tel:** 01747 825432<br>**Fax:** 01747 822204<br>**Email:** susan.lacey@farnfields.com<br>**Apply to:** Ms Susan Lacey | General rural practice with three departments (conveyancing, family, probate) across three offices. Private client & legal aid. Information technology led. | V 0<br>T 2<br>P 4<br>TS 65<br>WP no |
| **FASKEN MARTINEAU STRINGER SAUL LLP**<br>17 Hanover Square, London W1S 1HU<br>**Tel:** 020 7917 8500<br>**Fax:** 020 7917 8555<br>**Email:** info@fasken.co.uk<br>**Apply to:** Mr Steven Gordon | Fasken Martineau Stringer Saul LLP is a commercial law practice which has developed substantial legal capabilities in its practice areas and market expertise in certain industry sectors. | V 2<br>T 2<br>P 25<br>TS 95<br>WP no |
| **FBC SOLICITORS**<br>6-10 George Street, Snow Hill,<br>Wolverhampton WV2 4DN<br>**Tel:** 01902 311711<br>**Fax:** 01902 311102<br>**Email:** solicitors@fbc-sol.co.uk<br>**Apply to:** Mr James Sage | A long-established commercial firm dealing with corporate/commercial property, commercial litigation, employment, private client and family work. | V 3(09)<br>T 6<br>P 18<br>TS 140<br>WP no |
| **FEARON & CO**<br>Westminster House, 6 Faraday Road, Guildford,<br>Surrey GU1 1EA<br>**Tel:** 01483 540 840<br>**Fax:** 01483 540 844<br>**Email:** ajp@fearonlaw.com<br>**Apply to:** Mr A.J Phillips | | V 1(08)<br>T 2<br>P 2<br>TS 8<br>WP no |
| **FELLOWES**<br>21 Church Hill, Walthamstow, London E17 3AD<br>**Tel:** 020 8520 7392<br>**Fax:** 020 8509 0759<br>**Email:** info@fellowes.org<br>**Apply to:** Mr SRJ Fellowes | Long established general high street practice based in East London, covering conveyancing and probate with a franchise in family and criminal. Recruitment is open - no deadlines. | V 2<br>T 3<br>P 3<br>TS 28<br>WP no |
| **FENTONS**<br>485 Oldham Road, Failsworth,<br>Manchester M35 9FS<br>**Tel:** 0161 682 7101<br>**Fax:** 0161 683 4774<br>**Apply to:** Ms Sara Gray | Property, personal injury, employment, probate and wills, housing litigation. North Manchester - about five miles north of the city centre. | V 0<br>T 7<br>P 5<br>TS 110<br>WP no |
| **FENWICK ELLIOTT LLP**<br>Aldwych House, 71-91 Aldwych,<br>London WC2B 4HN<br>**Tel:** 020 7421 1986<br>**Fax:** 020 7421 1987<br>**Email:** recruitment@fenwickelliott.co.uk<br>**Apply to:** Mr Toby Randle | Fenwick Elliott is the largest specialist construction law firm in the UK. They are renowned for their pragmatic, personable and commercial approach. | V 1(08)<br>T 1<br>P -<br>TS -<br>WP yes |

**V** = Vacancies / **T** = Trainees / **P** = Partners / **TS** = Total Staff / **WP** = Work Placement

# Field Fisher Waterhouse LLP

35 Vine Street, London EC3N 2AA
**Tel:** 020 7861 4000
**Fax:** 020 7488 0084
**Email:** graduaterecruitment@ffw.com
**Web:** www.ffw.com

**The firm** Field Fisher Waterhouse LLP (FFW) is a mid-sized City law firm that provides a broad range of legal services to an impressive list of clients that range from small unlisted UK companies to multinationals and foreign corporations. We pride ourselves on offering creative solutions and practical advice for our clients in an ever-changing commercial world. Europe is our domestic market. We have offices in Brussels, Hamburg and London and an exclusive relationship with leading firms in Spain and Italy. We also have long-standing affiliations with firms in France, the Czech Republic, Hungary and Poland.

**Types of work** Throughout their training contract trainees have the opportunity to work within IP & technology, corporate and commercial, banking and finance, regulatory and real estate. We also offer trainee seats in a wide range of other areas including public sector, litigation, employment and travel and aviation.

**Who should apply** We are looking to recruit trainees from both law and non-law backgrounds who have a strong academic background, excellent communication skills, enthusiasm and the ability to work as part of a team.

**Training programme** We offer a six-seat training contract and our range of practice areas enable us to offer outstanding opportunities for training. Trainees are treated as a valued part of the team and are encouraged to assume early responsibility. Practical training is complemented by a comprehensive programme of in-house seminars, workshops and external courses, accompanied by regular feedback and a formal assessment at the end of each seat.

We invest highly in the development and training of all our trainees and provide good-quality work within a friendly, relaxed and supportive working environment. You will also have additional support from your fellow trainees, a buddy and a mentor who is a senior solicitor.

Benefits include: 25 days' holiday, life assurance, season ticket loan, medical insurance, GP service and pension, in addition to having two squash courts in our offices.

**When and how to apply** Please apply online for our summer vacation scheme and training contracts, via our website at www.ffw.com/careers.

Deadline for 2008 summer vacation scheme: 31 January 2008.

Deadline for 2010 training contracts: 31 July 2008.

**Work placements** Increasingly our trainees have come to the firm through our summer vacation scheme, which provides a useful way of getting an insider's view of FFW. We run two two-week schemes during July where you have the opportunity to spend a week in two different departments and take part in a variety of work and social activities.

**Sponsorship** Sponsorship and a £5,500 maintenance grant for the GDL and a £6,000 grant for the LPC.

| Vacancies | 20 |
|---|---|
| Trainees | 34 |
| Partners | 101 |
| Total staff | 640 |

**Work placement**   yes

**Apply to**
Lucie Ress, Graduate Recruitment

**Starting salary**
1st year: £33,000
2nd year: £36,500

**Minimum qualifications**
2.1 degree, ABB at A level

**Sponsorship**
GDL/LPC

**Offices**
London, Brussels, Hamburg

 Field Fisher Waterhouse

# Finers Stephens Innocent

179 Great Portland Street, London W1W 5LS
**Tel:** 020 7323 4000
**Fax:** 020 7580 7069
**Email:** personnel@fsilaw.com
**Web:** www.fsilaw.com

**The firm** Finers Stephens Innocent is an expanding practice in Central London providing a range of high quality legal services to corporate, commercial and private clients. The firm's philosophy includes close partner involvement and a cost-effective approach in all client matters. They have a working style which is unstuffy and informal, but still aspires to the highest quality of output, whilst offering a sensible work-life balance. The firm is a member of the Meritas International network of law firms.

**Types of work** Commercial property, company commercial, employment, private client, family, media, defamation. Please see the website for further details.

**Who should apply** The firm requires academic excellence in all applicants. It also looks for maturity, personality, a broad range of interests, initiative, strong communication skills and the ability to write clear English and to think like a lawyer. The firm has for several years given equal consideration to applicants whether applying straight from university or having followed another career previously. Trainees get early responsibility, client contact and close involvement in transactions and litigation matters.

**Training programme** Between offering you a training contract and the time you start, the firm aims to keep regularly in touch with you, including offering you some work experience with them. When you start they provide a careful induction programme, after which you complete four six-month seats in different departments, sharing a room with either a partner or lawyer. The firm has three training partners who keep a close eye on the welfare and progress of trainees. There are regular group meetings with trainees and an appraisal process which enables you to know how you are progressing as well as giving you a chance to provide feedback on your training. The firm runs a variety of in-house courses for trainees.

**When and how to apply** Write in with your CV and covering letter. We do not have an application form. We do not like long, stereotypical covering letters. We are looking for very good academic results, whatever discipline you have studied; for a demonstrated commitment to law; for evidence that you are a sociable person and that you have something to give to others. If you are an outstanding individualist who is also a team player then this is the firm for you.

**Open day** Open afternoon in June. Apply with similar information to above by 30 April 2008.

**Sponsorship** For LPC/CPE fees.

| | |
|---|---|
| Vacancies | 6 |
| Trainees | 11 |
| Partners | 36 |
| Total staff | 180 |

**Apply to**
Personnel Department

**Minimum qualifications**
2.1 degree

**Sponsorship**
CPE/LPC

**Offices**
London

Finers Stephens Innocent

# Fladgate Fielder

25 North Row, London W1K 6DJ
**Tel:** 020 7462 2299
**Fax:** 020 7629 4414
**Email:** trainees@fladgate.com
**Web:** www.fladgate.com

**The firm** Fladgate Fielder is an innovative, progressive and thriving law firm based in the heart of London's West End which prides itself on its friendly and professional working environment.

**Types of work** We provide a wide range of legal services to a portfolio of prestigious clients in the UK and overseas, including multinationals, major institutions and listed companies, clearing banks, lenders and entrepreneurs. Our lawyers have experience in most major areas of practice and we combine an accessible and responsive style of service with first-class technical skills and in-depth expertise.

We have a strong international dimension based on multilingual and multi-qualified lawyers working in London and complemented by access to an extensive network of overseas lawyers. We operate international 'desks' which serve continental Europe (with an emphasis on the Germanic countries), India, Israel, the US and the Middle East.

Our three main departments comprise property (which includes separate planning, construction and property litigation teams), corporate (which includes tax, intellectual property and employment groups) and litigation. These are supported by specialist cross-departmental teams that provide co-ordinated advice on a range of issues.

**Who should apply** We seek trainees with enthusiasm, leadership potential and excellent interpersonal skills. You must be able to work both independently and in a team and will be expected to show common sense and initiative. Awareness of the commercial interests of clients is essential.

You will have a minimum of a 2.1 degree, although not necessarily in law, together with three excellent A levels or equivalent. We are keen to attract candidates with language skills.

**Training programme** Typically, you will complete four six-month seats. Each seat will bring you into contact with new clients and colleagues, and you can expect to gain real hands-on experience of a variety of deals and projects, both large and small. In each seat you will work alongside senior lawyers who will supervise your development and ensure that you are involved in challenging and interesting work. In addition to on-the-job training, each department has a comprehensive training schedule of seminars and workshops covering a range of legal and skills training.

The firm has a modern culture and an open-door policy where trainees are given early responsibility and encouraged to achieve their full potential.

We offer a qualification bonus of £10,000 over two years to trainees retained upon qualification.

**When and how to apply** Apply by 31 July 2008 to begin in 2009 and 2010. Please apply using the firm's application form which will be available from March 2008 at www.fladgate.com.

| | |
|---|---|
| **Vacancies** | 8 |
| **Trainees** | 8 |
| **Partners** | 42 |
| **Total staff** | 197 |

**Apply to**
Mrs Annaleen Stephens,
HR Manager

**Starting salary**
1st year - £27,500
2nd year - £29,000

**Minimum qualifications**
2.1 degree

**Offices**
London

FLADGATE FIELDER
SOLICITORS

| Firm | Description | | |
|------|-------------|---|---|
| **FERDINAND KELLY**<br>21 Bennetts Hill, Birmingham B2 5QP<br>**Tel:** 0121 643 5228<br>**Fax:** 0121 632 5449<br>**Apply to:** The Recruitment Partner | Niche commercial firm in Birmingham city centre. Specialisms: commercial litigation, European law; commercial work generally, sometimes with an international element. | **V** 0<br>**T** 0<br>**P** 2<br>**TS** 5<br>**WP** no |
| **FIELD CUNNINGHAM & CO**<br>St Johns Court, 70 Quay Street,<br>Manchester M3 3EJ<br>**Tel:** 0161 834 4734<br>**Fax:** 0161 834 1772<br>**Apply to:** Mr SJ Hawkins | Field Cunningham & Co is a niche commercial property development practice specialising in residential and commercial property (particularly retail and leisure development) and secured property lending. | **V** 1<br>**T** 2<br>**P** 4<br>**TS** 30<br>**WP** no |
| **FIELD SEYMOUR PARKES**<br>PO Box 174, The Old Coroner's Court,<br>1 London Street, Reading RG1 4QW<br>**Tel:** 0118 951 6200<br>**Fax:** 0118 950 2704<br>**Email:** enquiry@fsp-law.com<br>**Apply to:** Mr Stuart Ironside | We are a dynamic Thames Valley practice with a growing client base, active in both commercial and private client work areas. | **V** 3<br>**T** 7<br>**P** 13<br>**TS** 105<br>**WP** yes |
| **FIELDINGS PORTER**<br>Silverwell House, Silverwell Street, Bolton BL1 1PT<br>**Tel:** 01204 387742<br>**Fax:** 01204 362129<br>**Email:** info@fieldingsporter.co.uk<br>**Apply to:** Ms Kathryn Gregory | Long established four office general practice dealing with a wide variety of work from high value commercial to PI and legal aid franchises. | **V** 3-4<br>**T** 5<br>**P** 12<br>**TS** 76<br>**WP** no |
| **FINN GLEDHILL**<br>1-4 Harrison Road, Halifax HX1 2AG<br>**Tel:** 01422 330000<br>**Fax:** 01422 342604<br>**Apply to:** The Training Principal | A Yorkshire general practice with two offices, undertaking both commercial and private client work. Has a legal aid franchise. | **V** 0<br>**T** 0<br>**P** 8<br>**TS** 60<br>**WP** no |
| **FISHER MEREDITH**<br>Blue Sky House, 405 Kennington Road,<br>London SE11 4PT<br>**Tel:** 020 7091 2700<br>**Fax:** 020 7091 2800<br>**Email:** michelle.matthias@fishermeredith.co.uk<br>**Apply to:** Ms Michelle Matthias | A large rights based law firm specialising in crime, family, immigration, mental health, actions against the police, housing, licensing, employment, community care and education with thriving property and small business sections. | **V** 5+[09]<br>**T** 14<br>**P** 9<br>**TS** 110<br>**WP** no |
| **FISHERS**<br>4-8 Kilwardby Street, Ashby De La Zouch,<br>Leicestershire LE65 2FU<br>**Tel:** 01530 412167<br>**Fax:** 01530 416146<br>**Email:** fishers@fisherslaw.co.uk<br>**Apply to:** Mr MCA Killin | A long established practice with strong client base and niche areas in company and commercial, commercial property, taxations and trusts. No training contracts available in 2008. | **V** 0-1<br>**T** 1<br>**P** 6<br>**TS** 58<br>**WP** no |
| **FLETCHER DERVISH**<br>582 Green Lanes, London N8 0RP<br>**Tel:** 020 8800 4615<br>**Fax:** 020 8802 2273<br>**Email:** law@fletcherdervish.com<br>**Apply to:** Mr D Dervish | Long established practice committed to high standard of work. Franchised in family, crime, housing, immigration with depts in P/I, consumer/general contract, property and wills/probate. | **V** 0<br>**T** 3<br>**P** 1<br>**TS** 20<br>**WP** no |

**V** = Vacancies / **T** = Trainees / **P** = Partners / **TS** = Total Staff / **WP** = Work Placement

# Foot Anstey

21 Derry's Cross, Plymouth, Devon PL1 2SW
**Tel:** 01752 675000
**Fax:** 01752 675500
**Email:** training@foot-ansteys.co.uk
**Web:** www.foot-ansteys.co.uk

**The firm** Based in the South West, Foot Anstey is committed to advising businesses, individuals and those requiring public funding. We are proud of our staff and our client base. We are determined to provide a first class service to our clients. Our trainees are supervised by some of the best legal minds in the profession. Our retention rate for trainees upon qualification is excellent. We provide a progressive, supportive and determined working environment and are committed to developing our staff.

We have been singled out by *The Lawyer* Rising 50 as "one to watch" but do not intend to sit on our laurels. We are committed to achieving our aim to be the premier law firm in the south west.

**Types of work** Our main areas of work include: commercial property, property and construction litigation, company and commercial, dispute resolution, banking, employment, insolvency, clinical negligence, criminal advocates, family and childcare, private client and residential property. We have an extensive range of clients from commercial, public and private sectors (acting for numerous local, regional and national companies and high net worth individuals). Key clients include: Associated Newspapers, Coors Brewery, Cornish Homes, Cotleigh Brewery, Gregory Distribution, Landmark Information Group, Lighthouse Group, Midas Group, Northcliffe Media Ltd, Plymouth Marine Laboratory, South West Highways, South West Venture Capital, Tamar Science Park, The Planning Inspectorate, The Wireless Group Plc, The Wrigley Company Ltd, and various Charities, local authorities and educational establishments. We hold major contracts with the Legal Services Commission.

**Who should apply** We welcome applications from all law and non-law graduates who have a strong academic background, excellent communication skills and the ability to work as part of a team. Trainees are welcomed into a friendly and supportive environment where they will find the quality and variety of work both challenging and rewarding.

**Training programme** Our wide range of legal services enable us to offer trainees experience in a wide range of disciplines throughout our four offices. Trainees undertake four seats of six months. Whenever possible (with the exception of the first seat) trainees are able to select their seats. All trainees attend an induction course. Individual monthly meetings are held with supervisors. Appraisals are conducted halfway through each seat. Regular feedback between supervisors and trainees ensures an open and friendly environment. The Professional Skills Course is taught externally. We have Lexcel and Investors in People accreditations and an excellent training and development programme.

Benefits include: Contributory pension scheme, 25 days' holiday.

**When and how to apply** By 31 July 2008 to begin a training contract in September 2010. Please send a covering letter and full CV to Louise Widley at the Plymouth office address or email it to training@foot-ansteys.co.uk or apply online at www.foot-ansteys.co.uk.

**Work placements** The deadline for the 2008 summer placement scheme is 31 March 2008.

**Sponsorship** £9600 grant available towards LPC and living expenses.

| | |
|---|---|
| Vacancies | 10 |
| Trainees | 16 |
| Partners | 28 |
| Total staff | 305 |

**Work placement** yes

**Apply to**
Louise Widley

**Starting salary**
1st year: £19,500
2nd year: £21,000

**Minimum qualifications**
Usually 2.1 degree

**Sponsorship**
LPC

**Offices**
Plymouth, Exeter, Taunton (2)

Foot Anstey
SOLICITORS

# Forbes Solicitors

73 Northgate, Blackburn BB2 1AA
**Tel:** 01254 580000
**Fax:** 01254 222216
**Email:** graduate.recruitment@forbessolicitors.co.uk
**Web:** www.forbessolicitors.co.uk

**The firm** Forbes is one of the largest practices in the North of England with 29 partners and over 350 members of staff based in nine offices. Fundamental to the practice is a strong commitment to quality, training and career development – a commitment underlined by the fact that Forbes was one of the first firms to be recognised as an Investor in People and our ISO 9001 accreditation.

The firm has a broad-based practice dealing with both commercial and private client work and can therefore provide a varied and exciting career. We are, however, especially noted for excellence in our company/commercial, civil litigation, defendant insurer, crime, family and employment departments. We have a number of higher court advocates and the firm holds many Legal Service Commission franchises.

For applicants looking for a 'city' practice without the associated hassles of working in a city, then Forbes could be for you. We can offer the best of both worlds - a large firm with extensive resources and support combined with a commitment to quality, people and the personal touch.

**Types of work** Company/commercial, civil litigation, defendant insurer, crime, family and employment services.

**Who should apply** Forbes looks for high-calibre recruits with strong local connections and good academic records, who are also keen team players. Candidates should have a total commitment to client service and identify with our philosophy of providing practical, straightforward legal advice.

**Training programme** A tailored training programme involves six months in four of the following: crime, civil litigation, defendant insurer, matrimonial and non-contentious/company commercial.

**When and how to apply** Applications (handwritten letter and CV) should be received by 31 July, two years before the planned September start date.

| Vacancies | 4 |
|---|---|
| Trainees | 15 |
| Partners | 29 |
| Total staff | 350+ |

**Apply to**
Graduate Recruitment Manager

**Starting salary**
Not less than the Law Society minimum

**Minimum qualifications**
2.1 degree

**Offices**
Accrington (x2), Blackburn (x3), Chorley, Leeds, Manchester, Preston

forbessolicitors.

# Foreman Laws

25 Bancroft, Hitchin SG5 1JW
**Tel:** 01462 458711
**Fax:** 01462 459242
**Email:** logic@foremanlaws.co.uk
**Web:** www.foremanlaws.co.uk

**The firm** At Foreman Laws we punch above our weight. At a relatively young 36 years, the firm currently has 12 partners and over 50 staff and we are constantly expanding.

We are 75% commercial but have a strong private client department. We provide all the legal needs to most business from contracts to share sales; from the purchase of the corner shop to the sale of companies worth £100 million. Our private clients require property asset management services, wills, trusts and tax planning, family and civil litigation. We do not undertake legal aid work.

Foreman Laws has a friendly, hard working and down to earth attitude. Partners, trainees, secretaries and support staff work alongside each other and there is an open door policy throughout the firm.

Hitchin itself is a vibrant, cosmopolitan market town. You will find an array of shops, café's and restaurants for any occasion. On top of this it is only 30 minutes to Kings Cross.

**Who should apply** We train to retain. Our trainees are our future and a local connection to Hitchin is desirable, though not essential. We are looking for candidates who possess intelligence, personality and excellent communication skills. Most importantly, you must be willing and eager to learn and possess a strong sense of humour.

Applicants must have at least a 2.1 degree though this does not have to be in law.

**Training programme** From day one we give trainees client contact and encourage them to develop their own case load. You will be supported along the way, not just by your supervisor but by all partners, fee earners, support staff and other trainees. Your aim should be to make yourself indispensable.

We offer four seats of six months each from the following:
Commercial property
Company
Residential property
Wills, trusts and tax planning
Family
Civil litigation

**When and how to apply** Please contact Tim Sellers at: 25 Bancroft, Hitchin, Herts SG5 1JW; email: tim.sellers@foremanlaws.co.uk; telephone: 01462 471 521.

| | |
|---|---|
| Vacancies | 2 |
| Trainees | 4 |
| Partners | 12 |
| Total staff | 55 |

**Apply to**
Tim Sellers

**Starting salary**
£16,000 (min)

**Minimum qualifications**
2.1 degree

**Offices**
Hitchin

FOREMAN LAWS
SOLICITORS

# Forsters LLP

31 Hill Street, London W1J 5LS
**Tel:** 020 7863 8333
**Web:** www.forsters.co.uk

**The firm** We are a young, successful firm committed to being the best at what we do. Based in Mayfair, in London's West End, Forsters was founded in 1998 and we have since doubled in size. We are known for our top-flight property and private client practices, but we also have thriving corporate, litigation and family law teams. The working atmosphere of the firm is informal, yet highly professional. We expect you to work hard, but believe that everyone should have a life outside work. It's also a friendly firm with a good social life.

**Types of work** The firm has a strong reputation for all aspects of commercial and residential property work. The groups handle investment funding, development, planning, construction, landlord and tenant, property taxation and residential investment and development. Forsters is also recognised as one of the leading proponents of private client work in London with a client base comprising a broad range of individuals and trusts in the UK and elsewhere. The corporate practice specialises in acquisitions and financing for technology, communication and media companies. The litigation group conducts commercial litigation and arbitration and advises on a broad spectrum of matters.

**Who should apply** We recruit graduates from a broad range of backgrounds and welcome both graduate and under-graduate applicants with a degree in any discipline. Our criteria are that you have a minimum of 320 UCAS points and have gained, or expect to gain, a 2.1 or higher degree classification. Beyond this, we are looking for ambitious, personable and motivated candidates who thrive on responsibility within a team environment.

**Training programme** Your training contract with Forsters will consist of six four-month seats. In your first year, you will usually have seats in three of the following departments: property, private client, company commercial or litigation. In your second year, the four-month pattern still applies, but if you have developed an area of particular interest, it may be possible to spend more time in the appropriate seat. As your training contract progresses, you will be given increasing responsibility. You will start working on your own files and will soon be talking to and meeting with clients. Supervision and guidance is always available but we are keen that you start playing a real role in the team. In addition to 'on the job' training there are regular in-house seminars on legal and commercial topics as well as training on our IT and in-house systems. You will also attend a bespoke Professionals Skills Course, provided by a leading training supplier and designed for Forsters.

**When and how to apply** All applications should be made online at www.forsters.co.uk. The application form can be accessed in the graduate section of our website. The closing date for training contracts commencing September 2010 is 31 July 2008.

**Work placements** We offer two-week placements during the summer vacation period for which we accept around 10 students each year. The closing date for online applications for the 2008 vacation scheme is 15 March 2008.

**Sponsorship** of fees for CPE/GDL and LPC, plus a maintenance grant of £5,000 per annum post-offer of employment.

| | |
|---|---|
| Vacancies | 5-6 |
| Trainees | 10 |
| Partners | 29 |
| Total staff | 190 |

**Work placement** Yes

**Apply to**
Miss Amy Sweetland

**Starting salary**
1st year: £30,000
2nd year: £32,000

**Minimum qualifications**
2.1 degree preferred
320 UCAS points (excluding General Studies)

**Sponsorship**
CPE/GDL & LPC

**Offices**
London

**FORSTERS**

## FLETCHERS SOLICITORS
160-162 Lord Street, Southport,
Merseyside PR9 OQA
**Tel:** 01704 546919
**Fax:** 01704 545588
**Email:** enquiries@fletcherssolicitors.co.uk
**Apply to:** Mr JC Owens

Matrimonial, employment, conveyancing, litigation, contract. Legal aid franchise, Investors in People and LEXEL accreditations held. A two office firm based in same town ie Southport.

| V | 2[09] |
|---|---|
| T | 2 |
| P | 4 |
| TS | 85 |
| WP | no |

## FLINT BISHOP
St Michaels Court, St Michaels Lane,
Derby DE1 3HQ
**Tel:** 01332 340211
**Fax:** 01332 207601
**Apply to:** Mrs Angie Whittingham

No 1 in the UK Diversity League table and this year nominations include The Regional Law Firm of The Year and Mould Breaking Firm of the Year - be part of our success.

| V | 4[09] |
|---|---|
| T | 8 |
| P | 22 |
| TS | 250 |
| WP | no |

## FOLLETT STOCK
Truro Business Park, Threemilestone, Truro,
Cornwall TR4 9NH
**Tel:** 01872 241700
**Fax:** 01872 245980
**Email:** nigel.fox@follettstock.co.uk
**Apply to:** Mr Martin Pearse

We are a young and dynamic niche commercial practice based in Cornwall servicing businesses throughout the South West. This year, our Managing Partner, Chris Lingard, won 'Partner of the Year' at the Lawyer Awards.

| V | 2[09] |
|---|---|
| T | 6 |
| P | 5 |
| TS | 45 |
| WP | yes |

## FORD & WARREN
Westgate Point, Westgate, Leeds LS1 2AX
**Tel:** 0113 243 6601
**Fax:** 0113 242 0905
**Email:** clientmail@forwarn.com
**Apply to:** Ms Debra Hinde

Ford & Warren is a commercial firm based in Leeds. Clients include the largest limited companies and PLCs and many from the public sector.

| V | 4 |
|---|---|
| T | 7 |
| P | 21 |
| TS | 200 |
| WP | no |

## FORD SIMEY
8 Cathedral Close, Exeter EX1 1EW
**Tel:** 01392 274126
**Fax:** 01392 410933
**Email:** sn@fordsimey.co.uk
**Apply to:** Ms Sonia Nye

General practice with specialist teams dealing with private client, family, personal injury and commercial. Welcomes non-law graduates.

| V | 2 |
|---|---|
| T | 3 |
| P | 14 |
| TS | 92 |
| WP | no |

## FOSTERS
William House, 19 Bank Plain, Norwich NR2 4FS
**Tel:** 01603 620508
**Fax:** 01603 624090
**Email:** alisonkirby@fosters-solicitors.co.uk
**Apply to:** Mr Chris Brown

Winner of UK Law Firm of the Year, Best Medium Sized Firm 1999 National Lawyer Awards. Award winning three year training contract. Applications ongoing.

| V | 4 |
|---|---|
| T | 11 |
| P | 11 |
| TS | 100 |
| WP | no |

## FOX HAYES LLP
118 North Street, Leeds LS2 7AN
**Tel:** 0113 249 6496
**Fax:** 0113 248 0466
**Email:** davidgill@foxhayes.co.uk
**Apply to:** Mr David Gill

We are a full service legal firm whose brand reflects a bold, pursuing, smart, agile, hungry to succeed attitude. Find out more from our website.

| V | 2[08] |
|---|---|
| T | 5 |
| P | 22 |
| TS | 200 |
| WP | no |

## FOX WILLIAMS
Ten Dominion Street, London EC2M 2EE
**Tel:** 020 7628 2000
**Fax:** 020 7628 2100
**Email:** cdenny@foxwilliams.com
**Apply to:** Miss Charlotte Denny

Fox Williams is an independent City law firm. Areas of specialism include; corporate, employment, dispute resolution, commerce and technology, property and partnership. We will be accepting applications from 1 November 2007.

| V | 5[08] |
|---|---|
| T | 8 |
| P | 17 |
| TS | 100 |
| WP | yes |

# Freeth Cartwright LLP

Cumberland Court, 80 Mount Street, Nottingham NG1 6HH
**Tel:** 0115 901 5504
**Fax:** 0115 859 9603
**Email:** carole.wigley@freethcartwright.co.uk
**Web:** www.freethcartwright.co.uk

**The firm** Freeth Cartwright LLP is a leading Midlands law firm. Tracing its origins back to 1805, the firm became Nottingham's largest firm in 1994, and has since pursued its dynamic strategy of becoming the law firm of the East Midlands, with successful offices now established in Derby, Leicester and Manchester. While Freeth Cartwright LLP is a heavyweight commercial firm, serving a wide variety of corporate and institutional clients, there is also a strong commitment to a broad range of legal services, which includes a substantial private client element. This enables us to give a breadth of experience in training which is not always available in firms of a similar size.

**Types of work** The firm covers a wide range of work and is organised into four divisions: property and construction, commercial services, private client and personal litigation.

**Who should apply** Freeth Cartwright LLP looks for people to bring their own perspective and individuality to the firm. So we are just as keen to recruit graduates from other disciplines as we are those with law degrees. We need people who can cope with the intellectual demands of life as a lawyer and who possess the wider personal skills which are needed in our diverse practice.

**Training programme** Freeth Cartwright LLP is committed to providing comprehensive training for all its staff, but particular emphasis is placed on the needs of trainee solicitors. We have a director of training and a training manager who supervise our training programme. This is based primarily on in-house training covering both technical matters and personal skills, supplemented with external courses where appropriate. More importantly, the firm endeavours to give the best possible experience during the training period, as we believe that informal training on the job is the most effective means of encouraging the skills required in a qualified solicitor. One of our senior members takes responsibility for all our trainees and their personal development. That member will oversee progress through the firm and will discuss performance based on feedback received on each assignment. Normally, during the training contract, you will have four six-month periods in different departments. The allocation of trainee solicitors to departments is discussed in advance and individual wishes are taken into account. Most of the training opportunities are available in our Nottingham offices, although it is now possible for trainees to spend at least one seat in another location.

**When and how to apply** Closing date for training contracts is 31 July. Applications should be made on the firm's online application form.

| | |
|---|---|
| Vacancies | 7 |
| Trainees | 15 |
| Members | 70 |
| Total staff | 509 |

**Work placement** no

**Apply to**
Carole Wigley, HR Manager

**Starting salary**
£20,000 (2007)

**Minimum qualifications**
None

**Sponsorship**
LPC

**Offices**
Nottingham, Leicester, Derby, Manchester

Freeth
Cartwright
LLP

# Freshfields Bruckhaus Deringer

65 Fleet Street, London EC4Y 1HS
**Tel:** 020 7936 4000
**Fax:** 020 7832 7001
**Email:** uktrainees@freshfields.com
**Web:** www.freshfields.com/uktrainees

**The firm** Freshfields Bruckhaus Deringer is a leading international law firm. Through our network of 27 offices in 16 countries, we provide first-rate legal services to corporations, financial institutions and governments around the world. Our lawyers work on high-profile, interesting and often ground-breaking work for clients such as Deutsche Bank, Hewlett Packard, Tesco and the Bank of England. We are recognised market leaders for a wide range of work.

**Types of work** Corporate; mergers and acquisitions; banking; dispute resolution; joint ventures; employment, pensions and benefits; asset finance; real estate; tax; capital markets; intellectual property; information technology; project finance; securities; antitrust, competition and trade; communications and media; construction and engineering; energy; environment; financial services; insolvency; insurance; international tax; investment funds; public international law.

**Who should apply** We are looking for people who have proven academic ability, an excellent command of spoken and written English, high levels of drive and determination, good team-working skills and excellent organisational ability.

**Training programme** Our trainee solicitors receive a thorough professional training in a very broad range of practice areas, an excellent personal development programme and the chance to work in one of our international offices or on secondment with a client in the UK or abroad. You will be working with and learning from one of the most talented peer groups in the legal world, and you will get the blend of support and freedom you need to evolve your career and take advantage of the opportunities our international network offers.

Your training will be unique to you. Flexibility is one of the hallmarks of our training programme and one of the features which most differentiates our training contract from others.

**When and how to apply** We are now accepting applications for training contracts to commence in August 2010 and February 2011. The deadline is 31 July 2008. Applications should be made on the firm's online form. See www.freshfields.com/uktrainees for details.

**Work placements** Easter and summer vacation schemes are available to students in their penultimate year. Applications are accepted between 20 November 2007 and 18 January 2008. Since we offer places as we receive applications, the sooner you apply after 20 November the better.

**Sponsorship** We pay our prospective trainees' tuition fees for the GDL and LPC and a maintenance grant of £6,250 to those studying the GDL and £7,250 to those studying the LPC.

Vacancies 100
Trainees 200 (London)
Partners 474
Total staff 5517

**Work placement** yes
*(see Insider Report on p101)*

**Apply to**
Deborah Dalgleish,
Head of UK Trainee
Recruitment

**Starting salary**
£38,000

**Minimum qualifications**
High 2.1 degree, any subject

**Sponsorship**
GDL/LPC

**Offices**
Amsterdam, Barcelona, Beijing, Berlin, Bratislava, Brussels, Budapest, Cologne, Dubai, Düsseldorf, Frankfurt, Hamburg, Hanoi, Ho Chi Minh City, Hong Kong, London, Madrid, Milan, Moscow, Munich, New York, Paris, Rome, Shanghai, Tokyo, Vienna, Washington DC

 FRESHFIELDS BRUCKHAUS DERINGER

# Furley Page LLP

39 St Margaret's Street, Canterbury, Kent CT1 2TX
**Tel:** 01227 863118
**Fax:** 01227 762829
**Email:** hr@furleypage.co.uk
**Web:** www.furleypage.co.uk

**The firm** Furley Page is a large regional law firm in Kent, providing a full range of services to private and commercial clients in the South East, particularly in Kent.

We have a strong team of business lawyers acting for many types of organisations, ranging from public companies to small businesses through to leading institutions in the charitable and educational fields. The wide diversity of issues encountered by the individual is reflected in the broad spectrum of services that we can offer to the private client.

We recognise that our success lies in the quality of staff that we employ, and that trainee recruitment and development are key to our future growth. Our aim is to have well-motivated employees through a balance of a modern and professional career with home life and external interests.

**Who should apply** A strong academic background is essential, together with good communication skills and an interest in business development.

**Training programme** The training principal will oversee the training programme and trainees will spend six months in each training seat, working with a training supervisor. Trainees will gain a wide range of experience and develop their professional skills laying the foundations for a successful future career in law.

**When and how to apply** Closing date for receipt of applications is 31 July 2008 for training contracts commencing in September 2010. All applications must be made on the official Furley Page graduate trainee application form which must be accompanied with a covering letter explaining why you should be considered for the post of graduate trainee solicitor. It is very important you remember to include your letter as this forms part of the selection process. For a copy of the official Furley Page graduate trainee application form either download the pdf from our website (www.furleypage.co.uk) or contact Human Resources on the above telephone number and ask for a graduate trainee application form.

**Sponsorship** A contribution of up to £2,000 towards the cost of the tuition fees for the LPC.

| Vacancies | 2 |
| Trainees | 4 |
| Partners | 20+ |
| Total staff | 120 |

**Apply to**
HR Manager

**Starting salary**
£16,995 (2007) with a review after one year

**Minimum qualifications**
2.1 degree

**Offices**
Canterbury, Chatham, Whitstable

| FRANCES LINDSAY & CO<br>27 High Street, Maidenhead, Berkshire SL6 1JG<br>**Tel:** 01628 634667<br>**Fax:** 01628 671133<br>**Email:** info@franceslindsay.co.uk<br>**Apply to:** Ms Frances Lindsay | Specialist family law practice. Non-legal aid. | V 0-1<br>T 1<br>P 1<br>TS 5<br>WP no |
|---|---|---|
| FRANKLINS SOLICITORS LLP<br>14 Castilian Street, Northampton NN1 1JX<br>**Tel:** 01604 828282<br>**Fax:** 01604 609639<br>**Email:** mlf@franklins-sols.co.uk<br>**Apply to:** Mr Michael Franklin | A well-established firm specialising in commercial, employment, domestic property, family and personal injury work, delivering a high quality service to all our clients. | V 0<br>T 12<br>P 9<br>TS 125<br>WP no |
| FREARSONS<br>48-50 Algitha Road, Skegness,<br>Lincolnshire PE25 2AW<br>**Tel:** 01754 762121<br>**Fax:** 01754 610074<br>**Email:** hf@frearsons.net<br>**Apply to:** Miss H Fisher | A general practice with a well established client base. Legal aid franchised in family. | V 0-1<br>T 1<br>P 4<br>TS 28<br>WP no |
| FREEMAN JOHNSON<br>11 Victoria Road, Darlington DL1 5SP<br>**Tel:** 01325 466221<br>**Fax:** 0845 389 3201<br>**Apply to:** Mr Kevin Campbell | Offices at Darlington, Durham and Spennymoor. All general private client work. Legal aid franchise in personal injury, matrimony and crimel. Some company commercial. | V 1<br>T 2<br>P 8<br>TS 45<br>WP yes |
| GAMLINS<br>31-37 Russell Road, Rhyl LL18 3DB<br>**Tel:** 01745 343500<br>**Fax:** 01745 343616<br>**Email:** gamlins@gamlins.co.uk<br>**Apply to:** Ms Sue Wilkinson | One of the largest firms in Wales specialising in commercial law, personal injury, litigation, family care law, probate, conveyancing and crime. A firm committed to information technology. | V Varies<br>T 4<br>P 6<br>TS 50<br>WP no |
| GAMMON BELL & CO<br>91 Leigh Road, Eastleigh SO50 9DQ<br>**Tel:** 023 80629009<br>**Fax:** 023 80612737<br>**Apply to:** The Recruitment Partner | Small general practice with two partners, three assistant solicitors, two managing clerks and one trainee. High street location. Established local clients. Emphasis on conveyancing and court work. | V 1<br>T 1<br>P 2<br>TS 25<br>WP no |
| GARDEN HOUSE SOLICITORS<br>23 London Road, Hertford SG13 7LG<br>**Tel:** 01992 422 128<br>**Fax:** 01992 422129<br>**Email:** patricia@gardenhousesolicitors.co.uk<br>**Apply to:** Mrs PE Ling | Garden House Solicitors specialise in representing claimants in personal injury cases. The firm also offers assistance in civil claims and wills and probate. | V 0<br>T 1<br>P 1<br>TS 4<br>WP yes |
| GEORGE GREEN<br>195 High Street, Cradley Heath,<br>West Midlands B64 5HW<br>**Tel:** 01384 410410<br>**Fax:** 01384 634237<br>**Email:** pbennett@georgegreen.co.uk<br>**Apply to:** Mr Paul Bennett | The leading Black Country commercial practice. | V 2[09]<br>T 5<br>P 10<br>TS 71<br>WP no |

# Gaby Hardwicke

33 The Avenue, Eastbourne, East Sussex BN21 3YD
**Tel:** 01323 435900
**Fax:** 01323 435901
**Email:** trainees@gabyhardwicke.co.uk
**Web:** www.gabyhardwicke.co.uk

**The firm** A major Sussex firm with 17 partners and a total staff of more than 180 in offices in Hastings, Bexhill and Eastbourne. Founded in 1886, Gaby Hardwicke has a dynamic corporate management style and in recent years has invested heavily in IT, training, personnel development and quality assurance. We have only one standard – excellence – and, as a result, we are fast expanding and have a reputation for a service which adds real value to every case.

**Types of work** Our three towns lie on the Sussex coast and have a combined population of 250,000, a significant proportion of whom are retired. About half of our work, therefore, is non-contentious private client, comprising residential conveyancing, wills, probate, trusts, etc. We do, however, have a very strong litigation team with specialist solicitors in employment, intellectual property, PI, family and commercial litigation. Indeed, the reputations of our commercial and litigation departments attract clients not only from the immediate locality, but also from much further afield. Our client base includes many small to medium (under £20 million) private companies and businesses, and we service their needs in both the contentious and non-contentious fields.

**Who should apply** Our minimum requirements for initial selection are: a 2.1 degree, or exceptionally, a 2.2 degree from a good university. In addition to academic ability, we expect our trainees to be dedicated, flexible and committed to playing a full part in the firm's success. We only offer training contracts to applicants of the highest calibre. After they qualify, trainees often stay a year or two to gain more experience and, to the very best, we offer long-term careers leading to full equity partnership.

**Training programme** We recruit one trainee each year and usually, therefore, have two at any one time. Each trainee has three seats spending six to 12 months in each. In the first year the emphasis is very much upon the inculcation of the culture of the firm, namely of approachable solicitors who care, who readily understand client's needs and concerns and provide positive, practical and realistic solutions. Trainees are at an early stage given all the responsibility we think they can handle. They have their own supervised caseload as well as assisting others with theirs, but we are always there with plenty of advice and support.

**When and how to apply** Training contracts commence on 1 September each year. Applications may be submitted up to 2 years in advance of commencement by sending a CV and covering letter to trainees@gabyhardwicke.co.uk.

| | |
|---|---|
| Vacancies | 1 |
| Trainees | 2 |
| Partners | 17 |
| Total staff | 180+ |

**Apply to**
Alisa Winters

**Starting salary**
£15,820 with a review after one year

**Minimum qualifications**
2.1 degree, or exceptionally, a 2.2 degree from a good university

**Offices**
Hastings, Bexhill, Eastbourne

# Geldards LLP

Dumfries House, Dumfries Place, Cardiff CF10 3ZF
**Tel:** 029 2023 8239
**Fax:** 029 2023 7268
**Email:** recruitment@geldards.co.uk
**Web:** www.geldards.com

**The firm** Geldards LLP is one of the leading regional law firms in the United Kingdom. The firm's offices are located in Cardiff, Derby and Nottingham. While continuing to expand the traditional areas of work in the company and commercial, commercial property, dispute resolution and private client departments, the firm has acquired particular expertise in a variety of niche areas of legal work. These include mergers and acquisitions, corporate finance and banking, intellectual property, public law, planning and environmental law, energy law, rail and transport law, construction contracts and building arbitration, employment law, insolvency, trusts and tax, secured lending, property litigation, clinical negligence and personal injury.

The firm's growth in recent years has been characterised by an expansion of its work for major stock exchange listed clients and for City of London-based organisations, and by the growing reputation of its work for public sector bodies.

**Types of work** Company/commercial, property, litigation and other smaller areas.

**Who should apply** Candidates who are motivated and hardworking, with a strong academic background. A sense of humour is essential, as is involvement in extracurricular activities and interests which show evidence of a balanced and well-rounded individual.

**Training programme** Training is divided into six four-month seats in the firm's main practice areas. Trainees are allocated to a particular team and are supervised by the lead partner or senior solicitors working within the team. An open-door policy applies and trainees are regarded very much as an integral part of the team to which they have been allocated. A dedicated partner within each office has responsibility for the trainees in that office. A senior partner monitors consistency, progress and development across the three offices. Training is reviewed every three months. Formal training will be a combination of external courses and internal seminars.

Early contact with clients is encouraged in both work and social environments, as is the acceptance of responsibility. The atmosphere is friendly and the firm encourages its own social and sporting functions outside the office.

**When and how to apply** Summer placement closing date: 1 March 2008. Training contracts closing date: end of July 2008 to start September 2010. Applications received online only at www.geldards.com.

**Work placements** Two one-week summer placements in Cardiff for no more than 10 each week. Two one-week summer placements in the East Midlands for no more than six each week.

**Sponsorship** Full funding towards the LPC plus £4,500 maintenance grant and £3,000 towards the CPE/GDL.

| | |
|---|---|
| Vacancies | 8 |
| Trainees | 16 |
| Partners | 54 |
| Total staff | 400 |

**Work placement** yes

**Apply**
Online

**Starting salary**
£19,000

**Minimum qualifications**
2.1 degree preferred

**Sponsorship**
GDL & LPC

**Offices**
Cardiff, Derby, Nottingham

**Geldards** LLP
law firm

# George Davies Solicitors LLP

Fountain Court, 68 Fountain Street, Manchester M2 2FB
**Tel:** 0161 236 8992
**Fax:** 0161 234 8846
**Email:** trainees@georgedavies.co.uk
**Web:** www.georgedavies.co.uk

**The firm** George Davies is an ambitious commercial law firm with a strong Manchester presence whilst acting at the same time for national clients. The firm aims to provide technical expertise and attention to detail in the areas of law in which it specialises. Our approach is proactive and commercial.

George Davies is determined to provide an excellent service to its clients and has, in recent years, expanded all of its practice teams by recruiting commercially driven and forward thinking people to maintain this commitment.

**Types of work** The core practice areas for George Davies are corporate/ commercial, insolvency, commercial property, healthcare/public sector, litigation, private client, sport and employment. We act for substantial owner managed businesses, national businesses and are on the panels of several banks. We do not do criminal or volume personal injury work.

**Who should apply** No rigid qualification requirements as such but we are seeking high achievers and all applicants will need to have a strong academic record. Applicants should be enthusiastic and demonstrate initiative, be able to handle responsibility and have a strong personality.

**Training programme** Trainees will complete four six-month seats, each one in a different department. Training seats are available in the corporate/ commercial, property, litigation, private client, sport and employment teams.

George Davies provides support for trainees at all times during the training programme with each trainee being assigned a partner in the team who guides the trainee to ensure the appropriate training is provided. Trainees will work closely with members of the teams and are encouraged to assess their development and discuss their progress.

**When and how to apply** By end of January 2008 for training contracts 2009. Apply in writing by letter with CV to Chris Wilkinson at the address above or by email to barbara.campbell@georgedavies.co.uk.

| | |
|---|---|
| Vacancies | 5 |
| Trainees | 10 |
| Partners | 15 |
| Total staff | 85 |

**Work placement** no

**Apply to**
Christopher Wilkinson

**Starting salary**
Above Law Society
recommended

**Offices**
Manchester

| GERSTEN & NIXON<br>National House, 60-66 Wardour Street,<br>London W1F 0TA<br>**Tel:** 020 7439 3961<br>**Fax:** 020 7734 2479<br>**Email:** hs@gernix.co.uk<br>**Apply to:** Mr Hugh Sullivan | Soho lawyers, established reputation in media, matrimonial, property and general commercial work, especially litigation. Maximum one trainee annually, top academic qualifications preferred. | V 0<br>T 1<br>P 3<br>TS 15<br>WP no |
|---|---|---|
| GILBERT STEPHENS<br>17 Southernhay East, Exeter EX1 1QE<br>**Tel:** 01392 424242<br>**Fax:** 01392 410925<br>**Email:** law@gilbertstephens.co.uk<br>**Apply to:** Mr Philip Luckham | A long-established highly respected firm offering a comprehensive range of legal services. The firm also has its own financial services department. | V 0<br>T 2<br>P 9<br>TS 60<br>WP no |
| GILL & CO<br>Trevian House, 422-426 Ley Street, Ilford,<br>Essex IG2 7BS<br>**Tel:** 020 8554 1011<br>**Fax:** 020 8554 6698<br>**Apply to:** Mrs GK Bhogal | | V 1[08]<br>T 1<br>P 2<br>TS 14<br>WP no |
| GILL AKASTER<br>Scott Lodge, Milehouse, Plymouth PL2 3DD<br>**Tel:** 01752 512000<br>**Fax:** 01752 513553<br>**Apply to:** Mrs Jacqui Ashley | Committed to providing a good all round service to its clients. Strong family and commercial departments. Legal aid franchise. | V 1-2[09]<br>T 1<br>P 13<br>TS 100<br>WP no |
| GILL TURNER TUCKER<br>Colman House, King Street, Maidstone ME14 1JE<br>**Tel:** 01622 759051<br>**Fax:** 01622 762192<br>**Email:** mjt@gillturnertucker.com<br>**Apply to:** Mr Michael Trigg | Established in 1949 we are a general practice with an emphasis on commercial and matrimonial work. | V 1<br>T 1<br>P 6<br>TS 25<br>WP no |
| GLAISYERS<br>6th Floor Manchester House, 18-20 Bridge Street,<br>Manchester M3 3BY<br>**Tel:** 0161 832 4666<br>**Fax:** 0161 832 1981<br>**Email:** kxh@glaisyers.com<br>**Apply to:** Miss Karen Hart | Medium sized practice that specialises in commercial/residential conveyancing, commercial litigation, personal injury, employment, debt collection, matrimonial and children/family law. | V 1-2<br>T 4<br>P 15<br>TS 90<br>WP yes |
| GLANVILLES<br>West Wing Cams Hall, Cams Hill, Fareham,<br>Hampshire PO16 8AB<br>**Tel:** 01329 282841<br>**Fax:** 01329 822052<br>**Email:** fareham@glanvilles.co.uk<br>**Apply to:** Ms Sue Craven | Five offices situated in South Hampshire and the Isle of Wight. Mix of commercial and private client work. Long established. | V 1<br>T 2<br>P 12<br>TS 120<br>WP no |
| GLOVERS<br>115 Park Street, London W1K 7DY<br>**Tel:** 020 7629 5121<br>**Fax:** 020 7491 0930<br>**Email:** central@glovers.co.uk<br>**Apply to:** Ms Mandy Rodgers | Friendly commercial firm in Mayfair. We encourage early responsibility and full involvement in all areas, including commercial litigation, banking, property and construction. | V 2<br>T 4<br>P 14<br>TS 46<br>WP no |

# Goodman Derrick LLP

90 Fetter Lane, London EC4A 1PT
**Tel:** 020 7404 0606
**Fax:** 020 7831 6407
**Email:** law@gdlaw.co.uk
**Web:** www.gdlaw.co.uk

**The firm** Goodman Derrick LLP is an established London law firm with a broad commercial practice and a particularly strong reputation for media work. We represent both UK and international clients. Our emphasis is on providing high quality yet practical legal advice tailored to our clients' business needs.

**Types of work** Our practice is focused on corporate, property and litigation work but the firm also has a particularly strong reputation for high profile media work. We provide a range of services throughout six departments: corporate; property; commercial litigation; family and private client; employment; and media. Within these departments we have specialists in IP/IT, franchising, construction, charities and film finance. The firm has an impressive client list acting for many public figures, public and large private companies, large retail chains, property companies, publishers, television companies, broadcasters and independent producers, charities and trade associations. We aim to offer a friendly but stimulating working environment where trainees are given maximum client contact and responsibility from the start.

**Who should apply** Applicants should have a minimum 2.1 degree (not necessarily law) and a strong academic background. In addition we look for trainees who are confident, motivated and practically-minded to suit our working environment.

**Training programme** We invest a lot of time and resource in our trainees and our training is aimed at producing solicitors with well-rounded knowledge, skills and abilities. Hands-on experience is supplemented by internal and external training courses.

Trainees undertake four seats of six months each selected from our six departments. Where possible these will include corporate, property and a litigation based seat, as we believe the skills learned in these practice areas are essential for a trainee's development. Some seats are combined (eg, family/private client and employment/media) enabling trainees to experience as many practice areas as possible.

Trainees are not assigned exclusively to any particular partner, but are treated as part of the department's team from day one, enabling them to experience the breadth of the department's work. Trainees are, however, supervised by and will share a room with a fee earner (usually a partner) to maximise their experience.

Trainees will play an active and essential role working with partners and fee earners on larger cases and transactions, but where possible trainees also run their own files. We like to encourage initiative and responsibility at an early stage. Trainees are also given maximum client contact.

**When and how to apply** The closing date for 2010 training contracts is 31 July 2008. Apply by online application form available on our website www.gdlaw.co.uk.

**Sponsorship** Funding for the LPC fees at the institution of your choice and a maintenance grant of £4,000 during the LPC.

| | |
|---|---|
| Vacancies | 3 |
| Trainees | 6 |
| Partners | 21 |
| Total staff | 90 |

Work placement  no

**Apply**
Online

**Starting salary**
1st year - £26,500
2nd year: £28,000

**Minimum qualifications**
2.1 degree

**Offices**
London

GOODMAN DERRICK LLP

# Gordons LLP

Riverside West, Whitehall Road, Leeds LS1 4AW
**Tel:** 0113 227 0100
**Fax:** 0113 227 0113
**Email:** karen.mills@gordonsllp.com
**Web:** www.gordonsllp.com

**The firm** Gordons LLP is one of Yorkshire's leading independent law firms. We have grown substantially in recent years as a result of mergers, key lateral hires and organic growth. We are a progressive, enthusiastic, committed law firm dedicated to delivering a comprehensive and integrated range of legal services to corporate and individual clients. We aim to be the law firm of choice in our region, providing a genuine alternative to the national firms.

**Types of work** As a result of our strong reputation and recognised expertise in both corporate and private work, Gordons' client base now extends far beyond the region as reflected in the recognition received in the leading legal directories.

**Who should apply** In recruiting trainees we are looking to select our solicitors and indeed partners of the future. We therefore require committed and loyal trainees who are keen to build a successful career in the region and specifically with us. We offer a broad-based training which gives early and increasing responsibility to trainees in a supportive environment. Applicants must therefore be willing to be challenged from week one.

Academically our entry standard is a 2.1 degree, though we will take a broader view encompassing A levels for those who just miss out on a 2.1. More importantly, the ability of applicants to present a well-researched, planned and drafted application is paramount. You would be surprised how many would-be trainees fail to demonstrate in their application an ability to communicate well in writing or good organisational skills.

The firm takes pride in its ability to build enduring working relationships with clients. We feel it is important to develop an understanding of our clients' needs in order that we can meet them. It is therefore essential that our trainees have the potential to be at ease with clients, be able to relate well to them in both a business and a social context, and most importantly inspire trust and confidence in the legal advice that they give. So interpersonal skills, a professional yet friendly manner and sound commercial awareness are criteria we use to measure the suitability of applicants.

At Gordons we endeavour to achieve a healthy work-life balance. We do not expect staff to work excessively long hours unless work requirements so dictate. The ability to relax and de-stress outside work is an important skill required of any potential trainee.

**Training programme** The training contract consists of four six-month placements. Usually all trainees have placements in commercial litigation, company/commercial and commercial property. We try where possible to meet the wishes of trainees in terms of the placements on offer, though such flexibility cannot always be accommodated. Trainees will spend time in both the Leeds and Bradford offices.

**When and how to apply** By 1 August 2008 to begin 2010. Online applications only via www.gordonsllp.com.

| | |
|---|---|
| Vacancies | 6 |
| Trainees | 12 |
| Partners | 38 |
| Total staff | 314 |

**Apply to**
Ms Karen Mills

**Starting salary**
£20,500

**Minimum qualifications**
2.1 degree

**Offices**
Leeds, Bradford

## GLP SOLICITORS
672 Bolton Road, Pendlebury, Swinton,
Manchester M27 8FH
**Tel:** 0161 793 0901
**Fax:** 0161 794 4779
**Email:** pendlebury@glplaw.com
**Apply to:** Mr S Fagelman

A modern progressive law firm specialising in personal injury, family law and conveyancing.

| | |
|---|---|
| V | 0-1 |
| T | 0 |
| P | 3 |
| TS | 9 |
| WP | no |

## GOODMAN RAY
450 Kingsland Road, London E8 4AE
**Tel:** 020 7254 8855
**Fax:** 020 7923 4345
**Email:** mail@goodmanray.com
**Apply to:** Mr Miles Honour

Family practice. East London area. No training contracts until further notice.

| | |
|---|---|
| V | 0 |
| T | 2 |
| P | 4 |
| TS | 17 |
| WP | no |

## GOODMANS
33 Rodney Street, Liverpool L1 9JF
**Tel:** 0151 707 0090
**Fax:** 0151 707 4600
**Email:** personnel@goodmanslaw.co.uk
**Apply to:** Ms Lynn Evans

High profile, client-focused practice covering a broad spectrum of legal work. We have a genuine commitment to training and development and offer excellent prospects.

| | |
|---|---|
| V | 2[09] |
| T | 2 |
| P | 7 |
| TS | 80 |
| WP | no |

## GOODSWENS
118 High Street, Redcar TS10 3DH
**Tel:** 01642 482424
**Fax:** 01642 471475
**Email:** law@goodswens.co.uk
**Apply to:** Mr MG Boyes

Goodswens is a long established general practice covering most areas of legal work. We regard ourselves as client-friendly, placing client care a top priority.

| | |
|---|---|
| V | Poss |
| T | 1 |
| P | 3 |
| TS | 18 |
| WP | no |

## GOODY BURRETT LLP
St Martin House, 63 West Stockwell Street,
Colchester CO1 1WD
**Tel:** 01206 577676
**Fax:** 01206 548704
**Email:** law@goodys.co.uk
**Apply to:** Mr BC Johnston

One of the oldest firms in Colchester (over 250 years), offer friendly, relaxed but professional legal services to private clients and companies.

| | |
|---|---|
| V | 1[08] |
| T | 1 |
| P | 5 |
| TS | 42 |
| WP | yes |

## GORDON DADDS
80 Brook Street, Mayfair, London W1K 5DD
**Tel:** 020 7493 6151
**Fax:** 020 7491 1065
**Email:** daviddruck@gordondadds.com
**Apply to:** Mr David Ruck

Medium-sized practice with UK and foreign clients. Departments: family, private client, litigation, property and company commercial.

| | |
|---|---|
| V | 2 |
| T | 2 |
| P | 10 |
| TS | 45 |
| WP | no |

## GORRARA HADEN SOLICITORS
Quadrant Court, 50 Calthorpe Road, Edgbaston,
Birmingham B15 1TH
**Tel:** 0121 452 8787
**Fax:** 0121 452 8788
**Apply to:** Mrs GP Haden

Gorrara Haden Solicitors is a niche commercial practice specialising in housing management work for local authorities and housing associations, and a recognised specialist for anti-social behaviour cases.

| | |
|---|---|
| V | 0 |
| T | 1 |
| P | 2 |
| TS | 12 |
| WP | no |

## GOSSCHALKS
Queens Gardens, Hull HU1 3DZ
**Tel:** 01482 324252
**Fax:** 01482 590290
**Email:** cjb@gosschalks.co.uk
**Apply to:** Mr Mark Teal

Purpose built city centre offices. Major national clients with emphasis on commercial and licensing work. Many partners recognised as specialists in their own field

| | |
|---|---|
| V | 3 |
| T | 7 |
| P | 33 |
| TS | 120 |
| WP | no |

**V** = Vacancies / **T** = Trainees / **P** = Partners / **TS** = Total Staff / **WP** = Work Placement

# Government Legal Service

**Tel:** 020 7649 6023
**Email:** glstrainees@tmpw.co.uk
**Web:** www.gls.gov.uk

**The firm** The Government Legal Service consists of around 1,950 qualified lawyers employed in about 30 separate government departments and bodies. There may be anything from 1 to over 400 lawyers in a single organisation.

**Types of work** Lawyers working in the Government Legal Service have one client, the government of the day. That client requires advice and support across an extraordinarily broad range of domestic and European matters. The GLS differs considerably from private practice. Our work offers a different perspective, intellectual stimulus and considerable diversity. Our objective is the public good and GLS lawyers have the opportunity to make a positive contribution to the wellbeing of the whole country. Our lawyers are given responsibility at an early stage of their career. We offer career development and training opportunities, allowing lawyers to progress to higher levels at a pace determined by their own performance. Sustained good performance is rewarded by additional salary increments. Our lawyers also have the opportunity to move between areas of responsibility within their department, or to other departments, in order to gain wider experience.

**Who should apply** We are looking for applicants who can demonstrate both the intellectual ability to work in a wide variety of legal fields and settings, and commitment to developing a career in the public sector. You will need strong analytical ability and excellent communication and interpersonal skills. Your background is unimportant.

**Training programme** Generally, trainee solicitors work in four different 'seats' over a two-year period in the department to which they are assigned, thereby gaining a broad view of government legal work. Occasionally, trainees may have the opportunity to spend time working in another government department. Pupil barristers spend the first six months or middle four months of their year's pupillage in chambers. Trainees and pupils are involved in a wide range of work conducted by their department, including high-profile cases, under the supervision of senior colleagues.

**When and how to apply** Trainees are recruited two years in advance. Penultimate-year law students and final-year non-law students should apply via the employer's application form (EAF), available on the GLS website, by 31 July 2008.

**Work placements** 60-70 placements are available each year. For Summer 2008, the closing date for receipt of applications (EAF) is 31 March 2008. Again, you can apply via the GLS website.

**Sponsorship** Sponsorship for the vocational year (LPC or BVC) is usually available to successful candidates. Sponsorship for the CPE may be available. Sponsorship for the vocational year is currently in the range of £5,000-£7,000. Course fees and 50% of the cost of course textbooks, where they are not included in the course fees, are also paid. All GLS trainees and pupils are salaried.

| | |
|---|---|
| Vacancies | 22-30 |
| Total lawyers | 1950 |
| Work placement | yes |
| Apply to | GLS Recruitment Team |
| Starting salary | Over £21,300 (in London) |
| Minimum qualifications | 2.1 degree in any subject |
| Sponsorship | LPC/BVC |
| Offices | Nationwide (but mostly London) |

| GOTELEE & GOLDSMITH<br>31-41 Elm Street, Ipswich IP1 2AY<br>**Tel:** 01473 211121<br>**Fax:** 01473 230387<br>**Email:** info@gotelee.co.uk<br>**Apply to:** Mrs Vicky Young | A well-established firm with a strong client base covering most areas of commercial private client and litigation work, including legal aid. | V 1[09]<br>T 3<br>P 13<br>TS 92<br>WP no |
|---|---|---|
| GOUGH-THOMAS & SCOTT<br>8 Willow Street, Ellesmere, Shropshire SY12 0AQ<br>**Tel:** 01691 622413<br>**Fax:** 01691 623226<br>**Apply to:** Mr MJ Kendall | Offices in Ellesmere and Oswestry, a young go ahead firm in a rural area dealing with general practice. | V 1[08]<br>T 1<br>P 4<br>TS 18<br>WP no |
| GRAHAM & ROSEN<br>8 Parliament Street, Hull HU1 2BB<br>**Tel:** 01482 323123<br>**Fax:** 01482 223542<br>**Email:** law@graham-rosen.com<br>**Apply to:** Mr ME Stewart | General practice including private client, personal injury, matrimonial and crime. Legal aid franchise. Member of network of European lawyers. | V 1-2<br>T 0<br>P 10<br>TS 60<br>WP yes |
| GRAYS<br>Duncombe Place, York YO1 7DY<br>**Tel:** 01904 634771<br>**Fax:** 01904 610711<br>**Email:** enquiries@grayssolicitors.co.uk<br>**Apply to:** Mrs L Rickatson | Matters handled include private client work, landed and settled estates, tax, trusts and probate, charities, litigation and agricultural, commercial and domestic conveyancing, and landlord and tenant work. | V 0<br>T 0<br>P 4<br>TS 30<br>WP no |
| GREENWICH COMMUNITY LAW CENTRE<br>187 Trafalgar Road, London SE10 9EQ<br>**Tel:** 020 8305 3350<br>**Fax:** 020 8858 5253<br>**Email:** info@gclc.co.uk<br>**Apply to:** The Recruitment Contact | A law centre providing free legal advice and representation in social welfare law. We have a 'not for profit' franchise in housing, immigration, employment and welfare rights. | V 0<br>T 0<br>P -<br>TS 12<br>WP no |
| GREENWOODS<br>Monkstone House, City Road,<br>Peterborough PEI 1JE<br>**Tel:** 01733 887700<br>**Fax:** 01733 887701<br>**Email:** rgearing@greenwoods.co.uk<br>**Apply to:** Miss Rosemary Gearing | Greenwoods is a leading regional firm offering a comprehensive range of legal services. Essentially a commercial practice. Welcomes applications from both law and non-law graduates. | V 2-3<br>T 6<br>P 11<br>TS 76<br>WP no |
| GREGG LATCHAMS WRH<br>7 Queen Square, Bristol BS1 4JE<br>**Tel:** 0117 906 9400<br>**Fax:** 0117 906 9401<br>**Email:** andrew.gregg@glwrh.co.uk<br>**Apply to:** Mr Andrew Gregg | Bristol based general practice with expertise in all areas of the law. | V 0<br>T 2<br>P 9<br>TS 75<br>WP no |
| GREGORY ABRAMS DAVIDSON LLP<br>20-24 Matthew Street, Liverpool L2 6RE<br>**Tel:** 0151 236 5000<br>**Fax:** 0151 330 2002<br>**Email:** lawline@gregoryabramsdavidson.com<br>**Apply to:** The Personnel Manager | Dynamic, forward-thinking practice that has achieved particular recognition for property, commercial, personal injury, family, crime and education law. A friendly yet challenging environment for trainees. | V 2[09]<br>T 4<br>P 4<br>TS 58<br>WP yes |

**V** = Vacancies / **T** = Trainees / **P** = Partners / **TS** = Total Staff / **WP** = Work Placement

| | | |
|---|---|---|
| **GREGORY ROWCLIFFE MILNERS**<br>1 Bedford Row, London WC1R 4BZ<br>**Tel:** 020 7242 0631<br>**Fax:** 020 7242 6652<br>**Email:** law@grm.co.uk<br>**Apply to:** Mr Tim Moloney | Long established private client, company/commercial and litigation practice with strongly developed Anglo-German, and other connections including Anglo-German trade organisations. | V 1[09]<br>T 2<br>P 13<br>TS 55<br>WP no |
| **GSC SOLICITORS**<br>31-32 Ely Place, London EC1N 6TD<br>**Tel:** 020 7822 2222<br>**Fax:** 020 7822 2211<br>**Email:** info@gscsolicitors.com<br>**Apply to:** Mr Clive Halperin | City practice with emphasis on intellectual property including music, copyright and trademarks, commercial property, corporate and commercial law, employment, litigation and general commercial work. | V 2[08]<br>T 3<br>P 8<br>TS 38<br>WP no |
| **GT STEWART SOLICITORS**<br>28 Grove Vale, East Dulwich, London SE22 8EF<br>**Tel:** 020 8299 6000<br>**Fax:** 020 8299 6009<br>**Email:** e.inegbu@gtstewart.co.uk<br>**Apply to:** Ms Esme Inegbu | Young firm committed to publicly funded criminal defence work. Particular expertise in youth work and judicial review. Many high and low profile cases. | V 1-2[09]<br>T 2<br>P 1<br>TS 21<br>WP no |
| **GUILDFORD BOROUGH COUNCIL**<br>Millmead House, Millmead, Guildford,<br>Surrey GU2 4BB<br>**Tel:** 01483 505050<br>**Fax:** 01483 444996<br>**Email:** lingardr@guildford.gov.uk<br>**Apply to:** Mr Richard Lingard | Local government in-house legal practice dealing primarily with planning, housing, public entertainment and taxi licensing, conveyancing, procurement, contracts and general local government law. | V 0<br>T 2<br>P -<br>TS 17<br>WP no |
| **GURNEY-CHAMPION & CO**<br>104 Victoria Road North, Southsea,<br>Hampshire PO5 1QE<br>**Tel:** 023 9282 1100<br>**Fax:** 023 9282 0447<br>**Email:** info@championlawyers.co.uk<br>**Apply to:** Mr N C A Gurney-Champion | Traditional high street practice, dealing with residential and commercial convincing, wills and probate, family, civil litigation and general business matters. Friendly and professional firm. | V 0<br>T 1<br>P 2<br>TS 8<br>WP no |
| **GWILYM HUGHES & PARTNERS**<br>Ashgrove, 26-30 Grosvenor Road, Wrexham,<br>Clwyd LL11 1BU<br>**Tel:** 01978 291456<br>**Fax:** 01978 291716<br>**Email:** wrexham@gwilymhughes.co.uk<br>**Apply to:** The Practice Manager | Leading regional firm, offering a complete and comprehensive service, with experts specialising in all aspects of private, commercial and legal aid work. | V 1[09]<br>T 7<br>P 10<br>TS 98<br>WP no |
| **GWYNNE HUGHES**<br>Council Chambers, 26 Alban Square,<br>Aberaeron SA46 0AL<br>**Tel:** 01545 570861<br>**Fax:** 01545 571121<br>**Email:** gwynnehughes@ukgateway.net<br>**Apply to:** Mr JD Gwynne Hughes | Family run practice established in 1943. Probate, conveyancing, matrimonial and civil litigation. Satellite office in New Quay (W. Wales). | V 1<br>T -<br>P 2<br>TS 12<br>WP no |
| **HACKING ASHTON LLP**<br>Berkeley Court, Borough Road,<br>Newcastle Under Lyme ST5 1TT<br>**Tel:** 01782 715555<br>**Fax:** 01782 715566<br>**Email:** c.wooliscroft@hackingashton.co.uk<br>**Apply to:** C R Woolliscroft | A commercial firm acting for UK and overseas clients. Most trainees will be required to work a trial period as paralegals. | V Poss 1<br>T 4<br>P 10<br>TS 38<br>WP no |

# Halliwells LLP

3 Hardman Square, Spinningfields, Manchester M3 3EB
**Tel:** 0870 365 8918
**Fax:** 0870 365 8919
**Email:** ekaterina.clarke@halliwells.com
**Web:** www.halliwells.com

**The firm** Halliwells is one of the largest independent commercial law firms in the northwest and specialises in providing a full range of legal services to the business community. With clients on a local, national and international level, Halliwells has high aspirations far beyond its regional boundaries. Over the last few years the firm has increased substantially in both size and turnover and is widely acknowledged as one of the country's most successfully managed practices.

**Types of work** Corporate (corporate, banking and tax), corporate recovery, dispute resolution (commercial litigation, insurance liability, regulatory and environmental and construction) business services (employment and intellectual property), real estate (property, planning and licensing) and private client. The firm acts for a number of well-known institutions and public companies.

**Who should apply** Penultimate-year law undergraduates or final-year non-law undergraduates. Applicants are expected to have a good academic background, a 2.1 degree, and exhibit the characteristics necessary to thrive in a busy commercial environment.

**Training programme** In conjunction with The College of Law, Halliwells offers their future trainee solicitors a place on a tailor-made LPC+. Halliwells LPC+ students study the core areas in groups with other corporate students. Elective groups are Halliwells exclusive and the electives are selected by Halliwells. On joining the firm, trainees from all offices take part in a tailored two-week induction programme. The training contract is structured into five seats to provide trainees with practical experience in a range of departments. In addition, trainees are encouraged to develop their legal knowledge and personal skills by attending the firm's regular in-house legal and skills workshops.

**When and how to apply** Before 31 July 2008 for contracts commencing in August 2010. Apply online at www.halliwells.com.

**Work placements** Operates for two-week sections throughout July and August. Applications to be made prior to 29 February 2008 in penultimate year of study for law students and final year of study for non-law students.

**Sponsorship** The firm will pay CPE and LPC course fees plus a maintenance grant of £6,500 per course.

| | |
|---|---|
| Vacancies | 38 |
| Trainees | 76 |
| Partners | 165 |
| Total staff | 1300 |

**Work placement**   yes
*(see Insider Report on p103)*

**Apply**
Online

**Starting salary**
£23,000 (2007)
£29,500 (London 2007)

**Minimum qualifications**
2.1 degree

**Sponsorship**
CPE/LPC

**Offices**
London, Manchester,
Liverpool, Sheffield

# Halliwells

# Hammonds

7 Devonshire Square, Cutlers Gardens, London EC2M 4YH
**Tel:** 0800 163498
**Email:** graduaterecruitment@hammonds.com
**Web:** www.hammonds.com/trainees

**The firm** Hammonds is one of Europe's largest corporate law firms and a member of the Global 100. In the UK alone, the firm advises over 30 FTSE 100 companies and over 90 FTSE All Share companies; it has also doubled the number of FTSE clients since 2003. The UK office network consists of a significant London presence, complemented by leading practices in the key commercial centres of Birmingham, Leeds and Manchester. An integrated European network includes offices in Berlin, Brussels, Madrid, Milan, Munich, Paris, Rome and Turin. There are also offices in Beijing and Hong Kong.

The firm has over 1,300 staff including 189 partners and 80 trainees. It is proud of the exceptional individuals it employs and a structured career progression path and tailored training programme are integral to the long term success of the business. The culture of the firm has always been to build from within. Many partners and senior fee earners originally trained with the firm.

As a full service law firm, Hammonds employs specialists in all areas of business law. The firm operates a distinct business sector approach and single partnership across its European network.

Trainees undertake six four-month seats supported by a two-tier supervision programme. Key to the firm's training contract is 'involvement and responsibility'. There is opportunity to consider an overseas seat from a choice of Berlin, Brussels, Hong Kong, Madrid, Paris or Turin. For those seeking an understanding of client business, the firm presently offers secondments with leading clients including Live Nation (Venues) UK Limited.

**Types of work** The firm has a broad practice area with opportunity to undertake seats in advertising, asset based lending, banking, business recovery and finance, commercial dispute resolution, commercial & IP, construction and engineering, corporate finance, employment, EU law, international project finance, media, pensions, planning, property, sports and tax strategies.

**Who should apply** Penultimate year law and non-law students.

**Training programme** The firm offers a unique training contract tailored to individual trainee needs. On arrival, trainees are involved in a three week induction programme in addition to receiving comprehensive department training and skills focus. The programme is supported by six four-month seats, two-tier supervision system and overseas and client secondment opportunities. Trainee development is key to the success of the business and the firm invests in bespoke training.

**When and how to apply** Applicants should complete the firm's online application form accessed via the website www.hammonds.com/trainees. Closing date for 2010 training contracts is 31 July 2008.

**Work placements** A two- week summer scheme is available at all UK offices. It provides the opportunity to gain experience in two practice areas. Applicants should complete the firm's online application form accessed via the website www.hammonds.com/trainees. Closing date is 31 January 2008.

**Sponsorship** Tuition fees and maintenance grant payable for both the GDL and LPC.

| Vacancies | 40 |
|---|---|
| Trainees | 80 |
| Partners | 183 |
| Total staff | 1300 |

**Work placement** yes

**Apply to**
Graduate Recruitment
Department

**Starting salary**
London
1st year: £35,000
2nd year: £38,000
Regions
1st year: 25,000
2nd year: £27,000

**Minimum qualifications**
2.1 degree, 280 UCAS points

**Sponsorship**
GDL/LPC

**Offices**
London, Birmingham, Leeds, Manchester, Beijing, Berlin, Brussels, Hong Kong, Madrid, Milan, Munich, Paris, Rome, Turin

# Hammonds

| | | | |
|---|---|---|---|
| **HADENS**<br>Leicester Buildings, Bridge Street,<br>Walsall WS1 1EL<br>**Tel:** 01922 720000<br>**Fax:** 01922 720023<br>**Email:** esmall@hadens.co.uk<br>**Apply to:** Mrs Elaine Small | General practice dealing with all aspects of commercial and private client work from two offices in the West Midlands. | V<br>T<br>P<br>TS<br>WP | 2⁽⁰⁹⁾<br>3<br>9<br>70<br>no |

| | | | |
|---|---|---|---|
| **HAINS & LEWIS**<br>2 Victoria Place, Haverford West,<br>Pembrokeshire SA61 2LP<br>**Tel:** 01437 764593<br>**Fax:** 01437 769434<br>**Email:** law@hainsandlewis.co.uk<br>**Apply to:** Miss V H Hains | General high street / legal aid practice - two branch office. 11 solicitors specialising in family, property, probate, public law, general civil litigation and some crime. | V<br>T<br>P<br>TS<br>WP | 0<br>0<br>2<br>42<br>no |

| | | | |
|---|---|---|---|
| **HAMILTON PRATT**<br>120 Edmund Street, Birmingham B3 2ES<br>**Tel:** 0121 237 2027<br>**Fax:** 0121 233 9686<br>**Apply to:** Mr JH Pratt | We are one of the top three franchise law firms worldwide. Over 20% of our work is international. | V<br>T<br>P<br>TS<br>WP | 1<br>1<br>3<br>10<br>no |

| | | | |
|---|---|---|---|
| **HANSELLS**<br>13-14 The Close, Norwich NR1 4DS<br>**Tel:** 01603 615731<br>**Fax:** 01603 633585<br>**Email:** timeagle@hansells.co.uk<br>**Apply to:** Mr Tim Eagle | Hansells is one of the largest firms in the county. Specialisms include charities, commercial property, employment, family, medical negligence, personal injury, residential property, wills and probate. | V<br>T<br>P<br>TS<br>WP | 1-2<br>7<br>15<br>130<br>yes |

| | | | |
|---|---|---|---|
| **HARBOTTLE & LEWIS LLP**<br>Hanover House, 14 Hanover Square,<br>London W1S 1HP<br>**Tel:** 020 7667 5000<br>**Fax:** 020 7667 5100<br>**Email:** kathy.beilby@harbottle.com<br>**Apply to:** Mrs Kathy Beilby | The firm specialises in the media, entertainment, leisure and aviation industries. Regarded by Legal 500 as a leading firm across all its industry areas. | V<br>T<br>P<br>TS<br>WP | 4<br>10<br>24<br>170<br>no |

| | | | |
|---|---|---|---|
| **HARDING EVANS LLP**<br>2 North Street, Newport, Gwent NP20 1TE<br>**Tel:** 01633 244233<br>**Fax:** 01633 246453<br>**Email:** dhm@hevans.com<br>**Apply to:** Mr David Morgan | We are the 8th largest practice in Wales and offer a broad range of practice areas. | V<br>T<br>P<br>TS<br>WP | 4<br>4<br>11<br>124<br>no |

| | | | |
|---|---|---|---|
| **THE HARDMAN PARTNERSHIP**<br>Seventh Floor, Blackfriars House, Parsonage,<br>Manchester M3 2JA<br>**Tel:** 0161 832 5748<br>**Fax:** 0161 832 5762<br>**Email:** lawyers@thehardmanpartnership.co.uk<br>**Apply to:** Mrs Susan Hardman | Niche commercial firm offering the full range of legal services to owner managed companies and high net worth individuals | V<br>T<br>P<br>TS<br>WP | 1-2⁽⁰⁹⁾<br>4<br>3<br>15<br>no |

| | | | |
|---|---|---|---|
| **HARPER & ODELL**<br>London Office, 111 St John Street,<br>London EC1V 4JA<br>**Tel:** 020 7490 0500<br>**Fax:** 020 7490 8040<br>**Email:** law@harperandodell.co.uk<br>**Apply to:** Mr RA Hussein | Long established firm with London offices specialising in personal injury, landlord and tenant and contractual claims, wills, administering wills and residential and commercial conveyancing. | V<br>T<br>P<br>TS<br>WP | 0<br>0<br>2<br>5<br>no |

**V** = Vacancies / **T** = Trainees / **P** = Partners / **TS** = Total Staff / **WP** = Work Placement

# Harvey Ingram LLP

20 New Walk, Leicester LE1 6TX
**Tel:** 0116 254 5454
**Fax:** 0116 255 4559
**Email:** claire.bingham@harveyingram.com
**Web:** www.harveyingram.com

**The firm** As one of the largest 20 firms in the Midlands, we offer comprehensive training in a range of legal services offered to clients both in the Midlands and throughout the UK. We place a high priority on our 'client-focused' approach and on giving commercial as well as technical legal advice.

**Types of work** We have a wide range of commercial clients, from quoted public companies to small family businesses. We have particularly strong property, commercial litigation, personal injury and employment law teams, and an excellent reputation for all types of commercial work. Allied to our commercial practice, we have renowned trust and probate and family teams catering for our significant private clients.

We also specialise in a variety of sectors including information technology, finance, insolvency, real estate, planning and construction, retail, intellectual property, pensions, family, sport and clinical negligence.

**Who should apply** We are looking for applicants with at least a 2.1 degree in any discipline, who are motivated, ambitious and demonstrate initiative and commitment to teamwork.

**Training programme** We believe that investing in people will contribute to the success and future growth of the firm and we pride ourselves in offering a carefully structured training programme. We offer six seats of four months, working with a range of lawyers from senior partners to more recently qualified solicitors. You will have the opportunity to work on all aspects of transactions, from major corporate and commercial cases through to gaining experience in intellectual property and personal injury claims. We can offer you unparalleled experience, real responsibility and client contact from day one.

You will receive a comprehensive induction, a well-structured training schedule, regular appraisals and excellent levels of support.

**When and how to apply** Applications need to be received prior to 31 July for a training contract to commence two years later. You will be required to submit an application form – this can be completed online via our website or by requesting a form personally.

**Work placements** We run a summer vacation scheme. Applications should be submitted before 30 April in the year you wish to participate.

**Sponsorship** If you are not eligible for local authority funding, we will pay LPC tuition fees for successful candidates.

| | |
|---|---|
| Vacancies | 3-4 |
| Trainees | 8 |
| Partners | 32 |
| Total staff | 200+ |

**Work placement**   yes

**Apply to**
Claire Bingham

**Starting salary**
No less than £19,000

**Minimum qualifications**
2.1 degree

**Sponsorship**
LPC

**Offices**
Leicester, Birmingham

Harvey Ingram LLP
solicitors

## HARRIS CARTIER LLP
Windsor Crown House, 7 Windsor Road, Slough,
Berks SL1 2DX
**Tel:** 01753 810710
**Fax:** 0870 6067344
**Email:** Fgrimmett@hclaw.co.uk
**Apply to:** Ms Fay Grimmett

A general practice, but with specialist niche areas of expertise including, in particular, expanding commercial, personal injury and clinical negligence departments. Excellent prospects for trainees.

| | |
|---|---|
| V | 2[08] |
| T | 4 |
| P | 9 |
| TS | 100 |
| WP | no |

## HARRIS WATERS & CO
406-408 High Road, Ilford, Essex IG1 1TW
**Tel:** 020 8478 0888
**Fax:** 020 8478 8668
**Email:** roger@harriswaters.com
**Apply to:** Mr R Waters

We are an expanding dynamic firm with a growing reputation for our professional yet warm and friendly services in family law, litigation, residential and commercial conveyancing.

| | |
|---|---|
| V | 1[08] |
| T | 1 |
| P | 2 |
| TS | 11 |
| WP | yes |

## HARRISON CLARK
5 Deansway, Worcester WR1 2JG
**Tel:** 01905 612001
**Fax:** 01905 20433
**Apply to:** Mrs Nikki Powell

Expanding progressive general practice with increasing commercial bias. Paralegals are recruited throughout the year and, if successful, training contracts are generally awarded after 12 months. Please refer to our website.

| | |
|---|---|
| V | 0 |
| T | 11 |
| P | 19 |
| TS | 130 |
| WP | no |

## HARROW SOLICITORS & ADVOCATES
5 Masons Avenue, Harrow, Middlesex HA3 5AH
**Tel:** 020 8863 0788
**Fax:** 020 8420 9998
**Apply to:** Mr Elvin Blades

Solicitors firm offering legal help to the public. Specialist help in criminal, debt, family, housing, immigration and nationality law.

| | |
|---|---|
| V | 0 |
| T | 6 |
| P | 4 |
| TS | 33 |
| WP | yes |

## HARROWELL SHAFTOE
1 St Saviourgate, York YO1 82Q
**Tel:** 01904 558600
**Fax:** 01904 617616
**Apply to:** Ms Barbara Collinson

One of North Yorkshire's largest law firms, serving business and individual clients throughout the region. Several of our legal teams also provide advice nationwide.

| | |
|---|---|
| V | 3[08] |
| T | 7 |
| P | 20 |
| TS | 175 |
| WP | yes |

## HART BROWN
Resolution House, Riverview, Walnut Tree Close,
Guildford GU1 4UX
**Tel:** 01483 887766
**Fax:** 01483 887750
**Email:** hr@hartbrown.co.uk
**Apply to:** Mr David Smith

With six offices, we are one of the largest firms based wholly in Surrey, offering training in three or four departments from civil, family, property, private client and commercial.

| | |
|---|---|
| V | 2 |
| T | 4 |
| P | 14 |
| TS | 110 |
| WP | no |

## HART READE
104 South Street, Eastbourne BN21 4LW
**Tel:** 01323 727321
**Fax:** 01323 721097
**Email:** info@hartreade.co.uk
**Apply to:** Mrs DA Breach

Established and respected high street firm which advises private and business clients on all main areas of law. Family Legal Services Commission franchise.

| | |
|---|---|
| V | 0 |
| T | 1 |
| P | 8 |
| TS | 72 |
| WP | no |

## HATCHERS
25 Castle Street, Shrewsbury SY1 1DA
**Tel:** 01743 248545
**Fax:** 01743 242979
**Email:** mail@hatchers.co.uk
**Apply to:** Mrs Jacinta Walmsley

General practice with some specialisms. Broad client base. Three offices in Central and North Shropshire. Specialisms: environment, agriculture, debt, PI, crime, family, private client, corporate and employment.

| | |
|---|---|
| V | 0 |
| T | 1 |
| P | 12 |
| TS | 80 |
| WP | no |

**V** = Vacancies / **T** = Trainees / **P** = Partners / **TS** = Total Staff / **WP** = Work Placement

# Hay & Kilner

30 Cloth Market, Newcastle Upon Tyne NE1 1EE
**Tel:** 0191 232 8345
**Fax:** 0191 261 7704
**Email:** ros.sparrow@hay-kilner.co.uk
**Web:** www.hay-kilner.co.uk

**The firm** Hay & Kilner is located in Newcastle upon Tyne's city centre. Newcastle is a thriving and exciting city with easy access to the beautiful countryside of Northumberland, the Lake District and Scotland.

Established in 1946, Hay & Kilner has grown organically to become one of the largest firms in Newcastle with 23 partners and 150 staff.

We provide a broad range of highly specialist services to both corporate and private clients. Young, modern and commercial in outlook, we aim to provide fast, efficient and practical advice to our clients.

We are committed to quality. We are ISO9001 accredited and Legal Aid franchise holders and are seeking Lexcel accreditation. As members of Eurojuris, we also have access to expertise from a network of quality accredited law firms throughout Europe.

**Types of work** Our main office is divided into three practice areas: commercial, litigation, and private client. We also have a branch office in Wallsend and a volume recoveries and re-mortgage operation, which trades as Wallers Solicitors and acts for a number of financial institutions.

**Who should apply** We are looking for intelligent, well motivated, commercially aware and outgoing individuals. Our minimum entry requirement is a 2.1 degree (or an expectation of one). We actively encourage applications from non-law graduates and we value outside interests and experience.

**Training programme** The training contract is usually divided into four six-month seats, generally including time in the three practice areas. During your training, you will have the opportunity to take responsibility for the conduct of files. You will also have client contact and will carry out advocacy where appropriate. In short, we will train you to be a complete solicitor.

The ethos of the firm is a wholly supportive one and throughout your training contract you will work closely with your supervisor and with other qualified fee earners.

You will meet with Bruce Howorth, your supervisor and training partner, on a six monthly basis. These appraisals provide the opportunity for a more detailed and structured review of your progress and allow us to plan your future training.

Along with a small number of other local commercial law firms, we have designed a commercial professional skills course for our trainees at the University of Northumbria. You will also be able to attend appropriate internal and external seminars and courses.

**When and how to apply** We aim to carry out interviews for training contracts two years in advance. Apply online at www.hay-kilner.co.uk.

Applications for the summer vacation scheme should be completed by 28 February and training contracts by 31 July. Please refer to our website for up to date details.

| | |
|---|---|
| Vacancies | 2 |
| Trainees | 4 |
| Partners | 23 |
| Total Staff | 150 |

**Work placement** yes

**Apply to**
Ms Ros Sparrow

**Starting salary**
Under review

**Minimum qualifications**
2.1 degree

**Offices**
Newcastle (head office)
Wallsend (branch office)

HAY ▲ KILNER
SOLICITORS

| **HATTON**<br>1 Sheaf Street, Daventry, Northants NN11 4AA<br>**Tel:** 01327 301201<br>**Fax:** 01327 706226<br>**Email:** jhatton@msn.com<br>**Apply to:** Mr Jonathan Hatton | Fraud, commercial and Chancery. | V 1-2<br>T 1<br>P 1<br>TS 6<br>WP yes |
| --- | --- | --- |
| **HAWKES HILL**<br>23 Winchester Road, Basingstoke,<br>Hampshire RG21 8UE<br>**Tel:** 01256 465404<br>**Fax:** 08707 438376<br>**Email:** a.hill@hawkes-hill.co.uk<br>**Apply to:** Mrs A Hill | No vacancies at present. | V 0<br>T 0<br>P -<br>TS -<br>WP no |
| **HAWKINS RUSSELL JONES**<br>7-8 Portmill Lane, Hitchin SG5 1AS<br>**Tel:** 01462 628888<br>**Fax:** 01462 631233<br>**Email:** david.heymans@hrjlaw.co.uk<br>**Apply to:** Mr David Heymans | Offices in Hitchin and Welwyn Garden City. Candidates should have a 2.1 degree and a local (Herts, Beds, Cambs, Bucks) connection. | V 0<br>T 2<br>P 14<br>TS 72<br>WP no |
| **THE HAWKSWELL KILVINGTON PARTNERSHIP**<br>Construction House, 1b South Park Way,<br>Wakefield 41 Business Park, Wakefield,<br>West Yorkshire WF2 0XJ<br>**Tel:** 01924 202170<br>**Fax:** 01924 380926<br>**Email:** ltankard@thkp.co.uk<br>**Apply to:** Mrs Louise Tankard | We are based south of Leeds in a modern business park. We have established a national reputation as a niche construction law practice. | V 0<br>T 2<br>P 3<br>TS 12<br>WP no |
| **HAYES + STORR**<br>18-19 Market Place, Fakenham, Norfolk NR21 9BH<br>**Tel:** 01328 863231<br>**Fax:** 01328 856696<br>**Apply to:** Mrs Christine Abel | Busy, friendly and expanding general practice in rural North Norfolk. Commercial, litigation, property and private client departments based over five branches. The quality of life option. | V 0<br>T 1<br>P 8<br>TS 60<br>WP no |
| **HC SOLICITORS LLP**<br>35 Thorpe Road, Peterborough PE3 6AG<br>**Tel:** 01733 565312<br>**Fax:** 01733 552748<br>**Email:** gwen.marshall@hcsolicitors.co.uk<br>**Apply to:** Ms Gwen Marshall | General practice firm with specialities in family care, crime and personal injury. Has legal aid franchise and Investors in People awards. Committed to IT solutions and training. | V 0<br>T 2<br>P 14<br>TS 97<br>WP no |
| **HCL HANNE & CO**<br>St. Johns Chambers, 1c St Johns Hill,<br>London SW11 1TN<br>**Tel:** 020 7228 0017<br>**Fax:** 020 7326 8300<br>**Apply to:** via website | Classic high street practice, with a strong commitment to publicly funded work and an overall service to clients. | V 1-2[08]<br>T 7<br>P 7<br>TS 50<br>WP no |
| **HEALD SOLICITORS**<br>471 Silbury Boulevard, Milton Keynes MK9 2AH<br>**Tel:** 01908 662277<br>**Fax:** 01908 675 667<br>**Email:** info@healdlaw.com<br>**Apply to:** Ms Mary Banham-Hall | Medium-sized firm in Milton Keynes and Bedford, specialising in commercial work and private client family, wills and trusts and personal injury. | V 2<br>T 2<br>P 6<br>TS 30<br>WP no |

**V** = Vacancies / **T** = Trainees / **P** = Partners / **TS** = Total Staff / **WP** = Work Placement

# HBJ Gateley Wareing LLP

One Eleven, Edmund Street, Birmingham B3 2HJ
**Tel:** 0121 234 0069
**Fax:** 0121 234 0079
**Email:** graduaterecruitment.england@hbj-gw.com
**Web:** www.hbjgateleywareing.com

**The firm** A 75 partner, UK commercial based practice with an excellent reputation for general commercial work and particular expertise in corporate, plc, commercial, employment, property, construction, insolvency, commercial dispute resolution, banking, tax and shipping.

The firm also offers individual clients a complete private client service including FSA approved financial advice. The firm is expanding (488 employees) and offers a highly practical, commercial and fast-paced environment. HBJ Gateley Wareing has built an outstanding reputation across the UK for its practical approach, sound advice and professional commitment to its clients. The firm is a full-range, multi-disciplinary legal business with expertise in many areas.

HBJ Gateley Wareing has an enviable reputation as a friendly and sociable place to work. We are committed to equality and diversity across the firm.

**Types of work** We work with major financial institutions, leading corporate companies and mid-market firms across a range of the UK's industrial sectors, however, the firm remains committed to building lasting relationships with smaller businesses and emerging entrepreneurs, helping them to grow and prosper.

**Who should apply** Second-year law students, final-year non-law students and graduates. Applicants should have (or be heading for) a minimum 2.1 degree, and should have at least three Bs (or equivalent) at A-level.

**Training programme** Four six-month seats with ongoing supervision and appraisals every three months. PSC taken internally. In-house courses on skills such as time management, negotiation, IT, drafting, business skills, marketing, presenting and writing in plain English.

**When and how to apply** To apply for a placement in England applications for next year's vacation placement scheme should be made by 11 February 2008 and the final closing date for 2010 training contract applications is 31 July 2008. Apply online at www.hbjgateleywareing.com. We do not accept written applications and CVs.

**Work placements** Two-week placements over the summer.

**Sponsorship** CPE/LPC and a LPC maintenance grant of £4,500.

**Vacancies** 11 (England)
**Trainees** 13 (Midlands)
**Partners** 75 (firmwide)
**Total staff** 488 (firmwide)

**Work placement** yes

**Apply**
Online only

**Starting salary**
£24,000 rising to £25,000
(September 2007)
(Midlands)

**Minimum qualifications**
2.1 degree and three Bs at
A level

**Sponsorship**
CPE/LPC

**Offices**
Birmingham, Edinburgh,
Glasgow, Leicester, London,
Nottingham,

HBJ Gateley Wareing

# Henmans LLP

5000 Oxford Business Park South, Oxford OX4 2BH
**Tel:** 01865 781000
**Fax:** 01865 778628
**Email:** welcome@henmansllp.co.uk
**Web:** www.henmansllp.co.uk

**The firm** Henmans LLP is the premier firm in Oxford, with more practice areas ranked in the top tier of the *Chambers* legal directory than any other Oxford firm. The firm has a national reputation in its specialist areas, handling commercial and personal matters for a wide range of clients both nationally and internationally. We also act for a large number of charities and insurers.

More than half of our senior lawyers are acknowledged as experts within their fields, so clients are confident of receiving the most authoritative advice available. Our belief is that the best advisers are those who thoroughly understand your concerns, so we work hard to ensure that we have a detailed appreciation of your business or personal questions, and can offer the best possible advice.

Our policy of bespoke services and controlled costs ensure that both corporate and private clients benefit from City level standards at competitive regional prices. We take highly qualified staff and make the best use of their talents, by encouraging them to achieve their full potential through training and development, irrespective of their background. This helped us to achieve the Investors in People Award in 2002 and a successful first review in October 2004.

**Types of work** The firm's core service of litigation is nationally recognised for its high quality. We also have an excellent reputation for our personal injury, clinical negligence, property, private client and charity work. The breakdown of work is as follows: professional negligence and commercial litigation: 24%; personal injury: 27%; property: 17%; private client (including family)/ charities/trusts: 25%; corporate/employment: 10%.

**Who should apply** Candidates should possess commercial awareness, sound academic accomplishment, intellectual capability, IT Literacy, good communication skills and thrive in an environment of team-working. We recruit from a diverse range of backgrounds and welcome applications from both law and non-law graduates. We value commitment, energy and enthusiasm both professionally and socially as an integral part of our culture.

**Training programme** Trainees are introduced to the firm with a detailed induction and overview of our client base. We provide four six-month seats within the areas of personal injury, property, family, professional negligence and commercial litigation, and private client departments. The firm provides an ongoing programme of in-house education and regular appraisals within its supportive and friendly environment.

**When and how to apply** Please apply by completing the training contract application form which can be found on our website at www.henmansllp.co.uk, where you will also find further information about the firm. The closing date for applications is 31 July 2008 for contracts to start in September 2010.

| | |
|---|---|
| Vacancies | 3 |
| Trainees | 6 |
| Partners | 23 |
| Total staff | 140 |

**Apply to**
Mrs Viv J Matthews
Head of HR

**Starting salary**
£20,000

**Minimum qualifications**
2.1 or high 2.2 degree with excellent A level grades and relevant experience

**Offices**
Oxford

HENMANS LLP

# Herbert Smith LLP

Exchange House, Primrose Street, London EC2A 2HS
**Tel:** 020 7374 8000
**Fax:** 020 7374 0888
**Email:** graduate.recruitment@herbertsmith.com
**Web:** www.herbertsmith.com

**The firm** We are a leading international legal practice, with more than 1,100 lawyers in our offices in Europe and Asia. In addition, we work closely with two premier European firms with which we have an alliance - the German firm Gleiss Lutz and the Dutch and Belgian firm Stibbe.

We have a diverse, blue-chip client base including FTSE 100 and Fortune 500 companies, major investment banks and governments. What makes Herbert Smith stand out is our culture: a collegial working environment, a pre-eminent market reputation in key practices and industry sectors, and an ambition to be consistently recognised as one of the world's leading law firms.

**Types of work** Herbert Smith is well known for advising on mergers, acquisitions and takeovers, as well as all forms of financing. Our specialist services include our energy, competition, insurance and intellectual property practices. Our reputation for domestic and international litigation, arbitration and alternative dispute resolution is unsurpassed in the UK and Asia.

**Who should apply** Applications are welcome from penultimate-year law students and final-year non-law students, or anyone wishing to commence a training contract in two years' time. The firm recruits from a wide range of universities, and the ratio of law and non-law graduates is broadly equal.

Trainee solicitors need common sense, self-confidence and intelligence to make their own way in a large firm. They are typically high achieving and intelligent, numerate and literate, with good interpersonal skills.

**Training programme** The Herbert Smith training programme is one of the most varied among leading City firms. Our priority is to provide a friendly, professional, team-based environment in which our lawyers can learn and develop their skills.

As a trainee, you will rotate around four seats of six months each, including one in litigation, one in corporate and a further non-contentious seat in either finance or real estate. You can also apply for a specialist seat such as IP, tax, trusts, EU and competition, employment, pensions and incentives or our advocacy unit. Alternatively you can apply to go on secondment to a client or to one of our international offices.

The firm's wide-ranging training and education programme is structured in two parts, both of which fulfil Solicitors Regulation Authority requirements and are tailored to the specific business objectives of Herbert Smith, the Professional Skills Course and the Legal Education Programme. In total, trainees can expect to spend some 30 days of training sessions during their contract. For further information, see our website at www.herbertsmith.com or call a member of the team on 020 7374 8000.

**When and how to apply** Herbert Smith is currently recruiting up to 100 students from any academic discipline to commence training contracts in September 2010 or March 2011. For a training contract students should complete the application form before 31 July 2008.

**Sponsorship**
£5,000 GDL outside London
£6,000 GDL London
£7,000 LPC

| | |
|---|---|
| **Vacancies** | up to 100 |
| **Trainees** | 181 (worldwide) |
| **Partners** | 233 (worldwide) |
| **Total staff** | Approx 2200 |

**Work placement** yes
*(see Insider Report on p105)*

**Apply to**
The Graduate Recruitment Team

**Starting salary**
1st year: £36,000
2nd year: £40,000

**Minimum qualifications**
2.1 degree

**Sponsorship**
CPE/GDL/LPC

**Offices**
Bangkok, Beijing, Brussels, Dubai, Hong Kong, London, Moscow, Paris, Shanghai, Singapore, Tokyo
Associated offices:
Amsterdam, Berlin, Frankfurt, Jakarta, Munich, New York, Prague, Stuttgart, Warsaw

Herbert Smith

| | | |
|---|---|---|
| **HEATH BUCKERIDGE**<br>23 Queen Street, Maidenhead, Berkshire SL6 1NB<br>**Tel:** 01628 671636<br>**Fax:** 01628 671922<br>**Email:** richard.buckeridge@heathbuckeridge.com<br>**Apply to:** Mr Richard Buckeridge | An established and successful general high street practice based in Maidenhead providing a wide range of professional legal services to both business and private clients. | V 0-1<br>T 1<br>P 2<br>TS 15<br>WP no |
| **HEMPSONS**<br>40 Villers Street, London WC2N 6NJ<br>**Tel:** 020 7839 0278<br>**Fax:** 020 7839 8212<br>**Email:** recruitment@hempsons.co.uk<br>**Apply to:** Trainee Solicitor Co-ordinator | Offices: London, Harrogate & Manchester, offering a full range of legal services to NHS and healthcare clients (both individuals and institutional) and charities. | V 6<br>T 6<br>P 30<br>TS 300<br>WP no |
| **HENRY'S SOLICITORS LIMITED**<br>72-74 Wellington Road South, Stockport, Cheshire SK1 3SU<br>**Tel:** 0161 477 8558<br>**Fax:** 0161 474 7667<br>**Apply to:** Mr Kieran Henry | A criminal and prison law specialist company with a fraud contract. We are one of the North West's leading criminal law providers. | V 1[09]<br>T 3<br>P -<br>TS 25<br>WP yes |
| **HEPTONSTALLS**<br>7-13 Gladstone Terrace, Goole DN14 5AH<br>**Tel:** 01405 765661<br>**Fax:** 01405 764201<br>**Email:** recruitment@heptonstalls.co.uk<br>**Apply to:** Miss Dorcas Sturgess | A friendly general practice firm with a strong emphasis on personal injury and medical negligence work. Applications should be made using the application form. | V 1-2<br>T 0<br>P 6<br>TS 98<br>WP no |
| **HEREFORDSHIRE DISTRICT COUNCIL**<br>Brockington, 35 Hafod Road, Hereford HR1 1SH<br>**Tel:** 01432 260299<br>**Fax:** 01432 260206<br>**Email:** pbailey@herefordshire.gov.uk<br>**Apply to:** Mrs PD Bailey | A multi-disciplinary in-house legal service with dedicated specialist reams providing comprehensive legal advice to the council and its external clients. | V 0<br>T 1<br>P 1<br>TS 25<br>WP no |
| **HERRINGTON & CARMICHAEL**<br>Riverside Way, Watchmoor Park, Camberley GU15 3YQ<br>**Tel:** 01276 686222<br>**Fax:** 01276 28041<br>**Email:** mp@herrington-carmichael.com<br>**Apply to:** Mr Peaty | Long established general practice with offices in Aldershot, Camberley, Bagshot and Wokingham. Private client and commercial work especially propertry and litigation. Quality Standards. | V 1-2[09]<br>T 2<br>P 10<br>TS 80<br>WP no |
| **HERTFORDSHIRE DISTRICT COUNCIL**<br>Brockington, 35 Hafod Road, Hereford HR1 1SH<br>**Tel:** 01432 260200<br>**Fax:** 01432 260206<br>**Apply to:** KJ O'Keefe | A busy legal practice serving both Herefordshire Council and a range of local public sector organisations. | V 0<br>T 1<br>P -<br>TS 31<br>WP yes |
| **HETHERTONS LLP SOLICITORS**<br>Northern House, 7-9 Rougier Street, York Y01 6HZ<br>**Tel:** 01904 625327<br>**Fax:** 01904 665850<br>**Email:** law@hethertons.co.uk<br>**Apply to:** The Staff Partner | General legal practice with offices in York, Boroughbridge and Doncaster. Private and publicly funded work and a comprehensive range of legal services. | V 0<br>T 0<br>P 3<br>TS 17<br>WP no |

**V** = Vacancies / **T** = Trainees / **P** = Partners / **TS** = Total Staff / **WP** = Work Placement

# Hewitsons

7 Spencer Parade, Northampton NN1 5AB
**Tel:** 01604 233233
**Fax:** 01604 627941
**Email:** carolinelewis@hewitsons.com
**Web:** www.hewitsons.com

**The firm** Hewitsons is ranked among the UK's foremost regional law firms with 44 partners and around 100 lawyers based at its main centres in Northampton and Cambridge, with a niche private client office in Essex.

**Types of work** The firm has a strong reputation in a range of specialisms and a national and international client base, particularly in Europe and across North America. Its areas of noted expertise include corporate and commercial work, technology, employment, competition law, property, construction, planning, environment, insolvency, bioscience, agriculture, tax, trusts and charities.

**Who should apply** The firm welcomes applications from candidates who have achieved a high standard of academic success, with a minimum of a 2.1 degree, and who are bright, personable, have initiative and enjoy working as part of a team.

**Training programme** Training contracts are offered at Northampton and Cambridge, where trainees complete four placements of six months each in a range of different legal specialisms. During each seat, the trainee is supervised closely by a partner or senior solicitor, and progress is monitored on a day-by-day basis as well as in a formal three-monthly review, carried out mid-seat and at end of seat. The firm provides a comprehensive induction programme specifically tailored for the needs of trainee solicitors. The Professional Skills Course is coupled with an extensive programme of trainee solicitors' seminars provided by specialist in-house lawyers.

**When and how to apply** Telephone the director of human resources, Caroline Lewis, on 01604 233233 or email carolinelewis@hewitsons.com. Applications for training contracts to start in September 2010 should be made between July and August 2008.

**Work placements** The firm operates a vacation scheme and placements are available throughout the year.

| | |
|---|---|
| Vacancies | 15 |
| Trainees | 15 |
| Partners | 44 |
| Total staff | 288 |

**Work placement**   yes

**Apply to**
Caroline Lewis

**Starting salary**
Under review

**Minimum qualifications**
2.1 degree

**Offices**
Northampton, Cambridge, Saffron Walden

# Hextalls LLP

28 Leman Street, London E1 8ER
**Tel:** 020 7488 1424
**Fax:** 020 7481 0232
**Email:** carmenshemilt@hextalls.com
**Web:** www.hextalls.com

**The firm** Hextalls is a long-established and forward-looking practice, with a strong team ethos. Hextalls has a broad domestic and international client base that includes major UK and global insurance companies, Lloyd's of London syndicates, domestic and foreign banks, shipping and other transport operators, owner-managed businesses, overseas governments, local authorities and high-net-worth individuals.

The core strength of the firm is the quality and enthusiasm of its people. It is through them that the firm is able to provide innovative solutions and consistently achieve excellent results for its clients. The firm's approach is to develop a close personal relationship with each client and to achieve a thorough understanding of their business. This enables the firm to deliver prompt and constructive legal advice and practical assistance on whatever issues arise.

**Types of work** Hextalls LLP provides a wide range of services, including commercial litigation and dispute resolution, commercial property, corporate and commercial law, employment, insurance and reinsurance, construction and engineering, insolvency and restructuring, shipping, transport, sport, travel and leisure, technology, media and telecoms.

**Who should apply** Applicants should have achieved three good A levels and a 2.1 degree or equivalent. Applications are also welcomed from candidates who are currently on, or have recently passed the LPC course. We are interested in applicants who are genuinely committed to servicing client needs through pragmatic use of the law and who are confident and commercially aware.

**Training programme** Trainees work closely with senior lawyers and with clients from the outset. Training is varied and you will spend six months in at least three different departments. Trainees are offered as much responsibility as they feel confident of handling. You will also be encouraged to participate in departmental meetings and seminars. You will receive regular appraisals and feedback.

**When and how to apply** You should send a comprehensive CV with a handwritten cover letter addressed to Carmen Shemilt by 31 July 2008 for training contracts to commence 2010.

**Work placements** One to two weeks of unpaid work experience during July and August. Closing date is 31 May 2008

**Sponsorship** The firm pays a contribution towards LPC course fees.

| | |
|---|---|
| Vacancies | 2 |
| Trainees | 7 |
| Partners | 20 |
| Total staff | 100 |

Work placement yes

Apply to
Carmen Shemilt

Starting salary
£25,000

Minimum qualifications
2.1 degree and 3 good A levels

Sponsorship
LPC

Offices
London

# Higgs & Sons

PO Box 15, Blythe House, 134 High Street, Brierley Hill DY5 3BG
**Tel:** 01384 342100
**Fax:** 01384 342178
**Email:** law@higgsandsons.co.uk
**Web:** www.higgsandsons.co.uk

**The firm** One of the leading law firms in the West Midlands providing cutting edge legal advice in a friendly and down-to-earth way to business and private paying clients across a wide variety of legal specialisations. Founded in 1875 we are committed to developing long term relationships with our clients. ISO9001 accredited.

**Types of work** For the business client: corporate and commercial, employment law, commercial litigation and commercial property work.

For the private client: wills, probate and trusts, employment law, personal injury, ULR and clinical negligence, conveyancing and civil litigation, matrimonial/family and motoring.

**Who should apply** LLB Graduates. Would prefer 2.1 degree but will consider a 2.2 and non-law.

**Training programme** A first-class structured programme, fully supervised, based on experience in at least four major disciplines with regular assessments. An open-door policy. Preferences balanced with firm's needs.

**When and how to apply** Deadline for September 2010 intake is by 18 August 2008. Apply by letter with CV to Margaret Dalton, Head of Human Resources, at the above address or online at www.higgsandsons.co.uk.

**Sponsorship** Professional Skills Course funded.

| | |
|---|---|
| **Vacancies** | 4 |
| **Trainees** | 10 |
| **Partners** | 26 |
| **Total staff** | 169 |

**Apply to**
Margaret Dalton

**Starting salary**
1st year: £20,000
2nd year: £22,000

**Minimum qualifications**
2.1 preferred (2.2 non-law considered)

**Offices**
Brierley Hill, Kingswinford, Stourbridge

HIGGS&SONS
SOLICITORS

# Hill Dickinson LLP

Pearl Assurance House, Derby Square, Liverpool L2 9XL
**Tel:** 0151 236 5400
**Fax:** 0151 236 2175
**Email:** recruitment@hilldickinson.com
**Web:** www.hilldickinson.com

**The firm** Hill Dickinson is one of the UK's leading independent law firms and is a national top 40 practice with offices in Liverpool, London, Manchester and Chester, and its associated firm Hill Dickinson International has offices in London and Greece.

**Types of work** Property & real estate: Hill Dickinson is a recognised leader in commercial property and related disciplines and in May 2006 the firm was awarded Property Law Firm of the Year 2006 at the Insider Property Awards North West. The team has an unparalleled portfolio of commercial property clients and is renowned for high-profile and complex deals.
Construction: The construction division has extensive expertise in all contentious and non-contentious legal issues affecting the industry and advises on building contracts across all types of developments.
Marine: The marine division, with experts in London, Liverpool and Manchester, is widely recognised as one of the UK's leaders in the field. Following a merger with Hill Taylor Dickinson on 1 November 2006 the firm is one of the top league marine firms.
Medico-legal: The firm has one of the UK's largest medico-legal practices acting on behalf of health authorities, NHS trusts and other health service bodies. The firm is a member of the National Health Service Litigation Authority's panel, which was the first licensed to provide health sector/ medical negligence elements within training contracts.
Commercial: The division provides advice on all aspects of commercial law including company formation, mergers and acquisitions, management buy-outs and buy-ins, venture capital, flotations, insolvency and banking.
Intellectual property & technology: The IP team, under the leadership of one of the UK's finest IP lawyers, is acknowledged to be at the forefront of the profession and has leading trademark-filing experience.
Private Client: The firm provides specialist advice on tax and estate planning, wills, trust, probate, financial planning matters, family law and advising charitable trusts. The firm is a lead adviser for Camelot.
Insurance: The leading UK insurance division acts on all aspects of insurance including EL/PL, transport, leisure and tourism, retail, regulatory, environment, fraud and negligence.

**Who should apply** Commercial awareness and academic ability are the key factors, together with a desire to succeed. Trainees are viewed as the partners of the future and we are looking for personable individuals with whom we want to work.

**Training programme** Trainees spend periods of six months in one of the practice groups and will be given the chance to specialise in specific areas. You will be given the opportunity to learn and develop communication and presentation skills, legal research, drafting, interviewing and advising, negotiations and advocacy. Trainees are encouraged to accept responsibility and are expected to act with initiative. The firm has an active social committee and a larger than usual selection of competitive sporting teams.

**When and how to apply** Closing date for 2010 is 31 July 2008. Apply via our online form at www. hilldickinson.com which opens on 1 November 2007.

**Work placements** Two-week structured scheme available for 2008. Apply online by March 31 2008.

| | |
|---|---|
| Vacancies | 17 |
| Trainees | 23 |
| Partners | 152 |
| Total staff | 1000 |

**Work placement** yes

**Apply**
Online

**Starting salary**
1st year (2007) - £22,000
2nd year (2007) - £24,000
London:
1st year (2007) - £30,000
2nd year (2007) - £32,000

**Minimum qualifications**
2.1 degree

**Sponsorship**
LPC

**Offices**
Liverpool, Manchester, London, Chester and Greece

HILL DICKINSON

**HEWITTS**
207 Newgate Street, Bishop Auckland DL14 7EL
**Tel:** 01388 604691
**Fax:** 01388 607899
**Email:** enquiries@hewitts.co.uk
**Apply to:** Ms Laura Saunders-Jerrom

General legal practice with five offices situated in rural South West Durham and Teeside.

| | |
|---|---|
| V | Poss[08] |
| T | 2 |
| P | 16 |
| TS | 103 |
| WP | no |

---

**HIBBERT DURRAD MOXON LLP**
144 Nantwich Road, Crewe, Cheshire CW2 6BG
**Tel:** 01270215117
**Fax:** 01270500494
**Email:** sb@hdmsolicitors.co.uk
**Apply to:** Mr SA Bailey

Long established and highly regarded South Cheshire practice with acknowledged expertise in agriculture, private client and criminal matters. High quality work for high quality clients.

| | |
|---|---|
| V | 1 |
| T | 2 |
| P | 7 |
| TS | 63 |
| WP | no |

---

**HILL & ABBOTT**
Threadneedle House, 9 & 10 Market Road, Chelmsford CM1 1XH
**Tel:** 01245 258892
**Fax:** 01245 490480
**Email:** info@hill-abbott.co.uk
**Apply to:** Mrs Marion Greenwood

General practice with specialisms in personal injury, family, child care and trusts.

| | |
|---|---|
| V | 0[09] |
| T | 1 |
| P | 7 |
| TS | 60 |
| WP | no |

---

**HILLIERS HRW**
132 Bedford Road, Kempston, Bedford MK42 8BQ
**Tel:** 01234 858 000
**Fax:** 01234 840816
**Email:** admin@hilliers-solicitors.co.uk
**Apply to:** Ms Su Jenkins

Offices at present in Bedfordshire & Hertfordshire. An extremely forward thinking firm in IT and all business matters.

| | |
|---|---|
| V | 2[08] |
| T | 6 |
| P | 5 |
| TS | 55 |
| WP | no |

---

**HILLYER MCKEOWN**
Durwen House, 7 Stanley Place, Chester, Cheshire CH1 2LU
**Tel:** 01244 345551
**Fax:** 01244 344749
**Email:** mail@law.uk.com
**Apply to:** Mr Steven J Harvey

The firm's four offices cover Chester/North Wales and the Wirral Pensinsula offering a broad range of commercial and private client services.

| | |
|---|---|
| V | 2 |
| T | 2 |
| P | 9 |
| TS | 60 |
| WP | no |

---

**HILTON NORBURY**
6-8 Upper Dicconson Street, Wigan WN1 2AD
**Tel:** 01942 241424
**Fax:** 01942 324188
**Apply to:** Ms Victoria S Hilton

Small high street general practice; family work emphasis on domestic violence, welfare, personal injury, conveyancing, wills and probate.

| | |
|---|---|
| V | 1 |
| T | 1 |
| P | 2 |
| TS | 10 |
| WP | yes |

---

**HKH KENWRIGHT & COX**
Mountsview House, 202-212 High Road, Ilford, Essex IG1 1QB
**Tel:** 020 8553 9600
**Fax:** 020 8553 9995
**Email:** hkh.sol@tiscali.co.uk
**Apply to:** Mr KS Mian

Specialist criminal and family firm. Handles residential and commercial conveyancing. Serious Fraud Panel Members. Private immigration and work permits. Legal Aid and private client base.

| | |
|---|---|
| V | 0 |
| T | 1 |
| P | 2 |
| TS | 19 |
| WP | yes |

---

**HLW COMMERCIAL LAWYERS LLP**
Commercial House, Commerical Street, Sheffield S1 2AT
**Tel:** 0114 276 5555
**Fax:** 0114 276 8066
**Email:** trainees@hlwlaw.co.uk

Founded in 1992 by former 'big firm' partners, hlw is an exclusively commercial practice serving the Yorkshire and wider business community.

| | |
|---|---|
| V | 2-3 |
| T | 6 |
| P | 19 |
| TS | 100 |
| WP | yes |

# Hodge Jones & Allen

180 North Gower Street, London NW1 2NB
**Tel:** 020 7388 0628
**Fax:** 020 7874 8305
**Email:** hja@hodgejonesallen.co.uk
**Web:** www.hodgejonesallen.co.uk

**The firm** Hodge Jones & Allen was founded in 1977 and its main areas of work include human rights, civil liberties, miscarriage of justice, inquests, criminal law, personal injury, clinical negligence, multi party actions, civil litigation, professional negligence, property, probate, wills & trusts, housing and family law.

The firm has been involved in a number of high-profile cases and is often involved in the news.

In April 2007, the firm relocated to its current premises, which have been fully refurbished. The premises are located a short walk away from Euston station, so the firm is now more centrally located in London and very accessible. The firm has good IT systems and comprehensive support departments. The firm has its own licensed bar.

**Types of work** Crime, personal injury, multi-party actions, public law, police actions, miscarriage of justice claims, human rights, medical negligence, family, housing, property, and wills and probate.

**Who should apply** Applications from both law and non-law graduates are welcome. You should be able to demonstrate a consistently high level of academic and personal achievement. We generally expect a upper second class degree.
We are looking for people who:
Communicate clearly and effectively
Have an excellent academic record
Are interested and committed to the work we do
Are hard working and dedicated
Understand and share the ethos of the firm
Have a record of achievement in extracurricular activities

**Training programme** Trainees have a full induction on joining Hodge Jones & Allen covering the work of the firm's main departments, procedural matters and professional conduct. Training consists of four six-month seats and trainees normally share an office with a partner who assists them and formally reviews their progress at least once during their seat. The training is well structured and the trainees have the benefit of a mentoring scheme. The firm provides good secretarial and clerking support so trainees can concentrate on legal work rather than administration. The firm has an excellent IT infrastructure and continues to invest heavily in IT to keep pace with innovation.

**When and how to apply** Applications are invited by 15 August 2008 for training contracts to begin in September 2009. All recruitment information is available on our website at www.hodgejonesallen.co.uk.

Applications are by application form only. The application form together with guidance notes and FAQs must be downloaded from our website. Unfortunately we are unable to accept applications in CV form.

**Sponsorship** Sponsorship contribution may be considered, but not generally available.

| Vacancies | 7 |
| Trainees | 14 |
| Partners | 20 |
| Total staff | 170 |

**Work placement** yes

**Apply to**
Personnel/HR Department

**Starting salary**
1st year - £20,000
2nd year - £22,000

**Minimum qualifications**
2.1 degree

**Offices**
London

hodge jones & allen
solicitors

# Holman Fenwick & Willan

Marlow House, Lloyds Avenue, London EC3N 3AL
**Tel:** 020 7488 2300
**Fax:** 020 7481 0316
**Email:** grad.recruitment@hfw.co.uk
**Web:** www.hfw.com

**The firm** Holman Fenwick & Willan is an international law firm and one of the world's leading specialists in maritime transportation, insurance, reinsurance and trade. It is a leader in the field of commercial litigation and arbitration, and also offers comprehensive commercial advice. Founded in 1883, the firm today is one of the largest operating in its chosen fields, with a team of 200 lawyers worldwide and a reputation for excellence and innovation.

**Types of work** Our range of services includes marine, admiralty and crisis management, insurance and reinsurance, commercial litigation and arbitration, international trade and commodities, energy, corporate and financial.

**Who should apply** Commercially minded undergraduates and graduates of all disciplines with good A levels (AAB) and who have, or can demonstrate they expect to receive, a good 2.1 degree. Good foreign languages or a scientific or maritime background are an advantage.

**Training programme** We will ensure that you gain valuable experience in a wide range of areas. We also organise formal training supplemented by a programme of in-house seminars and ship visits in addition to the Professional Skills Course.

**When and how to apply** Apply online via our website between 1 December 2007 and 31 July 2008 to begin September 2010.

**Work placements** Two summer schemes. Please see website for further details. Remuneration £250 per week. Applications accepted 1 December 2007 to 14 February 2008.

**Sponsorship** Fees paid and £6,000 maintenance grant for GDL and £7,000 for LPC.

| | |
|---|---|
| Vacancies | 10 |
| Trainees | 16 |
| Partners | 80+ |
| Total staff | 500 |

**Work placement** yes

**Apply to**
Rachel Frowde

**Starting salary**
£31,000 (September 2007)

**Minimum qualifications**
AAB at A level; minimum degree classification 2.1

**Sponsorship**
GDL/LPC

**Offices**
London, Paris, Rouen, Piraeus, Hong Kong, Singapore, Shanghai, Dubai, Melbourne

HOLMAN FENWICK & WILLAN

| | | | |
|---|---|---|---|
| **HMCS WEST MERCIA**<br>West Mercia Area, PO Box 2676, Comberton Pace,<br>Kidderminster DY10 1EW<br>**Tel:** 01562 514 000<br>**Fax:** 01562 514 009<br>**Email:** paul.bushell@hmcourts-service.gsi.gov.uk<br>**Apply to:** Mr Paul Bushell | Magistrates' court. | | V 0<br>T 2<br>P 0<br>TS 43<br>WP no |
| **HODDERS**<br>Po Box 344, 11 Station Road, Harlesden,<br>London NW10 4UD<br>**Tel:** 020 8965 9862<br>**Fax:** 020 8965 5803<br>**Apply to:** Ms Roz Stokes | A medium size four partner law firm<br>with offices in Northwest London,<br>Wembley, Battersea and High<br>Wycombe. For full details please see<br>our website. | | V 0<br>T 2<br>P 4<br>TS 65<br>WP no |
| **HOGAN & HARTSON**<br>Juxon House, 100 St Paul's Churchyard,<br>London EC4M 8BU<br>**Tel:** 020 7367 0200<br>**Fax:** 020 7367 0220<br>**Email:** graduaterecruitment@hhlaw.com<br>**Apply to:** Graduate Recruitment | We are a dynamic, full service, 'Top<br>30' global law firm with world scale<br>transactions and 1,000 lawyers in 22<br>offices worldwide. | | V 2-3<br>T 4<br>P 20<br>TS 115<br>WP no |
| **HOLDEN & CO**<br>32-33 Robertson Street, Hastings TN34 1HT<br>**Tel:** 01424 722422<br>**Fax:** 01424 720108<br>**Email:** law@holdenandco.co.uk<br>**Apply to:** Mr M Hunter | General high street practice of a legal<br>aid quality marked firm. | | V 1<br>T 1<br>P 1<br>TS 36<br>WP no |
| **HOLMES & HILLS INCORPORATING<br>YOUNG & CO**<br>Bocking End, Braintree, Essex CM7 9AJ<br>**Tel:** 01376 320 456<br>**Fax:** 01376 342 156<br>**Apply to:** Mrs Sue Bushell | Holmes & Hills offers a full range of<br>legal assistance from personal, family<br>and property services to<br>comprehensive support for your<br>business. | | V 0<br>T 2<br>P 12<br>TS 100<br>WP no |
| **HOOD VORES & ALLWOOD**<br>The Priory, Church Street, Dereham NR19 1DW<br>**Tel:** 01362 692424<br>**Fax:** 01362 698858<br>**Apply to:** Mr D Rose | Mid-Norfolk medium sized rural firm<br>able to offer excellent experience,<br>particularly in private client and<br>property work. Holds a CLS<br>exclusive contract for family work. | | V 1(09)<br>T 1<br>P 6<br>TS 35<br>WP no |
| **HOOPER & WOLLEN**<br>Carlton House, 30 The Terrace, Torquay TQ1 1BS<br>**Tel:** 01803 213251<br>**Fax:** 01803 296871<br>**Email:** lawyers@hooperwollen.co.uk<br>**Apply to:** Mrs Mary Lewis | Leading South Devon firm.<br>Departments include trust and<br>probate, conveyancing - domestic<br>and commercial, civil litigation,<br>personal injury, family and child care<br>and LSC franchise. | | V 1(08)<br>T 1<br>P 13<br>TS 92<br>WP yes |
| **HOPKINS SOLICITORS**<br>Crow Hill Drive, Mansfield,<br>Nottinghamshire NG19 7AE<br>**Tel:** 01623 468468<br>**Fax:** 01623 466200<br>**Email:** info@hopkins-solicitors.co.uk<br>**Apply to:** Mr John Bates | We have two offices in Mansfield and<br>two in Nottingham. We are a general<br>practice, specialising in personal<br>injury and commercial work. | | V 0<br>T 2<br>P 8<br>TS 50<br>WP no |

**V** = Vacancies / **T** = Trainees / **P** = Partners / **TS** = Total Staff / **WP** = Work Placement

# Howard Kennedy

19 Cavendish Square, London W1A 2AW
**Tel:** 020 7636 1616
**Fax:** 020 7491 2899
**Email:** trainee.recruitment@howardkennedy.com
**Web:** www.howardkennedy.com

**The firm** Howard Kennedy is a leading law firm located in the heart of London's West End, committed to providing practical commercial advice to our broad national and international client base.

**Types of work** Areas of expertise include aviation, banking, corporate, construction, employment, licensing, litigation, media and entertainment, property, property finance and private client.

**Training programme** Our training programme has been designed to ensure that each trainee gains practical experience of legal and non-legal skills in a friendly, informal working environment. Regular in-house seminars are held and trainees are quickly integrated and encouraged to have client contact to ensure that they develop business acumen. It is this commerciality and 'hands-on' approach which attracts clients and differentiates the firm from many of its larger competitors.

**When and how to apply** The next intake for trainees for the firm is 2010 and application forms will be available from the firm's website or HR department from January 2008 with a closing date for receipt of completed applications of 31 July 2008. There are no work placements available for 2008/2009.

For further information, please contact our Human Resources department on 020 7663 8722 or email trainee.recruitment@howardkennedy.com.

**Sponsorship** LPC and CPE sponsorship is considered.

| | |
|---|---|
| Vacancies | 4 |
| Trainees | 9 |
| Partners | 75 |
| Total staff | 335 |

Apply to
HR Assistant, The Human
Resources Department

**Starting salary**
Currently £29,500

**Sponsorship**
CPE/LPC discretionary

**Offices**
London

HOWARD KENNEDY

# Howes Percival LLP

Oxford House, Cliftonville, Northampton NN1 5PN
**Tel:** 01604 230400
**Fax:** 01604 620956
**Email:** katy.pattle@howespercival.com
**Web:** www.howespercival.com

**The firm** Howes Percival LLP is a leading commercial law firm with offices in Leicester, Milton Keynes, Northampton and Norwich. This year the firm won the Leicestershire Law Society Firm of the Year award and in 2006 won the UK Regional Firm of the Year award at the Legal Business Awards. Our working environment is progressive and highly professional, and our corporate structure means that fee-earners are rewarded on merit and can progress to associate or partner status quickly.

**Types of work** The firm is a recognised market leader in corporate law and undertakes all aspects of this work, including mergers and acquisitions, corporate finance (eg, private equity and AIM listings), IT and e-commerce, and banking. The firm also specialises in commercial property and environmental work, employment, commercial litigation, construction, IP and insolvency. Unusually for a firm outside of the City, Howes Percival LLP has an automotive unit, plus property litigation and arbitration teams.

The top-quality work that we do means that we are instructed by major companies such as ATS Euromaster Ltd and the National Geographic Channel.

Our write-up in the *Legal 500* reflects the top-quality work that is carried out by the firm.

**Who should apply** We are looking for ten well-educated, focused, enthusiastic, commercially aware graduates with a minimum 2.1 degree in any discipline. We welcome confident communicators with strong interpersonal skills who share our desire to be the best.

**Training programme** Trainees complete four six-month seats, each one in a different department. Trainees joining the Norwich office will remain at Norwich for the duration of their training contact. Within the East Midlands region there is the opportunity to gain experience in each of the three East Midlands offices.

Trainees report direct to a partner, and after three months and again towards the end of each seat will be formally assessed by the partner training them. Trainees will be given every assistance by the fee-earners in their department to develop quickly, and will be given responsibility as soon as they are ready.

Benefits include a contributory pension scheme and private health insurance.

**When and how to apply** The closing date for training contracts in 2010 is 31 July 2008. Our application form is online and can be found on the trainee page of our website.

**Work placements** These are available in June, July and August. Please apply in writing to Emma Kazmierczak, HR Assistant, at the above address (enclosing your CV) indicating which location you would prefer. The closing date is 30 April 2008.

**Sponsorship** LPC/GDL/maintenance grant.

| | |
|---|---|
| Vacancies | 10 |
| Trainees | 16 |
| Partners | 31 |
| Total staff | 300 |

**Work placement** yes
*(see Insider Report on p107)*

**Apply to**
Miss Katy Pattle,
HR Officer

**Starting salary**
1st year: £23,500
2nd year: £25,500

**Minimum qualifications**
2.1 degree

**Sponsorship**
LPC/GDL

**Offices**
Leicester, Milton Keynes,
Northampton, Norwich

| | | | |
|---|---|---|---|
| **HORWICH FARRELLY**<br>National House, 36 St Ann Street,<br>Manchester M60 8HF<br>**Tel:** 0161 834 3585<br>**Fax:** 0161 834 3630<br>**Email:** human.resources@horwichfarrelly.co.uk<br>**Apply to:** Kimby Priestley | Litigation specialists for both claimant and defendant and commercial. Expanding practice based in Manchester, but work is countrywide. | V<br>T<br>P<br>TS<br>WP | 0<br>11<br>10<br>300<br>no |
| **HORWOOD & JAMES**<br>7 Temple Square, Aylesbury,<br>Buckinghamshire HP20 2QB<br>**Tel:** 01296 487361<br>**Fax:** 01296 427155<br>**Email:** enquiries@horwoodjames.co.uk<br>**Apply to:** Mrs GEC Maison | Business and family lawyers, established in Aylesbury, Buckinghamshire, for over 200 years. | V<br>T<br>P<br>TS<br>WP | 1<br>1<br>5<br>32<br>no |
| **HOUGH HALTON & SOAL**<br>32 Abbey Street, Carlisle CA3 8RJ<br>**Tel:** 01228 524379<br>**Fax:** 01228 511249<br>**Apply to:** Mr JK Leiper | Well-established general practice including personal injury, family, employment, property, wills and probate. | V<br>T<br>P<br>TS<br>WP | 1-2<br>3<br>3<br>20<br>no |
| **HOWARD & OVER**<br>114 Albert Road, Devonport, Plymouth PL2 1AF<br>**Tel:** 01752 556606<br>**Fax:** 01752 607101<br>**Email:** admin@howard-over.co.uk<br>**Apply to:** Mrs SM Dyer | Offices at Devonport, Plymstock and Ivybridge. General practice with four partners and ten other fee-earners. The firm has a legal aid franchise in six categories. | V<br>T<br>P<br>TS<br>WP | 0<br>3<br>3<br>32<br>no |
| **HOWARTH GOODMAN**<br>8 King Street, Manchester M60 8HG<br>**Tel:** 0161 832 5068<br>**Fax:** 0161 819 7878<br>**Email:** sb@howarthgoodman.com<br>**Apply to:** Mr Steven Baddiel | Commercial property, employment, landlord and tenant, company, building contract disputes. | V<br>T<br>P<br>TS<br>WP | Poss[09]<br>1<br>4<br>50<br>yes |
| **HOWELL-JONES LLP**<br>75 Surbiton Road, Kingston Upon Thames KT1 2AF<br>**Tel:** 020 8549 5186<br>**Fax:** 020 8549 3383<br>**Email:** recruit@howell-jones.com<br>**Apply to:** Mr Bill Hatton | We are a long established firm offering a broad range of services including commercial, commercial litigation, personal injury, property, matrimonial and private client. | V<br>T<br>P<br>TS<br>WP | 2+[09]<br>4<br>11<br>45<br>no |
| **HOWELLS LLP**<br>15-17 Bridge Street, Sheffield S3 8NL<br>**Tel:** 0114 249 6666<br>**Fax:** 0114 249 6718<br>**Apply to:** The Personnel Department | One of the UK's largest suppliers of legally aided services. Three main departments of equal size: civil and community law, criminal and family. | V<br>T<br>P<br>TS<br>WP | 2<br>4<br>16<br>120<br>no |
| **HOWLETT CLARKE**<br>8-9 Ship Street, Brighton BN1 1AZ<br>**Tel:** 01273 326341<br>**Fax:** 01273 328857<br>**Email:** brighton@howlettclarke.co.uk<br>**Apply to:** Mrs P Austen | Long established general practice, providing a full range of legal services to the business community and private individuals, with an emphasis on client service. | V<br>T<br>P<br>TS<br>WP | 2<br>4<br>9<br>70<br>no |

# Hugh James

Hodge House, 114-116 St Mary Street, Cardiff CF10 1DY
**Tel:** 029 20224871
**Fax:** 029 20388222
**Email:** training.contracts@hughjames.com
**Web:** www.hughjames.com

**The firm** Hugh James is one of the UK's leading regional law firms and has experienced phenomenal growth and success since it was formed in 1960. It has for many years been one of only a handful of firms to dominate the legal scene in Wales. Hugh James is placed high in the table of the top law firms in the UK. The firm offers its clients a comprehensive service covering the whole of South Wales through its seven offices.

**Types of work** The practice is divided up into three divisions: property, corporate and banking, and claimant. Specialist terms have been established to service niche areas of the law and the firm has a multidisciplinary approach to the provision of legal services.

**Who should apply** Hugh James welcomes applications from law and non-law undergraduates with a good class degree. Candidates must exhibit first-class legal and practice skills, and good interpersonal and IT skills are essential. The majority of trainees are retained upon qualification and are seen as an integral part of the future of the firm. Hugh James is proud of the fact that most of its present partners were trained at the firm.

**Training programme** Trainees generally undertake four seats of not less than six months, which may be in any of the firm's offices. Broadly, experience will be gained in all four main work categories. The breadth of work dealt with by the firm enables it to ensure that over-specialisation is avoided.

**When and how to apply** By 31 July 2008 to begin 2010 on firm's application form.

**Work placements** Summer vacation scheme. Apply on firm's application form by 31 March 2008.

| | |
|---|---|
| Vacancies | 8 |
| Trainees | 18 |
| Partners | 50 |
| Total staff | 500+ |

**Work placement** yes

**Apply to**
Diane Brooks, HR Manager

**Minimum qualifications**
2.1 degree unless good reason why a 2.2 was achieved

**Offices**
Cardiff, Merthyr Tydfil

HUGH JAMES

| Firm | Description | | |
|------|-------------|---|---|
| **HSR LAW**<br>The Law Chambers, 8 South Parade, Doncaster, South Yorkshire DN1 2ED<br>**Tel:** 01302 347800<br>**Fax:** 01302 363466<br>**Email:** richard.allwood@hsrlaw.co.uk<br>**Apply to:** Mr Richard Allwood | Two offices organised in five teams: civil litigation/PI; family (franchised); private client; crime(franchised); business/agriculture. | **V** 0-1[08]<br>**T** 2<br>**P** 6<br>**TS** 42<br>**WP** no | |
| **HUGHES PADDISON**<br>10 Royal Crescent, Cheltenham GL50 3DA<br>**Tel:** 01242 574244<br>**Fax:** 01242 221631<br>**Apply to:** Ms Jane Brothwood | Mainly private client; one legal aid franchise area and large matrimonial department. | **V** 0<br>**T** 4<br>**P** 7<br>**TS** 32<br>**WP** no | |
| **HUMPHREYS & CO**<br>14 King Street, Bristol BS1 4EF<br>**Tel:** 0117 929 2662<br>**Fax:** 0117 929 2722<br>**Email:** lawyers@humphreys.co.uk<br>**Apply to:** The Staff Partner | Commercially orientated: intellectual property, employment, litigation, company/commercial, property, entertainment, insurance, negligence. Also private client work: industrial disease/personal injury litigation, residential property. | **V** 1-2<br>**T** 4<br>**P** 4<br>**TS** 30<br>**WP** yes | |
| **HUMPHRIES KIRK**<br>Glebe House, North Street, Wareham, Dorset BH20 4AN<br>**Tel:** 01929 552141<br>**Fax:** 01929 556701<br>**Email:** r.lewis@humphrieskirk.co.uk<br>**Apply to:** Mrs Rosemary Lewis | Specialised practice offering family, conveyancing, private client, PI, IP, construction, commercial litigation, company/commercial and commercial property work from offices in Dorset and Europe. | **V** 1[09]<br>**T** 2<br>**P** 15<br>**TS** 150<br>**WP** no | |
| **HUNT KIDD**<br>Alderman Fenwick's House, 98-100 Pilgrim Street, Newcastle-upon-tyne NE1 6SQ<br>**Tel:** 0191 232 3030<br>**Fax:** 0191 232 5600<br>**Email:** enquiries@huntkidd.co.uk<br>**Apply to:** Mr Richard Brown | City centre practice dealing with company law, commercial agreements, property development and a dedicated residential conveyancing team. | **V** 1-2[09]<br>**T** 4<br>**P** 4<br>**TS** 26<br>**WP** yes | |
| **HUNTERS**<br>9 New Square, Lincolns Inn, London WC2A 3QN<br>**Tel:** 020 7412 0050<br>**Fax:** 020 7412 0049<br>**Email:** paa@hunters-solicitors.co.uk<br>**Apply to:** Mr Paul Almy | Traditionally known for private client, charity and matrimonial work. Now a broadly based Lincoln's Inn practice with a significant presence in other fields. | **V** 2<br>**T** 5<br>**P** 21<br>**TS** 81<br>**WP** yes | |
| **HUNTON & WILLIAMS**<br>30 St Mary Axe, London EC3A 8EP<br>**Tel:** 020 7220 5700<br>**Fax:** 020 7220 5772<br>**Apply to:** Mrs Linda Felmingham | | **V** 2<br>**T** 4<br>**P** 9<br>**TS** 51<br>**WP** no | |
| **HUTCHINSON THOMAS**<br>119 London Road, Neath, West Glamorgan SA11 1LF<br>**Tel:** 01639 645061<br>**Fax:** 01639 646792<br>**Email:** reception@hutchinsonthomas.com<br>**Apply to:** Mrs Elizabeth Prosser | A large well-established provincial practice providing a wide range of legal services - very strong probate and conveyancing departments and a large contentious law department. | **V** 0<br>**T** 2<br>**P** 9<br>**TS** 50<br>**WP** yes | |

# IBB Solicitors

Capital Court, Windsor Road, Uxbridge UB8 1AB
**Tel:** 08456 381381
**Fax:** 08456 381341
**Web:** www.ibblaw.co.uk

**The firm** IBB Solicitors is a leading law firm in the West London providing a full range of services to an extensive business, institutional and private client community. IBB has established a consistent pattern of growth and now has 32 partners and a turnover in excess of £15 million.

**Types of work** Equal weight is given to each of our four client-facing groups – real estate, commercial, private client and community legal services. We act for commercial institutions, banks, charities, property developers and plcs, many of which are household names. Our clients also include a variety of locally based limited companies, professional partnerships and high net-worth individuals.

Our legally funded work is undertaken by specialist criminal defence and childcare teams. We are on the serious fraud panel. We have a well-established personal injury team which acts for a major trade union and other individuals.

Our private client group offers a range of services to high net-worth clients, ranging from residential property, divorce and ancillary relief to wills, trusts, probate, tax and financial services.

**Who should apply** We look for good academic results, a commitment to work in a regional firm and for individuals who can think on their feet and show us how they will make a difference.

**Training programme** Training with IBB offers the opportunity to complete four six-month seats in a wide range of areas of law within one or more of our practice groups. You will be given early responsibility, gain experience of dealing with clients and of assisting solicitors and partners on complex matters.

**When and how to apply** Recruitment for our 2009 and 2010 intake will take place between May and September 2008. The closing date for applications is 31 July 2008.

**Work placements** No formal scheme.

| | |
|---|---|
| Vacancies | 6 |
| Trainees | 12 |
| Partners | 32 |
| Total staff | 200 |

Work placement   no

Apply to
See website

Minimum qualifications
2.1 degree, first-time passes in all LPC papers

Offices
Uxbridge (Middlesex) x 2, Chesham (Buckinghamshire), Ingatestone (Essex)

# Ince & Co

International House, 1 St Katharine's Way, London E1W 1AY
**Tel:** 020 7481 0010
**Fax:** 020 7481 4968
**Email:** recruitment@incelaw.com
**Web:** www.incelaw.com

**The firm** From its origins in maritime law, the firm's practice today encompasses all aspects of the work areas listed below. Ince & Co is frequently at the forefront of developments in contract and tort law.

**Types of work** Aviation, business and finance, commercial disputes, energy, insurance and reinsurance, shipping and trade.

**Who should apply** Hard-working, competitive individuals with initiative who relish challenge and responsibility within a team environment. Academic achievements, positions of responsibility, sport and travel are all taken into account.

**Training programme** Trainees sit with four different partners for six months at a time throughout their training. Under close supervision, they are encouraged from an early stage to meet and visit clients, interview witnesses, liaise with counsel, deal with technical experts and handle opposing lawyers. They will quickly build up a portfolio of cases from a number of partners involved in a cross-section of the firm's practice and will see their cases through from start to finish. They will also attend in-house and external lectures, conferences and seminars on practical and legal topics.

**When and how to apply** By 31 July 2008 to begin 2010. Please apply online at www.incelaw.com.

**Work placements** Places for 2008: 15; duration: two weeks; remuneration: £250 per week; closing date: 14 February 2008.

**Sponsorship** LPC/GDL fees, £6,000 grant for study in London & Guildford, £5,500 grant for study elsewhere.

| Vacancies | 12 |
|---|---|
| Trainees | 21 |
| Partners | 79 |
| Total staff | 462 |

**Work placement**   yes
*(see Insider Report on p110)*

**Apply**
Online at www.incelaw.com

**Starting salary**
£31,000

**Sponsorship**
GDL/LPC

**Offices**
Dubai, Hamburg,
Hong Kong, Le Havre,
London, Paris, Piraeus,
Shanghai, Singapore

INCE
& CO
INTERNATIONAL
LAW FIRM

# Irwin Mitchell

Riverside East, 2 Millsands, Sheffield S3 8DT
**Tel:** 0870 1500 100
**Web:** www.irwinmitchell.com

**The firm** Irwin Mitchell (IM) was established over 90 years ago and is the fourth largest law firm, and the largest personal injury practice, in the UK. The practice employs more than 2300 staff - including over 1000 fee-earners, with offices in Birmingham, Glasgow, Leeds, London, Manchester, Newcastle, and Sheffield as well as the Spanish cities of Marbella and Madrid.

IM provide a comprehensive legal service with particular strengths in litigation throughout the practice. We have a truly distinctive profile with our reputation for progress and growth underpinned by our brand values - innovation, responsiveness, solutions and value. Our philosophy is to strive for constant improvement in everything we do.

No longer just a law firm which provides legal advice, but a business which offers legal and associated business solutions, we have embraced change to ensure that we can respond positively to our client needs. We have a strong customer service culture and a very high level of client retention.

**Types of work** We believe we are unique in the diversity of law we undertake - from commercial law to insurance law, from business crime to major and multi-claimant personal injury litigation, not forgetting our expanding private client department. Our reputation for being able to deal with novel and complex areas of law is built on the many and varied cases we have undertaken: the Barber pensions case, the British Coal and Asbestos multi-party litigation, Bahrain boat disaster and access to Herceptin case are only a few examples from a long and ever-growing list.

**Who should apply** We are looking for ambitious and well-motivated individuals who have a real commitment to the law and who can demonstrate a positive approach to a work-life balance. We recruit law and non-law graduates and view social ability as important to us as academic achievement. Foreign languages are an asset. Irwin Mitchell believes trainees to be an investment for the future and endeavours to retain trainees upon qualification.

**Training programme** We offer a structured induction programme to trainees joining the practice. Trainees then move to gain a broad range of experience in our specialist departments; your development will be encouraged through frequent reviews and feedback. Regular training events are held throughout the firm and the Professional Skills Course is financed and run by the firm in-house. Our trainees often move between offices as well as departments, giving them a wider experience of the firm.

**When and how to apply** Please visit our website www.irwinmitchell.com and complete our online application. This will be available from 3 December 2007.

**Work placements** We offer a one-week placement during the summer. This is an opportunity for potential applicants to get a foretaste of life at Irwin Mitchell.

Please see our website for details.

**Sponsorship** We meet fees for the GDL and LPC. We also offer a £4,500 maintenance grant.

| Vacancies | approx 20 |
|---|---|
| Trainees | 45 |
| Partners | 137 |
| Total staff | over 2000 |

**Work placement**   yes

**Apply to**
Claire England,
Graduate Recruitment
Officer

**Starting salary**
£19,000 (outside London)
(reviewed annually in
September)

**Minimum qualifications**
None

**Sponsorship**
GDL/LPC

**Offices**
Birmingham, Leeds, London,
Manchester, Newcastle,
Sheffield, Madrid, Marbella,
Glasgow

**HUTTONS**
16 St Andrew's Crescent, Cardiff CF10 3DD
**Tel:** 029 20378621
**Fax:** 029 20388450
**Email:** stuart.hutton@huttons-solicitors.co.uk
**Apply to:** Ms C Strowbridge

We are a young energetic practice specialising in litigation. We have a strong reputation for crime (including murder and fraud), medical negligence, personal injury and family.

| | |
|---|---|
| V | 1 |
| T | 1 |
| P | 5 |
| TS | 35 |
| WP | yes |

---

**IKIE SOLICITORS**
41 Lee High Road, London SE13 5NS
**Tel:** 020 8463 0808
**Fax:** 020 8463 0909
**Email:** ikiesolicitors@aol.com
**Apply to:** Mr A N Ikie

Small firm with particular focus in immigration law/practice. Services offered in general practice are as common in high street practices. Applicants must have a minimum 2:1 division degree.

| | |
|---|---|
| V | 0 |
| T | 2 |
| P | 2 |
| TS | 5 |
| WP | no |

---

**INGHAMS**
Guild Chambers, 4 Winckley Square, Preston, Lancashire PR1 3JJ
**Tel:** 01772 250931
**Fax:** 01772 823150
**Apply to:** Mr Bradley Burrow

We have seven offices on the Fylde coast and Preston. Our general practice is complimented by commercial work and significant litigation departments.

| | |
|---|---|
| V | Poss |
| T | 1 |
| P | 11 |
| TS | 100 |
| WP | no |

---

**IRENA SPENCE & CO**
68-70 Castle Street, Cambridge CB3 0AJ
**Tel:** 01223 713300
**Fax:** 01223 713 313
**Email:** mail@irenaspence.co.uk
**Apply to:** Ms Amelia Pugh

Small-medium general practice with 3 offices in the city of Cambridge and surrounding villages. Caseload is litigation and property mix particularly family, employment and personal injury.

| | |
|---|---|
| V | 0 |
| T | 2 |
| P | 5 |
| TS | 30 |
| WP | no |

---

**JA FORREST & CO**
10 Buckingham Palace Road, Westminster, London SW1W 0QP
**Tel:** 020 7233 9140
**Fax:** 0845 833 1075
**Email:** mail@jaforrest.com
**Apply to:** Mr JA Forrest

Small central London general practice. Applications should be by handwritten letter, with CV.

| | |
|---|---|
| V | 0 |
| T | 0 |
| P | 1 |
| TS | 3 |
| WP | yes |

---

**JA HUGHES**
Centenary House, 5-7 Tynewydd Road, Barry, South Glamorgan CF62 8HB
**Tel:** 01446 411000
**Fax:** 01446 411010
**Email:** timhackett@jahughes.com
**Apply to:** Mr TG Hackett

We are a high street practice founded in 1888. A forward looking 6 partner firm, coving a wide spectrum of law.

| | |
|---|---|
| V | 0 |
| T | 2 |
| P | 6 |
| TS | 40 |
| WP | yes |

---

**JACKSONS**
Innovation House, Yarm Road, Stockton-on-Tees TS18 3TN
**Tel:** 01642 356500
**Fax:** 01642 356501
**Email:** info@jacksons-cpl.com
**Apply to:** Mrs Rosemary Young

Jacksons' philosophy is based upon a modern approach to business, incorporating the most up to date information technology and a commercial style management structure.

| | |
|---|---|
| V | 0 |
| T | 2 |
| P | 11 |
| TS | 73 |
| WP | no |

---

**JACOBS & REEVES**
153 High Street, Poole, Dorset BH15 1AU
**Tel:** 01202 674425
**Fax:** 01202 681167
**Apply to:** Mr Peter Breeze

Well established firm with four offices in Poole/Bournemouth and Wimborne. Strong client base covering most areas of general practice, commercial, private client and litigation.

| | |
|---|---|
| V | 0-1[09] |
| T | 1 |
| P | 7 |
| TS | 50 |
| WP | no |

# Jeffrey Green Russell

Apollo House, 56 New Bond Street, London W1S 1RG
**Tel:** 020 7339 7000
**Fax:** 020 7339 7001
**Email:** humanresources@jgrlaw.co.uk
**Web:** www.jgrweb.com

**The firm** We are a medium-sized commercial law firm with strong international connections based in New Bond Street, London.

Our clients always come first; we are determined to excel on their behalf. We work hard to find the best and most cost-effective solutions to their problems. We try to be innovators, not imitators, providing a rapid and constructive response to our clients' increasingly specialised needs.

JGR is a founder member of ACL International, an association of commercial lawyers, providing members with access to an effective global legal service, beneficial for international business requirements.

**Types of work** With our diverse client base, we specialise in company/commercial and taxation, litigation, white collar crime, insurance litigation, property, gaming, licensing and leisure and private client.

Most of our clients are in commerce, finance and industry, and range in size from small businesses to multinational corporations. Their activities are wide-ranging and include banking, finance, technology, leisure and the licensed trade, insurance and property.

**Who should apply** We welcome intelligent, enthusiastic and ambitious individuals, who are not afraid of responsibility and are keen to learn from experienced lawyers who will guide them through their training period. Not only should they undertake work with diligence and care, and strive to develop negotiating skills, but they should also consider the variety of needs of both individual and corporate clients.

The firm feels that a friendly working environment is important to staff morale, and this is reflected by the approachable behaviour of all levels of staff. We welcome those who show a strong team spirit and take an interest in outside activities.

To maximise our efficiency and productivity, and to provide cost-effective services, the firm has for many years been making major investments in sophisticated office technology. Accordingly, applicants should have a keen interest in utilising office technology and be willing to develop these skills alongside their legal training to encourage the highest quality service with speed.

**Training programme** Trainees are supervised through the various departments, including company/commercial, litigation, property and licensing.

**When and how to apply** Please send your CV with a covering letter to the human resources manager by 31 July 2008 for training contracts beginning September 2010.

| | |
|---|---|
| Vacancies | 1-2 |
| Trainees | 4 |
| Partners | 18 |
| Total staff | 120 |

**Apply to**
Human Resources Manager

**Starting salary**
Competitive

**Minimum qualifications**
2.1 degree, any discipline

**Offices**
London

**JEFFREY**

**GREEN**

**RUSSELL**

Solicitors

| | | |
|---|---|---|
| **JAMES MURRAY SOLICITORS**<br>41 Merton Road, Bootle, Liverpool L20 7AP<br>**Tel:** 0151 933 3333<br>**Fax:** 0151 933 3343<br>**Email:** info@jamesmurray.law.co.uk<br>**Apply to:** Ms J Thomas | We offer training contracts on merit to in-house paralegals usually within one year. Vacancies arise through expansion and CWp received are kept on file. | V 0<br>T 5<br>P 5<br>TS 58<br>WP no |
| **JARMANS SOLICITORS**<br>Bell House, Bell Road, Sittingbourne ME10 4DH<br>**Tel:** 01795 472291<br>**Fax:** 01795 425411<br>**Email:** enquires@jarmans-solicitors.co.uk<br>**Apply to:** Ms Joyce Walsh | Partnership firm with 10 fee earners running a multi-skilled provincial practice. Long established with a progressive attitude to IT and client care. | V 0(08)<br>T 0<br>P 2<br>TS 21<br>WP no |
| **JAY VADHER & CO**<br>185 Romford Road, London E15 4JF<br>**Tel:** 020 8519 3000<br>**Fax:** 020 8519 3300<br>**Apply to:** Mr BND Vadher | High Street firm with litigation and conveyancing departments. CLS franchises. | V 1(09)<br>T 1<br>P 3<br>TS 8<br>WP no |
| **JEPSON & CO**<br>58 High Street,, Snainton, Scarborough,<br>Yorks YO13 9AL<br>**Tel:** 01723 859249<br>**Fax:** 01723 850249<br>**Email:** info@jepsonand.co.uk<br>**Apply to:** Mr BL Jepson | Rural general practice specialising in crime and family law. | V 0<br>T 2<br>P 2<br>TS 5<br>WP yes |
| **JEREMY ROBERTS & CO**<br>51-55 Park Road, Peterborough PE1 2TH<br>**Tel:** 01733 343943<br>**Fax:** 01733 313037<br>**Apply to:** Mr J Roberts | A small friendly high street solicitors in Petersborough specialising in family, criminal, employment, accident and general litigation with some conveyancing and general work. | V 1(09)<br>T 0<br>P 1<br>TS 8<br>WP yes |
| **JEREMY WOOD & CO SOLICITORS**<br>1A Princes Street, Yeovil, Somerset BA20 1EN<br>**Tel:** 01935 426047<br>**Fax:** 01935 427890<br>**Apply to:** Ms Tanya Hopkins | Office in Yeovil. All areas of work undertaken (excluding crime and public funding work). | V 0<br>T 1<br>P 3<br>TS 10<br>WP no |
| **JH POWELL & CO**<br>Cathedral Chambers, 2 Amen Alley,<br>Derby DE1 3GT<br>**Tel:** 01332 372211<br>**Fax:** 01332 290413<br>**Apply to:** Mr PJ Collinson | Long established general practice with commercial bias. No crime. City centre office. | V 1(09)<br>T 1<br>P 6<br>TS 20<br>WP no |
| **JOACHIM G REMDE SOLICITORS**<br>53 Chandos Place, London WC2N 4HS<br>**Tel:** 020 7812 6621<br>**Fax:** 020 7812 6677<br>**Email:** remde@mail.com<br>**Apply to:** Mr JG Remde | Specialised in looking after the legal needs of foreign nationals living in the UK under the status of non-domiciled residents (mainly Banking and Taxation Law). | V 0<br>T 0<br>P -<br>TS 2<br>WP no |

## JOBLING & KNAPE
19 Northumberland Street, Morecambe LA4 4AZ
**Tel:** 01524 416960
**Fax:** 01524 402515
**Apply to:** Mr D Harrison

A multi-discipline practice comprising four offices: Morecambe, Lancaster, Carnforth and Great Eccleston. Supported by IT for the future. Broad commercial private/legal aid client base.

| | |
|---|---|
| V | Poss |
| T | 0 |
| P | 5 |
| TS | 34 |
| WP | no |

## JOELSON WILSON & CO
30 Portland Place, London W1B 1LZ
**Tel:** 020 7580 5721
**Fax:** 020 7580 2251
**Email:** info@joelsonwilson.com
**Apply to:** Mr Paul Baglee

Founded in 1957, we undertake company/commercial, gaming/liquor licensing, litigation, property, employment, IP and international work for commercial clients, many in the leisure sector.

| | |
|---|---|
| V | 2[08] |
| T | 4 |
| P | 7 |
| TS | 45 |
| WP | no |

## JOHAR & CO
Beckville House, 66 London Road, Leicester LE2 OQD
**Tel:** 0116 2543345
**Fax:** 0116 2542370
**Email:** deepakjohar@johars.com
**Apply to:** Mr DK Johar

Franchised firm with IIP. General high street practice dealing with conveyancing, litigation, matrimonial, PI and immigration; clients both corporate and individual.

| | |
|---|---|
| V | 1 |
| T | 3 |
| P | 2 |
| TS | 25 |
| WP | no |

## JOHN A WHITE & CO
St John's House, 84 High Street, Huntingdon PE29 3DP
**Tel:** 01480 458885
**Fax:** 01480 451817
**Apply to:** Mr John White

General high street practice with interesting and wide ranging client base.

| | |
|---|---|
| V | 1 |
| T | 1 |
| P | 1 |
| TS | 16 |
| WP | no |

## JOHN CHAPMAN AND CO
152-154 Epsom Road, Sutton SM3 9EU
**Tel:** 020 8337 3801
**Fax:** 020 8330 4432
**Apply to:** Mr Andrew Larner

Conveyancing, wills and probate, litigation - personal injury, matrimonial, children. There are no vacancies at present.

| | |
|---|---|
| V | 0 |
| T | 0 |
| P | 4 |
| TS | 22 |
| WP | no |

## THE JOHNSON PARTNERSHIP
Cannon Courtyard, Long Row, Nottingham NG1 6JE
**Tel:** 0115 941 9141
**Fax:** 0115 947 0178
**Email:** mail@thejohnsonpartnership.co.uk
**Apply to:** Mr Bill Soughton

Criminal work. Vacancies start as work experience and possibly lead onto training contracts.

| | |
|---|---|
| V | 1-2 |
| T | 4 |
| P | 13 |
| TS | 80 |
| WP | no |

## JONES MORDEY DAVIES SOLICITORS
26-28 James Street, Cardiff Bay, Cardiff CF10 5EX
**Tel:** 029 20456780
**Fax:** 029 20456781
**Email:** nigel.jones@jmdlaw.co.uk
**Apply to:** Mr Nigel Jones

Personal injury, contract, probate, family, childcare, employment, professional negligence, commercial and residential conveyancing, business sales and acquisitions.

| | |
|---|---|
| V | 1[09] |
| T | 1 |
| P | 3 |
| TS | 15 |
| WP | yes |

## JR JONES SOLICITORS
58 Oxbridge Road, Ealing, London W5 2ST
**Tel:** 020 8566 2595
**Fax:** 020 8579 4288
**Email:** solicitors@jrjones.co.uk
**Apply to:** Mr T Raza

Prominent legal aid practice undertaking crime, medical negligence, personal injury, matrimonial, conveyancing, housing, immigration, landlord and tenant.

| | |
|---|---|
| V | 2 |
| T | 2 |
| P | 3 |
| TS | 39 |
| WP | yes |

**V** = Vacancies / **T** = Trainees / **P** = Partners / **TS** = Total Staff / **WP** = Work Placement

# Jones Day

21 Tudor Street, London EC4Y 0DJ
**Tel:** 020 7039 5959
**Fax:** 020 7039 5999
**Email:** recruit.london@jonesday.com
**Web:** www.jonesdaylondon.com/recruit

**The firm** Jones Day operates as one firm worldwide with 2,200 lawyers in 30 offices. Jones Day in London is a key part of this international partnership and has around 200 lawyers, including around 40 partners and 40 trainees. This means that we can offer our lawyers a perfect combination - the intimacy and atmosphere of a medium-sized City firm with access to both UK and multinational clients.

**Types of work** The principal areas of practice at Jones Day include: corporate finance and M&A transactions, investment funds, private equity and corporate tax planning, banking, capital markets and structured finance, business restructuring, litigation, intellectual property, tax and real estate. The London office also has teams of lawyers who are experienced in such areas as competition/antitrust, environmental, and employment and pensions law.

**Who should apply** We look for candidates with either a law or non-law degree, who have strong intellectual and analytical ability and good communication skills and who can demonstrate resourcefulness, drive, dedication and the ability to be a team player.

**Training programme** The firm operates a unique, non-rotational system of training which is designed to provide freedom, flexibility and responsibility from the start. Our trainees work across different practice areas simultaneously and are encouraged to assume their own workload, which allows for early responsibility, faster development of potential and the opportunity to compare and contrast different disciplines alongside one another. Because our trainees do not move to a different department every six months they don't miss the end of deals or trials that they have worked on. Work will vary from small cases which trainees may handle alone (under the supervision of a senior lawyer) to matters where they will assist a partner or an associate solicitor. The firm runs a structured training programme with a regular schedule of seminars to support the thorough practical training and regular feedback that trainees receive from the associates and partners they work with.

**When and how to apply** For September 2010/March 2011: Final-year law and non-law students - from November 2007; Penultimate-year law students - from June 2008, after penultimate-year exam results have been received.

Application deadline: 31 August 2008, but apply by 31 July to ensure an early interview date.

Applications should be submitted online with a CV and cover letter via our online application system.

**Work placements**
Christmas - non-law finalists or graduates - apply by 31 October.

Easter - penultimate or final-year non-law students - apply by 31 January.

Summer - penultimate or second-year law undergraduates - apply by 31 January.

Placements last for two weeks with an allowance of £400 per week. Students get to see how our non-rotational training system works in practice by taking on real work from a variety of practice areas. They also get to meet a range of lawyers at various social events.

**Sponsorship** CPE/GDL and LPC fees paid and £8,000 maintenance p.a.

| | |
|---|---|
| Vacancies | 15-20 |
| Trainees | 40 approx |
| Partners | 45 approx |
| Total staff | 371 |

**Work placement**  yes
*(see Insider Report on p109)*

**Apply to**
Jacqui Megson
Graduate Recruitment
Manager

**Starting salary**
£39,000 (2007)

**Minimum qualifications**
2.1 degree + AAB at A level

**Sponsorship**
CPE/GDL and LPC

**Offices**
London, Continental Europe, Asia, North America

| | | |
|---|---|---|
| **JW HUGHES & CO**<br>Bank House, Lancaster Square, Conwy,<br>Gwynedd LL32 8AD<br>**Tel:** 01492 593442<br>**Fax:** 01492 592587<br>**Apply to:** Mr DC Roberts | Established and busy general practice with well appointed offices in Conwy and Llandudno. Departmental structure dealing with areas of law in which the firm specialises. | V 1[08]<br>T 1<br>P 6<br>TS 34<br>WP no |
| **KAIM TODNER**<br>5 St Bride Street, London EC4A 4AS<br>**Tel:** 020 7353 6660<br>**Fax:** 020 7353 6661<br>**Email:** solicitors@kaimtodner.com<br>**Apply to:** Ms Deborah Rogers | Mainly criminal work, expanding mental health department and some family. Offices in central, north and south London. We only recruit for current year. | V 2[09]<br>T 14<br>P 7<br>TS 80<br>WP yes |
| **KAMRANS SOLICITORS**<br>2nd Floor, Waverley House, 14 Woodhouse Square, Leeds LS3 1AQ<br>**Tel:** 0113 245 5000<br>**Fax:** 0113 245 1741<br>**Apply to:** Mr A Iftikhar | Specialising in crime. Free advice and assistance at police stations. Advocacy in magistrate and crown courts. Also personal injury and employment departments. | V 1[08]<br>T 1<br>P 2<br>TS 7<br>WP no |
| **KANGS SOLICITORS**<br>2a Wake Green Road, Birmingham B13 9EZ<br>**Tel:** 0121 449 9888<br>**Fax:** 0121 449 8849<br>**Email:** enquiries@kangssolicitors.co.uk<br>**Apply to:** Mr H Kang | Niche criminal firm specialising in white collar crime/serious fraud work. Member of LSC specialist fraud panel. | V 1-2[09]<br>T 1<br>P 1<br>TS 10<br>WP no |
| **KCP LAW**<br>77 Hanworth Road, Hounslow, London TW3 1TT<br>**Tel:** 020 8572 1212<br>**Fax:** 020 8572 9114<br>**Email:** kirit@kcplaw.co.uk<br>**Apply to:** Mr Kirit Pankhania | Young dynamic and friendly practice focused on excellence in all areas inc. team development. Litigation bias progressive commercial specialisms. Positive attitude only. | V 0-2<br>T 1<br>P 1<br>TS 3<br>WP no |
| **KENNETH ELLIOTT & ROWE**<br>Enterprise House, 18 Eastern Road, Romford, Essex RM1 3PJ<br>**Tel:** 01708 757575<br>**Fax:** 01708 766674<br>**Email:** adam.carr@ker.co.uk<br>**Apply to:** Mr Adam Carr | General commercial firm. UK member LaWorld International Law Group. Also at: 24 Buckingham Gate, SW1E 6LB. | V Poss[09]<br>T 2<br>P 10<br>TS 65<br>WP yes |
| **KESTER CUNNINGHAM JOHN**<br>Beacon House, Kempson Way, Suffolk Business Park, Bury St Edmunds IP32 7AR<br>**Tel:** 01284 761233<br>**Fax:** 01284 702225<br>**Apply to:** Ms Camellia Dighe | The fourth largest law firm in East Anglia, and the fastest growing, providing a full range of legal services to its commercial and private clients. | V 6[09]<br>T 6<br>P 26<br>TS 200<br>WP yes |
| **KEVIN J COMMONS & CO**<br>2-6 Upper Jane Street, Workington, Cumbria CA14 4AY<br>**Tel:** 01900 604 698<br>**Fax:** 01900 609 439<br>**Email:** helen.mcneil@kjcommons.co.uk<br>**Apply to:** Ms Helen McNeil | Franchised firm in crime, family, PI and clinical negligence. Large criminal practice. Other areas covered - conveyancing & wills. Offices also in Carlisle and Whitehaven. | V Poss<br>T 5<br>P 2<br>TS 55<br>WP no |

**V** = Vacancies / **T** = Trainees / **P** = Partners / **TS** = Total Staff / **WP** = Work Placement

# Kendall Freeman

One Fetter Lane, London EC4A 1JB
**Tel:** 020 7583 4055
**Fax:** 020 7353 7377
**Email:** traineerecruitment@kendallfreeman.com
**Web:** www.kendallfreeman.com

**The firm** Kendall Freeman handles high-value and complex matters for clients in the corporate and public sectors, banks and the insurance and reinsurance industry. Its main practice areas are commercial litigation, corporate, employment, insolvency and restructuring, international law, insurance/reinsurance and energy and offshore engineering. We successfully compete and act alongside the largest international and UK firms.

**Who should apply** The firm seeks engaging and motivated individuals from law or non-law backgrounds with initiative, good commercial sense and who want to make their mark. Our trainees work hard and are rewarded with early responsibility and influence over the matters they work on. You will also have lots of client interaction so excellent people skills are vital. All of this coupled with a consistently strong academic background will enable you to provide focussed and effective commercial advice to clients. We also look for those who want to get involved in the life of the firm as a whole, be this socially or through contribution to the various committees. However, we also recognise the importance of your life outside work and actively encourage you to keep a good balance.

**Training programme** We believe supervised experience to be the best training and because of our size we can offer excellent training with high-quality work in a more personal environment. The firm soon gives trainees the chance to meet clients, be responsible for their own work and join in marketing and client development activities. Trainees spend six months in four of the firm's major practice areas and frequent workshops in each seat help develop basic skills in different practice areas. Regular structured feedback, reviews and constructive advice enable you to fulfil your true potential. A multi-level support network of people for you to talk to and bounce ideas off, ensures you have the correct level of guidance and support is never overstretched. Any suggestions or concerns can be voiced at a trainee solicitors' committee, which meets quarterly.

The firm won the LawCareers.Net/Trainee Solicitors Group 2004 award for best training at a medium-sized City law firm and was nominated for best recruiter at a medium City firm in 2006. We were also a winner in 9 out of 10 categories in the Lex 100 survey for 2006/7.

**When and how to apply** Applications must be made on the firm's online application form at http://trainee.kendallfreeman.com by 31 July 2008 to begin September 2010.

**Work placements** The firm offers a structured two-week placement to 10 students in July of each year. Applications should also be made using our online form with the closing date being 28 February 2008. The firm also hosts three open days in June of each year, enabling students to find out more about the firm and meet trainees, assistants and partners alike. Applications from all degree disciplines are welcome, but preference is given to second-year law students and final year non-law students. Please apply via the online form at the address above. Closing date is 16 May 2008.

**Sponsorship** CPE/GDL and LPC funding, plus a maintenance grant of £6,500 (London) / £6,000 (outside London).

| | |
|---|---|
| Vacancies | Up to 8 |
| Trainees | 17 |
| Partners | 19 |
| Total staff | 112 |

**Work placement** yes

**Apply to**
Trainee Recruitment

**Starting salary** (2007)
1st year - £34,000
2nd year - £36,000

**Minimum qualifications**
2.1 degree
At least 300 UCAS points

**Sponsorship**
CPE/GDL/LPC

**Offices**
London

KENDALL FREEMAN

# Kennedys

Longbow House, 14-20 Chiswell Street, London EC1Y 4TW
**Tel:** 020 7638 3688
**Fax:** 020 7614 3861
**Email:** personnel@kennedys-law.com
**Web:** www.kennedys-law.com

**The firm** Founded in 1899, Kennedys is one of the leading dispute resolution firms in the City of London and has experienced sustained growth in recent years. Our niche is dispute resolution, predominantly insurance funded, but increasingly by major companies in the construction, manufacturing, transport and banking fields. The firm has around 90 partners and over 500 people. We have six UK offices - three in the City and one each in Chelmsford, Belfast and Cambridge. Worldwide, the firm has offices in Hong Kong, Auckland, Dubai, New Delhi, Madrid and Sydney, and associated offices in New York, San Francisco, Paris, Karachi, Beirut, Dublin and Moscow.

**Types of work** We are one of the leading litigation firms in the City and the majority of our partners are dedicated to the conduct and resolution of disputes, whether by negotiation, litigation or arbitration/mediation. Our specialist litigation teams handle the whole spectrum of insurance work together with a large volume of work for the construction industry. We have expertise in the transportation sector and a fast-growing reputation for our work in the employment, healthcare and insolvency sectors. One of our unique selling points is the quality of service provided to the London insurance market sector. We recognise the need that clients have for an across-the-board service and are, therefore, geared up to do every class of work should that be required. We also recognise the need to be able to provide a full City service to clients, and are committed to the development of our property and commercial departments.

**Who should apply** We offer a vibrant and supportive working environment built upon our core values; we are approachable and responsive, we show respect for people, we are trustworthy and straightforward and we ensure that we deliver economic solutions for our clients. Our trainees experience early responsibility and client contact as we find that this produces excellent solicitors capable of running their own caseload once they qualify. We therefore recruit graduates who are confident, articulate and sociable, who are team players, self-aware and resourceful.

**Training programme** The purpose of the training contract is to give trainees a mix of experience and skills that will set you up in a legal career as a solicitor with Kennedys. Our ability to consistently offer the majority of trainees positions on qualification is attributable to producing newly qualified lawyers who are competent, confident and commercially driven. A balance of work experience, responsibility, supervision and formal training achieves this. We ensure that our trainee solicitors are given a sound training in the core disciplines. You are given a good level of responsibility early on, dealing with varied areas of work. We have an open-door policy, and partners and supervisors are readily accessible.

**When and how to apply** Kennedys recruits in the year of intake to ensure we select the right trainees for the firm and our teams.

We are now accepting online applications in the year of intake from LPC graduates and LPC students. Applications for our September 2008 intake should be submitted by 31 December 2007.

| | |
|---|---|
| Vacancies | 10 |
| Trainees | 24 |
| Partners | 90 |
| Total staff | 530 |

**Work placement** no

**Apply to**
Human Resources

**Starting salary**
£28,000

**Minimum qualifications**
2.1 degree, any discipline

**Offices**
London (3), Cambridge, Chelmsford, Belfast, Hong Kong, Auckland, New Delhi, Sydney, Madrid, Dubai

**Kennedys**
**Legal** advice in black and white

# Keoghs

2 The Parklands, Bolton BL6 4SE
**Tel:** 01204 677000
**Fax:** 01204 677111
**Email:** info@keoghs.co.uk
**Web:** www.keoghs.co.uk

**The firm** Keoghs is one of the UK's leading insurance litigation firms offering national coverage to clients and acts for the majority of the UK's major insurance companies. Keoghs also advises a diverse range of private and public sector organisations on employment, crime and regulatory issues.

The firm has grown considerably over recent years due to the high standard of service given to new and existing clients, which has enabled the firm to achieve ISO 9001 accreditation. Keoghs is driven by a firm wide commitment to excellence.

**Types of work** The main practice areas are personal injury litigation, commercial litigation and employment.

**Who should apply** The firm is looking to recruit the partners of the future and indeed many current partners and assistant solicitors joined the firm as trainees. Applicants should be able to demonstrate a high academic standard (at least a 2.1 degree, but not necessarily in law), an ability to work in a team, and good communication and decision-making skills. We welcome commercially aware, enthusiastic and self-motivated candidates with good IT skills and a sense of humour.

**Training programme** Trainees undertake a flexible programme of six-month periods in each of the firm's three main practice areas of defendant personal injury litigation, commercial litigation and employment work.

The trainee will work as part of a specialist team, receiving specific training from his or her departmental supervisor. The supervisor will also assess the trainee during and at the end of the placement to review progress and development of the trainee's drafting, research, communication, advocacy and negotiation skills.

The firm's training and development department runs a comprehensive programme of in-house training which is available to all trainees, designed to complement the compulsory Professional Skills Course.

**When and how to apply** Apply via the Keoghs website at www.keoghs.co.uk. Applications for 2010 should be received by 31 July 2008.

| | |
|---|---|
| Vacancies | 4 |
| Trainees | 6 |
| Partners | 30 |
| Total staff | 506 |

**Apply to**
HR Department

**Starting salary**
Market rate

**Minimum qualifications**
2.1 degree

**Offices**
Bolton, Coventry

# Keoghs

# Kimbells LLP

Power House, Harrison Close, Knowlhill, Milton Keynes MK5 8PA
**Tel:** 01908 668555
**Fax:** 01908 685085
**Email:** julie.bradley@kimbells.com
**Web:** www.kimbells.com

**The firm** We are a nice firm to work at! Based in Milton Keynes, England's fastest growing city, we were established about 20 years ago by a group of City lawyers wishing to combine top quality work with a good quality of life. That remains our underlying philosophy.

**Types of work** We act for several household names, including Scottish & Newcastle plc and London Luton Airport, as well as some of the largest UK pub chains.

Our core areas of work are brewing, corporate, commercial, IP/IT law, employment, commercial property and litigation. Clients range from FTSE 100 companies to entrepreneurs. We do not do any private client work.

**Who should apply** We look for candidates with a strong academic record and good people skills, and who have made a conscious decision that the right place for them is in a niche commercial law firm outside London. We are also happy to receive applications from mature candidates for whom the law may be a second career, if they bring with them a commercial acumen which will benefit our clients.

**Training programme** Our trainees are very important to us. We are small enough to listen to your wishes from the outset, and plan a bespoke programme accordingly. The norm is six months in four of our departments, but we do aim to be flexible and split seats will be considered. We hold reviews every three months to check that you are happy and on the right path. We give you a good training as we want you to stay with us on qualification and help shape our future.

And we do not chain our trainees to the desk or photocopier 24/7. All trainees are given an opportunity to network with other young professionals in the business community, and to play a full part in all our marketing activities. Because we are relatively small, you can expect an excellent level of responsibility and client contact from an early stage.

**When and how to apply** We have one vacancy for March 2009, two vacancies for September 2009 and vacancies for 2010. Please apply online.

**Work placements** We are happy to offer short placements to quality candidates at any time. Please refer to our website for more details.

**Sponsorship** Support towards LPC.

| | |
|---|---|
| Vacancies | 7 |
| Trainees | 6 |
| Partners | 11 |
| Total staff | 85 |

**Work placement** yes

**Apply to**
Julie Bradley

**Starting salary**
£25,000

**Minimum qualifications**
2.1 degree

**Sponsorship**
LPC

**Offices**
Milton Keynes

| **KINGSLEY BROOKES**<br>Estate Buildings, Railway Street,<br>Huddersfield HD1 1JY<br>**Tel:** 01484 302800<br>**Fax:** 01484 302870<br>**Apply to:** Mrs S Fenteman | A specialist criminal litigation firm, set up in 1998 with franchised office based in Huddersfield. | **V** 0<br>**T** 1<br>**P** 2<br>**TS** 8<br>**WP** no |
|---|---|---|
| **KINGSLEY NAPLEY**<br>Knights Quarter, 14 St Johns Lane,<br>London EC1M 4AJ<br>**Tel:** 020 7814 1200<br>**Fax:** 020 7702 5238<br>**Email:** swood@kingsleynapley.co.uk | Internationally recognised commercial law firm, with expertise in corporate and commercial work, criminal and commercial litigation and commercial property, immigration, employment, clinical negligence and family law. | **V** 0<br>**T** 0<br>**P** 36<br>**TS** 160<br>**WP** no |
| **KINGSLEY SMITH SOLICITORS LLP**<br>81/87/89 High Street, Chatham, Kent ME4 4EE<br>**Tel:** 01634 811118<br>**Fax:** 01634 831046<br>**Email:** mail@kslaw.co.uk<br>**Apply to:** Mrs Elizabeth Kingsley-Smith | We provide quality legal advice in a full range of legal services to individuals and businesses in the Medway towns and across Kent. | **V** 0<br>**T** 0<br>**P** 4<br>**TS** 20<br>**WP** no |
| **KIRBY SIMCOX**<br>36 High Street, Thornbury, Bristol BS35 2AJ<br>**Tel:** 01454 412706<br>**Fax:** 01454 411591<br>**Email:** a.harraway@kirbysimcox.co.uk<br>**Apply to:** Mrs Harraway | Large three office practice with one office in Bristol City centre, Kingswoood and Thornbury. | **V** 0<br>**T** 2<br>**P** 7<br>**TS** 65<br>**WP** no |
| **KIRWANS**<br>363 Woodchurch Road, Birkenhead,<br>Merseyside CH42 8PE<br>**Tel:** 0151 608 9078<br>**Fax:** 0151 609 0030<br>**Email:** david.kirwans@kirwanssolicitors.co.uk<br>**Apply to:** Mr DS Kirwan | High Street practice with LSC franchises in crime and family, also departments in personal injury, general civil, private client, serious fraud panel. LEXEL & Investor in People Accreditation. | **V** 2[09]<br>**T** 4<br>**P** 7<br>**TS** 79<br>**WP** no |
| **KITSON HUTCHINGS**<br>Hagley House, The Terrace, Torquay TQ1 1BN<br>**Tel:** 01803 202020<br>**Fax:** 01803 213532<br>**Apply to:** Ms Louise Mason | Established 1826. Serves private and commercial clients. Member SFLA, AVMA, APIL and Children Panel. Legal aid franchise. Investors in People. | **V** Poss<br>**T** 0<br>**P** 16<br>**TS** 90<br>**WP** no |
| **KJD**<br>Churchill House, Regent Road,<br>Stoke-on-Trent ST1 3RQ<br>**Tel:** 01782 202020<br>**Fax:** 01782 202040<br>**Email:** karen.duckworth@kjd.co.uk<br>**Apply to:** Mrs Karen Duckworth | A West Midlands commercial practice providing a range of specialist and general commercial advice. Corporate finance, commercial litigation, commercial property, employment and planning are its strengths. | **V** 1-2[09]<br>**T** 5<br>**P** 17<br>**TS** 54<br>**WP** yes |
| **KNIGHTS**<br>Regency House, 25 High Street,<br>Tunbridge Wells TN1 1UT<br>**Tel:** 01892 537311<br>**Fax:** 01892 526141<br>**Email:** knights@knights-solicitors.co.uk<br>**Apply to:** Mr Michael McNally | Primarily a litigation practice specialising in all aspects of property countryside and country sports law. Clients drawn from whole of England and Wales. Next recruiting 2009 to start 2011. | **V** 0<br>**T** 1<br>**P** 5<br>**TS** 14<br>**WP** yes |

# Kirkland & Ellis International LLP

30 St Mary Axe, London EC3A 8AF
**Tel:** 020 7469 2000
**Fax:** 020 7469 2001
**Email:** lontraineerecruit@kirkland.com
**Web:** www.kirkland.com

**The firm** Kirkland & Ellis International LLP is a leading international law firm with more than 1,300 lawyers representing global clients in complex corporate, restructuring, tax, litigation, dispute resolution and arbitration, and intellectual property and technology matters.

**Types of work** Corporate: Kirkland & Ellis is known for its ability to negotiate and close highly sophisticated transactions, representing private equity investors and public and private companies in mergers and acquisitions, securities, private equity and real estate transactions. Kirkland & Ellis is recognised as a global leader in private equity, having represented private investment funds, private equity groups and other participants in this industry for more than 25 years.

Restructuring: the restructuring practice group provides a broad range of business advisory and crisis management skills with extensive experience in UK, US and international insolvency matters. The group has earned a distinguished international reputation acting for a varied range of clients in complex corporate restructuring, work-out and bankruptcy planning, negotiation and litigation.

Tax: the firm's tax practice group provides its clients with the most creative tax planning available in a responsible and cost-efficient manner. The practice has developed a strong international reputation for providing sophisticated tax counseling and effectively representing its clients in tax disputes worldwide.

International Arbitration and Litigation: the firm represents multinational corporations, governments and government-owned entities in international arbitration and litigation cases around the world. Kirkland's lawyers are also recognised for their experience in the conduct of white collar crime investigations on a global basis.

Intellectual Property: Kirkland & Ellis represents some of the world's leading technology companies and brings its expertise to all areas of IP, patent litigation, trade mark matters, outsourcing, computer software, licensing, distribution, joint venture agreements, biotechnology, data protection and e-commerce issues, as well as competition law-related matters.

**Who should apply** We are seeking to recruit four trainee solicitors to work in the London office. Successful candidates will have a strong academic record and be motivated to work hard in a professional, friendly and growing team.

**Training programme** As one of a small number of trainees, you will be part of the firms growing expansion into Europe. A training contract at Kirkland & Ellis will allow you to very quickly become a valued team member, who is given early responsibility to work on complex and often multi-jurisdictional matters.

**When and how to apply** Apply by CV and covering letter, including academic results, by 31 July 2008 to begin training contracts in September 2010.

**Work placements** 2 x two week placements throughout the summer months.

**Sponsorship** Full sponsorship of GDL and LPC fees, plus a maintenance grant of £7,500 pa.

| | |
|---|---|
| Vacancies | 4 |
| Trainees | 0 |
| Partners | 523* |
| Total staff | 3000* |

* denotes worldwide figure

Work placement   yes

**Apply to**
Kate Osborne

**Starting salary**
1st year - £35,000
2nd year - £40,000

**Minimum qualifications**
2.1 degree

**Sponsorship**
GDL/LPC

**Offices**
Chicago, Hong Kong,
London, Los Angeles,
Munich, New York,
San Francisco,
Washington DC

# Kirkpatrick & Lockhart Preston Gates Ellis LLP

110 Cannon Street, London EC4N 6AR
**Tel:** 020 7648 9000
**Fax:** 020 7648 9001
**Email:** traineerecruitment@klgates.com
**Web:** www.klgates.com

**The firm** K&L Gates comprises approximately 1,400 lawyers in 22 offices located in North America, Europe and Asia, and represents capital markets participants, entrepreneurs, growth and middle market companies, leading FORTUNE 100 and FTSE 100 global corporations and public sector entities. Whilst our international practice requires lawyers with diverse backgrounds and skills, we come together in our shared values of investment and growth, both for the firm and the individual. We are committed to professional development and provide a cutting-edge training program. Our international clients are at the forefront of outstanding achievement. To remain competitive they look to us to provide pragmatic and innovative legal advice as well as creative solutions for their legal issues. Our continued success therefore rests on the ability of our lawyers not only to meet that challenge, but to then surpass their expectations.

**Types of work** K&L Gates is active in the areas of investment management and related funds work, mergers & acquisitions, private equity, real estate, intellectual property, music, digital media and sport, travel & leisure, construction, insurance coverage, securities enforcement, environmental matters and litigation and other forms of dispute resolution.

**Who should apply** We welcome applications from both law and non-law students. Law students should generally be in their penultimate year of study and non-law students should be in their final year of study. We also welcome applications from other relevant postgraduates or others who have satisfied the 'academic stage of training' as required by the law society. You should be highly motivated, intellectually curious, with an interest in commercial law and be looking for comprehensive training.

**Training programme** We ensure each trainee is given exceptional opportunities to learn, experience and develop so that they can achieve their maximum potential. Trainees spend four six-month seats in four of the following departments: corporate, dispute resolution and litigation, intellectual property; construction, tax and real estate. Each trainee sits with a supervisor and is allocated an individual mentor to ensure all round supervision and training. The firm has a thorough induction scheme which includes attendance at our First Year Academy in the US, and has won awards for its career development programme. Trainees are encouraged to participate fully in the activities of the firm. High importance is placed on the acquisition of business and professional skills, with considerable emphasis on client contact and early responsibility. The training programme consists of weekly legal education seminars, workshops and a full programme of skills electives. Language training is also available.

**When and how to apply** Apply between 1 November 2007 and 31 July 2008 to begin in September 2010. Applications must be made online at www.klgates.com/europe_recruitment/graduate/.

**Work placements** Our formal legal work placement scheme is open to penultimate year law students and final year non-law students, other relevant postgraduates or others who have satisfied the 'academic stage of training' as required by the law society.

**Sponsorship** GDL funding: fees paid plus £5,000 maintenance grant.
LPC funding: fees paid plus £7,000 maintenance grant.

| Vacancies | Up to 15 |
|---|---|
| Trainees | 21 |
| Partners | 54 |
| Total staff | 301 |

**Work placement**   yes

**Apply to**
Hayley Atherton

**Minimum qualifications**
2.1 degree

**Sponsorship**
GDL/LPC

**Offices**
Anchorage, Beijing, Berlin, Boston, Coeur D'Alene, Dallas, Harrisburg, Hong Kong, London, Los Angeles, Miami, Newark, New York, Orange County, Palo Alto, Pittsburgh, Portland, San Francisco, Seattle, Spokane, Taipei, Washington

## K&L|GATES

Kirkpatrick & Lockhart Preston Gates Ellis LLP

# Knight & Sons

The Brampton, Newcastle under Lyme ST5 0QW
**Tel:** 01782 619225
**Fax:** 01782 717260
**Email:** info@knightandsons.co.uk
**Web:** www.knightandsons.co.uk

**The firm** Knight & Sons is a medium-sized, commercially orientated firm with a strong private client department. The firm was founded in 1767 and continues to act for many of the older businesses and families of the Midlands, alongside a wide range of business clients nationally. We have 16 partners and approximately 150 members of staff. There is no such thing as a 'Knight & Sons clone' - we thrive on our different personalities, knowing how vital it is to be able to meet the needs of a wide range of clients. However, we are all down to earth in our approach, pragmatic, commercial, efficient and results driven.

**Types of work** The firm's main areas of work are commercial property (38%), corporate and commercial (17%), commercial litigation (24%), tax trust and private client (21%).

**Who should apply** The firm is keen to recruit trainees who will stay on once they have qualified. We like people with outstanding academic achievement, a commercial approach, drive and a 'can do' attitude, and who are computer literate; but apart from these attributes, whether you are sporty, arty or intellectual you have a fair chance with us. An outgoing personality is important, as is an ability to communicate well with others - colleagues and clients alike.

**Training programme** Trainees generally spend six months in each of the four main departments (litigation, commercial property, corporate and commercial and tax, trust and private client), but may also gain experience in the specialist units such as planning, environment, employment, personal injury, agriculture and charity. You will receive three-monthly reviews with your immediate training supervisor and the training principal. Your Professional Skills Course will be arranged and paid for by us. You will also be given the opportunity to attend Knight & Sons' internal workshops and seminars.The firm runs in-house skills-based programmes designed to enhance business and client care skills for all fee-earners. You may also be given the chance to develop your presentation skills by being involved in seminars given by us to clients or other professionals. The atmosphere is lively and a social committee organises events throughout the year, ranging from a summer ball to a quiz night.

**When and how to apply** By 31 July 2008 to begin 2010. Apply online by visiting our website at www.knightandsons.co.uk or make a handwritten application supported by a CV to Jane Selman, HR & Training Manager.

**Sponsorship** Interest-free loans may be available but are strictly subject to individual negotiation.

| | |
|---|---|
| Vacancies | 3 |
| Trainees | 4 |
| Partners | 16 |
| Total staff | 150 |

**Vacation scheme** yes

**Apply to**
Jane Selman

**Starting salary**
Above the Law Society minimum with six-monthly reviews

**Minimum qualifications**
2.1 degree

**Offices**
Newcastle under Lyme

## KOTECHA & CO
40b Station Road, North Harrow, Harrow,
Middlesex HA2 7SE
**Tel:** 020 8426 0014
**Fax:** 020 8863 1048
**Email:** info@kotechasolicitors.co.uk
**Apply to:** Ms Nayna Kotecha

Small friendly high street practice carrying out property work, wills & probate, matrimonial, landlord and tenant and personal injury.

| | |
|---|---|
| V | 1 |
| T | 1 |
| P | 2 |
| TS | 5 |
| WP | no |

## KPFD SOLICITORS
Norton House, 52 High Street South, Dunstable,
Bedfordshire LU6 3HD
**Tel:** 01582 477 320
**Fax:** 01582 604 280
**Apply to:** Mr Francis Domingo

A firm that specialises in criminal defence work that can provide the challenge and satisfaction of achievement in an increasingly demanding environment in criminal litigation.

| | |
|---|---|
| V | 1 |
| T | 1 |
| P | 3 |
| TS | 8 |
| WP | no |

## KSB LAW
Elan House, 5-11 Fetter Lane, London EC4A 1QD
**Tel:** 020 7822 7500
**Fax:** 020 7822 7600
**Email:** ksb@ksblaw.co.uk
**Apply to:** Miss Diana Oxford

KSB Law is a pioneering commercial law firm specialising in company commercial litigation, insolvency, property licensing, private client and employment.

| | |
|---|---|
| V | 2 |
| T | 2 |
| P | 22 |
| TS | 111 |
| WP | yes |

## KSL SOLICITORS
702a Kenton Road, Harrow, Middlesex HA3 9QP
**Tel:** 020 8206 2668
**Fax:** 020 8206 1666
**Email:** k.sheth@ksl-law.com
**Apply to:** Mr KK Sheth

| | |
|---|---|
| V | 0 |
| T | 0 |
| P | - |
| TS | - |
| WP | yes |

## KUIT STEINART LEVY
3 St Mary's Parsonage, Manchester M3 2RD
**Tel:** 0161 832 3434
**Fax:** 0161 832 6650
**Email:** ksllaw@kuits.com
**Apply to:** Mr Damian Bailey

Progressive commercial practice based in Manchester city centre with a large corporate and private client base - company/commercial, tax, property, litigation, licensing and banking.

| | |
|---|---|
| V | 3 |
| T | 7 |
| P | 19 |
| TS | 105 |
| WP | no |

## KUNDERT & CO
3 Copthall House, Station Square,
Coventry CV1 2FD
**Tel:** 024 7668 4928
**Fax:** 024 7625 1417
**Apply to:** Mr CJD Jones

General practice, two office locations in the centre of Coventry and at the north of the city. Mixed practice of contentious and non-contentious work.

| | |
|---|---|
| V | 0 |
| T | 2 |
| P | 5 |
| TS | 30 |
| WP | no |

## LA STEEL
Oxford Villa, 123 Dodworth Road, Barnsley,
South Yorkshire S70 2EJ
**Tel:** 01226 770 909
**Fax:** 01226 770 655
**Email:** enquiries@lasteelsolicitors.com
**Apply to:** Mr LA Steel

Specialists in civil litigation, including personal injury and employment law. A niche firm.

| | |
|---|---|
| V | 0 |
| T | 0 |
| P | 0 |
| TS | 8 |
| WP | yes |

## LACEYS
5 Poole Road, Bournemouth BH2 5QL
**Tel:** 01202 557256
**Fax:** 01202 551925
**Apply to:** Mr Mark Timberlake

A progressive Legal 500, Investors in People and Lexcel firm. Equally balanced between commercial and private. One of the largest mediation departments in the South.

| | |
|---|---|
| V | 0 |
| T | 2 |
| P | 8 |
| TS | 60 |
| WP | no |

# Langleys

Queens House, Micklegate, York YO1 6WG
**Tel:** 01904 610886
**Fax:** 01904 611086
**Email:** tracey.connor@langleys.com
**Web:** www.langleys.com

**The firm** Langleys is a dynamic and modern law firm. We are an unusual practice in that we have managed to successfully retain and develop the traditional private client services while also developing thriving commercial and insurance law departments. IIP and Lexcel accredited, Langleys believes investment in skilled legal and support personnel and their continued training and development is a vital factor in achieving ever-increasing levels of service. Langleys is committed to the provision of quality legal services and continually strives to exceed clients' expectations.

**Types of work** The firm's activities can be divided into four main areas: insurance claims, commercial, private client and residential conveyancing. Our clients range from national companies and public sector bodies to owner-managed businesses and private individuals, reflecting the broad range of services we offer as a practice.

**Who should apply** Langleys is looking for enthusiastic candidates with a strong academic background, commercial awareness and determination to succeed. Both law and non-law applicants are welcome.

**Training programme** Langleys tries to give all trainees a well-rounded experience. Trainees generally complete four six-month seats. We aim to provide exposure to a broad range of work and clients to enable trainees to qualify with the skills and knowledge they need to excel in their careers. Support and supervision is given throughout to enable trainees to take on as much responsibility as they can handle. The firm actively works towards retaining its trainees on qualification.

**When and how to apply** Electronically - please see our website for details. Apply by 28 February 2008 to begin September 2009.

**Work placements** We offer a short summer vacation scheme during the months of June, July and August. Applications should be made electronically - please see our website for details. Deadline is 28 February for placements in the summer of the same year.

| | |
|---|---|
| Vacancies | 6 |
| Trainees | 15 |
| Partners | 38 |
| Total staff | 325 |

**Work placement** yes

**Apply to**
Rachael Lowe

**Minimum qualifications**
2.1 degree preferred

**Sponsorship**
CPE/LPC

**Offices**
Lincoln, York

## :Langleys

## LADERMAN AND CO
4 The Shrubberies, George Lane,
London E18 1BD
**Tel:** 020 8530 7319
**Fax:** 020 8530 6805
**Apply to:** Mr Daniel C Laderman

| | |
|---|---|
| V | Poss |
| T | 2 |
| P | 2 |
| TS | 13 |
| WP | no |

## LAMPORT BASSITT
46 The Avenue, Southampton SO17 1AX
**Tel:** 023 80634931
**Fax:** 023 80222346
**Email:** e-mail@lamportbassitt.co.uk
**Apply to:** Mr John Newton

The firm concentrates on personal injury, commercial litigation, and general corporate/commercial work.

| | |
|---|---|
| V | 3 |
| T | 6 |
| P | 10 |
| TS | 80 |
| WP | no |

## LANDES HUTTON LLP
4-5 Market Place, Bexleyheath, Kent DA6 7DU
**Tel:** 020 8303 0168
**Fax:** 020 8303 9125
**Email:** mana.murray@landeshutton.co.uk
**Apply to:** Ms Maria Murray

Busy matrimonial and conveyancing practice in purpose-built, well-situated office, LIP accredited.

| | |
|---|---|
| V | 1[08] |
| T | 2 |
| P | 2 |
| TS | 14 |
| WP | yes |

## LANE & PARTNERS
15 Bloomsbury Square, London WC1A 2LS
**Tel:** 020 7242 2626
**Fax:** 020 7242 0387
**Email:** colin.hall@lane.co.uk
**Apply to:** Mr Colin M S Hall

The firm advises corporate clients on all relevant areas of law, and is well known for its arbitration, construction, litigation and aviation work.

| | |
|---|---|
| V | 2 |
| T | 4 |
| P | 19 |
| TS | 70 |
| WP | no |

## LANYON BOWDLER
Brodie House, Town Centre, Telford TF3 4DR
**Tel:** 01952 291222
**Fax:** 01952 292585
**Email:** grichards@lblaw.co.uk
**Apply to:** Mr Garry Richards

Medium sized general practice, with four offices, which carries out a significant amount of corporate and commercial, commercial property and commercial litigation work.

| | |
|---|---|
| V | 2-3[09] |
| T | 5 |
| P | 13 |
| TS | 155 |
| WP | no |

## LARCOMES LLP
168 London Road, North End,
Portsmouth PO2 9DN
**Tel:** 023 9244 8100
**Fax:** 023 9266 5701
**Apply to:** Mr Julian Quartermain

| | |
|---|---|
| V | 1 |
| T | 1 |
| P | 4 |
| TS | 53 |
| WP | no |

## LARGE & GIBSON
Kent House, 49 Kent Road, Southsea PO5 3EJ
**Tel:** 023 92296296
**Fax:** 023 92826134
**Email:** reception@largeandgibson.co.uk
**Apply to:** Mr RIM Wootton

Criminal, civil litigation, matrimonial, commercial and domestic conveyancing, company, charities, business sales and purchases for private and corporate clients.

| | |
|---|---|
| V | 0 |
| T | 0 |
| P | 2 |
| TS | 20 |
| WP | no |

## LAST CAWTHRA FEATHER LLP
Airedale House, 128 Sunbridge Road, Bradford,
West Yorkshire BD1 2AT
**Tel:** 01274 848800
**Fax:** 01274 390644
**Email:** enquiries@lcf.co.uk
**Apply to:** Mr Adrian McDonald

Last Cawthra Feather is a leading commercial firm in Bradford with a strong client base and reputation recognised throughout West Yorkshire.

| | |
|---|---|
| V | 1 |
| T | 5 |
| P | 12 |
| TS | 140 |
| WP | no |

# Latham & Watkins

99 Bishopsgate, London EC2M 3XF
**Tel:** 020 7710 1000
**Fax:** 020 7374 4460
**Email:** london.trainees@lw.com
**Web:** www.lw.com

**The firm** We are a major international law firm with an established London office. We are proud of the culture, the work and the people at our firm, and believe the key to our success is our 'one firm' culture with a spirit of teamwork and shared commitment to equality.

Latham & Watkins' award-winning London office is recognised for having the depth of experience to provide high-end legal services to local and multi-jurisdictional clients on complex, cross-border matters. We have over 150 lawyers in London who work closely with colleagues throughout the firm, drawing on the expertise of 1,900 attorneys located in 24 offices worldwide.

**Types of work** Our ability to field a team of the highest quality lawyers in a number of jurisdictions has led to our involvement in the largest and most complex cross-border transactions. Examples of our work include:
Securing a successful outcome for the Government of Barbados in its long running dispute with the Republic of Trinidad and Tobago in the first ever maritime boundary arbitration between two sovereign States under the UN Convention on the Law of the Sea.
Advising Nakilat on the largest ship financing ever undertaken with a view to transporting liquefied natural gas to established gas markets throughout the world.
Advising the underwriters on the first ever international high yield bond offering by a Pakistani corporate issuer (Pakistan Mobile Communications Limited).

Many of our practice areas are industry leaders and award winning, as are many of the partners. Legal Business awarded the firm the much coveted title of 'Law Firm of the Decade' in 2007.

We have strong capabilities in all areas including: banking and finance; corporate governance; debt and equity capital markets; employment; EU and competition law; IP; leveraged finance; litigation and ADR; mergers and acquisitions; private equity; project development and finance; public international law; real estate; restructuring and insolvency; tax; technology and outsourcing and venture capital and investment funds.

**Who should apply** Candidates should be entrepreneurial and thrive on early responsibility. Applicants with a strong academic background, excellent communication skills and a consistent record of personal and/or professional achievement will be rewarded with first class training in a stimulating environment.

**Training programme** The training programme will consist of four six-month seats and include the opportunity of an overseas seat. Preferences for practice areas within departments will be accommodated wherever possible.

**When and how to apply** Complete the online application form at www.lw.com. The deadline for submission is 31 July 2008.

**Work placements** Two-week summer scheme in August and a one-week Easter scheme.

**Sponsorship** GDL/LPC fees paid in full; £8,000 maintenance grant paid in each law school year.

| | |
|---|---|
| Vacancies | 10-15 |
| Trainees | 10 |
| Partners | 38 |
| Total staff | 265 |

**Work placement** yes
*(see Insider Report on p111)*

**Apply to**
Tracy Davidson

**Starting salary**
1st year - £37,500
2nd year - £38,500

**Minimum qualifications**
2.1 degree and 320 UCAS points

**Sponsorship**
GDL/LPC

**Offices**
24 offices in the EU, US and Asia

LATHAM&WATKINS LLP

# Lawrence Graham LLP

4 More london Riverside, London SE1 2AU
**Tel:** 020 7759 6694
**Fax:** 020 7173 8694
**Email:** graduate@lg-legal.com
**Web:** www.lg-legal.com

**The firm** We are a leading London-based firm with an outstanding reputation in commercial property transactions and mid-market corporate transactions. Our business is divided into four principal practice areas. The two main departments are real estate and business and finance. We also have a top-rated tax and private capital department and a highly regarded dispute resolution team. We famously combine a commercially driven environment with an open, unstuffy culture that results in an enjoyable place to work.

**Types of work** The bulk of our work consists of corporate transactions and major commercial property deals, so the ability to work as part of a team is essential. To support the major transactions, we have a full range of service departments which, because of their level of expertise, have thriving independent businesses of their own. The litigation department operates as a service department and has several specialist business areas independent of business and finance and real estate. Tax and private capital, though small in the context of the firm, is a leader in its field and has an enviable international reputation. More information on the different types of work can be found on our website.

**Who should apply** We are looking for individuals who can demonstrate a commitment to a career in the commercial application of law and an understanding of the rigours of professional practice. A strong academic track record with a minimum 2.1 degree, either expected or predicted, is a basic requirement. In addition, we expect a good record of achievement in other areas, indicative of the ability to succeed in a demanding career. Evidence of team-working skills and the ability to handle responsibility is also essential.

**Training programme** The objective of the two-year training contract is to develop competent all-round commercial lawyers who fully understand and have the ability to meet the quality standards demanded by the firm. Under partner supervision, you will be given early responsibility. Training is structured to facilitate the ability to manage your own files and interact with clients. In addition to the Professional Skills Course, there are departmental training and induction sessions. Formal appraisal sessions take place every three months providing the opportunity to discuss the progress of your training and receive feedback on your development as a lawyer. The two-year contract is divided into four six-month seats. Real estate, business and finance and contentious seats are compulsory. The final seat can either be in tax and private capital or back to real estate or business and finance, as they are the largest departments. After the first seat, seats are chosen in consultation with you, the objective being to develop broad skills in the commercial application of the law. Buy-in to the firm's ethos is essential. Strong personal ethics, a desire to work hard and give a quality client-orientated service along with a team orientation are part of the make-up of the firm.

**When and how to apply** Law degree – after second year results. Non-law degree – after final year results. Applications must be made on the firm's application form available online. The deadline for applications is 31 July 2008.

**Sponsorship** GDL and LPC plus maintenance grant.

| | |
|---|---|
| Vacancies | 25 |
| Trainees | 42 |
| Partners | 85 |
| Total staff | 500 |

**Work placement**   yes
*(see Insider Report on p113)*

**Apply to**
Graduate Recruitment Officer

**Starting salary**
£30,000 rising to £34,000 for the final year

**Minimum qualifications**
All disciplines 2.1

**Sponsorship**
GDL/LPC

**Offices**
London, Monaco

# Laytons

Carmelite, 50 Victoria Embankment, London EC4Y 0LS
**Tel:** 020 7842 8000
**Fax:** 020 7842 8080
**Email:** london@laytons.com
**Web:** www.laytons.com

**The firm** A commercial law firm whose primary focus is on developing dynamic business. The firm's offices in Guildford, London and Manchester provide excellent service to its commercial and private clients located throughout the UK. The firm's approach to legal issues is practical, creative and energetic. The firm believes in long-term relationships with clients by developing a thorough understanding of their businesses, their needs and objectives. Working together as one team, the firm is supportive and plays to each others' strengths.

**Types of work** Corporate and commercial, commercial property (including land development and construction), dispute resolution, debt recovery, insolvency, employment, intellectual property, technology and media, private client and trusts. Clients include: listed companies; privately owned companies; SMES; start-ups; and not-for-profit organisations.

**Who should apply** Successful candidates will be well-rounded individuals, commercially aware with a sound academic background (2.1 degree preferred), and enthusiastic and committed team members.

**Training programme** Generally, training seats are six months. The principal seats are corporate/commercial, property/construction and dispute resolution. The fourth seat will depend upon the circumstances of the particular office and may include employment, intellectual property, insolvency, private client or family law (this is a compulsory seat for trainees in our Manchester office). We always take into account the trainee's wishes as far as possible when allocating seats.

**When and how to apply** Not later than 31 August 2008 to begin September 2010. You should complete an application form (see www.laytons.com/recruitment) and submit it, together with your CV and a covering letter, to the recruitment partner at the office in which you wish to undertake your vacation placement or training contract. You can download an application form from our website, or alternatively please contact any of our recruitment partners.

**Work placements** Places for summer 2008: 6. Duration: 1 week. Closing date: 31 March 2008.

**Sponsorship** LPC and CPE funding: consideration given.

| | |
|---|---|
| Vacancies | 6 |
| Trainees | 12 |
| Partners | 34 |
| Total staff | 170 |

Work placement    yes

Apply to
Mr Stephen Cates &
Ms Lisa McLean

Starting salary
Market rate

Minimum qualifications
2.1 degree

Sponsorship
GDL/LPC

Offices
Guildford, London,
Manchester

LAYTONS
SOLICITORS

# LeBoeuf, Lamb, Greene & MacRae

No 1 Minster Court, Mincing Lane, London EC3R 7YL
**Tel:** 020 7459 5000
**Fax:** 020 7459 5099
**Email:** traineelondon@llgm.com
**Web:** www.llgm.com

**The firm** LeBoeuf, Lamb, Greene & MacRae is an international law firm with 750 lawyers worldwide, in offices across the US, Europe, Africa, the Middle East and Asia.

The London office of LeBoeuf Lamb is the firm's largest international office, with 35 partners and over 130 legal staff. The vast majority of our partners and associates are English qualified solicitors. In addition, we have significant US law capability.

**Types of work** In London, the firm advises a wide range of clients, including multinational corporations, financial institutions, governments and state owned entities, with interests in the UK and throughout Europe, Russia and the CIS, the Middle East, Africa and the US. Our London lawyers offer the full range of legal services from corporate and commercial advice, M&A and finance to litigation/arbitration, environment, insolvency, competition, employment, real estate, tax and intellectual property.

**Who should apply** We want outstanding people in the broadest possible sense. We welcome applications from people with varied and unusual backgrounds. Interpersonal skills are very important: we like confident, bright, engaging people. The London office is international in outlook and language skills are highly valued. In particular we are interested in candidates with French, Russian, Chinese and Arabic capabilities.

We like talented, motivated people who have commercial awareness and a genuine enthusiasm for the law, coupled with a desire to learn more. We want proactive people who will show initiative from day one.

**Training programme** Our training programme is comprehensive and covers an induction programme, participation in internal seminars and training sessions, and attendance at external courses, including the Professional Skills Course. Trainees have the opportunity to spend six months in four different areas. At least one seat will be spent in each of our mainstream practice areas of corporate and dispute resolution. Trainees will also typically spend six months working closely with one of our specialist teams gaining experience in areas such as capital markets, international arbitration, insurance regulatory, employment, environment, competition, IP/IT, real estate and tax. You can expect to be exposed to high quality work with early responsibility. In each seat you will sit with a partner or senior associate who will supervise your work. Six month secondments to Moscow and Paris are possible, along with the opportunity for secondment to our clients.

**When and how to apply** By 31 July 2008 to begin September 2010. Please visit www.llgm.com for our brochure and an application form.

**Work placements** The firm runs two-week summer vacation schemes throughout June and July for penultimate year law undergraduates and graduates of all disciplines. Places for 2008: 15. Remuneration: £300 per week. Closing date: 31 January 2008. Please visit www.llgm.com for more details and an application form.

**Sponsorship** Full payment of GDL/LPC fees and maintenance grant of £8,500 per annum.

| | |
|---|---|
| Vacancies | 20 |
| Trainees | 17 |
| Partners | 35 |
| Total staff | 220 |

**Work placement** yes

**Apply to**
Gail Sorrell

**Starting salary**
£40,000 rising to £45,000 in second year

**Minimum qualifications**
2.1 degree + AAB at A level or equivalent

**Sponsorship**
GDL/LPC

**Offices**
Albany, Almaty, Beijing, Boston, Brussels, Chicago, Hartford, Houston, Jacksonville, Johannesburg, London, Los Angeles, Moscow, New York, Paris, Riyadh, San Francisco, Washington DC

LEBOEUF LAMB

## LATIMER HINKS
5-8 Priestgate, Darlington DL1 1NL
**Tel:** 01325 341500
**Fax:** 01325 381072
**Apply to:** Ms Jacqui Jones

General long established practice providing legal services for commercial, agricultural and private clients in Durham, Teesside and North Yorkshire.

| V | Poss |
|---|---|
| T | 1 |
| P | 7 |
| TS | 56 |
| WP | no |

## LATIMER LEE
35 Bury New Road, Prestwich, Manchester M25 9JY
**Tel:** 0161 798 9000
**Fax:** 0161 773 6578
**Email:** customerservices@latimerlee.com
**Apply to:** Mr SR Latimer

Large local firm dedicated in providing exceptional work.

| V | 0 |
|---|---|
| T | 0 |
| P | - |
| TS | - |
| WP | yes |

## LAWSON & THOMPSON
30 Front Street, Newbiggin-By-The-Sea, Northumberland NE64 6PL
**Tel:** 01670 856060
**Fax:** 01670 812759
**Apply to:** Mr TJR Barker

High street practice with good local client base. Applications invited from ambitious, hardworking individuals with good sense of humour who are prepared to be a team players.

| V | 1 |
|---|---|
| T | 0 |
| P | 6 |
| TS | 30 |
| WP | no |

## LAWSON LEWIS & CO
11-12 Hyde Gardens, Eastbourne BN21 4PP
**Tel:** 01323 720142
**Fax:** 01323 725349
**Apply to:** Mr J H Sogno

Long established general practice in Sussex offering full range of legal services. Seek trainee who should be hardworking, able and possess good communication skills.

| V | 2(09) |
|---|---|
| T | 2 |
| P | 3 |
| TS | 60 |
| WP | no |

## LAYARD HORSFALL
64 High Street, Godalming, Surrey GU7 1DU
**Tel:** 01483 416134
**Fax:** 01483 428286
**Email:** info@layard.com
**Apply to:** Mr David Horsfall

Firm specialising in property law.

| V | 0 |
|---|---|
| T | 2 |
| P | 1 |
| TS | 3 |
| WP | no |

## LEATHES PRIOR
74 The Close, Norwich NR1 4DR
**Tel:** 01603 610911
**Fax:** 01603 281188
**Email:** info@leathesprior.co.uk
**Apply to:** Mr Martin Plowman

A firm of solicitors specialising in company and commercial work, franchising, employment, insolvency, conveyancing, wills and probate, matrimonial, common law, criminal and road traffic for private clients.

| V | 1-3 |
|---|---|
| T | 4 |
| P | 11 |
| TS | 55 |
| WP | no |

## LEE & PRIESTLEY
10-12 East Parade, Leeds LS1 2AJ
**Tel:** 0113 243 3751
**Fax:** 0113 246 7357
**Apply to:** Mrs Jackie Turner

General commercial practice which is expanding rapidly.

| V | 2(09) |
|---|---|
| T | 6 |
| P | 12 |
| TS | 100 |
| WP | no |

## LEECH & CO
First Floor Heron House, 11-12 Albert Square, Manchester M2 5HD
**Tel:** 0161 279 0279
**Fax:** 0161 279 1300
**Email:** emma.leech@leech.co.uk
**Apply to:** Ms Emma Leech

| V | Poss 2 |
|---|---|
| T | 3 |
| P | 7 |
| TS | 45 |
| WP | no |

**V** = Vacancies / **T** = Trainees / **P** = Partners / **TS** = Total Staff / **WP** = Work Placement

# Lee Bolton & Lee

1 The Sanctuary, Westminster, London SW1P 3JT
**Tel:** 020 7222 5381
**Fax:** 020 7222 7502
**Web:** www.leeboltonlee.com

**The firm** Lee Bolton & Lee is a medium-sized firm based in Westminster. It is associated with a firm of solicitors and parliamentary agents, Rees & Freres, who provide a specialist service in parliamentary, public and administrative law.

**Types of work** We offer extensive experience and advice across a wide spectrum of activities including commercial, property, private client, litigation, public law, charity and education work.

**Who should apply** We seek to recruit trainees with a good degree (2.1 or above), first-class communication skills, motivation, professionalism, initiative, enthusiasm and a sense of humour.

**Training programme** Trainees spend six months in four of six seats following induction – private client, property, litigation, commercial property, education and charity, and public law. Training is comprehensive and covers a full induction programme, participation in internal seminars and training sessions, and attendance at external courses including the Professional Skills Course.

**When and how to apply** Before 31 July to begin September two years later. Apply online.

**Sponsorship** Contribution towards cost of LPC – £4,000.

| | |
|---|---|
| Vacancies | 3 |
| Trainees | 6 |
| Partners | 13 |
| Total staff | 85 |

**Apply to**
Susie Hust

**Starting salary**
£25,000

**Minimum qualifications**
2.1 degree, any subject

**Sponsorship**
LPC

**Offices**
London

Lee Bolton & Lee
—— SOLICITORS ——

# Lester Aldridge LLP

Russell House, Oxford Road, Bournemouth BH8 8EX
**Tel:** 01202 786161
**Fax:** 01202 786110
**Email:** juliet.artal@la-law.com
**Web:** www.lesteraldridge.com

**The firm** Lester Aldridge LLP is a dynamic business providing both commercial and private client services. The firm has highly successful niche markets, including asset finance, marine, retail and care sector.

A key regional player, the firm has an impressive client repertoire supported by the recruitment of outstanding staff.

Lester Aldridge's positioning on the South Coast offers a positive working environment and a great work life balance; while providing opportunities to work with first class lawyers, impressive clients, and opportunity for City experience via LA's London office.

**Types of work** Corporate, banking and finance 32%; litigation 30%; private client 21%; commercial property 12%; investments 5%.

**Who should apply** Candidates should have a consistently strong academic record, be commercially aware and possess a broad range of interpersonal skills. Applicants should be highly motivated and have a desire to succeed working with teams to advise clients in dynamic and demanding industries.

**Training programme** Training consists of four six-month seats across the firm (preference will be accommodated where possible). Direct client involvement is encouraged and each trainee is assigned a mentor to provide guidance and encouragement. Appraisals are carried out with team leaders at the end of each seat, as are three-monthly group meetings with the Managing Partner, to ensure that trainees gain a range of work and experience.

**When and how to apply** Apply by 31 July 2008 to begin in 2010. Apply by letter, CV and completed application form.

**Sponsorship** LPC.

| | |
|---|---|
| Vacancies | 6 |
| Trainees | 13 |
| Partners | 31 |
| Total staff | 300 |

**Work placement**  yes

**Apply to**
Juliet Artal

**Starting salary**
£17,250 at present
(increasing by £500 after
each seat)

**Minimum qualifications**
2.1 degree

**Sponsorship**
LPC

**Offices**
Bournemouth (2),
Southampton,
Milton Keynes, London

LesterAldridge LLP

| | | | |
|---|---|---|---|
| **LEES & PARTNERS**<br>44/45 Hamilton Square, Birkenhead CH41 5AR<br>**Tel:** 0151 647 9381<br>**Fax:** 0151 666 1445<br>**Email:** jk@lees.co.uk<br>**Apply to:** Ms Joanna Kingston | Business and Property Services, Business Litigation, Claims, Clinical Negligence, Court of Protection, Family, Wills and Estates. Legal aid franchise and Investors in People. Offices in Birkenhead, Chester, Heswall and West Kirby. | **V** 1-2[09]<br>**T** 2<br>**P** 14<br>**TS** 100<br>**WP** no | |

| | | | |
|---|---|---|---|
| **LEIGH DAY & CO**<br>Priory House, 25 St John's Lane,<br>London EC1M 4LB<br>**Tel:** 020 7650 1200<br>**Fax:** 020 7253 4433<br>**Apply to:** Ms Frances Swaine | Severely injured claimants - clinical negligence, environmental, product liability, personal injury, public law, planning, community care and human rights. | **V** 0<br>**T** 7<br>**P** 18<br>**TS** 90<br>**WP** yes | |

| | | | |
|---|---|---|---|
| **LENNON & CO**<br>Chess Chambers, 2 Broadway Court,<br>Chesham HP5 1EG<br>**Tel:** 01494 773377<br>**Fax:** 01494 773100<br>**Apply to:** Mr Alan Lennon | General practice specialising in commercial/residential conveyancing; commercial work; all civil litigation including personal injury, professional and medical negligence, matrimonial and civil work, wills and probate. | **V** 0<br>**T** 3<br>**P** 6<br>**TS** 31<br>**WP** no | |

| | | | |
|---|---|---|---|
| **LEO ABSE & COHEN**<br>40 Churchill Way, Cardiff CF10 2SS<br>**Tel:** 02920 383252<br>**Fax:** 02920 345572<br>**Email:** rosemaryd@leoabse.co.uk<br>**Apply to:** Ms Hayley Jones | Established in the 1950s. A progressive and expanding law firm in South Wales offering a comprehensive range of legal services with particular emphasis on litigation. | **V** 0<br>**T** 4<br>**P** 13<br>**TS** 140<br>**WP** no | |

| | | | |
|---|---|---|---|
| **LEONARD & CO**<br>First Floor, Oakwood Court, 62a The Avenue,<br>Southampton SO17 1XS<br>**Tel:** 023 8023 4433<br>**Fax:** 023 8022 0460<br>**Email:** leonard.lawyers@btconnect.com<br>**Apply to:** Mr GM Leonard | Specialist litigation practice concentrating on childcare, family, crime, housing and immigration law. | **V** 1<br>**T** 2<br>**P** 3<br>**TS** 20<br>**WP** no | |

| | | | |
|---|---|---|---|
| **LESTER MORRILL**<br>27 Park Square West, Leeds LS1 2PL<br>**Tel:** 0113 245 8549<br>**Fax:** 0113 242 1965<br>**Email:** info@lmlaw.co.uk<br>**Apply to:** Mr RE Lester | Specialists in crime, clinical negligence, family and actions against the police. Franchised, I.I.P accredited. | **V** 1<br>**T** 1<br>**P** 5<br>**TS** 31<br>**WP** no | |

| | | | |
|---|---|---|---|
| **LEUNG & CO**<br>Albert House, 111 Victoria Street, Bristol BS1 6OX<br>**Tel:** 0117 920 9230<br>**Fax:** 0117 920 9239<br>**Email:** info@leung-solicitors.co.uk<br>**Apply to:** Miss WHA Leung | We are a general practice with emphasis in commercial properties, business immigration and licensing. | **V** 1[08]<br>**T** 1<br>**P** 1<br>**TS** 8<br>**WP** no | |

| | | | |
|---|---|---|---|
| **LIGHTFOOTS**<br>1-3 High Street, Thame, Oxfordshire OX9 2BX<br>**Tel:** 01844 268 301<br>**Fax:** 01844 214 984<br>**Email:** lparke@lightfoots.co.uk<br>**Apply to:** Ms Lesley Parke | One vacancy in each year. | **V** 0<br>**T** 2<br>**P** 3<br>**TS** 106<br>**WP** no | |

# Lewis Silkin LLP

5 Chancery Lane, Clifford's Inn, London EC4A 1BL
**Tel:** 020 7074 8000
**Fax:** 020 7864 1200
**Email:** train@lewissilkin.com
**Web:** www.lewissilkin.com

**The firm** Lewis Silkin is a commercial law firm with 45 partners. What distinguishes us is a matter of personality. For lawyers, we are notably informal, unstuffy…well, human really. We're 'people people': as committed and professional as any good law firm, but perhaps more adept at the inter-personal skills that make relationships work and go on working. We place a high priority on the excellent technical ability and commercial thinking of our lawyers and also on our relationships with clients. Our clients find us refreshingly easy to deal with. The firm has a friendly, lively style with a commitment to continuous improvement.

**Types of work** Lewis Silkin has a wide range of corporate clients and provides services through five departments: corporate, employment & incentives, litigation, property, housing and construction and media, brands & technology. The major work areas are: commercial litigation and dispute resolution; corporate services, which includes company commercial and corporate finance; defamation; employment; marketing services, embracing advertising and marketing law; property, construction and project finance; technology and communications, including IT, media and telecommunications.

We are UK leaders in employment law and have a strong reputation within social housing and the media and advertising sectors.

**Who should apply** We are looking for five trainees with keen minds and personalities, who will fit into a professional but informal team, to join us in September 2010.

**Training programme** We provide a comprehensive induction and training programme, with practical, hands-on experience from day one. You will sit with either a partner or senior associate giving you access to day-to-day supervision and guidance. The training contract consists of four six-month seats, working in four out of our five departments.

**When and how to apply** Applications for training contracts to commence in 2010 should be made between November 2007 and July 2008, via the firm's website. The closing date for applications is 31 July 2008.

**Work placements** There are three two-week vacation scheme sessions which take place during June and July giving 12 participants the opportunity to gain first-hand experience of life at Lewis Silkin. Applications should be made via the firm's website between November 2007 and the end of January 2008.

**Open days** Three open days will be held during summer 2008 to give participants an overview of the firm, our main areas of work and a chance to meet fellow trainees and partners of the firm. Applications should be made via the firm's website between November 2007 and the end of January 2008.

**Sponsorship** Funding for LPC fees provided plus £4,500 maintenance. Funding for GDL fees provided.

| | |
|---|---|
| Vacancies | 5 |
| Trainees | 12 |
| Partners | 45 |
| Total staff | 245 |

**Work placement** yes

**Apply**
Online

**Starting salary**
£31,000 (Sept 2007)

**Minimum qualifications**
2.1 degree, any subject

**Sponsorship**
GDL/LPC

**Offices**
London,
Oxford (small employment and incentives office)

**lewis**silkin

# Linklaters LLP

One Silk Street, London EC2Y 8HQ
**Tel:** 020 7456 2000
**Fax:** 020 7456 2222
**Email:** graduate.recruitment@linklaters.com
**Web:** www.linklaters.com/careers/ukgrads

**The firm** Linklaters LLP is the global law firm that advises the world's leading companies, financial institutions and governments on their most challenging transactions and assignments. This is an ambitious and innovative firm: the drive to create something new in professional services also shapes a very special offer to graduates.

There are approximately 2,000 lawyers at Linklaters; we work in 23 different countries with clients including over 50% of the FTSE-100. While many law firms have strengths in particular areas, we are strong across the full range of business law: this makes Linklaters a particularly rewarding place to train as a lawyer. It gives you more options when you qualify too.

Ask anyone from Linklaters what they most enjoy about the firm, and the answer is usually the same: 'It's the people'. Our people come from many different backgrounds. By working together, we achieve great things for clients, but we also fulfil our own ambitions as individuals. There is mutual benefit here, as well as mutual respect. We expect a lot of our trainees, but the rewards – personal and professional as well as financial – can be very high indeed.

**Types of work** Our work is divided into three main areas – corporate, finance & projects and commercial. We are equally strong across this full range of business law.

**Who should apply** The firm recruits graduates from both law and non-law disciplines. Non-law graduates spend a conversion year at law college taking the Graduate Diploma in Law (GDL). All trainees have to complete the Legal Practice Course (LPC) before starting their training contracts.

**Training programme** As part of our commitment to excellence in professional training, we have developed our own LPC course in partnership with The College of Law in London. The Linklaters LPC builds stronger links between theory and practice, making the transition to the training contract easier and smoother for everyone involved. Graduates in non-law disciplines spend a year at law school, taking the Graduate Diploma in Law. All trainees have to complete the Legal Practice Course before they begin their training contracts. Whichever route you take, we pay your way. The training contract itself is built around four six-month placements in different practice areas. As well as making you a well-rounded lawyer, it also gives you a good idea of what you might want to do after qualifying. There are opportunities for client secondments and overseas placements throughout your training contract (and beyond).

**When and how to apply** Training with Linklaters means working alongside some of the world's best lawyers on some of the world's most challenging deals. Full details of the opportunities (including our winter and summer vacation schemes) are available at www.linklaters.com/careers/ukgrads.

**Work placements** We run a Christmas vacation scheme for 30 final-year non-law students; and three summer schemes for a total of 80 penultimate-year law students. Our application deadline for Christmas is 18 November 2007 and for summer 20 January 2008.

**Sponsorship** We meet all costs for the GDL and LPC and offer a maintenance grant for both.

| | |
|---|---|
| Vacancies | 130 |
| Trainees | 250+ |
| Partners | 500+* |
| Total staff | 5000+* |

\* worldwide figures

**Work placement**   yes

**Apply to**
Charlotte Hart,
Graduate Recruitment

**Starting salary**
£36,000

**Minimum qualifications**
2.1 degree

**Sponsorship**
GDL/LPC

**Offices**
Amsterdam, Antwerp, Bangkok, Beijing, Berlin, Bratislava, Brussels, Bucharest, Budapest, Cologne, Dubai, Frankfurt, Hong Kong, Lisbon, London, Luxembourg, Madrid, Milan, Moscow, Munich, New York, Paris, Prague, Rome, São Paulo, Shanghai, Singapore, Stockholm, Tokyo, Warsaw

# Linklaters

# Lodders Solicitors LLP

Number 10, Elm Court, Arden Street, Stratford-upon-Avon, Warwickshire CV37 6PA
**Tel:** 01789 293259
**Fax:** 01789 268093
**Email:** lawyers@lodders.co.uk
**Web:** www.lodders.co.uk

**The firm** Lodders is a regional, established law firm based in Stratford-upon-Avon. The firm was founded over 150 years ago and has developed a strong client base both in the locality and nationally.

**Types of work** The principal office in Stratford-upon-Avon houses the main departments of the firm being private client, agriculture, commercial property, residential property, company/commercial and litigation and dispute resolution. In addition we have charity law, highways and planning specialists on staff. The branch office in Henley in Arden offers a smaller range of services to their local clients.

In terms of the work we undertake, you will find us listed in *Chambers 2007* as the leading firm in the Midlands in agriculture, and one of the leading firms in trusts and personal tax.

**Who should apply** We appreciate that people have different abilities and it takes a range of skills to make a business succeed, so we will be looking for candidates who display a number of key talents. You should be bright, enthusiastic, professional, commercially-minded, proactive, unafraid of responsibility, and interested in getting the little things right. You should be happy to get involved in the fabric of the firm, by attending the social events and meeting and entertaining clients. We like our trainees to be sociable, well-rounded people, who have a range of pursuits outside the office, and applicants should see their future in the Stratford-upon-Avon area.

**Training programme** Generally, you will spend six months in four departments but we are happy to accommodate any particular interests that you might wish to pursue. The choice is enviable and now includes the option of a seat for three months at Self, the financial planning and advice company with which we have close links. You can visit their web site at www.selfadvice.com.

In terms of the work that you will experience, the opportunities are wide and varied. You will work with both assistants and partners and will be involved in other fee earner's files as well as running your own.

The work that you carry out will be under the supervision of a partner in each department who operate an open door policy and are available to provide you with constructive feedback on your performance. This will ensure that you are progressing in the right direction.

We feel that your continued development is crucial to enable you to perform at the highest level and we support training both throughout your training contract and post qualification. You will have the opportunity to attend all in house seminars and any external seminars that may assist your development. We also encourage internal knowledge sharing involving inter-departmental seminars which will give you the chance to develop your presentation skills.

**When and how to apply** Applications should be made by 31 July 2008 to begin September 2010. Please send your CV together with a covering letter to Rebecca Whitehouse at the Stratford-upon-Avon address.

**Sponsorship** By agreement.

| | |
|---|---|
| Vacancies | 2 |
| Trainees | 5 |
| Partners | 15 |
| Total staff | 130 |

Work placement   no

Apply to
Rebecca Whitehouse

Starting salary
Under review

Minimum qualifications
2.1 degree but a 2.2 degree may be considered for exceptional candidates

Sponsorship
LPC

Offices
Stratford-upon-Avon,
Henley in Arden

# Lovells

Lovells LLP, Atlantic House, Holborn Viaduct, London EC1A 2FG
**Tel:** 020 7296 2000
**Fax:** 020 7296 2001
**Email:** recruit@lovells.com
**Web:** www.lovells.com/graduates

**The firm** Lovells is an international legal practice comprising Lovells LLP and its affiliated businesses with offices in the major financial and commercial centres across Europe, Asia and the United States.

**Types of work** Our international strength across a wide range of practice areas gives us an exceptional reputation not only for corporate, finance and dispute resolution, but also for other specialist areas including intellectual property, employment, EU/competition, insurance and tax.

**Who should apply** High-calibre candidates who can demonstrate strong academic/intellectual ability, ambition, drive, strong communication skills and interpersonal skills, and a professional/commercial attitude.

**Training programme** Trainees spend six months in four different areas of the practice to gain as much experience as possible. They have the option of spending time in their second year of training in an international office or on secondment to the in-house legal department of a major client. A comprehensive programme of skills training is run for trainees both in-house and externally that comprises the Professional Skills Course. Trainees are offered as much responsibility as they can handle as well as regular reviews, six-monthly appraisals and support. After qualification, continuous training and professional development remain a priority.

Benefits include: PPP medical insurance, life assurance, private health insurance, season ticket loan, in-house gym, staff restaurant, access to dentist, doctor and physiotherapist, lifestyle benefits.

**When and how to apply** Law students should apply over the summer after completion of their penultimate year and when they have their exam results (where applicable). Non-law students and postgraduates should apply in their final year. Applicants should visit our website at www.lovells.com/graduates and complete an application form online.

**Work placements** We offer up to 90 vacation placements over four highly regarded schemes lasting two or three weeks at Christmas, Easter and over the summer. Places are principally offered to penultimate-year law and final-year non-law students, but graduates and individuals considering a change of career are also welcome to apply.

The main feature of the programme is the broad insight into the work of the firm. Those attending a placement will experience two or three of our major sectors (corporate, finance, commerce and dispute resolution) and get involved in real work with real clients in much the same way as our trainees. This includes: drafting, attending meetings, doing legal research and, where possible, attending court. To complement this there is also a comprehensive programme of talks, workshops and social events.

For individuals gravitating towards law, the vacation placements provide the opportunity to gain exposure to life and work in a top City law firm and to see how well suited they would be to the firm.

**Sponsorship** GDL and LPC fees are paid, and a maintenance grant is also provided of £8,000 for all students reading the LPC and GDL in London and £7,000 for students reading the GDL elsewhere. In addition, £1,000 bonus on joining the firm; £1,000 advance in salary on joining; £500 for a first class degree result; £500 for getting the top overall marks within the Lovells LPC cohort; interest-free season ticket loan (for London Underground and overground services) during the LPC year.

| | |
|---|---|
| Vacancies | 90 |
| Trainees | 142 |
| Partners | 319 |
| Total staff | 3000 |

**Work placement** yes
*(see Insider Report on p115)*

**Apply to**
Natalya Taylor, Assistant Manager Graduate Recruitment

**Starting salary**
Year 1: £36,000
Year 2: £40,000

**Minimum qualifications**
2.1 degree

**Sponsorship**
GDL/LPC

**Offices**
Alicante, Amsterdam, Beijing, Brussels, Budapest, Chicago, Dubai, Düsseldorf, Frankfurt, Hamburg, Ho Chi Minh City, Hong Kong, London, Madrid, Milan, Moscow, Munich, New York, Paris, Prague, Rome, Shanghai, Singapore, Tokyo, Warsaw, Zagreb

# Lovells

## LUPTON FAWCETT
Yorkshire House, East Parade, Leeds LS1 5BD
**Tel:** 0113 280 2000
**Fax:** 0113 245 6782
**Email:** hr@luptonfawcett.com
**Apply to:** HR Manager

Lupton Fawcett is a well established integrated commercial law firm based in Leeds, the most important centre for legal services in the UK outside the City of London.

| | |
|---|---|
| V | 3 |
| T | 5 |
| P | 29 |
| TS | 190 |
| WP | yes |

## LUQMANI THOMPSON & PARTNERS
77-79 High Road, London N22 6BB
**Tel:** 020 8365 7800
**Fax:** 020 8826 0169
**Email:** luqthom@btinternet.com
**Apply to:** Ms Sally Thompson

London based firm specialising in immigration, education and civil actions against the immigration service.

| | |
|---|---|
| V | 0-1 |
| T | 2 |
| P | 3 |
| TS | 5 |
| WP | no |

## LYONS DAVIDSON
Victoria House, 51 Victoria Street, Bristol BS1 6AD
**Tel:** 0117 904 6000
**Fax:** 0117 904 6001
**Email:** info@lyonsdavidson.co.uk
**Apply to:** Mr Ben Morris

Substantial Bristol practice with offices in Birmingham, leeds, New Malden and Plymouth. Particular reputation in insurance litigation, property, corporate and planning/environment work. Very strong emphasis on training.

| | |
|---|---|
| V | 5-7 |
| T | 10 |
| P | 31 |
| TS | 750 |
| WP | yes |

## M & A SOLICITORS LLP
Kenneth Pollard House, 5-19 Cowbridge Road East, Cardiff CF11 9AB
**Tel:** 029 2066 5793
**Fax:** 029 2066 5798
**Email:** rsellek@manda.uk.com
**Apply to:** Miss RL Sellek

Niche firm specialising in corporate finance, commercial property and commercial advice.

| | |
|---|---|
| V | 3(08) |
| T | 6 |
| P | 9 |
| TS | 40 |
| WP | no |

## M OLUBI SOLICITORS
Unit 4, 2 Tunstall Road, London SW9 8BN
**Tel:** 0207 737 3400
**Fax:** 0207 737 3433
**Apply to:** Mr Moses Olubisose

South London busy and fast expanding solicitors require energetic hard working applicants for work experience and training contracts.

| | |
|---|---|
| V | 2 |
| T | 2 |
| P | - |
| TS | - |
| WP | yes |

## M S SOLICITORS LIMITED
9 Marlborough Place, Brighton BN1 1UB
**Tel:** 01273 609911
**Fax:** 01273 609944
**Email:** fiona@ms-solicitors.co.uk
**Apply to:** Miss Fiona Martin

Niche employment, housing and community care law practice seeking trainee solicitors on a yearly basis. Casework experience and IT skills essential. Recruiting in September.

| | |
|---|---|
| V | 0 |
| T | 0 |
| P | 3 |
| TS | 8 |
| WP | no |

## MACHINS
Victoria Street, Luton LU1 2BS
**Tel:** 01582 514000
**Fax:** 01582 535000
**Email:** postmaster@machins.co.uk
**Apply to:** The Personnel Officer

Machins' expertise spans the whole legal field with particular emphasis on commercial matters and a number of specialist areas including software contracts and aviation.

| | |
|---|---|
| V | 0 |
| T | 0 |
| P | 9 |
| TS | 80 |
| WP | no |

## MACKARNESS & LUNT
16 High Street, Petersfield GU32 3JJ
**Tel:** 01730 265111
**Fax:** 01730 267994
**Email:** mac@macklunt.co.uk
**Apply to:** Mrs Thelma Ball

A general practice firm dealing with property, litigation, probate and trusts, and other matters.

| | |
|---|---|
| V | 0 |
| T | 0 |
| P | 6 |
| TS | 35 |
| WP | no |

**V** = Vacancies / **T** = Trainees / **P** = Partners / **TS** = Total Staff / **WP** = Work Placement

# Mace & Jones

Drury House, 19 Water Street, Liverpool L2 0RP
**Tel:** 0151 236 8989
**Fax:** 0151 227 5010
**Web:** www.maceandjones.co.uk

**The firm** Mace & Jones is a leading regional practice in the North West with a national as well as a regional reputation for its commercial expertise, especially in employment, dispute resolution/insolvency, corporate and real estate. It also has one of the best private client teams in the region. The firm's clients range from national and multinational companies and public sector bodies to owner managed businesses and private individuals, reflecting the broad nature of the work undertaken. Sound practical advice is given always on a value-for-money basis.

**Types of work** Dispute resolution/insolvency 15%; real estate 25%; corporate 15%; employment 20%; personal injury/private client/family 25%

**Who should apply** Ability, motivation and the determination to succeed are a prerequisite. The trainee profile demonstrates the firms commitment to appointing trainees from a wide range of backgrounds and experiences.

**Training programme** Trainees complete an induction course to familiarise themselves with the work carried out by the firm's main departments, administration and professional conduct. Training consists of four six-month seats in the following departments: corporate, employment, dispute resolution/construction, real estate, family law, private client law. Strenuous efforts are made to ensure that trainees are able to select a training seat of their choice. Trainees are actively encouraged to participate in every aspect of the firm's activities and regularly act as mentors for undergraduates. The PSC is taught externally.

**When and how to apply** By 31 July 2008 to begin 1 September 2009. Apply by online application form at www.maceandjones.co.uk.

| | |
|---|---|
| Vacancies | 5-6 |
| Trainees | 11 |
| Partners | 36 |
| Total staff | 206 |

**Apply**
Online

**Starting salary**
£17,000

**Minimum qualifications**
2.1 degree

**Offices**
Liverpool, Manchester, Knutsford

# Macfarlanes

10 Norwich Street, London EC4A 1BD
**Tel:** 020 7831 9222
**Fax:** 020 7831 9607
**Email:** gradrec@macfarlanes.com
**Web:** www.macfarlanes.com

**The firm** Macfarlanes is a leading law firm in the City of London with a strong international outlook. The firm's success is founded on first-class lawyers, hard work and excellent training at all levels. Our commitment is to the quality of the work we do, the quality of our people and the quality of clients for whom we act. Getting this right has made us the successful firm we are today and we will continue to apply ourselves, our intellects, imagination and experience to provide a service to our clients which is second to none. Much of our work is international, and we act in complex cross-border transactions and international disputes. Many of our lawyers have spent time working abroad, and there are opportunities to work overseas on specific projects or take up secondments with foreign law firms with which we have established close relationships.

**Types of work** The firm has large corporate, property and litigation departments and, unusually for a City firm, a significant private client department. We serve a broad range of clients in the UK and overseas, from multinationals, quoted companies and banks to private individuals.

**Who should apply** Highly motivated, high-achieving graduates from any discipline with (or expecting) a strong 2.1 degree or higher, who are looking for top quality work and training in a cohesive firm where everyone's contribution counts and can be seen to count. We need people who can rise to a challenge and who will relish the opportunities and responsibilities that will be given to them.

**Training programme** We ask all trainees to study the LPC at BPP, Holborn branch in London. After the usual compulsory subjects studied with other students, we have created tailored electives, which aim to prepare students for seats in our wide range of practice areas. We seek to integrate what you study on the LPC with what is covered by our formal training programme during the training contract. Throughout the LPC year and in our week-long induction course at the start of your training contract, there are seminars to keep you up to date on the firm and its work and to prepare you so that you can be involved and effective from the moment you start your first seat. During the two-year training contract, trainees complete four six-month seats in different areas of practice to lay a broad foundation of practical experience. This is achieved through a combination of hands-on training involving real responsibility, continuous education and training in a broad range of legal topics, and the Professional Skills Course. Training will be given in both transactional and litigious work. The firm also provides language training to enable staff to maintain and improve language skills.

**When and how to apply** By 31 July 2008 to begin September 2010/March 2011.

**Work placements** 66 places available for 2008.

**Sponsorship** Fees in full and maintenance allowance.

| | |
|---|---|
| Vacancies | 30 |
| Trainees | 50 |
| Partners | 72 |
| Total staff | 528 |

**Work placement** yes
*(see Insider Report on p117)*

**Apply to**
Vicki Dimmick

**Starting salary**
£36,000

**Minimum qualifications**
2.1 degree

**Sponsorship**
GDL/LPC

**Offices**
London

MACFARLANES

# Maclay Murray & Spens LLP

151 St Vincent Street, Glasgow G2 5NJ
**Tel:** 0141 248 5011
**Fax:** 0141 248 5819
**Email:** trainee.recruitment@mms.co.uk
**Web:** www.mms.co.uk/traineeship

**The firm** Maclay Murray and Spens LLP is a full service commercial law firm. With over 550 people we are also one of the top 50 in the UK. This level of resource coupled with strong management and a clear vision of where we want to go as firm has resulted in impressive growth over the last few years. Although we are Scottish based, our success in that market has allowed us to invest in growing our London presence as well.

**Types of work** Maclay Murray & Spens LLP is a full service, independent, commercial law firm offering legal solutions and advice to clients throughout the UK and beyond. Our objective is to provide a consistently excellent quality of service across our entire service range and from all our offices. A full list of our clients and testimonials can be found on our website.

**Who should apply** We place great emphasis on teamwork and co-operation and make no secret of the fact that we want people who are hard working, enthusiastic and are able to respond to a challenge and responsibility. We are currently accepting applications for traineeships for 2009 and 2010.

**Training programme** At MMS trainees experience hands-on work from the outset. The degree of involvement in transactional work and contact with clients will vary according to department and case work, but rest assured, if we think you are capable of pushing forward the frontiers we will provide plenty of encouragement for you to do so.

Our two year traineeship consists of three seats, each lasting eight months, and will be based in our offices at One London Wall.

Trainees are allocated a mentor within their department and have regular appraisals throughout the traineeship.

During the traineeship we will support you to attend the Professional Skills Course. You will also have access to a wide range of seminars and training sessions. Each department has its own programme for trainees and qualified solicitors, and there are regular cross-departmental seminars. In addition, you will also be encouraged to attend seminars which we run for clients should they be relevant to your training. External courses can be attended where appropriate.

**When and how to apply** Please check our website for the most up to date information. To apply please follow the instructions on our website at www.mms.co.uk/traineeship and complete our standard application form.

**Work placements** Recruitment for our four-week Summer Placement Scheme will take place early 2008. Please fill out our standard application form and check the closing date which you will find at www.mms.co.uk/traineeship.

| Vacancies | 30 (UK wide) |
|---|---|
| Trainees | 60 |
| Partners | 72 |
| Total staff | 550 |

**Work placement** yes

**Apply to**
Trainee Recruitment

**Starting salary**
London: £30,000
Scotland: £17,000
(September 2007 figures)

**Minimum qualifications**
2.1 degree

**Offices**
Aberdeen, Edinburgh, Glasgow, London

mms | maclay murray & spens LLP

# Magrath & Co

66/67 Newman Street, London W1T 3EQ
**Tel:** 020 7495 3003
**Fax:** 020 7409 1745
**Email:** ben.sheldrick@magrath.co.uk
**Web:** www.magrath.co.uk

**The firm** Magrath & Co is a highly regarded independent law firm operating from modern offices in the heart of London's West End. Whilst we are renowned for our strengths in corporate immigration, the firm has also built a first-class reputation in the fields of employment and entertainment law.

Magrath & Co adopts a multi-disciplinary approach to the provision of legal services. This means the client always receives the very best partner led expertise designed to meet and deliver their objectives without departmental restrictions. This global view of our clients' needs is a fundamental part of the culture at Magrath & Co and one that marks the firm apart as one of the most innovative and progressive independent practices in the UK.

**Types of work** We act for a broad spectrum of clients ranging from major banks and listed companies to small family businesses and private clients. Our areas of expertise include corporate immigration, employment, media & entertainment, litigation, property and company commercial.

**Who should apply** We welcome applications from law and non-law graduates of high academic ability that can contribute enthusiasm and commitment to our team. We are looking for intelligence, versatility and personality combined with the desire to succeed. Candidates must also demonstrate an understanding and interest in our specialist services whilst sharing our passion to deliver the very highest levels of client service.

**Training programme** We provide high quality training that is designed to equip trainees with the skills required to become effective commercial solicitors. Training is generally divided into four seats of six months each covering, corporate immigration, employment, media & litigation (one seat) and property. Trainees' progress is closely monitored throughout the training contract and trainees are each assigned a training principal and a mentor. Our aim is to build on your natural talents and to develop these into the attributes required to make a highly effective business focused lawyer whatever area you ultimately decide to specialise in.

**When and how to apply** If you are interested in joining us in September 2008, please send us your CV and covering letter between January and April of 2008. Our interview process will take place before June 2008. Please address your applications for the attention Ben Sheldrick.

| | |
|---|---|
| Vacancies | 2 |
| Trainees | 4 |
| Partners | 11 |
| Total staff | 60 |

**Work placement** no

**Apply to**
Ben Sheldrick

**Starting salary**
Competitive

**Minimum qualifications**
1st or high 2.1 degree

**Offices**
London

magrath & co
solicitors

## MACKRELL TURNER GARRETT
9-11 Church Street West, Woking,
Surrey GU21 6DJ
**Tel:** 01483 755609
**Fax:** 01483 755818
**Email:** win.cummins@mtg.uk.net
**Apply to:** Mr Chris Appleyard

Founder member of Mackrell International and a long established firm. Mackrell Turner Garrett is committed to providing a tailor made efficient service to each of its clients.

| | |
|---|---|
| V | 2 |
| T | 2 |
| P | 13 |
| TS | 60 |
| WP | no |

## MACLEISH LITTLESTONE COWAN
11 Station Parade, High Street, Wanstead,
London E11 1QF
**Tel:** 020 8514 3000
**Fax:** 020 8530 3104
**Email:** nmacleish@mlclaw.co.uk
**Apply to:** Mr TN Macleish

Well established and expanding three office, six partner firm in Greater London and other locations. Commerical and General Practice. Community Legal Services franchisee (matrimonial).

| | |
|---|---|
| V | 1(08) |
| T | 2 |
| P | 6 |
| TS | 34 |
| WP | no |

## MACRAE & CO
Eagle Wharf, 59 Lafone Street, London SE1 2LX
**Tel:** 020 7378 7716
**Fax:** 020 7407 4318
**Email:** office@macraeco.com
**Apply to:** Mr LF MacRae

Commercial firm with predominantly international clientele.

| | |
|---|---|
| V | Poss |
| T | 1 |
| P | 3 |
| TS | 7 |
| WP | no |

## MAIDMENTS
Joule House, 49 The Crescent, Salford M5 4NW
**Tel:** 0870 403 4000
**Fax:** 0161 736 1551
**Email:** info@maidments.co.uk
**Apply to:** Ms Sally Shaw

"The national criminal law firm" specialising in defence of cases of serious crime and commercial fraud throughout country. Offices: Manchester, Birmingham, London, Leeds, Bolton, Sale, Salford.

| | |
|---|---|
| V | Poss |
| T | 2 |
| P | 6 |
| TS | 100 |
| WP | no |

## MAKIN DIXON SOLICITORS
3rd Floor, Sunbridge Chambers, 13-15 Sunbridge Road, Bradford, West Yorkshire BD1 2AY
**Tel:** 01274 747747
**Fax:** 01274 747277
**Email:** enquiries@makindixon.co.uk
**Apply to:** Mr IN Dixon

We are a team of specialist solicitors focused entirely on family law. We are an ever expanding firm with offices in Bradford and Keighley, covering all aspects of family law.

| | |
|---|---|
| V | 0 |
| T | 2 |
| P | 2 |
| TS | 20 |
| WP | yes |

## MALCOLM C FOY & CO
52 Hallgate, Doncaster DN1 3PB
**Tel:** 01302 340005
**Fax:** 01302 322283
**Email:** jo@malcolmcfoy.co.uk
**Apply to:** Mr Malcolm C Foy

General practice with offices in Doncaster and Rotherham. No criminal work undertaken. Legal aid franchise; specialising principally in commercial and civil litigation, matrimonial and personal injury.

| | |
|---|---|
| V | 0 |
| T | 5 |
| P | 3 |
| TS | 65 |
| WP | yes |

## MALCOLM COOKE & CO
2 Town Hall Street, Grimsby DN31 1HN
**Tel:** 01472 268888
**Fax:** 01472 268300
**Apply to:** The Recruitment Partner

General practice, but with emphasis on commercial and commercial property matters. The office is located centrally in Grimsby in its commercial hub.

| | |
|---|---|
| V | Poss |
| T | 2 |
| P | 2 |
| TS | 8 |
| WP | no |

## MALIK & MALIK
232 High Road, Willesden, London NW10 2NX
**Tel:** 020 8830 1991
**Fax:** 020 8830 3051
**Apply to:** Mr M Nazeer

Malik & Malik was established on 1/6/98. The firm deals with the following areas of law: crime, immigration & nationality, welfare benefits, conveyancing and personal injury.

| | |
|---|---|
| V | 2(08) |
| T | 4 |
| P | 2 |
| TS | 15 |
| WP | yes |

# Manches LLP

Aldwych House, 81 Aldwych, London WC2B 4RP
**Tel:** 020 7404 4433
**Fax:** 020 7430 1133
**Email:** sheona.boldero@manches.com
**Web:** www.manches.com

**The firm** Manches is a mid-size commercial law firm based in London and the Thames Valley which has been consolidating its expertise in four distinct industry sectors: property, construction, retail and media/technology. These reflect the firm's established client base. In parallel with the firm's core commercial practice, Manches continues to maintain its prestigious family law practice and is currently rated as the market leader in this area. Our approach to both clients and colleagues is one of pragmatism - aiming to communicate high-quality, succinct, practical solutions in a clear, timely and cost-effective manner, whilst also ensuring that clients enjoy working with us.

**Types of work** Commercial property, construction, family, IP/IT & media, corporate finance, employment, tax and commercial litigation and arbitration. Please see www.manches.com for more information on our specialist services.

**Who should apply** We like people who are individuals – characters, not clones! They should be intelligent with an excellent academic record but who are also practical in their approach. In addition we look for a genuine interest in commercial matters, the ability to be organised with outstanding attention to detail and good team players who are warm and personable and enjoy being sociable and meeting people.

**Training programme** After a comprehensive induction week, our trainees then learn almost entirely by practical 'on the job' training in each of four different seats. In addition the Professional Skills Course is run throughout the two years, so that elective choices can be matched to seats or areas of particular interest. We give trainees the opportunity where appropriate to run their own files from an early stage in their training contract so that they gain real experience at every stage of a transaction or case. We expect our trainees to be proactive and, where possible, manage their own learning and self-development by actively seeking out involvement in challenging work.

Newly qualified solicitors who stay on with the firm then enter into our structured Career Development Programme which runs all the way through to partnership level.

**When and how to apply** Please visit the Careers section of Manches website to apply online. Vacation scheme 2008 deadline is 31 January 2008 and training contracts 2010 deadline is 31 July 2008 (see website for confirmation or alteration of these dates).

**Work placements** Manches offers a limited number of summer placement scheme places during June and July. Students are placed in a department of their choice (subject to availability) and are supervised by a partner or an assistant solicitor. The aim is to give students the opportunity to join us for a normal busy working week, with some assessment exercises but the emphasis is getting involved in 'real work' of the type that a trainee would do and to experience first-hand the friendly culture and atmosphere at Manches.

**Sponsorship** Manches pays full fees and maintenance of £5000 per academic year to those students who have accepted an offer of a training contract and who are still to take or have only just started the GDL and/or LPC.

| | |
|---|---|
| Vacancies | 10 |
| Trainees | 20 |
| Partners | 48 |
| Total staff | 286 |

**Work placement** yes

**Apply to**
Mrs Sheona Boldero

**Starting salary**
£28,000 (London)

**Minimum qualifications**
2.1 degree

**Sponsorship**
GDL/CPE/LPC

**Offices**
London, Oxford

**MANCHES**

## MALLETTS

Market House, 17 Tuesday Market Place,
King's Lynn, Norfolk PE30 1JN
**Tel:** 01553 777 744
**Fax:** 01328 864 212
**Email:** info@malletts.com
**Apply to:** Mrs Sharon Mallett

Progressive dynamic firm specialising in serious crime,commercial litigation and family. Needs able and enthusiastic candidates.

| | |
|---|---|
| V | 1-2[08] |
| T | 2 |
| P | 6 |
| TS | 34 |
| WP | yes |

## MANBY STEWARD BOWDLER LLP

George House, St Johns Square,
Wolverhampton WV2 4BZ
**Tel:** 01902 578000
**Fax:** 01902 424321
**Apply to:** Mrs K Sandhu-Patel

Well established general practice with strong client base, the emphasis being on commercial work.

| | |
|---|---|
| V | 2[09] |
| T | 2 |
| P | 20 |
| TS | 145 |
| WP | no |

## MANDER HADLEY & CO

1 The Quadrant, Coventry CV1 2DW
**Tel:** 024 76631212
**Fax:** 024 76633131
**Email:** enquiries@manderhadley.co.uk
**Apply to:** Miss Sue Lane

Medium-sized firm located in Coventry city centre. Work undertaken includes civil and criminal litigation, matrimonial, conveyancing,commercial and company, probate, trusts, wills for private and corporate clients.

| | |
|---|---|
| V | 0 |
| T | 0 |
| P | 9 |
| TS | 46 |
| WP | no |

## MAPLES TEESDALE

21 Lincoln's Inn Fields, London WC2A 3DU
**Tel:** 020 7831 6501
**Fax:** 020 7405 3867
**Email:** enq@maplesteesdale.co.uk
**Apply to:** Mr Chris Wilkinson

The firm has been well established in London for over 200 years. Its core areas of practice are commercial property and construction.

| | |
|---|---|
| V | 2 |
| T | 6 |
| P | 9 |
| TS | 47 |
| WP | no |

## MARCH & EDWARDS

8 Sansome Walk, Worcester WR1 1LW
**Tel:** 01905 727800
**Fax:** 01905 727801
**Email:** enquiries@marchandedwards.co.uk
**Apply to:** Mr G C Salter

Friendly but professional practice based in a vibrant and expanding city. The firm has corporate and individual clients both regionally and nationally based.

| | |
|---|---|
| V | 1[08] |
| T | 1 |
| P | 6 |
| TS | 40 |
| WP | no |

## MARRIOTT HARRISON

12 Great James Street, London WC1N 3DR
**Tel:** 020 7209 2000
**Fax:** 020 7209 2001
**Apply to:** Ms Lynette Bridges

Leading corporate/media specialist law firm.

| | |
|---|---|
| V | 1-2[09] |
| T | 4 |
| P | 13 |
| TS | 54 |
| WP | no |

## MARRONS

1 Meridian South, Meridian Business Park,
Leicester LE19 1WY
**Tel:** 0116 289 2200
**Fax:** 0116 289 3733
**Email:** louisemee@marrons.net
**Apply to:** Mrs Louise Mee

Marrons is a niche planning and property development practice with a national reputation in the development industry for its legal expertise.

| | |
|---|---|
| V | 2 |
| T | 4 |
| P | 7 |
| TS | 32 |
| WP | no |

## MARTIN & HAIGH

12-18 Frances Street, Scunthorpe,
North Lincolnshire DN15 6NS
**Tel:** 01724 847888
**Fax:** 01724 280933
**Apply to:** Mrs RA Gilliatt

Friendly high street practice specialising in personal injury, family and property.

| | |
|---|---|
| V | 0 |
| T | 0 |
| P | 4 |
| TS | 37 |
| WP | no |

# Martineau Johnson

1 Colmore Square, Birmingham B4 6AA
**Tel:** 0870 763 2000
**Fax:** 0870 763 2001
**Email:** jennifer.seymour@martjohn.com
**Web:** www.graduates4law.co.uk and www.martineau-johnson.co.uk

**The firm** Martineau Johnson are a dynamic and passionate law firm that combines a commercial and vibrant atmosphere with a personal and caring attitude. Providing national and international advice to its clients, the firm is recognised as market leader in a wide variety of growing and intellectually challenging legal markets. Martineau Johnson looks for enthusiastic and committed individuals with good degrees, not necessarily in law, to contribute to its successful practice. The state of the art premises in the heart of Birmingham city centre, coupled with its expanding London office, provide trainees with an ideal base to gain experience in a variety of core and niche practice areas. As a founder member of Multilaw, an international network of law firms, opportunities also stretch far beyond the UK.

**Types of work** Core practice areas include corporate, bank and capital projects, private capital, commercial disputes, corporate finance and commercial property. We also have a strong reputation in many niche areas of practice: education, employment, intellectual property, trade and competition law, energy, capital, construction and charities.

**Who should apply** Trainees are vital to Martineau Johnson's future and no effort is spared to give the best possible experience and support to them, while treating them as individuals. In 2006 we were the first firm in Birmingham to offer NQ positions to our trainees - our retention rate is impressive with 100% of trainees qualifying in 2006 accepting roles in their preferred departments and specialisms. We look for good degrees (not necessarily in law) motivation, commercial flair, business skills and creativity.

**Training programme** Martineau Johnson work in partnership with trainees, providing them with mentoring, supervision, support and exposure to the key areas of the firm's practice. Trainees are actively encouraged to be an integral part of the team, delivering legal solutions to our clients while benefiting from quality work and flexible seat rotation in a small and friendly team environment. Generally, the firm's trainees are given experience in four main areas – corporate/commercial, commercial disputes management, commercial property and private client – and they are then given the opportunity to carry out further work in areas of their chosen specialisation. There is also a seat in our London office which all trainees have the opportunity to undertake.

Trainees benefit from a structured career training programme tailored to their personal development needs; it covers not only legal technical matters, but also a business and commercial approach which has never been more central to successful professional careers. In giving training and offering experience that matches the best City firms, Martineau Johnson offers a rare opportunity for trainees to lay great foundations for their legal career in a fast-moving, ever-changing but caring environment.

**When and how to apply** 1 April to 31 July 2008 to commence September 2010. Applicants should complete the firm's online application form. This is available at www.graduates4law.co.uk.

**Work placements** A mini vacation scheme is held during the summer months. Please submit online application form from 1 January 2008, closing date 23 April 2008, available at www.graduates4law.co.uk or contact Jennifer Seymour.

**Sponsorship** CPE - discretionary loan; LPC - fees are paid plus a maintenance grant of £4,500.

| | |
|---|---|
| Vacancies | 10-12 |
| Trainees | 21 |
| Partners | 42 |
| Total staff | 270 |

**Apply to**
Jennifer Seymour

**Starting salary**
£21,000 (September 2006)

**Minimum qualifications**
2.1 degree, not necessarily in law

**Sponsorship**
CPE/LPC

**Offices**
Birmingham, London

MARTINEAU JOHNSON

# Matthew Arnold & Baldwin

21 Station Road, Watford, Hertfordshire WD17 1HT
**Tel:** 01923 202020
**Fax:** 01923 215050
**Email:** trainee.recruitment@mablaw.co.uk
**Web:** www.mablaw.co.uk

**The firm** Matthew Arnold & Baldwin is one of the fastest growing law firms in the South East. The firm has more than doubled in size in the last five years and is in the 2007 Top Rising 50 medium-size law firms.

Through our network of offices in London, Milton Keynes and Watford our clients benefit from a truly integrated range of services and resources where the best possible team with the right level of expertise can deliver services swiftly and seamlessly. We have built our reputation on developing strong and successful business partnerships with clients and we pride ourselves on giving clients clear, practical advice and deliver solutions that are business driven to meet the needs of today's commercial organisations.

**Types of work** Matthew Arnold & Baldwin has an exciting, diverse, international client base. Their business clients, institutions and private clients benefit from the firm's clear commercial expertise and specialist advice that includes: banking and finance, corporate, employment, insolvency, real estate, and private client.

**Who should apply** We welcome applications from intelligent, enthusiastic and ambitious candidates. Not only will candidates need to be able to demonstrate a high level of academic achievement (minimum of a 2.1, not necessarily in law) they should also be excellent communicators, strong team players and possess common sense and initiative. Matthew Arnold & Baldwin's culture is collegiate and the ability of candidates to contribute positively to this working environment is very important.

**Training programme** We attribute the firm's success to the quality of our people, and the variety of their strengths and skills. At Matthew Arnold & Baldwin we encourage our trainees to take early responsibility. All trainees gain on-the job experience dealing directly with clients and assisting solicitors and partners on complex matters very early on in their training. The development of our trainees is further enhanced by attendance at in-house and external training courses.

The training contract consists of four six month seats. Wherever possible we try to accommodate trainees' wishes as regards seats, however, all trainees are required to undertake both contentious and non-contentious seats. We monitor our trainees' progress through a system of regular reviews and feedback on the job. Trainees are also encouraged to join in marketing and social events and to volunteer for external work in the firm's communities

We believe our trainees to be an investment for the future and we try, wherever possible, to retain them upon qualification.

**When and how to apply** Apply by 31 January 2008 for training contracts commencing in 2009. Please send a CV and covering letter to Sue Metselaar at trainee.recruitment@mablaw.co.uk.

| | |
|---|---|
| Vacancies | 4 |
| Trainees | 8 |
| Partners | 32 |
| Total staff | 265 |
| Work placement | no |

**Apply to**
Sue Metselaar

**Minimum qualifications**
2.1 degree

**Offices**
London, Milton Keynes, Watford

Matthew Arnold & Baldwin

| Firm | Description | V | T | P | TS | WP |
|---|---|---|---|---|---|---|
| **MARTIN CRAY AND CO**<br>177 Edward Street, Brighton BN2 0JB<br>**Tel:** 01273 673226<br>**Fax:** 01273 621715<br>**Email:** mcray@martincray.co.uk<br>**Apply to:** Mr MW Cray | The firm specialises in personal injury, family, probate, conveyancing and employment. | 1 | 2 | 2 | 22 | yes |
| **MARTIN MURRAY & ASSOCIATES**<br>152-156 High Street, Yiewsley,<br>West Drayton UB7 7BE<br>**Tel:** 01895 431332<br>**Fax:** 01895 448343<br>**Apply to:** Mr A Cosma | Martin Murray & Associates is a franchised firm and is one of the leading criminal practices in the Thames Valley. | 0 | 2 | 6 | 70 | no |
| **MARTIN SHEPHERD & CO**<br>753 High Road North, Finchley, London N12 8LG<br>**Tel:** 020 8446 4301<br>**Fax:** 020 8446 5117<br>**Email:** acd@martinshepherd.co.uk<br>**Apply to:** Ms Antoinette Doyle | A three branch North London general high street practice with a bias towards commercial work. | 1[08] | 1 | 6 | 35 | no |
| **MARTIN-KAYE SOLICITORS**<br>The Foundry, Euston Way, Telford TF3 4LY<br>**Tel:** 01952 272222<br>**Fax:** 01952 272223<br>**Email:** recruit@martinkaye.co.uk<br>**Apply to:** Mrs Alison Carter | A progressive practice in the expanding new town of Telford dealing with all aspects of commercial, corporate, IP, employment, litigation and property. Agency work undertaken. | Poss | 3 | 9 | 100 | no |
| **MASON BULLOCK**<br>4 Albion Place, Northampton NN1 1UD<br>**Tel:** 0845 257 1075<br>**Fax:** 0845 257 1076<br>**Email:** info@masonb.co.uk<br>**Apply to:** Mr Ian Mason | Strongly Christian emphasis and ethos; working for small/medium-sized enterprises and private clients of reasonable means: commercial/ litigation/ property/ wills/probate. Also voluntary organisations. | 0 | 0 | 2 | 9 | no |
| **MATRIX SOLICITORS**<br>Normanton Business Centre, 258 Normanton Road, Derby DE23 6WD<br>**Tel:** 01332 363 454<br>**Fax:** 01332 362338<br>**Apply to:** Mr Shamim Khan | Niche litigation, company/commercial, environmental and energy law and business immigration specialists in the centre of Derby. | 0 | 0 | 1 | 7 | yes |
| **MAUDSLEY WRIGHT & PEARSON**<br>1a East Square, Basildon, Essex SS14 1EN<br>**Tel:** 01268 527131<br>**Fax:** 01268 530089<br>**Email:** lawrencemaudsley@mwpsolicitors.co.uk<br>**Apply to:** Mr Lawrence Maudsley | Primarily legal aid practice covering crime, family, child protection, PI, employment matters. Also conveyancing, probate. Franchised. | 1[08] | 2 | 3 | 19 | yes |
| **MAX BITEL GREENE**<br>1 Canonbury Place, London N1 2NG<br>**Tel:** 020 7354 2767<br>**Fax:** 020 7226 1210<br>**Email:** office@mbg.co.uk<br>**Apply to:** Ms SM Trimmer | Small general practice with some commercial work and also an insolvency and sports law element. | 1 | 2 | 7 | 19 | no |

**V** = Vacancies / **T** = Trainees / **P** = Partners / **TS** = Total Staff / **WP** = Work Placement

# Maxwell Winward LLP

100 Ludgate Hill, London EC4M 7RE
**Tel:** 020 7651 0000
**Fax:** 020 7651 4800
**Email:** recruitment@maxwellwinward.com
**Web:** www.maxwellwinward.com

**The firm** Maxwell Winward is a 21 partner commercial firm. We specialise in a number of key areas in respect of which we carry out high quality work. The firm benefits from pooling its considerable knowledge from across its chosen sectors of specialisation to create a modern, focused law firm that is recognised as a compelling alternative to larger firms. Our unstuffy ethos encourages trainees to interact with and learn from everyone in the firm. Trainees are very much treated as one of the team, and the future solicitors of the firm.

**Types of work** The firm focuses on the specialist areas of real estate, construction, corporate and projects and dispute resolution. We act for a wide variety of clients in these sectors. As well as acting for high-profile, blue-chip clients on major developments and projects the firm also acts for a number of smaller clients. This allows the firm to offer a stimulating variety of experience to its trainees.

**Who should apply** We are looking to recruit graduates with at least a 2.1 in any discipline. It is important that the candidates are willing to learn and have enthusiasm, common sense and commercial awareness as well as a genuine interest in the firm's specialist areas.

**Training programme** The purpose of the training contract is to prepare the trainee for their future career at the firm. We see trainees as the life-blood of the firm and therefore our training programme is something on which we place a great deal of emphasis.

The varied nature of our work means that trainees will be given a wide range of experience from all of the different practice areas in the firm. The training contract will be split into four six-month seats in the different practice areas. Whilst we closely supervise the work of trainees, we are keen to ensure that they are given valuable practical experience and responsibility so that they gradually gain the confidence to deal with matters on their own.

We also arrange internal seminars for our trainees in order to give them formal training to complement the day to day informal training that comes with assisting on "real-life" matters.

**When and how to apply** By 31 July 2008 to begin September 2010. Send a CV and covering letter by post or email.

**Sponsorship** Contribution towards fees and maintenance for GDL and LPC.

| | |
|---|---|
| Vacancies | 4 |
| Trainees | 8 |
| Partners | 21 |
| Total staff | 100 |

**Apply to**
The Practice Manager

**Starting salary**
£29,000

**Minimum qualifications**
2.1 degree

**Sponsorship**
GDL/LPC

**Offices**
London

MAXWELL WINWARD

# Mayer Brown International LLP

11 Pilgrim Street, London EC4V 6RW
**Tel:** 020 7248 4282
**Fax:** 020 7782 8790
**Email:** graduaterecruitment@mayerbrownrowe.com
**Web:** www.mayerbrownrowe.com/london/careers/gradrecruit

**The firm** Mayer Brown International LLP is among the largest law practices in the world with over 500 partners and more than 1,400 lawyers worldwide. It has offices in Berlin, Brussels, Charlotte, Chicago, Cologne, Frankfurt, Hong Kong, Houston, Los Angeles, New York, Palo Alto, Paris and Washington DC. The international reach of the firm is further enhanced through an affiliated trade office in Beijing, a correspondent relationship with Mexican firm Jauregui, Navarette y Nader, an alliance with leading firm Tonucci & Partners and an alliance with leading Spanish firm Ramon & Cajal.

**Types of work** The firm advises leading financial and commercial companies around the world. Its client base includes many of the FTSE 100 and Fortune 500 companies together with other global leaders in target industries. The major emphasis in Europe is across industry sectors including chemicals, construction & engineering, energy, insurance & reinsurance, mining, pensions, pharmaceuticals & biotechnology, real estate, TMT and securitisation. Working within this framework core practice lines include corporate and securities (including M&A and corporate finance), litigation and dispute resolution, finance and banking, financial restructuring and insolvency, tax, environment, employment, pensions, intellectual property, outsourcing, advertising, music and publishing, antitrust and international trade.

**Who should apply** If you are looking for a leading international law practice that offers exposure to a multitude of blue-chip companies and a wide range of international work, combined with the confidence to know you have a place in its future, we'd like to hear from you. The practice is interested in motivated students with a good academic record and a strong commitment to law. Applications are welcomed from both law and non-law students.

**Training programme** Trainees will participate in a lively, energetic and positive business culture, spending time in four six-month seats including the corporate and litigation departments. Our culture of getting immersed in a client's business means that there are excellent secondment opportunities, and you will mix with lawyers and client staff at all levels. Trainees are given early responsibility, and a high level of contribution is expected and valued. In addition to the Professional Skills Course, our practice has a professional development and training programme, which covers subjects such as international law and the workings of the City. Three-monthly appraisals assist trainees in reaching their true potential.

Trainees are encouraged to join in the sports and social life and to be active members of the team from day one, so be prepared to get your hands dirty!

**When and how to apply** Non-law students should apply after 1 November in the final year of their degree. Law students should apply in July of their penultimate year of study. All other applicants should apply after 1 November in each recruitment year. The closing date for all applications is 31 July. Please apply online at our website.

**Work placements** There are 32 placements during the Easter and summer vacations. Students gain experience in two of our principal work groups, and the practice also organises a programme of seminars, visits and social events with trainees.

**Sponsorship** We pay all course fees for the GDL (if applicable) and the LPC, together with a maintenance grant of £6,500 (£7,000 for London and Guildford).

| | |
|---|---|
| Vacancies | 25-30 |
| Trainees | 56 |
| Partners | 101 |
| Total staff | 625 |

**Work placement** yes
*(see Insider Report on p119)*

**Apply**
Online

**Starting salary**
£36,000

**Minimum qualifications**
2.1 degree

**Sponsorship**
GDL/LPC

**Offices**
Berlin, Brussels, Charlotte, Chicago, Cologne, Frankfurt, Hong Kong, Houston, London, Los Angeles, New York, Palo Alto, Paris, Washington DC

MAYER·BROWN

# McDermott Will & Emery UK LLP

7 Bishopsgate, London EC2N 3AR
**Tel:** 020 7577 6900
**Fax:** 020 7577 6950
**Email:** graduate.recruitment@europe.mwe.com
**Web:** www.mwe.com

**The firm** McDermott Will & Emery UK LLP is a leading international law firm (among the top 20 in the US and globally). The firm has over 1,000 lawyers and offices in Boston, Brussels, Chicago, Düsseldorf, London, Los Angeles, Miami, Munich, New York, Orange County, Rome, San Diego, Silicon Valley and Washington DC.

Our client base includes some of the world's leading financial institutions, largest corporations, mid-cap businesses and individuals. As a firm we represent more than 75 of the companies in the Fortune 100, in addition to clients in the FTSE 100 and FTSE 250.

The firm is rated as one of the leading firms in the *American Lawyer's* Top 100 by a number of indicators, including gross revenues and profits per partner.

The London office was founded in 1998. It is already recognised as being in the top 10 of the 100-plus US law firms operating in London by the legal media. We have 80 lawyers at present in London, almost all of whom are English-qualified, and continue to have ambitious growth plans for London and for Europe.

We provide business-oriented legal advice to multinational and national corporates, financial institutions, investment banks and private clients. Most of our partners were head of practice at their former firms and are recognised as leaders in their respective fields by the most respected professional directories and market commentators.

**Types of work** Banking and finance, securitisation and structured finance, corporate including international corporate finance and mergers and acquisitions, private equity, EU competition, employment, IP, IT and e-business, litigation and arbitration, pensions and incentives, taxation, telecoms and US securities.

London is the hub for McDermott Will & Emery UK LLP's European expansion as we coordinate legal advice from here for our multinational clients across Europe and elsewhere.

**Who should apply** We are looking for the brightest, best and most entrepreneurial trainees. There are not too many 'right candidates' for us; you will need to convince us that you have made a deliberate choice.

**Training programme** The primary focus is to provide a practical foundation for your career with us. You will experience four to six seats over the two-year period. The deliberately small number of trainees means that we are able to provide a degree of flexibility in tailoring seats to the individual.

Our trainees do not get lost in the crowd; they are immediately part of a team and get support and regular feedback.

Benefits include: private medical and dental insurance, life insurance, permanent health insurance, season ticket loan, subsidised gym membership, employee assistance programme, 25 days' holiday.

**When and how to apply** By the end of 31 July 2008 to begin 2010 with CV and covering letter. Please see our website for our selection criteria.

**Sponsorship** GDL and LPC funding and maintenance grant.

| Vacancies | 4 |
| Trainees | 7 |
| Partners | 605* |
| Total staff | 2141* |

*denotes worldwide figure

**Apply to**
Áine Wood
Graduate Recruitment

**Starting salary**
£39,000

**Minimum qualifications**
First or high 2.1 degree

**Sponsorship**
GDL/LPC

**Offices**
Boston, Brussels, Chicago, Düsseldorf, London, Los Angeles, Miami, Munich, New York, Orange County, Rome, San Diego, Silicon Valley, Washington DC

McDermott
Will & Emery

# McGrigors LLP

5 Old Bailey, London EC4M 7BA
**Tel:** 020 7054 2500
**Email:** graduate.recruitment@mcgrigors.com
**Web:** www.mcgrigors.com

**The firm** McGrigors is a law firm based across the UK with 78 partners and 350 lawyers in total. As the only law firm in the UK that practices in all three jurisdictions, McGrigors has the strength and depth to commit to multiple, large, complex and high-value transactions simultaneously, and has earned an enviable reputation for providing excellent technical legal services, whilst at the same time being small enough to retain a friendly feel. The firm has a blue-chip client list which includes KPMG, Ministry of Defence, Royal Bank of Scotland, Fairview New Homes Ltd and BP.

**Types of work** Practice areas include banking and finance, commercial litigation, competition, construction procurement, contentious construction, corporate, dispute resolution, employment, energy, health and safety, human rights, intellectual property and commercial, planning and environment, projects/PPP, project finance, public law, public policy, real estate, tax litigation, and telecoms. McGrigors has a particular focus on a number of key industry sectors including energy and utilities, house builders, regeneration, financial services, infrastructure and public sector.

**Who should apply** We take on people regardless of background who have drive, ability, and confidence. Trainees need to prove that they are interested in business, not simply black letter law, as we pride ourselves on providing commercial solutions to clients. In addition, our trainees are highly visible in the firm and are expected to get actively involved, whether in business or social events.

**Training programme** Our training is based upon a standard rotation of six-month seats in four main practice areas. To widen trainees experience and enable them to see a broader range of legal work we encourage trainees to spend a seat in one of our other offices, and there are also opportunities for a secondment to a client. We were recently nominated as Best Trainer amongst Large City firms in the LawCareers.Net awards and our last Law Society Monitoring Visit concluded that training of trainee solicitors at McGrigors was, "excellent and of a very high standard".

Benefits: We offer private medical cover, life assurance, pension, a daily lunch allowance, 35 days holidays including bank holidays, season ticket loan, and plenty of social events throughout the year.

**When and how to apply** You should apply from December 2007 for summer placements in 2008, and from March 2008 for traineeships in 2010. Application is by a Word document which is downloaded from our website, www.mcgrigors.com. All other information concerning closing dates, where to send applications to and law fairs we are attending, is listed on our website under the careers section.

**Work placements** In London we offer placements in July and August, each lasting two weeks, when students will have an opportunity to visit two departments. In Scotland and Belfast we offer placements in June, July and August each lasting three weeks and students are based in one department. Information regarding remuneration and closing dates for application are available on www.mcgrigors.com together with testimonials of previous summer students.

**Sponsorship** CPE and LPC fees are paid plus maintenance of £6,000 for each year in England. We also provide shortfall funding up to £1,000 for those Scottish trainees who receive part or no funding.

**Vacancies** 12-15 (London)
15-20 (Scotland)

| | |
|---|---|
| Trainees | 67* |
| Partners | 78* |
| Total staff | 639* |

*denotes firm-wide figure

**Work placement** yes
*(see Insider Report on p121)*

**Apply to**
Georgina Bond - London
Margaret-Ann Roy - Scotland/Belfast

**Starting salary**
£32,000 - London
£18,000 - Scotland

**Minimum qualifications**
BBB at A level or equivalent/strong group of Highers with realistic estimate of 2.1 degree

**Sponsorship**
CPE/LPC

**Offices**
London, Edinburgh, Glasgow, Aberdeen, Belfast.
Baku, Azerbaijan and a satelite office in the Falkland Islands.

*McGrigors*

# Memery Crystal LLP

44 Southampton Buildings, London WC2A 1AP
**Tel:** 020 7242 5905
**Fax:** 020 7242 2058
**Email:** info@memerycrystal.com
**Web:** www.memerycrystal.com

**The firm** Memery Crystal LLP is a mid-sized law firm founded in 1978 by John Memery and Peter Crystal. The firm has grown from strength to strength and is now recognised as one of the UK's leading law firms in its specialist areas. The firm's ethos is that people come first, whether they are clients, members of the firm or fellow advisors; this philosophy has enabled the firm to bring out the best in its lawyers and its quality service to clients has been recognised through numerous awards.

**Types of work** The firm's main practice areas are corporate/commercial, dispute resolution and real estate. Within these areas, specialist groups deal with corporate finance (particularly AIM related transactions), employment, property litigation, tax, insolvency, construction and development, corporate crime, regulatory law and intellectual property.

**Who should apply** We are looking for candidates who:
Have achieved a high standard of education;
Show a willingness to take on responsibility;
Are commercially aware;
Respond to challenges;
Have the drive and ambition to succeed; and
Are seeking fulfilment and recognition in their chosen profession.

We want to recruit the very best candidates who would like to join our existing team of high achievers.

**Training programme** During your training you will have a balance of formal and practical training. Your development will be closely monitored with appraisals being carried out every three months. You will sit either with a partner, associate or senior assistant who will monitor your progress on a regular basis. During the course of your training contract, there will be a regular rotation of seats within the firm.

**When and how to apply** Apply via the online application form on our website (www.memerycrystal.com) at any time until 31 July 2008 to begin in September 2010.

**Sponsorship** The firm funds the CPE/GDL and the LPC.

| Vacancies | 5-6 |
| Trainees | 10 |
| Partners | 21 |
| Total staff | 107 |

**Apply**
Online

**Starting salary**
1st year - £27,000
2nd year - £28,000

**Sponsorship**
GDL/LPC

**Offices**
London

Memery Crystal

**MAXWELL HODGE**
18 Hoghton Street, Southport PR9 0PB
**Tel:** 01704 531991
**Fax:** 01704 537475
**Email:** carolhead@maxweb.co.uk
**Apply to:** Carol Head

Maxwell Hodge is a long established and progressive practice supplying a full range of legal services to private clients and commercial organisations.

| | |
|---|---|
| V | 0 |
| T | 1 |
| P | 19 |
| TS | 130 |
| WP | yes |

---

**MAYO WYNNE BAXTER**
Dial House, 221 High Street, Lewes,
E Sussex BN7 2AE
**Tel:** 01273 477071
**Fax:** 01273 478515
**Email:** ababey@mayowynnebaxter.co.uk
**Apply to:** Mr Ashley Babey

The merged firm was formed in April 2007 from two leading Sussex Firms. There are eight offices and we practice in commercial law, family, litigation, clinical negligence, trust and probate, crime and property.

| | |
|---|---|
| V | 4[09] |
| T | 4 |
| P | 32 |
| TS | 240 |
| WP | no |

---

**MCEWENS SOLICITORS**
9 Commercial Road, Swindon SN1 5NF
**Tel:** 01793 649249
**Fax:** 01793 649239
**Email:** anneg@mcewens.co.uk
**Apply to:** Ms Anne Goodenough

RTA and personal injury majority caseload. Some domestic and commercial, conveyancing, employment, matrimonial, commercial limited.

| | |
|---|---|
| V | 0-1 |
| T | 0 |
| P | - |
| TS | 40 |
| WP | no |

---

**MCHALE & COMPANY**
19/21 High Street, Altrincham,
Cheshire WA14 1QP
**Tel:** 0161 928 3848
**Fax:** 0161 928 3228
**Email:** siobhan.tench@mchaleandco.co.uk
**Apply to:** Ms Siobhan Tench

New and expanding firm offering specialist advice in the areas of conveyancing (commercial and domestic) employment, personal injury and crime.

| | |
|---|---|
| V | 2 |
| T | 4 |
| P | 2 |
| TS | 21 |
| WP | no |

---

**MCKEAGS**
One Carliol, Carliol Square, Newcastle Upon Tyne
NE18AF
**Tel:** 0191 2111800
**Fax:** 0191 2111835
**Email:** info@mckeags.co.uk
**Apply to:** Mr Malcolm Croudace

One of the more substantial practices in the North East. Offers a comprehensive range of legal services. Acts for an extensive business and private client base.

| | |
|---|---|
| V | 6[09] |
| T | 20 |
| P | 12 |
| TS | 300 |
| WP | no |

---

**MELDRUM YOUNG**
Riding House, 54-56 Cheapside, Luton,
Beds LU1 2HN
**Tel:** 01582 405577
**Fax:** 01582 452967
**Apply to:** Mrs Kathryn Archard

Specialised criminal practice, with CDS contract; duty scheme branch offices at St Albans and Watford.

| | |
|---|---|
| V | 2 |
| T | 3 |
| P | 3 |
| TS | 30 |
| WP | no |

---

**MELDRUM YOUNG SOLICITORS**
16 Station Road, Watford,
Hertfordshire WD17 1EG
**Tel:** 01923 231598
**Fax:** 01923 231599
**Apply to:** Mrs Elizabeth Johnston

A leading practice and culturally diverse team of dedicated criminal defence lawyers, fraud panel members, high cost cases department and 24hr police station assistance.

| | |
|---|---|
| V | 4 |
| T | 8 |
| P | 4 |
| TS | 106 |
| WP | yes |

---

**MERRIMAN WHITE**
14 Took's Court, London EC4A 1LB
**Tel:** 020 7421 1900
**Fax:** 020 7421 1901
**Apply to:** The Traineeship Co-ordinator

London and Guildford based. Broad range of work - especially commercial litigation, property and private client. Many international connections. Friendly atmosphere – direct fee earner contact/ supervision.

| | |
|---|---|
| V | 0 |
| T | 3 |
| P | 2 |
| TS | 40 |
| WP | yes |

---

**V** = Vacancies / **T** = Trainees / **P** = Partners / **TS** = Total Staff / **WP** = Work Placement

# MFG Solicitors LLP

Carlton House, Worcester Street, Kidderminster, Worcester DY10 1BA
**Tel:** 01562 820181
**Fax:** 01562 827893
**Email:** esther.withers@mfgsolicitors.com
**Web:** www.mfgsolicitors.com

**The firm** We are a large regional firm with a strong presence in Worcestershire, Shropshire and the West Midlands. With six main, one metro and three satellite offices and listed in the *Legal 500* with ISO 9001 quality standard, we are a dynamic regional firm with key strengths in both commercial and private client work areas. Our private client services include family, wills and probate and conveyancing, these services being offered from our offices in Worcester, Kidderminster, Wellington, Telford, and Bromsgrove. Our family lawyers are encouraged to develop special skills and join the child and family law panels with a regional reputation in ancillary relief matters and childcare issues.

Our commercial clients are offered the full range of corporate services, including acquisitions and disposals, shareholder agreements, partnership and company formations and mergers. These services are provided from Halesowen Bromsgrove and Telford offices. We also cater for the commercial property clients with a complete range of services for the commercial property and property developer clients with experienced lawyers in landlord and tenant issues both contentious and non-contentious.

Our specialist niche areas are tax and rural and agricultural affairs with nationally recognised experts in agricultural matters and tax affairs for the rural client. These services are provided from the Wellington, Worcester and Halesowen offices.

Other key services we offer are commercial litigation and employment, which are based at our Halesowen office.

We continue the development of teams of specialists working together in teams based at our main offices, this gives excellent opportunities for trainees to learn key skills in working as part of a team but while also working on matters individually whist under the supervision of a special lawyer.

**Types of work** Agricultural, commercial litigation, company commercial, commerical property, conveyancing, employment, family, landlord and tenant, mergers and acquisitions, personal injury, tax.

**Who should apply** We recruit between three to five trainees a year commencing in September of each year and we welcome applications from law and non-law degrees and from mature students. We expect a minimum of a 2.1 degree, a good academic track record and relevant work experience. We pride ourselves on our trainee retention and our flexibility towards a trainee's aspiration and our requirements.

**Training programme** We offer our trainees a well rounded training experience covering a minimum of three seats in different disciplines over the two year training contract period. The fourth seat is normally a repeat of a previous seat and would be in the chosen area that the trainee had expressed a desire to develop a career in. Our trainees are expected to become fully involved in client matters at an early stage and learning on the job is emphasised.

**When and how to apply** Candidates must apply in writing or complete our online application form by 31 March 2008 to begin training contracts in September 2009.

| | |
|---|---|
| Vacancies | 5 |
| Trainees | 4 |
| Partners | 29 |
| Total staff | 201 |

**Work placement** no

**Apply to**
Mrs Esther Withers

**Starting salary**
Law Society minimum

**Minimum qualifications**
2.1 degree

**Offices**
Bromsgrove, Halesowen, Kidderminster, Stourport, Telford, Wellington, Worcester

# Michelmores

Woodwater House, Pynes Hill, Exeter EX2 5WR
**Tel:** 01392 688688
**Fax:** 01392 360563
**Email:** enquiries@michelmores.com
**Web:** www.michelmores.com

**The firm** Michelmores is a dynamic Exeter and London based full service law firm providing first class service to a wide range of local, national and international clients including several central government departments. We have an established track record of attracting quality recruits at every level and our trainee solicitor retention rate is excellent. Combining state of the art technology in a new purpose built building with a management style which promotes the highest professional standards and an informal atmosphere, we have created a great place to work capable of attracting the very best lawyers. Our new offices provide an excellent working environment including a gym and a restaurant on site. We also have a thriving London office with four resident partners. The partnership has retained a collegiate style which helps to foster a happy law firm renowned for the enthusiasm of its lawyers from senior partner down to first year trainee. We have just been included in the lawyer "Rising 50" list of law firms nationally seen as rising stars.

**Types of work** We enjoy a high reputation for our work in the fields of company commercial, dispute resolution and commercial property while our private client department (including our family team) continues to thrive.

We are members of IAG International which is a network of foreign law firms and accountants and arrange for overseas secondments for trainees and solicitors.

**Who should apply** We welcome applications from both law and non-law graduates. We are looking for trainees with a strong academic background who are team players who genuinely want to share in our success and help us to continue to grow and improve.

**Training programme** As a Michelmores' trainee you will usually spend six months in each of our main departments (company commercial, litigation, commercial property and private client). You will work closely with a particular partner in each department and will be pleasantly surprised at the level of client exposure, responsibility and involvement that is afforded to you. Our trainees are given both the opportunity to handle work themselves while under supervision to work as part of a team. The quality of our training is high. You will be expected to attend relevant training sessions within the firm on areas such as marketing and IT skills and time management and will also be encouraged to attend conferences, seminars and courses. We offer the opportunity of spending part of your training contract in our London office.

**When and how to apply** You should apply on our trainee solicitor application form which is available on our website. Completed forms should arrive by 1st July 2008 for 2010 training contracts.

**Work placements** We run an annual vacation scheme in the early part of July for one week. Application forms are available on our website. Completed forms should arrive by 28 February 2008.

| | |
|---|---|
| Vacancies | 10 |
| Trainees | 10 |
| Partners | 32 |
| Total staff | 286 |

**Work placement**   yes

**Apply to**
Mr Tim Richards

**Starting salary**
1st year - £19,500
2nd year - £20,500

**Minimum qualifications**
Usually 2.1 degree

**Offices**
Exeter, London

Michelmores

| | |
|---|---|
| **METCALFE COPEMAN & PETTEFAR**<br>28-32 King Street, Kings Lynn PE30 1HQ<br>**Tel:** 01553 778102<br>**Fax:** 01553 766807<br>**Apply to:** Miss Alison Muir | A firm with four offices which undertakes some specialist commercial work as well as its general practice, which includes legal aid work. |
| | **V** 1[08]<br>**T** 4<br>**P** 15<br>**TS** 120<br>**WP** no |

| | |
|---|---|
| **METCALFES SOLICITORS**<br>46-48 Queen Square, Bristol BS1 4LY<br>**Tel:** 0117 929 0451<br>**Fax:** 0117 929 9551<br>**Email:** info@metcalfes.co.uk<br>**Apply to:** Ms Sammie Orchard | Niche commercial practice providing a quality, cost effective, partner led service to medium sized businesses, together with niche defendant and plaintiff personal injury practice. |
| | **V** 1<br>**T** 2<br>**P** 9<br>**TS** 55<br>**WP** no |

| | |
|---|---|
| **MEYRICK MILLS**<br>210-212 Calbonian Road, London N1 0SQ<br>**Tel:** 020 7837 1000<br>**Fax:** 020 7837 0603<br>**Email:** partners@meyrickmills.com<br>**Apply to:** Mr G Meyrick | General practice. |
| | **V** Poss<br>**T** 1<br>**P** 5<br>**TS** 7<br>**WP** no |

| | |
|---|---|
| **MIAN & CO**<br>The Citadel, 190 Corporation Street,<br>Birmingham B4 6QD<br>**Tel:** 0121 684 8000<br>**Fax:** 0121 684 8001<br>**Email:** mians@btinternet.com<br>**Apply to:** Mrs T S Mian | Long established criminal defence solicitors practice. Offices based directly opposite Birmingham magistrates court. Mainly legally aided work undertaken. |
| | **V** 0<br>**T** 1<br>**P** 2<br>**TS** 9<br>**WP** no |

| | |
|---|---|
| **MIDDLETON POTTS**<br>3 Cloth Street, Barbican, London EC1A 7NP<br>**Tel:** 020 7600 2333<br>**Fax:** 020 7600 0108<br>**Email:** recruitment@middletonpotts.co.uk<br>**Apply to:** Mr Stephen Morrall | City commercial law firm for international business clients including banks, insurance companies, commodity traders, ship owners and charterers, multinational corporations and foreign state institutions. |
| | **V** 1<br>**T** 4<br>**P** 12<br>**TS** 45<br>**WP** no |

| | |
|---|---|
| **MIDDLEWEEKS**<br>Swan Building, 20 Swan Street,<br>Manchester M4 5JW<br>**Tel:** 0161 839 7255<br>**Fax:** 0161 839 7243<br>**Apply to:** Barbara Cohen | A Manchester litigation practice which specialises in criminal litigation and which is highly regarded in that field, particularly in the area of white collar crime. |
| | **V** 0<br>**T** 2<br>**P** 2<br>**TS** 19<br>**WP** yes |

| | |
|---|---|
| **MILBURNS**<br>19 Oxford Street, Workington CA14 2AW<br>**Tel:** 01900 67363<br>**Fax:** 01900 65552<br>**Email:** jwood@milburns.org<br>**Apply to:** Mr James A Wood | Eight partner, three office firm with client base largely in West Cumbria. LSC Quality Marks in clinical negligence, PI and family. Strong non-contentious departments in all offices. |
| | **V** Poss[08]<br>**T** 2<br>**P** 8<br>**TS** 43<br>**WP** no |

| | |
|---|---|
| **MILLAN SOLICITORS**<br>1368 Leeds Road, Bradford,<br>West Yorkshire BD3 8ND<br>**Tel:** 01274 660 111<br>**Fax:** 01274 660 222<br>**Email:** goldie@millansolicitors.co.uk<br>**Apply to:** Miss GK Millan | Millan Solicitors is a family firm with family values. We are a young, dynamic, expanding firm specialising in residential property, commercial property, immigration and personal injury work. |
| | **V** 0<br>**T** 1<br>**P** 2<br>**TS** 5<br>**WP** yes |

# Mills & Reeve LLP

Francis House, 112 Hills Road, Cambridge CB2 1PH
**Tel:** 01223 222336
**Fax:** 01223 355848
**Email:** graduate.recruitment@mills-reeve.com
**Web:** www.mills-reeve.com

**The firm** We act for commercial organisations; ranging from PLCs to multinationals to start-ups, as well as more than 70 universities and colleges, more than 100 healthcare trusts and NHS bodies, and over 65 local government institutions. The firm also has a national centre of excellence in private client services.

Mills & Reeve has offices in Birmingham, Cambridge, London and Norwich.

For the fourth year running Mills & Reeve has been listed in the *Sunday Times* Top 100 Best Companies to Work For, which recognises that we put people at the centre of our business.

**Types of work** A major UK law firm renowned for its collegiate culture, strong competitive position and formidable reputation. Core sectors are: corporate and commercial, banking and finance, technology, insurance, real estate, healthcare, education and private client.

**Who should apply** We welcome applications from both law and non-law disciplines. We expect you to have already gained or be on course for a 2.1 degree or equivalent. You will be ready to accept early responsibility.

We recruit graduates who set high standards of achievement in both their academic and personal life. Our trainee solicitors should display energy, maturity, initiative and enthusiasm for their career and a professional approach to work.

**Training programme** Trainees complete six four-month seats and are recruited to the Birmingham, Cambridge and Norwich offices. Trainees can temporarily move to another office, including London, to complete a seat not practised in their base office. The firm will support the move with an accommodation allowance.

Trainees work alongside a partner or senior solicitor. Regular feedback is given to aid development. Performance is assessed by a formal review at the end of each seat.

We encourage early responsibility. Training is supported by a full induction, in-house training programme developed by our team of professional support lawyers and the professional skills course (PSC).

Job opportunities on qualification are good and a high proportion of trainees remain with the firm.

**When and how to apply** Apply online. Closing dates: 31 July 2008 for training contracts commencing in 2010; 31 January 2008 for summer placements in 2008.

**Work placements** Two-week placements run in the summer in Birmingham, Cambridge and Norwich offices. Applications should be made before 31 January 2008.

**Sponsorship** We fund the GDL and LPC course fees. Maintenance grant during GDL and LPC.

| | |
|---|---|
| Vacancies | 22 |
| Trainees | 23 |
| Partners | 79 |
| Total staff | 760 |

**Work placement**  yes
*(see Insider Report on p123)*

**Apply to**
Fiona Medlock

**Starting salary**
£23,000 rising to £24,00 in second year

**Minimum qualifications**
2.1 degree, any discipline

**Sponsorship**
GDL/LPC

**Offices**
Birmingham, Cambridge, Norwich, London

MILLS
—&—
REEVE

# Mishcon de Reya

Summit House, 12 Red Lion Square, London WC1R 4QD
**Tel:** 020 7440 7000
**Fax:** 020 7430 0691
**Email:** graduate.recruitment@mishcon.com
**Web:** www.mishcon.com

**The firm** Mishcon de Reya is a London-based commercial law firm that works with clients in building businesses, protecting assets, managing wealth and resolving disputes.

**Types of work** Organised internally into four key departments – corporate and commercial, dispute resolution, real estate and family. The firm also has a growing number of specialist groups which include: IP, banking and finance, defamation, employment, fraud, immigration, insolvency, private client, betting and gaming.

**Who should apply** Applications are welcome from penultimate-year law students, final-year non-law students and other graduates wishing to commence a training contract in two years time. The firm recruits from a wide range of universities.

Our trainees are typically high achieving and intelligent, with good interpersonal skills and outgoing personalities. Strength of character and the ability to think laterally are also important.

**Training programme** Trainees have the opportunity to experience four different seats of six months each. This will include one seat in the corporate and commercial department and one in the dispute resolution department. In the remaining seats you may work in our real estate department, family department or one of our specialist groups. Because of the relatively few training contracts offered, trainees can expect to be exposed to high-quality work with early responsibility. In order to support this, the firm has a wide-ranging training and education programme, and provides extensive internal training in addition to the Professional Skills Course.

Trainee performance is monitored closely and trainees can expect to receive regular feedback.

**When and how to apply** Applications can be submitted online at www.mishcon.com. Please check the website for closing dates.

**Work placements** Our summer scheme offers two-week placements in two of our four departments. Please refer to the website for closing dates.

**Sponsorship** Full LPC and CPE funding. Living allowance of £5,000 payable in the LPC year. Discretionary payments for other periods considered.

| | |
|---|---|
| Vacancies | 10-12 |
| Trainees | 17 |
| Partners | 55 |
| Total staff | 267 |

**Work placement** yes

**Apply to**
Graduate Recruitment

**Starting salary**
£30,000

**Minimum qualifications**
2.1 degree or higher

**Sponsorship**
CPE/LPC

**Offices**
London

Mishcon de Reya Solicitors

| Firm | Description | | |
|---|---|---|---|
| **MILNE MOSER**<br>100 Highgate, Kendal, Cumbria LA9 4HE<br>**Tel:** 01539 729786<br>**Fax:** 01539 723425<br>**Email:** solicitors@milnemoser.co.uk<br>**Apply to:** Mr D J Emmett | An old-established but progressive general practice with a legal aid franchise and estate agency undertaking all types of contentious and non-contentious work. | V 0<br>T 1<br>P 5<br>TS 30<br>WP no | |
| **MLM**<br>Pendragon House, Fitzalan Court, Newport Road, Cardiff CF24 0BA<br>**Tel:** 029 2046 2562<br>**Fax:** 029 2049 1118<br>**Email:** alex.pay@mlmsolicitors.com<br>**Apply to:** Mr Alex Pay | Seven partner commercial practice based in Cardiff. | V Varies[08]<br>T 3<br>P 7<br>TS 36<br>WP yes | |
| **MOGERS**<br>24 Queen Square, Bath BA1 2HY<br>**Tel:** 01225 750000<br>**Fax:** 01225 445208<br>**Apply to:** Mr S Treharne | Mogers are a medium size practice which specialises in private client work, ancillary commercial property and commercial work. | V 2[09]<br>T 2<br>P 7<br>TS 51<br>WP no | |
| **MOHAMMED & CO**<br>St John's House, 42 St John's Place, Preston PR1 3XX<br>**Tel:** 01772 888700<br>**Fax:** 01772 888345<br>**Apply to:** Mr Hanif Mohammed | | V 0<br>T 2<br>P 1<br>TS 13<br>WP yes | |
| **MOLESWORTHS BRIGHT CLEGG**<br>Octagon House, 25-27 Yorkshire Street, Rochdale OL16 1RH<br>**Tel:** 01706 356666<br>**Fax:** 01706 354681<br>**Email:** helen@molesworths.co.uk<br>**Apply to:** Ms Helen Humphreys | General provincial practice established over 100 years dealing with most areas of corporate and private client law. | V Varies[09]<br>T 0<br>P 7<br>TS 69<br>WP no | |
| **MONARCH AIRLINES LIMITED**<br>London Luton Airport, Luton LU2 9NU<br>**Tel:** 01582 398 043<br>**Fax:** 01582 401 306<br>**Email:** geoff.atkinson@flymonarch.com<br>**Apply to:** Mr Geoff Atkinson | Passengers airline providing charter and scheduled service flights to destinations worldwide. | V 0<br>T 2<br>P -<br>TS 5<br>WP no | |
| **MONRO FISHER WASBROUGH**<br>8 Great James Street, London WC1N 3DF<br>**Tel:** 020 7404 7001<br>**Fax:** 020 7404 7002<br>**Email:** law@monro-fisher.com<br>**Apply to:** Ms Anne Calder | Long established private client firm situated beside Gray's Inn, particularly specialising in taxation, trusts and estates, charity law, commercial and residential property. | V 1[09]<br>T 1<br>P 7<br>TS 40<br>WP no | |
| **MOOSA-DUKE SOLICITORS**<br>213 London Road, Leicester LE2 1ZE<br>**Tel:** 0116 220 6433<br>**Fax:** 0116 220 6432<br>**Email:** mail@moosaduke.com<br>**Apply to:** Mrs M Duke | Niche practice specialising in medical negligence and personal injury. LSC franchise for clinical negligence. | V 1[09]<br>T 2<br>P 1<br>TS 5<br>WP yes | |

**V** = Vacancies / **T** = Trainees / **P** = Partners / **TS** = Total Staff / **WP** = Work Placement

# Morgan Cole

Bradley Court, Park Place, Cardiff CF10 3DP
**Tel:** 029 2038 5385
**Fax:** 029 2038 5300
**Email:** recruitment@morgan-cole.com
**Web:** www.morgan-cole.com/careers

**The firm** Morgan Cole is a leading regional commercial law practice providing a comprehensive legal service to commercial clients in both the private and public sectors. The firm has a reputation for excellence and attracts a high quality of staff from all fields. The firm enjoys connections throughout the UK and USA, and is a founder member of the Association of European Lawyers, one of five leading UK law firms responsible for establishing a network of English-speaking lawyers throughout Europe.

**Types of work** The practice consists of seven practice areas: insurance, health and regulatory; dispute management; commercial; corporate; private client; employment, pensions and benefits; and commercial property. As a modern practice, we strive to meet the legal needs of clients in all sectors of industry. Within these practice areas the firm's work includes: acquisitions and disposals; commercial; corporate finance; employment; energy; information technology; insolvency; intellectual property; joint ventures; management buy-outs and buy-ins; partnerships; PFI; commercial property; construction; personal injury; professional indemnity; commercial litigation and alternative dispute resolution.

**Who should apply** Successful candidates should be commercially aware, self-motivated individuals with drive and initiative, and able to apply a logical and commonsense approach to solving client problems. The firm is seeking applications from graduates/undergraduates in both law and non-law subjects, preferably with a 2.1 degree, who are keen to stay on once they have qualified.

**Training programme** Trainees spend not less than six months in at least three different practice areas, and since each practice area handles a wide variety of work within its constituent teams, there is no danger of over-specialisation. Every effort is made to accommodate individual preferences with regard to seats consistent with balanced training.

**When and how to apply** By 31 July 2008 to begin September 2010. Applicants should complete the firm's online application form at www.morgan-cole.com/careers.

**Work placements** Vacation scheme held in our Oxford, Reading, Cardiff and Swansea offices between June and July. The application deadline date is 30 April 2008.

**Sponsorship** Full funding of CPE/GDL and LPC fees, as well as a contribution towards maintenance.

| | |
|---|---|
| Vacancies | 12 |
| Trainees | 24 |
| Partners | 47 |
| Total staff | 410 |

**Apply**
Online

**Starting salary**
The firm pays competitive salaries which are reviewed annually in line with market trends

**Minimum qualifications**
Preferably a 2.1 degree, law or non-law

**Sponsorship**
GDL/CPE/LPC

**Offices**
Croydon, Oxford, Reading, Bristol, Cardiff, Swansea

Morgan Cole

# Muckle LLP

Norham House, 12 New Bridge Street West, Newcastle upon Tyne NE1 8AS
**Tel:** 0191 244 2987
**Fax:** 0191 261 9520
**Email:** nsingh@muckle-llp.com
**Web:** www.muckle-llp.com

**The firm** Muckle LLP is a leading commercial law firm in the North East of England. We have an excellent client base of successful private and public companies, property developers, financial institutions, public sector and educational organisations, which recognise that our innovative commercial skills are a major benefit in enhancing our service delivery to them and in helping them achieve their aspirations.

The partners believe that the success and profitability of the firm must not be looked at in isolation from the wider North East community. In 2002 they set up the Robert Muckle Charitable Fund (now the Muckle Charitable Fund) and all members of the firm are encouraged as part of their personal development to help a wide variety of community projects.

In 2007 Muckle LLP and The Sage Gateshead were named as the best arts and business partnership in the North East. They won the accolade at The Journal's Culture Awards 2006.

In 2008 Muckle LLP will be moving to their new premises, Time Central, based at Gallowgate.

**Types of work** The firm is divided into four main groups – commercial, property, employment and dispute resolution. The specialist units within these groups are: banking, business restructuring and insolvency, business advisory services, corporate finance, intellectual property & technology, property development, planning, construction, employment, education and client wealth management.

**Who should apply** Graduates from any background, who expect to achieve a 2:1 degree. We are looking for highly motivated team players who want to build their careers in the North East and make a difference to their local community. Interpersonal skills and commerciality are considered essential as well as good academics.

**Training programme** We run an excellent training programme that focuses on the trainees' legal, IT, management and business development skills. Training for all staff has a high priority and we are an Investor in People. Trainees complete four six-month seats in different practice areas during their training contracts. Training is a combination of on-the-job experience, partner mentoring as well as in-house and external courses. Trainees are encouraged to join the social, charitable or graduate recruitment committees.

**When and how to apply** The deadline for applications for training contracts commencing in September 2010 is Thursday 31 July 2008. Interviews and an open day take place during August 2008. Applicants should fill in the online application form which is available on our website.

**Work placements** We offer up to 30 places on our summer vacation scheme which runs between June and August each year. Applications are made on the firm's online application form and should be submitted by Friday 8 February 2008.

**Sponsorship** Full LPC fees plus maintenance allowance.

| | |
|---|---|
| Vacancies | 4 |
| Trainees | 8 |
| Partners | 19 |
| Total staff | 132 |

**Work placement** yes

**Apply**
Online

**Starting salary**
A minimum of £24,000

**Minimum qualifications**
2.1 degree

**Sponsorship**
LPC

**Offices**
Newcastle upon Tyne

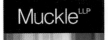

# Mundays LLP

Cedar House, 78 Portsmouth Road, Cobham, Surrey, KT11 1AN
**Tel:** 01932 590500
**Fax:** 01932 590220
**Email:** pauline.glynn@mundays.co.uk
**Web:** www.mundays.co.uk

**The firm** Mundays is one of Surrey's leading law practices, operating from modern offices in Cobham, with easy access to London and the M25. The practice has grown significantly over the past 10 years and continues to expand. Many of our lawyers have worked in the City but have chosen to relocate to a practice where we aim to offer a service as good as (if not better than) competitors in London at more economic rates, while enabling our lawyers to achieve a better work/life balance. We offer our diverse range of clients (both corporate and private) comprehensive, responsive and commercial advice, with separate departments working closely together as appropriate.

Culture: at Mundays, we have a relaxed, informal working style. Fee-earners have a willingness to share their knowledge and experience in the belief that, with hard work, our trainees of today are potentially our partners of the future.

**Types of work** The practice is divided into five principal departments: property, corporate/commercial, dispute resolution, private wealth and family. Within these departments we have specialisms in banking, employment, construction, insolvency and intellectual property.

**Who should apply** Candidates will need to demonstrate their confidence, ability to communicate and personality. They are also required to have (or expect to receive) at least a 2.1 degree (applications from law and non-law graduates are welcome) and 3 A levels or equivalent (AAB or better), and to demonstrate comparable performance in any postgraduate courses in law. We are looking for well-rounded individuals who are keen to develop their career with us as trainees and beyond.

**Training programme** Trainees typically spend periods of six months in each of the corporate/commercial, property and dispute resolution departments; where they spend the fourth period will depend on whether they wish to gain experience of another specialist area. Trainees are encouraged to take on responsibility from the beginning of their training through direct experience of dealing with matters and working alongside fee-earners. Progress is closely monitored and training given to reflect the needs of individual trainees.

**When and how to apply** Closing date for 2010 is 31 August 2008. Apply online at www.mundays.co.uk.

**Work placements** We do not run vacation placement schemes.

**Sponsorship** The practice will pay the cost of the LPC as well as a maintenance grant of £4,000.

| | |
|---|---|
| Vacancies | 3 |
| Trainees | 5 |
| Partners | 26 |
| Total staff | 155 |

**Apply to**
Pauline Glynn,
Human Resources Manager

**Starting salary**
1st year - £25,000
2nd year - £26,500

**Minimum qualifications**
2.1 degree

**Sponsorship**
LPC

**Offices**
Cobham

## MORGAN JONES & PETT

Grey Friars House, 18-20 Prince of Wales Road, Norwich NR1 1LB
**Tel:** 01603 877000
**Fax:** 01603 877007
**Email:** davidpett@m-j-p.co.uk
**Apply to:** Mr DR Pett

Specialist personal injury and clinical negligence firm. Also family and conveyancing departments. Offices in Norwich.

| V | T | P | TS | WP |
|---|---|---|----|----|
| 0 | 1 | 3 | 23 | no |

## MORRISH & CO

Oxford House, Oxford Row, Leeds LS1 3BE
**Tel:** 0113 245 0733
**Fax:** 0113 242 5168
**Email:** ken.cromar@morrishlaw.co.uk
**Apply to:** Mr Ken Cromar

City centre location close to law courts. Most types of legal work undertaken with particular specialisation in personal injury.

| V | T | P | TS | WP |
|---|---|---|----|----|
| 0 | 4 | 12 | 90 | no |

## MORRISON & FOERSTER

CityPoint, One Ropemaker Street, London EC2Y 9AW
**Tel:** 020 7920 4000
**Fax:** 020 7496 8500
**Email:** mmannell@mofo.com
**Apply to:** Ms Margaret Mannell

Morrison & Foerster is an international firm with over 1,000 lawyers across offices in the U.S., Europe and Asia. We take pride in promoting a diverse workplace.

| V | T | P | TS | WP |
|---|---|---|----|----|
| 3 | 5 | 16 | 95 | yes |

## MORTONS

110-112 High Street West, Sunderland SR1 1TX
**Tel:** 0191 514 4323
**Fax:** 0191 514 8100
**Email:** rrushton@mortonssolicitors.com
**Apply to:** The Practice Manager

Please apply to the Practice Manager in own handwriting and enclosing a full CV. We are committed until September 2009.

| V | T | P | TS | WP |
|---|---|---|----|----|
| 0 | 2 | 6 | 48 | no |

## MOWLL & MOWLL

Trafalgar House Gordon Road, Whitfield, Dover, Kent CT16 3PN
**Tel:** 01304 873344
**Fax:** 01304 873355
**Email:** enquiries@mowll.co.uk
**Apply to:** Mrs Valerie Scott

Established 130 years in Dover dealing with commercial property, company law, probate, conveyancing, family and civil litigation including employment.

| V | T | P | TS | WP |
|---|---|---|----|----|
| 0 | 1 | 4 | 26 | no |

## MULLIS & PEAKE

8-10 Eastern Road, Romford, Essex RM1 3PJ
**Tel:** 01708 762326
**Fax:** 01708 784041
**Email:** martyntrenery@mplaw.co.uk
**Apply to:** Mr Martyn Trenerry

We specialise in commercial work for business including company, employment and licensing. Private client includes litigation, accident claim, trust and probate, and advice to the elderly.

| V | T | P | TS | WP |
|---|---|---|----|----|
| Poss(08) | 2 | 9 | 70 | no |

## MUSA A PATEL & CO

71-73 Bradford Road, Dewsbury WF13 2EG
**Tel:** 01924 437800
**Fax:** 01924 488810
**Apply to:** Mr Musa Patel

Progressive firm catering for crime, conveyancing, immigration and matrimonial. Client base of various different ethnic origins and concentrating on legal aid work. Offices in Huddersfield, Bradford.

| V | T | P | TS | WP |
|---|---|---|----|----|
| 0 | 2 | 3 | 22 | no |

## MUSTOE SHORTER

6-8 Frederick Place, Weymouth DT4 8HQ
**Tel:** 01305 752700
**Fax:** 01305 778928
**Apply to:** The Staff Partner

Small company with the latest technology with offices in Dorchester and Weymouth dealing with most types of high street business.

| V | T | P | TS | WP |
|---|---|---|----|----|
| 0 | 3 | 7 | 50 | no |

**V** = Vacancies / **T** = Trainees / **P** = Partners / **TS** = Total Staff / **WP** = Work Placement

| | | |
|---|---|---|
| **MYERS LISTER PRICE**<br>5 + 7 Market Street, Altrincham,<br>Cheshire WA14 1QE<br>**Tel:** 0161 926 9969<br>**Fax:** 0161 926 1500<br>**Apply to:** Mr Michael Lister | Applications are invited from self motivated lawyers of partnership potential. This dynamic and highly accredited practice offers outstanding 'hands on' training and structured career progress. | V 2[09]<br>T 4<br>P 7<br>TS 53<br>WP yes |
| **NALDERS**<br>Farley House, Falmouth Road, Truro TR1 2HX<br>**Tel:** 01872 241414<br>**Fax:** 01872 242424<br>**Email:** post@nalders.co.uk<br>**Apply to:** Mr Ross Pascoe | One of the leading firms in Cornwall with seven offices and Lexcel accredited. Work covers civil litigation, PI, family, commercial, conveyancing, probate, financial services, employment. | V 1[09]<br>T 5<br>P 9<br>TS 115<br>WP no |
| **NANDY & CO**<br>72 Woodgrange Road, London E7 0QH<br>**Tel:** 020 8536 1800<br>**Fax:** 020 8536 1900<br>**Apply to:** Ms NR Welivitgodage | | V 0<br>T 0<br>P -<br>TS -<br>WP no |
| **NAPTHENS**<br>7 Winckley Square, Preston PR1 3JD<br>**Tel:** 01772 883883<br>**Fax:** 01772 254836<br>**Apply to:** Mr JM Woosnam | Large commercial property/corporate/commercial litigation/employment departments; also personal injury litigation and private client department with a significant trusts and probate portfolio. | V 2-3[09]<br>T 3<br>P 12<br>TS 70<br>WP no |
| **NASH & CO**<br>Beaumont House, Beaumont Park,<br>Plymouth PL4 9BD<br>**Tel:** 01752 664444<br>**Fax:** 01752 667112<br>**Email:** law@nash.co.uk<br>**Apply to:** Mrs Nicola Shelmerdine | For more information about Nash & Co please contact us or visit our website. | V 1<br>T 1<br>P 7<br>TS 70<br>WP no |
| **NEIL MYERSON SOLICITORS**<br>The Cottages, Regent Road, Altrincham WA14 1RX<br>**Tel:** 0161 941 4000<br>**Fax:** 0161 941 4411<br>**Email:** lawyers@neil-myerson.co.uk<br>**Apply to:** Mr Richard Lloyd | A commercial law firm based in South Manchester specialising in corporate law, commercial property, commercial litigation, employment and IT and internet law. | V 2[09]<br>T 4<br>P 6<br>TS 50<br>WP no |
| **NELSONS**<br>Pennine House, 8 Stanford Street,<br>Nottingham NG1 7BQ<br>**Tel:** 0115 958 6262<br>**Fax:** 0115 958 4702<br>**Email:** careers@nelsonslaw.co.uk<br>**Apply to:** HR Department | Nelsons is one of the largest law firms in the East Midlands, providing a full range of legal services to the corporate and private sectors. | V 0<br>T 0<br>P 34<br>TS 241<br>WP no |
| **NEWCASTLE UNDER LYME BOROUGH COUNCIL**<br>Civic Offices, Merrial Street, Newcastle,<br>Staffordshire ST5 2AG<br>**Tel:** 01782 717717<br>**Fax:** 01782 742215<br>**Email:** p.r.washington@newcastle-staffs.gov.uk<br>**Apply to:** Mr Paul R Washington | Local Authority | V 0<br>T 0<br>P -<br>TS 4<br>WP no |

# Nabarro

Lacon House, Theobald's Road, London WC1X 8RW
**Tel:** 020 7524 6000
**Fax:** 020 7524 6524
**Email:** graduateinfo@nabarro.com
**Web:** www.nabarro.com

**The firm** Nabarro is one of the country's leading commercial law firms. We have more than 400 lawyers offering a broad range of legal services to major national and international clients across a range of practice areas. We are known for having an open but highly professional culture, and expect our lawyers to have a life outside work.

**Types of work** The firm's areas of work include company and commercial law, real estate, planning, pensions and employment, corporate finance, IP/IT, commercial litigation, construction, PFI and environmental law. Our work includes complex financing and corporate agreements; property acquisitions and portfolio management; handling intellectual property rights; constructing high-profile commercial litigation and personal injury cases; and construction and engineering projects around the world.

**Who should apply** Those with a strong academic record and enthusiasm, self-motivation and commitment. Strong communication skills are essential.

**Training programme** Trainees will undertake six four-month seats to ensure maximum exposure to the firm's core practice areas (company commercial, real estate and litigation). We aim to retain all of our trainees on qualification. Trainees will have an opportunity to gain further experience by spending time in specialist areas (eg, pensions, IP/IT, tax, employment), possibly overseas in Brussels, or by completing a further seat in a core area. Trainees will return to the seat they wish to qualify into for the remaining four months of the contract. This will ensure a smooth transition from trainee to qualified solicitor.

We are completely commited to supporting and training our trainees. Once you have accepted a training contract with the firm we will keep in touch with you by assigning you a buddy (a current trainee) who will be a point of contact and will help you to feel a part of the firm. Each trainee will be assigned a mentor when they commence their training contract, who will be a partner. The mentor will be there to act as a sounding board and to assist the trainee during the two years. Trainees are assigned to a senior solicitor who will supervise their work. We have a Career Development Plan in place so that you will have a structured career path from trainee to partner.

**When and how to apply** Between 1 November and 31 July 2008 to commence September 2010 or January 2011. Apply using the firm's online application form at www.nabarro.com.

**Work placements** Three weeks under the supervision of a solicitor. Excellent and varied experience, training and social events enable you to find out what it is like to be a trainee and to meet a wide range of staff across the firm. The majority of our trainees come to us through our vacation scheme.

**Sponsorship** Full fees and maintenance grant of £7,000/£6,000 if studying the LPC in London and Guildford/elsewhere respectively; £6,000/£5,000 if studying the GDL in London and Guildford/elsewhere respectively.

| | |
|---|---|
| Vacancies | 35 |
| Trainees | 61 |
| Partners | 126 |
| Total staff | 945 |

**Work placement** yes
*(see Insider Report on p126)*

**Apply to**
Ms Jane Drew

**Starting salary**
London:
1st year - £36,000
2nd year - £40,000
Sheffield:
1st year - £25,000
2nd year - £28,000

**Minimum qualifications**
2.1 degree

**Sponsorship**
GDL/LPC

**Offices**
Brussels, London, Sheffield

NABARRO
CLARITY MATTERS

# Needham & James LLP

Needham & James House, Bridgeway, Stratford-Upon-Avon, Warwickshire CV37 6YY
**Tel:** 0845 630 8833
**Fax:** 0845 630 8844
**Email:** trainingcontracts@needhamandjames.com
**Web:** www.needhamandjames.com

**The firm** Needham & James is a medium-sized, Midlands-based commercial practice with a substantial private client department.

**Types of work** The firm has a strong commercial base offering a range of legal services in commercial property, banking, company law, employment law and dispute resolution. We also have expertise in several niche areas of law including social housing, agriculture and sports law. Our broad client base in the Midlands, across the UK and increasingly overseas includes small family run enterprises, larger publicly quoted companies, financial institutions, insurers, utility companies and venture capital firms, as well as local authorities, sports governing bodies, charitable trusts and private clients.

**Who should apply** We are looking for high calibre trainees who share our vision and dedication to our clients. We want people with an enthusiastic, 'can do' approach, keen to experience a wide range of work. Potential trainees will also have to demonstrate a high level of academic achievement, an analytical and enquiring mind and a sensitivity to clients' needs. Good interpersonal skills are a must. Candidates should normally have, or expect, at least a 2.1 honours degree (in any subject), and a minimum of 260 UCAS points from their best three A level results, excluding General Studies. Candidates with lesser qualifications who have achieved distinction in another field will always be considered. We are committed to recruiting the highest quality trainees, irrespective of background.

**Training programme** Our trainees take on significant personal responsibility at an early stage, and make an important contribution to client matters very quickly. All trainees are supervised by experienced lawyers who are themselves trained in trainee management. We strive to work in genuine partnership with our trainees and to assist them to develop their full potential.

The firm is organised into 13 fee earning teams: agriculture and rural affairs; banking and finance; commercial litigation; commercial property; company and commercial; employment; family; mergers and acquisitions; overseas property; private client litigation; residential property; social housing; wills and tax planning. A typical two-year training contract comprises four seats, each of six months' duration, with trainees visiting three or four teams during the contract. Trainees' preferences regarding the choice of seat are taken into account wherever possible, subject to the requirements of the business. Trainees are allocated a supervising partner or senior solicitor in each seat and exposed to a wide variety of work and clients. There is an informal appraisal after three months and a more formal written appraisal at the end of each six month period. The firm has a dedicated training partner who oversees the supervision and management of trainees.

**When and how to apply** Apply by 30 June 2008 for training contracts to commence in September 2010. Please complete the online application form, supported by an email with CV and covering letter to the address above. Late applications will not be considered. Shortlisted applicants are invited to attend an assessment day, after which offers are made. The firm can sometimes be flexible with regard to the commencement dates of training contracts for successful candidates.

**Work placements** Apply by email to the address above.

**Sponsorship** The firm will pay up to 50% of LPC fees.

| | |
|---|---|
| Vacancies | 5 |
| Trainees | 10 |
| Partners | 25 |
| Total staff | 180 |

**Work placement** yes

**Apply to**
Mr Andrew Owen

**Starting salary**
1st year: £22,000 minimum

**Minimum qualifications**
2.1 honours degree in any subject

**Sponsorship**
LPC

**Offices**
Birmingham,
Stratford-upon-Avon (head office), Moreton in Marsh, Shipston on Stour

Needham & James
*Solicitors*

# Norton Rose LLP

3 More London Riverside, London SE1 2AQ
**Tel:** 020 7283 6000
**Fax:** 020 7283 6500
**Email:** grad.recruitment@nortonrose.com
**Web:** www.nortonrose.com/graduate

**The firm** Norton Rose LLP is a constituent part of Norton Rose Group, a leading international legal practice offering a full business law service from offices across Europe, the Middle East and Asia.

Norton Rose Group comprises Norton Rose LLP and its affiliates and has over 1,000 lawyers operating from offices in Amsterdam, Athens, Bahrain, Bangkok, Beijing, Brussels, Dubai, Frankfurt, Hong Kong, Jakarta, London, Milan, Moscow, Munich, Paris, Piraeus, Prague, Rome, Shanghai, Singapre and Warsaw.

**Types of work** Knowing how our clients' businesses work and understanding what drives their iundustries is fundamental to us. Our lawyers share industry knowledge and sector expertise across borders, enabling us to support our clients anywhere in the world. We are strong in corporate finance, financial institutions, energy and infrastructure, transport and technology.

**Who should apply** The practice welcomes applications from individuals from law or non-law backgrounds who have good intellectual ability. All applicants must have at least 320 (26) UCAS points or equivalent/similar level qualifications and be on course for (or already achieved) a 2.1 degree or above. Candidates need to demonstrate a keen interest in the practice's areas of expertise as well as team work, commitment and a willingness to take responsibility.

**Training programme** Based on an innovative six-seat pattern, the Norton Rose LLP training contract is one of the most varied among leading City firms. Our flexible seat system allows trainees the widest possible exposure to different practice areas, in order to enable them to make the best and most informed choice of qualification area. There are also opportunities for trainees to spend up to eight months in an international office.

**When and how to apply** Apply before 31 July 2008 for training contracts commencing in September 2010/January 2011. If you are a non-law student or have already graduated, you should ideally aim to apply between January and March. Applications should be made online via our website at www.nortonrose.com/graduate.

**Work placements** Norton Rose LLP also offers placements in winter and during the summer for those considering a career in law. Remuneration is £250 per week. Further information and an application form may be found at www.nortonrose.com/graduate.

**Sponsorship** Full fees for GDL and LPC, plus a maintenance allowance of £6,000 and £7,000 (respectively).

| | |
|---|---|
| Vacancies | 55 |
| Trainees | 110 |
| Partners | 245 |
| Total staff | 1850 |

**Work placement** yes
*(see Insider Report on p125)*

**Apply to**
Karen Potts

**Starting salary**
£35,700

**Minimum qualifications**
2.1 degree

**Sponsorship**
GDL/LPC

**Offices**
Amsterdam, Athens, Bahrain, Bangkok, Beijing, Brussels, Dubai, Frankfurt, Hong Kong, Jakarta*, London, Milan, Moscow, Munich, Paris, Piraeus, Prague, Rome, Shanghai, Singapore, Warsaw
*Associate office

NORTON ROSE

| NEXUS SOLICITORS<br>18 Albert Square, Manchester M2 5PE<br>**Tel:** 0161 819 4900<br>**Fax:** 0161 819 4901<br>**Email:** cpugh@nexussolicitors.co.uk<br>**Apply to:** Mr Chris Pugh | We provide commercial legal services and business advice to SME's, plcs and high net worth individuals. Nexus is a commercial practice established in July 2000. | V 2[09]<br>T 4<br>P 9<br>TS 40<br>WP no |
|---|---|---|
| NICHOLAS SMITH<br>Portland Place, Halifax, West Yorkshire HX1 2QN<br>**Tel:** 01422 383380<br>**Fax:** 01422 383370<br>**Apply to:** Mr ANG Smith | 5 years old and growing. Local people should apply. | V 1<br>T 2<br>P 2<br>TS 20<br>WP no |
| NIJJAR SOLICITORS<br>Trinity Court 2nd Floor, 28 Newton Road,<br>Great Barr, Sandwell, Birmingham B43 6BW<br>**Tel:** 0870 446 1000<br>**Fax:** 0121 357 0123<br>**Apply to:** Mr JS Nijjar | The firm deals with serious crime, primarily in the Midlands but also across the country. | V 1[09]<br>T 1<br>P 2<br>TS 10<br>WP no |
| NK LEGAL SOLICITORS<br>255 Wilmslow Road, Rushorme,<br>Manchester M14 5LW<br>**Tel:** 0870 787 3945<br>**Fax:** 0161 249 3995<br>**Email:** info@nklegal.co.uk<br>**Apply to:** Mrs S Khan | A high street firm dealing with personal injury, conveyancing, immigration, employment, family, crime, civil litigation and wills. | V 0<br>T 2<br>P 2<br>TS 8<br>WP yes |
| NOBLE<br>21 High Street, Shefford, Bedfordshire SG17 5DD<br>**Tel:** 01462 814 055<br>**Fax:** 01462 814 155<br>**Apply to:** Mr Gareth Cotton | We are a busy criminal and mental health specilaist practice covering the Bedfordshire and N. Hertfordshire area. | V 0<br>T 0<br>P 3<br>TS 40<br>WP yes |
| NOCKOLDS<br>Market Square, Bishop's Stortford CM23 3UZ<br>**Tel:** 01279 755777<br>**Fax:** 01279 755149<br>**Email:** sts@nockolds.co.uk<br>**Apply to:** Mrs Sue Stevenson | General practice with branch office in Sawbridgeworth undertaking all types of legal work for a wide variety of private and commercial clients. | V 3[09]<br>T 6<br>P 8<br>TS 85<br>WP no |
| NORTH YORKSHIRE COUNTY COUNCIL<br>County Hall, Northallerton,<br>North Yorkshire DL7 8AD<br>**Tel:** 01609 780780<br>**Fax:** 01609 780447<br>**Email:** legal.services@northyorks.gov.uk<br>**Apply to:** Ms Catherine Whitehead | Provides legal advice to North Yorkshire County Council and other public bodies, expertise in all areas of public sector law. We have the Lexcel standard. | V 1<br>T 1<br>P -<br>TS 43<br>WP yes |
| NORTON PESKETT<br>148 London Road North, Lowestoft,<br>Suffolk NR32 1HF<br>**Tel:** 01502 533000<br>**Fax:** 01502 533001<br>**Apply to:** Mr TR Clifford | Medium sized firm with large private client workloads. Branch offices at Beccles, Gorleston, Great Yarmouth and Halesworth. | V 1<br>T 1<br>P 11<br>TS 133<br>WP no |

# Olswang

90 High Holborn, London WC1V 6XX
**Tel:** 020 7067 3000
**Fax:** 020 7067 3999
**Email:** traineesolicitor@olswang.com
**Web:** www.olswang.com

**The firm** Olswang is a leading law firm renowned for its ground-breaking work in the technology, media, communications and real estate industries. Founded in 1981, the firm has grown to a staff of nearly 600, including 80 partners and four European offices.

In 2007 the firm extended its international capability opening an office in Berlin which focuses on the real estate and finance industries. Olswang also has an established alliance with US law firm Greenberg Traurig LLP, as well as providing its services in over 80 countries through a network of like minded leading law firms.

The firm's sector focus supports the wealth of knowledge and interest among fee earners and attracts a distinct breadth of clients from across industries. The firm represents recognised brands and key industry players, as well as smaller, pioneering companies. These include Brixton plc, Dawnay, Day, eBay, International Cricket Council, ITV, Ladbrokes, MTV Networks Europe, Rotch Group, Sony BMG, The Guardian, Tottenham Hotspur FC, UBS, Vectura Group plc, Warner Music International and Woolworths.

The firm's strong management team and wider partnership is dedicated to its people and is committed to helping everyone realise their own potential. Olswang is proud to be ranked as a top 100 UK employer in *The Sunday Times* 100 Best Companies to Work For 2007, an achievement gained for the third year running.

**Types of work** Olswang's focus on media, communications, technology and real estate brings together cross-discipline teams drawn from our principal practice areas: advertising, banking, biosciences, commercial litigation, corporate & commercial, e-commerce, employment, EU & competition, film & TV finance and production, insolvency, intellectual property, IT, media litigation, music, private equity/venture capital, planning & construction, publishing, real estate, sport, tax, telecommunications and TV/broadcasting.

**Who should apply** Individuals with at least a 2.1 degree (or equivalent) in any discipline.

**Training programme** Training contracts are divided into four six-month seats. These will be arranged throughout the two years and will balance the needs of each individual with those of the firm. Full legal and non-legal training programmes are supplemented with on-the-job training to ensure all trainees receive the best training.

**When and how to apply** Apply by 31 July 2008 to begin September 2010 to Victoria Edwards, Recruitment Manager. Application is online via www.olswang.com.

**Work placements** Two two-week summer internship schemes during June and July.

**Sponsorship** Full fees for GDL and LPC. Where studies have been completed or students are more than three months into course, 25% of fees will be reimbursed.

| | |
|---|---|
| Vacancies | up to 24 |
| Trainees | 44 |
| Partners | 83 |
| Total staff | 585 |

**Work placement** yes
*(see Insider Report on p127)*

**Apply to**
Victoria Edwards

**Starting salary**
£35,000

**Minimum qualifications**
2.1 degree

**Sponsorship**
GDL/LPC

**Offices**
London, Berlin, Brussels, Reading

OLSWANG

# O'Melveny & Myers LLP

Warwick Court, 5 Paternoster Square, London EC4M 7DX
**Tel:** 020 7088 0000
**Fax:** 020 7088 0001
**Email:** graduate-recruitment@omm.com
**Web:** www.omm.com

**The firm** A top 20 global law firm staffed by over 1,000 lawyers in 13 offices, O'Melveny's clients include many of the world's largest financial institutions, leading private equity houses, investment banks and corporates. The London office is known for its entrepreneurial leadership and its commitment to excellence which underpin its approach to recruitment. The expertise of the team can also draw on the extensive reservoir of know-how and experience of the firm's offices around the world. The success achieved by the London office has been recognised in industry accolades and in the deals upon which it has been instructed - for example, it acted for GIC (Government of Singapore Investment Corporation Pte Ltd) on two of the largest M&A deals in Europe in 2006, being the successful consortium bids for BAA plc (£10.3 billion) and AB Ports plc (£2.8 billion).

**Types of work** The London office was effectively re-launched in 2004 and offers a full service transactions practice with a focus on private equity fund formation and deals and supported by leading tax, acquisition finance, regulatory, real estate and IP lawyers. As of July 2007 it has also established an adversarial and arbitration capacity with the hiring of a leading team from Watson, Farley & Williams. All lawyers in London are UK qualified with most having joined from Magic Circle and other leading UK law firms.

**Who should apply** The London office is seeking to recruit four to six high calibre graduates for training contracts each year. Successful candidates must be ambitious, have proven academic ability, high levels of drive and determination, good team working skills and sound commercial awareness. The office has a strong entrepreneurial and collegiate style.

**Training programme** We can take into account individual preferences when tailoring the training programme subject to the trainee completing the core competencies. Trainees will usually complete seats with partners or senior lawyers in each of our corporate, finance and funds formation practices and will also be able to obtain contentious experience in our litigation/arbitration practice and possibly in our competition/anti-trust practice (based partly in London and partly in our Brussels office). There will also be opportunities to work with our tax, IP and real estate practitioners. We encourage trainees to be proactive and take responsibility at an early stage. As a firm, O'Melveny & Myers places great importance on training for its lawyers at all levels which it views as key to the firm's ability to offer high quality legal services to its clients and so trainees will participate in the legal and non-legal skills training programme established by the London office. The Professional Skills Course is run by an external provider. Progress of each trainee is monitored with mid and end of seat reviews and feedback is given throughout each seat.

**When and how to apply** Applications can be made via www.cvmailuk.com. Closing date for September 2010 entry is 31 July 2008.

**Work placements** Vacation placements are available for two weeks between June and September. For 2008 summer vacation schemes, please apply by 1 February 2008 via www.cvmailuk.com.

**Sponsorship** GDL/LPC tuition fees incurred post recruitment plus a maintenance grant (currently £7,000 per annum).

| | |
|---|---|
| Vacancies | 4 |
| Trainees | 7 |
| Partners | 9 |
| Total staff | 76 |

**Work placement** yes

**Apply**
Online

**Starting salary**
1st year - £37,500
2nd year - £41,500
(2007)

**Minimum qualifications**
2.1 degree

**Sponsorship**
GDL/LPC

**Offices**
Beijing, Brussels, Century City, Hong Kong, London, Los Angeles, Newport Beach, New York, San Francisco, Shanghai, Silicon Valley, Tokyo and Washington DC

O'MELVENY & MYERS LLP

# Orrick, Herrington & Sutcliffe

Tower 42, Level 35, 25 Old Broad Street, London EC2N 1HQ
**Tel:** 020 7562 5000
**Fax:** 020 7628 0078
**Email:** recruitlondon@orrick.com
**Web:** www.orrick.com

**The firm** Orrick was founded in 1863 in San Francisco, California, and is now one of the world's leading international law firms with 980 lawyers in 18 offices located throughout the United States, Europe and Asia.

**Types of work** Orrick is known for its market-leading finance practices, as well as its corporate, restructuring, intellectual property and litigation practices. Orrick's London core practices are acquisition finance, arbitration and litigation, banking, capital markets, trade and asset finance, competition and European Union law, corporate and corporate finance, employment, energy and project finance, global bankruptcy and debt restructuring, international dispute resolution, private investment funds, real estate, structured finance and securitisation, and tax. Much of Orrick's client work involves cross-border transactions which have increased substantially in recent years with the development of the firm's European network consisting of offices in London, Paris, Milan, Rome and Moscow.

**Who should apply** If you set your standards high, have a strong work ethic and are a bright talented graduate of any discipline, you will be guaranteed broad based experience and Orrick could be for you. Applicants should have at least three A level passes at grades A and B and a 2.1 degree.

**Training programme** Orrick values team players and rewards collaboration over competition. We aim to give individuals the opportunity to flourish in a lively and supportive work environment and encourage interaction among lawyers across international offices at every level of experience within the firm. We support learning through a steadfast focus on training and a mentoring programme that will provide you with the right foundation for building your legal career and for working with clients. Trainees work closely with fee earners and gain practical experience in research, drafting, procedural and client-related skills.

Our two year training programme comprises four six-month seats in competition, corporate, employment, finance, litigation and real estate, with regular appraisals throughout. We also offer the opportunity to sit a six-month seat in either our Hong Kong or Paris offices. The firm has a dedicated training partner who oversees the supervision and management of trainees.

Trainees undertake the Professional Skills Course during their induction programme. In addition trainees have their own weekly training sessions with office-wide seminars covering the firm's practice areas.

**When and how to apply** Apply online at www.orrick.com/london/gradrecruitment by 31 July 2008 for 2010 training contracts.

**Sponsorship**
GDL: fees paid
LPC: fees paid plus maintenance

| | |
|---|---|
| Vacancies | 8 |
| Trainees | 13 |
| Partners | 14 |
| Total staff | 105 |
| (Figures for London office) | |

**Apply to**
Simon Cockshutt

**Starting salary**
1st year - £32,000 (2007)
2nd year - £36,000 (2007)

**Minimum qualifications**
2.1 degree

**Sponsorship**
GDL/LPC

**Offices**
Beijing, Hong Kong, London, Los Angeles, Milan, Moscow, New York, Orange County, Pacific Northwest, Paris, Rome, Sacramento, San Francisco, Shanghai, Silicon Valley, Taipei, Tokyo, Washington DC

ORRICK

## OGLETHORPE & BROATCH
6 Borrowdale Road, Keswick, Cumbria CA12 5DB
**Tel:** 01768 772125
**Fax:** 01768 774678
**Email:** info@oglethorpeandbroatch.co.uk
**Apply to:** Mr John Dunn

Not currently recruiting for 2004/2005.

| | |
|---|---|
| V | 0 |
| T | 0 |
| P | 3 |
| TS | 10 |
| WP | no |

## OGLETHORPE STURTON & GILLIBRAND
16 Castle Park, Lancaster LA1 1YG
**Tel:** 01524 846846
**Fax:** 01524 382247
**Email:** dlgillibrand@osg.co.uk
**Apply to:** Mr David Gillibrand

A well-established firm in serving the business and rural community based in North Lancashire and the South Lakes.

| | |
|---|---|
| V | 1-2 |
| T | 2 |
| P | 7 |
| TS | 46 |
| WP | no |

## OLDHAM MARSH PAGE FLAVELL
White House, 19 High Street, Melton Mowbray, Leicester LE13 0TZ
**Tel:** 01664 563162
**Fax:** 01664 568815
**Apply to:** Mr JS Mirfin

General market town practice including financial services, personal injury, matrimonial, crime. Legal aid franchise.

| | |
|---|---|
| V | Poss |
| T | 0 |
| P | 3 |
| TS | 30 |
| WP | no |

## OLDHAMS SOLICITORS
1 High Street, Baldock SG7 6AZ
**Tel:** 01462 895444
**Fax:** 01462 892476
**Email:** admin@oldhams.net
**Apply to:** Mrs Nicola Broe

We are a friendly practice specialising in the areas of immigration, crime, family, childcare and crime.

| | |
|---|---|
| V | 2 |
| T | 0 |
| P | 4 |
| TS | 16 |
| WP | no |

## O'NEILL PATIENT SOLICITORS
Chester House, 2 Chester Road, Hazel Grove, Stockport, Cheshire SK7 5NU
**Tel:** 0161 483 8555
**Fax:** 0161 483 0333
**Email:** enqs@oneillpatient.co.uk
**Apply to:** Mr Robin Higham

A young growing firm based in the South Manchester suburbs enjoying an enviable reputation for both private client and company/commercial work.

| | |
|---|---|
| V | 0 |
| T | 4 |
| P | 4 |
| TS | 180 |
| WP | no |

## ORCHARD BRAYTON GRAHAM LLP
24 Britton Street, London EC1M 5VA
**Tel:** 08708 747 477
**Fax:** 08708 747 577
**Email:** lisa.mills@orchardlaw.com
**Apply to:** Ms Lisa Mills

| | |
|---|---|
| V | 4 |
| T | 6 |
| P | 10 |
| TS | 49 |
| WP | yes |

## ORMERODS
Green Dragon House, 64-70 High Street, Croydon CR0 9XN
**Tel:** 020 8686 5000
**Fax:** 020 8680 0972
**Email:** enquiries@ormerods.co.uk
**Apply to:** Ms Maureen Walters

Large general practice in Croydon. Busy litigation practice: county and high court civil, criminal and matrimonial. Sizeable conveyancing (domestic and commercial) plus company and commercial, and probate.

| | |
|---|---|
| V | 2[(09)] |
| T | 3 |
| P | 8 |
| TS | 120 |
| WP | no |

## OSBORNES
Livery House, 9 Pratt Street, London NW1 0AE
**Tel:** 020 7485 8811
**Fax:** 020 7485 5660
**Email:** sandrahillard@osbornes.net
**Apply to:** Ms Sandra Hillard

A firm which undertakes all aspects of general practice, carried out to a high professional standard.

| | |
|---|---|
| V | 3 |
| T | 6 |
| P | 7 |
| TS | 57 |
| WP | yes |

# Osborne Clarke

2 Temple Back East, Temple Quay, Bristol BS1 6EG
**Tel:** 0117 917 3178
**Email:** graduate.recruitment@osborneclarke.com
**Web:** www.osborneclarke.com

**The firm** Osborne Clarke is one of Europe's most respected and dynamic law firms. The firm's success is the result of delivering excellent business-focused legal advice in an energetic, straightforward and efficient way.

Osborne Clarke advises market leading and high performing organisations on their UK and international legal needs from its City, national and European offices and the Osborne Clarke Alliance.

Our main areas of expertise include corporate, finance and property transactions and the full spectrum of business law services, including commercial contracts, employment, pensions, outsourcing and dispute resolution.

**Types of work** Banking, corporate, employment, pension & incentives, litigation/dispute resolution, property, commercial and tax.

**Who should apply** If you are a highly driven individual with good analytical, communication and organisational skills we would like to hear from you. Commercial acumen and the ability to build relationships with clients and colleagues are essential and foreign language skills are an advantage. Ideally, candidates should have grades A – B at A-level or equivalent, as well as a minimum 2.1 degree grade in any discipline. Applications are welcomed from candidates seeking a career change who can demonstrate strong commercial skills.

**Training programme** Our focus at Osborne Clarke is on developing a high performance culture and our aim is to develop trainees into legal business advisers. The Osborne Clarke trainee development programme offers legal, management and business skills training to develop the professional skills needed to progress as a lawyer in the firm.

The training contract is made up of four seats, each lasting six months in four different practice areas. Three of these seats are usually corporate, property and litigation. Trainees work closely with their training supervisors and fee earners in the department and can expect a high level of responsibility and client contact at an early stage in their training contract. Regular reviews and coaching sessions are held to ensure that trainees are reaching their potential. There are also opportunities for trainees to spend a seat in one of the firm's other offices including Germany or on a client secondment.

**When and how to apply** We welcome applications from candidates with either a law or non-law background. Applications should be made online by 31 July 2008.

**Sponsorship** The firm provides full funding for GDL and LPC tuition fees plus a maintenance grant for sponsored candidates.

| | |
|---|---|
| **Vacancies** | 20 |
| **Trainees** | 42 |
| **Partners** | 109 |
| **Total staff** | 677 |

**Work placement** yes
*(see Insider Report on p128)*

**Apply to**
Heather Stallabrass,
Graduate Recruitment
Officer

**Starting salary**
£30,000 - £34,000

**Minimum qualifications**
2.1 degree, any discipline

**Sponsorship**
GDL & LPC

**Offices**
Bristol, Cologne, London,
Munich, Silicon Valley,
Thames Valley.

Osborne Clarke

# Owen White

Senate House, 62-70 Bath Road, Slough SL1 3SR
**Tel:** 01753 876800
**Fax:** 01753 876876
**Email:** russell.ford@owenwhite.com
**Web:** www.owenwhite.com

**The firm** Owen White is a forward-thinking firm with a commitment to providing a first-class service to its clients and a happy and rewarding working environment for its employees. We expect employees to work hard but recognise that there is life outside Owen White. Outside interests are encouraged and we host exciting social activities for all staff. The partners have worked hard to establish a firm that can compete with other larger commercial firms, and have succeeded. Despite its size, Owen White is recommended by the *Legal 500* for housing association work, property development, employment and commercial litigation. We are particularly well respected in the area of franchising and are recommended in *Chambers* and the *Legal 500*'s top firms in the UK.

**Types of work** Our practice is primarily commercial. Principal areas of work are commercial property, litigation and a broad range of company/commercial matters. Many of our clients are involved in IT and this continues to be an expanding and exciting area of work for the firm. We have a national reputation in the fields of franchising and housing association work, and are a force within the Thames Valley in the area of employment law, handling difficult and high-profile cases.

**Who should apply** We are looking for articulate, bright trainees with academic ability, common sense and initiative. Academic achievement is clearly important, but a strong, interesting personality is also vital. Candidates should be able to demonstrate a general commercial awareness, and an understanding of the business as well as the legal world. Local connections are also helpful. The firm understands that during the training contract, support and encouragement are needed to ensure that you achieve your potential.

**Training programme** The training contract is divided into four six-month seats. Our trainees work closely with partners and solicitors, and receive hands-on training supported by external skills training as required by the Law Society. Trainees will work in a friendly, supportive atmosphere, with a genuine 'first-name terms' and open-door policy. Trainees will find that they are able to work very closely with the partners and are given a sensible level of very real responsibility, while receiving solid and friendly support throughout. We place an emphasis on teamwork at all levels and have a history of retaining our trainees once they qualify; indeed, most of the partners trained with the firm.

**When and how to apply** Applicants should complete the online application form on our website www.owenwhite.com. Please tell us about yourself and explain the contribution you can make and your reasons for choosing Owen White. Apply by 30 September 2008 to begin in 2010.

| | |
|---|---|
| Vacancies | 2 |
| Trainees | 5 |
| Partners | 7 |
| Total staff | 45 |

**Apply to**
Russell Ford

**Starting salary**
£20,000

**Minimum qualifications**
2.1 degree

**Offices**
Slough

OWEN WHITE
SOLICITORS

| | | |
|---|---|---|
| **OSMOND & OSMOND**<br>62-67 Temple Chambers, Temple Avenue,<br>London EC4Y OHP<br>**Tel:** 020 7583 3434<br>**Fax:** 020 7583 4242<br>**Email:** sarah@osmondandosmand.co.uk<br>**Apply to:** Miss Sarah Hastie | | V 0<br>T 2<br>P 2<br>TS 8<br>WP yes |
| **OWEN WHITE AND CATLIN**<br>74 Church Road, Ashford, Middlesex TW15 2TP<br>**Tel:** 01784 254188<br>**Fax:** 01784 257057<br>**Apply to:** Mrs JD Williamson | One of the largest practices covering all aspects of legal work in West London. Progressive and expanding firm and provides a wealth of opportunity for trainees. | V 4<br>T 0<br>P 7<br>TS 90<br>WP no |
| **OXLEY & COWARD**<br>34/46 Moorgate Street, Rotherham,<br>South Yorks S60 2HB<br>**Tel:** 01709 510999<br>**Fax:** 01709 512999<br>**Email:** mailbox@oxcow.co.uk<br>**Apply to:** Mr PW Hedley | An established (1791) franchised high street practice specialising in private, commercial and public funded areas of law with clients both local and national. | V 0<br>T 3<br>P 8<br>TS 80<br>WP yes |
| **OZANNES**<br>PO Box 186, Le Marchant Street, St Peter Port,<br>Channel Islands GY1 4HP<br>**Tel:** 01481 723 466<br>**Fax:** 01481 714 571<br>**Email:** tina.lepoidevin@ozannes.com<br>**Apply to:** Mrs Tina Le Poidevin | Ozannes is Guernsey's premier law firm for specialising in high value off-shore contentious and non-contentious work as well as servicing the local community's need for high street services. | V 1<br>T 2<br>P 13<br>TS 95<br>WP yes |
| **OZORAN TURKAN**<br>203 Green Lanes, Islington, London N16 9DJ<br>**Tel:** 020 7354 0802<br>**Fax:** 020 7704 9121<br>**Email:** ozoranturkan@aol.com<br>**Apply to:** Ms DM Ozoran | Small High Street frachised firm, three partners covering all areas of legal aid. | V 2<br>T 2<br>P 3<br>TS 20<br>WP no |
| **PARABIS LAW LLP**<br>30-36 Monument Street, London EC3R 8NB<br>**Tel:** 0870 084 8200<br>**Fax:** 0870 084 8300<br>**Email:** mail@plexuslaw.uk.com<br>**Apply to:** Ms S Killip | A medium sized insurance litigation practice including including specialisation in personal injury, professional indemnity, clinical negligence, and property work. | V 3[09]<br>T 6<br>P 21<br>TS 263<br>WP no |
| **PARDOES**<br>West Quay House, Northgate, Bridgwater TA6 3HJ<br>**Tel:** 01278 457891<br>**Fax:** 01278 429249<br>**Apply to:** Ms Lorraine Cox | The firm is a general practice, but with a commercial bias operating from a main office in Bridgwater, a new Yeovil Office and a regional motorway office at Taunton. | V 2<br>T 4<br>P 12<br>TS 100<br>WP no |
| **PARKER BULLEN**<br>45 Castle Street, Salisbury SP10 3SS<br>**Tel:** 01722 412 000<br>**Fax:** 01722 411 822<br>**Apply to:** Mr Mark Lello | A leading provider of company commercial, commercial property, litigation and private client services. | V 0<br>T 0<br>P 9<br>TS 66<br>WP no |

**V** = Vacancies / **T** = Trainees / **P** = Partners / **TS** = Total Staff / **WP** = Work Placement

# Palmers

19 Town Square, Basildon, Essex SS14 1BD
**Tel:** 01268 240000
**Fax:** 01268 240001
**Email:** recruitment@palmerslaw.co.uk
**Web:** www.palmerslaw.co.uk

**The firm** Founded in 1983, Palmers is a leading regional law firm providing a wide range of commercial and private client services from its three offices in Essex.

We pride ourselves on providing first class, cost-effective legal solutions to our clients and are highly regarded within the local area.

**Types of work** We have a legal aid franchise, (family & crime), and cover most areas of the law, including company, commercial, litigation, domestic and commercial property, tax, family, criminal, insolvency, employment, probate, wills, trusts & elderly client work. There is additional expertise in intellectual property and licensing.

**Training programme** Our trainee policy is to seek friendly, well-organised and enterprising people who welcome responsibility and who wish to play an active part within the firm. The training contract should be considered as the first period in a long relationship. Trainees usually sit in four seats of six months each across the practice and complete a comprehensive training programme, which includes full induction, attendance at relevant external courses, (including the Professional Skills Course), and regular review meetings with the Training Partner.

**When and how to apply** September 2010 training contracts: applications to be received by 31 July 2008.

September 2009 training contract applications may be submitted up until 31 December 2007.

Applications should be made using the firm's standard application form. This is available on our website; a copy will be posted on request.

**Work placements** 2008 summer work placements (1 July – 30 Sept 2008) – written applications with accompanying CVs to be received by 31 March 2008.

| | |
|---|---|
| Vacancies | 3 |
| Trainees | 5 |
| Partners | 10 |
| Total staff | 116 |

**Work placement** yes

**Apply to**
Mrs G Newman
HR Manager

**Starting salary**
Competitive

**Minimum qualifications**
2.1 degree (not necessarily in law)

**Offices**
Basildon,
South Woodham Ferrers,
Thurrock

**PALMERS**
SOLICITORS

# Pannone LLP

123 Deansgate, Manchester M3 2BU
**Tel:** 0161 909 3000
**Fax:** 0161 909 4444
**Email:** julia.jessop@pannone.co.uk
**Web:** www.pannone.com

**The firm** We are a full-service law firm located in central Manchester which continues to undergo rapid growth. Specialist departments serve a diverse client base which is split almost equally between business and private individuals. We pride ourselves on our ability to work in partnership with our clients and to offer practical and cost-effective solutions, meeting our clients' needs.

Committed to quality and client care, the firm was the first solicitors' practice to be awarded certification to the quality standard ISO 9001 and is a founder member of a European economic interest grouping, Pannone Law Group (although there is no opportunity for trainees to work abroad). The firm has held the Law Society's Lexcel accreditation since 1999 and a number of departments hold legal aid franchises.

Pannone LLP was again voted third in the *Sunday Times* 100 Best Companies to Work For in 2007 and is the highest-placed law firm in the survey.

**Types of work** Trainees at Pannone LLP benefit from the unusually wide range of law practised within the firm. The departments in which trainees will spend their time include corporate and commercial, commercial property, commercial litigation, employment, regulatory, personal injury, clinical negligence, family law, private client and construction. In many of these fields we are recognised as leading practitioners.

**Who should apply** We are a firm with a very distinct personality. We take great pride in providing legal services of the highest calibre, but we are also a very lively firm, and very down to earth. We therefore look for trainees of high academic standard who can organise themselves and others, can work in a team and have a life beyond the law. We are proud of being a Manchester firm and some connection with the North West is preferred. We welcome applications from both law and non-law graduates.

**Training programme** Trainees themselves choose from the above departments to complete four six-month seats. We offer a structured training programme and trainees' progress is closely monitored throughout each of their seats, with an induction programme, lunchtime seminars and departmental training sessions supplementing the main part of the training, which takes place through work in chosen departments. The Professional Skills Course is taken over the two years of the training contract and study leave is given.

**When and how to apply** Online application from November 2007. Closing date 13 July 2008. For September 2010 only.

**Work placements** One-week Easter and summer placements offered. Online application from November 2007. Closing date: 25 January 2008 (Easter), 16 May, 13 June and 13 July (Summer).

Application for training contracts is primarily through vacation placements.

**Sponsorship** Full grant for LPC fees.

Vacancies  14
Trainees  35
Partners  99
Total staff  707

Work placement  yes
*(see Insider Report on p129)*

Apply to
Mrs Julia Jessop

Starting salary
£22,000 (2007)

Minimum qualifications
2.1 degree

Sponsorship
LPC

Offices
Manchester

PANNONE
THE COMPLETE LAW FIRM

# Paris Smith & Randall LLP

1 London Road, Southampton SO15 2AE
**Tel:** 023 80482482
**Fax:** 023 80631835
**Email:** info@parissmith.co.uk
**Web:** www.parissmith.co.uk

**The firm** Paris Smith & Randall LLP is a well-established leading regional firm based in Southampton providing a variety of legal services to commercial, public sector and private clients. Paris Smith & Randall LLP has a reputation for first-class, practical legal advice which has been built over the last 185 years, and is unrivalled in Southampton. Today the firm has 24 LLP partners and employs more than 180 staff, including 72 lawyers and six trainees.

**Types of work** The main areas of the firm's work are in corporate and private client services. Paris Smith & Randall LLP's corporate services include commercial property, licensing, commercial litigation, company/commercial work, employment, public sector housing, secured lending and property litigation. Private client services consist of residential conveyancing, tax and estate planning, family, employment advice and personal litigation.

**Who should apply** Paris Smith & Randall LLP welcomes applications from law and non-law graduates with a strong academic background and at least a 2.2 honours degree. Applicants should have good commercial awareness, common sense and be able to demonstrate excellent communication skills. Creativity is encouraged, as well as initiative. Paris Smith & Randall LLP has a friendly and supportive environment and teamwork skills are essential. Trainees are regarded very much as the future of Paris Smith & Randall LLP and the firm is keen for trainees to remain as assistants after qualification and seeks highly motivated, loyal applicants with drive and ambition.

**Training programme** The training with Paris Smith & Randall LLP is flexible and is aimed to provide a balanced and practical grounding prior to qualification. The starting point is to spend six months in each seat, but this can be changed should the trainee wish to experience more seats during the contract. A special or particular interest in any field can be accommodated. Most trainees will do a seat in commercial property and company/commercial and litigation (whether it be commercial, personal, employment or family). Trainees receive three-monthly appraisals with their immediate supervisor (usually the head of department), and have monthly meetings with the training principal.

There is also a strong emphasis on acheiving a work/life balance. The active social committee arranges several events each year. The culture within the firm is friendly, relaxed and supportive.

**When and how to apply** By 31 July 2008 to begin 2010. Please send a CV and covering letter to Susie Warwick via post or email.

| | |
|---|---|
| Vacancies | 3 |
| Trainees | 6 |
| Partners | 24 |
| Total staff | 180 |

**Work placement**   yes

**Apply to**
Susie Warwick

**Minimum qualifications**
2.2 degree

**Offices**
Southampton

PARIS SMITH & RANDALL LLP
SOLICITORS

# Paul Hastings

8th Floor, Ten Bishops Sqaure, London E1 6EG
**Tel:** 020 3020 5204
**Fax:** 020 3020 5399
**Email:** melaniedamecourt@paulhastings.com
**Web:** www.paulhastings.com

**The firm** With 1,200 attorneys serving clients from 18 worldwide offices, Paul Hastings provides a full range of services to clients around the globe. We have established long standing partnerships with many of the world's top financial institutions, Fortune 500 companies and other leading corporations. We help clients anticipate market evolutions in order to create market advantage. Paul Hastings represents and advises clients across a full range of practices, industries and regions.

**Types of work** Paul Hastings's principal practice areas in London are corporate, finance, employment, real estate, tax and litigation.

**Who should apply** There is no such thing as a 'typical' Paul Hastings lawyer. We seek individuals with a wide variety of skills, who combine intellectual ability with enthusiasm, creativity and a demonstrable ability to thrive in a challenging environment. In addition, we expect you to show initiative and a willingness to make a positive contribution to the firm as a whole. People never thrive as individuals at Paul Hastings, only when they advance the common interest. When filling in the application form you should seek to demonstrate that you possess those qualities. We are looking for individuals with distinguished academic credentials. We expect candidates to have high level of achievement both at A level (or equivalent) and degree level. This would normally mean an upper second or first class degree and a majority of A grades at A level.

**Training programme** Our position as a leading international firm is built on our ability to understand, manage and complete transactions by drawing upon resources of our globally integrated practice areas. Our state-of-art telecommunications infrastructure links each of the Paul Hastings offices to the others and to our clients, facilitating the coordination of our transaction teams around the world.

We will provide you with a first class training and development programme, combining on-the-job training and various professional courses. We will monitor your progress on a formal and informal basis to ensure you receive ongoing training and have the opportunity to give feedback on the programme itself and on those areas that you consider are of most interest to you. Our trainee solicitors will spend time in four seats, including banking, corporate, employment, litigation, real estate, and tax. We recruit both law and non-law graduates.

**When and how to apply** Applicants should complete the online application form at www.paulhastings.com/Offices_London.aspx where you will also find details of application deadlines.

**Work placements** Formal two week placements available in July.

**Sponsorship** Full fees for LPC plus a maintenance grant whilst you are studying.

| | |
|---|---|
| Vacancies | 4 |
| Trainees | 8 |
| Partners | 10 |
| Total staff | 70 |

**Work placement** yes

**Apply to**
Mrs Melanie D'Amecourt

**Starting salary**
1st year: £40,000
2nd year: £45,000

**Minimum qualifications**
2.1 degree

**Sponsorship**
LPC

**Offices**
London

Paul*Hastings*

## PARKER RHODES
14 & 22 Moorgate Street, Rotherham,
South Yorks S60 2DA
**Tel:** 01709 511100
**Fax:** 01709 371917
**Email:** joyoddy@parker-rhodes.co.uk
**Apply to:** Mrs J Oddy

A leading general practice high street firm in the Rotherham area.

| | |
|---|---|
| V | 0 |
| T | 2 |
| P | 5 |
| TS | 49 |
| WP | no |

## PAUL NORTON & CO
154-156 Marsh Road, Leagrave, Luton LU3 2QL
**Tel:** 01582 494 970
**Fax:** 01582 494 854
**Email:** pnorton@pnac.co.uk
**Apply to:** Mr Allan Meek

Paul Norton & Co Solicitors is a dynamic, forward-thinking practice. Successful applicants are trained to be good solicitors in a friendly but challenging work environment.

| | |
|---|---|
| V | Poss |
| T | 1 |
| P | 1 |
| TS | 10 |
| WP | no |

## PAUL ROBINSON SOLICITORS
The Old Bank, 470/474 London Road,
Westcliff SS0 9LD
**Tel:** 01702 338338
**Fax:** 01702 354032
**Email:** info@paulrobinson.co.uk
**Apply to:** The Partnership Secretary

Established 1983. General practice undertaking all areas of law. Investor in people. Lexcel.

| | |
|---|---|
| V | 1[08] |
| T | 2 |
| P | 7 |
| TS | 70 |
| WP | no |

## PAYNE HICKS BEACH
10 New Square, Lincoln's Inn, London WC2A 3QG
**Tel:** 020 7465 4300
**Fax:** 020 7465 4400
**Email:** lstoten@phb.co.uk
**Apply to:** Miss Louise Stoten

A well known Inns of Court law firm which has particular expertise in private client and family law, and a good reputation in many corporate and commercial areas.

| | |
|---|---|
| V | 3 |
| T | 5 |
| P | 29 |
| TS | 140 |
| WP | no |

## PEARSON HINCHLIFFE
31 Queen Street, Oldham OL1 1RD
**Tel:** 0161 785 3500
**Fax:** 0161 624 2589
**Apply to:** Ms Joanne Ormston

| | |
|---|---|
| V | 2[08] |
| T | 5 |
| P | 10 |
| TS | 63 |
| WP | no |

## PEARSON MADDIN
Fountain House, 2 Kingston Road, New Malden,
Surrey KT3 3LR
**Tel:** 020 8949 9500
**Fax:** 020 8949 8011
**Apply to:** Mr Stewart Graham

A city firm in the suburbs without city prices. We offer a range of seats in commercial and private client areas.

| | |
|---|---|
| V | 1 |
| T | 2 |
| P | 5 |
| TS | 49 |
| WP | no |

## PEMBERTON GREENISH
45 Pont Street, London SW1X 0BX
**Tel:** 020 7591 3333
**Fax:** 020 7591 3300
**Email:** c.hall@pglaw.co.uk
**Apply to:** Ms Charlotte Hall

A niche practice specialising in property, including leasehold reform and collective enfranchisement and private client, plus related litigation and company commercial work.

| | |
|---|---|
| V | 2 |
| T | 4 |
| P | 14 |
| TS | 65 |
| WP | no |

## PENLEYS LLP
26 Long Street, Dursley, Gloucestershire GL11 4JA
**Tel:** 01453 541940
**Fax:** 01453 548527
**Email:** info@penleys.co.uk
**Apply to:** Mr David Knight

Private client practice: franchises for PI, mental health and family. Small market town. Wide variety of work. Excellent client base.

| | |
|---|---|
| V | 0 |
| T | 1 |
| P | 4 |
| TS | 23 |
| WP | no |

# Penningtons Solicitors LLP

Abacus House, 33 Gutter Lane, London EC2V 8AR
**Tel:** 020 7457 3000
**Fax:** 020 7457 3240
**Email:** trainingpost@penningtons.co.uk
**Web:** www.penningtons.co.uk

**The firm** Penningtons Solicitors LLP is a thriving, modern law firm with a 200-year history and a deep commitment to top-quality, partner-led legal services. Today, we're based in London and the Southeast with offices in London, Basingstoke, Godalming and Newbury. We advise on most areas of law, from personal injury claims to commercial property transactions to family trusts. Our main divisions are: business services, private individuals and commercial property. We know our trainee solicitors are happiest and most successful when busy with good-quality work. We believe in introducing trainees to challenging cases. We recognise the value of giving our trainees responsibility and allowing direct contact with clients. However, our experienced solicitors are always ready to give support when needed.

**Types of work** In the business sphere, we advise on matters relating to all aspects of commercial property, intellectual property, management buy-outs and buy-ins, mergers, acquisitions and joint ventures, as well as dispute resolution. We advise on information technology, business recovery, commercial contracts, agricultural and environmental law, and offer company secretarial services. We help families and individuals with advice on property, tax and estate planning, family law, general financial management, the administration of wills and trusts, charities, personal injury, clinical negligence and immigration. Many of our clients ask Penningtons to advise on both their private and commercial affairs.

**Who should apply** We seek high-calibre candidates with enthusiasm and resilience. A high standard of academic achievement is expected: three or more good A level passes and preferably a 2.1 or better at degree level, whether you are reading law or another discipline. Clarity of expression, written and oral, and reliability in research are important to us. There should be mental flair and flexibility. On the personal side, we look for enthusiasm and resilience (an ability to remain calm even if the client doesn't); self-confidence without arrogance; openness with discretion; a good team spirit; and, above all, integrity. We want people who will develop and assume comfortably the advisory role of a solicitor.

**Training programme** You will be given a thorough grounding in the law, spending time in the various areas of the firm's main divisions. We ensure a varied training is given, avoiding too specialised an approach before qualification. Nonetheless, the experience gained in each department gives you a solid foundation, equipping you to embark on your chosen specialisation at the end of your training contract with us. Our training programme includes in-house seminars covering specific areas of law as well as practical skills and the fostering of commercial awareness. Your time with us begins with an induction course to introduce you to the firm's main departments and office and accounting procedures. Thereafter, throughout the year, there are regular lectures and work sessions specifically for trainees. Additionally, the Professional Skills Course is provided.

**When and how to apply** Apply between 1 December 2007 and 31 July 2008 to begin in September 2010. Apply online via the recruitment section of our website at www.penningtons.co.uk.

**Work placement** Summer vacation scheme plus information days in the summer.

**Sponsorship** Full LPC fees plus a maintenance grant of £4,500.

| | |
|---|---|
| Vacancies | 14 |
| Trainees | 27 |
| Partners | 66 |
| Total staff | 420 |

**Work placement** yes

**Apply to**
Andrea Law

**Minimum qualifications**
2.1 degree preferred

**Sponsorship**
LPC

**Offices**
London, Basingstoke, Godalming, Newbury

**PENNINGTONS**
SOLICITORS

# Pinsent Masons

Citypoint, 1 Ropemaker Street, London EC2Y 9AH
**Tel:** 0845 300 3232
**Email:** graduate@pinsentmasons.com
**Web:** www.pinsentmasons.com/graduate

**The firm** Pinsent Masons is a top 15 UK law firm that is committed to sector-focused growth through its core sectors approach. This approach aligns the firm to specific business sectors to achieve market-leading positions. As a result, the firm has developed a successful and innovative approach to building strong corporate relationships. Offering a comprehensive range of services, the firm works with a substantial range of FTSE 100, FTSE 250, Fortune 500 and AIM quoted organisations, and public sector clients.

Internationally, Pinsents Masons has offices in Beijing, Brussels, Dubai, Hong Kong and Shanghai, as well as strategic alliances with firms in Austria, Czech Republic, Denmark, Dubai, Estonia, France, Germany, Holland, Hungary, India, Lithuania, Poland, Slovakia, Spain, Sweden and the USA.

**Types of work** The firm offers depth, scope and opportunity for its trainees in a culture of early responsibility and high-quality work. The firm's sector-based approach to business growth offers trainees a chance to get wide exposure to key industries as well as developing specialist legal expertise. Main areas of work include: banking & finance, corporate, dispute resolution & litigation, employment, insurance & reinsurance, international construction & energy, outsourcing, technology and commercial, pensions, projects, property, tax and UK construction & engineering.

**Who should apply** The firm welcomes applications from both law and non-law graduates. In addition to a strong academic background, the firm is looking for people who can combine a sharp mind with commercial acumen and strong people skills to work in partnership with their clients' businesses.

**Training programme** Trainees sit in four seats of six months across the practices, and are supervised by partners or associates. There are also opportunities for trainees to be seconded to clients. There is a supportive team culture, with early responsibility and contact with clients encouraged.

In addition to the training required by the Law Societies, the firm offers a broad-ranging and custom-made training programme designed to deliver superb technical and management skills that link with the needs of the business. This is the first stage in the firm's focused development programme that supports individuals on the route to partnership.

The firm has an open-door policy and informal atmosphere with a positive focus on work-life balance.

**When and how to apply** In England, by 31 July 2008 to begin September 2010/March 2011. In Scotland, by 21 October 2008 to begin September 2009. Applications are only accepted via the online application form at www.pinsentmasons.com/graduate.

**Work placements** 130 summer vacation schemes offered (two weeks' duration). Deadline for applications is 31 January 2008.

**Sponsorship** In England, full sponsorship is offered for the CPE and LPC fees, as well as a maintenance grant. In Scotland, financial assistance is offered for Diploma fees, together with a maintenance grant.

| | |
|---|---|
| Vacancies | 55 |
| Trainees | 112 |
| Partners | 260 |
| Total staff | 1500 |

Work placement    yes

Apply
Online

Starting salary
£30,000 - London (2006)
under review

Minimum qualifications
2.1 degree, any subject and
300 (24) UCAS points

Sponsorship
CPE & LPC (England)
Diploma fees (Scotland)

Offices
London, Birmingham,
Bristol, Edinburgh, Glasgow,
Leeds, Manchester

Pinsent Masons

# Piper Smith Watton LLP

31 Warwick Square, London SW1V 2AF
**Tel:** 020 7828 8000
**Fax:** 020 7828 8008
**Web:** www.pswlaw.co.uk

**The firm** Piper Smith Watton LLP is a progressive, forward thinking practice providing a broad range of specialist services for its commercial and private clients. PSW provides all of the capabilities and expertise associated with a larger firm but in a more personalised environment.

**Types of work** The firm is particularly well known for its commercial property work, including specialist retail services. Additionally the firm has a strong reputation within the travel industry. Corporate, litigation and private client departments (including family) ensure the firm's clients have access to a broad range of services.

**Who should apply** Individuals who have a strong academic record and a well rounded profile. We are keen to recruit trainees who have a keen interest in our practice, our business disciplines and our clients and can demonstrate their enthusiasm and abilities in contributing to the firm's success.

**Training programme** Four six-month seats in any of the following departments: corporate, commercial property, private client, litigation, family, travel.

**When and how to apply** Application form and details available on website. Apply by 1 December 2007 to begin training contracts in October 2008 and April 2009.

**Work placements** See website for details.

| | |
|---|---|
| Vacancies | 2 |
| Trainees | 4 |
| Partners | 8 |
| Total staff | 50 |

**Work placement** yes

**Apply to**
Graduate Recruitment

**Starting salary**
1st year - £22,000
2nd year - £24,000

**Minimum qualifications**
2.2 degree

**Offices**
London

PIPER ■ SMITH
WATTON   LLP

## PETER BROWN & CO
1st Floor, Comer House, 19 Station Road,
New Barnet, Herts EN5 1QJ
**Tel:** 020 8447 3277
**Fax:** 020 8447 3282
**Email:** info@peterbrown-solicitors.com
**Apply to:** Ms Fiona Brown

We are based in New Barnet and specialise in commercial and residential property and probate. Nearly all our work is from established clients or their recommendations.

| | |
|---|---|
| V | 0 |
| T | 1 |
| P | 3 |
| TS | 15 |
| WP | no |

## PETER SCAIFF LLP
23 Foregate Street, Worcester WR1 1UW
**Tel:** 01905 27505
**Fax:** 01905 29038
**Email:** mail@scaiff.co.uk
**Apply to:** Mr Peter Scaiff

General practice with emphasis on company commercial and litigation particularly personal injury and medical negligence.

| | |
|---|---|
| V | 1 |
| T | 1 |
| P | 5 |
| TS | 17 |
| WP | no |

## PETERS & PETERS
15 Fetter Lane, London EC4A 1BW
**Tel:** 020 7822 7777
**Fax:** 020 7822 7788
**Email:** law@petersandpeters.com
**Apply to:** Ms Jennifer Ansary

Practice recognised as a market leader in international and domestic commercial fraud, encompassing commercial / civil litigation and fraud and regulatory work. Highly recommended by leading directories.

| | |
|---|---|
| V | 2 |
| T | 4 |
| P | 12 |
| TS | 70 |
| WP | no |

## PHILLIPS
6 Wood Street, Mansfield,
Nottinghamshire NG18 1QA
**Tel:** 01623 658556
**Fax:** 01623 427530
**Apply to:** Mr Mark Marriott

Growing practice with contracts in criminal and family law. Aims to serve working class people with high quality and a smile.

| | |
|---|---|
| V | 0-1 |
| T | 2 |
| P | 2 |
| TS | 9 |
| WP | no |

## PICKERINGS SOLICITORS LLP
Etchell House, Etchell Court, Bonehill Road,
Tamworth, Staffs B78 3HQ
**Tel:** 01827 317070
**Fax:** 01827 317080
**Email:** recruitment@pickerings-solicitors.com
**Apply to:** Ms Sue Hatton

| | |
|---|---|
| V | 1 |
| T | 1 |
| P | 4 |
| TS | 33 |
| WP | no |

## PICTONS
28 Dunstable Road, Luton, Bedfordshire LU1 1DY
**Tel:** 01582 878544
**Fax:** 01582 878545
**Email:** yvonne.hardiman@pictons.co.uk
**Apply to:** Ms Yvonne Hardiman

Progressive practice with offices in Hemel Hempstead, Luton and Millton Keynes. Applications for training contracts are invited between 1 April & 31 July two years in advance.

| | |
|---|---|
| V | 6 |
| T | 6 |
| P | 15 |
| TS | 160 |
| WP | no |

## PITMANS
47 Castle Street, Reading RG1 7SR
**Tel:** 0118 958 0224
**Fax:** 0118 958 5097
**Email:** sobrien@pitmans.com
**Apply to:** Ms Susan O'Brien

Strong commercial practice in Thames Valley serving wide range of large and medium-sized corporate clients in commercial, property, litigation, intellectual property and various niche areas.

| | |
|---|---|
| V | 6 |
| T | 10 |
| P | 28 |
| TS | 210 |
| WP | yes |

## PJE SOLICITORS
115 Broadway, Pontypridd,
Rhondda Cynon Taf CF37 1BE
**Tel:** 01443 408647
**Fax:** 01443 493580
**Email:** mleyshon@pjesolicitors.co.uk
**Apply to:** Mr Mark David Leyshon

Well established firm. Strong litigation, employment, matrimonial and conveyancing client base. Aim to expand. 20 minutes from Cardiff. General practice serving valleys and city.

| | |
|---|---|
| V | 0-1 |
| T | 1 |
| P | 2 |
| TS | 10 |
| WP | no |

# Prettys

Elm House, 25 Elm Street, Ipswich IP1 2AD
**Tel:** 01473 232121
**Fax:** 01473 230002
**Email:** agage@prettys.co.uk
**Web:** www.prettys.co.uk

**The firm** Prettys is one of the largest and most successful legal practices in East Anglia. The firm is at the heart of the East Anglian business community, with the expanding high-technology corridor between Ipswich and Cambridge to the west, the UK's largest container port, Felixstowe, to the east and the City of London just 60 minutes away to the south. Our lawyers are approachable and pragmatic. We provide expert advice to national and regional businesses.

Prettys also has offices in Chelmsford. The firm is currently moving to larger premises in Chelmsford as it continues to expand. It provides an even closer link to London.

**Types of work** Our broad-based practice allows us to offer a full service to all our clients – corporate and private.

Business law services: company, commercial, shipping, transport, construction, intellectual property, information technology, property, property litigation, employment, insurance, professional indemnity, health and safety, work permits for executives.

Personal law services: French property, personal injury, clinical negligence, financial services, estates, conveyancing, family.

**Who should apply** Prettys' trainees are the future of the firm. Applicants should be able to demonstrate a desire to pursue a career in East Anglia. Trainees are given considerable responsibility early on and we are therefore looking for candidates who are well-motivated, enthusiastic and have a good commonsense approach. IT skills are essential.

**Training programme** A two-week induction programme will introduce you to the firm. Thereafter you will receive continuous supervision and three-monthly reviews. Training is in four six-month seats, with some choice in your second year. Trainees work closely with a partner, meeting clients and becoming involved in all aspects of the department's work. Frequent training seminars are provided in-house.

The Law Society's monitoring of training officer recently visited the firm and concluded: "Prettys offers a very strong commitment to training within a supportive environment."

**When and how to apply** Apply by 15 August 2008 to begin September 2010. Applicants should send in an application letter and CV by post or email.

| | |
|---|---|
| Vacancies | 6 |
| Trainees | 12 |
| Partners | 15 |
| Total staff | 140 |

**Work placement** yes

**Apply to**
Angela Gage

**Starting salary**
Above Law Society guidelines

**Minimum qualifications**
2.1 degree preferred in law or other relevant subject. Good A levels

**Offices**
Ipswich, Chelmsford

# PricewaterhouseCoopers Legal LLP

1 Embankment Place, London WC2N 6DX
**Tel:** 020 7212 1616
**Fax:** 020 7212 1570
**Web:** www.pwclegal.co.uk

**The firm** PricewaterhouseCoopers Legal LLP (formerly Landwell) is a member of the PricewaterhouseCoopers international network of firms. It is a niche law firm with close working relationships with the business specialisms of PricewaterhouseCoopers LLP ("PwC") as well as network firms across the world, giving the firm access to over 2,000 legal professionals in 40 countries.

The firm delivers services through key divisions including areas of specialisation such as corporate restructuring, M&A and private equity work, intellectual property, IT, employment, immigration, pensions, financial services, banking, commercial contracts, real estate and litigation (commercial and tax). Depending on the transaction type, the firm's lawyers work either on a domestic standalone basis or as part of a wider team of company lawyers from the international network. Its strong working relationship with PwC also enables its lawyers additionally to work in multi-competency teams of business advisers delivering complete solutions to a variety of complex business problems.

Clients include local, national and multinational companies; partnerships and LLPs; governments; and financial institutions. The firm recognises that today's lawyers must adapt to the changing needs of clients and must offer more than just legal services. By adopting a multi-disciplinary approach working alongside experts within PwC, solutions are not pigeon-holed under the disciplines of accountancy, tax and law, and PricewaterhouseCoopers Legal LLP (through its relationship with PwC) provides its clients with a single seamless offering of legal, tax and consultancy expertise. A diverse workforce enhances creativity and PricewaterhouseCoopers Legal LLP strives to achieve and maintain diversity throughout the firm.

**Who should apply** The firm wants to see applicants with a genuine interest in business law and the ambition to be part of a new model of legal practice. In return, it offers you something unique. The firm's relationship with PwC means you will work alongside experts in PwC as part of a multi-disciplinary team which differentiates PricewaterhouseCoopers Legal LLP from the majority of existing law firms. While the quality of the work and the excellence of the training can match those of any traditional law firm, the lawyers at PricewaterhouseCoopers Legal LLP spend a significant part of their time working alongside clients and other professionals as part of a unique approach to the provision of integrated business services.

**Training programme** A formal induction programme will introduce you to the firm. You will receive continuous supervision and three-monthly reviews. Training is in four six-month seats.

**When and how to apply** Complete our online application form at www.pwclegal.co.uk. Deadlines are as follows: 31 July 2008 for trainees starting in 2010; 31 March 2008 for the summer vacation programme in 2008.

**Work placements** The firm runs a summer vacation programme for two weeks in June and July, for which they welcome quality applications.

**Sponsorship** Trainee lawyers joining the firm are eligible to apply for a scholarship award to assist with the costs of the Graduate Diploma in Law Course and the Legal Practice Course. If successful, you will receive the total cost of the tuition and examination fees (from the date of signing your contract) and also a significant contribution towards your living expenses. More details can be found on the firm's website.

| | |
|---|---|
| Vacancies | 9 |
| Trainees | 12 |
| Partners | 13 |
| Total staff | 135 |

**Work placement** yes

**Apply**
Online

**Minimum qualifications**
280 UCAS points or equivalent
2.1 degree or equivalent

**Offices**
London

PRICEWATERHOUSE COOPERS LEGAL

# Pritchard Englefield

14 New Street, London EC2M 4HE
**Tel:** 020 7972 9720
**Fax:** 020 7972 9722
**Email:** wmorgan@pe-legal.com
**Web:** www.pe-legal.com

**The firm** A medium-sized City firm practising a mix of general commercial and non-commercial law with many German and French clients as well as clients based in North America and in the Far East. In addition to its strong commercial departments, the firm also undertakes family, personal injury and private client work, and is known for its strong international flavour.

**Types of work** All main areas of commercial practice including litigation, company commercial, corporate (including AIM and full listings) and banking (UK, German, French), employment, property, estates and trusts, personal injury and family. The firm acts for a range of clients, from large multinationals to small and medium-sized businesses as well as private individuals.

**Who should apply** We are looking for high academic achievers with either German or French as a second language.

**Training programme** An induction course acquaints trainees with the computer network, library and administrative procedures, and there is a formal in-house training programme. Four six-month seats make up most of your training. You can usually choose some departments and you could spend two six-month periods in the same seat. Over two years, you learn advocacy, negotiating, drafting and interviewing, attend court, use your language skills and meet clients. Occasional talks and seminars explain the work of the firm, and you can air concerns at bi-monthly lunches with the partners comprising the Trainee Panel. The Professional Skills Course is taken externally over two years. Quarterly drinks parties number among popular social events.

**When and how to apply** By 31 July 2008 to begin 2010. Apply online via www.pe-legal.com or complete an application form. Application packs can be obtained from Ms Wendy Morgan.

**Work placements** Two weeks, unpaid, summer only. Applicants must be fluent in German and/or French. Applications to be received between January and March. Please contact Ian Silverblatt (isilverblatt@pe-legal.com) enclosing a copy of your CV.

**Sponsorship** Full funding for LPC fees.

| | |
|---|---|
| Vacancies | 3-4 |
| Trainees | 6 |
| Partners | 23 |
| Total staff | 83 |

**Work placement** yes

**Apply to**
Wendy Morgan

**Starting salary**
Market rate

**Minimum qualifications**
2.1 degree plus fluent
German and/or French

**Sponsorship**
LPC

**Offices**
London

PRITCHARD ENGLEFIELD
SOLICITORS

| | | V/T/P/TS/WP |
|---|---|---|
| **PORTER DODSON**<br>Central House, Church Street, Yeovil,<br>Somerset BA20 1HH<br>**Tel:** 01935 424581<br>**Fax:** 01935 706063<br>**Email:** porterdodson@porter-dodson.co.uk<br>**Apply to:** Mrs Brenda Sherring | Expanding general practice working in specialist teams covering commercial (contentious and non-contentious) litigation, private client and property. Six offices in Somerset and Dorset. | V Poss[09]<br>T 6<br>P 25<br>TS 170<br>WP no |
| **PORTNER AND JASKEL LLP**<br>63-65 Marylebone Lane, London W1U 2RA<br>**Tel:** 020 7616 5300<br>**Fax:** 020 7935 0500<br>**Email:** info@portnerandjaskel.com<br>**Apply to:** Mr Mitchell Griver | Deals primarily with complex and interesting work providing a personalised service to substantial clients. Niche is commercial property, with fast expanding personal injury and clinical negligence departments. | V 1<br>T 1<br>P 7<br>TS 80<br>WP no |
| **POTHECARY WITHAM WELD**<br>70 St George's Square, London SW1V 3RD<br>**Tel:** 020 7821 8211<br>**Fax:** 020 7630 6484<br>**Email:** info@pwwsolicitors.co.uk<br>**Apply to:** Mrs A Lever | Main areas are charities (mostly RC) and individuals. Work covered includes company and commercial, residential and business property, trusts, wills, probate, civil litigation, employment and education. | V 2[08]<br>T 4<br>P 8<br>TS 48<br>WP no |
| **POWELL SPENCER & PARTNERS**<br>290 Kilburn High Road, London NW6 2DB<br>**Tel:** 020 7604 5600<br>**Fax:** 020 7328 1221<br>**Email:** enquiries@psplaw.co.uk<br>**Apply to:** Diana Du Bruyn | We are a litigation practice specialising in crime, family law, personal injury, clinical negligence, welfare rights, immigration and housing | V Poss 2<br>T 6<br>P 7<br>TS 75<br>WP yes |
| **PREMIER SOLICITORS LLP**<br>Mayfair House, 11 Lurke Street,<br>Bedford MK40 3HZ<br>**Tel:** 01234 358080<br>**Fax:** 01234 348112<br>**Apply to:** Mr Sunil Kambli | Main areas are commercial property, conveyancing, wills, probate, trusts, tax planning, company commercial, employment and notary services. | V 2<br>T -<br>P 3<br>TS 7<br>WP no |
| **THE PROJECTS PARTNERSHIP LIMITED**<br>53 Great Suffolk Street, London SE1 0DB<br>**Tel:** 020 7620 0888<br>**Fax:** 020 7620 0778<br>**Apply to:** Mr Graham Burns | Small niche firm specialising in public-private partnerships, PFI/projects, outsourcing and commercial contracts. Candidates should have an interest in this area. No contentious experience offered. | V Poss<br>T 3<br>P 3<br>TS 15<br>WP no |
| **PRYCE & CO**<br>6-8 East Street, Helen Street, Abingdon,<br>Oxfordshire OX14 5EW<br>**Tel:** 01235 523411<br>**Fax:** 01235 533283<br>**Email:** pryce.ab@virgin.net<br>**Apply to:** Mr Stuart Capel | Long established local practice with offices in both Abingdon and Wantage offering general practice with strong departments in agriculture and probate and trust work and LSC family franchise. | V 0-1[09]<br>T 1<br>P 1<br>TS 18<br>WP no |
| **PUNATAR & CO**<br>32 Junction Road, London N19 5RE<br>**Tel:** 020 7272 3330<br>**Fax:** 020 7272 3331<br>**Email:** lawyers@punatar.biz<br>**Apply to:** Ms Pritam Anand | Young, expanding firm involved primarily in publicly funded work, committed to providing high quality advice and representation. The firm is a member of the specialist fraud panel | V Varies<br>T 6<br>P 5<br>TS 24<br>WP yes |

# RadcliffesLeBrasseur

5 Great College Street, Westminster, London SW1P 3SJ
**Tel:** 020 7222 7040
**Fax:** 020 7222 6208
**Email:** gradrec@rlb-law.com
**Web:** www.rlb-law.com

**The firm** RadcliffesLeBrasseur combines traditional values of integrity and prompt response with a client-focused approach to everything it does. It has a wide and varied client base which includes healthcare services providers, public and private companies, property companies, charities, banks, institutions, public authorities and private individuals.

**Types of work** The firm is organised into departments and experts within them integrate their knowledge in the firm's specialist market-facing groups: health, corporate (including litigation), property, charities, tax and private client.

**Who should apply** Its aim is to recruit trainee solicitors who have a real prospect of becoming future partners. The firm seeks not just academic but also extracurricular activities, self-confidence, determination and a sense of humour.

**Training programme** All trainees are introduced to the firm with a full induction week.

If your training contract is in the London office, your two-year training is split into four six-month seats, three of which will be spent in one of the following departments: corporate, property, healthcare, litigation and dispute resolution, and tax and private client. Your fourth seat may be in one of the specialist departments such as residential property, employment or family law.

If your training contract is in the Leeds office, your two-year training is split into two 12-month seats. You will of course receive the necessary balance between contentious and non-contentious work, with the seats being in our property and healthcare departments.

We do not offer training contracts in our Cardiff office.

During training you will be encouraged to keep up to date on recent legal developments. Internal seminars are organised on a departmental basis as well as across the firm, and all trainees are expected to attend these as well as to contribute by formulating questions, giving briefings and encouraging legal debate among their colleagues. RadcliffesLeBrasseur has an excellent intranet with access to comprehensive and up-to-date legal sites which further assist you in keeping up to date with legal developments.

**When and how to apply** Closing date for our London-based training contracts is 31 July 2008 for contracts to commence September 2010. Apply by CV and covering letter. For further information, please contact graduate recruitment on gradrec@rlb-law.com. Applications for our Leeds-based training contracts are accepted between November 2007 and March 2008 for our intake in September 2009. Please send your CV and covering letter to our Westminster address.

**Work placements** (London only) Summer (June-September). Places for 2008: 12. Duration: two weeks. Remuneration: none. Closing date: 31 March 2008.

**Sponsorship** LPC fees.

| | |
|---|---|
| Vacancies | 5 |
| Trainees | 8 |
| Partners | 42 |
| Total staff | 210 |

**Work placement** yes

**Apply to**
Graduate Recruitment
c/o Human Resources

**Minimum qualifications**
2.1 degree

**Sponsorship**
LPC

**Offices**
London, Leeds, Cardiff

RadcliffesLeBrasseur

# Reed Smith Richards Butler LLP

Beaufort House, 15 St Botolph Street, London EC3A 7EE
**Tel:** 020 7247 6555
**Fax:** 020 7247 5091
**Email:** graduate.recruitment@reedsmith.com
**Web:** www.reedsmith.com

**The firm** Key to our success is our ability to build lasting relationships: with clients and with each other. United through a culture defined by commitment to professional development, team-work, diversity, pro bono and community support, we have grown to become one of the 15 largest law firms in the world. Our 21 offices span three continents and include almost 700 people in London and Birmingham (that's around 20% of our global presence). Our offices benefit from an international framework, but each one retains key elements of the local business culture.

Since 2001 we have enjoyed tremendous growth – we have more than doubled the size of our worldwide team of lawyers and in the same period trebled our revenue. Our international expansion continues to be dramatic and opens up increasing opportunities for our lawyers.

**Types of work** We are particularly well known for our work advising leading companies in the areas of financial services, life sciences, shipping, energy, trade and commodities, advertising, technology and media. We provide a wide range of commercial legal services for all these clients, including a full spectrum of corporate, commercial and financial services, dispute resolution, real estate and employment. Much of our work is multi-jurisdictional.

**Who should apply** We're looking for individuals with the drive and potential to become a world-class business lawyers. We want 'players' rather than 'onlookers' with a strong intellect, initiative, the ability to thrive in a challenging profession and the personal qualities to build strong relationships with colleagues and clients.

**Training programme** We offer a four-seat programme in which trainees are able to exercise much influence over the choice and timings of seats. There are many opportunities for secondments to clients and our overseas offices. Trainees also benefit from being able to take a wide range of courses in our award-winning corporate university, developed in partnership with the highly rated, Wharton School of the University of Pennsylvania. We have 30 vacancies for training contracts commencing in August 2010 and February 2011.

**When and how to apply** By 31 July 2008, for training contracts commencing in August 2010 and February 2011. Apply online via our website.

**Work placements** Our summer vacation programme allows delegates to spend two weeks in a department of their choice. In addition to shadowing associates and partners in the team, delegates participate in bespoke training sessions and practical exercises to build their skills and knowledge. They also enjoy a number of social events arranged for the group. We offer up to 40 places each year to applicants who will, on arrival, have completed at least two years of undergraduate study.

**Sponsorship** We pay for course fees and provide financial assistance for the LPC and GDL.

| | |
|---|---|
| Vacancies | 32 |
| Trainees | 57 |
| Partners | 108 |
| Total staff | 664 |
| (UK figures) | |

**Work placement** yes
*(see Insider Report on p131)*

**Apply to**
Mark Matthews

**Starting salary**
£30,000

**Minimum qualifications**
2.1 degree

**Sponsorship**
GDL/LPC

**Offices**
Abu Dhabi, Birmingham, Century City, Chicago, Dubai, London, Los Angeles, Munich, New York, Newark, Northern VA, Paris, Philadelphia, Piraeus, Pittsburgh, Richmond, San Francisco, Washington DC, Wilmington

**ReedSmith**
**Richards Butler**

## PUNCH ROBSON
35 Albert Road, Middlesbrough TS1 1NU
**Tel:** 01642 230700
**Fax:** 01642 353748
**Email:** disputes@punchrobson.co.uk
**Apply to:** Mr G Tyler

We are an ambitious, good quality firm acting for many substantial local commercial property and private clients. We also have both family and mental health specialist practitioners.

| | |
|---|---|
| V | 1-2[09] |
| T | 3 |
| P | 10 |
| TS | 50 |
| WP | no |

## R L EDWARDS SOLICITORS LTD
20/23 Nolton Street, Bridgend CF31 1DU
**Tel:** 01656 656861
**Fax:** 01656 668190
**Email:** bridgend.office@rledwards-partners.co.uk
**Apply to:** Mr JN Lewis

General practice serving the locality of the former County of Mid Glamorgan. Specialise in child care, mental health, personal injury, crime, housing, debt and welfare benefit.

| | |
|---|---|
| V | 1 |
| T | 2 |
| P | 6 |
| TS | 65 |
| WP | no |

## RATCLIFFE DUCE & GAMMER
49 & 51 London Street, Reading RG1 4PS
**Tel:** 0118 957 4291
**Fax:** 0118 939 3143
**Apply to:** Mrs Sarah Benfield

Long established legal aid franchised firm. Well known for its expertise in family law and private client work, but practising in all other legal areas.

| | |
|---|---|
| V | 2[09] |
| T | 3 |
| P | 7 |
| TS | 44 |
| WP | no |

## RATNA & CO
169a High Street North, London E6 1JB
**Tel:** 020 8470 8818
**Fax:** 020 8475 0131
**Apply to:** Mr Majid Shafiq

We are a small firm specialising in immigration, property, family and wills with some employment work.

| | |
|---|---|
| V | Poss |
| T | 1 |
| P | 2 |
| TS | 7 |
| WP | no |

## RAWAL & CO
310 Ballards Lane, London N12 0EY
**Tel:** 020 8445 0303
**Fax:** 020 8492 9385
**Apply to:** Ms Linda Burchill

Established high street franchised firm specialising in crime, housing, family and welfare benefit welcomes applications from law graduates for traineeship.

| | |
|---|---|
| V | 0 |
| T | 1 |
| P | 1 |
| TS | 7 |
| WP | no |

## RAWLINS DAVY
Rowland House, Hinton Road,
Bournemouth BH1 2EG
**Tel:** 01202 558844
**Fax:** 01202 557175
**Email:** enquiries@rawlinsdavy.com
**Apply to:** Mr E John Kennar

Well established local firm with offices in central Bournemouth, who have in recent years expanded to create a highly focused team of principally general commercial and commercial property lawyers.

| | |
|---|---|
| V | 0 |
| T | 2 |
| P | 8 |
| TS | 45 |
| WP | no |

## RAWSTORNE HERAN
27a Windsor Street, Stratford-Upon-Avon
CV37 6NL
**Tel:** 01789 267646
**Fax:** 01789 415335
**Email:** enquiries@rawstorneheran.co.uk
**Apply to:** Mrs Laura Mckenzie

A small high street litigation practice dealing mainly with criminal, mental health and family law. Both legal aid and private.

| | |
|---|---|
| V | 0-1 |
| T | 2 |
| P | 2 |
| TS | 7 |
| WP | yes |

## READ DUNN CONNELL
Manor Row Chambers, 35/37 Manor Row,
Bradford BD1 4PS
**Tel:** 01274 723858
**Fax:** 01274 728493
**Email:** info@readdunnconnell.co.uk
**Apply to:** Mr RE Anderson

Situated in centre of Bradford. Well established firm dealing in company and commercial; matrimonial; litigation and personal injury; property; trusts; probate and tax planning. Legal aid franchise.

| | |
|---|---|
| V | 0 |
| T | 1 |
| P | 5 |
| TS | 29 |
| WP | no |

**V** = Vacancies / **T** = Trainees / **P** = Partners / **TS** = Total Staff / **WP** = Work Placement

# Reynolds Porter Chamberlain LLP

Tower Bridge House, St Katharine's Way, London, E1W 1AA
**Tel:** 020 3060 6000
**Fax:** 020 3060 7000
**Email:** training@rpc.co.uk
**Web:** www.rpc.co.uk/training

WINNER LC'ⁿ
**AWARDS 2007**
BEST WORK PLACEMENT SCHEME
CITY FIRM

**The firm** RPC is a forward-thinking London-based law firm with a wide-ranging practice, some of the leading lawyers in their fields and some great clients. Based in brand new offices in the City, we work in an open, collaborative environment designed to bring out the best in our people and to ensure that the service we offer our clients is second-to-none.

As a trainee with RPC you will work side-by-side with more experienced lawyers. You will be immersed from the outset in real legal work, get hands-on experience, and be part of a strong, carefully planned system which will support you throughout your training contract.

In return for your commitment and hard work we promise open access to partners and all the support you need. For example we believe we are one of the first major law firms to implement open working right across the board, up to and including our CEO.

**Types of work** Comprehensive training is normally provided in the following areas of work: litigation; commercial property and corporate. We encourage our trainees to express preferences for the areas in which they would like to train.

**Who should apply** We appoint 15 trainees each year from law and non-law backgrounds. Although proven academic ability is important to us (we require a 2:1 degree or above), we also value flair, energy, business sense, commitment and the ability to communicate and relate well to others.

Recruitment takes place in the September two years before commencement of the training contract. Shortlisted candidates will be invited to one of our assessment days, during which they will have the opportunity to meet our existing trainees and partners.

**Training programme** As a trainee you will receive first rate training in a supportive working environment. You will work closely with a partner and be given real responsibility as soon as you are ready to handle it. At least six months will be spent in each of the main areas of the practice. In addition to the internally provided Professional Skills Course, the firm provides a complementary programme of in-house training. When you qualify, we hope you will stay with us and we endeavour to place you in the area of law which suits you best.

**When and how to apply** Please visit our website at www.rpc.co.uk/training to apply online for a training contract commencing in 2010. The deadline for training contract applications is 8 August 2008.

**Work placements** We run summer vacation schemes each year to enable prospective trainees to spend two weeks with us to get a feel for the firm's work and atmosphere. Please apply online at www.rpc.co.uk/training if you are interested in applying for a place on our summer vacation scheme. The application deadline is 29 February 2008.

**Sponsorship** Bursaries are available for the GDL, if applicable, and the LPC. Bursaries comprise course and examination fees and a grant of up to £6,500.

| | |
|---|---|
| Vacancies | 15 |
| Trainees | 30 |
| Partners | 65 |
| Total staff | 500 |

**Work placement** yes
*(see Insider Report on p133)*

**Apply to**
Kate Gregg

**Starting salary**
£31,000

**Minimum qualifications**
2.1 degree

**Sponsorship**
GDL/LPC

**Offices**
London

Reynolds Porter Chamberlain LLP

# Rickerbys

Ellenborough House, Wellington Street, Cheltenham, Gloucestershire GL50 1YD
**Tel:** 01242 224422
**Fax:** 01242 518428
**Web:** www.rickerbys.com

**The firm** One of the Southwest's leading law firms and one of a small number of firms to have achieved Lexcel. We advise a wide range of private and commercial clients, and with ambitious plans to develop the practice, now is an exciting time to join the team. Rickerbys regards its trainees as potential partners for the future. It has an excellent record of retaining trainees post-qualification and several of the current partners trained at Rickerbys.

**Types of work** Company/commercial (including e-commerce, information technology, construction and intellectual property), commercial property, education, employment, family, insolvency, litigation, private client and residential property.

**Who should apply** Successful candidates may come from various backgrounds, and we are happy to consider law or non-law graduates. We look for team players with a can-do attitude who possess strong communication and problem-solving skills and who are IT literate, able to work on their own initiative and have a strong commercial awareness.

**Training programme** Trainees have four six-month seats covering contentious and non-contentious law. They will be allocated a training supervisor who will oversee their work and development. They will receive regular feedback on progress and a formal performance review will be carried out during each seat. The training is very hands on. Under supervision trainees may conduct their own files and are often the first point of contact for clients.

**When and how to apply** By 31 July 2008 to begin October 2010. Apply by application form. Either request a recruitment pack by phoning Sophie Fry on 01242 246441, or visit our website at www.rickerbys.com.

**Work placements** One-week placements during July. Applications as per training contract, to be received by 31 May 2008.

**Sponsorship** £6,000 towards LPC fees if not already commenced studies. Full Professional Skills Course fees and time off.

| | |
|---|---|
| Vacancies | 3-4 |
| Trainees | 8 |
| Partners | 20 |
| Total staff | 188 |

**Work placement** yes

**Apply to**
Sophie Fry

**Starting salary**
No less than £21,800

**Minimum qualifications**
2.1 degree in law preferred but not essential

**Sponsorship**
LPC

**Offices**
Cheltenham

RICKERBYS solicitors

## REENA GHAI SOLICITORS
Stable Cottage, 42 High Street, Cranford,
Middlesex TW5 9RU
**Tel:** 020 8759 9959
**Fax:** 020 8759 9958
**Email:** contact@ghaiandco.com
**Apply to:** Ms Reena Ghai

Franchised legal aid department
specialising in crime, family and
welfare benefits.

| | |
|---|---|
| **V** | 0-1 |
| **T** | 2 |
| **P** | 1 |
| **TS** | 6 |
| **WP** | no |

## REES PAGE
8/12 Waterloo Road, Wolverhampton WV1 4BL
**Tel:** 01902 577777
**Fax:** 01902 577735
**Apply to:** Mr Andrew Lund

West Midlands practice supplying
legal services to corporate and
private clients. We are dedicated
practitioners with a friendly
philosophy to training and trainees.

| | |
|---|---|
| **V** | 0 |
| **T** | 2 |
| **P** | 8 |
| **TS** | 46 |
| **WP** | no |

## RENAISSANCE SOLICITORS
413 Hoe Street, London E17 9AP
**Tel:** 020 8521 1100
**Fax:** 020 8521 1123
**Apply to:** Mrs A E Nawaz

| | |
|---|---|
| **V** | 1 |
| **T** | 1 |
| **P** | 2 |
| **TS** | - |
| **WP** | yes |

## REYNOLDS COLMAN BRADLEY LLP
Gallery 4, Lloyds Building, 12 Leadenhall Street,
London EC3V 1LP
**Tel:** 0870 735 8364
**Fax:** 0870 735 8369
**Apply to:** Mr SJ Reynolds

Specialist professional negligence,
insurance, commercial and
construction litigation practice based
in Lloyds.

| | |
|---|---|
| **V** | 1 |
| **T** | 1 |
| **P** | 3 |
| **TS** | 7 |
| **WP** | yes |

## REYNOLDS JOHNS PARTNERSHIP
Apex House, 18 Hockerill Street,
Bishop's Stortford CM23 2DW
**Tel:** 01279 508626
**Fax:** 01279 503834
**Email:** nj@reynoldsjohns.co.uk
**Apply to:** Mr N Johns

| | |
|---|---|
| **V** | 0 |
| **T** | 0 |
| **P** | 2 |
| **TS** | 15 |
| **WP** | no |

## REYNOLDS PARRY-JONES
10 Easton Street, High Wycombe HP11 1NP
**Tel:** 01494 525941
**Fax:** 01494 530701
**Email:** robert.hill@rpj.uk.com
**Apply to:** Mr Robert Hill

Well established yet modern practice
with a heavy and varied workload in
the fields of company/commercial,
employment, private client, personal
injury and family law. 2006 Winner
Best Trainer (Small Firm) in
LawCareers.Net awards.

| | |
|---|---|
| **V** | 1 |
| **T** | 2 |
| **P** | 6 |
| **TS** | 38 |
| **WP** | no |

## RICHMONDS
Richmonds House, White Rose Way, Doncaster
DN4 5JH
**Tel:** 01302 762900
**Fax:** 01302 762801
**Apply to:** Ms Christine Burton

Three partner firm with two offices.
Doncaster: company commercial,
employment commercial litigation,
commercial property. Retford: private
client, personal injury, wills, trusts,
probate, conveyancing.

| | |
|---|---|
| **V** | 2[(09)] |
| **T** | 5 |
| **P** | 3 |
| **TS** | 48 |
| **WP** | yes |

## RN WILLIAMS & CO
53 Waterloo Road, Wolverhampton WV1 4QQ
**Tel:** 01902 429051
**Fax:** 01902 313435
**Email:** cr@rnwilliams.com
**Apply to:** Miss Richards

| | |
|---|---|
| **V** | 0 |
| **T** | 3 |
| **P** | 3 |
| **TS** | 17 |
| **WP** | no |

# Rooks Rider

Challoner House, 19 Clerkenwell Close, London EC1R 0RR
**Tel:** 020 7689 7000
**Fax:** 020 7689 7001
**Email:** lawyers@rooksrider.com
**Web:** www.rooksrider.com

**The firm** Rooks Rider is a long established London firm serving UK and International businesses as well as high net worth individuals.

The partnership is continually expanding the breadth of its expertise to respond to the changing needs of its clients. This allows us to deliver a wide range of expert services efficiently at short notice and always in a friendly way. Our aim is to provide creative and practical solutions specifically tailored to our client's needs. Our clients and their requirements always come first.

**Types of work** Rooks Rider is a full service firm operating through five departments: company and offshore structures; dispute resolution; family; private client; property.

Our strength is the ability to identify and address the tax planning opportunities of all transactions.

We handle the legal requirements of business whatever their stage of development from initial inception and incorporation through to floatation and beyond. Our clients cover a wide spectrum of commercial sectors.

Our dispute resolution team aims to resolve any dispute as quickly and cost efficiently as possible. We avoid sterile application of the law and judge our success by whether we achieve the client's objectives.

The private individual needs legal guidance on a wide variety of occasions, from the purchasing of property and the planning and management of finances to overcome the strains of modern family life to the business of winding up estates on death.

The firm has enjoyed a long involvement with the property world and we have developed the skills to handle all types of commercial and residential transactions. We therefore act for developers, investors and banks as well as private individuals and businesses.

**When and how to apply** Candidates should send a copy of their CV with a covering letter to Bernadette Sheridan, Head of Human Resources.

| | |
|---|---|
| Vacancies | Variable |
| Trainees | 4 |
| Partners | 17 |
| Total staff | 85 |

**Work placements** no

**Apply to**
Bernadette Sheridan

**Starting salary**
1st year - £24,000
2nd year - £25,000

**Minimum qualifications**
2.1 degree

**Offices**
London

ROOKS
RIDER
SOLICITORS

| | | |
|---|---|---|
| **ROBERT LIZAR**<br>159 Princess Road, Moss Side,<br>Manchester M14 4RE<br>**Tel:** 0161 226 2319<br>**Fax:** 0161 226 7985<br>**Email:** rlizar@robertlizar.com<br>**Apply to:** Ms Patricia Graham | Legal aid work in crime, actions against police, family, mental health, civil liberties. | V  Poss<br>T  0<br>P  6<br>TS 22<br>WP no |
| **ROBIN SIMON LLP**<br>2 St David's Court, David Street, Leeds LS11 5QA<br>**Tel:** 0870 839 0800<br>**Fax:** 0870 839 0900<br>**Email:** Matthew.Reynolds@robinsimonllp.com<br>**Apply to:** Mr Matthew Reynolds | Leading national and international commercial insurance and reinsurance practice in the city, Leeds, Manchester and Birmingham. | V  2[08]<br>T  4<br>P  10<br>TS 50<br>WP no |
| **ROBINSON JARVIS & ROLF (RJR SOLICITORS)**<br>18 Melville Street, Ryde, Isle of Wight PO33 2AP<br>**Tel:** 01983 562201<br>**Fax:** 01983 616602<br>**Email:** info@rjr.co.uk<br>**Apply to:** Mr Virgil Philpott | Established 1898 - serving the community on the Isle of Wight with four offices. The firm covers legal aid and private work. Currently one vacancy for 2008. | V  1<br>T  2<br>P  7<br>TS 50<br>WP no |
| **ROBINSONS**<br>10-11 St James Court, Derby DE1 1BT<br>**Tel:** 01332 291431<br>**Fax:** 01332 254142<br>**Email:** rob.styles@robinsons-solicitors.co.uk<br>**Apply to:** Mr Rob Styles | A general practice but with dominant company/commercial elements in Derby and Ilkeston. | V  Poss<br>T  4<br>P  7<br>TS 68<br>WP no |
| **ROBSON & CO**<br>147 High Street, Hythe CT21 5JN<br>**Tel:** 01303 267413<br>**Fax:** 01303 265157<br>**Email:** post@robson-co.co.uk<br>**Apply to:** Mr MJ Dearden | Friendly and supportive practice dealing in a range of non-contentious services including family law and P.I. in pretty Cinque Port Town. | V  0<br>T  0<br>P  -<br>TS -<br>WP no |
| **ROCHMAN LANDAU**<br>Accurist House, 44 Baker Street, London W1U 7AL<br>**Tel:** 020 7544 2424<br>**Fax:** 020 7544 2400<br>**Apply to:** Ms Philippa Dolan | An interesting and varied West End practice. Our clients range from antiques dealers and doctors to nationwide retail chains. | V  1[08]<br>T  3<br>P  11<br>TS 50<br>WP no |
| **THE ROLAND PARTNERSHIP**<br>St Mark's House, St Mary's Road, Sawtney,<br>Chester CH4 8DQ<br>**Tel:** 01244 659404<br>**Fax:** 01244 659535<br>**Email:** anne.hall@therolandpartnership.co.uk<br>**Apply to:** Mrs Anne Hall | Specialist solicitors based in Chester, leading firm in medical negligence and serious injury, also personal injury and conveyancing. LSC quality marked. | V  0<br>T  0<br>P  2<br>TS 21<br>WP yes |
| **ROLLITS**<br>Wilberforce Court, High Street, Hull HU1 1YJ<br>**Tel:** 01482 337250<br>**Fax:** 01482 326239<br>**Email:** neil.maidment@rollits.com<br>**Apply to:** Mr Neil Maidment | Recommended by leading law directories for corporate and commercial work, charity law, planning and environmental law, employment, commercial litigation, commercial property, intellectual property work and social housing. | V  3<br>T  5<br>P  21<br>TS 118<br>WP yes |

| **RONALDSONS**<br>45 Dereham Road, Norwich NR2 4HY<br>**Tel:** 01603 621113<br>**Fax:** 01603 766074<br>**Email:** richardronaldson@ronaldsons.com<br>**Apply to:** Mr Richard Ronaldson | The firm serves the community of Norwich and its surrounds by providing family law and residential conveyancing services. | V 1<br>T 1<br>P 1<br>TS 10<br>WP no |
|---|---|---|
| **ROSENBLATT**<br>9-13 St Andrew Street, London EC4A 3AF<br>**Tel:** 020 7955 0880<br>**Fax:** 020 7955 0888<br>**Email:** info@rosenblatt-law.co.uk<br>**Apply to:** Ms Tania MacLeod | Based in the City, our practice provides a comprehensive commercial law service to UK and overseas businesses. Corporate work, litigation and property are particular strengths. Deadline: 31/07 of each year. | V 4<br>T 8<br>P 13<br>TS 90<br>WP yes |
| **ROSLING KING SOLICITORS**<br>2-3 Hind Court, Fleet Street, London EC4A 3DL<br>**Tel:** 020 7353 2353<br>**Fax:** 020 7583 2035<br>**Email:** info@roslingking.co.uk<br>**Apply to:** Mr James Walton | Commercial firm, successfully competes with large City firms, specialising in property, banking, insurance and reinsurance, commercial litigation and dispute resolution, construction, company law and general commercial. | V 3<br>T 6<br>P 9<br>TS 75<br>WP no |
| **ROSS COATES SOLICITORS**<br>Unit 15 IP-City Centre, 1 Bath Street,<br>Ipswich IP2 8SD<br>**Tel:** 01473 695400<br>**Fax:** 01473 695500<br>**Email:** info@rosscoates.co.uk<br>**Apply to:** Mr Ross Coates | A young dynamic firm only ten years old, with emphasis on property and commercial work. Career opportunities for the young and enthusiastic trainee. | V 1-2<br>T 5<br>P 5<br>TS 45<br>WP no |
| **ROSS SOLICITOR**<br>40 Victoria Road, Swindon SN1 3AS<br>**Tel:** 01793 512960<br>**Fax:** 01793 432962<br>**Apply to:** Mr Robert Ross | Sole practitioner specialising in crime. | V 0<br>T 1<br>P 1<br>TS 11<br>WP no |
| **ROWLANDS SOLICITORS LLP**<br>3 York Street, Manchester M2 2RW<br>**Tel:** 0161 835 2020<br>**Fax:** 0161 835 2525<br>**Email:** recruitment@rowlands-solicitors.co.uk<br>**Apply to:** Ms Jane Parkin | A Manchester based general practice. Commercial, private client, litigation (personal injury, family, property, child care, coporate, employment, crime, wills, probate, inheritance tax, civil litigation). | V 5<br>T 10<br>P 26<br>TS 150<br>WP yes |
| **ROYDS**<br>2 Crane Court, 65 Carter Lane, London EC4V SHF<br>**Tel:** 020 7583 2222<br>**Fax:** 020 7583 2034<br>**Apply to:** Via online form only | Vibrant Central London commercial practice, established for over 100 years. The firm provides specialist expertise to a wide range of commercial organisations and individual clients. Apply via our online application form. | V 2[09]<br>T 5<br>P 19<br>TS 85<br>WP yes |
| **ROYTHORNE & CO**<br>10 Pinchbeck Road, Spalding PEII 1PZ<br>**Tel:** 01775 842500<br>**Fax:** 01775 725736<br>**Email:** roythorne@roythorne.co.uk<br>**Apply to:** Mr Paul Townshend | Major commercial 3 office practice in the East Midlands, specialising in agriculture and food law with additional highly regarded property, litigation, private client and corporate teams. | V 3-4[09]<br>T 3<br>P 20<br>TS 180<br>WP no |

**V** = Vacancies / **T** = Trainees / **P** = Partners / **TS** = Total Staff / **WP** = Work Placement

# Russell-Cooke

2 Putney Hill, London SW15 6AB
**Tel:** 020 8789 9111
**Fax:** 020 8788 1656
**Email:** traineeapplications@russell-cooke.co.uk
**Web:** www.russell-cooke.co.uk

**The firm** A medium-sized practice with offices in Central London, Putney and Kingston.

**Types of work** The City office deals primarily with commercial and contentious property and professional regulation. The Putney and Kingston offices have a range of specialist departments including company and commercial, commercial, construction and regulatory litigation, insolvency, employment, family, crime, medical negligence, personal injury, commercial and domestic conveyancing, charities, French property, private client, trusts, tax and childcare.

**Who should apply** Trainees will need at least two A grades and one B grade at A level and an upper second-class degree. Intellectual rigour, adaptability and the ability under pressure to handle a diverse range of people and issues efficiently and cost effectively are vital attributes.

**Training programme** Trainees are offered four seats lasting six months each. You will have the chance to manage your own caseload and deal directly with clients, with supervision tailored to your needs and those of your department and the clients in question.

**When and how to apply** Apply before 31 July 2008 to begin September 2010 with completed application form, CV and covering letter. A copy of our application form can be downloaded from our website at www.russell-cooke.co.uk.

| | |
|---|---|
| Vacancies | 8 |
| Trainees | 14-16 |
| Partners | 42 |
| Total staff | 310 |

**Apply to**
Jo Power

**Starting salary**
Not less than £28,000
(£30,000 in the second
year) plus bonus scheme

**Minimum qualifications**
2.1 degree and AAB grades
at A level

**Sponsorship**
LPC

**Offices**
Central London, Kingston-
upon-Thames, Putney

**RUSSELL-COOKE** SOLICITORS

| **RUNHAMS**<br>Salts Chambers, Salts Mill, Saltaire, Shipley,<br>West Yorkshire BD18 3LF<br>**Tel:** 01274 532233<br>**Fax:** 01274 534399<br>**Email:** ew@runhams.co.uk<br>**Apply to:** Mr Edward Wegorzewski | Busy, friendly practice based in World Heritage Site of Saltaire covering full range of private client/commercial and litigation work. | V 0-1<br>T 1<br>P 4<br>TS 32<br>WP no |
|---|---|---|
| **RUSSELL & CO**<br>32 The Boulevard, Crawley RH10 1XP<br>**Tel:** 01293 561965<br>**Fax:** 01293 521301<br>**Email:** post@russell-co-legal.co.uk<br>**Apply to:** Mr Colin Russell | Specialist personal injury/clinical negligence firm committed to positive resolution of victims' compensation claims, providing specialist training, but also able to provide experience of general practice during training. | V 1<br>T 1<br>P 2<br>TS 10<br>WP yes |
| **RUSSELL & RUSSELL**<br>Churchill House, Wood Street, Bolton BL1 1EE<br>**Tel:** 01204 399299<br>**Fax:** 01204 389223<br>**Apply to:** Mrs S Matthews | Long established firm undertaking criminal, conveyancing, PI, family, probate. Offices at Bolton, Atherton, Bury, Farnworth, Chester, Middleton, Horwich. | V 0<br>T 10<br>P 14<br>TS 165<br>WP no |
| **RUSSELL JONES & WALKER**<br>Swinton House, 324 Gray's Inn Road,<br>London WC1X 8DH<br>**Tel:** 020 7837 2808<br>**Fax:** 020 7837 2941<br>**Email:** enquiries@rjw.co.uk<br>**Apply to:** HR Officer (Graduate Recruitment) | | V 10<br>T 16<br>P 49<br>TS 630<br>WP no |
| **SA LAW**<br>60 London Road, St Albans,<br>Hertfordshire AL1 1NG<br>**Tel:** 01727 798000<br>**Fax:** 01727 798002<br>**Email:** info@salaw.com<br>**Apply to:** Mrs Gill Garrett | SA Law is one of the most dynamic legal practices in the South East offering speicalist commercial services supported by leading private client expertise. | V 2[09]<br>T 3<br>P 7<br>TS 70<br>WP no |
| **SAMUEL PHILLIPS LAW FIRM**<br>Gibb Chambers, 52 Westgate Road,<br>Newcastle upon Tyne NE1 5XU<br>**Tel:** 0191 232 8451<br>**Fax:** 0191 232 7664<br>**Email:** jennygoldstern@samuelphillips.co.uk<br>**Apply to:** Ms Jennifer Goldstein | Long established firm especially renowned for clinical negligence, personal injury, family/child care, employment, general litigation, private client, commercial property and litigation. | V 1<br>T 2<br>P 5<br>TS 44<br>WP yes |
| **SAMUELS**<br>18 Alexandra Road, Barnstaple, Devon EX32 8BA<br>**Tel:** 01271 343457<br>**Fax:** 01271 322187<br>**Email:** mail@samuels-solicitors.co.uk<br>**Apply to:** Mr Jan Samuel | A well-established firm with a strong client base covering most areas of commercial, private client and litigation work, including legal aid. | V 1[09]<br>T 1<br>P 3<br>TS 21<br>WP no |
| **SAMY & CO SOLICITORS**<br>29 High Street, Wealdstone, Harrow, Middlesex<br>HA3 5BY<br>**Tel:** 0208 861 2424<br>**Fax:** 0208 861 3939<br>**Email:** samy-co-solicitors@boltblue.com<br>**Apply to:** Mr PS Sivakumar | We specialise in crime, housing and welfare benefits and we are franchised in these areas by the LSC. In addition we do private practice in immigration. | V 0<br>T 2<br>P -<br>TS -<br>WP no |

**V** = Vacancies / **T** = Trainees / **P** = Partners / **TS** = Total Staff / **WP** = Work Placement

# Salans

Millennium Bridge House, 2 Lambeth Hill, London EC4V 4AJ
**Tel:** 020 7429 6000
**Fax:** 020 7429 6001
**Email:** london@salans.com
**Web:** www.salans.com

**The firm** Salans is an international law firm with full-service offices in the City of London, Almaty, Baku, Barcelona, Berlin, Bratislava, Bucharest, Budapest, Istanbul, Kiev, Madrid, Moscow, New York, Paris, Prague, Shanghai, St Petersburg and Warsaw. Our unique combination of international capability and domestic expertise enables us to provide a seamless, comprehensive service, meeting the needs of global and local clients alike.

**Types of work** Arbitration, banking, corporate and commercial, commercial property, emerging markets, litigation, employment law and re-structuring.

**Who should apply** Graduates in any discipline. The firm looks for applicants who are able to approach complex problems in a practical and commercial way.

Successful candidates will be able to demonstrate an ability and willingness to assume responsibility at an early stage and possess common sense and good judgement.

**Training programme** Trainees will spend six months in four different departments. Trainees are supervised at all times by a partner and encouraged to take an active part in the work of their department. The firm operates an in-house education scheme for both trainees and assistant solicitors. In addition, trainees will be offered the opportunity to attend external courses wherever possible.

Benefits include: private healthcare, pension, life assurance, critical illness cover, season ticket loan.

Further details about the firm and our recruitment process can be found on our website at www.salans.com.

**When and how to apply** From April 2008 to begin in September 2010. The closing date is 31 July 2008. Apply by letter (handwritten preferred) and CV addressed to Angela Butler, HR Manager.

**Sponsorship** LPC tuition fees paid.

**Work placements** Not available.

| | |
|---|---|
| Vacancies | 3-4 |
| Trainees | 7 |
| Partners | 154 |
| Total staff | 1300 |

**Apply to**
Angela Butler, HR Manager

**Starting salary**
£30,000 (2007)

**Minimum qualifications**
2.1 degree, any discipline
and ABB at A level

**Sponsorship**
LPC

**Offices**
Almaty, Baku, Barcelona, Berlin, Bratislava, Bucharest, Budapest, Istanbul, Kiev, London, Madrid, Moscow, New York, Paris, Prague, Shanghai, St Petersburg, Warsaw

 ❖ SALANS

| | | | |
|---|---|---|---|
| **SAS DANIELS**<br>30 Greek Street, Stockport SK3 8AD<br>**Tel:** 0161 475 7676<br>**Fax:** 0161 475 7677<br>**Email:** help@saslawyers.co.uk<br>**Apply to:** Mr Philip Smith | | **V** 0<br>**T** 4<br>**P** 19<br>**TS** 130<br>**WP** no |
| **SB SOLICITORS**<br>228a Whitechapel Road, London E1 1BJ<br>**Tel:** 020 7539 1900<br>**Fax:** 020 7539 1909<br>**Email:** sb_solicitor@yahoo.co.uk<br>**Apply to:** Mr S Bhuwanee | Growing two partner practice dealing with housing law, conveyancing (residential and commercial), litigation and construction work. | **V** 0<br>**T** 1<br>**P** 2<br>**TS** 4<br>**WP** yes |
| **SCHILLINGS**<br>41 Bedford Square, London WC1B 3HX<br>**Tel:** 020 7034 9000<br>**Fax:** 020 7034 9200<br>**Email:** legal@schillings.co.uk<br>**Apply to:** Ms Georgina Dancer | As a niche, west end firm specialising in media and entertainment work, we provide expert contentious/non-contentious services to media corporations, high profile individuals and celebrities. | **V** 2<br>**T** 4<br>**P** 6<br>**TS** 34<br>**WP** yes |
| **SCHOFIELD SWEENEY LLP**<br>Church Bank House, Church Bank,<br>Bradford BD1 4DY<br>**Tel:** 01274 306000<br>**Fax:** 01274 306111<br>**Email:** law@schoeys.com<br>**Apply to:** Mr Darren Birkinshaw | General commercial law firm. | **V** 2-3[08]<br>**T** 5<br>**P** 14<br>**TS** 80<br>**WP** yes |
| **SCOTT BAILEY**<br>63 High Street, Lymington, Hampshire SO41 9ZT<br>**Tel:** 01590 676933<br>**Fax:** 01590 679663<br>**Email:** law@scottbailey.co.uk<br>**Apply to:** Mr Nick Jutton | Progressive franchised high street firm in attractive location. | **V** 1[09]<br>**T** 1<br>**P** 4<br>**TS** 18<br>**WP** no |
| **SCOTT REES & CO**<br>Centaur House, Gardiners Place, Skelmersdale,<br>Lancs WN8 9SP<br>**Tel:** 01695 722222<br>**Fax:** 01695 733333<br>**Email:** info@scottrees.co.uk<br>**Apply to:** Ms Pauline Shaw | We are a progressive firm of solicitors specialising in personal injury, conveyancing, wills and probate and debt recovery, nationwide. Our office is based in Skelmersdale. | **V** 2[08]<br>**T** 6<br>**P** 7<br>**TS** 170<br>**WP** yes |
| **SCOTT ROWE SOLICITORS**<br>Chard Street, Axminster, Devon EX13 5DS<br>**Tel:** 01297 32345<br>**Fax:** 01297 35229<br>**Email:** sara.welch@scottrowe.co.uk<br>**Apply to:** Ms Sarah Welch | Well established West Country firm offering full range of legal services, seeks talented and hardworking trainee. The firm is Lexcel and Investors in People accredited. | **V** 1<br>**T** 3<br>**P** 3<br>**TS** 25<br>**WP** no |
| **SEDDONS**<br>5 Portman Square, London W1H 6NT<br>**Tel:** 020 7725 8000<br>**Fax:** 020 7935 5049<br>**Email:** postmaster@seddons.co.uk<br>**Apply to:** Mr Harvey Ingram | A commercial practice in London with corporate and individual business clients, media, property and litigation departments. | **V** 2[08]<br>**T** 4<br>**P** 16<br>**TS** 62<br>**WP** no |

**V** = Vacancies / **T** = Trainees / **P** = Partners / **TS** = Total Staff / **WP** = Work Placement

578 THE TRAINING CONTRACT & PUPILLAGE HANDBOOK

# Sewell Mullings and Logie

7 Dollar Street, Cirencester GL7 2AS
**Tel:** 01285 650000
**Fax:** 01285 649898
**Email:** jbb@sewellmullingsandlogie.co.uk

**The firm** Is your working environment important to you? Sewell Mullings and Logie is situated in the heart of the Cotswolds. It was founded in the late 18th century and over the years the firm has grown in size, breadth and depth of expertise.

However, we remain committed to a close individual relationship with our clients. We cover a wide variety of legal areas to suit the needs of our clients. We have a large local catchment area of the Cotswolds and North Wiltshire. We also act for clients throughout the British Isles and further afield.

We provide professional advice to individuals, partnerships, companies, trusts and charities at all levels. While both our history and geography result in a generous proportion of high-value work, we maintain our philosophy of looking after clients and their families with a wide range of backgrounds and financial standing.

**Types of work** We are divided into three specialised departments: private client, litigation (including family) and property. Sewell Mullings and Logie covers a wide range of private client work including domestic conveyancing, divorce and family matters, civil litigation, tax planning, wills, trusts and probate, as well as matters arising from the occupation and ownership of agricultural land. The firm also provides a complete service to small to medium-sized businesses including partnership advice, commercial conveyancing and employment.

The above is not an exhaustive list but provides an indication of the breadth of services we offer. The firm holds a Legal Services Commission franchise in family work.

**Who should apply** Those seeking a varied workload and early responsibility. Sewell Mullings and Logie looks for a good academic background. Trainees must also demonstrate good communication skills and common sense, and enjoy working with clients.

**Training programme** Trainees gain experience in three main areas: litigation, property and private client. Six months is spent in each seat. The final six months is a negotiated seat.

Sewell Mullings and Logie has an innovative approach to training. While trainees are encouraged to take responsibility for their own files, they will be closely supervised by an experienced member of staff within each department. Regular appraisals are arranged to assist progress within the firm.

**When and how to apply** Applications should be made by writing with a CV to Mr J B Bartholomew (not by email). Applications should be received by 15 April for entry in September of the following year.

| | |
|---|---|
| Vacancies | 1 |
| Trainees | 2 |
| Partners | 5 |
| Total staff | 45 |

**Apply to**
The Recruitment Partner

**Offices**
Cirencester

SEWELL,
MULLINGS
& LOGIE
Solicitors of Cirencester

# Shadbolt & Co LLP

Chatham Court, Lesbourne Road, Reigate RH2 7LD
**Tel:** 01737 226277
**Fax:** 01737 226165
**Email:** recruitment@shadboltlaw.com
**Web:** www.shadboltlaw.com

**The firm** Shadbolt & Co is an award-winning dynamic, progressive firm committed to high-quality work and excellence both in the UK and internationally. The atmosphere at the firm is friendly, relaxed and informal, and there are various social and sporting activities for staff. We are a lively and enterprising team who have a fresh and open approach to work. Our qualified staff have a high level of experience and industry knowledge, and some are widely regarded as leading practitioners in their field.

**Types of work** The firm is well known for its strengths in major projects, construction & engineering and dispute resolution & litigation, with established expansion into corporate & commercial, employment, commercial property and IT & e-commerce. The firm provides prompt personal service, and our client list includes some of the world's best-known names in the construction and engineering industries.

**Who should apply** Applicants must demonstrate that they are self-starters with a strong academic background and outside interests. Leadership, ambition, initiative, enthusiasm and good interpersonal skills are essential, as is the ability to play an active role in the future of the firm. Linguists are particularly welcome, as are those with supporting professional qualifications. We welcome non-law graduates.

**Training programme** Four six-month seats from construction & commercial litigation, arbitration & dispute resolution, major projects & construction, employment, corporate & commercial and commercial property. Where possible, individual preference is noted. Work has an international bias. There are opportunities for secondment to major clients and work in the overseas offices. Trainees are treated as valued members of the firm, expected to take early responsibility and encouraged to participate in all the firm's activities, including practice development. The firm is accredited by the Law Society as a provider of training and runs frequent in-house lectures. The Professional Skills Course is taught externally.

Benefits include 20 days' holiday per year (increasing to 25 on qualification) and the opportunity to 'buy' an additional five days' holiday per annum, optional private healthcare, permanent health insurance, group life assurance, paid study leave, season ticket loan, discretionary annual bonus of up to 5% of annual salary, paid professional memberships and subscriptions.

**When and how to apply** By 31 July 2008 for interviews in September 2008 and to commence employment in September 2010. Apply using the online application form no earlier than January 2008.

**Work placements** Places for 2008: six. Duration: two weeks. Remuneration (2008): £200 per week. Closing date: 28 February 2008. Interviews: March 2008. Apply using the online application form no earlier than January 2008.

**Sponsorship** Full LPC fees payable on commencement of training contract.

| | |
|---|---|
| Vacancies | 4 |
| Trainees | 8 |
| Partners | 25 |
| Total staff | 104 |

**Work placement** yes

**Apply to**
Andrea Pickett
Online application form

**Starting salary**
1st year (2007) - £29,000
2nd year (2007) - £33,000

**Minimum qualifications**
2.1 degree (occasional exceptions)

**Sponsorship**
LPC

**Offices**
Reigate, City of London, Paris
Associated offices:
Bucharest, Dar es Salaam

Shadbolt & Co LLP
Solicitors

# Sharpe Pritchard

Elizabeth House, Fulwood Place, London WC1V 6HG
**Tel:** 020 7405 4600
**Fax:** 020 7831 1284
**Email:** cv@sharpepritchard.co.uk
**Web:** www.sharpepritchard.co.uk

**The firm** We are a high-profile Central London firm with a long-established and extensive, but not exclusively, public sector client base providing broad areas of contentious and non-contentious practice.

**Types of work** Public sector, project work, planning, property, parliamentary, dispute resolution, including judicial review, are primary areas of the firm's practice. Others include employment, the environment, licensing, technology & construction and elections.

**Who should apply** Those candidates who combine an excellent academic track record - not limited to law graduates - with a lively personality and interesting all-round life experience are likely to get an interview. Trainees are expected to combine ability and high motivation with a positive outlook to fit into a very friendly professional working environment. Those who are intelligent, articulate and undaunted by advocacy or talking to a room full of people will thrive here.

**Training programme** Training is very much hands on. There is a high degree of client contact and in their time here trainees will have had broad experience of the firm's very varied workload. We encourage trainees to take on responsibility and become closely involved in making an effective contribution to the firm's success. There is a seat rotation through the departments and ready access to all levels of fee-earner, particularly partners.

**When and how to apply** Apply by August 31 2008 to begin August/ September 2010. Complete the application form on the firm's website in hard copy and send to Tracey Nottage at the firm's address.

**Work placements** On application.

**Sponsorship** Financial assistance is available for the LPC.

| | |
|---|---|
| Vacancies | 3 |
| Trainees | 6 |
| Partners | 18 |
| Total staff | 65 |

**Apply to**
Mr Ashley Baldock

**Starting salary**
1st year - £27,000 (2007)
2nd year - £28,000

**Minimum qualifications**
2.1 degree

**Sponsorship**
LPC

**Offices**
London

*SHARPE PRITCHARD*

# Shearman & Sterling LLP

9 Appold Street, London EC2A 2AP
**Tel:** 020 7655 5000
**Fax:** 020 7655 5500
**Email:** kdavies@shearman.com
**Web:** www.shearman.com

**The firm** Shearman & Sterling LLP is one of New York's oldest legal partnerships, which has transformed from a New York-based firm focused on banking into a diversified global institution.

Recognised throughout the globe, our reputation, skills and expertise are second to none in our field. Our London office, established in 1972, has become a leading practice covering all aspects of English and European corporate and finance law. We employ approximately 200 English and US-trained legal staff in London, and have more than 1,000 lawyers in 20 offices worldwide.

**Types of work** Banking, leveraged finance and structured finance; project finance; mergers and acquisitions; global capital markets; international arbitration and litigation; tax; financial institutions advisory and asset management; executive compensation and employee benefits; intellectual property; property; and EU and competition.

**Who should apply** Our firm's successful future development calls for people who will relish the hard work and intellectual challenge of today's commercial world. You will be a self-starter, keen to assume professional responsibility early in your career and determined to become a first-class lawyer in a first-class firm.

We want to recruit people who will stay with us; people who want to become partners in our continuing success story.

**Training programme** Our two-year training programme will equip you with all the skills needed to become a successful commercial lawyer. You will spend six months in each of four areas of practice, with an opportunity to spend six months in Abu Dhabi, New York or Singapore. You will be treated as an integral part of our London team from the outset. We will expect you to contribute creatively to all the transactions you are involved in. Ours is an informal yet professional atmosphere. Your enthusiasm, intellect and energy will be more important than what you wear to work.

We will provide you with a mentor, arrange personal and professional development courses and give you early responsibility.

**When and how to apply** By 31 July 2008 for training contracts starting in September 2010 (15 training contracts available). Please apply online at www.shearman.com.

**Work placements** We run a two-week vacation scheme for students, who will spend time in either one or two of our practice groups. The closing application date for vacation schemes in 2008 is 28 February 2008. Weekly remuneration for vacation work is £300.

**Sponsorship** We offer sponsorship for the GDL and LPC courses, together with a maintenance grant of £7,000.

| | |
|---|---|
| Vacancies | 15 |
| Trainees | 27 |
| Partners | 29 |
| Total staff | 300 |

**Work placement** yes
*(see Insider Report on p135)*

**Apply to**
Ms Kirsten Davies

**Starting salary**
£36,500

**Minimum qualifications**
2.1 degree

**Sponsorship**
GDL/LPC

**Offices**
Abu Dhabi, Beijing, Brussels, Düsseldorf, Frankfurt, Hong Kong, London, Mannheim, Menlo Park, Munich, New York, Paris, Rome, São Paulo, San Francisco, Shanghai, Singapore, Tokyo, Toronto, Washington DC

SHEARMAN & STERLING LLP

## SERGEANT & COLLINS
25 Oswald Road, Scunthorpe DN15 7PS
**Tel:** 01724 864215
**Fax:** 01724 280253
**Email:** sergeantcollins@tiscali.co.uk
**Apply to:** Mr P Wright

Traditional High Street practice dealing with conveyancing, probate, family work, crime and general business matters.

| | |
|---|---|
| V | 0 |
| T | 1 |
| P | 2 |
| TS | 15 |
| WP | no |

## THE SETHI PARTNERSHIP SOLICITORS
The Barn House, 38 Meadow Way, Eastcote, Ruislip HA4 8TB
**Tel:** 020 8866 6464
**Fax:** 020 8866 3232
**Email:** ritu@sethi.co.uk
**Apply to:** Mrs Ritu Sethi

General practice - specialising in property work, crime, matrimonial, litigation, immigration, civil litigation.

| | |
|---|---|
| V | 0 |
| T | 1 |
| P | 2 |
| TS | 25 |
| WP | yes |

## SFM LEGAL SERVICES
Alexander House, Kingsway North, Team Valley NE11 0JH
**Tel:** 0191 495 8900
**Fax:** 0191 495 8939
**Email:** mgraham@sfmnewcastle.co.uk
**Apply to:** Mr M Graham

Dynamic, modern firm specialising in private client work. The firm acts for hynetworth individuals in tax planning and trusts both onshore and offshore.

| | |
|---|---|
| V | 1[09] |
| T | 4 |
| P | 2 |
| TS | 60 |
| WP | yes |

## SHAKESPEARE PUTSMAN
Somerset House, Temple Street, Birmingham B25 DJ
**Tel:** 0121 237 3000
**Fax:** 0121 237 3087
**Apply to:** Mrs Sally Adey

Advice for businesses and individuals on matters including company and commercial law, property, employment, insurance, personal injury, litigation, intellectual property. Also has private client service.

| | |
|---|---|
| V | 6[09] |
| T | 14 |
| P | 44 |
| TS | 264 |
| WP | no |

## SHARP & PARTNERS
6 Weekday Cross, Nottingham NG1 2GF
**Tel:** 0115 959 0055
**Fax:** 0115 959 0099
**Apply to:** Mr GJ Tring

General practice based in centre of Nottingham with four branch offices and dealing with all aspects of legal work.

| | |
|---|---|
| V | 0-1 |
| T | 1 |
| P | 10 |
| TS | 60 |
| WP | no |

## SHEIKH & CO
208 Seven Sisters Road, London N4 3NX
**Tel:** 020 7263 5588
**Fax:** 020 7263 5522
**Apply to:** Mr SA Sheikh

General practice with 80% legal aid work. The firm expanded very rapidly within a year.

| | |
|---|---|
| V | 2 |
| T | 2 |
| P | 3 |
| TS | 28 |
| WP | yes |

## SHEPHERD HARRIS & CO
Nickel House, 96 Silver Street, Enfield, Middlesex EN1 3EL
**Tel:** 020 8363 8341
**Fax:** 020 8367 7440
**Apply to:** Mr Ian Godfrey

Medium sized general practice with franchise in crime, family, personal injury and consumer/general contract.

| | |
|---|---|
| V | 1 |
| T | 1 |
| P | 2 |
| TS | 30 |
| WP | no |

## SHERRARDS
45 Grosvenor Road, St Albans, Hertfordshire AL1 3AW
**Tel:** 01727 832830
**Fax:** 01727 832833
**Email:** jas@sherrards.com
**Apply to:** Mrs Julie Shields

A progressive firm with a strong bias towards commercial work and litigation, whilst retaining experienced private client departments.

| | |
|---|---|
| V | Poss[09] |
| T | 6 |
| P | 13 |
| TS | 49 |
| WP | no |

# Shoosmiths

The Lakes, Bedford Road, Northampton NN4 7SH
**Tel:** 08700 863223
**Fax:** 08700 863001
**Email:** join.us@shoosmiths.co.uk
**Web:** www.shoosmiths.co.uk

**The firm** Growing steadily with seven offices across the midlands and south of England, Shoosmiths is one of the big players outside London. The firm is run like a business - Shoosmiths is a progressive, forward-thinking law firm with a real spirit of enterprise. We really value our people by giving them the freedom, recognition and support to succeed, and our clients find us open, accessible and easy to work with.

**Types of work** Key areas include commercial property, disupte resolution, corporate and commercial, employment, intellectual property, banking, planning, private client and personal injury.

**Who should apply** You'll be open-minded and flexible and will care about your own personal development. One of your aims will be to become a rounded professional, as well as a successful solicitor – and you'll look to balance your career with a life outside of the office. Workwise, you'll care about the quality of service you give to clients (internal and external), and you'll want to make a real and direct contribution to the firm's commercial success.

**Training programme** With the 2007 LawCareers.Net Best Trainer award under our belt, we offer a training contract which revolves around real work. We only place one or two trainees in each department which means that you'll be listened to and valued, and will get much greater personal access to and attention from your partner and colleagues.

We also want you to use the two-year training contract with us as a time to try out new things, both at your desk and away from it. Our thinking is that if we allow you the freedom to innovate and experiment, you will develop really useful skills for your future career.

**When and how to apply** Please apply online at www.shoosmiths.co.uk. The closing date for training contract applications is 31 July each year.

**Work placements** We offer placements of up to two weeks during June, July and August. Please apply online via our website. The closing date for summer placement applications is 28 February each year.

**Sponsorship** GDL & LPC funding – we pay fees plus a maintenance grant.

| | |
|---|---|
| Vacancies | 17 |
| Trainees | 27 |
| Partners | 105 |
| Total staff | 1450 |

**Work placement**   yes
*(see Insider Report on p140)*

**Apply to**
Sally Stagles (via online system)

**Starting salary**
Competitive

**Minimum qualifications**
2.1 degree

**Sponsorship**
GDL & LPC

**Offices**
Solent, Northampton, Nottingham, Thames Valley, Milton Keynes, Birmingham, Basingstoke (not available for placement or training contract)

shoosmiths

# Shulmans

120 Wellington Street, Leeds LS1 4LT
**Tel:** 0113 245 2833
**Fax:** 0113 246 7326
**Email:** training@shulmans.co.uk
**Web:** www.shulmans.co.uk

**The firm** Shulmans is in the centre of Leeds, the very best place to train. Leeds, the second largest legal centre in the country, is a vibrant and thriving city – a brilliant place to live and work with facilities to match London, but without London's horrific living expenses.

Founded in 1981, Shulmans has grown to 11 partners and around 140 staff housed in modern offices, which are designed and fitted out to offer the very best facilities.

Young, modern and commercial in outlook, our philosophy is the provision of fast, efficient and practical advice for our clients, which mainly comprise the full range of commercial clients from an enviable list of plc and institutional clients to small new businesses. We are committed to quality and hold both the Investors in People and Lexcel awards.

**Types of work** Our core work, which is commercially based, includes all areas of corporate, company and commercial work, including corporate finance, property and development work and litigation.

The firm is a leading member of Interlegal, an association of law firms across the world, which provides an international element to the firm's work and the possibility of trainee solicitor exchanges with other law firms in the network – visit our website for more information.

**Who should apply** We want to attract the best because we regard ourselves as the best. We take pride in the very high skill levels of our staff and you will be expected to demonstrate professionalism, precision, commitment and hard work.

**Training programme** We take our responsibilities to trainees seriously. Today's trainees will be tomorrow's partners. From their first day, our trainees are immersed in the practical application of the law in a modern, commercial environment.

We take a structured and informed approach to career progression and only ever recruit trainees with the intention that they stay with us forever. In your first week you will find out what you need to do to become a partner and exactly how our career structure works.

Trainees can obtain career opportunities in a firm with high-quality clients and work, and can expect to gain experience in all areas of our work, including work on complex cases under supervision and full responsibility in some smaller cases.

**When and how to apply** We aim to make appointments two years prior to the start of a training contract. Refer to our website for up-to-date details.

**Work placements** A vacation placement scheme may be offered in 2008. Watch our website for details. Successful candidates will also be expected to complete a four-week period of paid internship in each of the two summers prior to the start of the training contract.

**Sponsorship** We have put together a unique salary and benefits package which includes our interest-free loan replacement scheme. This can provide funding up to £5,000 which can be written off during the training contract. Refer to our website for further details.

| | |
|---|---|
| Vacancies | 3 |
| Trainees | 7 |
| Partners | 11 |
| Total staff | 140 |

**Apply to**
Geraldine Shaw,
HR Manager

**Starting salary**
1st year: £18,000
2nd year: £19,500
(2006)

**Minimum qualifications**
2.2 degree

**Sponsorship**
See text

**Offices**
Leeds

# Sidley Austin LLP

Woolgate Exchange, 25 Basinghall Street, London EC2V 5HA
**Tel:** 020 7360 3600
**Fax:** 020 7626 7937
**Email:** ukrecruitment@sidley.com
**Web:** www.sidley.com

**The firm** Sidley Austin LLP is a full-service law firm with more than 1,600 lawyers and other professionals practising on four continents. The London office has over 100 lawyers and can offer experience in a range of international finance and corporate work across a broad range industries.

**Types of work** Corporate & securities, debt and equity capital markets, corporate reorganisations and bankruptcy, employment, financial services regulation, insurance, IP/IT, real estate and real estate finance, securitisation and structured finance and tax.

**Who should apply** The firm looks for enthusiastic individuals who can demonstrate a consistently strong academic record and who have a real interest in a legal career in international finance and corporate work.

**Training programme** Trainee solicitors generally will share an office and work closely with a partner or senior associate. We ensure that your experience is practical and you will be encouraged to take responsibility where appropriate. Your supervisor will provide feedback and advice as necessary and a more formal appraisal takes place at the end of each seat. Regular meetings with the Training Principal and the input of the partner with responsibility for work allocation ensure both quantity and quality of your work experience. Trainees are encouraged to participate in the firm training programme. Outside of work, the firm has a strong social calendar, headed by the social committee. Although we are expanding, the firm retains the intimacy and camaraderie of a smaller firm. The aim if that is you join the firm as trainee, it a long term commitment and the firm has an excellent record of keeping trainee solicitors on qualification.

**When and how to apply** By end of July 2008, to begin in a training contract in 2010.

**Sponsorship** GDL/CPE and LPC fees paid. Maintenance grant £7,000 per annum.

| | |
|---|---|
| Vacancies | 14 |
| Trainees | 14 |
| Partners | 41 |
| Total staff | 260 approx |

**Apply to**
Graduate Recruitment

**Starting salary**
1st year: £38,000
2nd year: £42,000

**Minimum qualifications**
2.1 degree plus A and B grades at A level

**Sponsorship**
CPE/LPC

**Offices**
Beijing, Brussels, Chicago, Dallas, Frankfurt, Geneva, Hong Kong, London, Los Angeles, New York, San Francisco, Shanghai, Singapore, Sydney, Tokyo, Washington DC

# Simmons & Simmons

CityPoint, One Ropemaker Street, London EC2Y 9SS
**Tel:** 020 7628 2020
**Fax:** 020 7628 2070
**Email:** recruitment@simmons-simmons.com
**Web:** www.simmons-simmons.com/traineelawyers

**The firm** Dynamic and innovative, Simmons & Simmons have a reputation for offering a superior legal service, wherever and whenever it is required. Our lawyers' high quality advice and the positive working atmosphere in our 21 international offices have won admiration and praise from both the legal community and our business clients.

**Types of work** We offer our clients a full range of legal services across numerous industry sectors. We have a particular focus on the world's fastest growing sectors, that is: energy & infrastructure; financial institutions; life sciences; and technology. We provide a wide choice of service areas in which our lawyers can specialise. These include corporate & commercial; communications, outsourcing & technology; dispute resolution; employment & benefits; EU & competition; financial markets; IP; projects; real estate; taxation & pensions.

**Who should apply** We look for a strong track record of achievements from our candidates. We are interested to find out about your academic successes but we will also explore your ability to form excellent interpersonal relations and work within a team environment, as well as your levels of motivation, drive and ambition. Show us evidence of a rich 'life experience' as well as examples of your intellectual capabilities and we will provide you with everything you need to become a successful member of our firm.

**Training programme** Our training programme is constantly evolving to build the skills you will need to be successful in the fast moving world of international business. We provide experience in a range of areas of law and a balanced approach to gaining the knowledge, expertise and abilities you will need to qualify in the practice area of your choice.

**When and how to apply** Applications should be made from 1 November 2007. All applicants should submit an online application form which can be found on our website at www.simmons-simmons.com/traineelawyers.

**Work placements** Our summer internship programme is one of our primary means of selecting candidates for a career at Simmons & Simmons. It provides us with the chance to test your suitability for a training contract. It is also a unique opportunity for you to get to know our firm, decide if we are the best firm for you and for you to prove your potential during your time with us. Undergraduates usually apply for internships in their penultimate year. However, we are also happy to offer internships to final year students, graduates, mature and international students and those changing career.

Open days: We run several open days throughout the year. Our open days provide you with a valuable opportunity to gain an insight into who we are and what we do.

Insight workshops: Our insight workshops are particularly suitable for candidates from non-law backgrounds. Our workshops will give you an insight into Simmons & Simmons and the commercial environment in which we operate.

**Sponsorship** We will cover your full tuition fees at law school and offer a maintenance allowance of up to £7,500.

| | |
|---|---|
| Vacancies | 50 |
| Trainees | 173 |
| Partners | 218 |
| Total staff | 2002 |

**Work placement** yes
*(see Insider Report on p137)*

**Apply to**
Anna King, Graduate
Recruitment Officer

**Starting salary**
£36,000 first and second seat
£40,000 third and fourth seat

**Minimum qualifications**
2.1 degree (or equivalent)

**Sponsorship**
GDL/LPC

**Offices**
Abu Dhabi, Amsterdam, Brussels, Dubai, Düsseldorf, Frankfurt, Hong Kong, Lisbon, London, Madeira, Madrid, Milan, New York, Oporto, Padua, Paris, Qatar, Rome, Rotterdam, Shanghai, Tokyo

Simmons & Simmons

## SHERRINGTON LAW, THE ACCIDENT SOLICITORS
Sherrington House, 66 Chorley Street,
Bolton BL1 4AL
**Tel:** 01204 361799
**Fax:** 01204 362988
**Email:** mailbox@sherringtons.com
**Apply to:** Mr TB Walters

A unique and leading firm specialising exclusively in accident cases on a nationwide basis, and dedicated to the pursuit of professionalism and results.

| | |
|---|---|
| V | Poss |
| T | 2 |
| P | 4 |
| TS | 90 |
| WP | no |

## SHRANKS
Ruskin House, 40/41 Museum Street,
London WC1A 1LT
**Tel:** 020 7831 6677
**Fax:** 020 7831 7627
**Email:** shrank@shranks.co.uk
**Apply to:** Mr Jeremy P Ticktum

Landlord and tenant, commercial property, company/commercial, residential conveyancing, personal injury, employment, general litigation, wills, trusts and probate.

| | |
|---|---|
| V | 0 |
| T | 1 |
| P | 2 |
| TS | 9 |
| WP | no |

## SILLS & BETTERIDGE
46 Silver Street, Lincoln LN2 1ED
**Tel:** 01522 542211
**Fax:** 01522 510463
**Email:** lgraham@sillslegal.co.uk
**Apply to:** Ms Liz Graham

A broadly based practice acting for a range of private and business clients and taking publicly funded work. Offices in Lincoln, Boston, Spilsby and Coningsby.

| | |
|---|---|
| V | 2 |
| T | 7 |
| P | 18 |
| TS | 120 |
| WP | no |

## SILVERBECK RYMER
Dempster Building, Atlantic Way,
Brunswick Bus Park, Liverpool L3 HUU
**Tel:** 0151 236 9594
**Fax:** 0151 227 1035
**Apply to:** Mr Ian Lamb

Major player within the insurance litigation sector, acting for claimant and liability claims department. 'Centre of excellence' for catastrophic injuries.

| | |
|---|---|
| V | 0-3[09] |
| T | 3 |
| P | 7 |
| TS | 218 |
| WP | no |

## SILVERMAN SHERLIKER LLP
7 Bath Place, London EC2A 3DR
**Tel:** 020 7749 2700
**Fax:** 020 7739 4309
**Email:** ncjl@silvermansherliker.co.uk
**Apply to:** Mr Nicholas Lakeland

A progressive and growing City law firm specialising in business law. A busy practice offering opportunities to candidates with motivation and self-reliance. There are three vacancies at present.

| | |
|---|---|
| V | 3[08] |
| T | 5 |
| P | 9 |
| TS | 28 |
| WP | no |

## SINTONS LLP
The Cube, Barrack Road,
Newcastle upon Tyne NE4 6DB
**Tel:** 0191 226 7878
**Fax:** 0191 226 7850
**Email:** k.simms@sintons.co.uk
**Apply to:** Mrs K Simms

Very highly regarded diverse, mid-sized city centre firm acting for businesses, entrepreneurs, organisations and individuals. Strengths: company & commercial, PI, commercial property and private client.

| | |
|---|---|
| V | 0 |
| T | 5 |
| P | 20 |
| TS | 140 |
| WP | yes |

## SLEE BLACKWELL
10 Cross Street, Barnstaple, Devon EX31 1BA
**Tel:** 01271 372 128
**Fax:** 01271 325 556
**Email:** julia.busfield@sleeblackwell.co.uk
**Apply to:** Mrs J Busfield

Thirteen partner firm with five offices throughout Devon. Predominantly commercial, property and litigation based.

| | |
|---|---|
| V | 0 |
| T | 1 |
| P | 13 |
| TS | 85 |
| WP | no |

## SMITH LLEWELYN PARTNERSHIP
18 Princess Way, Swansea SA1 3LW
**Tel:** 01792 464444
**Fax:** 01792 464726
**Email:** enquiries@smithllewelyn.com
**Apply to:** Mr Julian Thomas

South Wales' leading medical negligence, pharmaceutical product liability and personal injury firm; community legal service franchise in all areas committed to the victim.

| | |
|---|---|
| V | 1 |
| T | 2 |
| P | 4 |
| TS | 40 |
| WP | yes |

---

**V** = Vacancies / **T** = Trainees / **P** = Partners / **TS** = Total Staff / **WP** = Work Placement

# SJ Berwin LLP

10 Queen Street Place, London EC4R 1BE
**Tel:** 020 7111 2222
**Fax:** 020 7111 2000
**Email:** graduate.recruitment@sjberwin.com
**Web:** www.sjberwin.com/gradrecruit

**The firm** A pan-European, corporate-led City law firm which was established in 1982 in response to the dynamic, new entrepreneurial atmosphere of the UK and Europe. Since then it has grown to 170 partners and a staff of over 1,000. The firm has a wide range of departments, including corporate finance, real estate, litigation, employment, commercial, EU and competition, finance, intellectual property, media, construction, tax and financial services. Of these, corporate finance is the largest, generating around 50% of the annual turnover.

SJ Berwin has been named European Best Law Firm (Fund Formation) at the Private Equity Online Awards for the sixth year running and has also been named Law Firm of the Year for the EVCJ award for Venture Capital and Private Equity for the fourth successive year.

The client base is truly international and the firm has built up excellent links with other firms which specialise in different jurisdictions. As a European firm we have offices in Brussels, Paris, Madrid, Berlin, Frankfurt, Munich, Milan and Turin.

**Types of work** All aspects of commercial and corporate law with a wide range of national and international clients including blue-chip, private and public companies.

**Who should apply** We welcome applications for the summer vacation schemes from penultimate-year law students and non-law finalists and all graduates. Training contract applications are welcome from any discipline.

**Training programme** The traineeship is split into four six-month seats in a variety of departments, including two corporate seats. There are opportunities for seats in our overseas offices. Training is provided through a balance of hands-on, high-profile work and weekly training programmes, all suited to the demands of trainees and the departments. The legal and skills training programmes for qualified solicitors provide excellent opportunities for continual professional development.

The training department looks after trainee personnel issues, along with the trainee solicitor committee, to ensure a truly supportive system is in operation throughout the traineeship and into qualification.

**When and how to apply** Training contract applications should be made by 31 July 2008 to begin Autumn 2010. Vacation scheme applications should be made by 31 January 2008. Please apply online. The link to the application form is on our website at www.sjberwin.com/gradrecruit.

**Work placements** We run three two-week summer schemes with a full programme of workshops, talks and social events. Open days in December and January are also available.

| | |
|---|---|
| Vacancies | 50 |
| Trainees | 87 |
| Partners | 170 |
| Total staff | 1200 |

**Work placement** yes
*(see Insider Report on p139)*

**Apply to**
Graduate Recruitment Team

**Starting salary**
£36,000

**Minimum qualifications**
2.1 degree

**Sponsorship**
GDL/LPC

**Offices**
Berlin, Brussels, Frankfurt, London, Madrid, Milan, Munich, Paris, Turin

# Skadden, Arps, Slate, Meagher & Flom (UK) LLP

40 Bank Street, Canary Wharf, London E14 5DS
**Tel:** 020 7519 7000
**Fax:** 020 7519 7070
**Email:** graduate@skadden.com
**Web:** www.skadden.com

**The firm** Skadden is one of the leading law firms in the world with approximately 2,000 lawyers in 22 offices across the globe. Our clients include corporate, industrial and financial institutions and government entities.

The London office is the gateway to our European practice where we have some 250 lawyers dedicated to top-end, cross-border corporate transactions and international arbitration and litigation. We have handled matters in nearly every country in the greater European region, and in Africa and the Middle East. We consistently rank as a leader in all disciplines and amongst a whole host of accolades, we were recently voted 'Global Corporate Law Firm of the Year' (*Chambers and Partners*), 'Best US Law Firm in London' (*Legal Business*) and 'Best Trainer' in the US law firm in London category (LawCareers.Net Training & Recruitment Awards).

**Types of work** Lawyers across the European network focus primarily on corporate transactions, including domestic and cross-border mergers and acquisitions, private equity, capital markets, leveraged finance and banking, tax, corporate restructuring and energy and projects. We also advise in international arbitration and litigation and regulatory matters.

**Who should apply** We seek to recruit a small number of high-calibre graduates from any discipline to join our highly successful London office as trainee solicitors. We are looking for candidates who combine intellectual ability with enthusiasm, creativity and a demonstrable ability to rise to a challenge and to work with others towards a common goal.

**Training programme** The firm can offer you the chance to develop your career in a uniquely rewarding and professional environment. You will join a close-knit and diverse team in which you will be given ample opportunity to work on complex matters, almost all with an international aspect, whilst benefiting from highly personalised training and supervision in an informal and friendly environment.

The first year of your training contract will be divided into two six months seats where you will gain experience in corporate transactions and international litigation and arbitration. In the second year of your training contract, you will have the opportunity to discuss with us your prefernces for your remaining two seats. We also offer the opportunity for second year trainees to be seconded to our Hong Kong office for a six month seat.

**When and how to apply** Candidates must apply online at www.skadden.com by 31 July 2008 to begin training contracts in September 2010.

**Work placements** Skadden offers the opportunity for penultimate year law and non-law students to experience the culture and working environment of the firm through our two week vacation placements. Our vacation placements are paid and take place during Easter and over the course of the summer. The deadline for applications is 4 January 2008 for placements in 2008.

**Sponsorship** The firm pays for GDL and LPC course fees and provides a £8,000 grant for each year of these courses.

| | |
|---|---|
| Vacancies | 10* |
| Trainees | 7* |
| Partners | 23* |
| Total staff | 240* |
| * in London | |

**Work placement**   yes
*(see Insider Report on p141)*

**Apply**
Online

**Starting salary**
1st year - £40,000
2nd year - £43,000

**Minimum qualifications**
2.1 degree

**Sponsorship**
GDL/LPC

**Offices**
Beijing, Boston, Brussels, Chicago, Frankfurt, Hong Kong, Houston, London, Los Angeles, Moscow, Munich, New York Palo Alto, Paris, San Francisco, Singapore, Sydney, Tokyo, Toronto, Vienna, Washington DC, Wilmington

# Slaughter and May

One Bunhill Row, London EC1Y 8YY
**Tel:** 020 7600 1200
**Fax:** 020 7090 5000
**Web:** www.slaughterandmay.com

**The firm** An international law firm based in the City of London with clients ranging from the world's leading multinationals to venture capital start-ups. They include public and private companies, governments and non-governmental organisations, commercial and investment banks. Our lawyers devise solutions for complex, often transnational, problems and advise some of the world's brightest business minds. As well as our London and overseas offices, in order that we provide the best advice and service across the world, we nurture long-standing relationships with the leading independent law firms in other jurisdictions - relationships which are strengthened by exchanges of staff, know-how and technology, and which mean that individual lawyers at all levels work with their overseas counterparts as one team.

**Types of work** The firm's main activities are in the field of corporate, commercial and financing law. Our specialist groups - including tax, competition, financial regulation, dispute resolution, technology, media and telecommunications, intellectual property, commercial real estate, environment and pensions and employment - complement these main activities. We are organised into groups which undertake a general spread of work – we believe variety and challenge are essential for every lawyer.

**Who should apply** We are looking for intellectual capability (a good 2.1 ability or better), personality, common sense and the ability to communicate clearly. These qualities are personal to you, not the institution from which you gained your degree. While some of our trainees have read law at university, we welcome graduates from every discipline. More than 60 universities are represented among the lawyers who work in our firm.

**Training programme** It is the aim that every trainee recruited should continue his or her career with the firm. The training programme is designed to give a thorough grounding in the practice of being a solicitor, combining formal training with a high degree of hands-on experience. Trainees gain experience in a broad cross-section of the firm's practice by taking an active part in the work of four or five groups; they benefit from both the quality and the breadth of our work.

**When and how to apply** There is no closing date for receipt of applications for training contracts and we make no distinction between lawyers and non-lawyers in the timing of our recruitment. Our preferred method of application for training contracts and work experience schemes is by way of our online system at www.slaughterandmay.com. We will also accept postal applications - please send a CV and covering letter which should include a percentage breakdown of all examination results.

**Work placements** Christmas, Easter and summer schemes available for those considering a career as an English solicitor. The summer scheme is for students in the penultimate year of their first degree only. Applications for the summer scheme should arrive before 25 January 2008.

**Sponsorship** Maintenance grant, tuition and examination fees.

| | |
|---|---|
| Vacancies | 95 approx |
| Trainees | 182 |
| Partners | 133 |
| Total staff | 1300 approx |

**Work placement**   yes
*(see Insider Report on p143)*

**Apply to**
Charlotte Houghton,
Personnel Manager

**Starting salary**
£36,000 (May 2007) rising
to £40,000 in the second
year of training

**Minimum qualifications**
Good 2.1 ability, any
discipline

**Sponsorship**
CPE/LPC

**Offices**
London and overseas plus
'Best Friend' firms in all the
major jurisdictions

SLAUGHTER AND MAY

# Speechly Bircham LLP

6 St Andrew Street, London EC4A 3LX
**Tel:** 020 7427 6400
**Fax:** 020 7353 4368
**Email:** trainingcontracts@speechlys.com
**Web:** www.speechlys.com

**The firm** Speechly Bircham is a City law firm that provides a distinctive blend of advisory, transactional and disputes services in its five core areas of practice: corporate, private client, employment, property and construction. With over 180 lawyers, the firm acts for UK and international listed companies, banks and financial institutions, privately owned companies as well as high net worth individuals, families and trusts.

The firm's several discrete practice groups have an acknowledged reputation and performance which are competitive with those of larger firms. The structure of the firm and its ability to provide partner time and attention make it a good alternative to large City firms for many clients. The legal affairs of each client are managed by a single partner, responsible for ensuring that the service is delivered quickly and cost effectively.

Much of the firm's work has an international dimension, whether for UK clients doing business overseas, supervising and co-ordinating the work of foreign law firms, or advising overseas clients with business and financial interests in the UK.

The firm was also delighted to have been awarded 'Best Trainer - Medium City Firm' at the LawCareers.Net Training and Recruitment Awards 2007.

**Types of work** Speechly Bircham's principal practice areas are: banking and finance, commercial litigation, construction and engineering, corporate, corporate tax, employment, family, financial services, IP, technology and commercial, pensions, private client, private equity, property and property litigation.

**Who should apply** Both law and non-law graduates who are capable of achieving a 2.1 degree. The firm seeks intellectual individuals who enjoy a collaborative environment where they can make an impact.

**Training programme** The firm divides the training contract into four six-month seats. Emphasis is given to early responsibility and supervised client contact providing trainees with a practical learning environment.

**When and how to apply** No later than 31 July 2008 to commence September 2010. Further details on the firm and an application form can be found at www.speechlys.com.

**Work placements** The summer placement scheme (20 places) for students gives them the chance to experience a City legal practice. In a three-week placement, students will undertake real fee-earning work, which is likely to include research, drafting letters, attending client meetings and going to court. Students will be asked to research and present on a current topical issue at the end of their placements. Applications for summer placements to be received by 15 February 2008 for the 2008 intake.

**Sponsorship** GDL and LPC fees paid in full together with a maintenance grant.

| | |
|---|---|
| Vacancies | 10 |
| Trainees | 20 |
| Partners | 62 |
| Total staff | 278 |

**Work placement** yes
*(see Insider Report on p145)*

**Apply to**
Nicola Swann, Director of Human Resources

**Starting salary**
1st seat: £31,000
2nd seat: £32,000
3rd seat: £33,000
4th seat: £34,000
(September 2007)

**Minimum qualifications**
2.1 degree, any discipline

**Sponsorship**
GDL/LPC

**Offices**
London

SpeechlyBircham

| | | | |
|---|---|---|---|
| **SMITH PARTNERSHIP**<br>4th Floor, Celtic House, Friary Street,<br>Derby DE1 1LS<br>**Tel:** 01332 225 225<br>**Fax:** 01332 225 444<br>**Email:** dclark@smithpartnership.co.uk<br>**Apply to:** Mr David Clark | Smith Partnership is a young dynamic firm with offices throughout the East Midlands, practicing in a broad range of disciplines including public funded, private client and commercial law. | V<br>T<br>P<br>TS<br>WP | 1[09]<br>7<br>20<br>200<br>no |
| **SONN MACMILLAN**<br>19 Widegate Street, London E1 7HP<br>**Tel:** 020 7377 8889<br>**Fax:** 020 7377 8279<br>**Email:** emacmillan@sonnmacmillan.co.uk<br>**Apply to:** Mr Euan MacMillan | Specialist criminal defence firm, mainly legal aid work. Members of the Serious Fraud Panel. | V<br>T<br>P<br>TS<br>WP | 2[08]<br>4<br>2<br>12<br>no |
| **SOOKIAS & SOOKIAS**<br>5th Floor, 15 Brook's Mews, London W1K 4DS<br>**Tel:** 020 7465 8000<br>**Fax:** 020 7465 8001<br>**Email:** info@sookias.co.uk<br>**Apply to:** Barbara Lewin | Small West End solicitors specialising in commercial work including immigration, litigation, tax and company matters. | V<br>T<br>P<br>TS<br>WP | 0<br>0<br>4<br>20<br>no |
| **SOUTH BEDFORDSHIRE DISTRICT COUNCIL**<br>The District Offices, High Street North, Dunstable,<br>Bedfordshire LU6 1LF<br>**Tel:** 01582 472222<br>**Fax:** 01582 474016<br>**Apply to:** Mr AS Kang | SBDC offices are situated in Dunstable, Bedfordshire. Principle towns include Leighton Buzzard and Houghton Regis. Its administrative area covers a large part of rural bedfordshire. | V<br>T<br>P<br>TS<br>WP | 0<br>2<br>-<br>8<br>no |
| **SOUTHAMPTON CITY COUNCIL**<br>Corporate Legal Team, 1st Floor, Civic Centre,<br>Southampton SO14 7LT<br>**Tel:** 023 8083 2028<br>**Fax:** 023 80832 308<br>**Email:** sarita.riley@southampton.gov.uk<br>**Apply to:** Miss Sarita Riley | Local Government Legal Service - Unitary Authority | V<br>T<br>P<br>TS<br>WP | 0-1<br>1<br>-<br>50<br>no |
| **SOUTHERNS**<br>68 Bank Parade, PO Box 21, Burnley BB11 1UB<br>**Tel:** 01282 422711<br>**Fax:** 01282 470320<br>**Email:** evew@southernslaw.co.uk<br>**Apply to:** Mrs Eve Whittaker | General high street practice. Offices also in Nelson and Colne. Apply via our website. | V<br>T<br>P<br>TS<br>WP | 1[08]<br>4<br>9<br>60<br>no |
| **SPEAKEASY ADVICE CENTRE**<br>2-4 Arabella Street, Cardiff CF24 4TA<br>**Tel:** 029 2045 3111<br>**Fax:** 029 2045 1064<br>**Email:** kai.tan@speakeasyadvice.co.uk<br>**Apply to:** Mr Andrew Buchanan-Smith | Not-for-profit legal advice centre providing legal help and representation under legal aid franchise or on a pro bono basis regarding debt, benefits and related issues. | V<br>T<br>P<br>TS<br>WP | 0<br>0<br>-<br>15<br>no |
| **SPEARING WAITE**<br>27-41 Friar Lane, Leicester LE1 5RB<br>**Tel:** 0116 262 4225<br>**Fax:** 0116 251 2009<br>**Email:** info@spearingwaite.co.uk<br>**Apply to:** Mr WEB Spearing | One of the largest firms in Leicester specialising in commercial property, commercial, corporate, insolvency, litigation, employment, private client. An Investor in People and Lexcel accredited. | V<br>T<br>P<br>TS<br>WP | 3-4[08]<br>5<br>12<br>70<br>no |

# Squire Sanders & Dempsey

Tower 42, 25 Old Broad Street, London EC2N 1HQ
**Tel:** 020 7189 8000
**Fax:** 020 7189 8111
**Email:** eaustin@ssd.com
**Web:** www.ssd.com

**The firm** Squire Sanders was founded in 1890 and is one of the largest US-based international law firms. The London office offers a full set of services to UK, US and international clients investing or doing business in Europe or the UK, as well as to clients looking to do business around the world. A broad group of experienced UK and US lawyers advise clients on complex international and UK transactions in the communications, restructuring, finance, technology, real estate, transport, international trade, hospitality and leisure, private equity, energy and manufacturing sectors.

**Types of work** The main focus of the London office is corporate and commercial, often with a cross-border element. The work tends to be varied, challenging and exciting, often in multiple jurisdictions across Europe and the world. The London office works closely with the firm's offices in Europe, CEE, the CIS and the Middle East, and is an important centre of the firm's international practice, serving the needs of clients with businesses spanning the globe. Insolvency, communications, finance, tax and commercial litigation are other core areas of our practice. We have a mixture of domestic and overseas clients, typically multinational companies, UK plcs, UK limited companies and high net-worth individuals.

**Who should apply** We would like to hear from graduates of all disciplines who have, or would expect, a 2.1 degree from a good university. You should also be motivated and ambitious, and be able to work well in a team in an intimate working environment. It is an advantage for applicants to have language skills, but this is not essential.

**Training programme** The two-year training contract is divided into four six-month seats which cover the main practice areas in the London office. In most cases one of these seats comprises a secondment to one of our international offices. At the end of each seat your progress and performance will be reviewed in an appraisal with your training principal. We believe in giving trainees responsibility for files at an early stage of the development of their careers, subject to appropriate supervision, and for them to develop practical experience to go hand in hand with the theoretical training. Career progression can be rapid for bright and motivated trainees.

**When and how to apply** By 30 September 2008 to begin September 2010. Please send us your CV and a covering letter

**Work placements** We run open days during August. Apply by CV and covering letter between 1 January and 31 March of each year.

| | |
|---|---|
| Vacancies | 3-4 |
| Trainees | 7 |
| Partners | 282* |
| Total staff | 1720* |

*denotes worldwide figure

**Work placement** yes

**Apply to**
Elizabeth Austin

**Starting salary**
Market rate

**Minimum qualifications**
2.1 degree

**Offices**
*Europe*: Bratislava, Brussels, Bucharest*, Budapest, Dublin*, Frankfurt, Kiev*, London, Moscow, Prague, Warsaw.

*Americas*: Buenos Aires*, Caracas, Cincinnati, Cleveland, Columbus, Houston, Los Angeles, Miami, New York, Palo Alto, Phoenix, Rio de Janeiro, San Francisco, Santiago*, Santo Domingo, Tallahasssee, Tampa, Tysons Corner, Washington DC, West Palm Beach.

*Asia*: Beijing, Hong Kong, Shanghai, Tokyo

* associated office

SQUIRE SANDERS | LEGAL COUNSEL WORLDWIDE

# Stanley Tee LLP

High Street, Bishop's Stortford, Hertfordshire CM23 2LU
**Tel:** 01279 755200
**Fax:** 01279 758400
**Email:** rae@stanleytee.co.uk
**Web:** www.stanleytee.co.uk

**The firm** Established in 1915, Stanley Tee is a well-established and progressive firm of growing regional and national influence. We have a reputation for excellence based on the high calibre of our staff and a rigorous on-going recruitment policy. Our head offices are in Bishop's Stortford, Hertfordshire. We also have offices in Saffron Walden, Braintree and Great Dunmow, Essex and in Cambridge. The firm benefits from a strategic location close to the City of London and Stansted Airport and fast connections through its rail and motorway links with the Midlands and East Anglia.

**Types of work** We provide a broad spectrum of legal services to private and corporate clients (including insurance companies and publicly quoted companies) within our various departments: company and commercial, commercial property, conveyancing, litigation, crime and regulatory breach, family, employment and private client. Within these various departments the firm is involved in complex, high-value and widely publicised cases.

Our Home Counties location – close to London, yet enjoying a country setting – attracts an interesting cross-section of clients. On the one hand we act for many City-based clients, for whom we handle mostly commercial and litigious business. On the other hand, we represent a good many local – especially farming – clients, both public and private.

Full IT services are installed throughout the firm providing a stimulating, team-based work environment.

**Who should apply** We are looking for graduate trainees who are ambitious, highly motivated and who welcome a professional challenge. All applicants should be personable, self confident and able to inspire confidence in clients. They should also demonstrate the intellectual rigour and strength of character necessary to establish a firm foundation for a successful career.

**Training programme** On appointment, trainees are attached to individual partners as personal assistants. During their training period at our head office in Bishop's Stortford trainees will spend approximately six months with each of four different partners, thus gaining a variety of legal experience.

We regard trainee solicitors as part of the professional team and fundamental to the future progress of the firm. Initiative is encouraged and rewarded and, subject to ability, trainees will be actively entrusted with responsibility.

Although we make no formal commitment at the outset – nor ask for one – we often invite proven trainees to remain with us after training. It is our policy to recruit our assistant solicitors from our trainees. Many of our present assistant solicitors and most of our partners and associates trained with us.

**When and how to apply** All applications for trainee appointments should be addressed to Bob Elms, training partner, approximately 18 months before the proposed commencement of the training contract. Generally contracts start in September each year. Applications submitted after this time may still be considered. Where applications are received earlier we may consider offering the applicant the opportunity of summer vacation work. Application forms can be downloaded from our website.

**Sponsorship** Maintenance grant available for LPC. Full details available on application.

| | |
|---|---|
| Vacancies | 4 |
| Trainees | 8 |
| Partners | 17 |
| Total staff | 175 |

**Work placement** yes

**Apply to**
Bob Elms

**Starting salary**
£20,000 (2008)

**Sponsorship**
LPC

**Offices**
Bishop's Stortford,
Saffron Walden, Braintree,
Dunmow, Cambridge

STANLEY
TEE
LLP
SOLICITORS

# Stephenson Harwood

One St Paul's Churchyard, London EC4M 8SH
**Tel:** 020 7329 4422
**Fax:** 020 7329 7100
**Email:** graduate.recruitment@shlegal.com
**Web:** www.shlegal.com

**The firm** Established in the City of London in 1828, Stephenson Harwood has developed into an international practice, with a commercial focus and a wide client base.

**Types of work** Corporate (including corporate finance, funds, corporate tax, business technology); employment, pensions and benefits; banking and finance; dry and wet shipping litigation; dispute resolution; and real estate.

**Who should apply** Enthusiastic and committed individuals who have business awareness and a strong academic background which is demonstrated by a first or 2.1 degree, in any discipline, and 26 UCAS points (or equivalent).

You will have a stong desire to learn and the confirdence to take responsibility from the day you join us. You will also be able to demonstrate excellent communication and team working skills and, as well as an interest in law, you muct enjoy following modern business issues. Candidates must be eligible to work in the UK.

**Training programme** As the graduate intake is relatively small, we give trainees individual attention, coaching and monitoring. Your structured and challenging programme involves four six-month seats in areas of the firm covering contentious and non-contentious experience across any department within our practice groups: corporate, commercial litigation, banking and finance, employment, pensions and benefits, shipping and real estate. It may also involve a secondment to one of our overseas offices or to a client in London. These seats include on-the-job training and you will share an office with a partner or senior solicitor. In-house lectures complement your training and there is continuous review of your career development.

You will have the opportunity to spend six months abroad and have free language tuition where appropriate. You will be given your own caseload and as much responsibility as you can shoulder. The firm plays a range of team sports, has subsidised membership of a City health club (or a health club of your choice), and has privileged seats for concerts at the Royal Albert Hall and the London Coliseum and access to private views at the Tate Gallery.

**When and how to apply** 1 November – 31 July 2008 to begin 2010 (although non-law graduates should apply earlier). Apply online via the firm's website.

**Work placements** Summer only. 18 places available. Placements last for two weeks with an allowance of £260 per week. Application deadline is 17 February 2008.

**Sponsorship** For fees and maintenance awards.

| | |
|---|---|
| Vacancies | 12 |
| Trainees | 31 |
| Partners | 75 |
| Total staff | 545 |

**Work placement**   yes

**Apply to**
Romina Chambers

**Starting salary**
£35,000

**Minimum qualifications**
First or 2.1 degree

**Sponsorship**
CPE/LPC

**Offices**
London, Hong Kong, Guangzhou, Paris, Piraeus, Singapore, Shanghai
Associated offices in:
Greece, South Africa, Kuwait, Croatia, France, Romania

**STEPHENSON HARWOOD**

| | | | |
|---|---|---|---|
| **SPENCE & HORNE**<br>343 Mare Street, Hackney, London E8 1HY<br>**Tel:** 020 8985 2277<br>**Fax:** 020 8985 1177<br>**Apply to:** Miss A Spence | Small franchised legal aid practice specialising in immigration, family and housing with private clients in most other areas of law. | V<br>T<br>P<br>TS<br>WP | 0-2<br>1<br>2<br>8<br>yes |
| **STAFFURTH & BRAY**<br>York Road Chambers, York Road, Bognor Regis, W Sussex P021 1LT<br>**Tel:** 01243 864001<br>**Fax:** 01243 860708<br>**Email:** dwood@staffurth.co.uk<br>**Apply to:** Mr David Wood | General practice with offices in Bognor Regis covering all aspects of non-contentious work and litigation. | V<br>T<br>P<br>TS<br>WP | 0<br>4<br>5<br>45<br>no |
| **STAMP JACKSON AND PROCTER**<br>5 Parliament Street, Hull HU1 2AZ<br>**Tel:** 01482 324591<br>**Fax:** 01482 224048<br>**Email:** gen@sjplaw.co.uk<br>**Apply to:** Mrs Glynis Nesbitt | Providing a full range of commercial services to medium-sized businesses and public sector bodies; also dealing with personal injury/medical negligence litigation. | V<br>T<br>P<br>TS<br>WP | 2<br>5<br>8<br>65<br>yes |
| **STEELES**<br>3 The Norwich Business Park, Whiting Road, Norwich NR4 6DJ<br>**Tel:** 01603 598000<br>**Fax:** 01603 598111<br>**Email:** personnel@steeleslaw.co.uk<br>**Apply to:** Ms Ann Chancellor | A leading East Anglian general practice strongly focused on service excellence. High profile commercial client base. Offices in Norwich, London and Diss. | V<br>T<br>P<br>TS<br>WP | 6[09]<br>13<br>19<br>180<br>yes |
| **STEPHENS & SCOWN**<br>Curzon House, Southernhay West, Exeter EX1 1RS<br>**Tel:** 01392 210700<br>**Fax:** 01392 274010<br>**Email:** personnel@stephens-scown.co.uk<br>**Apply to:** Ms Heather Gibbs | The largest firm of solicitors with offices in Devon and Cornwall. Particular strengths include agriculture, corporate, family and litigation. Offices in Exeter, St Austell and Truro. | V<br>T<br>P<br>TS<br>WP | 2[08]<br>6<br>33<br>230<br>no |
| **STEPHENS & SON LLP**<br>Rome House, 37-41 Railway Street, Chatham, Kent ME4 4RP<br>**Tel:** 01634 811444<br>**Fax:** 01634 831532<br>**Email:** email@stephens-son.co.uk<br>**Apply to:** Miss Jacqueline Shicluna | One of the largest firms within the Medway Towns. The firm has achieved Lexcel + IIP. | V<br>T<br>P<br>TS<br>WP | 21[09]<br>2<br>7<br>47<br>no |
| **STEPHENSONS**<br>26 Union Street, Leigh WN7 1AT<br>**Tel:** 01942 777777<br>**Fax:** 01942 774397<br>**Apply to:** Mrs Janine Turner | Northwest regional full service practice. Serving small and medium sized businesses, public sector organisations, bulk referrals from banks and insurance companies, private individuals and LSC work. | V<br>T<br>P<br>TS<br>WP | 10<br>20<br>25<br>400<br>yes |
| **STEVENSDRAKE**<br>117-119 High Street, Crawley, West Sussex RH10 1YN<br>**Tel:** 01293 596900<br>**Fax:** 01293 596968<br>**Email:** jackie.darwin@stevensdrake.com<br>**Apply to:** Mrs Jackie Darwin | Niche commercial practice with strong property and commercial departments. Litigation and large specialist debt collection section. | V<br>T<br>P<br>TS<br>WP | 2[09]<br>4<br>9<br>65<br>no |

# Stevens & Bolton LLP

The Billings, Guildford GU1 4YD
**Tel:** 01483 302264
**Fax:** 01483 302254
**Email:** gradrec@stevens-bolton.co.uk
**Web:** www.stevens-bolton.co.uk

**The firm** We are among a small batch of firms offering lawyers and clients a real alternative to London from a south east base. Our client base is located all over the country, as well as overseas and we believe it would be the envy of some larger firms. To support our aim to become a nationally recognised firm, we sponsor the BlackRock Masters Tennis event at the Albert Hall. The event is broadcast on BBC TV and last year over 20 firms paid to take a corporate box.

Our business is both successful and profitable. The firm's work is 80% commercial, the remainder being private client work advising medium and high net-worth individuals. Clients include FTSE 100 businesses, subsidiaries of major international groups and growing, owner-managed companies. We receive instructions from household names such as Rentokil Initial plc, Hays plc, The BOC Group and Morse plc to name a few. In the last financial year revenue was a shade over £14 million and profit per equity partner stood at £305,000. To sum up, *Legal Business* described us as "...a City firm without the EC postcode".

Award winning: LawCareers.Net is the online resource for tomorrow's lawyers and we are proud that we have won three awards in the last four years; two for training and one for recruitment. Also in 2007 we won Corporate Law Firm of the Year Insider South East Dealmakers Awards.

**Who should apply** We'd like to hear from you if you have (or expect) a 2.1 or first class degree. Just as important is the kind of person you are. Tell us about your motivations, achievements, interests and hobbies – what gets you out of bed in the morning? Initiative is a quality that we look for too, so think about situations you have been in where your involvement has made a real difference.

**Training programme** Your training with us will see you working for six months at a time in four different areas of the firm. One seat will be corporate & commercial plus three others from real estate, dispute resolution, employment, tax and trusts and family. The majority of our trainees go on and qualify into their chosen areas of work in the firm.

Current salaries start at £24,500, rising to £26,500 for second year trainees. Other benefits include 25 days holiday, pension, private healthcare, life assurance and an interest free loan for rail travel or car parking (from day one.)

**When and how to apply** You can apply any time up to 30 September 2008 and we welcome applications from law and non-law students. Applications should be made by completing our online application form which is available from our website.

**Work placements** We will be running a vacation scheme in the summer of 2008. Please see our website for further information.

**Sponsorship** We pay the fees for the CPE/GDL and LPC, (if no grant is available), and £4,000 maintenance grant for each course of study.

| | |
|---|---|
| Vacancies | 4 |
| Trainees | 7 |
| Partners | 31 |
| Total staff | 150 |

**Work placement** yes

**Apply to**
Ms Julie Bounden,
Human Resources Manager

**Starting salary**
£24,500

**Minimum qualifications**
2.1 degree, 300 UCAS
points for A levels

**Sponsorship**
GDL/LPC

**Offices**
Guildford

| | |
|---|---|
| **STONE KING**<br>13 Queen Square, Bath BA1 2HJ<br>**Tel:** 01225 337599<br>**Fax:** 01225 335437<br>**Email:** sm@stoneking.co.uk<br>**Apply to:** Mrs Susan Murphy | General practice of seventeen partners. All solicitors/fee earners work in specialist units. Committed to publicly funded work. |

V 0
T 3
P 17
TS 130
WP no

| | |
|---|---|
| **STONE ROWE BREWER**<br>Stone House, 12/13 Church Street, Twickenham,<br>Middlesex TW1 3NJ<br>**Tel:** 020 8891 6141<br>**Fax:** 020 8744 1143<br>**Email:** info@srb.co.uk<br>**Apply to:** Mr John Andrews | General practice covering personal injury, commercial litigation, employment, family and conveyancing. Members of the Personal Injury Panel and the Employment Lawyers Association. |

V 1-2
T 4
P 5
TS 50
WP no

| | |
|---|---|
| **STONE WILDER**<br>195 St Helens Road, Hastings,<br>East Sussex TN34 2EA<br>**Tel:** 01424 712299<br>**Fax:** 01424 712302<br>**Email:** vkwilder@aol.com<br>**Apply to:** Ms VK Wilder | Trainee to provide assistance to modern progressive firm in areas of private client, European and commercial law. |

V 1
T 2
P 1
TS 9
WP yes

| | |
|---|---|
| **STONES**<br>Linacre House, Southernhay Gardens,<br>Exeter EX1 1UG<br>**Tel:** 01392 666777<br>**Fax:** 01392 666770<br>**Email:** bcs@stones-solicitors.co.uk<br>**Apply to:** Mrs Bronwen Courtenay-Stamp | One of the largest firms in Exeter with full range of clients from commercial to private individuals. Applicants should have a fluency in a foreign language. |

V 2[09]
T 4
P 23
TS 150
WP no

| | |
|---|---|
| **STORRAR COWDRY**<br>25 White Friars, Chester CH1 1NZ<br>**Tel:** 01244 400567<br>**Fax:** 01244 403377<br>**Email:** all@storrarcowdry.co.uk<br>**Apply to:** Mrs D Storrar | City centre general practice with good quality work. No criminal law. |

V 0
T 1
P 7
TS 24
WP no

| | |
|---|---|
| **STRINGFELLOW & GOWTHORPE**<br>41 North End Road, London W14 8SZ<br>**Tel:** 020 7371 3701<br>**Fax:** 020 7371 3744<br>**Apply to:** Mrs Claire Andoe | Specialist criminal defence team. |

V 1[08]
T 3
P 2
TS 15
WP no

| | |
|---|---|
| **SWEETMAN BURKE & SINKER**<br>158-160 The Broadway, West Ealing,<br>London W13 0TL<br>**Tel:** 020 8840 2572<br>**Fax:** 020 8567 8379<br>**Email:** info@sbs-law.co.uk<br>**Apply to:** Mr Peter Sweetman | We are looking for people who will initially work for one year as a paralegal and live within six miles of our practice. Family, crime, conveyancing and housing work. |

V Poss[09]
T 2
P 4
TS 16
WP yes

| | |
|---|---|
| **SYKES ANDERSON LLP**<br>Bury House, 31 Bury Street, London EC3A 5JJ<br>**Tel:** 020 7398 4700<br>**Fax:** 020 7283 6585<br>**Email:** catherine.smith@sykesanderson.com<br>**Apply to:** Ms Catherine Smith | A boutique commercial and civil firm in the City. Clients mainly owner-managed businesses and wealthy individuals with a few large corporates. Leasehold enfranchisement, French property and tax expertise. |

V 1[09]
T 2
P 5
TS 25
WP yes

# Taylor Vinters

Merlin Place, Milton Road, Cambridge CB4 0DP
**Tel:** 01223 225220
**Fax:** 01223 426523
**Email:** jo.douglas@taylorvinters.com
**Web:** www.taylorvinters.com

**The firm** Taylor Vinters is one of the largest firms in East Anglia, based in the city of Cambridge. It is the largest single-office firm in Cambridge. The firm represents a huge variety of clients, from long-established institutions such as the university to businesses involed in a wide range of activities, from landed estates to high-tech industries.

The firm came top of Chambers UK's quality league table for two consecutive years, 2004 and 2005, and also in 2005 was one of only six short listed for the prestigious Law Firm of the Year Award, the only finalist outside London.

**Types of work** Company commercial, intellectual property, commercial litigation, employment, commercial property, planning, agriculture, claimant personal injury, family and private client.

**Who should apply** Candidates should have energy, enthusiasm, intelligence, common sense, a friendly nature and a good sense of humour. Non-law degree graduates are welcomed.

**Training programme** The training contract comprises four-monthly seats in six of the above teams. Opportunities exist for exchanges with European network firms. There is an extensive in-house training programme within all departments and firm-wide. The Professional Skills Course is organised in-house.

The firm's training scheme was recently audited by the Law Society which reported: "This is an excellent training establishment. It is clear that the firm recognises the valuable part that trainees can play in the long term development of the firm. The training partner has devised a thorough training package which aims to produce high calibre solicitors who want to stay and develop their careers with the firm. The training programme goes far beyond what the vast majority of firms would consider".

**When and how to apply** Apply by 31 August 2008 to begin September 2010. The application form is available to print online.

**Work placements** Vacation placements are available, lasting one week. Apply by application form (again available online) by 31 March 2008 for Summer 2007.

| | |
|---|---|
| Vacancies | 5 |
| Trainees | 10 |
| Partners | 30 |
| Total staff | 200 |

**Work placement** yes

**Apply to**
Mr Paul Tapner

**Starting salary**
£20,000 (2007)

**Minimum qualifications**
2.1 degree

**Offices**
Cambridge

# Taylor Walton

28-44 Alma Street, Luton LU1 2PL
**Tel:** 01582 731161
**Fax:** 01582 457900
**Email:** jim.wrigglesworth@taylorwalton.co.uk
**Web:** www.taylorwalton.co.uk

**The firm** Strategically located in Hertfordshire and Bedfordshire, Taylor Walton is a major regional law practice advising both businesses and private clients. It has a progressive outlook, having invested heavily in effective IT systems, and is committed to staff training.

**Types of work** Taylor Walton's strengths are in commercial property, corporate work and commercial litigation. It still maintains a strong private client side to the practice and was one of the first firms in the country to specialise in relocation work, acting for many substantial companies in the relocation of their employees.

**Who should apply** Candidates need to show excellent intellectual capabilities, coupled with an engaging personality and an ambitious, mature attitude.

**Training programme** The training contract consists of four six-month seats. The training partner oversees the structural training alongside a supervisor, either a partner or senior solicitor, in each department. The firm does try to take trainees' own wishes in relation to seats into account.

In a regional law practice like Taylor Walton you will find client contact and responsibility coupled with supervision, management and training. There is an in-house training programme for all fee-earning members of staff, with regular outside speakers. At the end of each seat there is a post-seat appraisal with the trainee conducted by the training partner and the supervisor. The Professional Skills Course is taught externally.

The firm is friendly, with an open-door policy, and there are various sporting and social events.

**When and how to apply** Apply by 31 July 2008 to begin 2010. Apply by CV with covering letter.

| | |
|---|---|
| Vacancies | 5 |
| Trainees | 7 |
| Partners | 23 |
| Total staff | 200 |

**Apply to**
Mr Jim Wrigglesworth

**Minimum qualifications**
2.1 degree

**Sponsorship**
LPC

**Offices**
Harpenden, Luton, St Albans

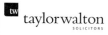

# Taylor Wessing LLP

Carmelite, 50 Victoria Embankment, Blackfriars, London EC4Y 0DX
**Tel:** 020 7300 7000
**Fax:** 020 7300 7100
**Web:** www.taylorwessing.com

**The firm** Taylor Wessing offers a full service to its clients providing a powerful source of legal support for commercial organisations doing business in Europe. We advise major corporations, medium-sized companies, financial and public institutions as well as growing enterprises and offer industry-focused advice by grouping together lawyers from different legal areas, but with in-depth sector experience. With our renowned expertise in intellectual property, we are particularly strong in knowledge-based industries, such as IT and telecommunications, life sciences and healthcare, media and entertainment, leisure, fashion and travel. Other core industries include construction and engineering, infrastructure projects and the banking and finance sectors.

Taylor Wessing is based primarily in the three largest economies in Europe, and has offices in other countries, including China where our Shanghai office serves a thriving Chinese market. Our clients also have the added benefit of our wide network of partner law firms. In Germany, we are one of the leading law firms, with a team of more than 250 lawyers.

**Types of work** Corporate, intellectual property, finance & projects, real estate, litigation & dispute resolution, employment & pensions and private client.

**Who should apply** High intellectual ability is paramount and we seek a minimum of ABB grades at A level and at least a 2.1 degree in any discipline. We look for team players who have excellent communication skills, energy, ambition, an open mind and a willingness to learn. You will also need to demonstrate a commitment to a career in law and a genuine interest in business.

**Training programme** As part of your training, you will spend six months in four different departments, including a seat in our corporate department. There is also the possibility of a secondment to another office or a client. All our trainees work closely with a number of partners and associates in the departments – so are directly involved in high-quality work from the start. At the beginning of the training and throughout you will have ongoing discussions about your interests and how they fit in with the growth and needs of the departments. There is support every step of the way, with regular feedback and appraisals in the middle and at the end of each seat. Not forgetting the essential Professional Skills Course, which is run in-house, along with other training courses as necessary during the two years.

**When and how to apply** All candidates need to apply via our online application form. The deadline for vacation schemes is 31 January 2008 and for training contracts is 31 July 2008.

**Work placements** Places for 2008: 40. Duration: two weeks. Remuneration: £250 per week. Closing date: 31 January 2008.

Our vacation schemes allow you to experience life as a trainee solicitor in a City law firm. You'll spend two weeks in two different departments gaining first-hand experience under the supervision of associates and partners. You'll also be assigned a buddy, attend departmental events and take part in numerous social activities. We also run open days in April and May.

**Sponsorship** GDL and LPC fees paid in full. Maintenance grant £7,000 per annum.

| | |
|---|---|
| Vacancies | 24 |
| Trainees | 48 |
| Partners | 264 |
| Total staff | approx 1000 |

**Work placement** yes
*(see Insider Report on p147)*

**Apply to**
Nichola Crilly, Graduate Recruitment Officer

**Starting salary**
1st year: £35,000
2nd year: £39,000

**Minimum qualifications**
2.1 degree

**Sponsorship**
GDL/LPC

**Offices**
Berlin, Brussels, Cambridge, Cologne, Düsseldorf, Frankfurt, Hamburg, London, Munich, Paris
Representative offices:
Alicante, Shanghai
Associated office:
Dubai

 TaylorWessing

# Teacher Stern Selby

37-41 Bedford Row, London WC1R 4JH
**Tel:** 020 7242 3191
**Fax:** 020 7242 1156
**Email:** r.raphael@tsslaw.com
**Web:** www.tsslaw.com

**The firm** We are not a large firm, but we pride ourselves on having the quality of clients and work normally attributed to larger practices. Established in central London in 1967, the firm is solid yet young, progressive and dynamic.

**Types of work** A commercial practice with a focus on transactional and contentious property-related matters, general commercial litigation, and commercial and corporate work. Our clients include heavyweight property investors – many from overseas - and lending institutions. We are well known in the media field as well as being a leading sports practice.

**Who should apply** Intelligent and committed trainees who have the confidence and personality to accept early responsibility. We prefer a 2.1 in any discipline.

**Training programme** Relevant training is provided in the corporate, property and litigation departments.

**When and how to apply** By 31 July 2008 to begin September 2010. Application is online via the website.

**Work placements** Summer scheme applied for in same manner. The closing date is 30 April 2008 for placements in summer 2008. Applicants for 2010 training contracts are encouraged to apply for vacation placements in 2008. Vacation scheme placements are only available to those who have applied for a training contract in 2010.

**Sponsorship** LPC.

| | |
|---|---|
| Vacancies | 3-4 |
| Trainees | 7 |
| Partners | 21 |
| Total staff | 99 |

**Work placement**  yes
*(see Insider Report on p152)*

**Apply to**
Mr Russell Raphael

**Starting salary**
£31,000 (2010)

**Minimum qualifications**
2.1 degree preferred

**Sponsorship**
LPC

**Offices**
London

| Firm | Description | V | T | P | TS | WP |
|---|---|---|---|---|---|---|
| **TALBOT & CO**<br>148 High Street, Burton-On-Trent, Staffordshire DE14 1JY<br>**Tel:** 01283 564716<br>**Fax:** 01283 510861<br>**Email:** tombramall@talbotco.co.uk<br>**Apply to:** Mr TJ Bramall | Long-established Legal 500 firm with extensive high-quality private client base. Particular expertise in wills, tax, trusts, estates and probate. Commercial/residential property and commercial/civil litigation, matrimonial, charities. City of London referrals. | 1[08] | 1 | 1 | 20 | yes |
| **TALBOT WALKER LLP**<br>16 Bridge Street, Andover, Hampshire SP10 1BJ<br>**Tel:** 01264 363354<br>**Fax:** 01264 721718<br>**Email:** employment@talbotwalker.co.uk<br>**Apply to:** Mr Gavin Burnett | Two member, two branch litigation firm with franchises in criminal, personal injury and clinical negligence. | Poss[09] | 2 | 2 | 35 | no |
| **TALFOURDS**<br>40 North Street, Hornchurch RM11 1EW<br>**Tel:** 01708 511000<br>**Fax:** 01708 511040<br>**Apply to:** Ms Jackie Shallow | Property and litigation based three partner firm with substantial commercial/private client base. | 1-2[08] | 2 | 5 | 35 | no |
| **TALLENTS SOLICITORS**<br>3 Middlegate, Newark NG24 1AQ<br>**Tel:** 01636 671881<br>**Fax:** 01636 700148<br>**Email:** roy.westerby@tallents.co.uk<br>**Apply to:** The Practice Manager | Offices in Newark, Mansfield and Southwell. | 0 | 1 | 7 | 51 | no |
| **TASSELLS**<br>20 West Street, Faversham, Kent ME13 7JF<br>**Tel:** 01795 533337<br>**Fax:** 01795 530375<br>**Email:** law@tassells-solicitors.co.uk<br>**Apply to:** Mr Stafford Day | Broad based general practice, undertaking all the usual non-contentious and contentious work. | 1[09] | 1 | 3 | 24 | yes |
| **TAYLOR & EMMET**<br>20 Arundel Gate, Sheffield S1 2PP<br>**Tel:** 0114 290 2200<br>**Fax:** 0114 290 2290<br>**Email:** info@tayloremmet.co.uk<br>**Apply to:** Ms Hannah Southern | Taylor & Emmet is a well established, three office firm based in Sheffield. It provides a wide range of business and personal legal services. No vacancies until 2009. | 3 | 11 | 7 | 145 | no |
| **TEMPLE HEELIS**<br>Bridge Mills, Stramongate, Kendal, Cumbria LA9 4HB<br>**Tel:** 01539 723757<br>**Fax:** 01539 727796<br>**Apply to:** Mrs Bridget Vickers | A progressive provincial practice with both LEXEL and Investors in People Awards. Specialising in bulk conveyancing and personal injury work. Leading lakeland lawyers. | 0 | 2 | - | - | yes |
| **TERRY JONES SOLICITORS & ADVOCATES**<br>Abbey House, Abbey Foregate, Shrewsbury SY2 6BH<br>**Tel:** 01743 285888<br>**Fax:** 01743 285900<br>**Email:** enquiries@terry-jones.co.uk<br>**Apply to:** Mrs Sharron Ditchburn | Dynamic forward thinking practice with state of the art technology providing a specialised personal service in most areas of law including public funded matters. | Poss | 5 | 2 | 90 | no |

**V** = Vacancies / **T** = Trainees / **P** = Partners / **TS** = Total Staff / **WP** = Work Placement

# Thomas Cooper

Ibex House, 42-47 Minories, London EC3N 1HA
**Tel:** 020 7481 8851
**Fax:** 020 7480 6097
**Email:** recruitment@thomascooperlaw.com
**Web:** www.thomascooperlaw.com

**The firm** Thomas Cooper is a firm of commercial lawyers specialising in international transportation, trade, finance and business affairs, banking and commercial work and litigation with about 80 partners and staff worldwide, of whom approximately 55 are in the London office. We also have offices in Singapore, Athens, Vancouver, Madrid and Paris.

**Who should apply** We wish to attract well-qualified graduates with good academic records who are articulate, clear thinking, well presented and ambitious. We want people who can solve problems and with enough drive to take things through to a successful conclusion. In addition to these qualities we want people who have a sense of humour and who can get along well with their colleagues and our clients. We are looking for a strong academic record and generally we will only recruit candidates with a 2.1 or better with good GCSE, AS and A level grades or Highers or International Baccalaureate (or equivalent).

We make no distinction between applicants with a law degree and those with a degree in any other subject. We particularly welcome applications from students with a foreign language or some other relevant skill.

**Training programme** At Thomas Cooper, we believe that the most effective training is a well-balanced and tailored mix of on-the-job learning and formal courses. The most valuable part of our training is the practical experience you will gain. In almost all cases, you will sit with and be closely supervised by a partner. Each trainee is allocated to a principal who is often the partner with whom he or she first sits and to whom you may speak at any time about any problem or concern which you have been unable to resolve. Your progress and work experience will be reviewed regularly and is formally assessed at the end of each six-month seat by the partner with whom you have just been sitting. Your principal (or the managing partner if you have just been sitting with your principal) will sit in at the meeting.

**When and how to apply** If you would like to apply for a training contract for Thomas Cooper, please do so by filling in our application form to be found on our website.

Applications for 2008 are now closed. Please visit our website in early 2008 to apply for the 2009 intake. There is generally one intake each year in September, although we sometimes accept candidates to start in March. We expect to recruit two or three candidates to start in September 2009. While there is not a strict closing date for applications you should aim to apply by 31 July 2008. After that we may close the application list at any time.

**Work placements** While we have no formal vacation scheme, we do accommodate students for work experience. Candidates should apply to Mr C R G Williams.

| | |
|---|---|
| Vacancies | 2 |
| Trainees | 6 |
| Partners | 25 |
| Total staff | 80 |

**Apply to**
Mr TJR Goode

**Starting salary**
1st year - £26,250
2nd year - £27,500

**Minimum qualifications**
3 Bs at A level (excluding General Studies)
2.1 degree

**Offices**
London, Athens, Madrid, Paris, Singapore, Vancouver

# Thomas Eggar

The Corn Exchange, Baffins Lane, Chichester PO19 1GE
**Tel:** 01243 813129
**Email:** mick.cassell@thomaseggar.com
**Web:** www.thomaseggar.com

**The firm** Thomas Eggar is rated as one of the top 100 law firms in the UK. Based in the Southeast, we are one of the country's leading regional law firms with a staff of over 400. As a firm we offer both private client and commercial services to a diverse range of clients, locally, nationally and internationally. These include high net-worth individuals, large national organisations, public service providers, small to medium enterprises and entrepreneurs. We also offer financial services through Thesis, the firm's investment management arm which is the largest solicitor-based investment management unit in the UK.

**Types of work** Apart from its strength in the private client sector, where it offers a comprehensive range of services, the firm handles property, commercial and litigation matters; among its major clients are banks, building societies and other financial institutions, railway and track operators and construction companies.

**Who should apply** The firm seeks very able trainees who exhibit good business acumen. It is looking for long-term investment and expects trainees to demonstrate their commitment to remain with the firm on a career basis once they have completed their contract. It makes no distinction during the selection process between candidates who have legal or other degrees.

**Training programme** Trainees would normally have four seats covering commercial property, commercial, litigation and private client. In order to give good exposure to the various specialisations, some of the seats are likely to be in different offices. A taxable travel allowance is paid monthly for the duration of the training contract.

**When and how to apply** Applications can be made up to 1 August 2008 for training contracts to commence in March 2009, September 2009 and March 2010. Applications should be in the form of a CV and covering letter and you should give details in the covering letter of your attachment to the Southeast region. During 2008 the application process will also adopt an online facility.

The Thomas Eggar website has an electronic version of the graduate brochure.

**Work placements** We run a very limited summer placement scheme in July and August each year; applications should be made with CV to Mick Cassell by 31 March 2008. Please give details of your accommodation plans in your covering letter. The placement can take place in any of our offices and lasts for one week.

**Sponsorship** We make a grant of 50% of the LPC fees and an interest-free loan to cover the balance; the loan is repayable over the period of the training contract.

| | |
|---|---|
| Vacancies | 6 |
| Trainees | 12 |
| Partners | 60 |
| Total staff | 429 |

**Work placement** yes

**Apply to**
Mick Cassell

**Starting salary**
We aim to pay the going rate for a Southeastern firm. A London weighting allowance is paid to those who undertake seats in our London office. A taxable travel allowance is paid to all trainees.

**Minimum qualifications**
2.1 degree is preferred in any discipline

**Sponsorship**
LPC

**Offices**
Chichester, Gatwick, London, Worthing

# Thomson Snell & Passmore

3 Lonsdale Gardens, Tunbridge Wells, Kent TN1 1NX
**Tel:** 01892 510000
**Fax:** 01892 549884
**Email:** recruitment@ts-p.co.uk
**Web:** www.ts-p.co.uk

**The firm** Thomson Snell & Passmore continues to be regarded as one of the premier law firms in the South East. The firm has a reputation for quality and a commitment to deliver precise and clear advice which is recognised and respected by both its clients and professional contacts. It has held the Lexcel quality mark since January 1999. The firm is vibrant and progressive, and enjoys an extremely friendly atmosphere. Its offices are located in the centre of Tunbridge Wells and in the Thames Gateway. The firm attracts clients both locally and nationally.

**Types of work** Commercial litigation: 14%. Corporate and employment: 14%. Commercial property: 14%. Private client: 24%. Personal injury/clinical negligence: 12%. Residential property: 15%. Family law: 7%.

**Who should apply** At Thomson Snell & Passmore we regard our trainees from the outset as future assistants, associates and partners. We are looking for people not only with strong intellectual ability, but also with enthusiasm, drive, initiative, strong interpersonal and teamworking skills.

**Training programme** Our induction course will help you to adjust to working life. As we are a founder member of Law South, your training is provided in-house with trainees from other member firms of Law South. Your two-year training contract is divided into four periods of six months each. You will receive a thorough grounding and responsibility with early client exposure. You will be monitored regularly, receive advice and assistance throughout and have appraisals every three months. Our training partner will coordinate your continuing education in the law, procedure, commerce, marketing, IT and presentation skills. Trainees enjoy an active social life which is encouraged and supported.

**When and how to apply** Apply by 31 July 2008 to begin September 2010. Applicants should apply by firm's own application form, available via website.

**Sponsorship** Grant and interest-free loan available for LPC.

| Vacancies | 5 |
|---|---|
| Trainees | 10 |
| Partners | 32 |
| Total staff | 200 |

**Apply to**
HR Manager

**Starting salary**
Competitive market rate for a South East regional firm

**Minimum qualifications**
2.1 degree, any discipline

**Offices**
Tunbridge Wells,
Thames Gateway

# Thomson Snell
# & Passmore

# Thring Townsend Lee & Pembertons Solicitors

6 Drakes Meadow, Penny Lane, Swindon SN3 3LL
**Tel:** 01793 410800
**Fax:** 01793 539040
**Email:** solicitors@ttuk.com
**Web:** www.ttuk.com

**The firm** With offices in Bath, Bristol, London and Swindon employing over 300 staff, Thring Townsend Lee & Pembertons provides a balanced portfolio of commercial, agricultural and private client services and has an impressive national and international client base.

The commitment from the management of the firm to employees and their career development has led to an open and friendly culture and a vibrant work ethic.

**Types of work** Agriculture: believed to be the largest stand-alone, specialist agriculture team in the country. Commercial property: an excellent reputation for specialist skills in strategic land and options and pension fund property and construction work. Corporate and commercial: acting for a wide variety of clients including many national and international household names. Litigation: a substantial practice with specialists in commercial litigation and claimant professional negligence work. The insolvency and corporate recovery department is one of the largest in the region and is attracting diverse and complex quality work. Personal injury: a niche practice specialising in catastrophic brain and spinal injuries and industrial disease claims. Family: leading the way in the Southwest for collaborative family law. Wills and probate, tax and trusts: advises private family trusts, substantial tax planning advice and estate administration. The team has particular expertise in issues surrounding the Mental Capacity Act. Private property: advising individuals and companies including investment landlords and clients resident abroad.

**Who should apply** We look for confident and well-rounded individuals who are pro-active, dedicated and commercially aware. We look for a minimum 2.1 degree and strong A levels but we are open to applications from students with a 2.2 degree who perhaps have something else to add such as relevant work or life experience.

**Training programme** We welcome graduates into a dynamic learning environment with an equal mix of structure and flexibility to cater for individual needs and career goals.

The firm operates a structured two-year training contract split into four six-month seats. Trainees can expect to gain experience within at least three different practice areas with both contentious and non-contentious exposure.

In addition, we offer our trainees:
- a dedicated partner supervisor
- mid-seat and end-seat appraisal feedback
- hands-on experience to develop client management skills
- in-house and external training courses
- regular social events including cinema, theatre, sports etc
- a competitive salary and benefits package reviewed annually
- a realistic and comfortable work life balance

**When and how to apply** Apply by July 31st 2008 with application form and CV.

| | |
|---|---|
| Vacancies | 9 |
| Trainees | 14 |
| Partners | 46 |
| Total staff | 304 |

**Work placement** no

**Apply to**
Pat Mapstone
01793 412502

**Starting salary**
1st year - £17,750
2nd year - £19,250
(under review)

**Minimum qualifications**
2.1 degree

**Offices**
Bath, Bristol, London, Swindon

Thring
Townsend
Lee & Pembertons

ttuk.com

**THACKRAY WILLIAMS**
Kings House, 32-40 Widmore Road,
Bromley BR1 1RY
**Tel:** 020 8290 0440
**Fax:** 020 8464 5282
**Apply to:** Ms Jane MacLeod

The largest firm in the Bromley and North Kent region. A vibrant and progressive general practice with a growing commercial side.

| | |
|---|---|
| V | 2[09] |
| T | 4 |
| P | 20 |
| TS | 145 |
| WP | no |

---

**THALES CORPORATE SERVICES LIMITED**
2 Dashwood Lang Road, Bourne Business Park,
Addlestone, Surrey KT15 2NX
**Tel:** 01932 824917
**Fax:** 01932 824898
**Email:** jennifer.eldred@thalesgroup.com
**Apply to:** Mrs Jennifer Eldred

Thales is a world leader in aerospace, defence and security systems. We offer training in the following areas: commercial property, litigation and commercial law.

| | |
|---|---|
| V | 0 |
| T | 2 |
| P | - |
| TS | 10000 |
| WP | no |

---

**THOMPSONS**
Congress House, Great Russell Street,
London WC1B 3LW
**Tel:** 020 7290 0000
**Fax:** 020 7637 0000
**Email:** traineeappointments@thompsons.law.co.uk
**Apply to:** The Managing Partner

Thompsons Solicitors is the largest trade union, employment rights and claimant personal injury firm in the UK.

| | |
|---|---|
| V | Poss[09] |
| T | 24 |
| P | 38 |
| TS | 800 |
| WP | no |

---

**THOMSON WEBB & CORFIELD**
16 Union Road, Cambridge CB2 1HE
**Tel:** 01223 578086
**Fax:** 01223 578050
**Email:** shollis@twclaw.co.uk
**Apply to:** Mr SA Hollis

Progressive Cambridge firm with expanding commercial and corporate teams, handling private and public company clients. Private client departments, including trusts, family and crime.

| | |
|---|---|
| V | 1 |
| T | 2 |
| P | 9 |
| TS | 39 |
| WP | no |

---

**THORPE & CO**
17 Valley Bridge Parade, Scarborough YO11 2JX
**Tel:** 01723 364321
**Fax:** 01723 500459
**Email:** info@thorpeandco.com
**Apply to:** The Recruitment Contact

General practice with four offices including domestic conveyancing, probate, family, personal injury and criminal work.

| | |
|---|---|
| V | 1 |
| T | 1 |
| P | 12 |
| TS | 55 |
| WP | no |

---

**THURSFIELDS**
14 & 27 Church Street, Kidderminster DY10 2AJ
**Tel:** 01562 820575
**Fax:** 01562 512496
**Email:** bheaselgrave@thursfields.co.uk
**Apply to:** Mr AW Heaselgrave

A well-established, friendly, busy and expanding regional firm. Strong client base, wide range of contentious/non-contentious work. Needs able, enthusiastic candidates seeking long term career.

| | |
|---|---|
| V | 0 |
| T | 4 |
| P | 16 |
| TS | 110 |
| WP | no |

---

**TICKLE HALL CROSS**
25 Hardshaw Street, St Helens,
Merseyside WA10 1RP
**Tel:** 01744 733333
**Fax:** 01744 746002
**Email:** he@ticklehallcross.co.uk
**Apply to:** Ms Helen Evans

Well established progressive firm offering a full range of legal services to the local business and private client community, seeks talented and hardworking trainees.

| | |
|---|---|
| V | 1 |
| T | 2 |
| P | 6 |
| TS | 40 |
| WP | no |

---

**TILLY BAILEY & IRVINE**
York Chambers, York Road, Hartlepool TS26 9DP
**Tel:** 01429 264101
**Fax:** 01429 274 796
**Apply to:** Mr RN Taylor

General practice in four offices in the North East of England

| | |
|---|---|
| V | 2-3[08] |
| T | 2 |
| P | 16 |
| TS | 146 |
| WP | no |

# TLT Solicitors

One Redcliff Street, Bristol, BS1 6TP
**Tel:** 0117 917 7777
**Fax:** 0117 917 7778
**Email:** graduate@TLTsolicitors.com
**Web:** www.TLTsolicitors.com

**The firm** Described by industry commentators as "the firm to watch", TLT remains one of the fastest growing law firms in the UK. Turnover has almost tripled since 2002. Headcount has risen three-fold to over 600. Growth for us provides the resources to be able to support our clients.

The firm is built around the needs of its clients. Around 60 percent of the firm's work is from outside of the South West region and TLT advises national and international businesses including Aardman Animations, Alfred McAlpine, Barclays, British Waterways Board, HBOS, GMAC RFC, Lloyds TSB Group, Merlin Entertainments, Punch Taverns, Orange and Somerfield. A high percentage of the firm's lawyers are identified as true experts in their respective fields and behind their legal advice is an insight and understanding of the commercial challenges clients face. The firm encourages and supports involvement in our wider community which includes 'pro bono' legal advice to a variety of charities and TLT staff volunteering.

**Types of work** TLT is a full-service UK law firm. It concentrates on providing industry focused multi-discipline integrated solutions. The firm's leading strengths are in the financial services and leisure sectors. Other chosen markets include retail, the built environment and technology and media. TLT's core legal specialisms are real estate, banking and finance, commercial, corporate, employment, dispute resolution and litigation. Client services are provided through dedicated, cross-firm specialist teams including banking and asset finance, construction, debt recovery (on behalf of lenders), environmental, insolvency and turnaround, IT and IP, total reward, property development, leisure, licensing, regulatory, retail, shipping, social housing and tax.

**Who should apply** Candidates with a strong academic background together with commitment and drive to succeed.

**Training programme** TLT's commitment to excellence will ensure that trainees benefit from a well-developed and challenging training programme. Training is delivered through four seats of six months' duration which are chosen in consultation with the trainee. In each seat the trainee will sit with a lawyer although their work will be drawn from all members of the team in order to gain the widest possible experience. Regular monitoring and development planning meetings ensure that trainees get the most out of their training and help them to identify their long-term career path from the varied specialisms on offer.

**When and how to apply** Completed TLT application forms to be received by 31 July 2008 to begin 2010. Apply online via website at www.TLTsolicitors.com.

**Work placements** Six paid Easter placements and 18 summer placements available, each lasting one week. Apply online by 31 January 2008 for placements in 2008.

**Sponsorship** CPE and LPC fees paid and a maintenance grant of £4,500 per annum.

| | |
|---|---|
| Vacancies | 10 |
| Trainees | 17 |
| Partners | 60 |
| Total staff | 600+ |

Work placement yes

Apply to
Human Resources

Starting salary
£24,000

Minimum qualifications
2.1 degree preferred, any discipline

Sponsorship
CPE/LPC

Offices
Bristol, London

# Tollers

2 Castilian Street, Northampton NN1 1JX
**Tel:** 01604 258558
**Fax:** 01604 258500
**Email:** mandy.lines@tollers.co.uk
**Web:** www.tollers.co.uk

**The firm** Established in 1877, Tollers is one of the oldest and most respected firms of solicitors in the region. With 21 partners and 237 staff, we operate a progressive, dynamic practice – well positioned both geographically and technically to meet all business and personal legal requirements. We have experienced tremendous growth in the last few years and aim to be recognised as an outstanding regional law firm.

**Types of work** Business legal services: commercial property, commercial litigation and dispute resolution, corporate/commercial, employment, planning and environment Issues, charity law and agricultural land.

Personal legal services: family law, residential property, trusts and estates and personal injury.

**Who should apply** We welcome applications from both law and non-law graduates. Candidates must be able to demonstrate intellectual ability (minimum 2.1 preferred), team skills, commercial acumen, resilience, initiative, enthusiasm and a sense of humour.

**Training programme** A typical training programme is divided into four seats of six months each. These are spent in different departments/offices within the firm. We place considerable emphasis on the structure and progress of your training and hold regular appraisals throughout the training contract in order that you should have constructive feedback. We make sure that you make an important contribution from the start, taking responsibility from your first day with us, within a well organised and supportive team-based environment. We are usually able to accommodate a trainee's choice of seats during the course of his/her training contract. Many of our current partners trained with the firm and, when recruiting trainees, we are looking for the partners of the future.

**When and how to apply** We aim to make appointments two years prior to the start of a training contract. Please refer to our website at www.tollers.co.uk for up-to-date details. Apply by using our online application form. The deadline for all training contract applications is 31 July each year. Please send the application form together with a short covering letter to mandy.lines@tollers.co.uk.

| | |
|---|---|
| Vacancies | 6 |
| Trainees | 12 |
| Partners | 21 |
| Total staff | 237 |

**Work placement**  no

**Apply to**
Mandy Lines

**Starting salary**
Competitive

**Minimum qualifications**
Normally a 2.1 degree
(occasional exceptions)

**Offices**
Northampton (2),
Milton Keynes, Kettering,
Corby

| **TINKLIN SPRINGALL**<br>Devonshire House, Elmfield Road,<br>Bromley BR1 1TF<br>**Tel:** 020 8290 6333<br>**Fax:** 020 8402 9222<br>**Apply to:** Mr RF Tinklin | A typical High Street practice covering conveyancing, litigation, probate and general matters. | V 1[08]<br>T 1<br>P 6<br>TS 40<br>WP no |
|---|---|---|
| **TINN CRIDDLE & CO**<br>6 High Street, Alford, Lincolnshire LN13 9DX<br>**Tel:** 01507 462882<br>**Fax:** 01507 462706<br>**Apply to:** Mr G Allen | Small, three office, country practice. | V 0<br>T 1<br>P 4<br>TS 10<br>WP no |
| **TINSDILLS**<br>Hays House, 25 Albion Street, Hanley,<br>Stoke on Trent ST1 1QF<br>**Tel:** 01782 262031<br>**Fax:** 01782 287571<br>**Email:** lawyers@tinsdills.co.uk | The firm has three offices located in North Staffordshire and one office in South Cheshire. The firm acts for private, corporate and institutional clients. | V Poss<br>T 3<br>P 13<br>TS 85<br>WP no |
| **TMJ LAW SOLICITORS**<br>5 Notre Dame Mews, Northampton NN1 2BG<br>**Tel:** 01604 608111<br>**Fax:** 01604 628777<br>**Email:** info@tmjlaw.co.uk<br>**Apply to:** Mr T J Synnott | An established but young and dynamic firm providing company and commercial expertise to a diversity of corporate and private clients using the latest IT solutions. | V 2<br>T 2<br>P 2<br>TS 12<br>WP yes |
| **TMJ LEGAL SERVICES LLP**<br>Foster House, 99 Raby Road,<br>Hartlepool TS24 8DT<br>**Tel:** 01429 235616<br>**Fax:** 01429 862859<br>**Email:** legal@tmjlegal.co.uk<br>**Apply to:** Mr KI Morgan | General legal aid practice specialising in personal injury and matrimonial/ children work. | V Poss<br>T 1<br>P 3<br>TS 39<br>WP yes |
| **TOFIELDS**<br>14 Figtree Lane, Sheffield S1 2DJ<br>**Tel:** 0114 272 2143<br>**Fax:** 0114 273 8280<br>**Email:** info@tofields.co.uk<br>**Apply to:** Mr S Stagg | Progressive city centre general practice. | V 0<br>T 1<br>P 7<br>TS 42<br>WP no |
| **TOLLER BEATTIE**<br>First Floor Queen's House, Queen Street,<br>Barnstaple, Devon EX32 8TB<br>**Tel:** 01271 341000<br>**Fax:** 01271 374762<br>**Email:** solicitors@tollerbeattie.co.uk<br>**Apply to:** Mr Robert H Beattie | Typical High Street clientele but with extra specialisms in environmental litigation, planning & commercial property which are unusual with such a firm. | V 1[09]<br>T 2<br>P 3<br>TS 40<br>WP yes |
| **TOUSSAINTS**<br>150 Soho Road, Birmingham B21 9LN<br>**Tel:** 0121 523 5050<br>**Fax:** 0121 523 3200<br>**Apply to:** Miss MM Toussaint | Busy high street office undertaking residential, commercial property, litigation, civil, crime and family work. | V 0<br>T 1<br>P 1<br>TS 3<br>WP no |

**V** = Vacancies / **T** = Trainees / **P** = Partners / **TS** = Total Staff / **WP** = Work Placement

# Travers Smith

10 Snow Hill, London EC1A 2AL
**Tel:** 020 7295 3000
**Fax:** 020 7295 3500
**Email:** graduate.recruitment@traverssmith.com
**Web:** www.traverssmith.com

**The firm** Travers Smith is a City firm with a major corporate and commercial practice. Although we are less than a quarter of the size of the dozen largest firms, we attract top-quality work but still offer a professional yet relaxed working environment providing the best of both worlds. A high proportion of the firm's work has an international dimension - to service this, we have opened an office in France as well as developing close working relationships with independent law firms that share our high standards.

**Types of work** The main areas of our practice are corporate law (including takeovers and mergers, financial services and regulatory laws), commercial law (which includes competition and intellectual property), dispute resolution, corporate recovery/insolvency, tax, employment, pensions, banking and real estate.

We offer a range of pro bono opportunities within individual departments and on a firm-wide basis. In particular, a group of trainees and assistant solicitors advise on a voluntary basis at a law centre in Central London and also at an advice clinic run out of the Inns of Court School of Law. The firm is an active member of the Caribbean Capital Cases Committee and has a long history of acting for prisoners on death row. The firm also takes on cases from the Bar Pro Bono Unit.

**Who should apply** We look for people who combine academic excellence with common sense; who are articulate, who think on their feet, who are determined and self-motivated and who take their work but not themselves seriously. Applications are welcome from law and non-law undergraduates/ graduates.

**Training programme** The firm has a comprehensive training programme which ensures that trainees experience a broad range of work. All trainee solicitors sit in rooms with partners and assistants, receive an individual and extensive training from experienced lawyers and enjoy client contact and the responsibility that goes with it from the beginning of their training contract.

Trainees gain six months' experience in each of the following departments - corporate, real estate/banking and dispute resolution/employment. The firm offers you a choice for your fourth seat in one of the remaining five departments. In addition, there is always one trainee in the firm's Paris office, which practises English law. The firm also operates an exchange programme for assistant solicitors with US and European law firms.

**When and how to apply** By 31 July 2008 to begin September 2010. Apply by CV and covering letter online or by post to Germaine VanGeyzel, Graduate Recruitment Manager.

**Work placements** Three summer schemes of two weeks each commencing 23 June, 7 July and 21 July 2008. Apply with CV and covering letter online or by post by 31 January 2008. The firm also offers a Christmas scheme of two weeks.

**Sponsorship** GDL and LPC paid in full plus maintenance of £7,000 per annum to those in London and £6,500 per annum to those outside London.

| | |
|---|---|
| Vacancies | 25 |
| Trainees | 36 |
| Partners | 66 |
| Total staff | 380 |

**Work placement**   yes
*(see Insider Report on p149)*

**Apply to**
Germaine VanGeyzel

**Starting salary**
£36,000

**Minimum qualifications**
2.1 degree and AAB at A level

**Sponsorship**
GDL/LPC

**Offices**
London, Paris

TRAVERS SMITH

# Trethowans

The Director General's House, Rockstone Place, Southampton SO15 2EP
**Tel:** 023 8032 1000
**Fax:** 023 8032 1001
**Email:** kate.lemont@trethowans.com
**Web:** www.trethowans.com

**The firm** A leading regional practice in the South of England, with two offices across Wiltshire and Hampshire, offering a comprehensive range of services (except criminal) for businesses and individuals throughout the UK. Commercial clients range from start-ups to larger corporates, with a particular emphasis on owner-managed businesses. Southampton remains the focus for the majority of the firm's corporate and commercial services. The commercial services offered are comparable to those of a London practice, but a competitive price structure and direct partner involvement are key bases for differentiation. Partners and fee-earners offer genuine expertise in their respective fields, and acknowledged reputations include property, employment, commercial/corporate work and licensing for national brand names. Private client work is undertaken across all sites with the Salisbury office at its core. Specialist areas include personal injury (head and spinal injuries), clinical negligence, family, residential property, wills, trusts and tax, probate, landed estates and agriculture.

The firm aims to adopt an open and forward-thinking approach to work and strongly believes in gaining and maintaining a thorough understanding of clients' objectives. Where necessary, specialist teams are built to ensure the optimum level of expertise. The firm has 24 partners and was the 11th practice of its size in the UK to achieve the Law Society's voluntary Lexcel Accreditation in 2002.

**Types of work** The breadth of the firm's practice areas provides a broad experience for trainees across a comprehensive range of areas: corporate, commercial, commercial property, commercial litigation, employment, personal injury, residential property, family, landed estates and private client work.

**Who should apply** Trainees should possess sound academic abilities and be able to demonstrate commercial acumen. Flexibility, ambition and enthusiasm are valued. Candidates should be good communicators and adopt a problem-solving approach to client work.

**Training programme** Our trainee solicitors normally undertake four separate specialist seats, each lasting six months. We offer a flexible approach in deciding trainees' seats to suit individual needs, while providing a broad training programme in accordance with the Law Society's guidelines. Trainees have their own desks and work closely with the supervising fee-earner/partner to whom they are responsible. They are considered an integral part of each team and become closely involved in the department's work to obtain first-hand legal experience.

Each trainee is appraised every six months by their supervisor and the Training Partner. This enables the trainee scheme to be continually evaluated and also ensures that the highest possible standards are maintained. Prospects for trainees are excellent – most trainees are offered a post as an assistant solicitor at the end of their training contract.

**When and how to apply** By 25 July 2008 for November 2010 entry. Applications by application form (available online) and covering letter.

**Sponsorship** Course fees paid for LPC.

| | |
|---|---|
| Vacancies | 3-4 |
| Trainees | 7 |
| Partners | 24 |
| Total staff | 160 |

**Apply to**
Kate Lemont

**Starting salary**
In excess of Law Society minimum

**Minimum qualifications**
2.1 degree

**Sponsorship**
LPC

**Offices**
Salisbury, Southampton

TRETHOWANS

# Trowers & Hamlins

Sceptre Court, 40 Tower Hill, London EC3N 4DX
**Tel:** 020 7423 8000
**Fax:** 020 7423 8001
**Email:** hking@trowers.com
**Web:** www.trowers.com

**The firm** Awarded Law Firm of the Year at the *Lawyer* awards 2007 and being one of only seven law firms who were ranked in the 2007 *Times* 100 Top Firms are two of the reasons why Trowers & Hamlins is a desirable law firm to train with. It does not stop there though. Of those seven, we were ranked second at number forty and it's easy to see why. Based in the City we are a medium sized international firm with offices in the UK and the Middles East, and are able to offer specialisms ranging from housing and urban regeneration to litigation, Islamic finance and international infrastructure projects. Our training contracts offer the prospect of work in our London, regional or Middle Eastern offices. As well as excellent client focused opportunities, we also offer the chance to get involved with many of our community projects and pro bono work. Sound good? Then read on.

**Types of work** Being the number one firm for social housing, you will not be surprised to learn that we cover a variety of property work (housing, public sector and commercial). But that's not all we do. We also have award winning projects and construction and structured finance teams and *Chambers & Partners* consistently confirms our status as one of the number one firms in the Middle East. Our other major practise areas include corporate, banking and finance, employment, litigation, tax, trusts and pensions and commercial property.

**Who should apply** Everyone knows that excellent academics are of course essential. However, we also believe in the merits of having a diverse workforce. Our commitment to this is demonstrated by our fifth place position in the 2006 Ethnicity League Table conducted by *The Lawyer* on behalf of the Commission for Racial Equality and the Black Solicitors Network. We look for candidates who can demonstrate a knowledge and passion for the law as well as commercial awareness but who are above all, individuals. If you possess excellent communication skills, are a strong and effective team player who wants to work in a fast paced, challenging and fulfilling environment then we want to hear from you.

**Training programme** We pride ourselves on the quality of the training that we are able to offer. During your time with us, you will rotate around four departments sitting with either a partner or senior solicitor who are easily accessible for supervision and guidance. In addition to this you will also be designated a mentor for the duration of your training contract to offer advice as you progress. Your performance will be formally evaluated through four end of seat appraisals and also half way through each seat. Client contact is encouraged from an early stage and you will find that you are quickly given real responsibility. Our dedication to training can further be demonstrated through our regular programme of lectures, workshops and our bespoke trainee lunch programme.

**When and how to apply** The deadline for training contracts to begin in March and September 2010 is 1 August 2008. Application is via our online application form which can be accessed on our website.

**Work placements** Places for 2008; 25-30; Duration: two weeks; Remuneration: £225pw London, £170pw Manchester; Application closing date: 1 March 2008; Open Day: June 2008

**Sponsorship** GDL and LPC fees paid together with a maintenance grant of £5,500 (£6000 for London) pa.

| | |
|---|---|
| Vacancies | 22 |
| Trainees | 39 |
| Partners | 106 |
| Total staff | 652 |

**Work placement** yes
*(see Insider Report on p151)*

**Apply to**
Hannah King, Graduate
Recruitment Officer

**Starting salary**
1st year: £29,000
2nd year: £31,000
(subject to review)

**Minimum qualifications**
2.1 degree

**Sponsorship**
GDL/LPC

**Offices**
Abu Dhabi, Bahrain, Cairo, Dubai, Exeter, London, Manchester, Sultanate of Oman

| | | |
|---|---|---|
| **TRANTERS**<br>29/31 Middle Hillgate, Stockport,<br>Cheshire SK1 3AY<br>**Tel:** 0161 480 7779<br>**Fax:** 0161 476 1926<br>**Email:** gill.hewitt@tranters-hr.com<br>**Apply to:** Ms Gill Hewitt | LAB franchised with specialist solicitors dealing with crime and accident claims with offices in South Manchester, Stockport and East Manchester. | **V** 4<br>**T** 4<br>**P** 6<br>**TS** 100<br>**WP** yes |
| **TRANTERS FREECLAIM SOLICITORS**<br>Alderman Gatley House, Hale Top, Civic Centre,<br>Wythenshawe, Manchester M22 5RW<br>**Tel:** 0161 437 9999<br>**Fax:** 0161 436 3332<br>**Apply to:** Mr JW Barstow | Specialist personal injury practice with a commitment to providing an interesting and challenging case load, excellent training and full support. | **V** 4<br>**T** 6<br>**P** 3<br>**TS** 47<br>**WP** yes |
| **TRIGGS READ & DART**<br>103 Boutport Street, Barnstaple, Devon EX31 1SY<br>**Tel:** 01271 346667<br>**Fax:** 01271 375379<br>**Apply to:** Ms Linda Fentiman | Expanding high street firm where solicitors specialise in one or two areas of practice to ensure high quality advice to all clients. | **V** 0-1<br>**T** 1<br>**P** 2<br>**TS** 49<br>**WP** no |
| **TROBRIDGES**<br>1 Ford Park Road, Mutley Plain, Plymouth PL4 6LY<br>**Tel:** 01752 664022<br>**Fax:** 01752 223761<br>**Apply to:** Mr CWG Matthews | We are a two office firm based in Plymouth providing a wide range of legal services with an emphasis on personal injury and family work. | **V** 2<br>**T** 2<br>**P** 3<br>**TS** 25<br>**WP** yes |
| **TRUEMANS**<br>Eden House, 38 St Aldates, Oxford OX1 1BN<br>**Tel:** 01865 722 383<br>**Fax:** 01865 792 024<br>**Email:** mtrueman@truemans.org.uk<br>**Apply to:** Mr M Trueman | Oxford city centre firm with excellent reputation. Higher court advocacy is a speciality. Full provision of high street services offered. | **V** 0<br>**T** 2<br>**P** 2<br>**TS** 18<br>**WP** no |
| **TUCKER TURNER KINGSLEY WOOD & CO**<br>18 Bedford Row, London WC1R 4EQ<br>**Tel:** 020 7242 3303<br>**Fax:** 020 7831 1732<br>**Apply to:** Mr P Davies | A general practice with a mix of institutional, corporate and private clients. A wide range of services are provided in these areas. | **V** 1-2<br>**T** 1<br>**P** 9<br>**TS** 33<br>**WP** yes |
| **TURBERVILLES**<br>122 High Street, Uxbridge UB8 1JT<br>**Tel:** 01895 201700<br>**Fax:** 01895 273519<br>**Email:** solicitors@turbervilles.co.uk<br>**Apply to:** Ms Norma Yeo | A progressive firm dealing with all aspects of law, with strong commercial and private practices. | **V** 1-2[09]<br>**T** 4<br>**P** 11<br>**TS** 67<br>**WP** no |
| **TV EDWARDS SOLICITORS**<br>Park House, 29 Mile End Road, London E1 4TP<br>**Tel:** 020 7791 1050<br>**Fax:** 020 7790 5101<br>**Email:** enquiries@tvedwards.com<br>**Apply to:** Ms Jenny Beck | Based in the East End of London, TV Edwards is a predominantly publicly-funded firm offering an extensive range of legal services. | **V** 0<br>**T** 7<br>**P** 6<br>**TS** 64<br>**WP** no |

**V** = Vacancies / **T** = Trainees / **P** = Partners / **TS** = Total Staff / **WP** = Work Placement

# Vertex Law LLP

39 Kings Hill Avenue, Kings Hill, West Malling, Kent ME19 4SD
**Tel:** 0870 084 4040
**Fax:** 0870 084 4041
**Email:** robert.dodgson@vertexlaw.co.uk
**Web:** www.vertexlaw.co.uk

**The firm** Vertex Law LLP is a dynamic legal business featuring some of the South East's most experienced corporate and commercial lawyers, recognised as leaders in their field. Vertex works on the principle that a law firm must evolve alongside its client's commercial needs. Staff welfare and reward are a key part of the ethos.

**Types of work** Vertex only serves a corporate and commercial client base and covers the following areas: commercial and finance, commercial property and environmental, dispute resolution, mergers and acquisitions, private and public equity and technology, with a fully outsourced and established relationship for the provision of employment, human resources, employee benefits and pensions advice.

**Who should apply** Vertex wish to attract trainees with excellent communication skills, a good academic record and a passion to work in a truly commercial environment.

**Training programme** A fully supervised and structured programme will involve four six month seats covering such areas as corporate, dispute resolution, technology and property which will include regular reviews by the relevant supervisors within each seat. Exposure to 'real' work, clients and the chance to develop relationships with the region's other leading advisors would come at an early stage, as will responsibility.

Benefits include: private medical insurance, life assurance, pension, paid professional memberships and subscriptions and 25 days holiday.

**When and how to apply** Apply online by 31 August 2008.

**Work placements** Vertex operates a vacation scheme open to those seeking training contracts and other students who are generally interested in gaining experience of life in a commercial legal business from June through to September each year each period lasting between two and four weeks.

**Sponsorship** Discretionary LPC funding on the basis of 50% fees paid and 50% interest free loan.

| | |
|---|---|
| Vacancies | 2 |
| Trainees | 2 |
| Partners | 8 |
| Total staff | 42 |

**Work placement**   yes

**Apply**
Online

**Starting salary**
First year: £22,000
Second year: £24,000

**Minimum qualifications**
2.1 degree (occasional exceptions)

**Sponsorship**
LPC

**Offices**
Kings Hill Business Park
(West Malling, Kent)

# Vinson & Elkins RLLP

City Point, 1 Ropemaker Street, London EC2Y 9UE
**Tel:** 020 7065 6000
**Fax:** 020 7065 6001
**Web:** www.velaw.com

**The firm** Vinson & Elkins is a leading US-based international law firm with more than 750 lawyers located in 12 cities across the globe. Over three decades ago, we became one of the first US law firms to establish a practice in London. Since then, we have built a dynamic office, doing work that has gained the respect of clients around the world.

Over the years, V&E has amassed a wealth of experience working on projects for clients in almost every country on the map. We are accustomed to working not only in well-defined markets, but also in less familiar and challenging environments, under developing local regimes or with poor communications and infrastructure. We know how to adapt to local customs, cultures and laws, enabling us to handle matters quickly and effectively.

We work in tandem with our clients, travelling wherever and whenever we're needed to get the job done. We know what it takes to make deals work and to win cases. That knowledge enables us to offer creative solutions for our clients engaged in leading-edge projects around the world.

**Types of work** Our clients are predominantly in the energy, finance and infrastructure sectors and the London office specialises in M&A, project development and finance, international arbitration and litigation, corporate and structured finance.

**Who should apply** We are looking to recruit ambitious individuals with strong academic results and sound commercial awareness. The ability to think laterally and creatively is essential.

**Training programme** The firm operates a non-rotational training system and trainees work in all practice areas throughout their two years. The training is designed to provide variety, flexibility and responsibility from the start. In 2006, V&E was named the 'Best Trainer – Medium City Firm' by LawCareers.Net. In 2007, the firm was nominated in the 'Best Trainer - US Firm in the City' category.

**When and how to apply** The deadline for applications is 31 August 2008 to begin training in 2010. Applications should be made by way of our application form, available from our website. Please note, we give preference to those students who have previously completed a vacation placement with us.

**Work placements** We view vacation placements as an important part of our recruitment process. For summer 2008 placements apply by 28 February 2008. Applications should be made by way of our application form, available from our website.

**Sponsorship** LPC fees paid plus a maintenance grant of up to £7,500.

| | |
|---|---|
| Vacancies | 2 |
| Trainees | 7 |
| Partners | 8 |
| Total staff | 49 |

**Work placement**   yes

**Apply to**
Mark Beeley

**Starting salary**
1st year: £40,000
2nd year: £42,000

**Minimum qualifications**
2.1 degree

**Sponsorship**
LPC

**Offices**
Austin, Beijing, Dallas, Dubai, Hong Kong, Houston, London, Moscow, New York, Shanghai, Tokyo, Washington DC

Vinson&Elkins RLLP

| | | | |
|---|---|---|---|
| **UNDERWOODS**<br>79 Marlowes, Hemel Hempstead,<br>Hertfordshire HP1 1LF<br>**Tel:** 01442 430900<br>**Fax:** 01442 239861<br>**Email:** underwoods@compuserve.com<br>**Apply to:** Mr Robert Males | Glowing reputation for quality service - innovative modern approach to client care, marketing and funding. | **V** 1-2[09]<br>**T** 1<br>**P** 3<br>**TS** 15<br>**WP** no | |
| **VAHIB & CO**<br>Alco House, 435 Green Lanes, Haringey,<br>London N4 1HA<br>**Tel:** 020 8348 0055<br>**Fax:** 020 8348 6655<br>**Email:** vahib@vahib.co.uk<br>**Apply to:** Mr Hassan Vahib | Established in 1999, this firm has expanded rapidly, successfully obtaining franchises in five categories of law (crime, family, immigration, housing and welfare benefits). | **V** 0-3<br>**T** 1<br>**P** 1<br>**TS** 22<br>**WP** no | |
| **VEALE WASBROUGH LAWYERS**<br>Orchard Court, Orchard Lane, Bristol BS1 5WS<br>**Tel:** 0117 925 2020<br>**Fax:** 0117 925 2025<br>**Apply to:** Ms Angela Parfitt | Friendly working environment, top class training and good quality commercial legal work. Modern IT infrastructure and excellent future prospects. | **V** 9<br>**T** 16<br>**P** 36<br>**TS** 260<br>**WP** yes | |
| **VINCENT SYKES**<br>4 West Street, Oundle, Peterborough PE8 4EF<br>**Tel:** 01832 272971<br>**Fax:** 01832 273115<br>**Email:** danielb@vincentsykes.co.uk<br>**Apply to:** Mr Daniel Berry | Two-partner firm in small town of Oundle, near Peterborough. Undertake general work with a bias to non-contentious work. | **V** 0<br>**T** 1<br>**P** 2<br>**TS** 10<br>**WP** yes | |
| **VIZARDS TWEEDIE**<br>Barnards Inn, 86 Fetter Lane, London EC4A 1AD<br>**Tel:** 020 7405 1234<br>**Fax:** 020 7405 4171<br>**Email:** info@vizardstweedie.co.uk<br>**Apply to:** Mrs Judith Cuxson | A long-established practice. Company and commercial work, commercial conveyancing, private client work including residential conveyancing, wills, trusts and probate, litigation and work for charities. | **V** 0<br>**T** 2<br>**P** 20<br>**TS** 51<br>**WP** no | |
| **VIZARDS WYETH**<br>Riverbridge House, Anchor Boulevard, Crossways,<br>Dartford, Kent DA2 6SL<br>**Tel:** 020 7400 9999<br>**Fax:** 020 7626 7788<br>**Apply to:** Miss Denise French | Defendant personal injury; residential and commercial conveyancing; wills and probate; family law, employment and commercial. | **V** 2<br>**T** 6<br>**P** 22<br>**TS** -<br>**WP** no | |
| **VODAFONE GROUP SERVICES**<br>Vodafone House, The Connection, Newbury,<br>Berkshire RG14 2FN<br>**Fax:** 01635 580 857<br>**Email:** nick.woodrow@vodafone.com<br>**Apply to:** Mr Nick Woodrow | Vodafone is the world's leading mobile telecommunications community, with offices across the globe. Vodafone's Newbury-based Group Legal function supports Vodafone's global initiatives. | **V** 1<br>**T** 2<br>**P** -<br>**TS** 70<br>**WP** yes | |
| **W BROOK & CO**<br>2a Doncaster Road, Goldthorpe, Rotherham,<br>South Yorks S63 9HQ<br>**Tel:** 01709 898697<br>**Fax:** 01709 881156<br>**Email:** wbrook@walterbrook.wanadoo.co.uk<br>**Apply to:** Mr W Brook | General practice including crime, family law/care, personal injury, domestic conveyancing. Franchised firm. | **V** 1[08]<br>**T** 1<br>**P** 2<br>**TS** 20<br>**WP** no | |

# Walker Morris

King's Court, 12 King's Street, Leeds LS1 2HL
**Tel:** 0113 283 2500
**Fax:** 0113 245 9412
**Email:** hellograduates@walkermorris.co.uk
**Web:** www.walkermorris.co.uk

**The firm** Large, commercial practice based in Leeds. One-office strategy to focus people and resources. The firm is one of the largest and most well respected in the North. It offers a full range of services to commercial and private clients, both nationally and internationally.

**Types of work** Company commercial; corporate; intellectual property; PFI/public sector; new media and convergence; corporate tax; commercial property; planning and environmental; CDR; insolvency; sports; employment; construction; regulatory services; and liquor licensing and gaming. Clients include major plc's and international clients.

**Who should apply** Bright, commercially minded and practical individuals who can get on with clients and team members, show a sense of humour and fun when the pressure is on, and adopt a commonsense approach to clients' problems.

**Training programme** Induction programme, four-month seats, choosing seats in the second year. Formal training includes lectures, workshops, seminars, videos and skills programmes. The Professional Skills Course is provided and IT training/workshops are also given. There is potential for secondments outside the firm.

**When and how to apply** By 31 July 2008 to begin September 2010. Applicants should complete the firm's application form, which is available online.

**Work placements** One-week structured vacation scheme is offered. 48 places are available. Closing date is 31 January 2008. Apply via online application form.

**Sponsorship** LPC and GDL fees plus £5,000 maintenance fees.

| | |
|---|---|
| Vacancies | 20 |
| Trainees | 35 |
| Partners | 52 |
| Total staff | 580 |

Work placement   yes
*(see Insider Report on p153)*

Apply to
Mr Tom Peel

Starting salary
£22,000

Minimum qualifications
2.1 degree

Sponsorship
GDL/LPC

Offices
Leeds

# Wallace LLP

One Portland Place, London W1B 1PN
**Tel:** 020 7636 4422
**Fax:** 020 7636 3736
**Email:** lawyers@wallace.co.uk
**Web:** www.wallace.co.uk

**The firm** Wallace is a commercial law practice which is widely respected for its reassuringly straightforward approach. We are a progressive and innovative firm with an enviable portfolio of domestic and international clients. We were shortlisted for Boutique Firm of the Year 2006 by *Legal Business* magazine.

**Types of work** Commercial, corporate, employment, leasehold enfranchisement, litigation (commercial), litigation (property), private client, property, technology/IP/media.

**Who should apply** We look for bright, articulate people who demonstrate practical awareness and commercial acumen. Wallace offers its people the training and freedom to develop and the opportunity to find their niche.

**When and how to apply** Apply by the end of January 2008 to begin a training contract in 2009. Send a CV and cover letter by post or email.

| | |
|---|---|
| Vacancies | 2 |
| Trainees | 4 |
| Partners | 10 |
| Total staff | 60 |

**Work placement** no

**Apply to**
Mrs Tricia Davenport

**Starting salary**
Market rate

**Minimum qualifications**
2.1 degree

**Offices**
London

WALLACE LLP

# Ward Hadaway

Sandgate House, 102 Quayside House, Newcastle upon Tyne NE1 3DX
**Tel:** 0191 204 4000
**Fax:** 0191 204 4098
**Email:** recruitment@wardhadaway.com
**Web:** www.wardhadaway.com

**The firm** Ward Hadaway is one of the UK's top 100 law firms and a major player in the north of England. We offer a comprehensive range of services delivered to the highest possible standards and all focused on securing the very best for our clients.

**Types of work** The firm is divided into five main departments - litigation, property, corporate, commercial and private client - with a number of cross-departmental units. The firm is commercially based, satisfying the needs of the business community in both business and private life. Clients vary from international plcs to local, private clients. The firm is on a number of national panels, for example the Arts Council, NHS (four panels), English Heritage, Department of Education and General Teaching Council.

**Who should apply** The usual academic and professional qualifications are sought. Ward Hadaway is keen to employ trainees who enjoy stimulating work and are capable of making a balanced contribution, often as part of a team. Sound commercial and business awareness is essential, as is the need to demonstrate strong communication skills, enthusiasm and flexibility. Candidates will be able to demonstrate excellent interpersonal and analytical skills.

**Training programme** The training contract is structured around four seats (property, corporate, commercial and private client), each of six months' duration. At regular intervals, and each time you are due to change seat, you will have the opportunity to discuss the experience you would like to gain during your training contract. The firm will always try to give high priority to your preferences. You will share a room with a partner or associate which will enable you to learn how to deal with different situations. Your practical experience will also be complemented by an extensive programme of seminars and lectures. All trainees are allocated a 'buddy', usually a second-year trainee or newly qualified solicitor, who can provide as much practical advice and guidance as possible during your training. The firm has an active social committee and offers a full range of sporting and social events.

**When and how to apply** By 31 July 2008 for a training contract to commence in September 2010 using the firm's application form.

**Work placements** Each summer between April and July of one week's duration. Apply by 28 February 2008.

**Sponsorship** CPE and LPC fees paid and £2,000 interest-free loan.

| | |
|---|---|
| Vacancies | 10 |
| Trainees | 20 |
| Partners | 57 |
| Total staff | 395 |

Work placement yes

Apply to
Tracy McCluskey
HR Executive

Starting salary
£19,500 (2006)

Minimum qualifications
2.1 degree

Sponsorship
LPC/CPE

Offices
Newcastle upon Tyne

wardhadaway

| WAINWRIGHT & CUMMINS                                                                                                                                                                                                                       | We look for candidates with practical experience of working for a criminal legal aid practice. Also someone who has made in roads into becoming an accredited police station representative. | V   | 0   |
|---|---|---|---|
| 413a Brixton Road, London SW9 7DG<br>**Tel:** 020 7737 9330<br>**Fax:** 020 7737 9331<br>**Email:** ajw@wainwrightcummins.co.uk<br>**Apply to:** Mr AJ Wainwright | | T | 2 |
| | | P | 2 |
| | | TS | 25 |
| | | WP | yes |

| WAKE SMITH | General practice serving both commercial and private clients. | V | 2 |
|---|---|---|---|
| 68 Clarkehouse Road, Sheffield S10 2LJ<br>**Tel:** 0114 266 6660<br>**Fax:** 0114 267 1253<br>**Apply to:** Ms Jo Barnett | | T | 4 |
| | | P | 15 |
| | | TS | 145 |
| | | WP | no |

| WALKER SMITH WAY SOLICITORS | With offices in Chester and Wrexham, a highly respected firm of specialists providing services to individuals, trade unions and businesses. | V | 3-4 |
|---|---|---|---|
| 26 Nicholas Street, Chester CH1 2PQ<br>**Tel:** 01244 357400<br>**Fax:** 01244 221150<br>**Email:** sarah.williams@wsw-law.com<br>**Apply to:** Mrs Sarah Williams | | T | 8 |
| | | P | 31 |
| | | TS | 165 |
| | | WP | no |

| WALLACE ROBINSON & MORGAN | Long established firm doing private client work, mainly conveyancing, probate, matrimonial, litigation and employment, together with company and commercial. Offices in Solihull, Dorridge and Marston Green. | V | 1-2(09) |
|---|---|---|---|
| 4 Drury Lane, Solihull B91 3BD<br>**Tel:** 0121 705 7571<br>**Fax:** 0121 705 9512<br>**Apply to:** Mr RP Hughes | | T | 5 |
| | | P | 6 |
| | | TS | 40 |
| | | WP | yes |

| WALTERS & PLASKITT | General high street practice with an emphasis on crime, family law and litigation. Action against the police, personal injury, legal aid and private clients. | V | Poss |
|---|---|---|---|
| Bews Corner, 2 Westport Road, Stoke-on-Trent ST6 4AW<br>**Tel:** 01782 819611<br>**Fax:** 01782 835747<br>**Apply to:** Mr M Plaskitt | | T | 1 |
| | | P | 5 |
| | | TS | 50 |
| | | WP | no |

| WANNOP & FOX | Medium sized mixed practice, largely private client but with some commercial property and general company/commercial work. Franchise in family and crime. | V | 1-2(09) |
|---|---|---|---|
| South Pallant House, 8 South Pallant, Chichester PO19 1TH<br>**Tel:** 01243 778844<br>**Fax:** 01243 788349<br>**Email:** info@wannopfox.com<br>**Apply to:** Mr Chris Gambs | | T | 4 |
| | | P | 6 |
| | | TS | 52 |
| | | WP | no |

| WANSBROUGHS | Market town practice with an emphasis on agriculture and insurance litigation. | V | 1(09) |
|---|---|---|---|
| Northgate House, Devizes SN10 1JX<br>**Tel:** 01380 723611<br>**Fax:** 01380 728213<br>**Email:** email@wansbroughs.com<br>**Apply to:** Mrs Sarah Lane | | T | 4 |
| | | P | 7 |
| | | TS | 102 |
| | | WP | no |

| WARD GETHIN | Conveyancing and commercial, private client, civil and personal injury, family, and crime. Legal aid contracts in family and membership of specialist panels. Additional office in Swaffham. | V | 1 |
|---|---|---|---|
| 8-12 Tuesday Market Place, King's Lynn PE30 1JT<br>**Tel:** 01553 660033<br>**Fax:** 01553 766857<br>**Email:** enquiries@wardgethin.co.uk<br>**Apply to:** Ms Sarah Scott | | T | 1 |
| | | P | 13 |
| | | TS | 96 |
| | | WP | no |

# Watson Burton LLP

1 St James' Gate, Newcastle upon Tyne NE99 1YQ
**Tel:** 0191 244 4301
**Fax:** 0191 244 4500
**Email:** margaret.cay@watsonburton.com
**Web:** www.watsonburton.com

**The firm** Watson Burton is a growing commercial practice based in Newcastle, Leeds and London. We work across the UK and Europe. Although Watson Burton is one of the North of England's longest-established firms, it has one of the youngest staff profiles. Our trainees, young solicitors and graduate assistants help to make us a lively and enthusiastic law firm.

**Types of work** The firm's main practice areas are commercial litigation, banking, commercial property, corporate, construction and engineering, professional indemnity, employment, commercial fraud, insolvency, regulatory, intellectual property and private client.

**Who should apply** Applicants are expected to be bright both academically and socially. We look for team players who can work with us and our clients, and bring inspiration and enthusiasm to the solving of legal problems.

**Training programme** Our trainees spend six months immersed in each of the three classical specialists: commercial litigation, commercial property and corporate with a fourth seat in one of these areas or another specialism. There are particular opportunities to pursue interests in employment and construction, in which we have established prominence. Our training programme includes both in-house and external seminars. Trainees are encouraged to assist in the firm's marketing from day one. Training at Watson Burton is meant to be enjoyable, demanding and productive. We invest time and money in our trainees with the aim of producing people who will take our practice forward and make their careers with Watson Burton.

**When and how to apply** Apply by 31 July 2008 to begin September 2010. Applications should be made by using the application form printed from our website (www.watsonburton.com), addressed to Mrs Margaret Cay.

**Work placements** 35 places are available for one-week placements during the months of July and August in either Newcastle or Leeds.

**Sponsorship** The firm pays LPC fees.

| | |
|---|---|
| Vacancies | 6 |
| Trainees | 15 |
| Partners | 40 |
| Total staff | 300 |

**Work placement** yes

**Apply to**
Margaret Cay

**Minimum qualifications**
2.1 degree + AAB at A level

**Sponsorship**
LPC

**Offices**
Newcastle upon Tyne,
Leeds, London

# Watson, Farley & Williams LLP

Earl Place, 15 Appold Street, London EC2A 2HB
**Tel:** 020 7814 8000
**Fax:** 020 7814 8017
**Email:** graduates@wfw.com
**Web:** www.wfw.com

**The firm** Watson, Farley & Williams was founded in 1982 in the City of London. It has grown rapidly to 68 partners and a total staff of over 420 since this time (220 fee-earners). We now have offices in London, Athens, Paris, New York, Singapore, Bangkok, Rome and Hamburg. We can advise on English, French, Thai, Italian, New York and US federal law. The close working relationship between our offices enables our clients, wherever they are based, to utilise the expertise of the whole firm. The firm is able to provide an integrated, multi-jurisdictional service in connection with those centres where offices are located, and worldwide through an extensive network of specialist correspondent lawyers. In each of our offices, our lawyers have expertise in the laws of the local jurisdictions, and a knowledge and understanding of local business customs and culture.

**Types of work** The firm is divided into four international practice groups: international corporate, international finance, international litigation and international tax. These groups are not divided by location but work together internationally. The international corporate group is divided into five sub-groups: corporate, Central and Eastern Europe, employment/immigration, EU competition/intellectual property and commercial property. The international finance group capabilities can broadly be split into specific shipping expertise including shipping finance, and general finance expertise. The international litigation group handles litigation and arbitration, with a particular emphasis on the banking, maritime, energy and aviation sectors. The firm has particular experience and specialisation in managing multi-jurisdiction ship finance enforcement proceedings. The international tax group advises in structuring tax-based transactions (both direct and indirect, and both asset and non-asset related) and their implications.

**Who should apply** The firm looks to recruit graduates who, in addition to a sound academic background, exhibit enthusiasm, ambition, self-assurance, initiative and commercial awareness.

**Training programme** Each trainee undertakes six four-month seats; we aim to seat trainees with a partner or a senior assistant from day one. Currently, a trainee can expect to spend a four-month period in Paris, Piraeus, Singapore or Bangkok. Each trainee will have at least one seat in one of our more specialised areas such as projects, tax, employment or EU competition. Trainees undertake professional skills training during their training contract. Compulsory courses are organised in-house as accredited Law Society courses and are tailored to meet the firm's main practice areas. We also hold regular in-house seminars at which we invite guest speakers and partners to speak. Additionally, each group holds seminars and workshops specifically for trainees spending time with them.

**When and how to apply** All applications for training contracts should be made online at our website at www.wfw.com/recruitment. The application deadline for training contracts is 31 July 2008.

**Work placements** Two-week placements will take place in April, June, July and August. All applications for vacation schemes should be made online via our website at www.wfw.com/recruitment. The application deadline for vacation placements is 24 February 2008.

**Sponsorship** Full payment of fees for CPE and/or LPC as applicable, plus maintenance grant.

| | |
|---|---|
| **Vacancies** | 12 |
| **Trainees** | 23 |
| **Partners** | 68 |
| **Total staff** | over 420 |

**Work placement**   yes
*(see Insider Report on p155)*

**Apply**
Online

**Starting salary**
£34,000 (September 2007)

**Minimum qualifications**
24 UCAS points and 2.1 degree, any discipline

**Sponsorship**
CPE/LPC

**Offices**
London, Paris, Piraeus, New York, Singapore, Bangkok, Rome, Hamburg

Watson, Farley & Williams
www.wfw.com

# Wedlake Bell

52 Bedford Row, London WC1R 4LR
**Tel:** 020 7395 3000
**Fax:** 020 7395 3100
**Email:** recruitment@wedlakebell.com
**Web:** www.wedlakebell.com

**The firm** Wedlake Bell is a medium-sized law firm providing legal advice to businesses and high net-worth individuals from around the world. Our services are based on a high degree of partner involvement, extensive business and commercial experience, and strong technical expertise. We have approximately 100 lawyers in Central London and Guernsey, and affiliations with law firms throughout Europe and in the United States.

**Types of work** For our business clients: banking and asset finance; corporate; corporate tax; business recoveries; commercial; intellectual property; information technology; media; commercial property; construction; residential property.

For private individuals: tax, trusts and wealth protection; offshore services; residential property.

**Who should apply** In addition to academic excellence, we look for commercial aptitude, flexibility, enthusiasm, a personable nature, confidence, mental agility and computer literacy in our candidates. Languages are not crucial.

**Training programme** Trainees have four seats of six months across the following areas: business recoveries; construction; commercial property; corporate; corporate tax; employment; media, IP and IT; pensions; private client; property litigation and residential property. As a trainee we encourage you to have direct contact and involvement with clients from an early stage. You will work within highly specialised teams and have a high degree of responsibility. You will be closely supervised by a partner or senior solicitor, and will become involved in high-quality and varied work. We are committed to the training and career development of our lawyers, and many of our trainees continue their careers with the firm, often through to partnership.

Wedlake Bell has an informal, creative and co-operative culture with a balanced approach to life.

**When and how to apply** By end of July 2008 to begin September 2010. Please visit our website to download an application form.

**Sponsorship** LPC fees paid and £4,000 maintenance grant where local authority grant not available.

**Work placements** Places for 2008: eight. Duration: three weeks in July. Remuneration: £200pw. Closing date: end of February.

| | |
|---|---|
| Vacancies | 7 |
| Trainees | 14 |
| Partners | 41 |
| Total staff | 200 |

**Work placement** yes

**Apply to**
Natalie King

**Starting salary**
£28,000 (2007)

**Minimum qualifications**
2.1 degree

**Sponsorship**
LPC

**Offices**
London, St Peter Port
(Guernsey)

**Wedlake Bell**

# Weightmans LLP

India Buildings, Water Street, Liverpool L2 0GA
**Tel:** 0151 227 2601
**Fax:** 0151 227 3223
**Email:** hr@weightmans.com
**Web:** www.weightmans.com

**The firm** Weightmans is a top 75 national law firm with offices in Birmingham, Leicester, Liverpool, London and Manchester.

With over 750 people in our dedicated teams, including over 90 partners, our aim is to be both the law firm and employer of choice.

**Types of work** We offer a comprehensive range of legal services to commercial, insurance and public sector clients, including insurance litigation, healthcare, professional indemnity, commercial property, commercial litigation and employment.

**Who should apply** We look to recruit up to 14 trainee solicitors each year. When considering training contract applications, we look for applicants from diverse backgrounds who can demonstrate an ability to achieve results. Above all, we value well-motivated candidates with a practical and pragmatic approach who can make a positive impact on a team.

**Training programme** Unlike many firms, we offer our trainees real legal experience during their training contract, including attendance at court and client meetings. Challenged from the outset, you will have the opportunity to demonstrate your talents across a range of seats. You will follow a focused training plan which will enable you to develop business as well as legal skills.

The quality of our training is an important commercial investment. Our retention rate is high and we want today's trainees to remain at Weightmans and be leaders in our future.

We pay a starting salary well above the minimum recommended by the Law Society, and this is reviewed every year to ensure that it is competitive. We also offer an excellent benefits package, which includes flexi-time, a pension, health cover, life assurance and 25 days holiday.

**When and how to apply** Apply before 31 July 2008. Our application form is available online at www.weightmans.com.

| | |
|---|---|
| **Vacancies** | Up to 14 |
| **Trainees** | 32 |
| **Partners** | Over 90 |
| **Total staff** | Over 750 |

**Work placement** no

**Apply to**
James See, Recruitment Manager

**Starting salary**
Well above the Law Society minimum

**Minimum qualifications**
2.1 degree preferred

**Sponsorship**
GDL/LPC

**Offices**
Birmingham, Leicester, Liverpool, London, Manchester

# Weil, Gotshal & Manges

One South Place, London EC2M 2WG
**Tel:** 020 7903 1074
**Fax:** 020 7903 0990
**Email:** graduate.recruitment@weil.com
**Web:** www.weil.com

**The firm** Weil, Gotshal & Manges is a leader in the marketplace for sophisticated, international legal services. With more than 1,100 lawyers across the US, Europe and Asia, the firm serves many of the most successful companies in the world in their high-stake matters and transactions.

**Types of work** Established in 1996, the London office now has over 110 lawyers. It has grown rapidly to become the second largest of the firm's 18 offices – it is the hub of our European practice.

Our key areas: private equity, M&A, business finance and restructuring, capital markets, securitisation, banking and finance, dispute resolution and tax.

Our expertise covers most areas: real estate, manufacturing, financial services, energy, telecommunications, pharmaceuticals, retailing and technology.

Due to the international nature of our business, our lawyers are experienced in working closely with colleagues from other offices – this ensures a coordinated approach to providing effective legal solutions efficiently.

**Who should apply** We are looking for trainees with the commercial acumen and energy to become legal experts providing high-quality client service and advice on complex international transactions. In addition, we need people who have a genuine contribution to make to the continued success in the development of our London office. We aim to recruit down-to-earth people with the intelligence, personality and drive to be happy and successful in an entrepreneurial environment.

**Training programme** Trainees who join the firm in 2010 will usually complete four six-month seats, one of which may be undertaken in an overseas office. In order to ensure our trainees receive adequate support and on-the-job training, they each work closely with senior associates and partners. The practical experience gained through exposure to client work is enhanced by regular internal seminars. Legal staff are also assisted by an excellent team of support staff. Weil, Gotshal & Manges aims to keep all trainees on qualification.

**When and how to apply** By employer's online application form by 31 July 2008 to begin September 2010.

**Work placements** Five vacation placements for Easter 2008 and 15 vacation placements for 2008. New for 2008: five vacation students will have the opportunity to spend three weeks in our New York office. Closing date by employer's online application form is 14 February 2008.

**Sponsorship** The firm will pay tuition fees and a maintenance allowance of £8,000 pa for GDL and LPC.

| | |
|---|---|
| Vacancies | 12 |
| Trainees | 21 |
| Partners | 24 |
| Total staff | 242 |

**Work placement**  yes
*(see Insider Report on p157)*

**Apply to**
Jillian Singh

**Starting salary**
£41,000

**Minimum qualifications**
2.1 degree

**Sponsorship**
GDL/LPC

**Offices**
Austin, Boston, Budapest, Dallas, Frankfurt, Houston, London, Miami, Munich, New York, Paris, Prague, Providence, Shanghai, Silicon Valley, Singapore, Warsaw, Washington DC, Wilmington

WEIL, GOTSHAL & MANGES

| **WARE & KAY**<br>Sentinel House, Peasholme Green, York YO1 7PP<br>**Tel:** 01904 716 000<br>**Fax:** 01904 716 100<br>**Email:** david.hyams@warekay.co.uk<br>**Apply to:** Mr David Hyams | Well established practice operating from prestigious city centre premises. Providing comprehensive range of legal services to private and business clients. There are currently no vacancies for positions at the firm. | V 2<br>T 4<br>P 6<br>TS 60<br>WP no |
|---|---|---|
| **WARNER GOODMAN LLP**<br>Portland Chambers, 66 West Street,<br>Fareham PO16 0JR<br>**Tel:** 01329 288121<br>**Fax:** 01329 822714<br>**Email:** recruitment@warnergoodman.co.uk<br>**Apply to:** The Human Resources Manager | A well-established medium-sized regional firm. Five offices Southampton/Portsmouth corridor. Legal aid franchise; member of specialist panels. | V 3<br>T 6<br>P 17<br>TS 240<br>WP no |
| **WARNERS**<br>Bankhouse, Bankstreet, Tonbridge TN9 1BD<br>**Tel:** 01732 770660<br>**Fax:** 01732 362452<br>**Email:** general@warners-solicitors.co.uk<br>**Apply to:** Mrs Sally Hardwick | Warners is a long established West Kent firm providing a quality service in the property, litigation, private client, and company and commercial fields. | V 2[09]<br>T 4<br>P 13<br>TS 125<br>WP no |
| **WATKINS SOLICITORS**<br>192-194 North Street, Bedminster, Bristol BS3 1JF<br>**Tel:** 0117 939 0350<br>**Fax:** 0117 939 0351<br>**Apply to:** Miss BJ Watkins | A progressive niche practice specialising in family, education and public law. | V 0<br>T 1<br>P 2<br>TS 7<br>WP yes |
| **WBW SOLICITORS**<br>Church House, Queen Street, Newton Abbot,<br>Devon TQ12 2QP<br>**Tel:** 01626 202404<br>**Fax:** 01626 202420<br>**Email:** dmhunt@wbw.co.uk<br>**Apply to:** Mrs Debbie Hunt | A well respected Devon based firm, strong clinical negligence, family, private client, civil litigation and commercial departments. Holders of legal aid franchise, ISO 9001, investors in people and Lexcel accredited. | V 0-3[09]<br>T 4<br>P 22<br>TS 140<br>WP no |
| **WELLERS**<br>Tenison House, Tweedy Road, Bromley BR1 3NF<br>**Tel:** 020 8464 4242<br>**Fax:** 020 8464 6033<br>**Apply to:** Mr NSG Harper | Main office Bromley. Additional office - 3rd Floor, 5 Lloyds Avenue, London EC3. Most areas of law covered on department basis. Established over 100 years. | V 1-2[09]<br>T 0<br>P 4<br>TS 37<br>WP no |
| **WENDY HOPKINS FAMILY LAW PRACTICE**<br>13 Windsor Place, Cardiff CF10 3BY<br>**Tel:** 029 20342233<br>**Fax:** 029 20343828<br>**Email:** enquiries@wendyhopkins.co.uk<br>**Apply to:** Ms MA Hamer | The first purely family law firm in Wales with expanding offices in Cardiff. Holds the legal aid franchise. Private and legal aid work. | V 2[08]<br>T 4<br>P 3<br>TS 26<br>WP no |
| **WEST LONDON LAW SOLICITORS**<br>Boundary House, Boston Road, Ealing,<br>London W7 2QE<br>**Tel:** 020 8434 3508<br>**Fax:** 020 8434 3740<br>**Email:** careers@westlondonlaw.com<br>**Apply to:** The Practice Manager | Small, friendly and busy niche High Court litigation practice. Applicants must be highly motivated, relish a high level of responsibility, be team players, have initiative and a 2:1 degree. | V 2<br>T 0<br>P 1<br>TS 7<br>WP yes |

# White & Case LLP

5 Old Broad Street, London, EC2N 1DW
**Tel:** 020 7532 1000
**Fax:** 020 7532 1001
**Email:** trainee@whitecase.com
**Web:** www.whitecase.com/trainee

**The firm** White & Case LLP is a global law firm with over 2,000 lawyers in the United States, Latin America, Europe, the Middle East, Africa and Asia. Through our unified network of 35 offices, we provide the full range of legal services of the highest quality in virtually every major commercial centre and emerging market. The firm works with international businesses, financial institutions and governments worldwide on corporate and financial transactions and dispute resolution proceedings. Our clients range from some of the world's longest-established and most respected names to many start-up visionaries.

**Types of work** Banking and capital markets; construction and engineering; corporate (including mergers and acquistions and private equity); dispute resolution (including litigation, arbitration and mediation); employment and benefits; energy, infrastructure, project and asset finance; intellectual property; public private partnership/private finance initiative; real estate; tax; and telecommunications.

**Who should apply** We welcome applications from candidates who are studying, or have obtained, either a law or a non-law degree, and who boast a strong academic record. They should be commercially minded and be keen to be involved in multi-jurisdictional work.

**Training programme** Trainees are an integral part of White & Case LLP and we take great interest in developing their potential. Following a comprehensive induction programme, trainees undertake four seats, each of six months in duration. To gain a greater understanding of our global network, our trainees are guaranteed to spend a seat in one of our overseas offices. Regardless of which office trainees are working in, they will be closely supervised by a senior associate or partner who will involve them from day one and ensure they receive high-quality, stimulating and rewarding work. We encourage trainees to take early responsibility and place an emphasis on providing practical hands-on training, together with plenty of support and feedback.

**When and how to apply** Candidates should apply for a training contract by completing the firm's online application form available at www.whitecase.com/trainee. We are currently recruiting for training contracts to start in August 2010 and February 2011. The closing date is 31 July 2008.

**Work placements** We offer one-week work experience placements during the Easter break and two-week placements during June, July and August. The aim of our placements is to allow candidates the opportunity to gain experience of how a global law firm operates and an understanding of the type of work our lawyers are involved in on a day-to-day basis. They will also be invited to attend a number of informal presentations, group exercises and social events. Apply by completing the firm's online application form available at www.whitecase.com/trainee by 31 January 2008.

**Sponsorship** Full fees for CPE and LPC plus £7,500 maintenance grant.

| | |
|---|---|
| Vacancies | 30-35 |
| Trainees | 55 |
| Partners | 68 |
| Total staff | 567 |

**Work placement** yes
(see *Insider Report on p158*)

**Apply to**
Emma Fernandes, Graduate Resourcing Manager

**Starting salary**
£41,000 rising by £1,000 every six months, plus sign-on bonus of £1,500

**Minimum qualifications**
2.1 degree

**Sponsorship**
CPE/LPC

**Offices**
Almaty, Ankara, Bangkok, Beijing, Berlin, Bratislava, Brussels, Budapest, Dresden, Düsseldorf, Frankfurt, Hamburg, Helsinki, Hong Kong, Istanbul, Johannesburg, London, Los Angeles, Mexico City, Miami, Milan, Moscow, Munich, New York, Palo Alto, Paris, Prague, Riyadh, São Paulo, Shanghai, Singapore, Stockholm, Tokyo, Warsaw, Washington DC

**WHITE & CASE**

# Wiggin LLP

95 The Promenade, Cheltenham, Gloucestershire GL50 1WG
**Tel:** 01242 224114
**Fax:** 01242 224223
**Email:** law@wiggin.co.uk
**Web:** www.wiggin.co.uk

**The firm** Wiggin is a boutique firm of solicitors specialising exclusively in film, TV, broadcast, new media, music, sport, gaming, technology and publishing, and has earned an international reputation for fresh thinking and innovative approaches. The *Financial Times* agrees, recently ranking us as one of the 'Most Innovative Law Firms' in the UK.

We offer a highly personalised relationship, working in partnership with our clients to address the complex legal challenges that the fast-evolving media industry presents. We have the knowledge and experience, as well as the commitment and confidence, to deliver straightforward and genuine advice motivated only by the need to achieve the best possible outcome for our clients.

Based out of our Cheltenham office, and also in London, and with blue-chip clients based all over the world (primarily London and the west coast of America) we go to where they need us to be.

**Types of work** Commercial media 57%; corporate 17%; litigation 22%; property 4%.

**Who should apply** If you want to experience high profile media issues in a forward-thinking environment then contact us. We're looking for you if you can demonstrate a passion for media and the law, strong academic ability and a commitment to success. One word of warning though, our seats are not for the faint-hearted. We need trainees that relish hard work and a challenge. We'll be at the law fairs, so come and see what we're all about.

**Training programme** Training is split into four seats and these will be allocated from commercial media (three seats), media litigation, corporate, employment and property. Although based at the Cheltenham office, you will be meeting clients in London and could end up on a six-month secondment there with the British Phonographic Industry (the record industry's trade association).

We don't want you to do the photocopying. Our trainees are encouraged to take an active role in transactions, assume responsibility and deal directly with clients. In-house seminars are held regularly and training reviews are held every three months. You'll get an experience just like your friends in the City but within the exciting and niche area of media law and within a firm small enough to recognise the importance of a personal approach.

Benefits: life assurance, private health cover, pension scheme, permanent health insurance, gym membership at corporate rates.

**When and how to apply** By 31 July 2008 to begin in September 2010. Apply online at www.wiggin.co.uk/recruitment.

**Sponsorship** GDL and LPC fees and £3,500 maintenance pa.

| | |
|---|---|
| Vacancies | 4 |
| Trainees | 8 |
| Partners | 14 |
| Total staff | 83 |

**Work placement** no

**Apply**
Online

**Starting salary**
c £26,500

**Minimum qualifications**
2.1 degree, law or non-law

**Sponsorship**
GDL/LPC

**Offices**
Cheltenham, London

| | | | |
|---|---|---|---|
| **WH DARBYSHIRE & SON**<br>252 Lytham Road, Blackpool FY1 6EX<br>**Tel:** 01253 346646<br>**Fax:** 01253 406069<br>**Apply to:** Miss Lynn S Williams | Two offices, 252 Lytham Road Blackpool and 51 Commonside, Ansdell. Main areas of expertise, personal injury, benefits, probate, domestic, commercial conveyancing, crime and matrimonial. Legal aid franchise. | V<br>T<br>P<br>TS<br>WP | 0<br>1<br>5<br>13<br>no |
| **WH MATTHEWS & CO**<br>11-13 Grove Road, Sutton, Surrey SM1 1DS<br>**Tel:** 020 8642 6677<br>**Fax:** 020 8643 3428<br>**Email:** sutton@whmatthews.com<br>**Apply to:** Mrs Deborah Mangnall | General practice although very strong private client base. Established in 1881. Seven out of the ten partners were trainees with the firm. | V<br>T<br>P<br>TS<br>WP | 3[09]<br>2<br>10<br>60<br>no |
| **WHETTER DUCKWORTH FOWLER**<br>95 High Street, Wheatley OX33 1XP<br>**Tel:** 01865 872206<br>**Fax:** 01865 872473<br>**Email:** fowler@wdfsolicitors.co.uk<br>**Apply to:** Mr RJ Fowler | A small provincial firm with two offices on the outskirts of Oxford with a staff of 25 including three partners providing publicly funded and private advice. | V<br>T<br>P<br>TS<br>WP | 1<br>2<br>3<br>25<br>yes |
| **WHITE & CO**<br>51 Alexandra Street, Southend-On-Sea SS1 1BW<br>**Tel:** 01702 340340<br>**Fax:** 01702 349564<br>**Email:** alison@whitesolicitors.co.uk<br>**Apply to:** Miss AM White | Specialist niche children's law practice serving predominantly publicly funded clients. | V<br>T<br>P<br>TS<br>WP | 1<br>1<br>1<br>7<br>no |
| **WHITEHEAD MONCKTON**<br>72 King Street, Maidstone ME14 1BL<br>**Tel:** 01622 698000<br>**Fax:** 01622 690050<br>**Email:** pammason@whitehead-monckton.co.uk<br>**Apply to:** Ms Pam Mason | Experience gained in two departments: commercial and personal client. Trainees encouraged to take on responsibility and use initiative. | V<br>T<br>P<br>TS<br>WP | Varies[09]<br>4<br>12<br>68<br>no |
| **WHITEHEADS SOLICITORS LIMITED**<br>PO Box m125, Chorley, Lancashire PR7 2GD<br>**Tel:** 01257 266008<br>**Fax:** 01257 249704<br>**Email:** info@whiteheadsols.co.uk<br>**Apply to:** Mr PJ Whitehead | Whiteheads provide specialised legal services in the whole field of housing management on a national basis to registered social landlords, local authorities and the police. | V<br>T<br>P<br>TS<br>WP | 0<br>2<br>2<br>23<br>no |
| **WHITTLES**<br>Assurance House, 23 Princess Street, Manchester M2 4ER<br>**Tel:** 0161 228 2061<br>**Fax:** 0161 236 1046<br>**Apply to:** Ms Julie Blackburn | Claimant personal injury, family, probate, trusts and employment work. Acting mainly for trades unions and staff federations. | V<br>T<br>P<br>TS<br>WP | 2[08]<br>4<br>10<br>165<br>no |
| **WILKINSON & BUTLER**<br>Peppercorn House, 8 Huntingdon Street, St Neots PE19 1BH<br>**Tel:** 01480 219229<br>**Fax:** 01480 472651<br>**Apply to:** Mr Dawson | An old established market town general practice handling all types of matters for private clients, commercial clients and legal aid. | V<br>T<br>P<br>TS<br>WP | 0<br>0<br>4<br>20<br>no |

**V** = Vacancies / **T** = Trainees / **P** = Partners / **TS** = Total Staff / **WP** = Work Placement

# Wilkin Chapman

New Oxford House, Town Hall Square, Grimsby DN31 1HE
**Tel:** 01472 262626
**Fax:** 01472 360198
**Email:** jwhittaker@wilkinchapman.co.uk
**Web:** www.wilkinchapman.co.uk

**The firm** Wilkin Chapman is a leading Lincolnshire law firm which has had sustained growth over the past few years and has recently expanded into East Yorkshire. Our lawyers work within departments and share their knowledge and specialisation with trainees, giving them the opportunity to contribute to cases and have responsibility for matters with appropriate supervision. Client service is of key importance throughout our business and excellent systems support lawyers in meeting high standards of client care.

**Types of work** We are exceptional as a regional practice as our lawyers work in highly specialised fields including corporate and commercial, agriculture, commercial property, private client, personal injury, employment and family. This gives an unusual breadth of law for trainees to mix within their training contracts yet undertake work of significant depth. Our clients range from plc to publicly funded with the majority in between: either companies, property developers, farmers or private individuals.

**Who should apply** Candidates should preferably have a 2.1 either in law or another discipline and be able to demonstrate a consistently good academic record. Our client-focussed approach means that we look for candidates who will be excellent communicators with a desire to achieve the best possible result for the client. There is excellent scope for career progression at Wilkin Chapman for strong candidates.

**Training programme** As a trainee you will undertake three seats, one of a year and two of six months. These are selected considering the areas of law of key interest to candidates. A mentoring programme is used to aid development and offer feedback.

**When and how to apply** Applications should be received by 31 July 2008 for entry in 2010 and should be made by letter and CV. Further information on the application process and the firm is available on our website at www.wilkinchapman.co.uk.

**Work placements** A limited number of two-day placements with the firm are available on application.

**Sponsorship** A £5,000 grant towards LPC and living expenses is available.

| | |
|---|---|
| Vacancies | 2 |
| Trainees | 4 |
| Partners | 33 |
| Total staff | 265 |

**Apply**
Mrs Julia Whittaker

**Starting salary**
Above Law Society guidelines

**Minimum qualifications**
2.1 degree

**Sponsorship**
LPC

**Offices**
Grimsby, Lincoln, Beverley, Louth, Horncastle, Cleethorpes

wilkin chapman
solicitors

# Wilsons Solicitors LLP

Steynings House, Summerlock Approach, Salisbury SP2 7RJ
**Tel:** 01722 412412
**Fax:** 01722 427610
**Email:** jo.ratcliffe@wilsonslaw.com
**Web:** www.wilsonslaw.com

**The firm** Wilsons is ranked as one of the leading private client law firms in the country and now has the largest team of private client lawyers outside London, eleven of whom are considered to be leaders in their fields. Private client business is our largest single area of work and it permeates the other areas of the firm, which include charity, family, tax and trusts, probate, agriculture, property, company commercial, employment and litigation teams. Our first-class reputation is based upon providing a quality service, a strategy which we have pursued consistently for over 30 years. Our clients include wealthy individuals, entrepreneurs, companies, landed estates, trust companies and charities and many have an international dimension to their interests. The work we do for our clients is best described as 'quirky' because of the particular issues they face.

**Types of work** Private client – The firm provides services to include tax planning, estate and succession planning, UK and offshore trust formation and advice, Wills, trust and estate administration. The litigation team advises clients on a wide range of matters, specialising in contentious trust, probate and property disputes.

The family team is regarded as one of the leading teams in the country handling divorces relating to landowners and offers considerable expertise in cross-jurisdictional divorces.

Charity – Wilsons has the largest and most highly ranked team of charity lawyers outside London, two of whom were formerly at the Charity Commission.

Commercial – The firm has a dedicated team of 20 lawyers specialising in employment, commercial property, corporate and intellectual property work.

Agriculture and rural affairs - During the last 20 years, the team of seven partners and eleven solicitors has developed a practice centred on advising rural businesses with a reputation for gaining exceptional results in selling land to developers.

Many of Wilsons' clients have substantial property interests and the firm deals with the purchase, letting and sales of their investment properties and all aspects of commercial property.

**Who should apply** We aim to employ the highest quality people. Our reputation relies upon this. We place considerable emphasis on teamwork and for this reason we look for applicants who are clear team players. Despite our national and international client base, we are situated 90 miles outside London. If quality of life is crucial to you, we would like to meet you.

**Training programme** A two-year training contract enables our trainees to sample four disciplines in six-month seats in our different sectors.

**When and how to apply** Applicants must apply by 31 July 2008 to begin training contracts in September 2010.

**Sponsorship** On joining us as a trainee we can offer you an interest free loan of up to £4,500 for the Legal Practice Course. If you stay with us for two years after qualifying we will write off the loan.

| | |
|---|---|
| Vacancies | 4 |
| Trainees | 8 |
| Partners | 30 |
| Total staff | 152 |

Work placement  yes

Apply to
Mrs Jo Ratcliffe

Starting salary
Market rate

Minimum qualifications
2.1 degree

Offices
Salisbury

WILSONS
LEGAL EXCELLENCE

## WILKINSON WOODWARD INC BOOCOCKS
11 Fountain Street, Halifax HX1 1LU
**Tel:** 01422 339600
**Fax:** 01422 339601
**Apply to:** Mrs Maureen Cawthorn

General practice with legal aid franchises. Clients vary from large companies to private individuals.

| | |
|---|---|
| V | 1-2 |
| T | 2 |
| P | 9 |
| TS | 85 |
| WP | no |

## WILLANS
28 Imperial Square, Cheltenham GL50 1RH
**Tel:** 01242 514707
**Fax:** 01242 519079
**Email:** info@willans.co.uk
**Apply to:** Ms Margaret Austen

Practice dealing with all types of commercial and private client work, except crime, from town centre offices.

| | |
|---|---|
| V | 1 |
| T | 2 |
| P | 12 |
| TS | 70 |
| WP | no |

## WILLS CHANDLER
76 Bounty Road, Basingstoke,
Hampshire RG21 3BZ
**Tel:** 01256 322911
**Fax:** 01256 327811
**Apply to:** Mr A Dodson

Typical high street firm undertaking a mix of work including matrimonial, litigation, probate and conveyancing. Old fashioned service, but modern systems.

| | |
|---|---|
| V | 1[09] |
| T | 1 |
| P | 4 |
| TS | 22 |
| WP | no |

## WILMER CUTLER PICKERING HALE & DORR
Alder Castle, 10 Noble Street, London EC2V 7QJ
**Tel:** 020 7645 2400
**Fax:** 020 7645 2424
**Email:** jobs@bhd.com
**Apply to:** The Recruiting Partner

A law firm dedicated to advising clients in the global technology industry and associated with two US firms: Brobeck Phleger & Harrison LLP and Hale and Dorr LLP.

| | |
|---|---|
| V | 2-4[08] |
| T | 2 |
| P | 10 |
| TS | 90 |
| WP | no |

## WILSON & BIRD
Ideal House, Exchange Street,
Aylesbury HP20 1QY
**Tel:** 01296 436766
**Fax:** 01296 393103
**Apply to:** Mrs J Majek

High street mixed practice. Legal aid franchise, strong crime, family and PI elements. Varied workload and experience.

| | |
|---|---|
| V | 1[08] |
| T | 2 |
| P | 1 |
| TS | 9 |
| WP | no |

## WILSON & CO
697 High Road, Tottenham, London N17 8AD
**Tel:** 020 8808 7535
**Fax:** 020 8880 3393
**Email:** info@wilsons-solicitors.org.uk
**Apply to:** Mr Simon Pugh

Large legal aid practice specialising in crime, immigration/refugee law and family law. No training contract vacancies at present - no speculative applications.

| | |
|---|---|
| V | 0 |
| T | 5 |
| P | 8 |
| TS | 69 |
| WP | no |

## WINCKWORTH SHERWOOD
35 Great Peter Street, Westminster,
London SW1P 3LR
**Tel:** 020 7593 5000
**Fax:** 020 7593 5099
**Email:** trainees@winckworths.co.uk
**Apply to:** Mr Hugh MacDougald

Public sector, charities and private client; a leading Westminster practice with further offices in the City, Oxford and Chelmsford. Specialist areas include parliamentary, housing, ecclesiastical.

| | |
|---|---|
| V | 4[09] |
| T | 10 |
| P | 24 |
| TS | 185 |
| WP | yes |

## WINDSOR BRONZITE
162 Millbrook Road East, Southampton SO15 1EB
**Tel:** 023 80634555
**Fax:** 023 80336365
**Apply to:** Mr PR Windsor

Personal injury, conveyancing, probate and private work.

| | |
|---|---|
| V | 0 |
| T | 2 |
| P | 3 |
| TS | 11 |
| WP | no |

**V** = Vacancies / **T** = Trainees / **P** = Partners / **TS** = Total Staff / **WP** = Work Placement

# Withers LLP

16 Old Bailey, London EC4M 7EG
**Tel:** 020 7597 6244
**Fax:** 020 7329 2534
**Email:** emma.macdonald@withersworldwide.com
**Web:** www.withersrecruitment.com

**The firm** Withers LLP is the first international law firm dedicated to the business and personal interests of successful people, their families, their businesses and their advisers.

**Types of work** The wealth of today's private client has increased in multiples and many are institutions in their own right. With our merger in 2002 we have been able to respond to these changing legal needs and offer integrated solutions to the international legal and tax needs of our clients. With 100 partners and 600 people we have unparalleled expertise in commercial and tax law, trusts, estate planning, litigation, charities, employment, family law and other legal issues facing high net worth individuals.

Withers' reputation in commercial law along with its status as the largest private client team in Europe and leading family team sets it apart from other City firms.

International exposure at Withers does not mean working in one of our foreign offices, although trainees can do seats abroad if they wish. A lot of the work done in London crosses numerous jurisdictions. Our international client base includes more than 15% of Britain's wealthiest citizens (based on the *Sunday Times* Rich List), at least 10% of the 50 wealthiest families based in Europe with US connections and a significant number of the *Forbes 400* list of Richest Americans.

**Who should apply** Each year we look for a diverse mix of trainees who are excited by the prospect of working with leaders in their field who are often in the public eye as spokespersons for the profession. Trainees should have a high degree of determination, ambition and be able to demonstrate business acumen and entrepreneurial flair.

**Training programme** Trainees spend six months in four different departments. Teams are small (files are typically handled by one senior fee earner and a trainee) so the client will know your name and will expect to engage with you on anything ranging from a property in Kensington to a revolutionary product they have invented. We also second our trainees to the client.

Buddy and mentor systems as well as on the job training ensure trainees are fully supported from the outset.

**When and how to apply** Apply online by July 31 2008 to begin training in August 2010. Interviews usually take place between April and September.

**Work placements** Our work experience scheme was nominated for 'Best Vacation Scheme' in 2006. We run our placements at Easter and over the summer in London. Apply online by 31 January 2008 for places in 2008.

**Sponsorship** Fees plus £5 000 maintenance for both the GDL and LPC are paid.

| | |
|---|---|
| Vacancies | 18 |
| Trainees | 35 |
| Partners | 100 |
| Total staff | 600 |

**Work placement** yes
*(see Insider Report on p159)*

**Apply to**
Emma MacDonald

**Starting salary**
1st year: £31,000
2nd year: £33,000

**Minimum qualifications**
2.1 degree, ABB at A level

**Sponsorship**
GDL/CPE/LPC

**Offices**
London, Milan, Geneva, New York, New Haven (Connecticut), Greenwich (USA)

**withers** LLP

# Wollastons

Brierly Place, New London Road, Chelmsford CM2 0AP
**Tel:** 01245 211211
**Fax:** 01245 354764
**Email:** graduate.recruitment@wollastons.co.uk
**Web:** www.wollastons.co.uk

**The firm** Wollastons is a dynamic, regional law firm, widely recognised as the leading, commercial practice in Essex. Wollastons has a strong reputation as a forward-thinking and energetic organisation, offering high levels of service to both businesses and private clients. The firm's first-class resources, including sophisticated IT, and the lively atmosphere attracts high calibre lawyers, keen to work in a modern, professional environment. The Investors in People accreditation demonstrates a strong commitment to staff development and training at all levels.

**Types of work** Main practice areas include corporate and commercial; commercial property; commercial disputes; employment; planning and property disputes; private client and family.

**Who should apply** Applications are welcomed from able and ambitious graduates with a 2.1 degree. Candidates should have a commercial outlook, be confident, outgoing and able to demonstrate a wide range of interests. A link with the Essex area would be desirable.

**Training programme** Trainees have four six-month seats. These will normally include: company and commercial; commercial disputes; commercial property and employment. Trainees sit with a partner or a senior solicitor and form an integral part of the team. Trainees are fully involved in a wide range of interesting work and, although work is closely checked, trainees are encouraged to take responsibility from an early stage. The firm is very friendly and informal and trainees receive a great deal of individual attention and support. Progress is kept under constant review with mid-seat and end of seat appraisals.

**When and how to apply** We start looking at trainee applications two years before the proposed start date but we also accept late applications depending on the vacancies remaining. Applications should be made using our online application form. Please see our website for more details.

| | |
|---|---|
| Vacancies | 2 |
| Trainees | 4 |
| Partners | 13 |
| Total staff | 103 |

**Apply to**
Jo Goode, Graduate
Recruitment Manager

**Starting salary**
1st year: £24,000
2nd year: £25,000
(for September 2009)

**Minimum qualifications**
2.1 degree

**Sponsorship**
LPC

**Offices**
Chelmsford

| | | |
|---|---|---|
| **WITHY KING**<br>5 & 6 Northumberland Buildings, Queen Square,<br>Bath BA1 2JE<br>**Tel:** 01225 425731<br>**Fax:** 01225 315562<br>**Email:** recruitment@withyking.co.uk<br>**Apply to:** Miss Charlotte Luton | Fast growing commercial and private client practice, with strong emphasis on personal approach. Excellent career prospects. | **V** 4-5<br>**T** 8<br>**P** 29<br>**TS** 200<br>**WP** no |
| **WOOD AWDRY & FORD**<br>Kingsbury House, Marlborough, Wiltshire SN8 1HU<br>**Tel:** 01672 512265<br>**Fax:** 01249 443666<br>**Email:** jmoor@woodawdryford.co.uk<br>**Apply to:** Mrs R Oswald Moor | Two vacancies in 2008. Seats offered in litigation, property, private client and matrimonial. Preference given to applicants with connections in South West England. | **V** 0<br>**T** 2<br>**P** 14<br>**TS** 80<br>**WP** no |
| **WOODFINES LLP**<br>Exchange Building, 16 St Cuthberts Street,<br>Bedford MK40 3JG<br>**Tel:** 01234 270600<br>**Fax:** 01908 202 152<br>**Email:** jegan@woodfines.co.uk<br>**Apply to:** Mr John Egan | A dynamic and expanding regional practice offering a comprehensive range of legal services. We see recruitment and training as the core of our development plan. | **V** 3[09]<br>**T** 6<br>**P** 22<br>**TS** 152<br>**WP** yes |
| **WOODHOUSE DAVIES & MARTIN**<br>137-141 High Street, New Malden KT3 4HA<br>**Tel:** 020 8949 1583<br>**Fax:** 020 8949 6165<br>**Email:** jrh@wdmlaw.co.uk<br>**Apply to:** Mr John Higdon | General practice in South West London/North Surrey | **V** 1<br>**T** 1<br>**P** 2<br>**TS** 17<br>**WP** no |
| **WORCESTERSHIRE COUNTY COUNCIL**<br>County Hall, Spetchley Road, Worcester WR5 2NP<br>**Tel:** 01905 766 335<br>**Fax:** 01905 766 677<br>**Email:** smallinson@worcestershire.gov.uk<br>**Apply to:** Mr SP Mallinson | Comprehensive legal service across all the County Council's functions including children's services, community care, highways and planning, property and trading standards. | **V** 0<br>**T** 1<br>**P** -<br>**TS** 28<br>**WP** no |
| **WORTHINGTONS**<br>28 Cheriton Gardens, Folkestone, Kent CT20 2AU<br>**Tel:** 01303 850206<br>**Fax:** 01303 246706<br>**Email:** bgk@weh.co.uk<br>**Apply to:** Mr BG Keating | Well established general provincial practice. Both private and legal aid. | **V** 0<br>**T** 0<br>**P** 3<br>**TS** 20<br>**WP** yes |
| **WORTLEY BYERS LLP**<br>Cathedral Place, Brentwood CM14 4ES<br>**Tel:** 01277 268368<br>**Fax:** 01277 268369<br>**Email:** jwinfield@wortleybyers.co.uk<br>**Apply to:** Mrs Jane Winfield | Wortley Byers LLP is based in Brentwood, Essex. Specialist work areas include business law, notarial services, employment and litigation, intellectual property law, property, environment law and planning. | **V** 2[09]<br>**T** 4<br>**P** 9<br>**TS** 65<br>**WP** no |
| **WRIGHT HASSALL LLP**<br>Olympus Avenue, Leamington Spa CV34 6BF<br>**Tel:** 01926 886688<br>**Fax:** 01926 885588<br>**Email:** humanresources@wrighthassall.co.uk<br>**Apply to:** Via online application | Leading law firm in the Midlands, strong commercial focus together with highly regarded private client services. Providing quality work/training within a supportive social environment. | **V** 4(10)<br>**T** 10<br>**P** 26<br>**TS** 186<br>**WP** yes |

**V** = Vacancies / **T** = Trainees / **P** = Partners / **TS** = Total Staff / **WP** = Work Placement

# Wragge & Co LLP

55 Colmore Road, Birmingham B3 2AS
**Tel:** 0800 096 9610
**Fax:** 0870 904 1099
**Email:** gradmail@wragge.com
**Web:** www.wragge.com/graduate

**The firm** Wragge & Co LLP is a major UK law firm providing a full service to some of the world's largest and most successful organisations.

At Wragge & Co cutting edge work for household names is our bread and butter. So, you may find yourself advising on multi-million pound cross border deals, high profile regeneration projects and complex disputes or working with bluechip clients like Marks & Spencer and British Airways. Working from London or Birmingham on national and international instructions, you will be part of a team passionate about providing the very best client service.

Wragge & Co is a relationship firm, taking time to form lasting relationships with clients to ensure we really understand what makes their businesses tick. Relationships and excellent client service are two of our driving forces. To make sure we get both right, you may find yourself on secondment, experiencing life and work as a client.

Relationships within the firm are just as important. We are a single team, working together to support colleagues and clients alike. This effort has been recognised in national employer surveys. Wragge & Co is the only firm ranked in both the Sunday Times 100 Best Companies to Work For and the Financial Times 50 Best Workplaces in the UK.

Benefits include prizes for first-class degree results and LPC distinction, £1,000 interest-free loan, pension scheme, life insurance, 25 days holiday a year, travel schemes, sports and social club, permanent health insurance, private medical insurance and corporate gym membership rates, plus a host of discounts on goods and services.

**Types of work** We have a national reputation in many areas, including dispute resolution, employment, antitrust, public law, tax, transport and energy and technology. We also have the UK's third largest real estate group and leading practices in corporate, construction, banking and pensions. Managing Intellectual Property magazine named us UK Law Firm of the Year. Our pensions team won the legal category of the FT Business Pension and Investment Provider Awards.

**When and how to apply** Applications are made online at www.wragge.com/graduate. The closing date is 31 July 2008 for training contracts commencing September 2010/March 2011. We will be recruiting 25 trainees into our Birmingham office and five into our London office. If you are a non-law student, please complete your application form as soon as possible, as we will be running assessment days over the forthcoming year.

**Work placements** Easter and summer vacation placements are run at Wragge & Co. Again, you can apply online at www.wragge.com/graduate. The closing date for applications is 31 January 2008.

**Sponsorship** The firm will provide your tuition fees for the LPC and GDL (where relevant) and a maintenance grant of £5,500 for each year of study for the LPC and GDL.

| Vacancies | 30 |
| Trainees | 64 |
| Partners | 110 |
| Total staff | 1017 |

**Work placement** yes
*(see Insider Report on p161)*

**Apply to**
Joanne Dowsett,
Graduate Recruitment
Advisor

**Starting salary**
1st year: £22,000
2nd year: £25,000
(to be reveiwed summer
2007)

**Minimum qualifications**
2.1 degree

**Sponsorship**
GDL/LPC

**Offices**
Birmingham, London

| | | | |
|---|---|---|---|
| **WRIGLEY CLAYDON**<br>29-33 Union Street, Oldham OL1 1HH<br>**Tel:** 0161 624 6811<br>**Fax:** 0161 624 3743<br>**Email:** jfm@wrigleyclaydon.com<br>**Apply to:** Mr John Mann | Medium general practice | **V** 1<br>**T** 0<br>**P** 6<br>**TS** 32<br>**WP** no | |
| **WRIGLEYS SOLICITORS LLP**<br>19 Cookridge Street, Leeds LS2 3AG<br>**Tel:** 0113 244 6100<br>**Fax:** 0113 244 6101<br>**Email:** thepartners@wrigleys.co.uk<br>**Apply to:** Mrs V M James | A specialist firm which concentrates on the financial affairs, property and assets of private individuals, charities, foundations, trustees and pension schemes. | **V** 1-2<br>**T** 3<br>**P** 17<br>**TS** 111<br>**WP** yes | |
| **YOUNG & PEARCE**<br>58 Talbot Street, Nottingham NG1 5GL<br>**Tel:** 0115 959 8888<br>**Fax:** 0115 947 5572<br>**Apply to:** Mr Richard Bates | Modern offices set in the centre of Nottingham. Fully computerised. Niche licensing and commercial, crime, family, civil litigation, BSI and legal aid franchise. | **V** 1<br>**T** 1<br>**P** 8<br>**TS** 33<br>**WP** yes | |
| **ZECKLER & CO**<br>75 Baker Street, London W1U 6RE<br>**Tel:** 020 7580 4546<br>**Fax:** 020 7580 4151<br>**Email:** rosanna@zeckler.co.uk<br>**Apply to:** Mr Andrew Selbo | Small, friendly, open-minded firm of competent, committed vocational lawyers. We aim to expand and select only on merit. Private and CLS work undertaken in diverse legal areas. | **V** 2<br>**T** 0<br>**P** 4<br>**TS** 12<br>**WP** yes | |

**V** = Vacancies / **T** = Trainees / **P** = Partners / **TS** = Total Staff / **WP** = Work Placement

# Barristers

# Training as a barrister

Barristers provide a specialist service in litigation and advocacy, and undertake advisory work. They prepare and present cases for trial, taking on a wide range of cases and clients (but usually specialising in only one practice area). Barristers also provide an independent advisory service on legal disputes or problems. Most legislation can be interpreted in numerous ways and barristers advise on how it may pertain to a particular case.

Generally, barristers work in private practice and are self-employed. However, they don't operate entirely in isolation: most of them pool their resources to form a 'set' of chambers, which enables them to share many of the costs involved in running a business. Each member of a set is known as a 'tenant' and has a say in the way in which the set is organised.

## Pupillage

Pupillage is essentially an apprenticeship whereby pupils observe a set at work and then practise under supervision. It's the final stage of training to be a barrister, where you put into practice everything you've learnt so far. Although you will be 'called to the Bar' on passing the Bar Vocational Course (BVC), pupillage is essential for all those wishing to go into practice.

### Structure

Pupillage usually takes a year to complete, with the year divided into two six-month periods known as 'sixes'. Each six is spent in a set of chambers (although there are a small number of places in companies and other institutions) under the guidance and supervision of a 'pupil supervisor', a junior barrister of at least five years' experience. It is not unheard of for each six to be spent in different chambers and/or with a different pupil supervisor.

### Content

To qualify as a barrister, pupils are required by the Bar Council to obtain sufficient practical experience of advocacy, conferences and negotiation, as well as legal research and the preparation of drafts and opinions.

The first six is spent shadowing and assisting the activities of the pupil supervisor. This involves attending court and case conferences, undertaking research, doing background reading and drafting documents. Thus, a pupil gains insight into how a case is prepared and argued, how a competent practitioner responds to developments as they occur and how pre-arranged tactics can be changed.

The second six sees a pupil take his or her first steps as a professional practitioner. Pupils are permitted to undertake their own cases for clients, under supervision. Inevitably, much of this work involves straightforward cases, but there is always the chance that an important or groundbreaking case may arise.

### How to apply

All pupillage providers must advertise all pupillage vacancies at www.pupillages.com. Vacancies are divided into two types: OLPAS and non-OLPAS.

OLPAS allows applicants to search and apply for pupillages online, and centralises applications into two seasons during which candidates can apply to chambers. The summer season runs from 3 March to 1 May and the autumn season runs from 28 August to 28 September. Using OLPAS you can apply to up to 24 pupillage providers each year (12 applications per season, two seasons per year) using just one application form. Check whether the chambers you are targeting accept applications for the summer season, autumn season or both. Also check whether your chosen chambers recruit one or two years in advance.

For non-OLPAS vacancies, recruitment is directly through chambers' own procedures, which are subject to the Bar Council's funding and advertising rules, as well as its common timetable. There is no limit on the number of applications allowed to be made to non-OLPAS providers.

The common timetable is intended to protect students concentrating on their final examinations from the pressure of deciding which offer to accept, and allows adequate time for interviews. It relates to both OLPAS and non-OLPAS recruitment, and states that:

- no offers can be made in the period 1 May to 31 July;
- no offers can be made before 31 July in an applicant's penultimate undergraduate year; and
- all offers must remain open for at least 14 days.

Remember that you must be a member of an Inn to take up your place on the BVC. You should have joined by 31 May of the year in which your BVC is due to commence. Further details about pupillages are available at www.barstandardsboard.org.uk.

### Tenancy

On satisfactory completion of pupillage, a pupil would ideally be offered a tenancy at the set in which he or she has trained. However, a quick comparison of the figures in the directory section concerning the ratio of pupillages to tenancies reveals that this does not necessarily happen. Inevitably, chambers cannot expand indefinitely and sometimes even the most gifted pupil is turned away. In such cases, pupils must work hard to secure a tenancy by any means possible (eg, by undertaking a third or even fourth six, or, as a last resort, becoming a 'squatter' (a non-member who uses a set as a base)).

# Career timetable

**First-year law degree students and second-year non-law degree students**

The key to this year is thinking ahead. Focus on getting top grades, do your homework on the Bar and get involved in achievement-type activities that will look good on your CV (eg, a Duke of Edinburgh award or captaining a sports team).

Research and apply for work experience (be it a mini-pupillage or a non-formal placement) in chambers for your summer holiday. Try to arrange a few stints in different chambers to give you an overview of the various work areas, unless you're unusually keen to specialise in one particular work area. Remember that without work experience, any application for pupillage is unlikely to be taken seriously. Not only will work experience give you a stronger CV, it'll also help you decide whether the Bar really is for you.

Join one of the four Inns of Court, which are non-academic societies that provide activities and support for barristers and student barristers. You must join an Inn before 31 May of the year in which you intend to commence the Bar Vocational Course (BVC), but it is a case of the earlier the better in terms of getting involved with the activities or using the facilities (eg, library and common rooms).

**Second-year law degree students and final-year non-law degree students**

Autumn term, Christmas vacation and spring term

Attend relevant careers events, including careers fairs, presentations and talks, and pupillage fairs. Look into funding possibilities for postgraduate training (eg, local education authority grants and Inn scholarships). Keep applying for mini-pupillages.

Non-law degree students should apply for a place on a conversion course, known as the Graduate Diploma in Law (GDL), before 1

February. Applications for full-time places must be made through the Central Applications Board (www.lawcabs.ac.uk). Although online applications are greatly preferred, you can phone 01483 451080 to request a hard-copy form. Applications for part-time courses must be made direct to the provider.

Summer vacation

Find out about pupillage applications. Look at the different BVC providers and check their application details. Gain further work experience.

**Final-year law degree students and GDL conversion course students**

Autumn term

Hot on the heels of your mini-pupillages, start making applications for year-long pupillage. Finalise your funding options and be clear about closing dates for funding applications. For more on funding, see "Financing the vocational courses".

The central BVC application system normally begins accepting applications for the first round in October. Late applications can be made until February, but with no guarantee of success. You can check the dates at www.bvconline.co.uk.

Spring term

Attend pupillage fairs, including the National Pupillage Fair, which is normally held in March. Apply for pupillage through OLPAS (summer season applications) in March/April. For more on how to apply, see "Training as a barrister".

Summer term

Check the progress of summer season OLPAS applications throughout May, June and July.

Obtain a certificate for completion of the academic stage of legal training.

### BVC year

If you were unsuccessful during your summer OLPAS season, apply again for pupillage through the autumn season in September/October.

Once you've successfully completed the BVC you'll be called to the Bar by your Inn. You'll also have to undertake 12 qualifying sessions (previously known as 'dining') before being called to the Bar.

### Pupillage

Pupillage is one year spent in an authorised training organisation (either barristers' chambers or another approved legal environment), usually split into two six-month periods referred to as 'sixes'.

#### First six

Without practising, you will observe and assist your pupil supervisor and other barristers in chambers. The intention is that the pupil shares their supervisor's daily professional life.

#### Second six

During these six months, you will be entitled to supply legal services and exercise rights of audience as a barrister. You may have cases and your own clients whom you'll represent in court. Now you start to build up your reputation as a barrister.

At the end of the second six, you must submit a certificate to the Bar Council Education and Training Department certifying that the second six has been satisfactorily completed. Provided that certain training conditions are met, you will be granted a full qualification certificate. Congratulations – you are a barrister!

# The Young Barristers' Committee

The Young Barristers' Committee (YBC) of the Bar Council was established in 1954 "to consider and make recommendations in regard to the younger members of the Bar". It was an "experiment for a period of one year in the first instance". More than 50 years on, it is flourishing as one of the main committees of the Bar Council.

The YBC exists to promote and represent the interests of the Young Bar, both within the Bar Council and more widely. The committee comprises those members of the Bar Council who were under seven years' call at the date of their election, plus a number of additional members who are co-opted to ensure good representation from the circuits and specialist Bar associations. The chairman and vice-chairman are elected annually, and the membership includes junior barristers in both self-employed and employed practice. Many YBC members also have a role in representing the YBC on other committees of the Bar Council.

## What do we do?

The YBC advises other committees of the Bar Council, and their subcommittees, on all matters that appear to the YBC to be of particular concern to young barristers or upon which advice is sought by other committees of the Bar Council.

Each year the YBC is involved in a variety of important issues affecting the Young Bar. Some of the major topics considered by the YBC in recent years include the compulsory funding of pupillage, the criminal justice system, proposals for direct access working, entry to the Bar, advocacy skills and training, judicial and silk appointments, and a range of issues connected with remuneration and fees for the Young Bar. Current projects are outlined below.

## Remuneration

The YBC meets regularly with government to press for improvements in publicly funded rates for young barristers, particularly in respect of magistrates' court fees and graduated fee cases. Recently, the chairman and other representatives from the committee have held meetings with the lord chancellor, the attorney general, the solicitor general and the Legal Services Commission. The YBC has also had significant involvement in the Carter Review in relation to the procurement of legal aid and has responded to the many consultation papers that have followed since.

## Education and training

The YBC takes a close interest in education and training for the Bar. It has assisted with the monitoring of Bar Vocational Course (BVC) providers and has contributed to a recent review of the BVC itself.

## International

The YBC helps to organise the annual International Weekend in London, during which it entertains young lawyers from jurisdictions worldwide. In June 2006 it hosted the biennial Anglo-Dutch Exchange and in June 2007, for the first time, an exchange with the Bar of Ireland. It regularly attends and speaks at conferences hosted by European Bars and the American Bar Association (Young Lawyers Division).

## Conferences

The YBC organises the Young Bar Forum at the annual Bar Conference and for the past three years has also hosted a conference for the Young Bar. Both events ensure that the YBC consults its constituency; they provide an opportunity for pupils and junior barristers to raise issues of concern to them and for the committee to hear about those issues.

## Young Bar Magazine

In July 2005 the YBC published its first ever *Young Bar Magazine*. The magazine was well-received and a second edition followed

in 2006, with plans for a 2007 edition to
follow. Copies are sent to all barristers under
10 years' call (including pupils) and are also
made available to BVC students.

### How can we help?

When you become a young barrister –
whether tenant, pupil or squatter – and you
feel that there are matters of general concern
to the Young Bar, please get in touch with the
YBC. Information about the committee, and
about qualifying and training as a barrister, is
available on the Bar Council's website
(www.barcouncil.org.uk). Alternatively, you
can contact the secretary, Gillian Dollamore,
at the General Council of the Bar, 289-293
High Holborn, London WC1V 7HZ
(gilliandollamore@barcouncil.org.uk).

*Sophie Shotton is the 2007 chair of the
Young Barristers' Committee. She specialises
in criminal law at 15 New Bridge Street,
London.*

# Clerks

Budding barristers: take heed! Clerks are the people who can make or break your career, furnish you with work or leave you twiddling your thumbs. You need them on your side. They wield enormous power and are an important source of knowledge and support.

The barrister-clerk relationship is as old as the profession itself and is an integral part of the whole process. Broadly speaking, the job of a clerk is to run the day-to-day business of chambers and organise barristers' caseloads. At the junior end of the job, a clerk will prepare papers, carry documents to and from court, and perform other administrative tasks. As the clerk becomes more senior, he or she will manage diaries, liaise between solicitors, clients and barristers, and bring business into the chambers.

Declan Redmond is senior clerk and chief executive at Wilberforce Chambers, a pre-eminent London chancery set. He is also chair of the Institute of Barristers' Clerks (IBC). With those credentials, it makes sense to listen to what he has to say.

Declan was encouraged to become a clerk by the husband of his college student liaison officer, who was himself a clerk. Declan joined Wilberforce in 1982, became first junior in 1992, deputy senior clerk in 1996 and senior clerk in 1998. Rising to even greater heights in 2002, he added chief executive to his senior clerk responsibilities.

Declan outlines what his role entails: "These days, I am doing much more strategic work, which means that I develop and implement business plans that have been agreed with members of chambers. Operation-wise, I have overall responsibility for all nine clerks and administration staff (including the finance and administration manager, marketing manager, receptionist and housekeepers). Importantly, I also manage client relationships, so that involves a lot of marketing. There is no typical day, which I really like. There are so many different things that can happen – if an important injunction comes in, it can change the way you work during that day. One phone call can change everything. But it's that variety which keeps you going."

The IBC was set up to protect clerks within the profession and to facilitate the exchange of views. Declan says: "It allows us all to get together and find out what's happening in the different sections of the Bar (eg, criminal and chancery). In addition, the Bar Council needs to know what the clerks are thinking, so representatives are often invited on to the Bar Council committees. Another important function is the education of clerks – we have college courses for junior clerks and we're about to start running senior managerial exams, all with a view to raising standards."

In terms of clerking, there is one very clear message that Declan has for the wannabe barrister: "As clerks, we build the practice of a new tenant up from nothing, calling on our own contacts and those of chambers that have built up over the years. Managing client relations is key to the job – the way a clerk answers the phone, offering a quality service to solicitors and professional clients alike, is very important indeed. If it all works in tandem, and you've got a good clerks team with a good reputation, that will bring work in. We go out to solicitors' offices (even as far as the Cayman Islands, sometimes!), particularly so when we have a new tenant starting. That person has no contacts, so we go out and talk about the junior end of chambers. We're basically saying, 'Look, this wonderful new person has started', and asking the solicitor to trust us to recommend the right person for the job. You of course hope that after a short while the new tenant will build his or her own practice. It's always a bit annoying if you've made an introduction and then you don't hear from that client again – that's when you have to start asking questions!"

And it's not just introductions to clients – the clerks act as a bridge between new tenants and QCs: "Although senior members of chambers may know you as a pupil, they don't really know how good you are when you start. We provide that link. If a QC wants a junior brought in, they will trust the clerk's judgment to suggest the right person." Clerks also negotiate client fees, with senior clerks dealing with the more complicated trials, "although we will bring junior clerks in early to help negotiate as there's nothing like experience".

Declan kindly explains the oft-mentioned 'cab rank rule': "When you go to get a cab from a taxi rank, provided certain conditions are met (ie, you are going to pay and the destination is agreed on), then he has to take you. In the world of barristers, if a solicitor phones up and asks for a particular barrister, and that person is available and certain conditions are met (eg, the pay is adequate and the specialism matches), then the barrister should take the case."

One feature of the job that Declan particularly enjoys is guiding someone's career from the very beginning: "You are dealing with up to 60 barristers who are all specialists, all highly intelligent, all highly trained, and your job is to help them get from an unknown to the top QC in the country (hopefully!). That is the goal as a clerk – you start with a promising pupil, take them as a new tenant, grow them into a QC and, ultimately, maybe get them to the bench. You have nearly as much invested in the career progression as the barrister. Clerks are very much a part of the organisation; there's no sense of 'us and them' anymore (or there shouldn't be!). It's gone from something of a gentlemen's club to being a fully fledged professional business now."

Declan has some final advice for the pupil or new tenant: "Seek the advice of the clerks. We are always happy to help. For example, we hold a lunch for the mini-pupils and keep in touch with pupils before and during pupillage. Once a person is a tenant, we have regular six-monthly reviews to discuss how things are going. Fantastic academics are not everything; if you don't know how to talk to clients or can't deal with staff, you're not going to succeed. A senior clerk will have seen 30 or 40 people come through chambers and will have a wealth of knowledge to share. Don't forget – they are the people who will be running your business for the next 20 to 30 years."

# Bar practice areas

# Admiralty and shipping

Shipping law is one of the most specialised areas of law, so its practitioners are always in demand. It falls into two areas: 'dry' shipping includes contractual issues, bill of lading and charterparty disputes, and disputes about damage to cargo, whereas 'wet' shipping usually involves casualties (eg, where a ship has sunk or collided with another vessel). Even when the world economy is slow, the shipping market remains buoyant and generally fares well because of its counter-cyclical nature.

Timothy Young QC is a member of 20 Essex Street, one of the country's foremost sets for shipping and commodities work. Called to the Bar in 1977, Tim had studied law at Magdalen College, University of Oxford. He remembers: "I was working for my university finals and I forgot to apply for the Bar finals course. They asked if I'd like to stay on to do a postgraduate degree, so I did."

Tim was then taken on as a law tutor for a few years at St Edmund Hall, Oxford, and planned to practise in Birmingham. He notes: "I had assiduously avoided anything to do with shipping. However, one night at dinner, I met the chap who was then the junior tenant in my chambers and he said, 'Birmingham?! Why do you want to go to Birmingham?! Why don't you come and do a pupillage in my chambers?' So I went along: I liked them and they quite liked me."

Of course, the career path is vastly different now. Tim doesn't even know where to begin in comparing his experiences as a pupil to those of budding barristers today. He says: "I didn't aim at shipping and it was a series of accidents. Accidents cannot happen these days. I come from another world: the dark ages."

Tim's just finished working on a case that he sees as the highlight of his career. Fittingly, it's a case known as *The Golden Victory*, after the vessel involved. He explains: "It was a long-term charter that was due to run until 2006. It had a little clause tucked away in it which said 'in the event of war between any of the following, including the United States, the United Kingdom and Iraq, we shall have the option to cancel this contract'. So my client, the charterer, terminated the charter in December 2001 (after 9/11) and the owners got an award saying that we'd repudiated the contract. Then there was a question of what the damages were. But by that time, America and Iraq *had* engaged in hostilities and so the question was whether it was legally relevant that there was this war. Back in 2001 you couldn't say it was probable that there would be a war, although maybe you could say it was possible."

Tim continues: "We had all sorts of evidence from professors of war and peace studies about the likelihood of war and fascinating insights into what was going on in the White House. We went all the way to the House of Lords on this point of law; whether events two years after a breach are legally relevant. It set the legal world alight. There are radically different views. I won it three-two with Lord Bingham against me. It was a bit of a victory!"

Although appearing before the country's most senior judges doesn't happen all the time, there's certainly no such thing as a typical day, notes Tim. So what does he actually do? He says: "Drink eight cups of coffee. If I'm in court I'll get in at 5:00am and go off to court and argue. If I'm just in chambers, I'm doing paperwork. I'll stop at about 11:00am and walk around, chat to colleagues, learn about other people's problems, canvas opinions and drink more coffee. The great thing about the Bar is that because we share only costs, not profits, we haven't got anybody looking over our shoulder saying we should be working. If we don't want to work, we can go and have half an hour talking about someone else's case. We're not answerable to our colleagues for our time."

It's this freedom that Tim clearly enjoys most about his career. Another highlight is the vast variety of work he sees. "In any one day," he explains, "I can deal with four or five cases. It keeps you young. I really wouldn't want to do another job."

And indeed, there's something special about admiralty work: "The thing about shipping is that actually you do find yourself getting involved in all sorts of things that may or may not have anything to do with water. At the moment I'm looking at a dispute involving a shipbuilding contract and the bribery of members of the government of a certain country. We look at why bits of metal break – from metallurgy through chemistry through physics. We do a lot of science. People ask me: 'I'm going to do law, shall I do Latin at A-level?' I say: 'Don't do Latin, do science!'"

As well as a broad academic interest, Tim suggests getting a good degree and building a broad CV. He says: "What we're not interested in is people who just work. We want people who've got a bit of fun about them. You do have to have a sense of humour and a bit of breadth. I would say broaden your CV, whether it's music, art or sport – anything other than pure work." Tim adds: "Learn the law of contract and tort well. What we do is contract law. We have bits and bobs of other things but when you look at the major contract cases, 60% of them come from our area. Commodities and shipping have been the powerhouse of commercial law."

But there's something much more subtle that's necessary for a successful career in shipping. Tim calls it precision and clarity of thought – something which is essential to every aspect of Tim's work: "Whether it's to do with construing a contract or working out a piece of chemistry, it's just a question of having the willingness and the modesty to know when you don't understand something and to ask for help."

Foresight doesn't go amiss either. Here's something Tim wishes he'd had back when he was considering a career at the Bar: "I wish I'd known quite how good it was so I wouldn't have spent two years thinking about becoming a solicitor! I just love it!"

# Chancery

Chancery work is split into two areas: **traditional** and **commercial chancery litigation. Traditional chancery includes real property, trusts and tax, while commercial chancery covers a wide range of finance and business disputes. Chancery work often has an international dimension, relating to asset tracing, cross-border insolvency and offshore trusts. Chancery barristers present cases before tribunals up to House of Lords level and draft a variety of documentation.**

David Mumford is a barrister of seven years' call at Maitland Chambers, one of the largest commercial chancery sets in London. He read classics at the University of Oxford, and did his conversion course at City University and his BVC at the Inns of Court School of Law. He explains: "I was always attracted to the idea that, at the Bar, one would be doing a job that had more intellectual demands on a day-to-day basis than many jobs, and so it was perhaps natural that I'd go to an area that might be said to be more academically oriented. But it only really became apparent to me that I was attracted to chancery work when I began studying – and enjoying – equity, contract and land law."

David did his pupillage at Maitland Chambers, where he enjoyed seeing the work of his pupil supervisors, who were generally barristers of 10 or 15 years' call. He says: "The work was reasonably large scale, as appropriate to barristers of that sort of call, and could be anything ranging from a property dispute to a fairly large commercial matter to some complicated trust problem. But it was broadly a representative cross-section of the work we do in chambers."

David has between 20 and 30 cases on his shelves that he describes as ongoing, in the sense that he's done work on them in the past and so far they haven't settled or been otherwise resolved. "Many will sit idle for months on end," says David. "In terms of what's actually on my desk and requiring something to be done in the immediate future, there'll probably be about four or five cases at any one time."

David describes a couple of his current cases: "I've been drafting particulars of claim in a fairly straightforward contractual dispute to do with the exporting of tinned tomatoes from Italy to England; and I'm just about to get involved in a big professional negligence claim against management consultants who advised on the restructuring of a brewer's supply chain."

David says: "Very rarely does your day involve sitting at your desk and doing one thing only. If I'm not in court, my day in chambers would normally involve me turning up to my room between 8:00am and 9:00am. Usually it'll be a question of setting about whatever piece of work I have on at that time, but during the course of the day solicitors will almost inevitably get in touch regarding another case and suddenly something that's been sitting on your shelf for months will go live. There's a very pleasing variety of work – the sorts of factual circumstances your cases involve, and the sorts of client, are very diverse, particularly with chancery work, where one might be doing a fight about co-ownership of a matrimonial home one day and a contractual dispute between two large corporations the next. Maitland is also a very friendly place and we tend to wander in and out of each others' rooms or grab a coffee or a sandwich together. If it's a day when there isn't court the next day, I'll normally hope to be leaving chambers by about 7:00pm."

Things are different when David's in court, however. It takes a lot of work to prepare for an interlocutory hearing or trial: "If that requires you to be in chambers until midnight preparing then that's what you have to do. Quite often you will have to get up pretty early the next morning, particularly if travelling to a far-flung county court or district registry."

More often in chambers than court, David notes: "The beauty of the job is that we are not in court every day and have the time to sit down quietly and really think about a problem between appearances; but equally we are not desk-bound. We get plenty of oral advocacy opportunities and one doesn't lose the sense that that is ultimately what the job is about." Moreover, solving people's problems is what excites him: "I find reading an entirely new set of facts, analysing what the issues are and trying to work out what the solution is very satisfying. I enjoy doing it whether it be with a view to advising, drafting a pleading or, ultimately, standing up in court and arguing about it."

Get ready for the flipside, though. David explains: "It can be very, very stressful, especially if you've got last-minute instructions to do a difficult hearing in front of a judge who is intimidating and well respected, and you simply don't have the time to be as prepared as you'd like to be. And even if you are well prepared, there is always an inherent element of unpredictability, particularly with live witness evidence. I'd be lying if I said there hadn't been hearings where things haven't gone quite as expected. That said, the stress makes it all the more exhilarating when it goes well."

The highlight of David's career to date was acting for a former actuary and director of Equitable Life in a professional negligence case against its former auditors, Ernst & Young, and board. David recalls what it was like: "It lasted some six months in the commercial court and there were about 15 different parties to it, many of them represented by QCs. It was a very daunting environment, particularly since it was a case that involved quite difficult allegations of professional negligence in the actuarial

context. It was difficult enough to get a handle on the concepts sufficiently to be able to argue them in court, and that just made something that was already intimidating even more scary. However, once the case got going and I got on my feet and did my opening, I really started to enjoy it. It was a thrilling experience and it got me a lot of exposure to good solicitors and barristers that otherwise I wouldn't have got that early on in my career."

For David, there's one thing that comes top of the list of skills you need to work at the Chancery Bar: intellectual ability. He says: "You have to have a strong academic record. You've got to be able to digest quickly quite complicated and diverse factual situations, together with what is sometimes quite obscure law, and work out what the issues really are. That requires you both to have good analytical skills and not to be daunted by things that may appear, initially at least, quite difficult. It's not pure intellectual ability, however: you've got not only to see the answer yourself, but have that sense for how to convey it in a way that other people will see it as being the answer too."

So, what should a budding barrister do to improve his or her chances of bagging a spot at the Chancery Bar? "Get a good degree with good grades behind it," advises David. "I would also say come and see what it's like: come and do mini-pupillages. There are a lot of misconceptions about the Chancery Bar. We have a lot of overlap with the Commercial Bar and a lot of the work that we do is not as dusty and old-fashioned as some people might think. And do what you can to practise your advocacy. Mooting is essential."

Above all, David says, you have to be informed about what the Chancery Bar is really like. "There's so much misinformation out there," he says. "It's sexier than you might have thought."

# Civil

**Civil law is that area of law involving relations between persons and organisations. It covers a very broad range of legal issues including those related to contract, tort, probate and trusts. More specifically, civil law covers disputes that range from employment to professional negligence, and from education to property.**

John Hobson is a barrister at Garden Court North Chambers in Manchester, a progressive set with a strong commitment to publicly funded work. John has enjoyed an interesting career path. He studied economics at the University of Sheffield, did a master's at the London School of Economics and then lectured for several years. "In my working life, I progressively got more interested in the representation of people," he says. "I was a trade union branch officer and later worked directly in the head office of the same union." All this experience led to a realisation that he wanted to be a barrister, and one representing individuals at that.

During a broad-based pupillage split between two sets, John saw "all kinds of basic criminal cases – representing shoplifters who had been arrested in Oxford Street to representing people in the youth courts across London". His pupillage also gave him the opportunity to do some civil work, which included representation in housing cases.

At eight years' call, John now focuses mainly on housing and employment. He says: "The emphasis in the work I've been doing is representing people in proceedings brought by public authorities. It's often about representing the individual against the state." He regularly does full final hearings in housing and cases at the employment tribunal that may last anything from a couple of days to several weeks: "I'm continually busy because there's work coming into chambers every day."

A case with which John is currently involved concerns the pensions of part-time female workers. He says: "The case involves representing women who were shut out of pension schemes over many years because of their part-time status and we're seeking remedy for them now. There are many claimants against many different private companies."

A recent highlight of John's career was representing a tenant against Manchester City Council in a high-profile case which involved a lot of media coverage for a number of reasons: "The case was about seeking to keep a mother and her children in her home, within the legal framework as it currently stands. It involved anti-social behaviour on the part of one of her three children. It wasn't a long case but it went to the Court of Appeal. It was about representing a vulnerable client and her family against a determined local authority."

Like most barristers, John finds his daily work depends on whether he's appearing in court. He says: "I could attend court in the morning for a trial that could be listed for a couple of days, or it might be a short application which sees you back in chambers in the afternoon. Then I might draft some paperwork or provide some advice to a solicitor over the phone." On other days, he'll work solely on papers in chambers but on occasion may be instructed to make an out-of-hours emergency application to the High Court by telephone. "This could involve a situation such as the provision of interim accommodation in a housing case where a substantive decision is to be challenged by way of judicial review."

John discusses what he enjoys about the job: "I like the variety of the work and the opportunity to combine many different skills, such as research, written, negotiation and advocacy skills, and the ability to get on with people at all levels. You're invariably drawing on those skills day in, day out whether you're working in court or in chambers." Many of the clients he works with are deeply vulnerable or facing situations such as eviction or a trial for breach of an injunction where the sanction may be imprisonment.

There are other skills essential to becoming a barrister. Commitment, hard work and thoroughness are key, says John: "I think that being thorough is important because if you miss something at first instance it may not be retrievable later on. And if you're on a case, you need to be fully prepared. Also, you need an incisive and analytical mind that's able to hone in on the important and salient points." However, the hard work does include late nights and early mornings, which John says are the least favourite aspect of his job.

If you're interested in civil work at the Bar, John advises the following: "Try and get as much exposure as possible to the life and work of a barrister – perhaps through mini-pupillages – to gain an insight into what's involved. I shadowed barristers working in publicly funded work. It's good experience to get the exposure in a safe environment like a mini-pupillage. I was definitely inspired by practitioners who were committed to their clients and who sought to secure the best possible outcome."

Another area to consider is the cost of the career path. "There's a lot of financial outlay involved," warns John. "But I'd say don't give up trying for as long as that's realistic. Remember that it's very competitive."

Since becoming a barrister, John has realised that his chosen career path was the right one. He says: "It has met, and gone beyond, my expectations. I always hoped to get this particular job in this type of chambers but I hadn't appreciated that I'd enjoy it as much as I do. It's representing people with concerns regarding key areas of their life, like housing, family or employment. It's also inspiring to be part of a chambers committed to the representation of people in such areas and to work alongside colleagues who are always seeking to develop the law."

Finally, John notes: "There's a lot of pressure on publicly funded work at the moment but there are still many committed people working within the field and, if that's what you're interested in doing, there are still the opportunities to work in that capacity."

# Commercial

**The Commercial Bar covers a broad range of practice areas that include banking and financial services, insolvency, insurance/ reinsurance and oil and gas law. Barristers will also handle matters for commercial clients that overlap with discrete areas of law such as employment, intellectual property and competition. Although advocacy is an important skill for a commercial barrister, the emphasis throughout pupillage is on developing a full understanding of commercial law principles.**

Nicola Allsop is a barrister at New Square Chambers, which offers a concentration of experience in chancery and commercial work. Nicola studied at the University of Bristol and then undertook the BVC at BPP in London before embarking on pupillage. Even during her undergraduate law degree, she knew that she wanted a commercial practice: "It was the area of law I enjoyed the most. I would look up points of law for my pupil masters; there was a considerable amount of paperwork. It was based a lot on academic research, a lot of work in the Inns of Court libraries and even going up to the Institute of Advanced Legal Studies in Russell Square. From a pupil's point of view, there were restrictions on how much I could get involved. There were numerous conferences, just not so much court work."

That's the main difference with Nicola's work now that she's a barrister of five years' call: "You go to court an awful lot more as a junior than as a pupil. The fundamental flaw in pupillage is that you're sitting with a pupil master who is usually 10 or 15 years' call and so, in the commercial context, that person does not go to court very often but, as a junior, I'm in court about three days a week."

So what's an average day like? Nicola explains: "I'll arrive in chambers at about 8:30am and I'll usually be in court in the morning on some sort of application, which will last for approximately an hour. That will be in either the High Court in front of a bankruptcy or companies registrar, or in front of the High Court applications judge in chancery, or in a London county court. It may be an application for an injunction in the context of a winding up petition or it might be a case management conference in a contractual dispute. Then I'll go back to chambers and have lunch at my desk. I'll check my diary and see if anything's come in. I always have a couple of opinions to be getting on with or preparation for the next hearing."

At any one time, Nicola will be working on a dozen cases but will have "another 20 which are liable to blow up but which I'm not actively doing any work on". At the moment, she's working on a very interesting shareholder dispute and recently did a trial which involved a misappropriated sports car: "It was a legal and factual dispute with plenty of scope for cross-examination and legal submission."

What Nicola enjoys most is learning about all the different businesses for which she acts. She says: "One day I might be learning about pig breeding, and the next day, it's the ins and outs of computer networking and firewalls. It gives me a far greater understanding of business and commerce and its interaction with the law. In terms of a career, I like the challenge of the work, the independence and the fact that I'm learning about other businesses that I wouldn't otherwise be involved with."

However, the nature of the profession can sometimes be quite frustrating. "There are still occasions on which I am instructed at short notice," she explains, "which sometimes means that I have to give up plans at the last minute."

In commercial law, Nicola notes that you

need thorough preparation: "There's often more law involved than for a criminal barrister, for example, who is more likely to go to court and argue over the facts of the case. In commercial, there's more scope to develop legal arguments." This requires a certain level of intelligence and what Nicola describes as "the ability to explain what can be quite complicated aspects of the law to lay clients so that they're able to make a decision as to the best way forward in a case". She continues: "You need to be a good communicator. And in commercial law especially, it's not just about being a good advocate in court, it's also about having good negotiating skills when dealing with opponents."

Nicola thinks that if you're interested in becoming a barrister, you should go and sit in court. You'll also need "to show an interest and have an awareness of recent legal developments. It doesn't hurt to read the law section in *The Times*. And, of course, do mini-pupillages".

Nicola herself did several mini-pupillages. Because she knew she wanted to practise commercial law, Nicola went directly to commercial sets: "I think it's important to do mini-pupillages in commercial sets. If someone applies to us and they've only done mini-pupillages in criminal sets, we might raise an eyebrow. I think it's essential to have a minimum of a good 2.1. If you haven't, then you'd need to consider doing a master's in a commercially related area of the law. Any business-related experience will help. I was quite well prepared coming into the profession because I'd done mini-pupillages."

Nicola has one final piece of advice for those about to embark on a career at the Bar: "There is an unbelievable amount of time spent waiting at the Bar; mainly waiting at court which can be frustrating." However, she sums up the profession as "extremely demanding but extremely rewarding – winning in court gives you a buzz like nothing else".

# Common law

The Common Law Bar remains an attractive option for those who believe that variety is the spice of life. Typically, common law chambers are multi-disciplinary and are divided into practice groups so that members can develop and maintain specialisations. Areas of practice can include actions against the police, employment law, discrimination law, landlord and tenant, personal injury, professional negligence, family law and criminal law.

Jack Ferro is a barrister at Crown Office Chambers, the largest civil common law set in London. Jack read law at the University of Oxford, where he started to think about entering the profession: "Establishing that I wanted to be a barrister was an evolutionary process. I was involved in public speaking and debating, and thought there'd be a touch of drama and theatre about a career at the Bar. I was also enjoying the academic study of the law, so that was another influence that led me towards the Bar."

Pupillage for Jack was spent at One Paper Buildings, which merged with Two Crown Office Row to become Crown Office Chambers. He recalls the intensity of that year: "You come in with what feels like zero knowledge and everyone else seems so competent and on top of things. It's hard to know how to contribute and not embarrass yourself! But then you get into the swing of things and in your second six you are appearing regularly in court. The end of pupillage is again quite stressful because you're in a vulnerable position and you're reliant on the assessment of others as to how much potential you've shown."

As part of Jack's common law practice, the largest area he covers is personal injury, for both claimants and defendants. He explains: "That's the most abundant source of court work for juniors. I also do product liability, construction, insurance and other general commercial matters. I'm in court on average three times a week, but it varies depending on the time of year and what settles. It's impossible to plan your week because you're often not getting your instructions until the last minute, and things collapse or something urgent might come in. As to the work itself, you've got to be flexible and think clearly in unexpected situations. You shouldn't be wedded to a particular way of thinking. It's better if you can assess the reality of a situation and build a case round that. And if there's a late development, you may have to return to first principles and re-evaluate your thinking."

Jack outlines what he's currently working on: "Today and yesterday I was working on a product liability case related to the construction of machinery that had trapped and seriously injured the claimant. The dispute centres on how to carve up liability among the machine's manufacturer, the person who introduced it to the UK, the person who bought it, the person who owned it at the time of the accident and the claimant's employer. That's the sharp end of the type of work I do! I've also earlier today been in a case management conference on a straightforward road traffic accident where liability is admitted."

Jack's "evil" career highlight is doing a case on his own against a QC who was "looking down his nose at me". Thankfully for Jack, by the middle of the second day, his opponent's evidence had collapsed and the client was thinking of suing the solicitor for negligence! More generally, Jack talks about "thriving on the adrenaline and thrill of being in a court situation where you don't know what's going to happen".

The best aspect of his career, as for many barristers, is autonomy: "I enjoy the freedom of not having a boss. You can devote your time to doing a piece of work thoroughly as you set your own working priorities and, conversely, can take time off when you feel you need it. It's also nice that as a barrister your papers come to you in semi-preparedness from the solicitor, so you don't have to do too much tedious leg work. And it appeals to my sense of the academic – you're looking at complicated problems and having to come up with imaginative answers. And, of course, you're flexing your advocacy muscles in court as well." While it can be difficult to plan your life outside the job, Jack thinks that things get better the more senior you become: "Now, if I feel that I'm at saturation point, I can tell the clerks not to take anything more on for me. I've been very satisfied with my work-life balance over the past couple of years."

Common law requires particular skills, says Jack: "The number one requirement is that you're a good advocate because you're in court all the time – more than if you were in commercial or chancery practice. If you don't have the ability to present persuasively, you're not going to get anywhere. Number two is academic ability; clients come to you for intelligent solutions to difficult problems. So you need to have persuasive, well-thought out arguments as well as advocacy skills."

Jack extols the virtues of mini-pupillages: "They're the closest you're ever going to get to seeing what this work entails and they're a way to differentiate yourself from others when it comes to applying for pupillage. Chambers are turning away huge numbers of well-qualified people at the paper stage, so you need to at least get to the point where you're being interviewed and you can sell yourself. If you've done a mini-pupillage at that chambers, it might be the thing that sets you apart. It also allows you to talk in an informed way – for example, what appealed about the work and what didn't. It's useful experience on which to hang your answers."

Finally, Jack talks about the nature of a career at the Bar: "It's inevitably a struggle when you're trying to get established, especially as you're not sure how to market yourself and you don't have a boss to feed you work. A lot comes from growing into the job; nobody takes to the environment immediately, but if you're well suited to it, it'll work out. I don't regret anything about the choices I've made."

# Construction

Contentious construction work often involves dispute resolution and encouraging the early settlement of disputes through mediation, other forms of alternative dispute resolution, adjudication, or litigation or arbitration. Other work includes advising on projects, insurance, health and safety, environmental matters and insolvency. Clients range from industry associations, public authorities and governmental bodies to major companies and partnerships.

Fiona Parkin is a barrister at Atkin Chambers, the first UK set to specialise in domestic and international construction law. Fiona did her LLB at the University of Exeter and her LLM at the University of Cambridge, followed by a spell lecturing at City University on the law conversion course. A "pretty grim" stint working in the City as a foreign exchange dealer saw Fiona return to the legal fold as a paralegal at Freshfields Bruckhaus Deringer. It was during this time, working on a technical case, that Fiona decided she wanted to pursue a technical area of the law at the Bar, and so applied to Atkin Chambers for pupillage. She was called to the Bar in 1993.

Of her pupillage experience, Fiona recalls: "Atkin Chambers is very friendly, so that helped enormously. It was hard work and stressful, because you are being assessed for an entire year. However, pupils here are encouraged to come along to social events, and taken out for drinks and dinner by the junior members of chambers, all of which serves to make things much easier!" Fiona outlines the type of work she did as a pupil: "You are shadowing your pupil supervisor. You do what he or she is doing, so you're working on interesting stuff right from the beginning and learning to apply academic law to real disputes. That is a big challenge and it takes a while to learn that the factual

circumstances surrounding a dispute are often just as significant as its legal framework. Our chambers ensures that pupils see a wide range of work. This can mean that there are periods when you accompany members if they are appearing in the Court of Appeal or House of Lords. We are also keen that pupils continue to develop their own style of advocacy, so all participate in our advocacy training programme."

Fiona enjoys a wide range of work, all of which has a technical element, and talks about some of the recent disputes she has acted on: "I have acted for major oil companies in relation to disputes arising out of the construction of oil rigs in the North Sea and in the Gulf of Mexico. I also acted for the House of Commons when a dispute arose in relation to the window package for installation in Portcullis House. I was also retained by the government of Gibraltar to advise it in connection with blocks of flats it had built to house over 1,000 Gibraltarians that leaked in the rain." She notes: "When you start out in our chambers, you are likely to experience a mixture of work. Some of it will be of comparatively small value – for example, advising on domestic house refurbishments that have gone wrong. However, it is also likely that you will be brought in as a junior member of a team working on a much larger project (often with an international angle that will involve overseas travel). It's great to start with a mixture because you learn how big cases involving complex factual and technical disputes are run, but you also learn from working on your own on smaller disputes. Whatever you're doing, everyone in chambers is always happy to help out with advice if you need it."

Revelling in the glamour of it all, Fiona is currently working on lots of disputes about sewerage works! The cases involve understanding why it is that sewerage works are not treating waste water to the required standard. Fiona is acting for the process engineering firms that installed, and in some cases designed, the technology responsible for treating the waste water: "It really is interesting! I have to try to understand water treatment and the biochemistry that underlies it. You're dealing with professional clients who know their stuff and expect you to know it too. You can't hide behind the fact that you're a lawyer and leave the technical detail to the experts – you're being paid to understand precisely why it is that something does not work. Certainly if the case goes all the way to trial, you need to have a clear understanding of the technology to ensure that you can conduct an effective cross-examination of the other side's expert witness. This means hard work, but the results are worth it. There is a real sense of achievement in understanding complex technical and scientific processes and being able to explain them to a judge."

Fiona enthuses about the enjoyment of continued learning, and not just about the law: "You are working as part of a team with others who are often regarded as world leaders in their chosen specialist field. This is exciting and stimulating. Working on the bigger cases also means that you are likely to be involved in some of the major infrastructure, power, water and civil engineering projects undertaken in this country and around the world. I enjoy the challenge of understanding how such projects are conceived, designed and implemented, and why it is that they have gone wrong. Even though I've been doing it for over 10 years, every new case is a fresh challenge because each case brings something new to learn about."

Fiona has a list of things that she enjoys about the job: "I work in a friendly and stimulating environment, with a great bunch of people. There is also nothing quite like the feeling of arguing and winning a case! I love working for myself too, as you have flexibility that you wouldn't have as a solicitor. I have three children, so if I don't want to work during August, I don't have to. I also think that the Bar is a great institution. Conversely, you learn to exist without much sleep, which is good training for when you have small children! And there are times when you have worked extremely hard on a case and believe that your client is right, but the judge doesn't agree. That can feel a bit miserable."

There are a number of skills needed to succeed in this field, says Fiona: "You need to have legal ability and enjoy acting as an advocate. You also need to be able to get on top of complex technical detail, sometimes in a comparatively short space of time. You certainly need to have stamina if you are working on a large case that is coming up to trial! Finally, you have to be able to interact well with all people from all walks of life."

As for advice, Fiona says: "Obviously, you stand the most chance of being offered a pupillage if you have done well at your chosen academic subjects – no amount of work experience or mini-pupillages will make up for a poor degree. However, when you come to doing mini-pupillages, I suggest you do them over a range of specialities to get a flavour of the sort of work that you would do during pupillage and tenancy, and to work out what you really want to do. I believe that in future, the Bar's strength is likely to lie in its specialisations. The trick is to find the specialist area of work that most interests you. If you are offered a pupillage, accept that there will be a steep learning curve that bar school is unlikely to have prepared you for. Although pupillage for me was undeniably hard work, the rewards once I was taken on made it all worthwhile!"

# Crime

At the Criminal Law Bar you may be called on to act for either the defence or the prosecution. Specialist criminal law chambers offer expertise in all areas, including child abuse and child sex offending, drug-related offences, fraud, human rights, mental illness, violent and sexual crime, and white collar crime. As might be expected, criminal barristers spend more time in court than almost any other sector of the Bar.

The international aspect of criminal law includes EU human rights, terrorism and war crimes, serious fraud, organised crime, drugs trafficking and money laundering. Practitioners in international criminal law regularly appear before foreign tribunals and international courts.

Kathryn Howarth is a barrister at 36 Bedford Row, one of London's largest sets with expertise in all aspects of the law, including criminal law. Kathryn's decision to become a barrister was motivated by a "sense of injustice in the world" and a desire to "do something about it", not to mention a love of TV lawyers ("more *Kavanagh QC* than *Judge John Deed* though!"). Kathryn studied law as an undergraduate at the University of Cambridge and then went on to complete a master's in law at the University of Toronto, specialising in international law and legal theory. Her view is that, while a master's degree isn't essential, "it can add another string to your bow and so can certainly help your pupillage application".

Kathryn has been involved in international human rights law and international criminal law for several years. While at university, she spent a summer working as an intern at the Jamaica Council for Human Rights, where she conducted interviews with defendants on death row. After her master's she spent a year in Sierra Leone working as an intern and then as a consultant at the Special Court for Sierra Leone. Prior to her pupillage she worked as a law clerk at the Prosecutor's Office of the War Crimes Chamber at the National Court of Bosnia and Herzegovina, and during her pupillage she went to Tanzania as part of a team from chambers defending at the International Criminal Tribunal for Rwanda. Her view is that "this type of international work is extremely rewarding and the type of experience that can help your application for pupillage to stand out among the crowd".

Pupillage at 36 Bedford Row was both a rewarding and challenging year. Kathryn explains: "I had a criminal pupil supervisor in my first six months, during which time I went to the Crown Court with her most days and observed lots of sex crime, violent crime and a lengthy double murder with three defendants. I also went to court with more junior members of chambers towards the end of the first six months and saw more junior work in the magistrates' and in the Crown Court." In her second six months Kathryn was in court in her own right, usually three to four times a week, including in the magistrates' court conducting trials and occasionally in the Crown Court for mentions.

Now, Kathryn's criminal practice means she is in court every day, although these days her time is increasingly spent in the Crown Court. She discusses how things break down: "I do a fairly even split of prosecution and defence work. Some days I'll do a number of mentions, for example a bail application, a sentence, a plea and case management hearing, or a mention in relation to another issue that has arisen in a case. Other days, I might be conducting a trial or an appeal against a conviction. I deal with a wide range of criminal offences; for example, I might conduct a trial in relation to theft, robbery, burglary or handling, or violent crime, or public order offences, or perhaps conduct a mention in relation to more serious matters such as sex crime or murder."

Kathryn talks about the best moments of her career so far: "Since pupillage, my highlights include my first trial at the magistrates' court (which I won), my first appeal against conviction at Luton Crown Court (which lasted three days during which I was appearing against two senior members of chambers), and of course my first jury trial! My international work has also been great to have been involved in, particularly some of the groundbreaking work at the Special Court for Sierra Leone, such as the first prosecutions for recruiting child soldiers."

Listen up – literally! Kathryn stresses the importance of keeping your ears open when in court: "It is important to be a good listener. If a judge asks a question you have to listen to what that question is and what he or she wants to know and give an accurate answer. In relation to witness handling you need to listen carefully to what the witness says; what they say and what they omit. If you are overly focused on your own pre-prepared questions and you're not listening to the witness's answers, it's easy to miss something important. You need to be reactive and that's not possible if you're not listening."

Kathryn has some advice about how to demonstrate a genuine interest in the Criminal Bar. She says: "I think that, in addition to mini-pupillages, it's a good idea to do some work experience with a criminal defence solicitor or the Crown Prosecution Service, or marshalling with a judge. That way you get a broader insight into what's involved in the work of those people that ultimately you will be working with or against. Also you should seize any opportunity to practise advocacy that you can."

Kathryn also thinks it's very important to know the chambers to which you are

applying. She says: "Look at their websites, see what sort of work they do and whether any members of chambers have been involved in notable cases. You can then tailor your application accordingly, showing that you know and have an interest in that chambers and its work."

Despite things not being exactly like on *Kavanagh QC*, Kathryn's view is that "if you do your research and take the time to talk to barristers about life at the Criminal Bar, then you won't get any nasty surprises, and you'll be well prepared for the reality of what is a very engaging and rewarding job".

# Employment

A popular misconception is that this area of law is just about employment contracts. In fact, employment lawyers can be expected to handle all areas of employment law, including discrimination, workplace monitoring and restructuring, and whistleblowing. There has been a massive increase in employment law cases in recent years due to a combination of new European legislation, Labour government policies and an increasing awareness by employees of their work-related rights.

Paul Michell is a barrister at Cloisters, a leading set with particular expertise in employment, equality, discrimination and human rights law. Paul's route to the Bar meandered via an English degree at the University of Cambridge and a number one single in Paraguay! He explains: "After university, I was a singer in a band, touring the world. Seven years later, I thought it was time to get serious (or end up looking a bit silly!). In fact, being a barrister is not a million miles away from being in a band: you're self-employed and there is an element of performance to both."

Paul did his first six at 39 Essex Street, doing mostly public law, and his second six at Cloisters. Then it was off to a tenancy at 4 King's Bench Walk for "five years of common law work" and finally back to Cloisters to focus on employment law. Paul talks about his practice: "There is massive variety. You might find yourself dealing with black letter law (such as an urgent injunction on a restrictive covenant), a claim for wrongful dismissal in the High Court or a sex discrimination case in Croydon. The clients are very varied as well. On average, you get more opportunity for advocacy (tribunal and court work) than other areas of civil law and you're not always appearing in front of judges."

Although "there is no typical day – that's what I like about it", Paul describes what a working day might include: "I could find myself attending conferences, going to hearings, drafting or giving advice. It's a good mixture." With Paul's caseload split between claimants and respondents fairly evenly, he discusses some of his recent work: "This week I'm acting for the Royal National Institute of Blind People in a whistleblowing case. Last week, I was working on a case which involved a woman who was psychiatrically very vulnerable, which was difficult because I had to avoid causing her distress during cross-examination, while at the same time getting the right answers for my client. You deal with a real mixture of people, so you have to tailor your questioning and attitude depending on who you're examining, who the tribunal is and what the case is about. There can be lots of courtroom drama. It can also be dry and dusty!"

Paul is excited about the prospect of going to the European Court of Justice (ECJ) later in the year with a cutting-edge case: "It's about associative disability discrimination. My client has a disabled son and she claims to have been discriminated against at work as a result. While associative discrimination has been prohibited in the UK in relation to race and in other contexts (for example, a white person could take action if discriminated against because he/she has a black partner), the UK legislation isn't clear on whether associative discrimination is actionable in relation to disability. So the tribunal has referred us to the ECJ to see if EC law prohibits associative discrimination and harassment in that context."

So what makes a good employment barrister? Common sense is particularly important, says Paul: "It can see you through an awful lot, not least because often you're in front of a tribunal where two out of the three adjudicators aren't lawyers. Common sense and lateral thinking is what they usually like, so you want them to be convinced that yours is the best way of doing things. You're there not just as a lawyer, but also as a persuader. And more so in employment, because you're up against a very proactive tribunal – you will get more questions than you would from a judge." And, of course, the old cliché remains true: "Preparation, preparation, preparation – you need to know your papers backwards and to keep up to date with employment law, which changes very rapidly. I sometimes think it's a shame we don't have a memory chip to plug in!"

Paul has some top tips on putting together an impressive CV: "We receive about 500 applications each year, of which we select about 80 to interview. To get into that group, you need to tick a variety of boxes. For example, you'll need to have some advocacy experience – if you get a chance to moot, do it and win; if you get a chance to do the Free Representation Unit, do it and win. Try and demonstrate skills that'll distinguish you from others. It's not enough to just have a good degree – what else makes you stand out? (In my case, sadly, it was being in a band!) We are also keen to see some commitment in the pro bono direction." And it's a question of 'do as I say, not as I do' in one respect: "I'd never been into a tribunal or a court before I applied for pupillage – I just liked the idea of 'defending the underdog', making some money and having some fun! My advice would be to try and learn more about how barristers work together, what the tribunals are like, what different chambers can offer – it's the only way you can get close to having an idea of what it's all about."

Overall, it's good to be an employment barrister, says Paul: "I enjoy the fact that, mostly, I have control over my job and hours. And it's a very good job for someone with a short attention span – you can get intensely involved and then move on! Employment also has a massive human interest side, whereby you're delving into people's lives. Winning usually feels good, but when you have a righteous case and you win, it feels very good indeed."

# European Union and international

**Barristers specialising in this area may appear before the International Court of Justice (ICJ), the World Trade Organisation, the European Court of Human Rights and other international and European tribunals. Matters that may be under dispute include those relating to boundaries, the interpretation of treaties, state responsibility, international investment, the environment and human rights.**

Josh Holmes is a barrister at Monckton Chambers, particularly known for its expertise in EU and competition, human rights, commercial, value added tax and customs law.

Josh read law at the University of Oxford and Harvard University, and was called to the Bar in 1997. Initially taking a pragmatic approach and choosing law because it is a versatile degree, Josh fell in love with the subject. He was always more attracted by the Bar: "As a self-employed barrister, you're responsible for your own practice and you have more freedom to decide how to develop your career."

Josh had a peripatetic journey from university to Monckton. He did his pupillage at Blackstone Chambers and at the European Commission in Brussels. After qualifying, he accepted a fellowship at New College, Oxford, and spent several years teaching in and researching EU and competition law. He was then offered a position at the European Court of Justice (ECJ) in Luxembourg, working as a *referendaire* (legal secretary) to the UK advocate general, Francis Jacobs. He explains: "I was *referendaire* from 2003 to 2005 and really enjoyed working at the heart of Europe. Each advocate general and judge has several *referendaires* whose job it is to help research the legal questions raised in cases before the court and to work on draft opinions and judgments."

Following his time in Luxembourg, Josh decided that he wanted to return to practice as a barrister. He chose Monckton as one of the two or three sets specialising in EU and competition law because he liked the forward-looking, dynamic atmosphere of the set. He explains his views on the route to practice: "In the field of EU law, it is helpful to have done something more than just an undergraduate degree before you start. That might be postgraduate study or work in a European institution – for example, doing a *stage* at the European Commission or working at the ECJ. Really, it's anything that can give you background and experience, and the chance to develop your language skills, which are important to EU law."

Josh's practice involves a large mixture of work at the UK and EU levels. He comments: "In the United Kingdom, it is mostly competition work and will involve either advising companies in their dealings with the Office of Fair Trading (OFT) or the sectoral regulators, or assisting the regulators themselves. The work is stimulating and challenging: it involves economic analysis as well as legal interpretation, and you quickly become familiar with the workings of particular industries. I've done a lot of work in relation to telecommunications and pharmaceuticals, for instance. On the EU side, my work has involved advising public authorities and companies on the interpretation of EU law, and representing companies being investigated by the European Commission in Brussels."

Of his experiences in court, Josh comments: "Working in the EU/competition field involves less court work than, say, criminal law. A greater proportion of the work is advisory. When you do appear before a court or tribunal, you are usually led by a silk, who does the advocacy. Your role is to help with preparing the written submissions, speaking notes for your leader or questions for cross-examination. There are still opportunities to present cases orally, but they are usually at the interlocutory stage rather than at the main hearing, or when representing clients before a regulatory authority like the OFT."

One of the high points of Josh's practice to date was acting for surfwear company Animal in a long-running IP dispute against sunglasses manufacturer Oakley. He says: "I was called in because several interesting points of European law had arisen at first instance. One of the issues was before the Court of Appeal. The case attracted a lot of attention, the attorney general intervened and it was very satisfying when we won. Another issue was referred to the ECJ. I drafted the written submissions, but unfortunately the litigation settled before the hearing in Luxembourg."

After his first two years, Josh is extremely positive about practice at the Bar: "I like the intellectual challenge and the fact that you're responsible for the advice you give. In a big law firm the opportunities to make strategic decisions are fewer and further between, particularly in the early years. I also enjoy the oral advocacy – that's important for anyone who wants to become a barrister." He accepts, however, that the Bar comes with a greater level of uncertainty: "You never know for sure what you will be working on next, but your confidence grows when you see the same clients returning with further instructions."

Finally, Josh offers his advice to those interested in practising EU law: "Try and gain relevant background experience so that you can show you are really interested, because it is highly specialised and chambers will want to know that you are going to stick at it and thrive. So the more experience the better. For example, you may want to try working with an NGO or EC institution, or gaining a graduate qualification. Most of the Inns of Court offer scholarships to do internships in Brussels or Luxembourg, which is an avenue well worth exploring and shows real commitment to the field." He adds, in reference to all fields of practice: "You have to have a firm degree of determination and you mustn't be easily put off; you've got to stick at it and see it through."

# Family

Family law barristers will deal with all legal matters relating to marriage, separation, divorce, cohabitation and all issues relating to children (eg, maintenance and access arrangements, and adoption both in England and internationally). Family law also encompasses financial negotiations, inheritance issues and prenuptial contracts. Some family law cases involve substantial assets and complex financial arrangements, or high-profile disputes involving well-known personalities.

Amy Jacobs is a barrister at St Ive's Chambers, a common law set in Birmingham. Amy studied modern and medieval languages at the University of Cambridge but made the choice to be a barrister. She did her CPE and BVC, and won a pupillage at St Ive's. In September 2006 she was taken on as a tenant.

During Amy's pupillage, she saw a little family work, "from urgent child protection order applications to care proceedings". She remembers: "In my second six they threw me in at the deep end. I did quite a lot of preliminary hearings and things like contact and residence, and then non-molestation orders. Gradually I did some care work." Now she works on more complex cases in the County Court. "It's a natural progression," she comments.

Amy has a general common law practice with a particular interest in criminal and family law: "I'm in court every day and the amount of family work I do fluctuates. Last week I had a five-day final hearing." She talks through the usual procedure for such a hearing: "It normally starts with reading the brief, which can vary in size. Last week it was two and a half lever-arch files. I'll speak with the solicitor first to make sure that from the client's perspective I know what's going on. When you get to court, the first port of call is to have a conference with the client to make sure that I understand their position and that it hasn't changed, but also to ensure that they understand what's going on and what's going to happen. With family law, the clients can be very vulnerable and emotionally tied up in the proceedings, so it's very important to make them feel that they're not being lost."

"Last week," says Amy, "it turned out that most of the parties were in agreement, or thereabouts, so most of the next day and a half was spent in negotiations to iron out the difficulties in what we wanted to do. A couple of times we had to see the judge to explain where we were in the proceedings. In the end he gave an indication of what his ruling would be if all of the allegations were proved. After that we were able to draw up an order and agree it. So there was a lot of to and fro between the parties."

Amy also works on many fact-finding hearings. "For example," she explains, "I had one where the father was my client and there were allegations that he had beaten the mother quite regularly and that he had also been violent towards the children. This was causing the oldest child to self-harm. We had to determine which of the allegations were true."

Her clients vary from parents to children's guardians, something which she finds "quite interesting because you're slightly removed. The guardian acts on behalf of the children. The local authority wants one thing and the parents want another, and it's the job of the guardian to make sure that the children's interests are what the court is looking at".

Although she's at the very start of her career, Amy is very pleased with one particular case: "I was acting for the husband and father. There were quite serious allegations against him but I believed him when he said he didn't do it. There was a lot of evidence against him and I didn't think he would come across very well in court. But in fact the court found that none of the allegations were true. I was pleased about that because often you have clients who you're not sure you believe when they say they didn't do it."

Working in chambers offers a sense of community, says Amy: "St Ive's has an open-door policy, so we pop in and out of each other's rooms if we've got a problem. It's almost a collegiate atmosphere with everyone helping each other out." The long hours can be a bit of a drag, though. Amy explains: "It's the unpredictability. There will be days when I don't have to be in court until 2:00pm and if I've got something light on the next day I can go home at 5:00pm or 6:00pm. But there are other days when I'm up at 5:00am and working before I go to court, working after court and working when I get home. It's a necessary part of the job but it's the thing that grates the most."

Amy sits on the pupillage interview panel at St Ive's, so she's grown to understand what makes a good candidate. She says: "Mini-pupillages are essential but you should also get some life experience. I think having voluntary work experience which exposes you to people who are vulnerable and from a different walk of life will stand you in good stead. You get the legal knowledge when you do your legal training and pupillage, but the ability to deal with people is something that you can gain from voluntary work."

During her school and university years, Amy herself did plenty of voluntary work. "I sat for hours with little old ladies making tea and dealt with people who are severely physically disabled. It does help to have that experience behind you when you're dealing with people who have problems. Life experience is a good thing. There are a lot of candidates who come straight through from school and university, and I think having

something other than a glowing academic career is ideal."

# Housing/landlord and tenant

**Housing/landlord and tenant law involves residential and commercial tenancies, and includes issues such as leasehold covenants, termination of tenancies, assignment of leases, nuisance, disrepair and dilapidation. Clients might include local authorities, housing associations, landlords and, of course, tenants.**

Daniel Bromilow is a barrister at 9 Stone Buildings, a chancery practice with expertise in a broad range of areas. Daniel studied law at the University of Cambridge and took the BVC at the Inns of Court School of Law. He says: "I really can't think of any other job I would want to do. I always leave decisions to the very last minute and really just fell into becoming a barrister. We had a law information evening at my college. A barrister turned up and he seemed very tanned in the middle of winter. I asked him where he'd been and he said he'd just been away for his second week-long skiing holiday. I thought that sounded good so I decided I'd give it a shot."

Now with 11 years' call, Daniel has developed a broad practice area covering chancery and civil work, but specialises in landlord and tenant, real property, and company and corporate insolvency law. Although now installed at 9 Stone Buildings, his pupillage was split between three other sets. During this time he practised company, entertainment, media and pensions law, and also did some general chancery work. He says: "I saw no landlord and tenant work during my pupillage, due to the nature of the work of my pupil masters. It was only something I started doing after I'd got tenancy."

Daniel's landlord and tenant work developed from simple beginnings. He says: "It started off with just straightforward possession hearings because I was the junior member and clients wanted someone cheap for a simple hearing. It was more a question of falling into it rather than making a determined effort to do it. The range of work I do now is slightly broader than the work I did as a pupil."

Daniel works on about a dozen landlord and tenant cases at any one time: "I'd say that there will be four or five short-term cases I'll be dealing with, maybe four or five medium-term cases that will last for up to a year, and then there will be four much longer cases in the background."

Litigation has only just begun on a particular case that has been rumbling on for years. Daniel explains: "It involves a site on a farm. The current owner's father originally let a traveller in a caravan occupy part of the field on the farm. Fifteen years later, after the farm had been inherited by the current owners, they decided they wanted to develop that field and they're trying to get possession. Because everything's been done on a very informal basis, it's difficult to say exactly what the legal relationships are. The real issue is to find out what people have done and how they've presented themselves and put that in a legal framework. It's not entirely straightforward. And then of course there are various statutes, such as the Mobile Homes Act 1983, and you have to look at it in the light of all those statutory frameworks."

Daniel remembers another recent case that proved pretty tricky. Indeed, the odds were stacked against him: "It was about service charges for long leases. There were a whole range of difficult technical points made by the other side. It was a difficult one because they raised so many different technical points and if they'd succeeded on any one of them, we would have lost. So we had to get a clean sweep or nothing. We won in the first instance. We won at the first appeal and we just found out that they've been refused permission to have a second appeal. The litigation lasted about two years because of the constant appeals and applications."

Daniel has three types of day. He could be in court, where he'll "hang around for an inordinate amount of time and then do the hearing – they're normally fairly short, although there are exceptions". Otherwise, he'll either be working from home or in chambers: "I don't think I could live as far away as I do if I had to come into London every day. I think it would kill me!"

That flexibility is something that all barristers relish, and Daniel's no exception. What's his favourite thing about being a barrister? "It is definitely being one's own boss," he says. "I think that's the thing that makes us different from others in the legal profession. It's the ability to work when you want and the fact that you don't have someone saying what you have to do. Despite the flexibility, you have to accept that you don't know exactly what you'll be doing. You might get instructed at very short notice. Just as you were thinking you'll be able to work from home for the next two days and then have a leisurely weekend, you'll get an urgent application that needs doing on the Thursday for a hearing on the Monday. So you've got the flexibility, but things keep cropping up at the last minute."

For budding barristers who are thinking about landlord and tenant work, Daniel has this advice: "Make sure you have some sort of training in the area before you start. There is a massive amount of primary legislation that governs the area and you just have to know all of it because you never know when a bit of it will become relevant in a case. When I started out I didn't know any of it. So I had to go on a steep learning curve to get the knowledge. My advice would be to try and flatten out that curve if you possibly can and get to know the area of law well in advance."

Interview practice is also a must, advises Daniel: "Get people to interview you – it doesn't matter who they are because the people who will interview you in real life will come from a range of backgrounds. Just practise interviews with anybody – even people on the bus!"

Although he seemed to fall into the practice area, Daniel says: "I'm glad I did. It's not always possible to take two weeks off a year for skiing though!"

# Human rights

In recent years human rights law has become a popular choice for both students and practitioners. University law faculties are increasingly offering human rights modules as part of their law degrees and more firms are boasting specialisms in the field. The introduction of the Human Rights Act 1998 has made the European Convention on Human Rights directly enforceable in the national courts.

Rabinder Singh QC is a barrister at Matrix Chambers, a high-profile barristers' organisation known for its modern way of working. Rabinder studied law at the University of Cambridge and then did a master's degree at the University of California at Berkeley, where he started to develop his interest in human rights law. "It's one of the most interesting areas of modern law," he says. "It's very topical, and provides an opportunity to help people whose lives may be affected." He was called to the Bar in 1989 and became a QC in 2002.

During his pupillage at 4-5 Gray's Inn Square (where he was a tenant from 1990 to 2000), Rabinder saw a range of work, from planning to administrative and even commercial law. He later moved into human rights law but has a broad practice which stretches to employment and media. Rabinder was actually a founding member of Matrix, which is so innovative an organisation that it is said to be the future of the Bar. Indeed, Matrix uses the word 'training' instead of 'pupillage'.

During the first half of Rabinder's career, there was no Human Rights Act: "It came into force in 2000 and it's made a huge difference to our legal system, particularly in public law. It arises virtually every day in my work." What he does in a typical day varies depending on whether he's scheduled to appear in court. He says: "I'm in court about half the time. On a typical court day I come in early and finish preparing for the hearing. Usually, my cases are in the higher courts. Afterwards, I come back and perhaps have a conference around 5:00pm, probably on the same case. I do some more work overnight, preparing for the next day of the hearing. If I'm not in court, I would usually be doing paperwork, either written advice or drafting a skeleton argument, or advising clients in meetings."

As a silk, Rabinder has worked on many high-profile cases, including some that were particularly groundbreaking. He notes: "The most important case I've done to date is a case called *Al-Skeini v Secretary of State for Defence*. This was a series of test cases, the most notorious of which arose from the death of a man called Baha Mousa. He was a civilian who was detained by British forces in Iraq and was killed in custody. In June 2007 the House of Lords decided that, in principle, the Human Rights Act applies to the actions of British Forces overseas."

The *Al-Skeini* ruling was a landmark decision and one that highlights what most excites Rabinder about working at the Bar: "I enjoy the combination of highly intellectual debate with the feeling that you've actually helped a particular client. The Mousa family's case illustrates that combination." However, there is something Rabinder doesn't like about his job: "Being kicked around by a grumpy judge in court! It doesn't happen often but it still happens."

As well as tolerating the odd irritable judge, Rabinder has some more tips for those considering a career at the Bar. He advises: "I'd say that it's very competitive but it's still worthwhile. There's a lot of hard law and it's not just about wearing your heart on your sleeve. Hard work is necessary at antisocial times, keeping on top of the latest legal developments and offering good client care."

Rabinder notes that, although the Bar is very competitive, it has been harder in the past: "At least we now have open competitive systems and it's not just an old boys' network. I would tell people to demonstrate diligence and to keep trying. By demonstrating their courage and perseverance, they will help themselves by showing the qualities needed for a successful career at the Bar."

For his final words on what it's like to practise human rights law in some of the highest courts in the land, Rabinder sums up by saying: "No matter how prepared you are, something unexpected always happens."

# Intellectual property

IP work can be divided into two main areas: hard and soft intellectual property. 'Hard' intellectual property relates to patents, while 'soft' intellectual property covers trademarks, copyright, design rights and passing-off. IP barristers will advise on issues that range from commercial exploitation to infringement disputes, and agreements that deal either exclusively with IP rights or IP rights in the wider context of larger commercial transactions.

Giles Fernando is a barrister at 11 South Square, a leading set whose members are dedicated to IP work. Giles studied law at the University of Oxford and then worked for a publishing company for two years. He says: "I always knew I wanted to be a barrister, but I wanted to get experience elsewhere first, which was valuable. Also, because I was a little young, it would have been difficult giving advice to people when I looked like their son." In fact, it was working in publishing that got him into intellectual property, "because there are all sorts of copyright issues that arise regularly. Also, at the time, the World Wide Web was emerging as a new publishing medium and raising new legal problems, so that sparked my interest".

Giles then obtained a pupillage at 11 South Square. He remembers: "The first trial I saw in pupillage was a copyright trial which ended up going to the House of Lords. It was very interesting and turned into one of the seminal cases on copyright infringement. I was lucky to see the case from the outset. That was the first time I'd seen the difference between the theoretical side of law and law in practice. The two are very different."

Now, Giles feels that his workload is spread evenly over all the various types of IP work. "You have to be very good at juggling," he says. "I had a case at the beginning of the year which became enormous. It took two or three months of my time. We do work silly hours – although not trainee solicitor hours – and you've got to be prepared to put in 60 hours a week when you start out."

Another consuming lawsuit was the *Douglas v Hello!* case in relation to the publication of unauthorised photographs of the wedding of Michael Douglas and Catherine Zeta-Jones. Giles worked on it for seven years and got the final judgment in May 2007. He says: "I saw that case right from the beginning. I got a call from my clerk when I was in the shower on a Tuesday morning. *OK!* had been granted an injunction overnight and we had just found out about it. The clerk called to say I needed to get down to court with a silk from my chambers to apply to set aside the injunction. We didn't succeed before that judge so we went straight to the Court of Appeal that evening. The two members of the Court of Appeal could not agree on the result so a new three-man court was convened for the following day. The trial in the end went on for 25 days, which is quite astonishing."

Next came all the appeals and, in fact, the case went to the highest appeal court in the land: the House of Lords. "At the end of the day," notes Giles, "we lost three-two which was quite frustrating, particularly as the two law lords in the minority gave very powerful judgments."

Giles enjoys the fact that he's in court regularly, but not every day. He says: "We're probably in court twice a week, but if we're not in court we'll be doing paperwork. I went down to court this morning on what I thought would be a short hearing. The judge decided it would be a good idea to have the trial expedited so it turned into a very lengthy hearing. I've come back to sort out the order from this morning and get on with my paperwork."

The thing Giles most enjoys, though, is cross-examination: "I think any barrister would say that's one of the most enjoyable aspects. It's what the job is all about. It all comes down to that moment in court. For the moment when you're cross-examining a witness, you have to know his area better than he does. You have to know in detail his life, his documents and his case. Once you leave the trial, you can forget it all. For the people who pretend that you can prepare it all on the back of an envelope, that's just a confidence trick on the public. The amount of preparation that goes into cross-examination is phenomenal."

Giles has another everyman answer for the aspect he enjoys least about the job. "Losing," he says. "I absolutely hate losing." However, he extracts a crucial strength from the process of losing: "You have to be very self-critical all the time, and that can be a bit of a burden. People who can't evaluate their performance and identify areas for improvement won't do very well. This is a profession in which you are constantly learning and you must be open to constructive criticism and be able to learn from the stars you are occasionally lucky enough to see in court."

Other character traits one needs include having an analytical mind and the ability to use it on the spot. "In intellectual property," says Giles, "the judges are quite interventionist, so you've got to be able to think on your feet. There's a lot of case law to grapple with, and a tide of legislation from Europe, so you've got to be up to date."

Giles sits on the pupillage interview panel at 11 South Square, so he knows what his chambers is looking for – or rather, what they are not. He says: "We interviewed a chap and asked him about his advocacy. He said he'd never done any. We asked: 'Have you done any mooting?' No. 'Have you done any debating?' No. We all wondered how he was going to persuade us that he wanted to be an advocate. There are a lot of people who think it would be nice to be a barrister, but don't really have the ambition and haven't done anything to show it. And it's expensive – you've got to borrow £20,000 or so. Why do that if you're not really sure?"

Giles thinks that it's best for budding barristers to ask themselves honestly whether they would be a barrister if they could do anything else. If the answer is an unequivocal yes, then you're on the right track. There are some things you can't ever learn, though. As Giles says: "I wish someone had taught me how to manage a clerk. Notionally the clerks are employed by us, but they're the ones who actually have all the power."

# Media law

**Media and entertainment barristers have clients in a variety of industry sectors, including theatre, film, music, publishing, broadcasting, sport and advertising. Barristers will advise and represent clients in court and other tribunals on matters that might include contract disputes, privacy and confidentiality, advertising standards, sponsorship, authorship and restraint of trade. Contract and IP law are often at the heart of disputes.**

Mark Vinall is a barrister at Blackstone Chambers, which specialises in commercial, public and employment law. He studied law with French law at the University of Oxford, a degree which included a year in Paris gaining insight into the fact that the answers reached by the English legal system "are not the only ones possible". Mark always knew that he wanted to be a barrister, and has found that the flexible reality suits him well: "Compared to a solicitor's life, your day can be more easily organised to suit you and there is more responsibility at an earlier stage. The buck stops here, in that *you* have to find the answer. But that's the great thing – you get the chance to think hard and get the answer, rather than having to subcontract out the interesting stuff to someone else."

Pupillage at Blackstone was characterised by its fair approach to assessment and retention, says Mark: "You're judged on a level playing field because you're seen by four different pupil supervisors and, in addition, everyone does certain pieces of assessed work for the same person. That gives you confidence that when a decision comes to be made, it'll be on a full and objective picture of what you can do rather than a more subjective basis. It also helped that in my year the pupils got on very well and were mutually supportive."

Mark's work is split into two kinds: court-based and desk-based. He discusses what that means on a day-to-day basis: "I will either be preparing for or attending trials and other hearings, or doing paperwork, such as drafting opinions, statements of case or skeleton arguments. As you'd expect, you tend to work much harder when you're coming up to, or you're in the middle of, a trial. In terms of how often you're in court, media is somewhere in the middle of the spectrum (with, I suppose, criminal at one end and tax at the other). At the beginning, you're unlikely to be doing media exclusively and unlikely to get much advocacy experience in that field. Most cases are important enough that the client doesn't want anyone too junior. So it's good to start off more broadly – all our very junior tenants do employment cases, whether or not they intend to continue with employment law, because they then get regular exposure to advocacy and running an entire case."

Mark expands on the sorts of legal issue that are covered by media and entertainment law. He says: "At one end, you've got soft intellectual property, such as performers' rights, copyright, moral rights – all the bits that give rise to income for pop stars and record companies! For example, I was junior counsel for the British Phonographic Industry in the recent Copyright Tribunal case, which decided how much composers and publishers should be paid for the use of their music online. At the other end of things is contract law that just happens to arise in an entertainment context; for example, a musician's record deal is just a specialised sort of contract. You need an understanding of how the industry works and the income streams to make sense of it. I was junior counsel for Seal's former manager in a case that involved contract issues, including what the contract meant, restraint of trade and undue influence. We had to assess whether a management deal was unreasonable, so we needed to sit down with industry experts to determine what terms would have been normal at the time."

Unsurprisingly, many cases have an online component: "I had an interesting case where we acted for a web-hosting company that was accused of trespassing on the claimant's domain name. More generally, almost every case these days involves email evidence and the use of 'metadata' [data showing when and by whom a document was created] is becoming more important."

For those who think media law is all celebrity clients and showbiz glamour, Mark injects a note of reality: "The work can be glamorous, meeting famous people and doing interesting things, but the two don't always go together. Famous people can have dull cases too!" Mark continues: "A great case is that perfect matrix of interesting issues of law, interesting facts and a great team to work with. With a mix of those three, you can't go far wrong."

Mark explains what he likes most and least about his career: "You get to be involved in the process of righting wrongs that have been done to people. Although media clients are not always the most obviously needy people, there are times when you're able to really help someone in trouble. The downside is the work-life balance – this is not the sort of job where you can leave the office at 5:00pm. You sometimes have to work late, or at short notice, or when you hoped to be doing something else. However, you can control it to some extent – you don't have to work stupid hours all the time."

So, what does it take to be successful in this field? Mark's view is that "you need the same skill set as for most barristers' work: a good understanding of the law, an ability to process, manage and retain complex facts, and an ability to explain things clearly to people". Over and above these strengths, media law also requires the development of "an interest in and understanding of how the various industries work".

The Free Representation Unit (FRU) is where it's at, says Mark: "I can't recommend FRU highly enough. Even if you don't see yourself going within a million miles of employment or social security law, you should be queuing up to do FRU. It's the best experience you can get! You get to do real cases of your own, you do all the advocacy (both submissions and witness handling) and you make the strategic decisions on how to run things, but there is help available if you need it." Mark's other top tip is a must-have book: "Every music lawyer I know has a copy of *All You Need to Know About the Music Business* by Donald S Passman. It's aimed at musicians, so they can understand what their lawyers and accountants are doing, but it gives you an idea of how the industry works and deals with difficult subject matter in a light-hearted way."

Mark offers a final word of advice on how to secure pupillage: "There is no getting away from the fact that you need a certain level of academic ability – this is difficult commercial and IP law – but in terms of the other things on your CV, it doesn't really matter what you do so long as you're doing it well. And don't forget, if you go to an interview claiming that you want to do a particular area of law, then you should have some sense of what that's all about and some of the hot issues."

# Personal injury

Personal injury (PI) law deals with compensation for accidents and diseases. This area of law is flourishing in light of the recognition of new types of physical and mental illness. The subject matter varies considerably and can range from controversial, high-profile disaster cases to road traffic accidents to health and safety cases involving what one lawyer describes as "trippers, slippers and whiplash". A related, specialised practice area of PI law is clinical negligence, which involves injuries suffered during medical procedures.

Cath Howells is a barrister at Exchange Chambers, a leading set with offices in Manchester and Liverpool. Cath has been at Exchange since her pupillage in 1989. She remembers: "As a pupil I did quite varied things. A lot of PI, but the scheme in chambers was to see a variety of work. So you see the senior work of your pupil supervisor and other senior members of chambers, including some high-profile criminal cases."

After watching her seniors at work for six months, Cath was ready for some of her own cases: "I think that towards the end of your first six you feel as if you can't learn anymore until you get on your feet and do it. And then when you get on your feet you feel that you haven't been paying attention for the last six months and you haven't really taken in things that you thought you knew, like where do you sit and whose turn it is to speak – all the practical things stump you." She did plenty of work, however: "Towards the end of your first six months you see a lot more junior work because that's what you'll be doing when you start on your feet, so it's a mixture of magistrates' court work and things like motoring court offences. At the end, I was in court almost every day."

But that was 17 years ago and Cath's practice has changed to focus solely on PI

and clinical negligence: "I'm in court two or three times a week, either for final or preliminary hearings. I have conferences two or three times a week and lots of paperwork too. The balance of my practice has changed. Also, my work has changed in terms of valuation. Before I could do an advice in a low-value case that would take an hour; now I very rarely assess a case that doesn't take me a day to do."

"One day last week," Cath says, "I had a case management conference in an asbestos case, where I was acting for the defendant. We were sorting out the best way forward for the claimant's case – what we could and couldn't agree on. Then I got back and had to do various aspects of paperwork in relation to that. In the afternoon I had a conference on a case with a chap who's got a severe back injury. There are real issues of whether he'll ever be able to get back to work."

In an 18-year career of highs and lows, a particular case stands out to Cath. She remembers: "Last year I was junior to Bill Braithwaite QC in a severe head injury case which lasted for 10 days in London. The claimant was a very promising student who was run over in a road traffic accident. She has a brain injury and is effectively immobile from the neck downwards. She can't speak anymore and needs to be spoon fed. Her parents have given the past five years of their life to care for her. There were lots of issues about who should look after her and who should pay for her care. We recovered £6.6 million. It was a fabulous result because we could see it really made a difference to her and her family. We had a fantastic relationship that built up with the family because I'd been involved in the case for three years. The judge said the parents deserved a medal for caring for her."

Such a case really brings home what working as a PI barrister is about. Cath explains: "I think PI gets a bad press because people think that it's ambulance chasing and you're making a claim for no good reason. People assume that it's all very straightforward. It isn't – the law is developing all the time."

Cath finds the area very intellectually demanding. She notes: "Over the last 12 months in PI litigation there's been a big issue as to how you quantify periodical payments, whether they should be earnings linked or retail prices index linked. There are real issues there that you have to work with to try and evaluate the best way to settle a claim. Another developing area is the issue of public funding, so whether the NHS or social services should fund the cost of someone's care package or whether the defendant should pay. There's an ethical issue there because you wonder why the state should have to pay if someone is insured. The defendants have been arguing that if there's public funding available to pay for care then you don't need care provided by the defendant. I don't see why taxpayers should pay to provide care to badly injured claimants, or why claimants should be dependent on state funding when there is insurance there to pay for it."

Although a career at the Bar requires long hours, it's worth it, argues Cath: "I love winning cases. I enjoy meeting the clients. I travel quite a bit over the whole country to meet people in their own homes, not just in solicitors' offices. People who've had severe spine or brain injuries don't know what to expect from a barrister and can feel a little in awe. If I can put them at ease, they can open up and talk about what effect an injury has had on their lives. That is incredibly satisfying because then you can work out the best way to help put their lives back together." The hours can take their toll though: "It is a 24 hour a day commitment. I don't think anything prepares you for it."

Cath is on the Exchange pupillage committee. Every year she sees 600 applications for a maximum of three pupillage places. She gives her advice on how to impress: "You have to use the application form as an advocacy exercise. You are using it to persuade someone of your cause. Don't be too wordy, too clever, or use expressions that you wouldn't normally use. Instead, use it as a way of demonstrating your skills as an advocate, but also let your personality shine through. You should have done mini-pupillages and advocacy, whether at university or Bar school, mooting or public speaking."

Finally, Cath says, don't give up. It's incredibly competitive but, if you make it through, it's worth it. PI is one area where you can really see the difference you make to a client: "You get a real thrill from getting a good result, not only in personal recognition for the job that you've done, but also for the client. Nothing beats the buzz of getting the right result."

# Planning/environment

**Planning law regulates the way property owners use and develop their property in the interests of the wider community. Local planning authorities are required to follow the national legal framework in their decision making. Planning law is often interwoven with other branches of the law such as environmental, local government and judicial review. Clients might include landowners, developers, local authorities, public and private utilities, government departments, amenity groups and individuals.**

**Environment law seeks to protect both humans and the physical environment against pollution and the impact of human activity on the natural world. Environment lawyers will find themselves involved in a wide range of matters, including in relation to health and safety risk management, contaminated land, waste, renewable energy, environmental finance, commercial and property transactions, and nuclear law.**

Tom Cosgrove is a barrister at 2-3 Gray's Inn Square, which is known for its planning expertise. Tom read law at the University of Cambridge, which was when he realised that the Bar was for him: "I had always considered being a lawyer, but at university a number of eminent barristers came to speak (my future head of chambers, Anthony Scrivener QC, being one of them), and I thought it sounded like good fun."

Tom made the most of his mini-pupillages, trying to get to the truth rather than being swayed by the sometimes unrealistic picture painted by many student guides (this one excepted, of course!). He says: "When you are doing a mini-pupillage, you should make a beeline for the junior members and pupils, and ask what they think about their own chambers. It's also worth asking them about which other chambers they think are the best in the field." Pupillage at 2-3 Gray's Inn Square was much as Tom had expected: "It's a nerve-wracking year, but you know you just have to go through it. I was fortunate with my pupil supervisor and the very friendly members here."

Specialising primarily in planning, environment and local government work, Tom discusses broadly what his planning work involves: "I act for both developers and local planning authorities on a full range of matters, including in relation to residential schemes, listed buildings and conservation. Part of the beauty of the job is that there isn't a typical day, but there is a distinction between a day in court or inquiry and a day in chambers or meeting clients. You certainly aren't working behind a computer every day; you might find yourself walking in an area of natural beauty doing a wind farm site visit, or you might be in the High Court."

Recent work includes a two-week planning inquiry where Tom was acting for Derbyshire Dales County Council: "It involved a contentious scheme whereby the developer wanted to convert a historic castle into luxury flats with additional new housing in the grounds. Prior to that, I worked on a case in Newmarket that involved a proposal to build the biggest horse hospital in Europe. Trainers came along to object and we had site visits at 4:00am to see the lads put the horses out, which was very interesting. Earlier this week, I had a High Court challenge acting for Horsham District Council in relation to the preservation of a tree, which involved legal questions of human rights and legitimate expectations. Tomorrow, I am starting an inquiry in Hampshire that centres on a big housing scheme on the edge of the M3 – about as far away from the Dales as you can get!" Tom also spends time in conferences with clients, discussing potential schemes and the practices that would serve them best.

Tom enthuses about the sense of satisfaction gained from winning a case: "Nothing beats that. I've had some good results, which is satisfying, although just as you think you're getting good, you come across someone who's better! There's no room for getting smug and you really do learn a lot from being beaten." He also notes the pleasure gained from making a positive difference to people's lives: "For example, there may be some monstrosity planned to be built that would block out lots of light – if you argue your case effectively and permission is refused, that is very satisfying." As ever, the advantages of the flexibility inherent in the job are mitigated by the "unsociable, weird hours that sometimes mean you have to let friends and family down".

There is a set of skills required in order to be a successful planning lawyer. Tom explains: "In terms of reading and preparing, you've got to put the hours in to get your head around the subject. You can't just turn up and cross-examine witnesses, many of whom are experts, no matter how brilliant you are. Also, you have to be able to get on with a diverse range of people, from very posh developers through to people who know nothing about the legal system. Finally, it is important that you have a range of advocacy styles. One day, you might be at a planning inquiry, where there's no room for highfalutin' legal terms, while the next day, you're in the High Court and need to be very succinct. These different styles tend to develop over time."

Tom has a lot of very practical advice for anyone interested in this field: "First, you should get as much experience as you possibly can. The obvious thing to do is go and sit in on a public planning inquiry at a council near you. They are advertised and anyone can attend; you can even get free copies of the documents. Next, you should be doing mini-pupillages, focusing

specifically on the three or four specialist planning sets. Finally, you should be doing research so that you are fully informed before your pupillage interviews. There are some good textbooks and guides that are useful if you're new to things. You need to show an interest in the topic, and there are always new developments to talk about (eg, wind farms, land disposal and nuclear waste). The Department for Communities and Local Government has a website [www.communities.gov.uk] that includes a planning section with news and free printouts, which should give you a feel for the area."

Finally, Tom offers a reality check about being a barrister in the early years: "Unless you are of very independent financial means, it can be quite tough. And those weird working hours mean that you may have to upset some friends along the way. But none of that would have put me off and it is really fun! I think that it is a privilege to be able to do it."

# Professional negligence

**Professional negligence covers the situation where a defendant is in breach of his or her duty of care to a claimant, and harm or loss has resulted. This particular type of negligence results from the fact that professional people present themselves as having greater than average abilities. The following professionals may be involved in professional negligence disputes: solicitors, accountants, financial services providers, surveyors and estate agents. Clinical negligence is a type of professional negligence that involves disputes between patients and healthcare providers (usually doctors) that centre on quality of care.**

Tiffany Scott is a barrister at Wilberforce Chambers, a set leading the way in commercial chancery work. She has a chancery-based practice spanning property, pensions, trusts and professional negligence. Tiffany says: "When I was at sixth form college, I was interested in the law and I went on a work experience placement for a week in a chambers in Guildford. It was a general common law set with a broad spread of work in different areas, like family, crime and personal injury. It put me off slightly because I didn't feel I was suited to that kind of work and I didn't know that there were specialist chancery or commercial chambers, or what chancery work involved. I knew about the conversion course which meant I didn't have to study law at university, so I went off and did a classics degree at Oxford instead."

After finishing her degree, Tiffany did the CPE. She says: "I went to the university law fair in my final year and learnt about chancery work, and I lined up several mini-pupillages then and during the CPE. I did investigate being a solicitor, but I think it was clear from my CV that I was leaning towards becoming a barrister, so I found it quite difficult to get work placements at good City firms." Tiffany went on to study the BVC at the Inns of Court School of Law.

When you're a student, professional negligence is usually a practice area buried within others. Tiffany says: "It isn't something that is really addressed as a subject area on either the CPE or the BVC – only in the peripheral sense when you study tort and contract. On the BVC, you start doing things like drafting pleadings, and it begins to fall into place a little bit. It's not something that you're taught as such."

Tiffany won a pupillage at Wilberforce Chambers. She describes her experience: "As a pupil, I saw a lot of property work. Professional negligence work goes along with each practice area, so it's in property work too. We structure our pupillages so that you sit with four pupil supervisors during your 12 months. I sat with barristers who did property and trusts, and someone who did more commercial aspects. I came across a little bit of professional negligence then."

Although Tiffany has chosen to keep her practice as broad as it was during pupillage, the level of work she sees now is very different. She notes: "In your early years of practice in the professional negligence sphere, you're more likely to get instructions from the claimant – that is, the person who's been on the receiving end of the negligence. The more experienced you get, the more you develop a relationship with the insurance companies representing the professionals and then you get more instructions from the defendants. The bigger the case, the more there is at stake and the more tactical decisions you've got to take."

Those decisions prove ever more complex: "Professional negligence litigation is largely about tactics. The law is relatively straightforward, but each case turns on its own facts, and there are many strategic and commercial decisions to take at each stage. That's why in many ways it's easier to do this kind of work when you're more senior and you've got more of a handle on tactics and practicalities; when you first start out, you're more concerned with what the law is and having to stay on top of that."

And Tiffany knows how hard one has to try to stay afloat. "At the moment," she explains, "I'm extremely busy. It's sometimes difficult to balance the court work with the paperwork. I've got a big fraud case on and I've got nine sets of papers waiting for me to deal with them. I've got another seven or eight cases bumbling along that pop up now and then. It's always either too much or too little!"

An average day includes several telephone conversations on several different cases. Tiffany describes a day in chambers as "trying to juggle all the cases I've got in the air". A professional negligence barrister will have a lot of pre-action hoops to jump through. Tiffany comments: "There's a good deal of preparatory work, such as drafting letters, before you even get to the proceedings." On other days, you'll be "attending court on an interim or substantive hearing".

Tiffany managed to bag work on a particularly groundbreaking case when she was a junior barrister. "It was a commercial case with many different aspects, including fraud and professional negligence," she remembers. "It went to the Court of Appeal on two occasions and it led to a clarification of the law. It was high profile and intellectually challenging work. The issues were really difficult. It was a very good experience for me and something I'm pleased to have on my CV."

As one of the members of her set's pupillage committee, Tiffany sees the applications and the interviewees. She's developed a keen

eye for what her chambers is looking for in a potential pupil. She says: "You've got to make sure you sell yourself on paper initially. I read so many applications where people don't sell themselves. Many people have good degrees these days so you've really got to make sure you bring out all your achievements or you can't get any credit for them. And be well-prepared for the interview. Research the kind of law that the chambers does. You can't just make blanket applications. You've got to show interest in the work that they do otherwise they won't be interested in you."

As for professional negligence work, you need a canny grasp of tactics and procedure. Tiffany says: "You've got to have a good understanding of how the insurance companies operate because they're always standing behind the professional. Whether you're acting for the professional or the claimant, you need to know what the insurance company will be interested in and how they're going to play the case."

Added to that, Tiffany emphasises the need for good commercial sense: "Behind every case that you do, there is a professional negligence case waiting to happen."

# Public law

The Public Law Bar spans the full range of administrative, public and constitutional law. A very broad range of work, including a great deal of advisory work, is undertaken in relation to judicial review and the powers and practices of various public bodies. Public law barristers can also be called upon to advise on matters such as the regulation of financial services or the organisation of the National Health Service.

Particular areas of expertise include civil liberties and human rights, commercial judicial review, community and healthcare law, disciplinary proceedings and internal administration of public bodies, education law, environmental law, housing law, planning law, prison law, social services and social security law, and other areas of judicial review (including asylum and immigration law).

Public law work has a European influence, with a steady stream of cases being referred to the European Court of Justice for preliminary rulings. Other cases may raise the issue of the application of the European Convention on Human Rights (ECHR).

Steven Kovats is a barrister at 39 Essex Street, a long-established civil set. Having ruled out being a doctor due to "not being able to stand the sight of blood", Steven read law at the University of Cambridge and did pupillage at 2 Garden Court (which became 39 Essex Street when the set moved). He discusses his experiences as a pupil: "I was very fortunate to be pupil to the then Treasury devil, so had 12 months of seeing very interesting cases, meeting very interesting people and doing very little work."

Now, Steven's practice is entirely public law focused, with the government as his main client. He explains: "Most of my work is for the Home Office, which is involved in more litigation than other departments because of asylum, criminal justice and prison system issues. I also do a fair amount of work that relates to the health system. European law comes up a lot, particularly in relation to immigration or the Department for Education and Skills [now the Department for Children, Schools and Families]. I have also been involved with some immigration cases in Luxembourg, although they don't come up that often."

With the government as a client, it makes it hard for Steven to talk with candour about the specifics of particular cases (although he mentions Zimbabwe and Iraq in passing!). However, he takes us through a couple of House of Lords criminal justice cases from 2006: "One was *Longworth*, which was all about whether someone on a conditional discharge was convicted for the purpose of being put on the sex offenders register. Another was *Clift*, which was concerned with Articles 5 and 14 of the ECHR, and whether the early release provisions to which each appellant was subject discriminated against him."

Steven is proud of his involvement with the training of new barristers: "The thing I'm most happy about in my career is running the pupillage system here for a number of years. I get more pleasure out of following people through the process, from first application to pupillage to tenancy, than from winning in court. That seems to me to be where you can have a real sense of achievement because you get to see someone developing, you gain a valuable asset for chambers and you often become good friends."

The least enjoyable part of the job is that of time wasted: "As with many jobs, there are a number of circumstances where you end up wasting time. For example, you're travelling around the country or waiting for a case to be called – that can be a most unsatisfactory part of the job, but not unique to being a barrister."

Steven discusses how best to approach the search for pupillage: "If you're applying for pupillage, you need to have a good track record in passing exams – there's no getting away from that. You need a clear head, good judgement and the ability to get on with people. If you want to come to the Bar (and you're not interested in doing family, criminal or tax law), you really should get a broad-based experience. I wouldn't advise anyone to say that they just want to do public law at an early stage, because you end up prematurely narrowing your options."

Advocacy skills are important, but only when employed in the right way, says Steven: "It is important that you are able to convey clearly what you mean, but advocacy in terms of rhetoric is no use whatsoever; in fact, it can do more harm than good in front of a judge. They can get very irritated if they think that someone is trying to pull a fast one. They prefer to be told what the situation is and left to make up their own minds." Developing such skills is imperative: "You will have difficulty getting pupillage without mooting or Free Representation Unit experience because you really won't know what you're letting yourself in for. It's no good being academically brilliant but not enjoying getting up and arguing – it's too late if you find that out in your second six. So it's much better to try it out and see if you like it. If you don't, there's no point in becoming a barrister."

Steven is also keen to see that someone is well rounded: "The thing we look for is people who have an interest in things outside the law – we wouldn't give pupillage to someone who sat in the library all day in order to pass exams, but had nothing else to offer. Other things might be anything from music to sport to a career in business."

Steven thinks that if you do your homework, you shouldn't be surprised by anything at the Bar, over and above the "great collection of historical portraits that are secreted about the Inns". He says: "The idea that it's some strange organisation like the Freemasons, where you're going to be initiated into something bizarre, is nonsense. However, one thing that you should consider is that there are already too many barristers and you shouldn't want to add to that unless you *really* want to be a barrister. If you can't imagine being anything else, then go for it. But be realistic – I'm constantly surprised by how many people waste their OLPAS applications by applying to a set that they simply won't get into. You should only apply to those where you have a realistic chance of being taken on."

# Revenue

**Tax law barristers advise and litigate on all aspects of commercial and personal tax issues. Corporate and business tax issues may concern company or group reconstructions, transfer pricing and the use of losses and capital allowances. Tax planning for individuals can encompass capital gains, inheritance and income tax. Typical cases might concern the sale of a family company or the creation and operation of trusts.**

**Barristers also advise on value added tax and other indirect taxes, including customs and excise duties, landfill tax and stamp duty. Work may involve detailed consideration of EU law and the fiscal laws of other jurisdictions.**

Hui Ling McCarthy is a tenant at Gray's Inn Tax Chambers, a leading set specialising in revenue law. Graduating from Durham University with a maths degree, Hui Ling first went to work for US investment bank Bear Stearns in its corporate finance department. However, her thoughts soon turned to other options: "I'd always been interested in law and knew the conversion course was available. It is taught especially well and I think there's an advantage to having studied all the subjects just a year before Bar school. I haven't felt at a disadvantage by not having a law degree – in fact, because of the complex nature of tax law, I've found it very useful to have done a technical degree that encourages a more structured way of thinking and complements this area of law. In my view, if you've done well in your first degree, no chambers will ever turn you away just because it wasn't in law."

The intellectual challenge of the Bar particularly appealed to Hui Ling: "If you're advising a client, particularly at the Tax Bar, there's lots of research and attention to detail. Sometimes you're very focused on one small point in isolation, rather than looking at a very general end product." She also feared that becoming a solicitor might be too much like working at a bank again, this time "analysing contracts instead of spreadsheets!"

Hui Ling discusses her time as a pupil: "It helped that this is a relatively small and friendly set, so I felt I could walk into anyone's room for advice. It was a bit like a driving exam; they want you to succeed and it's only you that can throw away your chance! It's worth looking at how many pupils a set takes on. Obviously there are no guarantees, but it makes for a pretty stressful year if there are four of you and you know from the outset that they only want to keep one. I also found it very helpful that I had worked before pupillage – I was already used to 12-hour days and working weekends! I also had experience of the commercial world, which helped with understanding the problems clients face and the pressure they're under – although your advice must be legally correct, it also needs to be workable for the client."

Hui Ling explains the sort of work that she is involved with: "I've been lucky to be brought in as a junior on lots of litigation so far, which is relatively rare for a new tenant at the Tax Bar. On the smaller cases, I am pretty much left to my own devices, liaising with the clients and generally running the case right up to the first draft of the skeleton argument. Right now, I am junioring on a couple of appeals to the High Court. One concerns the meaning of the word 'disposal' for the purposes of capital gains tax, so it's very conceptual. Another appeal concerns the availability of an allowable loss resulting from transactions involving life policies to set off against other profits. There is also a lot of advisory work, which constantly keeps you on your toes due to the complexity of the UK Tax Code and the necessity for absolute precision. A 'shall' instead of a 'may' could change the entire meaning of a clause!" Hui Ling also writes books and articles: "I enjoy the freedom to do my own research and writing that comes with spending a lot of time in chambers."

According to Hui Ling, there is a particular buzz to be had from those cases where "you think you're all set, only to be ambushed by the opposition with a new argument they have come up with at the last minute, which means that you have to rush away and work late into the night to find the answer for your reply the next morning. I love it when all the hard work pays off and your case comes together nicely on the day".

While there may not be as much court time in tax as in other branches of the Bar (eg, the Criminal Bar), you still have to be an exceptional advocate: "When you do appear, there is no room for error. You are often handling very technical arguments on complex points of law and have to know exactly what you want to say and how to say it. In essence, you need to be able to put your argument forward in a way that the court can grasp without the benefit of having done your research. So you need to have the skills, even if you aren't practising them that much. However, you also need to understand that you're not going to get lots of appeals in the particular niche in which you wish to specialise; rather, you have to be patient and persevere to shape your practice. No one is going to do it for you."

Hui Ling discusses the sort of skills and experience that are essential at the Tax Bar: "You have to be very academically capable, with an ability to understand and manipulate the legislation and get to grips with the case law. There's no room for showmanship or glossing over. It is very helpful to have an academic tax background, such as an LLM or a practical tax course, to give you an overview of how the tax regime operates as a whole. Even if you don't have enough time to attend a taught course, a professional body such as the Association of Taxation Technicians offers a useful qualification, which you can study at home to fit around a job or Bar school." Other useful experience might include doing a *stage* at the European Commission and any corporate work experience (particularly in the tax department of a firm of solicitors or accountants) that means you're not just a "brand-new graduate who is clueless about the business world".

Hui Ling attests to the value of getting involved with the Free Representation Unit (FRU): "At the beginning of your career, you mostly represent taxpayers so you very rarely get a chance to do any cross-examining. As a result, I found FRU training and working on a case incredibly useful because you get valuable real-life cross-examination experience, albeit in a different area of law. A lot of the exceptional barristers at the Tax Bar are those that have gone out of their way to get such skills."

And of course, it's a case of the more mini-pupillages the better, for a couple of reasons. Hui Ling explains: "If you have impressed at a mini-pupillage, you'll almost certainly be invited back for an interview. Even if you then miss out on that pupillage, if you received good feedback from your week in chambers, you at least know you were close, but simply unlucky that time. It's worth persevering; there's competition everywhere, so don't let that be the only reason to put you off choosing the Bar."

# Pupillage Directory

# How to use the barristers' index and directory

## Barristers' index
These tables are designed to allow you to shortlist sets of chambers by particular criteria. Further information about each set is contained within the pupillage directory.

The tables detail:
- the main location of the set;
- the number of annual pupillages at the set;
- the number of tenants and tenancies offered in the past three years;
- whether mini-pupillages are available;
- whether the set uses the OLPAS application system; and
- 19 specialisation work areas.

It should be noted that the information has been provided by the chambers themselves and has generally not been verified by us. We do not, therefore, claim that the information is fully accurate and comprehensive, only that it can be used as a starting point for shortlisting appropriate sets. Furthermore, although we have attempted to contact every recruiting chambers, some have not returned information and are therefore absent.

## Barristers' directory
The directory contains contact information and a brief practice description for all chambers that have provided information. It is therefore an essential reference guide to chambers that offer pupillages and mini-pupillages.

The basic entry includes an application address, telephone and fax numbers, email address (if available), the applications procedure (OLPAS or own system) and a brief description of the set, together with the number of pupillages per year, the number of tenants, the number of new tenants in the last three years and whether the set offers mini-pupillages. Those chambers that have a more detailed directory entry appear in bold in the regional indexes.

These resources should be used in conjunction with the section on the Bar practice areas, which features in-depth interviews with numerous barristers who are keen to pass on their advice about making it in the legal profession.

# Barristers' index

# Barristers' index

| | Location | Pupillages funded | Tenancies in the last three years | Number of tenants | Mini-pupillages offered | Apply through OLPAS |
|---|---|---|---|---|---|---|
| Albany Chambers | London | 3 | 8 | 17 | ✔ | |
| Albion Chambers | Bristol | 0 for 2008 | 4 | 49 | | |
| Angel Chambers | Swansea | 1 | 3 | 25 | ✔ | ✔ |
| **Arden Chambers** | London | 2 | 6 | 32 | ✔ | |
| **Atkin Chambers** | London | 3 | 6 | 36 | ✔ | ✔ |
| **Atkinson Bevan Chambers** | London | 2 | 6 | 40 | ✔ | ✔ |
| Atlantic Chambers | Liverpool | 1-2 | 6 | 59 | ✔ | |
| 2 Bedford Row | London | 4 | 4 | 63 | ✔ | ✔ |
| 7 Bedford Row | London | 3 | 7 | 83 | | ✔ |
| 9 Bedford Row | London | 3 | 6 | 55 | ✔ | ✔ |
| 42 Bedford Row | London | 2 | 5 | 59 | ✔ | ✔ |
| **25 Bedford Row** | London | 4 | 3 | 55 | ✔ | ✔ |
| 36 Bedford Row | London | 2 | 5 | 78 | ✔ | ✔ |
| 29 Bedford Row Chambers | London | 2 | 4 | 48 | ✔ | ✔ |
| 9-12 Bell Yard | London | 4 | 4 | 80 | ✔ | ✔ |
| Blackstone Chambers | London | 4-5 | 6 | 71 | ✔ | ✔ |
| 1 Brick Court | London | 2 | 2 | 20 | ✔ | |
| **4 Brick Court** | London | 2 | 6 | 37 | ✔ | ✔ |
| Brick Court Chambers | London | Normally 4 | 6 | 65 | ✔ | ✔ |
| Broadway House Chambers | Bradford | 1 | 3 | 38 | ✔ | ✔ |
| 18 Carlton Crescent | Southampton | 2 | 3 | 24 | ✔ | |
| **Carmelite Chambers** | London | 2-3 | 5 | 63 | ✔ | ✔ |
| 25-27 Castle Street | Liverpool | 1 | 4 | 29 | | ✔ |
| 1 Chancery Lane | London | 2 | 2 | 37 | ✔ | |
| Charter Chambers | London | 3 | 8 | 60 | ✔ | ✔ |
| Chartlands Chambers | Northampton | 1 | 1 | 13 | ✔ | |
| Chavasse Court Chambers | Liverpool | 1 | 7 | 34 | ✔ | |
| Citadel Chambers | Birmingham | 0 | 3 | 49 | ✔ | |
| Clarendon Chambers | London | 1 | 6 | 37 | | |
| Cloisters | London | 2 | 4 | 43 | ✔ | ✔ |
| College Chambers | Southampton | 1 | 8 | 22 | ✔ | |
| 12 College Place | Southampton | 2 | 5 | 42 | ✔ | |
| Coram Chambers | London | 3 | 4 | 54 | ✔ | ✔ |
| Cornwall Street Chambers | Birmingham | 1 | 6 | 48 | | |
| **Crown Office Chambers** | London | 4 | 7 | 79 | ✔ | |
| **One Crown Office Row** | London | 2 | 8 | 56 | ✔ | ✔ |
| Crown Office Row Chambers | Brighton | 2 | 8 | 34 | ✔ | ✔ |
| **Crown Prosecution Service** | York | 15-20 | | | ✔ | |
| Deans Court Chambers | Manchester | 2 | 7 | 75 | ✔ | ✔ |
| Devereux Chambers | London | 2 | | 42 | ✔ | ✔ |
| Doughty Street Chambers | London | 5 | 9 | 90 | ✔ | ✔ |

| Chancery | Civil | Commercial | Common | Construction | Crime | Employment | EU/international | Family | Human rights | IP | Landlord/tenant | Media | Personal injury | Planning | Prof negligence | Public | Revenue | Shipping |
|---|---|---|---|---|---|---|---|---|---|---|---|---|---|---|---|---|---|---|
|  | • | • |  |  | • | • |  | • |  |  | • |  | • |  |  | • |  |  |
|  | • | • | • |  | • | • |  | • |  |  | • |  | • |  |  | • |  |  |
| • | • |  | • |  | • | • |  | • |  |  | • |  | • |  |  | • |  |  |
|  |  |  |  |  |  |  |  |  | • |  | • |  |  | • | • |  |  |  |
|  | • | • |  | • |  |  | • |  |  |  |  |  |  | • | • |  |  |  |
| • | • |  | • |  | • | • |  | • |  |  | • |  | • |  | • | • |  | • |
|  | • | • | • |  | • | • |  | • |  |  |  |  | • |  | • |  |  |  |
|  | • |  | • |  | • | • |  |  | • |  | • |  | • |  |  | • |  |  |
| • | • | • |  |  | • | • | • | • | • |  | • |  | • |  | • | • |  |  |
|  |  |  |  |  | • |  |  | • |  |  |  |  |  |  |  |  |  |  |
|  | • | • |  |  |  | • | • |  | • |  |  | • |  |  |  | • |  |  |
|  |  |  |  |  |  |  |  |  | • |  |  |  |  |  |  |  |  |  |
|  | • |  |  |  |  |  | • | • | • |  | • |  | • |  |  | • |  | • |
|  | • |  |  |  | • | • |  | • |  |  | • |  | • | • | • |  |  |  |
|  | • |  |  |  | • | • |  | • |  |  | • |  | • | • | • |  |  |  |
|  |  |  |  |  | • |  |  |  |  |  |  |  |  |  |  |  |  |  |
|  | • |  |  |  | • | • |  | • |  |  | • |  | • |  |  | • |  |  |
|  | • | • | • |  |  |  |  |  |  |  | • |  | • |  | • | • |  |  |
|  | • |  |  |  | • | • |  | • |  |  |  |  | • |  |  | • |  |  |
|  | • |  |  |  | • |  |  | • |  |  |  |  |  |  |  |  |  |  |
|  | • |  |  |  | • | • |  | • |  |  |  |  |  |  |  |  |  |  |
|  | • | • | • |  | • | • |  | • |  |  | • |  | • |  |  |  |  |  |
|  | • |  |  |  | • | • |  | • | • |  |  | • | • |  | • | • |  |  |
| • | • |  | • | • | • |  |  | • |  |  | • |  | • | • |  |  |  |  |
|  |  |  |  |  |  |  |  | • |  |  |  |  | • |  |  |  |  |  |
| • | • | • | • |  | • |  |  | • |  |  | • |  | • | • | • | • |  |  |
|  | • | • | • | • |  |  |  |  |  |  |  |  | • |  | • |  |  |  |
|  | • |  | • |  |  | • |  | • | • |  |  |  | • | • | • | • |  |  |
|  | • |  | • |  | • |  |  | • |  |  |  |  |  |  |  |  |  |  |
|  |  |  |  |  | • |  |  |  |  |  |  |  |  |  |  |  |  |  |
| • | • | • | • |  | • |  |  | • |  |  | • |  | • | • | • |  |  |  |
|  | • | • | • |  |  | • |  |  |  |  |  |  | • | • | • |  | • |  |
|  | • |  |  |  | • | • |  |  | • |  | • | • | • | • |  | • |  |  |

# Barristers' index

| | Location | Pupillages funded | Tenancies in the last three years | Number of tenants | Mini-pupillages offered | Apply through OLPAS |
|---|---|---|---|---|---|---|
| 2 Dr Johnson's Buildings | London | Up to 4 | 8 | 36 | ✔ | |
| 2 Dyer's Buildings | London | 1 | 6 | 41 | ✔ | ✔ |
| East Anglian Chambers | Ipswich | 4 | 9 | 63 | ✔ | |
| Eastbourne Chambers | Eastbourne | 1 | 0 | 13 | ✔ | |
| Ely Place Chambers | London | 2 | 4 | 27 | ✔ | |
| Enterprise Chambers | London | 1 | 4 | 34 | ✔ | ✔ |
| **Erskine Chambers** | London | Up to 2 | 2 | 23 | ✔ | |
| One Essex Court | London | 4 | 9 | 60 | ✔ | ✔ |
| 5 Essex Court | London | 1 | 4 | 30 | ✔ | ✔ |
| Essex Court Chambers | London | 4 | 5 | 73 | ✔ | ✔ |
| 20 Essex Street | London | Up to 4 | 5 | 45 | ✔ | ✔ |
| **23 Essex Street** | London | 3 | 5 | 74 | ✔ | ✔ |
| **39 Essex Street** | London | 3 | 6 | 76 | ✔ | ✔ |
| **Exchange Chambers** | Liverpool | 1-2 | 12 | 100 | ✔ | |
| Falcon Chambers | London | 2 | 4 | 35 | ✔ | |
| **Farrar's Building** | London | 2 | 5 | 44 | ✔ | ✔ |
| Fenners Chambers | Cambridge | 1-2 | 3 | 40 | ✔ | ✔ |
| Field Court Chambers | London | 2 | 5 | 47 | ✔ | |
| 187 Fleet Street | London | 3 | 8 | 51 | ✔ | ✔ |
| Fountain Chambers | Middlesbrough | 1 | 11 | 30 | ✔ | |
| 8 Fountain Court | Birmingham | 2 | 3 | 26 | ✔ | |
| Fountain Court Chambers | London | Up to 4 | 6 | 63 | ✔ | ✔ |
| **Francis Taylor Building** | London | 2 | 2 | 36 | ✔ | |
| Furnival Chambers | London | 3 | 9 | 71 | ✔ | ✔ |
| 1 Garden Court | London | 2 | 5 | 53 | ✔ | |
| Garden Court Chambers | London | 6 | 28 | 107 | ✔ | ✔ |
| Garden Court North | Manchester | 2 | 5 | 23 | | ✔ |
| Garden Square | Leicester | 1 | 1 | 11 | ✔ | |
| **9 Gough Square** | London | 2 | 6 | 67 | ✔ | |
| Gough Square Chambers | London | 1 | 1 | 13 | ✔ | |
| 1 Gray's Inn Square | London | 6 | 6 | 60 | ✔ | ✔ |
| **4-5 Gray's Inn Square** | London | 3 | 3 | 48 | ✔ | ✔ |
| 14 Gray's Inn Square | London | 2 | 3 | 33 | ✔ | ✔ |
| Gray's Inn Tax Chambers | London | Up to 2 | 2 | 17 | ✔ | |
| Guildford Chambers | Guildford, Surrey | 2 | 5 | 26 | ✔ | |
| Guildhall Chambers | Bristol | Up to 2 | 5 | 65 | ✔ | |
| **Hailsham Chambers** | London | 1 | 6 | 43 | ✔ | |
| Harcourt Chambers | London | 1 | 4 | 36 | ✔ | ✔ |
| **Hardwicke Building** | London | 2 | 7 | 76 | ✔ | |
| **1 Hare Court** | London | 3 | 4 | 36 | ✔ | |
| 2 Hare Court | London | 2-3 | 5 | 53 | ✔ | ✔ |

| Chancery | Civil | Commercial | Common | Construction | Crime | Employment | EU/international | Family | Human rights | IP | Landlord/tenant | Media | Personal injury | Planning | Prof negligence | Public | Revenue | Shipping |
|---|---|---|---|---|---|---|---|---|---|---|---|---|---|---|---|---|---|---|
|  | • |  |  |  | • |  |  | • |  |  |  |  |  |  |  | • |  |  |
|  |  |  |  |  | • |  |  |  |  |  |  |  |  |  |  |  |  |  |
|  | • | • | • |  | • | • |  | • |  |  | • |  | • | • | • |  |  |  |
|  | • | • |  |  | • | • |  | • |  |  | • |  | • |  | • | • |  |  |
| • | • | • |  | • |  | • |  |  |  |  | • | • | • | • | • | • |  |  |
| • |  | • |  |  |  |  |  |  |  |  | • |  |  |  | • |  |  |  |
| • |  | • |  |  |  |  |  |  |  |  |  |  |  |  | • |  |  |  |
| • |  | • |  |  |  |  |  |  |  | • | • |  |  |  |  |  | • |  |
|  | • |  |  |  | • |  |  | • |  |  |  |  | • |  | • | • |  |  |
|  | • | • |  |  |  | • | • | • | • |  |  | • |  |  | • | • | • | • |
|  |  | • |  |  |  |  |  | • | • |  |  |  |  |  |  | • |  | • |
|  |  |  |  |  | • |  |  |  |  |  |  |  |  |  |  |  |  |  |
|  | • |  |  | • | • |  |  |  |  |  |  |  | • | • | • |  |  |  |
| • | • | • |  |  | • |  | • | • | • | • | • |  | • | • | • | • | • |  |
| • |  |  |  |  |  |  |  |  |  |  | • |  |  |  | • |  |  |  |
|  | • | • | • |  | • |  |  | • |  |  |  |  | • |  | • |  |  |  |
| • | • | • | • |  | • |  |  | • |  |  |  |  | • |  | • |  |  |  |
| • | • | • | • |  | • |  |  | • |  | • |  |  | • |  | • | • |  |  |
|  |  |  |  |  | • |  |  |  |  |  |  |  |  |  |  |  |  |  |
|  | • |  | • |  | • |  |  | • |  |  |  |  | • |  | • | • |  |  |
|  | • |  |  |  | • |  |  | • |  |  |  |  | • |  | • |  |  |  |
| • | • | • |  |  | • | • | • |  |  |  |  | • |  |  | • | • |  |  |
|  |  |  |  |  |  |  | • | • | • |  |  |  |  |  |  |  |  |  |
|  |  |  |  |  | • |  |  |  |  |  |  |  |  |  |  |  |  |  |
|  |  |  |  |  |  |  |  | • | • |  |  |  |  |  |  |  |  |  |
|  | • |  | • |  | • | • | • | • | • |  | • |  | • | • | • | • |  |  |
|  | • |  |  |  | • |  | • | • | • |  | • |  | • |  |  | • |  |  |
|  | • |  |  |  | • |  |  |  |  |  |  |  | • |  |  |  |  |  |
| • | • |  |  |  | • |  |  | • |  |  | • |  | • |  | • | • |  |  |
|  | • | • |  |  | • |  |  |  |  |  |  |  | • |  | • |  |  |  |
|  | • | • |  |  |  | • | • |  |  |  | • |  |  | • | • | • |  |  |
|  | • | • |  |  |  | • |  |  |  |  |  |  | • |  | • | • |  |  |
|  |  |  |  |  |  |  |  |  |  |  |  |  |  |  |  |  | • |  |
| • | • |  | • |  | • | • |  | • |  |  |  |  | • |  | • | • |  |  |
| • | • | • |  |  | • |  |  |  |  |  | • |  | • |  | • |  |  |  |
|  | • | • |  |  |  |  |  |  |  |  |  |  | • |  | • |  |  |  |
|  | • | • |  |  |  |  |  |  |  |  |  |  | • |  | • |  |  |  |
| • | • | • | • | • |  | • |  | • | • | • |  |  | • |  | • | • |  | • |
|  |  |  |  |  |  |  |  | • |  |  |  |  |  |  |  |  |  |  |
|  |  |  |  |  | • |  |  |  |  |  |  |  |  |  |  |  |  |  |

# Barristers' index

| | Location | Pupillages funded | Tenancies in the last three years | Number of tenants | Mini-pupillages offered | Apply through OLPAS |
|---|---|---|---|---|---|---|
| 3 Hare Court | London | 2 | 5 | 29 | ✔ | ✔ |
| **Henderson Chambers** | London | 1-3 | 3 | 40 | ✔ | ✔ |
| **Hogarth Chambers** | London | 1 | 1 | 26 | ✔ | |
| Hollis Whiteman Chambers | London | 4-5 | 4 | 53 | ✔ | ✔ |
| India Buildings | Liverpool | 1 | 12 | 45 | ✔ | |
| 1 Inner Temple Lane | London | 2 | 5 | 29 | ✔ | ✔ |
| Iscoed Chambers | Swansea | 2 | 5 | 33 | ✔ | ✔ |
| **11 KBW** | London | 2-3 | 6 | 51 | ✔ | ✔ |
| KCH Chambers | Nottingham | 1 | 4 | 41 | ✔ | ✔ |
| **Keating Chambers** | London | 4 | 7 | 49 | ✔ | ✔ |
| Kenworthy's Chambers | Manchester | 2 | 12 | 45 | ✔ | |
| King Street Chambers | Leicester | 1 | 7 | 21 | ✔ | |
| 8 King Street Chambers | Manchester | 1-2 | 6 | 39 | ✔ | ✔ |
| King's Bench Chambers | Plymouth | 1 | 2 | 22 | ✔ | ✔ |
| **1 King's Bench Walk** | London | 2 | 4 | 54 | ✔ | ✔ |
| 2 King's Bench Walk | London | 3 | 10 | 55 | | |
| 4 King's Bench Walk | London | 2 | 6 | 40 | | ✔ |
| 5 King's Bench Walk | London | 2 | 5 | 43 | ✔ | |
| **6 King's Bench Walk** | London | 4 | 6 | 52 | ✔ | ✔ |
| 6 King's Bench Walk | London | 2 | 2 | 31 | ✔ | |
| **7 King's Bench Walk** | London | Up to 4 | 4 | 44 | ✔ | ✔ |
| **12 King's Bench Walk** | London | 3 | 8 | 55 | ✔ | ✔ |
| 13 King's Bench Walk | London | 2 | 3 | 50 | ✔ | ✔ |
| Kings Chambers | Manchester | 3 | 10 | 69 | ✔ | ✔ |
| Lamb Building | London | 3 | 10 | 51 | ✔ | |
| Lamb Chambers | London | 2 | 5 | 50 | ✔ | ✔ |
| **Landmark Chambers** | London | 6 | 6 | 63 | ✔ | ✔ |
| 9 Lincoln's Inn Fields | London | 2 | 4 | 50 | ✔ | ✔ |
| Littleton Chambers | London | 2 | 6 | 42 | ✔ | |
| Maidstone Chambers | Maidstone, Kent | 0 | 2 | 13 | ✔ | |
| **Maitland Chambers** | London | 3 | 6 | 64 | ✔ | |
| **Matrix Chambers** | London | 2 | 3 | 59 | | |
| 1 Mitre Court Buildings | London | 3 | 5 | 56 | ✔ | ✔ |
| Mitre House Chambers | London | 0 | 4 | 28 | ✔ | ✔ |
| Monckton Chambers | London | 2 | 5 | 44 | ✔ | ✔ |
| New Bailey Chambers | Preston | 2 | 8 | 32 | ✔ | |
| New Court Chambers | London | 1 | 4 | 20 | ✔ | ✔ |
| New Court Chambers | Newcastle Upon Tyne | 2 | 1 | 36 | ✔ | |
| 3 New Square | London | 1 | 2 | 16 | ✔ | ✔ |
| **4 New Square** | London | Up to 4 | 5 | 57 | ✔ | ✔ |
| 8 New Square | London | 1 | 2 | 25 | ✔ | ✔ |

| Chancery | Civil | Commercial | Common | Construction | Crime | Employment | EU/international | Family | Human rights | IP | Landlord/tenant | Media | Personal injury | Planning | Prof negligence | Public | Revenue | Shipping |
|---|---|---|---|---|---|---|---|---|---|---|---|---|---|---|---|---|---|---|
|  | • | • | • |  |  | • | • |  |  |  |  |  | • |  | • |  |  |  |
|  | • | • | • | • |  | • |  | • | • |  | • |  | • | • | • | • |  |  |
| • |  | • |  |  |  |  |  |  |  | • |  | • |  |  |  |  |  |  |
|  | • | • |  | • |  | • |  | • |  |  | • |  | • |  | • | • |  |  |
|  |  |  |  | • |  |  |  |  |  |  |  |  |  |  |  |  |  |  |
| • | • | • |  | • |  | • |  | • |  |  | • |  | • | • | • | • |  |  |
|  | • |  |  |  |  |  |  |  | • |  |  |  |  |  |  |  |  |  |
|  | • | • |  |  | • | • |  | • |  |  |  |  |  |  | • |  |  |  |
|  | • | • | • |  | • | • | • | • | • |  | • |  | • | • | • | • |  |  |
| • | • | • |  |  | • | • |  | • |  |  | • |  | • |  | • | • |  |  |
| • | • | • | • | • | • | • |  | • |  |  | • |  | • |  | • | • |  |  |
|  | • |  |  |  |  |  |  | • |  |  |  |  |  |  |  |  |  |  |
|  |  |  | • |  |  | • | • | • |  |  | • |  | • |  | • | • |  |  |
|  |  | • |  |  |  | • | • | • |  |  | • |  | • |  | • | • |  |  |
|  |  |  |  |  | • |  |  | • |  |  |  |  |  |  |  |  |  |  |
|  | • | • |  |  | • | • | • | • |  |  | • |  | • |  |  |  |  |  |
|  | • |  |  |  | • | • | • | • |  |  |  |  |  |  | • |  |  |  |
|  | • | • |  |  |  | • |  |  |  |  | • |  |  | • |  | • |  | • |
|  | • |  |  |  |  | • |  |  |  |  | • |  | • |  |  |  |  |  |
| • | • | • |  |  | • | • |  |  |  |  |  |  | • | • | • | • | • |  |
| • | • | • | • | • |  | • |  | • |  | • |  |  | • | • | • | • | • |  |
| • | • |  | • | • |  | • |  |  |  |  | • |  | • | • | • |  |  |  |
| • | • |  | • |  |  | • |  |  | • |  | • |  | • | • | • | • |  |  |
|  |  |  |  | • |  |  |  |  |  |  |  |  |  |  |  |  |  |  |
| • | • | • |  |  |  | • | • | • |  |  | • | • | • |  |  |  |  |  |
| • | • | • | • | • | • | • | • | • |  |  | • | • | • |  | • |  | • |  |
| • | • |  |  |  |  |  |  |  | • |  | • | • |  |  |  |  |  |  |
|  | • | • |  | • | • | • | • | • |  |  | • |  | • |  | • | • | • |  |
|  | • |  |  |  | • | • |  | • |  |  | • |  |  | • |  |  |  |  |
|  | • | • |  |  | • | • | • | • |  |  | • |  | • |  | • | • | • |  |
| • | • | • | • |  | • | • |  |  |  |  | • |  | • |  | • |  |  |  |
|  |  |  |  |  |  | • |  |  |  |  |  |  |  |  |  |  |  |  |
|  | • |  |  |  | • |  |  | • |  |  |  |  | • |  |  |  |  |  |
|  |  |  |  |  |  |  |  |  |  | • |  |  |  |  |  |  |  |  |
| • | • | • | • | • |  | • |  |  |  |  |  | • |  | • |  |  |  |  |

# Barristers' index

| | Location | Pupillages funded | Tenancies in the last three years | Number of tenants | Mini-pupillages offered | Apply through OLPAS |
|---|---|---|---|---|---|---|
| **New Square Chambers** | London | 2 | 2 | 46 | ✔ | |
| 2 New Street Chambers | Leicester | 1 | 3 | 13 | ✔ | ✔ |
| New Walk Chambers | Leicester | Up to 4 | 6 | 23 | ✔ | |
| Nicholas Street Chambers | Chester | 1 | 5 | 34 | ✔ | |
| **No 5 Chambers** | Birmingham | 2 | 63 | 196 | ✔ | |
| Northampton Chambers | Northampton | 2 | 6 | 10 | ✔ | ✔ |
| **24 Old Buildings** | London | 2 | 3 | 31 | ✔ | |
| Old Court Chambers | Middlesbrough | 1 | 3 | 20 | | |
| 15 Old Square | London | 1 | 2 | 12 | ✔ | |
| **10 Old Square** | London | 1 | 3 | 29 | ✔ | |
| **Old Square Chambers** | London | 3 | 4 | 62 | ✔ | ✔ |
| Oriel Chambers | Liverpool | up to 2 | 11 | 57 | ✔ | ✔ |
| Outer Temple Chambers | London | 2 | 6 | 63 | ✔ | |
| Pallant Chambers | Chichester | Up to 2 | 7 | 21 | ✔ | |
| 1 Paper Buildings | London | 2 | 5 | 41 | | |
| 2 Paper Buildings | London | 4 | 6 | 48 | ✔ | ✔ |
| 3 Paper Buildings | London | 5-6 | 10 | 130 | ✔ | |
| 4 Paper Buildings | London | 2 | 3 | 47 | ✔ | ✔ |
| 5 Paper Buildings | London | 3 | 5 | 41 | ✔ | ✔ |
| 5 Paper Buildings | London | 2 | 4 | 37 | ✔ | |
| Paradise Chambers | Sheffield | 2 | 2 | 43 | ✔ | |
| Park Court Chambers | Leeds | 1 | 5 | 58 | ✔ | ✔ |
| Park Lane Chambers | Leeds | 1 | 5 | 41 | ✔ | |
| 9 Park Place | Cardiff | 2 | 7 | 50 | ✔ | |
| **30 Park Place** | Cardiff | 2 | 4 | 57 | ✔ | ✔ |
| 33 Park Place | Cardiff | 1 | 8 | 47 | ✔ | ✔ |
| 37 Park Square | Leeds | 0 | 6 | 35 | ✔ | |
| 1 Pump Court | London | 23 | 10 | 72 | ✔ | |
| 2 Pump Court | London | 1 | 6 | 39 | ✔ | ✔ |
| **4 Pump Court** | London | 2 | 6 | 51 | ✔ | |
| 6 Pump Court | London | 2-3 | 5 | 40 | ✔ | ✔ |
| 5 Pump Court Chambers | London | 2 | 7 | 35 | ✔ | |
| **Pump Court Tax Chambers** | London | Up to 3 | 2 | 25 | ✔ | |
| **Quadrant Chambers** | London | 4 | 5 | 41 | ✔ | |
| **Queen Elizabeth Building** | London | 3 | 5 | 31 | ✔ | ✔ |
| **Radcliffe Chambers** | London | Up to 2 | 4 | 45 | ✔ | ✔ |
| 3 Raymond Buildings | London | 3 | 5 | 44 | ✔ | ✔ |
| 5RB | London | 2 | 4 | 29 | ✔ | ✔ |
| **18 Red Lion Court** | London | 5 | 5 | 86 | ✔ | ✔ |
| Regency Chambers | Peterborough | 1-2 | 3 | 18 | ✔ | ✔ |
| Renaissance Chambers | London | 2 | 3 | 48 | ✔ | ✔ |

| Chancery | Civil | Commercial | Common | Construction | Crime | Employment | EU/international | Family | Human rights | IP | Landlord/tenant | Media | Personal injury | Planning | Prof negligence | Public | Revenue | Shipping |
|---|---|---|---|---|---|---|---|---|---|---|---|---|---|---|---|---|---|---|
| • |  | • |  |  |  |  |  |  |  | • | • |  |  |  | • | • | • |  |
|  | • | • | • |  |  | • |  | • |  |  | • |  | • | • | • | • |  |  |
| • | • | • |  | • | • | • | • | • |  |  | • |  | • | • | • | • |  |  |
|  |  | • |  | • | • | • |  | • |  |  | • |  | • | • | • | • |  |  |
| • | • | • | • | • | • | • |  | • |  |  | • |  | • | • | • | • | • |  |
|  | • | • | • |  | • |  |  | • |  |  | • |  | • | • | • | • |  |  |
| • |  | • |  |  | • | • | • |  |  |  | • |  |  |  |  |  |  |  |
|  | • | • | • |  | • | • |  | • |  |  | • |  | • | • | • | • |  |  |
|  |  |  |  |  | • |  |  |  |  |  |  |  |  |  |  |  | • |  |
|  |  |  |  |  |  | • |  |  |  |  |  |  | • | • | • |  |  |  |
| • | • | • | • | • | • | • |  | • |  |  | • |  | • | • | • |  |  |  |
| • | • | • | • |  | • | • | • | • |  |  | • |  | • |  | • |  |  |  |
| • |  |  |  |  | • | • |  | • |  |  | • |  | • |  |  |  |  |  |
|  | • |  |  |  | • |  |  | • |  |  |  |  | • |  |  |  |  |  |
|  |  |  |  |  | • |  |  |  |  |  |  |  |  |  |  |  |  |  |
| • | • | • | • | • | • |  |  | • |  |  | • |  | • |  | • | • |  |  |
| • | • |  |  | • | • | • |  | • |  |  | • |  | • |  | • |  |  |  |
|  |  | • |  |  |  |  |  |  |  |  | • |  |  |  |  |  |  |  |
| • |  | • |  |  |  | • |  | • |  |  | • |  |  |  | • |  |  |  |
| • | • | • | • |  | • | • |  | • |  |  | • |  | • |  | • |  |  |  |
| • | • | • | • |  | • |  |  | • |  |  | • |  | • |  |  |  |  |  |
| • | • |  |  |  | • |  |  | • |  |  | • |  | • |  | • |  |  |  |
| • | • |  |  |  | • |  |  | • |  |  | • |  |  | • |  |  |  |  |
| • | • | • |  | • | • | • |  | • |  |  | • |  | • | • | • | • |  |  |
| • | • | • |  |  | • | • | • |  | • |  | • |  | • | • | • | • |  |  |
| • | • | • | • |  | • | • |  | • |  |  | • |  | • | • | • |  |  |  |
|  | • |  |  |  | • |  |  | • |  |  | • |  |  |  |  | • |  |  |
|  |  |  |  |  | • |  |  | • |  |  |  |  |  |  |  |  |  |  |
|  | • | • | • | • |  |  |  | • |  |  |  |  | • |  | • |  |  |  |
|  | • |  |  |  | • | • |  | • |  |  |  |  | • | • |  | • |  |  |
| • | • | • |  |  | • | • |  | • |  |  | • |  | • |  | • |  |  |  |
|  |  |  |  |  |  |  |  |  |  |  |  |  |  |  |  |  | • |  |
|  |  | • |  |  |  |  |  |  |  |  |  | • |  |  | • |  |  | • |
|  |  |  |  |  |  |  |  | • |  |  |  |  |  |  |  |  |  |  |
| • |  | • |  |  |  |  |  |  |  |  |  |  |  |  |  |  |  |  |
|  |  |  |  |  | • |  |  |  |  |  |  |  |  | • |  | • |  |  |
|  | • |  |  |  |  |  |  | • | • | • |  | • |  |  | • |  |  |  |
|  |  |  |  |  | • |  |  |  |  |  |  |  |  |  |  |  |  |  |
|  | • |  | • |  | • | • |  | • |  |  | • |  | • | • | • |  |  |  |
|  | • |  |  |  |  |  |  | • | • |  | • |  | • |  | • | • |  |  |

# Barristers' index

| | Location | Pupillages funded | Tenancies in the last three years | Number of tenants | Mini-pupillages offered | Apply through OLPAS |
|---|---|---|---|---|---|---|
| **Ropewalk Chambers** | Nottingham | 2 | 3 | 38 | ✔ | |
| Rougemont Chambers | Exeter | 2 | 6 | 24 | ✔ | |
| **Selborne Chambers** | London | Up to 2 | 4 | 21 | ✔ | |
| 3 Serjeants' Inn | London | 2 | 7 | 41 | ✔ | ✔ |
| **Serle Court** | London | 2 | 4 | 48 | ✔ | |
| **3-4 South Square** | London | Up to 4 | 5 | 46 | ✔ | |
| 11 South Square | London | 1 | 2 | 17 | ✔ | ✔ |
| 5 St Andrew's Hill | London | 2 | 4 | 45 | ✔ | ✔ |
| **3 Stone Buildings** | London | 2 | 2 | 26 | ✔ | ✔ |
| 4 Stone Buildings | London | 2 | 3 | 27 | ✔ | |
| **5 Stone Buildings** | London | 2 | 2 | 24 | ✔ | |
| 9 Stone Buildings | London | 1 | 4 | 28 | ✔ | |
| 11 Stone Buildings | London | 2 | 3 | 50 | ✔ | ✔ |
| Stone Chambers | London | 1 | 3 | 25 | ✔ | ✔ |
| St Ive's Chambers | Birmingham | 2 | 6 | 59 | ✔ | |
| St James's Chambers | Manchester | 2 | 5 | 28 | ✔ | |
| 18 St John Street | Manchester | Up to 4 | 6 | 54 | ✔ | |
| St John's Buildings | Manchester | 2 | 10 | 105 | ✔ | ✔ |
| St John's Chambers | Bristol | 2 | 22 | 77 | ✔ | ✔ |
| St Mary's Family Law Chambers | Nottingham | 1 | 3 | 20 | ✔ | ✔ |
| St Paul's Chambers | Leeds | 0 | 4 | 44 | ✔ | |
| **St Philips Chambers** | Birmingham | Up to 4 | 9 | 171 | ✔ | |
| 1 Stanley Place | Chester | 1 | 7 | 35 | ✔ | |
| Stour Chambers | Canterbury, Kent | 1 | 5 | 12 | ✔ | |
| Tanfield Chambers | London | 3 | 6 | 65 | ✔ | ✔ |
| Temple Chambers | Cardiff | 2 | 3 | 42 | ✔ | |
| 55 Temple Chambers | London | Up to 4 | 9 | 15 | ✔ | ✔ |
| 1 Temple Gardens | London | 2 | 6 | 56 | ✔ | ✔ |
| 2 Temple Gardens | London | 2-3 | 9 | 49 | ✔ | ✔ |
| 3 Temple Gardens | London | 2 | 4 | 26 | ✔ | ✔ |
| 3 Temple Gardens | London | 3 | 5 | 53 | ✔ | ✔ |
| 3 Temple Gardens | London | 1 | 5 | 39 | ✔ | ✔ |
| Thomas More Chambers | London | 1 | 3 | 30 | | ✔ |
| Tooks Chambers | London | 3 | 5 | 60 | ✔ | ✔ |
| Trinity Chambers | Newcastle Upon Tyne | 1-2 | 10 | 50 | ✔ | ✔ |
| Unity Street Chambers | Bristol | 1 | 2 | 13 | ✔ | |
| 3 Verulam Buildings | London | 3 | 6 | 58 | ✔ | ✔ |
| Walnut House | Exeter | 1 | 3 | 21 | ✔ | |
| **Westgate Chambers** | Lewes | 3 | 18 | 46 | ✔ | |
| **Wilberforce Chambers** | London | 2 | 6 | 46 | ✔ | |
| 15 Winckley Square | Preston | 2 | 4 | 45 | ✔ | ✔ |

| Chancery | Civil | Commercial | Common | Construction | Crime | Employment | EU/international | Family | Human rights | IP | Landlord/tenant | Media | Personal injury | Planning | Prof negligence | Public | Revenue | Shipping |
|---|---|---|---|---|---|---|---|---|---|---|---|---|---|---|---|---|---|---|
| • | • | • |   |   |   | • |   |   |   |   | • |   | • | • | • | • |   |   |
| • | • | • | • | • | • | • | • | • | • |   | • |   | • | • | • | • |   |   |
| • | • | • |   |   |   |   |   |   |   |   | • |   |   | • | • |   |   |   |
|   |   |   | • |   | • | • | • |   |   |   |   |   |   |   | • |   |   |   |
| • |   | • |   |   |   |   |   |   |   |   | • |   |   |   | • | • |   |   |
| • | • | • |   |   |   |   | • |   |   |   |   |   |   |   | • | • |   |   |
|   |   |   |   |   |   |   |   |   |   | • |   |   |   |   |   |   |   |   |
|   | • |   |   |   | • |   |   |   |   |   |   |   |   |   |   |   |   |   |
| • | • | • |   |   |   |   |   |   |   |   | • |   |   |   | • |   | • |   |
| • |   | • |   |   |   |   |   |   |   |   | • |   |   |   | • |   | • |   |
| • | • |   | • |   |   |   | • |   |   |   | • |   |   |   | • |   | • |   |
| • |   | • |   |   |   | • |   |   |   |   | • |   |   |   | • |   | • |   |
| • |   | • |   |   |   | • |   |   |   | • | • | • |   |   | • |   |   |   |
| • | • | • |   |   | • | • |   | • |   |   | • |   | • | • | • |   | • |   |
| • | • | • | • |   | • | • |   | • |   | • | • |   | • |   | • |   |   |   |
| • | • | • |   |   | • | • | • | • |   | • | • |   | • |   | • | • |   | • |
| • | • | • | • | • | • | • | • | • |   | • | • |   | • | • | • | • |   | • |
|   |   |   |   |   |   |   |   | • |   |   |   |   |   |   |   |   |   |   |
| • | • | • |   | • | • | • |   | • |   | • |   |   | • | • | • | • | • |   |
| • | • | • | • | • | • | • |   | • |   |   | • |   | • | • | • | • |   |   |
|   | • | • |   | • | • |   |   | • |   |   | • |   | • |   | • |   |   |   |
|   | • | • |   | • |   |   |   | • |   |   | • |   | • |   | • |   |   |   |
|   | • |   |   | • |   |   |   | • |   |   | • |   | • |   | • |   |   |   |
|   | • |   |   | • |   |   |   | • |   |   | • |   | • |   | • |   |   |   |
|   | • |   |   | • |   |   |   | • |   |   | • |   | • |   | • | • |   |   |
|   | • |   | • |   | • | • |   |   | • |   | • |   | • |   | • | • |   |   |
|   | • | • |   |   | • | • | • | • |   |   |   | • | • |   | • | • |   |   |
|   |   |   |   |   | • |   |   | • |   |   |   |   |   |   |   |   |   |   |
|   | • |   |   | • |   |   |   | • |   |   |   |   | • | • | • | • |   |   |
|   | • |   |   | • |   |   |   | • |   |   | • |   | • | • | • | • |   |   |
|   | • | • |   | • | • |   | • | • |   |   |   |   | • |   |   | • |   |   |
|   | • |   |   | • | • |   |   | • |   |   |   |   |   |   |   | • |   |   |
| • | • | • | • |   | • | • |   | • |   |   | • |   | • |   | • | • |   |   |
| • | • |   | • |   | • | • |   | • |   | • |   |   | • |   | • |   |   |   |
| • |   | • |   |   |   |   |   | • |   |   | • |   |   |   | • |   |   |   |
|   | • |   |   |   | • | • |   | • |   |   | • |   | • |   | • | • |   |   |
|   | • |   |   |   | • | • |   | • |   |   | • |   | • |   |   |   |   |   |
| • | • | • |   |   |   |   |   | • |   | • | • |   |   | • | • |   | • |   |
| • | • |   |   |   | • | • |   | • |   |   | • |   | • |   | • |   |   |   |

| | Location | Pupillages funded | Tenancies in the last three years | Number of tenants | Mini-pupillages offered | Apply through OLPAS |
|---|---|---|---|---|---|---|
| York Chambers | York | 2 | 6 | 50 | ✔ | |
| Young Street Chambers | Manchester | 1 | 30 | 47 | ✔ | |

| Chancery | Civil | Commercial | Common | Construction | Crime | Employment | EU/international | Family | Human rights | IP | Landlord/tenant | Media | Personal injury | Planning | Prof negligence | Public | Revenue | Shipping |
|---|---|---|---|---|---|---|---|---|---|---|---|---|---|---|---|---|---|---|
|  | • |  | • |  | • | • |  | • |  |  |  |  | • |  | • |  |  |  |
| • | • |  | • |  | • | • |  | • |  |  | • |  | • |  | • |  |  |  |

# Pupillage directory

# Arden Chambers

2 John Street, London WC1N 2ES
**Tel:** 020 7242 4244
**Fax:** 020 7242 3224
**Email:** clerks@ardenchambers.com
**Web:** www.ardenchambers.com

**Description of Chambers** Andrew Arden QC and six of the current members founded Arden Chambers in April 1993 in order to provide a specialist centre for the practice of housing and local government law building on the authorative publications edited or authored by Andrew Arden and now also by other members of chambers.

Today, chambers specialises in all aspects of housing, local government and property law. We offer the combined experience of more than 30 barristers (ten of whom are regarded as leaders in their respective fields by *Chambers UK: A Client's Guide to the UK Legal Profession 2007*).

**Areas of work** Housing, local government and property.

**Who should apply** Candidates with an interest in or experience of housing law, property law and local government/public law.

**Pupillage programme** We offer two pupillages annually for 12 months. Each pupil is allocated a coordinator for the whole of that period who is responsible for the pupil's overall education and training and arranges individual supervisors in consultation with the pupil. Pupils can expect to spend time with at least four supervisors.

**When and how to apply** Apply by 31 July 2008 to begin October 2009 on the chambers application form and equal opportunities monitoring form.

**Mini-pupillages** Limited number available during each year. Apply by CV and covering letter.

**Sponsorship/funding** £10,000 award for first six months, guaranteed earnings for second six months, subject to clawback.

| | |
|---|---:|
| Pupillages funded | 2 |
| Tenants | 32 |
| Tenancies in last 3 yrs | 6 |

Mini-pupillages     yes

Applications contact
Mr Jonathan Manning

Remuneration for pupillage
£20,000

ARDEN

CHAMBERS

# Atkin Chambers

1 Atkin Building, Gray's Inn, London WC1R 5AT
**Tel:** 020 7404 0102
**Fax:** 020 7405 7456
**Email:** clerks@atkinchambers.com
**Web:** www.atkinchambers.com

**Description of Chambers** Atkin Chambers was the first set to specialise in the law relating to domestic and international construction and engineering projects. Atkin Chambers has a significant and growing international practice at all levels of seniority. Chambers success in this area has recently been recognised by the grant of the Queen's Award for Enterprise 2005 in the category of International Trade. Atkin Chambers is the first and only chambers to receive this award. Chambers intends to continue to grow and consolidate its position in both the domestic and international markets.

Atkin Chambers is committed to recruiting pupils and tenants (generally from its own pupils) that will participate in its continued success in domestic and international work.

**Areas of work** Atkin Chambers is a leader in its field: technology and construction law. Members of Chambers are regularly instructed to advise and act as advocates in relation to some of the largest and most complex domestic and international disputes in the areas of Chambers' expertise. Members of Atkin Chambers have been involved in many of the largest high-profile domestic and international disputes in the fields of construction, technology, power, energy, computers and telecommunications of recent years, both in court and in international and domestic arbitration. Members of Chambers are regular participants as advocates, advisers or tribunals in all forms of alternative dispute resolution.

**Who should apply** Applicants for pupillage should have a first-class degree or a good 2.1 degree. Postgraduate qualifications are viewed favourably but are not essential. Applications from non-law graduates are welcomed.

**Pupillage programme** Atkin Chambers takes recruitment to pupillage and tenancy extremely seriously. The pupillage award – equivalent to the sums paid by other much larger sets of Chambers – reflects this.

The pupillage year is structured to provide all of the Bar Council's minimum training requirements and the additional training Chambers considers is necessary for successful entry into the high-quality commercial work of its practice. Atkin Chambers provides its own advocacy training and assessment in addition to that provided by the Inns.

Full and up-to-date details of the structure and goals of Atkin Chambers' pupillage training programme may be reviewed on our website.

**When and how to apply** Atkin Chambers is a member of OLPAS.

**Mini-pupillages** Six mini-pupillages are offered each year. Applications by letter with CV should be received by 30 November 2008. Mini-pupillages will be offered to candidates who have achieved or have clear potential to achieve the academic standards required of pupils.

**Sponsorship/funding** Three fully funded pupillages of £42,500 per pupil for 12 months are available. Funding for the BVC year by way of drawdown is available. Atkin Chambers is committed to applying equal opportunities good practice.

| | |
|---|---|
| Pupillages funded | 3 |
| Tenants | 36 |
| Tenancies in last 3 yrs | 6 |
| Mini-pupillages | yes |
| Apply through OLPAS | |
| Remuneration for pupillage | £42,500 |
| Minimum qualifications | 2.1 degree |

Atkin Chambers Barristers

# Atkinson Bevan Chambers

2 Harcourt Buildings, Temple, London EC4Y 9DB
**Tel:** 020 7353 2112
**Fax:** 020 7353 8339
**Email:** clerks@2hb.co.uk
**Web:** www.2hb.co.uk

**Description of Chambers** With four QCs, one Senior Treasury Counsel and 35 juniors, Atkinson Bevan Chambers is one of the leading specialist criminal sets in the Temple. We are committed to maintaining a balance of high-quality defence and prosecution work in London and on the Western and South Eastern circuits, and we have been awarded the Quality Mark for the Bar accreditation in recognition of the importance we place on our procedures in practice management. We offer a friendly and relaxed environment in which to complete pupillage.

**Areas of work** Members of Chambers are involved in all kinds of criminal cases, ranging from high-profile and sensitive matters requiring specialist expertise such as murder and terrorism to more routine offences found every day in the magistrates' and crown courts. Many of our barristers have developed particular expertise in such areas as commercial, revenue and VAT fraud, drug cases, corruption, child abuse and sexual offences, and multi-handed police and undercover operations. We are represented on the Attorney General's panel of prosecution advocates, which covers work for, among others, HM Revenue & Customs, the Department of Environment, Food and Rural Affairs, and the Health and Safety Executive. Members are regularly briefed by the Serious Fraud Office. We also regularly cover criminal confiscation work within Chambers.

**Who should apply** We are committed to a policy of equal opportunities and aim to recruit articulate and confident candidates, regardless of their background, who can demonstrate drive and determination and who are committed to a future at the Criminal Bar. We look for applicants who can balance intellectual excellence with common sense and pragmatism. We take the recruitment of our pupils very seriously and every pupil is selected on the basis that they are a potential tenant.

**Pupillage programme** Pupils are assigned one pupil supervisor for each six-month period. During the first six non-practising months pupils attend court with their pupil supervisor on a daily basis, and complete research and written work as directed. Effort is taken to ensure that the pupil has contact with, and the opportunity to work for, tenants of all levels of seniority within Chambers. During the second six months pupils conduct cases in court alone and can expect to develop their own busy practice. In-house advocacy training is provided during pupillage, along with regular written assessments by the pupil supervisor and feedback from instructing solicitors.

**When and how to apply** Chambers recruits through the summer season of OLPAS.

**Mini-pupillages** We offer mini-pupillages during Easter and summer, subject to availability. Applicants must be aged 18 and over. Applications must be made by way of a form which may be downloaded from our website.

**Sponsorship/funding** We offer two funded 12-month pupillages commencing in October with awards of up to £15,000 each for the first six months and guaranteed earnings of £6,000 in the second six months.

| | |
|---|---|
| Pupillages funded | 2 |
| Tenants | 40 |
| Tenancies in last 3 yrs | 6 |
| Mini-pupillages | yes |
| Apply through OLPAS | |
| Remuneration for pupillage | Up to £15,000 |

Community Legal Service

Criminal Defence Service

## ALBANY CHAMBERS
46 Bedford Row, London WC1R 4LR
**Tel:** 020 7242 5468
**Fax:** 020 7242 4009
**Email:** albanychambers@aol.com
**Apply to:** Miss Pamela Lawrence

| | |
|---|---|
| PF | 3 |
| T | 17 |
| TL3Y | 8 |
| MP | yes |

## ALBION CHAMBERS
Broad Street, Bristol BS1 1DR
**Tel:** 0117 927 2144
**Fax:** 0117 926 2569
**Email:** clerks@albionchambers.co.uk

A large Western Circuit set with 4 silks and 45 juniors covering the full range of criminal, civil and family work and many specialist areas.

| | |
|---|---|
| PF | 0 for 2008 |
| T | 49 |
| TL3Y | 4 |
| MP | no |

## ANGEL CHAMBERS
96 Walter Road, Swansea SA1 5QA
**Tel:** 01792 464623
**Fax:** 01792 648 501
**Email:** clerk@angelchambers.co .uk
**Apply through OLPAS**

Busy Common law set specialising in crime, family and civil law.

| | |
|---|---|
| PF | 1 |
| T | 25 |
| TL3Y | 3 |
| MP | yes |

## ATLANTIC CHAMBERS
4-6 Cook Street, Liverpool L2 9QU
**Tel:** 0151 236 4421
**Fax:** 0151 236 1559
**Email:** pupillage@atlanticchambers.co.uk
**Apply through OLPAS**

Atlantic Chambers provides specialist advice and advocacy to a range of clients from publicly-funded individuals to international commercial organisations as our pupils discover.

| | |
|---|---|
| PF | 1-2 |
| T | 59 |
| TL3Y | 6 |
| MP | yes |

## 2 BEDFORD ROW
London WC1R 4BU
**Tel:** 020 7440 8888
**Fax:** 020 7242 1738
**Email:** tkendal@2bedfordrow.co.uk
**Apply through OLPAS**

Criminal set covering London and the South Eastern circuit, defending and prosecuting at all levels and all work.

| | |
|---|---|
| PF | 4 |
| T | 63 |
| TL3Y | 4 |
| MP | yes |

## 7 BEDFORD ROW
Chambers of Kate Thirlwall QC,
London WC1R 4BU
**Tel:** 020 7242 3555
**Fax:** 020 7242 2511
**Email:** clerks@7br.co.uk
**Apply through OLPAS**

A leading common law set practising a mix of civil and criminal work both in London and on the Midland Circuit. Three generously-funded 12-month pupillages offered each year.

| | |
|---|---|
| PF | 3 |
| T | 83 |
| TL3Y | 7 |
| MP | no |

## 9 BEDFORD ROW
London WC1R 4AZ
**Tel:** 020 7489 2727
**Fax:** 020 7489 2828
**Email:** clerks@9bedfordrowr.co.uk
**Apply through OLPAS**

| | |
|---|---|
| PF | 3 |
| T | 55 |
| TL3Y | 6 |
| MP | yes |

## 42 BEDFORD ROW
London WC1R 4JL
**Tel:** 020 7831 0222
**Fax:** 020 7831 2239
**Email:** clerks@42br.com
**Apply through OLPAS**

| | |
|---|---|
| PF | 2 |
| T | 59 |
| TL3Y | 5 |
| MP | yes |

PF = Pupillages funded / T = Tenants / TL3Y = Tenancies in last 3 years / MP = Mini pupillages offered

# 25 Bedford Row

London WC1R 4HD
**Tel:** 020 7067 1500
**Fax:** 020 7067 1507
**Email:** clerks@25bedfordrow.com
**Web:** www.25bedfordrow.com

**Description of Chambers** 25 Bedford Row specialises in defence advocacy, with members of chambers frequently defending in the highest profile cases. Chambers is housed in a modern, fully networked building which includes a suite of conference rooms and video conferencing facilities. 25 Bedford Row's facilities allow practioners and solicitors to conduct remote conferences with 61 prisons and secure units in the UK and conduct global conferences from London. The clerking team offers a 24-hour service for emergencies and in December 1999 the set was the first chambers to be awarded the Bar Mark, the Bar Council's kite mark for quality assurance.

Central to our philosophy is a belief that everyone should have equal access to the best representation and we continue our commitment to publicly funded representation. Where appropriate, members undertake pro bono work through the Bar Council Pro Bono Scheme.

**Areas of work** 25 Bedford Row is a defence advocacy set, with specialisms in business litigation, crime and civil liberties and human rights. Members also have expertise in a number of areas of civil law which impact on criminal defence, including civil actions against the police, environmental law and sports law.

**Who should apply** Chambers seeks pupils which share its values of professionalism, integrity and a strong commitment to providing the best possible defence for all. Chambers continues to welcome applicants with strong advocacy skills and experience.

**Pupillage programme** Pupils undergo an in-house advocacy training programme and a one-week placement with one of Chambers' solicitors. Each year Chambers organises additional experiences for pupils; in previous years these have included placements with the Crown Prosecution Service and prison visits.

Each year pupils submit an essay on a given topic for the Michael Jaffa Award; the winning entry receives £750.

**When and how to apply** OLPAS Summer Season to begin in the autumn of the following year. 25 Bedford Row is a member of the online pupillage application system (OLPAS) and will only accept applications for pupillage through this system.

**Mini-pupillages** Chambers provides mini pupillages during Easter and Summer of each year. Applications are accepted and considered in January of each year. Application is by CV and covering letter and should be addressed to Liam Pepper.

**Sponsorship/funding** Each pupil receives a grant of £9,000 during their first, non-practising, six months. During the second practising six months, pupils have a guaranteed income of £9,000.

| | |
|---|---|
| Pupillages funded | 4 |
| Tenants | 55 |
| Tenancies in last 3 yrs | 3 |
| Mini-pupillages | yes |
| Apply through OLPAS | |
| Remuneration for pupillage | £18,000 |

# 4 Brick Court

Chambers of Miss Janet Mitchell, Ground Floor, Temple, London EC4Y 9AD
**Tel:** 020 7832 3200
**Fax:** 020 7797 8929
**Email:** clerks@4bc.co.uk
**Web:** www.4bc.co.uk

**Description of Chambers** 4 Brick Court is recognised by its clients as a leading family law set.

**Areas of work** Chambers specialise in family, and to a much lesser degree, civil, immigration and criminal law. The family practitioners have considerable expertise in childcare law, with an emphasis on public and private work. Practitioners are also instructed in ancillary relief matters. The immigration team covers both Home Office and appellant work. The small amount of criminal work is principally for the defence. We also undertake general civil work. Chambers offers a friendly and supportive environment in which to do pupillage, as we believe our pupils are the future, and great emphasis is attached to their training.

**Who should apply** We encourage applications from those who wish to practice family law. We look for ambitious, intellectually able applicants with good communication skills. Applicants should have the minimum degree requirement of 2.1 together with a consistently good academic record. Applicants should either have or be awaiting the results of their BVC.

**Pupillage programme** During their pupillage, each pupil will have two supervisors. In addition they will assist other members in a number of matters in a variety of practice areas. Opportunities exist for pupils to become involved in interesting and high profile work. In their second six they will appear in court regularly developing their court room skills.

**When and how to apply** Chambers is a member of OLPAS and accepts applications in the year prior to entry. Apply for the OLPAS summer season 2008 (April/May deadline) to begin October 2009.

**Mini-pupillages** A limited number of mini-pupillage and student placements are available. Due to the limited number of places available not all applicants will be successful. Apply in writing to the Practice Manager for an application form. Chambers operates an equal opportunities policy.

**Sponsorship/funding** Chambers maintains a policy of gradual expansion. Chambers currently provides two funded pupillages of £12,000 per year each.

| | |
|---|---|
| Pupillages funded | 2 |
| Tenants | 37 |
| Tenancies in last 3 yrs | 6 |

Mini-pupillages       yes

Apply through OLPAS

Remuneration for pupillage
£12,000

Minimum qualifications
2.1 degree

## 36 BEDFORD ROW
36 Bedford Row, London WC1R 4JH
**Tel:** 020 7421 8000
**Fax:** 020 7421 8080
**Email:** clerks@36bedfordrow.co.uk
**Apply through OLPAS**

| | |
|---|---|
| PF | 2 |
| T | 78 |
| TL3Y | 5 |
| MP | yes |

## 29 BEDFORD ROW CHAMBERS
29 Bedford Row, London WC1R 4HE
**Tel:** 020 7404 1044
**Fax:** 020 7831 0626
**Email:** clerks@29bedfordrow.co.uk
**Apply through OLPAS**

A leading set of chambers specialising in matrimonial finance and family law.

| | |
|---|---|
| PF | 2 |
| T | 48 |
| TL3Y | 4 |
| MP | yes |

## 9-12 BELL YARD
9-12 Bell Yard, London WC2A 2JR
**Tel:** 020 7400 1800
**Fax:** 020 7400 1850
**Email:** clerks@bellyard.co.uk
**Apply through OLPAS**

Criminal defence and prosecution (inc CPS, HMCE, DTI, SFO); police disciplinary boards; work for Westminster City Council; and some other work.

| | |
|---|---|
| PF | 4 |
| T | 80 |
| TL3Y | 4 |
| MP | yes |

## BLACKSTONE CHAMBERS
Blackstone House, Temple, London EC4Y 9BW
**Tel:** 020 7583 1770
**Fax:** 020 7822 7350
**Email:** pupillage@blackstonechambers.com
**Apply through OLPAS**

Blackstone Chambers is known for its formidable strengths in commercial, public, employment and European law. It is rated as one of the Legal 500 and Chambers UK top barristers' chambers.

| | |
|---|---|
| PF | 4-5 |
| T | 71 |
| TL3Y | 6 |
| MP | yes |

## 1 BRICK COURT
Chambers of Andrew Caldecott QC, Temple, London EC4Y 9BY
**Tel:** 020 7353 8845
**Fax:** 020 7583 9144
**Email:** clerks@onebrickcourt.com
**Apply to:** Mr David Glen

One of two leading specialist sets in defamation, confidence and privacy law, reporting law and all media-related work including human rights law.

| | |
|---|---|
| PF | 2 |
| T | 20 |
| TL3Y | 2 |
| MP | yes |

## BRICK COURT CHAMBERS
7-8 Essex Street, London WC2R 3LD
**Tel:** 020 7379 3550
**Fax:** 020 7379 3558
**Email:** lyana.peniston@brickcourt.co.uk
**Apply through OLPAS**

Brick Court Chambers is a leading set of chambers with particular expertise in commercial, EU and public law. We normally offer four pupillage awards each year.

| | |
|---|---|
| PF | Normally 4 |
| T | 65 |
| TL3Y | 6 |
| MP | yes |

## BROADWAY HOUSE CHAMBERS
9 Bank Street, Bradford BD1 1TW
**Tel:** 01274 722560
**Fax:** 01274 370708
**Email:** clerks@broadwayhouse.co.uk
**Apply through OLPAS**

A progressive common law set of chambers in a dominant position within Bradford but servicing within the West Yorkshire conurbation

| | |
|---|---|
| PF | 1 |
| T | 38 |
| TL3Y | 3 |
| MP | yes |

## 18 CARLTON CRESCENT
Southampton SO15 2ET
**Tel:** 023 8063 9001
**Fax:** 023 8033 9625
**Email:** clerks@18carltoncrescent.co.uk
**Apply to:** Ms Sally Carter

A general common law set with specialist teams offering a high standard of advocacy in criminal, general civil, employment and family work. Two funded pupillages.

| | |
|---|---|
| PF | 2 |
| T | 24 |
| TL3Y | 3 |
| MP | yes |

**PF** = Pupillages funded / **T** = Tenants / **TL3Y** = Tenancies in last 3 years / **MP** = Mini pupillages offered

# Carmelite Chambers (Richard Ferguson QC)

9 Carmelite Street, London EC4Y 0DR
**Tel:** 020 7936 6300
**Fax:** 020 7936 6301
**Email:** clerks@carmelitechambers.co.uk
**Web:** www.carmelitechambers.co.uk

**Description of Chambers** Carmelite Chambers is well established as one of the leading sets specialising in criminal law. Members of Chambers defend at all levels in London, throughout England and Wales and overseas, and are experienced in advising parties from the commencement of the investigation, including issues arising from international judicial assistance.

**Areas of work** Members of Chambers have been instructed in most of the high profile cases in the last ten years including the current spate of terrorist cases and the Iraqi court martials. Chambers has considerable experience in high-profile cases involving murder, corporate manslaughter, terrorism, police corruption, drug trafficking, sexual offences and internet pornography, as well as those involving child witnesses, and has increasingly specialised in commercial fraud and international money laundering. Individual tenants also provide specialist expertise in associated fields including immigration, licensing, health and safety, and prison law.

**Who should apply** Chambers selects as pupils articulate and well-motivated individuals of high intellectual ability who can demonstrate sound judgement and a practical approach to problem solving. Candidates are expected to have a first-class or good second-class degree. But mere intellectual ability is only part of it: a successful candidate must have the confidence and ambition to succeed, the common sense to recognise the practical advice a client really needs, and an ability to get on well with clients, solicitors and other members of Chambers – and the clerks.

**Pupillage programme** Chambers normally offers five or six 12-month pupillages starting in October. The year is divided into two six-month periods (although pupils are assigned to a different pupil supervisor for each of the three months to ensure experience in different areas of crime). Chambers pays for the 'Advice to Counsel' course and runs its own weekly in-house advocacy training.

The set aims to give all pupils the knowledge, skills and practical experience they need for a successful career at the Bar. It believes that it is important for all pupils to see as much as possible of the different kinds of work in Chambers. This enables pupils to judge whether their work suits them, and allows different members of Chambers to assess the pupils. Each pupil therefore normally spends time with two or more pupil supervisors within any six-month period. If other members of Chambers have particularly interesting cases in court, pupils will be encouraged to work and attend court with them. All pupils work in their pupil supervisors' rooms, read their papers, attend their conferences and write draft opinions and accompany their pupil supervisors to court. Pupils are treated as part of the Chambers and are fully involved in the activities of Chambers while they are with Carmelite Chambers. Chambers operates a compulsory in-house advocacy course which pupils must pass before being permitted to practise in their second six months. Pupils can therefore expect to be well prepared for an exceptionally busy second six.

**When and how to apply** Apply through OLPAS.

**Sponsorship/funding** Twelve-month pupils will be sponsored through a combination of an award scheme, guaranteed earnings and additional earnings. No clerks' fees or deductions are taken from earnings.

| | |
|---|---|
| Pupillages funded | 2-3 |
| Tenants | 63 |
| Tenancies in last 3 yrs | 5 |
| Mini-pupillages | yes |
| Apply through OLPAS | |
| Remuneration for pupillage | |
| Award and guaranteed earnings | |
| Minimum qualifications | |
| 2.1 degree | |

# Crown Office Chambers

2 Crown Office Row, Temple, London EC4Y 7HJ
**Tel:** 020 7797 8100
**Fax:** 020 7797 8101
**Email:** clerks@crownofficechambers.com
**Web:** www.crownofficechambers.com

**Description of Chambers** Crown Office Chambers is one of the foremost sets of chambers specialising in civil common law work. Formed by the merger of One Paper Buildings and Two Crown Office Row, both long-established sets with many leading and highly regarded practitioners, we are now a set of 79 members, including 13 silks. We have high-calibre teams of counsel in a number of areas of work, ranging from county court disputes to large and complex litigation, and have state-of-the-art facilities.

**Areas of work** A wide range of common law and commercial work, with particular specialisms in construction, commercial contracts, insurance and reinsurance, personal injury, health and safety, product liability, professional negligence and clinical negligence.

**Who should apply** The members of Crown Office Chambers pride themselves on their professionalism, an astute and business-orientated awareness of the practical needs of solicitors and clients, combined with an approachable and 'unstuffy' attitude to their work. We look for the same in our pupils, all of whom are regarded as having strong tenancy potential. Pupils are welcomed as an integral part of Chambers from the moment they arrive, and are expected to display the motivation, dedication and intelligence which are the hallmarks of a first-class barrister. Academically, we look for a first or upper second-class honours degree (not necessarily in law), and a flair for the oral and written presentation of complex legal arguments. You will be expected to work hard and to show strong commitment to your work, but in a friendly and relaxed Chambers environment.

**Pupillage programme** Pupils sit with two pupil supervisors in their first six months, and one in their second, but are likely to work with a number of different members of Chambers practising in different fields of work over the course of the year. They appear in court regularly during their second six, generally handling applications and small trials in the county courts, affording ample opportunity to develop advocacy skills. Chambers also organises a series of advocacy training sessions.

**When and how to apply** Apply by 30 April 2008 to begin October 2009 on Chambers' application form, downloadable from the Chambers website at www.crownofficechambers.com.

**Mini-pupillages** Mini-pupillages are available throughout the year – contact the mini-pupillage administrator enclosing a copy of your CV.

**Sponsorship/funding** Up to four pupillages offered per year, each with an award of £35,000, part of which may be forwarded during the BVC year.

| | |
|---|---|
| Pupillages funded | 4 |
| Tenants | 79 |
| Tenancies in last 3 yrs | 7 |
| Mini-pupillages | yes |
| Apply via website | |
| Remuneration for pupillage | |
| £35,000 | |
| Minimum qualifications | |
| 2.1 degree (not necessarily in law) | |

**25-27 CASTLE STREET**
Liverpool L2 4TA
**Tel:** 0151 227 5661
**Fax:** 0151 236 4054
**Email:** mail@25castlestreet.co.uk
**Apply through OLPAS**

| | |
|---|---|
| PF | 1 |
| T | 29 |
| TL3Y | 4 |
| MP | no |

---

**1 CHANCERY LANE**
1 Chancery Lane, London WC2A 1LF
**Tel:** 0845 634 66 66
**Fax:** 0845 634 66 67
**Email:** jfensham@1chancerylane.com
@1chancerylane.com
**Apply to:** Ms Jenny Fensham

Comprehensive professional negligence practice offering pupils opportunity to develop wide-ranging litigation skills and work as part of a team. Also PI, property, travel.

| | |
|---|---|
| PF | 2 |
| T | 37 |
| TL3Y | 2 |
| MP | yes |

---

**CHARTER CHAMBERS**
Two Dr Johnson's Buildings, Temple, London EC4Y 7AY
**Tel:** 020 7618 4400
**Fax:** 020 7618 4401
**Email:** clerks@charterchambers.com
**Apply through OLPAS**

Work: mainly criminal (prosecution and defence), public, prison law, immigration, family, employment. Second six pupils conduct a substantial amount of work in their own right.

| | |
|---|---|
| PF | 3 |
| T | 60 |
| TL3Y | 8 |
| MP | yes |

---

**CHARTLANDS CHAMBERS**
3 St Giles Terrace, Northampton NN1 2BN
**Tel:** 01604 603322
**Fax:** 01604 603388
**Email:** chartlands.chambers@btopenworld.com
**Apply to:** Mr Matthew Robinson

Common law chambers. Principal field: family law. Also: immigration, general civil litigation.

| | |
|---|---|
| PF | 1 |
| T | 13 |
| TL3Y | 1 |
| MP | yes |

---

**CHAVASSE COURT CHAMBERS**
18 Queen Avenue, Liverpool L2 4TX
**Tel:** 0151 229 2030
**Fax:** 0151 229 2039
**Apply to:** The Pupillage Committee

Established and well respected set. Crime and family at all levels.

| | |
|---|---|
| PF | 1 |
| T | 34 |
| TL3Y | 7 |
| MP | yes |

---

**CITADEL CHAMBERS**
190 Corporation Street, Birmingham B4 6QD
**Tel:** 0121 233 85 00
**Fax:** 0121 233 8501
**Apply to:** Mr Timothy Hannam

Chambers is a large criminal set. Chambers also undertakes work in the spheres of licensing, family, common law, employment and landlord & tenant.

| | |
|---|---|
| PF | 0 |
| T | 49 |
| TL3Y | 3 |
| MP | yes |

---

**CLARENDON CHAMBERS**
1 Plowden Buildings, Temple, London EC4Y 9BU
**Tel:** 020 7353 0003
**Fax:** 020 7353 9213
**Email:** clerks@clarendonchambers.com
**Apply to:** The Pupillage Committee

Chambers has not yet decided its pupillage policy for 2007.

| | |
|---|---|
| PF | 1 |
| T | 37 |
| TL3Y | 6 |
| MP | no |

---

**CLOISTERS**
First Floor, 1 Pump Court, Temple, London EC4Y 7AA
**Tel:** 020 7827 4000
**Fax:** 020 7827 4100
**Email:** pupillage@cloisters.com
**Apply through OLPAS**

Informal, award-winning Chambers at the cutting edge of employment, PI, clinical negligence, human rights, public law, commercial, media and sports law.

| | |
|---|---|
| PF | 2 |
| T | 43 |
| TL3Y | 4 |
| MP | yes |

---

**PF** = Pupillages funded / **T** = Tenants / **TL3Y** = Tenancies in last 3 years / **MP** = Mini pupillages offered

# One Crown Office Row

Temple, London EC4Y 7HH
**Tel:** 020 7797 7500
**Fax:** 020 7797 5550
**Email:** mail@1cor.com
**Web:** www.1cor.com

**Description of Chambers** This is a long-established and leading civil set of 56 members including 16 silks. It counts among its members and former members the fomer lord chief justice, Lord Woolf, four lords justices of appeal, 10 High Court judges and three former chairmen of the Bar.

**Areas of work** The set has particular strengths in clinical and professional negligence, environmental and public law and human rights (it runs the unique and well-received free update service at www.humanrights.org.uk which has over 800 commentaries on human rights cases). The *Chambers & Partners* directory describes the set's clinical negligence practice as follows: 'This "fantastic set of chambers" contains, without doubt, many of the "leaders in the field". It continues to dominate the market through its contingent of experienced silks and juniors and can handle with ease both claimant and defendant work'. It also has in-depth expertise in public inquiries, disciplinary tribunals, personal injury, professional negligence, medical and specialist crime, matrimonial finance, employment, VAT, costs and sports law.

**Who should apply** Chambers looks to recruit lawyers who have a keen interest in the areas of work in which members practise. Academic prowess is important, with a normal requirement of a first or upper second class degree. A sound grounding in legal principle is expected. Chambers retains a strong reputation for the advocacy skills of its members and demonstration of an aptitude for advocacy is helpful to an applicant's chances. This may be shown in a number of ways, for instance mooting, debating and work in the voluntary legal services sector. We recognise that work at the Bar demands high levels of commitment and look for signs that applicants have that quality by examining, for example, whether they have done mini-pupillages or in some other way established that the Bar, with all its challenges and hurdles, is for them. Chambers does not, however, discriminate between those with first degrees in law and those who have converted to law after their first degree.

**Pupillage programme** We offer up to two 12-month pupillages. Each pupillage is split between at least two pupil supervisors. Pupils can expect to gain a wide experience of court and paperwork and have opportunities to help and accompany other members of Chambers (including silks) on interesting cases.

**When and how to apply** Chambers is a member of the centralised pupillage application system, OLPAS, and recruits through its summer season – all details are at www.pupillages.com. Full details of the selection process are at www.1cor.com.

**Mini-pupillages** We offer places for 14 mini-pupils during June and July each year with applications closing at the end of February. Applications should be addressed to Mr Owain Thomas. Travel and other expenses will be reimbursed to mini-pupils up to a maximum of £150 per week.

**Sponsorship/funding** Each pupil receives an annual award of £37,500 paid as a £18,750 grant in the first six months and as £18,750 of guaranteed earnings in the second six. We also fund all necessary training courses for pupils. Pupils may draw down up to 20% of the award in advance to assist in funding their Bar Vocational Course.

| | |
|---|---|
| Pupillages funded | 2 |
| Tenants | 56 |
| Tenancies in last 3 yrs | 8 |
| Mini-pupillages | yes |
| Apply to | Mr William Edis |
| Remuneration for pupillage | £37,500 |
| Minimum qualifications | 2.1 degree |

Community
Legal Service

# Crown Prosecution Service

Enquiries: legal.trainees@cps.gsi.gov.uk
**Tel:** 01904 545621
**Fax:** 01904 545560
**Web:** www.cps.gov.uk

**Description of organisation** The Crown Prosecution Service is the Government Department responsible for prosecuting people in England and Wales who have been charged with a criminal offence. We employ approximately 9,000 staff throughout the country including caseworkers & administrators and around 3,000 lawyers, of which 750 are barristers.

**Areas of work** As the principal prosecuting authority in England and Wales, we are responsible for advising the police on cases for prosecution, making the charging decision, preparing cases for court and presenting them in court. We handle over 1.3 million magistrates' court cases and 115,000 Crown court cases every year. Our work includes advice to the police, legal research, attendance at hearings in the Magistrates' and Crown Courts, case preparation and management and liaison with victims and witnesses.

**Who should apply** The CPS is an equal opportunities employer. Our policies including the need to guard against false assumptions based on sex or marital status, gender reassignment, sexual orientation, colour, race, religion, ethnic or national origin, work pattern, age or disability, are followed at all stages of the recruitment and selection procedure. We are also a Disability Symbol user – all those with a disability who satisfy the minimum criteria for advertised vacancies will be invited for interview.

Many of our pupils do not come through the 'traditional' route but have worked and studied part-time over many years – often after having left school with minimal qualifications. We do not take account of academic qualifications. Minimum entry criteria will be specified for each advertised post.

**Pupillage programme** Pupils are assigned to an individual trained supervisor who is an experienced crown prosecutor and is responsible for the pupil's daily work and personal development. Induction is tailored to the needs of the individual. Further learning and development opportunities are provided as required.

Training is provided in criminal litigation. Pupils work under supervision, handling all cases, from straightforward summary pleas to trials and appeals. We recommend that pupils spend at least a month in chambers during the first six. This is negotiated locally as appropriate. Pupils are appraised every six months and after secondment, depending on the length of the secondment.

**When and how to apply** Opportunities in local offices are advertised when available. These will generally be for immediate start and applicants will need to have BVC results. We also advertise national pupillages. The application procedure is set out in the advertisements but will usually comprise an application form, a written or oral exercise and an assessment centre or interview.

We do not accept speculative applications.

**Sponsorship/funding** At present the Law Scholarship Scheme, which provides sponsorship for the academic stages including law degree, GDL and BVC is available to internal applicants only.

Pupillages funded  15-20
(variable)
Total staff  9000

Mini-pupillages  yes

Applications contact
see details in
advertisements

Remuneration for pupillage
£18,425 (national)
£19,441 (London)
Pay award pending

Minimum qualifications
BVC

## COLLEGE CHAMBERS
19 Carlton Crescent, Southampton SO15 2ET
**Tel:** 023 8023 0338
**Fax:** 023 8023 0376
**Email:** clerks@college-chambers.co.uk
**Apply to:** Mr Gary Self

Rapidly expanding set of chambers with wide work base. Emphasis on all forms of civil litigation.

| | |
|---|---|
| PF | 1 |
| T | 22 |
| TL3Y | 8 |
| MP | yes |

## 12 COLLEGE PLACE
Southampton SO15 2FE
**Tel:** 023 8032 0320
**Fax:** 023 8032 0321
**Email:** clerks@12cp.co.uk
**Apply to:** The Pupillage Secretary

A medium-sized, multi-disciplinary set which prides itself on being friendly and approachable. Chambers has a reputation for providing a high quality, client-focussed service.

| | |
|---|---|
| PF | 2 |
| T | 42 |
| TL3Y | 5 |
| MP | yes |

## CORAM CHAMBERS
9-11 Fulwood Place, London WC1V 6HG
**Tel:** 020 7092 3700
**Fax:** 020 7092 3701
**Email:** mail@coramchambers.co.uk
**Apply through OLPAS**

Chambers is a family law set committed to the principle and implementation of equal opportunities and to the promotion of pro bono and human rights work.

| | |
|---|---|
| PF | 3 |
| T | 54 |
| TL3Y | 4 |
| MP | yes |

## CORNWALL STREET CHAMBERS
85-87 Cornwall Street, Birmingham B3 3BY
**Tel:** 0121 233 7500
**Fax:** 0121 233 7501
**Email:** clerks@cornwallstreet.co.uk
**Apply to:** Miss Laura Kasasian

Principally crime, family and common law but with specialists in other fields. Pupils gain wide experience in 1st six and enjoy regular work thereafter.

| | |
|---|---|
| PF | 1 |
| T | 48 |
| TL3Y | 6 |
| MP | no |

## CROWN OFFICE ROW CHAMBERS
Blenheim House, 119 Church Street,
Brighton BN1 1WH
**Tel:** 01273 625625
**Fax:** 01273 698888
**Email:** clerks@1cor.com
**Apply through OLPAS**

A long-established, busy set committed to expansion in Sussex. Up to 2 12 month pupillages available each year.

| | |
|---|---|
| PF | 2 |
| T | 34 |
| TL3Y | 8 |
| MP | yes |

## DEANS COURT CHAMBERS
24 St John Street, Manchester M3 4DF
**Tel:** 0161 214 6000
**Fax:** 0161 214 6001
**Email:** clerks@deanscourt.co.uk
**Apply through OLPAS**

A leading set of chambers on the Northern Circuit. 11 silks. Excellent facilities. Well funded pupillages with a view to a tenancy.

| | |
|---|---|
| PF | 2 |
| T | 75 |
| TL3Y | 7 |
| MP | yes |

## DEVEREUX CHAMBERS
Devereux Court, London WC2R 3JH
**Tel:** 020 7353 7534
**Fax:** 0870 622 0045
**Email:** mailbox@devchambers.co.uk
**Apply through OLPAS**

A substantial set with particular strengths in the fields of employment, insurance/reinsurance, commercial and personal injury/clinical negligence. We seek intelligence, enthusiasm, stamina and a sense of humour.

| | |
|---|---|
| PF | 2 |
| T | 42 |
| TL3Y | - |
| MP | yes |

## DOUGHTY STREET CHAMBERS
10-11 Doughty Street, London WC1N 2PG
**Tel:** 020 7404 1313
**Fax:** 020 7404 2283
**Email:** enquiries@doughtystreet.co.uk
**Apply through OLPAS**

While at the forefront of many cutting-edge domestic and international human rights cases, we operate across a whole range of different areas of law.

| | |
|---|---|
| PF | 5 |
| T | 90 |
| TL3Y | 9 |
| MP | yes |

---

**PF** = Pupillages funded / **T** = Tenants / **TL3Y** = Tenancies in last 3 years / **MP** = Mini pupillages offered

# Erskine Chambers

33 Chancery Lane, London WC2A 1EN
**Tel:** 020 7242 5532
**Fax:** 020 7831 0125
**Email:** clerks@erskine-chambers.co.uk
**Web:** www.erskine-chambers.co.uk

**Description of Chambers** Erskine Chambers is widely recognised as the leading specialist company law set and undertakes litigation and advisory work in all areas in which company law arises.

**Areas of work** Company and related commercial law, including, in particular, shareholder disputes, corporate insolvencies, directors' duties, takeovers, corporate reconstructions, loan capital and banking securities, financial services, accounting and auditing, professional negligence and corporate fraud.

**Who should apply** Intellectually able students, ordinarily with a first or upper second-class degree and preferably some knowledge or experience of company law.

**Pupillage programme** Each pupil will spend three months with one pupil supervisor before moving to another pupil supervisor. Increasingly they will begin to work for other members of Chambers. There are opportunities throughout for pupils to become involved in particularly interesting or high-profile work being done by members of Chambers.

**When and how to apply** By 30 April 2008 to begin in 2009 or for deferred pupillage in 2010/11. Apply on Chambers' standard application form available from the above address.

**Mini-pupillages** Available throughout the year.

**Sponsorship/funding** Up to two awards of up to £40,000 may be made each year in respect of the 12-month pupillage period.

| | |
|---|---|
| Pupillages funded | up to 2 |
| Tenants | 23 |
| Tenancies in last 3 yrs | 2 |

Mini-pupillages                yes

**Applications contact**
Mr Stephen Horan

**Remuneration for pupillage**
Up to £40,000 for the 12-month period

**Minimum qualifications**
2.1 degree (ordinarily)

| | | |
|---|---|---|
| **2 DR JOHNSON'S BUILDINGS**<br>Temple, London EC4Y 7AY<br>**Tel:** 020 7936 2613<br>**Fax:** 020 7353 9439<br>**Email:** clerks@2drj.com<br>**Apply to:** Mr Silas Reid | A medium-sized busy and friendly set. 70% crime, 30% family and civil. Up to four funded 12 month pupillages. | PF Up to 4<br>T 36<br>TL3Y 8<br>MP yes |
| **2 DYER'S BUILDINGS**<br>Holborn, London EC1N 2JT<br>**Tel:** 020 7404 1881<br>**Fax:** 020 7404 1991<br>**Email:** pupillage@2dyersbuildings.com<br>**Apply through OLPAS** | Pupils are trained by experienced supervisors in all areas of criminal law, practice and procedure in this busy criminal set with many specialisations. | PF 1<br>T 41<br>TL3Y 6<br>MP yes |
| **EAST ANGLIAN CHAMBERS**<br>5 Museum Street, Ipswich IP1 1HQ<br>**Tel:** 01473 346120<br>**Fax:** 01473 346123<br>**Email:** cbull@ealaw.co.uk<br>**Apply to:** Carol Bull | East Anglian Chambers is now based at four sites, Ipswich, Colchester, Norwich and Chelmsford, and offers a wide range of opportunities | PF 4<br>T 63<br>TL3Y 9<br>MP yes |
| **EASTBOURNE CHAMBERS**<br>5 Chiswick Place, Eastbourne BN21 4NH<br>**Tel:** 01323 642102<br>**Fax:** 01323 641402<br>**Apply to:** Miss Rebecca Upton | Small criminal and general common law set. | PF 1<br>T 13<br>TL3Y 0<br>MP yes |
| **ELY PLACE CHAMBERS**<br>30 Ely Place, London EC1N 6TD<br>**Tel:** 020 7400 9600<br>**Fax:** 020 7400 9630<br>**Email:** admin@elyplace.com<br>**Apply to:** Mr Scott Pearman | We advise on contractual, tortious and property disputes including defamation, employment and civil police actions. Pupils can expect a friendly, supportive environment with broad exposure to civil work. | PF 2<br>T 27<br>TL3Y 4<br>MP yes |
| **ENTERPRISE CHAMBERS**<br>9 Old Square, Lincoln's Inn, London WC2A 3SR<br>**Tel:** 020 7405 9471<br>**Fax:** 020 7242 1447<br>**Email:** london@dial.pipex.com<br>**Apply through OLPAS** | Enterprise Chambers is a progressive set specialising in modern commercial chancery litigation. In addition to London, it has thriving annexes in Leeds and Newcastle. | PF 1<br>T 34<br>TL3Y 4<br>MP yes |
| **ONE ESSEX COURT**<br>Ground Floor, Temple, London EC4Y 9AR<br>**Tel:** 020 7583 2000<br>**Fax:** 020 7583 0118<br>**Email:** clerks@oeclaw.co.uk<br>**Apply through OLPAS** | Applications for pupillage must be made through OLPAS except where an applicant is exempt under the OLPAS rules. For mini-pupillages, contact Miss Sally Brown (sbrown@oeclaw.co.uk). | PF 4<br>T 60<br>TL3Y 9<br>MP yes |
| **5 ESSEX COURT**<br>5 Essex Court, Temple, London EC4Y 9AH<br>**Tel:** 020 7410 2000<br>**Fax:** 020 7410 2010<br>**Email:** barristers@5essexcourt.co.uk<br>**Apply through OLPAS** | Among the leading police civil law sets in the country. Members of chambers specialise in personal injury, employment and public law. | PF 1<br>T 30<br>TL3Y 4<br>MP yes |

**PF** = Pupillages funded / **T** = Tenants / **TL3Y** = Tenancies in last 3 years / **MP** = Mini pupillages offered

# 23 Essex Street

London WC2R 3AA
**Tel:** 020 7413 0353
**Fax:** 020 7413 0374
**Email:** clerks@23ES.com
**Web:** www.23ES.com

**Description of Chambers** 23 Essex Street is ranked as one of the leading sets of Chambers specialising in criminal law, with 75 tenants including 11 silks.

**Areas of work** Our expertise covers all areas of the criminal law and all members of Chambers appear regularly, prosecuting and defending, at all levels in all of the main court centres of London and the South-East circuit. Members of Chambers have appeared in many of the major criminal trials in recent years. In addition, we are particularly strong in our conduct of IP crime, commercial frauds and white collar crime, and we have a thriving practice in related areas of regulatory work, with members of Chambers conducting cases for and before such bodies as the General Medical Council, Lloyds, the FSA, the Environment Agency and the CAA. We also undertake public inquiries, professional disciplinary tribunals, extradition, licensing, coroners' courts and courts martial.

**Who should apply** Applicants should be able to demonstrate that their intellectual ability is matched by their flair for advocacy, their presentation and communication skills and their originality of thought. We encourage applications from those who have engaged in mooting and debating, and those who have worked for the FRU.

**Pupillage programme** We offer three structured 12-month pupillages each year. We have prepared and published on our website a detailed document setting out our policy on the selection of pupils, including details of our pre-interview selection criteria, interview procedure, organisation of pupillage itself and the criteria and procedure for the selection of junior tenants.

**When and how to apply** Chambers is a member of OLPAS and we recruit exclusively through the summer season.

**Mini-pupillages** Non–assessed mini-pupillages are available between June and August (inclusive). Each mini-pupil will be assigned to a junior member of Chambers for the week and must expect to travel to courts in London and throughout the Southeast.

Please apply in writing, enclosing a CV, to Daniel Fugallo on or after 1 April 2008.

**Sponsorship/funding** We offer three 12-month pupillages each year, all funded at £22,000 pa (comprising £12,000 payable monthly in advance over six months plus a guaranteed minimum second six months' earnings of £10,000).

Sponsored students are accepted.

| | |
|---|---|
| Pupillages funded | 3 |
| Tenants | 75 |
| Tenancies in last 3 yrs | 5 |
| Mini-pupillages | yes |
| Apply through OLPAS | |
| Remuneration for pupillage | £22,000 |

23 essex street

# 39 Essex Street

London WC2R 3AT
**Tel:** 020 7832 1111
**Fax:** 020 7353 3978
**Email:** clerks@39essex.com
**Web:** www.39essex.com

**Description of Chambers** 39 Essex Street is a long-established civil set. We currently have 76 members, including 23 QCs. Chambers has several members on each of the attorney general's A, B and C panels for civil litigation. Chambers prides itself on its friendly and professional atmosphere. Chambers is fully networked and our clerking and administrative services are of a high standard. We work very hard. But we also have extensive social, sporting and professional development activities.

**Areas of work** Commercial and construction law: construction and engineering; general commercial; insurance and reinsurance; employment; media, entertainment and sports.

Administrative and public law: all aspects of judicial review; local government; mental health and community care; environmental and planning; human rights; European Union regulation.

Common law: personal injury; clinical negligence; professional negligence; product liability; health and safety; toxic torts.

**Pupillage programme** We take up to three 12-month pupils a year. During the pupillage year, each pupil will be rotated among four pupil supervisors, covering a broad range of Chambers' work. The pupils will also do a number of assessed pieces of written work for other members of Chambers. There is also an in-house advocacy course. Pupils work only 9:00 to 18:00 Monday to Friday.

**When and how to apply** Chambers is a member of OLPAS. Applicants should consult the OLPAS timetable.

**Mini-pupillages** Mini-pupillage is an important part of our selection process. We urge anyone who wishes to apply for pupillage at 39 Essex Street to apply to us for mini-pupillage. Due to the limited number of places available, not all mini-pupillage applicants will be successful. Applicants should be in their final year before undertaking the BVC, save in exceptional circumstances. Applications are made between 1 September and 30 November. Selection takes place between 1 December and 14 December. The deadline for acceptance of offers is mid-January. Mini-pupillages take place from mid-January until July.

**Sponsorship/funding** Each 12-month pupillage comes with an award, £40,000 for 2008-09. Of this, up to £8,000 may be drawn down during the year before pupillage commences. Awards and offers are all conditional on passing the BVC. Junior tenants receive an interest-free loan of £30,000, which is repaid out of earnings during the first 12 months.

| | |
|---|---|
| Pupillages funded | 3 |
| Tenants | 76 |
| Tenancies in last 3 yrs | 6 |
| Mini-pupillages | yes |
| Apply through OLPAS | |
| Remuneration for pupillage | |
| £40,000 (2008-09) | |
| Minimum qualifications | |
| 2.1 degree | |

# Exchange Chambers

Pearl Assurance House, Derby Square, Liverpool L2 9XX
**Tel:** 0845 300 7747
**Fax:** 0151 236 3433
**Email:** info@exchangechambers.co.uk
**Web:** www.exchangechambers.co.uk

**Description of Chambers** Exchange Chambers is a leading set with offices in both Manchester and Liverpool. Chambers comprises 100 tenants including 13 silks. A flexible team-based structure is in place, ensuring that specialists are available in all areas of law. Members are instructed by solicitors across England and Wales. A mediation service and fully accredited training for solicitors are part of our service.

**Areas of work** All types of personal injury claims are dealt with including catastrophic injury to brain and spine and clinical negligence. The commercial and Chancery team deals in company, commercial, insolvency, real property as well as trusts, wills and tax. Specialist areas also include intellectual property, shipping, employment, human rights, insurance, European law, tax/VAT and pensions. The criminal department undertakes a balance of prosecution and defence work. HM Revenue & Customs, DTI, DWP and the Health and Safety Executive instruct it. The team also specialises in fraud work including that under the Proceeds of Crime Act. The family team practises in all areas of family law but particularly in large ancillary relief cases.

**Who should apply** A successful candidate is likely to have a fine intellect, a capacity for sustained hard work under pressure, integrity, sound judgement, an ability to relate appropriately to the very widest cross-section of the population, clarity of thought, confidence, enthusiasm and broadness of mind. We encourage all applications regardless of age, sex, race, religion, marital status, sexual orientation, ethnic origin, disability and social background. While we take into account A levels, we believe more recent evidence of academic achievement is of greater significance. We accept that class of degree alone should not be regarded as an infallible indicator of likely success in practice. We are always prepared to consider a range of intellectual ability criteria when we assess the potential of candidates.

**Pupillage programme** Normally two funded pupillages are offered annually. Throughout the 12-month pupillage a main pupil supervisor is in place together with several sub-pupil supervisors who offer guidance in the main practice areas. Regular reviews and feedback sessions are undertaken and are seen as an essential part of pupillage. Pupillages are generally offered with a view to tenancy.

**When and how to apply** For applications for pupillage commencing in autumn 2008 Chambers' application form is to be found on our website at www.exchangechambers.co.uk.

**Mini-pupillages** Chambers encourages applications for mini-pupillage and this is regarded as a helpful way of seeing prospective applicants for pupillage. Applications for mini-pupillage can be made by letter and CV, sent to Chambers and marked "Mini-pupillage". We try to give mini-pupils an idea of all the areas of work covered by Chambers during the period of the mini-pupillage.

**Sponsorship/funding** Chambers surpasses the Bar Council's funding requirements and offers provision for the period after the completion of pupillage with a guarantee that each pupil who is granted a tenancy total receipts of £75,000 net of VAT by way of interest-free loan during the first two years of practice. We hope that the receipts of most tenants will exceed this sum.

| | |
|---|---|
| Pupillages funded | 1–2 |
| Tenants | 100 |
| Tenancies in last 3 yrs | 12 |
| Mini-pupillages | yes |

**Apply**
On Chambers' website

**Minimum qualifications**
2.1 degree (except in exceptional circumstances)

**Locations**
Liverpool and Manchester

| | | |
|---|---|---|
| **ESSEX COURT CHAMBERS**<br>24 Lincoln's Inn Fields, London WC2A 3EG<br>**Tel:** 020 7813 8000<br>**Fax:** 020 7813 8080<br>**Email:** clerksroom@essexcourt.net<br>**Apply through OLPAS** | We are a leading set of commercial barristers advising on international and domestic commercial law, and appearing as counsel in litigation and commercial arbitration worldwide. | PF  4<br>T  73<br>TL3Y 5<br>MP yes |
| **20 ESSEX STREET**<br>20 Essex Street, London WC2R 3AL<br>**Tel:** 020 7842 1200<br>**Fax:** 020 7842 1270<br>**Email:** pupillage@20essexst.com<br>**Apply through OLPAS** | 20 Essex Street specialises in commercial, EU and public international law and was Chambers & Partners' Commercial Chambers of the Year 2005. | PF  Up to 4<br>T  45<br>TL3Y 5<br>MP yes |
| **FALCON CHAMBERS**<br>Falcon Court, London EC4Y 1AA<br>**Tel:** 020 7353 2484<br>**Fax:** 020 7353 1261<br>**Email:** pupillage@falcon-chambers.com | At Falcon Chambers, we specialise in all aspects of real property. Up to two funded pupillages (6 or 12 months) are available each year. | PF  2<br>T  35<br>TL3Y 4<br>MP yes |
| **FENNERS CHAMBERS**<br>3 Madingley Road, Cambridge CB3 OEE<br>**Tel:** 01223 368761<br>**Fax:** 01223 313007<br>**Email:** clerks@fennerschambers.co.uk<br>**Apply through OLPAS** | We cover almost every area of work but aim for longer term specialisation. We take a maximum of two pupils annually to ensure good training. | PF  1-2<br>T  40<br>TL3Y 3<br>MP yes |
| **FIELD COURT CHAMBERS**<br>5 Field Court, Gray's Inn, London WC1R 5EF<br>**Tel:** 020 7405 6114<br>**Fax:** 020 7831 6112<br>**Email:** clerks@fieldcourt.co.uk<br>**Apply to:** Mr Adrian Davis | Formed from the merger of two established sets, 2 Field Court and 17 Bedford Row, these chambers cover a wide range of civil, family and public law work. | PF  2<br>T  47<br>TL3Y 5<br>MP yes |
| **187 FLEET STREET**<br>London EC4A 2AT<br>**Tel:** 020 7430 7430<br>**Fax:** 020 7430 7431<br>**Apply through OLPAS** | A high-profile, long-established chambers whose members defend and prosecute for all agencies in each area of the criminal law (especially serious crime and corporate fraud). | PF  3<br>T  51<br>TL3Y 8<br>MP yes |
| **FOUNTAIN CHAMBERS**<br>Cleveland Business Centre, 1 Watson Street,<br>Middlesbrough TS1 2RQ<br>**Tel:** 01642 804040<br>**Fax:** 01642 804060<br>**Email:** clerks@fountainchambers.co.uk<br>**Apply to:** Mr Harvey Murray | Fountain Chambers is well-established in Teesside & provides an excellent service in the areas of criminal, family and common law work. One 12-month pupillage offered annually. | PF  1<br>T  30<br>TL3Y 11<br>MP yes |
| **8 FOUNTAIN COURT**<br>Steelhouse Lane, Birmingham B4 6DR<br>**Tel:** 0121 236 5514<br>**Fax:** 0121 236 8225<br>**Email:** clerks@no8chambers.co.uk<br>**Apply to:** The Pupillage Committee | We are a mixed common law set covering criminal, family and all types of civil work including some chancery. Currently one pupillage annually. | PF  2<br>T  26<br>TL3Y 3<br>MP yes |

**PF** = Pupillages funded / **T** = Tenants / **TL3Y** = Tenancies in last 3 years / **MP** = Mini pupillages offered

# Farrar's Building

Temple, London EC4Y 7BD
**Tel:** 020 7583 9241
**Fax:** 020 7583 0090
**Email:** chambers@farrarsbuilding.co.uk
**Web:** www.farrarsbuilding.co.uk

**Description of Chambers** Farrar's Building is a long-established set with an excellent reputation for providing high-quality service for claimants and defendants in a wide range of work. Members appear in courts and tribunals in all parts of the UK. Chambers retains strong links with Wales, with a number of silks practicing predominantly on that circuit. We have strong connections and draw significant amounts of work from the Northern and North-eastern Circuits. We are a friendly and reliable set. Experience is shared in informal practice groups. We pride ourselves on the way we are efficiently clerked and administered by an experienced and long-established team.

**Areas of work** Farrar's Building is a specialist set with particular expertise in five main areas of practice: personal injury; employment; serious and white collar crime; health & safety; and inquiries & disciplinary tribunals. Members of Chambers have appeared in many of the leading cases in these fields and are recommended in *Chambers & Partners*, and *Legal 500*. Over the last 20 years, Chambers has gained an excellent reputation from our involvement in many of the high-profile public inquiries, including those into the King's Cross fire, North Wales Child Abuse, the Paddington, Ladbroke Grove and Hatfield rail crash inquiries and 'Bloody Sunday'.

**Who should apply** Candidates must be able to demonstrate a high level of intellectual ability, advocacy in debates or moots, ethical awareness and a commitment to pursuing a career at the Bar. We are looking for dedicated people, who are ready for the hard work and responsibility of practice, to maintain Chambers as a dominant force. Members of chambers have many and varied outside interests and we welcome applications from candidates who can demonstrate interests and pursuits outside of the law.

**Pupillage programme** We offer two 12-month pupillages, organised in three four-month periods with pupil supervisors whose practices focus on different areas of specialisation. The pupil supervisor for the 'middle' four months will focus on preparing pupils for taking their own caseload and supporting them when it arrives. We provide pupils with a networked computer and access to online law reports, email and word processing facilities. We fund pupils' attendance at the Bar Conference and circuit advocacy courses. In recent years many pupils have attended an Advanced Civil Advocacy course in Florida.

**When and how to apply** Apply through OLPAS for the 2009 summer session.

**Mini-pupillages** Farrar's Building offers three days work experience at certain time of the year to suitably qualified students (18+). Please apply in the time specified on the website by sending an application (with CV) to tbarton@farrarsbuilding.co.uk.

**Sponsorship/funding** Each 12-month pupillage currently comes with an award of £20,000, £5,000 of which can be drawn down the year before pupillage. Unlike many other sets, Chambers wishes pupils to have the incentive of receiving earnings from their own work in the second six months. In previous years, diligent pupils have earned between £10,000 and £15,000. Awards and offers are all conditional on passing the BVC.

| | |
|---|---|
| Pupillages funded | 2 |
| Tenants | 44 |
| Tenancies in last 3 yrs | 5 |
| Mini-pupillages | yes |
| Apply through OLPAS | |

**Remuneration for pupillage**
£20,000 plus second six earnings (recent pupils achieving c. £10,000)

**Minimum qualifications**
2.1 degree

# Francis Taylor Building

Francis Taylor Building, Inner Temple, London EC4Y 7BY
**Tel:** 020 7353 8415
**Fax:** 020 7353 7622
**Email:** clerks@ftb.eu.com
**Web:** www.ftb.eu.com

**Description of Chambers** Francis Taylor Building (formerly at 2 Harcourt Buildings) is a long-established and leading set of public law chambers, specialising in planning, environmental, licensing, administrative and parliamentary work; all increasingly influenced by EC law and the European Convention of Human Rights. Members of Chambers undertake specialist advisory work and appear regularly at planning inquiries, the High Court, the Court of Appeal, the House of Lords, the Lands Tribunal and sometimes before Select Committee in Parliament. They also appear at the ECJ. From the Head of Chambers to the most junior tenant, the workload is wide and varied. There are 14 Queen's Counsel in Chambers and most junior tenants find themselves working on cases as junior to a silk on a fairly regular basis.

**Areas of work** Planning; environmental; public; administrative; local government; transport and works orders; highways law; parliamentary proceedings; rating; European and Human Rights law; ecclesiastical law; listed buildings, conservation and trees; energy; common land and village greens; education; landlord and tenant; licensing; restrictive covenants and easements; minerals; statutory nuisance; advertising; compulsory purchase and compensation; employment; health and safety; and consumer law.

**Who should apply** Prospective pupils should demonstrate a high intellectual ability and have a degree of at least upper second level. They should have an interest in the field in which Chambers practises.

**Pupillage programme** Three pupil supervisors – four months each.
*What will you do as a pupil?*
The first six months - Pupils usually sit in their pupil-supervisors' rooms and experience all aspects of their professional lives. During the first six months pupils read their pupil-supervisors' instructions and papers, research relevant law, attempt their own draft pleadings and opinions for discussion, and attend with them at Court and in conference with solicitors and lay clients.
Arrangements for pupils to spend a month in a common law set of chambers to enable them to see the criminal and civil courts in action.
The second six months - Pupils are expected to undertake a certain amount of written work for, and attend at Court with, other members of Chambers as well as their pupil-supervisors. In recent years second-six pupils have also been briefed to appear in a variety of courts and tribunals, including the High Court, County Court and Planning inquiries. Pro bono work for FRU, Law For All, the Bar Pro Bono Unit and others is actively encouraged.
*What are the prospects of tenancy?* Since 2000, Chambers has recruited six junior tenants. There can, of course, be no guarantee that a new tenant will be recruited from each new year's intake. Chambers recognizes its responsibility to those who are not offered a tenancy and does its best to ensure that suitable positions are found elsewhere. In recent years, some of its former pupils have obtained tenancies in other chambers; others have joined major firms of solicitors or worked as lawyers in central and local government.

**When and how to apply** Apply by 31 January 2008 to begin September/October 2009. Chambers' application form available on the website or by application to Ms Saira Kabir Sheikh.

**Mini-pupillages** Apply to Mr Alexander Booth.

**Sponsorship/funding** Two awards of not less than £35,000.

Pupillages funded 2
Tenants 36
Tenancies in last 3 yrs 2

Mini-pupillages yes

Applications contact
Ms Saira Kabir Sheikh

Remuneration for pupillage
Not less than £35,000

Minimum qualifications
2.1 degree

**ftb**

Francis Taylor Building

Community
Legal Service

## FOUNTAIN COURT CHAMBERS
Temple, London EC4Y 9DH
**Tel:** 020 7583 3335
**Fax:** 020 7353 0329
**Email:** chambers@fountaincourt.co.uk
**Apply through OLPAS**

A leading set of chambers specialising in commercial work. Up to four funded pupillages offered through OLPAS. Mini pupillages also available. Further details on website.

PF Up to 4
T 63
TL3Y 6
MP yes

---

## FURNIVAL CHAMBERS
Chambers of Andrew Mitchell QC,
32 Furnival Street, London EC4A 1JQ
**Tel:** 020 7405 3232
**Fax:** 020 7405 3322
**Email:** pupillage@furnivallaw.co.uk
**Apply through OLPAS**

Furnival Chambers is a young, energetic and progressive leading criminal set and the leading set in the field of asset forfeiture and confiscation.

PF 3
T 71
TL3Y 9
MP yes

---

## 1 GARDEN COURT
Ground Floor, Temple, London EC4Y 9BJ
**Tel:** 020 7797 7900
**Fax:** 020 7797 7929
**Email:** clerks@1gc.com
**Apply to:** Pupillage Committee

1 Garden Court is a leading set in the family law field. All of our membesr work with specialist family practice teams.

PF 2
T 53
TL3Y 5
MP yes

---

## GARDEN COURT CHAMBERS
57-60 Lincoln's Inn Fields, London WC2A 3LS
**Tel:** 020 7993 7600
**Fax:** 020 7993 7700
**Email:** info@gclaw.co.uk
**Apply through OLPAS**

We are a civil liberties Chambers specialising in human rights, family, immigration, criminal defence, employment, personal injury and housing work.

PF 6
T 107
TL3Y 28
MP yes

---

## GARDEN COURT NORTH
22 Oxford Court, Manchester M2 3WQ
**Tel:** 0161 236 1840
**Fax:** 0161 236 0929
**Email:** clerks@gcnchambers.co.uk
**Apply through OLPAS**

A leading civil liberties chambers outside London providing high quality representation in our specialist areas particularly to those disadvantaged by discrimination and inequality.

PF 2
T 23
TL3Y 5
MP no

---

## GARDEN SQUARE
96A New Walk, Leicester LE1 6RD
**Tel:** 0116 2987500
**Fax:** 0116 2987501
**Email:** clerks@gardensquarechambers.com

A newly-formed set, specialising in criminal law and related matters. Members appear in all levels of the courts.

PF 1
T 11
TL3Y 1
MP yes

---

## GOUGH SQUARE CHAMBERS
6-7 Gough Square, London EC4A 3DE
**Tel:** 020 7353 0924
**Fax:** 020 7353 2221
**Email:** gsc@goughsq.co.uk
**Apply to:** Mr Jonathan Goulding

A friendly set of chambers specialising in consumer law.

PF 1
T 13
TL3Y 1
MP yes

---

## 1 GRAY'S INN SQUARE
Ground Floor, London WC1R 5AA
**Tel:** 020 7405 8946
**Fax:** 020 7405 1617
**Email:** clerks@1gis.law.co.uk
**Apply through OLPAS**

PF 6
T 60
TL3Y 6
MP yes

---

PF = Pupillages funded / T = Tenants / TL3Y = Tenancies in last 3 years / MP = Mini pupillages offered

# 9 Gough Square

London EC4A 3DG
**Tel:** 020 7832 0500
**Fax:** 020 7353 1344
**Web:** www.9goughsquare.co.uk

**Description of Chambers** We are a large common law set comprising 67 members, having been established for over 50 years. Although we continue to expand, our aim is to retain the friendly and relaxed atmosphere that continues to attract pupils and lateral recruits as it did in the past. We believe that a firm commitment to pupillage is the best way to perpetuate the growth and success of Chambers, and as evidence of this we have taken on seven tenants from our pupils in the last three years.

**Areas of work** Chambers has a strong reputation in personal injury and professional negligence, having been involved in a number of high-profile cases, for example the *British Coal* respiratory disease litigation, the *Marchioness* disaster and the *Kegworth* air crash. We have a strong criminal team whose work includes serious fraud and white collar crime. Members of Chambers were involved in the *Carl Bridgwater* murder case and subsequent inquiry, and in the *Blue Arrow* fraud trial. Chambers has extensive experience in family work, particularly for local authorities, and was involved in the *Climbie* inquiry. Civil actions against the police feature prominently, which corresponds with our expertise in civil and criminal advocacy. Chambers' employment, property and commercial teams also thrive.

**Who should apply** Chambers seeks candidates of high intellectual ability, usually evidenced by at least a 2.1 degree, but who can also demonstrate a commitment to the Bar and a flair for advocacy combined with common sense and sound judgement. We operate an equal opportunities code which is designed to support diversity in recruitment.

**Pupillage programme** We offer two pupillages for 12 months. All pupils are funded. Each pupil has three pupil supervisors so that the pupil sees as broad an area of practice as possible. Pupillage incorporates formal training and regular reviews in addition to the traditional experience offered by a pupil supervisor.

**When and how to apply** Chambers recruits once per year. The closing date for applications for pupillage for the following year is 30 April. There is no application form. Applications should be made by CV (three copies) and a covering letter together with one academic reference. Applications should be addressed to Chambers and be marked "Pupillage Application".

**Mini-pupillages** We offer assessed mini-pupillages. For the period 1 July to 30 September, the deadline for applications is 1 May. They should be made to Cleo Perry accompanied by a CV and covering letter and marked "Mini-pupillage Application".

**Sponsorship/funding** Each pupil will receive £35,000 by way of award and guaranteed minimum receipts, which includes a BVC award of £8,000 available on application.

| | |
|---|---|
| Pupillages funded | 2 |
| Tenants | 67 |
| Tenancies in last 3 yrs | 6 |

Mini-pupillages      yes

**Applications contact**
Dan Lawson

**Remuneration for pupillage**
£35,000 including a BVC
award of £8,000

**Minimum qualifications**
2.1 degree

# 4-5 Gray's Inn Square

Gray's Inn, London WC1R 5AH
**Tel:** 020 7404 5252
**Fax:** 020 7242 7803
**Email:** clerks@4-5.co.uk
**Web:** www.4-5.co.uk

**Description of Chambers** 4-5 Gray's Inn Square is a leading set of chambers specialising in a wide range of work, including in particular public law and judicial review, planning and environmental law, commercial law, employment and human rights. A distinctive feature of Chambers is the large number of barristers who practise at the intersection of these various specialisms. We believe our strong reputation owes a lot to this unusual diversity. We are a large set, comprising 48 tenants (12 QCs and 36 juniors), and take a modern and innovative approach to the changing market for legal services. We have well-established links with the academic world and have a number of leading lawyers and academics among our associate tenants. We are fully committed to the Bar's responsibilities as a profession and members of Chambers frequently undertake work in a pro bono capacity. We pride ourselves on being not only a high-quality set, but a friendly one.

**Areas of work** General public law (including judicial review applications for and against local government and human rights challenges); planning and environmental law (including inquiries, statutory appeals and judicial review applications) on behalf of developers and planning authorities, and all aspects of domestic and EU environmental law; employment law (including unfair dismissal, domestic and EU sex discrimination, race, disability and other prohibited discrimination and trade union law); commercial law (including fraud, banking, shipping, regulatory work, insurance and reinsurance); professional negligence (including actions involving property, education and solicitors); education.

**Who should apply** We have a rigorous selection procedure for pupillage. To obtain a first interview, candidates must show first-class academic ability (though not necessarily a first-class degree) and strong evidence of advocacy potential. Successful interview candidates will be expected to demonstrate exceptional legal problem-solving and advocacy ability.

**Pupillage programme** Pupils will receive a thorough training in the full range of Chambers' work during their pupillage. During the pupillage, pupils will generally be assigned to three or four different members of Chambers (pupil supervisors) to ensure they see the full range of work in which Chambers specialises. There may be some opportunity for pupils to gain advocacy experience by appearing in employment tribunals or in court. To gain additional advocacy experience pupils may take cases for the Free Representation Unit, which can be done both prior to and during pupillage.

**When and how to apply** Apply through OLPAS summer season, even if OLPAS exempt. Candidates should see Chambers' website for full information.

**Mini-pupillages** We welcome applications for mini-pupillages. Chambers also holds an annual open day and again full details can be found on our website.

**Sponsorship/funding** We normally offer up to three 12-month pupillages, each carrying an award of at least £35,000 (2007 figure) with the possibility to draw down up to £10,000 in the BVC year at Chambers' discretion.

| | |
|---|---|
| Pupillages funded | 3 |
| Tenants | 48 |
| Tenancies in last 3 yrs | 3 |
| Mini-pupillages | yes |
| Apply through OLPAS | |
| Remuneration for pupillage | |
| Minimum £35,000 (2007 figure) | |

4-5
Gray's Inn Square

| | | |
|---|---|---|
| **14 GRAY'S INN SQUARE**<br>Gray's Inn, London WC1R 5JP<br>**Tel:** 020 7242 0858<br>**Fax:** 020 7242 5434<br>**Email:** clerks@14graysinnsquare.co.uk<br>**Apply through OLPAS** | A leading family law set, with some tenants also practising in other areas of civil law. Two funded 12-month pupillages are offered each year. | PF 2<br>T 33<br>TL3Y 3<br>MP yes |
| **GRAY'S INN TAX CHAMBERS**<br>3rd Floor, Gray's Inn Chambers, Gray's Inn,<br>London WC1R 5JA<br>**Tel:** 020 7242 2642<br>**Fax:** 020 7831 9017<br>**Email:** clerks@taxbar.com<br>**Apply to:** Miss Hui Ling McCarthy | One of the leading sets of chambers specialising in revenue law (domestic, European and international). Members undertake all aspects of tax litigation and advice. | PF Up to 2<br>T 17<br>TL3Y 2<br>MP yes |
| **GUILDFORD CHAMBERS**<br>Stoke House, Leapale Lane, Guildford,<br>Surrey GU1 4LY<br>**Tel:** 01483 539131<br>**Fax:** 01483 300542<br>**Email:** clerks@guildfordbarristers.com<br>**Apply to:** The Pupillage Committee | A mixed common law set serving the South East. | PF 2<br>T 26<br>TL3Y 5<br>MP yes |
| **GUILDHALL CHAMBERS**<br>22-26 Broad Street, Bristol BS1 2HG<br>**Tel:** 0117 930 9000<br>**Fax:** 0117 930 3898<br>**Email:** info@guildhallchambers.co.uk | Friendly progressive set in the centre of Bristol. Fully networked computer system (pupils provided with PCs). Specialised practice groups. | PF Up to 2<br>T 65<br>TL3Y 5<br>MP yes |
| **HARCOURT CHAMBERS**<br>Churchill House, 3 St Aldates Courtyard,<br>38 St Aldates, London OX1 1BN<br>**Tel:** 01865 791559<br>**Fax:** 01865 791585<br>**Apply through OLPAS** | | PF 1<br>T 36<br>TL3Y 4<br>MP yes |
| **2 HARE COURT**<br>Temple, London EC4Y 7BH<br>**Tel:** 020 7353 5324<br>**Fax:** 020 7353 0667<br>**Email:** clerks@2harecourt.com<br>**Apply through OLPAS** | We are recognised as a leading criminal set, with an even mix of prosecution and defence work. We offer up to three fully-funded twelve-month pupillages per year. | PF 2-3<br>T 53<br>TL3Y 5<br>MP yes |
| **3 HARE COURT**<br>Temple, London EC4Y 7BJ<br>**Tel:** 020 7415 7800<br>**Fax:** 020 7415 7811<br>**Email:** clerks@3harecourt.com<br>**Apply through OLPAS** | Commercial/common law set which undertakes consitutional, human rights and criminal appeals in the Privy Council. We offer two funded 12-month pupillages each year. | PF 2<br>T 29<br>TL3Y 5<br>MP yes |
| **HOLLIS WHITEMAN CHAMBERS**<br>Third and Fourth Floor, Queen Elizabeth Building,<br>London EC4Y 9BS<br>**Tel:** 020 7583 5766<br>**Fax:** 020 7353 0339<br>**Email:** barristers@holliswhiteman.co.uk<br>**Apply through OLPAS** | Large chambers specialising in criminal law and professional disciplinary bodies - pupils can expect to be involved in high profile cases at an early stage. | PF 4-5<br>T 53<br>TL3Y 4<br>MP yes |

**PF** = Pupillages funded / **T** = Tenants / **TL3Y** = Tenancies in last 3 years / **MP** = Mini pupillages offered

# Hailsham Chambers

4 Paper Buildings, Ground Floor, Temple, London EC4Y 7EX
**Tel:** 020 7643 5000
**Fax:** 020 7353 5778
**Email:** clerks@hailshamchambers.com
**Web:** www.hailshamchambers.com

**Description of Chambers** Hailsham Chambers has been established for many years at 4 Paper Buildings and has a distinguished common law lineage that includes the former law lord the late Lord Diplock and the former lord chancellor the late Lord Hailsham of St Marylebone. We are proud of our tradition but are committed to remaining one of the most forward-thinking sets of chambers in London. Members of Hailsham Chambers provide advice and representation in a diverse range of specialities before all levels of courts and tribunals in England and Wales.

**Areas of work** Hailsham Chambers has six main practice areas: professional negligence, medical law, professional disciplinary and employment, costs, personal injury and commercial litigation. We have leading practitioners and experts in all these fields and are recognised by the legal directories as a leading set for professional and medical negligence. Our work ethos is to provide the highest possible standards of advocacy, advice and service. This is complemented by the support given by members of Hailsham Chambers to each other within our specialist team and across Chambers.

**Who should apply** We want motivated candidates committed to providing their best and determined to succeed. Usually a minimum 2.1 degree is required but special circumstances will be considered. Hailsham Chambers adheres to and supports the Bar Council's policies on equal opportunity and non-discrimination.

**Pupillage programme** We provide a 12-month period of intensive and high quality training in a relaxed atmosphere. Pupils are likely to spend time with three different pupil supervisors, one for each of the first and second three months, and one for the second six months. The pupil supervisors' respective practices will cover two or more of Chambers' areas of specialisation, including clinical disputes or professional negligence in particular. Pupils are encouraged to work with different members of Chambers and to undertake work for the FRU or other pro bono work. In the second six months pupils accept instructions and attend court on their own account. Formal and informal feedback is provided and regarded as crucial for the learning process. A mentor is always available to discuss pupillage in the strictest confidence.

**When and how to apply** For 12-month pupillage commencing October 2009 apply on Chambers' own application form which will be available to download from our website at www.hailshamchambers.com from January 2008. Closing date for applications 1 April 2008. Alternatively you can write to the receptionist (or telephone) to request a copy of the form once available.

**Mini-pupillages** Hailsham Chambers offers mini-pupillages throughout the year (although vacation periods are best avoided) to those who have started university and can show a real interest in pursuing a legal career. To apply please send a copy of your CV together with a covering letter to Luke Wygas.

**Sponsorship/funding** We are offering one 12-month pupillage commencing in October 2009 with an award of £35,000 plus £5,000 guaranteed earnings.

| | |
|---|---|
| Pupillages funded | 1 |
| Tenants | 43 |
| Tenancies in last 3 yrs | 6 |
| Mini-pupillages | yes |

Apply to
The Receptionist

Remuneration for pupillage
£40,000

Minimum qualifications
2.1 degree

**hailsham**chambers

# Hardwicke Building

Lincoln's Inn, London WC2A 3SB
**Tel:** 020 7242 2523
**Fax:** 020 7691 1234
**Email:** clerks@hardwicke.co.uk
**Web:** www.hardwicke.co.uk

**Description of Chambers** Hardwicke is an established and successful civil set with a growing reputation for high quality in our various specialist areas. We now have 11 members recommended by *Chambers & Partners* and 14 in the *Legal 500*, in areas as diverse as shipping, commercial litigation, insurance and reinsurance; professional negligence; education; public law; housing, property law and real estate litigation; personal injury, clinical negligence and healthcare.

We successfully strive to anticipate and meet the needs of our clients and to provide clear and concise specialist legal assistance coupled with excellent customer service.

Hardwicke is an ambitious and commercially-minded and managed Chambers. Our 21st century facilities were designed specifically with the needs of a modern chambers in mind. Chambers makes considerable strategic use of information technology and e-communication, including Blackberries, video-conferencing and its award-winning website, all of which promote the accessibility of its barristers to clients throughout the UK and overseas.

Divided into work-based and client-focused teams, Hardwicke comprises specialist counsel at all levels of seniority who provide a comprehensive service. Pupils' preferred areas of practice can therefore be accommodated within reason although we encourage our pupils to gain as broad an experience as possible and to avoid specialisation too soon.

Our pupils will find themselves in court regularly throughout their 2nd six and will receive in-house advocacy training to supplement this and help make their first time in court less nerve-wracking! We also encourage our pupils to work for FRU.

Our work is intellectually demanding and our remuneration package is generous. We therefore require pupils of the highest academic calibre, personality and ambition, who have the potential to make a real contribution to the future of chambers.

**Areas of work** Hardwicke Building operates in distinct and active teams focusing on: commercial litigation; insurance & reinsurance; intellectual property; education; property; housing & public law; personal injury & clinical negligence; employment; and family.

**When and how to apply** Application on Chambers' own application form (write to Sarah Taylor, the Secretary of the Pupillage Committee for a copy, marking the envelope 'Pupillage 2009') or download from www.hardwicke.co.uk/pupillage.

**Mini-pupillages** Mini-pupillages are available: up to eight per quarter. Applications with CV and covering letter to the Pupillage Secretary marked 'Mini-Pupillage' or to mini-pupillage@hardwicke.co.uk. Closing dates: TBC. See the website for further details. Student visits are not available.

**Sponsorship/funding** Up to £35,000.

| | |
|---|---|
| Pupillages funded | 2 |
| Tenants | 76 |
| Tenancies in last 3 yrs | 7 |
| Mini-pupillages | yes |
| Applications contact | Sarah Taylor |
| Remuneration for pupillage | Up to £35,000 |

Hardwicke Building

# 1 Hare Court

Temple, London EC4Y 7BS
**Tel:** 020 7797 7070
**Fax:** 020 7797 7435
**Email:** clerks@1hc.com
**Web:** www.1hc.com

**Areas of work** The first set of Chambers to specialise in family law, we moved from 1 Mitre Court Buildings to new premises at 1 Hare Court in 2002 and we now have eight silks and 28 juniors. The majority of members work in the area of ancillary relief. While some members of Chambers are involved in child law, the opportunity for our pupils to see child cases is relatively limited. Former members of Chambers include two previous presidents of the Family Division, two lords justice of appeal and two High Court judges of the Family Division. Current members of Chambers have acted in almost all the recent cases of importance in the field of matrimonial finance, including *White*, *Parlour*, *Miller/MacFarlarne* and *Charman*. Chambers' clients tend to be high net worth individuals, and include well-known personalities from the worlds of entertainment, finance and sport.

We expect that applicants will have a strong academic record. In addition to the professional work undertaken by members of Chambers, we have a long-standing tradition of contributing to legal works. *Rayden on Divorce*, which is the principal practitioners' textbook, was renamed *Rayden & Jackson* as a tribute to the former head of Chambers Joseph Jackson QC, who edited the work for many years. Current members of Chambers continue to edit *Rayden & Jackson*, as well as many other leading books, and we regularly contribute articles to the specialist press. Candidates who demonstrate the potential to carry on this strong intellectual tradition will impress.

A pupillage at 1 Hare Court offers training in advocacy, advice and drafting in every aspect of family work, particularly ancillary relief. During the last three years we have taken on four junior tenants. Our strong reputation and the quality of training available mean that those pupils who are not taken on stand a good prospect of finding a professional opportunity elsewhere, frequently in other specialist chambers. Unlike some other sets, and to ensure that we recruit only the very best, we do entertain applications for tenancy from those who have conducted their pupillage elsewhere.

**Who should apply** Candidates should be able to show that they have a potential flair for advocacy, presentational and analytical skills and the ability to develop sound judgement, as well as having a strong academic record. Given the emphasis on financial work, some aptitude and interest in commercial and financial matters is desirable. However, Chambers' work remains rooted in human problems and a sympathetic but perceptive response to those problems is essential.

**When and how to apply** We recruit pupils once a year. Apply by 8 June 2008 for pupillages starting in October 2009 in writing, with a CV, to the chairman of the tenancies and pupillage committee. References may be helpful. Those invited for an interview are likely to be interviewed on a Saturday. Chambers is not a member of OLPAS but does keep to the OLPAS timetable for the communication and acceptance of offers.

**Mini-pupillages** Mini-pupillages are available during term time only. Applicants must be at least at undergraduate level and have some interest in family law. Applications in writing, marked "Mini-pupillage" accompanied by a CV to the chairman of the tenancies and pupillage committee.

**Sponsorship/funding** Up to three fully funded pupillages.

| | |
|---|---|
| Pupillages funded | 3 |
| Tenants | 36 |
| Tenancies in last 3 yrs | 4 |
| Mini-pupillages | yes |

**Remuneration for pupillage**
Up to £25,000 maximum per pupillage

**Minimum qualifications**
2.1 degree

1 HARE COURT

# Henderson Chambers

2 Harcourt Buildings, Temple, London EC4Y 9DB
**Tel:** 020 7583 9020
**Fax:** 020 7583 2686
**Email:** clerks@hendersonchambers.co.uk
**Web:** www.hendersonchambers.co.uk

**Description of Chambers** We are a leading common law and commercial set with 40 tenants. Two of our door tenants (Clive Stanbrook QC OBE and Phillip Bentley QC) practise from the Brussels office of the US law firm McDermott Will & Emery.

**Areas of work** We are recognised by all leading directories as pre-eminent in the field of product liability litigation. Health and safety litigation is another chambers forte and chambers is ranked joint number one in this area by *Chambers & Partners*. Consumer, information technology, public law and public enquiries are other areas in which we are recognized leaders. We undertake a broad range of other work, including: business and commercial; employment; property; judicial review; personal injury; clinical and other professional negligence; railway law; environmental law; construction and engineering; telecommunications; consumer credit; financial services; insurance; human rights; housing; education; sport; competition; and EU law. Our extensive inquiry work includes Clapham, Southall, Marchioness, Ladbroke Grove and Shipman.

**Who should apply** We are proud of the friendly atmosphere within Chambers and seek exceptional pupils who are both personable and have a record of academic excellence usually evidenced by a first or upper second class degree. Chambers' junior tenants have predominantly been recruited from pupils over the last 10 years and we continue to seek to expand.

**Pupillage programme** Pupillages are for 12 months and usually with two different pupil supervisors for six months each. Pupils are given the opportunity to work in Brussels to experience European practice at first hand and are expected to attend court regularly during their second six months.

**When and how to apply** We are part of the OLPAS system and abide by its closing date for the summer season. Applications for pupillage commencing in October 2009 will be required by about 30 April 2008. Queries about pupillage should be addressed to Adam Heppinstall.

**Mini-pupillages** Applications for mini-pupillages should be addressed to Ross Fentem.

**Sponsorship/funding** We offer a maximum of three, and usually two, funded 12-month pupillages with minimum remuneration of £42,500. This consists of an award of £35,000 and guaranteed minimum earnings of £7,500 during the second six months. One further pupillage may be available on Bar Council approved and agreed terms. We also consider applications for third six pupillages.

| | |
|---|---|
| Pupillages funded | 1-3 |
| Tenants | 40 |
| Tenancies in last 3 yrs | 3 |
| Mini-pupillages | yes |
| Apply through OLPAS | |

Remuneration for pupillage
£42,500 for 12 months
(£35,000 award, £7,500
guaranteed earnings)

HENDERSON
CHAMBERS

# Hogarth Chambers

5 New Square, Lincoln's Inn, London WC2A 3RJ
**Tel:** 020 7404 0404
**Fax:** 020 7404 0505
**Email:** barristers@hogarthchambers.com
**Web:** www.hogarthchambers.com

**Description of Chambers** Hogarth Chambers is a 26-member set, offering a comprehensive range of legal services, ranging from advice and representation in court proceedings to specialised non-contentious advice in all aspects of intellectual property, information technology, media and entertainment and chancery/commercial law. Chambers is widely recognised as a leading set in the fields of intellectual property, information technology and media and entertainment law. The *Legal 500* recommends us as a leading set for IP and media and entertainment, saying "Hogarth Chambers is strong on IP matters affecting broadcasting and on copyright generally". *Chambers and Partners* refers to Hogarth Chambers as "an up and coming set which handles media and entertainment work and IT work, in addition to its substantial IP caseload". Hogarth Chambers was also recently nominated as Chambers of the Year at *The Lawyer* Awards 2006.

**Areas of work** Members of Hogarth Chambers specialise in four core areas: intellectual property, information technology, media and entertainment and chancery/commercial law. Members of Chambers also have expertise in alternative dispute resolution, mediation and arbitration in all its practice areas.

**Who should apply** Hogarth seeks pupils with an excellent academic background, who have an ability to communicate clearly and persuasively both orally and on paper, who are commercially aware and who have a desire to succeed. We take into account further and higher degrees, practical experience in commerce or industry, other legal experience, participation in moots or debates, authorship of articles and lecturing and tutoring activity. Demonstrating an interest in the work that Hogarth Chambers undertakes is also important.

**Pupillage programme** Hogarth Chambers offers IP pupillages and mixed practice pupillages. We endeavour to make pupillage at Hogarth rewarding and educational. Pupils are encouraged to experience the range of work undertaken in chambers. Therefore, a twelve-month pupillage will involve a pupil sitting with at least four pupil masters. Pupils will also sit with other members of chambers either for a set period or on occasion for the duration of an interesting case. This circulation of pupils is important both to them, because they see the variety of ways in which barristers work, and to us, as more members of chambers can assess a pupil's merits. Pupils also take part in Hogarth's regular in-house group meetings, at which we discuss recent developments in the law.

**When and how to apply** Closing date is 27 June 2008 to begin September/October 2009. Hogarth is non-OLPAS. Contact kwilliams@hogarthchambers.com for an application form or download one from our website at www.hogarthchambers.com.

**Mini-pupillages** We offer 16 three-day, assessed mini-pupillage placements throughout the year (excluding court vacation periods). There are two opportunities to apply; 14 September 2007 and 7 March 2008. Application is by CV and covering letter, addressed to Kathryn Williams.

**Sponsorship/funding** Up to £35,000 award, of which £5,000 may be drawn down during Bar School. We also fund all necessary training courses.

| | |
|---|---|
| Pupillages funded | 1 |
| Tenants | 26 |
| Tenancies in last 3 yrs | 1 |
| Mini-pupillages | yes |

Applications contact
Miss Kathryn Williams

Remuneration for pupillage
Up to £35,000

Minimum qualifications
Science/Law qualification
and IP interest

| | | |
|---|---|---|
| **INDIA BUILDINGS**<br>India Buildings, Water Street, Liverpool L2 0XG<br>**Tel:** 0151 243 6000<br>**Fax:** 0151 243 6040 | India Buildings is a long-established set of chambers providing high quality advocacy and advice in all aspects of criminal, civil and family work. | PF 1<br>T 45<br>TL3Y 12<br>MP yes |
| **1 INNER TEMPLE LANE**<br>Temple, London EC4Y 1AF<br>**Tel:** 020 7427 4400<br>**Fax:** 020 7427 4427<br>**Email:** clerks@1itl.com<br>**Apply through OLPAS** | Specialist criminal law chambers prosecuting and defending the full range of criminal work. | PF 2<br>T 29<br>TL3Y 5<br>MP yes |
| **ISCOED CHAMBERS**<br>86 St Helen's Road, Swansea SA1 4BQ<br>**Tel:** 01792 652988<br>**Fax:** 01792 458089<br>**Email:** clerks@iscoedchambers.co.uk<br>**Apply through OLPAS** | Chambers is a long-established set, the largest in Swansea with a broad range of practice areas. Chambers has a broad client base including private and publicly funded work including CFAs. | PF 2<br>T 33<br>TL3Y 5<br>MP yes |
| **KCH CHAMBERS**<br>1 Oxford Street, Nottingham NG1 5BH<br>**Tel:** 0115 9418851<br>**Fax:** 0115 9414169<br>**Email:** clerks@kch.co.uk<br>**Apply through OLPAS** | Busy, friendly Chambers with Barmark and excellent administrative support. Mixed common law work with specialist teams - crime, family, civil, employment, personal injury and immigration. | PF 1<br>T 41<br>TL3Y 4<br>MP yes |
| **KENWORTHY'S CHAMBERS**<br>Arlington House, Bloom Street, Salford, Manchester M3 6AJ<br>**Tel:** 0161 832 4036<br>**Fax:** 0161 832 0370<br>**Email:** maria@kenworthysbarristers.co.uk<br>**Apply to:** Mrs Maria Rushworth | Progressive set with a strong emphasis on Crime, Family, Immigration, Civil, Employment & Housing. | PF 2<br>T 45<br>TL3Y 12<br>MP yes |
| **KING STREET CHAMBERS**<br>65-67 King Street, Leicester LE1 6RP<br>**Tel:** 0116 254 7710<br>**Fax:** 0116 247 0145<br>**Email:** clerks@kingstreetchambers.com<br>**Apply to:** Miss Tracey Paskins | An established and friendly common law set serving the Midland Circuit. Chambers is committed to the training of pupils and to equal opportunities. | PF 1<br>T 21<br>TL3Y 7<br>MP yes |
| **8 KING STREET CHAMBERS**<br>Manchester M2 6AQ<br>**Tel:** 0161 834 9560<br>**Fax:** 0161 834 2733<br>**Apply through OLPAS** | A leading civil and commercial chambers with a broad range of expertise, particularly in commercial, personal injury, employment and family law. | PF 1-2<br>T 39<br>TL3Y 6<br>MP yes |
| **KING'S BENCH CHAMBERS**<br>115 North Hill, Plymouth PL4 8JY<br>**Tel:** 01752 221551<br>**Fax:** 01752 664379<br>**Email:** clerks@kingsbenchchambers.co.uk<br>**Apply through OLPAS** | General common law set covering all of the West Country, predominantly Devon and Cornwall. | PF 1<br>T 22<br>TL3Y 2<br>MP yes |

**PF** = Pupillages funded / **T** = Tenants / **TL3Y** = Tenancies in last 3 years / **MP** = Mini pupillages offered

# 11 KBW

Temple, London EC4Y 7EQ
**Tel:** 020 7632 8500
**Fax:** 020 7583 9123
**Email:** chalas@11kbw.com
**Web:** www.11kbw.com

**Description of Chambers** Chambers was founded in 1981 by 10 practitioners, led by Alexander Irvine QC, and since then has expanded, primarily by recruitment from those carrying out pupillage in Chambers, to the current numbers, taking on tenants at a rate of about one a year on average.

Chambers seeks to provide a very high quality of service to solicitors and clients, and the standards expected of pupils are accordingly challenging. Twelve-month pupils are selected only where we consider that they will have a reasonable prospect of proving their worth during pupillage so as to be taken on as a tenant at the end. If taken on as a tenant, there is considerable scope for specialisation within one or more of the areas of practice in which Chambers specialises. All areas of practice give rise to difficult and interesting issues of law, and Chambers seeks to recruit pupils of ability with a real interest in legal problems.

As a set of chambers we are comparatively young and we aim to be friendly and forward-looking. We encourage applications from candidates irrespective of sex, race, religion or belief, disability or sexual orientation.

**Areas of work** Members of Chambers practise principally in three areas: employment law, public law (including EU and human rights law) and commercial law.

**Pupillage programme** Chambers usually takes two or three funded pupils in October of each year for 12-month pupillages. The Chambers award for funded pupils in 2009 is £40,000.

**When and how to apply** Applications for pupillage should be made through OLPAS.

**Mini-pupillages** Chambers offers one-week mini-pupillages to students who are considering applying to us for a full pupillage. There is considerable demand for the limited number of mini-pupillage places we have available, and accordingly they are offered on a selective basis. We strongly recommend an assessed mini-pupillage to pupils applying through OLPAS.

| | |
|---|---|
| Pupillages funded | 2-3 |
| Tenants | 51 |
| Tenancies in last 3 yrs | 6 |
| Mini-pupillages | yes |

Apply through OLPAS

Remuneration for pupillage
£40,000

Minimum qualifications
2.1 degree

# Keating Chambers

15 Essex Street, London WC2R 3AA
**Tel:** 020 7544 2600
**Fax:** 020 7544 2700
**Email:** clerks@keatingchambers.com
**Web:** www.keatingchambers.com

**Description of Chambers** Keating Chambers is a leading commercial set specialising in construction, technology and related professional negligence disputes. These disputes often relate to high-profile projects in the UK and overseas and typically involve complex issues in the law of tort, contract and restitution. Chambers is based in modern premises outside the Temple.

**Areas of work** Our members are involved in disputes of all shapes and sizes: from residential building works at the junior end to multi-million pound projects for the construction of airports, dams, power stations and bridges at a more senior level. Much of Chambers' work now also includes rapidly developing areas such as information technology, telecommunications and energy. Members of Chambers act as advocates in litigation and arbitration throughout the UK and often act at hearings elsewhere in Europe and throughout Asia, Africa and the Caribbean. Some of our members are involved in EU law. Chambers' area of practice is dynamic and challenging. The relevant principles of law are constantly developing and the technical complexity of disputes requires thorough analytical skills. New and alternative methods of dispute resolution are often used, and several of our members are frequently appointed as mediators, arbitrators, and adjudicators. In their first years of practice, tenants can expect earnings equivalent to those in other top sets of chambers.

**Who should apply** Chambers' selection criteria:
Intellectual Ability: A very good academic record. The ability rapidly to master and retain complex and extensive information, to identify and memorise essentials, to produce pragmatic and practical solutions and to respond quickly to intellectual challenge.
Motivation: A high level of drive and determination. A desire to practise commercial law.
Relationships: The ability to have sustained collaborative relationships with a wide range of colleagues, members of professional teams and clients.
Temperament: The ability to sustain attention while working with complex material for long hours against deadlines; to remain calm and to retain priorities whilst meeting unexpected challenges; to be confident and objective in challenging circumstances.
Impact: Articulate, confident, perceptive and sensitive to situations.

**Pupillage programme** Pupils are normally allocated four supervisors to ensure that each pupil sees a variety of work in Chambers. We also have an active pupillage education programme. We recruit tenants in the first instance from those who have completed pupillage with us.

**When and how to apply** Chambers invites applications for pupillage starting in October 2009. All applications are to be made through OLPAS in the 2008 summer season.

**Mini-pupillages** Details of funded and unfunded mini-pupillages can be found on our website.

**Sponsorship/funding** Up to four 12 month pupillages available with an award of up to £42,500. Those who are offered pupillage will be entitled to an advance of £15,000 towards the BVC year.

Pupillages funded  4
Tenants  49
Tenancies in last 3 yrs  7

Mini-pupillages  yes

Apply through OLPAS

Remuneration for pupillage
Up to £42,500

Minimum qualifications
2.1 degree

# 1 King's Bench Walk

Temple, London EC4Y 7DB
**Tel:** 020 7936 1500
**Fax:** 020 7936 1590
**Email:** clerks@1kbw.co.uk
**Web:** www.1kbw.co.uk

**Description of Chambers** 1KBW is an established and progressive set of chambers occupying fine premises in the Inner Temple. Although we can trace a distinguished history as far back as the 17th century, we recognise that we cannot rely on the past to carry us forward into the future. As a modern set of Chambers we provide not only legal advice and advocacy of the highest level, but also efficient administration in order to give excellent standards of service to professional and lay clients alike. At 1KBW we are truly committed to maintaining and improving our standards in line with the ever-changing needs of our client base.

As one of the larger sets of around 54 members, we can provide the client with an extensive choice of individuals or teams of Counsel and yet are small enough to retain the best of the more traditional sets of chambers.

More information on Chambers and individual members can be found on our website at www.1kbw.co.uk or by e-mail from our Chambers' Director sgray@1kbw.co.uk.

**Areas of work** The work at 1KBW is principally divided into two practice areas: family and crime. Although long acknowledged as one of the leading family law sets in the country, we have consciously decided to continue with this mix of practice, believing it to be important for the advocate to have as wide an experience as possible, particularly at the beginning of his or her career.

**Who should apply** We are looking for pupils who are personable, self-confident and have the ability to inspire confidence in our clients. They will be focused, intelligent and enthusiastic individuals with a good academic record and a commitment to providing excellent standards of client care.

**Pupillage programme** During your pupillage at 1KBW you will be allocated to three separate supervisors in order to ensure that you see the full range of Chambers work. You will be expected to participate in monthly advocacy sessions with other members of Chambers and you will be offered the opportunity to take part in monthly 'pupillage surgeries' at which you will have the opportunity to discuss any aspect of your pupillage with a more senior member of Chambers. Chambers' policy is to recruit from current pupils. We regard our pupils and junior tenants as an investment in our future.

**When and how to apply** Chambers retains its membership of the Bar Council OLPAS scheme, sifting applications and carrying out interviews in the season. We offer two pupillages of 12 months' duration annually, commencing in October. Chambers has set aside substantial funds to assist pupils throughout their time with us.

**Mini-pupillages** Applications for mini-pupillage should be made online via our website. There is no need to send a copy of your CV. We regret that we are unable to accept applications other than those made in this way. If you do not have access to the Internet you may obtain a copy of the form by writing to the Chambers Director, enclosing a SAE.

| | |
|---|---|
| Pupillages funded | 2 |
| Tenants | 54 |
| Tenancies in last 3 yrs | 4 |
| Mini-pupillages | yes |
| Apply through OLPAS | |
| Remuneration for pupillage £50,000 | |
| Minimum qualifications 2.1 degree | |

# 6 King's Bench Walk

Temple, London EC4Y 7DR
**Tel:** 020 7583 0410
**Fax:** 020 7353 8791
**Email:** clerks@6kbw.com
**Web:** www.6kbw.com

**Description of Chambers** Situated in the heart of the Temple, the Chambers of Roy Amlot QC is recognised as a leading set in the field of criminal law. Our practice covers all areas of criminal law, from terrorism and murder at the Old Bailey to road traffic offences at the magistrates' court. A continuing policy of careful expansion has ensured that we can offer expertise at every level of call. We are also fortunate to have a skilled and dedicated team of clerking and administrative staff headed by Andrew Barnes.

**Areas of work** We specialise in criminal law. Members of Chambers are involved in high-profile cases and frequently appear in the House of Lords and Court of Appeal and Privy Council, as well as the Administrative and Crown courts. We undertake work in all manner of criminal cases, for both defence and prosecution, primarily in central London. In addition to crime, our practice also covers extradition, judicial review and defamation. Members of chambers have recently appeared in many of the highest profile cases including the trial of the 21/7 bombers, the Damilola Taylor murder, the 'Cash for Honours' enquiry and the Hatfield Rail Disaster trial.

**Who should apply** We are committed to equal opportunities and aim to select the best and brightest applicants, regardless of their background, for pupillage with us. We look for academic excellence, proven public-speaking ability and a commitment to the criminal law. Every pupil is selected on the basis that they are potential tenants, so we also look for people with whom we feel we could spend the rest of our working lives.

**Pupillage programme** Pupils are assigned to one pupil supervisor for each six-month period. We ensure that both have contrasting practices to allow pupils to have the widest possible exposure to all aspects of criminal law. We have a training programme that continues throughout the 12 months of pupillage. It centres on advocacy, taught by members of Chambers who are experienced advocacy teachers, with exercises ranging from cross-examination skills through to mock trials in front of district judges. The culmination of the training during the first six is a mock trial held before a resident judge at the Old Bailey. In addition, the course also covers ethics, dealing with clients and the more prosaic completion of legal aid and claims forms. The programme has been consistently praised by the Bar Council, and ensures that every pupil we have is well equipped to face the challenge of their first days in court.

**When and how to apply** We recruit exclusively through the summer season of OLPAS.

**Mini-pupillages** We offer non-assessed mini-pupillages throughout the year. Demand is high, and so applicants should apply early. Applications, in the form of a CV and covering letter, should be sent to Robin McCoubrey.

**Sponsorship/funding** We offer four funded 12-month pupillages commencing in October, each with an award of at least £12,000 together with substantial earnings during the second six months of pupillage.

| | |
|---|---|
| Pupillages funded | 4 |
| Tenants | 52 |
| Tenancies in last 3 yrs | 6 |
| Mini-pupillages | yes |

**Applications contact**
Mark Weekes

**Remuneration for pupillage**
At least £12,000 award in first six, plus substantial earnings in second six.

# 7 King's Bench Walk

Temple, London EC4Y 7DS
**Tel:** 020 7910 8300
**Fax:** 020 7910 8400
**Email:** clerks@7kbw.co.uk
**Web:** www.7kbw.co.uk

**Description of Chambers** 7 King's Bench Walk is a specialist commercial set with a reputation for excellence and intellectual rigour. The vast majority of our work is in the commercial courts and in commercial arbitrations in London, although members also appear in other courts and other jurisdictions. The general character of Chambers' work is of an international flavour.

**Areas of work** Commercial law. The core of our work is shipping, insurance and reinsurance disputes. In addition, Chambers' work typically includes sale of goods and international trade, professional negligence, commercial fraud, banking, energy, oil and gas, conflicts of laws, EU and competition law.

**Who should apply** Candidates with strong analytical and intellectual abilities. We do not typically interview candidates who do not have a first or a good upper second-class degree. Chambers typically recruits three pupils per year.

**Pupillage programme** Pupils are allocated a pupillage supervisor for the first two to three months and will change pupillage supervisor more frequently thereafter. A large component of pupillage is assisting in the preparation of trials and applications and attending court with the pupil supervisor. It will also involve drafting statements of case, researching the law, advices and attending conferences. Chambers also organises advocacy exercises for its pupils.

**When and how to apply** OLPAS summer season 2008 to begin October 2009 or October 2010.

**Mini-pupillages** Applications in the form of a covering letter and CV are to be made to the Mini-pupillage Secretary either by post or e-mail. The CV should give a breakdown of all university examination results achieved to date. Applications for mini-pupillages in the period from 1 June to 30 September (excluding August) must be received by 31 March; applications for mini-pupillages in the period 1 October to 31 January must be received by 31 July; applications for mini-pupillages in the period 1 February to 31 May must be received by 30 November.

**Sponsorship/funding** Pupillages are fully funded, with awards of at least £42,000 for 12 months.

| | |
|---|---|
| Pupillages funded | Up to 4 |
| Tenants | 44 |
| Tenancies in last 3 yrs | 4 |
| Mini-pupillages | yes |

Apply through OLPAS

Remuneration for pupillage
At least £42,000

Minimum qualifications
Good 2.1 degree

# 12 King's Bench Walk

Temple, London EC4Y 7EL
**Tel:** 020 7583 0811
**Fax:** 020 7583 7228
**Email:** chambers@12kbw.co.uk
**Web:** www.12kbw.co.uk

**Description of Chambers** 12 King's Bench Walk is one of the best-known and respected civil sets of barristers' chambers in London. Our 55 barristers (including eight silks) offer a wealth of expertise and skill in a wide range of legal fields. 12KBW's expertise is reflected in the prominence of its members in areas outside their practice. Among our members are the recent chairman of the Personal Injury Bar Association (PIBA) and the recent president of the Association for Personal Injury Lawyers (APIL). One of our members sits on the Ogden committee and another is vice chairman of the Remuneration Committee of the Bar Council and is a member of the Costs Sub-committee of the Civil Justice Council and chairman of sittings of the Funding Review Panel of the Legal Services Commission. 12KBW won the Personal Injury Silk of the Year Award at the Chambers Bar Awards 2006.

**Areas of work** 12KBW is the premier personal injury set and is proud of its unrivalled PI focus. 12KBW is instructed by both claimants and defendants in numerous intellectually challenging or high-value PI cases and continues to be the dominant set in all forms of industrial disease work. 12KBW also possesses an impressive and burgeoning employment practice. This has enabled 12KBW to remain at the cutting edge of the PI/employment law nexus, an area of increasing significance. 12KBW has a significant strength in clinical negligence including injuries at birth, catastrophic brain damage and injuries caused by pharmaceutical products. 12KBW's well-deserved reputation in this area is now recognised by its inclusion in the *Legal 500* and *Chambers UK* as a leading set. Additional areas of work undertaken by specialist teams within chambers include professional negligence and insurance. 12KBW acts for a wide variety of clients in both the public and private sectors, all major insurance companies and trade unions.

**Who should apply** Academically successful candidates will normally have a 2.1 degree from a good university. In addition, Chambers looks for an aptitude for advocacy, evidence of non-academic achievements, motivation, a positive and enthusiastic personality and a commitment to the Bar.

**Pupillage programme** 12KBW is committed to providing the best training to its pupils. Pupils are usually allocated to three or four pupil supervisors throughout the year. Chambers ensures that pupils are given every opportunity to get to know other members. It is expected that pupils will spend time with junior members doing the type of work pupils would expect to have in the early years of practice.

**When and how to apply** Chambers is a member of OLPAS and recruitment is strictly via the summer OLPAS season.

**Mini-pupillages** We offer four sessions spaced throughout the year where six successful candidates are offered a three-day mini-pupillage. Applications are by email or letter, addressing our criteria and enclosing a CV to the mini-pupillage officer, Neil Seligman, email: seligman@12kbw.co.uk.
Session dates for 2008 will be published on our website.

**Sponsorship/funding** We usually offer up to three pupillages a year, each of 12 months' duration. An award of £30,000 is available for each pupillage, payable as a £20,000 grant and £10,000 in guaranteed earnings [£10,000 of the grant may be drawn down during the Bar Vocation Course].

| | |
|---|---|
| Pupillages funded | 3 |
| Tenants | 55 |
| Tenancies in last 3 yrs | 8 |
| Mini-pupillages | yes |
| Apply through OLPAS | |
| Remuneration for pupillage | £30,000 |
| Minimum qualifications | 2.1 degree |

**12**
12 King's Bench Walk

| | | |
|---|---|---|
| **2 KING'S BENCH WALK**<br>Ground Floor, Temple, London EC4Y 7DE<br>**Tel:** 020 7353 1746<br>**Fax:** 020 7583 2051<br>**Email:** clerks@2kbw.com | General common-law chambers, primarily based on the Western Circuit | PF 3<br>T 55<br>TL3Y 10<br>MP no |
| **4 KING'S BENCH WALK**<br>Second Floor, Temple, London EC4Y 7DL<br>**Tel:** 020 7822 7000<br>**Fax:** 0870 803 1901<br>**Email:** clerks@4kbw.co.uk<br>**Apply through OLPAS** | Chambers is 40 strong, including three silks. Our practice base is nationwide encompassing all common law work, particularly on the South eastern and Midland Circuits. | PF 2<br>T 40<br>TL3Y 6<br>MP no |
| **5 KING'S BENCH WALK**<br>Temple, London EC4Y 7DM<br>**Tel:** 020 7353 5638<br>**Fax:** 020 7353 6166<br>**Email:** clerks@5kbw.co.uk<br>**Apply through OLPAS** | Applicants through OLPAS only. | PF 2<br>T 43<br>TL3Y 5<br>MP yes |
| **6 KING'S BENCH WALK**<br>Chambers of Sibghat Kadri QC, Temple, London EC4Y 7DR<br>**Tel:** 020 7583 0695<br>**Fax:** 020 7353 1726<br>**Apply to:** Miss SD Stamford | Multi-racial set. Of particular concern to all practitioners are those areas of law which deal with the liberty and rights of the individual. | PF 2<br>T 31<br>TL3Y 2<br>MP yes |
| **13 KING'S BENCH WALK**<br>First Floor, Temple, London EC4Y 7EN<br>**Tel:** 020 7353 7204<br>**Fax:** 020 7583 0252<br>**Email:** clerks@13kbw.co.uk<br>**Apply through OLPAS** | An established common law set of chambers practising in chancery/commercial, employment and personal injury and, from its Oxford annexe, crime. | PF 2<br>T 50<br>TL3Y 3<br>MP no |
| **KINGS CHAMBERS**<br>36 Young Street, Manchester M3 3FT<br>**Tel:** 0161 832 9082<br>**Fax:** 0161 835 2139<br>**Email:** clerks@kingschambers.com<br>**Apply through OLPAS** | One of the largest and most successful sets outside London, specialising in common law, commercial & chancery and planning & public law. | PF 3<br>T 69<br>TL3Y 10<br>MP yes |
| **LAMB BUILDING**<br>Ground Floor, Temple, London EC4Y 7AS<br>**Tel:** 020 7797 7788<br>**Fax:** 020 7353 0535<br>**Email:** clerks@lambbuilding.co.uk<br>**Apply to:** Chambers Administration | Common law set, tenants covering a broad range of specialities. Extensive education/advocacy training offered. Friendly unstuffy set. Apply on standard form from chambers' website. | PF 3<br>T 51<br>TL3Y 10<br>MP yes |
| **LAMB CHAMBERS**<br>Lamb Building, Temple, London EC4Y 7AS<br>**Tel:** 020 7797 8300<br>**Fax:** 020 7797 8308<br>**Email:** info@lambchambers.co.uk<br>**Apply through OLPAS** | A long-established and forward-looking set of chambers specialising in mainstream civil litigation and structured in three specialist groups: commercial, property and personal injury/clinical negligence. | PF 2<br>T 50<br>TL3Y 5<br>MP yes |

PF = Pupillages funded / T = Tenants / TL3Y = Tenancies in last 3 years / MP = Mini pupillages offered

# Landmark Chambers

180 Fleet Street, London EC4A 2HG
**Tel:** 020 7430 1221
**Fax:** 020 7421 6060
**Email:** clerks@landmarkchambers.co.uk
**Web:** www.landmarkchambers.co.uk

**Description of Chambers** Landmark Chambers is the UK's leading chambers specialising in the inter-related fields of planning, environmental, property and public & administrative law. Chambers is unique in its ability to offer individuals with true expertise in all of these areas of practice. Many of our members of chambers are recognised by *Chambers & Partners* and *Legal 500* as leaders in their fields. We were ranked 17th overall in *Chambers & Partners 2007*.

**Areas of work** We act for a wide variety of clients in both the public and private sectors. Planning and environmental work includes appearances both at planning inquiries and in the courts. Our clients may be private sector developers, local authorities or NGOs. Our success can be seen in the buildings, infra-structure projects, and protection of our environment in a way that touches our everyday lives. Our public law work covers all aspects of central government activities, local government law (including finance), regulatory bodies, human rights, European law, education, health, mental health, housing, social security and social services, public procurement, negligence and dishonesty in public office. Property work comprises all aspects of landlord and tenant and real property issues, including commercial litigation involving property and property-related torts. Property work often stretches into the area of environmental law which is an ever-increasing area of our work.

**Pupillage programme** Chambers is a member of OLPAS. We offer up to three pupillages a year, each of 12 months' duration. An award of £37,500 is available to each pupil, payable monthly in arrears. Up to £7,500 may be taken as an early drawdown prior to the start of your pupillage year. The pupillage year here is divided into four equal parts with each part being spent with a different pupil supervisor. Wherever possible we take into consideration any interests that you may have in a particular area of law. We encourage you to work for others and we will often send you to work with a Silk or senior junior on longer more complex cases. These arrangements enable you to see a wide variety of work and allow more members of Chambers to get to know you. In your second six months you will be in court on average twice a week on your own account, usually in the county court on small applications, thus gaining valuable advocacy experience. Any money earned by you in your second six is in addition to your pupillage award. During the year there are four formal exercises (three written and one oral) along with individual feedback via your pupil supervisor. Chambers is committed to its policy on diversity and welcomes applications from candidates who believe they may come from a minority group.

**Mini-pupillages** We offer a limited number of mini-pupillages lasting between 3-5 days. Please see our web site for up to date information. Applications for mini-pupillage should be emailed to Charles Banner cbanner@landmarkchambers.co.uk and marked 'mini-pupillage application'. They should be accompanied by a CV. Mini-pupillages are not assessed and do not form part of the pupillage application process.

We also hold two or three Open Days each year for prospective pupils who may not be able to come for mini-pupillage. Please check our website regularly for details. The next Open Days will be held on 27 February and 7 March 2008.

| | |
|---|---:|
| Pupillages funded | 3 |
| Tenants | 63 |
| Tenancies in last 3 yrs | 6 |
| Mini-pupillages | yes |
| Apply through OLPAS | |
| Remuneration for pupillage | |
| £37,500 | |
| Minimum qualifications | |
| 2.1 degree | |

**Landmark**
Specialists in Planning, Property and Public Law

# Maitland Chambers

7 Stone Buildings, Lincoln's Inn, London WC2A 3SZ
**Tel:** 020 7406 1200
**Fax:** 020 7406 1300
**Email:** pupillage@maitlandchambers.com
**Web:** www.maitlandchambers.com

**Description of Chambers** Maitland Chambers is the largest commercial Chancery set in London. We are instructed in a wide range of cases – from major international litigation involving multinational companies to county court disputes over the family home. Much of our work is done in London, though we frequently advise and appear for clients in other parts of the United Kingdom and abroad.

**Areas of work** Maitland Chambers undertakes a full range of commercial Chancery work, including: arbitration and mediation; banking, building society work, mortgages and security guarantees; charities; civil fraud and related trust claims; commercial law and contractual disputes; company law; energy; insolvency; insurance and reinsurance; intellectual property; landlord and tenant; media and entertainment law; partnership disputes; pensions; private international law; pre-emptive remedies; probate, administration, wills and intestacy, family provision; professional negligence; property law; restitution; sports law; trusts, settlements and taxation.

**Who should apply** The typical recruit has a first-class mind and a sense of commercial practicality, and will enjoy and be stimulated by the challenge of advocacy. Academically we look for a first or upper second-class honours degree. Pupils must have an aptitude for and general enjoyment of complex legal argument. Your aptitude for and enjoyment of advocacy can be tested by mooting and debating. If you undertake the CPE and/or the BVC year in London, work for the Free Representation Unit is strongly recommended. We encourage both law students and non-law students to apply.

**Pupillage programme** We offer up to three 12-month pupillages, all of which are funded. All pupils in Chambers are regarded as potential tenants. Pupils sit with at least three different barristers but spend their first few months in Chambers (October to Christmas) with one pupil supervisor in order that the pupil can find his or her feet and establish a point of contact which we hope will endure throughout the pupil's time in Chambers.

**When and how to apply** Chambers in not a member of OLPAS and the closing date for 2009-10 applications is 4 February 2008. Visit our website at www.maitlandchambers.com from January 2008 for up-to-date information.

**Mini-pupillages** Applications are considered twice a year; persons seeking a mini-pupillage in the period June to November should apply by 30 April and those seeking a place for the period December to May should apply by 31 October. Applications should be made with a covering letter and CV (listing all university grades) and clearly marked "Mini-pupillage" to the pupillage secretary. Mini-pupils are accepted only after they have completed at least a year of an undergraduate law degree or after part of the CPE course.

**Sponsorship/funding** A pupillage award (£40,000 for pupillage starting in October 2009) is offered to all pupils in Chambers. Up to £10,000 of the award may be drawn down in advance during the BVC year. Income guarantee: Maitland Chambers operates an income guarantee scheme during the first two years of practice and also operates a loan scheme to assist with cash flow during the first six months of tenancy (details are available on request).

Pupillages funded | up to 3
Tenants | 64
Tenancies in last 3 yrs | 6

Mini-pupillages | yes

Applications contact
Ms Valerie Piper

Remuneration for pupillage
£40,000

Minimum qualifications
2.1 degree

# Matrix Chambers

Griffin Building, Gray's Inn, London WC1R 5LN
**Tel:** 020 7404 3447
**Fax:** 020 7404 3448
**Email:** matrix@matrixlaw.co.uk
**Web:** www.matrixlaw.co.uk

**Description of Chambers** Matrix is a dynamic legal practice set up in anticipation of the complex challenges facing the law in the new century. The lawyers who make up Matrix aim to innovate in the way legal services are delivered and to move beyond traditional divisions – between practitioners and academics, private and public law, and domestic and international law. They are also committed to collaborative ventures that will break down traditional divisions within the legal profession itself.

**Areas of work** The members of Matrix practise in a range of different areas of UK public and private law, the law of the European Union and the ECHR, and public international law. Matrix was established to bring together practitioners who recognise that these disciplines are becoming increasingly influenced by common principles of constitutional, European and international law.

We act for private and public clients and have particular expertise in areas including: commercial; competition; crime; data protection; discrimination; education; employment; environmental; extradition; fraud; freedom of information; human rights; immigration, nationality and asylum; international arbitration; local government; public and administration; media; mutual assistance; prison and social welfare.

**Pupillage programme** We are committed to providing a stimulating, balanced and comprehensive 12-month training schedule which is split roughly into quarters. The training committee tends to choose who will supervise in the first quarter, while trainees are finding their feet, but after this consideration is taken into account of the direction the trainee would like to follow. This is usually in the form of at least two pieces of written advice and at least one oral advocacy exercise.

**When and how to apply** Please check our website for information on how to apply for a traineeship.

**Mini pupillages** We currently do not offer mini-pupillages, but for up-to-date information and details on opportunities available and how to apply please visit the opportunities section of our website at www.matrixlaw.co.uk.

**Sponsorship/funding** Matrix offers up to two traineeships each year carrying an award of £35,000 per trainee. £7,500 of this is payable to those yet to complete the Bar School year with the remaining £27,500 to be paid during the 12-month traineeship.

| | |
|---|---|
| Pupillages funded | 2 |
| Tenants | 59 |
| Tenancies in last 3 yrs | 3 |

Apply to
Check website for
application details

Remuneration for pupillage
£35,000

| **9 LINCOLN'S INN FIELDS**<br>9 Lincoln's Inn Fields, London WC2A 3BP<br>**Tel:** 020 7831 4344<br>**Fax:** 020 7831 9945<br>**Email:** chambers@9lif.co.uk<br>**Apply through OLPAS** | A leading set with a strong reputation in all areas of criminal law. | PF 2<br>T 50<br>TL3Y 4<br>MP yes |
|---|---|---|
| **LITTLETON CHAMBERS**<br>3 King's Bench Walk North, Temple,<br>London EC4Y 7HR<br>**Tel:** 020 7797 8600<br>**Fax:** 020 7797 8699<br>**Email:** info@littletonchambers.co.uk<br>**Apply to:** Mr Gerard Hickie | Recognised as a leading set in employment, commercial, professional negligence and ADR. We see pupillage as a major step to tenancy, provide structured, tailored and appraised training. | PF 2<br>T 42<br>TL3Y 6<br>MP yes |
| **MAIDSTONE CHAMBERS**<br>33 Earl Street, Maidstone, Kent ME14 1PF<br>**Tel:** 01622 688592<br>**Fax:** 01622 683305<br>**Email:** clerks@maidstonechambers.co.uk<br>**Apply to:** Pupillage Committee | Currently expanding, applications invited for 3rd six/squatters only with a view to a tenancy.. | PF 0<br>T 13<br>TL3Y 2<br>MP yes |
| **1 MITRE COURT BUILDINGS**<br>Temple, London EC4Y 7BS<br>**Tel:** 020 7452 8900<br>**Fax:** 020 7452 8999<br>**Email:** clerks@1mcb.com<br>**Apply through OLPAS** | Chambers has expanded from its radical beginnings to a progressive and friendly set. Strong specialist teams in ciminal defence, housing, immigration and family. | PF 3<br>T 56<br>TL3Y 5<br>MP yes |
| **MITRE HOUSE CHAMBERS**<br>15-19 Devereux Court, London WC2R 3JJ<br>**Tel:** 020 7842 1300<br>**Fax:** 020 7307 7139<br>**Email:** mitrehse@dircon.co.uk<br>**Apply through OLPAS** | Progressive set with a strong commitment to civil liberties. Main areas include: criminal, family, civil litigation, with particular emphasis on employment, housing, actions against the police and judicial review. | PF 0<br>T 28<br>TL3Y 4<br>MP yes |
| **MONCKTON CHAMBERS**<br>1-2 Raymond Buildings, Gray's Inn,<br>London WC1R 5NR<br>**Tel:** 020 7405 7211<br>**Fax:** 020 7405 2084<br>**Email:** chambers@monckton.com<br>**Apply through OLPAS** | One of the English Bar's leading civil practices, and currently has 44 members. We are a modern set, committed to providing practical and effective advice of the highest quality. | PF 2<br>T 44<br>TL3Y 5<br>MP yes |
| **NEW BAILEY CHAMBERS**<br>Marshall House, Ringway, Preston PR1 2QD<br>**Tel:** 01772 258087<br>**Fax:** 01772 880100<br>**Email:** clerks@newbailey.co.uk | Provincial common law set. | PF 2<br>T 32<br>TL3Y 8<br>MP yes |
| **NEW COURT CHAMBERS**<br>3 Broad Chare, Quayside,<br>Newcastle Upon Tyne NE1 3DQ<br>**Tel:** 0191 232 1980<br>**Fax:** 0191 232 3730<br>**Email:** bryandickson59@newcourt-chambers.co.uk<br>**Apply to:** Chambers Director | | PF 2<br>T 36<br>TL3Y 1<br>MP yes |

**PF** = Pupillages funded / **T** = Tenants / **TL3Y** = Tenancies in last 3 years / **MP** = Mini pupillages offered

# 4 New Square

Lincoln's Inn, London WC2A 3RJ
**Tel:** 020 7822 2000
**Fax:** 020 7822 2001
**Email:** barristers@4newsquare. com
**Web:** www.4newsquare.com

**Areas of work** Professional negligence and indemnity; chancery and commercial law; construction and engineering; insurance and reinsurance; financial services and banking; product liability; clinical negligence; employment.

**When and how to apply** Chambers is a member of OLPAS, and applications for pupillage are accepted through that scheme. The relevant dates and deadlines for applications (for both the summer and autumn seasons) should be obtained from OLPAS.

Students are encouraged to apply to us for a mini-pupillage and those selected are invited to spend a period of three days with us. The purpose of this mini-pupillage is for the applicant to see us and the work that we do and for us to assess his/her potential as a pupil and a prospective tenant. Mini-pupils are paid £100 to cover expenses. Instructions for applying for a mini-pupillage can be found on the website at www. 4newsquare.com. Chambers has a good record of recruiting from its pupils.

**Sponsorship/funding** Chambers offers up to four 12-month pupillages, with awards of £45,000, comprising an award of £37,500 ( up to a third of which can be drawn down during the BVC year) and guaranteed earnings of £7,500. Chambers has a good record of recruiting from its pupils. We guarantee that junior tenants  will earn a minimum of £150,000 in total, net of Chambers' expenses, during their first three years of tenancy, in addition to their pupillage awards.

Pupillages funded  up to 4
Tenants  61
Tenancies in last 3 yrs  5

Mini-pupillages  yes

Applications contact
Ms Catherine Culley

Remuneration for pupillage
£45,000

Minimum qualifications
Good 2.1 degree

FOUR NEW SQUARE

# New Square Chambers

12 New Square, Lincoln's Inn, London WC2A 3SW
**Tel:** 020 7419 8000
**Fax:** 020 7419 8050
**Email:** pupillage@newsquarechambers.co.uk
**Web:** www.newsquarechambers.co.uk

**Description of Chambers** New Square Chambers offers a concentration of experience in Chancery and commercial work and related international matters. We have 46 members, 8 silks and 38 juniors.

**Areas of work** New Square Chambers undertakes a full range of commercial and Chancery work including: charities; civil fraud; company law (including directors' disqualification proceedings and shareholders' disputes); highways and rights of way; housing; insolvency; intellectual property; landlord and tenant; partnership law; pensions; probate, administration of estates, wills and intestacy and family provision; professional negligence; property law; revenue; trusts; settlements and taxation. A considerable amount of our work has an international element. Several member of Chambers have established practices in overseas jurisdictions, including Antigua, the Bahamas, Bermuda, the British Virgin Islands, the Caymans, the Channel Islands, Gibraltar, Hong Kong and Singapore, and before the Privy Council. Our members' international practices span the full range of Chambers' work, including trusts, land, insolvency and public law, in litigious and non-contentious contexts. The editors of *Lewin on Trusts* and *Shareholders' Rights* are all members of Chambers.

**Pupillage programme** At New Square Chambers, we aim to recruit bright and enthusiastic pupils with a proven academic background. Consequently, applicants will usually have a first or good upper second degree, although this need not be in law. Despite our size we are an informal and friendly set, and encourage our pupils to take an active part in the life of Chambers. Pupils undertake four 'seats' of three months, each with a different pupil supervisor, in order to experience the full range of Chambers' work. In addition, pupils are given the opportunity to learn something of the practices of other members of Chambers during their pupillage. The Bar Council's recent Monitoring of Pupillage Review concluded that New Square Chambers "stood out in its pupil arrangements of an exceptional standard".

**When and how to apply** Chambers offers two 12-month pupillages, terminable after six months on either side, which carry with them an award of £35,000. Chambers is not a member of OLPAS and applications for pupillage commencing in 2009 should be made on our application form which is available at www.newsquarechambers.co.uk. The closing date is 15 February 2008. Applications should be submitted via email in accordance with Chambers' pupillage policy which may also be found on our website.

**Mini-pupillages** A limited number of mini-pupillages are available, usually lasting for three days. Applicants must have at least completed the second year of their law degree or, if they are not yet studying law, the third year of their degree. As with pupillage applicants, we require applicants for mini-pupillage to be of at least a high 2.1 or first-class standard.
Applications may only be made by email to minipupillage@newsquarechambers.co.uk between 1 August and 30 September in any given year and must be made in the manner prescribed in our Mini-pupillage Policy which can be found in Appendix I to the Chambers' Pupillage Policy (2003). Applications not made in the prescribed manner may not receive a response. Please refer to our website for further details or telephone Ms Shelley White in Chambers on 020 7419 8000.

| | |
|---|---|
| Pupillages funded | 2 |
| Tenants | 46 |
| Tenancies in last 3 yrs | 3 |
| Mini-pupillages | yes |

**Applications contact**
Chambers

**Remuneration for pupillage**
£35,000

**Minimum qualifications**
2.1 degree

NEW SQUARE CHAMBERS▪

# No5 Chambers

Steelhouse Lane, Birmingham B4 6DR
**Tel:** 0870 203 5555
**Fax:** 0121 606 1501
**Email:** shirleyt@no5.com
**Web:** www.no5.com

| | |
|---|---|
| Pupillages funded | 2 |
| Tenants | 196 |
| Mini-pupillages | yes |

**Apply to**
Shirley Titmarsh

**Remuneration for pupillage**
Grant of £20,000 in first six months plus earnings averaging £20,000 in second six

**Description of Chambers** Throughout its 100 year history, No5 Chambers has established a reputation for breaking new ground and continues to be regarded as a progressive and forward-thinking set, maintaining its success in traditional sectors of law whilst offering specialist advice and representation at the cutting edge of newly evolving areas.

In response to an increase in its client requirements, No5 Chambers continues to develop new areas and recruit specialists into its groups so it is well placed to provide expertise at all levels on a national and international level. With offices in Birmingham, London and Bristol, the Chambers is divided into nine main practice groups (crime, personal injury, clinical negligence, planning, family, commercial & chancery, agriculture, regulatory and employment), each with a dedicated clerking team and additional marketing resources.

Despite recent changes in the structure and funding of barristers' work, No5 has defended and expanded its market share, with members of Chambers enjoying above average earnings for practitioners in their fields. The barristers continue to innovate to ensure that obstacles to the Bar become opportunities.

**Who should apply** No5 Chambers is an equal opportunities employer and welcomes applications from all sections of the community.

**Pupillage programme** No5 Chambers seeks to offer up to two, 12-month pupillages each year based in its Birmingham Chambers. A considerable investment is made by No5 Chambers, with its pupillages being offered with a view to tenancy provided appropriate benchmark requirements are met.

Pupillage training is tailored to suit the needs and interests of each individual, although some time will be spent in each practice group during the first six months to ensure familiarity with any work likely to be encountered during the second six months.

Throughout the 12-month period, pupils are regularly and carefully monitored by the recruitment committee to ensure that they are progressing appropriately and that all their training needs are being met. Pupils can expect their workload during the second six months to be varied and challenging.

**When and how to apply** Applications for entrance in Autumn 2009 will be considered from 01 January 2008 onwards. The closing date for applications is 4pm on 12 May 2008.

Candidates should obtain a copy of the Chambers' application form from the website (www.no5.com) or from Shirley Titmarsh (shirleyt@no5.com). Applications through OLPAS are not accepted.

**Sponsorship/funding** An award of £20,000 is made during the first six months of a pupillage and pupils can earn an average of £20,000 during the second six months. In addition, loans are available if required, and bursaries or advances for the BVC year will also be considered.

CHAMBERS

BIRMINGHAM · LONDON · BRISTOL

| | | | |
|---|---|---|---|
| **NEW COURT CHAMBERS**<br>Temple, London EC4Y 9BE<br>**Tel:** 020 7583 5123<br>**Fax:** 020 7353 3383<br>**Email:** pupillages@newcourtchambers.net<br>**Apply through OLPAS** | Chambers is now a specialist family set: children and finance, public and private. Long established base of local authorities as professional clients. Friendly atmosphere. | PF<br>T<br>TL3Y<br>MP | 1<br>20<br>4<br>yes |
| **3 NEW SQUARE**<br>Lincoln's Inn, London WC2A 3RS<br>**Tel:** 020 7405 1111<br>**Fax:** 020 7405 7800<br>**Email:** clerks@3newsquare.co.uk<br>**Apply through OLPAS** | A specialist intellectual property chambers which is regularly recommended as a leading set for patent, trademark, copyright, media and entertainment law. | PF<br>T<br>TL3Y<br>MP | 1<br>16<br>2<br>yes |
| **8 NEW SQUARE**<br>Chambers of Mark Platts-Mills QC, Lincoln's Inn, London WC2A 3QP<br>**Tel:** 020 7405 4321<br>**Fax:** 020 7405 9955<br>**Email:** clerks@8newsquare.co.uk<br>**Apply through OLPAS** | The largest specialist intellectual property, media and entertainment chambers in the UK, covering a broad range of work, from technical patent to high profile media cases. | PF<br>T<br>TL3Y<br>MP | 1<br>25<br>2<br>yes |
| **2 NEW STREET CHAMBERS**<br>2 New Street, Leicester LE1 5NA<br>**Tel:** 0116 262 5906<br>**Fax:** 0116 251 2023<br>**Email:** clerks@2newstreet.co.uk<br>**Apply through OLPAS** | A specialist family and civil law set, well established, over 80 years old and practising throughout the Midland circuit. A minimum 2:1 degree required. | PF<br>T<br>TL3Y<br>MP | 1<br>13<br>3<br>yes |
| **NEW WALK CHAMBERS**<br>27 New Walk, Leicester LE1 6TE<br>**Tel:** 0116 255 9144<br>**Fax:** 0116 255 9084<br>**Email:** mryan@newwalkchambers.law.co.uk<br>**Apply to:** Mr Michael Ryan | Chambers continues to enjoy a strong work base coupled with expertise in its specialist areas. Application form on website. | PF<br>T<br>TL3Y<br>MP | Up to 4<br>23<br>6<br>yes |
| **NICHOLAS STREET CHAMBERS**<br>22 Nicholas Street, Chester CH1 2NX<br>**Tel:** 01244 323886<br>**Fax:** 01244 347732<br>**Apply to:** Mr J Cullen | A long established common law set offering advice and advocacy services across the North West, with particular strengths in crime, family and personal injury. | PF<br>T<br>TL3Y<br>MP | 1<br>34<br>5<br>yes |
| **NORTHAMPTON CHAMBERS**<br>22 Albion Place, Northampton NN1 1UD<br>**Tel:** 01604 636271<br>**Fax:** 01604 232931<br>**Email:** james@northampton-chambers.co.uk<br>**Apply through OLPAS** | Small, well-established, friendly set. Mainly criminal and family work for local solicitors. Good quality work for junior tenants. | PF<br>T<br>TL3Y<br>MP | 2<br>10<br>6<br>yes |
| **OLD COURT CHAMBERS**<br>Newham House, 96-98 Borough Road, Middlesbrough TS12HJ<br>**Tel:** 01642 23 25 23<br>**Fax:** 01642 23 28 96<br>**Email:** clerks@oldcourtchambers.com<br>**Apply to:** Mr John Constable | | PF<br>T<br>TL3Y<br>MP | 1<br>20<br>3<br>no |

PF = Pupillages funded / **T** = Tenants / **TL3Y** = Tenancies in last 3 years / **MP** = Mini pupillages offered

# XXIV Old Buildings

24 Old Buildings, Lincoln's Inn, London WC2A 3UP
**Tel:** 020 7691 2424
**Fax:** 0870 460 2178
**Email:** clerks@xxiv.co.uk
**Web:** www.xxiv.co.uk

**Description of Chambers** XXIV Old Buildings is a commercial Chancery chambers of 31 barristers based in Lincoln's Inn.

**Areas of work** Members are instructed in a wide variety of commercial Chancery areas, with particular emphasis on business matters (both litigation and transactional matters, including mergers and acquisitions); company and financial services with related pension law aspects; insolvency; property; trusts and estates work; international and offshore – particularly in relation to trusts and offshore structures with the closely associated fields of fraud, breach of fiduciary duty and asset recovery. Professional liability is covered in all these fields, particularly in relation to solicitors, accountants, professional trustees and financial managers and advisers.

We are particularly respected for our practice in the international and offshore fields, covering both traditional Chancery work as well as major commercial litigation. Many of us frequently advise and appear in other jurisdictions (eg, the BVI, the Cayman Islands, the Bahamas, Malaysia, Hong Kong, Gibraltar and the Isle of Man).

Uniquely for a London chambers, we have a permanent office in Geneva, which deals almost exclusively with offshore disputes.

We also have a niche practice in aviation and travel law, specialising mainly in aircraft leasing and insurance/reinsurance issues.

**Pupillage programme** We like to recruit our junior members from those who have undertaken pupillage with us. We are therefore careful that our pupils acquire all the skills necessary to make them successful commercial Chancery barristers. During a 12-month pupillage, a pupil will have, on average, four pupil supervisors with whom they will spend the majority of their time. Each year we are looking for two pupils with a first or 2.1 degree, though not necessarily in law, who have an enthusiasm for the type of work we do, sound judgement and the application required to succeed in a very competitive and intellectually demanding environment.

**When and how to apply** Send your CV to Helen Galley, secretary of the Pupillage Committee, at XXIV Old Buildings, 24 Old Buildings, London, WC2A 3UP; telephone: 020 7691 2424; email: clerks@xxiv.co.uk.

You can also find out more about XXIV Old Buildings at www.xxiv.co.uk. Our website also contains guidance on pupillage and mini-pupillage applications.

**Sponsorship/funding** Each pupil will be paid £37,500.

| | |
|---|---|
| Pupillages funded | 2 |
| Tenants | 31 |
| Tenancies in last 3 yrs | 3 |
| Mini-pupillages | yes |

**Applications contact**
Helen Galley

**Remuneration for pupillage**
£37,500

**Minimum qualifications**
2.1 degree

Twenty Four Old Buildings

# 10 Old Square

Ground Floor, Lincoln's Inn, London WC2A 3SU
**Tel:** 020 7405 0758
**Fax:** 020 7831 8237
**Web:** www.tenoldsquare.com

**Description of Chambers** Chambers is a leading Chancery set which enjoys the highest reputation in the specialist areas of: commercial property, including real property litigation; landlord and tenant; credit and security agreements; and trusts, including probate and administration of estates, capital taxation, private international law and equitable remedies. Related areas of practice include company and insolvency law, banking, commercial litigation, partnerships and professional negligence.

**Who should apply** We are looking for a potential tenant. Candidates should have a real enthusiasm for the sort of work in which we specialise, be of proven high academic ability and possess excellent powers of analysis, reasoning and presentation. In addition, the successful candidate will demonstrate sound judgement and energy.

**Pupillage programme** The pupillage is structured so that the pupil can see the full range of the work of members of Chambers. The pupil will have one pupil supervisor for the first six months and another for the second six months. The pupil will sit with two other members of Chambers during the 12 months under the supervision of their pupil supervisor. The pupil's progress is closely monitored and is subject to formal review at the end of the third, fifth, eighth and eleventh months of the pupillage.

**When and how to apply** For pupillage commencing October 2009 candidates must apply by 30 April 2008. Applications must be made on the Chambers' application form, which will be available from the clerks' room or on the Chambers' website from 1 March 2008. Interviews will be conducted at the end of June, followed by assessed mini-pupillages for shortlisted candidates during the first two weeks in July.

We offer either one 12-month pupillage or two six-month pupillages.

**Mini-pupillages** Apply by application form available from Robert Arnfield.

**Sponsorship/funding** £40,000 (subject to upward review), with the option of drawing down up to a quarter in the previous year.

| | |
|---|---|
| Pupillages funded | 1 |
| Tenants | 29 |
| Tenancies in last 3 yrs | 3 |
| Mini-pupillages | yes |
| Remuneration for pupillage | |
| £40,000 | |
| Minimum qualifications | |
| 2.1 degree | |

# Old Square Chambers

10-11 Bedford Row, London WC1R 4BU
**Tel:** 020 7269 0300
**Fax:** 020 7405 1387
**Email:** clerks@oldsquare.co.uk
**Web:** www.oldsquare.co.uk

**Description of Chambers** Although highly motivated and ambitious, we consider ourselves to be a relaxed set. One attraction of the Bar is that Chambers is a collection of individuals rather than a corporate hierarchy. Tenants span the age range and a number are in their second career, having started their working life as academics, trade union officials or solicitors.

We have an annex in Bristol comprising 14 tenants which is regarded not as a separate set but as an extension of Chambers. There is an option for pupils to undertake pupillage in Bristol. London pupils will generally spend a week in Bristol and longer visits can be arranged.

We have a system of special interest groups in Chambers which provides a vehicle for in-house discussions on recent developments in the law, external training for others and marketing opportunities. Pupils are encouraged to be involved in the various groups.

We have a well-regarded clerking and administration team: our clerks are experienced and work to clear lines of responsibility; in your second six a clerk will look after your work and diary.

**Areas of work** Employment, personal injury, product liability, environmental and clinical law.

**Who should apply** We assess candidates on a number of criteria. These may change from year to year but generally include: intellectual ability (measured by academic or other achievement), potential as an advocate, interest in Chambers' fields of practice, ability to cope with hard work and pressure, and interpersonal skills.

**Pupillage programme** In general we offer two 12-month pupillages (preferably one in Bristol), funded generously. You will experience a wide variety of work in our different specialisms and there is also the opportunity to work closely with silks on complex and sometimes high-profile cases.

In the second six you will undertake your own court and advisory work.

We aim to recruit tenants from our pupils.

**When and how to apply** As per OLPAS (summer season). We would prefer you to have undertaken a mini-pupillage at Old Square Chambers before applying for a pupillage.

**Mini-pupillages** Apply online at www.oldsquare.co.uk/minipupillage1.asp.

**Sponsorship/funding** 2009 award will be £30,000 guaranteed minimum earnings which may be exceeded depended on earnings in second six. A draw down system facility is available for BVC on application.

| | |
|---|---|
| Pupillages funded | 2 |
| Tenants | 62 |
| Tenancies in last 3 yrs | 4 |
| Mini-pupillages | yes |
| Apply through OLPAS | |
| Remuneration for pupillage | £30,000 |
| Minimum qualifications | 2.1 degree preferred |

OLD SQUARE
CHAMBERS

## 15 OLD SQUARE
Lincoln's Inn, London WC2A 3UE
**Tel:** 020 7242 2744
**Fax:** 020 7831 8095
**Email:** taxchambers@15oldsquare.co.uk
**Apply to:** Dr Timothy Lyons QC

The chambers specialise in revenue law.

| | |
|---|---|
| PF | 1 |
| T | 12 |
| TL3Y | 2 |
| MP | yes |

---

## ORIEL CHAMBERS
14 Water Street, Liverpool L2 8TD
**Tel:** 0151 236 7191
**Fax:** 0151 227 5909
**Email:** clerks@oriel-chambers.co.uk
**Apply through OLPAS**

We are a prominent, busy, friendly set who offer the successful applicant an excellent grounding in all the areas of specialisation covered.

| | |
|---|---|
| PF | up to 2 |
| T | 57 |
| TL3Y | 11 |
| MP | yes |

---

## OUTER TEMPLE CHAMBERS
222 Strand, London WC2R 1BA
**Tel:** 020 7353 6381
**Fax:** 020 7583 1786
**Email:** pupillage@outertemple.com
**Apply to:** Miss Victoria Jearum

| | |
|---|---|
| PF | 2 |
| T | 63 |
| TL3Y | 6 |
| MP | yes |

---

## PALLANT CHAMBERS
12 North Pallant, Chichester PO19 1TQ
**Tel:** 01243 784538
**Fax:** 01243 780861
**Email:** clerks@pallantchambers.co.uk
**Apply to:** Mr Neil Maton

Primarily a family & civil law set with a small criminal team. Strong connections with public authorities.

| | |
|---|---|
| PF | Up to 2 |
| T | 21 |
| TL3Y | 7 |
| MP | yes |

---

## 1 PAPER BUILDINGS
1st Floor, Temple, London EC4Y 7EP
**Tel:** 020 7353 3728
**Fax:** 020 7353 2911
**Email:** clerks@onepaperbuildings.com
**Apply to:** Mr Barnaby Shaw

1 Paper Buildings is predominantly a criminal set working on the south eastern circuit (Cambridgeshire, Norfolk) and western circuit (Hampshire, Dorset). Two pupillages available.

| | |
|---|---|
| PF | 2 |
| T | 41 |
| TL3Y | 5 |
| MP | no |

---

## 2 PAPER BUILDINGS
First Floor, Temple, London EC4Y 7ET
**Tel:** 020 7556 5500
**Fax:** 020 7583 3423
**Email:** briefsin@2pb.co.uk
**Apply through OLPAS**

A well established, busy and friendly criminal law chambers, offering 12-month pupillages. Second six pupils will be in court each working day.

| | |
|---|---|
| PF | 4 |
| T | 48 |
| TL3Y | 6 |
| MP | yes |

---

## 3 PAPER BUILDINGS
First Floor, Temple, London EC4Y 7EU
**Tel:** 020 7583 8055
**Fax:** 020 7353 6271
**Email:** clerks@3paper.co.uk

With centres in London, Bournemouth, Bristol, Winchester and Oxford and committed specialist barristers, Three Paper Buildings prides itself on being a genuine 'one-stop shop'.

| | |
|---|---|
| PF | 5-6 |
| T | 130 |
| TL3Y | 10 |
| MP | yes |

---

## 4 PAPER BUILDINGS
First Floor, Temple, London EC4Y 7EX
**Tel:** 020 7583 0816
**Fax:** 020 7353 4979
**Email:** clerks@4pb.com
**Apply through OLPAS**

For many years, these chambers have had a reputation for high quality advice and advocacy in family and civil law.

| | |
|---|---|
| PF | 2 |
| T | 47 |
| TL3Y | 3 |
| MP | yes |

---

PF = Pupillages funded / T = Tenants / TL3Y = Tenancies in last 3 years / MP = Mini pupillages offered

# 30 Park Place

Cardiff CF10 3BS
**Tel:** 029 2039 8421
**Fax:** 029 2039 8725
**Email:** clerk@30parkplace.law.co.uk
**Web:** www.30parkplace.com

**Description of Chambers** 30 Park Place is a common law set of chambers with 57 members including 11 QCs. It is the largest set on the Wales Circuit and is located in the centre of Cardiff. It was founded in 1970. It is, therefore, a well established set that is committed to continuing development and progress. It was the first set to be awarded the Bar Council's 'BarMark' in South Wales and it also holds the Legal Services Commission's 'Quality Mark'.

**Areas of work** The advice and representation provided by '30' extend across the legal spectrum. Junior members generally engage in a wide variety of work to ensure a broad experience of advocacy while developing their own specialities. The main areas of work include administrative law, European law, Chancery, commercial, company, construction, crime (both prosecution and defence), education, family, immigration, personal injury and professional negligence.

**Who should apply** Both law and non-law graduates are encouraged to apply and all applicants should have a good first degree. A strong desire to succeed and a commitment to the profession are essential. Pupils are expected to have an aptitude for legal argument and should be able to provide evidence of their experience at public speaking and debate.

**Pupillage programme** Normally two 12-month pupillages are offered each year, both of which are funded. The pupillage is divided into two six-month periods, each with a different pupil supervisor practising in different areas of law. Pupillage is not offered with a view to tenancy; therefore, at the end of their pupillage, it is up to pupils to satisfy Chambers that they merit election.

**When and how to apply** 30 Park Place is currently a member of OLPAS, but please check Chambers' website.

**Mini pupillages** Mini-pupillages are assessed and are often oversubscribed. Potential applicants therefore need to apply in plenty of time. Mini-pupils are only accepted once a student has either commenced their law degree or is in the final year of a non-law degree when they have to decide to take the CPE. Applications with a full CV together with a letter saying why they want to undertake a mini-pupillage at '30' should be sent to the pupillage secretary.

**Sponsorship/funding** A pupillage award of £10,000 is paid during the first six months. Chambers then guarantees earnings of at least £6,000 during the second six months

| | |
|---|---|
| Pupillages funded | 2 |
| Tenants | 57 |
| Tenancies in last 3 yrs | 4 |
| Mini-pupillages | yes |

Apply through OLPAS

Remuneration for pupillage
£10,000 award in first six;
£6,000 guaranteed earnings
in secnd six

# 4 Pump Court

Temple, London EC4Y 7AN
**Tel:** 020 7842 5555
**Fax:** 020 7583 2036
**Email:** chambers@4pumpcourt.com
**Web:** www.4pumpcourt.com

**Description of Chambers** 4 Pump Court is one of London's leading sets of Chambers, with a reputation for excellence in advocacy. We believe we offer an exceptionally friendly and relaxed environment in which to complete pupillage.

**Areas of work** The work of Chambers covers virtually every aspect of commercial and common law, but with particular emphasis on insurance and reinsurance, professional negligence, construction and information technology.

**Who should apply** We look for candidates with sound academic qualifications (minimum 2.1), impressive academic references and the ability to express themselves clearly and attractively, on paper as well as orally.

**Pupillage programme** During their first six months, each pupil is assigned to two barristers for three months each. During their second six months, each pupil has only one pupil supervisor, but will usually be conducting his or her own cases as well.

**When and how to apply** By 31 January 2008 to begin October 2009. The application form is available on request (to Mrs Kathryn Webb) or on the Chambers' website.

**Mini-pupillages** Limited places available throughout the year upon application by email with CV to minipupillage@4pumpcourt.com.

**Sponsorship/funding** Usually two funded pupillages with awards of £42,000, of which up to £14,000 may be advanced during the Bar Vocational Course. Any fees earned in the second six months are in addition to the award.

| | |
|---|---|
| Pupillages funded | 2 |
| Tenants | 51 |
| Tenancies in last 3 yrs | 6 |
| Mini-pupillages | yes |

Applications contact
Mrs Kathryn Webb

Remuneration for pupillage
£42,000

Minimum qualifications
2.1 degree

**5 PAPER BUILDINGS**
First Floor, Temple, London EC4Y 7HB
**Tel:** 020 7583 6117
**Fax:** 020 7353 0075
**Email:** clerks@5pb.co.uk
**Apply through OLPAS**

We are a leading set, specialising in criminal law. Commercial fraud is an acknowledged strength. Other expertise includes trading law, public inquiries and disciplinary tribunals.

PF 3
T 41
TL3Y 5
MP yes

---

**5 PAPER BUILDINGS**
Ground Floor, Temple, London EC4Y 7HB
**Tel:** 020 7815 3200
**Fax:** 020 7815 3201
**Email:** clerks @5paper.com
**Apply to:** Mr Robert Harrap

Two pupillages available each year. Barmark award. Range of corporate and private clients. Four specialist practice groups. Applications on Chambers' application form only.

PF 2
T 37
TL3Y 4
MP yes

---

**PARADISE CHAMBERS**
26 Paradise Square, Sheffield S1 2DE
**Tel:** 0114 273 8951
**Fax:** 0114 276 0848
**Email:** pupillage@paradise-sq.co.uk
**Apply to:** via website

Established, respected and busy common law set. History of pupils being accepted for tenancy. Private and public clients.

PF 2
T 43
TL3Y 2
MP yes

---

**PARK COURT CHAMBERS**
16 Park Place, Leeds LS1 2SJ
**Tel:** 0113 243 3277
**Fax:** 0113 242 1285
**Email:** clerks@parkcourtchambers.co.uk
**Apply through OLPAS**

We are one of the busiest and most prestigious sets outside London with 11 silks and 47 juniors undertaking heavy criminal, civil and family work.

PF 1
T 58
TL3Y 5
MP yes

---

**PARK LANE CHAMBERS**
19 Westgate, Leeds LS1 2RD
**Tel:** 0113 228 5000
**Fax:** 0113 228 1500
**Email:** clerks@parklanechambers.co.uk
**Apply to:** Mr Simon Thorp

One of the leading civil sets in the north eastern circuit with established teams in the fields of personal injury, clinical negligence, family, chancery and commercial work.

PF 1
T 41
TL3Y 5
MP yes

---

**9 PARK PLACE**
9 Park Place, Cardiff CF10 3DP
**Tel:** 029 2038 2731
**Fax:** 029 2022 2542
**Apply to:** Mr Gwydion Hughes

9 Park Place is a leading set offering a wide spectrum of legal specialisation. Chambers offers two funded pupillages each year.

PF 2
T 50
TL3Y 7
MP yes

---

**33 PARK PLACE**
Chambers of Graham Walters, Cardiff CF10 3TN
**Tel:** 029 2023 3313
**Fax:** 029 2022 8294
**Email:** andrew.thomas@33parkplace.com
**Apply through OLPAS**

PF 1
T 47
TL3Y 8
MP yes

---

**37 PARK SQUARE**
Leeds LS1 2NY
**Tel:** 0113 243 9422
**Fax:** 0113 242 4229
**Email:** chambers@no37.co.uk

A friendly, progressive common law set that recruits pupils with a view to tenancy. Minimum of 2.1 in qualifying law degree. Very competent on the BVC. Srong connections to the North East desirable.

PF 0
T 35
TL3Y 6
MP yes

---

**PF** = Pupillages funded / **T** = Tenants / **TL3Y** = Tenancies in last 3 years / **MP** = Mini pupillages offered

# Pump Court Tax Chambers

16 Bedford Row, London WC1R 4EF
**Tel:** 020 7414 8080
**Fax:** 020 7414 8099
**Email:** pupils@pumptax.com
**Web:** www.pumptax.com

**Description of Chambers** Pump Court Tax Chambers is the largest set specialising in tax law (26 members, 10 silks).

**Areas of work** Members of Chambers undertake litigation and advisory work in all areas of tax law, both personal and corporate. Members appear in courts at all levels from the tax tribunals to the House of Lords and the European Court of Justice.

**Who should apply** Anyone interested in practising in an area of law requiring an analytical mind and a grasp of other areas of law, especially trusts and contract. Tax planning provides a unique opportunity to use legal skills in a creative manner while tax litigation often involves novel points of law.

**Pupillage programme** Chambers offers 12 months' pupillages but will also consider applications for first or second sixes. Pupils generally spend their first ten weeks with one pupil supervisor followed by four to six weeks with three other supervisors. They also spend time with silks and senior juniors. This allows them to see a wide variety of work and also gives members at different levels of seniority the opportunity to give them feedback.

**When and how to apply** Chambers keeps its membership of OLPAS under review and has chosen not to participate in OLPAS for pupillages starting in October 2009. Applications should be made by CV and covering letter, marked for the attention of the Pupillage Secretary, and be either posted or emailed to pupils@pumptax.com by 18 February 2008. Further details are available on our website.

**Mini-pupillages** We welcome applications for both assessed and unassessed mini-pupillages. Unassesed mini-pupillages of two to three days' duration are available throughout the year. Assessed mini-pupillages last for five days and are available during certain weeks in the summer, advertised on our website. For both types of mini-pupillage, please apply by CV and covering letter, marked for the attention of the Pupillage Secretary by post or email.

**Sponsorship/funding** Pupils are given up to £20,000 for each six months, £8,000 of which can be drawn down during Bar school.

| | |
|---|---|
| Pupillages funded | up to 3 |
| Tenants | 26 |
| Tenancies in last 3 yrs | 2 |
| Mini-pupillages | yes |

Apply by CV

Remuneration for pupillage
£20,000 per six months

Minimum qualifications
2.1 degree

PUMP COURT TAX CHAMBERS

# Quadrant Chambers

Chambers of Lionel Persey QC & Simon Rainey QC, Quadrant House, 10 Fleet Street, London EC4Y 1AU
**Tel:** 020 7583 4444
**Fax:** 020 7583 4455
**Email:** pupillage@quadrantchambers.com
**Web:** www.quadrantchambers.com

**Description of Chambers** Quadrant Chambers is one of the foremost and longest-established sets of chambers specialising in commercial law. Chambers has kept abreast of the latest technological advances in information and computer technology. Quadrant Chambers offers a first-class service at sensible fee rates, and has a staff renowned for their openness and fairness.

**Areas of work** The challenging and rewarding work of Chambers encompasses the broad range of commercial disputes, embracing arbitration, aviation, banking, shipping, international trade, insurance and reinsurance, professional negligence, entertainment and media, environmental and construction law. Over 70% of Chambers' work involves international clients.

**Who should apply** Quadrant Chambers seeks high-calibre pupils with good academic qualifications (at least a 2.1 degree), who exhibit good written and verbal skills.

**Pupillage programme** Chambers offers a maximum of four funded pupillages of 12 months' duration (reviewable at six months). Pupils are moved among several members of Chambers and will experience a wide range of high-quality commercial work. Outstanding pupils are likely to be offered a tenancy at the end of their pupillage.

**When and how to apply** See website for details or contact Chambers.

**Mini-pupillages** Mini-pupillages are encouraged so that potential pupils can experience the work of Chambers before committing themselves to an application for full pupillage.

**Sponsorship/funding** Awards of £37,500 are available for each funded pupillage - part of which may be forwarded during the BVC, at the pupillage committee's discretion.

| | |
|---|---|
| Pupillages funded | 4 |
| Tenants | 41 |
| Tenancies in last 3 yrs | 5 |
| Mini-pupillages | yes |
| Applications | See website |
| Remuneration for pupillage | £37,500 |
| Minimum qualifications | 2.1 degree |

quadrant
chambers

# Queen Elizabeth Building

Temple, London EC4Y 7BS
**Tel:** 020 7797 7070
**Fax:** 020 7797 7435
**Email:** clerks@qeb.co.uk
**Web:** www.qeb.co.uk

**Areas of work** QEB is a leading set of family law chambers with particular expertise in high-profile ancillary relief work. There is immense experience in all aspects of family law including: jurisdictional disputes, foreign divorces, pre-marital agreements, civil partnerships, injunctions both financial and domestic, public and private law child work, adoption, child abduction, Inheritance Act claims and disputes between former cohabitees. Cases tend to involve substantial assets and complex financial arrangements. Members of Chambers have been involved in many of the most important cases of legal principle. They also often act for high-profile figures in the public eye. In addition some members practise in general common law with particular emphasis on personal injury and professional negligence work. We have been established for over 80 years. Six former members of Chambers are current High Court Judges in the Family Division and one has recently been appointed a Lord Justice of Appeal. Members of Chambers are consistently highly rated in the legal directories.

**Who should apply** The practice of family law is infinitely varied and clients come from all walks of life. International and conflict of laws issues arise increasingly often. An ability to deal not only with complex financial disputes, often involving commercial issues, but also with child-related or other emotionally fraught and sensitive situations, is essential. We are looking for applicants with a strong academic record (minimum 2.1 law or non-law degree save in exceptional circumstances), good legal and analytical skills, and also those who can demonstrate an ability to communicate sensitively with a wide range of people at a critical time in their lives.

**Pupillage programme** A pupillage at QEB offers top-quality training and very good financial support in a busy, friendly environment. A 12-month pupillage involves three pupil supervisors, but pupils are also encouraged to work with other tenants at all levels to gain a broad experience of our work. All our pupils are automatically considered candidates for tenancy and new tenants are only recruited from QEB pupils. Our reputation is such that where a pupil is not taken on, he or she is usually well placed elsewhere.

**When and how to apply** Chambers is a part of the OLPAS system and we recruit through the summer season. Please consult the latest OLPAS handbook or website for details of the timetable.

**Mini-pupillages** Applications for mini-pupillages are to be made in writing with enclosed CV to the Mini-Pupillage Secretary. Chambers has recently adopted a timetable for mini-pupillage applications. Please consult our website at www.qeb.co.uk for full details.

**Sponsorship/funding** Maximum £25,000 pa (plus earnings)

| | |
|---|---|
| Pupillages funded | Up to 3 |
| Tenants | 31 |
| Tenancies in last 3 yrs | 5 |

Mini-pupillages      yes

Apply through OLPAS

Remuneration for pupillage
£25,000 (plus earnings)

Minimum qualifications
2.1 degree save in
exceptional circumstances

| | | |
|---|---|---|
| **1 PUMP COURT**<br>Lower Ground Floor, Temple, London EC4Y 7AB<br>**Tel:** 020 7842 7070<br>**Fax:** 020 7353 4944<br>**Apply through OLPAS** | Chambers is a democratic collective and does not have a traditional head of chambers. Chambers prides itself on representing those disadvantaged by poverty or discrimination. | PF 23<br>T 72<br>TL3Y 10<br>MP yes |
| **2 PUMP COURT**<br>First Floor, Temple, London EC4Y 7AH<br>**Tel:** 020 7353 5597<br>**Fax:** 020 7583 2122<br>**Apply through OLPAS** | Well-established and friendly set of chambers, specialising in all aspects of criminal and family law. | PF 1<br>T 39<br>TL3Y 6<br>MP yes |
| **6 PUMP COURT**<br>First Floor, Temple, London EC4Y 7AR<br>**Tel:** 020 7797 8400<br>**Fax:** 020 7797 8401<br>**Email:** clerks@6pumpcourt.co.uk<br>**Apply through OLPAS** | Chambers' work is divided between four specialist groups: criminal law, planning and environmental law, civil litigation and family law. Chambers also has an annexe in Maidstone. | PF 2-3<br>T 40<br>TL3Y 5<br>MP yes |
| **5 PUMP COURT CHAMBERS**<br>Ground Floor, Temple, London EC4Y 7AP<br>**Tel:** 020 7353 2532<br>**Fax:** 020 7353 5321<br>**Email:** clerks@5pumpcourt.com | Chambers is a long-established common law set. Tenants undertake work within one or more of the three practice teams - criminal, family and civil. | PF 2<br>T 35<br>TL3Y 7<br>MP yes |
| **3 RAYMOND BUILDINGS**<br>Gray's Inn, London WC1R 5BH<br>**Tel:** 020 7400 6400<br>**Fax:** 020 7400 6464<br>**Email:** chambers@3raymondbuildings.com<br>**Apply through OLPAS** | Leading set with a national and international reputation. Expertise in crime, commercial fraud, extradition, public and administrative law, licensing, human rights, environmental/health and safety. | PF 3<br>T 44<br>TL3Y 5<br>MP yes |
| **5RB**<br>5 Raymond Buildings, Gray's Inn, London WC1R 5BP<br>**Tel:** 020 7242 2902<br>**Fax:** 020 7831 2686<br>**Email:** pupillage@5RB.com<br>**Apply through OLPAS** | Chambers is particularly well known for expertise in all areas of media and entertainment law, intellectual property and sports law. | PF 2<br>T 29<br>TL3Y 4<br>MP yes |
| **REGENCY CHAMBERS**<br>Cathedral Square, Peterborough PE1 1XW<br>**Tel:** 01733 315215<br>**Fax:** 01733 315851<br>**Email:** clerks@regencychambers.law.co.uk<br>**Apply through OLPAS** | General common law chambers. | PF 1-2<br>T 18<br>TL3Y 3<br>MP yes |
| **RENAISSANCE CHAMBERS**<br>Gray's Inn Chambers, Gray's Inn, London WC1R 5JA<br>**Tel:** 020 7404 1111<br>**Fax:** 020 7430 1522<br>**Email:** clerks@renaissancechambers.co.uk<br>**Apply through OLPAS** | Chambers specialises in all aspects of family law (public and private); immigration and refugee law; administrative law; local government and general common law. | PF 2<br>T 48<br>TL3Y 3<br>MP yes |

PF = Pupillages funded / **T** = Tenants / **TL3Y** = Tenancies in last 3 years / **MP** = Mini pupillages offered

# Radcliffe Chambers

11 New Square, Lincoln's Inn, London WC2A 3QB
**Tel:** 020 7831 0081
**Fax:** 020 7405 2560
**Email:** clerks@radcliffechambers.com
**Web:** www.radcliffechambers.com

**Description of Chambers** Radcliffe Chambers was formed on 5 June 2006 on the merger of 11 Old Square and 11 New Square. We have 45 barristers, including 5 Queen's Counsel, and are one of the largest commercial Chancery chambers in the country, with over 40 recommendations in the current editions of *The Legal 500* and *Chambers* directories, covering the leading areas of commercial and Chancery practice.

**Areas of work** The barristers at Radcliffe Chambers practise in the fields of banking and financial services; charities; company and commercial; consumer credit and mortgages; insolvency; pensions; planning, environment and local government; professional negligence; property; and trusts and estates, as well as a number of other specialist areas. We provide advice in contentious and non-contentious matters within these and associated areas of work, and appear as advocates before all levels of courts and tribunals.

**Who should apply** We are seeking to recruit candidates with excellent academic ability (at least a good 2.1 degree, although not necessarily in law) and effective communication skills who demonstrate a strong interest in Chambers' core areas of work. We aim to recruit junior tenants from our own pupils and, for this reason, only offer pupillage to candidates whom we believe have a realistic prospect of being offered tenancy.

**Pupillage programme** We are offering up to two pupillages to start in October 2009 with an award of £37,500. Radcliffe Chambers carries on the tradition and high standards set by 11 New Square and 11 Old Square. We believe that we provide our pupils with excellent training under the supervision of experienced and successful practitioners. Our pupils may anticipate having up to four pupil supervisors during their pupillage and will see a wide range of commercial and Chancery work, both advisory and in court. During their second six, pupils are likely to have the opportunity to undertake their own court work and any fees earned will be in addition to the pupillage award.

We aim to equip our pupils for successful practice at the junior Bar and we pride ourselves on the quality of training that we provide. Pupillage at Radcliffe Chambers is a rewarding and varied experience in a commercially-aware, forward-thinking and friendly environment.

**When and how to apply** We are a member of OLPAS and applications should be made in the summer season.

**Mini-pupillages** We offer a number of two-day, unassessed mini-pupillages throughout the year for those with a strong interest in our core areas of practice. A full CV with a covering letter should be addressed to: Christopher Buckley, Radcliffe Chambers, 11 New Square, Lincoln's Inn, London WC2A 3QB. Please mark the envelope "Mini-pupillage".

Further details of Chambers generally and of pupillage and mini-pupillages can be found at www.radcliffechambers.com and specific enquiries about pupillage should be made in the first instance to Christopher Buckley.

| | |
|---|---|
| Pupillages funded | Up to 2 |
| Tenants | 45 |
| Tenancies in last 3 yrs | 4 |
| Mini-pupillages | yes |

Apply through OLPAS

Remuneration for pupillage
£37,500

Minimum qualifications
2.1 degree

Radcliffe Chambers

# 18 Red Lion Court

London EC4A 3EB
**Tel:** 020 7520 6000
**Fax:** 020 7520 6248
**Email:** pupillage@18rlc.co.uk
**Web:** www.18rlc.co.uk

**Description of Chambers** 18 Red Lion Court is one of the country's leading criminal sets, comprising 17 silks and 69 juniors, and offers one of the most comprehensive cross-sections of expertise in the field of criminal law.  The UK *Legal 500* 2006 calls us "one of the largest and most respected crime sets", while the *Chambers Guide to the Legal Profession* 2007 notes that 18 Red Lion Court is "home to some of the most cogent, eloquent and outstandingly prepared advocates". We have a reputation for friendliness and approachability.

**Areas of work** We cover the whole range of crime, defending and prosecuting at all levels. We are particularly strong in the areas of commercial fraud, Inland Revenue and VAT offences, money laundering, corruption, drug trafficking and sex cases, including child abuse and obscene publications. Individual members are involved in international human rights cases from Rwanda to Santa Monica. Others have written well-respected practitioner texts on a wide range of topics. Chambers' work is centred primarily on the Southeastern circuit with an emphasis on London and East Anglia. Much of the East Anglian work is serviced by our annexe in Chelmsford.

**Who should apply** Chambers is looking for pupils with the potential to develop into first-class advocates. Pupils are selected for a combination of marked intellectual ability, together with good judgement and independent personalities. Candidates should ordinarily obtain at least a 2.1 in their first degree.

**Pupillage programme** In addition to experiencing a broad range of work, all pupils participate in our in-house advocacy programme. Nearly all our pupils obtain tenancies with us or elsewhere. Pupils and tenants in their first six months do not pay rent or clerks' fees.

**When and how to apply** Chambers is a member of OLPAS, and recruits in the summer season.

**Mini-pupillages** Applications for unassessed mini-pupillages should be made to Jamie Sawyer. The closing date is the end of March 2008 for mini-pupillages from May to October 2008.

**Sponsorship/funding** Five pupillages are offered, each carrying an award/guaranteed earnings package of at least £16,500.

| | |
|---|---|
| Pupillages funded | 5 |
| Tenants | 86 |
| Tenancies in last 3 yrs | 5 |
| Mini-pupillages | yes |
| Apply through OLPAS | |

Remuneration for pupillage
Award/guaranteed earnings
of at least £16,500.

# Ropewalk Chambers

24 The Ropewalk, Nottingham NG1 5EF
**Tel:** 0115 947 2581
**Fax:** 0115 947 6532
**Email:** clerks@ropewalk.co.uk
**Web:** www.ropewalk.co.uk

**Description of Chambers** Ropewalk Chambers has an established nationwide reputation with a professional client base throughout England & Wales and receives instructions from firms in every major city, including London. We are one of the few solely civil provincial sets. Our 38 tenants offer a rare depth of quality and experience enhanced through the development of teams of barristers within four dedicated practice groups - personal injury and clinical negligence; health and safety at work; business and property; planning, environment and local government.

**Areas of work** Ropewalk Chambers is perhaps best known in the field of personal injury and clinical negligence. Over the years we have appeared in some of the highest-profile litigation in this field. We undertake personal injury claims ranging from catastrophic injuries and group litigation through disease and employers' liability claims to minor accidents. Some members of Chambers have developed a particular specialisation in costs litigation. Members appear in cases across the whole spectrum of clinical negligence litigation from birth injuries/cerebral palsy to dental negligence. In health and safety at work, we specialise in regulatory work, inquests and tribunals, both inquisitorial and disciplinary. Members of Chambers routinely defend corporate clients, employers and individuals in criminal prosecutions. Chambers also enjoys a strong reputation for commercial litigation, employment and property litigation. Members of our planning group have appeared in major planning enquiries. Further details of our areas of work are available on our website.

**Who should apply** We recruit pupils with a view to their becoming tenants of Ropewalk Chambers. We are looking for candidates with an excellent academic background showing clear legal ability. However, applicants will also have to demonstrate that that they have the personality, enthusiasm, stamina and commitment to succeed at the Bar.

**Pupillage programme** We recognise that the future lies in providing the very best training for prospective barristers. We consider it essential that significant investment is made in pupils, both financially and in terms of training and guidance, to ensure the traditions and ethos of Ropewalk Chambers are upheld by our future tenants. Pupils have one pupil supervisor who will have overall responsibility for the pupil for the whole year, but the pupil will be moved within Chambers to experience different types of practice. The process is supervised by the pupillage committee. We pride ourselves on the flexibility of our pupillages which can be adapted to meet the needs of each pupil. We have a regular appraisal system. In the second six months pupils can expect to have substantial court work. Further details, including reports from former pupils, are available on our website.

**When and how to apply** By 30 April 2008 for pupillages starting in October 2009 on Chambers' own application form which can be downloaded from our website at www.ropewalk.co.uk from the end of January 2008. We do not operate within OLPAS.

**Mini-pupillages** Please see website for mini-pupillage policy.

**Sponsorship/funding** Annual award of £25,000. Comprised of £12,500 by way of grant in the first six months and £12,500 by way of guaranteed receipts in the second six months.

| | |
|---|---|
| Pupillages funded | 2 |
| Tenants | 38 |
| Tenancies in last 3 yrs | 3 |
| Mini-pupillages | yes |
| Applications | Via website |
| Remuneration for pupillage | £25,000 |

| | | |
|---|---|---|
| **ROUGEMONT CHAMBERS**<br>8 Colleton Crescent, Exeter EX2 4DG<br>**Tel:** 01392 208484<br>**Fax:** 01392 208204<br>**Email:** clerks@rougemontchambers.co.uk<br>**Apply to:** Mr John Lloyd | A busy progressive civil-based set based in the West Country. One 12 month and one second-six pupilllage offered each year. | PF 2<br>T 24<br>TL3Y 6<br>MP yes |
| **3 SERJEANTS' INN**<br>3 Serjeants' Inn, London EC4Y 1BQ<br>**Tel:** 020 7427 5000<br>**Fax:** 020 7353 0425<br>**Email:** admin@3serjeantsinn.com<br>**Apply through OLPAS** | Our specialities are principally medical law, police law and construction. We are a friendly forward-thinking set; pupillage with us is generally testing but enjoyable. | PF 2<br>T 41<br>TL3Y 7<br>MP yes |
| **11 SOUTH SQUARE**<br>Second Floor, Gray's Inn, London WC1R 5EY<br>**Tel:** 020 7405 1222<br>**Fax:** 020 7242 4282<br>**Email:** clerks@11southsquare.com<br>**Apply through OLPAS** | 11 South Square is a leading set of barristers chambers specialising in intellectual property law, but is additionally well-known for its information technology and media and entertainment work. | PF 1<br>T 17<br>TL3Y 2<br>MP yes |
| **5 ST ANDREW'S HILL**<br>London EC4V 5BY<br>**Tel:** 020 7332 5400<br>**Fax:** 020 7489 7847<br>**Email:** clerks@5sah.co.uk<br>**Apply through OLPAS** | A friendly common law set of chambers formerly at 1 Harcourt Buildings. Now in new premises with first rate facilities. Pupils enjoy these, gain wide experience, and have reasonable tenancy prospects. | PF 2<br>T 45<br>TL3Y 4<br>MP yes |
| **4 STONE BUILDINGS**<br>Lincoln's Inn, London WC2A 3XT<br>**Tel:** 020 7242 5524<br>**Fax:** 020 7831 7907<br>**Email:** clerks@4stonebuildings.com<br>**Apply to:** Mr David Goddard | 4 Stone Buildings specialise in litigation and advisory work in the fields of company law, commercial law, financial services regulation, insolvency and international trusts. | PF 2<br>T 27<br>TL3Y 3<br>MP yes |
| **9 STONE BUILDINGS**<br>Lincoln's Inn, London WC2A 3NN<br>**Tel:** 020 7404 5055<br>**Fax:** 020 7405 1551<br>**Email:** clerks@9stonebuildings.com | Rooted in chancery practice, chambers offers advocacy, drafting and advice in a broad range of commercial, insolvency, private client and property matters. | PF 1<br>T 28<br>TL3Y 4<br>MP yes |
| **11 STONE BUILDINGS**<br>Lincoln's Inn, London WC2A 3TG<br>**Tel:** 020 7831 6381<br>**Fax:** 020 7831 2575<br>**Email:** pupillage@11stonebuildings.com<br>**Apply through OLPAS** | Up to 2 pupillages available. Work split between commercial, company, insolvency, property and trusts. Broad client base, UK and international. | PF 2<br>T 50<br>TL3Y 3<br>MP yes |
| **STONE CHAMBERS**<br>4 Field Court, Gray's Inn, London WC1R 5EF<br>**Tel:** 020 7440 6900<br>**Fax:** 020 7242 0197<br>**Email:** clerks@stonechambers.com<br>**Apply through OLPAS** | Stone Chambers is a specialist shipping and general commercial set. We offer advocacy and advisory services in our chosen fields. | PF 1<br>T 25<br>TL3Y 3<br>MP yes |

**PF** = Pupillages funded / **T** = Tenants / **TL3Y** = Tenancies in last 3 years / **MP** = Mini pupillages offered

# Selborne Chambers

10 Essex Street, London WC2R 3AA
**Tel:** 020 7420 9500
**Fax:** 020 7420 9555
**Email:** clerks@selbornechambers.co.uk
**Web:** www.selbornechambers.co.uk

**Description of Chambers** Selborne Chambers comprises 21 established barristers (three silks and 18 juniors), many of whom are rightly recognised as being among the most talented in their field. Since its foundation in June 2002, we have established ourselves as one of the leading commercial and property sets at the London Bar. Our reputation as a centre of excellence has been built on a core set of values and coherence of purpose that are recognised duly by clients and the legal press alike.

**Areas of work** We act for a wide range of institutional and private clients in this and other jurisdictions. Our main areas of practice are:

Commercial disputes – banking; commercial contracts; financial services; insurance; guarantees; partnership; professional negligence.
Company – directors' duties and disqualification; insolvency; shareholders' disputes.
Property – commercial, residential and agricultural, landlord and tenant; covenants; conveyancing disputes and other contractual issues; easements; equitable interests; mortgages and charges; planning; registered land; options.
Chancery – bankruptcy; fraud, tracing and associated interlocutory remedies; intellectual property; trusts and equitable obligations and remedies; probate and wills.

**Who should apply** "Keeping small means that the set can afford to cherry-pick from applicants" – *The Lawyer*. Chambers seeks pupils who are ambitious and determined, with exceptional intellectual ability (minimum 2.1) and common sense.

**Pupillage programme** All pupils will undertake a structured pupillage encompassing all four principal practice areas. Unlike in many commercial sets, our pupils can expect regular court appearances in their own right during their second six months. Advocacy training will be provided. It is Chambers' intention to recruit a junior tenant annually, ideally from its pupils.

**When and how to apply** Chambers intends to offer up to two 12-month pupillages (reviewable after six months) to commence in October 2009. Applications are by way of covering letter and CV (with full examination results to date) which are to be received by the pupillage secretary no later than 30 April 2008. Full details at www.selbornechambers.co.uk

**Mini-pupillages** Mini-pupillages normally last for two days and are available for students approaching the final year of a law degree or who have/ are about to commence the GDL. Application is by CV and covering letter, clearly marked "Mini-pupillage application".

**Sponsorship/funding** An award of £40,000 is offered to each successful applicant, of which £8,500 comprises guaranteed second six earnings. Up to £10,000 of the pupillage award may be drawn down during the BVC year.

| | |
|---|---|
| **Pupillages funded** | Up to 2 |
| Tenants | 21 |
| Tenancies in last 3 yrs | 4 |
| **Mini-pupillages** | yes |
| **Applications contact** | |
| The Pupillage Secretary | |
| **Remuneration for pupillage** | |
| £40,000 | |
| **Minimum qualifications** | |
| 2.1 degree | |

SELBORNE
CHAMBERS

# Serle Court

6 New Square, Lincoln's Inn, London WC2A 3QS
**Tel:** 020 7242 6105
**Fax:** 020 7405 4004
**Email:** pupillage@serlecourt.co.uk
**Web:** www.serlecourt.co.uk

**Description of Chambers** '....Commercial powerhouse of the Chancery Bar....' *Chambers & Partners Guide to the UK Legal Profession 2006.* Serle Court is one of the leading commercial chancery sets with 48 barristers including 13 silks. Widely recognised as a leading set, Chambers is recommended in 20 different areas of practice by the legal directories. Chambers has a stimulating and inclusive work environment and a forward looking approach.

**Areas of work** Litigation, arbitration, mediation and advisory services across the full range of chancery and commercial practice areas including: banking, civil fraud, commercial litigation, company, financial services, insolvency, insurance and reinsurance, partnership, professional negligence, property, regulatory and disciplinary, trusts and probate.

**Who should apply** We are interested in well-rounded candidates from any background. Chambers looks for highly motivated individuals with first class intellectual ability, combined with a practical approach, sound judgment and the potential to become excellent advocates. Serle Court has a reputation for 'consistent high quality' and for having 'responsive and able team members' and seeks the same qualities in pupils.

**Pupillage programme** Pupils sit with different pupil supervisors in order to experience a broad range of work. Two pupils are recruited each year and Chambers offers an excellent preparation for successful practice, a genuinely friendly and supportive environment, the opportunity to learn from some of the leading barristers in their field and a real prospect of tenancy.

**When and how to apply** Application deadline is 4 February 2008 for pupillage to begin in 2009, although do check our website in case this changes. Contact pupillage@serlecourt.co.uk for an application form or download one from our website at www.serlecourt.co.uk.

**Mini-pupillages** About 30 available each year. Apply online at www.serlecourt.co.uk.

**Sponsorship/funding** Serle Court offers awards of £40,000 for 12 months, of which up to £12,500 can be drawn down during the BVC year. It also provides an income guarantee worth up to £100,000 over the first two years of practice.

| | |
|---|---|
| Pupillages funded | 2 |
| Tenants | 48 |
| Tenancies in last 3 yrs | 4 |
| Mini-pupillages | yes |
| Apply via website | |
| Remuneration for pupillage | |
| £40,000 | |
| Minimum qualifications | |
| 2.1 degree | |

serle court

# 3-4 South Square

Gray's Inn, London WC1R 5HP
**Tel:** 020 7696 9900
**Fax:** 020 7696 9911
**Email:** pupillage@southsquare.com
**Web:** www.southsquare.com

**Description of Chambers** Chambers is an established successful commercial set, which is involved in high-profile international and domestic commercial litigation. Members of Chambers have been involved in some of the most important commercial cases of the last decade including Barings, BCCI, Enron, Global Crossing, Lloyds, Marconi, Maxwell, NTL, Railtrack and TXU.

**Areas of work** 3-4 South Square has a pre-eminent reputation in insolvency and restructuring law and specialist expertise in banking, financial services, company law, professional negligence, domestic and international arbitration, mediation, European Union law, insurance/reinsurance law and general commercial litigation.

**Who should apply** We actively seek to recruit the highest calibre of candidates who must be prepared to commit themselves to establishing a successful practice and maintaining Chambers' position at the forefront of the modern Commercial Bar. The minimum academic qualification is a 2.1 degree. A number of our members have degrees in law, and some have the BCL or other postgraduate qualifications. Others have non-law degrees and have gone on to take the Diploma in Law.

**Pupillage programme** Pupils are welcomed into all areas of Chambers' life and are provided with an organised programme designed to train and equip them for practice in a dynamic and challenging environment. Pupils sit with a number of pupil supervisors for periods of six to eight weeks.

We look to recruit at least one tenant every year from our pupils and it is the policy of Chambers to assist new tenants to establish careers in the early stages of practice.

**When and how to apply** The deadline for pupillages commencing in October 2009 is 31 January 2008. Applications should be by CV with covering letter addressed to the pupillage secretary.

**Mini-pupillages** Chambers offers up to 10 funded mini-pupillages each carrying an award of £500. Those interested in applying for a 12-month pupillage are strongly encouraged to apply for a mini-pupillage in the previous year. Please see our website for further details.

Chambers also offers unfunded mini-pupillages of two days' duration. Again please see our website for further details.

**Sponsorship/funding** The current level of pupillage award for a 12-month pupillage is £40,000 (reviewed annually). A proportion of the pupillage award may be paid during the BVC year.

| | |
|---|---|
| Pupillages funded | up to 4 |
| Tenants | 46 |
| Tenancies in last 3 yrs | 5 |
| Mini-pupillages | yes |

**Applications contact**
The Pupillage Secretary

**Remuneration for pupillage**
£40,000 (reviewable annually)

**Minimum qualifications**
2.1 degree

**3/4 SOUTH SQUARE**

| | | |
|---|---|---|
| **ST IVE'S CHAMBERS**<br>Whittall Street, Birmingham B4 6DH<br>**Tel:** 0121 236 0863<br>**Fax:** 0121 236 6961<br>**Email:** stives.chambers@btinternet.com | Busy, friendly common law chambers with modern facilities. Specialist groups: crime; family; environmental and regulatory; property; commercial/employment; personal injury. | PF 2<br>T 59<br>TL3Y 6<br>MP yes |
| **ST JAMES'S CHAMBERS**<br>68 Quay Street, Manchester M3 3EJ<br>**Tel:** 0161 834 7000<br>**Fax:** 0161 834 2341<br>**Email:** pupillages@stjameschambers.co.uk | Chambers is offering two funded pupillage: a civil pupillages: a civil pupillage with an emphasis on PI and employment, and a chancery and commercial pupillage. Applications can be downloaded online. | PF 2<br>T 28<br>TL3Y 5<br>MP yes |
| **18 ST JOHN STREET**<br>Manchester M3 4EA<br>**Tel:** 0161 278 1800<br>**Fax:** 0161 835 2051<br>**Email:** pupils@18sjs.com<br>**Apply to:** The Chambers Manager | Chambers was founded in 1973 and has developed into a strong mixed set practising in the principal specialist groups: crime, civil, family, chancery/commercial. | PF Up to 4<br>T 54<br>TL3Y 6<br>MP yes |
| **ST JOHN'S BUILDINGS**<br>24-28a St John Street, Manchester M3 4DJ<br>**Tel:** 0161 214 1500<br>**Fax:** 0161 835 3929<br>**Email:** clerk@stjohnsbuildings.co.uk<br>**Apply through OLPAS** | A leading Manchester/Preston common law set with a strong reputation and acknowledged collegial culture. Family, PI/clinical negligence, crime employment, commercial and mental health. Modern, efficient and friendly. | PF 2<br>T 105<br>TL3Y 10<br>MP yes |
| **ST JOHN'S CHAMBERS**<br>101 Victoria Street, Bristol BS1 1DW<br>**Tel:** 0117 921 3456<br>**Fax:** 0117 929 4821<br>**Email:** clerks@stjohnschambers.co.uk<br>**Apply through OLPAS** | St John's Chambers offers an excellent service through highly specialised practice groups - chancery commercial, personal injury, family and crime with particular expertise in local government work, professional negligence, planning, environment and employment matters. | PF 2<br>T 77<br>TL3Y 22<br>MP yes |
| **ST MARY'S FAMILY LAW CHAMBERS**<br>50 High Pavement, Nottingham NG1 1HW<br>**Tel:** 0115 950 3503<br>**Fax:** 0115 958 3060<br>**Email:** clerks@smc.law.co.uk<br>**Apply through OLPAS** | A well established specialist family law set practising throughout the East Midlands, and beyond. Further expansion is expected. | PF 1<br>T 20<br>TL3Y 3<br>MP yes |
| **ST PAUL'S CHAMBERS**<br>St Paul's House, 23 Park Square, Leeds LS1 2ND<br>**Tel:** 0113 245 5866<br>**Fax:** 0113 245 5807<br>**Email:** clerks@stpaulschambers.com<br>**Apply to:** Secretary of Pupillage Committee | Founded in 1982, St Paul's Chambers now comprises 39 tenants working in complementary areas of expertise, in order to provide a consistent service across a broad range of legal fields. | PF 0<br>T 44<br>TL3Y 4<br>MP yes |
| **1 STANLEY PLACE**<br>Stanley Place, Chester CH1 2LU<br>**Tel:** 01244 348282<br>**Fax:** 01244 342336<br>**Email:** clerks@sedanhouse.co.uk<br>**Apply to:** Mr Huw Roberts | Busy, medium-sized, provincial set undertaking work of a wide description. Members are divided into criminal, civil and family teams (with some overlapping). | PF 1<br>T 35<br>TL3Y 7<br>MP yes |

**PF** = Pupillages funded / **T** = Tenants / **TL3Y** = Tenancies in last 3 years / **MP** = Mini pupillages offered

# 3 Stone Buildings

Ground Floor, Lincoln's Inn, London WC2A 3XL
**Tel:** 020 7242 4937
**Fax:** 020 7405 3896
**Email:** clerks@3sb.law.co.uk
**Web:** www.3stonebuildings.com

**Description of Chambers** The Chambers of Geoffrey Vos QC is a chancery and commercial set, specialising in financial and property litigation and advice. The majority of Chambers' work takes place in London, although a large number of Chambers' clients come from overseas and members of Chambers have appeared in a number of foreign jurisdictions in recent years. Chambers has a New York annexe.

**Areas of work** Individuals in Chambers specialise in areas including commercial, insurance, company and insolvency litigation; pensions (both litigation and advisory work); professional (except medical) negligence; real property and landlord and tenant; revenue law and tax planning; and intellectual property. Members of Chambers have been involved in many recent cases with high public profiles in the City and elsewhere, such as *Equitable Life*, *Barings*, *The Premier League*, *Chris Evans*, *Guinness*, *Maxwell*, and *Lloyds*.

**Who should apply** Applicants should be interested in the areas of work identified above, have strong intellectual abilities, good communication skills and an ability to work hard under pressure. A good personality also helps. An upper second at degree level (not necessarily in law) is normally required to gain an interview.

**Pupillage programme** Chambers offers two 12-month pupillages. Offers of pupillage will be conditional upon passing Bar finals at the first attempt. Normally pupils divide their pupillage into four periods of three months with different pupil supervisors. However, we are prepared to be flexible in pupillage arrangements and pupils' interests are taken into account as far as possible.

**When and how to apply** Through OLPAS (summer season).

**Mini-pupillages** These are offered throughout the year subject to availability.

**Sponsorship/funding** Awards are available of up to £40,000.

| | |
|---|---|
| Pupillages funded | 2 |
| Tenants | 26 |
| Tenancies in last 3 yrs | 2 |
| Mini-pupillages | yes |
| Apply through OLPAS | |
| Remuneration for pupillage | |
| up to £40,000 | |
| Minimum qualifications | |
| 2.1 degree (not necessarily in law) | |

# 5 Stone Buildings

Lincoln's Inn, London WC2A 3XT
**Tel:** 020 7242 6201
**Fax:** 020 7831 8102
**Email:** clerks@5sblaw.com
**Web:** www.5sblaw.com

**Description of Chambers** 5 Stone Buildings is one of the outstanding sets of Chancery chambers with many distinguished present and former members, including a number of current and former law lords. We have 24 members, of whom five are silks. Chambers is consistently ranked highly in the legal directories and the vast majority of our members are recommended practitioners (more than three-quarters of those over 10 years' call).

When compared to the largest chancery sets, chambers is relatively small. However, we believe that our size and ethos enables us to ensure that pupils and young tenants are trained and clerked properly and are well prepared for the problems and opportunities which practice will throw at them. All members of chambers, however senior, are always willing to assist other members, however junior, and to provide advice and guidance when requested.

Generous terms are offered to junior tenants in their first years of practice, including heavily subsidised rent and an income guarantee.

**Areas of work** Members' work covers a wide span of civil law with an emphasis on chancery work, from specialist trust, pension and revenue work through to real property, professional negligence, banking and general commercial litigation. Chambers is instructed by a wide range of solicitors, from the largest city firms to sole practitioners outside London. Many members have practices involving work from the major offshore financial centres.

**Who should apply** Applicants should normally have at least a 2.1 degree. Our policy is only to offer pupillages to candidates whom we believe to be potential tenants. We welcome applications from law and non-law graduates alike.

**Pupillage programme** We aim to offer two twelve month pupillages each year and to recruit tenants from our pupils. Pupils will normally sit with at least three pupil supervisors during that period with a view to experiencing a wide range of work. Pupils are given regular feedback as to how they might improve or refine their work

**When and how to apply** Chambers is not a member of OLPAS. Applications for pupillage commencing in October 2009 must be made in writing on chambers' application form, which can be downloaded from our website at www.5sblaw.com. Applications should be addressed to "the Pupillage Committee" or sent by email to agirling@5sblaw.com. Applications must be received by 30 April 2008. Any offers of pupillage will be made after 31 July 2008.

**Mini-pupillages** We offer a limited number of mini-pupillages each year for periods of three to five days. Details and a timetable for applications can be found on our website at www.5sblaw.com.

**Sponsorship/funding** Up to £40,000 per pupillage, £10,000 of which can be drawn down during the BVC year.

| | |
|---|---|
| Pupillages funded | 2 |
| Tenants | 24 |
| Tenancies in last 3 yrs | 2 |
| Mini-pupillages | yes |

Applications contact
Ms Anne Girling

Remuneration for pupillage
Up to £40,000

Minimum qualifications
2.1 degree

# St Philips Chambers

55 Temple Row, Birmingham B2 5LS
**Tel:** 0121 246 7000
**Fax:** 0121 246 7001
**Email:** pupillage@st-philips.com
**Web:** www.st-philips.com

**Description of Chambers** Large, busy, successful, diverse and forward-thinking, Chambers comprises six main practice groups within which members' individual practices flourish. Chambers is enhanced by a dedicated and professional staff team, a wealth of facilities and state-of-the-art premises.

**Areas of work** Commercial, crime, employment, landlord/tenant, planning/environment, Chancery, construction, family, professional negligence, civil, personal injury and public law.

**Who should apply** Chambers seeks candidates of the highest calibre with both excellent academic credentials and well-rounded personalities.

**Pupillage programme** Pupils will spend the first four months with one pupil supervisor, but will see a variety of junior work in the last two months of the first six. During the second six months pupils can expect to be in court four days a week doing a variety of civil, crime and family work, although close supervision will continue.

**When and how to apply** Apply by 20 June 2008 to begin 5 October 2009. Interviews are likely to take place on Saturday 18 July 2008. Application form available from Emily Smith, recruitment coordinator, or online.

**Mini-pupillages** Available on application (CV and covering letter) to Emily Smith, recruitment coordinator.

**Sponsorship/funding** £20,000 in first six months; £15,000 minimum guaranteed receipts in second six. A proportion of this sum may be drawn during the BVC year in exceptional circumstances.

Pupillages funded   Up to 4
Tenants   171
Tenancies in last 3 yrs   9

Mini-pupillages   yes

Apply to
Pupillage Administrator

Remuneration for pupillage
£20,000 first six; £15,000 guaranteed receipts second six

Minimum qualifications
2.1 degree

## STOUR CHAMBERS
Mill Studio, 17a Stour Street, Canterbury,
Kent CT1 2NR
**Tel:** 01227 764899
**Fax:** 01227 764941
**Email:** clerks@stourchambers.co.uk
**Apply to:** Pupillage & Tenancy Co-ordinator

Chambers' specialisations are crime, family, civil and employment law. Applications must be made on Chambers' application form.

| | |
|---|---|
| PF | 1 |
| T | 12 |
| TL3Y | 5 |
| MP | yes |

## TANFIELD CHAMBERS
2nd Floor, Temple, London EC4Y 7BY
**Tel:** 020 7421 5300
**Fax:** 020 7421 5333
**Email:** clerks@tanfieldchambers.co.uk
**Apply through OLPAS**

An established common law set specialising in all aspects of employment, family, personal injury and property law. Three 12-month pupillages offered each year.

| | |
|---|---|
| PF | 3 |
| T | 65 |
| TL3Y | 6 |
| MP | yes |

## TEMPLE CHAMBERS
32 Park Place, Cardiff CF10 3BA
**Tel:** 01633 267403
**Fax:** 01633 253441
**Email:** clerks@temple-chambers.co.uk
**Apply to:** Mr Richard Miller

Chambers undertakes prosecution and defence work. The family team has a wide breadth of experience in public and private child law together with financial matters.

| | |
|---|---|
| PF | 2 |
| T | 42 |
| TL3Y | 3 |
| MP | yes |

## 55 TEMPLE CHAMBERS
Temple Avenue, London EC4Y 0HP
**Tel:** 020 7353 7400
**Fax:** 020 7353 7100
**Email:** templechambers55@aol.com
**Apply through OLPAS**

| | |
|---|---|
| PF | Up to 4 |
| T | 15 |
| TL3Y | 9 |
| MP | yes |

## 1 TEMPLE GARDENS
First Floor, Temple, London EC4Y 9BB
**Tel:** 020 7583 1315
**Fax:** 020 7353 3969
**Email:** clerks@1templegardens.co.uk
**Apply through OLPAS**

General common law. Chambers is instructed by a wide range of solicitors including those representing government departments, insurance companies and trade unions.

| | |
|---|---|
| PF | 2 |
| T | 56 |
| TL3Y | 6 |
| MP | yes |

## 2 TEMPLE GARDENS
Temple, London EC4Y 9AY
**Tel:** 020 7822 1200
**Fax:** 020 7822 1300
**Email:** clerks@2tg.co.uk
**Apply through OLPAS**

2tg is a common law and commercial chambers. We specialise in banking, clinical negligence, employment, insurance, personal injury and professional negligence.

| | |
|---|---|
| PF | 2-3 |
| T | 49 |
| TL3Y | 9 |
| MP | yes |

## 3 TEMPLE GARDENS
Second Floor, Temple, London EC4Y 9AU
**Tel:** 020 7583 1155
**Fax:** 020 7353 5446
**Email:** clerks@3templegardens.co.uk
**Apply through OLPAS**

| | |
|---|---|
| PF | 2 |
| T | 26 |
| TL3Y | 4 |
| MP | yes |

## 3 TEMPLE GARDENS
Chambers of Donald Gordon & Paul Williams,
Third Floor, Temple, London EC4Y 9AU
**Tel:** 020 7583 0010
**Fax:** 020 7353 3361
**Email:** clerks@e3tg.co.uk
**Apply through OLPAS**

Busy Common Law set - particular strength in criminal defence. First six months pupils will gain experience in all areas of chambers work.

| | |
|---|---|
| PF | 1 |
| T | 39 |
| TL3Y | 5 |
| MP | yes |

**PF** = Pupillages funded / **T** = Tenants / **TL3Y** = Tenancies in last 3 years / **MP** = Mini pupillages offered

## 3 TEMPLE GARDENS
Lower Ground Floor, Temple, London EC4Y 9AU
**Tel:** 020 7353 3102
**Fax:** 020 7353 0960
**Email:** clerks@3tg.co.uk
**Apply through OLPAS**

Chambers is well-established, specialising in all areas of criminal law. Chambers has achieved accreditation to Barmark as issued by the General Council of the Bar.

| | |
|---|---|
| PF | 3 |
| T | 53 |
| TL3Y | 5 |
| MP | yes |

## THOMAS MORE CHAMBERS
7 Lincoln's Inn Fields, London WC2A 3BP
**Tel:** 020 7404 7000
**Fax:** 020 7831 4606
**Email:** clerks@thomasmore.co.uk
**Apply through OLPAS**

A small and dynamic common law set with an excellent reputation. We offer a broad and challenging pupillage, with exceptional prospects for the successful candidate.

| | |
|---|---|
| PF | 1 |
| T | 30 |
| TL3Y | 3 |
| MP | no |

## TOOKS CHAMBERS
8 Warner Yard, London EC1R 5EY
**Tel:** 020 7841 6100
**Fax:** 020 7841 6199
**Email:** clerks@tooks.co.uk
**Apply through OLPAS**

Tooks Chambers offers a broad range of both civil and criminal work. We are strongly committed to equal opportunities and welcome applications from women and black people.

| | |
|---|---|
| PF | 3 |
| T | 60 |
| TL3Y | 5 |
| MP | yes |

## TRINITY CHAMBERS
The Custom House, Quayside,
Newcastle Upon Tyne NE1 3DE
**Tel:** 0191 232 1927
**Fax:** 0191 232 7975
**Email:** info@trinitychambers.co.uk
**Apply through OLPAS**

Busy provincial set with sites in Newcastle and Middlesborough with significant specialisations including those indicated. Chambers has Barmark and Investors in People accreditation.

| | |
|---|---|
| PF | 1-2 |
| T | 50 |
| TL3Y | 10 |
| MP | yes |

## UNITY STREET CHAMBERS
5 Unity Street, Bristol BS1 5HH
**Tel:** 0117 906 9789
**Fax:** 0117 906 9799
**Email:** chambers@unitystreetchambers.com
**Apply to:** The Pupillage Secretary

| | |
|---|---|
| PF | 1 |
| T | 13 |
| TL3Y | 2 |
| MP | yes |

## 3 VERULAM BUILDINGS
London WC1R 5NT
**Tel:** 020 7831 8441
**Fax:** 020 7831 8479
**Email:** chambers@3vb.com
**Apply through OLPAS**

3VB is a leading set of commercial chambers with a progressive culture and a range of work spanning the domestic and international commercial fields.

| | |
|---|---|
| PF | 3 |
| T | 58 |
| TL3Y | 6 |
| MP | yes |

## WALNUT HOUSE
63 St. David's Hill, Exeter EX4 4DW
**Tel:** 01392 279751
**Fax:** 01392 412080
**Email:** clerks@walnuthouse.co.uk
**Apply to:** Chairman Pupillage Committee

General common law set with emphasis on crime, family, employment and persoanl injury. Maximum of two pupillages available.

| | |
|---|---|
| PF | 1 |
| T | 21 |
| TL3Y | 3 |
| MP | yes |

## 15 WINCKLEY SQUARE
Preston PR1 3JJ
**Tel:** 01772 252828
**Fax:** 01772 258520
**Email:** clerks@15winckleysq.co.uk
**Apply through OLPAS**

| | |
|---|---|
| PF | 2 |
| T | 45 |
| TL3Y | 4 |
| MP | yes |

PF = Pupillages funded / T = Tenants / TL3Y = Tenancies in last 3 years / MP = Mini pupillages offered

# Westgate Chambers

64 High Street, Lewes BN7 1XG
**Tel:** 01273 480510
**Fax:** 01273 483179
**Email:** clerks@westgate-chambers.co.uk
**Web:** www.westgate-chambers.co.uk

**Description of Chambers** Westgate Chambers is an established provincial set on the South Coast with members approaching 50 at all levels of seniority, including one in silk. We possess both BarMark and The Legal Services Quality Mark for the Bar, and more recently have attained BS EN ISO9001:2000.

**Areas of work** Chambers' work is predominately criminal and we have specialists in white collar crime, drugs, homicide and serious sexual offences operating in all courts at all levels. We prosecute for the CPS, HM Revenue & Customs, local councils, the Department for Work and Pensions and various other agencies.

In addition to our strong criminal emphasis, Chambers has an expanding specialist family section covering all aspects of family law, including public law, childcare work, private law Children Act applications, divorce, ancillary relief and applications under related legislation.

**Who should apply** Chambers operates a policy for equal opportunities at every level and aims to recruit the best candidates irrespective of background. Successful candidates will demonstrate a commitment to the independent Bar and a flair for advocacy combined with superb presentational and analytical skills. A strong academic record will also be considered.

**Pupillage programme** Pupillages are divided into three periods of four months' supervision, during which pupils will receive advocacy training and guidance throughout, including a mock trial exercise. Pupils will receive a £15,000 grant and will be provided with two written assessments for each section of their pupillage.

**When and how to apply** Three funded pupillages are offered each October. Applicants should apply the preceding year, by no later than 31 May. Applications should be addressed to the pupillage secretary, and must include a CV with a handwritten covering letter.

**Mini-pupillages** We actively encourage mini-pupillages, and preference may be given to candidates who have completed one. Please apply in writing to the senior clerk. Student visits are not available.

| | |
|---|---|
| Pupillages funded | 3 |
| Tenants | 46 |
| Tenancies in last 3 yrs | 18 |
| Mini-pupillages | yes |

Apply to
Pupillage Secreatry

Remuneration for pupillage
£15,000 grant and
guaranteed earnings

# Wilberforce Chambers

8 New Square, Lincoln's Inn, London WC2A 3QP
**Tel:** 020 7306 0102
**Fax:** 020 7306 0095
**Email:** pupillage@wilberforce.co.uk
**Web:** www.wilberforce.co.uk

**Description of Chambers** Wilberforce Chambers is a leading commercial chancery set of Chambers and is involved in some of the most commercially important and cutting edge litigation and advisory work undertaken by the Bar today. Members are recognised by the key legal directories as leaders in their fields. Instructions come from top UK and international law firms, providing a complex and rewarding range of work for international companies, financial institutions, well-known names, sports and media organisations, pension funds, commercial landlords and tenants, and private individuals. Our clients demand high intellectual performance and client-care standards but in return the reward is a successful and fulfilling career at the Bar. Chambers has grown in size in recent years but retains a united and friendly "family" atmosphere.

**Areas of work** Practice areas include property, pensions, private client, trust and taxation, professional negligence, general commercial litigation, banking, company, financial services, intellectual property and information technology, sports and media and charities.

**Who should apply** We look to offer two 12-month pupillages. You should possess high intellectual ability, excellent communication skills and a strong motivation to do commercial chancery work. You need to be mature and confident, have the ability to work with others and analyse legal problems clearly, demonstrating commercial and practical good sense. We look for people who have real potential to join Chambers as tenants at the end of their pupillage with us, and we take great care in our selection process and put effort into providing an excellent pupillage. We have a minimum requirement of a 2.1 degree in law or another subject, and we have a track record of taking on CPE students.

**Pupillage programme** We operate a well-structured pupillage programme aimed at providing you with a broad experience of Commercial Chancery practice under several pupil supervisors with whom you will be able to develop your skills. We aim to reach a decision about tenancy after approximately 9-10 months, but all pupils are expected to stay with us for the remainder of their pupillage on a full pupillage award.

**When and how to apply** We usually interview in March, receiving applications during January and February, but please visit our website for further information regarding the closing date for applications in 2008. We operate an initial long-list general interview before selecting a short-list of candidates for a more in-depth interview that will include analysis and discussion of a legal problem. Application forms are available on our website.

**Mini-pupillages** We encourage potential candidates for pupillage to undertake a minipupillage with us in order to learn how our Chambers operates, to meet members of Chambers and to see the type of work that we do – but a mini-pupillage is not a prerequisite for pupillage. We run three separate mini-pupillage weeks (two in December and one in July). Please visit our website for an application form and for further information.

**Sponsorship/funding** We offer a generous and competitive pupillage award which we review annually with the intention that it should be in line with the highest awards available. The award is currently £40,000 for 12 months and is paid in monthly instalments. A proportion of the award (up to £13,500) can be drawn down during the BVC year.

Pupillages funded    2
Tenants    46
Tenancies in last 3 yrs   6

Mini-pupillages    yes

Apply
Online via our website

Remuneration for pupillage
£40,000 (2008/2009)

Minimum qualifications
2.1 degree

WILBERFORCE CHAMBERS

| | | |
|---|---|---|
| **YORK CHAMBERS**<br>14 Toft Green, York YO1 6JT<br>**Tel:** 01904 620048<br>**Fax:** 01904 610056<br>**Email:** clerks@yorkchambers.co.uk<br>**Apply to:** Chairman of the Pupillage Committee | A broad-based pupillage with wide experience of differing areas of chambers practice. | PF 2<br>T 50<br>TL3Y 6<br>MP yes |
| **YOUNG STREET CHAMBERS**<br>76 Quay Street, Manchester M3 4PR<br>**Tel:** 0161 833 0489<br>**Fax:** 0161 835 3938<br>**Email:** skilvington@young-street-chambers.com<br>**Apply to:** Mr David James | Chambers is recognised as a leading set on the Northern Circuit. Pupillages are offered with a specific team (with a view to tenancy). | PF 1<br>T 47<br>TL3Y 30<br>MP yes |

**PF** = Pupillages funded / **T** = Tenants / **TL3Y** = Tenancies in last 3 years / **MP** = Mini pupillages offered

**780** THE TRAINING CONTRACT & PUPILLAGE HANDBOOK

# Useful Information

# Glossary

**ADR** Alternative dispute resolution, which comprises various methods for resolving problems without going to court.

**Advocacy** The act of arguing or pleading in favour of something. A key skill for lawyers.

**Affidavit** A written statement, the truth of which must be sworn before an officer of the court.

**Annulment** A legal decree that states that a marriage was never valid.

**Appeal** A request to a supervisory court, usually composed of a panel of judges, to overturn the legal ruling of a lower court.

**Arbitration** A method of alternative dispute resolution in which the disputing parties agree to abide by the decision of an arbitrator.

**Articles** The predecessor to the training contract.

**Articles of incorporation** A document that must be filed in order for a company to incorporate. Among the things it must include are the name and address of the corporation, its general purpose, and the number and type of shares of stock to be issued.

**Assistant solicitor** Next step on the career ladder after the two-year training period.

**Associated office** (Usually overseas) office with which a firm has an arrangement to share work and to second trainees.

**Associate solicitor** Next step on the career ladder after working as an assistant solicitor.

**Bad faith** Dishonesty or fraud in a transaction, such as entering into an agreement with no intention of honouring its terms.

**Bail** The money a defendant pays as a guarantee that he or she will show up in court at a later date.

**Bankruptcy** Another term for insolvency.

**The Bar** Informal term used to refer to the barristers' branch of the legal profession.

**Bar Council** Official body overseeing the barristers' branch of the profession.

**Bar Standards Board** Independent board responsible for regulating barristers in England and Wales.

**Barrister** A lawyer who has been called to the Bar and who appears in court to argue a client's case.

**Beneficiary** Person named in a will or insurance policy to receive money or property; person who receives benefits from a trust.

**Board of directors** The group of people elected by a corporation's shareholders to make major business decisions for the company.

**Bolt-on** A department (or even an entire smaller firm) that joins an existing firm. Generally the larger firm will not have practised in the specialist area in which the newcomers excel.

**Bond** A document with which one party promises to pay another within a specified amount of time.

**Boutique** Small niche firm offering specialist advice on a few areas of law.

**Brief** Details of a client's case, prepared by a solicitor and given to the barrister who argues it in court.

**Burden of proof** The duty of a party in a case to convince the judge or jury that enough facts exist to prove the allegations in question.

**BVC** The Bar Vocational Course, the stage between degree and pupillage.

**Call to the Bar** A formal ceremony following completion of the BVC during which you are given the title of barrister.

**Carter reforms** Lord Carter's proposed changes to the way legal aid is funded, which have been met with widespread criticism across the profession.

**Case law** The law created by judges when deciding individual cases. Also known as 'common law'.

**Caveat emptor** Latin for 'buyer beware', giving the buyer full responsibility for determining the quality of the goods in question.

**Chambers** Offices of a group of barristers.

**Chinese walls** Procedures enforced within firms to restrict access to certain information and so avoid any awkward conflicts of interest.

**Citizens Advice Bureau** A charity service offering legal and financial advice to the public.

**The City** The commercial and financial area in the centre of London.

**Codicil** A supplement to a will.

**Collateral** An asset that a borrower agrees to give up if he or she fails to repay a loan.

**Common law** The law created by judges when deciding individual cases. Also known as 'case law'.

**Contentious** Legal situation where a dispute has arisen.

**Contingency fee** A fee arrangement in which the lawyer is paid out of any damages that are awarded.

**Contract** An agreement between two or more parties in which an offer is made and accepted, and each party benefits.

**Copyright** A person's right to prevent others from copying works that he or she has written, authored or otherwise created.

**Corporate finance** This area of law involves advising clients on mergers and acquisitions, takeovers, stock exchange flotations and the like.

**Corporation** An independent entity created to conduct a business.

**Counsel** Barrister(s) acting for one of the parties in a legal action.

**CPE** Common Professional Exam, a conversion course for non-law graduates. More often referred to as the GDL.

**CPS** The Crown Prosecution Service is responsible for prosecuting criminal cases investigated by the police in England and Wales. Employs solicitors and barristers.

**Creditor** An individual (or institution) to whom money is owed.

**Damages** The financial compensation awarded to someone who suffered an injury or was harmed by someone else's wrongful act.

**Debtor** Person who owes money.

**Decision** The judgment rendered by a court.

**Deed** A written legal document that describes a property and outlines its boundaries.

**Defamation** The publication of a statement that injures a person's reputation. Libel and slander are defamation.

**Defendant** In criminal cases, the person accused of the crime. In civil matters, the person or organization that is being sued.

**Devilling** Doing paperwork for other members of chambers.

**Dining** Occasions when the Inns of Court invite student members to dine with them, providing the opportunity to make valuable contacts.

**Due diligence** Investigation carried out to establish an accurate picture of a company's finances and market position.

**Due process** The concept that laws and legal proceedings must be fair.

**ECHR** The European Convention on Human Rights of 1950 for the protection of human rights within the member states of the Council of Europe.

**Encumbrance** Any claim or restriction on a property's title.

**Equity partner** A partner at a firm who owns a share of the business (and is liable for its failures).

**Escrow** Money or documents, such as a deed or title, held by a third party until the conditions of an agreement are met.

**Estate** All the property that a person owns.

**Evidence** The various testimony and documents presented in court to prove an alleged fact.

*Ex parte* Latin term meaning 'by or for one party'. Refers to situations in which only one party appears before a judge.

**Executor** Person named in a will to oversee and manage an estate.

**Expert witness** A witness with a specialized knowledge of a subject who is allowed to discuss an event in court even though he or she was not present.

# Glossary

**Fee earner** A lawyer at a firm for whose time the firm charges.

**First six** The first six months of pupillage. During this stage the pupil will train under a barrister but will not have rights of audience.

*Force majeure* When parties to a commercial agreement are excused from performance of the contract due to events that are beyond their control.

**Franchise** A business relationship in which an owner (the franchisor) licenses others (the franchisees) to operate outlets.

**FTSE** The Financial Times Stock Exchange. The FTSE 100 is an index of the top 100 companies in the country, based on share value and turnover.

**GDL** Graduate Diploma in Law, a conversion course for non-law students. Formerly known as the PGDL. See also CPE.

**GLS** The Government Legal Service provides legal services across the spectrum of the government's activities. Employs solicitors and barristers.

**Good faith** Honestly and without deception.

**Human Rights Act 2000** Statute that requires public authorities to act in a way that is compatible with the rights guaranteed by the ECHR and requires the courts to read and give effect to primary legislation in a way that is compatible with the convention rights.

**Hung jury** A jury that is unable to reach a verdict.

*In camera* Latin for 'in chambers'. Refers to a hearing or inspection of documents that takes place in private, often in a judge's chambers.

**In-house** Refers to a lawyer who works within a company (not a law firm) as a salaried employee.

**Inns of Court** Collective name of the four legal societies in London that have the exclusive right of admission to the Bar.

**Interlocutory order** Temporary order issued during the course of litigation. Typically cannot be appealed because it is not final.

**Intestate** To die without a will.

**IPOs** Initial public offerings (listing companies on the stock exchange).

**JLD** Part of the Law Society, the Junior Lawyers Division is a group for students, trainees and newly qualified solicitors. It supersedes the Trainee Solicitors' Group (TSG) and the Young Solicitors Group (YSG).

**Judgment** A court's official decision on the matter before it.

**Jurisdiction** A court's authority to rule on the questions of law at issue in a dispute.

**Law clinic** A free legal advice centre, usually staffed by volunteer lawyers.

**Law Commission** An independent body set up in 1965 to keep the law of England and Wales under review and to recommend reform where needed.

**Law Society** Official body representing solicitors in England and Wales.

**Lawyer** Umbrella term used to refer to both barristers and solicitors.

**Legal aid** A scheme which gives to persons whose disposable income and capital fall within the limits prescribed advice, assistance and/or representation in legal proceedings.

**Legal Services Bill** A bill that would open up the legal market by allowing lawyers to form new business structures and permitting corporations (eg, Tesco) to move into the legal services market.

**Legal Services Commission** The body that runs the legal aid scheme in England and Wales.

**Liability** Legal responsibility, duty or obligation.

**Libel** Defamatory written statements or materials.

**LLB** Letters written after someone's name, showing that he or she has the degree of Bachelor of Laws.

**LLC** A limited liability company is a business structure that is a hybrid of a partnership and a corporation.

**LLD** Letters written after someone's name, showing that he or she has a doctorate in law.

**LLM** Letters written after someone's name, showing that he or she has the degree of Master of Laws.

**LLP** A limited liability partnership is essentially a hybrid between general and limited partnerships. An LLP allows partners not to be personally liable for the negligent acts of the other partners.

**Lockstep** A system by which partners' pay is decided by time served as partner in predictable sequence. Pay rises in a series of steps (eg, after one, three, five, seven and 10 years).

**LPC** The Legal Practice Course is the vocational stage between degree and training contract.

**M&A** Mergers and acquisitions. A merger occurs where two or more companies join as one. An acquisition is the takeover of one company by another.

**Magic circle** Term used to refer to the top five UK law firms: Allen & Overy, Clifford Chance, Freshfields Bruckhaus Deringer, Linklaters and Slaughter and May.

**MDP** Multi-disciplinary partnership. A combination firm offering a full range of professional services, particularly law and accountancy functions.

**Mediation** A method of alternative dispute resolution in which a neutral third party helps resolve a dispute.

**Mini-pupillage** Work experience within a set of chambers.

**Ministry of Justice** The body created in 2007 to take control of prisons, judges and courts, and probation, mostly from the Department for Constitutional Affairs.

**Moot** A mock trial, designed to test advocacy skills.

**Negligence** A failure to use the degree of care that a reasonable person would use given a certain set of circumstances.

**Niche firm/chambers** Firm or set that specializes in a certain area of law.

**Non-contentious** Legal situation where there is no dispute.

**Notary** An official authorized to certify deeds, contracts, copies of documents, etc.

**No win, no fee** An agreement whereby a solicitor acting in a claim is entitled to be paid his fee only if he wins. Such payment is usually made by the losers or their insurance company. Also known as a 'conditional fee'.

**Paralegal** Support staff within the legal profession whose work often closely resembles that of a solicitor.

**Partnership** An association of two or more people who agree to share in the profits and losses of a business venture.

**Patent** A document issued to an inventor, detailing ownership, rights and the nature of the invention.

**Perjury** A crime in which a person knowingly makes a false statement while under oath in court.

**Piercing the corporate veil** The concept through which a corporation's shareholders, who are usually protected from liability for the corporation's activities, may be held responsible for certain actions.

**Plaintiff** The person who initiates a lawsuit.

**Pleadings** The allegations by each party of their claims and defences.

**Power of attorney** The authority to act legally for another person.

**Precedent** A previously decided case that is considered binding in the court where it was issued and in all lower courts in the same jurisdiction.

*Prima facie* Latin for 'at first view'. Refers to the minimum amount of evidence a plaintiff must have to avoid having a case dismissed.

**Pro bono** The giving of free legal advice and services.

**Profits per partner** A firm's total profit divided by the number of partners at the firm. The best benchmark for comparing how successful firms are.

**PSC** Professional Skills Course, which must be passed while training to qualify as a solicitor.

**Punitive damages** Money awarded to a victim that is intended to punish a defendant and stop the person or business from repeating the type of conduct that caused the injury in question.

# Glossary

**Pupil barrister** A trainee barrister who is effectively practising, but is not yet fully qualified. Also known as a 'pupil'.

**Pupillage** The training period before qualifying as a barrister.

**Pupil supervisor** A barrister who oversees an individual's training during pupillage.

**QC** 'Queen's Counsel', a barrister who has been appointed Counsel to Her Majesty on the advice of the Lord Chancellor. Also known as a 'silk'.

**Receivership** The process of appointment by a court of a receiver to take custody of the property, business, rents and profits of a party to a lawsuit pending a final decision.

**Salaried partner** Unlike an equity partner, still an employee of a firm, though with enhanced status, influence and responsibilities.

**Seats** Periods of training during a training contract.

**Second six** The second six months of pupillage. The pupil continues to train under a barrister but has rights of audience in all courts.

**Secondment** Placement with a law firm's client.

**Settlement** The resolution or compromise by the parties in a civil case.

**SIF** The Solicitors Indemnity Fund, covering liability for claims made against its members.

**Silk** Another term for QC.

**Slander** Defamatory verbal statements.

**Solicitor** A lawyer who provides clients with skilled advice and representation. Mostly works in private practice.

**Sponsorship** The payment of your GDL and/or LPC fees by a firm if they've already offered you a training contract.

**Square mile** London's financial centre, as defined by London's old medieval walls.

**Squatter** A barrister who remains in chambers after pupillage but not as a tenant.

**Sponsorship** The payment of your GDL and/or LPC fees by a firm if they've already offered you a training contract.

*Stare decisis* Latin for 'to stand by that which is decided'. Refers to the principle of adhering to precedent when deciding a case.

**Subpoena** An order compelling a person to appear to testify or produce documents.

**Tenant** A barrister based in a particular set of chambers after pupillage.

**Title** Ownership of property.

**Tort** A civil wrong that results in an injury to a person or property.

**Trademark** A word, name or symbol used to identify products sold or services provided by a business.

**Training contract** The two-year pre-qualification training period for a solicitor. Formerly known as 'articles'.

**Transaction** A deal arranged by two sets of lawyers.

**TSG** The Trainee Solicitors' Group. It has been superseded by the JLD.

**Vacation scheme** Paid, formal work experience within a law firm. Also known as a 'work placement scheme'.

**White-collar crime** Term referring to financial crimes, such as fraud or insider dealing, committed primarily by persons at management level.

**White-shoe firm** A traditional, 'well-heeled' and established US firm.

**Woolf Report** Report by Lord Woolf on the civil justice system, which led to reform through the Civil Procedure Rules 1998.

**Work placement scheme** Paid, formal work experience within a law firm, usually for one or two weeks. Also known as a 'vacation scheme'.

**YSG** The Young Solicitors' Group. It has been superseded by the JLD.

# Useful addresses

**Association of Graduate Careers Advisory Services**
AGCAS Administration Office, Millennium House, 30 Junction Road, Sheffield S11 8XB
**Tel:** 0114 251 5750
**Fax:** 0114 251 5751
**Web:** www.agcas.org.uk

**Association of Law Costs Draftsmen**
Church Cottage, Church Lane, Stuston, Diss, Norfolk IP21 4AG
**Tel:** 01379 741404
**Fax:** 01379 742 702
**Email:** enquiries@alcd.org.uk
**Web:** www.alcd.org.uk

**Association of Taxation Technicians**
12 Upper Belgrave Street, London SW1X 8BB
**Tel:** 020 7235 2544
**Fax:** 020 7235 4571
**Email:** info@att.org.uk
**Web:** www.att.org.uk

**Association of Women Barristers**
1 Pump Court, Temple, London EC4Y 7AB
**Tel:** 020 7842 7070
**Fax:** 020 7353 4944
**Email:** janehoyal@aol.com  (Chair)
**Web:** www.womenbarristers.co.uk

**Association of Women Solicitors**
114 Chancery Lane, London WC2A 1PL
**Tel:** 020 7320 5793
**Email:** enquiries@womensolicitors.org.uk
**Web:** www.womensolicitors.org.uk

**Bar Association for Commerce, Finance and Industry**
BACFI, PO Box 4352, Edlesborough, Dunstable, Bedfordshire LU6 9EF
**Tel/Fax:** 01515 222 244
**Email:** secretary@bacfi.org
**Web:** www.bacfi.org

**Bar Education and Training Office**
289–293 High Holborn, London WC1V 7HZ
**Tel:** 020 7611 1444
**Fax:** 020 7831 9217
**Email:** mbooker@barcouncil.org.uk
**Web:** www.barstandardsboard.org.uk

**Bar Lesbian and Gay Group (BLAGG)**
Secretary, Bar Lesbian & Gay Group, PO Box 7324, London N1 9QS
**Email:** info@blagg.org
**Web:** www.blagg.org

**Black Solicitors Network**
Zainab Kemsley, Policy Executive, The Law Society, 113 Chancery Lane, London WC2A 1PL
**Tel:** 020 7316 5773
**Fax:** 020 7831 0170
**Email:** bsn@lawsociety.org.uk
**Web:** www.blacksolicitorsnetwork.co.uk

**British Institute of Verbatim Reporters**
Mary Sorene, 73 Alicia Gardens, Kenton, Harrow, Middlesex HA3 8JD
**Email:** sec@bivr.org.uk
**Web:** www.bivr.org.uk

**British Council**
10 Spring Gardens, London SW1A 2BN
**Tel:** 020 7930 8466
**Fax:** 020 7389 6347
**Email:** general.enquiries@britishcouncil.org
**Web:** www.britishcouncil.org

**Career Development Loans**
**Tel:** 0800 585505
**Web:** www.lifelonglearning.co.uk/cdl

**Central Applications Board**
PO Box 84, Guildford, Surrey GU3 1YX
**Tel:** 01483 451080
**Web:** www.lawcabs.ac.uk

**Central Law Training Ltd**
Wrens Court, 52-54 Victoria Road, Sutton Coldfield, Birmingham B72 1SX
**Tel:** 0121 355 0900
**Fax:** 0121 355 5517
**Email:** cis@centlaw.com
**Web:** www.clt.co.uk

# Useful addresses

**Chartered Institute of Patent Agents**
95 Chancery Lane, London WC2A 1DT
**Tel:** 020 7405 9450
**Fax:** 020 7430 0471
**Email:** mail@cipa.org.uk
**Web:** www.cipa.org.uk

**Chartered Institute of Taxation**
12 Upper Belgrave Street, London SW1X 8BB
**Tel:** 020 7235 9381
**Fax:** 020 7235 2562
**Email:** post@tax.org.uk
**Web:** www.tax.org.uk

**Citizens Advice Bureaux**
Head Office, Myddleton House, 115-123
Pentonville Road, London N1 9LZ
**Tel:** 020 7833 2181
**Fax:** 020 7833 4371
**Web:** www.citizensadvice.org.uk

**Commercial Bar Association**
3 Verulam Buildings, Gray's Inn, London
WC1R 5NT
**Tel:** 020 7404 2022
**Fax:** 020 7404 2088
**Email:** admin@combar.com
**Web:** www.combar.com

**Council for Licensed Conveyancers**
16 Glebe Road, Chelmsford, Essex CM1 1QG
**Tel:** 01245 349599
**Fax:** 01245 314300
**Web:** www.conveyancer.org.uk

**Criminal Bar Association**
289-293 High Holborn, London WC1V 7HZ
**Tel:** 020 7242 1289
**Email:** jbradley@barcouncil.org.uk
**Web:** www.criminalbar.com

**The Crown Office**
25 Chambers Street, Edinburgh EH1 1LA
**Tel:** 0131 226 2626
**Fax:** 0131 225 7473
**Email:** ps/COPFS@scotland.gsi.gov.uk
**Web:** www.crownoffice.gov.uk

**Crown Prosecution Service**
7th Floor, 50 Ludgate Hill, London EC4M 7EX
**Tel:** 020 7796 8000
**Fax:** 020 7710 3447
**Web:** www.cps.gov.uk

**Department for Education and Skills (DfES)**
Sanctuary Buildings, Great Smith Street, London
SW1P 3BT
**Tel:** 0870 000 2288
**Email:** info@dfes.gsi.gov.uk
**Web:** www.dfes.gov.uk

**The Directory of Social Change**
24 Stephenson Way, London NW1 2DP
**Tel:** 020 7391 4800
**Fax:** 020 7391 4808
**Email:** enquiries@dsc.org.uk
**Web:** www.dsc.org.uk

**Local Government Employers**
Local Government House, Smith Square, London
SW1P 3HZ
**Tel:** 020 7187 7373
**Fax:** 020 7664 3030
**Email:** info@lge.gov.uk
**Web:** www.lge.gov.uk

**Employment Law Bar Association**
2nd Floor, 2-3 Cursitor Street, London EC4A 1NE
**Tel:** 020 7242 1289
**Fax:** 020 7242 1107
**Email:** enquiries@elba.org.uk
**Web:** www.elba.org.uk

**European Commission**
8 Storey's Gate, London SW1P 3AT
**Tel:** 020 7973 1992
**Fax:** 020 7973 1900/1910
**Email:** reijo.kemppinen@ec.europa.eu
**Web:** www.cec.org.uk

**The Faculty of Advocates**
Parliament House, Edinburgh EH1 1RF
**Tel:** 0131 226 5071
**Web:** www.advocates.org.uk

**Family Law Bar Association**
289-293 High Holborn, London WC1V 7HZ
**Tel:** 020 7242 1289
**Fax:** 020 7831 7144
**Email:** charris@barcouncil.org.uk
**Web:** www.flba.co.uk

**Foreign and Commonwealth Office (FCO)**
King Charles Street, London, SW1A 2AH
**Tel:** 020 7008 1500
**Web:** www.fco.gov.uk

**Free Representation Unit**
Sixth Floor, 289-293 High Holborn, London
WC1V 7HZ
**Tel:** 020 7611 9555
**Email:** admin@freerepresentationunit.org.uk
**Web:** www.freerepresentationunit.org.uk

**General Council of the Bar (Bar Council)**
289-293 High Holborn, London WC1V 7HZ
**Tel:** 020 7242 0082
**Fax:** 020 7831 9217
**Web:** www.barcouncil.org.uk

**General Social Care Council (GSCC)**
Goldings House, 2 Hay's Lane, London SE1 2HB
**Tel:** 020 7397 5100
**Fax:** 020 7397 5101
**Email:** info@gscc.org.uk
**Web:** www.gscc.org.uk

**Government Legal Service**
GLS Legal Trainee Recruitment Team, Chancery
House, 53-64 Chancery Lane, London WC2A 1QS
**Tel:** 020 7649 6023
**Fax:** 020 7210 3288
**Email:** glsqualified@tmpw.co.uk
**Web:** www.gls.gov.uk

**Graduate Prospects Ltd**
Prospects House, Booth Street East, Manchester
M13 9EP
**Tel:** 0161 277 5200
**Fax:** 0161 277 5210
**Web:** www.prospects.ac.uk

**The Grants Register**
Palgrave Macmillan, Houndmills, Basingstoke,
Hampshire RG21 6XS
**Tel:** 01256 329242
**Fax:** 01256 479476
**Web:** www.grants.ord.sa.gov.au

**The Home Office**
Direct Communications Unit, 2 Marsham Street,
London SW1P 4DF
**Tel:** 020 7035 4848
**Fax:** 020 7035 4745
**Email:** public.enquiries@homeoffice.gsi.gov.uk
**Web:** www.homeoffice.gov.uk

**HM Revenue & Customs (HMRC)**
**Web:** www.hmrc.gov.uk

**Gray's Inn**
Treasury Office, 8 South Square, London
WC1R 5ET
**Tel:** 020 7458 7800
**Fax:** 020 7458 7801
**Email:** info@graysinn.org.uk
**Web:** www.graysinn.org.uk

**Inner Temple**
The Honourable Society of the Inner Temple,
Treasury Office, Inner Temple, London EC4Y 7HL
**Tel:** 020 7797 8250
**Fax:** 020 7797 8178
**Email:** enquiries@innertemple.org.uk
**Web:** www.innertemple.org.uk

**Lincoln's Inn**
The Honourable Society of Lincoln's Inn, Treasury
Office, Lincoln's Inn, London WC2A 3TL
**Tel:** 020 7405 1393
**Fax:** 020 7831 1839
**Email:** mail@lincolnsinn.org.uk
**Web:** www.lincolnsinn.org.uk

**Middle Temple**
Treasury Office, Middle Temple Lane, London
EC4Y 9AT
**Tel:** 020 7427 4800
**Fax:** 020 7427 4801
**Email:** mastertreasurer@middletemple.org.uk
**Web:** www.middletemple.org.uk

**The Institute of Barristers**
289-293 High Holborn, London WC1V 7HZ
**Tel:** 020 7831 7144
**Fax:** 020 7242 1107

**The Institute of Barristers' Clerks**
289-293 High Holborn, London WC1V 7HZ
**Tel:** 020 7831 7144
**Fax:** 020 7831 7144
**Email:** admin@barristersclerks.co.uk
**Web:** www.barristersclerks.com

**Institute of Career Guidance (ICG)**
3rd Floor, Copthall House, 1 New Road,
Stourbridge DY8 1PH
**Tel:** 01384 376 464
**Web:** www.icg-uk.org

**Institute of Chartered Accountants in England
and Wales (ICAEW)**
Chartered Accountants Hall, PO Box 433, Moorgate
Place, London EC2P 2BJ
**Tel:** 020 7920 8100
**Fax:** 020 7920 0547
**Web:** www.icaew.co.uk

**Institute of Chartered Secretaries &
Administrators**
16 Park Crescent, London W1B 1AH
**Tel:** 020 7580 4741
**Fax:** 020 7323 1132
**Email:** info@icsa.co.uk
**Web:** www.icsa.org.uk

**Institute of Legal Cashiers & Administrators**
2nd Floor, Marlowe House, 109 Station Road,
Sidcup, Kent DA15 7ET
**Tel:** 020 8302 2867
**Fax:** 020 8302 7481
**Email:** info@ilca.org.uk
**Web:** www.ilca.org.uk

**Institute of Legal Executives (ILEX)**
Kempston Manor, Kempston, Bedfordshire
MK42 7AB
**Tel:** 01234 841000
**Fax:** 01234 840373
**Email:** info@ilex.org.uk
**Web:** www.ilex.org.uk

**Institute of Trademark Attorneys**
Canterbury House, 2-6 Sydenham Road, Croydon,
Surrey CR0 9XE
**Tel:** 020 8686 2052
**Fax:** 020 8680 5723
**Email:** tm@itma.org.uk
**Web:** www.itma.org.uk

**Intellectual Property Bar Association**
(Chair: Richard Miller QC) 3 New Square,
Lincoln's Inn, London WC2A 3RS
**Tel:** 020 7405 1111
**Fax:** 020 7405 7800
**Email:** miller@3newsquare.co.uk
**Web:** www.ipba.co.uk

**Law Centres Federation**
Third Floor, 293-299 Kentish Town Road, London
NW5 2TJ
**Tel:** 020 7428 4400
**Fax:** 020 7428 4401
**Email:** info@lawcentres.org.uk
**Web:** www.lawcentres.org.uk

**The Law Commission**
Conquest House, 37-38 John Street, Theobalds
Road, London WC1N 2BQ
**Tel:** 020 7453 1220
**Fax:** 020 7453 1297
**Email:** chief.executive@lawcommission.gsi.gov.uk
**Web:** www.lawcom.gov.uk

**Law Society**
113 Chancery Lane, London WC2A 1PL
**Tel:** 020 7242 1222
**Fax:** 020 7831 0344
**Email:** info.services@lawsociety.org.uk
**Web:** www.lawsociety.co.uk

**Law Society Consumer Complaints Service**
Victoria Court, 8 Dormer Place, Leamington Spa,
Warwickshire CV32 5AE
**Tel:** 0845 608 6565
**Web:** www.oss.lawsociety.org.uk

**Law Society of Northern Ireland**
40 Linenhall Street, Belfast BT2 8BA
**Tel:** 028 9023 1614
**Fax:** 028 9023 2606
**Email:** info@lawsoc-ni.org
**Web:** www.lawsoc-ni.org

**Law Society of Scotland**
26 Drumsheugh Gardens, Edinburgh EH3 7YR
**Tel:** 0131 226 7411
**Fax:** 0131 225 2934
**Email:** lawscot@lawscot.org.uk
**Web:** www.lawscot.org.uk

**Legal Action Group**
242 Pentonville Road, London N1 9UN
**Tel:** 020 7833 2931
**Fax:** 020 7837 6094
**Email:** lag@lag.org.uk
**Web:** www.lag.org.uk

**Legal Aid Practitioners Group**
10 Greycoat Place, London SW1P 1SB
**Tel:** 020 7960 6068
**Fax:** 020 7960 6168
**Email:** kate@lapg.co.uk
**Web:** www.lapg.co.uk

**Lord Chancellor's Department**
Selbourne House, 54 Victoria Street, London
SW1E 6QW
**Tel:** 020 7210 8500
**Email:** general.queries@dca.gsi.gov.uk
**Web:** www.dca.gov.uk

**The Magistrates Association**
28 Fitzroy Square, London W1T 6DD
**Tel:** 020 7387 2353
**Fax:** 020 7383 4020
**Email:** information@magistrates-association.org.uk
**Web:** www.magistrates-association.org.uk

**National Offender Management Service**
Home Office, 3rd Floor, Peel Building, 2 Marsham
Street, London SW1P 4DF
**Tel:** 020 7035 4848
**Email:** noms@homeoffice.gsi.gov.uk
**Web:** www.noms.homeoffice.gov.uk

**Online Pupillage Application System (OLPAS)**
Any careers-related queries or advice on answering
questions should be sought from the Bar Council at
the details below.
**Tel:** 020 7242 0082
**Email:** pupillage@barcouncil.org.uk
**Web:** www.pupillages.com

**Personal Injuries Bar Association**
39 Essex Street, London WC2R 3AT
**Tel:** 020 7832 1111
**Email:** william.norris@39essex.com
(Chair: William Norris QC)
**Web:** www.piba.org.uk

**Planning and Environmental Bar Association**
2 Harcourt Buildings, London EC4Y 9DB
**Tel:** 020 7353 8415
**Fax:** 020 7353 7622
**Email:** rpurchas@2hb.law.uk
**Web:** www.peba.info

**Police Graduate Liaison Office**
Room 446, Home Office, 50 Queen Anne's Gate,
London SW1H 9AT
**Tel:** 0845 608 3000
**Web:** www.ca.courses-careers.com/police2

**Property Bar Association**
(Chair: Nicholas Dowding QC) c/o Hardwicke Building,
New Square, Lincoln's Inn, London WC2A 3SB
**Tel:** 020 7691 3700
**Fax:** 020 7691 1234
**Email:** propertybar@hardwicke.co.uk
**Web:** www.propertybar.org.uk

**Revenue Bar Association**
RBA Secretary, Pump Court Tax Chambers,
16 Bedford Row, London WC1R 4EF
**Tel:** 020 7414 8080
**Fax:** 020 7414 8099
**Email:** rba@pumptax.com
**Web:** www.revenue-bar.org

**Society of Asian Lawyers**
c/o Saima Hanif, 4-5 Gray's Inn Square, Gray's Inn,
London WC1R 5AH
**Tel:** 020 7404 5252
**Fax:** 020 7242 7803
**Email:** info@societyofasianlawyers.com
**Web:** www.societyofasianlawyers.com

**Technology & Construction Bar Association**
(Chair: Paul Darling QC) Keating Chambers,
15 Essex Street, London WC2R 3AU
**Tel:** 020 7544 2600
**Fax:** 020 7240 7722
**Email:** pdarling@keatingchambers.com
**Web:** www.tecbar.org.uk

**Trainee Solicitors' Group**
The Law Society, 114 Chancery Lane, London
WC2A 1PL
**Tel:** 020 7320 5794
**Fax:** 020 7316 5697
**Email:** info@tsg.org
**Web:** www.tsg.org

**Universities and Colleges Admission Service**
UCAS Enquiries, UCAS, Rosehill, New Barn Lane,
Cheltenham, Gloucestershire, GL52 3LZ
**Tel:** 01242 222444
**Fax:** 01242 544960
**Email:** enquiries@ucas.ac.uk
**Web:** www.ucas.com

**Young Solicitors' Group**
The Law Society, 114 Chancery Lane, London
WC2A 1PL
**Tel:** 020 7320 5794
**Fax:** 020 7831 0170
**Email:** policy@ysg.org
**Web:** www.ysg.org

# Useful websites

| | |
|---|---|
| www.barcouncil.org.uk | The Bar Council's official website |
| www.barprobono.org.uk | Details of the Bar Pro Bono Unit |
| www.careers.civil-service.gov.uk | Civil service career opportunities |
| www.chambersandpartners.com | UK and US legal directories |
| www.criminal-law.co.uk | Offers weekly updates on criminal law matters |
| www.doctorjob.com | Interactive careers magazine |
| www.inbrief.co.uk | Online version of the *Inbrief* legal magazine |
| www.justice.org.uk | Independent human rights organization website |
| www.LawCareers.Net | The most comprehensive online guide to becoming a lawyer |
| www.lawgazette.co.uk | Online version of the Law Society magazine |
| www.lawsociety.org.uk | The Law Society's official website |
| www.lawstudents.org.uk | Directory with links to other useful legal websites |
| www.lcan.org.uk | Legal information and services for undergraduates and graduates |
| www.lectlaw.com | Online law library |
| www.legalweek.com | Online version of the independent news magazine |
| www.mootingnet.org.uk | Information and support for mooters in England and Wales |
| www.lawworks.org.uk | Information on the Solicitors Pro Bono Group |
| www.prospects.ac.uk | Graduate careers website |
| www.pupillages.com | Online application process for OLPAS chambers and details of all pupillage vacancies in England and Wales |
| www.rollonfriday.com | Irreverent legal news site |
| www.spr-consilio.com | Legal resource provider |
| www.students.probonogroup.org.uk | Works in conjunction with the Solicitors Pro Bono Group |
| www.support4learning.org.uk | Information on grants, loans and other funds for students in further education |
| www.thelawyer.com | Online version of the independent news magazine |
| www.tsg.org | The Trainee Solicitors' Group official website |
| www.venables.co.uk | Comprehensive legal directory |
| www.waterlowlegal.com | Law information resource |
| www.worldlegalforum.com | Guide to law firms around the globe |

# Other useful sources of information

**Blackstone's Guide to Becoming a Solicitor (by Nicola Laver)**

Published by Oxford University Press, Great Clarendon Street, Oxford OX2 6DP
**Tel:** 01865 556 767
**Fax:** 01865 556 646

---

**Chambers & Partners Directory**
*An A-Z business directory of law firms (and solicitors), chambers (and barristers) aimed primarily at commercial clients.*

Published by Chambers & Partners Publishing, Saville House, 23 Long Lane, London EC1A 9HL
**Tel:** 020 7606 8844
**Fax:** 020 7606 0906

---

**Chambers & Partners Directory – A Guide to the Legal Profession: Student Edition**
*A student edition of the above directory aimed at helping students find the right firm in which to train.*

Published by Chambers & Partners Publishing, Saville House, 23 Long Lane, London EC1A 9HL
**Tel:** 020 7606 8844
**Fax:** 020 7606 0906

---

**Dee Allen's Success Strategies to Help You Get the Law Job You Want**
*Unconventional strategies to help you get a career in the law.*

Published by Bruno Wells Publications c2003

---

**Hobsons European Placement Guide**

Published by Hobsons, Challenger House, 42 Alder Street, London E1 1EE
**Tel:** 020 7958 5000

---

**LaCareers.Net Guide to Best in Law**
*A stylish, annual magazine featuring detailed profiles of those firms that won the LawCareers.Net Training and Recruitment Awards. Available from university careers services.*

Published by Globe Business Publishing Ltd, New Hibernia House, Winchester Walk, London Bridge, London SE1 9AG
**Web:** www.bestinlaw.co.uk

---

**LawCareers.Net**
*The most comprehensive online guide to becoming a lawyer. The site includes details of over 1,000 firms, 200 chambers, all law courses as well as up-to-date news, features and editorial.*

**Web:** www.LawCareers.Net

---

**LawCareers.Net Launchpad to Law**
*An approachable, glossy magazine packed with advice about how a non-law student can become a lawyer, along with profiles of those who've made it. Available from university careers services..*

Published by Globe Business Publishing Ltd, New Hibernia House, Winchester Walk, London Bridge, London SE1 9AG
**Web:** www.launchpadtolaw.co.uk

---

**Law Society Directory of Solicitors and Barristers**
*An official and comprehensive listing of all law firms, solicitors and barristers practising in the United Kingdom.*

Published by the Law Society, 113 Chancery Lane, London WC2A 1PL
**Tel:** 020 7242 1222
**Fax:** 020 7831 0344

---

**Law Society Gazette**
*The Law Society's own weekly magazine for the profession.*

Available on subscription from the Law Society, 113 Chancery Lane, London WC2A 1PL
**Tel:** 020 7242 1222
**Fax:** 020 7831 0344
**Web:** www.lawgazette.co.uk

---

**The Lawyer**
*A weekly newspaper for the legal profession.*

Available on subscription from The Lawyer, St Giles House, 50 Poland Street, London W1F 7AX
**Tel:** 020 7292 3716
**Fax:** 020 7970 4292
**Web:** www.the-lawyer.com
**Email:** lawcirc@centaur.co.uk

---

**Lawyer2B**
*Student version of the above paper, aimed at the recruitment market.*

Available on subscription from The Lawyer, St Giles House, 50 Poland Street, London W1F 7AX
**Tel:** 020 7292 3716
**Fax:** 020 7970 4292
**Web:** www.lawyer2b.com
**Email:** lawcirc@centaur.co.uk

---

**The Legal 500**
*Corporate clients' guide to UK law firms and barristers chambers, with analysis of the market and recommendations by subject area.*

Published by Legalease, Kensington Square House, 12-14 Ansdell Street, London W8 5BN
**Tel:** 020 7396 9292
**Fax:** 020 7396 9300
**Web:** www.legal500.com

---

**Legal Week**
*A weekly newspaper for the legal profession. Periodically includes student supplements and special reports.*

Available on subscription from Legal Week, Incisive Media, Level Three, 32-34 Broadwick Street, London W1A 2HG
**Tel:** 020 7316 9000
**Fax:** 020 7316 9278
**Web:** www.legalweek.com

# Other useful sources of information

**Prospects Focus on Law**
*A guide to training opportunities in both the solicitors' and barristers' professions, as well as information on postgraduate studies.*

Published by CSU Ltd, Prospects House, Booth Street East, Manchester M13 9EP
**Tel:** 0161 277 5200
**Fax:** 0161 277 5210
**Web:** www.prospects.ac.uk/law

**Pupillages & Awards Handbook**
*A directory of chambers offering pupillages.*

Available from The General Council of the Bar, 2/3 Cursitor Street, London EC4A 1NE
**Tel:** 020 7 440 4000

**Target Law**
*A magazine-format journal containing information regarding legal training and life as a trainee/pupil.*

Published by GTI Specialist Publishers, The Barns, Preston Crowmarsh, Wallingford, Oxfordshire OX10 6SL
**Tel:** 01491 826262
**Fax:** 01491 833146

**tsgLIFE**
*The Trainee Solicitors' Group magazine. NB The TSG is to be replaced by the Junior Lawyers' Division in January 2008.*

Published by Waterlow Professional Publishing, Paulton House, 8 Shepherdess Walk, London N1 7LB
**Tel:** 020 7490 0049
**Fax:** 020 7253 1308

**Waterlows**
*A comprehensive listing of all the law firms and individual solicitors practising in the UK.*

Published by Waterlow Professional Publishing, Paulton House, 8 Shepherdess Walk, London N1 7LB
**Tel:** 020 7490 0049
**Fax:** 020 7253 1308

# Index of advertisers